COMMITMENT TO EQUITY HANDBOOK

COMMITMENT TO EQUITY HANDBOOK

Estimating the Impact of Fiscal Policy
on Inequality and Poverty

Second Edition

VOLUME 1

Fiscal Incidence Analysis: Methodology,
Implementation, and Applications

Nora Lustig

EDITOR

CEQ INSTITUTE AT TULANE UNIVERSITY
New Orleans

BROOKINGS INSTITUTION PRESS
Washington, D.C.

Published by Brookings Institution Press
1775 Massachusetts Avenue, NW
Washington, DC 20036
www.brookings.edu/bipress

Co-published by Rowman & Littlefield
An imprint of The Rowman & Littlefield Publishing Group, Inc.
4501 Forbes Boulevard, Suite 200, Lanham, Maryland 20706
www.rowman.com

86-90 Paul Street, London EC2A 4NE

The Brookings Institution is a nonprofit organization devoted to research, education,
and publication on important issues of domestic and foreign policy. Its principal
purpose is to bring the highest quality independent research and analysis to bear on
current and emerging policy problems.

The Commitment to Equity (CEQ) Institute at Tulane University, founded by Nora
Lustig in 2015, works to reduce inequality and poverty through comprehensive and
rigorous tax and benefit incidence analysis, and active engagement with the policy
community.

British Library Cataloguing in Publication Information Available

Library of Congress Cataloging-in-Publication Data

ISBN: 978-0-8157-4046-9 (paperback)
ISBN: 978-0-8157-4047-6 (electronic)

♾™ The paper used in this publication meets the minimum requirements of American
National Standard for Information Sciences—Permanence of Paper for Printed Library
Materials, ANSI/NISO Z39.48-1992

To Anthony Atkinson (1944–2017), one of the most brilliant thinkers on the topics of inequality, poverty, and social injustice

For Antonio, my beloved husband and companion

For Carlos Javier and Liliana, our wonderful children

CONTENTS

Volume 1

PART I
Methodology

Chapter 1
The *CEQ Assessment*©: Measuring the Impact of Fiscal Policy on Inequality and Poverty
Nora Lustig and Sean Higgins

Chapter 2

Analytic Foundations: Measuring the Redistributive Impact
of Taxes and Transfers

Ali Enami, Nora Lustig, and Rodrigo Aranda

Chapter 3
Measuring the Redistributive Impact of Taxes and Transfers in the Presence of Reranking
Ali Enami

Chapter 4

Can a Poverty-Reducing and Progressive Tax and Transfer System Hurt the Poor?

Sean Higgins and Nora Lustig (*reproduced from* Journal of Development Economics)

Chapter 9

Analyzing the Impact of Fiscal Policy on Ethno-Racial Inequality

Rodrigo Aranda and Adam Ratzlaff

PART III
Applications
Included in First Edition

Chapter 10
Fiscal Policy, Income Redistribution, and Poverty Reduction in Low- and Middle-Income Countries
Nora Lustig

Chapter 11
Argentina: Taxes, Expenditures, Poverty, and Income Distribution
Dario Rossignolo

Chapter 15
El Salvador: The Impact of Taxes and Social Spending on Inequality and Poverty

Margarita Beneke de Sanfeliu, Nora Lustig, and Jose Andres Oliva Cepeda

Chapter 16
Ghana and Tanzania: The Impact of Reforming Energy Subsidies, Cash Transfers, and Taxes on Inequality and Poverty

Stephen D. Younger

Chapter 17
Fiscal Policy, Inequality, and Poverty in Iran: Assessing the Impact and Effectiveness of Taxes and Transfers

Ali Enami, Nora Lustig, and Alireza Taqdiri (*reproduced from* Middle East Development Journal)

Chapter 18
Tunisia: Fiscal Policy, Income Redistribution, and Poverty Reduction

Nizar Jouini, Nora Lustig, Ahmed Moummi, and Abebe Shimeles

Chapter 19
Uganda: The Impact of Taxes, Transfers, and Subsidies on Inequality and Poverty

Jon Jellema, Nora Lustig, Astrid Haas, and Sebastian Wolf

Added to Second Edition

Chapter 20

China: The Impact of Taxes and Transfers on Income Inequality, Poverty, and the Urban-Rural and Regional Income Gaps in China

Nora Lustig and Yang Wang

Chapter 21
Argentina: Fiscal Policy, Income Redistribution
and Poverty Reduction in Argentina   862
Juan Cruz Lopez Del Valle, Caterina Brest Lopez, Joaquin Campabadal,
Julieta Ladronis, Nora Lustig, Valentina Martinez Pabon,
and Mariano Tommasi

PART IV
The *CEQ (Commitment to Equity) Assessment* Tools
Available only online at www.ceqinstitute.org, under "Handbook."

1. Planning for a CEQ Assessment[©]: Data and Software Requirements
CEQ Institute

9. CEQ Assessment: Checking Protocol
Sandra Martinez-Aguilar, Adam Ratzlaff, Maynor Cabrera,
Cristina Carrera, and Sean Higgins

10. CEQ Training Tools
CEQ Institute

10.a CEQ Training PPT Presentations

10.b CEQ Training Videos

PART V
CEQ Data Center on Fiscal Redistribution
CEQ Institute
Available only online at www.ceqinstitute.org.

1. Description

2. CEQ Standard Indicators

3. CEQ Data Visualization

4. CEQ Indicators and the Sustainable Development Goals

5. CEQ Master Workbooks

6. CEQ Do Files and Replication Codes

6.a CEQ Assessments: Constructing Income Concepts and for Running CEQ Stata Package to Complete Master Workbook

6.b Frontier Topics

7. CEQ Harmonized Microdata

8. CEQ Metadata Table

9. Comparison of Income Concepts in Databases with Indicators of Fiscal Redistribution

PART VI
CEQ Microsimulation Tools
Available only online at www.ceqinstitute.org.

1. CEQ Desktop Tax Simulator
Ali Enami, Patricio Larroulet, and Nora Lustig

2. CEQ Markdown Statistical Code for Microsimulating the Short-run Impact of COVID-19 on Inequality and Poverty
Federico Sanz

3. CEQ Statistical Code for Microsimulating the Long-run Impact of COVID-19 on Human Capital and Intergenerational Mobility
Guido Neidhöfer and Patricio Larroulet

CONTENTS

Volume 2

Alternative Methods to Value Transfers in Kind: Health, Education, and Infrastructure

Chapter 2
The Market Value of Public Education: A Comparison of Three Valuation Methods
Sergei Soares

Chapter 3
Redistribution through Education: Assessing the Long-Term Impact of Public Spending
Sergio Urzua

Chapter 4
The Market Value of Owner-Occupied Housing and
Public Infrastructure Services 116
Sergei Soares

Fiscal Incidence of Corporate Taxes

Chapter 5
Taxes, Transfers, and Income Distribution in Chile:
Incorporating Undistributed Profits 135
Bernardo Candia and Eduardo Engel

Redistributive Impact of Contributory Pensions

Chapter 6

The Within-System Redistribution of Contributory Pension Systems: A Conceptual Framework and Empirical Method of Estimation

Carlos Grushka

Fiscal Redistribution and Sustainability

Chapter 7

Intertemporal Sustainability of Fiscal Redistribution: A Methodological Framework

Jose Maria Fanelli

Political Economy of Redistribution

LIST OF ILLUSTRATIONS

Tables

FOREWORD

François Bourguignon

Since the pioneering fiscal incidence analysis developed by Charles Stauffacher (1941)[1] for the United States in the 1930s and Tibor Barna (1945)[2] for the United Kingdom in 1937, the quality and richness of data have improved considerably; indicators for measuring income inequality, poverty, and the incidence of redistribution instruments have become more rigorous; and standard practices for evaluating redistribution in developed countries have emerged. The public interest for the issue of redistribution has recently been revived by the observed increase in disposable income inequality in numerous countries. Comparative data on redistribution are now regularly published in Organisation for Economic Cooperation and Development (OECD) reports,[3] and household survey–based microsimulation models, pioneered by Guy Orcutt at the Brookings Institution in the late 1950s[4] and now available in most high-income countries, enable analysts to evaluate the potential impact of each of the many redistribution instruments available to governments.

In the last decade, these methodologies have been extended to, and adapted for, low- and middle-income countries. This has been one of the most important contributions of the Commitment to Equity (CEQ) Institute, founded—as a project, first—in 2008 by Nora Lustig. In the past, numerous isolated attempts had been made to evaluate the incidence in a few middle-income countries of specific aspects of their redistributive systems, including cash transfers, indirect subsidies, public education

Paris School of Economics January 2022

[1] Charles Stauffacher, "The Effects of Government Expenditures and Tax Withdrawals upon Income Distribution, 1930–39," in *Public Policy: A Yearbook of the Graduate School of Public Policy*, ed. C. J. Friedrich and Edward S. Mason (Harvard University Press, 1941).

[2] Tibor Barna, *Redistribution of Incomes through Public Finance* (Oxford University Press, 1945).

[3] See, for example, "Growing Unequal" (2008), "Divided We Stand: Why Inequality Keeps Rising" (2011), and "In It Together: Why Less Inequality Benefits All" (2015).

[4] Guy Orcutt, "A New Type of Socio-Economic System," *Review of Economics and Statistics* 39, no. 2 (1957): 116–23.

expenditures, indirect taxes, and the like. But no attempt had been made to construct a framework that would both enable the study of most redistributive fiscal instruments together and be systematically applicable to a variety of developing countries until the CEQ Institute took on this ambitious task. Developing and adapting the micro-based concepts and indicators needed to rigorously evaluate redistribution in a developing country context, researchers at the institute also designed the appropriate tools to compute these indicators and apply them to a diverse array of countries—over sixty overall at this stage!

The *CEQ Handbook* combines what they have learned from a conceptual and an analytical point of view, the practical tools they have developed, and some of the applications of these concepts and methods to a variety of countries and issues. All the questions a research team or a government administration would ask when trying to evaluate the distributional impact of its fiscal revenue and expenditure system as a whole or of a single instrument are answered in this most valuable volume.

Even more, the *CEQ Handbook* innovates in the discipline of incidence analysis in several major respects and emphasizes several properties of redistribution systems that are often ignored. For instance, an interesting discussion is offered of the concept of "progressivity" of a single fiscal instrument when integrated into a system comprised of many others. Since the impact of a tax or a transfer on inequality or poverty depends on the other fiscal instruments in place, understanding the full context is of obvious importance in the policy debate on that particular tax or transfer. Equally interesting and useful is the use of alternative income concepts to measure the overall inequality and poverty and the demonstration of how different concepts may lead to different conclusions about the distributional incidence of the fiscal system. Thus, a system may be progressive and/or poverty reducing when viewed from the perspective of the familiar concept of "disposable income" but regressive and/or poverty increasing when indirect taxes are added into the picture, as they are in the CEQ "consumable income" concept. The Handbook tackles more complex issues as well, providing, for instance, a thorough consideration of how some combinations of taxes and transfers can modify the income ranking of households or people and lead in some cases to counterintuitive results in measures of redistribution.

In addressing the issue of redistribution, the *CEQ Handbook* puts more emphasis on the role of indirect taxes and subsidies than a typical tax-benefit incidence analysis in a developed country. This is because direct taxation and overall cash transfers weigh much less in total income in low- and middle-income countries, which, in turn, increases the relative importance of indirect taxation and subsidies for redistribution. This change in emphasis is most welcome as indirect taxation and subsidies often hide unwanted redistributive effects. For instance, indirect subsidies to basic goods such as food and energy are seen as key instruments for relieving poverty in many developing countries. They indeed reduce poverty, but as they also benefit the nonpoor by reducing their consumption bill, they prove a rather costly redistribution instrument. Likewise, it is also crucial to investigate whether cash transfers to the poor, which have gained importance in developing countries, may more than offset the effect of regressive indirect taxes on poverty.

The phenomenon of informality, which differentiates incidence analysis in developing and developed countries, also receives more conceptual and empirical emphasis in the CEQ methodology. In developing countries, numerous small production units escape legislation and thus do not pay labor taxes or make social security contributions. They also evade indirect taxation on the sale of their output—but they pay the value added taxes (VAT) on inputs bought from the formal sector. This formal/informal dualism makes incidence analysis intricate. Some general equilibrium framework is needed to figure out the impact of indirect taxation and subsidies on consumer prices, in order to determine the incidence of taxes on "consumable income." Informality makes this computation difficult because informality is imprecisely observed. In this respect, it is not clear that the IMF's or the World Bank's general equilibrium modules, used by the CEQ to perform that computation, take satisfactorily into account the complication arising from informality. This is a topic that requires further investigation and the CEQ Institute should pursue it in future editions of this Handbook.

There are other valuable additions to standard incidence analysis practice in the *CEQ Handbook*. One concerns the treatment of pensions and the oversimplifying assumption in many studies and micro-simulation models that pensions paid by the public sector are essentially cash transfers from the public sector—a problem that has plagued OECD incidence analyses for a long time. Of course, this ignores the fact that some of the beneficiaries have contributed during their active lifetime to social security in a kind of forced savings so that their pension may simply be the return on these savings. Making explicit the distinction between contributory and noncontributory pension benefits as suggested in the *CEQ Handbook* is most helpful. And the same applies to other benefits such as healthcare, which may be granted free of contribution in some cases and as counterpart of contributions in others. Here, too, the differences with respect to standard incidence analysis in developed countries may be substantial.

The inclusion of primary and secondary public educational expenditures in fiscal incidence analysis is another major difference. These expenditures are generally ignored when measuring redistribution in developed countries, possibly because primary and secondary schooling are practically universal and, in many countries, publicly funded. Their redistributive impact thus seems limited (this is much less true of subsidies to tertiary education). Things are different in most low- and middle-income countries where schooling is far from universal. Considering the cost to the government of public education as a transfer to households with children in public schools may thus be necessary, although it can involve a variety of complications, as the Handbook acknowledges. First, the value placed by parents on the schooling of their children, that is, their "willingness to pay" for schooling, might differ from the cost of pupils in public schools. Second, the current practice ignores differences in school quality, a potentially important source of inequality. Third, and most crucially, it is not clear that an increase in the cost of schooling, aimed precisely at equalizing quality across schools, could be considered as a net gain in the standard of living of families with children in school and therefore in more redistribution. Although it will be a gain for the child when entering the labor force in the future, it is not certain that this gain will then be shared with parents.[5] In this second edition of the *CEQ Handbook*, valuable innovations have been made in the measurement of the incidence of public educational expenditures on social welfare and inequality. They take care of the first two previous points, i.e., willingness to pay and school quality, as well as some others. Yet, the intergenerational dimension of the incidence of public education spending is still to be tackled.

This edition of the *CEQ Handbook* also improves on the measurement of the redistributive incidence of another type of in-kind benefit—namely, the impact of public health care systems. In particular, a method is proposed that takes into account the distributional impact of public spending on health outcomes rather than merely allocating health expenditures to users.

The CEQ incidence analysis methodology is also notable for its attention to the diversity of the redistributive instruments that are available and the extent of their impact on inequality and poverty. In this regard, the *CEQ Master Workbook©*, a multi-sheet Excel file that presents standardized results of exhaustive fiscal incidence analyses, should hugely facilitate country comparisons. It not only shows the distributional incidence of taxes and transfers based on a specific core income concept, such as disposable, consumable, or final income, but also provides crucial information for evaluating the actual reach of incidence estimates. It thus informs the metadata of the household survey used for the estimation, including the list of available income components, taxes paid, and transfers received; clarifies the assumptions used to estimate nonreported taxes and transfers; and specifies the amounts of each individual tax or transfer in administrative accounts so as to compare them with the equivalent amounts as reported in the survey or imputed by the analyst, as well as to judge the actual coverage of the incidence analysis and identify potential biases. Finally, combined with a user-written software in Stata (commonly known as "ado files"), a final spreadsheet includes the more detailed original indicators on the progressivity of the various fiscal instruments and their redistributive effectiveness as defined in the theoretical part of the Handbook.

With the notable expansion in coverage, the CEQ Institute's Data Center is thus becoming the repository of rigorous incidence analyses conducted on a wide variety of countries according to the methodology described in the Handbook and presented in the *CEQ Master Workbook* format. At present, the CEQ Data Center already has comparative inequality and poverty indicators as well as the structure of redistributive fiscal instruments for over sixty countries, including the United States. Quite clearly, the CEQ has the potential for becoming for the distributional incidence analysis of fis-

---

[5] A full argument along these lines may be found in François Bourguignon and Halsey Rogers, "Distributional Effects of Educational Improvements: Are We Using the Wrong Model?," *Economics of Education Review* 26, no. 6 (2007): 735–46.

cal policies the equivalent of the renowned Luxembourg Income Study (LIS), which releases harmonized microdata from national household surveys, a little along the lines of, but with a broader outreach than, EUROMOD,[6] a tax-benefit model that includes the twenty-eight members of the European Union. An important difference is that—whenever permissions have been duly granted by the proper authorities—microdata in the CEQ Data Center is downloadable,[7] which is not the case in LIS, where customer programs are run onsite, or EUROMOD, where users do not have direct access to the data, or the computer code used to simulate the fiscal systems. In the CEQ Data Center, whenever authorized, the income concepts and specific taxes and transfers, along with the computer code used to allocate them, will be made available so users can replicate or modify them at will.

This Handbook and the achievement it represents are certainly not the end of the huge undertaking the CEQ Institute began a decade ago. Many improvements of fiscal incidence analysis are under way and will be incorporated in the next edition of this Handbook. Of particular importance is developing ways to combine survey and administrative data, especially on taxes but possibly on transfers too. So is creating tools for the systematic updating of incidence analysis either with more recent data or, perhaps more importantly, changes in the fiscal instruments—an operation that may require some "nowcasting" work so as to make the database temporally consistent with the fiscal reform. Making the whole dataset and full calculation module available for microsimulation work by policymakers, observers, and analysts, so that they can transparently change the rules governing specific fiscal instruments and easily evaluate the distributional consequences, is also crucial. Such microsimulation models, which are now available in most OECD countries, differ somewhat from the pure incidence analysis of the *CEQ Handbook* in the sense that all taxes and transfers are systematically computed on the basis of official rules. This facilitates the simulation of reforms of the fiscal system, as well as easier updating of the incidence analysis when the government modifies the way some taxes or transfers are calculated. While such models are available in practically all developed countries, the *CEQ Handbook* and the work at the CEQ Institute have prepared the way for this to become the case in less advanced economies.

Another step that needs to be taken is the inclusion of some basic behavioral response to the existing fiscal instruments and reforms in it. It is not clear that it is so easy to include behavioral responses concerning labor supply or consumption because economic models and the databases used to estimate such models are often weak and in any case results are very imprecise. Nevertheless, an area of first importance is tax evasion and the incomplete take-up of benefits, as both introduce an important wedge between the official rules in fiscal system and their actual impact on personal incomes

---

[6] See https://www.euromod.ac.uk/.

[7] Since the first edition, harmonized microdata have now become available for a number of countries in Harvard Dataverse: https://dataverse.harvard.edu/dataverse/ceqmicrodata.

and their distribution. The CEQ Institute is planning to incorporate models of these behavioral responses into the CEQ basic framework for the next edition of its Handbook.

This *CEQ Handbook* must thus be seen not only as a significant achievement in and of itself, but also as the successful first stage of an ambitious project that aims to acquire full mastery of redistribution through fiscal policy in low- and middle-income countries. But while the CEQ institute is moving on to broaden the application of its tools and extending their reach, it is crucial that the material in this Handbook receives the attention it deserves among academics and think tanks, as well as policymakers and all observers of socioeconomic conditions who, like the members of the CEQ Institute, are committed to equity.

ACKNOWLEDGMENTS
CEQ HANDBOOK

Nora Lustig

Acknowledgments to the Second Edition

The *CEQ Handbook* has continued to grow and, we hope, improve. From a working paper published in 2013, it has now expanded to two volumes. The first edition now became Volume 1: Fiscal Incidence Analysis: Methodology, Implementation, and Applications. It contains all the chapters included in the first edition published in 2018 with important updates. Volume 2: Methodological Frontiers in Fiscal Incidence Analysis includes entirely new material.

To those acknowledged in the first edition, I would like to add the following.

Like the first edition of this Handbook, the second edition is the result of teamwork. For their exceptional help with its production, I would like to thank CEQ Institute's collaborators Beenish Amjad, Ali Enami, Patricio Larroulet, and Federico Sanz. Valuable contributions to the CEQ Data Center on Fiscal Redistribution and parts IV and VI of Volume 1 were provided by Beenish Amjad, Caterina Brest Lopez, Maynor Cabrera, Cristina Carrera, Samantha Greenspun, Maya Goldman, Sean Higgins, Ian Houts, Jon Jellema, Patricio Larroulet, Carlos Martin del Campo, Haley Renda, Federico Sanz, and Stephen Younger, as well as Tulane's graduate students Valentina Martinez Pabon, Siyu Quan, and Mart Trasberg, and research assistant Emilia Nordgren. Chapters in Volume 2 greatly benefited from the peer reviews by Laurent Bach, Seth Benzell, Augusto de la Torre, Nicholas Barr, Douglas Harris, Felix Rioja, and Steven Slutsky.

I would once again like to thank all members of Tulane University's community acknowledged in the first edition with the addition of Brian Edwards, Dean of the School of Liberal Arts since 2018, for his steadfast support of the CEQ Institute. For their valuable help on multiple fronts, my gratitude also goes to the Department of Economics Chair Douglas Harris and Executive Secretary Erin Callhover. My special thanks again to Ludovico Feoli, Director of Tulane's Center for Interamerican Policy and Research and of the CEQ Institute's Policy Area, for his generosity and insightful contributions to everything that the CEQ Institute does, including this Handbook.

My thanks also to our partners and collaborators at the Brookings Institution, the Center for Global Development, the Global Development Network, the French Development Agency, the Inter-American Development Bank, the Inter-American Dialogue, the International Monetary Fund, Oxfam, UNDEP, UNICEF, and the World Bank.

All authors of this Handbook are grateful to Bill Finan, editorial director of Brookings Institution Press, and to the rest of the staff at the press; and, to production editor Angela Piliouras and the rest of the Westchester Publishing Services staff.

And on behalf of the entire team that contributed to this Handbook, I would like to express our special gratitude to the Bill & Melinda Gates Foundation for its generous and continued support. Our thanks also to the National Science Foundation (NSF) for supporting the upgrading of the CEQ Data Center on Fiscal Redistribution.

Acknowledgments to the First Edition

This Handbook has its origins in the 2013 publication "Commitment to Equity Assessment (CEQ): Estimating the Incidence of Social Spending, Subsidies and Taxes. Handbook," by Nora Lustig and Sean Higgins, published as CEQ Working Paper 1. We acknowledge the very valuable contributions of many individuals and organizations in the acknowledgments to the *CEQ Handbook 2013* below. In May 2015, the Commitment to Equity (CEQ) Institute was created at Tulane University. A key output of the Institute is this new edition of the Handbook, and because the methodological changes are significant, the previous edition is no longer available online. As happened with its 2013 "ancestor," this Handbook was written with invaluable inputs and suggestions that have helped transform the 2013 version into the expansive edited volume that it now is. Here we will gratefully acknowledge those who have enabled the culmination of this project. We, the authors in this Handbook, remain fully responsible for any remaining errors or omissions and offer our sincere apologies to those whose names were inadvertently left out.

As editor of this Handbook, I want to acknowledge the support from Ludovico Feoli, Director of the Center for Inter-American Policy and Research (CIPR) and of the CEQ Institute's Policy Area, without whose invaluable contributions and support the CEQ Institute, and this Handbook in particular, would not have been possible. I am also very grateful to Tulane's Department of Economics and its Chair, James Alm; the Roger Thayer Stone Center for Latin American Studies and its Director, Thomas Reese; and staff at the School of Liberal Arts, Sponsored Projects Administration, the Office of the General Counsel, as well as other university staff. In particular, I want to acknowledge Samantha Greenspun, Director of Grants and Project Management of the CEQ Institute, for her crucial inputs—both substantive and managerial—at every step of the production of this Handbook. I am also indebted to our partners, the Center for Global Development (CGD) and the Inter-American Dialogue (IAD), for their continuous support. CGD's former president Nancy Birdsall and IAD's Ariel Fiszbein, Peter

Hakim, and Michael Shifter have all been CEQ enthusiasts and helped make this Handbook come true in multiple ways.

François Bourguignon, Jean-Yves Duclos, Jon Jellema, and Stephen D. Younger have provided numerous crucial methodological and technical contributions. We as authors are also particularly indebted to James Alm, Stefano Barbieri, Francisco Ferreira, Peter Lambert, Santiago Levy, Jorge Martinez-Vazquez, and Angel Melguizo for their invaluable comments on specific chapters and sections. Additionally, Maynor Cabrera, Sandra Martinez-Aguilar, Estuardo Moran, and Adam Ratzlaff and Tulane University's Economics Ph.D. students Ali Enami, Rodrigo Aranda, and Yang Wang; research assistants Cristina Carrera and Ruoxi Li also provided exceptional contributions, especially to part IV of this Handbook. We are also grateful to Tulane undergraduate students Jacob Edelson, Nicole Florack, Xinghao Gong, Jenny Huang, and David Roberts, as well as to Marc Brooks, Israel Martinez, Luis F. Munguia, Itzel Orozco, Xavi Recchi, and Hilda Vlachopoulou. We also thank editors Rebecca Disrud and Sefira Fialkoff.

The Handbook has also become what it is thanks to the enthusiastic dedication of the many teams that have applied the CEQ methodology since 2009. We are particularly grateful to these research associates for their patience and persistence as we have worked to ensure that we have the strongest methodology possible. Their names and those of the countries they work on can be found here. We want to thank as well the members of the CEQ Advisory Board (http://www.commitmentoequity.org/our-team/).

We are very grateful to World Bank staff, including Francisco Ferreira, Alan Fuchs, Gabriela Inchauste, Luis Felipe Lopez-Calva, Maria Ana Lugo, Miguel Martinez, Blanca Moreno-Dodson, Carlos Rodriguez, Jaime Saavedra, Carolina Sanchez-Paramo, and Carlos Silva Jauregui, and all the participants in the joint CEQ–World Bank projects for continuing to support the growth of the CEQ and make possible the implementation of *CEQ Assessments* in an increasing number of countries. In particular, we want to thank Gabriela Inchauste and Luis Felipe Lopez-Calva for spearheading the application of the CEQ tools at the World Bank and their insightful comments and suggestions.

This Handbook has also benefited greatly from the collaboration with the Inter-American Development Bank's (IDB) Gender and Diversity Division. Thanks to the vision and financial support of its Senior Advisor, Judith Morrison, and the dedication of her collaborators Diana Ortiz, Maria Olga Pena, and Adam Ratzlaff, the CEQ methodology, software, and results include an analysis of the impact of fiscal policy on inequality between ethnic and racial groups and within them. We want to also thank IDB's Carola Pessino for her intellectual contributions, insights, and support since the CEQ project's inception back in 2008. We are also very grateful to the African Development Bank, the Asian Development Bank, the Economic Research Forum, the Fundacion Salvadoreña para el Desarrollo Economico y Social (FUSADES), the Instituto Centroamericano de Estudios Fiscales (ICEFI), the International Fund for Agricultural Development (IFAD), the International Growth Center, the International Monetary

Fund, the Organisation for Economic Co-operation and Development (OECD), and the United Nations Development Programme (UNDP) for partnering with CEQ to apply the methodology and broaden the coverage of countries.

We would also like to thank the EUROMOD team, especially Holly Sutherland and Daria Popova, for clarifying the assumptions made by EUROMOD. Similarly, we appreciate the feedback from colleagues at the Institute of Fiscal Studies (IFS), especially David Philips and Laura Abramovsky, and we are likewise grateful to the LIS team, especially Janet Gornick, Branko Milanovic, and Teresa Munzi, for clarifying the assumptions made by LIS and the process used to harmonize microdata. We are also indebted to Facundo Alvaredo, Lucas Chancel, and Thomas Piketty at the Paris School of Economics' World Inequality Lab for very useful discussions.

In addition, we are indebted to our peer reviewers who provided invaluable comments, as well as to the editorial director Bill Finan, the managing editor Janet Walker, and other staff at the Brookings Institution Press, and the senior production editor Melody Negron and the rest of the Westchester Publishing Services staff for their guidance and support. Marie Breaux and her staff should be thanked for their excellent intellectual property rights advice.

Last but never least, we would like to thank the Bill & Melinda Gates Foundation. This Handbook has been possible thanks to the foundation's generous financial and substantive support. The team we have worked with has provided many opportunities for us to brainstorm, helpful introductions to individuals and organizations, and useful administrative advice. In particular, we would like to thank Rodrigo Salvado, Vishal Gujadhur, and Jessica Brinton, who have been highly supportive Program Officers. We are also indebted to Becky Clifford, Program Coordinator, who is always efficient and pleasant. And, of course, we are grateful to Gargee Ghosh, Director of Development Policy and Finance, for her unwavering guidance and support.

Acknowledgments to the Online Edition (2013)

Launched in 2008, the Commitment to Equity (CEQ) framework was designed to analyze the impact of taxation and social spending on inequality and poverty in individual countries and to provide a roadmap for governments, multilateral institutions, and nongovernmental organizations in their efforts to build more equitable societies. Led by Nora Lustig, the CEQ is a project of the Center for Inter-American Policy and the Department of Economics, Tulane University, and the Inter-American Dialogue, with Peter Hakim as Co-Director.

This Handbook was written with invaluable inputs and suggestions from a large number of people. Jim Alm, Carola Pessino, and John Scott provided essential contributions and guidance from the project's inception in 2008. We would also like to thank the Tulane University's Center for Inter-American Policy and Research and, in particular, Ludovico Feoli, its Director, for his constant support. Specific sections of this

Handbook relied substantially on inputs and feedback from others. We are very grateful to Gary Burtless, David Phillips, and Paolo Verme for authoring boxes. The section on Inequality of Opportunity is based on a write-up sent to the authors by Norbert Fiess. The section on Fiscal Mobility Matrices is based on a paper written by the authors (Higgins and Lustig, 2013) which benefited greatly from conversations with and comments from François Bourguignon, Satya Chakravarty, Nachiketa Chattopadhyay, Jean-Yves Duclos, Francisco Ferreira, Gary Fields, James Foster, Peter Lambert, Darryl McLeod, John Roemer, Jon Rothbaum, Shlomo Yitzhaki, and participants in the Symposium on Ultra-Poverty hosted by the Institute for International Economic Policy at George Washington University, Washington, D.C., March 22–23, 2012; "Well-Being and Inequality in the Long Run: Measurement, History and Ideas," hosted by Universidad Carlos III de Madrid and the World Bank, Madrid, June 1, 2012; the annual meeting of the Latin American and Caribbean Economic Association (LACEA), Lima, November 1–3, 2012; the XX Meetings of the Research Network on Inequality and Poverty (NIP), Washington, D.C., May 6, 2013; and the annual meetings of the Society for the Study of Economic Inequality (ECINEQ), Bari, Italy, July 24, 2013.

Important recent revisions have been largely guided by the feedback received from the World Bank team and the Advisory Committee of the CEQ and World Bank project on *The Distributional Impact of Fiscal Policy*. In particular, we are very grateful to Jaime Saavedra, as well as to Gabriela Inchauste and her collaborator Catherine Lee; to peer reviewers Shubham Chaudhuri, Andrew Dabalen, Luis F. Lopez-Calva, and Luis Serven from the World Bank; and to advisors François Bourguignon, Gary Burtless, David Coady, Robert Gillingham, Jorge Martinez-Vasquez, Cormac O'Dea, David Phillips, Ian Preston, Sally Wallace, and Stephen D. Younger. We are also highly indebted to Jean-Yves Duclos. We are also thankful to Mariellen Jewers and Emily Travis for their research assistance.

We are also greatly indebted to the members of the CEQ-Latin America Advisory Board. In particular, we wish to thank Jere Behrman, Nancy Birdsall, Otaviano Canuto, Mauricio Cardenas, Fernando Carrera Castro, Miguel Luis Castilla, Louise Cord, Rolando Cordera, Augusto de la Torre, Ludovico Feoli, Francisco Ferreira, Ariel Fiszbein, Juan Alberto Fuentes Knight, Juan Carlos Gomez Sabaini, Carol Graham, Rebeca Grynspan, Martin Hopenhayn, Santiago Levy, Luis F. Lopez-Calva, Mario Marcel, Jonathan Menkos, Carmelo Mesa-Lago, Judith Morrison, Hugo Noe Pino, Jose Antonio Ocampo, Daniel Ortega, Tamara Ortega Goodspeed, Guillermo Perry, Jeffrey Puryear, David Roodman, Ana Maria Sanjuan, Michael Shifter, Vito Tanzi, and Andras Uthoff.

The Handbook has also benefited enormously from the country teams' important contributions to the methodological discussions and revisions. For that, we are grateful to Shamma Alam, Rythia Afkar, Florencia Amabile, Nisha Arunatilake, Marisa Bucheli, Margarita Beneke de Sanfeliu, Maynor Cabrera, Eliana Carranza, Andres Castañeda, Dante Contreras, Camilo Gomez Osorio, George Gray Molina, Carlos

Hurtado, Veronica Paz Arauco, Miguel Jaramillo, Jon Jellema, Wilson Jimenez, Cristina Llerena, Mashekwa Maboshe, Yusuf Mansur, Marcela Melendez, Hilcias Estuardo Moran, Jose Andres Oliva, Claudiney Pereira, Julio Ramirez, Maximo Rossi, Jaime Ruiz-Tagle, Pablo Sauma, Nistha Sinha, Barbara Sparrow, William Swanson, Juan Diego Trejos, Eyasu Tsehaye, Paolo Verme, Matthew Grant Wai-Poi, Tassew Woldehanna, Ingrid Woolard, Ernesto Yañez, and Precious Zikhali.

At numerous conferences and workshops, many individuals contributed to discussions on the methodological issues explored here, and others provided comments on earlier versions of the Handbook; we would like to thank in particular Maria Socorro Bautista, Andrew Berg, Benedict Clements, Chistian Daude, Manuel Deshon, Norbert Fiess, Robert Gillingham, Samantha Greenspun, Margaret Grosh, Friederike Koehler, Kathy Lindert, Maria Ana Lugo, Christina Malmberg-Calvo, Angel Melguizo, Emiro Molina, Jose Molinas, Judith Morrison, Ahmed Moummi, Eduardo Ortiz-Juarez, Jacob Ricker-Gilbert, Jamele Rigolini, Tomas Rosada, Eliana Rubiano, Whitney Ruble, Pablo Sanguinetti, Abebe Shimeles, Tim Smeeding, Dan Teles, Teresa Ter-Minassian, Erwin Tiongson, Dominique van de Walle, Renato Vargas, Adam Wagstaff, and Quentin Wodon, as well as participants in the Commitment to Equity Workshops (hosted by Tulane University and CIPR, New Orleans, October 2010; Universidad Torcuato di Tella, Buenos Aires, December 2010; and the Inter-American Dialogue, Washington, D.C., November, 2011), the Workshop on Fiscal Incidence in LAC (World Bank, Washington, D.C., May 2012), Fiscal Policy for an Equitable Society (World Bank, Washington, D.C., June 2013), Fiscal Incidence Analysis for Selected African Countries (African Development Bank, Tunis, August 12, 2013).

We are indebted to Shaohua Chen for answering our incessant questions about the methodologies used by the World Bank's PovcalNet, to Guillermo Cruces, Leonardo Gasparini, Leonardo Lucchetti, and Leonardo Tornarolli for answering similar questions about CEDLAS and the World Bank's Socio-Economic Database for Latin America and the Caribbean (SEDLAC), to David Phillips for answering questions about the Institute for Fiscal Studies' research, to Abdelkrim Araar and Jean-Yves Duclos for answering our questions about their Distributional Analysis Stata Package (DASP) and providing us with additional ado files, to Rafael Osorio, Sergei Soares, and Pedro Souza at the Instituto de Pesquisa Econômica Aplicada for providing us with the Stata code to implement their methodology to correct for underestimation of the number of cash transfer beneficiaries, and to the Fiscal Affairs department at the International Monetary Fund for providing us with the Stata code to estimate the indirect effects of price increases using input-output tables.

Since its inception, the CEQ has received financial support from Tulane University's Center for Inter-American Policy and Research, the School of Liberal Arts, and the Stone Center for Latin American Studies, as well as the Canadian International Development Agency (CIDA), the Development Bank of Latin America (CAF), the General Electric Foundation, the Inter-American Development Bank (IADB), the International Fund for Agricultural Development (IFAD), the Norwegian Ministry of Foreign Affairs, the United Nations Development Programme's Regional Bureau for Latin America and the Caribbean (UNDP/RBLAC), and the World Bank.

Of course, the authors remain fully responsible for any remaining errors or omissions.

ABSTRACTS—VOLUME 1

Volume 1 of this Handbook is a unique manual that explains in detail the theory and practical methods of fiscal incidence analysis. It also includes multiple new contributions developed by the Commitment to Equity (CEQ) Institute for determining the impact of fiscal policy on inequality and poverty. Policymakers, social planners, and economists are presented with a step-by-step guide to applying fiscal incidence analysis as well as country studies, or *CEQ Assessments*, that illustrate the process. Volume 1 has six parts. Part I, Methodology, describes what a *CEQ Assessment*© is and presents the theoretical underpinnings of fiscal incidence analysis and the indicators used to assess the distributive impact and effectiveness of fiscal policy. Part II, Implementation, presents the methodology on how taxes, subsidies, and social spending should be allocated. It includes a step-by step guide to completing the *CEQ Master Workbook*©, a multi-sheet Excel file that houses detailed information on the country's fiscal system and the results used as inputs for policy discussions, academic papers, and policy reports. Part III, Applications, presents applications of the CEQ framework to low- and middle-income countries and includes simulations of policy reforms. Parts IV, V, and VI are available online only. Part IV, *The CEQ Assessment* Tools, contains guidelines for the implementation of *CEQ Assessments*, including the data and software requirements, recommendations for the composition of the team, and a thorough protocol of quality control. Part V includes all the components of the CEQ Data Center on Fiscal Redistribution.[1] Part VI contains the CEQ Institute's microsimulation tools. Given the characteristics of their content, there are no abstracts for parts IV–VI. A description can be found in the Introduction.

---

[1] https://commitmentoequity.org/datacenter/

Part I. Methodology

Chapter 1. The *CEQ Assessment*©: Measuring the Impact of Fiscal Policy on Inequality and Poverty

Nora Lustig and Sean Higgins

This chapter presents key analytical insights in fiscal redistribution theory. The chapter also discusses the basics of fiscal incidence analysis used in *CEQ Assessments*. The chapter describes the set of indicators used to answer the following four key questions: How much income redistribution and poverty reduction is being accomplished through fiscal policy? How equalizing and pro-poor are specific taxes and government spending? How effective are taxes and government spending in reducing inequality and poverty? What is the impact of fiscal reforms that change the size and/or progressivity of a particular tax or benefit? Finally, the chapter illustrates how these questions may be answered with examples from existing *CEQ Assessments*.

JEL Codes: H22, D31, D63, I32, I38

Keywords: handbook, taxes and transfers, fiscal incidence, poverty, inequality

Chapter 2. Analytic Foundations: Measuring the Redistributive Impact of Taxes and Transfers

Ali Enami, Nora Lustig, and Rodrigo Aranda

This chapter provides a theoretical foundation for analyzing the redistributive effect of taxes and transfers when the ranking of individuals by prefiscal income remains unchanged. Typically, the redistributive effect is measured by the so-called concentration curve or the Kakwani coefficient. We show that in a world with more than a single fiscal instrument, however, the simple rule that progressive taxes or transfers are always equalizing does not necessarily hold, and offer alternative rules that survive theoretical scrutiny. In particular, we show that the sign of the marginal contribution unambiguously predicts whether a tax or a transfer is equalizing or not.

JEL Codes: H22, D31, A23

Keywords: marginal contribution, progressivity, inequality, multiple taxes and transfers

Chapter 3. Measuring the Redistributive Impact of Taxes and Transfers in the Presence of Reranking

Ali Enami

This chapter provides a theoretical foundation for analyzing the redistributive effect of taxes and transfers when the ranking of individuals by prefiscal income changes as a result of fiscal redistribution. Through various examples, this chapter shows how reranking—a common feature in all actual fiscal systems—reduces the predictive power of simple measures of progressivity in assessing the actual effect of taxes and transfers on inequality.

JEL Codes: H22, D31, A23.

Keywords: marginal contribution, vertical equity, reranking

Chapter 4. Can a Poverty-Reducing and Progressive Tax and Transfer System Hurt the Poor?

Sean Higgins and Nora Lustig (*reproduced from* Journal of Development Economics)

To analyze anti-poverty policies in tandem with the taxes used to pay for them, comparisons of poverty before and after taxes and transfers are often used. We show that these comparisons, as well as measures of horizontal equity and progressivity, can fail to capture an important aspect: that a substantial proportion of the poor are made poorer (or non-poor made poor) by the tax and transfer system. We illustrate with data from seventeen developing countries: in fifteen, the fiscal system is poverty-reducing and progressive, but in ten of these at least one-quarter of the poor pay more in taxes than they receive in transfers. We call this fiscal impoverishment, and axiomatically derive a measure of its extent. An analogous measure of fiscal gains of the poor is also derived, and we show that changes in the poverty gap can be decomposed into our axiomatic measures of fiscal impoverishment and gains.

JEL Codes: I32, H22

Keywords: poverty, horizontal equity, progressivity, fiscal impoverishment

Chapter 5. Measuring the Effectiveness of Taxes and Transfers in Fighting Inequality and Poverty

Ali Enami

This chapter introduces new indicators that measure the effectiveness of the elements of a fiscal system in reducing inequality and poverty. The new indices are generally divided into two families—impact effectiveness (IE) and spending effectiveness (SE) indicators—and are applicable in any context (i.e., inequality and poverty). Moreover, a variation of the former, known as the fiscal impoverishment and gains effectiveness indicator (FI/FGP), which is applicable only in the context of poverty, is separately introduced. IE and SE indicators are similar in that they both compare the performance of a tax or transfer in reducing inequality or poverty with respect to its theoretically maximum potential. For IE indicators, we keep the amount of money raised (or spent) constant and compare the actual performance of a tax (or transfer) with its potential performance. For SE indicators, we keep the impact of a tax (or transfer) on inequality or poverty constant and compare the actual size of a tax (or transfer) with the theoretically minimum amount of tax (or transfer) that would create the same impact.

JEL Codes: D31, H22, I38

Keywords: inequality, poverty, fiscal incidence, marginal contribution, effectiveness indicator

Part II. Implementation

Chapter 6. Allocating Taxes and Transfers and Constructing Income Concepts: Completing Sections A, B, and C of the *CEQ Master Workbook*©

Ali Enami, Sean Higgins and Nora Lustig

This chapter presents a step-by-step guide to applying the incidence analysis used to prepare *CEQ Assessments*. We define income concepts before and after taxes, transfers, and subsidies; discuss the methodological assumptions used to construct them; explain how taxes, transfers, and subsidies should be allocated at the household level; and suggest what to do when information on who paid or received certain taxes and/or transfers, or how much they paid or received, is not included in the household survey. This chapter is the basis for completing sections B and C of the *CEQ Master Workbook*.

JEL Codes: H22, D31, D63, I32, I38

Keywords: handbook, taxes and transfers, fiscal incidence, poverty, inequality

Chapter 7. Constructing Consumable Income: Including the Direct and Indirect Effects of Indirect Taxes and Subsidies

Jon Jellema and Gabriela Inchauste

This chapter presents a step-by-step guide to applying the incidence analysis of indirect taxes and subsidies used in *CEQ Assessments*. We define the Consumable Income concept as Disposable Income plus the benefits received when subsidized items are purchased minus the taxes paid when taxed items are purchased. We discuss how the direct effects of indirect taxes and subsidies on either welfare or purchasing power can be estimated. We review a "price-shifting" model for estimating the magnitude of the indirect effects of indirect taxes and subsidies and demonstrate how to use an input-output matrix together with a household expenditure survey to allocate the indirect burden across households. The methods in this chapter form the basis for constructing the *CEQ Assessment's* Consumable Income concept.

JEL Codes: H22, H24, H26, D31, D63, I32, I38

Keywords: handbook, indirect taxes, subsidies, fiscal incidence, poverty, inequality

Chapter 8. Producing Indicators and Results, and Completing Sections D and E of the *CEQ Master Workbook*© Using the *CEQ Stata Package*©

Sean Higgins and Caterina Brest Lopez

This chapter describes the indicators and results used in a *CEQ Assessment*, describes sections D and E of the *CEQ Master Workbook*, and describes how the indicators and results can be produced and exported to the *CEQ Master Workbook* using the *CEQ Stata Package*.

JEL Codes: H22, D31, D63, I32, I38

Keywords: handbook, taxes and transfers, fiscal incidence, poverty, inequality

Chapter 9. Analyzing the Impact of Fiscal Policy on Ethno-Racial Inequality

Rodrigo Aranda and Adam Ratzlaff

An important element of inequality in nearly every country derives from circumstances that are outside an individual's control. These include gender, place of birth, and, particularly important in many countries, race or ethnicity. This chapter expands on the CEQ analysis by examining how to measure fiscal incidence across ethno-racial lines in an effort to determine if governments effectively reduce ethno-racial inequalities. The chapter examines how to measure ethno-racial inequality and what indicators are useful in determining the impact of fiscal interventions across groups. Additionally, this chapter provides information on Section F of the *CEQ Master Workbook* and instructions on how to use the ceqrace.ado Stata command to complete the CEQ analysis across ethno-racial lines.

JEL Codes: H22, D31, D63, I32, I38

Keywords: handbook, taxes and transfers, fiscal incidence, poverty, inequality, ethnic and racial inequality

Part III. Applications

Chapter 10. Fiscal Policy, Income Redistribution, and Poverty Reduction in Low- and Middle-Income Countries

Nora Lustig

Using comparative fiscal incidence analysis, this chapter examines the impact of fiscal policy on inequality and poverty in twenty-nine low- and middle-income countries for circa the year 2010. Success in fiscal redistribution is driven primarily by redistributive efforts (share of social spending to GDP in each country) and the extent to which transfers are targeted to the poor and direct taxes are targeted to the rich. While fiscal policy always reduces inequality, this is not the case with poverty. While spending on preschool and primary school is pro-poor (the per capita transfer declines with income) in almost all countries, pro-poor secondary school spending is less prevalent, and tertiary education spending tends to be progressive only in relative terms (equalizing, but not pro-poor). Health spending is always equalizing except for in Jordan.

JEL Codes: H22, H5, D31, I3

Keywords: fiscal incidence, social spending, inequality, poverty, developing countries

Chapter 11. Argentina: Taxes, Expenditures, Poverty, and Income Distribution

Dario Rossignolo

Using standard fiscal incidence analysis, this chapter estimates the impact of tax and expenditure policies on income distribution and poverty in Argentina with data from the National Household Survey on Incomes and Expenditures 2012–13. The results show that fiscal policy has been a powerful tool in reducing inequality and poverty, but that the unusually high levels of public spending may make the programs unsustainable.

JEL Codes: H2, I3. D3

Keywords: taxes, public expenditures, inequality, poverty

Chapter 12. Brazil: Fiscal Policy and Ethno-Racial Poverty and Inequality

Claudiney Pereira

Fiscal policy played an important role in reducing poverty and inequality in Brazil over the last fifteen years, but how much redistribution and poverty reduction is being accomplished across ethnic groups? How was the ethno-racial divide affected by fiscal policy? We estimate the effects of taxes and social spending on inequality and poverty among ethnic groups using a household survey. We find that direct transfers have similar effects on inequality across ethnic groups, but that the reduction is larger for pardos after adding monetized in-kind benefits (health and education). However, the income ratio between whites and non-whites is virtually unchanged. Poverty is reduced after direct transfers, but the reduction is higher for whites despite the prevalence of poverty being at least twice as high among pardos, blacks, and indigenous peoples. The positive effects on poverty are tempered by a deleterious effect from indirect taxes. In addition, per capita transfers are on average higher for whites, and benefits can be twice as large as those for non-whites. Fiscal interventions did not have a significant impact in reducing the divide between whites and non-whites in Brazil.

JEL Codes: D31, H22, I32, 054

Keywords: fiscal policy, great divide, Brazil, inequality, ethno-racial

Chapter 13. Chile: The Impact of Fiscal Policy on Inequality and Poverty

Sandra Martinez-Aguilar, Alan Fuchs, Eduardo Ortiz-Juarez, and Giselle Del Carmen

This chapter applies a comprehensive tax-benefit incidence analysis to estimate the distributional effects of fiscal policy in Chile in 2013. Four results are indicative of an overall positive net effect of fiscal interventions on poverty and inequality. First, subsidies exert a positive, yet modest effect on poverty and inequality, whereas direct transfers are progressive, equalizing, and reduce the poverty headcount by 4 to 5 percentage points, depending on the poverty line used. Second, although social contributions are unequalizing and poverty-increasing, direct taxes on personal income are equalizing and poverty-neutral, whereas indirect taxes are poverty-increasing but exert a counterintuitive, yet feasible equalizing effect known as Lambert's conundrum. Third, social spending on tertiary education is slightly equalizing but it is not pro-poor, contrary to the effects of social spending on basic and secondary education and health, which are not only equalizing but also pro-poor. Finally, the net effect of Chile's tax/transfer system leaves fewer individuals impoverished relative to the number of fiscal gainers, and the magnitude of monetary fiscal gains is significantly higher than that of fiscal impoverishment.

JEL Codes: D31, I32

Keywords: fiscal policy and inequality, income inequality, poverty, social assistance, taxation

Chapter 14. The Dominican Republic: Fiscal Policy, Income Redistribution, and Poverty Reduction

Jaime Aristy-Escuder, Maynor Cabrera, Blanca Moreno-Dodson, and Miguel E. Sanchez-Martin

This chapter assesses whether the limited redistributive effect of fiscal policy in the Dominican Republic has slowed improvements in poverty and inequality during a period of strong economic growth. Departing from the Commitment to Equity methodology for fiscal incidence analysis, this chapter introduces new methodological considerations and addresses the time gap between the current fiscal structure (2013) and the latest available household survey (2007) by deflating public revenue and spending data to

2007 prices. Results show that fiscal policy in the Dominican Republic is overall progressive given that, compared to other countries, the fiscal system achieves intermediate levels of inequality reduction (5 Gini points) through direct and indirect taxes, transfers and subsidies, and that it generates very little horizontal inequality. At the same time, the impact of direct transfers on poverty reduction is modest, due to the limited cash amounts granted, and there seems to be scope for boosting revenue and enhancing progressivity by revising tax exemptions and indirect electricity subsidies.

JEL Codes: D31, H23, H32, I32

Keywords: fiscal incidence, income inequality, poverty, conditional cash transfers, taxation

Chapter 15. El Salvador: The Impact of Taxes and Social Spending on Inequality and Poverty

Margarita Beneke de Sanfeliu, Nora Lustig, and Jose Andres Oliva Cepeda

Using the CEQ's methodology, we conducted a fiscal impact study to estimate the effect of taxes, social spending, and subsidies on inequality and poverty in El Salvador. Taxes are progressive, but given their volume, their impact is limited. Direct transfers are concentrated on poor households, but their budget is small, so their effect is also limited; a significant portion of the subsidies goes to households in the upper income deciles, so although their budget is greater, their impact is low. The component that has the greatest effect on inequality is spending on education and health. Therefore, the impact of fiscal policy is limited and low when compared with other countries with a similar level of per capita income. There is room for improvement using current resources.

JEL Codes: D31, H22, I14

Keywords: fiscal incidence, poverty, inequality, El Salvador

Chapter 16. Ghana and Tanzania: The Impact of Reforming Energy Subsidies, Cash Transfers, and Taxes on Inequality and Poverty

Stephen D. Younger

The chapter explains methods developed by the CEQ Institute to simulate policy changes and uses them to assess the distributional consequences of three types of policy reform in Ghana and Tanzania: removal of energy subsidies, expansion of conditional cash transfer programs, and shifts in the balance between indirect and direct taxation. The methods are simple to implement and provide a first-order approximation to the true distributional effects. In both countries energy subsidies are substantial and popular, but regressive despite the use of lifeline tariffs for electricity consumption. Their removal would reduce inequality but also increase poverty by a nontrivial amount because the poor do garner some benefit from the subsidies. A simultaneous expansion of cash transfer programs could offset the poverty consequences at significantly lower fiscal cost than that of the energy subsidies. In both countries, direct taxes are more progressive than indirect taxes, yet shifting taxation from indirect to direct taxes has relatively little effect on inequality and poverty because the incidence of the two is not as different as, for instance, the difference between taxes and a strongly progressive expenditure like conditional cash transfers.

JEL Codes: D31, H22, I14

Keywords: fiscal incidence, poverty, inequality, subsidy reform, Ghana, Tanzania

Chapter 17. Iran: Fiscal Policy, Inequality, and Poverty in Iran: Assessing the Impact and Effectiveness of Taxes and Transfers

Ali Enami, Nora Lustig, and Alireza Taqdiri (*reproduced from* Middle East Development Journal)

Using the Iranian Household Expenditure and Income Survey for 2011–12, we estimate the impact and effectiveness of various components of Iran's fiscal system on reducing inequality and poverty. We utilize marginal contribution analysis to determine the impact of each component, and we introduce newly developed indicators of effectiveness to calculate how well various taxes and transfers are operating to reduce inequality and poverty. We find that the fiscal system reduces the poverty head-count ratio by 10.5 percentage points and inequality by 0.0854 Gini points. Transfers are generally more effective in reducing inequality than taxes, while taxes are especially effective in raising revenue without causing poverty to rise. Although transfers are not targeted toward the poor, they reduce poverty significantly. The main driver is the Targeted-Subsidy Program (TSP), and we show through simulations that the poverty reducing impact of TSP could be enhanced if resources were more targeted to the bottom deciles.

JEL Codes: D31, H22, I38

Keywords: Incidence analysis; marginal contribution; effectiveness; energy subsidy reform; Iran

Chapter 18. Tunisia: Fiscal Policy, Income Redistribution, and Poverty Reduction

Nizar Jouini, Nora Lustig, Ahmed Moummi, and Abebe Shimeles

Using the National Survey of Consumption and Household Living Standards for 2010, this chapter estimates the incidence of the government's taxation and spending in Tunisia. Taking into account the impact of direct taxes and transfers, indirect taxes and subsidies, and the monetized value of in-kind transfers in education and health services, the Gini coefficient falls from 0.43 (before taxes and transfers) to 0.35 (after taxes and transfers), mainly due to taxes (30 percent of the decrease) and in-kind services

(30 percent of the decrease). Most of the equalization is produced by personal income taxes and contributions to social security. Direct taxes are progressive, and the VAT is regressive. Cash transfers contribute little to redistribution. Although direct transfers are strongly progressive and equalizing, their share in the budget remains very limited (only 0.2 percent). Subsidies are equalizing, though much less so than cash transfers, because benefits to the non-poor are higher than their population share (that is, subsidies are progressive but only in relative terms). Primary and secondary education are strongly redistributive and equalizing whereas tertiary education is progressive only in relative terms because the poor still have limited access. Health spending is progressive.

JEL Codes: H22, I38, D31

Keywords: fiscal policy, fiscal incidence, social spending, inequality, poverty, taxes, Tunisia

Chapter 19. Uganda: The Impact of Taxes, Transfers, and Subsidies on Inequality and Poverty

Jon Jellema, Nora Lustig, Astrid Haas, and Sebastian Wolf

This paper uses the 2012–13 Uganda National Household Survey to analyze the redistributive effectiveness and impact of Uganda's revenue collection instruments and social spending programs on poverty and inequality. Fiscal policy, including many of its constituent tax and spending elements, is inequality-reducing in Uganda, but the impact of fiscal policy on inequality is modest. The reduction of inequality due to fiscal policy in Uganda is lower than in other countries with similar levels of initial inequality—a result tied to generally low levels of spending. The impact of fiscal policy on poverty is negligible, though the combination of very sparse coverage of direct transfer programs and nearly complete coverage of indirect tax instruments means that many poor households are net payers into, rather than net recipients from, the fiscal system. As Uganda looks ahead to increased revenues from taxation and concurrent investments in productive infrastructure, it should take care to protect the poorest households from further impoverishment from the fiscal system.

JEL Codes: H22, I38, D31

Keywords: fiscal incidence, poverty, inequality, fiscal policy, Uganda

Chapter 20. China: The Impact of Taxes and Transfers on Income Inequality, Poverty, and the Urban-Rural and Regional Income Gaps in China

Nora Lustig and Yang Wang

China is characterized by high prefiscal urban-rural, regional, and overall inequality. Applying standard fiscal incidence analysis, we estimate the redistributive effect of taxes and social spending on income distribution and poverty. In particular, we estimate the effect of direct and indirect taxes, direct cash transfers, contributory pensions, indirect subsidies, and in-kind transfers (education and health) on overall inequality and poverty, the urban-rural income gap, and income inequality between regions. The results show that the fiscal system is inequality-reducing for the country as a whole and between regions. However, the urban-rural gap rises and the postfiscal headcount ratio is higher than prefiscal poverty in rural areas. Both are undesirable outcomes, given that rural residents are poorer. They are largely explained by the considerably lower contributory pensions received by rural residents.

JEL Codes: D31, H22, I38

Keywords: poverty and inequality in China, urban-rural gap, regional disparity, taxes, transfers, incidence analysis

Chapter 21. Argentina: Fiscal Policy, Income Redistribution and Poverty Reduction in Argentina

Juan Cruz Lopez Del Valle, Caterina Brest Lopez, Joaquin Campabadal, Julieta Ladronis, Nora Lustig, Valentina Martinez Pabon, and Mariano Tommasi

We implement a fiscal incidence analysis for Argentina with data from the 2017 national household survey. We find that Argentina's fiscal system reduces inequality and poverty more than is the case in many other comparable countries. This result is driven primarily by the size of the state (as measured by social spending to GDP) and less so by the progressivity of the fiscal system. While there are spending items that are quite progressive and even pro-poor, taxes are unequalizing, and a number of subsidies disproportionately benefit the rich.

JEL Codes: E62, D6, H22, H23, I14, I24, I32

Keywords: fiscal policy, inequality, poverty, incidence, public economics

INTRODUCTION

Nora Lustig

The CEQ Handbook has continued to grow and, we hope, improve. From a paper-length online document published in 2013, the second edition of the Handbook has now expanded to two volumes. The first edition now became Volume 1: Fiscal Incidence Analysis: Methodology, Implementation, and Applications. Volume 1 contains all the chapters included in the 2018 first edition plus some new ones. Of the existing chapters, several were subject to important updates which are listed at the end of section 1 of this Introduction. Volume 2—Methodological Frontiers in Fiscal Incidence Analysis—includes chapters on alternative methods to estimate the incidence of spending on education, health, and infrastructure; the incidence of corporate taxes; the distributive impact of contributory pensions; the sustainability of fiscal redistribution; and the political economy of the provision of public goods.

1 About Volume 1: Fiscal Incidence Analysis: Methodology, Implementation, and Applications

Volume 1 is a unique manual that explains in detail the method and practice of fiscal incidence analysis. It also includes multiple new contributions developed by the Commitment to Equity (CEQ) Institute for determining the impact of fiscal policy on inequality and poverty. Policymakers, social planners, and economists are presented with a step-by-step guide to applying fiscal incidence analysis as well as country studies (called *CEQ Assessments*©) to illustrate.[1]

Taxation and public spending are key policy levers that the state has in its power to change the distribution of income determined both by market forces and institutions

---

[1] Volume 1 of this Handbook has its origins in the 2013 publication "Commitment to Equity Assessment (CEQ): Estimating the Incidence of Social Spending, Subsidies and Taxes. Handbook," by Nora Lustig and Sean Higgins, which had been published as CEQ Working Paper 1. Because the methodological changes are significant, the previous edition is no longer available online, but can be obtained upon request.

and by the prevailing distribution of wealth, property, and power. Rooted in the field of Public Finance, fiscal incidence analysis is the most commonly used method to measure the distributional impact of a country's taxes and public spending. Fiscal incidence has a long tradition in public policy analysis. The tax incidence literature includes empirical estimates going back more than half a century as reflected in the pioneer work of Musgrave (1959), Musgrave, Case, and Leonard (1974), Musgrave and others (1951), Pechman and Okner (1974), Bourguignon and Morrisson (1980), and Pechman (1985). Similarly, on the expenditure side, there is a long tradition using the accounting approach (see, for example, Meerman, 1979; Selowsky, 1979). See also the studies mentioned in the Foreword to this Handbook by François Bourguignon. Several authors have incorporated behavioral responses to the fiscal incidence framework (see, for example, Gertler and Glewwe, 1990; Gertler and van der Gaag, 1990; Sahn and Younger, 2000; van de Walle, 2003; Younger and others, 1999). Useful methodological guidelines for fiscal incidence analysis can be found in, for example, Bourguignon and da Silva (2003), Demery (2000), Duclos and Araar (2006), and Martinez-Vazquez (2008). For a summary, also see Lustig (2020b).

Fiscal incidence analysis is designed to measure who bears the burden of taxes and who receives the benefits of government spending—in particular, of social spending—and who the gainers and losers of particular tax reforms or changes to welfare programs are. In essence, fiscal incidence analysis is the method utilized to allocate taxes and public spending to households so that one can compare incomes before taxes and transfers with incomes after them, and calculate the relevant indicators of prefiscal and postfiscal inequality and poverty, among others.

Fiscal incidence analysis can be used to assess the redistributive impact of a fiscal system as a whole or changes of specific fiscal instruments. In particular, fiscal incidence analysis is used to address the following questions: Who bears the burden of taxation and who receives the benefits of public spending? How much income redistribution is being accomplished through taxation and public spending? What is the impact of taxation and public spending on poverty and the poor? How equalizing are specific taxes and government welfare programs? How progressive are spending on education and health? How effective are taxes and government spending in reducing inequality and poverty? Who are the losers and winners of tax and welfare programs reforms? A sample of key indicators meant to address these questions are discussed here. Real-time analysis of winners and losers plays an important role in shaping the policy debate in a number of countries.

In practice, fiscal incidence analysis is the method utilized to allocate taxes and public spending to households so that one can compare incomes before taxes and transfers with incomes after them. Standard fiscal incidence analysis looks only at what is paid and what is received without assessing the behavioral responses that taxes and public spending may trigger in individuals or households. This is often referred to as the "accounting approach." Although in theory the method is quite straightforward, its application can be fraught with complications. The salient ones are discussed in Volume 1 of this Handbook.

Volume 1 has six parts. Part I, Methodology, describes what a *CEQ Assessment*© is and presents the theoretical underpinnings of fiscal incidence analysis and the indicators used to assess the distributive impact and effectiveness of fiscal policy. Part II, Implementation, presents the methodology on how taxes, subsidies, and social spending should be allocated. It includes a step-by step guide to completing the *CEQ Master Workbook*© (available online in part IV of this Volume; CEQ Institute, 2022), a multi-sheet Excel file that houses detailed information on the country's fiscal system and fiscal incidence results. Part III, "Applications," presents applications of the CEQ framework to low- and middle-income countries and includes simulations of policy reforms.

Parts IV, V, and VI are available online only. Part IV, "The *CEQ Assessment Tools*" contains guidelines for the implementation of *CEQ Assessments*, including the data and software requirements, recommendations for the composition of the team, and a thorough protocol of quality control. It also includes guidelines on how to organize the fiscal incidence database to generate the CEQ Harmonized Microdata. Part IV also contains the *CEQ Assessment*'s main tools: the *CEQ Master Workbook (MWB)* (a blank version of the multi-sheet Excel file that houses detailed information on the country's economic, political, and social context, description of microdata, the country's fiscal system and the results of the fiscal incidence analysis used as inputs for policy discussions, academic papers, and policy reports; CEQ Institute, 2022), and the *CEQ Stata Package* with user-written software to complete the results section of the *CEQ MWB*. It also includes examples of "do files" in Stata for constructing the income concepts and completed MWB and for constructing income concepts with corrections for undercoverage and underreporting of top incomes. There are two "demos" of completed Master Workbooks and do files in part IV: one for Ghana (consumption-based survey) and Mexico (income-based survey). Part V includes all the components of the CEQ Data Center on Fiscal Redistribution.[2] Part VI contains the CEQ Institute's microsimulation tools.

A detailed description of the six parts is found in section 5 of this Introduction.

Of the changes made in the second edition, readers should note important updates introduced in chapter 6, "Allocating Taxes and Transfers and Constructing Income Concepts: Completing Sections A, B, and C of the *CEQ Master Workbook*©" (Enami, Higgins, and Lustig, 2022). As indicated by its title, chapter 6 describes the methods used to allocate taxes and transfers to households and construct each one of the income concepts to analyze the impact of fiscal policy on inequality and poverty. Since the publication of the first edition in 2018, some of these methods have been subject to change, and the information included in the CEQ Data Center on Fiscal Redistribution

---

[2] https://commitmentoequity.org/datacenter/

has incorporated them. We have also eliminated some inaccuracies and sharpened the definitions of income concepts.

Chapter 8, "Producing Indicators and Results, and Completing Sections D and E of the *CEQ Master Workbook©* Using the *CEQ Stata Package©*" (Higgins and Brest Lopez, 2022), has also been subject to important updates. This chapter describes the indicators and results used in a CEQ Assessment, describes sections D and E of the *CEQ Master Workbook*, and describes how the indicators and results can be produced and exported to the *CEQ Master Workbook* using the *CEQ Stata Package*.

In addition, the online-only part IV, "The *CEQ Assessment* Tools," has been thoroughly updated. Volume 1 also has two new additional online-only parts: part V, the CEQ Data Center on Fiscal Redistribution, an information and monitoring system where results are presented at increasing levels of detail (from summary indicators to microdata), and part VI, which contains the CEQ Institute's microsimulation tools.

Although meant to be a guide to completing a *CEQ Assessment*, this Volume of the Handbook can also be used as a stand-alone reference for those interested in methodological and practical approaches to carry out incidence analysis and assess the impact of fiscal policy on poverty and shared prosperity. In addition, it can be used as a textbook for advanced undergraduate and graduate courses on public finance and income redistribution.

2 The Relevance of Fiscal Incidence Analysis in Today's World

The world is an unequal place. Income and wealth inequality among and within countries is pervasive. Unequal opportunities translate into earnings inequality. Concentration of power and wealth translates into unfair social contracts. Societies have two main ways to change this: first, by expanding poor people's access to assets—in particular, human capital—and bargaining power to level the playing field; second, by redistributing income through taxes and transfers. In both instances, the power of the state to redistribute assets, income, and wealth through fiscal policy plays a key role.[3]

By adopting the Sustainable Development Goals (SDGs) in September 2015, countries worldwide have committed to make the world more just. They have committed to eradicating poverty and hunger, reducing inequality, and achieving healthy lives, quality education, gender equality, and sustainable development. Countries have also committed to promoting full-employment growth, decent work, peaceful societies, and accountable institutions, as well as strengthening global partnerships for sustainable development. One key factor necessary to achieve these goals will be the availability of fiscal resources to deliver the social protection, social services, and infrastructure embedded in them. A significant portion of these resources is expected to come from the countries' own fiscal systems, complemented by transfers from the countries that are

---

[3] For a historical analysis of fiscal redistribution, see the excellent book by Lindert (2004).

better off. As is typical with these exercises, the proposals shy away from acknowledging that goals have trade-offs: for example, that devoting resources to eradicating hunger may mean that fewer resources are available for infrastructure investment (or vice versa), that raising additional revenues domestically may hurt a significant portion of the poor or abate economic growth, or that protecting the elderly may mean protecting less of the young (or vice versa). The *CEQ Assessments*—as a first approximation—can contribute to quantifying some of these trade-offs.

Governments are increasingly interested in assessing how effective their current fiscal policies are in promoting growth, expanding opportunities, and accelerating poverty reduction. More generally, governments need to gauge how well they can achieve their own distributional objectives and those implicit in the SDGs. How can we know if fiscal effort and the allocation of fiscal resources are consistent with the adopted social equity goals? Who bears the costs of financing expanded social protection systems, social services, and infrastructure? What are the fiscal trade-offs that governments face in the quest toward achieving these goals? Do investments in education and health truly benefit the users of these services? Fiscal incidence analysis is one of the key tools that can shed light on questions as fundamental as these.

Since the publication of the first edition of the Handbook in 2018 and following a proposal submitted by Oxfam, the CEQ Institute, and the World Bank to the Inter Agency and Expert Group (IAEG)-SDGs 2020 Comprehensive Review, in March 2020, the United Nations Statistical Commission ratified the adoption of the indicator 10.4.2, the Redistributive Impact of Fiscal Policy, to monitor the distributional impact of taxes and transfers. Indicator 10.4.2 equals the difference between prefiscal and postfiscal income inequality (as measured by the Gini coefficient). Developed by the CEQ at Tulane University, the Redistributive Impact of Fiscal Policy indicator is already being used by both the World Bank and the IMF to guide their own programs and policy advice to countries. The indicator is also included in the Commitment to Reducing Inequality Index developed by Development Finance International and Oxfam. With its inclusion among the SDG indicators, policy analysts, policymakers, and policy advocates throughout the world will be given the opportunity to systematically track progress in fiscal policy's contribution to more equitable societies.[4]

3 Fiscal Incidence in Practice: The *Commitment to Equity Assessment*

The *CEQ Assessment*© is a diagnostic tool that uses fiscal incidence analysis to determine the extent to which fiscal policy reduces inequality and poverty in a particular

---

[4] For more details, see the blogpost by Nora Lustig, Chiara Mariotti, and Carolina Sanchez-Paramo: https://blogs.worldbank.org/opendata/redistributive-impact-fiscal-policy-indicator-new-global-standard-assessing-government

country. The *CEQ Assessment* is designed to address the following four main questions:

1. How much income redistribution and poverty reduction is being accomplished through fiscal policy?[5]
2. How equalizing and pro-poor are specific taxes and government spending?
3. How effective are taxes and government spending in reducing inequality and poverty?
4. What is the impact of fiscal reforms that change the size and/or progressivity of a particular tax or benefit?

There are, of course, additional questions for which the *CEQ Assessments* can be used. For example, they can be used to guide policymakers in terms of what could be done to increase redistribution and poverty reduction through changes in taxation and spending in specific countries.

To measure the redistributive effect and poverty impact of taxes and benefits, the core building block of fiscal incidence analysis is the definition and construction of a prefiscal income concept and a post-fiscal income concept—that is, income after taxes net of transfers. The construction of income concepts refers to the method of allocating the burden of taxes and the benefits of government spending to each household. In the CEQ framework we begin by defining prefiscal income: the income of individuals before taking into account taxes paid and benefits received. Prefiscal income is the income by which individuals are initially ranked to assess the incidence of taxes and transfers across the income distribution. As shown in figure I.1, there are four core income concepts.

Figure I.1 is a very stylized version of the income concepts whose definition is presented in detail in Figures 6-1 and 6-2 and Table 6-5 in chapter 6 of this Volume. As discussed at length in chapter 1 in this Volume, in the CEQ framework, depending on the assumptions made regarding old-age pensions from a contributory social security system, we define two categories of prefiscal income: Market Income and Market Income plus Pensions. If pensions are treated as deferred income (hereafter, Pensions as Deferred Income, or PDI scenario), the prefiscal income is Market Income plus Pensions; and, if pensions are treated as government transfers (hereafter, Pensions as Government Transfers, or PGT scenario), the prefiscal income is Market Income.

The CEQ framework, which aims to be as comprehensive as possible, enables one to estimate the combined impact of taxes and transfers. The analysis also includes the estimated marginal contribution of each individual intervention to the reduction in inequality and poverty. The use of a common methodology makes the results compa-

---

[5] Throughout this Handbook, "fiscal policy," "fiscal instruments," "taxes and government spending," "revenue collection and government spending," "taxes and transfers," "taxes and benefits," and "net fiscal system" are used interchangeably.

FIGURE I.1

Fiscal Incidence Analysis: Core Income Concepts

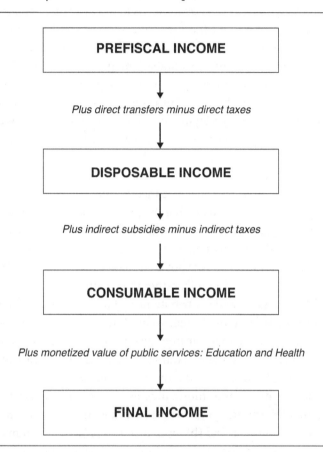

rable across countries. This approach has been effective in providing a sound evidence base and spurring national policy dialogues. For instance, the *CEQ Assessments* have led to additional diagnostic work and policy changes in Armenia regarding tax policy, in Ethiopia regarding the coverage of transfers and the minimum threshold of taxable income, and in Indonesia regarding subsidy policy.[6]

At the outset, it is important to recognize some important caveats. First, the analysis excludes some important categories of taxes and spending, such as spending on infrastructure, corporate income taxes, defense, and other public goods because it is difficult to assign these benefits or burdens to any single individual, as the economic burden (in the case of corporate taxes) or benefit (in the case of spending on public goods) are diffuse. Existing methodologies are yet not fully developed to credibly incorporate the economic incidence of those categories of taxes and spending. Second,

---

[6] See interviews with Tassew Woldehanna and Gabriela Inchauste in CEQ Institute (2016).

by considering only the *redistributive* effects of taxes and transfers, at this point the CEQ framework does not offer a full analysis of whether specific taxes or expenditures are *desirable*. When one type of tax or expenditure is found to be more progressive than another, the temptation is to conclude that the former is preferable. However, redistribution is only one of many criteria that matter when making public policy. Good tax policy will aim to be efficient in addition to equitable, and public spending will aim to meet a state's minimal functions by investing in necessary public goods in addition to improving equity. By assessing the equity of taxes and spending, the results of the approach are one input to public policymaking—one that should be weighed with other evidence before deciding whether a tax or a benefit is desirable in its present form or should be reformed.

It is important to keep in mind that the fiscal incidence analysis used in the *CEQ Assessments* is point-in-time and does not incorporate behavioral or general equilibrium effects. That is, no claim is made that the prefiscal income (i.e., the income before taxes and transfers) equals the true counterfactual income in the absence of taxes and transfers. It is a first-order approximation that measures the average incidence of fiscal interventions. However, the analysis is not a mechanically applied accounting exercise. The incidence of taxes is the economic, rather than statutory, incidence. It is assumed that individual income taxes and contributions by both employees and employers, for instance, are borne by labor in the formal sector. Individuals who are not contributing to social security are assumed to pay neither direct taxes nor contributions. The burden of consumption taxes is fully shifted forward to consumers. In the case of consumption taxes, the analyses take into account the lower incidence associated with own-consumption, rural markets, and informality. Finally, it is important to note that the CEQ results cannot inform the trade-offs between spending on (a) current transfers to alleviate poverty in the present and (b) investments in physical and human capital that could lead to large impacts on well-being in the future through higher economic growth.

In spite of the comprehensive methodology described in Volume 1 of this Handbook, there is still important work to be done to sharpen the methods, broaden the scope of the analysis, and enhance the policy tools. Some of these issues are addressed in Volume 2 of this Handbook (see "About Volume 2" below) and ongoing work in the CEQ Institute. For example, the ongoing research agenda for 2021–23 includes correcting for undercoverage and underreporting of top incomes in fiscal incidence analysis (see, for example, Lustig, 2020a, Flachaire and others, 2021, and Lustig and Martinez Pabon, forthcoming), measuring the impact of fiscal policy on multidimensional poverty, introducing gender-differentiated analysis (see, for example, Greenspun, 2019 and Bargain, 2022), incorporating microsimulation tools in the CEQ fiscal incidence analysis, and microsimulation methods to measure the short- and long-term impact of COVID-19 on inequality, poverty, and intergenerational mobility (see, for example, Lustig and others, 2021 and Neidhöfer, Lustig, and Tommasi, 2021). Other topics shall be developed further in the future. For example, taxes and transfers trigger behav-

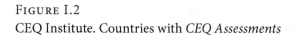

Figure I.2
CEQ Institute. Countries with *CEQ Assessments*

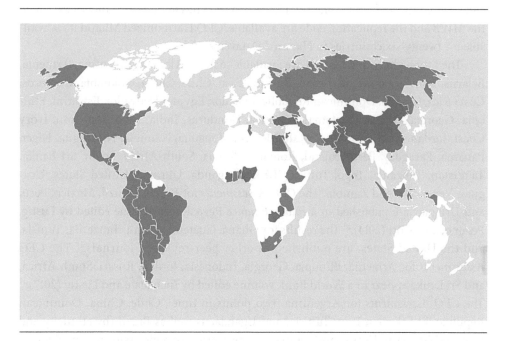

ioral responses that, in the current "accounting framework," are ignored. These behavioral responses may imply important trade-offs in terms of efficiency, effectiveness, and sustainability of the fiscal redistribution compact.[7] To expand the knowledge and methodological frontiers, the CEQ Institute is continuously working with scholars and partners. As new work becomes available, it will be made available through, for example, the CEQ Institute's Working Paper series.

Until the launch of the CEQ project in 2008,[8] work that analyzed the incidence of both government revenue and spending simultaneously—including net indirect taxes and spending on in-kind services—in middle- and low-income countries was not frequent. The CEQ project has changed this. Often in collaboration with other institutions, the CEQ Institute has completed or is in the process of completing over sixty *CEQ Assessments* that span all regions of the world as shown in the map in figure I.2.[9]

---

[7] See chapter 1 in this Volume (Lustig and Higgins, 2022) for citations on incidence analysis that incorporates behavioral responses in partial and general equilibrium frameworks.

[8] The project was initially launched at the Inter-American Dialogue with a focus on Latin America only.

[9] This information is as of January 2022. Please visit www.ceqinstitute.org for the most up-to-date coverage. Note that there are countries with partial fiscal incidence analysis for which there may be

As of January 2022, there are *CEQ Assessments* available for fifty-eight countries. "Available" means that the results are featured in the CEQ Standard Indicators. Of the fifty-eight, the CEQ Data Center on Fiscal Redistribution has forty-five countries for which the *MWB* and the replication code are available. CEQ Harmonized Microdata is available for twenty-six countries in Harvard Dataverse.

The fifty-eight countries that are available include: Albania, Argentina, Armenia, Belarus, Bolivia, Botswana, Brazil, Burkina Faso, Chile, China, Colombia, Comoros, Costa Rica, Croatia, Dominican Republic, Ecuador, Egypt, El Salvador, Eswatini, Ethiopia, Georgia, Ghana, Guatemala, Guinea, Honduras, India, Indonesia, Iran, Ivory Coast, Jordan, Kenya, Lesotho, Mali, Mexico, Mongolia, Namibia, Nicaragua, Niger, Panama, Paraguay, Peru, Poland, Romania, Russia, South Africa, Spain, Sri Lanka, Tajikistan, Tanzania, Togo, Tunisia, Turkey, Uganda, Ukraine, United States, Uruguay, Venezuela, and Zambia. The *CEQ Assessments* for Bolivia, Brazil, Mexico, Peru, and Uruguay are published in a *Public Finance Review* special issue edited by Lustig, Pessino, and Scott (2014).[10] The results for Ghana, Guatemala, Iran, Tanzania, Tunisia, and the United States, are published in other peer-reviewed journals.[11] The *CEQ Assessments* for Armenia, Ethiopia, Georgia, Indonesia, Jordan, Russia, South Africa, and Sri Lanka appear in a World Bank volume edited by Inchauste and Lustig (2017).[12] The *CEQ Assessments* for Argentina (two points in time), Chile, China, Dominican Republic, El Salvador, Iran, Tunisia, and Uganda, as well as Brazil (by ethnicity and race) and Ghana and Tanzania (comparing the impacts of policy reforms) are chapters in this Volume.[13] Studies for the remaining countries are available in the Publications at www.commitmentoequity.org,[14] and/or the results are in the CEQ Data

---

a paper but were not included in the CEQ Data Center. The converse is also true: there are some countries for which there is data in the CEQ Standard Indicators but there is no paper (e.g., India).

[10] Lustig, Pessino, and Scott (2014). Argentina: Lustig and Pessino (2014); Bolivia: Paz Arauco and others (2014); Brazil: Higgins and Pereira (2014); Mexico: Scott (2014); Peru: Jaramillo (2014); Uruguay: Bucheli and others (2014).

[11] Ghana: Younger, Osei-Assibey, and Oppong (2017); Guatemala: Cabrera, Lustig, and Moran (2015); Tanzania: Younger, Myamba, and Mdadila (2016); United States: Higgins and others (2016).

[12] Inchauste and Lustig (2017). Armenia: Younger and Khachatryan (2017); Ethiopia: Hill and others (2017); Georgia: Cancho and Bondarenko (2017); Indonesia: Jellema, Wai-Poi, and Afkar (2017); Jordan: Alam, Inchauste, and Serajuddin (2017); Russia: Lopez-Calva and others (2017); South Africa: Inchauste and others (2017); and Sri Lanka: Arunatilake, Inchauste, and Lustig (2017).

[13] Argentina: Rossignolo (2022) (chapter 11) and Lopez del Valle and others (2022) (chapter 21); Chile: Martinez-Aguilar and others (2022) (chapter 13); China: Lustig and Wang (2022) (chapter 20); Dominican Republic: Aristy-Escuder and others (2022) (chapter 14); El Salvador: Beneke de Sanfeliu, Lustig, and Oliva Cepeda (2022) (chapter 15); Iran: Enami, Lustig, and Taqdiri (2019) (chapter 17); Tunisia: Jouini and others (2022) (chapter 18); and Uganda: Jellema and others (2022) (chapter 19).

[14] Albania: Davalos et.al (2018); Belarus: Bornukova, Shymanovich, and Chubrik. (2017); Bolivia: Paz Arauco and others (2014); Botswana: International Monetary Fund: African Department

Center.[15] There are also several multi-country studies that illustrate the powerful insights one obtains when comparing the redistributive effort across countries (see, for example, chapter 10 in this Volume; Lustig, 2022).[16]

4 Main Messages

There are two main messages from Volume 1's part I on Methodology. First, analyzing the tax and spending sides simultaneously is not only desirable but necessary. Taxes can be unequalizing, but the impact of government spending so equalizing that the unequalizing effect of taxes is more than compensated for (chapter 2). Taxes can be regressive, but when combined with transfers make the system more equalizing than without the regressive taxes (chapters 2 and 3).[17] Second, to assess the impact of the fiscal system on people's standard of living, it is crucial to measure the effect of taxation and spending not only on inequality but also on poverty: the net fiscal system can be equalizing but impoverishing (chapter 4). Transfers can be equalizing, but when combined with taxes, postfiscal poverty can be higher than prefiscal poverty.[18]

Part III on Applications of the CEQ framework includes a summary of results for a sample of twenty-nine low and middle-income countries around the world

---

(2018); Brazil: Higgins and Pereira (2014); Burkina Faso: World Bank (2018); Comoros: Belghith et.al (2018); Costa Rica: Sauma and Trejos (2014); Croatia: Inchauste and Rubil (2017); Ecuador: Llerena et.al (2015); Egypt: Ibarra and others (2019); eSwatini: International Monetary Fund: African Department (2020); Guinea: Batana et.al (2019); Honduras: Icefi (2017a); Kenya: Pape Utz and Lange (2018); Lesotho: Houts and Massara (2020); Mali: Hounsa, Coulibaly, and Sanoh (2019); Mexico (2012): Scott and others (2012); Mexico (2014): Scott and others (2014); Mongolia: Freije-Rodriguez and Yang (2018); Namibia: Sulla et.al (2017); Nicaragua: ICEFI (2017b); Niger: Hounsa, Coulibaly, and Sanoh (2019); Paraguay: Gimenez et.al (2017); Poland: Goraus and Inchauste (2016); Romania: Inchauste and Militaru (2018); Spain: Gomez Bengoechea and Quan (2020); Tajikistan: Dalmacio et.al. (2021); Turkey: Cuevas, Lucchetti and Nebiler (2020); Ukraine: Bornukova, Leshchenko, and Matytsin (2019); Zambia: International Monetary Fund: African Department (2017).

[15] Colombia: Melendez and Martinez (2015); El Salvador: Oliva (2020a, 2020b, 2020c); India: Khundu and Cabrera (2020); Mexico: Scott (2020a, 2020ba); Togo: Jellema and Tassot (2020); Venezuela: Molina (2016); Panama (2016): Martinez-Aguilar (2019).

[16] Birdsall, Lustig, and Meyer (2014); Higgins and Lustig (2016) (reproduced in chapter 4 of Volume 1 of this Handbook); Inchauste and Lustig (2017); Lustig (2015, 2016a, 2016b, 2017a, 2017b, 2022). Also, see the dozens of CEQ Working Papers available at www.commitmentoequity.org.

[17] This result is known as the Lambert's conundrum (Lambert, 2001) and will be extensively discussed in chapters 2 (Enami, Lustig, and Aranda,2022) and 3 (Enami, 2022a).

[18] In this context, it is important to note that the typical indicators of poverty such as the headcount ratio, poverty gap ratio, or the squared poverty gap ratio (and any other) may show a reduction in postfiscal poverty even if a number of poor people have been made worse off by the fiscal system. This is formally proved in chapter 4, which reproduces Higgins and Lustig (2016).

(chapter 10).[19] The results show that fiscal systems are always equalizing but the extent of redistribution is quite heterogeneous. In contrast, fiscal systems are not always poverty reducing. In fact, fiscal policy is impoverishing more frequently than one would have thought, especially if one focuses on the "cash portion" of the fiscal system (direct taxes, direct transfers, indirect taxes, and indirect subsidies). In Armenia, Bolivia, Ethiopia, Ghana, Guatemala, Honduras, Nicaragua, Sri Lanka, Tanzania, and Uganda fiscal policy *increases* the incidence of poverty (even extreme poverty in some of the cases), meaning that a significant number of the market income poor (non-poor) are made poorer (poor) by taxes and transfers (chapters 4 and 10).[20] This startling result is primarily the consequence of high consumption taxes on basic goods.

Direct taxes and direct transfers are always equalizing. The impact of net indirect taxes (indirect taxes minus indirect subsidies) is equalizing in nineteen countries out of the twenty-nine low- and middle-income countries analyzed in chapter 10. Government spending on education and health is always equalizing, and its contribution to the reduction in inequality is rather large. This result is not surprising given that the use of government services is monetized at a value equal to average government cost. While the results concerning the distribution of the benefits of in-kind services in education and health are encouraging from the equity point of view, it is important to note that they may be due to factors one would prefer to avoid. The more intensive use of services in education and health on the part of the poorer portions of the population, for example, may be caused by the fact that, in their quest for quality, the middle classes (and, of course, the rich) chose to use private providers. This situation leaves the poor with access to second-rate services. In addition, if the middle classes opt out of public services, they may be much more reluctant to pay the taxes needed to improve both the coverage and quality of services than they would be if services were used universally.

There are two main lessons for policymakers that emerge from the analysis. First, the fact that specific fiscal interventions can have countervailing effects underscores the importance of taking a coordinated view of both taxation and spending rather than pursuing a piecemeal policy reform. Efficient regressive taxes (such as the value added tax), when combined with generous well-targeted transfers, can result in a net fiscal system that is equalizing and poverty-reducing. Second, governments should design their tax and transfers system so that the after taxes and transfers incomes (or consumption) of the poor are not lower than their incomes (or consumption) before fiscal interventions. If the policy community is seriously committed to eradicating income/

---

[19] The twenty-nine low- and middle-income countries are Argentina, Armenia, Bolivia, Brazil, Chile, Colombia, Costa Rica, Dominican Republic, Ecuador, El Salvador, Ethiopia, Georgia, Ghana, Guatemala, Honduras, Indonesia, Iran, Jordan, Mexico, Nicaragua, Peru, Russia, South Africa, Sri Lanka, Tanzania, Tunisia, Uganda, Uruguay, and Venezuela. These countries represent about a fifth of the world's extreme poor population and a sixth of total population.

[20] Higgins and Lustig (2016) (reproduced in chapter 4 in Volume 1); Lustig (2022) (chapter 10 in Volume 1).

consumption poverty, governments will need to explore ways to redesign taxation and transfers so that the poor do not end up as net payers.

5 Organization of Volume 1

As stated above, Volume 1 has six parts. Part I ("Methodology") describes what a *CEQ Assessment* is and presents the theoretical underpinnings of fiscal incidence analysis and the indicators used to assess the distributive impact and effectiveness of fiscal policy. Part II ("Implementation") presents the methodology on how taxes, subsidies, and social spending should be allocated. It includes a step-by step guide to completing the *CEQ Master Workbook*, a multi-sheet Excel file that houses detailed information on the country's fiscal system and the results used as inputs for policy discussions, academic papers, and policy reports. Part III ("Applications") presents applications of the CEQ framework to low- and middle-income countries and includes simulations of policy reforms. Part IV ("The *CEQ Assessment* Tools"), available online only, contains the *CEQ Master Workbook* (CEQ Institute, 2022) and the *CEQ Stata Package* with user-written software to complete it. It also contains a completed Master Workbook and "do files" for Ghana and Mexico as examples. In addition, this part features guidelines for the implementation of *CEQ Assessments*, including a thorough protocol of quality control. Part V includes all the components of the CEQ Data Center on Fiscal Redistribution.[21] Part VI contains the CEQ Institute's microsimulation tools.

Part I, on methodology used in the *CEQ Assessment*, has five chapters. Chapter 1 by Nora Lustig and Sean Higgins (2022) presents key analytical insights in fiscal redistribution theory. The chapter also discusses the basics of fiscal incidence analysis used in *CEQ Assessments*. The *CEQ Assessments* rely on the fiscal incidence method known as the "accounting approach" because it ignores behavioral responses and general equilibrium effects. Because pensions frequently tend to be a combination of deferred income and government transfer, there is a section dedicated to how contributory pensions should be considered in fiscal incidence analysis. Finally, the chapter describes the set of indicators used to answer the four key questions outlined above and illustrates with examples from existing *CEQ Assessments*.

For the interested reader, the formulation of the mathematical conditions for the net fiscal system to be equalizing in the case of multiple fiscal interventions and in the absence of reranking is presented in chapter 2 by Ali Enami, Nora Lustig, and Rodrigo Aranda. Chapter 2 also derives the conditions that must prevail for a particular tax or transfer to be equalizing and shows that in the world of multiple interventions, some of these conditions defy our preconceptions and intuition.

The conditions derived in chapter 2 assume no reranking: that is, households occupy the same place in the ranking from poorest to richest with prefiscal and with postfiscal income; individuals do not change their position in the postfiscal income

---

[21] https://commitmentoequity.org/datacenter/.

ordering. In other words, the poorest individual in the prefiscal income scale will continue to be the poorest individual in the postfiscal income scale, the second poorest individual in the prefiscal income scale will continue to be the second poorest individual in the postfiscal income scale, and so on, all the way up to the richest individual. Chapter 3 by Ali Enami (2022a) discusses how the conditions derived in chapter 2 change in the presence of reranking.

A fundamental question in the policy discussion is whether a particular fiscal intervention (or a particular combination of them) is equalizing or unequalizing. In a world with a single fiscal intervention (and no reranking), it is sufficient to know whether a particular intervention is progressive or regressive to give an unambiguous response using the typical indicators of progressivity such as the Kakwani index.[22] Chapter 2 demonstrates, however, that in a world with more than one fiscal intervention (even in the absence of reranking), this one-to-one relationship between the progressivity of a particular intervention and its effect on inequality breaks down. For instance, depending on certain characteristics of the fiscal system, a tax that is regressive based on any typical indicator can exert an equalizing force over and above that which would prevail in the absence of that regressive tax.

As shown in chapter 3, reranking, which is practically universal in real-life fiscal systems, *destroys* (as a mathematical truth, that is) the public finance dictum that

> if the combined redistributive impact of tax and spending is progressive then the higher the level of tax and spending in a country the larger is the redistributive impact. Similarly, for a given level of tax and spending, the more revenue collection is concentrated in more redistributive taxes (progressive income taxes) and the more spending is concentrated in more redistributive transfers (well targeted social transfers), the greater the redistributive impact of fiscal policy. (Bastagli, Coady, and Gupta, 2015, p. 57)

If there is reranking, in order to determine whether a fiscal system, a particular tax or transfer, or a particular policy change is inequality-increasing or inequality-reducing— and by how much—one must resort to numerical calculations. In particular, one must calculate the inequality indicator that would prevail with and without the specific intervention or policy change.

Chapter 4 by Sean Higgins and Nora Lustig is a reproduction of a 2016 article published in the *Journal of Development Economics*. The article shows how the typical measures of poverty, horizontal equity, and progressivity can fail to capture an important characteristic that, unfortunately, a rather large number of fiscal systems have:

---

[22] The Kakwani index for taxes is defined as the difference between the concentration coefficient of the tax and the Gini for market income. For transfers, it is defined as the difference between the Gini for market income and the concentration coefficient of the transfer. See, for example, Kakwani (1977).

namely, that a substantial proportion of the poor are made poorer (or non-poor made poor) by the tax and transfer system. The chapter axiomatically derives a measure of this phenomenon, which the authors call "fiscal impoverishment." They illustrate with specific examples how in countries in which the fiscal system is poverty-reducing and equalizing, a significant number of the poor pay more in taxes than they receive in transfers. The chapter also derives an analogous measure of fiscal gains to the poor and shows that changes in the poverty gap can be decomposed in the two axiomatic measures of fiscal impoverishment and fiscal gains to the poor.

Chapter 5 by Ali Enami (2022b) introduces the new CEQ Effectiveness indicators. The chapter begins by discussing the shortcomings of the old CEQ Effectiveness indicators. Then it proceeds to introduce the new indicators known as the Impact and Spending Effectiveness indicators. A variation of the former indicator, known as the FI-FGP Effectiveness indicator, is also introduced; it is specific to the measurement of the performance of a fiscal system (or its components) in reducing poverty and uses the two concepts of Fiscal Impoverishment and Fiscal Gain to the Poor introduced in chapter 4. In all indicators, the observed performance of a tax or transfer is compared to its maximum potential. The Impact Effectiveness indicator holds the monetary size of a tax or transfer constant and asks how much more reduction in inequality or poverty could be theoretically achieved if the tax or transfer is allocated in the most mathematically optimum way (given the inequality or poverty indicator of choice). The Spending Effectiveness indicator holds the effect of a tax or transfer on inequality or poverty constant and asks what is the minimum amount of tax or transfer that can achieve the same effect (again, using the most mathematically optimum way of allocating the tax or transfer).

Part II, on implementing the *CEQ Assessment*, has four chapters. Chapter 6 by Ali Enami, Sean Higgins, and Nora Lustig presents a step-by-step guide to applying the incidence analysis used to prepare *CEQ Assessments*. The chapter (a) defines the core income concepts before and after taxes, transfers, and subsidies, (b) discusses the methodological assumptions used to construct them, (c) explains how taxes, transfers, and subsidies should be allocated at the household level, and (d) suggests what to do when information on who paid certain taxes and/or received certain transfers, or how much they paid or received, is not included in the household survey.

Chapter 7 by Jon Jellema and Gabriela Inchauste (2022) presents a step-by-step guide to constructing the Consumable Income concept[23] when one takes into account not only the direct but also the indirect effect (through input prices) of indirect taxes and subsidies. The chapter reviews a "price-shifting" model for estimating the magnitude of the indirect effects of indirect taxes and subsidies and demonstrates how to use an input-output matrix together with a household expenditure survey to allocate the indirect burden across households.

---

[23] "Consumable income" is the concept and the name used in Canada's Social Policy Simulation Database Model (SPSD/M), one of the main sources used to produce the distribution of household income accounts and evaluate the impact of changes in tax and spending policies.

Chapter 8 by Sean Higgins and Caterina Brest Lopez (2022) presents the results and indicators used in a *CEQ Assessment* and describes in great detail how indicators (such as prefiscal inequality and poverty, concentration coefficients, incidence curves, and so on) and results can be produced and automatically exported to the relevant sections of the *CEQ Master Workbook* using the *CEQ Stata Package*. In particular, this chapter describes how to calculate the (marginal) contribution of a particular tax or transfer (or any combination of them) to the reduction in inequality and poverty, as discussed in chapters 1, 2, and 3. It also describes how to calculate the suite of CEQ effectiveness and efficiency indicators proposed by Ali Enami in chapter 5. The ensemble of CEQ indicators is calculated by the commands of the *CEQ Stata Package* and automatically exported to the results sections (sections E, "Output Tables," and D, "Summary of Results") of the *CEQ Master Workbook*, described below.

The CEQ analysis provides researchers with a comprehensive and comparable set of indicators to determine the impacts of fiscal intervention on poverty and inequality. However, inequality may take many different forms beyond the income dimension. Race, gender, location, and parental characteristics can have important implications for the economic and social outcomes of individuals. In an effort to determine if government fiscal interventions are exacerbating or reducing ethno-racial inequalities in Latin America, the Inter-American Development Bank (IDB) partnered with the CEQ Institute to finance the adoption of the CEQ analysis to explore the impacts of fiscal policies on ethno-racial inequality in the Latin America and Caribbean region (LAC). Chapter 9 by Rodrigo Aranda and Adam Ratzlaff (2022) describes what measures should be used to determine the impact of fiscal policy on indicators of ethno-racial inequality, as well as how the indicators and results can be produced and exported to the *CEQ Master Workbook* using corresponding instructions in the *CEQ Stata Package*. Lustig, Morrison, and Ratzlaff (2019) present results for a set of Latin American countries.

Part III, which includes applications of the *CEQ Assessment*, has twelve chapters with country and cross-country studies in which the CEQ methodology has been applied. In chapter 10, Nora Lustig presents comparative results for twenty-nine low- and middle-income countries and the United States. Chapters 11 through 15 and chapters 18 through 21 present *CEQ Assessments* for Argentina (Dario Rossignolo, 2022), Brazil by race (Claudiney Pereira, 2022), Chile (Sandra Martinez-Aguilar, Alan Fuchs, Eduardo Ortiz-Juarez, and Giselle Del Carmen, 2022), Dominican Republic (Jaime Aristy-Escuder, Maynor Cabrera, Blanca Moreno-Dodson, and Miguel E. Sanchez-Martin, 2022), El Salvador (Margarita Beneke de Sanfeliu, Nora Lustig, and Jose Andres Oliva Cepeda, 2022), Tunisia (Nizar Jouini, Nora Lustig, Ahmed Moummi, and Abebe Shimeles, 2022), Uganda (Jon Jellema, Astrid Haas, Nora Lustig, and Sebastian Wolf, 2022), China (Nora Lustig and Yang Wang, 2022), and an updated and comprehensive assessment for Argentina (Juan Cruz Lopez Del Valle, Caterina Brest Lopez, Joaquin Campabadal, Julieta Ladronis, Nora Lustig, Valentina Martinez Pabon, and Mariano Tommasi, 2022). Stephen D. Younger shows how the CEQ framework can be used to simulate policy reforms with an application to Ghana and Tanzania in chapter 16. In chapter 17, Ali Enami, Nora Lustig, and Alireza Taqdiri (2019) apply the new effectiveness indicators described in chapter 5 to Iran. Except for the new chapters 20 and 21, and the published version of chapter 17, the rest of the chapters in part III are identical to the versions published in the first edition of the Handbook in 2018. It is important to note that in addition to the applications included in this Volume of the Handbook, there are many more country-based and cross-country analyses in the CEQ Working Paper series.

Part IV, "The *CEQ Assessment* Tools," includes ten items: (1) Planning for a *CEQ Assessment*: Data and Software Requirements. (2) Planning for a *CEQ Assessment*: Recommended Team Composition and Timeline. (3) *CEQ Assessment: CEQ Master Workbook (MWB)*, details follow. (4) *CEQ Master Workbook*: Examples, Ghana 2012 (consumption-based) and Mexico 2012 (income-based). (5) CEQ Do Files in Stata for Constructing Income Concepts: Examples, Ghana 2012 (consumption-based) and Mexico 2012 (income-based). (6) *CEQ Stata Package* and Do Files to Run It, details follow. (7) *CEQ Assessment*: Sample Stata Code for Measuring the Indirect Effects of Indirect Taxes and Subsidies, which shows sample software to construct the so-called Consumable Income concept (described in chapter 1) incorporating the indirect effects of indirect taxes and subsidies. (8) *CEQ Assessment: Constructing the CEQ Harmonized Microdata,* which provides guidelines on how to organize the fiscal incidence database in a manner that facilitates the running of the *CEQ Stata Package*; the instructions also are used to generate a harmonized database to enable granular comparison across countries and implement changes in allocation assumptions and policy changes. (9) *CEQ Assessment*: Checking Protocol, a detailed checking protocol to ensure that results are as free as possible of egregious mistakes. (10) CEQ Training Tools, which includes videos and PowerPoint presentations used in training workshops.

The *CEQ Master Workbook (MWB)* (in the online-only part IV of this Volume; CEQ Institute, 2022) is a multi-sheet Excel file that houses country-background information, description of the microdata, budgetary data, and description of the fiscal system, methodology, and the results of the fiscal incidence analysis as well as the full set of indicators used as inputs for policy discussions, academic papers, and policy reports. The *CEQ MWB* consists of six sections: section A, "Country Context"; section B, "Data"; section C, "Methodology"; section D, "Summary of Results"; section E, "Output Tables"; and section F, "Results by Ethnicity and Race."

Sections A, B, and C are meant to be filled by the *CEQ Assessment's* team. Section A, "Country Context," contains information on the macroeconomic, political, and socioeconomic context, as well as the evolution of inequality and poverty over time. It also includes information on whether the country experienced a natural disaster, civil strife, or a financial crisis, and whether there was an election or any other special situation that could have affected fiscal policy in the year of the analysis. Section B, "Data," includes a description of the microdata and the fiscal data utilized in the fiscal incidence analysis. For the microdata, section B includes a detailed description of the survey(s) being used to conduct the analysis, such as sample size, coverage, and questionnaire, including, for example, the exact survey questions used to construct each component of the income concepts. In the fiscal data section, the team needs to compile the budget information from administrative registries and summarize the characteristics of the fiscal interventions (such as direct taxes, consumption taxes, excise taxes, cash transfers, subsidies, and in-kind transfers) that will be included in the analysis. Section C, "Methodology," presents the methodology followed to construct the income concepts and key assumptions made in the allocation process, and compares survey-based totals with those from administrative registries for validation purposes.

The instructions on how to complete sections A, B, and C are included in chapter 6. If the incidence analysis includes the indirect effects of indirect taxes and subsidies, the instructions on how to complete section C are in chapter 7. The order of the sections has been chosen having the *user* (rather than the producer) of the *CEQ Assessment* in mind. Producers of a *CEQ Assessment* should start with section B, the data and information required to implement an assessment and may wish to complete section A at the end.

Section E of the *CEQ MWB* contains the ensemble of indicators used in *CEQ Assessments*, described in chapter 1 and in more detail in chapter 8. Section D presents the results in a user-friendly manner to be used both in policy dialogues and in scholarly research. Section E is automatically populated by the commands in the *CEQ Stata Package* described below. Section D, in turn, is automatically populated with information from section E through "linking" commands embedded in the *CEQ MWB*. The linking commands import information from section E and paste it in the relevant cells in section D. Section F of the *CEQ MWB* includes the indicators of the CEQ analysis by ethnicity or race and is also automatically populated by the commands in the *CEQ Stata Package* whenever the researcher has generated the prefiscal and postfiscal income concepts by ethnicity and/or race.

The *CEQ Stata Package* contains user-written software that automates the process of producing and uploading CEQ results in sections E and F of the *CEQ MWB* and ensures the quality of these estimates. The *CEQ Stata Package* greatly enhances the reproducibility and scalability of *CEQ Assessments* because it helps produce results for additional countries or years more quickly and less expensively. In addition, it will greatly reduce the marginal cost of robustness checks testing the sensitivity of one's results to various assumptions. The *CEQ Stata Package* is accompanied by a set of do files to run it. Before running the *CEQ Stata Package*, the user should read the *Constructing the CEQ Harmonized Microdata* document (also found in part IV) to make appropriate use of the software. This step is important because the *CEQ Stata Package* assumes that variables are named in a particular way. If variables are not written in a way that is consistent with the *CEQ Stata Package*, the researcher may run into difficulties while trying to run it.

Part V, the CEQ Data Center on Fiscal Redistribution, is an information and monitoring system where results are presented at increasing levels of detail. It includes a collection of spreadsheets containing the summary indicators required to assess the redistributive impact of fiscal policy, known as the CEQ Standard Indicators. This information is periodically updated to reflect new data points and indicators. The CEQ Data Visualization draws from the summary indicators and includes interactive graphs using state-of-the-art data visualization techniques. This tool also includes Country Profile pages that highlight inequality, poverty, and net payer/net beneficiary indicators for every country assessed to date. The Data Center includes the CEQ-based indicators incorporated as targets of the Sustainable Development Goals. Data Center information may be disaggregated by gender, race, ethnicity, and other categories. The site also includes the completed CEQ Master Workbooks, which are multi-sheet spreadsheet "books" that store detailed fiscal system information and the calculated fiscal incidence indicators for assessed countries. Both the Standard Indicators and Master Workbooks are publicly available for download directly from the website. The CEQ Harmonized Microdata—with prefiscal and postfiscal incomes and all fiscal interventions at the household level for each country—is published in the CEQ Dataverse on Harvard Dataverse. It is available through open access but only for those countries that allow access to this data. The Data Center also includes the CEQ Data Center Metadata Table, a key metadata document with detailed information about the data availability and allocation methods and assumptions used for each assessment, organized by country, year, and study. Finally, the CEQ Data Center features the do files in the construction of income concepts of the assessed countries as well as replication codes used to explore methodological frontiers such as alternative methods to value in-kind transfers, correction methods for underreporting and undercoverage of top incomes, gender disaggregated analysis, and fiscal policy and multidimensional poverty.

Part VI features the CEQ microsimulation tools. The CEQ Fiscal Policy Simulator is an Excel-based tool used to simulate the impact in taxes and transfers on incomes by decile as a "desktop" option—that is, without having to go back to the microdata. The CEQ Markdown Statistical Code for Microsimulating the Short-Run Impact of COVID-19 on Inequality and Poverty can be used to replicate the analysis of the economic shock caused by COVID (or other systemic shocks with similar characteristics) on living standards in different settings. Finally, the CEQ Statistical Code for Microsimulating the Long-Run Impact of COVID-19 on Human Capital and Intergenerational Mobility can be used to assess the impact of school closures on the intergenerational persistence of education and inequality dynamics in the future.

6 Implementing a *CEQ Assessment*: How to Use Volume 1

For those interested in implementing a *CEQ Assessment* (the fiscal incidence study that uses the Commitment to Equity methodological framework), **the recommendation is to read chapter 1 (methodological basics; chapter 6 (how to allocate taxes and transfer to construct the income concepts); and, chapter 8 (description of indicators to analyze results). If the researcher plans to include the indirect effects of**

indirect taxes and subsidies in the fiscal incidence analysis, chapter 7 should be consulted in tandem with chapter 6. Be sure to read **the updated** chapter 6 included in the 2nd edition, since some of the methodological recommendations were subject to change. We have also eliminated some inaccuracies and sharpened the definitions of income concepts.

To produce a *CEQ Assessment*, one must have access to a recent household survey, disaggregated government budget data on revenues and expenditures, and a detailed description of the characteristics of fiscal policy instruments that will be included in the analysis. For more information, see section 7 below and chapter 6 in this Volume. The user-written software (commonly known as "ado files") required to produce all the results was written in Stata.[24]

After reading the above, it is advisable to follow these steps:

Step 1: Getting Ready

- Read chapter 1. (*Note*: if you are interested in the mathematical derivations of results discussed in chapter 1, read chapters 2, 3, and 4.)
- Obtain a recent household survey following the data requirements explained in section 7 of chapter 1 and prepare it for use.
- Open the *CEQ MWB* (in part IV, available online only) and complete sheet B3 of the *CEQ Master Workbook* (government revenues and spending from administrative accounts).

Step 2: Constructing the Income Concepts and Completing Sections B and C of the CEQ Master Workbook

- Read chapter 6. Recall that in the 2nd edition this chapter introduces some significant changes in the methodological recommendations.
- Open the *CEQ MWB* and fill out the rest of section B.
- To facilitate the use of the *CEQ Stata Package* described in Step 3, read the document *Constructing the CEQ Harmonized Microdata* included in part IV of this Volume (online only). This step is important because the *CEQ Stata Package* assumes that variables are named in a particular way. If variables are not written in a way that is consistent with the *CEQ Stata Package*, the researcher may run into difficulties while trying to run it.
- Write the code to allocate taxes and transfers to each household and construct the income concepts for both the PDI and PGT scenarios. Based on the information included in the primary household survey (and, whenever applicable, in the complementary surveys), as well as on the detailed description of the fiscal system, choose the allocation methods that you will use to allocate taxes and transfers to each household.
- If you are using an input-output table to estimate the indirect effects of indirect taxes and subsidies, read chapter 7 in this Volume and use the sample software in part IV.

---

[24] To take advantage of the automatic features included in the *CEQ Stata Package*, Stata 14 or a newer version is required.

- Complete the construction of income concepts and fill out section C of *CEQ MWB*.
- Compare totals and structure (for example, the ratio of total personal income tax to total disposable income [or private consumption if you do not have income in your survey]) from administrative accounts and those that emerge from your calculations using the household survey. This is done using the information that you input in sheet C1 in the *CEQ MWB*. It will show you how your "economy" differs when you use administrative versus survey-based data (see details in chapter 6).

    (*Note*: This step is probably the most time-consuming of all both because obtaining budget data can be quite challenging and because constructing the income concepts requires making many thoughtful decisions on how to allocate taxes and transfers to individual households.)

Step 3: Producing Results
- Read chapter 8.
- Install the *CEQ Stata Package*. To install it, include the following Stata code in a .do file or enter it into Stata's command prompt:

    ```
    update all
    ssc install ceq, replace
    ```
- Fill out section E of the *CEQ MWB* using the *CEQ Stata Package* and the .do files to run it.
- Remember that you will need to create two sets of section E: one for the scenario in which contributory pensions are considered deferred income (PDI) and one for the scenario in which contributory pensions are considered government transfers (PGT). You need two sets of E sheets because the following income concepts are different for each scenario: Market Income, Market Income plus Pensions, Net Market Income, and Gross Income. Disposable Income, Consumable Income, and Final Income are the same in both. For details, see chapter 6, and figure 6-2 and table 6-5.
- Follow the linking instructions to automatically populate section D. To populate the D section see the general linking Instructions that appear on the sheet called "Linking" in the D section of the *CEQ MWB* and follow the detailed instructions in the "Instructions Linking" document in part IV of this Volume. Like everything else, you can download this document from www.ceqinstitute.org and clicking on the Handbook tab. When completing the linking with section D, two sets of section D sheets will be created, one for each scenario.
- As mentioned in chapter 6, if the pension system had a deficit in the year of the survey, one can generate a third scenario (in addition to PDI and PGT), in which contributory pensions are partially a transfer (the amount of the deficit). If you choose to estimate this third scenario, this requires a separate run of the *CEQ Stata Package* commands and a separate set of sections E and D results.
- If you are testing the robustness of specific assumptions (see chapter 6), you will need to complete separate sets of sections E and D for each test. The ceqassump command

provides a preliminary way to check robustness on the main *CEQ Assessment* results without producing sections E and D in their entirety.

- If you are using an input-output table to estimate the indirect effects of indirect taxes and subsidies, use the sample software in part IV.
- If you are planning to produce a *CEQ Assessment* by ethnic or racial group (or by rural-urban or other regional breakdown), read chapter 9 and fill out section F of the *CEQ MWB* using the *CEQ Stata Package.*
- If you are planning to correct your data for undercoverage and underreporting (especially in the upper tail), you should run the *CEQ* Stata Package with the corrected income concepts and present results separately in sections E and D of a new MWB. This way you will still be able to compare your uncorrected results with the existing ones for other countries.

Step 4: Checking Results
- Complete section A of the *CEQ MWB*; you will use some of the information (e.g., inequality and poverty trends from existing sources) to check the accuracy of the CEQ results.
- Using the *Checking Protocol* in part IV as a guide, do a thorough quality control.
- We highly recommend that consult with other experts if your results appear sensible.
- You should not use or publish results until the checking process is completed. Experience shows that errors are not uncommon the first time around.

Step 5: Presenting Results
- To present results, see the chapters with applications of CEQ in part III as well as the chapters in Inchauste and Lustig (2017) and the working papers published by the CEQ Institute more generally.
- You may find it useful to compare your country's results with others from the same region or with similar GDP per capita. The Standard Indicators in the CEQ Data Center on Fiscal Redistribution can be used for this purpose.

7 *CEQ Assessment:* **Data Requirements**

A *CEQ Assessment* requires a household income survey and expenditure (HIES), a household income (employment) survey, or a household budget survey (HBS), and a (preferably audited) confirmed national budget (of the same year as the HIES).

More specifically, it requires the following:

1. Recent household survey (possible options: income, income-expenditure, expenditure, employment, LSMS, etc.) representative at the national level
   - The household roster and the expenditures module—hopefully in raw or semi-cleaned, item-by-item form—are necessities.

- The health and education modules are somewhere in between necessary and very desirable. (When health and/or education are not covered in the HIES, we would appreciate having a reference to a secondary survey that does capture utilization of those services, such as the Demographic and Health Surveys.).
- The remaining modules are often useful—we can determine taxpayer status from other questions in the labor module, for example—and if they are available, we would definitely like to have them.
- If there are any official (or even just generally accepted) practices/methods for calculating household expenditures, household size, per-adult equivalent scales, and the national poverty line, it is important to know them.

2. Detailed description of each tax and spending item to be included in the analysis
3. Audited or confirmed budget and administrative data for year of the survey (see also chapter 6 in this Volume):

3a. Revenues:
- Personal income and payroll tax revenues and, if available, number of individuals and/or households who pay them.
- Corporate income tax revenues.
- Other income tax revenues.
- Indirect tax revenues disaggregated by type and product (VAT, excise, customs, etc.) as well as by taxable base (In the best-case scenario we would get official estimates of the magnitude/sales value of the taxable base for each tax as well.).
- Non–tax revenues.
- Social security contributions and expenditures broken down by type (national health insurance, national pension, national unemployment insurance, etc.).
- If not included in social security contributions, contributory pension contributions.

3b. Expenditures:
- Expenditures and number of beneficiaries on direct transfers (cash or near-cash) broken down by program; often this requires participation of the executing agency.
- Subsidy expenditures by good or service being subsidized.
- Public housing or subsidized housing expenditures and number of beneficiaries if available.
- Education expenditures *and* enrollment levels broken down by schooling level: preschool, primary, secondary, and tertiary (at least).
- Health expenditures; please provide whatever general breakdown of the spending is available. For example, spending on hospitals versus clinics, or spending on hospitalized patients versus outpatients, or spending on wages versus goods and services. We would be particularly interested in any information on co-pays or other payments from households required to access public health services.

Additionally, we would be interested in spending channeled through health insurance schemes, including the payments by households to participate in these schemes. Any spending of these areas occurring outside the general government can be described outside the table itself in the column for notes.

4. Most updated Input-output table, SAM (social accounting matrix), or SUT (supply and use table) available; beyond the information available in the country, the researcher may want to consult OECD (https://www.oecd.org/sti/ind/input-outputta bles.htm) and World Input-Output Database (https://www.rug.nl/ggdc/valuechain /wiod/).

8 About Volume 2: Methodological Frontiers in Fiscal Incidence Analysis

As mentioned above, in spite of the comprehensive methodology described in Volume 1, there is still important work to be done to sharpen the methods, broaden the scope of the analysis, and enhance the policy tools. Some of these topics are addressed in Volume 2, which includes a collection of chapters whose purpose is to expand the knowledge and methodological frontiers to sharpen the analysis of fiscal policy's redistributive impact even further. Topics include alternative approaches to value in-kind education and health services; alternative methods to evaluate spending on infrastructure; corporate taxes and taxation on capital incomes; intertemporal fiscal incidence and the redistributive consequences of social insurance pensions; fiscal redistribution, macroeconomic stability, and growth; and the political economy of fiscal redistribution.

In the current CEQ framework, and following conventions in the field, in-kind benefits from free government services in education and health are valued at the average cost of provision. Such an approach ignores the fact that the "true" value to consumers and the returns to investments in human capital may be quite different from what they cost the government due to, for example, poor quality and waste. In Volume 2, chapter 1, Jeremy Barofsky and Stephen Younger (2022) describe and compare three approaches to measuring the distributional consequences of government health spending: average cost of provision, willingness to pay, and health outcomes, and provide example applications for each of these methods using a national cross-section from Ghana for 2012/13. Sergei Soares (2022a; chapter 2) compares three methods for valuing education services and illustrates their distributive impact with data for Brazil. The methods are valuing educational services with the conventional cost of provision approach; valuing educational services using labor market outcomes as the measure of their worth; and matching private educational expenditures, paid for by students or their parents, with equivalent public education services, and then valuing the latter according to the price of the former. Sergio Urzua (2022; chapter 3) uses private returns to schooling to measure the incidence of spending on public education and incorporates behavioral responses to public subsidies regarding school enrollment. The author applies the proposed methodology to Chile and Ghana.

Our current method does not measure the incidence of investment in infrastructure such as water and sanitation, rural roads, large-scale projects, and so on. This is an important limitation because especially in low-income countries, a significant portion of the budget is allocated toward infrastructure. In chapter 4 in Volume 2, Sergei Soares (2022b) suggests using hedonic prices as a way to find the market value for public infrastructure such as piped water, garbage collection, piped gas, and sewerage. The author applies the methodology using data for Brazil for several years to impute rental values for owner occupied housing and the associated infrastructure services.

We do not include corporate taxes or taxes on capital income in our current framework. Ignoring the impact of corporate taxes is problematic because they represent an important share of government revenues. In Volume 2, Bernardo Candia and Eduardo Engel (2022; chapter 5) present a method for incorporating the incidence of corporate taxes and taxes on capital incomes more broadly by incorporating incomes accrued (but not received) in the taxpayers' corporations and companies in the definition of prefiscal income.

Given that contributory pensions are partly government transfers and partly deferred incomes, the current approach recommends producing results for two "extreme" scenarios: all contributory pensions are deferred income (Pensions as Deferred Income, or PDI), and all contributory pensions are pure government transfers (Pensions as Government Transfers, or PGT). Ideally, one would like to know which scenario reflects actual situations more accurately. Carlos Grushka (2022; chapter 6 in Volume 2) proposes a method to determine the extent to which pensions are a government transfer or deferred income when only cross-section household surveys are available. The author applies the proposed approach using data for Argentina.

The current framework estimates the redistributive effect of taxes and transfers without assessing its sustainability from the macroeconomic, demographic, and natural capital perspectives. Without information on the sustainability of fiscal redistribution profiles, it is difficult to make comprehensive policy recommendations.[25] In Volume 2, Jose Maria Fanelli (2022; chapter 7) proposes a methodological framework to study the linkages between fiscal redistributions, fiscal sustainability, and the government's wealth constraint. Ramiro Albrieu and Jose Maria Fanelli (2022; chapter 8) apply it to Latin America.

The extent of fiscal redistribution depends on politics. Stefano Barbieri and Koray Caglayan (2022; chapter 9 in Volume 2) analyze the public provision of public goods and income redistribution in a median voter framework.

9   About the CEQ Institute

The CEQ Institute works to reduce inequality and poverty through comprehensive and rigorous tax and benefit incidence analysis, as well as active engagement with the

---

[25] See Fanelli (2018).

policy community. Building on the achievements of the CEQ project,[26] directed by Nora Lustig since 2008, the CEQ Institute was founded in May 2015 at Tulane University with Professor Lustig at its helm. The Institute has four main areas of work: (a) development of research methods and policy tools, (b) a data center, (c) advisory and training services, and (d) bridges to policy.

The four areas were chosen to fulfill the Institute's main goals:

1. To improve the methodological instruments, policy tools, and database to evaluate how consistent and effective revenue collection and spending practices are with global equity goals;
2. To establish an information system designed to monitor progress in fiscal redistributive efforts to achieve equity goals;
3. To mainstream the use of *CEQ Assessments* by reaching out to the policy community through partnerships, training programs, and policy forums;
4. To disseminate findings through an active communication and advocacy program undertaken in conjunction with key partners in the research, philanthropic, and social activist communities.

In October of 2015, the Bill & Melinda Gates Foundation awarded a five-year grant of $4.9 million to support the CEQ Institute in achieving its goals. This was followed by an award of $1.182 million in May of 2021 designed to measure fiscal equity in the post-COVID world. The CEQ Project had benefited from a previous grant from the Gates Foundation in the amount of $581,162. The three grants have been partially used to fund (among other components) in part the production of the two editions of this Handbook. The Institute has also received financial support from the Millennium Challenge Corporation, the National Science Foundation, and the United Nations Development Programme's Regional Bureau for Latin America and the Caribbean (UNDP/RBLAC).[27]

Tax and benefit incidence studies using the CEQ methodology have been completed in a wide array of low- and middle-income countries in all regions of the world. Results are published in the CEQ Working Paper series and the CEQ Data Center and are available at www.commitmentoequity.org. The Institute's studies have been published in leading peer-reviewed journals such as the *Journal of Development Economics*, the *Journal of Economic Inequality, Public Finance Review*, the *Review of Income*

---

[26] The CEQ project was first launched at the Inter-American Dialogue in Washington, DC, under the leadership of Nora Lustig. Since 2009 the project has been based at Tulane University. The Center for Global Development and the Inter-American Development Bank are partners of the initiative.

[27] During its early stages at the Inter-American Dialogue, the CEQ project received financial support from the Canadian International Development Agency (CIDA), the General Electric Foundation, and the Norwegian Ministry of Foreign Affairs.

and Wealth, and *World Development* as well as leading geographic area journals such as the *African Development Review, Economia* (for Latin America) and the *Middle East Development Journal.*

The indicators on the redistributive impact of fiscal policy are available in the CEQ Institute's Data Center on Fiscal Redistribution (at www.commitmentoequity.org). The CEQ Data Center on Fiscal Redistribution is an information and monitoring system where results of the fiscal incidence studies are presented at increasing levels of detail. Unless otherwise specified, the results were generated by the CEQ Institute and its collaborators applying the methodological framework described in this Handbook. The CEQ Data Center is described in detail in the section below.

Initially focused on Latin America, the Institute's geographic scope has grown continuously and, as of November 2021, it includes sixty countries (with a full set of Standard Indicators for fifty-eight of them) in Africa, Asia, the Americas, and Europe. Since there is more than one point in time for some countries, the coverage is for seventy-six country studies.

The fiscal incidence analyses are implemented in collaboration with local teams, and collaborators are invited to become nonresident research associates of the CEQ Institute. The studies are often produced in partnership with multilateral organizations such as (in alphabetical order) the Asian Development Bank (ADB), the African Development Bank (AfDB), the Inter-American Development Bank (IADB), the International Fund for Agricultural Development (IFAD), the International Monetary Fund (IMF), the Latin American Development Bank (CAF), the Organisation for Economic Co-operation and Development (OECD), the United Nations Development Programme (UNDP), UNICEF, and the World Bank; bilateral aid organizations such as the Agence Française de Développement (AFD) and the US Millennium Challenge Corporation (MCC); and other research and advocacy institutions such as (in alphabetical order) India's Centre for Budget and Governance Accountability (CBGA), El Salvador's FUSADES, the Middle East's Economic Research Forum, the Global Development Network (GDN), the UK's Institute of Fiscal Studies (IFS), Central America's ICEFI, OXFAM, the Paris School of Economics (PSE), Tanzania's REPAL, the University of Capetown, and the University of Ghana. The Institute has partnered with Latin American institutions to create Fiscal Equity Labs in Argentina (with the Center for the Study of Human Development in Universidad de San Andres), Brazil (Universidad Federal Fluminense), and Mexico (Public Policy Lab at the Center for Research and Teaching in Economics, CIDE).

The CEQ Institute research program has pushed the methodological frontier to develop effective tools for analysts, policymakers, and influencers working to enhance the equity of fiscal systems and has generated a series of important contributions. For example, the Institute's research has shown that typical progressivity indicators are not necessarily accurate in predicting whether a tax or a subsidy improves equity or not, a problem that can be avoided by using the marginal contribution indicator (Lustig and

Higgins, 2022) (chapter 1 in this Volume);[28] it has shown that treating contributory pensions as pure transfers can exaggerate the redistributive impact of fiscal systems and distort policy recommendations (chapter 1 in this Volume); it has demonstrated that standard poverty indicators can be misleading to the extent that fiscal system interventions impoverish the poor (Higgins and Lustig, 2016) (reproduced as chapter 4 in this Volume); and it has shown that typical indicators of effectiveness can produce the wrong conclusions and proposed new ones that yield consistent rankings of policy interventions (chapter 5 in this Volume).

In addition, the CEQ Institute continues to explore how to measure the incidence of in-kind benefits in education, health, and infrastructure; the indirect effects of indirect taxes and subsidies on inputs in the presence of informality; the impact of fiscal policy on multidimensional poverty; fiscal incidence that incorporates intra-household dynamics; correction methods for misreporting and undercoverage in the upper tail; measuring the redistributive impact of contributory pensions; incorporating the incidence of corporate taxes in the fiscal incidence exercise; microsimulation methods to nowcast impacts of systemic shocks; microsimulation methods to assess the effects of reforms on taxes and transfers; intertemporal fiscal incidence analysis (macro-sustainability, demographic transitions, and depletion of natural resources); political economy of fiscal redistribution; child-centered fiscal incidence analysis; and fiscal redistribution and different levels of government.

The CEQ methodology has been taken up by organizations working to improve fiscal equity around the world, including the World Bank, the Inter-American Development Bank (IADB) and the IMF. Such organizations are the most effective vehicle for advancing our theory of change because they reach the greatest number of countries, engage their governments directly, and have influence over those governments as a result of their roles. The Institute has also worked with the French Development Agency (AFD), the European Union, the Organization for Economic Co-operation and Development (OECD), Oxfam, UNICEF and others. The relevance of the Institute's work has been highlighted by the adoption of our "Redistributive Impact of Fiscal Policy" indicator by the United Nations (SDG 10.4.2) to monitor progress in the reduction of global inequality as part of the Sustainable Development Goals, specifically SDG 10, "Reduce Inequality within and among Countries." We also collaborated with Save the Children and UNICEF to develop a new and more precise indicator 1.b.1, which is

---

[28] The marginal contribution is used to measure whether taxes and transfers (at the aggregate category level or for specific interventions) are equalizing or unequalizing (and, poverty reducing or poverty increasing). For example, the marginal contribution of a VAT is calculated as the difference between the Gini coefficient without the VAT (but all the rest of taxes and transfers in place) and the Gini coefficient that includes the VAT. If this difference is positive (negative), the VAT exercises an equalizing (unequalizing) effect. For details see chapters 1 (Lustig and Higgins, 2022) and 8 (Higgins and Brest Lopez, 2022) in this Volume.

the main component for the ambitious SDG 1, "End Poverty in All It Its Forms Everywhere."

10 About the CEQ Data Center on Fiscal Redistribution

The CEQ Data Center on Fiscal Redistribution is an information and monitoring system in which results of the fiscal incidence studies are presented at increasing levels of detail. Unless otherwise specified, the results were generated by the CEQ Institute and its collaborators applying the methodological framework described in this Handbook.

The CEQ Data Center includes a collection of spreadsheets containing the summary indicators required to assess the redistributive impact of fiscal policy, known as the CEQ Standard Indicators. This information is periodically updated to reflect new data points and indicators. The CEQ Data Visualization draws from the summary indicators and includes interactive graphs using state-of-the-art data visualization techniques. This tool also includes Country Profiles pages that highlight inequality, poverty, and net payer/net beneficiary indicators for every country assessed to date. In addition, the Data Center includes the CEQ-based indicators incorporated as targets of the Sustainable Development Goals. For some countries, Data Center information is disaggregated by gender, race, ethnicity, and other categories.

The site also includes the completed CEQ Master Workbooks, which are multisheet spreadsheet "books" that store detailed fiscal system information and the calculated fiscal incidence indicators for assessed countries. Both the Standard Indicators and Master Workbooks are publicly available for download directly from the website. The CEQ Harmonized Microdata—with prefiscal and postfiscal incomes and all fiscal interventions at the household level for each country—is published in the CEQ Dataverse on Harvard Dataverse. It is available through open access but only for those countries that allow access to this data. The Data Center also includes the CEQ Data Center Metadata Table, a key metadata document with detailed information about the data availability and allocation methods and assumptions used for each assessment, organized by country, year, and study.

CEQ Standard Indicators

This is a database in spreadsheet format describing who bears the burden of various taxes and who benefits from transfer programs, subsidies, and public spending on health and education. Indicators include, among others. Gini Coefficient and Poverty Indicators before and after taxes and transfers, Incidence by Decile and Income Category, Marginal Contributions for each fiscal intervention, Indexes of Progressivity and Pro-Poorness, Indicators of Impact and Spending Effectiveness, and Key Assumptions. The indicators are described in chapters 1 (Lustig, 2022) and 8 (Higgins and Brest Lopez,

2022) in Volume 1 of the *CEQ Handbook*. The references and data sources for each study are listed in the last two sheets.

CEQ Master Workbook (MWB)

The *CEQ MWB* (in part IV of Volume 1 of this Handbook, available online; CEQ Institute, 2022) is a multi-sheet Excel file that houses country-background information, description of the microdata, budgetary data, and description of the fiscal system, methodology, and the results of the fiscal incidence analysis as well as the full set of indicators used as inputs for policy discussions, academic papers, and policy reports. The *CEQ MWB* consists of six sections: section A, Country Context; section B, Data; section C, Methodology; section D, Summary of Results; section E, Output Tables; and Section F, Compendium of Results by Ethnicity and Race. The contents of the *CEQ MWB* and how to generate them are described in chapters 5 (Enami 2022a), 6 (Enami, Higgins, and Lustig, 2022), 7 (Jellema and Inchauste, 2022) and 8 (Higgins and Brest Lopez), and part IV in Volume 1 of the *CEQ Handbook*.

CEQ Harmonized Data

The CEQ Harmonized Data is a dataset that contains microdata at the household/individual level with the income concepts (e.g., Market Income, Disposable Income, Consumable Income, and Final Income) and the fiscal policy components used to generate the income concepts (i.e., personal income taxes, cash transfers, value added taxes, and so on) from countries with non-binding intellectual property restrictions. While the fiscal components are made available with the detail suitable for each country, the Harmonized Microdata Data also combines them into categories that facilitate cross-country comparisons (e.g., direct taxes, cash transfers, indirect taxes, and so on). The Harmonized Microdata is published in the CEQ Dataverse on Harvard Dataverse with their respective metadata or read-me files. For a subset of countries, there are Extended Harmonized Microdata (EHM) which include additional variables such as a disaggregation of market income by source, labor market information, and/or use of financial services. The guidelines on how to generate the CEQ Harmonized Microdata are in Part IV of Volume 1 of the second edition of the CEQ Handbook.

CEQ Data Center Metadata Table

The CEQ Data Center Metadata Table is a metadata multi-sheet Excel file with detailed information about the data availability and allocation methods and assumptions used for each CEQ Assessment, organized by country, year, and study. For each country study, the Metadata Table includes name of partner institution (if applicable), data availability per country study and levels of disaggregation, basic information on household survey, year of PPP conversion factors, allocation method for each fiscal intervention, whether study includes the indirect effects of indirect taxes and transfers, and valuation methods used for health benefits.

References

Alam, Shamma A., Gabriela Inchauste, and Umar Serajuddin. 2017. "The Distributional Impact of Fiscal Policy in Jordan," in *The Distributional Impact of Taxes and Transfers: Evidence from Eight Low- and Middle-Income Countries*, edited by Gabriela Inchauste and Nora Lustig (Washington: World Bank).

Albrieu, Ramiro and Fanelli, Jose Maria. 2022. "Fiscal Redistribution, Sustainability, and Demography in Latin America" chap. 8 in *Commitment to Equity Handbook: Estimating the Impact of Fiscal Policy on Inequality and Poverty*, 2nd ed., Vol. 2, edited by Nora Lustig (Brookings Institution Press and CEQ Institute, Tulane University). Free online version available at www .commitmentoequity.org.

Aranda, Rodrigo, and Adam Ratzlaff. 2022. "Analyzing the Impact of Fiscal Policy on Ethno-Racial Inequality," chap. 9 in *Commitment to Equity Handbook: Estimating the Impact of Fiscal Policy on Inequality and Poverty*, 2nd ed., Vol. 1, edited by Nora Lustig (Brookings Institution Press and CEQ Institute, Tulane University). Free online version available at www.commitmentoequity.org.

Aristy-Escuder, Jaime, Maynor Cabrera, Blanca Moreno-Dodson, and Miguel E. Sanchez Martin. 2022. "The Dominican Republic: Fiscal Policy, Income Redistribution, and Poverty Reduction," chap. 14 in *Commitment to Equity Handbook: Estimating the Impact of Fiscal Policy on Inequality and Poverty*, 2nd ed., Vol. 1, edited by Nora Lustig (Brookings Institution Press and CEQ Institute, Tulane University). Free online version available at www .commitmentoequity.org.

Arunatilake, Nisha, Gabriela Inchauste, and Nora Lustig. 2017. "The Incidence of Taxes and Spending in Sri Lanka," in *The Distributional Impact of Taxes and Transfers: Evidence from Eight Low- and Middle-Income Countries*, edited by Gabriela Inchauste and Nora Lustig (Washington: World Bank).

Barbieri, Stefano, and Caglayan, Koray. 2022. "On the Political Economy of Redistribution and Provision of Public Goods," chap. 9 in *Commitment to Equity Handbook: Estimating the Impact of Fiscal Policy on Inequality and Poverty*, 2nd ed., Vol. 2, edited by Nora Lustig (Brookings Institution Press and CEQ Institute, Tulane University). Free online version available at www.commitmentoequity.org.

Bargain, Olivier. 2022. "Income Sources and Intrahousehold Distribution: A Methodological Framework and Applications for Argentina and South Africa." Draft for comments (CEQ Institute, Tulane University).

Barofsky, Jeremy, and Younger, Stephen. 2022. "The Effect of Government Health Expenditure on the Income Distribution: A Comparison of Valuation Methods in Ghana," chap. 1 in *Commitment to Equity Handbook: Estimating the Impact of Fiscal Policy on Inequality and Poverty*, 2nd ed., Vol. 2, edited by Nora Lustig (Brookings Institution Press and CEQ Institute, Tulane University). Free online version available at www.commitmentoequity.org.

Bastagli, Francesca, David Coady, and Sanjeev Gupta. 2015. "Fiscal Redistribution in Developing Countries: Overview of Policy Issues and Options," in *Inequality and Fiscal Policy*, edited by Benedict Clements, Ruud Mooji, Sanjeev Gupta, and Michael Keen (Washington: International Monetary Fund).

Batana, Yele Maweki, Mahunan Thierry Hounsa, Akakpo Domefa Konou, and Bienvenue Tien. 2019. "Incidence of Fiscal Policies on Poverty and Inequality in Guinea" (Washington: World Bank).

Beneke de Sanfeliu, Margarita, Nora Lustig, and Jose Andres Oliva Cepeda. 2022. "El Salvador: The Impact of Taxes and Social Spending on Inequality and Poverty," chap. 15 in *Commitment to Equity Handbook: Estimating the Impact of Fiscal Policy on Inequality and Poverty*, 2nd ed., Vol. 1, edited by Nora Lustig (Brookings Institution Press and CEQ Institute, Tulane University). Free online version available at www.commitmentoequity.org.

Birdsall, Nancy, Nora Lustig, and Christian Meyer. 2014. "The Strugglers: The New Poor in Latin America?" *World Development* 60, August, pp. 132–46.

Bornukova, Kateryna, Nataliia Leshchenko, and Mikhail Matytsin. 2019. "Fiscal Incidence in Ukraine: A Commitment to Equity Analysis." Policy Research working paper, no. WPS 8765 (Washington: World Bank).

Bornukova, Kateryna, Gleb Shymanovich, and Alexander Chubrik. 2017. "Fiscal Incidence in Belarus: A Commitment to Equity Analysis." Policy Research working paper no. WPS 8216 (Washington: World Bank).

Bourguignon, François, and Christian Morrisson. 1980. "Progressivité et incidence de la redistribution des revenus en pays développés." *Revue economique*, pp. 197–233.

Bourguignon, Francois, and Luiz Pereira da Silva. 2003. *The Impact of Economic Policies on Poverty and Income Distribution: Evaluation Techniques and Tools* (Washington: World Bank and Oxford University Press), © World Bank (https://openknowledge.worldbank.org/handle/10986/15090) License: CC BY 3.0 IGO.

Bucheli, Marisa, Nora Lustig, Maximo Rossi, and Florencia Amabile. 2014. "Social Spending, Taxes and Income Redistribution in Uruguay," in "The Redistributive Impact of Taxes and Social Spending in Latin America," edited by Nora Lustig, Carola Pessino, and John Scott, special issue, *Public Finance Review* 42, no. 3, pp. 413–33.

Cabrera, Maynor, Nora Lustig, and Hilcias E. Moran. 2015. "Fiscal Policy, Inequality, and the Ethnic Divide in Guatemala." *World Development* 76, pp. 263–79.

Cancho, Cesar, and Elena Bondarenko. 2017. "The Distributional Impact of Fiscal Policy in Georgia," in *The Distributional Impact of Taxes and Transfers: Evidence from Eight Low- and Middle-Income Countries*, edited by Gabriela Inchauste and Nora Lustig (Washington: World Bank).

Candia, Bernardo, and Engel, Eduardo. 2022. "Taxes, Transfers and Income Distribution in Chile: Incorporating Undistributed Profits," chap. 5 in *Commitment to Equity Handbook: Estimating the Impact of Fiscal Policy on Inequality and Poverty*, 2nd ed., Vol. 2, edited by Nora Lustig (Brookings Institution Press and CEQ Institute, Tulane University). Free online version available at www.commitmentoequity.org.

CEQ Institute. 2016. "CEQ Snapshot No. 2," November (http://us12.campaign-archive1.com/?u=960e58866948cf8683d79637c&id=6128048d0f).

———. 2022. "*CEQ Assessment: CEQ Master Workbook*," available online only in part IV of the *Commitment to Equity Handbook: Estimating the Impact of Fiscal Policy on Inequality and Poverty*, 2nd ed., Vol. 1, edited by Nora Lustig (Brookings Institution Press and CEQ Institute, Tulane University). Free online version available at www.commitmentoequity.org.

Dalmacio F., Benicio, Jon Jellema, Maya Goldman, and William Seitz. 2021. "The Effects of Fiscal Policy on Poverty and Inequality in Tajikistan." CEQ Working Paper 108 (CEQ Institute, Tulane University), February.

Davalos, Maria E., Monica Robayo-Abril, Esmeralda Shehaj, and Aida Gjika. 2018. "The Distributional Impact of the Fiscal System in Albania," Policy Research Working Paper, WPS 8370 (Washington: World Bank).

Demery, Lionel. 2000. *Benefit Incidence: A Practitioner's Guide* (Washington: World Bank).

Duclos, J.-Y., and A. Araar. 2006. *Poverty and Equity: Measurement, Policy and Estimation with DAD* (London: Kluwer Academic Publishers).

Enami, Ali. 2022a. "Measuring the Redistributive Impact of Taxes and Transfers in the Presence of Reranking," chap. 3 in *Commitment to Equity Handbook: Estimating the Impact of Fiscal Policy on Inequality and Poverty*, 2nd ed., Vol. 1, edited by Nora Lustig (Brookings Institution Press and CEQ Institute, Tulane University). Free online version available at www.commitmentoequity.org.

———. 2022b. "Measuring the Effectiveness of Taxes and Transfers in Fighting Poverty and Reducing Inequality," chap. 5 in *Commitment to Equity Handbook: Estimating the Impact of Fiscal Policy on Inequality and Poverty*, 2nd ed., Vol. 1, edited by Nora Lustig (Brookings Institution Press and CEQ Institute, Tulane University). Free online version available at www.commitmentoequity.org.

Enami, Ali, Sean Higgins, and Nora Lustig. 2022. "Allocating Taxes and Transfers, Constructing Income Concepts, and Completing Sections A, B, and C of *CEQ Master Workbook*," chap. 6 in *Commitment to Equity Handbook: Estimating the Impact of Fiscal Policy on Inequality and Poverty*, 2nd ed., Vol. 1, edited by Nora Lustig (Brookings Institution Press and CEQ Institute, Tulane University). Free online version available at www.commitmentoequity.org.

Enami, Ali, Nora Lustig, and Rodrigo Aranda. 2022. "Analytic Foundations: Measuring the Redistributive Impact of Taxes and Transfers," chap. 2 in *Commitment to Equity Handbook: Estimating the Impact of Fiscal Policy on Inequality and Poverty*, 2nd ed., Vol. 1, edited by Nora Lustig (Brookings Institution Press and CEQ Institute, Tulane University). Free online version available at www.commitmentoequity.org.

Enami, Ali, Nora Lustig and Alireza Taqdiri. (2019). Fiscal policy, inequality, and poverty in Iran: assessing the impact and effectiveness of taxes and transfers. *Middle East Development Journal* 11, no. 1, pp. 49–74.

Fanelli, Jose Maria. 2018. "Inter-Temporal Sustainability of Fiscal Redistribution: A Methodological Framework," CEQ Working Paper 77 (Commitment to Equity [CEQ] Institute, Tulane University), March.

———. 2022. "Inter-Temporal Sustainability of Fiscal Redistribution: A Methodological Framework," chap. 7 in Commitment to Equity Handbook: Estimating the Impact of Fiscal Policy on Inequality and Poverty, 2nd ed., Vol. 2, edited by Nora Lustig (Brookings Institution Press and CEQ Institute, Tulane University). Free online version available at www.commitmentoequity.org.

Flachaire, Emmanuel, Nora Lustig, and Andrea Vigorito. 2021. "Underreporting of Top Incomes and Inequality: An Assessment of Correction Methods Using Linked Survey and Tax Data."

Freije-Rodriguez, Samuel, and Judy Yang. 2018. "Mongolia: Distributional Impact of Taxes and Transfers." Policy Research working paper, no. WPS 8639 (Washington: World Bank).

Gertler, Paul, and Paul Glewwe. 1990. "The Willingness to Pay for Education in Developing Countries: Evidence from Rural Peru." *Journal of Public Economics* 42, no. 3, pp. 251–75.

Gertler, Paul, and Jacques van der Gaag. 1990. *The Willingness to Pay for Medical Care: Evidence from Two Developing Countries* (Johns Hopkins University Press for the World Bank).

Gimenez, Lea, Maria Ana Lugo, Sandra Martinez-Aguilar, Humberto Colman, Juan Jose Galeano, and Gabriela Farfan. 2017. "Paraguay: Analisis del Sistema Fiscal y su Impacto en la Pobreza y la Equidad." CEQ Working Paper 74 (Ministerio de Hacienda de Paraguay, World Bank, and CEQ Institute, Tulane University), October.

Gomez Bengoechea, Gonzalo, and Siyu Quan. 2020. "Fiscal Incidence in Spain in 2016." CEQ Working Paper 95 (CEQ Institute, Tulane University).

Goraus, Karolina, and Gabriela Inchauste. 2016. "The Distributional Impact of Taxes and Transfers in Poland." Policy Research Working Paper, WPS 7787 (Washington: World Bank).

Greenspun, Samantha, 2019. "A Gender-Sensitive Fiscal Incidence Analysis for Latin America: Brazil, Colombia, the Dominican Republic, Mexico, and Uruguay." Unpublished doctoral dissertation (Tulane University, Graduate Program in Latin American Studies). ProQuest Dissertations Publishing, 27672416.

Grushka, Carlos. 2022. "The Within-System Redistribution of Contributory Pension Systems: Conceptual Framework and Empirical Method of Estimation," chap. 6 in *Commitment to Equity Handbook: Estimating the Impact of Fiscal Policy on Inequality and Poverty*, 2nd ed., Vol. 2, edited by Nora Lustig (Brookings Institution Press and CEQ Institute, Tulane University). Free online version available at www.commitmentoequity.org.

Higgins, Sean, and Caterina Brest Lopez. 2022. "Producing Indicators and Results, and Completing Sections D and E of *CEQ Master Workbook* using the *CEQ Stata Package*," chap. 8 in *Commitment to Equity Handbook: Estimating the Impact of Fiscal Policy on Inequality and Poverty*, 2nd ed., Vol. 1, edited by Nora Lustig (Brookings Institution Press and CEQ Institute, Tulane University). Free online version available at www.commitmentoequity.org.

Higgins, Sean, and Nora Lustig. 2016. "Can a Poverty-Reducing and Progressive Tax and Transfer System Hurt the Poor?" *Journal of Development Economics* 122, September, pp. 63–75.

Higgins, Sean, Nora Lustig, Whitney Ruble, and Timothy M. Smeeding. 2016. "Comparing the Incidence of Taxes and Social Spending in Brazil and the United States." *Review of Income and Wealth* 62, pp. S22–46.

Higgins, Sean, and Claudiney Pereira. 2014. "The Effects of Brazil's Taxation and Social Spending on the Distribution of Household Income," in "The Redistributive Impact of Taxes and Social Spending in Latin America," edited by Nora Lustig, Carola Pessino, and John Scott, special issue, *Public Finance Review* 42, no. 3, pp. 346–67.

Hill, Ruth, Gabriela Inchauste, Nora Lustig, Eyasu Tsehaye, and Tassew Woldehanna. 2017. "A Fiscal Incidence Analysis for Ethiopia," in *The Distributional Impact of Taxes and Transfers. Evidence from Eight Low- and Middle-Income Countries*, edited by Gabriela Inchauste and Nora Lustig (Washington: World Bank).

Hounsa, Iry, Mohamed Coulibaly, and Aly Sanoh. 2019. "The Redistributive Effects of Fiscal Policy in Mali and Niger." Policy Research working paper, no. WPS 8887 (Washington: World Bank).

Houts, Ian, and Alexander Massara. 2020. "CEQ Master Workbook: Lesotho (2016)," CEQ Data Center on Fiscal Redistribution (CEQ Institute, Tulane University, and the World Bank), August 19.

ICEFI. 2017a. "Incidencia de la politica fiscal en el ambito rural de Centro America: el caso de Honduras," CEQ Working Paper 51 (CEQ Institute, Tulane University, IFAD and Instituto Centroamericano de Estudios Fiscales).

———. 2017b. "Incidencia de la politica fiscal en la desigualdad y la pobreza en Nicaragua," CEQ Working Paper 52 (CEQ Institute, Tulane University, IFAD and Instituto Centroamericano de Estudios Fiscales).

Inchauste, Gabriela, and Nora Lustig. 2017. "Overview," in *The Distributional Impact of Taxes and Transfers: Evidence from Eight Low- and Middle-Income Countries*, edited by Gabriela Inchauste and Nora Lustig (Washington: World Bank).

Inchauste, Gabriela, Nora Lustig, Mashekwa Maboshe, Catriona Purfield, and Ingrid Wollard. 2017. "The Distributional Impact of Fiscal Policy in South Africa," in *The Distributional Impact of Taxes and Transfers: Evidence from Eight Low- and Middle-Income Countries*, edited by Gabriela Inchauste and Nora Lustig (Washington: World Bank).

Inchauste, Gabriela, and Eva Militaru. 2018. "The Distributional Impact of Taxes and Social Spending in Romania." Policy Research working paper no. WPS 8565 (Washington: World Bank).

Inchauste, Gabriela, and Ivica Rubil. 2017. "The Distributional Impact of Taxes and Social Spending in Croatia." Policy Research working paper, WPS 8203 (Washington: World Bank).

International Monetary Fund, African Department. 2017. "Zambia: Selected Issues," International Monetary Fund Country Report No. 17/328 (Washington: IMF).

———. 2018. "Botswana: 2018 Article IV Consultation-Press Release; Staff Report; and Statement by the Executive Director for Botswana" (Washington: IMF).

———. 2020. "Kingdom of Eswatini: 2019 Article IV Consultation—Press Release; Staff Report; and Statement by the Executive Director for the Kingdom of Eswatini" (Washington: IMF).

Jaramillo, Miguel. 2014. "The Incidence of Social Spending and Taxes in Peru," in "The Redistributive Impact of Taxes and Social Spending in Latin America," edited by Nora Lustig, Carola Pessino, and John Scott, special issue, *Public Finance Review* 42, no. 3, pp. 391–412.

Jellema, Jon. 2020. "CEQ Master Workbook: Ivory Coast (2015)." CEQ Data Center on Fiscal Redistribution (CEQ Institute, Tulane University, and the World Bank), November 16.

Jellema, Jon, Astrid Haas, Nora Lustig, and Sebastian Wolf. 2022. "Uganda: The Impact of Taxes, Transfers, and Subsidies on Inequality and Poverty," chap. 19 in *Commitment to Equity Handbook: Estimating the Impact of Fiscal Policy on Inequality and Poverty*, 2nd ed., Vol. 1, edited by Nora Lustig (Brookings Institution Press and CEQ Institute, Tulane University). Free online version available at www.commitmentoequity.org.

Jellema, Jon, and Gabriela Inchauste. 2022. "Constructing Consumable Income: Including the Direct and Indirect Effects of Indirect Taxes and Subsidies," chap. 7 in *Commitment to Equity Handbook: Estimating the Impact of Fiscal Policy on Inequality and Poverty*, 2nd ed., Vol. 1, edited by Nora Lustig (Brookings Institution Press and CEQ Institute, Tulane University). Free online version available at www.commitmentoequity.org.

Jellema, Jon, and Caroline Tassot. 2020. "CEQ Master Workbook: Togo (2015)." CEQ Data Center on Fiscal Redistribution (CEQ Institute, Tulane University), October 19.

Jellema, Jon, Matthew Wai-Poi, and Rythia Afkar. 2017. "The Distributional Impact of Fiscal Policy in Indonesia," in *The Distributional Impact of Taxes and Transfers: Evidence from Eight Low- and Middle-Income Countries*, edited by Gabriela Inchauste and Nora Lustig (Washington: World Bank).

Jouini, Nizar, Nora Lustig, Ahmed Moummi, and Abebe Shimeles. 2022. "Tunisia: Fiscal Policy, Income Redistribution, and Poverty Reduction," chap. 18 in *Commitment to Equity Handbook: Estimating the Impact of Fiscal Policy on Inequality and Poverty*, 2nd ed., Vol. 1, edited by Nora Lustig (Brookings Institution Press and CEQ Institute, Tulane University). Free online version available at www.commitmentoequity.org.

Kakwani, Nanak C. 1977. "Measurement of Tax Progressivity: An International Comparison." *Economic Journal* 87, no. 345, pp. 71–80.

Khundu, Sridhar, and Maynor Cabrera. 2020. "CEQ Master Workbook: India (2011)." CEQ Data Center on Fiscal Redistribution (CEQ Institute, Tulane University, and Centre for Budget and Governance Accountability), June 22.

Lambert, Peter. 2001. *The Distribution and Redistribution of Income*, 3rd ed. (Manchester University Press).

Lara Ibarra, Gabriel, Nistha Sinha, Rana Nayer Safwat Fayez, and Jon Jellema. 2019. "Impact of Fiscal Policy on Inequality and Poverty in the Arab Republic of Egypt." Policy Research working paper no. WPS 8824 (Washington: World Bank).

Lindert, Peter. 2004. *Growing Public: Social Spending and Economic Growth since the Eighteenth Century*, vols. 1–2 (Cambridge University Press).

Llerena Pinto, Freddy Paul, Maria Christina Llerena Pinto, Roberto Carlos Saa Daza, and Maria Andrea Llerena Pinto. 2015. "Social Spending, Taxes and Income Redistribution in Ecuador." CEQ Working Paper 28 (Center for Inter-American Policy and Research and Department of Economics, Tulane University, and Inter-American Dialogue).

Lopez-Calva, Luis Felipe, Nora Lustig, Mikhail Matytsin, and Daria Popova. 2017. "Who Benefits from Fiscal Redistribution in Russia?," in *The Distributional Impact of Taxes and Transfers: Evidence from Eight Low- and Middle-Income Countries*, edited by Gabriela Inchauste and Nora Lustig (Washington: World Bank).

Lustig, Nora. 2015. "The Redistributive Impact of Government Spending on Education and Health: Evidence from 13 Developing Countries in the Commitment to Equity Project," in *Inequality and Fiscal Policy*, edited by Benedict Clements, Ruud Mooji, Sanjeev Gupta, and Michael Keen (Washington: International Monetary Fund).

———. 2016a. "Fiscal Policy, Inequality, and the Poor in the Developing World." Tulane University Economics Working Paper 1612, October.

———. 2016b. "Inequality and Fiscal Redistribution in Middle-Income Countries: Brazil, Chile, Colombia, Indonesia, Mexico, Peru and South Africa." *Journal of Globalization and Development* (doi: 10.1515/jgd-2016-0015).

———. 2017a. "Fiscal Redistribution and Ethnoracial Inequality in Bolivia, Brazil and Guatemala." *Latin American Research Review. Special Issue: Enduring and/or New Forms of Inequality in a Globalizing World* 52, no. 2, pp. 208–20 (http://doi.org/10.25222/larr.90).

———. 2017b. "El impacto del sistema tributario y el gasto social en la distribucion del ingreso y la pobreza en America Latina. Una aplicacion del marco metodologico del proyecto Compromiso con la Equidad (CEQ)." *El Trimestre Economico* 335 (July–September).

———. 2018. "Measuring the Distribution of Household Income, Consumption and Wealth: State of Play and Measurement Challenges," in *For Good Measure: Advancing Research on Well-Being Metrics Beyond GDP*, edited by Martine Durand, Jean-Paul Fitoussi, and Joseph E. Stiglitz, OECD report by the High Level Expert Group on Measuring Economic Performance and Social Progress (Paris: OECD).

———. 2020a. "The Missing Rich in Household Surveys: Causes and Correction Methods." CEQ Working Paper 75 (Commitment to Equity [CEQ] Institute, Tulane University).

———. 2020b. "Measuring the Distributional Impact of Taxation and Public Spending: The Practice of Fiscal Incidence Analysis," In *Oxford Research Encyclopedia of Economics and Finance* (Oxford University Press).

———. 2022. "Fiscal Policy, Income Redistribution, and Poverty Reduction in Low- and Middle-Income Countries," chap. 10 in Commitment to Equity Handbook: Estimating the Impact of Fiscal Policy on Inequality and Poverty, 2nd ed., Vol. 1, edited by Nora Lustig (Brookings Institution Press and CEQ Institute, Tulane University). Free online version available at www .commitmentoequity.org.

Lustig, Nora, and Sean Higgins. 2016. "Inequality and Fiscal Redistribution in Middle Income Countries: Brazil, Chile, Colombia, Indonesia, Mexico, Peru and South Africa." *Journal of Globalization and Development* 7, no. 1, pp. 17–60 (doi:10.1515/jgd-2016-0015).

———. 2022. "The *CEQ Assessment*: Measuring the Impact of Fiscal Policy on Inequality and Poverty," chap. 1 in *Commitment to Equity Handbook: Estimating the Impact of Fiscal Policy on Inequality and Poverty*, 2nd ed., Vol. 1, edited by Nora Lustig (Brookings Institution Press and CEQ Institute, Tulane University). Free online version available at www.commitmentoequity .org.

Lustig, N., and V. Martinez Pabon. Forthcoming. "Do We Know How Much Inequality There Is?" Draft for comments (CEQ Institute, Tulane University).

Lustig, Nora, Valentina Martinez Pabon, Guido Neidhöfer, and Mariano Tommasi. 2021. "Short and Long-Run Distributional Impacts of Covid-19 in Latin America." CEQ Working Paper 96 (Commitment to Equity [CEQ] Institute, Tulane University), June.

Lustig, Nora, Judith Morrison, and Adam Ratzlaff. 2019. *Splitting the Bill: Taxing and Spending to Close Ethnic and Racial Gaps in Latin America* (Washington: Inter-American Development Bank) (https://publications.iadb.org/publications/english/document/Splitting_the_Bill _Taxing_and_Spending_to_Close_Ethnic_and_Racial_Gaps_in_Latin_America.pdf).

Lustig, Nora, and Carola Pessino. 2014. "Social Spending and Income Redistribution in Argentina in the 2000s: The Rising Role of Noncontributory Pensions." *Public Finance Review* 42, no. 3 (http://pfr.sagepub.com/content/early/2013/10/24/1091142113505193.full.pdf+html).

Martinez-Aguilar, Sandra. 2019. "CEQ Master Workbook: Panama (2016)." CEQ Data Center on Fiscal Redistribution (CEQ Institute, Tulane University, and the Economic Co-operation and Development), January 16.

Martinez-Aguilar, Sandra, Alan Fuchs, Eduardo Ortiz-Juarez, and Giselle Del Carmen. 2022. "Chile: The Impact of Fiscal Policy on Inequality and Poverty," chap. 13 in *Commitment to Equity Handbook: Estimating the Impact of Fiscal Policy on Inequality and Poverty*, 2nd ed., Vol. 1, edited by Nora Lustig (Brookings Institution Press and CEQ Institute, Tulane University). Free online version available at www.commitmentoequity.org.

Martinez-Vazquez, Jorge. 2008. "The Impact of Budgets on the Poor: Tax and Expenditure Benefit Incidence Analysis," chap. 5 in *Public Finance for Poverty Reduction Concepts and Case Studies from Africa and Latin America*, edited by Blanca Moreno-Dodson and Quentin Wodon (Washington: World Bank).

Meerman, Jacob. 1979. *Public Expenditure in Malaysia: Who Benefits and Why* (Oxford University Press for the World Bank).

Melendez, Marcela, and Valentina Martinez. 2015. "CEQ Master Workbook: Colombia. Version: December 17, 2015," CEQ Data Center on Fiscal Redistribution (CEQ Institute, Tulane University and Inter-American Development Bank).

Molina, Emiro. 2016. "CEQ Master Workbook: Venezuela. Version: November 15, 2016," CEQ Data Center on Fiscal Redistribution (CEQ Institute, Tulane University).

Musgrave, Richard. 1959. *The Theory of Public Finance* (New York: McGraw-Hill).

Musgrave, Richard A., J. J. Carroll, L. D. Cook, and L. Frane. 1951. "Distribution of Tax Payments by Income Groups: A Case Study for 1948." *National Tax Journal* 4 (March), pp. 1–53.

Musgrave, Richard, Karl Case, and Herman Leonard. 1974. "The Distribution of Fiscal Burdens and Benefits." *Public Finance Quarterly* 2, no. 3, pp. 259–311.

Neidhöfer, Guido, Nora Lustig, and Mariano Tommasi. 2021. "Intergenerational Transmission of Lockdown Consequences: Prognosis of the Longer-Run Persistence of COVID-19 in Latin America." *Journal of Economic Inequality* 19, ppP. 571–98.

Oliva, Jose Andres. 2020a. "CEQ Master Workbook: El Salvador (2013)." CEQ Data Center on Fiscal Redistribution (CEQ Institute, Tulane University, and Inter-American Development Bank), June.

———. 2020b. "CEQ Master Workbook: El Salvador (2015)." CEQ Data Center on Fiscal Redistribution (CEQ Institute, Tulane University, and Inter-American Development Bank), June.

———. 2020c. "CEQ Master Workbook: El Salvador (2017)." CEQ Data Center on Fiscal Redistribution (CEQ Institute, Tulane University and Inter-American Development Bank), June.

Pape, Utz Johann, and Simon Lange. 2018. "Fiscal incidence Analysis for Kenya: Using the Kenya Integrated Household Budget Survey 2015–16" (Washington: World Bank Group).

Paz Arauco, Veronica, George Gray Molina, Wilson Jimenez Pozo, and Ernesto Yañez Aguilar. 2014. "Explaining Low Redistributive Impact in Bolivia," in "The Redistributive Impact of Taxes and Social Spending in Latin America," edited by Nora Lustig, Carola Pessino, and John Scott, special issue, *Public Finance Review* 42, no. 3, pp. 326–45.

Paz Arauco, Veronica, Wilson Jimenez, and Ernesto Yañez. 2020. "CEQ Master Workbook: Bolivia (2015)." CEQ Data Center on Fiscal Redistribution (CEQ Institute, Tulane University), December.

Pereira, Claudiney. 2022. "Brazil: Fiscal Policy and Ethno-Racial Poverty and Inequality," chap. 12 in *Commitment to Equity Handbook: Estimating the Impact of Fiscal Policy on Inequality and Poverty*, 2nd ed., Vol. 1, edited by Nora Lustig (Brookings Institution Press and CEQ Institute, Tulane University). Free online version available at www.commitmentoequity.org.

Pechman, Joseph A. 1985. *Who Paid the Taxes, 1966–1985* (Brookings Institution Press).

Pechman, Joseph A., and Benjamin A. Okner. 1974. *Who Bears the Tax Burden?* (Brookings Institution Press).

Rossignolo, Dario. 2022. "Argentina: Taxes, Expenditures, Poverty, and Income Distribution," chap. 11 in *Commitment to Equity Handbook: Estimating the Impact of Fiscal Policy on Inequality and Poverty*, 2nd ed., Vol. 1, edited by Nora Lustig (Brookings Institution Press and CEQ Institute, Tulane University). Free online version available at www.commitmentoequity.org.

Sahn, D., and S. Younger. 2003. "Estimating the Incidence of Indirect Taxes in Developing Countries," in *The Impact of Economic Policies on Poverty and Income Distribution: Evaluation Techniques and Tools*, edited by F. Bourguignon and L. A. Pereira da Silva (Oxford University Press).

Sahn, David E., and Stephen D. Younger. 2000. "Expenditure Incidence in Africa: Microeconomic Evidence." *Fiscal Studies* 21, no. 3, pp. 329–47.

Sauma, Juan, and Diego Trejos. 2014. "Social Public Spending, Taxes, Redistribution of Income, and Poverty in Costa Rica." CEQ Working Paper No. 18 (Center for Inter-American Policy and Research and Department of Economics, Tulane University and Inter-American Dialogue).

Scott, John. 2014. "Redistributive Impact and Efficiency of Mexico's Fiscal System," in "The Redistributive Impact of Taxes and Social Spending in Latin America," edited by Nora Lustig, Carola Pessino, and John Scott, special issue, *Public Finance Review* 42, no. 3, pp. 368–90.

Scott, John, Sandra Martinez-Aguilar, Enrique de la Rosa, and Rodrigo Aranda. 2020a. "CEQ Master Workbook: Mexico (2012)." CEQ Data Center on Fiscal Redistribution (CEQ Institute, Tulane University), July 28.

———. 2020b. "CEQ Master Workbook: Mexico (2014)." CEQ Data Center on Fiscal Redistribution (CEQ Institute, Tulane University). July 28, 2020.

Selowsky, Marcelo. 1979. *Who Benefits from Government Expenditures? A Case Study of Colombia* (Oxford University Press).Soares, Sergei. 2022a. "The Market Value of Public Education: A Comparison of Three Valuation Methods" chap. 2 in *Commitment to Equity Handbook: Estimating the Impact of Fiscal Policy on Inequality and Poverty*, 2nd ed., Vol. 2, edited by Nora Lustig (Brookings Institution Press and CEQ Institute, Tulane University). Free online version available at www.commitmentoequity.org.

———. 2022b. "The Market Value of Owner Occupied Housing and Public Infrastructure Services" chap. 4 in *Commitment to Equity Handbook: Estimating the Impact of Fiscal Policy on Inequality and Poverty*, 2nd ed., Vol. 2, edited by Nora Lustig (Brookings Institution Press and CEQ Institute, Tulane University). Free online version available at www.commitmentoequity.org.

Sulla, Victor, Precious Zikhali, Philip M. Schuler, and Jon Jellema. 2017. "Does Fiscal Policy Benefit the Poor and Reduce Inequality in Namibia? The Distributional Impact of Fiscal Policy in Namibia." World Bank Working Paper No. 116029 (Washington: World Bank),.

Urzua, Sergio. 2022. "Estimating the Value of Education Services" chap. 3 in *Commitment to Equity Handbook: Estimating the Impact of Fiscal Policy on Inequality and Poverty*, 2nd ed., Vol. 2, edited by Nora Lustig (Brookings Institution Press and CEQ Institute, Tulane University). Free online version available at www.commitmentoequity.org.

Van de Walle, Dominique. 2003. "Behavioral Incidence Analysis of Public Spending and Social Programs," in *The Impacts of Economic Policies on Poverty and Income Distribution. Evaluation Techniques and Tools*, edited by François Bourguignon and Luiz. A. Pereira da Silva, pp. 69–83 (Washington: World Bank).

World Bank. 2018. "Burkina Faso: Fiscal Incidence, Inequality, and Poverty." Report 132876-BF (Washington: World Bank).

Younger, Stephen D. 2022. "Ghana and Tanzania: The Impact of Reforming Energy Subsidies, Cash Transfers, and Taxes on Inequality and Poverty," chap. 16 in *Commitment to Equity Handbook: Estimating the Impact of Fiscal Policy on Inequality and Poverty*, 2nd ed., Vol. 1, edited by Nora Lustig (Brookings Institution Press and CEQ Institute, Tulane University). Free online version available at www.commitmentoequity.org.

Younger, Stephen D., and Artsvi Khachatryan. 2017. "Fiscal Incidence in Armenia," in *The Distributional Impact of Taxes and Transfers: Evidence from Eight Low- and Middle-Income Countries*, edited by Gabriela Inchauste and Nora Lustig (Washington: World Bank).

Younger, Stephen D., Flora Myamba, and Kenneth Mdadila. 2016. "Fiscal Incidence in Tanzania." *African Development Review* 28, no. 3, pp. 264–76.

Younger, Stephen D., Eric Osei-Assibey, and Felix Oppong. 2017. "Fiscal Incidence in Ghana." *Review of Development Economics* 21, no. 4, pp. e47–e66 (doi:10.1111/rode.12299).

PART I

Methodology

Chapter 1

THE *CEQ ASSESSMENT*©

Measuring the Impact of Fiscal Policy on Inequality and Poverty

Nora Lustig and Sean Higgins

Introduction

Taxation and public spending are key policy levers the state has in its power to change the distribution of income determined by the prevailing distribution of wealth, property, and power, market forces, and institutions. As stated in the introduction, the purpose of this Volume is to present a step-by-step guide to applying the incidence analysis used in *Commitment to Equity (CEQ) Assessments*. Developed by the Commitment to Equity Institute at Tulane University, the *CEQ Assessment* is a diagnostic tool that uses fiscal incidence analysis to determine the extent to which fiscal policy reduces inequality and poverty in a particular country.

The *CEQ Assessment* is designed to address the following four questions:

1. How much income redistribution and poverty reduction is being accomplished through fiscal policy?[1]
2. How equalizing and pro-poor are specific taxes and government spending?
3. How effective are taxes and government spending in reducing inequality and poverty?
4. What is the impact of fiscal reforms that change the size and/or progressivity of a particular tax or benefit?

---

[1] Throughout this Handbook, "fiscal policy," "fiscal instruments," "taxes and government spending," "revenue collection and government spending," "taxes and transfers," "taxes and benefits," and the "net fiscal system" are used interchangeably.

Volume 1 guides researchers and policy analysts in the completion of the *CEQ Master Workbook© (MWB)* (available online in part IV of Volume 1 of this Handbook; CEQ Institute, 2022), a multi-sheet Excel file that contains all the information used in a *CEQ Assessment*: detailed information on the country's economic, political, and social context; description of microdata; the country's fiscal system; and the results of the fiscal incidence analysis used as inputs for policy discussions, academic papers, and policy reports. The *CEQ Stata Package* (which can be installed directly through Stata) includes a suite of user-written Stata commands that automatically produces and fills out the results section (section E) of the *CEQ Master Workbook* (available online in part IV of this Volume).[2] The Handbook can also be used as a stand-alone document for those interested in learning or teaching methodological and practical approaches to carry out fiscal incidence analysis.

This chapter presents key analytical insights in fiscal redistribution theory, such as the fundamental equation that links the redistributive effect to the size and redistributive effects of taxes and benefits; how to calculate the contribution of each fiscal instrument (or combinations of them) to the change in inequality and poverty; and the implications of reranking (for the interested reader, their mathematical formulation is presented in detail in chapter 2 [Enami, Lustig, and Aranda, 2022] and chapter 3 [Enami, 2022a] in this Volume). The chapter also discusses the basics of fiscal incidence analysis used in *CEQ Assessments*. The *CEQ Assessments* rely on the fiscal incidence method known as the "accounting approach" because it ignores behavioral responses and general equilibrium effects. Because pensions frequently tend to be a combination of deferred income and government transfer, there is a section dedicated to discussing how contributory pensions should be considered in fiscal incidence analysis. Finally, the chapter describes the set of indicators used to answer the four key questions outlined above and illustrates with examples from existing *CEQ Assessments* (a detailed description of indicators is in chapter 8 of this Volume [Higgins and Brest Lopez, 2022]).

Instructions for the implementation of a *CEQ Assessment* in practice are in chapter 6 (Enami, Higgins, and Lustig, 2022) and chapter 8 in part II of this Volume. Chapter 6 is a guide on how to allocate taxes and transfers to households and construct the income concepts. Chapter 8 shows how to use the *CEQ Stata Package* to produce the suite of indicators used in fiscal incidence analysis (section E of the *MWB* [available online in part IV of Volume 1]). In addition, chapter 7 in this Volume (Jellema and Inchauste, 2022) explains how to allocate taxes and transfers when considering the indirect effects of indirect taxes and subsidies. Chapter 9 (Aranda and Ratzlaff, 2022), also in this Volume, describes how to use the *CEQ Stata Package* to produce indicators

---

[2] Higgins, Aranda, and Li (2022) (in part IV of this Volume, available only online at www.ceq institute.org). Descriptions of how to use the *CEQ Stata Package* are in chapters 8 and 9 of this Volume.

disaggregated by ethnicity, race, location, gender, and so on (section F of the *MWB* [available online in part IV of Volume 1]).

Part III includes applications of the *CEQ Assessment* tool to specific countries and cross-country comparisons. Part IV of Volume 1 ("The *CEQ Assessment* Tools"), available online only, contains a blank version of the *CEQ Master Workbook* and the *CEQ Stata Package* with user-written software to complete it. It also contains a completed Master Workbook and "do files" for Ghana and Mexico as examples. In addition, this part features guidelines for the implementation of *CEQ Assessments*, including a thorough protocol of quality control. Part V includes all the components of the CEQ Data Center on Fiscal Redistribution.[3] Part VI contains the CEQ Institute's microsimulation tools. Volume 2 of this Handbook includes chapters on alternative methods to estimate the incidence of spending on education, health, and infrastructure, including the incidence of corporate taxes; to measure the distributive impact of contributory pensions; to assess the sustainability of fiscal redistribution; and to consider the political economy of the provision of public goods.

1 The Theory of Fiscal Redistribution: Key Analytical Insights

As stated above, taxation and public spending are key policy levers that the state has in its power to change both the distribution of income as determined both by market forces and institutions and the prevailing distribution of wealth and property. In this Handbook, "fiscal redistribution" refers precisely to the process by which the state collects revenues from individuals and households (primarily through taxes) and spends these revenues on benefits (for example, cash transfers, price subsidies, and in-kind benefits such as education and health) intended for specific individuals and households. In so doing, the state changes the postfiscal income distribution and poverty rates that would have prevailed in the absence of fiscal policy. Because of behavioral responses and general equilibrium effects, fiscal policy can also change the prefiscal income distribution and poverty rates. While at this point the *CEQ Assessments* do not estimate the counterfactual prefiscal income with these second-round effects in place, it is important to note that the analytical insights presented here and in chapters 2, 3, 4 (a reprint of Higgins and Lustig, 2016), and 5 (Enami, 2022b) in this Volume apply to fiscally induced income redistribution regardless of the method used to estimate its extent. That is, regardless of whether fiscal redistribution is calculated using run-of-the-mill fiscal incidence analysis, microsimulation methods, or partial or general equilibrium modeling, the theoretical results discussed below and in the next four chapters of this Volume apply.

In addition to the taxes and benefits currently included in the *CEQ Assessments*, the state, of course, also spends on public goods, and collects revenues from and spends on subsidies that benefit corporations as well. While spending on public goods and taxing

---

[3] https://commitmentoequity.org/datacenter/

and subsidizing corporations also have redistributive effects, these forms of revenue collection and spending are not considered in the *CEQ Assessment* tool (at least, not for the moment). A proposal for how to incorporate the incidence of taxes on corporate income is presented by Bernardo Candia and Eduardo Engel (2022) (chapter 5 in Volume 2 of the Handbook).

To measure the redistributive effect and poverty impact of taxes and benefits, the core building block of fiscal incidence analysis is the definition and construction of a prefiscal income concept and a postfiscal income concept—that is, income after taxes net of transfers. The construction of postfiscal income refers to the method of allocating the burden of taxes and the benefits of government spending to households. Although this procedure may sound very simple, allocating taxes and transfers to households is the most challenging task of fiscal incidence analysis. Below we present a brief description of the fiscal incidence method used in *CEQ Assessments*. Chapter 6 in this Volume is devoted to explaining the approaches to be followed in practice, while part III includes applications.

1.1 The Fundamental Equation of the Redistributive Effect

In his seminal book *The Distribution and Redistribution of Income: A Mathematical Analysis*, Lambert defined the redistributive effect as the difference between inequality for postfiscal income and prefiscal income.[4] Lambert shows that the redistributive effect of the net fiscal system is equal to the weighted sum of the redistributive effect of taxes and transfers, where the redistributive effect of the tax system is defined as the difference between inequality of post-tax and Market Income; the redistributive effect of the benefit system is defined as the difference between inequality of post-transfer income and Market Income; and the weights are equal to the ratios of taxes and benefits divided by total prefiscal (market) income, respectively.[5]

In mathematical terms,

$$RE_N = \frac{(1-g)RE_t + (1+b)RE_B}{1-g+b},$$

where RE_N, RE_t, and RE_B are the change in the Gini indices for the net fiscal system, taxes (only) and benefits (only), respectively; and g and b are the total tax and benefit ratios—that is, total taxes and total benefits divided by total prefiscal (original) income,

---

[4] Lambert (2001).

[5] See Lambert (2001, equation 11.29, p. 277). This equation can be applied to the so-called S-Gini family of indicators of which the Gini coefficient is one particular case. For the description of S-Gini indicators see, for example, Duclos and Araar (2006). Other inequality indicators cannot necessarily be neatly decomposed into a weighted sum of the redistributive effect of taxes and transfers.

respectively. Actually, Lambert's formulation measures the redistributive effect with the Reynolds-Smolensky index,[6] which in the absence of reranking of households (that is, when households occupy the same place in the ranking from poorest to richest whether they are ranked by prefiscal income or by postfiscal income) equals the difference between the prefiscal and postfiscal Gini coefficient.

We will call this the "fundamental equation of the redistributive effect."[7] It is a fundamental equation because it lies at a heart of two essential implications. The first implication is that to correctly estimate the redistributive effect of fiscal policy, it is essential to analyze taxes *and* benefits in tandem. The second implication is that whether a tax or a transfer exercises an equalizing or unequalizing force no longer depends only on the progressivity or regressivity of the intervention vis-à-vis prefiscal income.

From the fundamental equation[8] one can formally derive the key condition that must be fulfilled for a net fiscal system to be equalizing:

$$RE_t > -\frac{(1+b)}{(1-g)}RE_B.$$

This condition shows, for example, how taxes could be unequalizing $RE_t < 0$, but that given the ratios of taxes g and transfers b and the equalizing effect of transfers $RE_B > 0$, the unequalizing effect of taxes would be more than compensated. While many authors have already stressed the importance of analyzing the redistributive impact of taxes and transfers in tandem,[9] it is important to emphasize that to do so is *essential*.

1.2 Lambert's Conundrum

Lambert's fundamental equation of the redistributive effect has another implication that has been largely overlooked in the literature. The equation can be used to show that relying on the typical indicators of progressivity such as the Kakwani index (described below and in chapter 2 in this Volume) to predict whether a tax or a transfer will exert an equalizing effect is wrong. Taxes, for instance, can be regressive according to the Kakwani index, but when combined with transfers (or, with other taxes), they can make the system more equalizing than without the regressive taxes. This startling

---

[6] For a definition, see Duclos and Araar (2006) and chapter 2 in this Volume.

[7] In this Volume's chapter 2, we reproduce Lambert's formulation and extend it to the case of multiple taxes and transfers. We show how if the redistributive effect is measured with the Gini coefficient, the fundamental equation can be expressed using the Kakwani index for taxes and transfers. In chapter 3 in this Volume, Ali Enami shows how these conditions are affected if taxes and transfers rerank households.

[8] Lambert (2001).

[9] See, for example, Bastagli, Coady, and Gupta (2015, p. 57) and Engel, Galetovi, and Raddatz (1999).

result, which was first identified by Lambert,[10] has been largely ignored in applied fiscal incidence analysis. We proceed to explain how such a counterintuitive result is possible.

Suppose one observes that fiscal policy has an equalizing effect. Can one measure the influence of specific taxes (direct versus indirect, for example) or transfers (direct transfers versus indirect subsidies or in-kind transfers, for example) on the observed result?[11] A fundamental question in the policy discussion is whether a particular fiscal intervention (or a particular combination of them) is equalizing or unequalizing. In a world with a single fiscal intervention and no reranking, it is sufficient to know whether a particular intervention is progressive or regressive to give an unambiguous response using the typical indicators of progressivity such as the Kakwani index (chapter 2 in this Volume).[12] In a world with more than one fiscal intervention, this one-to-one relationship between the progressivity of a particular intervention and its effect on inequality breaks down. As Lambert so eloquently demonstrates,[13] depending on certain characteristics of the fiscal system, a regressive tax can exert an equalizing force over and above that which would prevail in the absence of that regressive tax.[14] *The reader should note that this result can occur in the absence of reranking*—that is, even if the order in which households are ranked by per capita income in the prefiscal situation remains intact in the postfiscal situation.

An example borrowed from Lambert helps illustrate this point in the case of a regressive tax (table 1-1).[15] The table shows that "taxes may be regressive in their original income . . . and yet the net system may exhibit more progressivity" than the progressive benefits alone. The redistributive effect for taxes (leaving out the transfers) in this example is equal to −0.0517, highlighting their regressivity.[16] Yet, the redistributive effect for the net fiscal system is 0.25, higher than the redistributive effect for benefits *only* equal to 0.1972. If taxes are regressive vis-à-vis the original income but progres-

---

[10] Lambert (1985, 2001).

[11] Note that the influence of specific interventions may not be equalizing, even if the overall effect of the net fiscal system is.

[12] The Kakwani index for taxes is defined as the difference between the concentration coefficient of the tax and the Gini for Market Income. For transfers, it is defined as the difference between the Gini for Market Income and the concentration coefficient of the transfer. See, for example, Kakwani (1977).

[13] Lambert (2001).

[14] See Lambert (2001, pp. 277–78). Also, for a derivation of all the mathematical conditions that can be used to determine when adding a regressive tax is equalizing or when adding a progressive transfer is unequalizing, see chapter 2 in Volume 1 of this Handbook.

[15] Lambert (2001).

[16] Since there is no reranking, the Reynolds-Smolensky coefficient equals the difference between the Ginis before and after the fiscal intervention.

TABLE 1-1
Lambert's Conundrum

	1	2	3	4	Total
Original income x	10	20	30	40	100
Tax liability $t(x)$	6	9	12	15	42
Benefit level $b(x)$	21	14	7	0	42
Post-benefit income	31	34	37	40	142
Final income	25	25	25	25	100

Source: Lambert (2001, table 11.1, p. 278).

sive with respect to the less unequally distributed post-transfers income, regressive taxes exert an equalizing effect over and above the effect of progressive transfers.[17]

Note that Lambert's conundrum is not equivalent to the well-known result we mentioned above: that efficient regressive taxes can be fine as long as, when combined with transfers, the net fiscal system is equalizing.[18] The surprising aspect of Lambert's conundrum is that a net fiscal system *with* a regressive tax (vis-à-vis prefiscal income) is *more* equalizing than *without* it.[19] The implications of Lambert's conundrum in real fiscal systems are quite profound: in order to determine whether a particular intervention (or a particular policy change) is inequality increasing or inequality reducing—and by how much—one must resort to numerical calculations that include the whole system. As Lambert mentions, the conundrum is "not altogether farfetched."[20] Two renowned studies in the 1980s found this type of result for the United States and the

---

[17] Note that Lambert (2001) uses the terms "progressive" and "regressive" in a way that is different from other authors in the theoretical and empirical incidence analysis literature. Thus, he calls "regressive" transfers that are equalizing. See definitions in earlier chapters of his book.

[18] As Higgins and Lustig (2016) mention, efficient taxes that fall disproportionately on the poor, such as a no-exemption value-added tax, are often justified with the argument that "'spending instruments are available that are better targeted to the pursuit of equity concerns' (Keen and Lockwood, 2010, p. 141). Similarly, Engel et al. (1999, p. 186) assert that 'it is quite obvious that the disadvantages of a proportional tax are moderated by adequate targeting' of transfers, since 'what the poor individual pays in taxes is returned to her.'" Ebrill, Keen, and Summers (2001, p. 105) argue that "a regressive tax might conceivably be the best way to finance pro-poor expenditures, with the net effect being to relieve poverty."

[19] It can also be shown that if there is reranking, a pervasive feature of net tax systems in the real world, making a tax (or a transfer) more progressive can *increase* post-tax and transfers inequality. In Lambert's example, regressive taxes not only enhance the equalizing effect of transfers, but making taxes more progressive (that is, more disproportional in the Kakwani sense) would result in higher(!) inequality; any additional change (toward more progressivity) in taxes or transfers would just cause reranking and an increase in inequality.

[20] Quotations are from Lambert (2001, p. 278).

United Kingdom.[21] While it did not make its appearance in a 1990s study for Chile,[22] it did in the 2015 *CEQ Assessment* for Chile,[23] as discussed in chapter 13 in this Volume (Martinez-Aguilar and others, 2022).

The counterintuitive result embedded in Lambert's conundrum is the consequence of path dependency: a particular tax can be regressive vis-à-vis Market Income but progressive vis-à-vis the income that would prevail if all the other fiscal interventions were already in place.[24] As shown in chapter 2 in this Volume, there are other counterintuitive results; for instance, adding a regressive transfer to a system with an existing regressive transfer could reduce inequality by more than if one does not add the new regressive transfer.

Given path dependency, how should one calculate the sign and order of magnitude of a particular tax's or transfer's influence on the redistributive effect? There are several ways of calculating the contribution of a particular fiscal intervention to the change in inequality (or poverty). The most commonly used in the literature is the *sequential contribution*. The sequential contribution is calculated as the difference between inequality indicators with fiscal interventions ordered in a path according to their presumed institutional design.[25] For example, if direct transfers are subject to taxation, the sequential contribution of personal income taxes is the difference between Gross Income (Market Income plus transfers), on the one hand, and Disposable Income (Market Income plus transfers minus personal income taxes), on the other.

However, while it may be easy to identify based on institutional design a certain hierarchy for some taxes and transfers in the income construction tree, it will be difficult for others. To assume that Market Income plus (taxable) transfers—that is, Gross Income—occurs before (i.e., should come first in the hierarchical sequence) direct taxes seems quite reasonable. However, in which place of the hierarchy do the benefits derived from access to public education and health services belong? While for purposes of the *CEQ Assessments* we define income concepts following a particular accounting framework (more on this below) and place education benefits (together with health benefits) at the end of the accounting exercise, this does not mean that we think that this sequence responds to a particular institutional design.

If it is not possible to establish a precise hierarchy or sequence in the income construction tree according to a particular institutional design, then the contribution to fiscal redistribution of the taxes and transfers for which establishing a hierarchy is not

---

[21] O'Higgins and Ruggles (1981) for the United Kingdom; Ruggles and O'Higgins (1981) for the United States.

[22] Engel, Galetovi, and Raddatz (1999). These authors showed that the Chilean system was equalizing in spite of featuring regressive indirect taxes. They did not discuss whether there was a "Lambert conundrum."

[23] Martinez-Aguilar and Ortiz-Juarez (2016).

[24] See the discussion on path dependency in chapter 7 of Duclos and Araar (2006).

[25] OECD (2011) used this method, for example.

feasible is path dependent: that is, there will be as many contributions as the possibilities to place the tax or the transfer of interest in a sequence. For instance, the contribution of benefits from public education could be calculated by comparing the change in inequality it induces vis-à-vis Market Income inequality, Gross Income inequality, or Disposable Income inequality. Each one would be equally valid because education benefits do not depend on any of these income concepts but on whether the household has school-aged children. The size of the contribution of this benefit will be different for each path.

Given path dependency, the result obtained by the sequential method can thus be wrong. In theory, path dependency would require measuring the total average contribution by considering all the possible paths and taking, for example, the so-called Shapley value (used in game theory)[26] or applying methods that combine the sequential and Shapley-value approaches where the latter is applied on the subset of fiscal interventions for which an institutionally defined hierarchical path cannot be determined.[27] Applying the latter is complex, and results are sensitive to the assumptions made about the hierarchy of interventions. A sensible alternative is to use what in the statistical literature is known as the *marginal contribution*.[28] In our context, the marginal contribution of a tax (or transfer) is calculated by taking the difference between the inequality (or poverty) indicator *without* the tax (or transfer) and *with* it.[29] For example, the marginal contribution of direct taxes is the difference between the Gini for Gross Income (Market Income plus transfers) and the Gini for Disposable Income (Market Income plus transfers minus direct taxes).[30]

The marginal contribution has a straightforward policy interpretation because it is equivalent to asking the question: Would inequality be higher, the same, or lower with the tax (or transfer) than without it?[31] It is important to note as well that the notion of marginal contribution is general. That is, it can be applied not only to any inequality indicator but to poverty indicators as well. The basic issue is always the same:

---

[26] For an analysis of the Shapley value and its properties, see, for example, Shorrocks (2013).

[27] See, for example, Sastre and Trannoy (2002) and Sastre and Trannoy (2008).

[28] The term "marginal" here is not to be confused with the term "marginal" used in defining a derivative in calculus.

[29] The *marginal contribution* should not be confused with the *marginal incidence*, the latter being the incidence of a small change in spending. Note that, because of path dependency, adding up the marginal contributions of each intervention will not be equal to the total change in inequality. Clearly, adding up the sequential contributions will not equal the total change in inequality either. An approach that has been suggested to calculate the contribution of each intervention in such a way that they add up to the total change in inequality is to use the Shapley value. The studies analyzed here do not have estimates for the latter.

[30] Note that if certain fiscal interventions come in bundles (for example, a tax that kicks in only if a certain transfer is in place), the marginal contribution can be calculated for the net tax (or the net benefit) in question.

[31] Or, equivalently, by replacing the existing tax (transfer) by one that is distributionally neutral.

one must compare the size of the indicator without the fiscal instrument in place with the indicator that *does* include the latter. One drawback of the marginal contribution in the context of inequality measures is that it does not satisfy the aggregation principle: that is, the sum of the marginal contributions of all the taxes and transfers will not equal—except by accident—the total redistributive effect. At this point, we are ready to give up the aggregation principle in exchange for always obtaining the correct answer as to whether a tax or a transfer exerts an equalizing or unequalizing influence.

1.3 The Wildcard: Reranking of Households

Reranking refers to the phenomenon whereby fiscal interventions arbitrarily alter the relative position of individuals (or households) across the distribution. In other words, reranking occurs if individual A was poorer than individual B before a fiscal intervention, but B is poorer than A after the intervention. The definition of horizontal equity postulates that the prefiscal policy income ranking should be preserved (Duclos and Araar, 2006). In other words, if individual A was poorer than individual B before the fiscal interventions, individual A should continue to be poorer than individual B after the interventions.

In Volume 1's chapter 2, Enami, Lustig, and Aranda reproduce Lambert's formulation and extend it to the case of multiple taxes and transfers. In chapter 3 in this Volume, Enami shows how conditions are affected if taxes and transfers rerank households (when households occupy a different spot in the ranking with prefiscal rather than with postfiscal income). It is important to note that if there is reranking, the *fundamental equation* can no longer be interpreted as a measure of the fiscally induced change in *inequality*. To illustrate, let's think of the hypothetical case in which taxes and transfers cause extreme reranking: that is, households switch places in such a way that the prefiscal richest becomes the postfiscal poorest, the second prefiscal richest becomes the second postfiscal poorest, and so on. In such a situation, the change in inequality will be zero. However, the redistributive effect will be positive and equal to the weighted sum described above, but where RE_N, RE_t, and RE_B are the Reynolds-Smolensky indices for the net fiscal system, taxes (only) and benefits (only), respectively.[32]

In other words, reranking introduces the equivalent of a "wildcard": the only way to know if the net fiscal system is equalizing or not is by empirical estimation. One cannot predict whether a net fiscal system is equalizing by relying on the size and progressivity of taxes and transfers. Most if not all fiscal systems in real life feature some degree of reranking of households. The order of magnitude can vary; below we present an indicator to measure reranking and illustrate with examples from existing *CEQ*

---

[32] In fact, in the presence of reranking the fundamental equation measures the change induced to what in the literature Is often called "vertical equity." Reranking is considered a form of horizontal inequity. See, for example, Duclos and Araar (2006).

Assessments. Reranking is interpreted as a measure of fiscally induced horizontal inequality.[33] The more reranking there is, the more horizontal inequity.

It can also be shown that if there is reranking—which as we say is a pervasive feature of net fiscal systems in the real world—making a tax more progressive (vis-à-vis Market Income) can result in an *increase* in postfiscal inequality. Let's go back to Lambert's table 1-1 to illustrate. Make the tax more progressive and see what happens. In Lambert's example, not only do regressive taxes enhance the equalizing effect of transfers, but making taxes more progressive (in other words, more disproportional in the Kakwani sense) would result in higher(!) inequality; any additional change (toward more progressivity) in taxes or transfers would just cause reranking and an increase in inequality.

In other words, reranking destroys the public finance dictum that

> if the combined redistributive impact of tax and spending is progressive then the higher the level of tax and spending in a country the larger is the redistributive impact. Similarly, for a given level of tax and spending, the more revenue collection is concentrated in more redistributive taxes (progressive income taxes) and the more spending is concentrated in more redistributive transfers (well targeted social transfers), the greater the redistributive impact of fiscal policy.[34]

If there is reranking, in order to determine whether a particular intervention (or a particular policy change) is inequality increasing or inequality reducing—and by how much—one must resort to numerical calculations that include the full set of components of the fiscal system being analyzed. In particular, one must calculate the inequality indicator that would prevail with and without the specific intervention (or policy change).[35]

Therefore, indices that rely on concentration measures that use prefiscal income as a classifier (i.e., the income by which households are ranked), such as the Kakwani index of progressivity, can mathematically produce sign-inconsistent cases in the presence of reranking and/or the Lambert conundrum.[36] While it is mathematically possible for a component of fiscal policy to be progressive (regressive) based on the

---

[33] Duclos and Araar (2006).

[34] Bastagli, Coady, and Gupta (2015, p. 57).

[35] The same applies to poverty indicators or any other indicator of interest. The difficulties are compounded when one wants to compare the impact of net fiscal systems across countries because the original distributions (that is, the income distribution before taxes and transfers) differ. For a discussion comparing systems when the original distribution must be taken into account, see Lambert (2001) and Duclos and Araar (2006).

[36] This sign-inconsistency can occur with other indices of progressivity that rely on concentration measures that use prefiscal income as the classifier such as the Suits and the Reynolds-Smolensky indeces.

Kakwani index yet unequalizing (equalizing), how frequently does this occur in actual fiscal systems? Enami, Lustig, and Larroulet (forthcoming) show that in a sample of 39 countries obtained from the CEQ Data Center, "for everything but indirect taxes, inconsistent results appear only in three cases. That is, the risk of a Kakwani index yielding a misleading result is minimal. However, in the case of indirect taxes, we find that in 22 country cases the two indicators do not have the same sign. That is, in roughly 25 percent of our sample there is sign-inconsistency: regressive indirect taxes, based on the Kakwani index, are equalizing (i.e., the marginal contribution is positive)."

2 Fiscal Incidence Analysis at a Glance

As stated above, taxation and public spending are key policy levers that the state has in its power to change the distribution of income. The tool proposed here—the *CEQ Assessment*—relies on state-of-the art fiscal incidence analysis to address the following four questions:

1. How much income redistribution and poverty reduction is being accomplished through fiscal policy?[37]
2. How equalizing and pro-poor are specific taxes and government spending?
3. How effective are taxes and government spending in reducing inequality and poverty?
4. What is the impact of fiscal reforms that change the size and/or progressivity of a particular tax or benefit?

Rooted in the field of Public Finance, fiscal incidence analysis is one of the most commonly used methods to measure the distributional impact of a country's taxes and public spending. Fiscal incidence analysis is designed to measure who bears the burden of taxes and who receives the benefits of government spending—in particular, of social spending—and who are the gainers and losers of particular tax reforms or changes to welfare programs. In practice, fiscal incidence analysis is the method utilized to allocate taxes and public spending to households so that one can compare incomes before taxes and transfers with incomes after them, and calculate the relevant indicators of prefiscal and postfiscal inequality and poverty, among others.

Without attempting to provide an exhaustive literature review here, it is worth mentioning that the tax incidence literature includes a long list of studies going back to the middle of the twentieth century—mainly on the US tax system—starting with the pioneer work of Musgrave and others (1951) and Musgrave (1959), and the Tax Foundation (1960); and, subsequently, by Musgrave, Case, and Leonard (1974), Pechman

---

[37] As stated at the outset, throughout this Handbook, "fiscal policy," "fiscal instruments," "taxes and government spending," "revenue collection and government spending," "taxes and transfers," and "taxes and benefits" are used interchangeably.

and Okner (1974), and Pechman (1985). On the expenditure side, early studies on its incidence can be found in Peacock (1954), Gillespie (1965), and the Tax Foundation (1967).[38] These studies, as does our current framework to produce *CEQ Assessments*, belong to the so-called accounting approach to fiscal incidence analysis.[39] That is, they ignore behavioral responses, general equilibrium effects, and intertemporal effects. While ignoring behavioral responses and general equilibrium effects is a limitation of the accounting approach, the effects calculated with this method are considered a reasonable approximation of the short-run welfare impact.

An alternative to the accounting approach is to model behavioral responses in the incidence analysis. This can be done in a partial equilibrium or general equilibrium framework.[40] Intertemporal effects and lifetime tax incidence can also be done as long as there is the necessary data because results depend critically on the lifetime earnings profile of household members.[41]

As Martinez-Vazquez (2008) and this Handbook forcibly argue, from a policy viewpoint, net fiscal incidence is the relevant equity measure that government authorities

---

[38] To this early work one should add, for example, Meerman (1979) and Selowsky (1979) who analyzed the incidence of public spending in Malaysia and Colombia, respectively. The Tax Foundation (1967) study, actually, looks at both taxes and expenditures. In some tax incidence work, taxes are measured as taxes net of cash transfers.

[39] For more recent descriptions and applications, and discussions on the limitations of standard incidence analysis, see also, for example, Adema and Ladaique (2005); Alleyne and others (2004); Atkinson (1983); Barr (2004); Barros and others (2009); Bastagli, Coady, and Gupta (2015); Bergh (2005); Birdsall, de la Torre, and Menezes (2008); Bourguignon and Pereira da Silva (2003); Breceda, Rigolini, and Saavedra (2008); Dilnot, Kay, and Keen (1990); Ferreira and Robalino (2010); Fiszbein and others (2009); Goñi, Lopez, and Serven (2011); Grosh and others (2008); Gupta and others (2015); Kakwani (1977); Lambert (2001); Lora (2006); Martinez-Vazquez (2008); Morra Imas and Rist (2009); O'Donnell and others (2008); Bibi and Duclos (2010); Shah (2003); Suits (1977); van de Walle (1992); van de Walle and Nead (1995); World Bank (2000/2001, 2006, 2009, 2011). The readings mentioned in the above paragraph or other sections of this chapter (including footnotes) are meant neither to be an exhaustive list nor to represent the history of thought in fiscal incidence analysis. The cited readings are meant to give the reader a sample of references to early work on fiscal incidence analysis as well as of its evolution.

[40] For partial equilibrium analysis, see, for example, Coady (2006); Gertler and Glewwe (1990); Gertler and van der Gaag (1990); McClure (1970); Mieszkowski (1967); Musgrave (1959); Ravallion and Chen (2015); Rolph (1954); van de Walle (1998 and 2004); and Younger and others (1999). An example of fiscal incidence analysis in a general equilibrium framework is the article by Devarajan and Hossain (1998) for the Philippines. For estimates of the spillover effects of cash transfer programs, see Barrientos and Sabates-Wheeler (2009); Angelucci and De Giorgi (2009). There are other spillover effects through the externalities that a better educated and healthier population generates on society as a whole.

[41] See, for example, the fiscal incidence analysis in an intertemporal setting for the United States by Fullerton and Rogers (1991) and Slemrod (1992).

need to use in judging particular policies. For instance, an increase in value-added taxes (VAT) may be rejected on equity grounds as being regressive, but it may be desirable from an equity standpoint if the resulting revenues are used to finance primary-school services in poor neighborhoods. Taxes may be progressive, but if transfers to the poor are not large enough, they may worsen poverty. However, until the launch of the Commitment to Equity (CEQ) project in 2008,[42] work that analyzed the incidence of both government revenue and spending simultaneously—including net indirect taxes and spending on in-kind services—was less common. Since the launching of the CEQ project, this has changed quite strikingly, as evidenced by the publication of the country studies included in the Applications section (part III) of Volume 1 as well as in the following publications: Alam, Inchauste, and Serajuddin (2017); Arunatilake, Inchauste, and Lustig (2017); Bucheli and others (2014); Cabrera, Lustig, and Moran (2015); Cancho and Bondarenko (2017); Higgins and Lustig (2016); Higgins and Pereira (2014); Higgins and others (2016); Hill and others (2017); Inchauste and Lustig (2017); Inchauste and others (2017); Jaramillo (2014); Jellema, Wai-Poi, and Afkar (2017); Lopez-Calva and others (2017); Lustig (2015, 2016); Lustig, Pessino, and Scott (2014); Paz Arauco and others (2014); Scott (2014); Younger and Khachatryan (2017); Younger, Myamba, and Mdadila (2016); Younger, Osei-Assibey, and Oppong (2017); and numerous others included in the CEQ Working Paper series (with over 100 publications) available at www.ceqinstitute.org. Often in collaboration with other institutions, the CEQ Institute has completed or is in the process of completing over sixty *CEQ Assessments* that span all regions of the world as shown in the map featured in the homepage of www.ceqinstitute.org. As of January 2022, there are *CEQ Assessments* available for fifty-eight countries. Available means that the results are featured in the CEQ Standard Indicators. Of the fifty-eight, the CEQ Data Center on Fiscal Redistribution has forty-five countries for which the *MWB* and the replication code are available. CEQ Harmonized Microdata is available for twenty-six countries in Harvard Dataverse.[43]

As stated above, fiscal incidence analysis is used to assess the distributional impact of a country's taxes, transfers, and subsidies. Essentially, fiscal incidence analysis consists of allocating taxes (for example, personal income tax, payroll taxes, other direct taxes such as property taxes, VAT, sales taxes, and excise taxes) and public spending (for example, cash transfers, education, health, and housing spending, and consumption subsidies) to households so that one can compare incomes before taxes and transfers (prefiscal income) with incomes after taxes, transfers, and subsidies (post-

---

[42] The project was initially launched at the Inter-American Dialogue with a focus on Latin America only.

[43] This information is as of January 2022. Please visit www.ceqinstitute.org for the most up-to-date coverage. Note that there are countries with partial fiscal incidence analysis for which there may be a paper but were not included in the CEQ Data Center. The converse is also true: there are some countries for which there are data in the CEQ Standard Indicators but there is no paper (e.g., India).

fiscal income).[44] "Transfers" in CEQ language refer to both cash transfers and near cash transfers such as school breakfasts and uniforms, as well as benefits in kind such as free government services in education and healthcare.[45] "Subsidies" refer to the benefit obtained in the form of a below–market price when purchasing a good or service.

Usually, fiscal incidence analysis looks only at what is paid and what is received without assessing the behavioral responses that taxes and public spending may trigger on individuals or households. This is often referred to as the "accounting" approach. Put simply, the accounting approach consists of starting from an income concept and, depending on the fiscal intervention under study, allocating the proper amount of a tax or a transfer to each household or individual. If the fiscal intervention is a direct tax (transfer) and one starts the analysis from pretax (pre-transfer) income, the post-tax (post-transfer) income is calculated by subtracting (adding) the tax paid (transfer received).

More formally, define the before taxes and transfers income of household h as I_h and taxes as T_i (where i refers to the range of taxes whose incidence is being analyzed) and transfers or benefits B_j (where j refers to the range of transfers whose incidence is being analyzed); define the "allocator" of tax i to household h as S_{ih} (or the share of net tax i borne by unit h); then, post-tax income of household h can be defined as Y_h:

$$Y_h = I_h - \Sigma_i\, T_i S_{ih} + \Sigma_j\, B_j S_{jh}$$

Although the method is quite straightforward, its application can be fraught with complications. Some of these complications arise because actual or economic incidence can be quite different from statutory incidence. As stated by Lustig (2020):

Statutory incidence refers to the rate of taxation established by law and where the tax is proximately levied. For example, in statutory terms, an excise tax might be collected from consumers. However, as formally shown by Harberger (1962) many decades ago, the actual burden in welfare terms—that is, the economic incidence— of a tax may be quite different from who mails the check to the tax authorities. In the case of an excise tax, the economic burden may fall entirely on the consumer, entirely on the producer, or on both, depending on demand (or supply) elasticities. In partial equilibrium analysis (and in competitive economies where markets clear), if demand is completely inelastic (or supply perfectly elastic), consumers will bear the entire burden of an excise tax: the price of the good at the cash register will increase exactly in the amount of the tax. If, on the other hand, demand is perfectly elastic (or supply completely inelastic), producers will: the prices on the shelf will not change but the price that producers receive will be reduced

---

[44] In addition to the studies cited here and other studies in www.commitmentoequity.org, see, for example, Förster and Whiteford (2009), Immervoll and Richardson (2011), and OECD (2011).
[45] "Transfers" in this Handbook are also called "benefits" and "government spending."

exactly in the amount of the tax. Beyond these two limiting cases, the fundamental principle is that taxes tend to be borne by the more inelastic consumers (or, more generally, demanders) or producers (or, more generally, suppliers). In the case of payroll taxes, for instance, the more inelastic labor supply versus labor demand is, the more is the employer able to transfer the burden of employer's payroll taxes to workers in the form of lower wages: i.e., the burden is shifted backward to workers. Likewise, the burden of a tax on inputs (such as a gasoline tax on retailers) will be borne by the consumer in the form of higher prices the more inelastic his/her demand for the taxed good is vis-à-vis the supply elasticity.[46]

In sum, the economic incidence depends on the elasticity of demand and/or supply of a factor or a good: the burden of taxes is borne by those who cannot easily adjust to the change in price induced by the tax. The economic incidence of taxes will also be affected by how revenues are used. In a general equilibrium analysis (which is necessary when taxes impact large parts of the economy), the economic incidence is also sensitive to a large number of elasticities. In open economies, the extent of factor mobility will affect on whom the burden of taxes fall. Finally, in a dynamic context, the long run economic incidence will ultimately depend on how taxes affect capital accumulation and marginal productivities of factors of production. (p. 5)

Actual incidence can also differ from statutory incidence because, for example, there is tax evasion or informality, or the take up of a transfer program is above or below what is stated by the law. Another source of difficulty is that the data to calculate the actual incidence are usually incomplete or absent.

Chapter 6 in part II of this Volume is dedicated to explaining how to carry out incidence analysis in practice and complete a *CEQ Assessment* using the *CEQ Master Workbook* (available online in part IV of this Volume) as the repository of "input" data. The chapter also provides detailed recommendations on how to address a wide range of challenges stemming from lack of information and measurement error. Chapter 7 describes how to extend the incidence analysis incorporating the indirect effects (through inputs) of indirect taxes and subsidies. Chapter 8 presents the CEQ indicators and describes how to generate the results using the *CEQ Stata Package*. The indicators are automatically transferred to the relevant sections of *CEQ Master Workbook* as the repository of "output" data.

Fiscal incidence analysis can be partial or comprehensive. Partial fiscal incidence analysis assesses the impact of one or several fiscal policy interventions: for example, income taxes or use of public education and health services. Comprehensive fiscal incidence analysis assesses the impact of the revenue and spending sides simultaneously:

---

[46] For an analysis of the economic incidence of taxes, see, for example, Atkinson and Stiglitz (2015); Chetty, Looney, and Kroft (2009); Kotlikoff and Summers (1987); Salanie (2011).

namely, the impact of direct and indirect taxes, cash and in-kind transfers, and indirect subsidies. Incidence analysis can use income or consumption (per capita or equivalized) to measure household welfare. Additionally, there is point-in-time versus lifetime fiscal incidence analysis. The analysis can assess a current system or estimate the potential or actual effects of particular reforms. It can use the statutory incidence or the economic one. It can make different tax-shifting assumptions and about the value of in-kind benefits. The analysis can assess the average incidence of a tax or benefit, or it can assess the incidence on the margin, the distribution of an increase in the spending of public education to increase primary enrollment.

In terms of data, incidence studies use microdata from household surveys combined with budget data from fiscal accounts and other administrative registries. Since in practice surveys will not include information on every tax paid or transfer received (or, if the information exists, it may be inaccurate), that information must be generated in a consistent and methodologically sound way. Frequently, the information will have to be generated using a variety of assumptions to check the sensitivity of the results to assumptions that cannot be externally validated.

In addition to assessing the impact of fiscal policy on the personal distribution of income, one may be interested in how taxes and transfers affect the welfare of different morally or institutionally relevant social groups, such as groups of individuals differentiated by gender, ethnicity, or location.

2.1 Allocating Taxes and Transfers to Individuals: The Art of Fiscal Incidence Analysis

As stated above, fiscal incidence analysis consists of allocating taxes (personal income tax and consumption taxes, in particular) and public spending (social spending and consumption subsidies, in particular) to households or individuals so that one can compare incomes before taxes and transfers with incomes after taxes and transfers. Transfers include both cash transfers and benefits in kind, such as free government services in education and healthcare. Transfers also include consumption subsidies such as food, electricity, and fuel subsidies. The building block of fiscal incidence analysis is the construction of income concepts. That is, starting from prefiscal income, each new income concept is constructed by adding (for transfers) and subtracting (for taxes) to the previous income concept. Figure 1-1 presents a stylized version of how to construct the income concepts. However, in practice one needs to use the detailed definition of income concepts presented in this Volume's chapter 6, and in figure 6-2 and table 6-5.

As discussed below, social insurance contributory pensions are in general (and depending on the history of contributions and life expectancy of individuals) partly deferred income and therefore should have a portion of them added to Market Income (and contributions subtracted from factor income); and partly government transfer and therefore a portion of them should be included with the rest of government transfers

FIGURE 1-1

Income Concepts under the Two Scenarios in *CEQ Assessments*: Pensions as
Deferred Income (PDI) and Pensions as Government Transfer (PGT)

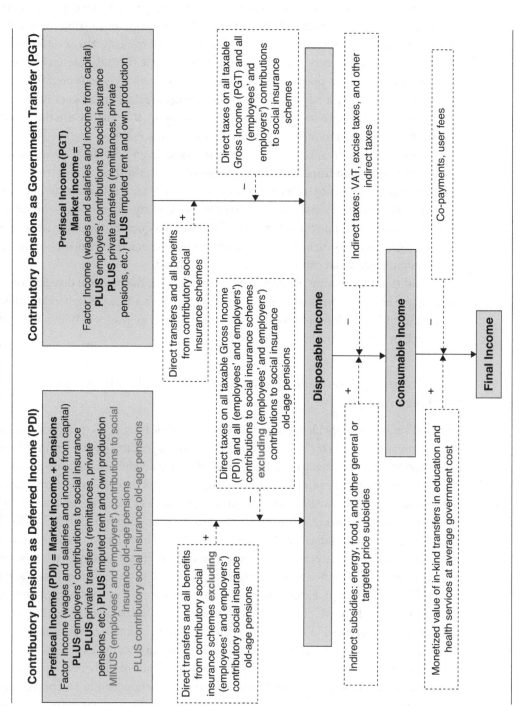

(and contributions treated as any other direct tax). However, since at this point there is no conventional method to determine which portion should be allocated to prefiscal income and which to government transfers when the only information available is a cross-section household survey, this Volume recommends calculating the impact of the net fiscal system under the two extreme scenarios: (1) contributory pensions are pure deferred income (also known as "replacement income") and (2) contributory pensions are a pure government transfer. In chapter 6 of Volume 2 of this Handbook, Carlos Grushka (2022) proposes an approach to determine which scenario may be more appropriate when one has access to cross-section data only.

As stated, the basic incidence analysis used in *CEQ Assessments* is point-in-time rather than lifecycle and does not incorporate behavioral or general equilibrium modeling. That is, we do not claim that the prefiscal income obtained from this exercise equals the true counterfactual income in the absence of taxes and transfers. It is a first-order approximation (and in a variety of settings a first-order approximation is all one may need).[47] Despite being a standard incidence analysis that does not incorporate second-round or general equilibrium effects, the analysis is not a mechanically applied accounting exercise. We analyze the incidence of taxes by their (assumed) economic rather than their statutory incidence. For instance, we assume that individual income taxes and contributions (both by employee and employer) are borne by labor in the formal sector and that consumption taxes (on both final goods and inputs, using input-output tables for the latter) are fully shifted forward to consumers. This is equivalent to assuming that the supply of labor and demand for goods and services are perfectly inelastic.[48] In the case of consumption taxes, furthermore, we take into account the lower incidence associated with own-consumption (i.e., direct consumption of goods and services produced by the household such as corn products cooked from corn grown by peasant households) and tax avoidance/evasion due to informality (i.e., employees or self-employed who are not registered in the administrative system and do not pay taxes or contributions to the social security system) or other reasons. Old-age contributory pensions are not automatically assumed to always be a government transfer, a subject that is discussed in more detail below.

---

[47] Coady and others (2006), for instance, state, "The first order estimate is much easier to calculate, provides a bound on the real-income effect, and is likely to closely approximate a more sophisticated estimate. Finally, since one expects that short-run substitution elasticities are smaller than long-run elasticities, the first-order estimate will be a better approximation of the short-run welfare impact" (p. 9).

[48] The economic incidence, strictly speaking, depends on the elasticity of demand and/or supply of a factor or a good, and the ensuing general equilibrium effects. In essence, the accounting approach implicitly assumes zero demand price and labor supply elasticities, and zero elasticities of substitution among inputs, which may not be far-fetched assumptions for analyzing effects in the short-run, especially when changes are small.

Even though the *CEQ Assessments* do not model behavioral, lifecycle, or general equilibrium effects, the method and resulting studies are among the most comprehensive and comparable tax-benefit incidence analyses available for middle-income and low-income countries to date.

We attempt to cover a very broad spectrum of taxes and government spending. Taxes include personal income and payroll taxes, other direct taxes such as property taxes, and consumption taxes. Spending on public goods such as defense and corporate taxes and subsidies are not included in *CEQ Assessments* (at least, not at this point).

Spending covers direct cash and near-cash direct transfers, indirect subsidies (especially on food, housing, energy, and agricultural inputs), and benefits from public spending on education and health. Throughout the Handbook, we refer to "transfers," "benefits," and "social spending" interchangeably; "transfers" is intended to include indirect subsidies (which includes housing subsidies) and in-kind benefits from public spending on education and health.

As a rule, if taxes and transfers are explicitly available in the surveys, one should use this information unless there are reasons to believe that it is not reliable. However, the information on direct and indirect taxes, transfers in cash and in-kind, and subsidies is often not collected in household surveys. In order to allocate the benefits of transfers and burden of taxation to individuals included in the household surveys, the CEQ Assessments make use of administrative data on revenues and government expenditures as well as knowledge about how the tax and transfer programs work, and allocate these taxes and transfers following methods that are described below. Thus, one of the most important aspects of CEQ is a detailed description of how each component of income is calculated (for example, directly identified in the survey or simulated) and the methodological assumptions that are made while calculating it. These are included in section C of the *Master Workbook* (available online in Volume 1) and compiled for all available countries in the Metadata Table in Volume 1's part V (available online only).

In many cases, the authors must choose a method based on the institutional structure of the country and the data available. CEQ relies on local experts as a crucial part of the research team for precisely this reason. In many cases, the researcher must exercise judgment based on his or her knowledge of the country's institutions, spending, and revenue collection, as well as on the availability and quality of the data. It is of the utmost importance to always describe what method was used for a particular tax or transfer, the reasoning for using this method, and—whenever possible—the sensitivity of the results to using alternative methods.

When taxes and transfers can be obtained directly from the household survey, we call this the "direct identification method." When the direct identification method is not feasible, there are several options—namely, *inference, imputation, simulation,* and *prediction,* which are described in detail in chapter 6 in this Volume. If the primary survey being used for the *CEQ Assessment* does not have the necessary information, these methods can be used in an *alternate survey*, then benefits or taxes can be matched back into the main survey. As a last resort, one can use secondary sources: for example, incidence or concentration shares by quintiles or deciles that have been calculated by other authors. Finally, if none of these options can be used for a specific category, the analysis for that category will have to be left blank.

One of the biggest challenges for the *CEQ Assessments* has to do with how to treat the differences in scale and structure between survey-based values and administrative registries. The causes for these differences are multiple including differences in definitions, but most prominently measurement errors due to under-reporting of certain income categories (for example, income from capital) and under-sampling of the rich in the surveys and measurement errors in national accounts. Whatever the cause, the overriding principle followed in the CEQ is that—unless there are good reasons not to—the information in the surveys is taken as valid and given precedence over and above the information from administrative registries. However, whenever the team has sufficient evidence to believe that totals in the survey are less credible than those in administrative registries, the latter should be used and the rationale properly documented (more on this in chapter 6 in this Volume).

CEQ is not the only methodological framework for applying fiscal incidence analysis. EUROMOD, based in the University of Essex, and LATAX, a multi-country flexible tax microsimulation model housed in the Institute of Fiscal Studies, are two alternatives. Their characteristics are described in appendixes to chapter 6 in this Volume.

Because the process of allocating taxes and transfers relies on assumptions that one cannot truly test or uses definitions for which there is no overriding consensus, it is recommended that robustness checks be carried out to assess the reliability of results. For example, use consumption instead of income, use equivalized income instead of per capita income, change assumptions about tax evasion or program take-up, assume ratios of taxes and transfers to Disposable Income are the same in the surveys as in national accounts, and so on.

2.2 Old-Age Social Insurance Contributory Pensions: A Government Transfer or Deferred Income?

In assessing the extent to which there is fiscal redistribution, it is important to be able to distinguish fiscal redistribution in a cross-section versus fiscal redistribution over the life-cycle (that is, to take into account the redistribution that takes place for the same individual as she or he faces different circumstances). Although this distinction, in theory, affects several fiscal interventions (such as contributory health and unemployment compensation), the assumptions made about pensions have perhaps the most significant consequences in terms of the order of magnitude of redistribution. The treatment of pensions from government-sponsored social insurance compulsory pension schemes (henceforth, contributory pensions) poses a particular challenge. Should contributions be treated as a tax or a form of "forced saving"? Should income from contributory pensions be treated as a government transfer or deferred income (consumption)? This decision can have a significant impact on assessing the redistributive power of a fiscal system especially in countries with a high proportion of retirees and large spending on social security. See, for example, discussion in chapter 10 of this Volume (Lustig, 2022) of the large difference in the size of the redistributive effect observed for countries in the European Union, the United States, Argentina, Russia, and other countries in which the old-age social insurance pension system covers a large proportion of workers and the retirement age population is relatively high.

In the incidence analysis literature, one can find both approaches: in some cases contributory pensions are considered deferred income,[49] while in others—especially in systems with a large subsidized component—they are considered a pure government transfer.[50] We believe that treating income from contributory pensions as a pure transfer is misleading. In populations with a large proportion of retirees, prefiscal income will be zero or close to zero for a large number of individuals. The fiscally induced inequality and poverty reduction will be overestimated because the system will feature many "false poor." To make this point clearer, let's assume a pensioner had been earning a high wage during her working years and that, privately, she could have saved enough so that at the time of retirement, her pension would have been at an x percent replacement ratio. Let's assume that instead she receives a pension from the social security system and that this is her only income. If her pension is treated as a pure government transfer, she will have been ranked among high wage–earners during her working years and fall to the prefiscal destitute poor during retirement. This does not make sense. Part or all of her pension would be the equivalent of what she would have earned from saving the equivalent of her contributions in a private scheme.[51]

Some may argue that in the absence of a government-sponsored program, individuals would not save enough for their old age and could become much poorer, and so treating pensions as a transfer makes sense. However, the government's role could be just that of a "piggy bank"[52] forcing individuals to save during their working years to ensure an

---

[49] Alvaredo and others (2015); Breceda, Rigolini, and Saavedra (2008); Immervoll and others (2009).
[50] Goñi, Lopez, and Serven (2011); Immervoll and others (2009); Lindert, Skoufias, and Shapiro (2006); Silveira and others (2011).
[51] Also, although any government tax or transfer might generate behavioral change, social security is special in the sense that it is a lifelong contract between a working individual and society. Although a conditional cash transfer (CCT) or other cash transfer will likely induce some behavioral changes, not having a government-sponsored retirement plan would generate major behavioral changes in a significant part of the population. Bosch and Campos-Vazquez (2014); Camacho, Conover, and Hoyos (2014); Garganta and Gasparini (2015).
[52] Barr (2001).

income stream during retirement. Accordingly, many countries place social security in a separate budget, protected from the politics governing other public expenditures.

Thus, as long as there is a government-sponsored old-age pension system with a mandatory savings component during individuals' working years, pensions should not be treated as a pure government transfer (at least, not in full). Independently of whether a system is fully funded or pay-as-you-go, or whether it is a defined benefit or defined contributions system,[53] the redistribution and transfer components of a pension from a government-sponsored system have to be calculated against what would have happened if the contributions had been placed in an interest-bearing individual account whose accrued assets would be used to finance consumption during retirement years through an annuity or in some other way. In addition, to be consistent, contributions have to be treated as "forced savings" and not a tax, to avoid double counting of this income (when it is earned as labor income and then later as retirement income).[54]

Let us illustrate with a simple set of formulas. Let us assume that there are only two types of individuals: working and retired. For simplicity, we also assume that only workers contribute to the system.[55] Given that we need to develop a framework that can be applied to cross-section household surveys, the individual during working years and the individual during retirement are not the same in the following.

Let us define:

Y_f = factor income during working years (grossed up for employer contributions to pensions)

s = rate of contributions to contributory pensions (as a proportion of factor income) during working period made by worker (as stated, in this stylized presentation we assume that the employer does not make contributions). For simplicity and more easily interpreted formulas, we assume the interest rate $r = 0$, so the return to saving is denoted sY_f.[56]

---

[53] See, for example, Barr (2012) for a description of pension systems.

[54] It is important to note that here we are ignoring within-system redistribution (i.e., from pensioners who receive less than what the private sector annuity counterfactual would yield to those who receive more but where this difference is funded from the savings obtained from those who receive less).

[55] In reality, contributions often also come from the employer (and, in some cases, the government). As discussed in detail in chapter 6 of Volume 1, we assume that the contributions made by the employer are shifted in total to the worker in the form of lower wages. See, for example, Melguizo and Gonzalez-Paramo (2013). This is not relevant for the purposes of the stylized presentation we make here because we assume that employers are not making any contributions.

[56] If the interest rate were not equal to zero, the income from pensions would be equal to $(1 + r)sY_f$, which is the annuity (or some other payment form) that would have been generated by the contributions sY_f made by the retirees over their lifetime and the returns rsY_f (with "r" equal to the interest rate) on those contributions in a purely private system.

$Y_m = (1 - s)Y_f + Y_o =$ Market Income[57] during working years, where $Y_o =$ other income during working years (for example, private transfers, remittances, and alimony)[58]

$Y =$ Disposable Income during working years

$Y' =$ Disposable Income during retirement which is equal to pensions plus any other income. (Here we assume that other sources of income—e.g., remittances—except for other government transfers, are zero for simplicity.)

$C =$ consumption during working years

$C' =$ consumption during retirement

$\omega =$ proportion of deficit in the pension system allocated to each pensioner

$B, B' =$ direct transfers during working years, direct transfers during retirement (these are other direct transfers during retirement, different from the transfers due to within-system redistribution or those that emanate from the deficit of the social security system)

$T, T' =$ direct taxes during working years (these taxes do not include contributions to the old-age pensions of the social security system), direct taxes during retirement (these taxes are unrelated to the within-system redistribution of the social security system)

In *CEQ Assessments* we have decided to do the following. In the "pensions as deferred income" (PDI) scenario, we assume that contributions during working years are a form of "forced saving" and define the prefiscal income as factor income plus private transfers AND plus income from contributory old-age public pensions LESS contributions to the old-age public pension systems (see figure 1-1). This way one avoids double counting since this saving is treated as income/consumption during retirement.[59]

During retirement, income from contributory pensions are assumed to be equal to the private saving counterfactual, and thus in the "pensions as deferred income"

---

[57] Note that as described in detail in chapter 6 of Volume 1, this "Market Income" will not be identical to the "Market Income" obtained for the scenario in which pensions are treated as a government transfer.

[58] For simplicity, we ignore imputed rent for owner occupied housing and consumption of own production. These two are considered part of prefiscal income in our empirical studies as described in detail in chapter 6 of Volume 1.

[59] Note that in the analyses that use income-based surveys, the "double-counting" problem does not occur with other forms of savings since we do not include dissaving (either through selling of assets, withdrawing from savings, or borrowing) as part of income. In the analyses that use consumption-based surveys, although dissaving is implicit in observed consumption, so is saving; thus, there is no double-counting issue either. This is so because observed consumption, by definition, will be equal to the portion of income consumed during the period plus dissaving (amounts borrowed or withdrawn from bank accounts, or revenues from selling of assets) minus saving.

(PDI) scenario, contributory pensions are considered part of prefiscal income and, thus, added to factor income (independently of whether contributory pensions are subject to taxation or not). If the only income a retiree receives is income from contributory pensions, then Y′ (Disposable Income) is implicitly assumed to be equal to sY_f minus any taxes paid on contributory pensions plus any other transfers. In other words, Market Income is Disposable Income plus any taxes paid on contributory pensions, if such taxation exists, minus government transfers. In pensions' jargon, this scenario is equivalent to assuming a fully funded defined contributions system.

Table 1-2 summarizes CEQ practice in the case in which contributory pensions are considered deferred income (PDI).[60] For simplicity, here and in all the scenarios below, we assume that there are no retirees in the household during working years and that there are no working members in the household during retirement. However, in practice, we take into account the fact that—especially in developing countries—households will be frequently composed of both working members and retirees.

Comparing the Market Income of the working and retired in table 1-2, it is obvious why Market Income should be net of contributions to contributory pensions in the pensions as deferred income scenario: otherwise, sY_f would be double counted as part of the working individual's Market Income as well as part of the retired individual's Market Income. When reading the results for the consumption-based scenario, it is useful to read the table "backwards" by beginning at Disposable Income, then subtracting out benefits and adding taxes (the opposite of the usual operation of adding benefits and subtracting taxes) to arrive at Market Income, etc.

In order to compare the results of a *CEQ Assessment* with exercises in which people assume that contributions are a tax and pensions are a pure transfer, we suggest calculating such a scenario in the *CEQ Assessment* as well. We call it the Pensions as Government Transfers (PGT) scenario. In this case, Market Income for pensioners equals zero or other income if there is one, and the transfer equals the entire pension.[61] Contributions paid during the year of the survey are equal to sY_f and are treated as a pure tax.[62] Table 1-3 summarizes the CEQ practice when contributory pensions are considered a pure government transfer and contributions a pure tax.

Note that in the two scenarios—PDI and PGT—Disposable Income is identical (Figure 1-1).

---

[60] In the original paper-length online-only version of the Handbook (Lustig and Higgins, 2013), this scenario was called the "benchmark" case.

[61] In Lustig and Higgins (2013) this scenario was called the "sensitivity analysis scenario."

[62] This scenario should not be viewed as a special case of the general framework developed above, but rather a scenario we construct to compare with the typical assumptions made in other exercises (for example, EUROMOD). As such, it is inconsistent (on purpose) with the general framework in which contributions are deferred income even if a portion of the transfer is subsidized, since this scenario is based on a different conceptualization.

TABLE 1-2
Scenario with Pensions as Deferred Income (PDI) in CEQ Assessments

	Factor income	Contributions to old-age social security system (forced saving)	Market income	Tax	Transfer	Disposable income
Income-based scenario						
Working	Y_f	sY_f	$Y_m = (1-s)Y_f + Y_o$	T	B	$Y = Y_m - T + B$
Retirement	0	0	sY_f	T'	B'	$Y' = sY_f - T' + B'$
Consumption-based scenario						
Working	Y_f	sY_f	$C + T - B$	T	B	C
Retirement	0	0	$C' + T' - B'$	T'	B'	C'

Note: Pensions are treated as deferred income and contributions as forced saving.

TABLE 1-3
Scenario with Pensions as Government Transfer (PGT) in *CEQ Assessments*

	Factor income	Contributions to old-age social security system (forced saving)	Market income	Tax	Transfer	Disposable income
				Income-based scenario		
Working	Y_f	0	$Y_m = Y_f + Y_o$	$T + sY_f$	B	$Y = Y_m - T - sY_f + B$
Retirement	0	0	0	T	$B + sY_f$	$Y' = sY_f - T' + B'$
				Consumption-based scenario		
Working	Y_f	0	$C + T + sY_f - B$	$T + sY_f$	B	C
Retirement	0	0	$C' + T' - B' - sY_f$	T	$B + sY_f$	C'

Note: Pensions are treated as a government transfer and contributions as a tax.

Summing-up, in CEQ we propose running two scenarios:

1. A scenario in which old-age contributory public pensions are treated as pure deferred income. As stated, we call this scenario "pensions as deferred income," or PDI. In the PDI scenario, the income from these pensions is added to factor income to generate the prefiscal income AND contributions to old-age contributory pensions are subtracted from factor income. In the PDI scenario, the prefiscal income (that is, the starting income concept by which households are ranked to calculate the incidence of taxes and transfers) is called "Market Income plus Pensions."

2. A scenario in which old-age contributory public pensions are treated as a pure government transfer. As stated, we call this scenario "pensions as government transfer," or PGT. In the PGT scenario, the income from these pensions is added to the rest of government cash transfers AND contributions to old-age contributory pensions are added to direct taxes. In the PGT scenario, the prefiscal income (that is, the starting income concept by which households are ranked to calculate the incidence of taxes and transfers) is called "Market Income."

The PDI and PGT scenarios describe two "extreme" situations. In practice, pensions are probably a combination of deferred income and a government transfer. In chapter 6 of Volume 2, Carlos Grushka (2022) proposes an approach to determine which scenario may be appropriate when one has access to cross-section data only.

The income concepts for the two scenarios are presented in figure 1-1, which was shown earlier in the chapter but for the readers' convenience is repeated again on page **31**.

It is important to note that the above formulations do not calculate the within-system redistribution (intragenerational lifetime redistribution). If there is within-system (within-cohort) redistribution, people are implicitly taxed, or receive a transfer, at the time of retirement. If their pension is below what they would have received had the contributions been privately saved at the market expected return, the difference is the tax; in contrast, for the retirees whose pension is above what they would have received in the private savings counterfactual, the difference is a transfer. In a system that is actuarially fair, this tax and transfer process occurs implicitly. In a system that is actuarially fair at the system level as well as at the level of each individual, there is neither redistribution within the system nor from other revenue sources. This would be, in the social security systems' jargon, equivalent to a fully funded defined contribution system. However, if the system is not actuarially fair, in addition to within-system redistribution, there is a redistribution process that takes place when government revenues (for example, taxes) are used to finance the deficit of the social security system. This corresponds to our hybrid scenario described below. Ideally, one would like to be able to estimate the within-system redistribution. In practice, however, it is quite challenging to calculate the annualized income that would correspond to the accumulated contributions and their respective return in the private saving counterfactual from cross-section household surveys since one does not know either the history

FIGURE 1-1

Income Concepts under the Two Scenarios in *CEQ Assessments*: Pensions as
Deferred Income (PDI) and Pensions as Government Transfer (PGT)

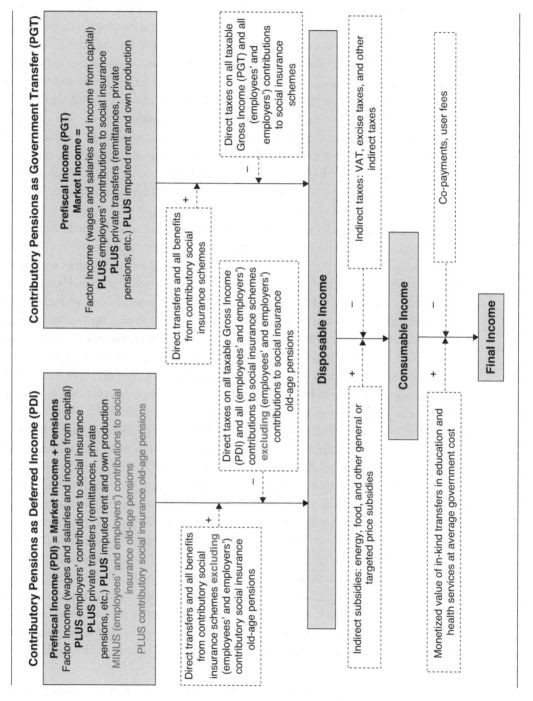

of contributions of individuals who are receiving a pension at the time of the survey or their life expectancy.

It is also important to note that the formulations under the scenarios presented here do not calculate the implicit tax burden on future generations for the case in which the social security deficit is financed not by current taxes but through debt.

Another clarification worth making is that if pensions of public servants have a component that is a transfer (i.e., noncontributory; whether partial or in full), this does not immediately mean that they should be treated as a pure transfer; this depends on whether pension income is part of the labor contract of public servants. For example, if the public servants' remuneration in the private sector during their working years would have been higher but their pension benefits lower or more subject to uncertainty, this would be the case in which pensions—although in the government's bookkeeping might appear as a transfer—are actually a component of wages of public employees, a component that is paid at retirement.

A hybrid scenario—relevant when the contributory pension system is in deficit and part of pensions are funded out of general revenue—is to assume that a portion of pensions are deferred income and a portion are a government transfer. In this scenario, we still assume that contributions are a form of "forced saving" during working years. Hence, *all* income concepts—including Market Income plus Pensions—are net of the contribution. This again avoids the double-counting issue. We allocate the portion of contributory pensions represented by the system's deficit to each individual receiving a contributory pension during retirement, proportionally to his or her observed pension income. Since pension income equals the gross returns to saving during working years, the portion of the pension considered a transfer is equal to $\omega s Y_f$, where ω is the portion of the contributory pension system funded by deficit spending. In other words, if D equals the deficit of old-age pensions system, i.e., total spending on social security old-age pensions less total revenues from contributions to contributory pensions in the year of the survey, then ω equals D divided by total spending on social security old-age pensions in the year of the survey.[63]

Since in most consumption-only surveys we do not know how much of the income comes from pensions, and since many households are made up in practice of some retired individuals and some nonretired ones (so we cannot just set the proportion of the pension that is a transfer as $\omega C'$), we attempt to estimate pension income. For example, in the *CEQ Assessment* for Indonesia, $s Y_f$ was estimated as follows. Individuals potentially making contributions to (as well as those potentially receiving income from) the pension system were identified using individual characteristics such as relationship to household head, age, education, sector of work, and, most important, participation in other benefit schemes for civil servants. Contribution and benefit amounts were estimated using parameters from an imputed wage regression carried out in a secondary labor force survey.[64]

---

[63] Note that one might also want to use the actuarial deficit rather than the actual one if an estimate is available.

[64] Jellema, Wai-Poi, and Afkar (2017).

Table 1-4 summarizes CEQ practice in the scenario where a portion of pensions are considered as deferred income and a portion as a government transfer because is a deficit in the social security system in the year of the survey.

2.3 Policy Simulations

The CEQ Handbook describes how to estimate the distributional impact of a system of taxes, cash transfers, and in-kind services using microdata. Once this is done for the existing public finance system, one might want to explore further issues to get a fuller understanding of the impacts of tax and spending policy, as well as the opportunities and risks of policy change. What is the impact of a particular set of reforms to the system on the incomes and spending power of different types of households and on the government's revenue or spending? What about the potential behavioral impacts of the existing system or of reforms to it? These are the kinds of issues that are typically examined using tax-and-transfer microsimulation and other models.[65] Policy simulations in CEQ are done "manually." See Volume 1's chapter 16 by Stephen D. Younger (2022) on how one can use CEQ to simulate the elimination of energy subsidies in Ghana and Tanzania and the impact of compensatory cash transfers.

2.4 Caveats: No Behavioral Responses, No Intertemporal Effects, and No Spillover Effects

At this point, CEQ considers only first-order effects (also known as "partial equilibrium analysis"). We do not account for behavioral or general equilibrium effects, although it is worth noting that our economic incidence assumptions (for example, on who bears the burden of payroll or consumption taxes) are consistent with a general equilibrium model in which one assumes zero demand price and labor supply elasticities and zero elasticities of substitution among inputs. As said above, these may not be farfetched assumptions for analyzing effects in the short run. "The first order estimate is much easier to calculate, provides a bound on the real-income effect, and is likely to closely approximate a more sophisticated estimate. Finally, since one expects that short-run substitution elasticities are smaller than long-run elasticities, the first-order estimate will be a better approximation of the short-run welfare impact."[66] Box 1-1 provides more detail on the accuracy of these first-order approximations. In some contexts,

---

[65] Two salient examples are EUROMOD and LATAX, descriptions of which are presented in chapter 6 of this Volume. See also Bourguignon and Pereira da Silva (2003), Bourguignon and Spadaro (2006), and Urzua (2012). For further information on the different types of model that can be developed, and the data requirements for each of these, see O'Donoghue (2014, chaps. 1–9).

[66] Coady and others (2006, p. 9).

TABLE 1-4
Scenario Where Pensions are Partly Deferred Income and Partly a Government Transfer (Hybrid) in *CEQ Assessments*

	Factor income	Contributions to old-age social security system (forced saving)	Market income	Tax	Transfer	Disposable income
			Income-based scenario			
Working	Y_f	sY_f	$Y_m = (1-s)Y_f + Y_o$	T	B	$Y = Y_m - T + B$
Retirement	0	0	$(1-\omega)sY_f$	T′	$B' + \omega sY_f$	$Y' = sY_f - T' + B'$
			Consumption-based scenario			
Working	Y_f	sY_f	$C + T - B$	T	B	C
Retirement	0	0	$C' + T' - B' - \omega sY_f$	T′	$B' + \omega sY_f$	C′

Note: Pensions are treated as partially deferred income and partially a government transfer; contributions as forced saving.

Box 1-1

Ignoring Behavioral Responses to Tax and Expenditure Policies: Implications
Stephen D. Younger

Many incidence analyses, including standard CEQ analyses, ignore households' behavioral responses to taxes and expenditures. This greatly simplifies the analysis as it obviates the need for demand estimation, but it may also prove to be misleading. As it turns out, the estimate of a tax's cost or an expenditure's benefit used in the simple approach of a standard incidence analysis is usually a first-order approximation to the true cost or benefit. The question of how misleading this analysis is then boils down to asking: How good is a first-order approximation?

Consider an *ad valorem* indirect tax of t percent. In competitive markets, this will raise the price of the good(s) taxed by t percent. A standard measure of the cost of such a tax to consumers is the compensating variation: the amount of additional expenditure a consumer would need to keep her utility constant in the face of the price increase:

$$CV = e(p^1, u^0) - e(p^0, u^0) = \int_{p_0}^{p_1} x^c(p, u^0) dp,$$

where $e(\ )$ is the expenditure function; p^1 is a vector of prices inclusive of the tax, which is what we usually observe; p^0 is a vector of prices without the tax; u is utility; and x^c is the compensated demand function. The second equality shows that the compensating variation is equal to the area under the compensated demand curve. If we take a Taylor expansion of this function around p^1 and allow all prices to vary with the tax, we have

$$CV \approx \sum_i x_i^c(p^1, u^0) \Delta p_i + \frac{1}{2} \sum_i \sum_j \frac{\partial x_i^c(p^1, u^0)}{\partial p_j} \Delta p_i \Delta p_j + \cdots$$

If we limit our interest to the change in one price only, this reduces to

$$CV \approx x_i^c(p^1, u^0) \Delta p_i + \frac{1}{2} \frac{\partial x_i^c(p^1, u^0)}{\partial p_i} * \Delta p_i^2 + \cdots$$

The first term of the expansion is what a standard incidence analysis uses to estimate the cost of a tax to consumers: the ex post quantity consumed times the difference in prices, which is the tax rate. The second term is a linear approximation of the behavioral response—the change in (compensated) demand induced by the price change. Higher-order terms approximate any nonlinearity in the demand function. The accuracy of standard incidence methods thus depends on the size of the higher-order terms.

A figure can help assess this accuracy. The figure below shows the compensating variation for a single tax on good i, which is the area to the left of the

(continued)

Box 1-1 (continued)

FIGURE B1-1

Variation for a Single Tax on Good i

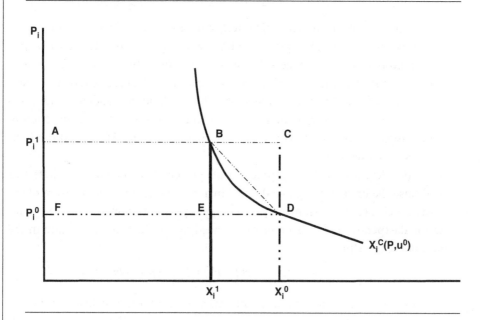

demand curve from P_i^0 to P_i^1. The first-order approximation is area ABEF. The second-order term is BDE. And higher-order terms capture the eye-shaped area between the demand curve and the line segment BD.

The first-order approximation captures the largest share of the compensating variation, as it should. It is straightforward to show that the ratio of the second-order term to the first-order increases with the size of the price change and the demand elasticity. That is, the first-order approximation is more accurate for smaller price changes and for more inelastic demands.

It is worth noting that many of the tax and expenditure policies that a typical incidence analysis evaluates do in fact have inelastic demands: VAT taxes all consumption; income tax falls on labor supply; excises are often levied on products with inelastic demand like petroleum or tobacco. On the expenditure side, demands for the health and education services governments provide are often inelastic. All of this suggests that the first-order approximations to the compensating variation are adequate. On the other hand, the price changes tend to be non-marginal.

behavioral responses can be quite significant, so results based on first-order approximation must be taken with great caution.[67]

It is important to note that the first-order effects *do* take into account both the direct effects of indirect taxes and subsidies and the indirect effects on final goods' prices of indirect taxes/subsidies applied to inputs. For the latter, one uses input-output matrices, described in chapter 7 in this Volume. Indirect effects should not be confused with general equilibrium effects because the indirect effects measured with input-output tables still do not incorporate behavioral responses to changes in relative prices.

If a team decides to depart from partial equilibrium analysis, the decision should be carefully explained and the exercise done as an additional sensitivity analysis so that there still exists a standard *CEQ Assessment* (without behavioral responses or general equilibrium effects) to allow results to be compared with those for other countries.[68]

CEQ analyzes cross-sectional data and thus provides a point-in-time perspective on the incidence of taxation and social spending. While some work has focused on intertemporal effects and lifetime tax incidence, we do not due to data limitations. In particular, "The lifetime perspective requires much more data over long periods of time, because results depend critically on the whole shape of the lifetime earnings profile."[69] Compared to a lifetime perspective, we are therefore likely overstating the progressivity of income taxes and the regressivity of consumption taxes. We take some solace in findings that replacing annual income with a longer-term income average did not significantly reduce the measured degree of inequality in the United States,[70] as well as findings that "the lifetime incidence of the entire U.S. tax system is strikingly similar to the annual incidence."[71]

CEQ does not incorporate spillover effects—such as the effect of cash transfers on local employment or property prices due to the difficulty in estimating their magnitudes and the beneficiaries or payers.[72]

3 *CEQ Assessment*: Indicators

The indicators used in a *CEQ Assessment* can be categorized by the questions a *CEQ Assessment* is designed to address. The main indicators are reviewed here and described in more detail, including their mathematical formulas when applicable, and instructions on producing the indicators using the *CEQ Stata Package* in chapter 8 in this Volume.

---

[67] Ravallion and Chen (2015).

[68] For work on incidence analysis accounting for behavioral effects, see, for example, Coady (2006) and Ravallion and Chen (2015).

[69] Fullerton and Rogers (1991, p. 277).

[70] Slemrod (1992).

[71] Fullerton and Rogers (1991, p. 277).

[72] For estimates of the spillover effects of cash transfer programs, see Angelucci and De Giorgi (2009) and Barrientos and Sabates-Wheeler (2009).

3.1. How Much Income Redistribution and Poverty Reduction Is Being Accomplished in Each Country through the Fiscal System (Taxes, Social Spending, and Subsidies)?

We use various indicators to answer this question, further organized by the following sub-questions.

3.1.1. Does the Fiscal System Reduce Inequality?

First, we compare inequality for the different income concepts described earlier in this chapter.[73] Doing so allows us to trace how inequality evolves as different transfers and taxes are added to and subtracted from income. For example, comparing Market and Disposable Income inequality shows how much redistribution is achieved by direct transfers and taxes, while comparing Disposable and Consumable Income inequality shows how much redistribution is achieved by indirect subsidies and taxes, and comparing Consumable and Final Income inequality shows how much redistribution is achieved by in-kind transfers in the form of education, health, and other public spending. Finally, comparing Market and Final Income inequality shows the extent to which the fiscal system is redistributive as a whole: that is, incorporating the cash and in-kind components altogether.

The inequality measures used in CEQ include the Gini, S-Gini, Theil, and 90/10 indices.[74] In addition, we measure how ex-ante inequality of opportunity varies across income concepts, where inequality is measured using the mean log deviation.[75] We also decompose the change in inequality between income concepts into that of vertical equity and horizontal inequity (reranking), where the latter is measured by the Atkinson-Plotnick index of reranking.[76]

3.1.2 Does the Fiscal System Decrease Poverty?

We can again assess the impact of the fiscal system by tracing out the change in poverty across income concepts. The poverty measures we use are members of the FGT class of poverty measures,[77] and include the headcount index, which measures the proportion of the population that is poor; the poverty gap ratio, which measures the depth of poverty; and the squared poverty gap ratio, which measures the severity of poverty. We measure poverty for a number of poverty lines, including commonly used "international poverty lines," national extreme and moderate poverty lines, and any other extreme and moderate poverty line that is relevant, such as the lines estimated

---

[73] For more detail about these concepts, see chapter 6 in this Volume.

[74] For a comprehensive discussion of inequality indexes and their properties see, for example, Duclos and Araar (2006).

[75] See Ferreira and Gignoux (2011).

[76] See Duclos and Araar (2006).

[77] Foster, Greer, and Thorbecke (1984).

by the UN Economic Commission for Latin American and the Caribbean (in the case of countries in Latin America), and a relative poverty line set as a percent of median income (commonly 50 or 60 percent). If the 2005 International Comparison Project (ICP) is used for purchasing power parity (PPP) adjustments, these lines are commonly set at $1.25, $2.50, and $4 per person per day.[78] If the 2011 ICP is used, $1.90 is the official World Bank extreme poverty line.[79] Researchers at the World Bank have proposed to use of $3.20 in 2011 PPP for lower middle-income countries and $5.50 in 2011 PPP for upper middle-income countries[80] and a global societal—or weakly relative—poverty line equal to $1 + 0.5 times the median consumption (or, in its absence, the median household per capita income) from the country's household survey.[81]

Note that in some regions, other poverty lines are commonly used by the World Bank.

We also use dominance tests to assess whether poverty is unambiguously lower in one income distribution than another for a range of poverty lines and broad class of poverty measures.[82]

In addition to directly measuring the change in poverty caused by taxes and transfers, we assess whether various groups (for example, income deciles) are net payers to the fiscal system or net receivers of transfers on average. These averages provide an overall picture of who tends to benefit more from or pay more to the fiscal system across the income distribution, but could overlook substantial variation within each decile.

3.1.3 Does the Fiscal System Make the Poor Poorer or the Non-Poor Poor?

Even if a tax and transfer system unambiguously reduces poverty and inequality and is progressive, it can make a substantial portion of the poor poorer, or non-poor poor.[83] This startling result occurs because poverty indicators are anonymous in the sense that we do not know whether a particular individual with a set postfiscal income had a lower or higher prefiscal income. Figure 1-2 illustrates this issue. The dark gray areas refer to poor (non-poor) individuals who were made poorer (poor) by the prevailing combination of taxes and transfers. In contrast, the light gray areas are prefiscal poor individuals who were made less poor.

We thus use the measure of Fiscal Impoverishment[84] to assess the extent to which the tax and transfer system makes some of the poor poorer and some of the non-poor

---

[78] Chen and Ravallion (2010); Ferreira and others (2013).

[79] Ferreira and others (2016).

[80] Jolliffe and Prydz (2016).

[81] Jolliffe and Prydz (2017). For a thorough discussion of the advantages and limitations of proposed international poverty lines, see Lustig and Silber (2016).

[82] Atkinson (1987); Foster and Shorrocks (1988).

[83] Higgins and Lustig (2016).

[84] Derived in Higgins and Lustig (2016).

FIGURE 1-2

Fiscal Impoverishment and Fiscal Gains to the Poor

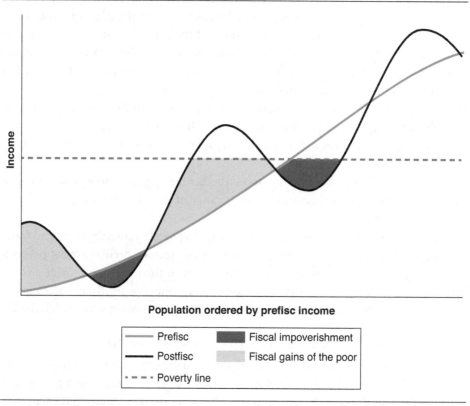

Source: Higgins and Lustig (2016).

poor.[85] As shown by Higgins and Lustig (2016), the poverty gap ratio can be exactly decomposed into the measure of fiscal impoverishment and fiscal gains to the poor. When using these measures, please cite the Higgins and Lustig (2016) article, which is reprinted as chapter 4 in this Volume for the reader's convenience.

3.2 How Equalizing and Pro-Poor Are Specific Taxes and Government Spending?

3.2.1 Is a Particular Tax or Transfer Equalizing (Unequalizing)?

To determine whether a particular tax or transfer is equalizing or unequalizing, we use the marginal contribution of that tax or transfer to inequality. In essence, the marginal contribution equals the difference between the inequality indicator measured without

---

[85] Higgins and Lustig (2016).

the tax or transfer of interest but with all the other components of fiscal policy in place MINUS the same indicator with all the components including the one whose effect we are considering. If this difference is positive (negative), then the tax or transfer is equalizing (unequalizing): that is, inequality is higher (lower) without the tax or transfer of interest than with it. If the difference equals zero, the tax or transfer is "neutral" (in other words, it does not affect inequality or poverty). So, for example, let's say one would like to know whether the value-added tax (VAT) is unequalizing. One would calculate, for instance, the Gini coefficient with a new income concept defined as Consumable Income (see figure 1-1) less VAT and would subtract the Gini coefficient for Consumable Income. If the difference is positive (negative), the VAT is equalizing (unequalizing). Box 1-2 defines the marginal contribution in more formal terms.

We measure progressivity using concentration coefficients and Kakwani coefficients;[86] chapter 2 in this Volume shows why a progressive tax or transfer is not necessarily equalizing (as explained earlier in this chapter). By comparing the sign of the marginal contribution with the Kakwani coefficient, we can determine if a tax or transfer is equalizing despite being regressive or unequalizing despite being progressive. Note that this can happen for two reasons: due to Lambert's conundrum, which can occur even in the absence of reranking, or due to reranking.[87]

3.2.2 What is the Contribution of a Tax or a Transfer to the Fiscally Induced Change in Inequality and Poverty?

We once again use the marginal contribution for this, comparing the size of the marginal contribution of a particular tax or transfer to the overall inequality or poverty reduction caused by the fiscal system. Note, however, that this does not provide a direct decomposition of the total effect into a sum of its parts from each tax or transfer. Attempting to do such a decomposition encounters path dependency issues.[88]

3.2.3 What Is the Impact of Fiscal Reforms That Change the Size and Progressivity of a Particular Tax or Spending Program?

The indicator used to answer this question is the derivative of the MC of a tax or transfer with respect to its size and progressivity. For more detail, see chapter 2 and chapter 3 in this Volume.[89]

---

[86] The Kakwani coefficient is described in chapter 2 in this Volume.

[87] The implications of reranking are explained in more detail in chapter 3 in this Volume.

[88] Shorrocks (2013). While using something like a Shapley value would ensure that the sum of the individual contributions adds up to the total redistributive effect, a Shapley value does not lend itself to a clear policy interpretation. By contrast, the marginal contribution does: it tells us what would be the influence of a particular tax or transfer or a change in that tax or transfer on inequality.

[89] Mathematical expressions of these in the absence and presence of reranking are described in chapters 2 and 3, respectively, in this Volume.

Box 1-2

Marginal Contribution

Ali Enami

We use T and B to refer to "Taxes" and "Benefits," where T can refer to any combination of direct and indirect taxes, and B can refer to any combination of direct transfers, indirect subsidies, and in-kind transfers from public spending on health and education. The indicators can also be defined for combinations of taxes and transfers, which is why we write "T (and/or B)" throughout. We calculate the Marginal Contribution (MC) of any combination of taxes or benefits as follows:

$$MC_{T(and/or\,B)}^{End\,income} = Index_{End\,income\backslash T\,(and/or\,B)} - Index_{End\,income}.$$

"Index" refers to any inequality or poverty indices that one may use in the calculation of the marginal contribution. For example, we use the Gini index as a measure of inequality. The subscript of the index, that is "End income," refers to the income concept with respect to which we calculate the marginal contribution to the index of a tax or benefit. For example, $Gini_{Disposable\,Income}$ means the Gini coefficient of disposable income, and if we use it for $Gini_{End\,income}$, it implies that we are interested in calculating the marginal contribution of a tax or benefit to the disposable income Gini. "End income\T (and/or B)" refers to the income concept that is equivalent to the End income prior to the tax or benefit of interest. For example, "Disposable Income\Direct Taxes" equals disposable income plus direct taxes (to have the income concept *prior to* subtracting out direct taxes). Intuitively,

$$MC_{T(and/or\,B)}^{End\,income}$$

is how much the value of $Index_{End\,income}$ would have changed if T (and/or B) were removed from the fiscal system. It should be noted that the End income does not have to be one of the CEQ core income concepts.

An example is that if we want to calculate the marginal effect of indirect taxes with respect to disposable income (since indirect taxes have not yet been subtracted out of disposable income), the end income concept would be "Disposable Income minus Indirect Taxes." The MC in this case would be calculated as follows:

$$MC_{Indirect\,Taxes}^{Disposable\,Income\,minus\,Indirect\,Taxes} = Index_{Disposable\,Income}$$
$$- Index_{Disposable\,Income\,minus\,Indirect\,Taxes}.$$

On the other hand, if we were calculating the MC of *direct* taxes with respect to disposable income, since disposable income is already net of direct taxes, the end income would be disposable income, while the end income without the fiscal intervention would require taking disposable income and *adding back in* direct taxes, so we would have:

$$MC_{Direct\ Taxes}^{Disposable\ Income} = Index_{Disposable\ Income\ plus\ Direct\ taxes} - Index_{Disposable\ Income}.$$

In calculating MC, what matters is that we have two income concepts that are different from each other only because of one component or a bundle of taxes and/or transfers. In other words, one can use components of a fiscal system separately and also in different combinations (bundles) to perform a marginal contribution analysis. An example would be to evaluate the inequality-reducing effect of different taxes in a system separately and then the whole taxation system together as one entity. Regardless of how a component or bundle is set up, we consider the difference for a particular inequality index between these two income concepts (the End income with and without that specific component or bundle) as the MC of that fiscal intervention.

While the above examples are all about the Gini index, the concept of marginal contribution is applicable to any inequality or poverty index.

3.2.4 Is a Particular Spending Item Pro-Poor?

Once it has been established that the marginal contribution of a fiscal intervention to inequality is positive (that is, the fiscal intervention is equalizing), we can determine whether it is pro-poor by comparing its concentration curve to the original income Lorenz curve. (The concentration coefficient also serves as a summary indicator of whether the concentration curve is above [coefficient less than Gini] or below [coefficient greater than Gini] the original income Lorenz, and above [coefficient less than 0] or below [coefficient greater than 0] the 45-degree line of perfect equality. Concentration *curves* provide a better assessment, however, as they could cross the Lorenz curve or 45-degree line, which is not revealed by the concentration *coefficient*.)

The pro-poorness of public spending here is defined using concentration coefficients (also called "quasi-Ginis").[90] In keeping with conventions, spending is defined as regressive whenever the concentration coefficient is higher than the Gini for Market Income. When this occurs, it means that the benefits from that spending as a share

---

[90] A concentration coefficient is calculated in a way analogous to the Gini coefficient. Let p be the cumulative proportion of the total population when individuals are ordered in increasing income values using Market Income, and let $C(p)$ be the concentration curve—that is, the cumulative proportion of total program benefits (of a particular program or aggregate category) received by the poorest p percent of the population. Then, the concentration coefficient of that program or category is defined as $2\int_0^1 (p - C(p))dp$.

FIGURE 1-3
Progressivity of Transfers: A Diagrammatic Representation

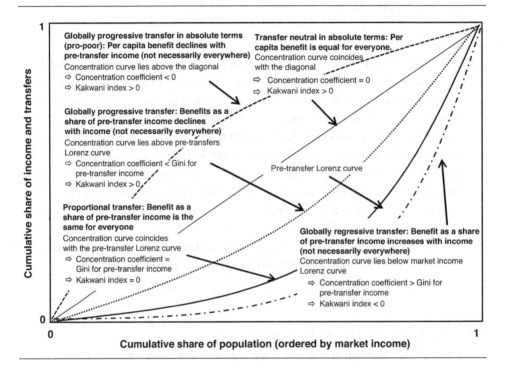

of Market Income *tend* to rise with Market Income.[91] Spending is progressive when-ever the concentration coefficient is lower than the Gini for Market Income. This means that the benefits from that spending as a share of Market Income tend to fall with Mar-ket Income. Within progressive spending, spending is neutral in absolute terms—spending per capita is the same across the income distribution—whenever the concen-tration coefficient is equal to zero. Spending is defined as *pro-poor* whenever the concentration coefficient is not only lower than the Gini but its value is also negative. Pro-poor spending implies that the *per capita* government spending on the transfer *tends* to fall with Market Income.[92] Any time spending is pro-poor or neutral in abso-lute terms, it is by definition progressive. The converse, of course, is not true.[93] The taxonomy of transfers is synthesized in figure 1-3.

---

[91] For global regressivity/progressivity to occur, it is not a necessary condition for the share of the benefit to rise/fall at each and every income level. When the latter occurs, the benefit is regressive/progressive *everywhere*. Whenever a benefit is *everywhere* regressive/progressive, it will be *glob-ally* regressive/progressive, but the converse is not true.

[92] This case is also sometimes called "progressive in absolute terms."

[93] As mentioned above, care must be taken not to infer that any spending that is progressive (re-gressive) will automatically be equalizing (unequalizing).

For the analysis of pro-poorness and progressivity (as that shown in figure 1-3 or by concentration coefficients), households are ranked by per capita prefiscal income (Market Income or Market Income plus Pensions, depending on the scenario), and no adjustments are made to their size because of differences in the composition by age and gender.[94] If the country's poverty data are usually presented in equivalized income, it is advisable to estimate the indicators of pro-poorness and progressivity ranking household per equivalized income as well. In some analyses, the pro-poorness of education spending, for example, is determined using children—not all members of the household—as the unit of analysis. Since poorer families typically have more children, they would naturally benefit more from spending per child. As a result, pro-poor concentration curves may simply reflect this, rather than imply that poorer families receive more resources per child.

3.3 How Effective Are Taxes and Government Spending in Reducing Inequality and Poverty?

In addition to their impact on inequality and poverty, a question of interest to, especially, policymakers is whether specific taxes or transfers (or their combination) are effective. In CEQ, effectiveness is viewed as whether the tax or the transfer generates as much reduction in inequality (and poverty) as it could potentially do or, conversely, whether one could achieve the same reduction in inequality and poverty with a smaller mobilization of fiscal resources (a tax or a transfer) by optimally allocating it. "Optimal" and the "highest potential" in this context refer the theoretically maximum potential, which is explained in more detail below. The indices proposed below are classified into two broad categories: Impact Effectiveness (IE) and Spending Effectiveness (SE) indicators. IE and SE indicators are similar in the sense that they both compare the performance of a tax or transfer in reducing inequality or poverty with respect to its theoretically maximum potential. For IE indicators, we keep the amount of money raised (or spent) constant and compare the actual and potential performance of a tax (or transfer) to each other. For SE indicators, we keep the impact of a tax (or transfer) on inequality or poverty constant and compare the actual size of a tax (or transfer) with the theoretically minimum amount of tax (or transfer) that would create the same impact. All this is discussed in detail in Volume 1's chapter 5 by Ali Enami (2022b).

In addition to these new proposed indicators, there are of course the conventional indicators of coverage and leakages, discussed below.

---

[94] Recall that in a number of countries the Market Income concept is derived from consumption data and will not be exactly the same as the Market Income that would be derived with income data. Also, for the purposes of robustness and comparisons, in some countries the calculations are performed using equivalized income as well.

3.3.1 Impact and Spending Effectiveness Indicators

Ali Enami (chapter 5 in this Volume) derived new effectiveness indicators whose main goal is to provide policymakers with meaningful but easy to interpret indices: the CEQ Impact Effectiveness and Spending Effectiveness Indicators.[95] Policy analysts and policymakers are interested in what is called a tax's or a transfer's "bank for the buck": that is, how much inequality or poverty reduction is obtained given the amount collected and spent. In developing these indicators, Enami ensured that they fulfill the mathematical requirements for producing proper ranking of taxes and transfers. Specifically, the new indicators ensure that, everything else being equal, an intervention with a higher marginal contribution (MC) to the reduction of inequality (or poverty) has a higher ranking and that an intervention with higher potential to reduce inequality (or poverty) yet with a lower realized effect gets a lower ranking. Enami, Lustig, and Taqdiri (2019) presents an application of the indicators to the case of Iran in chapter 17 of this Volume.

Impact effectiveness (IE)

As discussed in chapter 5 in this Volume, IE is defined as the ratio of the observed marginal contribution of a tax (transfer) to the optimum marginal contribution of that tax (transfer) if the tax (transfer) was distributed in a way that maximizes its inequality- or poverty-reducing impact. In the case of a tax, to maximize the inequality-reducing impact of a tax of a given size, we would need to tax the richest person until her pretax income equals the pretax income of the second richest person; then, both would be taxed until their pretax income equals the pretax income of the third richest person, and so on until there is no more of the tax to be allocated. In the case of a transfer, the procedure would be analogous but moving from the poorest person and giving him enough of a transfer until his income equals that of the second poorest, and so on. If the indicator of interest is a Gini or S-Gini index, the IE indicator is identical to what is proposed by Fellman, Jantti, and Lambert.[96]

---

[95] The spending effectiveness indicator previously suggested (Lustig and Higgins, 2013) was defined as follows: $CEQ\ Old\ Effectiveness\ Indicator = \dfrac{Change\ in\ Gini\ as\ a\ Result\ of\ Transfers}{Transfers/GDP}$ As shown by Enami (chapter 5 in this Volume), however, this indicator suffers from some fundamental shortcomings. The most important is that the indicator would fail to rank transfers (and taxes) properly. If, for example, a transfer is scaled up proportionally, one would expect—everything else being equal—the effectiveness indicator to remain constant. The reduction in Gini, however, is a nonlinear function of the transfer, so if the transfer is multiplied by two, the reduction in Gini would not necessarily be multiplied by two. As a result, bigger programs could be ranked worse because of this nonlinearity and not because they are less effective at reducing inequality.
[96] Fellman, Jantti, and Lambert (1999, pp. 115–26).

The IE indicator shows the relative realized power of a tax and/or transfer in reducing inequality or of a transfer (or combined tax-transfer system) in reducing poverty. (Since taxes can only increase poverty, the poverty reduction indicator is defined only for benefits or for combined tax-transfer systems that have a positive marginal contribution.) An example shows how to interpret this indicator: if the IE of a transfer is equal to 0.7, it means the transfer has realized 70 percent of its potential power in reducing inequality. Therefore, the higher the value of this indicator, the more effective a transfer is in fulfilling its potential to reduce inequality. An advantage of the IE is that its value does not depend on whether one uses change in Gini or percentage change in Gini.

For poverty, one calculates the IE only for benefits or combined tax-benefit systems that reduce poverty. For taxes, the denominator is always zero because taxes can only increase poverty (so the optimal effect of a tax on poverty is zero).

Spending effectiveness (SE)

As discussed in chapter 5 in this Volume, the SE indicator is defined as the ratio of the minimum amount of a tax (transfer) that is required to be collected (spent) in order to create the observed marginal contribution of the tax (transfer), if the tax (transfer) is instead redistributed optimally. This indicator shows how much less tax (transfer) is required to achieve the same observed outcome (in terms of inequality reduction) if the tax (transfer) is collected (spent) in an optimal way. For example, a value of 70 percent for SE of a transfer means that the same MC can be achieved by spending only 70 percent of the current resources if the resources are spent optimally (if the objective function is to maximize equality). We calculate this indicator only for the taxes and transfers with a positive MC (as a result, the SE of taxes on poverty reduction is undefined).

We also measure effectiveness of achieving fiscal gains to the poor and avoiding fiscal impoverishment[97] using the fiscal impoverishment and gains effectiveness described in box 1-3 by Ali Enami, Sean Higgins, and Stephen D. Younger.

In addition to the impact and spending indicators, in the *CEQ Assessments* we estimate additional poverty reduction effectiveness indicators.[98]

3.3.2 Effectiveness Indicators for Transfers: Definitions of Coverage, Errors of Exclusion, and Errors of Inclusion

To generate the concepts of coverage, errors of inclusion or leakages, and errors of exclusion, we can think of separating the population into two groups based on poverty

---

[97] See Higgins and Lustig (2016) on these concepts.
[98] From Beckerman (1979) and Immervoll and others (2009).

Box 1-3

Fiscal Impoverishment and Gains Effectiveness Indicators

Ali Enami, Sean Higgins, and Stephen D. Younger

H ere, we introduce effectiveness indicators that are specific to the effect of taxes and transfers on fiscal impoverishment (FI) and fiscal gains to the poor (FGP). Axiomatic indicators for FI and FGP are derived in Higgins and Lustig (2016) and described earlier in this chapter, and instructions on how to calculate them with the *CEQ Stata Package* are in chapter 8 of this Volume. Consider a set of policies that may include both benefits and taxes. We measure the effectiveness of these policies at reducing poverty without making many of the poor poorer as

$$Effectiveness_{FI/FGP} = \left[\left(\frac{B}{T+B} \right) \left(\frac{FGP\_MC_{T\,and\,B}^{End\,income}}{B} \right) \right]$$
$$+ \left[\left(\frac{T}{T+B} \right) \left(1 - \frac{FI\_MC_{T\,and\,B}^{End\,income}}{T} \right) \right].$$

where T and B are the size of total taxes and transfers (both positive values), $FGP\_MC_{T\,and\,B}^{End\,income}$ is the marginal contribution of the net system (i.e., T and B) to FGP (always a non-negative value), and $FI\_MC_{T\,and\,B}^{End\,income}$ is the marginal contribution of the net system (i.e., T and B) to FI (always a non-negative value).

Note that T and B are the maximum possible reduction or increase in the FGP and FI indicators. In other words, if taxes are all paid by the poor and no benefits reach the poor, $FI\_MC_{T\,and\,B}^{End\,income}$ becomes equal to T. Similarly, if all transfers go to the poor (only up to the point that brings them out of poverty) and the poor pay no taxes, the value of $FGP\_MC_{T\,and\,B}^{End\,income}$ becomes equal to B. As a result, both $\left(\frac{FGP\_MC_{T\,and\,B}^{End\,income}}{B} \right)$ and $\left(1 - \frac{FI\_MC_{T\,and\,B}^{End\,income}}{T} \right)$ are bounded between zero and 1. More-over, the higher the value of each of these two components, the more effective the bundle of taxes and transfers is from the poverty reduction perspective. The weights $\left(\text{i.e.,} \left(\frac{B}{T+B} \right) \text{ and } \left(\frac{T}{T+B} \right) \right)$ also add up to one. Therefore, the whole indicator is bounded between zero and one, and the higher the value of the indicator, the more effective the bundle of taxes and transfers is in reducing poverty.

For analyzing bundles that include only taxes, including a single tax, the indicator reduces to

$$Tax\,Effectiveness_{FI} = 1 - \frac{FI\_MC_P^{End\,income}}{T}.$$

For policies that include only benefits, it reduces to

$$Transfer\ Effectiveness_{FGP} = \frac{FGP\_MC_B^{End\ income}}{B}.$$

Note that taxes can only hurt and transfers can only help the poor, and even though both above indicators have positive values, one should not compare the effectiveness of a tax to a transfer in reducing poverty.

These indicators vary between zero and one and the higher the value of the indicator, the better. In addition, the *Effectiveness*$_{FI/FGP}$ indicator (and its special cases for tax effectiveness and transfer effectiveness) satisfies the following axioms:

1. FI Monotonicity: if a person experiencing FI has a larger decrease in postfiscal income, the measure must decrease.

2. FGP Monotonicity: if a person experiencing FGP has a larger increase in postfiscal income, the measure must not decrease, and must increase if that person's postfiscal income was still below the poverty line prior to this additional increase.

3. Weak Monotonicity in B: if B increases and all else equal, the measure must not increase.

4. Weak Monotonicity in T: if T increases and all else equal, the measure must not decrease.

5. Focus: if the pre- and post-incomes of all individuals experiencing FI and FGP are the same in two scenarios, and T and B are the same, the measure is the same.

6. Normalization: if the government performs as well as possible, so FGP = B and FI = 0, then the measure equals 1. If the government performs as poorly as possible, so FGP = 0 and FI = T, then the measure equals 0.

7. Continuity in individual prefiscal incomes, postfiscal incomes, and the poverty line, as well as continuity in FI, FGP, T, B.

8. Permutability.

9. Subgroup consistency.

10. Scale Invariance in FI, FGP, T, and B.

status and two groups based on whether they receive benefits. This results in four total groups, which we call group A, B, C, and D and represent with the 2×2 matrix shown in table 1-5.

We can then define the indicators of coverage, leakages, and errors of exclusion as follows:

TABLE 1-5
Conceptualizing Coverage Indicators

	Receives benefits	Does not receive benefits
Poor	A	B
Non-poor	C	D

Coverage: the total number of households that receive benefits[99] divided by the total number of households in the country, or $(A+C)/(A+B+C+D)$.

Coverage of the poor: the total number of *poor* households that receive benefits divided by the total number of *poor* households in the country, or $A/(A+B)$.

Errors of exclusion: the total number of *poor* households that do not receive benefits divided by the total number of *poor* households in the country, or $B/(A+B)$.

Leakages (also known as "errors of inclusion"): the total number of *non-poor* households that nevertheless receive benefits divided by the total number of households that receive benefits, or $C/(A+C)$.

Proportion of beneficiary households that are poor: the total number of poor households receiving benefits divided by the total number of households receiving benefits, or $A/(A+C)$.

The above definitions can then be modified in any combination of the following ways to generate additional indicators of coverage, leakages, and errors of exclusion:

- Replacing total number of households with "total number of direct beneficiaries" or "total number of individuals" (that is, "direct and indirect beneficiaries");
- Replacing "total number of" with "benefits received by," where benefits can be defined at either the household or per capita (dividing by the number of members in the household) levels;
- Computing the mean benefits accruing to households in each group A, B, C, and D;
- Further disaggregating the population not just into *poor* and *non-poor* but into various income groups;

---

[99] For the indicators at the household level, a beneficiary household will be a household that receives a benefit whether one can or cannot identify who within the household is the recipient of the benefit.

- Replacing "poor and "non-poor" with "eligible for the program" (also called "target") and "not eligible for the program" if clear eligibility criteria are available, and potentially further disaggregating eligible and non-eligible by income group.

Each of these definitions can be measured among *households*, which is how we define them here for illustration. Alternatively, they can be measured among *direct beneficiaries* (the individuals within the household who directly receive benefits) and among *individuals* or equivalently among *direct and indirect beneficiaries*, where "direct and indirect beneficiaries" are defined as all individuals within a beneficiary household. For example, a household may have five total members and two members who report directly receiving benefits from a particular program. For the household-level calculations, the household counts as one; for the direct beneficiaries calculation, there are two direct beneficiaries; and for the individual-level calculation, there are five individuals (or "direct and indirect beneficiaries").

In sections D and E of the *CEQ Master Workbook* (available online in part IV of this Volume), we compute all of the measures discussed here; for more detail, see Volume 1's chapter 8.

Acknowledgments

The authors are very grateful to François Bourguignon, Francisco Ferreira, Alvaro Forteza, Carlos Grushka, Santiago Levy, Angel Melguizo, Rafael Rofman, Sergei Soares, and Sergio Urzua for their invaluable insights and comments. We are also very grateful to Patricio Larroulet for his invaluable help in updating chapter 1 for the 2nd edition of the Handbook.

References

Adema, Willem, and Maxime Ladaique. 2005. "Net Social Expenditure, 2005 Edition: More Comprehensive Measures of Social Support," Employment and Migration Working Papers 29 (OECD Social).

Alam, Shamma A., Gabriela Inchauste, and Umar Serajuddin. 2017. "The Distributional Impact of Fiscal Policy in Jordan," in *The Distributional Impact of Taxes and Transfers: Evidence from Eight Low- and Middle-Income Countries*, edited by Gabriela Inchauste and Nora Lustig (Washington: World Bank).

Alleyne, Dillon, James Alm, Roy Bahl, and Sally Wallace. 2004. "Tax Burden in Jamaica," Working Paper 04-34 (Georgia State University International Studies Program).

Alvaredo, Facundo, Anthony Atkinson, Thomas Piketty, and Emmanuel Saez. 2015. "The World Top Incomes Database" (http://topincomes.g-mond.parisschoolofeconomics.eu/).

Angelucci, Manuela, and Giacomo De Giorgi. 2009. "Indirect Effects of an Aid Program: How Do Cash Transfers Affect Ineligibles' Consumption?" Working Paper 71 (International Policy Center, Gerald R. Ford School of Public Policy, University of Michigan).

Aranda, Rodrigo, and Adam Ratzlaff. 2022. "Analyzing the Impact of Fiscal Policy on Ethno-Racial Inequality," chap. 9 in *Commitment to Equity Handbook: Estimating the Impact of Fiscal Policy on Inequality and Poverty*, 2nd ed., Vol. 1, edited by Nora Lustig (Brookings Institution Press and CEQ Institute, Tulane University). Free online version available at www.commitmentoequity.org.

Arunatilake, Nisha, Gabriela Inchauste, and Nora Lustig. 2017. "The Incidence of Taxes and Spending in Sri Lanka," in *The Distributional Impact of Taxes and Transfers: Evidence from Eight Low- and Middle-Income Countries*, edited by Gabriela Inchauste and Nora Lustig (Washington: World Bank).

Atkinson, Anthony B. 1983. *Social Justice and Public Policy* (MIT Press).

———. 1987. "On the Measurement of Poverty." *Econometrica* 55, no. 4, pp. 749–64.

Barr, Nicholas. 2001. "The Truth about Pension Reform." *Finance and Development* 38, no. 3, pp. 6–9.

———. 2004. *Economics of the Welfare State*, 4th ed. (Oxford University Press).

———. 2012. "Credit Crisis and Pensions: International Scope," in *The Future of Multi-Pillar Pensions*, edited by Lans Bovenberg, Casper van Ewijk, and Ed Westerhout (Cambridge University Press).

Atkinson, Anthony B., and Joseph E. Stiglitz. 2015. "Lectures on Public Economics." (Princeton University Press).

Barrientos, Armando, and Rachel Sabates-Wheeler. 2009. "Do Transfers Generate Local Economy Effects?" Working Paper 106 (Brooks World Poverty Institute, University of Manchester).

Barros, Ricardo, Francisco Ferreira, Jose Molinas Vegas, and Jaime Saavedra Chanduvi. 2009. *Measuring In-equality of Opportunities in Latin America and the Caribbean* (Washington: World Bank).

Bastagli, Francesca, David Coady, and Sanjeev Gupta. 2015. "Fiscal Redistribution in Developing Countries: Overview of Policy Issues and Options," in *Inequality and Fiscal Policy*, edited by Benedict Clements, Ruud Mooji, Sanjeev Gupta, and Michael Keen (Washington: International Monetary Fund).

Beckerman, Wilfred. 1979. "The Impact of Income Maintenance Payments on Poverty in Britain, 1975." *Economic Journal* 89, pp. 261–79.

Bergh, Andreas. 2005. "On the Counterfactual Problem of Welfare State Research: How Can We Measure Redistribution?" *European Sociological Review* 21, no. 4, pp. 345–57.

Bibi, Sami, and Jean-Yves Duclos. 2010. "A Comparison of the Poverty Impact of Transfers, Taxes and Market Income across Five OECD Countries." *Bulletin of Economic Research* 62, no. 4, pp. 387–406.

Birdsall, Nancy, Augusto de la Torre, and Rachel Menezes. 2008. *Fair Growth: Economic Policies for Latin America's Poor and Middle-Income Majority* (Brookings Institution Press).

Bosch, Mariano, and Raymundo M. Campos-Vazquez. 2014. "The Trade-Offs of Welfare Policies in Labor Markets with Informal Jobs: The Case of the 'Seguro Popular' Program in Mexico." *American Economic Journal: Economic Policy* 6, no. 4, pp. 71–99.

Bourguignon, François, and Luiz A. Pereira da Silva, eds. 2003. *The Impact of Economic Poverty and Income Distribution* (Washington: World Bank).

Bourguignon, François, and Amadeo Spadaro. 2006. "Microsimulation as a Tool for Evaluating Redistribution Policies." *Journal of Economic Inequality* 4, no. 1, pp. 77–106.

Breceda, Karla, Jamele Rigolini, and Jaime Saavedra. 2008. "Latin America and the Social Contract: Patterns of Social Spending and Taxation." Policy Research Working Paper 4604 (Washington: World Bank, World Bank Latin American and Caribbean Region Poverty Department Poverty Reduction and Economic Management Division).

Bucheli, Marisa, Nora Lustig, Maximo Rossi, and Florencia Amabile. 2014. "Social Spending, Taxes and Income Redistribution in Uruguay," in "The Redistributive Impact of Taxes and Social Spending in Latin America," edited by Nora Lustig, Carola Pessino, and John Scott, special issue, *Public Finance Review* 42, no. 3, pp. 413–33.

Cabrera, Maynor, Nora Lustig, and Hilcias E. Moran. 2015. "Fiscal Policy, Inequality and the Ethnic Divide in Guatemala." *World Development* 76, December, pp. 263–79.

Camacho, Adriana, Emily Conover, and Alejandro Hoyos. 2014. "Effects of Colombia's Social Protection System on Workers' Choice between Formal and Informal Employment." *World Bank Economic Review* 28, no. 3, pp. 446–66.

Cancho, Cesar, and Elena Bondarenko. 2017. "The Distributional Impact of Fiscal Policy in Georgia," in *The Distributional Impact of Taxes and Transfers: Evidence from Eight Low- and Middle-Income Countries*, edited by Gabriela Inchauste and Nora Lustig (Washington: World Bank).

Candia, Bernardo, and Eduardo Engel. 2022. "Taxes, Transfers, and Income Distribution in Chile: Incorporating Undistributed Profits," chap. 5 in *Commitment to Equity Handbook: Estimating the Impact of Fiscal Policy on Inequality and Poverty*, 2nd ed., Vol. 2, edited by Nora Lustig (Brookings Institution Press and CEQ Institute, Tulane University). Free online version available at www.commitmentoequity.org.

CEQ Institute. 2022. "*CEQ Assessment: CEQ Master Workbook*," available online only in part IV of the *Commitment to Equity Handbook: Estimating the Impact of Fiscal Policy on Inequality and Poverty*, 2nd ed., Vol. 1, edited by Nora Lustig (Brookings Institution Press and CEQ Institute, Tulane University). Free online version available at www.commitmentoequity.org.

Chen, Shaohua, and Martin Ravallion. 2010. "The Developing World Is Poorer than We Thought, but No Less Successful in the Fight against Poverty." *Quarterly Journal of Economics* 125, no. 4, pp. 1577–1625.

Chetty, Raj, Adam Looney, and Kory Kroft. 2009. "Salience and Taxation: Theory and Evidence." *American Economic Review* 99, no. 4, pp. 1145–77.

Coady, David. 2006. "The Distributional Impacts of Indirect Tax and Public Pricing Reforms," in *Analyzing the Distributional Impact of Reforms: A Practitioner's Guide to Pension, Health, Labor Markets, Public Sector Downsizing, Taxation, Decentralization and Macroeconomic Modeling*, edited by A. Coudouel and S. Paternostro (Washington: World Bank).

Coady, David, Moataz El-Said, Robert Gillingham, Kangni Kpodar, Paulo Medas, and David Newhouse. 2006. "The Magnitude and Distribution of Fuel Subsidies: Evidence from Bolivia, Ghana, Jordan, Mali, and Sri Lanka," International Monetary Fund Working Paper 06/247.

Devarajan, Shantayanan, and Shaikh I. Hossain. 1998. "The Combined Incidence of Taxes and Public Expenditures in the Philippines." *World Development* 26, no. 6, pp. 963–77.

Dilnot, Andrew, John Kay, and Michael Keen. 1990. "Allocating Taxes to Households: A Methodology." *Oxford Working Papers* 42, no. 1, pp. 210–30.

Duclos, Jean-Yves, and Abdelkrim Araar, 2006. *Poverty and Equity: Measurement, Policy and Estimation with DAD*. Economic Studies in Inequality, Social Exclusion and Well-Being 2 (New York: Springer, IDRC).

Ebrill, Liam, Michael Keen, and Victoria P. Summers. 2001. *The Modern VAT* (Washington: International Monetary Fund).

Enami, Ali. 2022a. "Measuring the Redistributive Impact of Taxes and Transfers in the Presence of Reranking," chap. 3 in *Commitment to Equity Handbook: Estimating the Impact of Fiscal Policy on Inequality and Poverty*, 2nd ed., Vol. 1, edited by Nora Lustig (Brookings Institution Press and CEQ Institute, Tulane University). Free online version available at www.commitmentoequity.org.

———. 2022b. "Measuring the Effectiveness of Taxes and Transfers in Fighting Inequality and Poverty," chap. 5 in *Commitment to Equity Handbook: Estimating the Impact of Fiscal Policy on Inequality and Poverty*, 2nd ed., Vol. 1, edited by Nora Lustig (Brookings Institution Press and CEQ Institute, Tulane University). Free online version available at www.commitmentoequity.org.

Enami, Ali, Sean Higgins, and Nora Lustig. 2022. "Allocating Taxes and Transfers, Constructing Income Concepts, and Completing Sections A, B, and C of *CEQ Master Workbook*," chap. 6 in *Commitment to Equity Handbook: Estimating the Impact of Fiscal Policy on Inequality and Poverty*, 2nd ed., Vol. 1, edited by Nora Lustig (Brookings Institution Press and CEQ Institute, Tulane University). Free online version available at www.commitmentoequity.org.

Enami, Ali, Patricio Larroulet, and Nora Lustig. (Forthcoming). "How Accurate is the Kakwani Index in Predicting Whether a Tax or a Transfer is Equalizing? An Empirical Analysis." *Journal of Income Distribution*. Special issue in honor of Professor Nanak K. Kakwani, edited by Dr. Jacques Silber and Dr Hyun Son.

Enami, Ali, Nora Lustig, and Rodrigo Aranda. 2022. "Analytic Foundations: Measuring the Redistributive Impact of Taxes and Transfers," chap. 2 in *Commitment to Equity Handbook: Estimating the Impact of Fiscal Policy on Inequality and Poverty*, 2nd ed., Vol. 1, edited by Nora Lustig (Brookings Institution Press and CEQ Institute, Tulane University). Free online version available at www.commitmentoequity.org.

Enami, Ali, Nora Lustig, and Alireza Taqdiri. 2019. Fiscal Policy, Inequality, and Poverty in Iran: Assessing the Impact and Effectiveness of Taxes and Transfers. *Middle East Development Journal* 11 no. 1, pp. 49–74.

Engel, Eduardo, Alexander Galetovi, and Claudio Raddatz. 1999. "Taxes and Income Distribution in Chile: Some Unpleasant Redistributive Arithmetic." *Journal of Development Economics* 59, no. 1, pp. 155–92.

Fellman, Johan, Markus Jantti, and Peter J. Lambert. 1999. "Optimal Tax-Transfer Systems and Redistributive Policy." *Scandinavian Journal of Economics* 101, no. 1, pp. 115–26.

Ferreira, Francisco H. G., Shaohua Chen, Andrew Dabalen, Yuri Dihkanov, Nada Hamadeh, Dean Jolliffe, Ambar Narayan, Espen Prydz, Ana Revenga, Prem Sangraula, Umar Serajuddin, and Nobuo Yoshida. 2016. "A Global Count of the Extreme Poor in 2012: Data Issues, Methodology and Initial Results," Policy Research Working Paper 7432 (Washington: World Bank).

Ferreira, Francisco H. G., and Jeremie Gignoux. 2011. "The Measurement of Educational Inequality: Achievement and Opportunity," Policy Research Working Paper 5873 (Washington: World Bank).

Ferreira, Francisco H. G., Julian Messina, Jamele Rigolini, and Renos Vakis. 2013. *Socio-Economic Mobility and the Rise of the Middle Class in Latin America and the Caribbean* (Washington: World Bank Regional Flagship Report for Latin America and the Caribbean).

Ferreira, Francisco H. G., and David Robalino. 2010. "Social Protection in Latin America: Achievements and Limitations," Policy Research Working Paper 5305 (Washington: World Bank).

Fiszbein, Ariel, Norbert Schady, Francisco Ferreira, Margaret Grosh, Nial Kelleher, Pedro Olinto, and Emmanuel Skoufias. 2009. *Conditional Cash Transfers: Reducing Present and Future Poverty* (Washington: World Bank).

Förster, Michael, and Peter Whiteford. 2009. "How Much Redistribution Do Welfare States Achieve? The Role of Cash Transfers and Household Taxes," *CESifo DICE Report* 7, no. 3 (Ifo Institute–Leibniz Institute for Economic Research at the University of Munich), pp. 34–41.

Foster, James, Joel Greer, and Erik Thorbecke. 1984. "A Class of Decomposable Poverty Measures." *Econometrica* 52, no. 3, pp. 761–66.

Foster, James, and Anthony F. Shorrocks. 1988. "Poverty Orderings." *Econometrica* 56, no. 1, pp. 173–77.

Fullerton, Don, and Diane Lim Rogers. 1991. "Lifetime versus Annual Perspectives on Tax Incidence." *National Tax Journal* 44, no. 3, pp. 277–87.

Garganta, Santiago, and Leonardo Gasparini. 2015. "The Impact of a Social Program on Labor Informality: The Case of AUH in Argentina." *Journal of Development Economics* 115 (July), pp. 99–110.

Gertler, Paul, and Paul Glewwe. 1990. "The Willingness to Pay for Education in Developing Countries: Evidence from Rural Peru." *Journal of Public Economics* 42, no. 3, pp. 251–75.

Gertler, Paul, and Jacques van der Gaag. 1990. *The Willingness to Pay for Medical Care: Evidence from Two Developing Countries* (Johns Hopkins University Press for the World Bank).

Gillespie, W. Irwin. 1965. "The Effect of Public Expenditures on the Distribution of Income," in *Essays in Fiscal Federalism*, edited by Richard A. Musgrave, 122–86 (Washington: Brookings Institution).

Goñi, Edwin, J. Humberto Lopez, and Luis Serven. 2011. "Fiscal Redistribution and Income Inequality in Latin America." *World Development* 39, no. 9, pp. 1558–69.

Grosh, Margaret, Carlo del Ninno, Emil Tesliuc, and Azedine Ouerghi. 2008. *For Protection and Promotion: The Design and Implementation of Effective Safety Nets* (Washington: World Bank).

Grushka, Carlos. 2022. "The Within-System Redistribution of Contributory Pension Systems: A Conceptual Framework and Empirical Method of Estimation," chap. 6 in *Commitment to Equity Handbook: Estimating the Impact of Fiscal Policy on Inequality and Poverty*, 2nd ed., Vol. 2, edited by Nora Lustig (Brookings Institution Press and CEQ Institute, Tulane University). Free online version available at www.commitmentoequity.org.

Gupta, Sanjeev, Michael Keen, Benedict Clements, and Ruud de Mooij, eds. 2015. *Inequality and Fiscal Policy* (Washington: International Monetary Fund).

Harberger, Arnold Carl. 1962. "The Incidence of the Corporation Income Tax." *Journal of Political Economy* 70, pp. 215–0.

Higgins, Sean, Rodrigo Aranda, Caterina Brest Lopez, Ruoxi Li, Beenish Amjad, Patricio Larroulet, Roy McKenzie. 2022. "CEQ Assessment: CEQ Stata Package," in part IV in *Commitment to Equity Handbook: Estimating the Impact of Fiscal Policy on Inequality and Poverty*, 2nd. ed., Vol. 1, edited by Nora Lustig (Brookings Institution Press and CEQ Institute, Tulane University). Available online only at www.ceqinstitute.org.

Higgins, Sean, and Caterina Brest Lopez. 2022. "Producing Indicators and Results, and Completing Sections D and E of *CEQ Master Workbook* using the *CEQ Stata Package*," chap. 8 in

Commitment to Equity Handbook: Estimating the Impact of Fiscal Policy on Inequality and Poverty, 2nd ed., Vol. 1, edited by Nora Lustig (Brookings Institution Press and CEQ Institute, Tulane University). Free online version available at www.commitmentoequity.org.

Higgins, Sean, and Nora Lustig. 2016. "Can a Poverty-Reducing and Progressive Tax and Transfer System Hurt the Poor?" *Journal of Development Economics* 122, pp. 63–75.

Higgins, Sean, Nora Lustig, Whitney Ruble, and Timothy Smeeding. 2016. "Comparing the Incidence of Taxes and Social Spending in Brazil and the United States." *Review of Income and Wealth* 62, no. S1, pp. S22–S46 (doi:10.1111/roiw.12201).

Higgins, Sean, and Claudiney Pereira. 2014. "The Effects of Brazil's Taxation and Social Spending on the Distribution of Household Income," in "The Redistributive Impact of Taxes and Social Spending in Latin America," edited by Nora Lustig, Carola Pessino, and John Scott, special issue, *Public Finance Review* 42, no. 3, pp. 346–67.

Hill, Ruth, Gabriela Inchauste, Nora Lustig, Eyasu Tsehaye, and Tassew Woldehanna. 2017. "A Fiscal Incidence Analysis for Ethiopia," in *The Distributional Impact of Taxes and Transfers: Evidence from Eight Low- and Middle-Income Countries*, edited by Gabriela Inchauste and Nora Lustig (Washington: World Bank).

Inchauste, Gabriela, and Nora Lustig, eds. 2017. *The Distributional Impact of Taxes and Transfers: Evidence from Eight Low- and Middle-Income Countries*, edited by Gabriela Inchauste and Nora Lustig (Washington: World Bank).

Inchauste, Gabriela, Nora Lustig, Mashekwa Maboshe, Catriona Purfield, and Ingrid Wollard. 2017. "The Distributional Impact of Fiscal Policy in South Africa," in *The Distributional Impact of Taxes and Transfers: Evidence from Eight Low- and Middle-Income Countries*, edited by Gabriela Inchauste and Nora Lustig (Washington: World Bank).

Immervoll, Herwig, Horacio Levy, Jose Ricardo Nogueira, Cathal O'Donoghue, and Rozane Bezerra de Siqueira. 2009. "The Impact of Brazil's Tax-Benefit System on Inequality and Poverty," in *Poverty, Inequality, and Policy in Latin America*, edited by Stephan Klasen, and Felicitas Nowak-Lehmann, 271–302 (MIT Press).

Immervoll, Herwig, and Linda Richardson. 2011. "Redistribution Policy and Inequality Reduction in OECD Countries: What Has Changed in Two Decades?" IZA Discussion Paper 6030.

Jaramillo, Miguel. 2014. "The Incidence of Social Spending and Taxes in Peru," in "The Redistributive Impact of Taxes and Social Spending in Latin America," edited by Nora Lustig, Carola Pessino, and John Scott, special issue, *Public Finance Review* 42, no. 3, pp. 391–412.

Jellema, Jon, and Gabriela Inchauste. 2022. "Constructing Consumable Income: Including the Direct and Indirect Effects of Indirect Taxes and Subsidies," chap. 7 in *Commitment to Equity Handbook: Estimating the Impact of Fiscal Policy on Inequality and Poverty*, 2nd ed., Vol. 1, edited by Nora Lustig (Brookings Institution Press and CEQ Institute, Tulane University). Free online version available at www.commitmentoequity.org.

Jellema, Jon, Matthew Wai-Poi, and Rythia Afkar. 2017. "The Distributional Impact of Fiscal Policy in Indonesia," in *The Distributional Impact of Taxes and Transfers: Evidence from Eight Low- and Middle-Income Countries*, edited by Gabriela Inchauste and Nora Lustig (Washington: World Bank).

Jolliffe, Dean and Espen Beer Prydz. 2016. "Estimating International Poverty Lines from Comparable National Thresholds." Policy Research Working Paper 7606 (Washington: World Bank).

———. 2017. "Societal Poverty. A Relative and Relevant Measure." Policy Research Working Paper 8073 (Washington: World Bank).

Kakwani, Nanak C. 1977. "Measurement of Tax Progressivity: An International Comparison." *Economic Journal* 87, no. 345, pp. 71–80.

Keen, Michael, and Ben Lockwood. 2010. "The Value Added Tax: Its Causes and Consequences." *Journal of Development Economics* 92, no. 2, pp. 138–51.

Kotlikoff, Laurence, and Lawrence H. Summers 1987. "Tax Incidence," in *Handbook of Public Economics*, vol. 2, edited by A. J. Auerbach and M. Feldstein (Amsterdam: Elsevier).

Lambert, Peter. 1985. "On the Redistributive Effect of Taxes and Benefits." *Scottish Journal of Political Economy* 32, no. 1, pp. 39–54.

———. 2001. *The Distribution and Redistribution of Income*, 3rd ed. (Manchester University Press).

Lindert, Kathy, Emmanuel Skoufias, and Joseph Shapiro. 2006. "Redistributing Income to the Poor and Rich: Public Transfers in Latin America and the Caribbean." Social Protection Discussion Paper 0605 (Washington: World Bank).

Lopez-Calva, Luis Felipe, Nora Lustig, Mikhail Matytsin, and Daria Popova. 2017. "Who Benefits from Fiscal Redistribution in Russia?," in *The Distributional Impact of Taxes and Transfers: Evidence from Eight Low- and Middle-Income Countries*, edited by Gabriela Inchauste and Nora Lustig (Washington: World Bank).

Lora, Eduardo, ed. 2006. *The State of State Reforms in Latin America* (Washington: World Bank).

Lustig, Nora. 2015. "The Redistributive Impact of Government Spending on Education and Health: Evidence from 13 Developing Countries in the Commitment to Equity Project," in *Inequality and Fiscal Policy*, edited by Benedict Clements, Ruud Mooji, Sanjeev Gupta, and Michael Keen (Washington: International Monetary Fund).

———. 2016. "Inequality and Fiscal Redistribution in Middle Income Countries: Brazil, Chile, Colombia, Indonesia, Mexico, Peru and South Africa." *Journal of Globalization and Development* 7, no. 1, pp. 17–60 (doi:10.1515/jgd-2016-0015).

———. 2020. "Measuring the Distributional Impact of Taxation and Public Spending: The Practice of Fiscal Incidence Analysis." *Oxford Research Encyclopedia of Economics and Finance* (Oxford University Press).

———. 2022. "Fiscal Policy, Income Redistribution, and Poverty Reduction in Low- and Middle-Income Countries," chap. 10 in *Commitment to Equity Handbook: Estimating the Impact of Fiscal Policy on Inequality and Poverty*, 2nd ed., Vol. 1, edited by Nora Lustig (Brookings Institution Press and CEQ Institute, Tulane University). Free online version available at www.commitmentoequity.org.

Lustig, Nora, and Sean Higgins. 2013. "Commitment to Equity Assessment (CEQ): Estimating the Incidence of Social Spending, Subsidies and Taxes. Handbook." CEQ Working Paper 1 (New Orleans: Center for Inter-American Policy and Research, Department of Economics, Tulane University, and Inter-American Dialogue).

Lustig, Nora, Carola Pessino, and John Scott, eds. 2014. "The Redistributive Impact of Taxes and Social Spending in Latin America," special issue, *Public Finance Review* 42, no 3, pp. 287–303.

Lustig, Nora, and Jacques Silber. 2016. Introduction, "Global Poverty Lines," special issue, *Journal of Economic Inequality* 14, no. 2, pp. 129–140.

Martinez-Aguilar, Sandra, Alan Fuchs, Eduardo Ortiz-Juarez, and Giselle Del Carmen. 2022. Chile: "The Impact of Fiscal Policy on Inequality and Poverty," chap. 13 in *Commitment to Equity Handbook: Estimating the Impact of Fiscal Policy on Inequality and Poverty*, 2nd ed., Vol. 1, edited by Nora Lustig (Brookings Institution Press and CEQ Institute, Tulane University). Free online version available at www.commitmentoequity.org.

Martinez-Aguilar, Sandra, and Eduardo Ortiz-Juarez. 2016. "CEQ Master Workbook: Chile. Version: October 7, 2016," CEQ Data Center on Fiscal Redistribution (CEQ Institute, Tulane University and the World Bank).

Martinez-Vazquez, Jorge. 2008. "The Impact of Budgets on the Poor: Tax and Expenditure Benefit Incidence Analysis," in *Public Finance for Poverty Reduction: Concepts and Case Studies from Africa and Latin America*, edited by Blanca Moreno-Dodson and Quentin Wodon, Directions in Development (Washington: World Bank).

McClure, Charles E. 1970. "Tax Incidence, Macroeconomic Policy, and Absolute Prices." *Quarterly Journal of Economics* 84, pp. 254–67.

Meerman, Jacob. 1979. *Public Expenditure in Malaysia: Who Benefits and Why* (Oxford University Press for the World Bank).

Melguizo, Angel, and Jose M. Gonzalez-Paramo. 2013. "Who Bears the Social Security Taxes? A Meta-Analysis Approach." *SERIEs—Journal of the Spanish Economic Association* 4, no. 3, pp. 247–71.

Mieszkowski, Peter. 1967. "On the Theory of Tax Incidence." *Journal of Political Economy* 75 (June), pp. 250–62.

Morra Imas, Linda G., and Ray C. Rist. 2009. *The Road to Results: Designing and Conducting Effective Development Evaluations* (Washington: World Bank).

Musgrave, Richard. 1959. *The Theory of Public Finance* (New York: McGraw-Hill).

Musgrave, Richard A., J. J. Carroll, L. D. Cook, and L. Frane. 1951. "Distribution of Tax Payments by Income Groups: A Case Study for 1948." *National Tax Journal* 4 (March), pp. 1–53.

Musgrave, Richard, Karl Case, and Herman Leonard. 1974. "The Distribution of Fiscal Burdens and Benefits." *Public Finance Quarterly* 2, no. 3, pp. 259–311.

O'Donnell, Owen, Eddy Van Doorslaer, Adam Wagstaff, and Magnus Lindelow. 2008. *Analyzing Health Equity Using Household Survey Data: A Guide to Techniques and Their Implementation*, WBI Learning Resources (Washington: World Bank).

O'Donoghue, Cathal, ed. 2014. *Handbook of Microsimulation*. Book Series: Contributions to Economic Analysis, Volume 293, series edited by Badi H. Baltagi and Efraim Sadka (West Yorkshire, UK: Emerald Insight).

OECD. 2011. *Divided We Stand: Why Inequality Keeps Rising* (Paris: OECD Publishing).

O'Higgins, Michael, and Patricia Ruggles. 1981. "The Distribution of Public Expenditures and Taxes among Households in the United Kingdom." *Review of Income and Wealth* 27, no. 3, pp. 298–326.

Paz Arauco, Veronica, George Gray-Molina, Wilson Jimenez, and Ernesto Yañez. 2014. "Explaining Low Redistributive Impact in Bolivia," in "The Redistributive Impact of Taxes and Social Spending in Latin America," edited by Nora Lustig, Carola Pessino, and John Scott, special issue, *Public Finance Review* 42, no 3, pp. 326–45.

Peacock, Alan T., ed. 1954. *Income Redistribution and Social Policy* (London: Jonathan Cape).

Pechman, Joseph A. 1985. *Who Paid the Taxes, 1966–1985* (Brookings Institution).

Pechman, Joseph A., and Benjamin A. Okner. 1974. *Who Bears the Tax Burden?* (Brookings Institution).

Ravallion, Martin, and Shaohua Chen. 2015. "Benefit Incidence with Incentive Effects, Measurement Errors and Latent Heterogeneity: A Case Study for China." *Journal of Public Economics* 128 (August), pp. 124–32.

Rolph, Earl R. 1954. *The Theory of Fiscal Economics* (University of California Press).

Ruggles, Patricia, and Michael O'Higgins. 1981. "The Distribution of Public Expenditure among Households in the United States." *Review of Income and Wealth* 27, no. 2, pp. 137–64.

Sastre, Mercedes, and Alain Trannoy. 2002. "Shapley Inequality Decomposition by Factor Components: Some Methodological Issues." *Journal of Economic Theory* 9, pp. 51–89.

———. 2008. "Changing Income Inequality in Advanced Countries: A Nested Marginalist Decomposition Analysis." Unpublished paper.

Salanie, Bernard. 2011. *The Economics of Taxation*, 2nd ed. (MIT Press).Scott, John. 2014. "Redistributive Impact and Efficiency of Mexico's Fiscal System," in "The Redistributive Impact of Taxes and Social Spending in Latin America," edited by Nora Lustig, Carola Pessino, John Scott, special issue, *Public Finance Review* 42, no. 3, pp. 368–90.

Selowsky, Marcelo.1979. *Who Benefits from Government Expenditures? A Case Study of Colombia* (Oxford University Press).

Shah, Anwar, ed. 2003. *Handbook on Public Sector Performance Reviews* (Washington: World Bank).

Shorrocks, Anthony F. 2013. "Decomposition Procedures for Distributional Analysis: A Unified Framework Based on the Shapley Value." *Journal of Economic Inequality* 11, no. 1, pp. 99–126.

Silveira, Fernando Gaiger, Jhonatan Ferreira, Joana Mostafa, and Jose Aparecido Carlos Ribeiro. 2011. "Qual o impacto da tributação e dos gastos publicos sociais na distribuição de renda do Brasil? Observando os dois lados da moeda," in *Progressividade da Tributação e Desoneração da Folha de Pagamentos Elementos para Reflexão*, edited by Jose Aparecido Carlos Ribeiro, Alvaro Luchiezi Jr., and Sergio Eduardo Arbulu Mendonça (Brasilia: IPEA).

Slemrod, Joel. 1992. "Taxation and Inequality: A Time-Exposure Perspective," in *Tax Policy and the Economy*, vol. 6, edited by James M. Poterba (MIT Press).

Suits, Daniel B. 1977. "Measure of Tax Progressivity." *American Economic Review* 67, no. 4, pp. 747–52.

Tax Foundation, Inc. 1960. "Allocation of the Tax Burden by Income Class." Project Note No. 45, May.

———. 1967. *Tax Burdens and Benefits from Government Expenditures by Income Class, 1961 and 1965* (New York: Tax Foundation, Inc.).

Urzua, Carlos M., ed. 2012. *Fiscal Inclusive Development: Microsimulation Models for Latin America* (Mexico: IDRC-PNUD-ITESM).

van de Walle, Dominique. 1992. "The Distribution of the Benefits from Social Services in Indonesia, 1978–87." Policy Research Working Paper 871 (Washington: World Bank, Country Economics Department).

———. 1998. "Assessing the Welfare Impacts of Public Spending." *World Development* 26 (March), pp. 365–79.

———. 2004. "Testing Vietnam's Public Safety Net." *Journal of Comparative Economics* 32, no. 4, pp. 661–79.

van de Walle, Dominique, and Kimberly Nead, eds. 1995. *Public Spending and the Poor: Theory and Evidence* (published for the World Bank by John Hopkins University Press).

World Bank. 2000/2001. *World Development Report 2000/2001: Attacking Poverty* (published for the World Bank by Oxford University Press).

———. 2006. *Country Policy and Institutional Assessments*, Operations Policy and Country Services (http://siteresources.worldbank.org/IDA/Resources/CPIA2006Questionnaire.pdf).

———. 2009. *The World Bank's Country Policy and Institutional Assessment, An Evaluation* (http://siteresources.worldbank.org/EXTCPIA/Resources/cpia_full.pdf).

———. 2011. "CPIA Public Sector Management and Institutions Cluster Average" (http://data.worldbank.org/indicator/IQ.CPA.PUBS.XQ).

Younger, Stephen D. 2022. "Ghana and Tanzania: The Impact of Reforming Energy Subsidies, Cash Transfers, and Taxes on Inequality and Poverty," chap. 16 in *Commitment to Equity Handbook: Estimating the Impact of Fiscal Policy on Inequality and Poverty*, 2nd ed., Vol. 1, edited by Nora Lustig (Brookings Institution Press and CEQ Institute, Tulane University). Free online version available at www.commitmentoequity.org.

Younger, Stephen D., and Artsvi Khachatryan. 2017 "Fiscal Incidence in Armenia," in *The Distributional Impact of Taxes and Transfers. Evidence from Eight Low- and Middle-Income Countries*, edited by Gabriela Inchauste and Nora Lustig (Washington: World Bank).

Younger, Stephen D., Flora Myamba, and Kenneth Mdadila. 2016. "Fiscal Incidence in Tanzania." *African Development Review* 28, no. 3, pp. 264–76 (doi:10.1111/1467-8268.12204).

Younger, Stephen D., Eric Osei-Assibey, and Felix Oppong. 2017. "Fiscal Incidence in Ghana." *Review of Development Economics,* January 11 (doi:10.1111/rode.12299).

Younger, Stephen D., David Sahn, Stephen Haggblade, and Paul Dorosh. 1999. "Tax Incidence in Madagascar: An Analysis Using Household Data." *World Bank Economic Review* 13, no. 2, pp. 303–31.

Chapter 2

ANALYTIC FOUNDATIONS
Measuring the Redistributive Impact of Taxes and Transfers

Ali Enami, Nora Lustig, and Rodrigo Aranda

Introduction

Suppose we observe that income inequality after taxes and transfers is lower than prefiscal income inequality. Can this finding be related to the characteristics of the tax and transfer system in terms of the usual indicators of progressivity and size? As shown below, once one leaves the world of a single fiscal intervention, the relationship between inequality outcomes and the size and progressivity of fiscal interventions is complex and at times counterintuitive. In particular, in a system of multiple taxes and transfers, the simple relationship between the size of a tax (or transfer) and its progressivity, on the one hand, and its impact on inequality, on the other, no longer holds.

We start this chapter with a review of the simplest case: a single fiscal intervention. The first section shows the conditions for a tax or a transfer to be equalizing. We draw, primarily, on Lambert (2001) and Duclos and Araar (2007). The second section presents the conditions for the net fiscal system to be equalizing in the case of multiple fiscal interventions. We also derive the conditions that must prevail for a particular tax or transfer to be equalizing and see that in the world of multiple interventions, some of these conditions defy our preconceptions and intuitions.

Both sections of this chapter assume no reranking—that is, individuals do not change their original position in the postfiscal income ordering. In other words, the poorest individual in the prefiscal income scale will continue to be the poorest individual in the postfiscal income scale, the second poorest individual in the prefiscal income scale will continue to be the second poorest individual in the postfiscal income scale, and so on, all the way up to the richest individual. These sections also assume that there is dominance: that is, the prefiscal and postfiscal Lorenz curves do not cross. They also assume that, when comparing systems with different taxes and transfers, the respective postfiscal Lorenz curves do not cross either. Finally, these sections assume a constant prefiscal income distribution—that is, that the conditions apply to a particular country at a specific point in time. Comparisons across countries and over time will usually feature different prefiscal income distributions and are not the subject of this chapter.

Chapter 3 of this Volume (Enami, 2022) discusses how the conditions derived in sections 1 and 2 below change in the presence of reranking. The implications of relaxing the assumption of dominance or having different prefiscal income distributions will be the subject of future work. Throughout this chapter, the traditional Gini coefficient is used as our measure of inequality, but the ideas presented here can be easily extended to all members of the S-Gini family. However, while the idea of "marginal" analysis (introduced in this chapter) can be applied to other measures of inequality, the type of decomposition that we rely on in this chapter and the next one may not be applicable for other measures of inequality, such as the Theil index.

1 The Fiscal System and Income Redistribution: The Case of a Single Tax or a Single Transfer

In this section, we focus on a fiscal system with a single tax or transfer. Here we define concepts that we use throughout this chapter to analyze the effect of a tax or a transfer on the income distribution. We should first clarify that the word "single" does not mean that a system has only one tax, but rather that the same conditions apply when all taxes are combined into a single category.[1]

1.1 A Single Tax

We start by presenting some notations and definitions that will be used throughout the chapter:

x = pretax income

$f(x)$ = pretax income distribution

$T(x)$ = tax liability at income x

$x - T(x)$ = post-tax income

$t(x) = T(x)/x$ = tax rate at income x

$t'(x)$ = marginal tax rate at income x

---

[1] This section draws from Lambert (2001) and Duclos and Araar (2007).

Let's assume that the tax schedule adheres to a typical pattern of starting at a zero rate and that it follows a sequence of fixed and increasing marginal tax rates.[2] Let's also assume that both the tax liability and post-tax income increase with pretax income:

(2-1)
$$0 \leq T(x) < x$$

(2-2)
$$0 \leq t'(x) < 1.$$

Condition 2-2 rules out reranking; that is, no pair of individuals switches places after the tax has been imposed.

Now, let's define the following terms:

$T =$ total taxes paid $= \sum_i T(x_i)$

$X =$ total pretax (and pre-transfers) income $= \sum_i x_i$

$g =$ total tax ratio $= T/X$; thus, $(1-g) = (X-T)/X$ and $g/(1-g) = T/(X-T) =$ total tax as a share of pretax income

$$g = \frac{\int_i T(x_i) f(x_i) dx_i}{\int_i x_i\, f(x_i) dx_i} = \text{total tax ratio (continuous version)}$$

$L_X(p)$, $L_{X-T}(p) =$ Lorenz curve of pretax income and post-tax income, respectively (ranked by original income)

$C_{X-T}(p)$, $C_T(p) =$ concentration curve of post-tax income and taxes, respectively (ranked by original income)[3]

In all preceding formulas p has a value between zero and one and represents quantile p of income distribution in which $100p$ percent of individuals are below it.

It can be shown that the Lorenz curve of pretax income is the weighted average of the concentration curve of taxes and the concentration curve of post-tax income:

(2-3)
$$L_X(p) = g\, C_T(p) + (1-g)\, C_{X-T}(p).$$

Because of conditions 2-1 and 2-2, the ranking of people by pretax and post-tax income is exactly the same. Thus, condition 2-3 can be rewritten simply as the weighted average of the concentration curve of taxes and the Lorenz curve of post-tax income:

---

[2] Lambert (2001).

[3] Recall that concentration curves plot the cumulative shares of post-tax income and taxes by positions in pretax income distribution (in notational terms, if there is no superscript, they are ranked by pretax income). The reader should recall that a concentration coefficient is calculated in the same manner as the Gini coefficient. The difference is the same as that between the Lorenz and concentration curves: the cumulative distribution of the tax (in this case) is plotted against the cumulative distribution of the population ranked by original income and *not* the tax.

$$(2\text{-}3)' \qquad\qquad L_X(p) = g\, C_T(p) + (1-g)\, L_{X-T}(p).$$

1.1.1 Equalizing, Neutral, and Unequalizing Net Fiscal Systems: Conditions for the One-Tax Case

In this section, we review conditions that allow us to determine whether a fiscal system with only a single tax is equalizing, neutral, or unequalizing.

Concentration and Lorenz curves

When the post-tax income Lorenz curve lies everywhere above the pretax income Lorenz curve—that is, $L_{X-T}(p) \geq L_X(p)$—the tax is equalizing (and vice versa).

Equation 2-3′ implies that the post-tax income Lorenz curve lies completely above the pretax income Lorenz curve if and only if the concentration curve of taxes lies completely below the pretax income Lorenz curve,[4] i.e.,

$$(2\text{-}4) \qquad\qquad L_{X-T}(p) \geq L_X(p) \Leftrightarrow C_T(p) \leq L_X(p),$$

for all p, and with strict inequality for some p.

In other words, the distribution of post-tax income is less unequal than the pretax income distribution if and only if the tax is distributed more unequally than the income to which it applies, or put another way, if and only if the concentration curve of taxes lies completely below the pretax income Lorenz curve. This condition is shown on figure 2-1, which features the Lorenz curves for pretax and post-tax income and the concentration curve for taxes. In other words, if the average tax rate $t(x)$ is increasing with income *everywhere*, then taxes are distributed more unequally than pretax income. Thus, an everywhere progressive tax will always be equalizing.

Given equation 2-4, it is easy to see that the condition for a tax to be unequalizing is $C_T(p) \geq L_X(p)$. This condition will occur if $t(x)$ decreases with income—that is, if taxes are regressive everywhere. However, just as in the case of progressive taxes, it is not necessary for taxes to be regressive everywhere to be unequalizing. Finally, in the case of a proportional tax—that is, when $T(x)/x$ is the same for all x—the distribution of post-tax and pretax income will be exactly the same and $C_T(p) = L_X(p)$.

In sum, incomes are *less* unequal after a tax than before the tax if and only if the tax is distributed more unequally than the income to which it applies. Incomes are *more* unequal after a tax than before the tax if and only if the tax is distributed more equally than the income to which it applies. A proportional tax will have the same distribution as the pretax income and leave the distribution of income unchanged. A poll tax, which taxes all individuals by the same absolute amount, will

---

[4] This is true because if $0 < g < 1$, the weights by definition sum to one. Hence $L_X(p)$ must lie between $C_T(p)$ and $C_{X-T}(p)$ by necessity.

FIGURE 2-1

Lorenz Curve of Pretax Income and Post-Tax Income and Concentration Curve of Tax

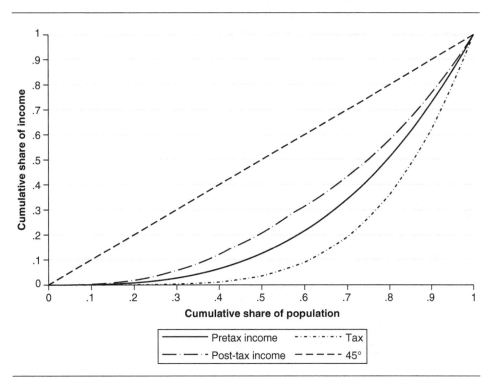

feature a concentration curve coincidental with the diagonal; that is, it will be very unequalizing.[5]

If condition 2-2 is *everywhere* observed, plotting the average tax rate $T(x)/x$ against values (or quantiles) of pretax income will be sufficient to determine whether a tax system is *everywhere* progressive (tax rates rise with income), neutral (tax rates are the same for all incomes—a flat tax), or regressive (tax rates decrease with income). For example, if we are sure that condition 2-2 is strictly observed within deciles, we can determine whether a tax system is progressive, regressive, or neutral by plotting the incidence of the tax by decile as we do in figure 2-2.

Globally progressive taxes and taxes that are everywhere progressive

Note, however, that taxes do not have to be progressive everywhere for the distribution of post-tax income to be less unequal than the pretax income distribution.

---

[5] Although not impossible in principle, taxes in absolute terms (that is, per capita) rarely decline with income in the real world. If such a tax were to exist, its concentration curve would lie above the diagonal and be extremely unequalizing.

FIGURE 2-2
Average Tax Rate by Pretax Income: A Progressive, Neutral, and Regressive Tax

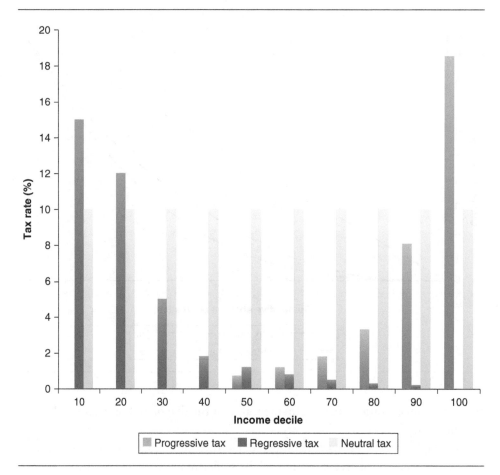

A necessary and sufficient condition for a tax to be equalizing is for it to be globally progressive—that is, that $C_T(p) \leq L_X(p)$ for all p and strict inequality for some p and for any distribution of pretax income.

The toy example in table 2-1 illustrates the difference between a tax that is progressive everywhere and one that is globally progressive only.

The Kakwani index

To assess whether a tax is equalizing or not, one can also use the Kakwani index of progressivity.[6] Kakwani's index of progressivity of tax t is defined as the difference

---

[6] Kakwani was among the first to propose a measure of tax progressivity based on "disproportionality," that is, by the extent to which a tax distribution was not proportional to the distribution of pretax income. See Kakwani (1977).

TABLE 2-1

An Everywhere Progressive Tax and a Globally Progressive Tax

Everywhere progressive tax

Population	Pretax income ($)	Lorenz curve pretax (%)	Average tax rate, % (everywhere progressive)	Tax paid ($)	Post-tax income ($)	Lorenz curve post-tax (%)	Difference between post- and pretax Lorenz curves (%)
1	10.00	10	0	0.00	10.00	13	2.50
2	20.00	30	10	2.00	18.00	35	5.00
3	30.00	60	20	6.00	24.00	65	5.00
4	40.00	100	30	12.00	28.00	100	0.00
Total	100.00		20	20.00	80.00		

Globally progressive tax

Population	Pretax income ($)	Lorenz curve pretax (%)	Average tax rate, % (not everywhere progressive)	Tax paid ($)	Post-tax income ($)	Lorenz curve post-tax (%)	Difference between post- and pretax Lorenz curves (%)
1	10.00	10	0	0.00	10.00	13	2.50
2	20.00	30	18	3.60	16.40	33	3.00
3	30.00	60	12	3.60	26.40	66	6.00
4	40.00	100	32	12.80	27.20	100	0.00
Total	100.00		20	20.00	80.00		

Notes: The globally progressive tax panel (the bottom panel) has a post-tax Lorenz curve that is above the pretax Lorenz curve (just like the top panel), but the tax rate does not always increase with income (see highlighted cells).

TABLE 2-2
Conditions for Equalizing, Neutral, and Unequalizing Taxes

Tax	Sufficient	Necessary and sufficient
Equalizing	$t'(x) \geq 0$ for all x with some $t'(x) > 0$	$C_T(p) \leq L_X(p)$ for all p and for any distribution of pretax income
		or
		$\Pi_T^K > 0$
Neutral	$t'(x) = 0$ for all x	$C_T(p) = L_X(p)$ for all p and for any distribution of pretax income
		or
		$\Pi_T^K = 0$
Unequalizing	$t'(x) \leq 0$ for all x with some $t'(x) < 0$	$C_T(p) \geq L_X(p)$ for all p and for any distribution of pretax income
		or
		$\Pi_T^K < 0$

between the concentration coefficient (C_T) of the tax and the Gini coefficient of pretax income (G_X), or

$$(2\text{-}5) \qquad \Pi_T^K = C_T - G_X,$$

where C_T is the concentration coefficient of the tax t and G_X is the Gini coefficient of pretax income. The conditions for a tax to be equalizing, neutral, or unequalizing are $\Pi_T^K > 0$, $\Pi_T^K = 0$, and $\Pi_T^K < 0$, respectively.

Table 2-2 presents a summary of the conditions described above. Of course, if the tax meets the sufficient condition, it implies that the necessary condition is met, too (but not vice versa). Since we assumed there is no reranking, the disproportionality measures such as the concentration curves and the Kakwani index translate immediately into measures of redistribution.

If there is reranking, the link between inequality and measures of disproportionality is no longer straightforward because with reranking we need to use equation 2-3—that is, $L_X(p) = g\, C_T(p) + (1-g)\, C_{X-T}(p)$—instead of equation 2-3'. Note that in equation 2-3, the post-tax income Lorenz curve has been replaced by the post-tax income concentration curve (the distribution of post-tax income with individuals ranked by pretax income). Because we are no longer comparing two income distributions with the presence of reranking, some of the "redistribution" will not be actual redistribution; instead, the tax will be reordering individuals. The consequences of reranking will be further discussed in chapter 3 of this Volume.[7]

---

[7] See also Urban (2009).

FIGURE 2-3

A Diagrammatic Representation of Progressivity of Taxes

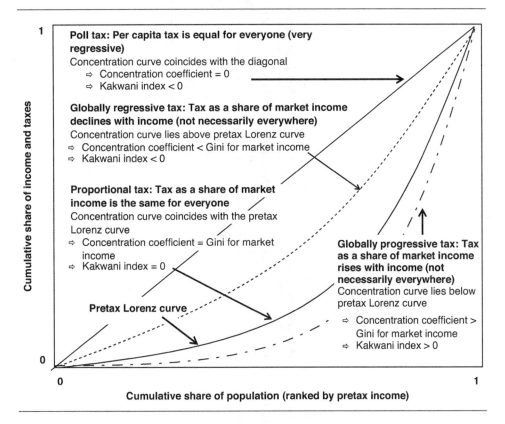

In addition, because we assume that the post-tax income Lorenz curve dominates the pretax income Lorenz curve, we can be sure that the Kakwani index will give an unambiguous ordering of different taxes in terms of progressivity (the implication of no dominance is left for future work). However, it is important not to extrapolate from progressivity to impact on inequality when comparing taxes of different sizes. We discuss this issue in the following subsection on comparing taxes (1.1.2).

Measures of progressivity of a tax are presented diagrammatically in figure 2-3.

1.1.2 Comparing Two Taxes of Different Sizes

We have just shown how progressivity determines whether a tax in a single tax system is equalizing or not. Does this mean that the more unequally distributed a tax is (that is, the more progressive), the more equalizing it is? The following example will show that this is not necessarily the case.[8] In table 2-3, we present two hypothetical taxes taken from Duclos and Tabi (1996), A and A'. We can see that tax A' is more unequally distributed (that is,

---

[8] This section draws from Lambert (2001) and Duclos and Araar (2007).

TABLE 2-3
Redistributive Effect and the Progressivity and Size of Taxes

Individual	Gross income Income ($)	Gross income Distribution (%)	Tax A = 50.5% Tax ($)	Tax A = 50.5% Distribution (%)	Net income under A Income ($)	Net income under A Distribution (%)	Tax A' = 1% Tax ($)	Tax A' = 1% Distribution (%)	Net income under A' Income ($)	Net income under A' Distribution (%)
1	21	21	1	2	20	40	0	0	21	21
2	80	79	50	98	30	60	1	100	79	79
Total	101	100	51	100	50	100	1	100	100	100

Source: Duclos and Tabi (1996, table 1).

more progressive) than tax A, or using the terminology presented in the previous section, that the concentration curve of tax system A lies completely above the concentration curve of tax system A′ (that is, A is less disproportional than A′). Yet, the post-tax distribution is more unequal under tax system A′. How can that be? Notice that tax system A′ collects a lower share of post-tax income than system A. The higher tax ratio in A more than compensates for its lower progressivity to the point that the redistributive effect in A is higher.

The extent of disproportionality is not sufficient to compare the redistributive effect across different taxes. What indicators can we use? There are three options: comparing the post-tax Lorenz curves, comparing the residual progression functions, or comparing the Reynolds-Smolensky (R-S) indices if one wishes to use a scalar instead of a function. In the absence of reranking and if there is Lorenz dominance, the three approaches are equivalent.

The first condition is straightforward. If the Lorenz curve of post-tax income A dominates the Lorenz curve of post-tax income A′, inequality will be reduced more greatly under the former than the latter.

"Residual progression" is defined as the elasticity of post-tax income with respect to pretax income (that is, the percentage change in post-tax income per 1 percent change in pretax income) and can be written as follows:

$$(2\text{-}6) \qquad RP_{X-T} = [\partial(X - T(X))/\partial X]\,[X/((X - T(X)))],$$

and

$$(2\text{-}7) \qquad RP_{X-T} = (1 - T'(x))/(1 - T(x)/x).$$

If $RP_{X-T} < 1$ everywhere, the tax is progressive everywhere. To determine if tax A is more equalizing than tax A′, compare the residual progression for tax A and A′. If RP_{X-T} for tax A lies completely below the RP_{X-T} of tax A′, the former will generate a higher reduction in inequality than the latter.

Finally, the Reynolds-Smolensky (R-S) index is defined as

$$(2\text{-}8) \qquad \Pi_T^{RS} = G_X - C_{X-T} = g/(1-g)(C_T - G_X) = [g/(1-g)]\Pi_T^K,$$

where C_{X-T} is the concentration coefficient of post-tax income, G_X is the Gini coefficient of pretax income, C_T is the concentration coefficient of tax T, and Π_T^K is the Kakwani index of progressivity of tax T defined as $C_t - G_x$ (see section 1.1.1).

To see this equality, note the following. Lerman and Yitzhaki prove that

$$C_Q = \frac{2cov(Q, F_X)}{\mu_Q}.$$

where $cov(Q, F_X)$ is the covariance between income concept or component Q and ranking of individuals with respect to the original income (that is, X).[9] Moreover, μ_Q is the average value of income concept or component Q among all individuals. Similarly,

$$G_X = \frac{2cov(X, F_X)}{\mu}.$$

Therefore, we have the following:

$$G_X - C_{X-T} = G_X - \frac{2cov(X - T, F_X)}{\mu(1-g)} = G_X - \frac{2cov(X, F_X)}{\mu(1-g)} + \frac{2cov(T, F_X)}{\mu(1-g)}$$

$$= G_X - \left(\frac{1}{1-g}\right)\frac{2cov(X, F_X)}{\mu} + \left(\frac{g}{1-g}\right)\frac{2cov(T, F_X)}{\mu g}$$

$$= G_X - \left(\frac{1}{1-g}\right)G_X + \left(\frac{g}{1-g}\right)C_T$$

$$= \left(\frac{g}{1-g}\right)(C_T - G_X).$$

Under no reranking, it turns out that the R-S index is identical to the redistributive effect (RE)—that is, the change in inequality between pretax and post-tax income distribution measured in Gini points.[10]

With no reranking,

$$C_{X-T} = G_{X-T}.$$

Therefore:

$$(2\text{-}8)'\qquad RE = G_X - G_{X-T} = g/(1-g)(C_T - G_X) = \Pi_T^{RS} = \left[g/(1-g)\right]\Pi_T^{K}.$$

The R-S index, Π_T^{RS}, is greater than, equal to, or less than 0, depending on whether the tax is equalizing, neutral, or unequalizing, respectively. The larger the R-S index, the more equalizing the tax. Thus, we can use Π_T^{RS} to order different taxes individually based on their redistributive effects.

The R-S index (Π_T^{RS}) shows exactly how the redistributive effect does not depend *only* on the extent of progressivity. It is an increasing function of the latter *and* the tax ratio g.[11] Therefore, either making a given tax more progressive or raising the tax ratio of a progressive tax can increase the redistributive effect. In the case of a regressive tax, either making the tax less regressive or lowering the tax ratio will make its effect less unequalizing. We summarize these conditions in table 2-4.

---

[9] Lerman and Yitzhaki (1989).

[10] This result can be generalized to a wide range of inequality measures of the S-Gini family. See also Lambert (2001) and Duclos and Araar (2007).

[11] See Lambert (2001).

TABLE 2-4
Conditions for the Redistributive Effect and Progressivity and Size of Taxes

	Necessary and sufficient conditions
Tax A is more **equalizing** than Tax A′ *if*	$L^A_{X-T}(p) \geq L^{A'}_{X-T}(p)$ for all p, with strict inequality for some p, and for any distribution of pretax income, or $RP^A_{X-T}(p) \leq RP^{A'}_{X-T}(p)$ for all p, with strict inequality for some p, and for any distribution of pretax income.
Tax A is more **unequalizing** than Tax A′ *if*	$L^A_{X-T}(p) \leq L^{A'}_{X-T}(p)$ for all p, with strict inequality for some p, and for any distribution of pretax income, or $RP^A_{X-T}(p) \geq RP^{A'}_{X-T}(p)$ for all p, with strict inequality for some p, and for any distribution of pretax income.

We have developed table 2-4 assuming there is no reranking. If there is reranking, the link between the progressivity and size of a tax and its redistributive effect is no longer straightforward, and thus comparisons are no longer straightforward either. (We will return to the consequences of reranking in chapter 3 of this Volume.) In addition, the three conditions in table 2-4 are equivalent under the assumption that the post-tax Lorenz curve under a specific tax dominates the post-tax Lorenz curve under another tax. We have left the discussion of the implications of no dominance for future work.

Note also that the conditions for comparing the redistributive effect between different taxes characterized by different degrees of progressivity and size were defined for the case in which the pretax income distribution is always the same. The comparison of the redistributive effect of taxes (and transfers) in cases when the original income distributions are not the same is left for future work.[12]

More importantly, when there is more than one intervention, the neat relationship between the size and progressivity of a fiscal intervention and its redistributive effect (i.e., equation 2-8′) no longer holds. That is the case even without reranking, with dominance and when the original distribution is constant. As we will see in section 2 of this chapter, a tax can be regressive using any of the necessary or sufficient conditions in table 2-2 and still exert an equalizing influence on the post-tax and transfer income distribution, by which we mean that, in the absence of such a tax, the reduction in inequality would be smaller than with the tax in place. Before we turn to this topic, however, we will present the analogous conditions for a single transfer.

---

[12] Interested readers can refer to Dardanoni and Lambert (2000).

1.2 A Single Transfer

The word "single" here does not mean that the conditions derived in this section apply to a system with only one transfer. In the case of multiple transfers, however, they need to be aggregated into one category in order for the conditions to apply.

Transfers here encompass a wide spectrum of benefits provided by the government, such as cash transfers, school food programs, consumption subsidies, and access to free public services. We will use the words "transfer" and "benefit" interchangeably and use the abbreviation B for both.

We will also use the following definitions:

x = pre-transfer income

$B(x)$ = transfer at income x

$x + B(x)$ = post-transfer income

$B(x)/x = b(x)$ = average benefit rate at income x

$b'(x)$ = marginal benefit rate

B = total transfers = $\sum_i B(x_i)$

b = total transfers ratio = B/X

Using the last equation, we have the following two equations:

$$(1 + b) = (X + B)/X$$
$$b/(1 + b) = B/(X + B)$$

$L_X(p)$, $L_{X+B}(p)$ = Lorenz curve of pre-transfer income and post-transfer income, respectively (ranked by original income)

$C_{X+B}(p)$, $C_B(p)$ = Concentration curve of post-transfer income and transfer, respectively (ranked by original income)

It can be shown that

(2-9) $$L_X(p) = (1 + b)\, C_{X+B}(p) - b\, C_B(p),$$

which implies that

(2-10) $$L_X(p) \geq C_{X+B}(p) \Leftrightarrow C_{X+B}(p) \geq C_B(p).$$

If we assume no reranking, that is,

$$-1 \leq b'(x),$$

FIGURE 2-4

A Progressive Transfer: Lorenz Curve of Pre-Transfer Income, Concentration Curve of an Equalizing Transfer, and Lorenz Curve of Post-Transfer Income

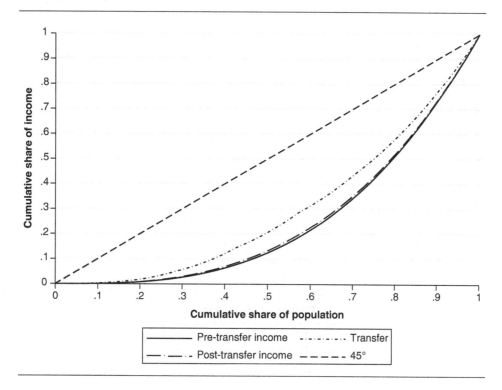

where $b'(x)$ is the increase in benefits that occurs as pre-transfer income X rises, the ranking of people by pre-transfer and post-transfer income does not change. Thus, equation 2-10 can be rewritten as

$$(2\text{-}10)' \qquad L_X(p) \geq L_{X+B}(p) \Leftrightarrow L_{X+B}(p) \geq C_B(p).$$

Under no reranking, incomes are less unequal after transfers than before if and only if transfers are distributed more *equally* than the income to which they apply. If the average transfer rate $b(x)$ decreases with income *everywhere*, then transfers are distributed more equally than pre-transfer income. This scenario is shown in figure 2-4.

For instance, although cash transfers are very unlikely to be regressive, this is not the case with subsidies, contributory pensions, and spending on tertiary education, which are sometimes regressive in the real world. An everywhere regressive transfer will fulfill the following condition:

$$(2\text{-}10)'' \qquad L_X(p) \leq L_{X+B}(p) \Leftrightarrow L_{X+B}(p) \leq C_B(p).$$

When 2-10″ occurs, benefits will be unequalizing.

FIGURE 2-5

A Pro-Poor Transfer: Lorenz Curve of Pre-Transfer Income, Concentration Curve of an Equalizing Transfer, and Lorenz Curve of Post-Transfer Income

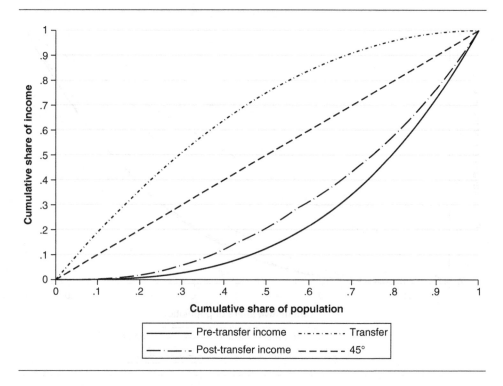

However, equalizing transfers may not be pro-poor. As long as the relative size of the transfer declines with income, a transfer will be equalizing. However, to be pro-poor, the *absolute* size of the transfer also needs to decline with income (although not so much that the marginal benefit is less than −1). That is, the share of a transfer going to the rich can be higher than the share going to the poor even if a transfer is equalizing (or progressive).

Figure 2-5 shows the concentration curve for a transfer that is both equalizing and pro-poor.

1.2.1 Fiscal Systems: Comparing Two Single-Transfer Systems of Different Sizes

So far, we have shown that in a system with only one transfer and no reranking, a progressive transfer is equalizing. Does this mean that the more progressive a transfer is (that is, the more progressive or disproportional), the more equalizing it is? Table 2-5 shows that this need not be the case: transfer A is not only more progressive but also more pro-poor than A′, yet the post-transfer distribution is considerably more equal with transfer A than with transfer A′.

TABLE 2-5
Redistributive Effect and the Progressivity of Transfers

Population	Gross income		Transfer A		Net income under A		Transfer A'		Net income under A'	
	Income	Distribution (%)	Transfer	Distribution (%)	Income	Distribution (%)	Transfer	Distribution (%)	Income	Distribution (%)
1	21	21	50	98	71	47	1	100	22	22
2	80	79	1	2	81	53	0	0	80	78
Total	101	100	51	100	152	100	1	100	102	100

Population	Gross income		Transfer A		Net income under A		Transfer A'		Net income under A'	
	Income	Distribution (%)	Transfer	Distribution (%)	Income	Distribution (%)	Transfer	Distribution (%)	Income	Distribution (%)
1	21	21	50	98	71	47	1	100	22	22
2	80	79	1	2	81	53	0	0	50	78
Total	101	100	51	100	152	100	1	100	72	100

TABLE 2-6

Conditions for Equalizing, Neutral, and Unequalizing Transfers

A transfer is	Sufficient	Necessary and sufficient
Equalizing, if	$-1 < b'(x) \leq 0$ for all x and $b'(x) < 0$ for some x	$C_B(p) \geq L_X(p)$ for all p, with strict inequality for some p, and for any distribution of pretax income
Neutral, if	$b'(x) = 0$ for all x	$C_B(p) = L_X(p)$ for all p and for any distribution of pretax income
Unequalizing, if	$b'(x) \geq 0$ for all x and $b'(x) > 0$ for some x	$C_B(p) \leq L_X(p)$ for all p, with strict inequality for some p, and for any distribution of pretax income

As with taxes, the redistributive effect of a transfer depends not only on its progressivity but also on its relative size. That is, under no reranking,

$$(2\text{-}11) \qquad RE = G_X - G_{X+B} = b/(1+b)[G_X - C_B] = \rho_B^{RS} = [b/(1+b)]\rho_B^K,$$

where ρ_B^{RS} and ρ_B^K are the R-S index and Kakwani index of the benefit B, respectively.[13] This equation highlights the fact that the redistributive effect does not depend *only* on the extent of progressivity (disproportionality) of the transfer. Rather, the redistributive effect depends on both the extent of progressivity *and* the relative size of the transfer, $b/(1+b)$, which equals the total transfer divided by the post-transfer total income. Therefore, either making a given transfer more progressive or raising the relative size of a progressive transfer can increase the redistributive effect. The R-S index can also be used to compare the redistributive effect across transfers.

As in the case of taxes, the R-S is a summary index and thus will not alert us to cases in which a transfer is more redistributive in some parts of the distribution and less in others. Additionally, as with taxes, one can use the residual progression to compare the redistributive effect of transfers across the entire distribution.

We summarize these results and present the conditions under which a transfer exerts an equalizing force on the pre-transfer distribution of income in table 2-6.

In the case of transfers, the literature tends to distinguish between a relatively progressive transfer and a transfer that is progressive in absolute terms.[14] The former is defined by the following condition: $b'(x) \leq 0$ for all x and $b'(x) < 0$ for some x. This condition is sufficient for a transfer to be equalizing. However, this condition does not need to be fulfilled in order for a transfer to be equalizing. As mentioned previously, the necessary and sufficient condition is $C_B(p) \geq L_X(p)$ for all p, with strict inequality for some p, and for any distribution of pretax income, or for $\rho_B^K > 0$.

---

[13] The proof of this formula is similar to equation 2-8 explained earlier.

[14] Such a distinction is not made in the case of taxes because no one expects per capita taxes to increase with income.

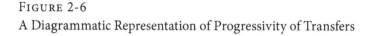

FIGURE 2-6

A Diagrammatic Representation of Progressivity of Transfers

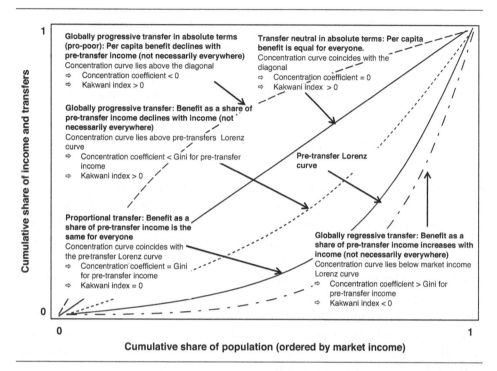

In the case of a transfer that is progressive in absolute terms, the concentration curve $C_B(p)$ is compared not to the $L_X(p)$ but rather to the population shares or the diagonal. When the transfer tends to decline with income in per capita terms, that is, $B(x)$, transfers are called "progressive" in absolute terms. They are also sometimes called "pro-poor."

In figure 2-6, we present hypothetical concentration curves for progressive, neutral (proportional), and regressive transfers. Among the progressive transfers, we distinguish between the transfers that are progressive in relative and in absolute terms. A simple way to identify a transfer that is progressive in absolute terms is by the sign of its concentration coefficient, which will be negative.

2 The Fiscal System and Income Redistribution: Multiple Taxes and Transfers

This section derives the conditions for fiscal redistribution in a world of multiple fiscal interventions.[15] We first derive the conditions for the simple one tax–one transfer case

---

[15] The word "multiple" is used as opposed to the word "single." In the case of a "single" tax or transfer, we deal either with only one tax or transfer or with a group of taxes or transfers that are combined and treated as one incident.

TABLE 2-7
Lambert's Conundrum

Individual	1	2	3	4	Total
Original income x	10	20	30	40	100
Tax liability (T)	6	9	12	15	42
Benefit level (B)	21	14	7	0	42
Post-benefit income	31	34	37	40	142
Final income	25	25	25	25	100

Source: Lambert (2001, p. 278, table 11.1).

and, subsequently, for the case with multiple taxes and transfers. Suppose we observe that postfiscal income inequality is lower than prefiscal income inequality. Can we relate this finding to the characteristics of specific taxes and transfers in terms of indicators of progressivity and size? As demonstrated in the following section, once we leave the world of a single fiscal intervention, the relationship between inequality outcomes and the size and progressivity[16] of fiscal interventions is complex and at times counterintuitive. In particular, the relative size and progressivity of a fiscal intervention by itself can no longer tell us if inequality would be higher or lower without it. We will show that, under certain conditions, a fiscal system that includes a regressive tax can be *more* equalizing than a system that excludes it.[17] In the same vein, a fiscal system that includes a progressive transfer can be *less* equalizing than a system that excludes it.

The so-called Lambert's conundrum helps to illustrate this point in the case of a regressive tax.[18] Table 2-7 shows that "taxes may be regressive in their effect on original income . . . and yet the net system may exhibit more progressivity" than the progressive benefits alone.[19] The R-S index for taxes in this example is equal to −0.0517, highlighting their regressivity.[20] Yet, the R-S index for the net fiscal system is 0.25, higher than the R-S index for benefits equal to 0.1972. If taxes are regressive in relation to the original income,[21] but progressive with respect to the less unequally distributed post-transfers (and subsidies) income, regressive taxes exert an equalizing effect over and above the effect of progressive transfers.[22]

---

[16] Using, for example, the Kakwani index of progressivity.

[17] See also Lambert (2001, p. 278), for the same conclusion.

[18] Lambert (2001, p. 278).

[19] Lambert (2001, p. 278).

[20] Since there is no reranking, the R-S index equals the difference between the Ginis before and after the fiscal intervention.

[21] Note that original income is in fact the "tax base" in this example.

[22] Note that Lambert uses the terms "progressive" and "regressive" in a way that differs from that of other authors in the theoretical and empirical incidence analysis literature. Thus, he calls transfers that are equalizing "regressive." See definitions in earlier chapters of his book (2001).

Note that Lambert's conundrum is not equivalent to the well-known (and frequently repeated) result that efficient regressive taxes can be fine as long as the net fiscal system is equalizing when combined with transfers.[23] The surprising aspect of Lambert's conundrum is that a net fiscal system *with* a regressive tax (in relation to prefiscal income) can be *more* equalizing than *without* the tax.[24]

The implications of Lambert's conundrum for real fiscal systems are quite profound. In order to determine whether a particular intervention (or a particular policy change) is inequality-increasing or inequality-reducing—and by how much—one must resort to numerical calculations that include the whole system. As Lambert mentions, his example is "not altogether farfetched."[25] For example, two renowned studies in the 1980s found this type of result for the United States and the United Kingdom.[26] Moreover, two recent studies for Chile found that although the value-added tax (VAT) is regressive, it is equalizing.[27] The conundrum, however, can occur with transfers as well: a transfer may be progressive but unequalizing, as was the case for contributory pensions in the *CEQ Assessment* for Colombia.[28] In this analysis, the Kakwani index for contributory pensions was positive but unequalizing in the sense that the reduction in inequality would have been higher without the contributory pensions (and the rest of the fiscal interventions) in place.

Estimating the sign and order of magnitude of the contribution of a particular intervention to the change in inequality will depend on the particular question one is

---

[23] As Higgins and Lustig (2016, p. 63) mention, "Efficient taxes that fall disproportionately on the poor, such as a no-exemption value-added tax, are often justified with the argument that 'spending instruments are available that are better targeted to the pursuit of equity concerns' (Keen and Lockwood, 2010, p. 141)." Similarly, Engel, Galetovic, and Raddatz (1999, p. 186) assert that "it is quite obvious that the disadvantages of a proportional tax are moderated by adequate targeting" of transfers, because "what the poor individual pays in taxes is returned to her." Ebrill, Keen, and Summers (2001, p. 105) argue that "a regressive tax might conceivably be the best way to finance pro-poor expenditures, with the net effect being to relieve poverty."

[24] It can also be shown that if there is reranking (a pervasive feature of net tax systems in the real world), making a tax (or a transfer) more progressive can *increase* post-tax and transfer inequality. In Lambert's example, not only do regressive taxes enhance the equalizing effect of transfers, but making taxes more progressive (that is, more disproportional in the Kakwani sense) would result in *higher* inequality. Any additional change (toward more progressivity) in taxes or transfers would just cause reranking and an increase in inequality.

[25] Lambert (2001, p. 278).

[26] See O'Higgins and Ruggles (1981) for the United Kingdom and Ruggles and O'Higgins (1981) for the United States.

[27] See Martinez-Aguilar and others (2022) (chapter 13 in this Volume) and Engel, Galetovic, and Raddatz (1999). Although Engel and his coauthors were not aware of this characteristic of the Chilean system when they published their article, in a recent interaction, Engel concluded that the Chilean system featured regressive albeit equalizing indirect taxes.

[28] Lustig and Melendez (2016).

interested in. For example, if one is interested in answering the question "What if we remove or introduce a particular intervention?," one should estimate the "marginal" contribution by taking the difference in the indicators of interest (for example, the Gini coefficient) that would prevail with and without the specific intervention.[29] Another possibility is to view the "without" case as substituting a tax or transfer with an alternative tax or transfer that is distribution- or poverty-neutral (but it cannot be both since each would imply a different "counterfactual").

Note, however, that the sum of all the marginal contributions will not equal the total redistributive effect (except by a fluke)[30] because there is path dependency in how interventions affect the net fiscal system and the marginal effect.[31] Essentially, the path in which the fiscal intervention of interest is introduced last is just one of the possible paths. To obtain the average contribution of a specific intervention, one would need to consider all the possible (and institutionally valid) paths and use an appropriate formula to average them. One commonly used approach is to calculate the Shapley value. The Shapley value fulfills the efficiency property: that is, the sum of all the individual contributions is equal to the total effect.[32] Moreover, if some particular paths are irrelevant, the Shapley formula can be modified to exclude them (without losing the efficiency property introduced earlier). We shall return to the Shapley value and its use in appendix 2A.[33]

In the following section, we first turn to deriving the conditions that ensure that a net fiscal system is equalizing. Next, we derive the conditions that must prevail in order for the marginal contribution of a tax or a transfer to be equalizing. As mentioned earlier, we first derive the conditions for the simple one tax–one transfer case and, subsequently, for the case with multiple taxes and transfers.

2.1 Equalizing, Neutral, and Unequalizing Net Fiscal Systems

The next two subsections discuss the conditions for a net system to have an equalizing marginal effect. We begin with the simple case of one tax and one transfer, and then we extend it to the case of a system with multiple taxes and transfers.

---

[29] The same applies to poverty indicators or any other indicator of interest.

[30] This is also the case for the vertical equity and reranking components of redistributive effect.

[31] Note that here we use the terms "marginal contribution" and "marginal effect" interchangeably.

[32] See the discussion of path dependency in chapter 7 of Duclos and Araar (2007). See also Bibi and Duclos (2010).

[33] For a review of the decomposition techniques in economics, see Fortin and others (2011). For a review of the Shapley decomposition, see also Shorrocks (2013).

2.1.1 Conditions for the One Tax–One Transfer Case

As shown by Lambert,[34] the redistributive effect (measured by the change in Gini co-efficients) is equal to the weighted sum of the redistributive effect of taxes and transfers:

(2-12) $$\Pi_N^{RS} = \frac{(1-g)\Pi_T^{RS} + (1+b)\rho_B^{RS}}{1-g+b},$$

where Π_N^{RS}, Π_T^{RS}, and ρ_B^{RS} are the Reynolds-Smolensky indices for the net fiscal system, taxes, and benefits, respectively; and g and b are the total tax and benefit ratios—that is, total taxes and total benefits divided by total prefiscal (original) income, respectively.[35] There are two features to note. First, the weights sum to more than unity so the redistributive effect is not a weighted *average*. This fact is not innocuous: it lies at the heart of Lambert's conundrum. Second, recall that in the absence of rerank-ing, the Reynolds-Smolensky index is identical to the redistributive effect measured as the difference between the Gini coefficients. As we will see later in chapter 3 of this Volume, if there is reranking, equation 2-12 will no longer be equal to the redistribu-tive effect.

Using equation 2-12, we can derive the general condition for the case in which the combination of one tax and one transfer (that is, the net fiscal system) is equalizing, neutral, or unequalizing. As noted, when there is no reranking, Π_N^{RS} is equal to the change in the Gini coefficient (that is, $G_X - G_{X-T+B}$). If $G_X - G_{X-T+B} > 0$, the net fiscal system is equalizing, which simply means that equation 2-12 must be positive. Since the denominator is positive by definition, the condition implies that the numerator has to be positive. In other words,

(2-13) $$\Pi_N^{RS} = \frac{(1-g)\Pi_T^{RS} + (1+b)\rho_B^{RS}}{1-g+b} > 0 \Leftrightarrow (1-g)\Pi_T^{RS} + (1+b)\rho_B^{RS} > 0$$

(2-14) $$\Leftrightarrow \Pi_T^{RS} > -\frac{(1+b)}{(1-g)}\rho_B^{RS}$$

(2-15) $$\Leftrightarrow \Pi_T^{K} > -\frac{(b)}{(g)}\rho_B^{K},$$

where Π_T^{K} and ρ_B^{K} are the Kakwani index of the tax and transfer, respectively, and $1-g$ is positive.

Therefore, we can state the following conditions:

---

[34] Lambert (2001, p. 277, equation 11.29).

[35] It is important to note that the tax relative sizes or ratios have to be those that are calculated in the actual data of the fiscal incidence analysis, which are not necessarily equal to the ratios of taxes or transfers to GDP obtained from administrative accounts.

Condition 2-16:

If and only if

$$\Pi_T^{RS} > -\frac{1+b}{1-g}\rho_B^{RS}\left(, \text{ or } \rho_B^{RS} > -\frac{1-g}{1+b}\Pi_T^{RS}\right), \text{ or }$$

$$\Pi_T^{K} > -\frac{(b)}{(g)}\rho_B^{K}\left(, \text{ or } \rho_B^{K} > -\frac{(g)}{(b)}\Pi_T^{K}\right),$$

the net fiscal system reduces inequality.

Condition 2-17:

If and only if

$$\Pi_T^{RS} = -\frac{1+b}{1-g}\rho_B^{RS}\left(, \text{ or } \rho_B^{RS} = -\frac{1-g}{1+b}\Pi_T^{RS}\right), \text{ or }$$

$$\Pi_T^{K} = -\frac{(b)}{(g)}\rho_B^{K}\left(, \text{ or } \rho_B^{K} = -\frac{(g)}{(b)}\Pi_T^{K}\right),$$

the net fiscal system leaves inequality unchanged.

Condition 2-18:

If and only if

$$\Pi_T^{RS} < -\frac{1+b}{1-g}\rho_B^{RS}\left(, \text{ or } \rho_B^{RS} < -\frac{1-g}{1+b}\Pi_T^{RS}\right), \text{ or }$$

$$\Pi_T^{K} < -\frac{(b)}{(g)}\rho_B^{K}\left(, \text{ or } \rho_B^{K} = < -\frac{(g)}{(b)}\Pi_T^{K}\right),$$

the net fiscal system increases inequality.

As shown in table 2-8, a system that combines a regressive tax with a regressive or neutral transfer or a neutral tax with a regressive transfer can never be equalizing. A system that combines a progressive tax with a neutral or progressive transfer or a neutral tax with a progressive transfer is always equalizing. Combining a neutral tax and a neutral transfer leaves inequality unchanged. A regressive tax combined with a progressive transfer or a progressive tax combined with a regressive transfer can be equalizing if and only if condition 2-16 holds.

2.1.2 Conditions for the Multiple Taxes and Transfers Case

Let's assume there are n taxes and m transfers in a fiscal system. Equation 2-12 can be written as

(2-19)
$$\Pi_N^{RS} = \frac{\sum_{i=1}^{n}(1-g_i)\Pi_{T_i}^{RS} + \sum_{j=1}^{m}(1+b_j)\rho_{B_j}^{RS}}{1-\sum_{i=1}^{n}g_i + \sum_{j=1}^{m}b_j}.$$

TABLE 2-8
Net Fiscal System: Conditions for the One Tax–One Transfer Case

		Transfer		
		Regressive $\rho_B^K < 0$	Neutral $\rho_B^K = 0$	Progressive $\rho_B^K > 0$
Tax	Regressive $\prod_T^K < 0$	Always unequalizing	Always unequalizing	Equalizing if and only if condition 2-16 holds
	Neutral $\prod_T^K = 0$	Always unequalizing	No change in equality	Always equalizing
	Progressive $\prod_T^K > 0$	Equalizing if and only if condition 2-16 holds	Always equalizing	Always equalizing

The condition for the net system to be equalizing is that the Reynolds-Smolensky index for the net fiscal system should be higher than zero—that is,

$$(2\text{-}20) \qquad \prod_N^{RS} > 0,$$

that is,

$$(2\text{-}21) \qquad \frac{\sum_{i=1}^{n}(1-g_i)\prod_{T_i}^{RS} + \sum_{j=1}^{m}(1+b_j)\rho_{B_j}^{RS}}{1 - \sum_{i=1}^{n} g_i + \sum_{j=1}^{m} b_j} > 0,$$

assuming, of course, that the denominator is positive,

$$(2\text{-}22a) \qquad \Leftrightarrow \sum_{i=1}^{n}(1-g_i)\prod_{T_i}^{RS} > - \sum_{j=1}^{m}(1+b_j)\rho_{B_j}^{RS},$$

or equivalently,

$$(2\text{-}22b) \qquad \Leftrightarrow \sum_{i=1}^{n} g_i \prod_{T_i}^{K} > - \sum_{j=1}^{m} b_j \rho_{B_j}^{K}.$$

Therefore, we can state the following conditions:

Condition 2-23:
   If and only if

$$\sum_{i=1}^{n}(1-g_i)\prod_{T_i}^{RS} > - \sum_{j=1}^{m}(1+b_j)\rho_{B_j}^{RS}, \quad \text{or} \quad \sum_{i=1}^{n} g_i \prod_{T_i}^{K} > - \sum_{j=1}^{m} b_j \rho_{B_j}^{K},$$

   the net fiscal system reduces inequality.

Condition 2-24:
   If and only if

$$\sum_{i=1}^{n}(1-g_i)\prod_{T_i}^{RS} = - \sum_{j=1}^{m}(1+b_j)\rho_{B_j}^{RS}, \quad \text{or} \quad \sum_{i=1}^{n} g_i \prod_{T_i}^{K} = - \sum_{j=1}^{m} b_j \rho_{B_j}^{K},$$

   the net fiscal system leaves inequality unchanged.

Condition 2-25:
   If and only if

$$\sum_{i=1}^{n}(1-g_i)\Pi_{T_i}^{RS} < -\sum_{j=1}^{m}(1+b_j)\rho_{B_j}^{RS}, \quad \text{or} \quad \sum_{i=1}^{n}g_i\Pi_{T_i}^{K} < -\sum_{j=1}^{m}b_j\rho_{B_j}^{K},$$

the net fiscal system increases inequality.

2.2 Equalizing, Neutral, and Unequalizing Taxes or Transfers

Whereas the previous section looked at the net system and provided conditions for the whole system to be equalizing, this section focuses on only one tax or only one transfer in the system. The question is whether that specific component leads to a more equalizing total system. The first case is a simple system with only one transfer (or one tax) in place and determines the conditions for the addition of a tax (or a transfer) to make the system more equal. In the following subsection, a more general case with multiple taxes and transfer is analyzed.

2.2.1 Conditions for the One Tax–One Transfer Case

In a scenario where there is one tax and one transfer, conditions to assess whether adding a regressive (or progressive) transfer or tax exerts an unequalizing (or equalizing) effect do not necessarily hold as described in section 1 on "The Fiscal System and Income Redistribution: The Case of a Single Tax or a Single Transfer," and introducing these interventions could even derive nonintuitive results. For example, adding a regressive transfer to a regressive tax could result in a more equal system or adding a progressive transfer to a progressive tax could decrease equality. The toy examples in tables 2-9 and 2-10 illustrate the two nonintuitive cases just mentioned.[36]

The main factor in these nonintuitive examples is that progressivity is (usually) calculated with respect to the original income, and it is perfectly possible for a transfer (for example) to be progressive with respect to the original income yet regressive with respect to the "original income plus tax." Such a transfer, therefore, would decrease equality if it were added to this system. Given these results, we derive the conditions under which the marginal contribution of a single tax or benefit can be unequalizing, neutral, or equalizing.

Is the marginal contribution of a single tax equalizing?

This section addresses the question of whether a tax is equalizing, unequalizing, or neutral, and if it is equalizing or unequalizing, by how much. To answer the question of whether the tax exerts an equalizing or unequalizing force over and above the

---

[36] In the toy examples, we assume that the tax and transfer ratios are equal. (It would be very easy to show that the results occur when the ratios are not equal so we chose the "most difficult" assumption.)

TABLE 2-9

Toy Example: Adding a Regressive Transfer to a Regressive Tax Can Exert an Equalizing Effect

Individual	1	2	3	4	Total	Gini
Original income	10.00	20.00	30.00	40.00	100.00	0.2500
Tax (regressive)	9.00	10.00	2.00	0.00	21.00	n.c.
Original income minus tax	1.00	10.00	28.00	40.00	79.00	0.4272
Benefit (regressive)	0.30	3.50	7.00	10.20	21.00	n.c.
Original income plus benefit	10.30	23.50	37.00	50.20	121.00	0.2752
Original income minus tax plus benefit	1.30	13.50	35.00	50.20	100.00	0.4205

n.c. = Not calculated.

TABLE 2-10

Toy Example: Adding a Progressive Transfer to a Progressive Tax Can Exert an Unequalizing Effect

Individual	1	2	3	4	Total	Gini
Original income	10.00	20.00	30.00	40.00	100.00	0.2500
Tax (progressive)	0.00	1.55	3.10	4.65	9.30	n.c.
Original income minus tax	10.00	18.45	26.90	35.35	90.70	0.2329
Benefit (progressive)	1.00	1.80	2.80	3.70	9.30	n.c.
Original income plus benefit	11.00	21.80	32.80	43.70	109.30	0.2495
Original income minus tax plus benefit	11.00	20.25	29.70	39.05	100.00	0.2340

n.c. = Not calculated.

one prevailing in the system without the tax, we must assess whether the marginal contribution of the tax is positive or negative.

Before continuing, it should be noted that there are three instances in which the word "marginal" is used in incidence analysis:[37]

1. *The marginal contribution or effect* of a fiscal intervention (or of a change in a particular intervention): this is the subject of this section of the chapter. It is calculated as the difference between the indicator of choice (for example, the Gini) without the intervention of interest (or the change in the intervention of interest) and with the intervention. So, for example, if we are interested in the marginal contribution of direct

---

[37] For an extensive review of the literature on analyzing the concept of tax incidence, see Fullerton and Metcalf (2002).

taxes when going from Market Income to Disposable Income, we take the difference of, for example, the Gini without direct taxes and the Gini of Disposable Income (which includes the effect of direct taxes).

2. *The derivative of the marginal contribution* with respect to progressivity or size of the intervention: this is, so to speak, the marginal effect of progressivity or size on the marginal contribution. In the case of the derivative with respect to the relative size, this is also known as the *marginal incidence for the intensive margin.*

Both of the above definitions assume that the behavior of individuals is unchanged and unaffected by changes in the taxes or transfers.

3. *The extensive margin* is the last instance for the application of the phrase "margin." To calculate the extensive margin, one needs to estimate the predicted expansion in, for example, users of a service or beneficiaries of a cash transfer or payers of a tax, when the size of the intervention is increased. Researchers have followed different approaches in calculating this type of marginal effect.

One way to estimate the effect of an expansion on the extensive margin is by comparing results of average incidence analyses over time. For example, in Mexico, Lopez-Calva and others (f2018) found that concentration curves for tertiary education moved conspicuously toward the diagonal from 1992 to 2010; that is, the extensive margin was progressive. Because of identification problems, care must be taken not to ascribe a causal effect from the expansion of tertiary education to the fact that the extensive margin is progressive. However, one can argue that more spending has probably had something to do with the progressive extensive margin.

As shown by Lambert,[38] the general condition for the tax to be equalizing (when it is added to a system with a benefit in place) is derived from the following inequality:

$$(2\text{-}26) \qquad \qquad \Pi_N^{RS} > \rho_B^{RS}.$$

Substituting the expression in equation 2-12 for the left-hand side gives

$$(2\text{-}27) \qquad \qquad \frac{(1-g)\Pi_T^{RS} + (1+b)\rho_B^{RS}}{1-g+b} > \rho_B^{RS}$$

$$(2\text{-}28) \qquad \qquad \Leftrightarrow \Pi_T^{RS} > -\frac{g}{1-g}\rho_B^{RS}$$

$$(2\text{-}29) \qquad \qquad \Leftrightarrow \Pi_T^{K} > -\frac{b}{1+b}\rho_B^{K}.$$

---

[38] Lambert (2001, p. 278).

Therefore, we can state:

Condition 2-30:

If and only if

$$\Pi_T^{RS} > -\frac{g}{1-g}\rho_B^{RS}\left(, \text{ or } \rho_B^{RS} > -\frac{1-g}{g}\Pi_T^{RS}\right), \text{ or}$$

$$\Pi_T^{K} > -\frac{b}{1+b}\rho_B^{K}\left(, \text{ or } \rho_B^{K} > -\frac{1+b}{b}\Pi_T^{K}\right),$$

adding the tax reduces inequality. This is exactly the condition derived by Lambert.[39]

Condition 2-31:

If and only if

$$\Pi_T^{RS} = -\frac{g}{1-g}\rho_B^{RS}\left(, \text{ or } \rho_B^{RS} = -\frac{1-g}{g}\Pi_T^{RS}\right), \text{ or}$$

$$\Pi_T^{K} = -\frac{b}{1+b}\rho_B^{K}\left(, \text{ or } \rho_B^{K} = -\frac{1+b}{b}\Pi_T^{K}\right),$$

adding the tax leaves inequality unchanged.

Condition 2-32:

If and only if

$$\Pi_T^{RS} < -\frac{(g)}{(1-g)}\rho_B^{RS}\left(, \text{ or } \rho_B^{RS} < -\frac{1-g}{g}\Pi_T^{RS}\right), \text{ or}$$

$$\Pi_T^{K} < -\frac{(b)}{(1+b)}\rho_B^{K}\left(, \text{ or } \rho_B^{K} < -\frac{(1+b)}{(b)}\Pi_T^{K}\right),$$

adding the tax increases inequality.

From conditions 2-30, 2-31, and 2-32, we can immediately derive some conclusions, summarized in table 2-11. As expected, adding a regressive tax to a system with a regressive transfer can never be less unequalizing. Similarly, adding a progressive tax to a progressive transfer is always more equalizing. However, the unexpected result—which goes back to Lambert's conundrum—is that adding a regressive tax to a system with a progressive transfer can be *more* equalizing if and only if condition 2-30 holds. Note that all of the inequality comparisons are made with respect to a system without the tax (that

---

[39] Lambert (2001, p. 278, equation 11.30).

TABLE 2-11
Marginal Contribution of a Tax

		System with a transfer that is		
		Regressive $\rho_B^K < 0$	Neutral $\rho_B^K = 0$	Progressive $\rho_B^K > 0$
Adding a tax that is	**Regressive $\prod_T^K < 0$**	Always more unequalizing	Always unequalizing	More equalizing only if condition 2-30 holds
	Neutral $\prod_T^K = 0$	Always more unequalizing	No change in inequality	Always more equalizing
	Progressive $\prod_T^K > 0$	More equalizing only if condition 2-30 holds	Always equalizing	Always more equalizing

is, a system that has only a transfer in place). The other example of a nonintuitive result is that a neutral tax is unequalizing when it is added to a progressive tax. To understand the logic behind these cases, note that the progressivity is calculated with respect to the original income (without any tax or transfer), whereas for a tax to be equalizing when it is added to a system that has a transfer in place, it has to be progressive with respect to the "original income plus transfer."

Is the marginal contribution of a single transfer equalizing?

Adding a transfer to a system that has a tax in place is equalizing if

$$(2\text{-}33) \qquad \prod_N^{RS} > \prod_T^{RS}.$$

Substituting for the left-hand side and rearranging the preceding inequality we have

$$(2\text{-}34) \qquad \Leftrightarrow \prod_T^{RS} < \frac{(1+b)}{b}\rho_B^{RS}$$

$$(2\text{-}35) \qquad \Leftrightarrow \prod_T^K < \frac{(1-g)}{g}\rho_B^K.$$

Therefore, we can state the following conditions.

Condition 2-36:
    If and only if

$$\prod_T^{RS} < \frac{1+b}{b}\rho_B^{RS}\left(, \text{ or } \rho_B^{RS} > \frac{b}{1+b}\prod_T^{RS}\right), \quad \text{or} \quad \prod_T^K < \frac{1-g}{g}\rho_B^K\left(, \text{ or } \rho_B^K > \frac{g}{1-g}\prod_T^K\right),$$

does adding the transfer reduce inequality.

TABLE 2-12
Marginal Contribution of a Transfer

		Adding a transfer that is		
		Regressive $\rho_B^K < 0$	Neutral $\rho_B^K = 0$	Progressive $\rho_B^K > 0$
A system with a tax that is	Regressive $\prod_T^K < 0$	Less unequalizing if and only if condition 2-36 holds	Always less unequalizing	Always less unequalizing
	Neutral $\prod_T^K = 0$	Always unequalizing	No change in equality	Always equalizing
	Progressive $\prod_T^K > 0$	Always less equalizing	Always less equalizing	More equalizing if and only if condition 2-36 holds

Condition 2-37:
    If and only if

$$\prod_T^{RS} = \frac{1+b}{b} \rho_B^{RS} \left(, \text{ or } \rho_B^{RS} = \frac{b}{1+b} \prod_T^{RS}\right), \quad \text{or} \quad \prod_T^K = \frac{1-g}{g} \rho_B^K \left(, \text{ or } \rho_B^K = \frac{g}{1-g} \prod_T^K\right),$$

does adding the transfer leave inequality unchanged.

Condition 2-38:
    If and only if

$$\prod_T^{RS} > \frac{1+b}{b} \rho_B^{RS} \left(, \text{ or } \rho_B^{RS} < \frac{b}{1+b} \prod_T^{RS}\right), \quad \text{or} \quad \prod_T^K > \frac{1-g}{g} \rho_B^K \left(, \text{ or } \rho_B^K < \frac{g}{1-g} \prod_T^K\right),$$

does adding the transfer increase inequality.

Some conclusions can be immediately derived from conditions 2-36 through 2-38. Adding a progressive transfer to a system with a regressive tax always reduces inequality. Similarly, adding a regressive transfer to a system with a progressive tax increases inequality. However, somewhat counterintuitively, adding a regressive transfer to a system with a regressive tax does not always increase inequality (see the toy example in table 2-9). Similarly, adding a progressive transfer to a system with a progressive tax does not always increase equality (see the toy example in table 2-10). These two results (as shown in table 2-12) are essentially similar to Lambert's conundrum discussed earlier. Note that when comparing the change in equality, the reference point is the system with only a tax and without any transfer and not the original distribution of income.

2.2.2 Conditions for the Multiple Taxes and Transfers Case

This section generalizes the preceding discussion for a system with only one tax and one transfer. In the following subsections, we focus on the conditions for a tax or transfer to have an equalizing marginal contribution in a system with multiple other taxes and transfers.

In the presence of multiple taxes and transfers, is the marginal contribution of a tax equalizing?

Assuming no reranking, for a tax to be equalizing (if it is added to a system with other taxes and transfers in place), the following inequality has to hold:

$$(2\text{-}39) \qquad\qquad \Pi_N^{RS} > \Pi_{N\setminus T_k}^{RS}.$$

In other words, the redistributive effect is larger with the tax of interest than without it.

The element on the right-hand side shows the change in the Gini coefficient (from prefiscal to postfiscal income) when all taxes and transfers other than tax T_k are in place. Without loss of generality and for simplicity, we will set $k=1$. Using equation 2-13, we have

$$\frac{\sum_{i=1}^{n}(1-g_i)\Pi_{T_i}^{RS} + \sum_{j=1}^{m}(1+b_j)\rho_{B_j}^{RS}}{1 - \sum_{i=1}^{n}g_i + \sum_{j=1}^{m}b_j} > \frac{\sum_{i=2}^{n}(1-g_i)\Pi_{T_i}^{RS} + \sum_{j=1}^{m}(1+b_j)\rho_{B_j}^{RS}}{1 - \sum_{i=2}^{n}g_i + \sum_{j=1}^{m}b_j}.$$

The analysis goes similarly. After some rearranging, we have

$$(2\text{-}40a) \qquad \Pi_{T_1}^{RS} > \left(\frac{-g_1}{1-g_1}\right)\left(\frac{\sum_{i=2}^{n}(1-g_i)\Pi_{T_i}^{RS} + \sum_{j=1}^{m}(1+b_j)\rho_{B_j}^{RS}}{1 - \sum_{i=2}^{n}g_i + \sum_{j=1}^{m}b_j}\right),$$

or equivalently,

$$(2\text{-}40b) \qquad \Pi_{T_1}^{K} > -\left(\frac{\sum_{i=2}^{n}g_i\Pi_{T_i}^{K} + \sum_{j=1}^{m}b_j\rho_{B_j}^{K}}{1 - \sum_{i=2}^{n}g_i + \sum_{j=1}^{m}b_j}\right).$$

Therefore, for T_1 to be equalizing when $(n-1)$ taxes and m benefits are already in place, the following conditions apply:

Condition 2-41:
   If and only if

$$\Pi_{T_1}^{RS} > \left(\frac{-g_1}{1-g_1}\right)\left(\frac{\sum_{i=2}^{n}(1-g_i)\Pi_{T_i}^{RS} + \sum_{j=1}^{m}(1+b_j)\rho_{B_j}^{RS}}{1 - \sum_{i=2}^{n}g_i + \sum_{j=1}^{m}b_j}\right), \text{ or}$$

$$\Pi_{T_1}^{K} > -\left(\frac{\sum_{i=2}^{n}g_i\Pi_{T_i}^{K} + \sum_{j=1}^{m}b_j\rho_{B_j}^{K}}{1 - \sum_{i=2}^{n}g_i + \sum_{j=1}^{m}b_j}\right),$$

then adding T_1 reduces the inequality.

Condition 2-42:

If and only if

$$\Pi_{T_1}^{RS} = \left(\frac{-g_1}{1-g_1} \right) \left(\frac{\sum_{i=2}^{n}(1-g_i)\Pi_{T_i}^{RS} + \sum_{j=1}^{m}(1+b_j)\rho_{B_j}^{RS}}{1 - \sum_{i=2}^{n}g_i + \sum_{j=1}^{m}b_j} \right), \text{ or}$$

$$\Pi_{T_1}^{K} < -\left(\frac{\sum_{i=2}^{n}g_i\,\Pi_{T_i}^{K} + \sum_{j=1}^{m}b_j\rho_{B_j}^{K}}{1 - \sum_{i=2}^{n}g_i + \sum_{j=1}^{m}b_j} \right),$$

then adding T_1 increases the inequality.

Condition 2-43:

If and only if

$$\Pi_{T_1}^{RS} < \left(\frac{-g_1}{1-g_1} \right) \left(\frac{\sum_{i=2}^{n}(1-g_i)\Pi_{T_i}^{RS} + \sum_{j=1}^{m}(1+b_j)\rho_{B_j}^{RS}}{1 - \sum_{i=2}^{n}g_i + \sum_{j=1}^{m}b_j} \right), \text{ or}$$

$$\Pi_{T_1}^{K} = -\left(\frac{\sum_{i=2}^{n}g_i\,\Pi_{T_i}^{K} + \sum_{j=1}^{m}b_j\,\rho_{B_j}^{K}}{1 - \sum_{i=2}^{n}g_i + \sum_{j=1}^{m}b_j} \right),$$

then adding T_1 does not change the inequality.

In the presence of multiple taxes and transfers, is the marginal contribution of a transfer equalizing?

Assuming no reranking, the following inequality should hold:

(2.44) $$\Pi_N^{RS} > \Pi_{N\backslash B_k}^{RS}.$$

Assuming $k=1$ and substituting for both sides of the inequality, we have

$$\frac{\sum_{i=1}^{n}(1-g_i)\Pi_{T_i}^{RS} + \sum_{j=1}^{m}(1+b_j)\rho_{B_j}^{RS}}{1 - \sum_{i=1}^{n}g_i + \sum_{j=1}^{m}b_j} > \frac{\sum_{i=1}^{n}(1-g_i)\Pi_{T_i}^{RS} + \sum_{j=2}^{m}(1+b_j)\rho_{B_j}^{RS}}{1 - \sum_{i=1}^{n}g_i + \sum_{j=2}^{m}b_j}.$$

After some rearranging, we have

(2.45a) $$\rho_{B_1}^{RS} > \left(\frac{b_1}{1+b_1} \right) \left(\frac{\sum_{i=1}^{n}(1-g_i)\Pi_{T_i}^{RS} + \sum_{j=2}^{m}(1+b_j)\rho_{B_j}^{RS}}{1 - \sum_{i=1}^{n}g_i + \sum_{j=2}^{m}b_j} \right),$$

or equivalently,

(2-45b) $$\rho_{B_1}^{K} > \left(\frac{\sum_{i=1}^{n}g_i\,\Pi_{T_i}^{K} + \sum_{j=2}^{m}b_j\,\rho_{B_j}^{K}}{1 - \sum_{i=1}^{n}g_i + \sum_{j=2}^{m}b_j} \right).$$

Therefore, for B_1 to be equalizing when n taxes and $(m-1)$ benefits are already in place, the following conditions apply:

Condition 2-46:
  If and only if

$$\rho_{B_1}^{RS} > \left(\frac{b_1}{1+b_1} \right) \left(\frac{\sum_{i=1}^{n}(1-g_i)\Pi_{T_i}^{RS} + \sum_{j=2}^{m}(1+b_j)\rho_{B_j}^{RS}}{1-\sum_{i=1}^{n}g_i + \sum_{j=2}^{m}b_j} \right), \text{ or}$$

$$\rho_{B_1}^{K} > \left(\frac{\sum_{i=1}^{n}g_i\,\Pi_{T_i}^{K} + \sum_{j=2}^{m}b_j\rho_{B_j}^{K}}{1-\sum_{i=1}^{n}g_i + \sum_{j=2}^{m}b_j} \right),$$

then adding B_1 reduces inequality.

Condition 2-47:
  If and only if

$$\rho_{B_1}^{RS} = \left(\frac{b_1}{1+b_1} \right) \left(\frac{\sum_{i=1}^{n}(1-g_i)\Pi_{T_i}^{RS} + \sum_{j=2}^{m}(1+b_j)\rho_{B_j}^{RS}}{1-\sum_{i=1}^{n}g_i + \sum_{j=2}^{m}b_j} \right), \text{ or}$$

$$\rho_{B_1}^{K} = \left(\frac{\sum_{i=1}^{n}g_i\,\Pi_{T_i}^{K} + \sum_{j=2}^{m}b_j\rho_{B_j}^{K}}{1-\sum_{i=1}^{n}g_i + \sum_{j=2}^{m}b_j} \right),$$

then adding B_1 does not change inequality.

Condition 2-48:
  If and only if

$$\rho_{B_1}^{RS} < \left(\frac{b_1}{1+b_1} \right) \left(\frac{\sum_{i=1}^{n}(1-g_i)\Pi_{T_i}^{RS} + \sum_{j=2}^{m}(1+b_j)\rho_{B_j}^{RS}}{1-\sum_{i=1}^{n}g_i + \sum_{j=2}^{m}b_j} \right), \text{ or}$$

$$\rho_{B_1}^{K} < \left(\frac{\sum_{i=1}^{n}g_i\,\Pi_{T_i}^{K} + \sum_{j=2}^{m}b_j\rho_{B_j}^{K}}{1-\sum_{i=1}^{n}g_i + \sum_{j=2}^{m}b_j} \right),$$

then adding B_1 increases inequality.

Table 2-13 presents the marginal contributions for broad categories of fiscal interventions for eight countries for which *CEQ Assessments* were performed. The redistributive effect shown here is from Market Income to Final Income, which includes the monetized value of transfers in kind in the form of public spending on education and health.[40] The main results can be summarized as follows. Direct taxes and transfers as well as indirect subsidies are equalizing in all countries. Indirect taxes are equalizing in four countries: Brazil, Chile, Sri Lanka, and South Africa. Given that indirect taxes

---

[40] For the definitions of income concepts and how they are calculated, see chapter 1 by Lustig and Higgins (2022) in this Volume.

TABLE 2-13

Marginal Contributions: Results from *CEQ Assessments*

	Lower-middle-income economies			Upper-middle-income economies				
	Georgia (2013)	Indonesia (2012)	Sri Lanka (2010)	Brazil (2009)	Chile (2013)	Jordan (2010)	Russia (2010)	South Africa (2010)
Redistributive effect (from Gini market income plus pensions) to *final* income	0.1244	0.0238	0.0278	0.1221	0.0740	0.0230	0.0629	0.1758
Marginal contribution								
Direct taxes	0.0221	…	0.0025	0.0143	0.0120	0.0071	0.0139	0.0430
Direct transfers	0.1002	0.0037	0.0041	0.0148	0.0190	0.0052	0.0203	0.0517
Indirect taxes	−0.0141	−0.0022	0.0006	0.0113	0.0040	−0.0014	−0.0009	0.0127
Indirect subsidies	0.0004	0.0014	0.0051	0.0005	0.0023	0.0042	0.0001	…
Education	0.0199	0.0194	0.0105	0.0509	0.0321	0.0155	0.0207	0.0490
Health	0.0077	0.0031	0.0056	0.0292	0.0135	−0.0087	0.0127	0.0433
Kakwani								
Direct taxes	0.1819	…	0.5458	0.2490	0.4520	0.5941	0.1042	0.1254
Direct transfers	0.7063	0.6397	0.7572	0.5069	0.8243	0.5497	0.5927	1.0421
Indirect taxes	−0.2298	−0.0420	−0.0063	−0.0179	−0.0273	−0.0664	−0.0724	−0.0828
Indirect subsidies	0.3716	0.0560	0.3056	0.8373	0.4969	0.1512	0.2128	…
Education	0.5414	0.3630	0.3892	0.7087	0.6641	0.4784	0.4978	0.8169
Health	0.6360	0.2730	0.3963	0.6914	0.5930	0.0557	0.3740	0.8275

(continued)

TABLE 2-13   (continued)

| | Lower-middle-income economies | | | | Upper-middle-income economies | | | | |
	Georgia (2013)	Indonesia (2012)	Sri Lanka (2010)	Brazil (2009)	Chile (2013)	Jordan (2010)	Russia (2010)	South Africa (2010)
				Relative size				
Direct taxes	9.8%	. . .	0.5%	4.2%	2.3%	1.3%	0.0704	15.0%
Direct transfers	19.4%	0.7%	0.6%	5.1%	2.7%	1.3%	0.0467	5.4%
Indirect taxes	12.8%	6.8%	7.4%	12.9%	10.3%	3.1%	0.0803	14.1%
Indirect subsidies	0.4%	8.2%	2.0%	0.1%	0.5%	3.5%	0.0009	. . .
Education	4.3%	6.2%	3.2%	10.6%	5.2%	3.6%	0.0445	6.9%
Health	1.9%	1.6%	1.6%	4.8%	3.2%	3.4%	0.0419	5.5%

. . . = Not applicable.

Sources: Higgins and Pereira (2014); Martinez-Aguilar and others (2022); Alam and others (2017); Afkar and others (2017); Arunatilake and others (2017); Cancho and Bondarenko (2017); Inchauste and others (2017); Lopez-Calva (2017).

are regressive in all countries, these four countries display a (Lambert) conundrum in which a regressive tax is equalizing and the fiscal system would be more unequal in the absence of it. Lambert's conundrum, thus, is much more common than one might anticipate. Education and health spending are always equalizing except for health spending in Jordan. In Jordan, health spending is progressive but unequalizing, demonstrating another example of the conundrum.

2.3 The Derivative of Marginal Contribution with Respect to Progressivity and Size

Section 2.2 showed the conditions that must prevail for the marginal contribution of a tax or a transfer to be equalizing, neutral, or unequalizing. How will the marginal contribution of a particular tax or transfer be affected if its progressivity or size is changed? This is a relevant question in terms of policymaking, especially in the realistic context where leaders want to adjust the progressivity or relative size of an existing intervention given a pre-existing fiscal system—for example, making cash transfers more progressive or increasing the level of collection of a VAT or, more generally, expanding any pilot program.

This question can be answered by taking the derivative of the particular tax or transfer of interest with respect to progressivity and size. The reader should bear in mind that while the derivative yields the marginal effect of changing the progressivity or size of a particular intervention, the word "marginal" in this context does not have the same meaning or interpretation as it does when one is talking about marginal contributions in a joint distribution. The marginal contribution or effect in the latter sense was discussed previously throughout this chapter. This section presents the conditions for the marginal effect in the "partial derivative sense."

2.3.1 The Derivatives for the Case of a Marginal Change in Taxes

We will define M_{T_i} as the marginal contribution of tax T_i. The marginal contribution of a tax ($T_i = T_1$ is chosen without loss of generality) in the case of multiple taxes and benefits is defined as follows:

$$M_{T_1} = G_{N\backslash T_1} - G_N,$$

or

(2-49a)
$$M_{T_1} = G_{X - \sum_{i=2}^{n} T_i + \sum_{j=1}^{m} B_j} - G_{X - \sum_{i=1}^{n} T_i + \sum_{j=1}^{m} B_j}$$

$$= \left(G_X - G_{X - \sum_{i=1}^{n} T_i + \sum_{j=1}^{m} B_j} \right) - \left(G_X - G_{X - \sum_{i=2}^{n} T_i + \sum_{j=1}^{m} B_j} \right)$$

$$\underset{\substack{\smile \\ \text{Assuming no-reranking}}}{=} \Pi^{RS}_{X - \sum_{i=1}^{n} T_i + \sum_{j=1}^{m} B_j} - \Pi^{RS}_{X - \sum_{i=2}^{n} T_i + \sum_{j=1}^{m} B_j}$$

$$= \frac{\sum_{i=1}^{n} g_i \Pi^{K}_{T_i} + \sum_{j=1}^{m} b_j \rho^{K}_{B_j}}{1 - \sum_{i=1}^{n} g_i + \sum_{j=1}^{m} b_j} - \frac{\sum_{i=2}^{n} g_i \Pi^{K}_{T_i} + \sum_{j=1}^{m} b_j \rho^{K}_{B_j}}{1 - \sum_{i=2}^{n} g_i + \sum_{j=1}^{m} b_j},$$

or

$$(2.49b) \qquad = \frac{g_1\left[\left(1-\sum_{i=2}^{n} g_i + \sum_{j=1}^{m} b_j\right)\Pi_{T_1}^{K} + \left(\sum_{i=2}^{n} g_i \Pi_{T_i}^{K} + \sum_{j=1}^{m} b_j \rho_{B_j}^{K}\right)\right]}{\left(1-\sum_{i=1}^{n} g_i + \sum_{j=1}^{m} b_j\right)\left(1-\sum_{i=2}^{n} g_i + \sum_{j=1}^{m} b_j\right)}.$$

What are the derivatives of the marginal contribution of a tax with respect to its progressivity and size? Manipulating equation 2-49b, we obtain[41]

$$(2.50) \qquad \frac{\partial M_{T_1}}{\partial \Pi_{T_1}^{K}} = \frac{g_1}{1-\sum_{i=1}^{n} g_i + \sum_{j=1}^{m} b_j}.$$

Note that the derivative 2-50 is always positive given the usual assumption about the total size of taxes and transfers—that is,

$$1-\sum_{i=1}^{n} g_i + \sum_{j=1}^{m} b_j > 0.$$

The following shows the derivative of the marginal effect with respect to the size of a tax:

$$(2\text{-}51) \qquad \frac{\partial M_{T_1}}{\partial g_1} = \frac{\left[\Pi_{T_1}^{K}\left(1-\sum_{i=1}^{n} g_i + \sum_{j=1}^{m} b_j\right)\right] - \left[(-1)\left(\sum_{i=1}^{n} g_i \Pi_{T_i}^{K} + \sum_{j=1}^{m} b_j \rho_{B_j}^{K}\right)\right]}{\left(1-\sum_{i=1}^{n} g_i + \sum_{j=1}^{m} b_j\right)^2}$$

$$= \frac{\left[\Pi_{T_1}^{K}\left(1-\sum_{i=1}^{n} g_i + \sum_{j=1}^{m} b_j\right)\right] + \left[\left(\sum_{i=1}^{n} g_i \Pi_{T_i}^{K} + \sum_{j=1}^{m} b_j \rho_{B_j}^{K}\right)\right]}{\left(1-\sum_{i=1}^{n} g_i + \sum_{j=1}^{m} b_j\right)^2}$$

To sign derivative 2-51, please note that it is equal to[42]

$$= \frac{\Pi_{T_1}^{K} + \Pi_{X-\sum_{i=1}^{n} T_i + \sum_{j=1}^{m} B_j}^{RS}}{1-\sum_{i=1}^{n} g_i + \sum_{j=1}^{m} b_j}.$$

Since the denominator is always positive, the sign depends only on the numerator, which is the Kakwani index of tax $(\Pi_{T_1}^{K})$ and the R-S index of the net system with $T_1\left(\Pi_{X-\sum_{i=1}^{n} T_i + \sum_{j=1}^{m} B_j}^{RS}\right)$; that is, the following condition ensures the derivative is positive:

Condition MT1:

$$\Pi_{T_1}^{K} > -\Pi_{X-\sum_{i=1}^{n} T_i + \sum_{j=1}^{m} B_j}^{RS}.$$

Table 2-14 shows what the ultimate sign will be. Here the assumption is that there is no reranking, so the R-S index being positive is equivalent to the fiscal system being equalizing.

---

[41] Here we hold the relative size of T_1 and everything else constant.

[42] Here we hold the progressivity of T_1 and everything else constant.

TABLE 2-14

The Sign of the Derivative of a Tax's Marginal Contribution with Respect to Its Relative Size

		The tax of interest: T_1		
		Regressive $\Pi^K_{T_1} < 0$	Neutral $\Pi^K_{T_1} = 0$	Progressive $\Pi^K_{T_1} > 0$
The whole system (including T_1)	**Unequalizing** $\Pi^{RS}_{X - \sum_{i=1}^n T_i + \sum_{j=1}^m B_j} < 0$	Negative (more unequalizing)	Negative (more unequalizing)	Positive (less unequalizing), if and only if condition MT1 holds
	Neutral $\Pi^{RS}_{X - \sum_{i=1}^n T_i + \sum_{j=1}^m B_j} = 0$	Negative (more unequalizing)	Zero	Positive (more equalizing)
	Equalizing $\Pi^{RS}_{X - \sum_{i=1}^n T_i + \sum_{j=1}^m B_j} > 0$	Positive (more equalizing), if and only if condition MT1 holds	Positive (more equalizing)	Positive (more equalizing)

The following expression shows that when the marginal effect of progressivity on the marginal contribution of a tax is more than its relative size,

$$(2\text{-}52) \qquad \frac{\partial M_{T_1}}{\partial \Pi^K_{T_1}} > \frac{\partial M_{T_1}}{\partial g_1}$$

$$\Leftrightarrow \frac{g_1}{1 - \sum_{i=1}^n g_i + \sum_{j=1}^m b_j} > \frac{\Pi^K_{T_1}\left(1 - \sum_{i=1}^n g_i + \sum_{j=1}^m b_j\right) + \left(\sum_{i=1}^n g_i \Pi^K_{T_i} + \sum_{j=1}^m b_j \rho^K_{B_j}\right)}{\left(1 - \sum_{i=1}^n g_i + \sum_{j=1}^m b_j\right)^2}$$

$$\Leftrightarrow g_1 > \Pi^K_{T_1} + \frac{\sum_{i=1}^n g_i \Pi^K_{T_i} + \sum_{j=1}^m b_j \rho^K_{B_j}}{1 - \sum_{i=1}^n g_i + \sum_{j=1}^m b_j}$$

$$(2\text{-}53) \qquad \Leftrightarrow g_1 > \Pi^K_{T_1} + \Pi^{RS}_{X - \sum_{i=1}^n T_i + \sum_{j=1}^m B_j}.$$

Formula 2-52 for the simple case of one tax and one transfer is

$$M_T = G_{X+B} - G_{X-T+B} \underset{\text{Assuming no reranking}}{\equiv} \Pi^{RS}_{X-T+B} - \rho^{RS}_{B_j} = \frac{g\Pi^K_T + b\rho^K_B}{1 - g + b} - \rho^{RS}_{B_j}.$$

The derivatives with respect to progressivity and size are shown as follows:

$$\frac{\partial M_T}{\partial \Pi^K_T} = \frac{g}{1 - g + b}$$

and

$$\frac{\partial M_T}{\partial g} = \frac{\left[\Pi^K_T(1 - g + b)\right] + \left[g\Pi^K_T + b\rho^K_B\right]}{(1 - g + b)^2} = \frac{\Pi^K_T + \Pi^{RS}_{X-T+B}}{1 - g + b}$$

The following (i.e., equation 2-53a) shows the condition under which the derivative of the marginal contribution of a tax with respect to its progressivity would be greater than the derivative with respect to its size:

$$\frac{\partial M_T}{\partial \Pi_T^K} > \frac{\partial M_T}{\partial g}$$

$$\Leftrightarrow \frac{g}{1-g+b} > \frac{\left[\Pi_T^K(1-g+b)\right]+\left[g\Pi_T^K+b\rho_B^K\right]}{(1-g+b)^2}$$

(2-53a)
$$\Leftrightarrow g > \Pi_T^K + \Pi_{X-T+B}^{RS}$$

2.3.2 The Derivatives for the Case of a Marginal Change in Transfers

The marginal contribution M_{B_i} of a transfer B_i ($B_i = B_1$ is chosen without the loss of generality) in the case of multiple taxes and benefits can be similarly written in this format as

$$M_{B_1} = G_{N \backslash B_1} - G_N,$$

or

$$M_{B_1} = G_{X - \sum_{i=1}^{n} T_i + \sum_{j=2}^{m} B_j} - G_{X - \sum_{i=1}^{n} T_i + \sum_{j=1}^{m} B_j}$$

$$= \left(G_X - G_{X - \sum_{i=1}^{n} T_i + \sum_{j=1}^{m} B_j}\right) - \left(G_X - G_{X - \sum_{i=1}^{n} T_i + \sum_{j=2}^{m} B_j}\right)$$

$$\underset{\text{Assuming no reranking}}{=} \Pi_{X - \sum_{i=1}^{n} T_i + \sum_{j=1}^{m} B_j}^{RS} - \Pi_{X - \sum_{i=1}^{n} T_i + \sum_{j=2}^{m} B_j}^{RS}$$

$$= \frac{\sum_{i=1}^{n} g_i \Pi_{T_i}^K + \sum_{j=1}^{m} b_j \rho_{B_j}^K}{1 - \sum_{i=1}^{n} g_i + \sum_{j=1}^{m} b_j} - \frac{\sum_{i=1}^{n} g_i \Pi_{T_i}^K + \sum_{j=2}^{m} b_j \rho_{B_j}^K}{1 - \sum_{i=1}^{n} g_i + \sum_{j=2}^{m} b_j},$$

or

(2-54)
$$= \frac{b_1 \left[\left(1 - \sum_{i=1}^{n} g_i + \sum_{j=2}^{m} b_j\right)\rho_{B_1}^K - \left(\sum_{i=1}^{n} g_i \Pi_{T_i}^K + \sum_{j=2}^{m} b_j \rho_{B_j}^K\right)\right]}{\left(1 - \sum_{i=1}^{n} g_i + \sum_{j=1}^{m} b_j\right)\left(1 - \sum_{i=1}^{n} g_i + \sum_{j=2}^{m} b_j\right)}.$$

The derivatives with respect to progressivity and size are expressed in equations 2-55 and 2-56, respectively. The derivative with respect to progressivity is as follows:

(2-55)
$$\frac{\partial M_{B_1}}{\partial \rho_{B_1}^K} = \frac{b_1}{1 - \sum_{i=1}^{n} g_i + \sum_{j=1}^{m} b_j}.$$

Note that the derivative 2-55 is always positive given the usual assumption about the total size of taxes and transfers, that is,

$$1 - \sum_{i=1}^{n} g_i + \sum_{j=1}^{m} b_j > 0$$

TABLE 2-15

The Sign of the Derivative of the Marginal Contribution of a Transfer with Respect to Its Relative Size

		The transfer of interest: B_1		
		Regressive $\rho_{B_1}^K < 0$	Neutral $\rho_{B_1}^K = 0$	Progressive $\rho_{B_1}^K > 0$
The whole system (including B_1)	Unequalizing $\Pi_{X-\Sigma_{i=1}^n T_i + \Sigma_{j=1}^m B_j}^{RS} < 0$	Positive (more equalizing), if and only if condition MB1 holds	Positive (more equalizing)	Positive (more equalizing)
	Neutral $\Pi_{X-\Sigma_{i=1}^n T_i + \Sigma_{j=1}^m B_j}^{RS} = 0$	Negative (more unequalizing)	Zero	Positive (more equalizing)
	Equalizing $\Pi_{X-\Sigma_{i=1}^n T_i + \Sigma_{j=1}^m B_j}^{RS} > 0$	Negative (more unequalizing)	Negative (more unequalizing)	Positive (more equalizing), if and only if condition MB1 holds

The derivative with respect to size is as follows:

$$\frac{\partial M_{B_1}}{\partial b_1} = \frac{\left[\rho_{B_1}^K\left(1-\sum_{i=1}^n g_i + \sum_{j=1}^m b_j\right)\right] - \left[(+1)\left(\sum_{i=1}^n g_i \Pi_{T_i}^K + \sum_{j=1}^m b_j \rho_{B_j}^K\right)\right]}{\left(1-\sum_{i=1}^n g_i + \sum_{j=1}^m b_j\right)^2}$$

(2-56)
$$= \frac{\left[\rho_{B_1}^K\left(1-\sum_{i=1}^n g_i + \sum_{j=1}^m b_j\right)\right] - \left(\sum_{i=1}^n g_i \Pi_{T_i}^K + \sum_{j=1}^m b_j \rho_{B_j}^K\right)}{\left(1-\sum_{i=1}^n g_i + \sum_{j=1}^m b_j\right)^2}.$$

To sign the preceding derivative, please note that it is equal to

$$= \frac{\rho_{B_1}^K - \Pi_{X-\Sigma_{i=1}^n T_i + \Sigma_{j=1}^m B_j}^{RS}}{1-\sum_{i=1}^n g_i + \sum_{j=1}^m b_j}.$$

Because the denominator is always positive, the sign depends only on the numerator, which is the Kakwani index of transfer ($\rho_{B_1}^K$) and R-S index of the net system with $B_1 \left(\Pi_{X-\Sigma_{i=1}^n T_i + \Sigma_{j=1}^m B_j}^{RS}\right)$. The following condition ensures the derivative is positive.

Condition MB1:

$$\rho_{B_1}^K > \Pi_{X-\Sigma_{i=1}^n T_i + \Sigma_{j=1}^m B_j}^{RS}.$$

Table 2-15 shows what the ultimate sign will be. Here, we assume that there is no reranking, so the R-S index being positive is equivalent to the fiscal system being equalizing.

Expression 2-57 shows the scenario in which the effect of progressivity on the marginal effect of a benefit is more than its relative size:

(2-57)
$$\frac{\partial M_{B_1}}{\partial \rho_{B_1}^K} > \frac{\partial M_{B_1}}{\partial b_1} \Leftrightarrow \frac{b_1}{1 - \sum_{i=1}^n g_i + \sum_{j=1}^m b_j}$$

$$> \frac{\left[\rho_{B_1}^K \left(1 - \sum_{i=1}^n g_i + \sum_{j=1}^m b_j\right)\right] - \left(\sum_{i=1}^n g_i \Pi_{T_i}^K + \sum_{j=1}^m b_j \rho_{B_j}^K\right)}{\left(1 - \sum_{i=1}^n g_i + \sum_{j=1}^m b_j\right)^2}$$

$$\Leftrightarrow b_1 > \rho_{B_1}^K - \frac{\sum_{i=1}^n g_i \Pi_{T_i}^K + \sum_{j=1}^m b_j \rho_{B_j}^K}{1 - \sum_{i=1}^n g_i + \sum_{j=1}^m b_j}$$

(2-58)
$$\Leftrightarrow b_1 > \rho_{B_1}^K - \Pi_{X - \sum_{i=1}^n T_i + \sum_{j=1}^m B_j}^{RS}.$$

In order to have an equivalent condition for the simple case of one tax and one transfer similar to equation 2-58, note the following equations introduced earlier:

$$\frac{\partial M_B}{\partial \rho_B^K} = \frac{b}{1 - g + b}$$

and

$$\frac{\partial M_B}{\partial b} = \frac{\left[\rho_B^K (1 - g + b)\right] - (g \Pi_T^K + b \rho_B^K)}{(1 - g + b)^2} = \frac{\rho_B^K - \Pi_{X - T + B}^{RS}}{1 - g + b}.$$

Equation 2-59 shows the condition under which the derivative of marginal contribution with respect to a transfer's progressivity would be greater than the derivative with respect to its size:

$$\frac{\partial M_B}{\partial \Pi_B^K} > \frac{\partial M_B}{\partial b}$$

(2-59)
$$\Leftrightarrow b > \rho_B^K - \Pi_{X - T + B}^{RS}$$

2.4 The Sensitivity of Marginal Contribution Analysis to the Use of the Conventional Gini Index

Thus far, we have focused on the conventional Gini coefficient to determine whether a specific tax or transfer is equalizing. The application of this index implies a normative choice with regard to how individuals from different parts of an income distribution are weighted (Gini puts more weight on the middle of the income distribution). One may prefer to weight more heavily the gains that accrue to lower deciles (or the higher ones) and, therefore, can opt for the family of S-Gini indexes (or Extended Gini) to calculate the marginal contribution of the components of a fiscal system.[43] The final conclusion about a tax (or transfer) having a positive marginal contribution (that is, an equalizing

---

[43] See Yitzhaki and Schechtman (2005) for a mathematical review of these indicators.

effect) could change if the concentration curve of that tax (or transfer) crosses the Lorenz curve of the total system without that tax (or transfer). In other words, in the case of no dominance, one would expect the results to depend on the normative choice of how to weight individuals. In the following explanation, we clarify this issue further.

In section 1, we discussed the application of the concentration and Lorenz curves in determining whether a tax or transfer is (everywhere) progressive or not. A similar analysis can be applied to the concept of the marginal contribution. Suppose we define the Lorenz curve of "the final income without a specific tax (T_1)" as $L(p)_{X-\sum_{i=2}^{n}T_i+\sum_{j=1}^{m}B_j}$. Then the specific tax that is being analyzed has an equalizing effect (in the marginal contribution sense), regardless of the normative choice of how to weigh individuals if and only if

$$(2\text{-}60) \quad \begin{cases} L(p)_{X-\sum_{i=2}^{n}T_i+\sum_{j=1}^{m}B_j} \geq C(p)_{T_1}^{X-\sum_{i=2}^{n}T_i+\sum_{j=1}^{m}B_j} \quad \forall p \text{ and,} \\[2mm] L(p)_{X-\sum_{i=2}^{n}T_i+\sum_{j=1}^{m}B_j} > C(p)_{T_1}^{X-\sum_{i=2}^{n}T_i+\sum_{j=1}^{m}B_j} \quad \text{for some } p. \end{cases}$$

where

$$C(p)_{T_1}^{X-\sum_{i=2}^{n}T_i+\sum_{j=1}^{m}B_j}$$

is the concentration curve of T_1 when individuals are ranked with respect to their Final Income without T_1.

Similarly, for the case of a transfer (B_1), we have the following condition:

$$(2\text{-}61) \quad \begin{cases} L(p)_{X-\sum_{i=1}^{n}T_i+\sum_{j=2}^{m}B_j} \leq C(p)_{B_1}^{X-\sum_{i=1}^{n}T_i+\sum_{j=2}^{m}B_j} \quad \forall p \text{ and,} \\[2mm] L(p)_{X-\sum_{i=1}^{n}T_i+\sum_{j=2}^{m}B_j} < C(p)_{B_1}^{X-\sum_{i=1}^{n}T_i+\sum_{j=2}^{m}B_j} \quad \text{for some } p. \end{cases}$$

If these conditions do not hold for some p—that is, if there is at least one crossing of the two curves—then the conclusion about whether a specific tax or transfer is equalizing depends on how one weights individuals in different parts of an income distribution. Therefore, it is important to use graphical representations and the sensitivity analysis (that is, using S-Gini indexes with different values for the normative parameter of weighting instead of the conventional Gini) in the context of the inequality (and poverty) analysis. These tools help to determine how much the results of an analysis using a specific index hinge on the underlying normative choice of using that specific indicator.

References

Afkar, Rythia, Jon Jellema, and Mathew Wai-Poi. 2017. "The Distributional Impact of Fiscal Policy in Indonesia," in *The Distributional Impact of Fiscal Policy: Experience from Developing Countries*, edited by Gabriela Inchauste and Nora Lustig (Washington: World Bank).

Alam, Shamma A., Gabriela Inchauste, and Umar Serajuddin. 2017. "The Distributional Impact of Fiscal Policy in Jordan," in *The Distributional Impact of Fiscal Policy: Experience from*

Developing Countries, edited by Gabriela Inchauste and Nora Lustig (Washington: World Bank).

Arunatilake, Nisha, Gabriela Inchauste, and Nora Lustig. 2017. "The Incidence of Taxes and Spending in Sri Lanka," in *The Distributional Impact of Fiscal Policy: Experience from Developing Countries*, edited by Gabriela Inchauste and Nora Lustig (Washington: World Bank).

Bibi, Sami, and Jean-Yves Duclos. 2010. "A Comparison of the Poverty Impact of Transfers, Taxes and Market Income across Five OECD Countries." *Bulletin of Economic Research* 62, no. 4, pp. 387–406.

Cancho, Cesar, and Elena Bondarenko. 2017. "The Distributional Impact of Fiscal Policy in Georgia," in *The Distributional Impact of Fiscal Policy: Experience from Developing Countries*, edited bynGabriela Inchauste and Nora Lustig (Washington: World Bank).

Dardanoni, Valentino, and Peter Lambert. 2000. "Progressivity Comparisons." *Journal of Public Economics* 86, no. 1, pp. 99–122

Duclos, Jean-Yves, and Abdelkrim Araar. 2007. "Poverty and Equity: Measurement, Policy and Estimation with DAD," in *Springer Science & Business Media*, vol. 2 (New York: Springer).

Duclos, Jean-Yves, and Martin Tabi. 1996. "The Measurement of Progressivity, with an Application to Canada." *Canadian Journal of Economics* part 1 (April), pp. S165–S170.

Ebrill, Liam, Michael Keen, and Victoria P. Summers. 2001. *The Modern VAT* (Washington: International Monetary Fund).

Enami, Ali. 2022. "Measuring the Redistributive Impact of Taxes and Transfers in the Presence of Reranking," chap. 3 in *Commitment to Equity Handbook: Estimating the Impact of Fiscal Policy on Inequality and Poverty*, 2nd ed., Vol. 1, edited by Nora Lustig (Brookings Institution Press and CEQ Institute, Tulane University). Free online version available at www .commitmentoequity.org.

Engel, Eduardo, Alexander Galetovic, and Claudio E. Raddatz. 1999. "Taxes and Income Distribution in Chile: Some Unpleasant Redistributive Arithmetic." *Journal of Development Economics* 59, no. 1, pp. 155–92.

Fortin, Nicole, Thomas Lemieux, and Sergio Firpo. 2011. "Decomposition Methods in Economics," in *Handbook of Labor Economics*, 4th ed., edited by David Card and Orley Ashenfelter (North Holland: Elsevier).

Fullerton, Don, and Gilbert E. Metcalf. 2002. "Tax Incidence," in *Handbook of Public Economics*, vol. 4, edited by Alan J. Auerbach and Martin Feldstein (North Holland: Elsevier).

Higgins, Sean, and Nora Lustig. 2016. "Can a Poverty-Reducing and Progressive Tax and Transfer System Hurt the Poor?" *Journal of Development Economics* 122, pp. 63–75.

Higgins, Sean, and Claudiney Pereira. 2014. "The Effects of Brazil's Taxation and Social Spending on the Distribution of Household Income," in "The Redistributive Impact of Taxes and Social Spending in Latin America," edited by Nora Lustig, Carola Pessino, and John Scott, special issue, *Public Finance Review* 42, no. 3, pp. 346–67.

Inchauste, Gabriela, Nora Lustig, Mashekwa Maboshe, Catriona Purfield, and Ingrid Wollard. 2017. "The Distributional Impact of Fiscal Policy in South Africa," in *The Distributional Impact of Fiscal Policy: Experience from Developing Countries*, edited by Gabriela Inchauste and Nora Lustig (Washington: World Bank).

Kakwani, Nanak C. 1977. "Measurement of Tax Progressivity: An International Comparison." *Economic Journal* 87, no. 345, pp. 71–80.

Keen, Michael, and Ben Lockwood. 2010. "The Value Added Tax: Its Causes and Consequences." *Journal of Development Economics* 92, no. 2, pp. 138–51.

Lambert, Peter. 2001. *The Distribution and Redistribution of Income*, 3rd ed. (Manchester University Press).

Lerman, Robert I., and Shlomo Yitzhaki. 1989. "Improving the Accuracy of Estimates of Gini Coefficients." *Journal of Econometrics* 42, no. 1, pp. 43–47.

Lopez-Calva, Luis Felipe, Nora Lustig, Mikhail Matytsin, and Daria Popova. 2017. "Who Benefits from Fiscal Redistribution in Russia?," in *The Distributional Impact of Fiscal Policy: Experience from Developing Countries*, edited by Gabriela Inchauste and Nora Lustig (Washington: World Bank).

Lopez-Calva, Luis Felipe, Nora Lustig, John Scott, and Andres Castañeda. 2018. "Gasto social, redistribucion del ingreso y reduccion de la pobreza en Mexico: Evolucion y comparacion con Argentina, Brasil y Uruguay," in *Politica social y bienestar: Mexico desde el año 2000*, edited by Rodolfo de la Torre, Eduardo Rodriguez-Oreggia, and Isidro Soloaga (Mexico D.F.: CIDE-FCE).

Lustig, Nora, and Sean Higgins. 2022. "The *CEQ Assessment*: Measuring the Impact of Fiscal Policy on Inequality and Poverty," chap. 1 in *Commitment to Equity Handbook: Estimating the Impact of Fiscal Policy on Inequality and Poverty*, 2nd ed., Vol. 1, edited by Nora Lustig (Brookings Institution Press and CEQ Institute, Tulane University). Free online version available at www.commitmentoequity.org.

Lustig, Nora, and Marcela Melendez. 2016. "The Impact of Taxes and Transfers on Inequality and Poverty in Colombia," CEQ Working Paper 24 (New Orleans: Tulane University and Inter-American Dialogue: CEQ Institute, Center for Inter-American Policy and Research, and Tulane Department of Economics).

Martinez-Aguilar, Sandra, Alan Fuchs, Eduardo Ortiz-Juarez, and Giselle Del Carmen. 2022. "Chile: The Impact of Fiscal Policy on Inequality and Poverty," chap. 13 in *Commitment to Equity Handbook: Estimating the Impact of Fiscal Policy on Inequality and Poverty*, 2nd ed., Vol. 1, edited by Nora Lustig (Brookings Institution Press and CEQ Institute, Tulane University). Free online version available at www.commitmentoequity.org.

O'Higgins, Michael, and Patricia Ruggles. 1981. "The Distribution of Public Expenditures and Taxes among Households in the United Kingdom." *Review of Income and Wealth* 27, no. 3, pp. 298–326.

Owen, Guilliermo. 1977. "Values of Games with a Priori Unions," in *Mathematical Economics and Game Theory*, edited by Rudolph Henn and Otto Moeschlin (Berlin and Heidelberg: Springer).

Ruggles, Patricia, and Michael O'Higgins. 1981. "The Distribution of Public Expenditure among Households in the United States." *Review of Income and Wealth* 27, no. 2, pp. 137–64.

Sastre, Mercedes, and Alain Trannoy. 2001. "Une decomposition de l'evolution de l'inegalite en France avec une perspective internationale 1985–1995," in *Inegalites Economiques, Rapport pour le Conseil d'Analyse Economique*, 315–32 (Paris: La Documentation Française, Paris).

———. 2002. "Shapley Inequality Decomposition by Factor Components: Some Methodological Issues." *Journal of Economics* 77, no. 1, pp. 51–89.

———. 2008. "Changing Income Inequality in Advanced Countries: A Nested Marginalist Decomposition Analysis." THEMA working paper.

Shapley, Lloyd S. 1952. "A Value for n-Person Games," No. RAND-P-295 (Santa Monica, Calif.: Rand Corporation).

Shorrocks, Anthony F. 2013. "Decomposition Procedures for Distributional Analysis: A Unified Framework Based on the Shapley Value." *Journal of Economic Inequality* 11, no.1, pp. 99–126.

Urban, Ivica. 2009. "Kakwani Decomposition of Redistributive Effect: Origins, Critics and Upgrades," Working Paper 148 (Society for the Study of Economic Inequality [ECINEQ]).

Yitzhaki, Shlomo, and Edna Schechtman. 2005. "The Properties of the Extended Gini Measures of Variability and Inequality." *Metron-International Journal of Statistics* 63, no. 3, pp. 401–33.

Appendix 2A

The Shapley Value

Despite its seeming simplicity, the question "How much does inequality increase (or decrease) due to a particular source of income?" does not have a straightforward answer. In fact, the answer will be different depending on (1) what other sources of income are available to the society, (2) whether any particular meaningful order of allocating different sources of income exists, and (3) whether any theoretical basis for aggregating income sources exists.

To better understand why information about "the other sources of income" (regarding the first point) is important, imagine the following simple example. There are two individuals, *I* and *J*, who need a taxi. They live on the same street but at different distances from the place that they need to get to in the taxi. If each of them gets a taxi separately, they will need to pay $10 and $15, respectively. But if they share the ride, they have to pay $15 together. How should they divide the cost? Now, assume a third person joins them, who lives between the two initial passengers and who would have to pay $12 if he were to get a taxi on his own. If they all three go together, their fare remains $15 and unchanged from the previous case when only *I* and *J* shared the ride. Going from the first case to the second case, individuals *I* and *J*'s share of the taxi fare should change because a third person has joined them. This example makes it clear that it is perfectly possible that based on a particular circumstance or depending on how an inequality index is defined, individual shares of each income source in creating or reducing inequality can depend on information about all other sources of income. This situation is why the Shapley value was initially formulated by Lloyd Shapley (1952).

Now, focusing on the second and third points of our original question, if there is no particular order for how the income sources are assigned and all income sources are perceived in the most disaggregated way (no aggregation hierarchy), then the "simple Shapley value" is the way to calculate the effect of each individual source. This formula is discussed later in this appendix in section 1, on the simple Shapley value.

If there is a particular order for how some sources of income will be allocated (for example, if taxes cannot be first), then the problem can be easily reduced to the case of simple Shapley. Imagine we have five sources of income and source numbers 1 and 2 are always first and the other sources (3, 4, and 5) are always last. The inequality will change in two steps. First, when sources 1 and 2 are added, the amount of change in inequality can be decomposed between these two sources using the simple Shapley formula. Then, in the second step, inequality will change due to the remaining sources. This change can be decomposed again between the remaining sources using the simple Shapley formula. The total change will be then equal to the individual shares.

Finally, if there is no particular order, but there is an aggregation scheme (for example, taxes, benefits, and so on), then a two-stage, or hierarchy-Shapley, value should be used, which is discussed in section 2. The general idea of this two-stage methodology is to determine the contribution of different groups (such as a group of taxes versus a group of transfers) in the first step and then to determine the share of each individual fiscal incidence from the total contribution of its group.

1 Simple Shapley Value

There are two ways to calculate simple Shapley values. Each results in different outcomes and therefore has different theoretical implications. Sastre and Trannoy call these methods "zero income decomposition" (ZID) and "equalized income decomposition" (EID).[44] The difference between the two formulas is the way that they answer a simple but fundamental question: What should be considered the reference point? In ZID (as the word "zero" implies), we always calculate changes in inequality by using zero allocation of a particular source of income as the reference point. In EID, the reference point is a hypothetical state in which a particular source is divided evenly among all people, so here change in inequality occurs because we deviate from this (hypothetical) equalized distribution of income. To see this point more clearly, assume we have three individuals and their income from a specific source is $10, $20, and $30, respectively. In order to determine the contribution of this source of income to inequality, ZID compares the Gini after this source of income is added to the scenario when this source is not added. EID, on the other hand, compares the Gini after this source of income is added to a scenario in which everybody would receive $20 from this source.

Sastre and Trannoy (2002) prefer EID over ZID due to a major theoretical difference. To better understand the difference, discussing a simple question is enlightening: If there were a source of income that was distributed evenly among members of a society, what should be the share of this source in creating inequality? Sastre and Trannoy argue that the answer is zero because this particular source does not create any inequality. Only EID produces zero value for such a source; ZID would result in a non-zero value.

The preceding justification for preferring EID over ZID is, however, not as tenable if one deals with taxes and transfers as other types of income (using a broad definition

---

[44] Sastre and Trannoy (2002, p. 54).

of income to include negative sources as a type of income). An evenly distributed tax (that is, a lump-sum tax) is regressive, or pro-rich (poor people pay the same tax as rich people so their tax rate is much higher given their lower income), and an evenly distributed transfer (that is, a lump-sum transfer) is progressive, or pro-poor (because poor people get the same amount of money as rich people but relative to their lower income, they are receiving higher benefits). A regressive tax is considered a cause of increasing inequality, and a progressive transfer is considered a cause of reducing inequality, so accordingly one would expect to see a negative Shapley value for a lump-sum tax and a positive Shapley value for a lump-sum transfer, which is only possible through the ZID approach. The EID method would give zero shares to these taxes and transfers.

The other problem with the EID approach is that it cannot be used to decompose changes in the inequality index if the starting value of the index is not zero and the sum of the total sources of income is not zero (for example, if taxes are not equal to transfers due to inefficiency in the fiscal system). This problem is explained in more detail when the EID formula is introduced.

Table 2A-1 shows the simple Shapley value calculated using the ZID and EID approaches for a specific example of three sources of income: a Market Income (M), an equalized tax (T), and a (non-equalized) transfer (R). We assume that Market Income is always first, so we are interested only in the share of the tax and transfer in changing the Gini index (as a measure of inequality) between Market Income and total income.

As is clear from table 2A-1, the ZID approach produces a negative share (that is, inequality increases) for a regressive (pro-rich) tax, which is in line with the literature. It seems reasonable to use these two different approaches in their appropriate contexts. When the sources of income do not include any form of income redistribution (taxes or transfers), using EID has more theoretical justification. On the other hand, if one is only performing an incidence analysis (that is, if only taxes and transfers are included in the analysis), then ZID is the better approach. In cases where both income and redistribution sources are involved, using a two-step approach in ordering different sources can solve the problem. If one can argue that all sources of earned income come first, after which taxes and transfers are added, then a two-step decomposition (as explained earlier) can be employed, with the EID approach for the first step (when only earned incomes are considered), followed by the ZID approach for the second step (when only taxes and transfers are considered).

Because both approaches have merits depending on the circumstances, they are both introduced mathematically in the following sections.

1.1 Simple Shapley Value: ZID Approach

Define a value function V that uses different income sources as input and produces one value as output. The Gini coefficient is an example of such value function. If there are n sources of income and m individuals in the society, then V can be defined as V:

TABLE 2A-1

Comparison of ZID and EID Approaches in Calculating the Shapley Value
When an Equalized (Regressive) Tax Is Involved

Individual	Market income	Tax (equalized)	Transfer	Final income
1	1	−5	9	5
2	20	−5	7	22
3	30	−5	5	30
4	40	−5	3	38
5	50	−5	1	46
Total	**141**	**−25**	**25**	**141**
Average	**28.2**	**−5**	**5**	**28.2**

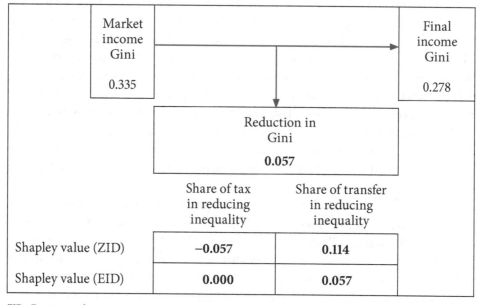

	Market income Gini 0.335			Final income Gini 0.278
		Reduction in Gini **0.057**		
	Share of tax in reducing inequality	Share of transfer in reducing inequality		
Shapley value (ZID)	**−0.057**	**0.114**		
Shapley value (EID)	**0.000**	**0.057**		

ZID = Zero income decomposition; EID = Equalized income decomposition.

$R^{m \times n} \to R$. The set of sources of income is $N = \{\underline{I}_1, \underline{I}_2, \ldots, \underline{I}_n\}$ where each $\underline{I}_i$ is itself a $(m \times 1)$ vector of values for all individuals in the society. Therefore, $V(\underline{I}_1, \underline{I}_2, \ldots, \underline{I}_n)$ is, for example, the Gini coefficient when all sources of income are distributed in the society and $V(\underline{I}_1, \underline{0}, \ldots, \underline{0})$ is the Gini coefficient when only source I_1 (and none of the other sources) is distributed. The Shapley value is a weighted average of all possible cases in which we can demonstrate the effect of adding one source to the value function. For example, $V(\underline{I}_1, \underline{I}_2, \ldots, \underline{I}_n) - V(\underline{0}, \underline{I}_2, \ldots, \underline{I}_n)$ and $V(\underline{I}_1, \underline{0}, \ldots, \underline{0}) - V(\underline{0}, \underline{0}, \ldots, \underline{0})$ are two of many ways to measure the effect of adding $\underline{I}_1$ to the value function. If all of these different ways result in the same value, there is no need to use a complicated weighted average. But for many indexes, including the Gini, this is not the case. While it is easy to list all of the possible ways of calculating the effect of adding a particular source to the value function, determining the weights requires more attention. Before introducing the formula for the weights, let's start with an intuitive example.

Assume we are interested in determining the weight of path $V(I_1, I_2, I_3, I_4, I_5, 0, \ldots, 0) - V(0, I_2, I_3, I_4, I_5, 0, \ldots, 0)$. This path determines how much V changes when we add I_1 given that I_2, I_3, I_4, and I_5 are already added and sources I_6 through I_n will not be added. The Shapley value is determined based on the permutation of sources, or put another way, order matters. In other words, we need to ask how many times we can permute sources I_2 through I_5 (which is $4! = 24$) and then add I_1 and permute sources $I_6 = 0$ through $I_n = 0$ (which is $(n - (4 + 1))!$). We have to multiply all these numbers to get the total number of permutations, that is, $(4!) \times [(n - (4 + 1))!]$. Two important points should be noted. First, even though none of the sources from 6 through n would be added for this path, the number of their permutations matters. Second, for any path, we always calculate the permutation of previously added sources (sources other than the one that we are interested in) together and then multiply it by the number of permutations of sources that are not added. For example, if we were calculating the weight of path $V(I_1, 0, 0, I_4, I_5, I_6, I_7, 0, \ldots, 0) - V(0, 0, 0, I_4, I_5, I_6, I_7, 0, \ldots, 0)$, the number of permutations is exactly equal to the previous case—that is, $(4!) \times [(n - (4 + 1))!]$. One should note that 4 is the number of income sources that are added already and $[n - (4 + 1)]$ is the number of income sources that will not be added. Therefore, what matters is the number of added sources, not which source is added. The number of permutations is the weight of each path. The total number of permutations, $n!$, is used (as the denominator) so that the weights add up to one. With this explanation, the ZID formula can now be formally introduced.

Assume we are interested in finding the Shapley value of income source i. Define set S_{I_i} as the set of subsets of set $N - \{I_i\}$ (that is, a set that includes all sources of income except for source I_i). Note that the empty set, $\varnothing$, and $N - \{I_i\}$ itself are considered two subsets of $N - \{I_i\}$ and therefore included in S_{I_i}. Each element in S_{I_i} represents a different path through which the effect of adding I_i to V can be measured. These elements (which are themselves a set) represent income sources that are added before I_i is added. Because all of the possible paths are represented by elements of S_{I_i}, a summation over these elements with appropriate weights would result in the Shapley value. The resulting formula is therefore

$$(2A\text{-}1) \qquad Sh_{I_i}^{ZID} = \sum_{S \in S_{I_i}} \left(\frac{(s!) \times ((n - s - 1)!)}{n!} (V^{ZID}(S \cup I_i) - V^{ZID}(S)) \right).^{48}$$

First, note that in this formula, S represents an element of set S_{I_i}. Second, s is the dimensionality of each element of S that enters in the summation, and n is the dimensionality of set N. It should be noted that s is the number of income sources that are already added, and $n - s - 1$ is the number of sources that will not be added. Third, $V^{ZID}(S \cup I_i)$ means the value function V allocates zero to any income source that is not included in set S (and it is not I_i). For example, if $= \{I_2, I_3, I_4, I_5\}$, then

$$V^{ZID} = V(\underset{\sim}{0}, \underset{\sim}{I_2}, \underset{\sim}{I_3}, \underset{\sim}{I_4}, \underset{\sim}{I_5}, \underset{\sim}{0}, \ldots, \underset{\sim}{0}).$$

1.2 Simple Shapley Value: EID Approach

Using the same notation as in the previous section, the Shapley formula using the EID approach is

(2A-2) $$Sh_{I_i}^{EID} = \sum_{S \in S_{I_i}} \left(\frac{(s!) \times ((n-s-1))!}{n!} (V^{EID}(S \cup I_i) - V^{EID}(S)) \right).^{49}$$

The only difference here is that $V^{EID}(S)$ means the value function V allocates the average income to all individuals in the society for any income source that is not included in S. For example, if $S = \{I_2, I_3, I_4, I_5\}$, then the corresponding value function is

$$V^{EID} = V((\mu_{I_1} \times \underset{\sim}{1}), \underset{\sim}{I_2}, \underset{\sim}{I_3}, \underset{\sim}{I_4}, \underset{\sim}{I_5}, (\mu_{I_6} \times \underset{\sim}{1}), \ldots, (\mu_{I_n} \times \underset{\sim}{1}))$$

where $\underset{\sim}{1}$ is a $(m \times 1)$ vector of ones and μ_{I_i} is the average value of income source i.

Note how the EID formula would run into problems if one tried to use it to explain a change in a value function (for example, the Gini coefficient) between a reference point that is not zero and an end point that has a different per capita income in comparison to the reference point (that is, the sum of taxes and transfers is not zero). Assume the same example that is shown in table 2A-1. When total taxes and transfers are the same, the per capita values are also equal, and they cancel each other out, so the reference point remains the Market Income—that is,

$$V(Market\ Income, (\mu_{Tax} \times 1), (\mu_{Transfer} \times 1)) = V(Market\ Income, 0, 0)$$
$$when\ \mu_{Tax} = -\mu_{Transfer}.$$

If the sum of taxes and transfers is not zero, the reference point is no longer Market Income and has a different value for the Gini coefficient, which results in the decomposition differing from the value we want to explain. Table 2A-2 shows this problem in a simple example. The sum of the EID Shapley values does not add up to the change in the Gini coefficient that we would like to explain.

2 Hierarchy-Shapley Value

According to Sastre and Trannoy, the "Shapley value does not satisfy the principle of independence of the aggregation level."[45] The following example demonstrates this shortcoming. Assume in our previous example in table 2A-1 that the equalized tax is in fact the combination of two independent taxes and we recalculate the simple (ZID) Shapley values for two taxes and one transfer. As is clear from

---

[45] Sastre and Trannoy (2002, p. 54).

TABLE 2A-2
Example of EID Failing to Decompose the Change in Gini

Individual	Market income	Tax	Transfer	Final income
1	1	−1	6	6
2	20	−2	4	22
3	30	−3	3	30
4	40	−4	2	38
5	50	−5	1	46
Total	**141**	**−15**	**16**	**142**
Average	**28.2**	**−3**	**3.2**	**28.4**

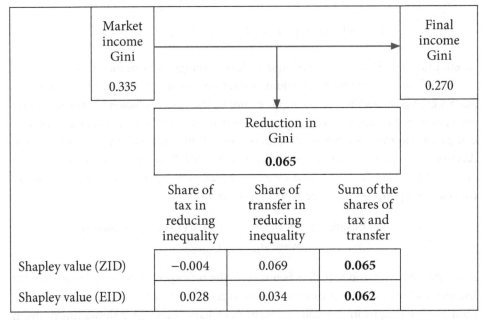

	Share of tax in reducing inequality	Share of transfer in reducing inequality	Sum of the shares of tax and transfer
Shapley value (ZID)	−0.004	0.069	**0.065**
Shapley value (EID)	0.028	0.034	**0.062**

Gini value of the market income is not zero; the sum of taxes and transfers is not zero.

ZID = Zero income decomposition; EID = Equalized income decomposition.

table 2A-3, the Shapley values for these taxes would not add up to the Shapley value of the equalized tax in table 2A-1. Moreover, the Shapley value of the transfer is different.

Given that no new tax has been added and that the only change is that some additional information about the sources of taxes has been included in the analysis, it is inconvenient that the Shapley value for transfers has also changed. Different solutions have been suggested to solve this problem. Sastre and Trannoy in particular introduce two methods, "Nested Shapley" and "Owen Decomposition."[46] Both of these solutions

---

[46] Sastre and Trannoy (2002, p. 54).

TABLE 2A-3

New Shapley Values (ZID) When Taxes Are Divided into Two Groups

Individual	Market income	Tax1	Tax2	Transfer	Final income
1	1	0	−5	9	5
2	20	−1	−4	7	22
3	30	−2	−3	5	30
4	40	−3	−2	3	38
5	50	−4	−1	1	46
Total	141	−10	−15	25	141
Average	28.2	−2	−3	5	28.2

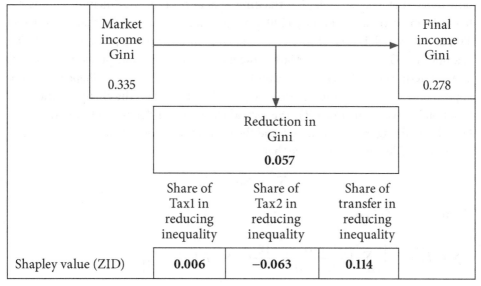

	Market income Gini		Final income Gini
	0.335		0.278

	Reduction in Gini
	0.057

	Share of Tax1 in reducing inequality	Share of Tax2 in reducing inequality	Share of transfer in reducing inequality
Shapley value (ZID)	**0.006**	**−0.063**	**0.114**

ZID = Zero income decomposition.

use a type of hierarchy, which is why they are called "hierarchy-Shapley values here." In the following sections, unless otherwise specified, no distinction between ZID and EID approaches is made, and the formulas can be used for both cases.

2.1 Hierarchy-Shapley Value: Nested Shapley

Using notations from the previous section, now assume each source of income I_i is the summation of a subset of sources, that is, $I_i = I_{i1} + I_{i2} + \cdots + I_{ik}$. It is assumed that this hierarchy has a particular theoretical basis. Define set $N_{I_i} = \{I_{i1}, I_{i2}, \ldots, I_{ik}\}$ as the set of all incomes that comprise income source I_i. We are particularly interested in one of these sub-sources, the nested Shapley value of I_{ij}. Define set $NS_{I_{ij}}$ as the set of subsets of set $N_{I_i} - \{I_{ij}\}$ (analogous to set S_{I_i}, defined in previous sections). According to Sastre and Trannoy (2002), nested Shapley can be viewed as a two-step procedure. In the first step, we assume that the second layer does not exist, and we calculate the simple Shapley value for all sources I_i. In the second step, we decompose the Shapley value of each source I_i between its sub-sources. The nested Shapley value of source I_{ij} (which is an element of I_i) is then equal to

$$(2A-3) \qquad NSh_{I_{ij}} = \sum_{S \in NS_{I_{ij}}} \left(\frac{(s!) \times ((k-s-1)!)}{k!} (V(S \cup I_{ij}) - V(S)) \right)$$
$$+ \frac{1}{k}(Sh_{I_i} + V(I_i) - V(0)).$$

Elements of this formula are either introduced above or in the previous sections. The only remaining item is k, which is the dimensionality of set N_{I_i}. Equation 2A-3 is different from Sastre and Trannoy (2002) because we do not assume that the value of $V(0)$ is zero, which is crucial when the inequality in the starting point is not zero (for example, the Gini value of the Market Income is not zero in our previous examples). The first term is exactly the same formula introduced for the simple Shapley, which is applied only to the set of sources that are part of N_{I_i} to explain the change in the value function between $V(0)$ and $V(I_i)$. The second term is the difference between the Shapley value of the aggregated source I_i and the value of function V when only aggregated source I_i is added. It is clear to see that

$$(2A-4) \qquad\qquad\qquad \sum_{j=1}^{k} NSh_{I_{ij}} = Sh_{I_i}.$$

The proof is as follows:

$$\sum_{j=1}^{k} NSh_{I_{ij}} = \sum_{j=1}^{k} \left\{ \sum_{S \in NS_{I_{ij}}} \left(\frac{(s!) \times ((k-s-1)!)}{k!} (V(S \cup I_{ij}) - V(S)) \right) \right\}$$
$$+ \sum_{j=1}^{k} \frac{1}{k}(Sh_{I_i} + V(I_i) - V(0)) \rightarrow \sum_{j=1}^{k} NSh_{I_{ij}}$$
$$= \sum_{j=1}^{k} \left\{ \sum_{S \in NS_{I_{ij}}} \left(\frac{(s!) \times ((k-s-1)!)}{k!} (V(S \cup I_{ij}) - V(S)) \right) \right\} + Sh_{I_i} + V(I_i) - V(0).$$

Note that in the second term, the summation over k and $(1/k)$ cancel each other. Now note that the term inside the braces is equal to $Sh_{I_{ij}}$ if one decomposes the change in V between $V(0)$ and $V(I_i)$. The summation over the Shapley value of all j income concepts that are part of I_i is simply equal to the total change in the value function between $V(0)$ and $V(I_i)$. This means the preceding equation could be written as follows:

$$\rightarrow \sum_{j=1}^{k} NSh_{I_{ij}} = V(I_i) - V(0) + Sh_{I_i} + V(I_i) - V(0),$$

and therefore,

$$\to \sum_{j=1}^{k} NSh_{I_{ij}} = Sh_{I_i}.$$

Note that the value of j has to be at least 1 (that is, one income inside each income group) and if all income groups have $j=1$, then the nested Shapley is reduced to the simple Shapley.

This nested Shapley formula, however, suffers from a few theoretical problems. First, the choice of decomposing $V(I_i) - V(0)$ between sub-elements of I_i (the first term in equation 2A-3) is arbitrary. One can choose any element of set S_{I_i}. Let's call it O_j and then decompose $V(I_i \cup O_j) - V(O_j)$ between elements of I_i such that the decomposition also satisfies equation 2A-4. Equation 2A-3 can then be generalized as

$$(2A\text{-}5) \quad NSh_{I_{ij}} = \sum_{S \in NS_{I_{ij}}} \left(\frac{(s!) \times ((k-s-1)!)}{k!} (V(O_j \cup S \cup I_{ij}) - V(O_j \cup S)) \right)$$

$$+ \frac{1}{k}(Sh_{I_i} - V(O_j \cup I_i) + V(O_j)) \quad \textit{for any arbitrarily chosen } O_j \in S_{I_i}.$$

The value of $NSh_{I_{ij}}$ would change with the choice of O_j.

The second theoretical problem with equation 2A-3 is that $Sh_{I_i} + V(I_i) - V(0)$ is divided evenly between all k sub-elements of I_i. There is no particular reason to do so, and any weighting scheme works as long as the weights add up to unity. In fact, one might argue that assigning similar weights is not in line with the idea of decomposition, which tries to allocate an appropriate share to each element depending on how important the element is. Using a weighting scheme that gives more weight to more important elements results in equation 2A-6:

$$(2A\text{-}6) \quad NSh_{I_{ij}} = \sum_{S \in NS_{I_{ij}}} \left(\frac{(s!) \times ((k-s-1)!)}{k!} (V(O_j \cup S \cup I_{ij}) - V(O_j \cup S)) \right)$$

$$+ \left(\frac{\sum_{S \in NS_{I_{ij}}} \left(\frac{(s!) \times ((k-s-1)!)}{k!} (V(O_j \cup S \cup I_{ij}) - V(O_j \cup S)) \right)}{V(I_i \cup O_j) - V(O_j)} \right.$$

$$\left. \times (Sh_{I_i} + V(O_j \cup I_i) - V(O_j)) \right) \quad \textit{for any arbitrarily chosen } O_j \in S.$$

The weighting scheme in equation 2A-6 uses the relative importance of element I_{ij} in explaining the gap between $V(O_j \cup I_i)$ and $V(O_j)$, that is, $V(O_j \cup I_i) - V(O_j)$. While this modified weighting scheme has a much better theoretical ground, the fact that $NSh_{I_{ij}}$ depends on the choice of O_j is still problematic.

The following example helps to better visualize this problem. We use the same example as in table 2A-3, but the results should be compared to table 2A-1. Regardless of how we decompose the Shapley value of the total tax between its elements, the Shapley value of the transfer remains unchanged and equal to the value in table 2A-1 (the ZID

Shapley value). However, depending on which formula is used for the decomposition for taxes, the Shapley values of Tax 1 and Tax 2 change, though they always add up to the Shapley value of total tax. Among the four different methods, 2A-6′ is preferred to 2A-3′ and 2A-6″ is preferred to 2A-5′ because of their modified weighting scheme, but there is no theoretical basis for any preference between 2A-6′ and 2A-6″. Note that in table 2A-4, values for 2A-5′ and 2A-6′ happen to be the same by pure luck and that this is not a general rule.

In the following formulas, $N_{Tax} = \{Tax1, Tax2\}$ and NS_{Taxj} is the set of all subsets of $N_{Tax} - \{Taxj\}$. Moreover, M represents the Market Income and $V(\bullet)$ represents the Gini coefficient function. The following formulas are derived from the original formulas discussed in the specific example in table 2A-4.

(2A-3)′
$$NSh_{Taxj} = -\left[\sum_{S \in NS_{Taxj}} \left(\frac{\left(V(M \cup S \cup Taxj) - V(M \cup S)\right)}{2} \right) + \frac{1}{2}\left(Sh_{Tax} + V(M \cup Tax) - V(M)\right) \right]$$

(2A-5)′
$$NSh_{Taxj} = -\left[\sum_{S \in NS_{Taxj}} \left(\frac{\left(V(O_j \cup S \cup Taxj) - V(O_j \cup S)\right)}{2} \right) + \frac{1}{2}\left(Sh_{Tax} + V(O_j \cup Tax) - V(O_j)\right) \right]$$
$$Where\ O_j = \{Market\ Income + Transfer\}$$

(2A-6)′
$$NSh_{Taxj} = \sum_{S \in NS_{Taxj}} \left(\frac{\left(V(M \cup S \cup Taxj) - V(M \cup S)\right)}{2} \right)$$
$$+ \left(\frac{\sum_{S \in NS_{Taxj}} \left(\frac{\left(V(M \cup S \cup Taxj) - V(M \cup S)\right)}{2} \right)}{V(M \cup Tax) - V(M)} \times \left(Sh_{Tax} + V(M \cup Tax) - V(M)\right) \right)$$

(2A-6)″
$$NSh_{Taxj} = \sum_{S \in NS_{Taxj}} \left(\frac{\left(V(O_j \cup S \cup Taxj) - V(O_j \cup S)\right)}{2} \right)$$
$$+ \left(\frac{\sum_{S \in NS_{Taxj}} \left(\frac{\left(V(O_j \cup S \cup Taxj) - V(O_j \cup S)\right)}{2} \right)}{V(O_j \cup Tax) - V(O_j)} \times \left(Sh_{Tax} + V(O_j \cup Tax) - V(O_j)\right) \right)$$
$$Where\ O_j = \{Market\ Income + Transfer\}$$

Nested Shapley Values (ZID) Using Different Methods of Weighting and
Reference Points

Individual	Market income	Tax1	Tax2	Transfer	Final income
1	1	0	−5	9	5
2	20	−1	−4	7	22
3	30	−2	−3	5	30
4	40	−3	−2	3	38
5	50	−4	−1	1	46
Total	**141**	**−10**	**−15**	**25**	**141**
Average	**28.2**	**−2**	**−3**	**5**	**28.2**

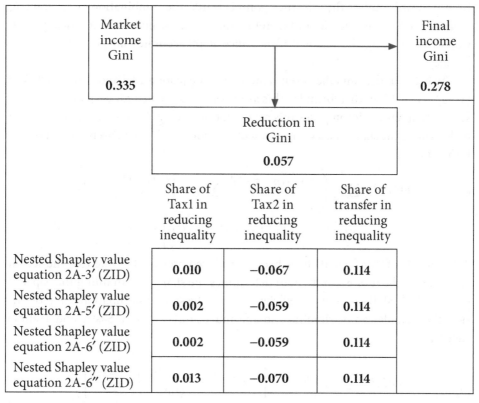

	Market income Gini				Final income Gini
	0.335				**0.278**
		Reduction in Gini **0.057**			
		Share of Tax1 in reducing inequality	Share of Tax2 in reducing inequality	Share of transfer in reducing inequality	
Nested Shapley value equation 2A-3′ (ZID)		**0.010**	**−0.067**	**0.114**	
Nested Shapley value equation 2A-5′ (ZID)		**0.002**	**−0.059**	**0.114**	
Nested Shapley value equation 2A-6′ (ZID)		**0.002**	**−0.059**	**0.114**	
Nested Shapley value equation 2A-6″ (ZID)		**0.013**	**−0.070**	**0.114**	

ZID = Zero income decomposition.

2.2 Hierarchy-Shapley Value: Owen Decomposition

In order to avoid the problem of the reference point in the nested Shapley value, one can use the Owen value.[47] Intuitively, the Owen value can be viewed as a Shapley value of different nested Shapley values: that is, all possible reference points are included. Therefore, the Owen value is not subject to the theoretical shortcomings of the nested Shapley, and accordingly, it has some advantages. Sastre and Trannoy (2002) disagree with this argument because they believe that reference points other than $V(0)$ imply that income elements are combined at a different aggregation level. This argument loses its ground, however, as soon as we try to use the nested Shapley value to explain, for example, changes in the Gini index between market and final income. Because Market Income is on the same aggregation level as total tax but not Tax 1, using the nested Shapley implies the combination of two elements from two different aggregation levels. In other words, unless the reference point is "null," the combination of different aggregation levels is inevitable, and therefore the Owen method is a theoretically better way of calculating the Shapley value since it incorporates all possible reference points.[48]

To better understand the Owen value, consider equation 2A-1 and particularly V^{ZID} $(S \cup I_i) - V^{ZID}(S)$ in that formula. This argument is calculated for each element of the summation. Owen decomposes this argument (for every element of the summation) to determine the share of each sub-element. The formula for the Owen decomposition is therefore

$$(2A\text{-}7) \qquad OSh_{I_{ij}}^{ZID} = \sum_{S \in S_{I_i}} \left(\frac{(s!) \times ((n-s-1)!)}{n!} \sum_{S' \in NS_{I_{ij}}} \left\{ \frac{(s'!) \times ((k-s'-1)!)}{k!} \right. \right.$$
$$\left. \left. \times (V^{ZID}(S \cup S' \cup I_i) - V^{ZID}(S \cup S')) \right\} \right).$$

All elements of this formula have been introduced previously. Note that the second summation (the inside summation) determines the share of I_{ij} in filling the gap V^{ZID} $(S \cup I_i) - V^{ZID}(S)$. Because the coefficient outside the second summation can move inside, the formula can be simplified to a formula similar to what Sastre and Trannoy suggest:

$$(2A\text{-}7)' \qquad OSh_{I_{ij}}^{ZID} = \sum_{S \in S_{I_i}} \left(\sum_{S' \in NS_{I_{ij}}} \left\{ \frac{(s'!)(s!)((k-s'-1)!)((n-s-1)!)}{k!n!} \right\} \right).$$
$$\times (V^{ZID}(S \cup S' \cup I_i) - V^{ZID}(S \cup S'))$$

---

[47] Owen (1977).

[48] Sastre and Trannoy (2002) use a formula similar to equation 2-43, which suffers from a second theoretical problem (assigning equal weights to all sub-elements of one source), which is discussed in previous sections.

TABLE 2A-5
Owen Values (ZID)

Individual	Market income	Tax1	Tax2	Transfer	Final income
1	1	0	−5	9	5
2	20	−1	−4	7	22
3	30	−2	−3	5	30
4	40	−3	−2	3	38
5	50	−4	−1	1	46
Total	141	−10	−15	25	141
Average	28.2	−2	−3	5	28.2

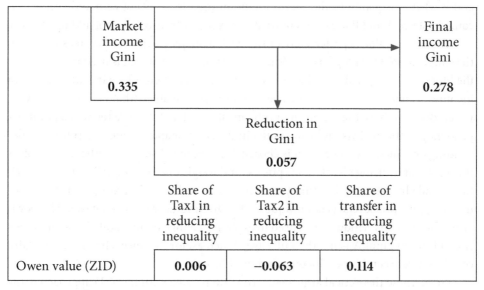

ZID = Zero income decomposition.

Note that one can easily use V^{EID} in the preceding formula. Using the same example as in table 2A-3, the Owen values for the case of two taxes and one transfer are calculated in table 2A-5 and can be compared with the values in tables 2A-1 and 2A-4.

It should be noted that the Owen value of the transfer is the same as in table 2A-1, as expected. Comparing Owen values from table 2A-5 to those in table 2A-4, the Owen value of each tax component is between its nested Shapley value for equations 2A-6′ and 2A-6″. This outcome is expected because the Owen value incorporates all possible reference points and is intuitively a type of (weighted) average value. As a result, the Owen value is a more conservative estimate than the nested Shapley values for the share of each component.

3 Concluding Remarks

Of the different methods for estimating the Shapley value for income sources, there are better theoretical justifications for using the ZID approach than EID and for using the Owen value instead of the nested Shapley for performing an incidence analysis (which is focused mainly on different sources of taxes and transfers). This conclusion stands in contrast to the suggestions by Sastre and Trannoy (2002) and Duclos and Araar (2007). ZID is preferred over EID for two main reasons. First, ZID allocates a negative (or positive) value to a lump-sum tax (or transfer) that is by definition regressive (or progressive) and therefore increases (or decreases) inequality. EID will assign a zero value to such a tax (or transfer). Second, ZID decomposition is always exact; in contrast, EID will not be exact if we decompose a change in inequality between states A and B where inequality in the beginning point (that is, A) is not zero and average income in states A and B are different (that is, taxes and transfers do not add up to zero).

The Owen value is preferred over the nested Shapley value for two reasons. First, the simple nested Shapley formula (that is, equation 2A-3), which is used more often in the literature, assigns identical weights to different sub-items of a particular source of income. Second, even the modified version of nested Shapley (that is, equation 2A-6), which does not have the weighting problem, still suffers from the reference point dependency problem. This problem results in different Shapley values for sub-items depending on which reference point is chosen. The Owen value, on the other hand, solves this problem by using all reference points (and weighting them equally). The only critique made by Sastre and Trannoy (2002) for this technique (mixing items from different aggregation levels) is not unique to the Owen value. Moreover, nested Shapley is also subject to this critique if it is used to explain a change in inequality between points A and B when point A is not the null case,[49] such as, for instance, changes in the Gini coefficient between Market Income and total income.

Given these theoretical arguments, the Owen value with the ZID approach is the best option when the fiscal system under study includes mainly taxes and transfers, which is true for most cases. This method ensures that the decomposition is exact and that every single source of income receives its appropriate share based on how much it contributes to the reduction (or escalation) of inequality. Moreover, when using the Owen value, there is no problem regarding the choice of the reference point.

For a more in-depth discussion of the theory and application of the Shapley value see a series of papers by Sastre and Trannoy (2001, 2002, 2008).

---

[49] The null case is where no source of income is distributed in the society.

Chapter 3

MEASURING THE REDISTRIBUTIVE IMPACT OF TAXES AND TRANSFERS IN THE PRESENCE OF RERANKING

Ali Enami

Introduction

In chapter 2 of this Volume of the Handbook, Enami, Lustig, and Aranda (2022) discussed how to measure the redistributive impact of taxes and transfers in a system where there is no reranking: that is, the position of individuals ordered by their income remains identical in the prefiscal and postfiscal situations. This chapter introduces the possibility of reranking in a fiscal system into the analysis of a tax or transfer's marginal contribution in reducing (increasing) inequality. As will become clear in this chapter, when a fiscal system creates reranking in individuals, it is much harder to use simple rules to determine whether a specific tax or transfer is equalizing or not. The complicated math introduced here shows that, in contrast to such measures as progressivity, the marginal contribution analysis is the only straightforward way of determining whether a tax or transfer is equalizing. It should be noted that the analysis in this chapter is focused on the traditional Gini index but can be similarly extended to the S-Gini indexes. The idea of marginal contribution analysis can also be extended to other measures of inequality, but one should be cautious about the fact that the type of decomposition that we use in this chapter may not be applicable to other indexes (for example, the Theil index).

The best way to see how introducing reranking would create new problems is through a simple example. Chapter 2 in this Volume of the Handbook, in which reranking was not present, introduced a simple rule that held that if a system has only one tax and that tax is progressive, then the postfiscal system is unambiguously more equal. Although this "progressive-means-equalizing" rule of thumb is one of the most commonly used rules, chapter 2 in this Volume showed that this rule is not always correct when a system is not composed of only one tax or one transfer (see for example,

TABLE 3-1

Example of an Unequalizing Progressive Tax in the Presence of Reranking

Individual	Original income	Tax	End income
1	10.00	0.00	10.00
2	11.00	2.00	9.00
3	12.00	4.00	8.00
4	13.00	6.00	7.00
Total	46.00	12.00	34.00
Average	11.50	3.00	8.50
Gini	0.0540	n.c.	0.0740

n.c. Not calculated for the purposes of this chapter.

the so-called Lambert conundrum). This chapter shows that in the presence of reranking, this rule is not always correct even in a system with only one tax (transfer). In other words, this chapter shows that a progressive tax could create a more unequal post-fiscal system (using Gini as the measure of inequality). Table 3-1 shows an example where the Gini increases from 0.054 to 0.074 after introducing a progressive tax into the system.

1 Notations

This section provides the definitions of notations that will be used throughout this chapter. The notations are generally similar to those in other chapters in this Volume, but some minor modifications have been made to meet the requirements of the topics covered here.

1.1 Gini and Concentration Coefficients

This chapter uses G_Q and C_Q^G for the "Gini coefficient of the income concept Q" and the "concentration coefficient of income concept Q with respect to the income concept G." Note how the Gini and concentration coefficients are calculated using the covariance formula:

$$G_Q = \frac{2cov(Q, F_Q)}{\mu_Q}.$$

and

$$C_Q^G = \frac{2cov(Q, F_G)}{\mu_Q},$$

where F_Q is the normalized rank of individuals when they are ranked by income concept Q and μ_Q is the average value of the income concept Q. The normalized rank is calculated simply as follows. Assume there are n individuals who are ranked by income Q from 1 to n, where n is the rank of the individual with the highest income. The normalized rank of individual j is simply equal to j/n. Therefore, the normalized rank ranges from $1/n$ to 1. Similarly, F_G is the normalized rank of individuals if they are ranked by income concept G.

Chapter 2 in this Volume uses a simpler notation, C_Q, for the concentration coefficient, which implies that the "original income ranking of households" is used in its calculation. This chapter uses the superscript X to represent that individuals are ranked by their original income:

$$C_Q = C_Q^X = \frac{2cov(Q, F_X)}{\mu_Q}.$$

The covariance formula helps to explain why the concentration coefficient can be negative. For example, if the ranking of individuals with income concept Q is exactly the opposite of those with income concept X, then C_Q^X would be negative. On the other hand, the Gini coefficient for income concept Q, G_Q, is always non-negative since it uses the same income concept to calculate the Gini index as it uses to rank individuals.

1.2 Reynolds-Smolensky and Kakwani Indexes

As in section 1.1, I use the following formulas for the R-S and Kakwani indexes of a tax (T) or transfer (B) when they are calculated with respect to the original income ranking of households. For a tax,

$$\Pi_T^{RS} = G_X - C_{X-T}^X = \frac{2cov(X, F_X)}{\mu_X} - \frac{2cov(X-T, F_X)}{\mu_X(1-g)}$$

$$\Pi_T^K = C_T^X - G_X = \frac{2cov(T, F_X)}{\mu_X g} - \frac{2cov(X, F_X)}{\mu_X}$$

and for a transfer,

$$\rho_B^{RS} = G_X - C_{X+B}^X = \frac{2cov(X, F_X)}{\mu_X} - \frac{2cov(X+B, F_X)}{\mu_X(1+b)}$$

$$\rho_B^K = G_X - C_B^X = \frac{2cov(X, F_X)}{\mu_X} - \frac{2cov(B, F_X)}{\mu_X b}$$

where $g(b)$ is the total taxes (transfers) collected, divided by the total amount of original income (that is, X). For example,

$$g = \frac{T}{X}$$

and

$$b = \frac{B}{X}.$$

In this chapter, I also use a modified version of these two indicators (the R-S and Kakwani indexes), which allows the basis for ranking to be different from the original income. Whenever I use these new indexes, the superscript shows the income concept for the ranking. For example, if I used income concept Q for the ranking, I would have the following formulas: for a tax,

$$\Pi_T^{RSQ} = C_X^Q - C_{X-T}^Q$$
$$\Pi_T^{KQ} = C_T^Q - C_X^Q,$$

and for a transfer,

$$\rho_B^{RSQ} = C_X^Q - C_{X+B}^Q$$
$$\rho_B^{KQ} = C_X^Q - C_B^Q.$$

The relationship between the R-S and Kakwani indexes is as follows: for a tax,

$$\Pi_T^{RSQ} = \frac{g}{1-g} \Pi_T^{KQ},$$

and for a transfer,

$$\rho_B^{RSQ} = \frac{b}{1+b} \rho_B^{KQ}.$$

1.3 The Relationship between the Redistributive Effect, Vertical Equity, and Reranking

To understand how reranking affects a fiscal system, it is helpful to decompose the redistributive effect (RE), which is the change in Gini from the original income to the end income, into the vertical equity (VE) and the reranking (RR) components. The following derivation shows explicitly that RR always reduces VE and is therefore always an unequalizing component. The presence of RR in a fiscal system implies a form of inefficiency in redistributive policy because the same level of reduction in inequality could be achieved with a lower level of income redistribution through taxes and transfers if RR were to be eliminated.

For the purpose of simplicity, I bundle all of the taxes in a system together and all of the transfers (benefits) together and use just one tax (T) and one transfer (B) in the following.

The RE (that is, the change in Gini) can be decomposed into two elements,[1] as follows:

$$(3\text{-}1) \qquad G_X - G_{X-T+B} = \underbrace{(G_X - C^X_{X-T+B})}_{Vertical\ Equity} + \underbrace{(C^X_{X-T+B} - G_{X-T+B})}_{Reranking\ (non-positive)}.$$

These indexes are known as the Reynolds-Smolensky index of progressivity and VE[2] and the Atkinson-Plotnick index of RR.[3] According to Lambert,[4] in the absence of RR, the change in Gini can be simply calculated using the following formula (assuming only one tax and one transfer or, alternatively, grouping all taxes together as well as all transfers):

$$G_X - C^X_{X-T+B} = \frac{(1-g)\Pi^{RS}_T + (1+b)\rho^{RS}_B}{1-g+b}.$$

If reranking is allowed, the change in Gini will be equal to

$$(3\text{-}2) \qquad G_X - G_{X-T+B} = \frac{(1-g)\Pi^{RS}_T + (1+b)\rho^{RS}_B}{1-g+b} + \left(G_X - C^{X-T+B}_X\right)$$

$$+ \left(\frac{(1-g)\left(\Pi^{RS}_T - \Pi^{RS^{X-T+B}}_T\right) + (1+b)\left(\rho^{RS}_B - \rho^{RS^{X-T+B}}_B\right)}{1-g+b}\right).$$

---

[1] See Duclos and Araar (2007). Note that the component called VE in equation 2.3.1 is not exactly pure and could include a "horizontal inequality" component. This component captures the "negative" behavior of a fiscal system that treats individuals who are exactly the same in different ways (Duclos and Araar, 2007). Here it is assumed that people are not exactly the same, so the horizontal inequality does not exist. Note that the phrase "exactly the same" is not limited to the amount of original income and includes other elements such as number of children and even subjective measures. If people have exactly the same original income, the derivations here are still valid, so we assume people are not exactly the same in other dimensions, but we allow them to have identical original income.

[2] Reynolds and Smolensky (2013).

[3] Atkinson (1979); Plotnick (1981, 1982).

[4] See Lambert (2001, p. 277).

The proof is as follows:

We know that the change in Gini can be decomposed into two elements:

$$(3\text{-}3) \qquad G_X - G_{X-T+B} = (G_X - C^X_{X-T+B}) + (C^X_{X-T+B} - G_{X-T+B}).$$

As mentioned previously, Lambert proves the following inequality:[5]

$$(3\text{-}4) \qquad G_X - C^X_{X-T+B} = \frac{(1-g)\Pi^{RS}_T + (1+b)\rho^{RS}_B}{1-g+b}.$$

Now, focusing on the second term in equation 3-3, that is, the RR term, we know from equation 3-4 that

$$(3\text{-}5) \qquad C^X_{X-T+B} = G_X - \frac{(1-g)\Pi^{RS}_T + (1+b)\rho^{RS}_B}{1-g+b}.$$

Now, focusing on G_{X-T+B},

$$(3\text{-}6) \qquad G_{X-T+B} = \frac{2Cov(X-T+B, F_{X-T+B})}{\mu_X(1-g+b)} \rightarrow$$

$$G_{X-T+B} = \frac{2Cov(X-T, F_{X-T+B})}{\mu_X(1-g+b)} + \frac{2Cov(X+B, F_{X-T+B})}{\mu_X(1-g+b)} - \frac{2Cov(X, F_{X-T+B})}{\mu_X(1-g+b)}$$

$$= \underbrace{\left(\frac{(1-g)}{(1-g+b)}\right)\frac{2Cov(X-T, F_{X-T+B})}{\mu_X(1-g)}}_{A} + \underbrace{\left(\frac{(1+b)}{(1-g+b)}\right)\frac{2Cov(X+B, F_{X-T+B})}{\mu_X(1+b)}}_{B}$$

$$\underbrace{- \frac{2Cov(X, F_{X-T+B})}{\mu_X(1-g+b)}}_{C}.$$

To make it simpler to follow the next steps, I examine each one of the three terms in equation 3-6 in turn.

$$A = \left(\frac{(1-g)}{(1-g+b)}\right)\frac{2Cov(X-T, F_{X-T+B})}{\mu_X(1-g)} - \left(\frac{(1-g)}{(1-g+b)}\right)\frac{2Cov(X, F_{X-T+B})}{\mu_X}$$

$$+ \left(\frac{(1-g)}{(1-g+b)}\right)\frac{2Cov(X, F_{X-T+B})}{\mu_X}.$$

Note that I just added and subtracted the same term in the preceding equation at the end.

---

[5] See Lambert (2001, p. 277).

It is important to note that the first two terms in the preceding formula would add up to

$$-\left(\frac{(1-g)}{(1-g+b)}\right)\Pi_T^{RS^{X-T+B}}.$$

The third term is equal to

$$\left(\frac{(1-g)}{(1-g+b)}\right)C_X^{X-T+B}.$$

Therefore,

(3-7) $$A=-\left(\frac{(1-g)}{(1-g+b)}\right)\Pi_T^{RS^{X-T+B}}+\left(\frac{(1-g)}{(1-g+b)}\right)C_X^{X-T+B}.$$

Analogously for B,

(3-8) $$B=-\left(\frac{(1+b)}{(1-g+b)}\right)\rho_B^{RS^{X-T+B}}+\left(\frac{(1+b)}{(1-g+b)}\right)C_X^{X-T+B}.$$

And similarly for C,

(3-9) $$C=-\left(\frac{1}{(1-g+b)}\right)C_X^{X-T+B}.$$

The following formula puts the preceding parts together (that is, it uses 3-7, 3-8, and 3-9 in equation 3-6).

(3-10) $$G_{X-T+B}=A+B+C=-\left[\frac{(1-g)\Pi_T^{RS^{X-T+B}}+(1+b)\rho_B^{RS^{X-T+B}}}{1-g+b}\right]+C_X^{X-T+B}.$$

Finally, the following formula puts all the parts together (that is, it uses 3-4, 3-5, and 3-10 in 3-3):

$$G_X-G_{X-T+B}=\frac{(1-g)\Pi_T^{RS}+(1+b)\rho_B^{RS}}{1-g+b}+(G_X-C_X^{X-T+B})$$

$$+\left(\frac{(1-g)\left(\Pi_T^{RS}-\Pi_T^{RS^{X-T+B}}\right)+(1+b)\left(\rho_B^{RS}-\rho_B^{RS^{X-T+B}}\right)}{1-g+b}\right)$$

Q.E.D.

It should be noted that since the RR term is always non-positive, the following expression is always negative:

$$(G_X - C_X^{X-T+B}) + \left(\frac{(1-g)\left(\Pi_T^{RS} - \Pi_T^{RS^{X-T+B}} \right) + (1+b)\left(\rho_B^{RS} - \rho_B^{RS^{X-T+B}} \right)}{1-g+b} \right) \leq 0.$$

Also, equation 3-2 can be further simplified:

$$(3\text{-}11) \qquad G_X - G_{X-T+B} = (G_X - C_X^{X-T+B}) + \left(\frac{(1-g)\Pi_T^{RS^{X-T+B}} + (1+b)\rho_B^{RS^{X-T+B}}}{1-g+b} \right).$$

1.4 Marginal Contribution

Based on equation 3-11, I can now derive the formula for the marginal contribution of a tax (or transfer).

For simplicity, I define income concepts Z and $Z\backslash T_1$ as follows:

$$Z = X - \sum_{i=1}^{n} T_i + \sum_{j=1}^{m} B_j$$

$$Z\backslash T_1 = X - \sum_{i=2}^{n} T_i + \sum_{j=1}^{m} B_j.$$

In the general case, I define the marginal contribution of Tax 1 (without the loss of generality) as follows:

$$M_{T_1} = G_{Z\backslash T_1} - G_Z.$$

The interpretation of this formula is straightforward: the marginal contribution of a tax is equal to the change in the Gini index when this tax is added to the rest of the taxes and transfers in the system.

By adding and subtracting G_X in the above equation, we would have

$$M_{T_1} = G_{Z\backslash T_1} - G_Z + G_X - G_X,$$

which can then be rewritten as

$$(3\text{-}12) \qquad M_{T_1} = (G_X - G_Z) - (G_X - G_{Z\backslash T_1}).$$

Using a generalized version of equation 3-11, we can rewrite equation 3-12 as follows:

$$(3\text{-}13) \quad M_{T_1} = \left\{ (G_X - C_X^Z) + \left(\frac{\sum_{i=1}^{n}(1-g_i)\Pi_{T_i}^{RS^Z} + \sum_{j=1}^{m}(1+b_j)\rho_{B_j}^{RS^Z}}{1 - \sum_{i=1}^{n}g_i + \sum_{j=1}^{m}b_j} \right) \right\}$$
$$- \left\{ (G_X - C_X^{Z\backslash T_1}) + \left(\frac{\sum_{i=2}^{n}(1-g_i)\Pi_{T_i}^{RS^{Z\backslash T_1}} + \sum_{j=1}^{m}(1+b_j)\rho_{B_j}^{RS^{Z\backslash T_1}}}{1 - \sum_{i=2}^{n}g_i + \sum_{j=1}^{m}b_j} \right) \right\}.$$

Similarly, the marginal contribution of a benefit can be defined as follows:

$$(3\text{-}14) \quad M_{B_1} = \left\{ (G_X - C_X^Z) + \left(\frac{\sum_{i=1}^{n}(1-g_i)\Pi_{T_i}^{RS^Z} + \sum_{j=1}^{m}(1+b_j)\rho_{B_j}^{RS^Z}}{1 - \sum_{i=1}^{n}g_i + \sum_{j=1}^{m}b_j} \right) \right\}$$
$$- \left\{ (G_X - C_X^{Z\backslash B_1}) + \left(\frac{\sum_{i=1}^{n}(1-g_i)\Pi_{T_i}^{RS^{Z\backslash B_1}} + \sum_{j=2}^{m}(1+b_j)\rho_{B_j}^{RS^{Z\backslash B_1}}}{1 - \sum_{i=1}^{n}g_i + \sum_{j=2}^{m}b_j} \right) \right\}.$$

Note that derivations 3-13 and 3-14 use a modified R-S index that ranks individuals by income concepts other than by the original income. One can suggest alternative formulas that are based on the ranking with respect to the original income. The following examples provide such derivations.

Beginning with equation 3-12,

$$M_{T_1} = (G_X - G_Z) - (G_X - G_{Z\backslash T_1})$$
$$= \left[(G_X - C_Z^X) + (C_Z^X - G_Z) \right] - \left[(G_X - C_{Z\backslash T_1}^X) + (C_{Z\backslash T_1}^X - G_{Z\backslash T_1}) \right],$$

we can rearrange the above terms to have

$$M_{T_1} = \overbrace{\left[(G_X - C_Z^X) - (G_X - C_{Z\backslash T_1}^X) \right]}^{\text{Contribution of } T_1 \text{ to vertical equity}} + \overbrace{\left[(C_Z^X - G_Z) - (C_{Z\backslash T_1}^X - G_{Z\backslash T_1}) \right]}^{\text{Contribution of } T_1 \text{ to reranking}}.$$

Using the relationship between VE and the R-S index of the taxes and transfers (calculated with respect to the original income ranking of households), we can rewrite the above equation as follows:

$$M_{T_1} = \left[\left(\frac{\sum_{i=1}^{n}(1-g_i)\Pi_{T_i}^{RS} + \sum_{j=1}^{m}(1+b_j)\rho_{B_j}^{RS}}{1 - \sum_{i=1}^{n}g_i + \sum_{j=1}^{m}b_j} \right) - \left(\frac{\sum_{i=2}^{n}(1-g_i)\Pi_{T_i}^{RS} + \sum_{j=1}^{m}(1+b_j)\rho_{B_j}^{RS}}{1 - \sum_{i=2}^{n}g_i + \sum_{j=1}^{m}b_j} \right) \right]$$
$$+ \underbrace{\left[(C_Z^X - G_Z) - (C_{Z\backslash T_1}^X - G_{Z\backslash T_1}) \right]}_{\text{Contribution of } T_1 \text{ to reranking}}.$$

Now, simplifying the above equation we have

$$
(3\text{-}15) \quad M_{T_1} = \left[\left(\frac{\left[\left(1-\sum_{i=2}^{n} g_i + \sum_{j=1}^{m} b_j\right)(1-g_1)\Pi_{T_1}^{RS}\right] + \left[(g_1)\left(\sum_{i=2}^{n}(1-g_i)\Pi_{T_i}^{RS} + \sum_{j=1}^{m}(1+b_j)\rho_{B_j}^{RS}\right)\right]}{\left(1-\sum_{i=1}^{n} g_i + \sum_{j=1}^{m} b_j\right)\left(1-\sum_{i=2}^{n} g_i + \sum_{j=1}^{m} b_j\right)}\right) \right]
$$
$$
+ \underbrace{\left[(C_Z^X - G_z) - (C_{Z\backslash T_1}^X - G_{Z\backslash T_1})\right]}_{\text{Contribution of } T_1 \text{ to reranking}},
$$

which can be also written as follows:

$$
(3\text{-}16) \quad M_{T_1} = \left[\left(\frac{[(1-g_1)\Pi_{T_1}^{RS}] + \left[(g_1) \overbrace{(G_X - C_{Z\backslash T_1}^X)}^{\text{VE of the system without } T_1}\right]}{\left(1-\sum_{i=1}^{n} g_i + \sum_{j=1}^{m} b_j\right)}\right) \right] + \underbrace{[(C_Z^X - G_Z) - (C_{Z\backslash T_1}^X - G_{Z\backslash T_1})]}_{\text{Contribution of } T_1 \text{ to reranking}}.
$$

Similarly, for a transfer we have the following formulas:

$$
(3\text{-}17) \quad M_{B_1} = \left[\left(\frac{\left[\left(1-\sum_{i=1}^{n} g_i + \sum_{j=2}^{m} b_j\right)(1+b_1)\rho_{B_1}^{RS}\right] - \left[(b_1)\left(\sum_{i=1}^{n}(1-g_i)\Pi_{T_i}^{RS} + \sum_{j=2}^{m}(1+b_j)\rho_{B_j}^{RS}\right)\right]}{\left(1-\sum_{i=1}^{n} g_i + \sum_{j=1}^{m} b_j\right)\left(1-\sum_{i=1}^{n} g_i + \sum_{j=2}^{m} b_j\right)}\right) \right]
$$
$$
+ \underbrace{\left[(C_Z^X - G_Z) - (C_{Z\backslash B_1}^X - G_{Z\backslash B_1})\right]}_{\text{Contribution of } B_1 \text{ to reranking}}
$$

or

$$
(3\text{-}18) \quad M_{B_1} = \left[\left(\frac{[(1+b_1)\rho_{B_1}^{RS}] - \left[(b_1) \overbrace{(G_X - C_{Z\backslash B_1}^X)}^{\text{VE of the system without } B_1}\right]}{\left(1-\sum_{i=1}^{n} g_i + \sum_{j=1}^{m} b_j\right)}\right) \right] + \underbrace{[(C_Z^X - G_Z) - (C_{Z\backslash B_1}^X - G_{Z\backslash B_1})]}_{\text{Contribution of } B_1 \text{ to reranking}}.
$$

In the rest of this chapter, I rely mainly on equations 3-13, 3-15, and 3-16 for the analysis related to the marginal contribution of a tax, and 3-14, 3-17, and 3-18 for the analysis related to the marginal contribution of a transfer. Equations 3-13 and 3-14 give us a rule of thumb for cases of multiple taxes and transfers and for cases when the tax or transfer of interest does not change the end income ranking of individuals (as will become clearer later in this chapter). These two equations, however, rely on the calculation of the R-S and Kakwani indexes with respect to the end income ranking of individuals, which is an inferior method compared to calculating them by the original income ranking because the indicators based on the end income ranking are dependent, whereas the indicators based on the original income ranking are independent. In other words, any change in a tax (size, progressivity, introducing or removing a tax) can change the R-S index of a transfer if the end income ranking is used in the calculation of this index. Moreover, the previous chapter in this Volume (Enami, Lustig, and Aranda, 2022) uses only the original income ranking, so using equations 3-15, 3-16, 3-17, and 3-18 would provide comparable results. When there is no RR (as in the previous chapter), the value of the R-S and Kakwani indexes is the same no matter which ranking is used.

1.5 Vertical Equity

Vertical Equity (VE) is defined as follows:

$$VE_Z = G_X - C_Z^X.$$

This formula uses the original income both as the starting point and as a basis for ranking, but we can generalize it to use any other income concept for the purpose of ranking:

$$VE_{L,M}^Q = C_L^Q - C_M^Q.$$

2 In the Presence of Reranking, Is the Marginal Contribution of a Tax Equalizing?

This section examines the marginal contribution of a tax and identifies conditions that make a tax equalizing. The conditions are derived for different scenarios, beginning with a system that has only one tax, then a system that has only a transfer, and finally a system with multiple taxes and transfers (besides the specific tax that is of the interest of the analysis).

2.1 The Case of Only One Tax

Although a progressive tax in a system with no reranking is always equalizing, this is not the case when there is RR (see table 3-1). Since there is only one tax, equation 3-13 can be simplified as follows:

(3-19) $$M_T = (G_X - C_X^{X-T}) + \prod_T^{RS^{X-T}}.$$

Using equation 3-16, we have the following:

(3-20) $$M_T = \Pi_T^{RS} + (C_{X-T}^X - G_{X-T}).$$

Because equation 3-20 is easier to use, I will focus on it. Note that the RR term is always non-positive; that is,

$$C_{X-T}^X - G_{X-T} \leq 0.$$

For a tax to be equalizing, equation 3-20 has to be positive:

$$M_T = \Pi_T^{RS} + (C_{X-T}^X - G_{X-T}) > 0$$

or

(3-21) $$\Pi_T^{RS} > (G_{X-T} - C_{X-T}^X)$$

or

(3-22) $$\Pi_T^K > \left(\frac{1-g}{g}\right)(G_{X-T} - C_{X-T}^X).$$

Note that the right-hand side of equation 3-22 is always non-negative[6] and reaches its minimum (that is, zero) when the ranking of individuals before and after adding the tax remains the same. Therefore, a progressive tax (which is defined as a tax where $\Pi_T^K > 0$) is equalizing only when equation 3-22 holds. However, a regressive tax ($\Pi_T^K < 0$) is always unequalizing. Surprisingly, however, a neutral tax ($\Pi_T^K = 0$) can be unequalizing when it creates RR.

Table 3-2 identifies the effect of adding a tax to a system that has no other tax or transfer in place.

Table 3-3 shows that adding a neutral tax (where progressivity is calculated with respect to households ranked by the original income) could be unequalizing.

---

[6] This can be shown intuitively. For any income value, the deviation of highest and lowest income from the average and their rank from the average rank is the highest. The underlying covariance formula multiplies these deviations for each person and adds them together. Since Gini multiplies the largest deviation of income by the largest deviation of rank (for example, for a person with the highest or lowest income) and then adds these values, Gini is bigger than any other concentration coefficient that uses rankings that do not rank by the income concept of interest.

TABLE 3-2
Marginal Contribution of a Tax without Another Tax or Transfer in Place

	Adding a tax that is	
Regressive $\prod_T^K < 0$	Neutral $\prod_T^K = 0$	Progressive $\prod_T^K > 0$
Always unequalizing	Always no change in equality or unequalizing	Equalizing if and only if equation 3-22 holds

TABLE 3-3
Addition of a Neutral Tax with an Unequalizing Effect

Individual	Original income (OI)	Tax (T)	OI–T
1	1.00	0.00	1.00
2	11.00	0.00	11.00
3	12.00	10.00	2.00
4	13.00	0.00	13.00
Total	37.00	10.00	27.00
Average	9.25	2.50	6.75
Gini	0.2500	n.c.	0.4167
C^X	n.c.	0.2500	n.c.
$\prod_T^{K^X}$	. . .	0.0000	. . .

Note: In calculating progressivity, households' rank with respect to their original income is used.

n.c. = Not calculated; . . . = Not applicable.

2.2 The Case of Adding a Tax to a System That Has a Transfer in Place

Because there is only one transfer in place and only one tax is added, equation 3-13 can be simplified as follows:

$$M_T = \left\{ (G_X - C_X^{X-T+B}) + \left(\frac{(1-g)\prod_T^{RS^{X-T+B}} + (1+b)\rho_B^{RS^{X-T+B}}}{1-g+b} \right) \right\} - \left\{ (G_X - C_X^{X+B}) + \rho_B^{RS^{X+B}} \right\}.$$

The preceding equation can be simplified one more step, as

$$M_T = (C_X^{X+B} - C_X^{X-T+B}) + \left(\frac{(1-g)\prod_T^{RS^{X-T+B}} + (1+b)\rho_B^{RS^{X-T+B}}}{1-g+b} \right) - \rho_B^{RS^{X+B}}$$

or

$$M_T = (C_X^{X+B} - C_X^{X-T+B}) + \left(\frac{(1-g)\Pi_T^{RS^{X-T+B}} + g\rho_B^{RS^{X-T+B}}}{1-g+b} \right) + \left(\rho_B^{RS^{X-T+B}} - \rho_B^{RS^{X+B}} \right).$$

Recalling the notation section and the definitions of $\rho_B^{RS^{X-T+B}}$ and $\rho_B^{RS^{X+B}}$, which are equal to $(C_X^{X-T+B} - C_{X+B}^{X-T+B})$ and $(C_X^{X+B} - G_{X+B})$, respectively, we can rewrite the preceding equation as follows:

$$(3\text{-}23) \qquad M_T = \left(\frac{(1-g)\Pi_T^{RS^{X-T+B}} + g\rho_B^{RS^{X-T+B}}}{1-g+b} \right) + \left(G_{X+B} - C_{X+B}^{X-T+B} \right).$$

Now, notice that based on equation 3-23, if ranking of the households does not change before and after adding the tax, the last parentheses become equal to zero. As discussed previously, the last set of parentheses is generally a non-negative term and reaches its minimum when ranking of individuals before and after adding the tax remains the same.

Now, using these generally defined Kakwani indexes, equation 3-23 can be written as follows:

$$(3\text{-}24) \qquad M_T = \left(\frac{g\Pi_T^{K^{X-T+B}} + \frac{gb}{1+b}\rho_B^{K^{X-T+B}}}{1-g+b} \right) + \left(G_{X+B} - C_{X+B}^{X-T+B} \right).$$

For a tax to be equalizing, equation (3-24) should be positive, that is,

$$(3\text{-}25) \qquad M_T = \left(\frac{g\Pi_T^{K^{X-T+B}} + \frac{gb}{1+b}\rho_B^{K^{X-T+B}}}{1-g+b} \right) + (G_{X+B} - C_{X+B}^{X-T+B}) > 0.$$

Using the preceding condition, table 3-4 helps to determine whether adding a tax to a system with a transfer in place would reduce inequality.

The most counterintuitive result is that adding a regressive tax to a regressive transfer, where progressivity is calculated with respect to the Final Income ranking of households, can reduce inequality. The following examples illustrate this case and other counterintuitive results.

Table 3-5 shows that adding a regressive tax to a fiscal system with a regressive transfer (where progressivity is calculated with respect to households ranked by original income) could be equalizing.

TABLE 3-4
Marginal Contribution of a Tax with a Transfer in Place

		To a system with a transfer that, with respect to the end income ranking, is		
		Regressive $\rho_B^{K^{X-T+B}} < 0$	Neutral $\rho_B^{K^{X-T+B}} = 0$	Progressive $\rho_B^{K^{X-T+B}} > 0$
Adding a tax that, with respect to the end income ranking, is	**Regressive** $\Pi_T^{K^{X-T+B}} < 0$	More equalizing if and only if condition 3-25 holds	More equalizing if and only if condition 3-25 holds	More equalizing if and only if condition 3-25 holds
	Neutral $\Pi_T^{K^{X-T+B}} = 0$	More equalizing if and only if condition 3-25 holds	More equalizing if and only if condition 3-25 holds	Always equalizing
	Progressive $\Pi_T^{K^{X-T+B}} > 0$	More equalizing if and only if condition 3-25 holds	Always equalizing	Always equalizing

Note: In calculating progressivity, households' rank with respect to their original income is used.

TABLE 3-5
Addition of a Regressive Tax with an Equalizing Effect to a Fiscal System with a Regressive Transfer

Individual	Original income (OI)	Benefit (B)	OI + B	Tax (T)	OI − T	End income (EI)
1	10.00	0.90	10.90	1.00	9.00	9.90
2	11.00	0.00	11.00	0.20	10.80	10.80
3	12.00	1.10	13.10	2.20	9.80	10.90
4	13.00	0.00	13.00	4.10	8.90	8.90
Total	46.00	2.00	48.00	7.50	38.50	40.50
Average	11.50	0.50	12.00	1.88	9.63	10.13
Gini	0.0543	n.c.	0.0448	n.c.	0.0422	0.0426
C^{X-T+B}	−0.0109	0.3	0.0021	−0.2167	0.0292	n.c.
$\Pi_T^{K^{X-T+B}}$ or $\rho_B^{K^{X-T+B}}$	. . .	−0.3109	. . .	−0.2058	. . .	. . .

Note: In calculating progressivity, households' rank with respect to their end income is used.

n.c. = Not calculated; . . . = Not applicable.

TABLE 3-6

Addition of a Regressive Tax with an Equalizing Effect to a Fiscal System
with a Neutral Transfer

Individual	Original income (OI)	Benefit (B)	OI + B	Tax (T)	OI − T	End income (EI)
1	1.00	0.00	1.00	0.00	1.00	1.00
2	11.00	0.00	11.00	1.10	9.90	9.90
3	12.00	2.00	14.00	3.00	9.00	11.00
4	13.00	0.00	13.00	1.00	12.00	12.00
Total	37.00	2.00	39.00	5.10	31.90	33.90
Average	9.25	0.50	9.75	1.28	7.98	8.48
Gini	0.2500	n.c.	0.2628	n.c.	0.2657	0.2515
C^{X-T+B}	0.2500	0.2500	0.2500	0.2402	0.2516	n.c.
$\Pi_T^{K^{X-T+B}}$ or $\rho_B^{K^{X-T+B}}$	...	0.0000	...	−0.0098	...	...

Note: In calculating progressivity, households' rank with respect to their end income is used.

n.c. = Not calculated; . . . = Not applicable.

Table 3-6 shows that adding a regressive tax to a fiscal system with a neutral transfer (where progressivity is calculated with respect to households ranked by original
income) could be equalizing.

Table 3-7 shows that adding a regressive tax to a fiscal system with a progressive
transfer (where progressivity is calculated with respect to households ranked by original income) could be equalizing.

Table 3-8 shows that adding a neutral tax to a fiscal system with a regressive transfer (where progressivity is calculated with respect to households ranked by original
income) could be equalizing.

Table 3-9 shows that adding a neutral tax to a fiscal system with a neutral transfer
(where progressivity is calculated with respect to households ranked by original income) could be equalizing.

Table 3-10 shows that adding a neutral tax to a fiscal system with a progressive
transfer (where progressivity is calculated with respect to households ranked by original income) could be equalizing.

Table 3-11 shows that adding a progressive tax to a fiscal system with a regressive
transfer (where progressivity is calculated with respect to households ranked by original income) could be unequalizing.

Although equation 3-23 is derived using the R-S index that is calculated with respect to the end income ranking of households, one can calculate a similar derivation

TABLE 3-7

Addition of a Regressive Tax with an Equalizing Effect to a Fiscal System with a Progressive Transfer

Individual	Original income (OI)	Benefit (B)	OI + B	Tax (T)	OI – T	End income (EI)
1	1.00	0.10	1.10	0.00	1.00	1.10
2	11.00	0.00	11.00	1.10	9.90	9.90
3	12.00	1.10	13.10	3.00	9.00	10.10
4	13.00	0.00	13.00	1.00	12.00	12.00
Total	37.00	1.20	38.20	5.10	31.90	33.10
Average	9.25	0.30	9.55	1.28	7.98	8.28
Gini	0.2500	n.c.	0.2487	n.c.	0.2657	0.2485
C^{X-T+B}	0.2500	0.1667	0.2474	0.2402	0.2516	n.c.
$\Pi_T^{K^{X-T+B}}$ or $\rho_B^{K^{X-T+B}}$	...	0.0833	...	–0.0098	...	...

Note: In calculating progressivity, households' rank with respect to their end income is used.

n.c. = Not calculated; ... = Not applicable.

TABLE 3-8

Addition of a Neutral Tax with an Equalizing Effect to a Fiscal System with a Regressive Transfer

Individual	Original income (OI)	Benefit (B)	OI + B	Tax (T)	OI – T	End income (EI)
1	1.00	0.00	1.00	0.00	1.00	1.00
2	11.00	0.00	11.00	1.00	10.00	10.00
3	12.00	2.00	14.00	3.00	9.00	11.00
4	13.00	0.10	13.10	1.00	12.00	12.10
Total	37.00	2.10	39.10	5.00	32.00	34.10
Average	9.25	0.53	9.78	1.25	8.00	8.53
Gini	0.2500	n.c.	0.2628	n.c.	0.2656	0.2515
C^{X-T+B}	0.2500	0.2738	0.2513	0.2500	0.2500	n.c.
$\Pi_T^{K^{X-T+B}}$ or $\rho_B^{K^{X-T+B}}$	...	–0.0238	...	0.0000	...	...

Note: In calculating progressivity, households' rank with respect to their end income is used.

n.c. = Not calculated; ... = Not applicable.

TABLE 3-9

Addition of a Neutral Tax with an Equalizing Effect to a Fiscal System with a Neutral Transfer

Individual	Original income (OI)	Benefit (B)	OI + B	Tax (T)	OI − T	End income (EI)
1	1.00	0.00	1.00	0.00	1.00	1.00
2	11.00	0.00	11.00	2.00	9.00	9.00
3	12.00	2.00	14.00	4.00	8.00	10.00
4	13.00	0.00	13.00	2.00	11.00	11.00
Total	37.00	2.00	39.00	8.00	29.00	31.00
Average	9.25	0.50	9.75	2.00	7.25	7.75
Gini	0.2500	n.c.	0.2628	n.c.	0.2672	0.2500
C^{X-T+B}	0.2500	0.2500	0.2500	0.2500	0.2500	n.c.
$\Pi_T^{K^{X-T+B}}$ or $\rho_B^{K^{X-T+B}}$	...	0.0000	...	0.0000	...	...

Note: In calculating progressivity, households' rank with respect to their end income is used.

n.c. = Not calculated; ... = Not applicable.

TABLE 3-10

Addition of a Neutral Tax with an Equalizing Effect to a Fiscal System with a Progressive Transfer

Individual	Original income (OI)	Benefit (B)	OI + B	Tax (T)	OI − T	End income (EI)
1	1.00	0.10	1.10	0.00	1.00	1.10
2	11.00	0.00	11.00	1.00	10.00	10.00
3	12.00	2.00	14.00	3.00	9.00	11.00
4	13.00	0.00	13.00	1.00	12.00	12.00
Total	37.00	2.10	39.10	5.00	32.00	34.10
Average	9.25	0.53	9.78	1.25	8.00	8.53
Gini	0.2500	n.c.	0.2602	n.c.	0.2656	0.2471
C^{X-T+B}	0.2500	0.2024	0.2474	0.2500	0.2500	n.c.
$\Pi_T^{K^{X-T+B}}$ or $\rho_B^{K^{X-T+B}}$	...	0.0476	...	0.0000	...	...

Note: In calculating progressivity, households' rank with respect to their end income is used.

n.c. = Not calculated; ... = Not applicable.

TABLE 3-11

Addition of a Progressive Tax with an Unequalizing Effect to a Fiscal System with a Regressive Transfer

Individual	Original income (OI)	Benefit (B)	OI + B	Tax (T)	OI − T	End income (EI)
1	10.00	30.00	40.00	1.00	9.00	39.00
2	11.00	0.00	11.00	1.00	10.00	10.00
3	12.00	0.00	12.00	1.00	11.00	11.00
4	16.00	0.00	16.00	2.00	14.00	14.00
Total	49.00	30.00	79.00	5.00	44.00	74.00
Average	12.25	7.50	19.75	1.25	11.00	18.50
Gini	0.0969	n.c.	0.2880	n.c.	0.0909	0.3041
C^{X-T+B}	0.0051	0.7500	0.2880	0.0500	0.0000	n.c.
$\Pi_T^{K^{X-T+B}}$ or $\rho_B^{K^{X-T+B}}$	. . .	−0.7449	. . .	0.0449	. . .	. . .

Note: In calculating progressivity, households' rank with respect to their end income is used.

n.c. = Not calculated; . . . = Not applicable.

using the R-S index that is calculated with respect to the original income ranking, as shown in the following equation:

$$M_T = \left(\frac{(1-g)\Pi_T^{RS} + g\rho_B^{RS}}{1-g+b} \right) + \left[\underbrace{\left(C_{X-T+B}^X - G_{X-T+B} \right)}_{\text{Reranking in the whole system}} - \underbrace{\left(C_{X+B}^X - G_{X+B} \right)}_{\text{Reranking before the tax is added}} \right].$$

Because both terms in the brackets are non-positive, the bracket could be positive, zero, or negative. For the tax to be equalizing, the following condition should hold:

$$\left(\frac{(1-g)\Pi_T^{RS} + g\rho_B^{RS}}{1-g+b} \right) + \left[\left(C_{X-T+B}^X - G_{X-T+B} \right) - \left(C_{X+B}^X - G_{X+B} \right) \right] > 0$$

or

$$(3\text{-}26) \quad \left(\frac{g\Pi_T^K + \dfrac{gb}{1+b}\rho_B^K}{1-g+b} \right) + \overbrace{\left[\underbrace{\left(C_{X-T+B}^X - G_{X-T+B} \right)}_{\text{Reranking after the tax is added}} - \underbrace{\left(C_{X+B}^X - G_{X+B} \right)}_{\text{Reranking before the tax is added}} \right]}^{\text{Marginal effect of the tax on reranking}} > 0.$$

TABLE 3-12
Marginal Contribution of a Tax with a Transfer in Place

		To a system with a transfer that, with respect to the original income ranking, is		
		Regressive $\rho_B^K < 0$	Neutral $\rho_B^K = 0$	Progressive $\rho_B^K > 0$
Adding a tax that, with respect to the original income ranking, is	**Regressive** $\Pi_T^K < 0$	Equalizing if and only if condition 3-26 holds	Equalizing if and only if condition 3-26 holds	Equalizing if and only if condition 3-26 holds
	Neutral $\Pi_T^K = 0$	Equalizing if and only if condition 3-26 holds	Equalizing if and only if condition 3-26 holds	Equalizing if and only if condition 3-26 holds
	Progressive $\Pi_T^K > 0$	Equalizing if and only if condition 3-26 holds	Equalizing if and only if condition 3-26 holds	Equalizing if and only if condition 3-26 holds

Note: In calculating progressivity, households' rank with respect to their original income is used.

As shown in table 3-12, using the traditional Kakwani index (that is, when the index is calculated with respect to the original income ranking of households) would not result in any certainty about whether the addition of a tax reduces inequality.

Table 3-12 contains some counterintuitive cases that the following examples will help to explain. Table 3-13, for instance, shows that adding a regressive tax to a fiscal system with a regressive transfer (where progressivity is calculated with respect to households ranked by original income) could be equalizing.

Table 3-14 shows that adding a regressive tax to a fiscal system with a neutral transfer (where progressivity is calculated with respect to households ranked by original income) could be equalizing.

Table 3-15 shows that adding a regressive tax to a fiscal system with a progressive transfer (where progressivity is calculated with respect to households ranked by original income) could be equalizing.

Table 3-16 shows that adding a neutral tax to a fiscal system with a regressive transfer (where progressivity is calculated with respect to households ranked by original income) could be equalizing.

Table 3-17 shows that adding a neutral tax to a fiscal system with a regressive transfer (where progressivity is calculated with respect to households ranked by original income) could be unequalizing.

TABLE 3-13

Addition of a Regressive Tax with an Equalizing Effect to a Fiscal System with a Regressive Transfer

Individual	Original income (OI)	Benefit (B)	OI + B	Tax (T)	OI − T	End income (EI)
1	1.00	0.00	1.00	0.10	0.90	0.90
2	11.00	0.00	11.00	1.00	10.00	10.00
3	12.00	2.00	14.00	3.00	9.00	11.00
4	13.00	0.40	13.40	1.00	12.00	12.40
Total	37.00	2.40	39.40	5.10	31.90	34.30
Average	9.25	0.60	9.85	1.28	7.98	8.58
Gini	0.2500	n.c.	0.2627	n.c.	0.2688	0.2587
C^X	0.2500	0.3333	0.2551	0.2304	0.2531	0.2587
Π_T^K or ρ_B^K	. . .	−0.0833	. . .	−0.0196	. . .	. . .

Note: In calculating progressivity, households' rank with respect to their original income is used.

n.c. = Not calculated; . . . = Not applicable.

TABLE 3-14

Addition of a Regressive Tax with an Equalizing Effect to a Fiscal System with a Neutral Transfer

Individual	Original income (OI)	Benefit (B)	OI + B	Tax (T)	OI − T	End income (EI)
1	1.00	0.00	1.00	0.10	0.90	0.90
2	11.00	0.00	11.00	1.00	10.00	10.00
3	12.00	2.00	14.00	3.00	9.00	11.00
4	13.00	0.00	13.00	1.00	12.00	12.00
Total	37.00	2.00	39.00	5.10	31.90	33.90
Average	9.25	0.50	9.75	1.28	7.98	8.48
Gini	0.2500	n.c.	0.2628	n.c.	0.2688	0.2529
C^X	0.2500	0.2500	0.2500	0.2304	0.2531	0.2529
Π_T^K or ρ_B^K	. . .	0.0000	. . .	−0.0196	. . .	. . .

Note: In calculating progressivity, households' rank with respect to their original income is used.

n.c. = Not calculated; . . . = Not applicable.

TABLE 3-15

Addition of a Regressive Tax with an Equalizing Effect to a Fiscal System
with a Progressive Transfer

Individual	Original income (OI)	Benefit (B)	OI + B	Tax (T)	OI − T	End income (EI)
1	1.00	1.00	2.00	0.10	0.90	1.90
2	11.00	0.00	11.00	1.00	10.00	10.00
3	12.00	2.00	14.00	3.00	9.00	11.00
4	13.00	0.40	13.40	1.00	12.00	12.40
Total	37.00	3.40	40.40	5.10	31.90	35.30
Average	9.25	0.85	10.10	1.28	7.98	8.83
Gini	0.2500	n.c.	0.2376	n.c.	0.2688	0.2302
C^X	0.2500	0.0147	0.2302	0.2304	0.2531	0.2302
Π_T^K or ρ_B^K	...	0.2353	...	−0.0196	...	...

Note: In calculating progressivity, households' rank with respect to their original income is used.

n.c. = Not calculated; . . . = Not applicable.

TABLE 3-16

Addition of a Neutral Tax with an Equalizing Effect to a Fiscal System
with a Regressive Transfer

Individual	Original income (OI)	Benefit (B)	OI + B	Tax (T)	OI − T	End income (EI)
1	1.00	0.00	1.00	0.00	1.00	1.00
2	11.00	0.00	11.00	1.00	10.00	10.00
3	12.00	2.00	14.00	3.00	9.00	11.00
4	13.00	0.10	13.10	1.00	12.00	12.10
Total	37.00	2.10	39.10	5.00	32.00	34.10
Average	9.25	0.53	9.78	1.25	8.00	8.53
Gini	0.2500	n.c.	0.2628	n.c.	0.2656	0.2515
C^X	0.2500	0.2738	0.2513	0.2500	0.2500	0.2515
Π_T^K or ρ_B^K	...	−0.0238	...	0.0000	...	...

Note: In calculating progressivity, households' rank with respect to their original income is used.

n.c. = Not calculated; . . . = Not applicable.

Table 3-18 shows that adding a neutral tax to a fiscal system with a neutral transfer (where progressivity is calculated with respect to households ranked by original income) could be unequalizing.

Table 3-19 shows that adding a neutral tax to a fiscal system with a neutral transfer (where progressivity is calculated with respect to households ranked by original income) could be equalizing.

TABLE 3-17

Addition of a Neutral Tax with an Unequalizing Effect to a Fiscal System with a Regressive Transfer

Individual	Original income (OI)	Benefit (B)	OI + B	Tax (T)	OI – T	End income (EI)
1	1.00	0.00	1.00	0.00	1.00	1.00
2	11.00	0.00	11.00	1.00	10.00	10.00
3	12.00	2.00	14.00	5.00	7.00	9.00
4	13.00	0.10	13.10	1.00	12.00	12.10
Total	37.00	2.10	39.10	7.00	30.00	32.10
Average	9.25	0.53	9.78	1.75	7.50	8.03
Gini	0.2500	n.c.	0.2628	n.c.	0.3000	0.2671
C^X	0.2500	0.2738	0.2513	0.2500	0.2500	0.2516
Π_T^K or ρ_B^K	. . .	−0.0238	. . .	0.0000	. . .	. . .

Note: In calculating progressivity, households' rank with respect to their original income is used.

n.c. = Not calculated; . . . = Not applicable.

TABLE 3-18

Addition of a Neutral Tax with an Unequalizing Effect to a Fiscal System with a Neutral Transfer

Individual	Original income (OI)	Benefit (B)	OI + B	Tax (T)	OI – T	End income (EI)
1	1.00	0.00	1.00	0.00	1.00	1.00
2	11.00	0.00	11.00	1.00	10.00	10.00
3	12.00	2.00	14.00	5.00	7.00	9.00
4	13.00	0.00	13.00	1.00	12.00	12.00
Total	37.00	2.00	39.00	7.00	30.00	32.00
Average	9.25	0.50	9.75	1.75	7.50	8.00
Gini	0.2500	n.c.	0.2628	n.c.	0.3000	0.2656
C^X	0.2500	0.2500	0.2500	0.2500	0.2500	0.2500
Π_T^K or ρ_B^K	. . .	0.0000	. . .	0.0000	. . .	. . .

Note: In calculating progressivity, households' rank with respect to their original income is used.

n.c. = Not calculated; . . . = Not applicable.

TABLE 3-19

Addition of a Neutral Tax with an Equalizing Effect to a Fiscal System
with a Neutral Transfer

Individual	Original income (OI)	Benefit (B)	OI + B	Tax (T)	OI − T	End income (EI)
1	1.00	0.00	1.00	0.00	1.00	1.00
2	11.00	0.00	11.00	1.00	10.00	10.00
3	12.00	2.00	14.00	3.00	9.00	11.00
4	13.00	0.00	13.00	1.00	12.00	12.00
Total	37.00	2.00	39.00	5.00	32.00	34.00
Average	9.25	0.50	9.75	1.25	8.00	8.50
Gini	0.2500	n.c.	0.2628	n.c.	0.2656	0.2500
C^X	0.2500	0.2500	0.2500	0.2500	0.2500	0.2500
Π_T^K or ρ_B^K	. . .	0.0000	. . .	0.0000	. . .	. . .

Note: In calculating progressivity, households' rank with respect to their original income is used.

n.c. = Not calculated; . . . = Not applicable.

TABLE 3-20

Addition of a Neutral Tax with an Equalizing Effect to a Fiscal System
with a Progressive Transfer

Individual	Original income (OI)	Benefit (B)	OI + B	Tax (T)	OI − T	End income (EI)
1	1.00	0.00	1.00	0.00	1.00	1.00
2	11.00	0.10	11.10	1.00	10.00	10.10
3	12.00	2.00	14.00	3.00	9.00	11.00
4	13.00	0.00	13.00	1.00	12.00	12.00
Total	37.00	2.10	39.10	5.00	32.00	34.10
Average	9.25	0.53	9.78	1.25	8.00	8.53
Gini	0.2500	n.c.	0.2615	n.c.	0.2656	0.2485
C^X	0.2500	0.2262	0.2487	0.2500	0.2500	0.2485
Π_T^K or ρ_B^K	. . .	0.0238	. . .	0.0000	. . .	. . .

Note: In calculating progressivity, households' rank with respect to their original income is used.

n.c. = Not calculated; . . . = Not applicable.

Table 3-20 shows that adding a neutral tax to a fiscal system with a progressive transfer (where progressivity is calculated with respect to households ranked by original income) could be equalizing.

Table 3-21 shows that adding a neutral tax to a fiscal system with a progressive transfer (where progressivity is calculated with respect to households ranked by original income) could be unequalizing.

TABLE 3-21

Addition of a Neutral Tax with an Unequalizing Effect to a Fiscal System
with a Progressive Transfer

Individual	Original income (OI)	Benefit (B)	OI + B	Tax (T)	OI − T	End income (EI)
1	1.00	0.00	1.00	0.00	1.00	1.00
2	11.00	0.10	11.10	1.00	10.00	10.10
3	12.00	2.00	14.00	5.00	7.00	9.00
4	13.00	0.00	13.00	1.00	12.00	12.00
Total	37.00	2.10	39.10	7.00	30.00	32.10
Average	9.25	0.53	9.78	1.75	7.50	8.03
Gini	0.2500	n.c.	0.2615	n.c.	0.3000	0.2656
C^X	0.2500	0.2262	0.2487	0.2500	0.2500	0.2484
Π_T^K or ρ_B^K	...	0.0238	...	0.0000	...	...

Note: In calculating progressivity, households' rank with respect to their original income is used.

n.c. = Not calculated; ... = Not applicable.

TABLE 3-22

Addition of a Progressive Tax with an Unequalizing Effect to a Fiscal System
with a Regressive Transfer

Individual	Original income (OI)	Benefit (B)	OI + B	Tax (T)	OI − T	End income (EI)
1	1.00	0.00	1.00	0.00	1.00	1.00
2	11.00	0.00	11.00	1.00	10.00	10.00
3	12.00	2.00	14.00	5.00	7.00	9.00
4	13.00	0.10	13.10	1.10	11.90	12.00
Total	37.00	2.10	39.10	7.10	29.90	32.00
Average	9.25	0.53	9.78	1.78	7.48	8.00
Gini	0.2500	n.c.	0.2628	n.c.	0.2985	0.2656
C^X	0.2500	0.2738	0.2513	0.2570	0.2483	0.2500
Π_T^K or ρ_B^K	...	−0.0238	...	0.0070	...	...

Note: In calculating progressivity, households' rank with respect to their original income is used.

n.c. = Not calculated; ... = Not applicable.

Table 3-22 shows that adding a progressive tax to a fiscal system with a regressive transfer (where progressivity is calculated with respect to households ranked by original income) could be unequalizing.

Table 3-23 shows that adding a progressive tax to a fiscal system with a neutral transfer (where progressivity is calculated with respect to households ranked by original income) could be unequalizing.

TABLE 3-23

Addition of a Progressive Tax with an Unequalizing Effect to a Fiscal System with a Neutral Transfer

Individual	Original income (OI)	Benefit (B)	OI + B	Tax (T)	OI − T	End income (EI)
1	10.00	1.00	11.00	0.00	10.00	11.00
2	11.00	1.10	12.10	0.00	11.00	12.10
3	12.00	1.20	13.20	0.00	12.00	13.20
4	13.00	1.30	14.30	5.00	8.00	9.30
Total	46.00	4.60	50.60	5.00	41.00	45.60
Average	11.50	1.15	12.65	1.25	10.25	11.40
Gini	0.0543	n.c.	0.0543	n.c.	0.0793	0.0702
C^X	0.0543	0.0543	0.0543	0.7500	−0.0305	−0.0219
Π_T^K or ρ_B^K	...	0.0000	...	0.6957	...	...

Note: In calculating progressivity, households' rank with respect to their original income is used.

n.c. = Not calculated; . . . = Not applicable.

Table 3-24 shows that adding a progressive tax to a fiscal system with a progressive transfer (where progressivity is calculated with respect to households ranked by original income) could be unequalizing.

2.3 The Case of Adding a Tax to a System with Multiple Taxes and Transfers in Place

Recall from equation 3-13 that

$$M_{T_1} = \left\{ (G_X - C_X^Z) + \left(\frac{\sum_{i=1}^{n}(1-g_i)\Pi_{T_i}^{RS^Z} + \sum_{j=1}^{m}(1+b_j)\rho_{B_j}^{RS^Z}}{1 - \sum_{i=1}^{n}g_i + \sum_{j=1}^{m}b_j} \right) \right\}$$
$$- \left\{ \left(G_X - C_X^{Z\backslash T_1}\right) + \left(\frac{\sum_{i=2}^{n}(1-g_i)\Pi_{T_i}^{RS^{Z\backslash T_1}} + \sum_{j=1}^{m}(1+b_j)\rho_{B_j}^{RS^{Z\backslash T_1}}}{1 - \sum_{i=2}^{n}g_i + \sum_{j=1}^{m}b_j} \right) \right\}.$$

For T_1 to be equalizing, this equation has to be positive;[7] that is,

$$(3\text{-}27) \quad \left\{ (G_X - C_X^Z) + \left(\frac{\sum_{i=1}^{n}(1-g_i)\Pi_{T_i}^{RS^Z} + \sum_{j=1}^{m}(1+b_j)\rho_{B_j}^{RS^Z}}{1 - \sum_{i=1}^{n}g_i + \sum_{j=1}^{m}b_j} \right) \right\}$$
$$- \left\{ \left(G_X - C_X^{Z\backslash T_1}\right) + \left(\frac{\sum_{i=2}^{n}(1-g_i)\Pi_{T_i}^{RS^{Z\backslash T_1}} + \sum_{j=1}^{m}(1+b_j)\rho_{B_j}^{RS^{Z\backslash T_1}}}{1 - \sum_{i=2}^{n}g_i + \sum_{j=1}^{m}b_j} \right) \right\} > 0.$$

---

[7] Recall from the notation section that $Z = X - \sum_{i=1}^{n}T_i + \sum_{j=1}^{m}B_j$ and $Z\backslash T_1 = X - \sum_{i=2}^{n}T_i + \sum_{j=1}^{m}B_j$.

TABLE 3-24

Addition of a Progressive Tax with an Unequalizing Effect to a Fiscal System with a Progressive Transfer

Individual	Original income (OI)	Benefit (B)	OI + B	Tax (T)	OI − T	End income (EI)
1	1.00	0.10	1.10	0.00	1.00	1.10
2	11.00	0.00	11.00	1.00	10.00	10.00
3	12.00	2.00	14.00	5.00	7.00	9.00
4	13.00	0.00	13.00	1.10	11.90	11.90
Total	37.00	2.10	39.10	7.10	29.90	32.00
Average	9.25	0.53	9.78	1.78	7.48	8.00
Gini	0.2500	n.c.	0.2602	n.c.	0.2985	0.2609
C^X	0.2500	0.2024	0.2474	0.2570	0.2483	0.2453
$\prod_T^K$ or ρ_B^K	...	0.0476	...	0.0070	...	...

Note: In calculating progressivity, households' rank with respect to their original income is used.

n.c. = Not calculated; . . . = Not applicable.

If adding this specific tax does not change the end income ranking of households (that is, if end income rankings are the same before and after adding the tax), then ranking with respect to Z and Y is the same, which simplifies the whole equation to

$$\left(1 - \sum_{i=2}^{n} g_i + \sum_{j=1}^{m} b_j\right)(1 - g_1)\prod_{T_1}^{RS^Z} > -g_1\left(\sum_{i=2}^{n}(1 - g_i)\prod_{T_i}^{RS^{Z\backslash T_1}} + \sum_{j=1}^{m}(1 + b_j)\rho_{B_j}^{RS^{Z\backslash T_1}}\right),$$

which is equal to

$$\prod_{T_1}^{RS^Z} > -\frac{g_1}{(1 - g_1)}\left(\frac{\sum_{i=2}^{n}(1 - g_i)\prod_{T_i}^{RS^{Z\backslash T_1}} + \sum_{j=1}^{m}(1 + b_j)\rho_{B_j}^{RS^{Z\backslash T_1}}}{1 - \sum_{i=2}^{n}g_i + \sum_{j=1}^{m}b_j}\right)$$

or

$$\prod_{T_1}^{RS^Z} > -\frac{g_1}{(1 - g_1)}\left(C_X^{Z\backslash T_1} - G_{Z\backslash T_1}\right)$$

or

(3-28)
$$\prod_{T_1}^{K^Z} < \left(C_X^{Z\backslash T_1} - G_{Z\backslash T_1}\right).$$

The term on the right-hand side is the modified VE term, which was introduced in the notation section as

$$VE_{X, Z\backslash T_1}^{Z\backslash T_1} = C_X^{Z\backslash T_1} - G_{Z\backslash T_1}.$$

TABLE 3-25

Marginal Contribution of a Tax with Multiple Taxes and Transfers in Place

		To a system with multiple taxes and transfers where its vertical equity (with respect to the final income ranking) is		
		Negative $VE^{Z \backslash T_1}_{X, Z \backslash T_1} < 0$	**Zero** $VE^{Z \backslash T_1}_{X, Z \backslash T_1} = 0$	**Positive** $VE^{Z \backslash T_1}_{X, Z \backslash T_1} > 0$
Adding a tax that, with respect to the final incomes ranking (Z), is	**Regressive** $\Pi^{KZ}_T < 0$	Equalizing if and only if condition 3-29 holds	Always equalizing	Always equalizing
	Neutral $\Pi^{KZ}_T = 0$	Always unequalizing	No change in inequality	Always equalizing
	Progressive $\Pi^{KZ}_T > 0$	Always unequalizing	Always unequalizing	Equalizing if and only if condition 3-29 holds

Note: $Z = X - \sum^n_{i=1} T_i + \sum^m_{j=1} B_j$ and $Z \backslash T_1 = X - \sum^n_{i=2} T_i + \sum^m_{j=1} B_j$. The new tax does not change the end income ranking of individuals.

Thus, equation 3-28 can be written as follows:

(3-29) $$\Pi^{KZ}_{T_1} < VE^{Z \backslash T_1}_{X, Z \backslash T_1}.$$

Table 3-25 shows how one can determine whether adding a tax to a system of taxes and transfers reduces inequality when the new tax does not change the end income ranking of households. For the results in table 3-25 to hold, the tax that we are interested in should not have any effect on the end income ranking of households. If that is not the case, then equation 3-27 cannot be simplified much further and the effect of adding such a tax cannot be determined using a simple rule of thumb from the table.

As an alternative, one can use the progressivity with respect to the original income in the analysis. For this purpose, we need to use equation 3-16:

$$M_{T_1} = \left[\frac{\left[(1-g_1) \Pi^{RS}_{T_1} \right] + \left[(g_1) \overbrace{\left(G_X - C^X_{X \backslash T_1} \right)}^{VE \text{ of the system without } T_1} \right]}{\left(1 - \sum^n_{i=1} g_i + \sum^m_{j=1} b_j \right)} \right] + \underbrace{\left[\left(C^X_Z - G_Z \right) - \left(C^X_{X \backslash T_1} - G_{X \backslash T_1} \right) \right]}_{\text{Contribution of } T_1 \text{ to reranking}}.$$

For a tax to be equalizing when it is added to a system of taxes and transfers, the following condition should hold:

$$(3\text{-}30) \quad M_{T_1} = \left[\left(\frac{\left[(1-g_1)\Pi_{T_1}^{RS}\right]+\left[(g_1) \overbrace{\left(G_X - C_{X\backslash T_1}^X\right)}^{\text{VE of the system without } T_1}\right]}{\left(1-\sum_{i=1}^{n}g_i+\sum_{j=1}^{m}b_j\right)}\right)\right] + \underbrace{\left[(C_Z^X - G_Z)-\left(C_{X\backslash T_1}^X - G_{X\backslash T_1}\right)\right]}_{\text{Contribution of } T_1 \text{ to reranking}} > 0$$

or

$$(3\text{-}31) \quad M_{T_1} = \left[\left(\frac{\left[g_1\Pi_{T_1}^{K}\right]+\left[(g_1) \overbrace{\left(G_X - C_{X\backslash T_1}^X\right)}^{\text{VE of the system without } T_1}\right]}{\left(1-\sum_{i=1}^{n}g_i+\sum_{j=1}^{m}b_j\right)}\right)\right] + \underbrace{\left[(C_Z^X - G_Z)-\left(C_{X\backslash T_1}^X - G_{X\backslash T_1}\right)\right]}_{\text{Contribution of } T_1 \text{ to reranking}} > 0.$$

3 In the Presence of Reranking, Is the Marginal Contribution of a Transfer Equalizing?

This section is similar to the previous one, so I have presented only the minimum derivations except in cases of significant differences.

3.1 The Case of Only One Transfer

As in section 2.1, we begin with the following equation (using equation 3-18):

$$(3\text{-}32) \qquad\qquad M_B = \rho_B^{RS} + (C_{X+B}^X - G_{X+B}).$$

For a transfer to be equalizing, equation 3-32 has to be positive; that is,

$$M_B = \rho_B^{RS} + (C_{X+B}^X - G_{X+B}) > 0$$

Or

$$(3\text{-}33) \qquad\qquad \rho_B^{RS} > (G_{X+B} - C_{X+B}^X)$$

or

TABLE 3-26
Marginal Contribution of a Transfer with No Other Tax or
Transfer in Place

Regressive $\rho_B^K < 0$	Neutral $\rho_B^K = 0$	Progressive $\rho_B^K > 0$
Always unequalizing	Always no change in equality or unequalizing	Equalizing if and only if equation 3-34 holds

TABLE 3-27
Addition of a Neutral Transfer with Unequalizing Results

Individual	Original income (OI)	Benefit (B)	OI + B
1	1.00	0.00	1.00
2	11.00	0.00	11.00
3	12.00	10.00	22.00
4	13.00	0.00	13.00
Total	37.00	10.00	47.00
Average	9.25	2.50	11.75
Gini	0.2500	n.c.	0.3457
C^X	n.c. ·	0.2500	n.c.
$\rho_B^{K^X}$	...	0.0000	...

Note: In calculating progressivity, households' rank with respect to their original income is used.

n.c. = Not calculated; . . . = Not applicable.

$$(3\text{-}34) \qquad \rho_B^K > \left(\frac{1+b}{b} \right) (G_{X+B} - C_{X+B}^X).$$

As in the previous section, the right-hand side is non-negative and reaches zero if the transfer does not change the ranking of individuals. Table 3-26 identifies the effect of adding a transfer to a system that has no other tax or transfer in place.

To see how a neutral transfer can be unequalizing in the presence of reranking, refer to table 3-27.

3.2 The Case of Adding a Transfer to a System That Has a Tax in Place

Because there is only one tax in place and only one transfer is added, equation 3-14 can be simplified as follows:

$$M_B = \left\{ (G_X - C_X^{X-T+B}) + \left(\frac{(1-g)\Pi_T^{RS^{X-T+B}} + (1+b)\rho_B^{RS^{X-T+B}}}{1-g+b} \right) \right\}$$
$$- \left\{ \Pi_T^{RS^{X-T}} + (G_X - C_X^{X-T}) \right\}.$$

As in section 2.2, this equation can then be simplified as follows:

(3-35) $$M_B = \left(\frac{-b\Pi_T^{RS^{X-T+B}} + (1+b)\rho_B^{RS^{X-T+B}}}{1-g+b} \right) + \left(G_{X-T} - C_{X-T}^{X-T+B} \right)$$

or

(3-36) $$M_B = \left(\frac{\dfrac{-bg}{1-g}\Pi_T^{K^{X-T+B}} + b\rho_B^{K^{X-T+B}}}{1-g+b} \right) + \left(G_{X-T} - C_{X-T}^{X-T+B} \right).$$

For a transfer to be equalizing, equation 3-36 should be positive; that is,

(3-37) $$M_B = \left(\frac{\dfrac{-bg}{1-g}\Pi_T^{K^{X-T+B}} + b\rho_B^{K^{X-T+B}}}{1-g+b} \right) + \left(G_{X-T} - C_{X-T}^{X-T+B} \right) > 0.$$

Using the preceding condition, table 3-28 helps to determine whether adding a transfer to a system with a tax in place would increase the equality. Note that $G_{X-T} - C_{X-T}^{X-T+B}$ is a non-negative term that reaches zero if adding the benefit does not change the ranking.

Table 3-28 includes some counterintuitive cases that the following examples will show are indeed possible. Table 3-29, for instance, shows that adding a regressive transfer to a fiscal system with a regressive tax (where progressivity is calculated with respect to households ranked by original income) could be equalizing.

Table 3-30 shows that adding a regressive transfer to a fiscal system with a neutral tax (where progressivity is calculated with respect to households ranked by original income) could be equalizing.

Table 3-31 shows that adding a neutral transfer to a fiscal system with a neutral tax (where progressivity is calculated with respect to households ranked by original income) could be equalizing.

Table 3-32 shows that adding a regressive transfer to a fiscal system with a progressive tax (where progressivity is calculated with respect to households ranked by original income) could be equalizing.

TABLE 3-28

Marginal Contribution of a Transfer with a Tax in Place

		Adding a transfer that, with respect to the end income ranking, is		
		Regressive $\rho_B^{K^{X-T+B}} < 0$	Neutral $\rho_B^{K^{X-T+B}} = 0$	Progressive $\rho_B^{K^{X-T+B}} > 0$
To a system with a tax that, with respect to the end income ranking, is	Regressive $\Pi_T^{K^{X-T+B}} < 0$	Equalizing if and only if condition 3-37 holds	Always equalizing	Always equalizing
	Neutral $\Pi_T^{K^{X-T+B}} = 0$	Equalizing if and only if condition 3-37 holds	Equalizing if and only if condition 3-37 holds	Always equalizing
	Progressive $\Pi_T^{K^{X-T+B}} > 0$	Equalizing if and only if condition 3-37 holds	Equalizing if and only if condition 3-37 holds	Equalizing if and only if condition 3-37 holds

Note: In calculating progressivity, households' rank with respect to their original income is used.

TABLE 3-29

Addition of a Regressive Transfer with an Equalizing Effect to a Fiscal System with a Regressive Tax

Individual	Original income (OI)	Benefit (B)	OI + B	Tax (T)	OI − T	End income (EI)
1	10.00	2.10	12.10	1.00	9.00	11.10
2	11.00	1.05	12.05	1.00	10.00	11.05
3	12.00	0.00	12.00	1.90	10.10	10.10
4	13.00	0.00	13.00	2.80	10.20	10.20
Total	46.00	3.15	49.15	6.70	39.30	42.45
Average	11.50	0.79	12.29	1.68	9.83	10.61
Gini	0.0543	n.c.	0.0155	n.c.	0.0235	0.0227
C^{X-T+B} $\Pi_T^{K^{X-T+B}}$	−0.0435	0.5833	−0.0033	−0.1679	−0.0223	n.c.
or $\rho_B^{K^{X-T+B}}$	. . .	−0.6268	. . .	−0.1244	. . .	. . .

Note: In calculating progressivity, households' rank with respect to their original income is used.

n.c. = Not calculated; . . . = Not applicable.

TABLE 3-30

Addition of a Regressive Transfer with an Equalizing Effect to a Fiscal System with a Neutral Tax

Individual	Original income (OI)	Benefit (B)	OI + B	Tax (T)	OI − T	End income (EI)
1	1.00	0.10	1.10	0.00	1.00	1.10
2	11.00	0.00	11.00	1.00	10.00	10.00
3	12.00	1.90	13.90	3.00	9.00	10.90
4	13.00	0.10	14.00	1.00	12.00	13.00
Total	37.00	3.00	40.00	5.00	32.00	35.00
Average	9.25	0.75	10.00	1.25	8.00	8.75
Gini	0.2500	n.c.	0.2600	n.c.	0.2656	0.2614
C^{X-T+B}	0.2500	0.3833	0.2600	0.2500	0.2500	n.c.
$\rho_T^{K\,X-T+B}$ or $\rho_B^{K\,X-T+B}$	...	−0.1333	...	0.0000	...	...

Note: In calculating progressivity, households' rank with respect to their end income is used.

n.c. = Not calculated; ... = Not applicable.

TABLE 3-31

Addition of a Neutral Transfer with an Equalizing Effect to a Fiscal System with a Neutral Tax

Individual	Original income (OI)	Benefit (B)	OI + B	Tax (T)	OI − T	End income (EI)
1	1.00	1.00	2.00	0.00	1.00	2.00
2	11.00	3.00	14.00	1.00	10.00	13.00
3	12.00	4.40	16.40	3.00	9.00	13.40
4	13.00	5.00	18.00	1.00	12.00	17.00
Total	37.00	13.40	50.40	5.00	32.00	45.40
Average	9.25	3.35	12.60	1.25	8.00	11.35
Gini	0.2500	n.c.	0.2500	n.c.	0.2656	0.2500
C^{X-T+B}	0.2500	0.2500	0.2500	0.2500	0.2500	n.c.
$\Pi_T^{K\,X-T+B}$ or $\rho_B^{K\,X-T+B}$	...	0.0000	...	0.0000	...	...

Note: In calculating progressivity, households' rank with respect to their end income is used.

n.c. = Not calculated; ... = Not applicable.

TABLE 3-32

Addition of a Regressive Transfer with an Equalizing Effect to a Fiscal System with a Progressive Tax

Individual	Original income (OI)	Benefit (B)	OI + B	Tax (T)	OI – T	End income (EI)
1	1.00	1.00	2.00	0.00	1.00	2.00
2	11.00	3.00	14.00	1.00	10.00	13.00
3	12.00	8.00	20.00	3.00	9.00	17.00
4	13.00	6.00	19.00	1.10	11.90	17.90
Total	37.00	18.00	55.00	5.10	31.90	49.90
Average	9.25	4.50	13.75	1.28	7.98	12.48
Gini	0.2500	n.c.	0.2682	n.c.	0.2641	0.2590
C^{X-T+B}	0.2500	0.2778	0.2591	0.2598	0.2484	n.c.
$\prod_T^{K^{X-T+B}}$ or $\rho_B^{K^{X-T+B}}$	...	−0.0278	...	0.0098	...	...

Note: In calculating progressivity, households' rank with respect to their end income is used.

n.c. = Not calculated; . . . = Not applicable.

Table 3-33 shows that adding a neutral transfer to a fiscal system with a progressive tax (where progressivity is calculated with respect to households ranked by original income) could be equalizing.

Table 3-34 shows that adding a progressive transfer to a fiscal system with a progressive tax (where progressivity is calculated with respect to households ranked by original income) could be unequalizing.

Although equation 3-35 is derived using the R-S index calculated with respect to the end income ranking of households, one can calculate a similar derivation using the R-S index calculated with respect to the original income ranking, as shown in the following equation:

$$M_B = \left(\frac{-b\prod_T^{RS} + (1+b)\rho_B^{RS}}{1-g+b} \right) + \left[(C_{X-T+B}^X - G_{X-T+B}) - (C_{X-T}^X - G_{X-T}) \right].$$

Because both terms in the brackets are non-positive, the bracket could be positive, zero, or negative. For the tax to be equalizing, the following condition should hold:

$$\left(\frac{-b\prod_T^{RS} + (1+b)\rho_B^{RS}}{1-g+b} \right) + \left[(C_{X-T+B}^X - G_{X-T+B}) - (C_{X-T}^X - G_{X-T}) \right] > 0.$$

Table 3-33

Addition of a Neutral Transfer with an Equalizing Effect to a Fiscal System with a Progressive Tax

Individual	Original income (OI)	Benefit (B)	OI + B	Tax (T)	OI − T	End income (EI)
1	10.00	11.00	21.00	8.90	1.10	12.10
2	11.00	12.10	23.10	10.00	1.00	13.10
3	12.00	13.20	25.20	10.00	2.00	15.20
4	13.00	14.30	27.30	12.10	0.90	15.20
Total	46.00	50.60	96.60	41.00	5.00	55.60
Average	11.50	12.65	24.15	10.25	1.25	13.90
Gini	0.0543	n.c.	0.0543	n.c.	0.1700	0.0513
C^{X-T+B}	0.0543	0.0543	0.0543	0.0585	0.0200	n.c.
$\Pi_T^{K^{X-T+B}}$ or $\rho_B^{K^{X-T+B}}$	...	0.0000	...	0.0042	...	...

Note: In calculating progressivity, households' rank with respect to their end income is used.

n.c. = Not calculated; ... = Not applicable.

Table 3-34

Addition of a Progressive Transfer with an Unequalizing Effect to a Fiscal System with a Progressive Tax

Individual	Original income (OI)	Benefit (B)	OI + B	Tax (T)	OI − T	End income (EI)
1	10.00	7.00	17.00	1.00	9.00	16.00
2	11.00	9.00	20.00	1.00	10.00	19.00
3	12.00	9.00	21.00	1.90	10.10	19.10
4	13.00	9.00	22.00	2.80	10.20	19.20
Total	46.00	34.00	80.00	6.70	39.30	73.30
Average	11.50	8.50	20.00	1.68	9.83	18.33
Gini	0.0543	n.c.	0.0500	n.c.	0.0235	0.0331
C^{X-T+B}	0.0543	0.0441	0.0500	0.2351	0.0235	n.c.
$\Pi_T^{K^{X-T+B}}$ or $\rho_B^{K^{X-T+B}}$	...	0.0102	...	0.1807	...	...

Note: In calculating progressivity, households' rank with respect to their end income is used.

n.c. = Not calculated; ... = Not applicable.

TABLE 3-35

Marginal Contribution of a Transfer with a Tax in Place

		Adding a transfer that, with respect to the original income ranking, is		
		Regressive $\rho_B^K < 0$	Neutral $\rho_B^K = 0$	Progressive $\rho_B^K > 0$
To a system with a tax that, with respect to the original income ranking, is	**Regressive** $\Pi_T^K < 0$	Equalizing if and only if condition 3-38 holds	Equalizing if and only if condition 3-38 holds	Equalizing if and only if condition 3-38 holds
	Neutral $\Pi_T^K = 0$	Equalizing if and only if condition 3-38 holds	Equalizing if and only if condition 3-38 holds	Equalizing if and only if condition 3-38 holds
	Progressive $\Pi_T^K > 0$	Equalizing if and only if condition 3-38 holds	Equalizing if and only if condition 3-38 holds	Equalizing if and only if condition 3-38 holds

Note: In calculating progressivity, households' rank with respect to their original income is used.

or

$$(3\text{-}38) \quad \left(\frac{-\dfrac{gb}{1-g}\Pi_T^K + b\rho_B^K}{1-g+b} \right) + \left[\overbrace{\underbrace{(C_{X-T+B}^X - G_{X-T+B})}_{\text{Reranking after the transfer is added}} - \underbrace{(C_{X-T}^X - G_{X-T})}_{\text{Reranking before the transfer is added}}}^{\text{Marginal effect of the transfer on reranking}} \right] > 0.$$

As table 3-35 shows, using Kakwani indexes calculated with respect to the original income ranking of households cannot give a definitive answer about the marginal effect of a transfer in any of the cases.

Table 3-36 shows that adding a regressive transfer to a fiscal system with a regressive tax (where progressivity is calculated with respect to households ranked by original income) could be equalizing.

Table 3-37 shows that adding a neutral transfer to a fiscal system with a regressive tax (where progressivity is calculated with respect to households ranked by original income) could be equalizing.

Table 3-38 shows that adding a neutral transfer to a fiscal system with a regressive tax (where progressivity is calculated with respect to households ranked by original income) could be unequalizing.

TABLE 3-36

Addition of a Regressive Transfer with an Equalizing Effect to a Fiscal System with a Regressive Tax

Individual	Original income (OI)	Benefit (B)	OI + B	Tax (T)	OI − T	End income (EI)
1	1.00	1.00	2.00	0.00	1.00	2.00
2	11.00	0.00	11.00	1.10	9.90	9.90
3	12.00	3.00	15.00	3.00	9.00	12.00
4	13.00	2.10	15.10	1.00	12.00	14.10
Total	37.00	6.10	43.10	5.10	31.90	38.00
Average	9.25	1.53	10.78	1.28	7.98	9.50
Gini	0.2500	n.c.	0.2512	n.c.	0.2657	0.2526
C^X	0.2500	0.2582	0.2512	0.2402	0.2516	0.2526
Π_T^K or ρ_B^K	. . .	−0.0082	. . .	−0.0098	. . .	. . .

Note: In calculating progressivity, households' rank with respect to their original income is used.

n.c. = Not calculated; . . . = Not applicable.

TABLE 3-37

Addition of a Neutral Transfer with an Equalizing Effect to a Fiscal System with a Regressive Tax

Individual	Original income (OI)	Benefit (B)	OI + B	Tax (T)	OI − T	End income (EI)
1	1.00	1.00	2.00	0.00	1.00	2.00
2	11.00	0.10	11.10	1.10	9.90	10.00
3	12.00	3.00	15.00	3.00	9.00	12.00
4	13.00	2.10	15.10	1.00	12.00	14.10
Total	37.00	6.20	43.20	5.10	31.90	38.10
Average	9.25	1.55	10.80	1.28	7.98	9.53
Gini	0.2500	n.c.	0.2500	n.c.	0.2657	0.2513
C^X	0.2500	0.2500	0.2500	0.2402	0.2516	0.2513
Π_T^K or ρ_B^K	. . .	0.0000	. . .	−0.0098	. . .	. . .

Note: In calculating progressivity, households' rank with respect to their original income is used.

n.c. = Not calculated; . . . = Not applicable.

TABLE 3-38
Addition of a Neutral Transfer with an Unequalizing Effect to a Fiscal System
with a Regressive Tax

Individual	Original income (OI)	Benefit (B)	OI + B	Tax (T)	OI − T	End income (EI)
1	1.00	0.00	1.00	1.00	0.00	0.00
2	11.00	0.00	11.00	1.10	9.90	9.90
3	12.00	5.00	17.00	3.00	9.00	14.00
4	13.00	0.00	13.00	1.00	12.00	12.00
Total	37.00	5.00	42.00	6.10	30.90	35.90
Average	9.25	1.25	10.50	1.53	7.73	8.98
Gini	0.2500	n.c.	0.2976	n.c.	0.2985	0.3071
C^X	0.2500	0.2500	0.2500	0.0779	0.2840	0.2792
Π_T^K or ρ_B^K	...	0.0000	...	−0.1721	...	...

Note: In calculating progressivity, households' rank with respect to their original income is used.

n.c. = Not calculated; ... = Not applicable.

TABLE 3-39
Addition of a Progressive Transfer with an Unequalizing Effect to a Fiscal System
with a Regressive Tax

Individual	Original income (OI)	Benefit (B)	OI + B	Tax (T)	OI − T	End income (EI)
1	1.00	0.10	1.10	1.00	0.00	0.10
2	11.00	0.00	11.00	1.10	9.90	9.90
3	12.00	5.00	17.00	3.00	9.00	14.00
4	13.00	0.00	13.00	1.00	12.00	12.00
Total	37.00	5.10	42.10	6.10	30.90	36.00
Average	9.25	1.28	10.53	1.53	7.73	9.00
Gini	0.2500	n.c.	0.2951	n.c.	0.2985	0.3042
C^X	0.2500	0.2304	0.2476	0.0779	0.2840	0.2764
Π_T^K or ρ_B^K	...	0.0196	...	−0.1721	...	...

Note: In calculating progressivity, households' rank with respect to their original income is used.

n.c. = Not calculated; ... = Not applicable.

Table 3-39 shows that adding a progressive transfer to a fiscal system with a regressive tax (where progressivity is calculated with respect to households ranked by original income) could be unequalizing.

Table 3-40 shows that adding a regressive transfer to a fiscal system with a neutral tax (where progressivity is calculated with respect to households ranked by original income) could be equalizing.

TABLE 3-40

Addition of a Regressive Transfer with an Equalizing Effect to a Fiscal System with a Neutral Tax

Individual	Original income (OI)	Benefit (B)	OI + B	Tax (T)	OI − T	End income (EI)
1	1.00	1.00	2.00	0.00	1.00	2.00
2	11.00	2.90	13.90	1.00	10.00	12.90
3	12.00	4.40	16.40	3.00	9.00	13.40
4	13.00	4.95	17.95	1.00	12.00	16.95
Total	37.00	13.25	50.25	5.00	32.00	45.25
Average	9.25	3.31	12.56	1.25	8.00	11.31
Gini	0.2500	n.c.	0.2505	n.c.	0.2656	0.2506
C^X	0.2500	0.2519	0.2505	0.2500	0.2500	0.2506
Π_T^K or ρ_B^K	...	−0.0019	...	0.0000	...	...

Note: In calculating progressivity, households' rank with respect to their original income is used.

n.c. = Not calculated; ... = Not applicable.

TABLE 3-41

Addition of a Neutral Transfer with an Equalizing Effect to a Fiscal System with a Neutral Tax

Individual	Original income (OI)	Benefit (B)	OI + B	Tax (T)	OI − T	End income (EI)
1	1.00	1.00	2.00	0.00	1.00	2.00
2	11.00	3.00	14.00	1.00	10.00	13.00
3	12.00	4.40	16.40	3.00	9.00	13.40
4	13.00	5.00	18.00	1.00	12.00	17.00
Total	37.00	13.40	50.40	5.00	32.00	45.40
Average	9.25	3.35	12.60	1.25	8.00	11.35
Gini	0.2500	n.c.	0.2500	n.c.	0.2656	0.2500
C^X	0.2500	0.2500	0.2500	0.2500	0.2500	0.2500
Π_T^K or ρ_B^K	...	0.0000	...	0.0000	...	...

Note: In calculating progressivity, households' rank with respect to their original income is used.

n.c. = Not calculated; ... = Not applicable.

Table 3-41 shows that adding a neutral transfer to a fiscal system with a neutral tax (where progressivity is calculated with respect to households ranked by original income) could be equalizing.

Table 3-42 shows that adding a neutral transfer to a fiscal system with a neutral tax (where progressivity is calculated with respect to households ranked by original income) could be unequalizing.

TABLE 3-42

Addition of a Neutral Transfer with an Unequalizing Effect to a Fiscal System with a Neutral Tax

Individual	Original income (OI)	Benefit (B)	OI + B	Tax (T)	OI − T	End income (EI)
1	10.00	0.00	10.00	4.50	5.50	5.50
2	20.00	2.00	22.00	9.00	11.00	13.00
3	30.00	100.00	130.00	27.00	3.00	103.00
4	40.00	2.00	42.00	18.00	22.00	24.00
Total	100.00	104.00	204.00	58.50	41.50	145.50
Average	25.00	26.00	51.00	14.63	10.38	36.38
Gini	0.2500	n.c.	0.4657	n.c.	0.3765	0.5215
C^X	0.2500	0.2500	0.2500	0.2500	0.2500	0.2500
Π_T^K or ρ_B^K	...	0.0000	...	0.0000	...	...

Note: In calculating progressivity, households' rank with respect to their original income is used.

n.c. = Not calculated; ... = Not applicable.

TABLE 3-43

Addition of a Progressive Transfer with an Unequalizing Effect to a Fiscal System with a Neutral Tax

Individual	Original income (OI)	Benefit (B)	OI + B	Tax (T)	OI − T	End income (EI)
1	10.00	0.10	10.10	4.50	5.50	5.60
2	20.00	2.00	22.00	9.00	11.00	13.00
3	30.00	100.00	130.00	27.00	3.00	103.00
4	40.00	2.00	42.00	18.00	22.00	24.00
Total	100.00	104.10	204.10	58.50	41.50	145.60
Average	25.00	26.03	51.03	14.63	10.38	36.40
Gini	0.2500	n.c.	0.4651	n.c.	0.3765	0.5206
C^X	0.2500	0.2490	0.2495	0.2500	0.2500	0.2493
Π_T^K or ρ_B^K	...	0.0010	...	0.0000	...	...

Note: In calculating progressivity, households' rank with respect to their original income is used.

n.c. = Not calculated; ... = Not applicable.

Table 3-43 shows that adding a progressive transfer to a fiscal system with a neutral tax (where progressivity is calculated with respect to households ranked by original income) could be unequalizing.

Table 3-44 shows that adding a regressive transfer to a fiscal system with a progressive tax (where progressivity is calculated with respect to households ranked by original income) could be equalizing.

Table 3-44

Addition of a Regressive Transfer with an Equalizing Effect to a Fiscal System with a Progressive Tax

Individual	Original income (OI)	Benefit (B)	OI + B	Tax (T)	OI − T	End income (EI)
1	1.00	1.00	2.00	0.00	1.00	2.00
2	11.00	2.90	13.90	1.00	10.00	12.90
3	12.00	4.40	16.40	3.00	9.00	13.40
4	13.00	4.95	17.95	1.05	11.95	16.90
Total	37.00	13.25	50.25	5.05	31.95	45.20
Average	9.25	3.31	12.56	1.26	7.99	11.30
Gini	0.2500	n.c.	0.2505	n.c.	0.2649	0.2500
C^X	0.2500	0.2519	0.2505	0.2550	0.2492	0.2500
Π_T^K or ρ_B^K	...	−0.0019	...	0.0050	...	...

Note: In calculating progressivity, households' rank with respect to their original income is used.

n.c. = Not calculated; ... = Not applicable.

Table 3-45

Addition of a Neutral Transfer with an Unequalizing Effect to a Fiscal System with a Progressive Tax

Individual	Original income (OI)	Benefit (B)	OI + B	Tax (T)	OI − T	End income (EI)
1	10.00	0.00	10.00	4.40	5.60	5.60
2	20.00	2.00	22.00	9.00	11.00	13.00
3	30.00	100.00	130.00	27.00	3.00	103.00
4	40.00	2.00	42.00	18.00	22.00	24.00
Total	100.00	104.00	204.00	58.40	41.60	145.60
Average	25.00	26.00	51.00	14.60	10.40	36.40
Gini	0.2500	n.c.	0.4657	n.c.	0.3750	0.5206
C^X	0.2500	0.2500	0.2500	0.2517	0.2476	0.2493
Π_T^K or ρ_B^K	...	0.0000	...	0.0017	...	...

Note: In calculating progressivity, households' rank with respect to their original income is used.

n.c. = Not calculated; ... = Not applicable.

Table 3-45 shows that adding a neutral transfer to a fiscal system with a progressive tax (where progressivity is calculated with respect to households ranked by original income) could be unequalizing.

Table 3-46 shows that adding a progressive transfer to a fiscal system with a progressive tax (where progressivity is calculated with respect to households ranked by original income) could be unequalizing.

TABLE 3-46

Addition of a Progressive Transfer with an Unequalizing Effect to a Fiscal System with a Progressive Tax

Individual	Original income (OI)	Benefit (B)	OI + B	Tax (T)	OI – T	End income (EI)
1	10.00	0.10	10.10	4.40	5.60	5.70
2	20.00	2.00	22.00	9.00	11.00	13.00
3	30.00	100.00	130.00	27.00	3.00	103.00
4	40.00	2.00	42.00	18.00	22.00	24.00
Total	100.00	104.10	204.10	58.40	41.60	145.70
Average	25.00	26.03	51.03	14.60	10.40	36.43
Gini	0.2500	n.c.	0.4651	n.c.	0.3750	0.5197
C^X	0.2500	0.2490	0.2495	0.2517	0.2476	0.2486
$\prod_T^K$ or ρ_B^K	...	0.0010	...	0.0017	...	...

Note: In calculating progressivity, households' rank with respect to their original income is used.

n.c. = Not calculated; . . . = Not applicable.

3.3 The Case of Adding a Transfer to a System with Multiple Taxes and Transfers in Place

Recall from equation 3-14 that

$$M_{B_1} = \left\{ (G_X - C_X^Z) + \left(\frac{\sum_{i=1}^n (1-g_i)\prod_{T_i}^{RS^Z} + \sum_{j=1}^m (1+b_j)\rho_{B_j}^{RS^Z}}{1 - \sum_{i=1}^n g_i + \sum_{j=1}^m b_j} \right) \right\} - \left\{ \left(G_X - C_X^{Z \backslash B_1}\right) + \left(\frac{\sum_{i=1}^n (1-g_i)\prod_{T_i}^{RS^{Z \backslash B_1}} + \sum_{j=2}^m (1+b_j)\rho_{B_j}^{RS^{Z \backslash B_1}}}{1 - \sum_{i=1}^n g_i + \sum_{j=2}^m b_j} \right) \right\}.$$

For B_1 to be equalizing, this equation has to be positive; that is,

$$(3\text{-}39) \quad \left\{ (G_X - C_X^Z) + \left(\frac{\sum_{i=1}^n (1-g_i)\prod_{T_i}^{RS^Z} + \sum_{j=1}^m (1+b_j)\rho_{B_j}^{RS^Z}}{1 - \sum_{i=1}^n g_i + \sum_{j=1}^m b_j} \right) \right\} - \left\{ \left(G_X - C_X^{Z \backslash B_1}\right) + \left(\frac{\sum_{i=1}^n (1-g_i)\prod_{T_i}^{RS^{Z \backslash B_1}} + \sum_{j=2}^m (1+b_j)\rho_{B_j}^{RS^{Z \backslash B_1}}}{1 - \sum_{i=1}^n g_i + \sum_{j=2}^m b_j} \right) \right\} > 0.$$

If adding this specific transfer does not change the end income ranking of individuals (that is, if end income rankings are the same before and after adding the tax), then ranking with respect to Z and $Z\backslash B_1$ is the same, which simplifies the whole equation to

$$\left(1 - \sum_{i=1}^{n} g_i + \sum_{j=2}^{m} b_j\right)(1+b_1)\rho_{B_1}^{RS^Z} > b_1\left(\sum_{i=1}^{n}(1-g_i)\Pi_{T_i}^{RS^{Z\backslash B_1}} + \sum_{j=2}^{m}(1+b_j)\rho_{B_j}^{RS^{Z\backslash B_1}}\right),$$

which is equal to

$$\rho_{B_1}^{RS^Z} > \frac{b_1}{1+b_1}\left(\frac{\sum_{i=1}^{n}(1-g_i)\Pi_{T_i}^{RS^{Z\backslash B_1}} + \sum_{j=2}^{m}(1+b_j)\rho_{B_j}^{RS^{Z\backslash B_1}}}{1 - \sum_{i=1}^{n} g_i + \sum_{j=2}^{m} b_j}\right)$$

or

$$\rho_{B_1}^{RS^Z} > \frac{b_1}{1+b_1}\left(C_X^{Z\backslash B_1} - G_{Z\backslash B_1}\right)\frac{1}{2}$$

or

(3-40)
$$\rho_{B_1}^{KZ} > \left(C_X^{Z\backslash B_1} - G_{Z\backslash B_1}\right).$$

As mentioned in section 2.3, the term on the right-hand side is

$$VE_{X,\,Z\backslash B_1}^{Z\backslash B_1} = C_X^{Z\backslash B_1} - G_{Z\backslash B_1}.$$

Thus,

(3-41)
$$\rho_{B_1}^{KZ} > VE_{X,\,Z\backslash B_1}^{Z\backslash B_1}.$$

Therefore, we can use table 3-47 to determine the marginal effect of adding a transfer to a system with multiple taxes and transfers when the end income ranking of households does not change because of this additional transfer.

It is crucial that for the preceding results to hold, the transfer that we are interested in should not have any effect on the end income ranking of households. If that is not the case, then equation 3-39 cannot be simplified much further, and the effect of adding such a transfer cannot be determined using a simple rule of thumb from table 3-47.

TABLE 3-47

Marginal Contribution of a Transfer with Multiple Taxes and Transfers in Place

		To a system with multiple taxes and transfers where its vertical equity (with respect to the final income ranking) is		
		Negative $VE_{X,\,Z\backslash B_1}^{Z\backslash B_1} < 0$	**Zero** $VE_{X,\,Z\backslash B_1}^{Z\backslash B_1} = 0$	**Positive** $VE_{X,\,Z\backslash B_1}^{Z\backslash B_1} > 0$
Adding a transfer that, with respect to the final incomes ranking (Z), is	**Regressive** $\rho_B^{KZ} < 0$	Equalizing if and only if condition 3-41 holds	Always unequalizing	Always unequalizing
	Neutral $\rho_B^{KZ} = 0$	Always equalizing	No change in inequality	Always unequalizing
	Progressive $\rho_B^{KZ} > 0$	Always equalizing	Always equalizing	Equalizing if and only if condition 3-41 holds

Note: $Z = X - \sum_{i=1}^{n} T_i + \sum_{j=1}^{m} B_j$ and $Z\backslash B_1 = X - \sum_{i=1}^{n} T_i + \sum_{j=2}^{m} B_j$. Adding the new transfer does not change the end income ranking of individuals.

As an alternative, one can use the progressivity with respect to the original income in the analysis. For this purpose, we need to use equation 3-18:

$$M_{B_1} = \left[\frac{[(1+b_1)\rho_{B_1}^{RS}] - \left[(b_1) \overbrace{\left(G_X - C_{Z\backslash B_1}^{X}\right)}^{VE\ of\ the\ system\ without\ B_1} \right]}{\left(1 - \sum_{i=1}^{n} g_i + \sum_{j=1}^{m} b_j\right)} \right] + \underbrace{\left[(C_Z^X - G_Z) - \left(C_{Z\backslash B_1}^{X} - G_{Z\backslash B_1}\right) \right]}_{Contribution\ of\ B_1\ to\ reranking}.$$

For a transfer to be equalizing when it is added to a system of taxes and transfers, the following condition should hold:

$$(3\text{-}42)\quad M_{B_1} = \left[\frac{[(1+b_1)\rho_{B_1}^{RS}] - \left[(b_1) \overbrace{\left(G_X - C_{Z\backslash B_1}^{X}\right)}^{VE\ of\ the\ system\ without\ B_1} \right]}{\left(1 - \sum_{i=1}^{n} g_i + \sum_{j=1}^{m} b_j\right)} \right] + \underbrace{\left[(C_Z^X - G_Z) - \left(C_{Z\backslash B_1}^{X} - G_{Z\backslash B_1}\right) \right]}_{Contribution\ of\ B_1\ to\ reranking} > 0$$

or

$$(3\text{-}43) \quad M_{B_1} = \left[\left(\frac{[b_1 \rho_{B_1}^K] - \left[(b_1) \overbrace{\left(G_X - C_{Z\backslash B_1}^X \right)}^{\text{VE of the system without } B_1} \right]}{\left(1 - \sum_{i=1}^{n} g_i + \sum_{j=1}^{m} b_j \right)} \right) \right] + \underbrace{\left[\left(C_Z^X - G_Z \right) - \left(C_{Z\backslash B_1}^X - G_{Z\backslash B_1} \right) \right]}_{\text{Contribution of } B_1 \text{ to reranking}} > 0.$$

4 Is the Total System More Equal? The Case of Adding a Tax and a Transfer

After examining the marginal contribution of taxes and transfers in the previous two sections, this section examines the total redistributive effect of all taxes and transfers. For simplicity, I bundle all of the taxes together and all of the transfers together and treat them as if there were only one tax and one transfer in the system. Recall that the change in the Gini is equal to

$$G_X - G_{X-T+B} = (G_X - C_X^{X-T+B}) + \left(\frac{(1-g)\Pi_T^{RS^{X-T+B}} + (1+b)\rho_B^{RS^{X-T+B}}}{1-g+b} \right).$$

Then, for the whole system to be equalizing, we would need the following condition to hold:

$$(3\text{-}44) \qquad (G_X - C_X^{X-T+B}) + \left(\frac{(1-g)\Pi_T^{RS^{X-T+B}} + (1+b)\rho_B^{RS^{X-T+B}}}{1-g+b} \right) > 0$$

or

$$(3\text{-}45) \qquad (G_X - C_X^{X-T+B}) + \left(\frac{g\Pi_T^{K^{X-T+B}} + b\rho_B^{K^{X-T+B}}}{1-g+b} \right) > 0.$$

Note that the first term is non-negative. Therefore, we have the following case in table 3-48, which shows the effect of the total system in the case of one tax and one transfer and when progressivity is calculated with respect to the end income ranking of households.

The following examples display the counterintuitive cases.

Table 3-49 shows that adding a regressive tax and a regressive transfer (where progressivity is calculated with respect to households ranked by original income) to a fiscal system could be equalizing.

TABLE 3-48

Effect of the Total System with One Tax and One Transfer (using modified Kakwani index)

		If the transfer with respect to the end income ranking is		
		Regressive $\rho_B^{K^{X-T+B}} < 0$	Neutral $\rho_B^{K^{X-T+B}} = 0$	Progressive $\rho_B^{K^{X-T+B}} > 0$
If the tax with respect to the end income ranking is	Regressive $\Pi_T^{K^{X-T+B}} < 0$	Equalizing if and only if 3-45 holds	Equalizing if and only if equation 3-45 holds	Equalizing if and only if equation 3-45 holds
	Neutral $\Pi_T^{K^{X-T+B}} = 0$	Equalizing if and only if equation 3-45 holds	Equalizing if and only if equation 3-45 holds	Always equalizing
	Progressive $\Pi_T^{K^{X-T+B}} > 0$	Equalizing if and only if equation 3-45 holds	Always equalizing	Always equalizing

Note: In calculating progressivity, households' rank with respect to their original income is used.

TABLE 3-49

Addition of a Regressive Tax and a Regressive Transfer with an Equalizing Effect to a Fiscal System

Individual	Original income (OI)	Benefit (B)	OI + B	Tax (T)	OI − T	End income (EI)
1	1.00	12.10	13.10	1.00	0.00	12.10
2	11.00	0.00	11.00	0.00	11.00	11.00
3	12.00	0.00	12.00	10.00	2.00	2.00
4	13.00	0.00	13.00	1.00	12.00	12.00
Total	37.00	12.10	49.10	12.00	25.00	37.10
Average	9.25	3.03	12.28	3.00	6.25	9.28
Gini	0.2500	n.c.	0.0372	n.c.	0.4500	0.2109
C^{X-T+B}	−0.2095	0.7500	0.0270	−0.5417	−0.0500	n.c.
$\Pi_T^{K^{X-T+B}}$ or $\rho_B^{K^{X-T+B}}$	...	−0.9595	...	−0.3322	...	...

Note: In calculating progressivity, households' rank with respect to their end income is used.

n.c. = Not calculated; ... = Not applicable.

TABLE 3-50
Addition of a Regressive Tax and a Neutral Transfer with an Equalizing Effect
to a Fiscal System

Individual	Original income (OI)	Benefit (B)	OI + B	Tax (T)	OI – T	End income (EI)
1	1.00	0.10	1.10	0.10	0.90	1.00
2	11.00	1.10	12.10	1.10	9.90	11.00
3	12.00	1.20	13.20	1.20	10.80	12.00
4	13.00	1.30	14.30	3.40	9.60	10.90
Total	37.00	3.70	40.70	5.80	31.20	34.90
Average	9.25	0.93	10.18	1.45	7.80	8.73
Gini	0.2500	n.c.	0.2500	n.c.	0.2404	0.2371
C^{X-T+B}	0.2095	0.2095	0.2095	0.0431	0.2404	n.c.
$\Pi_T^{K^{X-T+B}}$ or $\rho_B^{K^{X-T+B}}$	...	0.0000	...	–0.1664	...	...

Note: In calculating progressivity, households' rank with respect to their end income is used.

n.c. = Not calculated; ... = Not applicable.

Table 3-50 shows that adding a regressive tax and a neutral transfer (where progressivity is calculated with respect to households ranked by original income) to a fiscal system could be equalizing.

Table 3-51 shows that adding a neutral tax and a regressive transfer (where progressivity is calculated with respect to households ranked by original income) to a fiscal system could be equalizing.

Table 3-52 shows that adding a neutral tax and a neutral transfer (where progressivity is calculated with respect to households ranked by original income) to a fiscal system could be equalizing.

As an alternative, we can use the formula based on the Kakwani index calculated with respect to the original income ranking of households:

$$G_X - G_{X-T+B} = \left(G_X - C_{X-T+B}^X\right) + \left(C_{X-T+B}^X - G_{X-T+B}\right),$$

which can be written as

$$G_X - G_{X-T+B} = \left(\frac{(1-g)\Pi_T^{RS} + (1+b)\rho_B^{RS}}{1-g+b}\right) + \left(C_{X-T+B}^X - G_{X-T+B}\right).$$

TABLE 3-51

Addition of a Neutral Tax and a Regressive Transfer with an Equalizing Effect to a Fiscal System

Individual	Original income (OI)	Benefit (B)	OI + B	Tax (T)	OI − T	End income (EI)
1	1.00	10.10	11.10	0.40	0.60	10.70
2	11.00	0.00	11.00	4.40	6.60	6.60
3	12.00	0.00	12.00	4.80	7.20	7.20
4	13.00	0.00	13.00	5.20	7.80	7.80
Total	37.00	10.10	47.10	14.80	22.20	32.30
Average	9.25	2.53	11.78	3.70	5.55	8.08
Gini	0.2500	n.c.	0.0366	n.c.	0.2500	0.0998
C^{X-T+B}	−0.1959	0.7500	0.0069	−0.1959	−0.1959	n.c.
$\Pi_T^{K^{X-T+B}}$ or $\rho_B^{K^{X-T+B}}$	. . .	−0.9459	. . .	0.0000	. . .	. . .

Note: In calculating progressivity, households' rank with respect to their end income is used.

n.c. = Not calculated; . . . = Not applicable.

TABLE 3-52

Addition of a Neutral Tax and a Neutral Transfer with an Equalizing Effect to a Fiscal System

Individual	Original income (OI)	Benefit (B)	OI + B	Tax (T)	OI − T	End income (EI)
1	1.0000	0.2000	1.2000	0.0000	1.0000	1.2000
2	11.0000	2.2000	13.2000	1.0148	9.9852	12.1850
3	12.0000	2.4000	14.4000	3.0000	9.0000	11.4000
4	13.0000	2.6000	15.6000	2.8154	10.1846	12.7850
Total	37.0000	7.4000	44.4000	6.8302	30.1698	37.5698
Average	9.2500	1.8500	11.1000	1.7076	7.5425	9.3925
Gini	0.2500	n.c.	0.2500	n.c.	0.2365	0.2365
C^{X-T+B}	0.2365	0.2365	0.2365	0.2365	0.2365	n.c.
$\Pi_T^{K^{X-T+B}}$ or $\rho_B^{K^{X-T+B}}$	. . .	0.0000	. . .	0.0000	. . .	. . .

Note: In calculating progressivity, households' rank with respect to their end income is used.

n.c. = Not calculated; . . . = Not applicable.

TABLE 3-53

Effect of the Total System with One Tax and One Transfer (using traditional Kakwani index)

		If the transfer with respect to the original income ranking is		
		Regressive $\rho_B^K < 0$	Neutral $\rho_B^K = 0$	Progressive $\rho_B^K > 0$
If the tax with respect to the original income ranking is	**Regressive** $\Pi_T^K < 0$	Always unequalizing	Always unequalizing	Equalizing if and only if equation 3-47 holds
	Neutral $\Pi_T^K = 0$	Always unequalizing	Never equalizing	Equalizing if and only if equation 3-47 holds
	Progressive $\Pi_T^K > 0$	Equalizing if and only if equation 3-47 holds	Equalizing if and only if equation 3-47 holds	Equalizing if and only if equation 3-47 holds

Note: In calculating progressivity, households' rank with respect to their original income is used.

For the total system to be equalizing, we need to have

$$(3\text{-}46) \qquad \left(\frac{(1-g)\Pi_T^{RS} + (1+b)\rho_B^{RS}}{1-g+b} \right) + \left(C_{X-T+B}^X - G_{X-T+B} \right) > 0$$

or

$$(3\text{-}47) \qquad \left(\frac{g\Pi_T^K + b\rho_B^K}{1-g+b} \right) + \left(C_{X-T+B}^X - G_{X-T+B} \right) > 0.$$

Note that the latter term is always non-positive. Therefore, we have the following cases.

Table 3-53 shows the effect of the total system in the case of one tax and one transfer and when progressivity is calculated with respect to the original income ranking of households. The relatively counterintuitive cases in table 3-53 are presented in the following examples.

Table 3-54 shows that adding a neutral tax and a neutral transfer (where progressivity is calculated with respect to households ranked by original income) to a fiscal system could be unequalizing.

Table 3-55 shows that adding a neutral tax and a progressive transfer (where progressivity is calculated with respect to households ranked by original income) to a fiscal system could be unequalizing.

TABLE 3-54
Addition of a Neutral Tax and a Neutral Transfer with an Unequalizing Effect
to a Fiscal System

Individual	Original income (OI)	Benefit (B)	OI + B	Tax (T)	OI − T	End income (EI)
1	2.00	0.00	2.00	1.00	1.00	1.00
2	2.00	1.00	3.00	1.00	1.00	2.00
3	2.00	1.00	3.00	1.00	1.00	2.00
4	2.00	0.00	2.00	1.00	1.00	1.00
Total	8.00	2.00	10.00	4.00	4.00	6.00
Average	2.00	0.50	2.50	1.00	1.00	1.50
Gini	0.0000	n.c.	0.1000	n.c.	0.0000	0.1667
C^X	0.0000	0.0000	0.0000	0.0000	0.0000	0.0000
$\prod_T^K$ or ρ_B^K	. . .	0.0000	. . .	0.0000	. . .	. . .

Note: In calculating progressivity, households' rank with respect to their original income is used.

n.c. = Not calculated; . . . = Not applicable.

TABLE 3-55
Addition of a Neutral Tax and a Progressive Transfer with an Unequalizing Effect
to a Fiscal System

Individual	Original income (OI)	Benefit (B)	OI + B	Tax (T)	OI − T	End income (EI)
1	2.00	1.00	3.00	1.00	1.00	2.00
2	2.00	0.00	2.00	1.00	1.00	1.00
3	2.00	0.00	2.00	1.00	1.00	1.00
4	2.00	0.00	2.00	1.00	1.00	1.00
Total	8.00	1.00	9.00	4.00	4.00	5.00
Average	2.00	0.25	2.25	1.00	1.00	1.25
Gini	0.0000	n.c.	0.0833	n.c.	0.0000	0.1500
C^X	0.0000	−0.7500	−0.0833	0.0000	0.0000	−0.1500
$\prod_T^K$ or ρ_B^K	. . .	0.7500	. . .	0.0000	. . .	. . .

Note: In calculating progressivity, households' rank with respect to their original income is used.

n.c. = Not calculated; . . . = Not applicable.

Table 3-56 shows that adding a progressive tax and a neutral transfer (where progressivity is calculated with respect to households ranked by original income) to a fiscal system could be unequalizing.

Table 3-57 shows that adding a progressive tax and a progressive transfer (where progressivity is calculated with respect to households ranked by original income) to a fiscal system could be un-equalizing.

TABLE 3-56

Addition of a Progressive Tax and a Neutral Transfer with an Unequalizing Effect to a Fiscal System

Individual	Original income (OI)	Benefit (B)	OI + B	Tax (T)	OI − T	End income (EI)
1	2.00	1.00	3.00	0.00	2.00	3.00
2	2.00	1.00	3.00	0.00	2.00	3.00
3	2.00	1.00	3.00	0.00	2.00	3.00
4	2.00	1.00	3.00	1.00	1.00	2.00
Total	8.00	4.00	12.00	1.00	7.00	11.00
Average	2.00	1.00	3.00	0.25	1.75	2.75
Gini	0.0000	n.c.	0.0000	n.c.	0.1071	0.0682
C^X	0.0000	0.0000	0.0000	0.7500	−0.1071	−0.0682
Π_T^K or ρ_B^K	...	0.0000	...	0.7500	...	...

Note: In calculating progressivity, households' rank with respect to their original income is used.

n.c. = Not calculated; ... = Not applicable.

TABLE 3-57

Addition of a Progressive Tax and a Progressive Transfer with an Unequalizing Effect to a Fiscal System

Individual	Original income (OI)	Benefit (B)	OI + B	Tax (T)	OI − T	End income (EI)
1	2.00	1.00	3.00	0.00	2.00	3.00
2	2.00	0.00	2.00	0.00	2.00	2.00
3	2.00	0.00	2.00	0.00	2.00	2.00
4	2.00	0.00	2.00	1.00	1.00	1.00
Total	8.00	1.00	9.00	1.00	7.00	8.00
Average	2.00	0.25	2.25	0.25	1.75	2.00
Gini	0.0000	n.c.	0.0833	n.c.	0.1071	0.1875
C^X	0.0000	−0.7500	−0.0833	0.7500	−0.1071	−0.1875
Π_T^K or ρ_B^K	...	0.7500	...	0.7500	...	...

Note: In calculating progressivity, households' rank with respect to their original income is used.

n.c. = Not calculated; ... = Not applicable.

5 The Effect of a Marginal Change in One Tax or Transfer on the Equalizing (Unequalizing) Effect of a Whole System

This section focuses on the derivatives of the marginal contribution of a tax or transfer (that is, M_{T_1} or M_{B_1}), with respect to its progressivity or relative size, to determine whether such a marginal change would increase the equalizing effect of the whole system. What differentiates this section from chapter 2 in this Volume (the case of no reranking) is that the progressivity is calculated with respect to both the end income ranking and the original income ranking of households. In this section, therefore, I will discuss three derivatives (with respect to the relative size and two types of Kakwani indexes).

Before calculating the derivatives, I need to point out an important simplifying assumption. The derivatives represent a very minor change in a tax or transfer, and therefore it is safe to assume that the end income ranking of households would not change. This is not the case, of course, if we deviate from the case of a very "marginal" change in a tax or transfer.

It should also be noted that, conceptually, the derivatives of a marginal contribution with respect to either relative size or Kakwani indexes are equivalent to the derivatives of the redistributive effect or Gini of the end income with respect to these two variables, which should be easily seen in the following equation:[8]

$$M_{T_1} = G_{Z \setminus T_1} - G_Z = \overbrace{(G_X - G_Z)}^{RE} - (G_X - G_{Z \setminus T_1}).$$

Note that the Gini of the Final Income is the only term on the right-hand side that has T_1 in it; that is, G_Z and the rest of the terms are constants in any derivative with respect to the relative size or Kakwani index of T_1 (and they would drop out). Also note that while the sign of the derivatives of G_Z is different from RE and M_{T_1}, these derivatives are of the same size and equivalent interpretation. To provide a more intuitive explanation, we show the following three statements in the example below are equivalent.

EXAMPLE: DUE TO A MARGINAL CHANGE IN A TAX'S RELATIVE SIZE (OR ITS PROGRESSIVITY),

- the end Gini decreased by 0.2.
- the redistributive effect of the total system increased by 0.2.
- the marginal contribution of that tax (to reducing inequality) increased by 0.2.

5.1 The Case of a Marginal Change in a Tax

This section focuses on the derivatives of the marginal contribution of a tax with respect to its relative size (g), Kakwani index calculated with respect to the original income ranking of households and Kakwani index calculated with respect to the end income ranking of households ($\Pi_T^{K^Z}$).

---

[8] Recall from the notation section that $Z = X - \sum_{i=1}^n T_i + \sum_{j=1}^m B_j$ and $Z \setminus T_1 = X - \sum_{i=2}^n T_i + \sum_{j=1}^m B_j$.

To calculate the derivative of M_{T_1} with respect to g_1, we have two formulas to work with. Using equation 3-13, we get

$$M_{T_1} = \left\{ (G_X - C_X^Z) + \left(\frac{\sum_{i=1}^{n}(1-g_i)\Pi_{T_i}^{RS^Z} + \sum_{j=1}^{m}(1+b_j)\rho_{B_j}^{RS^Z}}{1 - \sum_{i=1}^{n} g_i + \sum_{j=1}^{m} b_j} \right) \right\}$$
$$- \left\{ \left(G_X - C_X^{Z\backslash T_1} \right) + \left(\frac{\sum_{i=2}^{n}(1-g_i)\Pi_{T_i}^{RS^{Z\backslash T_1}} + \sum_{j=1}^{m}(1+b_j)\rho_{B_j}^{RS^{Z\backslash T_1}}}{1 - \sum_{i=2}^{n} g_i + \sum_{j=1}^{m} b_j} \right) \right\}$$

or

$$M_{T_1} = \left\{ (G_X - C_X^Z) + \left(\frac{\sum_{i=1}^{n} g_i \Pi_{T_i}^{K^Z} + \sum_{j=1}^{m} b_j \rho_{B_j}^{K^Z}}{1 - \sum_{i=1}^{n} g_i + \sum_{j=1}^{m} b_j} \right) \right\}$$
$$- \left\{ \left(G_X - C_X^{Z\backslash T_1} \right) + \left(\frac{\sum_{i=2}^{n} g_i \Pi_{T_i}^{K^{Z\backslash T_1}} + \sum_{j=1}^{m} b_j \rho_{B_j}^{K^{Z\backslash T_1}}}{1 - \sum_{i=2}^{n} g_i + \sum_{j=1}^{m} b_j} \right) \right\}.$$

Therefore,

$$\frac{\partial M_{T_1}}{\partial g_1} = \frac{\partial(-C_X^Z)}{\partial g_1} + \frac{\left(1-\sum_{i=1}^{n} g_i + \sum_{j=1}^{m} b_j\right)\left(\Pi_{T_1}^{K^Z} + \frac{\partial \Pi_{T_1}^{K^Z}}{\partial g_1} g_1 + \sum_{i=2}^{n} g_i \frac{\partial \Pi_{T_i}^{K^Z}}{\partial g_1} + \sum_{j=1}^{m} b_j \frac{\partial \rho_{B_j}^{K^Z}}{\partial g_1}\right) + \left(\sum_{i=1}^{n} g_i \Pi_{T_i}^{K^Z} + \sum_{j=1}^{m} b_j \rho_{B_j}^{K^Z}\right)}{\left(1-\sum_{i=1}^{n} g_i + \sum_{j=1}^{m} b_j\right)^2}$$

or

$$\frac{\partial M_{T_1}}{\partial g_1} = \frac{\partial(-C_X^Z)}{\partial g_1} + \frac{\left(\Pi_{T_1}^{K^Z} + \frac{\partial \Pi_{T_1}^{K^Z}}{\partial g_1} g_1 + \sum_{i=2}^{n} g_i \frac{\partial \Pi_{T_i}^{K^Z}}{\partial g_1} + \sum_{j=1}^{m} b_j \frac{\partial \rho_{B_j}^{K^Z}}{\partial g_1}\right) + (C_X^Z - G_Z)}{1 - \sum_{i=1}^{n} g_i + \sum_{j=1}^{m} b_j}.$$

Note that if a new reranking were to occur due to the marginal change in g_1, then all terms ordered by Z would change, thus making it impossible to derive any general conclusion. However, our assumption about no further reranking (with respect to the end income ranking of households) would simplify the above derivative to the following equation:

$$\frac{\partial M_{T_1}}{\partial g_1} = \frac{\Pi_{T_1}^{K^Z} + (C_X^Z - G_Z)}{1 - \sum_{i=1}^{n} g_i + \sum_{j=1}^{m} b_j} = \frac{C_{T_1}^Z - G_Z}{1 - \sum_{i=1}^{n} g_i + \sum_{j=1}^{m} b_j}.$$

The sign of this derivative is ambiguous. A closer look at the numerator reveals that it follows the same idea as the traditional Kakwani index. In other words, if the concentration curve of a tax (with respect to the end income concept) happens to be below the Gini of the end income, then a marginal increase in the size of that tax would increase the value of the marginal contribution of that tax (to reducing inequality). The other obvious case is that when the concentration coefficient of a tax (with respect to the end income ranking of households) is negative, it makes the derivative unambiguously negative. This happens, for example, if the poorer a household is (with respect to the end income ranking of households), the more tax dollars it pays.

An equivalent formula can be derived from equation 3-16. From this equation, we have

$$M_{T_1} = \left[\left(\frac{g_1\left(\Pi^K_{T_1} - G_X - C^X_{Z\backslash T_1}\right)}{\left(1 - \sum_{i=1}^n g_i + \sum_{j=1}^m b_j\right)} \right) \right] + \left[\left(C^X_Z - G_Z\right) - \left(C^X_{Z\backslash T_1} - G_{Z\backslash T_1}\right) \right].$$

The derivative therefore is equal to

$$\frac{\partial M_{T_1}}{\partial g_1} = \frac{\left(\Pi^K_{T_1} - G_X - C^X_{Z\backslash T_1}\right)\left(1 - \sum_{i=1}^n g_i + \sum_{j=1}^m b_j\right) + g_1\left(\Pi^K_{T_1} - G_X - C^X_{Z\backslash T_1}\right)}{\left(1 - \sum_{i=1}^n g_i + \sum_{j=1}^m b_j\right)^2} + \frac{\partial(C^X_Z - G_Z)}{\partial g_1}$$

or

$$\frac{\partial M_{T_1}}{\partial g_1} = \frac{\left(\Pi^K_{T_1} - G_X - C^X_{Z\backslash T_1}\right)\left(1 - \sum_{i=2}^n g_i + \sum_{j=1}^m b_j\right)}{\left(1 - \sum_{i=1}^n g_i + \sum_{j=1}^m b_j\right)^2} + \frac{\partial(C^X_Z - G_Z)}{\partial g_1}.$$

Unlike the previous derivative, however, there is no reasonable simplifying assumption to take care of the last term,

$$\frac{\partial(C^X_Z - G_Z)}{\partial g_1}.$$

In order to calculate the derivative with respect to the Kakwani index when this index is calculated with respect to the original income ranking of households, one needs to use equation 3-16 and the transformation of the R-S index to the Kakwani index as mentioned previously:

$$M_{T_1} = \left[\left(\frac{g_1\left(\Pi^K_{T_1} - G_X - C^X_{Z\backslash T_1}\right)}{\left(1 - \sum_{i=1}^n g_i + \sum_{j=1}^m b_j\right)} \right) \right] + \left[\left(C^X_Z - G_Z\right) - \left(C^X_{Z\backslash T_1} - G_{Z\backslash T_1}\right) \right].$$

Therefore,

$$\frac{\partial M_{T_1}}{\partial \Pi_{T_1}^K} = \frac{g_1}{1 - \sum_{i=1}^n g_i + \sum_{j=1}^m b_j} + \frac{\partial (C_Z^X - G_Z)}{\partial \Pi_{T_1}^K}.$$

The sign of this derivative is ambiguous as well. The value of this derivative depends on the distribution of postfiscal income and how the progressivity is changed (that is, the latter term in the derivative cannot be simplified any further in the general case).

Finally, the derivative with respect to the Kakwani index when this index is calculated with respect to the end income ranking of households can be calculated using equation 3-13 and transformation of the R-S index to Kakwani index; that is,

$$M_{T_1} = \left\{ (G_X - C_X^Z) + \left(\frac{\sum_{i=1}^n g_i \Pi_{T_i}^{KZ} + \sum_{j=1}^m b_j \rho_{B_j}^{KZ}}{1 - \sum_{i=1}^n g_i + \sum_{j=1}^m b_j} \right) \right\}$$
$$- \left\{ \left(G_X - C_X^{Z \setminus T_1} \right) + \left(\frac{\sum_{i=2}^n g_i \Pi_{T_i}^{KZ \setminus T_1} + \sum_{j=1}^m b_j \rho_{B_j}^{KZ \setminus T_1}}{1 - \sum_{i=2}^n g_i + \sum_{j=1}^m b_j} \right) \right\}.$$

Therefore,

$$\frac{\partial M_{T_1}}{\partial \Pi_{T_1}^{KZ}} = \frac{\partial (-C_X^Z)}{\Pi_{T_1}^{KZ}} + \frac{g_1 + \sum_{i=2}^n g_i \dfrac{\partial \Pi_{T_i}^{KZ}}{\partial \Pi_{T_1}^{KZ}} + \sum_{j=1}^m b_j \dfrac{\partial \rho_{B_j}^{KZ}}{\partial \Pi_{T_1}^{KZ}}}{1 - \sum_{i=1}^n g_i + \sum_{j=1}^m b_j}.$$

Using the simplifying assumption that increase in the progressivity is unchanged in the final ranking (Z), the preceding derivative would be simplified to

$$\frac{\partial M_{T_1}}{\partial \Pi_{T_1}^{KZ}} = \frac{g_1}{1 - \sum_{i=1}^n g_i + \sum_{j=1}^m b_j}.$$

This derivative is always positive. Therefore, making a tax more progressive, when progressivity is calculated with respect to the end income ranking of households, is always equalizing (with or without reranking), assuming that no change in the end income ranking of households occurs as a result of a marginal increase in the progressivity of that tax. It is worth noting that the value of this derivative is equal to the one calculated in chapter 2 in this Volume for the derivative of the marginal effect with respect to the traditional Kakwani index. This outcome is of course expected as these two types of Kakwani indexes are the same when there is no reranking.

5.2 The Case of a Marginal Change in a Transfer

This section provides the derivatives of the marginal contribution of a transfer with respect to its relative size (b), the Kakwani index calculated with respect to the original income ranking of households (ρ_B^K), and the Kakwani index calculated with respect to the end income ranking of households (ρ_B^{KZ}). Because there is no specific methodological difference between this section and the previous one, only the formulas for these derivatives are presented. First, the derivative of marginal contribution of a transfer with respect to its relative size (b):

$$\frac{\partial M_{B_1}}{\partial b_1} = \frac{\partial(-C_X^Z)}{\partial b_1} + \frac{\left(\rho_{B_1}^{KZ} + \frac{\partial \rho_{B_1}^{KZ}}{\partial b_1} b_1 + \sum_{i=1}^n g_i \frac{\partial \Pi_{T_i}^{KZ}}{\partial b_1} + \sum_{j=2}^m b_j \frac{\partial \rho_{B_j}^{KZ}}{\partial b_1} \right) - (C_X^Z - G_Z)}{1 - \sum_{i=1}^n g_i + \sum_{j=1}^m b_j}.$$

With the simplifying assumption that the end income ranking of households (Z) would not change as a result of a marginal change in the relative size of the transfer, we have

$$\frac{\partial M_{B_1}}{\partial b_1} = \frac{\rho_{B_1}^{KZ} - (C_X^Z - G_Z)}{1 - \sum_{i=1}^n g_i + \sum_{j=1}^m b_j} = \frac{G_Z - C_{B_1}^Z}{1 - \sum_{i=1}^n g_i + \sum_{j=1}^m b_j}.$$

The sign of this derivative is ambiguous, but it would be positive if, for example, the concentration curve of a benefit (with respect to the end income ranking of households) happened to be above the Gini curve of the end income. Also, a negative concentration coefficient of a benefit (with respect to the end income ranking of households) would result in a positive sign for the preceding derivative, which happens when the poorer a household is, the higher the dollar value of the transfer it receives.

As an alternative, and using the traditional Kakwani index, we would have

$$\frac{\partial M_{B_1}}{\partial b_1} = \frac{\left(\rho_{B_1}^{RS} - G_X - C_{Z \backslash B_1}^X \right) \left(1 - \sum_{i=1}^n g_i + \sum_{j=2}^m b_j \right)}{\left(1 - \sum_{i=1}^n g_i + \sum_{j=1}^m b_j \right)^2} + \frac{\partial(C_Z^X - G_Z)}{\partial b_1}.$$

The derivative with respect to ρ_B^K would be equal to

$$\frac{\partial M_{B_1}}{\partial \rho_B^K} = \frac{b_1}{1 - \sum_{i=1}^n g_i + \sum_{j=1}^m b_j} + \frac{\partial(C_Z^X - G_Z)}{\partial \rho_B^K}.$$

The sign of this derivative is ambiguous since the last term cannot be simplified any further.

Finally, the derivative with respect to ρ_B^{KZ} would be equal to

$$\frac{\partial M_{B_1}}{\partial \rho_B^{K^Z}} = \frac{\partial(-C_X^Z)}{\partial \rho_B^{K^Z}} + \frac{\left(b_1 + \sum_{i=1}^{n} g_i \frac{\partial \prod_{T_i}^{K^Z}}{\partial \rho_B^{K^Z}} + \sum_{j=2}^{m} b_j \frac{\partial \rho_{B_j}^{K^Z}}{\partial \rho_B^{K^Z}}\right)}{1 - \sum_{i=1}^{n} g_i + \sum_{j=1}^{m} b_j}.$$

Applying the simplifying assumption of no change in the final ranking (Z) results in the following formula:

$$\frac{\partial M_{B_1}}{\partial \rho_B^{K^Z}} = \frac{b_1}{1 - \sum_{i=1}^{n} g_i + \sum_{j=1}^{m} b_j}.$$

Unlike all preceding derivatives, this one has a positive sign, which means that making a transfer more progressive, when progressivity is calculated with respect to the end income ranking of households, will always reduce inequality as long as the end income ranking does not change. As in the case of a tax explained in section 5.1, this derivative is equal to the one calculated in chapter 2 of this Volume for the derivative of the marginal contribution with respect to the Kakwani index in the absence of reranking in the system.

The main message of this chapter is that in the presence of reranking, indicators of progressivity do not provide any insight into whether a tax or transfer reduces inequality in the marginal contribution sense. Mathematical derivations and various examples throughout this chapter are intended to make this message clear. The complicated and usually inconclusive math can be entirely avoided if the marginal contribution analysis is employed. In other words, there is no shortcut to answering fiscal policy questions other than performing simulations and accounting for all components (taxes and transfers) of a fiscal system.

6 Lambert's Conundrum Revisited

Chapter 2 of this Volume introduced the Lambert conundrum in which a regressive tax exerts an equalizing effect. Similarly, a progressive tax can increase inequality. This chapter shows that reranking can also result in a similar outcome especially for progressive taxes and transfers. Since reranking always happens in the real world, it is important to decompose the role of reranking in producing these odd outcomes from what one would describe as a pure Lambert conundrum. This section introduces a decomposition designed to achieve this goal.

To gain an introduction to this decomposition technique, assume that we are dealing with a regressive tax that has an equalizing effect. We would like to know how much change (reduction) in Gini happens before individuals are reranked and how much it happens after they are reranked.

TABLE 3-58

Using an Actual Tax, T, to Simulate a Hypothetical Tax, T^{NR}, That Does Not Create Reranking

Individual	X + B	T	X + B − T	T^{NR}	X + B − T^{NR}
1	11	0	11	0	11
2	12	0	12	0	12
3	13	2	11	1	12
4	14	4	10	2	12

$$MC_T = G_{X+B} - G_{X-T+B} = \overbrace{\left(G_{X+B} - G_{X-T^{NR}+B}\right)}^{\text{Change in Gini before reranking begins}} + \overbrace{\left(G_{X-T^{NR}+B} - G_{X-T+B}\right)}^{\text{Change in Gini after reranking begins}},$$

where MC_T is the marginal contribution of a tax (we assume the system has only one tax and one transfer), G_{X+B} is the Gini before tax, and G_{X-T+B} is the Gini after the tax is added to the fiscal system. Finally, $G_{X-T^{NR}+B}$ is the Gini of a simulated distribution of income in which we begin adding taxes to people but only up to the point that they are not reranked. Table 3-58 shows how this simulation works.

In the pure Lambert conundrum, for example, the latter term of the decomposition equation would be zero because there would be no reranking. Moreover, if the simulated tax, T^{NR}, is still regressive and equalizing, we can conclude that the Lambert conundrum does not depend on the reranking. However, the size of the total reduction in Gini may significantly depend on the reranking, and the above decomposition would identify the relative importance of it.

Generalizing this decomposition to the case of any tax or transfer in a fiscal system with numerous other taxes and transfers, we would have the following equations:

$$M_{T_1} = \left(G_{Z\backslash T_1} - G_{Z_{T_1^{NR}}}\right) + \left(G_{Z_{T_1^{NR}}} - G_Z\right)$$

$$M_{B_1} = \left(G_{Z\backslash B_1} - G_{Z_{B_1^{NR}}}\right) + \left(G_{Z_{B_1^{NR}}} - G_Z\right),$$

where Z is the end income (Market Income minus all taxes plus all transfers) and $Z\backslash T_1$ ($Z\backslash B_1$) is the end income without including $T_1(B_1)$. Finally, $Z_{T_1^{NR}}(Z_{B_1^{NR}})$ is the end income when the simulated $T_1^{NR}(B_1^{NR})$ is used instead of the actual $T_1(B_1)$.

References

Atkinson, Anthony Barnes. 1979. *Horizontal Equity and the Distribution of the Tax Burden* (London: Social Science Research Council).

Duclos, Jean-Yves, and Abdelkrim Araar. 2007. *Poverty and Equity: Measurement, Policy and Estimation with DAD*, vol. 2 (New York: Jointly published by Springer and International Research Development Center).

Enami, Ali, Nora Lustig, and Rodrigo Aranda. 2022. "Analytic Foundations: Measuring the Redistributive Impact of Taxes and Transfers," chap. 2 in *Commitment to Equity Handbook: Estimating the Impact of Fiscal Policy on Inequality and Poverty*, 2nd ed., Vol. 1, edited by Nora Lustig (Brookings Institution Press and CEQ Institute, Tulane University). Free online version available at www.commitmentoequity.org.

Lambert, Peter. 2001. *The Distribution and Redistribution of Income* (Manchester University Press).

Plotnick, Robert. 1981. "A Measure of Horizontal Inequity." *Review of Economics and Statistics* 63, no. 2, pp. 283–88.

———. 1982. "The Concept and Measurement of Horizontal Inequity." *Journal of Public Economics* 17, no. 3, pp. 373–91 (doi:10.1016/0047-2727(82)90071-8).

Reynolds, Morgan, and Eugene Smolensky. 2013. *Public Expenditures, Taxes, and the Distribution of Income: The United States, 1950, 1961, 1970* (London: Academic Press).

Chapter 4

CAN A POVERTY-REDUCING AND PROGRESSIVE TAX AND TRANSFER SYSTEM HURT THE POOR?

Sean Higgins and Nora Lustig

This chapter is a reprint of an article published in the *Journal of Development Economics*, which can be accessed in its published form at http://dx.doi.org /10 1016/j.jdeveco.2016.04.001. The article is published Open Access funded by the Bill & Melinda Gates Foundation, under Creative Commons license CC BY 4.0. If you use material from this chapter, including but not limited to using the fiscal impoverishment measure, please cite the following article: Sean Higgins and Nora Lustig. 2016. "Can a Poverty-Reducing and Progressive Tax and Transfer System Hurt the Poor?" *Journal of Development Economics* 122, September, pp. 63–75.

Abstract

To analyze anti-poverty policies in tandem with the taxes used to pay for them, comparisons of poverty before and after taxes and transfers are often used. We show that these comparisons, as well as measures of horizontal equity and progressivity, can fail to capture an important aspect: that a substantial proportion of the poor are made poorer (or non-poor made poor) by the tax and transfer system. We illustrate with data from seventeen developing countries: in fifteen, the fiscal system is poverty-reducing and progressive, but in ten of these at least one-quarter of the poor pay more in taxes than they receive in transfers. We call this fiscal impoverishment, and axiomatically derive a measure of its extent. An analogous measure of fiscal gains of the poor is also derived, and we show that changes in the poverty gap can be decomposed into our axiomatic measures of fiscal impoverishment and gains.

Keywords: poverty, horizontal equity, progressivity, fiscal impoverishment

1 Introduction

Anti-poverty policies are often evaluated in isolation from the taxes used to pay for them.[1] If, however, taxes cancel out the benefits of transfers for many poor households,

---

[1] We focus on anti-poverty policies that are redistributive in nature, one of the three categories of anti-poverty policies described in Ghatak (2015).

so that some poor pay more in taxes than they receive in transfers, the objective of these policies might be compromised. This is especially important when poverty traps exist at the individual level (e.g., Ghatak, 2015; Ravallion, 2015): a tax and transfer system in which many poor pay more in taxes than they receive in transfers risks pushing the transiently poor into chronic poverty by shifting their after tax and transfer incomes below their individual-specific poverty trap thresholds.

Recently, the connection between anti-poverty policies and the taxes used to pay for them has come into the spotlight in the debates over the United Nations' Post-2015 Sustainable Development Goals. In recognition of the resources necessary to achieve these ambitious development goals, and partly as a consequence of austerity in advanced countries (and thus lower anticipated flows of international aid to developing countries), much of the discussion has focused on how developing countries should collect the revenue necessary to achieve the goals.[2] Influential organizations such as the International Monetary Fund and World Bank emphasize the importance of efficient taxes with minimal exemptions (International Monetary Fund, 2013; World Bank, 2013). When concerns are raised about these taxes—such as a no-exemption value added tax—falling disproportionately on the poor, many argue that higher tax burdens on the poor are acceptable if they are accompanied by sufficiently large targeted transfers: "spending instruments are available that are better targeted to the pursuit of equity concerns" (Keen and Lockwood, 2010, p. 141). Similarly, Engel et al. (1999, p. 186) assert that "it is quite obvious that the disadvantages of a proportional tax are moderated by adequate targeting" of transfers, since "what the poor individual pays in taxes is returned to her." These taxes "might conceivably be the best way to finance pro-poor expenditures, with the net effect being to relieve poverty" (Ebrill et al., 2001, p. 105).

How can we be sure that what the poor individual pays in taxes is returned to her? Even if the net effect of taxes and transfers is to relieve poverty, are some poor made worse off? When taxes and transfers are analyzed in tandem to determine how they affect the poor, it is common to compare poverty before taxes and transfers ("pre-fisc") to poverty after taxes and transfers ("post-fisc"). As we show in this paper, however, a fiscal system can be unambiguously poverty-reducing for a range of poverty lines and any poverty measure, yet still make a substantial proportion of the poor worse off. This phenomenon does not only occur with regressive taxes: we show that taxes and transfers can be globally progressive, unambiguously equalizing, and unambiguously poverty-reducing and *still* make many poor worse off. In other words, conventional tools used to measure how the poor are affected by the tax and transfer system are inadequate to measure whether some of the poor pay more in taxes than they receive in transfers, a phenomenon we call fiscal impoverishment (FI).

We also show that in practice, there are a number of countries with poverty-reducing and progressive tax and transfer systems that nevertheless make a substantial proportion of the poor poorer (or non-poor poor), illustrating with data from seventeen

---

[2] See, for example, the focus on domestic resource mobilization in United Nations (2015).

developing countries.[3] In fifteen of these countries, post-fisc poverty is unambiguously lower than pre-fisc poverty (measured with any poverty line up to $1.25 per person per day in low and lower-middle income countries and $2.50 per day in upper-middle income countries)[4] and the tax and transfer system is globally progressive and unambiguously equalizing, i.e., we would conclude that the tax and transfer system unambiguously benefits the poor using conventional measures, potentially overlooking impoverishment. In all of these countries, some degree of FI occurs, and in ten of them we find that at least one-quarter of the poor pay more in taxes than they receive in transfers.

In light of the debate about financing anti-poverty policies and the Sustainable Development Goals, it is necessary to fill this gap in the measurement arsenal and develop a measure of this phenomenon that adheres to certain properties. We axiomatically derive a measure of FI, as well as an analogous measure for fiscal gains of the poor (FGP), which captures the extent to which some poor receive more in transfers than they pay in taxes.[5] We then show how a commonly used measure of poverty that overlooks the extent of FI, the poverty gap, can be decomposed into FI and FGP components using our axiomatic measures, again illustrating with data from seventeen developing countries. Because the extent of FI and FGP depend on the particular poverty line used, we also propose dominance criteria that can be used to determine whether one fiscal system (such as the one that would occur after a proposed reform) causes unambiguously less FI or more FGP than another (such as the current system) over a range of poverty lines. We analyze FI and FGP over a range of poverty lines in Brazil, which is a pertinent example due to the coexistence of high tax burdens on the poor

---

[3] Our illustration uses results provided to us by the authors of country studies conducted as part of the Commitment to Equity (CEQ) Institute, located at Tulane University (www.commitmenttoequity .org). The countries included are Armenia (Younger and Khachatryan, forthcoming), Bolivia (Paz Arauco et al., 2014), Brazil (authors' calculations), Chile (Martinez-Aguilar and Ortiz-Juarez, 2015), the Dominican Republic (Aristy-Escuder et al., forthcoming), Ecuador (Llerena Pinto et al., 2015), El Salvador (Beneke et al., 2015), Ethiopia (Hill et al., forthcoming), Ghana (Younger et al., 2015), Guatemala (Cabrera et al., 2015), Indonesia (Afkar et al., forthcoming), Mexico (Aranda and Scott, 2015), Peru (Jaramillo et al., 2015), Russia (Lopez-Calva et al., forthcoming), South Africa (Inchauste et al., forthcoming), Sri Lanka (Arunatilake et al., forthcoming), and Tunisia (Shimeles et al., forthcoming). For an overview of the impact of taxes and social spending on inequality and poverty in many of these countries, see Lustig (2015).

[4] The $1.25 per person per day poverty line (in 2005 US dollars adjusted for purchasing power parity) is approximately equal to the median poverty line of the fifteen poorest countries for which poverty line data are available, and the $2.50 line to the median of the world's low and middle income countries excluding the fifteen poorest (Chen and Ravallion, 2010).

[5] Our axioms are adapted from the axiomatic poverty and mobility measurement literatures (see Foster, 2006, and Zheng, 1997, for surveys of axiomatic poverty measurement and Fields, 2001, for a survey of axiomatic mobility measurement). Our resulting measure can be viewed as a censored directional version of the mobility measure derived by Fields and Ok (1996).

(Baer and Galvão, 2008; Goñi et al., 2011) and lauded poverty-reducing cash transfer programs: a large-scale conditional cash transfer program that reaches over one-fourth of all Brazilian households and a non-contributory pension program for the elderly poor that reaches one-third of all elderly (Levy and Schady, 2013, table 1).

Section 2 uses hypothetical and empirical examples to show that common tools to assess how the tax and transfer system affects the poor can fail to capture FI. Section 3 axiomatically derives a measure that does capture FI; it then proposes a partial FI ordering that can be used to compare the level of FI induced by two fiscal systems for any poverty line. Section 4 derives an analogous measure and partial ordering for FGP and shows that the poverty gap can be decomposed into our axiomatic measures of FI and FGP. Section 5 uses data from seventeen developing countries to illustrate the axiomatic measures and poverty gap decomposition. Section 6 concludes, and the formal axioms and proofs are collected in the appendix.

2 The Problems with Conventional Measures

Through a number of examples, we illustrate and explain the problems with conventional measures of poverty, horizontal equity, and progressivity. Of course, these measures are still quite important for assessing a tax and transfer system; we merely aim to show that they do not capture everything we are interested in. First, in section 2.1 we show the problem with poverty measures when they are used to compare poverty before and after taxes and transfers. Although comparisons of pre-fisc and post-fisc poverty are common in empirical studies (e.g., DeFina and Thanawala, 2004; Hoynes et al., 2006), poverty measures can overlook fiscal impoverishment because they obey the anonymity axiom (which is usually taken as an innocuous and desirable axiom): the tax and transfer system can reduce poverty while simultaneously making a substantial portion of the poor poorer, or making some non-poor poor. The anonymity axiom is not the only culprit for the shortcomings of existing measures, however, in section 2.2 we show that measures designed to incorporate information about individuals' pre-fisc positions, such as measures of horizontal equity and progressivity, can also fail to capture FI.[6] To show that these shortcomings of conventional measures are not confined to contrived hypothetical examples, but rather occur frequently in practice, in section 2.3 we present examples from seventeen developing countries: in ten, the tax and transfer system is poverty-reducing and progressive, but hurts a substantial portion of the poor by pushing them deeper into poverty.

---

[6] Other measures that are sometimes used, such as the percent of income gained or lost by each pre-fisc income decile, overlook FI for a distinct reason: they average over individuals, so for example the poorest decile could gain income on average while a substantial number of poor within the first decile lose income. We do not include these measures in this paper since the reason they overlook FI is obvious.

2.1 Poverty Measures

Suppose the change in poverty caused by the fiscal system will be evaluated over a range of poverty lines, including lines greater than 6 and less than or equal to 10. Suppose there are three individuals in society with pre-fisc incomes of 5, 8, and 20, and (retaining the order of the individuals) post-fisc incomes 9, 6, and 18. For any poverty line in the range we are considering, and for any poverty measure in a broad class of measures, poverty has either not changed or decreased. This is because the poorest individual in the pre-fisc income distribution has an income of 5 and the second-poorest 8, while in the post-fisc distribution, the poorest has an income of 6 and the second-poorest 9. Poverty comparisons do not take into account that the poorest individual in the post-fisc distribution, with an income of 6, is not the poorest individual in the pre-fisc distribution who has an income of 5, but instead had an income of 8 in the pre-fisc distribution and paid 2 more in taxes than she received in transfers. Depending on the exact poverty line chosen within the range we are considering, this individual was either pre-fisc poor and lost income to the fiscal system, or pre-fisc nonpoor and pushed into poverty by the fiscal system.

It is clear, then, that poverty measures are inadequate to measure whether some of the poor pay more in taxes than they receive in transfers. Stochastic dominance tests, which are used to determine whether poverty is unambiguously lower in one income distribution than another for any poverty line and a broad class of poverty measures (Atkinson, 1987; Foster and Shorrocks, 1988), are also inadequate. This is because poverty measures and stochastic dominance tests are anonymous with respect to pre-fisc income: they compare the pre- and post-fisc income distributions without paying attention to the specific pre-fisc to post-fisc trajectory of particular individuals' incomes. The anonymity axiom, normally considered an innocuous and desirable property, becomes problematic when we are concerned with how the fiscal system affects the poor: in the words of Amiel and Cowell (1994, p. 448–9), "anonymity itself may be questionable as a welfare criterion when the social-welfare function is to take into account something more than the end-state distribution of incomes." Anonymity implies that poverty measures fail to take into account individuals' initial positions, and thus whether some are being made poorer by the tax and transfer system.[7]

---

[7] Amiel and Cowell (1994) also point out that the respect for income dominance axiom is only equivalent to the monotonicity axiom when anonymity is imposed. In the example from the previous paragraph, the post-fisc income distribution first order stochastically dominates the pre-fisc distribution on the domain from 0 to the maximum poverty line, so it would be evaluated as superior by any measure satisfying poverty focus and respect for income dominance (or, equivalently, poverty focus and both monotonicity and anonymity). It would not necessarily be evaluated as superior by a measure satisfying poverty focus and monotonicity but not anonymity, however. Other concerns with the anonymity axiom have also been pointed out: for example, it can clash with the Pigou–

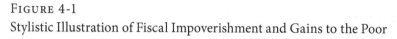

FIGURE 4-1

Stylistic Illustration of Fiscal Impoverishment and Gains to the Poor

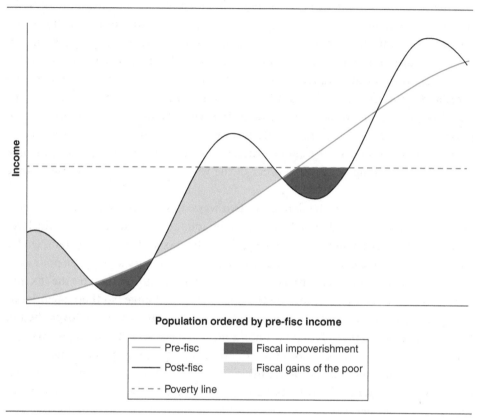

To illustrate visually, figure 4-1 shows a stylistic representation of the pre- and post-fisc incomes of a population ordered by pre-fisc income. The orange curve represents pre-fisc income, blue post-fisc income, and dashed gray the poverty line; because some individuals receive more in transfers than they pay in taxes, while others pay more in taxes than they receive in transfers, the post-fisc income curve is sometimes above and sometimes below the pre-fisc income curve. Although post-fisc poverty is lower than pre-fisc poverty because the losses of some poor are more than compensated by the gains of other poor, there is FI. The extent of FI is shown by the dark-shaded areas, while the light-shaded areas represent the extent of FGP (using the measures we axiomatically derive in sections 3 and 4).

Dalton transfer axiom when there are households of different types (Ebert, 1997) and with the subgroup sensitivity axiom, an extension of the Pigou–Dalton transfer axiom to subgroups (Subramanian, 2006).

2.2 Horizontal Equity and Progressivity

Anonymity is not the only reason conventional measures overlook fiscal impoverishment: non-anonymous measures such as horizontal equity and progressivity, which are designed to incorporate information about an individual's pre-fisc position, can fail to capture FI because they are not concerned with whether her net tax burden (taxes paid minus transfers received) is positive or negative. Denote income before taxes and transfers by $y_i^0 \in \mathbb{R}_+$ and income after taxes and transfers by $y_i^1 \in \mathbb{R}_+$ for each $i \in S$, where S is the set of individuals in society. Consider a range of potential poverty lines $Z \subset \mathbb{R}_+$. Each individual's income before or after taxes and transfers is arranged in the vector y^0 or y^1, both ordered in ascending order of pre-fisc income y_i^0—even if reranking occurs, the order of the y^1 vector reflects the pre-fisc income ranking.

Horizontal equity can be defined in two ways: the reranking definition, which requires that no pair of individuals switch ranks, and the classical definition, which requires that pre-fisc equals are treated equally by the tax and transfer system. Under either definition, the existence or absence of horizontal equity among the poor does not tell us whether FI has occurred. Even if some are impoverished by the tax and transfer system, the ranking among the poor may not change (so there is horizontal equity by the reranking definition) and pre-fisc equals may be impoverished to the same degree (so there is classical horizontal equity): e.g., $Z = (6, 10]$, $y^0 = (1, 1, 7, 7, 13)$, $y^1 = (3, 3, 6, 6, 11)$. Nor does horizontal inequity among the poor necessarily imply FI, because there could be reranking among the poor or unequal treatment among pre-fisc equals when the tax and transfer system lifts incomes of some of the poor without decreasing incomes of any poor: e.g., $Z = (6, 10]$, $y^0 = (5, 5, 6, 20)$, $y^1 = (5, 7, 6, 18)$.

A tax and transfer system is everywhere progressive when net taxes (i.e., taxes minus benefits), relative to pre-fisc income, increase with income (Duclos, 1997; Lambert, 1988). The tax and transfer system can be progressive (and unambiguously equalizing) but cause fiscal impoverishment: e.g., $Z = (6, 10]$, $y^0 = (1, 3, 7, 13)$, $y^1 = (3, 4, 6, 11)$; net taxes relative to pre-fisc income increase with income, but the third individual whose income falls from 7 to 6 is fiscally impoverished; thus, progressivity is not a sufficient condition to ensure that FI does not occur. Nor is progressivity a necessary condition for the absence of FI: e.g., $Z = (6, 10]$, $y^0 = (1, 3, 7, 14)$, $y^1 = (1, 5, 8, 11)$, which involves no FI but is not everywhere progressive because net taxes first decrease with income when moving from the poorest to the second-poorest, then increase with income thereafter.

Table 4-1 summarizes the examples presented in sections 2.1 and 2.2 to show that conventional tools—specifically, poverty measures (and stochastic dominance tests) and measures of or tests for horizontal equity and progressivity—can overlook FI.

TABLE 4-1

Summary of the Problems with Conventional Measures

Measure	Issue	Example with $Z = (6, 10]$
Poverty (and stochastic dominance)	$\downarrow$ poverty $\nRightarrow$ no FI (anonymity)	$y^0 = (5, 8, 20)$, $y^1 = (9, 6, 18)$
Horizontal equity	Horizontally equitable $\nRightarrow$ no FI	$y^0 = (1, 1, 7, 7, 13)$, $y^1 = (3, 3, 6, 6, 11)$
	No FI $\nRightarrow$ horizontally equitable	$y^0 = (5, 5, 6, 20)$, $y^1 = (5, 7, 6, 18)$
Progressivity	Progressive $\nRightarrow$ no FI	$y^0 = (1, 3, 7, 13)$, $y^1 = (3, 4, 6, 11)$
	No FI $\nRightarrow$ progressive	$y^0 = (1, 3, 7, 14)$, $y^1 = (1, 5, 8, 11)$

2.3 Real-World Examples

The problems with conventional measures are not limited to contrived hypothetical examples. In a number of countries, we observe an unambiguous reduction in poverty and a globally progressive tax and transfer system, while a significant proportion of the poor are fiscally impoverished. Using the income concepts from Higgins et al. (2015), we compare market income (before taxes and transfers) to post-fiscal income (after direct and indirect taxes, direct cash and food transfers, and indirect subsidies) in seventeen developing countries. We use post-fiscal income as the after taxes and transfers income concept even though taxes are used to fund more than just direct cash and food transfers and indirect subsidies from the government (e.g., they are used to fund public goods and services, many of which also reach the poor) because this is the income concept relevant for measuring poverty: it is "disposable money and near-money income" that should be compared to the poverty line when the latter is based on "a poverty budget for food, clothing, shelter, and similar items" (Citro and Michael, 1995, p. 212, 237). For low and lower-middle income countries, we use a poverty line of \$1.25 per person per day; for upper middle income countries, \$2.50 per day. Table 4-2 column 1 shows the pre-fisc (market income) poverty headcount and column 2 shows the change in poverty from the pre-fisc to the post-fisc income distribution; countries in which poverty increased due to the fiscal system are excluded.[8]

---

[8] Although the table only shows poverty for a particular poverty line and poverty measure, it is also true that the post-fisc distribution first order stochastically dominates the pre-fisc distribution from 0 to the poverty line used for each country, meaning that poverty unambiguously fell for all poverty lines up to \$1.25 or \$2.50 and all poverty measures in a broad class.

TABLE 4-2
Poverty, Inequality, and Fiscal Impoverishment in Developing Countries

Country (survey year)	(1) Pre-fisc poverty headcount (%)	(2) Change in poverty headcount (p.p.)	(3) Pre-fisc inequality (Gini)	(4) Reynolds-Smolensky (post-fisc w.r.t. profisc)	(5) Change in inequality (ΔGini)	(6) Fiscally impoverished as % of population	(7) Fiscally impoverished as % of post-fisc poor
Panel A: Upper-middle income countries, using a poverty line of $2.50 per day							
Brazil (2008–2009)	16.8	–0.8	57.5	4.6	–3.5	5.6	34.9
Chile (2013)	2.8	–1.4	49.4	3.2	–3.0	0.3	19.2
Ecuador (2011–2012)	10.8	–3.8	47.8	3.5	–3.3	0.2	3.2
Mexico (2012)	13.3	–1.2	54.4	3.8	–2.5	4.0	32.7
Peru (2011)	13.8	–0.2	45.9	0.9	–0.8	3.2	23.8
Russia (2010)	4.3	–1.3	39.7	3.9	–2.6	1.1	34.4
South Africa (2010–2011)	49.3	–5.2	77.1	8.3	–7.7	5.9	13.3
Tunisia (2010)	7.8	–0.1	44.7	8.0	–6.9	3.0	38.5
Panel B: Lower-middle income countries, using a poverty line of $1.25 per day							
Armenia (2011)	21.4	–8.4	47.4	12.9	–9.2	6.2	52.3
Bolivia (2009)	10.9	–0.5	50.3	0.6	–0.3	6.6	63.2
Dominican Republic (2007)	6.8	–0.9	50.2	2.2	–2.2	1.0	16.3
El Salvador (2011)	4.3	–0.7	44.0	2.2	–2.1	1.0	27.0
Guatemala (2010)	12.0	–0.8	49.0	1.4	–1.2	7.0	62.2
Indonesia (2012)	12.0	–1.5	39.8	1.1	–0.8	4.1	39.2
Sri Lanka (2009–2010)	5.0	–0.7	37.1	1.3	–1.1	1.6	36.4

Sources: For Brazil, authors' calculations. For other countries, provided to us by the authors of the studies cited in footnote 3.

Notes: p.p. = percentage points. w.r.t. = with respect to. Ethiopia and Ghana are not included in the table because poverty with a $1.25 per day poverty line increased from pre-fisc to post-fisc income (and hence they do not illustrate shortcomings of conventional measures). Country classifications are from the World Bank for the year of the survey.

Moving to the progressivity of the tax and transfer system and change in inequality in each country, column 3 shows the pre-fisc Gini coefficient and column 4 shows the Reynolds and Smolensky (1977) index, which is a summary indicator corresponding to tests of global progressivity; the Reynolds-Smolensky equals the pre-fisc Gini minus the concentration coefficient of post-fisc income with respect to pre-fisc income, and thus globally progressive systems have a positive Reynolds-Smolensky index. Column 5 shows the change in inequality, with negative numbers indicating that inequality fell as a result of the tax and transfer system.[9]

Since we do not derive an axiomatic measure of FI until section 3, here we use two intuitively appealing measures likely to have policy traction. Column 6 shows the percent *of the population* that are fiscally impoverished and column 7 the percent *of the post-fisc poor* that are fiscally impoverished. Although all of the countries in table 4-2 experienced a reduction in poverty and inequality due to the tax and transfer system, the amount of FI varies greatly between countries. In ten countries—Armenia, Bolivia, Brazil, El Salvador, Guatemala, Indonesia, Mexico, Russia, Sri Lanka, and Tunisia—between one-quarter and two-thirds of the post-fisc poor lost income to the fiscal system.[10] In other countries, this figure is much lower, at 13.3% of the post-fisc poor in South Africa (but, due to the high proportion of the total population that is poor, still 5.9% of the total population) and 3.2% of the post-fisc poor in Ecuador.

Even when poverty increases from pre-fisc to post-fisc income and hence we know that FI has occurred (as in Ghana and Ethiopia), it is impossible to tell its extent without explicit measures like the ones we propose in section 3. A stark example of this comes from Ethiopia, where looking at poverty and progressivity numbers alone greatly masks the extent of FI: the headcount ratio at $1.25 per day increases from 31.9% to 33.2% of the population, while squared poverty gap and Gini coefficient fall as a result of taxes and transfers (World Bank, 2015). Nevertheless, applying our measures to the same data, Hill et al. (forthcoming) find that 28.5% of Ethiopians and over 80% of the post-fisc poor experience FI.

Even if we add the value of public spending on education and health (imputed at their government cost to families who report a child attending public school or who report using public health facilities), fiscal impoverishment is still high in several countries: in Armenia, Ethiopia, Indonesia, Tunisia, and Russia, between 25 and 50% of those who are fiscally impoverished before adding in benefits from public spending on

---

[9] We test global progressivity by dominance of the concentration curve of post-fisc with respect to pre-fisc income over the pre-fisc Lorenz curve, and test unambiguously equalizing by comparing the post-fisc and pre-fisc Lorenz curves.

[10] If we instead scale down taxes so that they equal the transfers included in our analysis, which we avoid in the main analysis for the reasons mentioned above in defense of post-fiscal income as the after taxes and transfers income concept, FI is lower: for example, in Brazil 10.8% of the post-fisc poor are fiscally impoverished using this method.

health and education are still fiscally impoverished when these benefits are included as transfers.

3 Measures of Fiscal Impoverishment

To assess anti-poverty policies in tandem with the taxes used to finance them, it is important to have measures of the extent of fiscal impoverishment. In the last section, we provided a glimpse of FI in several developing countries using two simple, straightforward, and intuitive measures that—given these features—can be useful for policy discussions. These two measures also have drawbacks, however. To illustrate their limitations, we begin by providing more detail about the two measures. For a particular poverty line $z \in Z$, there is *fiscal impoverishment* if $y_i^1 < y_i^0$ and $y_i^1 < z$ for some individual $i \in S$. In other words, the individual could be poor before taxes and transfers and made poorer by the fiscal system, or non-poor before taxes and transfers but poor after. Both straightforward measures count the number of individuals who meet this condition (and are thus fiscally impoverished) in the numerator. The proportion *of the population* who are fiscally impoverished (column 6 of table 4-2) divides this numerator by the number of individuals in society, while the proportion *of the post-fisc poor* who are fiscally impoverished (column 7) divides it by the number who are post-fisc poor (with $y_i^1 < z$).

In the context of poverty measurement, Sen (1976, p. 219) proposes a monotonicity axiom requiring that, all else equal, "a reduction in income of a person below the poverty line must increase the poverty measure." We propose a similar axiom for FI measures requiring that a larger decrease in post-fisc income for an impoverished person, all else equal, must increase the FI measure. Monotonicity is violated by the straightforward measures, which do not increase when an impoverished person becomes more impoverished because she counts as one impoverished individual in the measure's numerator regardless of how much income she loses to the fiscal system.[11]

3.1 Axioms

We propose eight properties desirable for a robust measure of FI; we describe these properties here and formally define them in the appendix. Throughout, we assume that income is measured in real terms and has been converted to a common currency such as US dollars adjusted for purchasing power parity, thereby simplifying away concerns about inflation or currency conversions if comparing FI over time or across countries.

---

[11] Another simple tool to examine FI is the $q \times q$ transition matrix P, whose typical element p_{kl} represents the probability of being in post-fisc income group $l \in \{1, \ldots, q\}$ for an individual in pre-fisc income group $k \in \{1, \ldots, q\}$. Measures based on P also fail to satisfy FI monotonicity and have the large drawback of not capturing FI among the poorest pre-fisc group ($k = 1$).

Our **FI monotonicity** axiom described above implies not only that the FI measure must be strictly increasing in the extent to which an impoverished individual is impoverished (ceteris paribus), but also that the measure must be strictly increasing in the number of individuals that are impoverished, holding fixed the amount of FI experienced by others. The **focus** axiom, analogous to Sen's (1981) focus axiom for poverty measurement, says that different income changes to the non-impoverished—provided that they remain non-impoverished—leave the FI measure unchanged. Given the focus axiom, it is natural to impose a **normalization** that if no one is impoverished, the FI measure equals zero. Note that this normalization axiom is not instrumental to our result: if we did not impose it, our result would be that our axioms uniquely determine a measure of FI up to a linear (rather than proportional) transformation.[12]

Similar to Chakravarty's (1983) **continuity** axiom for poverty measures, we require the FI measure to be continuous in pre-fisc income, post-fisc income, and the poverty line (since we may want to assess FI for a range of possible poverty lines). This is stronger than Foster and Shorrocks's (1991) restricted continuity axiom which only requires the measure to be continuous in incomes *below* the poverty line and left-continuous *at* the poverty line, thus allowing the measure to jump discontinuously at the poverty line; see Zheng (1997) and Permanyer (2014) for arguments in favor of using the stronger continuity axiom in the contexts of unidimensional and multidimensional poverty measures.

Because "the names of income recipients do not matter" (Zheng, 1997, p. 131), we impose a **permutability** axiom requiring that if we take each individual's pre- and post-fisc income pair and (keeping each pre- and post-fisc income pair as a bundle) shuffle these around the population, FI is unchanged. We use the term "permutability" rather than symmetry or anonymity because—although both have been used in the same way we use permutability above (e.g., Cowell, 1985; Fields and Fei, 1978; Plotnick, 1982)—symmetry and anonymity have also taken on different definitions. Symmetry can instead mean, for two income distributions X and Y and a distance measure d, that $d(X, Y) = d(Y, X)$; the two income distributions are treated symmetrically: losses are not distinguishable from gains (Ebert, 1984; Fields and Ok, 1999). Anonymity can instead mean that the measure compares the cumulative distribution of pre-fisc income, F_0, to that of post-fisc income, F_1, without regard to where a particular individual at position j in F_0 ended in F_1 (e.g., Bourguignon, 2011a,b). In other words, an anonymous measure would compare the pre-fisc income of the jth poorest individual in F_0 to the post-fisc income of the jth poorest individual in F_1, even though "they are not necessarily the same individuals" because of reranking (Bourguignon, 2011a, p. 607).

---

[12] It is also possible to normalize by the measure's upper bound so that it always lies on the interval [0, 1] by specifying an axiom that if everyone loses all of their income to the fiscal system (the maximum possible FI), the measure of FI equals 1. We prefer to avoid normalizing in this way so that the class of axiomatic FI measures is more general.

Next, we must decide whether our measure of FI should be absolute or relative (recalling that we assume income to be in real terms of a constant currency, so arguments about inflation or currency exchange should not affect the decision). Suppose each poor individual's pre-fisc income increases by $1, taxes and transfers are held fixed, and the price of one essential good in the basic goods basket, normalized to have one unit in the basket, also increases by $1 per unit.[13] Each poor individual remains the same distance below the poverty line; that distance represents the amount of additional income she needs to afford adequate nutrition and other basic necessities. For those who experience FI, it is the absolute increase in the distance between that individual's income and the poverty line that matters in terms of the quantity of basic goods she can buy. Hence, we assume that if all pre- and post-fisc incomes increase by $1 and the poverty line also increases by $1, FI should remain unchanged. We thus impose **translation invariance.**

Given our above argument for absolute measures, we also impose **linear homogeneity:** if all incomes and the poverty line are multiplied by the same factor, the measure of FI changes by that factor. Instead, specifying homogeneity of degree zero (scale invariance) would be incompatible with translation invariance for the reasons explored in Zheng (1994). Since we assume income is expressed in real terms and a common currency, our measure is nevertheless insensitive to inflation or currency changes. The translation invariance and linear homogeneity axioms have been used together in axiomatic derivations of measures of inequality (Kolm, 1976), poverty (Blackorby and Donaldson, 1980), economic distance (Chakravarty and Dutta, 1987; Ebert, 1984), and mobility (Fields and Ok, 1996; Mitra and Ok, 1998).[14]

Our final axiom is based on a concept introduced to the poverty literature by Foster et al. (1984, p. 761), who argue that "at the very least, one would expect that a decrease in the poverty level of one subgroup ceteris paribus should lead to less poverty for the population as a whole." Similarly, it would be desirable for a measure of FI if a decrease in the measured FI for one subgroup of the population and no change in the measured FI for all other subgroups results in a decrease in the measured FI of the entire population. Hence, we impose a **subgroup consistency** axiom analogous to the one used for poverty measurement by Foster and Shorrocks (1991). In his survey of axiomatic poverty measurement, Zheng (1997, p. 137) notes that subgroup consistency "has gained wide recognition in the literature."

---

[13] To avoid inflation in this thought experiment, assume that there is an offsetting fall in the price of a good *not* in the basic good basket and not consumed by the poor.

[14] By requiring translation invariance and linear homogeneity, we are deriving a measure of *absolute* FI; from there, the measure can nevertheless be modified to obtain other types of desired measures such as a scale invariant measure. This is similar to the approach taken by Fields and Ok (1996), who axiomatically derive a measure of absolute mobility from which other desired measures such as mobility proportional to income can be obtained.

3.2 An Axiomatic Measure of Fiscal Impoverishment

PROPOSITION 1. *A measure satisfying FI monotonicity, focus, normalization, continuity, permutability, translation invariance, linear homogeneity, and subgroup consistency is uniquely determined up to a proportional transformation, and given by*

(1) $$f(y^0, y_i^0; z) = \kappa \sum_{i \in S} (\min\{y_i^0, z\} - \min\{y_i^0, y_i^1, z\}).$$

The summand for individual i behaves as follows. For an individual who was poor before taxes and transfers and is impoverished ($y_i^1 < y_i^0 < z$), it is equal to her fall in income, $y_i^0 - y_i^1$. For an individual who was non-poor before taxes and transfers and is impoverished ($y_i^1 < z \leq y_i^0$), it equals her post-fisc poverty gap, or the amount that would need to be transferred to her to move her back to the poverty line (equivalently, to prevent her from becoming impoverished), $z - y_i^1$. For a non-impoverished pre-fisc non-poor individual ($y_i^0 \geq z$ and $y_i^1 \geq z$) it equals $z - z = 0$. For a non-impoverished pre-fisc poor individual ($y_i^0 < z$ and $y_i^1 \geq y_i^0$) it equals $y_i^0 - y_i^0 = 0$. Hence, f sums the total amount of FI, multiplied by a factor of proportionality. This constant can be chosen based on the preferences of the practitioner: for example, $\kappa = 1$ gives total FI (the dark-shaded area in figure 4-1), while $\kappa = |S|^{-1}$ gives per capita FI.[15]

3.3 Fiscal Impoverishment Dominance Criteria

Having identified the existence of FI in a country, a useful implementation of our FI measure would be to compare the degree of FI in two situations, e.g. by comparing the current fiscal system to a proposed reform. The choice of poverty line might, however, influence our conclusion about which situation entails higher FI. We thus present a partial FI ordering that can be used to determine if FI is unambiguously lower in one situation than another for any poverty line and any measure that satisfies FI monotonicity, focus, normalization, continuity, permutability, translation invariance, linear homogeneity, and subgroup consistency. Since we have already shown that a FI measure satisfies these axioms if and only if it takes the form in (1), a simple way to test for FI dominance for any measure satisfying those axioms and any poverty line in the domain of poverty lines Z is to simply compare the curves $f(y^0, y^1; z)$ and $f(x^0, x^1; z)$ across Z. Interestingly, if the minimum poverty line being considered is 0 (so $Z = [0, z^+]$, where z^+ is the maximum poverty line), there is an alternative (equivalent) way to test whether FI is unambiguously lower in one situation than another that uses a dominance test

---

[15] We do not impose a population invariance axiom; this axiom is commonly imposed but is criticized by Hassoun and Subramanian (2012). A subset of measures of form (1) are population invariant: choosing $\kappa = |S|^{-1}$ gives a measure that satisfies population invariance, while $\kappa = 1$ gives a measure that does not.

already developed in the mobility literature: Foster and Rothbaum's (2014) second order downward mobility dominance.

PROPOSITION 2. *The following are equivalent.*

a) *FI is unambiguously lower in (y^0, y^1) than (x^0, x^1) for any poverty line in $[0, z^+]$ and any measure satisfying FI monotonicity, focus, normalization, continuity, permutability, translation invariance, linear homogeneity, and subgroup consistency.*

b) $f(y^0, y^1; z) < f(x^0, x^1; z) \ \forall z \in [0, z^+]$.

c) (y^0, y^1) *second order downward mobility dominates* (x^0, x^1) *on* $[0, z^+]$.

4 Fiscal Gains of the Poor

Most likely, we will be interested in more than just the extent to which some poor are not compensated for their tax burden with transfers: we will also want to know about the gains of other poor families, and the way in which a comparison of poverty before and after taxes and transfers can be decomposed into the losses and gains of different poor households. In this section, we formally define fiscal gains of the poor, briefly present the axioms for a measure of FGP analogous to those in section 3.2 for a measure of FI, and present an axiomatic measure and partial ordering of FGP. We then show that a commonly used measure of poverty, the poverty gap, can be decomposed into our axiomatic measures of FI and FGP.

4.1 An Axiomatic Measure of Fiscal Gains of the Poor

There are *fiscal gains of the poor* if $y_i^0 < y_i^1$ and $y_i^0 < z$ for some individual $i \in S$. The individual may or may not receive enough in net transfers to be post-fisc non-poor (i.e., it is possible that $z \leq y_i^1$ or $y_i^1 < z$). Consider a pre-fisc poor individual who receives more in transfers than she pays in taxes. If she is given even more transfer income, while the pre- and post-fisc incomes of all others experiencing FGP do not change, FGP should not decrease; if she would have remained in poverty post-fisc without the additional transfer income, FGP should increase with the additional transfer. We impose these conditions in the **FGP monotonicity** axiom; we also impose FGP analogues of the other axioms from section 3.2.

PROPOSITION 3. *A measure satisfying FGP monotonicity, focus, normalization, continuity, permutability, translation invariance, linear homogeneity, and subgroup consistency is uniquely determined up to a proportional transformation, and given by*

(2) $$g(y^0, y_i^0; z) = \kappa \sum_{i \in S} (\min\{y_i^1, z\} - \min\{y_i^0, y_i^1, z\}).$$

An individual who is pre-fisc poor and gains income from the tax and transfer system, but remains post-fisc poor ($y_i^1 < y_i^0 < z$), contributes the amount of her income gain, $y_i^1 - y_i^0$, to the measure of FGP. A pre-fisc poor individual that gains income and as a result has post-fisc income above the poverty line ($y_i^0 < z < y_i^1$) contributes the amount of net transfers that pulled her pre-fisc income to the poverty line, $z - y_i^0$. Someone who is pre-fisc poor and does not gain income ($y_i^1 \leq y_i^0 < z$) contributes $y_i^1 - y_i^1 = 0$. Someone who is pre-fisc non-poor ($z < y_i^0$) also contributes 0 (for her, the summand equals $z-z$ if she remains non-poor or $y_i^1 - y_i^1$ if she loses income and becomes poor). For $\kappa = 1$, g equals the light-shaded area in figure 4-1.

As with fiscal impoverishment orderings, a fiscal gain partial ordering can be used to make unambiguous FGP comparisons for any poverty line and any measure satisfying our axioms. The ordering compares $g(y^0; y^1; z)$ to $g(x^0, x^1; z)$ for all $z \in Z$, and for $Z = [0, z^+]$ coincides with Foster and Rothbaum's (2014) second order upward mobility dominance (the proof proceeds similarly to the proof of Proposition 2 for FI).

4.2 Decomposition of the Difference between Pre-Fisc and Post-Fisc Poverty

The most common measures of poverty used in both policy circles and scholarly papers (e.g., Chen and Ravallion, 2010; Ravallion, 2012) are the poverty headcount ratio, which enumerates the proportion of the population that is poor, and the poverty gap, which takes into account how far the poor fall below the poverty line. The latter might be expressed in absolute terms, summing the gap between each poor person's income and the poverty line, in which case it can be thought of as the total amount that would need to be given to the poor to eliminate poverty (if targeting were perfect). Or it can be normalized, dividing the absolute poverty gap by the poverty line and population size, for example, to create a scale- and population-invariant measure. We use a general definition of the poverty gap that encompasses its absolute and normalized forms:

(3) $$p(y; z) = v(S, z) \sum_{i \in S} (z - y_i) \mathbb{I}(y_i < z),$$

where $v(S, z)$ is a normalization factor. Two special cases are the *absolute poverty gap*, where $v(S, z) = 1$, and the *poverty gap ratio*, where $v(S, z) = (z|S|)^{-1}$. For simplicity and because a comparison of pre- and post-fisc poverty usually occurs for a fixed population and given poverty line, we assume that S and z are fixed in what follows.

PROPOSITION 4. *A change in the poverty gap before and after taxes and transfers is equal to the difference between the axiomatic measures of FI and FGP from (1) and (2), multiplied by a constant.*

Given the assumption that the population and poverty line are fixed, $v(S, z)$ is a constant that we denote $\bar{v}$. The poverty gap in (3) can be rewritten as $p(y; z) =$

$\bar{v} \Sigma_{i \in S}(z - y_i)\mathbb{I}(y_i < z) = \bar{v} \Sigma_{i \in S}(z - \min\{y_i, z\})$, so we have $p(y^1; z) = p(y^0; z) = \bar{v} \Sigma_{i \in S}$ $(z - \min\{y_i^1, z\}) - \bar{v} \Sigma_{i \in S}(z - \min\{y_i^0, z\})$, or

$$p(y^1; z) = p(y^0; z) = \bar{v}\left[\sum_{i \in S} \min\{y_i^0, z\} - \min\{y_i^0, y_i^1, z\} \right.$$

$$\left. - \sum_{i \in S} \min\{y_i^1, z\} - \min\{y_i^0, y_i^1, z\} \right]$$

$$= \frac{\bar{v}}{\kappa}[f(y^1, y^0; z) - g(y^1, y^0; z].$$

Comparisons of pre- and post-fisc poverty are often used to assess whether the tax and transfer system helps or hurts the poor. This decomposition can be used to dig deeper into that net effect and observe the extent to which a net reduction in poverty masks the offsetting gains of some poor and impoverishment of others at the hands of the (possibly progressive) tax and transfer system.

5 Illustration

5.1 Results for Seventeen Developing Countries

We saw in section 2 that in fifteen of seventeen developing countries for which we have data, the tax and transfer system is poverty-reducing and progressive but, in many cases, fiscally impoverishes a significant proportion of the poor. In table 4-3, we present FI and FGP results for these countries using the axiomatic measures derived in sections 3 and 4. Column 1 gives total FI (i.e., the axiomatic measure from (1) with $\kappa = 1$) and column 2 total FGP, both expressed in millions of 2005 US dollars per year using purchasing power parity adjusted exchange rates. Because the axiomatic measure with $\kappa = 1$ is population variant, FI and FGP tend to be higher in more populous countries; these absolute amounts of FI and FGP can be useful, for example, in comparisons to the size of a country's main cash transfer program, as we show for Brazil below. To ease interpretation and comparison across countries, column 3 shows FI expressed as a percent of FGP, while columns 4 and 5 show FI and FGP per capita (where per capita refers to dividing by the entire population), normalized by the poverty line; each of these is population invariant.

There is large heterogeneity in the extent to which some poor are hurt by the tax and transfer system relative to the extent to which other poor gain, despite that the same range of policies, including direct taxes, direct cash and near-cash transfers, indirect consumption taxes, and indirect subsidies were considered in each country study. Among the upper-middle income countries, FI as a percent of FGP (using a poverty line of $2.50 per day) ranges from less than 1% in Ecuador to 40% in Tunisia. In low and lower-middle income countries, FI as a percent of FGP (using a poverty line of $1.25 per day) is even higher in some countries, reaching 55% in Guatemala and 81% in Bolivia; in Ethiopia and Ghana—the two countries in which post-fisc poverty is higher than pre-fisc poverty—FI exceeds FGP.

Column 6 shows the change in the poverty gap ratio from pre-fisc to post-fisc income, which by Proposition 4 can be decomposed into FI per capita minus FGP per capita, both normalized by the poverty line like the poverty gap ratio. This decomposition reveals some interesting traits of each country's tax and transfer system. For example, Ecuador achieves the same FGP per capita as Brazil but with nearly no FI, compared to substantial FI in Brazil; as a result, the poverty gap is reduced by more in Ecuador. The difference in FI might be attributable to the the multiple consumption taxes levied at the state and federal levels in Brazil: these are high and often cascading, and consumption tax exemptions for basic goods are almost nonexistent (Corbacho et al., 2013), compared to a system that exempts food, basic necessities, and medicine in Ecuador (Llerena Pinto et al., 2015). Interestingly, most of those experiencing FI are *not* excluded from the safety net; they *do* receive government transfers or subsidies: 65% of the impoverished in Brazil receive cash transfers from Bolsa Familia, for example. It is also noteworthy that Peru, one of the countries in which *less than* a quarter of the post-fisc poor experience FI, nevertheless redistributes low amounts to the poor, and thus has a low reduction in the poverty gap; this is consistent with Jaramillo's (2014, p. 391) finding that Peru's low poverty reduction induced by fiscal policy is "associated with low social spending rather than with inefficient spending." Among three lower-income countries that each reduce the poverty gap ratio by about 0.3 percentage points (El Salvador, Guatemala, and Indonesia), Guatemala has high FI but also higher FGP, while El Salvador has lower FGP but very low FI, and Indonesia falls in the middle. We do not attempt to answer whether a lower-FI, lower-FGP or higher-FI, higher-FGP system is preferable from a welfare perspective, but note that this decomposition enables a substantially richer analysis than the typical comparison of poverty before and after taxes and transfers.

5.2 Results for a Range of Poverty Lines in Brazil

So far, the FI and FGP results we have presented use a fixed poverty line ($1.25 in low and lower-middle income countries and $2.50 in upper-middle income countries). We now extend the analysis to a range of poverty lines, focusing the illustration on data from Brazil, using the Pesquisa de Orçamentos Familiares (Family Expenditure Survey) 2008–2009. The precise direct and indirect taxes, direct cash and food transfers, and indirect subsidies included in our analysis are described in detail in Higgins and Pereira (2014).

As we stated in section 2.3, the tax and transfer system in Brazil is unambiguously poverty-reducing for any poverty line up to $2.50 per person per day, globally progressive, and unambiguously equalizing.[16] This is shown in figure 4-2, where cumulative

---

[16] Nevertheless, the tax and transfer system reduces poverty by less than its potential under the type of optimal redistribution considered by Fellman et al. (1999), which follows a lexicographic

FIGURE 4-2

Conventional Tools to Assess the Tax and Transfer System in Brazil

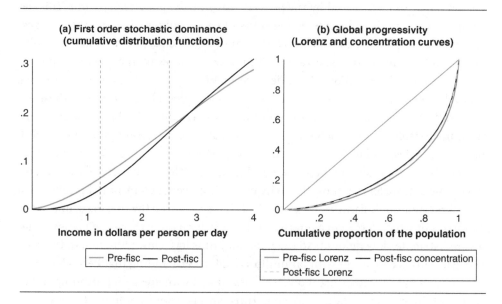

distribution functions reveal that the post-fisc distribution first order stochastically dominates the pre-fisc distribution on the domain [0, 2.5], which implies an unambiguous reduction in poverty for any poverty line in this domain and any measure in a broad class (Atkinson, 1987; Foster and Shorrocks, 1988);[17] the post-fisc concentration curve with respect to pre-fisc income dominates the pre-fisc Lorenz curve, which implies global progressivity (in the income redistribution sense; see Duclos, 2008); and the post-fisc Lorenz curve dominates the pre-fisc Lorenz curve, which implies that the fiscal system is unambiguously equalizing (Atkinson, 1970). If, however, we extend the maximum poverty line to, say, $4 per person per day—a poverty line frequently used by the World Bank when studying middle-income Latin American countries (e.g.,

---

maximin principle. Replacing the actual tax system with optimal taxes of this type (which, in total, equal the size of actual taxes), and replacing the actual distribution of Bolsa Familia benefits with the optimal one (redistributing all transfers this way would completely eliminate poverty, so we only optimally redistribute Bolsa Familia for illustration), the lowest income in the population would be $1.92 per day, the post-fisc poverty gap ratio would be 2.7% of the poverty line rather than 5.5%, and the post-fisc Gini would be 45.3 rather than 53.9.

[17] We verify that this first order dominance is statistically significant at the 5% level using the asymptotic sampling distribution derived by Davidson and Duclos (2000) with a null hypothesis of non-dominance; the result is also robust to the type of data contamination considered in Cowell and Victoria-Feser (2002).

Ferreira et al., 2013)—poverty is no longer unambiguously lowered by the fiscal system: for poverty lines above about $3 per day, the poverty headcount is higher after taxes and transfers than before. We would thus know that FI occurred using conventional measures and a poverty line above $3 per day, but would still be unaware of its extent without FI measures.[18]

Using the $2.50 line, we know that 5.6% of Brazil's population and over one-third of its post-fisc poor experience FI (table 4-2); these impoverished individuals pay a total of $676 million more in taxes than they receive in transfers annually (table 4-3), which is equivalent to 10% of the 2009 budget of Bolsa Familia, Brazil's flagship anti-poverty program that reaches over one-fourth of the country's population. While substantial in size, this FI is dwarfed by FGP from Brazil's transfer programs, which totals over $3.5 billion. The absolute poverty gap, or the minimum amount that would need to be transferred to the poor to eliminate poverty if transfers were perfectly targeted, falls from $12.4 billion before taxes and transfers to $9.6 billion after. The change in the absolute poverty gap, $2.8 billion, looks impressive, but masks differential trends in two groups of the poor: those who gain (a total of $3.5 billion) and those who lose (a total of $676 million), as revealed by the decomposition of the change in the poverty gap derived in section 4.

Figure 4-3 shows how this decomposition and our axiomatic measures of total FI and FGP in Brazil vary with the poverty line. For low poverty lines, FI is essentially non-existent: at $1.25 per day, for example, total FI is $28 million per year, or 0.4% of the 2009 budget of Bolsa Familia (figure 4-3a). This is not surprising in light of the unconditional component of the government cash transfer program Bolsa Familia, available to households with income below 70 reais per person per month ($1.22 per day), regardless of whether the household has children or elderly members, and without conditions. At higher poverty lines, FI begins to increase more rapidly, and at a poverty line of $2.88 the rate of increase of FI exceeds the rate of increase of FGP: this can be seen by comparing the slopes of the solid curves in figure 4-3a, or by looking at the point where the difference between the two curves (plotted as the dashed curve in figure 4-3a) is at its maximum. By Proposition 4, this is also the point at which the absolute poverty gap reduction acheived by the fiscal system reaches its maximum, as seen by the dashed curve in figure 4-3b.

At this poverty line of $2.88 per day, where maximum poverty reduction is achieved, the difference between the pre-fisc and post-fisc poverty gaps is $2.9 billion. The eligibility cut-off for the conditional component of Bolsa Familia, available to families with children who comply with certain education and health requirements, is $2.45 per person per day. Just above this line, a number of families still receive benefits due to

---

[18] It is easy to show that if the post-fisc distribution does not first order stochastically dominate the pre-fisc distribution on the domain from 0 to the maximum poverty line, then FI has occurred.

TABLE 4-3

Fiscal Impoverishment and Gains of the Poor in Developing Countries

Country (survey year)	(1) Total FI ($ millions per year)	(2) Total FGP ($ millions per year)	(3) FI as % of FGP	(4) Per capita FI as % of z	(5) Per capita FGP as % of z	(6) Change in poverty gap ratio (p.p.)
Panel A: Upper-middle income countries, using a poverty line of $2.50 per day						
Brazil (2008–2009)	676.0	3503.6	19.3	0.39	2.02	−1.63
Chile (2013)	2.0	93.3	2.1	0.01	0.59	−0.58
Ecuador (2011–2012)	1.1	277.8	0.4	0.01	2.00	−1.99
Mexico (2012)	227.7	1446.5	15.7	0.21	1.35	−1.14
Peru (2011)	53.7	177.0	30.3	0.20	0.65	−0.45
Russia (2010)	84.9	1561.4	5.4	0.07	1.24	−1.17
South Africa (2010–2011)	186.6	5964.0	3.1	0.41	12.96	−12.56
Tunisia (2010)	20.8	52.0	40.0	0.23	0.59	−0.35
Panel B: Low and lower-middle income countries, using a poverty line of $1.25 per day						
Armenia (2011)	6.3	117.9	5.3	0.44	8.17	−7.74
Bolivia (2009)	25.9	32.2	80.6	0.55	0.68	−0.13
Dominican Republic (2007)	4.4	105.1	4.2	0.02	0.53	−0.51
El Salvador (2011)	1.2	11.1	11.1	0.04	0.39	−0.35
Ethiopia (2010–2011)	408.9	392.8	104.1	1.18	1.13	0.05
Ghana (2013)	25.9	9.9	262.1	0.22	0.08	0.13
Guatemala (2010)	20.7	37.8	54.9	0.33	0.61	−0.27
Indonesia (2012)	150.2	531.5	28.3	0.13	0.47	−0.34
Sri Lanka (2009–2010)	4.4	25.5	17.1	0.05	0.27	−0.23

Sources: For Brazil, authors' calculations. For other countries, provided to us by the authors of the studies cited in footnote 3.

Notes: p.p. = percentage points, z denotes the poverty line. "$ millions" denotes millions of 2005 US dollars, at purchasing power parity adjusted exchange rates. Country classifications are from the World Bank for the year of the survey.

FIGURE 4-3

FI, FGP, and Poverty Gaps in Brazil for Various Poverty Lines

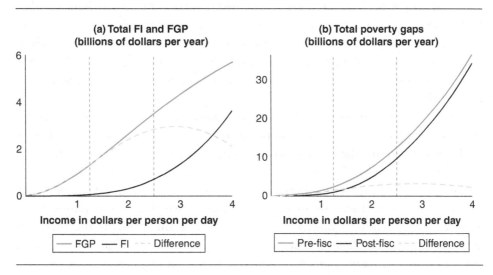

program leakages, variable and mismeasured income, or components of income we are measuring that are not taken into account in the estimation of eligible income; not far above the line, however, families become much less likely to receive the program and we see a simultaneous deceleration of fiscal gains and acceleration of impoverishment.

6 Conclusions

Anti-poverty policies are increasingly being discussed in the same breath as the taxes used to pay for them. One example is the focus on mobilizing domestic resources to finance the policies necessary to achieve the United Nations' Post-2015 Sustainable Development Goals. To analyze transfers, subsidies, and taxes together, poverty comparisons and progressivity measures are often used. These measures, however, can lead us to conclude that the tax and transfer system unambiguously benefits the poor, when in fact a substantial number of poor are not compensated with transfers for their tax burdens. Indeed, we observe this in a number of developing countries: out of seventeen developing countries for which we have data, fifteen have tax and transfer systems that unambiguously reduce poverty and are globally progressive, but in ten of these at least one-quarter of the poor pay more in taxes than they receive in transfers and subsidies. In Brazil, for example, over one-third of the post-fisc poor experience fiscal impoverishment, paying a total of $676 million more in taxes than they receive in transfers and subsidies.

Given this shortcoming of conventional criteria and the debate about anti-poverty policies and the taxes used to pay for them, we propose a set of axioms that should be met by a measure of FI, and show that these uniquely determine the measure up to a proportional transformation. We also propose a partial ordering to determine when one fiscal system, such as that under a proposed reform, induces unambiguously less FI than another, such as the current system, over a range of possible poverty lines. To obtain a complete picture of the fiscal system's effect on the poor, we propose an analogous measure of fiscal gains of the poor, and show that the difference between the pre-fisc and post-fisc poverty gaps can be decomposed into our axiomatic measures of FI and FGP.

Our results can be extended to comparisons between two points in time or before and after a policy reform, rather than pre- and post-fisc. In comparison to the tools used to assess whether the tax and transfer system hurts the poor, tools from the literatures on pro-poor growth and policy reforms (tax and subsidy reforms, trade liberalization, etc.) suffer from similar limitations. For pro-poor growth,[19] poverty measures and stochastic dominance tests are often used to assess whether poverty is unambiguously reduced over time; it directly follows from the first row of table 4-1 that these will not necessarily capture that some of the poor become poorer over time. Hence, growth can appear unambiguously pro-poor even if a significant proportion of the poor are immiserized. Growth incidence curves (Ravallion and Chen, 2003) and related pro-poor partial orderings (Duclos, 2009) can fail to capture impoverishment for the same reason that stochastic dominance tests do: they are anonymous with respect to initial income. Although their non-anonymous counterparts (Bourguignon, 2011a; Grimm, 2007; Van Kerm, 2009) resolve this issue in theory, in practice—to become graphically tractable—they average within percentiles, and hence impoverishment can still be overlooked if within some percentiles, some poor are "hurting behind the averages" (Ravallion, 2001, p. 1811).

For consumption tax and subsidy reform, Besley and Kanbur (1988) derive poverty-reducing conditions for reallocating food subsidies; these results are extended to commodity taxes and a broader class of poverty measures by Makdissi and Wodon (2002) and Duclos et al. (2008). Again, by the first row of table 4-1, unambiguous poverty reduction does not guarantee that a substantial portion of the poor are not hurt by the reform. Studies that evaluate indirect tax reform with measures that take pre-fisc positions into account but average within groups, such as the percent gain or loss caused by the reform for each income or expenditure decile (Mirrlees et al., 2011, chapter 9), can again overlook FI that occurs within each group.

---

[19] Here, we are using the poverty-reducing or weak absolute definition of pro-poor (in the respective taxonomies of Kakwani and Son (2008) and Klasen (2008)), by which "growth is pro-poor if the poverty measure of interest falls" (Kraay, 2006, p. 198). We could instead adopt a relative definition of pro-poor growth (Kakwani and Pernia, 2000); growth-adjusted stochastic dominance tests can be used to determine when growth is unambiguously relatively pro-poor (Duclos, 2009), and it can be shown that this type of dominance can also occur despite a significant portion of the poor becoming poorer.

In the literature on trade liberalization, Harrison et al. (2003, p. 97) note that "even the most attractive reforms will typically result in some households losing," and recent efforts to measure welfare impact at the household level have been made following Porto (2006). Nevertheless, because results are presented at some aggregate level (e.g., by state or percentile), impoverishment due to trade reform could still be overlooked. For example, Nicita's (2009, p. 26) finding that "on average all income groups benefited from [Mexico's] trade liberalization, but to a varying extent" does not tell us the extent to which some households within each group were made worse off by the reform.

In each of these cases, our axiomatically derived FI measure could be used to quantify the impoverishment of those becoming poorer over time or the extent to which losers are hurt by policy reforms. Our decomposition could be used to examine the extent to which a decrease in poverty over time or due to a reform balances out the gains and losses of different households. Doing so, we will cease to overlook cases where growth, policy reform, or the tax and transfer system is poverty-reducing and progressive, yet hurts a substantial proportion of the poor.

Acknowledgments

For detailed comments on earlier versions of the paper, we are grateful to Francesco Andreoli, Alan Barreca, Jean-Yves Duclos, John Edwards, Charles Kenny, Peter Lambert, Darryl McLeod, Mauricio Reis, Kathleen Short, Rafael Salas, Jay Shimshack, Harry Tsang, Paolo Verme, two anonymous referees, and Maitreesh Ghatak, the editor. For applying our measures to microdata in a number of developing countries and sharing the results with us for this paper, we are grateful to the many country study authors we cite in the paper. We thank Claudiney Pereira for collaboration on the analysis of Brazilian data and Ruoxi Li, Sandra Martinez-Aguilar, Adam Ratzlaff, Mel Reitcheck, and William Smith for research assistance. Work on this project was partially completed when S. Higgins was visiting Haas School of Business at UC Berkeley and the Center for Economic Studies at El Colegio de México with funding from the Fulbright–García Robles Public Policy Initiative. This paper is part of a larger project that received funding from the Bill & Melinda Gates Foundation (grant numbers OPP1097490 and OPP1335502). These institutions and funders are gratefully acknowledged.

References

Afkar, R., Jellema, J., Wai-Poi, M., forthcoming. The distributional impact of fiscal policy in Indonesia, in: Inchauste, G., Lustig, N. (Eds.), The Distributional Impact of Fiscal Policy: Experience from Developing Countries. World Bank, Washington, D.C.

Amiel, Y., Cowell, F., 1994. Monotonicity, dominance and the Pareto principle. Economics Letters 45, 447–450.

Aranda, R., Scott, J., 2015. CEQ Master Workbook for Mexico. Mimeo.

Aristy-Escuder, J., Cabrera, M., Sánchez-Martin, M.E., forthcoming. An analysis of fiscal policy and income redistribution in the Dominican Republic. CEQ Working Paper 37.

Arunatilake, N., Hewawasam, J., Gunasekara, N., forthcoming. The distributional impact of fiscal policy in Sri Lanka, in: Inchauste, G., Lustig, N. (Eds.), The Distributional Impact of Fiscal Policy: Experience from Developing Countries. World Bank, Washington, D.C.

Atkinson, A.B., 1970. On the measurement of inequality. Journal of Economic Theory 2, 244–263.

Atkinson, A.B., 1987. On the measurement of poverty. Econometrica 55, 749–764.

Baer, W., Galvão, A.F., 2008. Tax burden, government expenditures and income distribution in Brazil. Quarterly Review of Economics and Finance 48, 345–358.

Beneke, M., Lustig, N., Oliva, J.A., 2015. El impacto de los impuestos y el gasto social en la desigualded y la pobreza en El Salvador. CEQ Working Paper 26.

Besley, T., Kanbur, R., 1988. Food subsidies and poverty alleviation. The Economic Journal 98, 701–719.

Blackorby, C., Donaldson, D., 1980. Ethical indices for the measurement of poverty. Econometrica 48, 1053–1060.

Bourguignon, F., 2011a. Non-anonymous growth incidence curves, income mobility and social welfare dominance. Journal of Economic Inequality 9, 605–627.

Bourguignon, F., 2011b. Status quo in the welfare analysis of tax reforms. Review of Income and Wealth 57, 603–621.

Cabrera, M., Lustig, N., Morán, H., 2015. Fiscal policy, inequality, and the ethnic divide in Guatemala. World Development 76, 263–279.

Chakravarty, S.R., 1983. A new index of poverty. Mathematical Social Sciences 6, 307–313.

Chakravarty, S.R., Dutta, B., 1987. A note on measures of distance between income distributions. Journal of Economic Theory 41, 185–188.

Chen, S., Ravallion, M., 2010. The developing world is poorer than we thought, but no less successful in the fight against poverty. Quarterly Journal of Economics 125, 1577–1625.

Citro, C.F., Michael, R.T., 1995. Measuring Poverty: A New Approach. National Academy Press, Washington, D.C.

Corbacho, A., Cibils, V.F., Lora, E., 2013. More than Revenue: Taxation as a Development Tool. Palgrave Macmillan, New York.

Cowell, F.A., 1985. Measures of distributional change: An axiomatic approach. Review of Economic Studies 52, 135–151.

Cowell, F.A., Victoria-Feser, M.P., 2002. Welfare rankings in the presence of contaminated data. Econometrica 70, 1221–1233.

Davidson, R., Duclos, J.Y., 2000. Statistical inference for stochastic dominance and for the measurement of poverty and inequality. Econometrica 68, 1435–1464.

Debreu, G., 1960. Topological methods in cardinal utility theory, in: Arrow, K.J., Karlin, S., Suppes, P. (Eds.), Mathematical Methods in the Social Sciences. Stanford University Press, Palo Alto, pp. 16–26.

DeFina, R.H., Thanawala, K., 2004. International evidence on the impact of transfers and taxes on alternative poverty indexes. Social Science Research 33, 311–338.

Duclos, J.Y., 1997. Measuring progressivity and inequality. Research on Economic Inequality 7, 19–37.

Duclos, J.Y., 2008. Horizontal and vertical equity, in: Durlauf, S.N., Blume, L.E. (Eds.), The New Palgrave Dictionary of Economics. Palgrave Macmillan, New York.

Duclos, J.Y., 2009. What is pro-poor? Social Choice and Welfare 32, 37–58.

Duclos, J.Y., Makdissi, P., Wodon, Q., 2008. Socially improving tax reforms. International Economic Review 49, 1505–1537.

Ebert, U., 1984. Measures of distance between income distributions. Journal of Economic Theory 32, 266–274.

Ebert, U., 1997. Social welfare when needs differ: An axiomatic approach. Economica 64, 233–244.

Ebrill, L.P., Keen, M., Summers, V.P., 2001. The Modern VAT. International Monetary Fund, Washington, D.C.

Engel, E.M.R.A., Galetovic, A., Raddatz, C.E., 1999. Taxes and income distribution in Chile: Some unpleasant redistributive arithmetic. Journal of Development Economics 59, 155–192.

Fellman, J., Jäntti, M., Lambert, P.J., 1999. Optimal tax-transfer systems and redistributive policy. The Scandinavian Journal of Economics 101, 115–126.

Ferreira, F.H.G., Messina, J., Rigolini, J., López-Calva, L.F., Lugo, M.A., Vakis, R., 2013. Economic Mobility and the Rise of the Latin American Middle Class. The World Bank, Washington, D.C.

Fields, G.S., 2001. Distribution and Development. Russell Sage Foundation and MIT Press, Cambridge.

Fields, G.S., Fei, J.C.H., 1978. On inequality comparisons. Econometrica 46, 303–316.

Fields, G.S., Ok, E.A., 1996. The meaning and measurement of income mobility. Journal of Economic Theory 71, 349–377.

Fields, G.S., Ok, E.A., 1999. Measuring movement of incomes. Economica 66, 455–471.

Foster, J., 2006. Poverty indices, in: de Janvry, A., Kanbur, R. (Eds.), Poverty, Inequality and Development: Essays in Honor of Erik Thorbecke. Kluwer Academic, Norwell, pp. 41–66.

Foster, J., Greer, J., Thorbecke, E., 1984. A class of decomposable poverty measures. Econometrica 52, 761–766.

Foster, J., Rothbaum, J., 2014. The mobility curve: Measuring the impact of mobility on welfare. Working Paper.

Foster, J., Shorrocks, A.F., 1988. Poverty orderings. Econometrica 56, 173–177.

Foster, J., Shorrocks, A.F., 1991. Subgroup consistent poverty indices. Econometrica 59, 687–709.

Ghatak, M., 2015. Theories of poverty traps and anti-poverty policies. World Bank Economic Review 29, S77–S105.

Goñi, E., López, J.H., Servén, L., 2011. Fiscal redistribution and income inequality in Latin America. World Development 39, 1558–1569.

Gorman, W.M., 1968. The structure of utility functions. Review of Economic Studies 35, 367–390.

Grimm, M., 2007. Removing the anonymity axiom in assessing pro-poor growth. Journal of Economic Inequality 5, 179–197.

Harrison, G.W., Rutherford, T.F., Tarr, D.G., 2003. Trade liberalization, poverty and efficient equity. Journal of Development Economics 71, 97–128.

Hassoun, N., Subramanian, S., 2012. An aspect of variable population poverty comparisons. Journal of Development Economics 98, 238–241.

Higgins, S., Lustig, N., Ruble, W., Smeeding, T.M., 2015. Comparing the incidence of taxes and social spending in Brazil and the United States. Review of Income and Wealth, advance online publication. doi:10.1111/roiw. 12201.

Higgins, S., Pereira, C., 2014. The effects of Brazil's taxation and social spending on the distribution of household income. Public Finance Review 42, 346–367.

Hill, R., Inchauste, G., Lustig, N., Tsehaye, E., Woldehanna, T., forthcoming. A fiscal incidence analysis for Ethiopia, in: Inchauste, G., Lustig, N. (Eds.), The Distributional Impact of Fiscal Policy: Experience from Developing Countries. World Bank, Washington, D.C.

Hoynes, H.W., Page, M.E., Stevens, A.H., 2006. Poverty in America: Trends and explanations. Journal of Economic Perspectives 20, 47–68.

Inchauste, G., Lustig, N., Maboshe, M., Purfield, C., Woolard, L, forthcoming. The distributional impact of fiscal policy in South Africa, in: Inchauste, G., Lustig, N. (Eds.), The Distributional Impact of Fiscal Policy: Experience from Developing Countries. World Bank, Washington, D.C.

International Monetary Fund, 2013. Fiscal Monitor: Taxing Times. International Monetary Fund, Washington, D.C. URL: https://www.imf.org/external/pubs/ft/fm/2013/02/pdf/fm1302.pdf.

Jaramillo, M., 2014. The incidence of social spending in Peru. Public Finance Review 42, 391–412.

Jaramillo, M., de la Flor, L., Sparrow, B., 2015. Are ethnic groupings invisible for fiscal policy in Peru? An incidence analysis of taxes and transfers on indigenous and non-indigenous Peruvians. Mimeo.

Kakwani, N.C., Pernia, E.M., 2000. What is pro-poor growth? Asian Development Review 18, 1–16.

Kakwani, N.C., Son, H.H., 2008. Poverty equivalent growth rate. Review of Income and Wealth 54, 643–655.

Keen, M., Lockwood, B., 2010. The value added tax: Its causes and consequences. Journal of Development Economics 92, 138–151.

Klasen, S., 2008. Economic growth and poverty reduction: Measurement issues using income and non-income indicators. World Development 36, 420–445.

Kolm, S.C., 1976. Unequal inequalities I. Journal of Economic Theory 12, 416–442.

Kraay, A., 2006. When is growth pro-poor? Evidence from a panel of countries. Journal of Development Economics 80, 198–227.

Lambert, P.J., 1988. Net fiscal incidence progressivity: Some approaches to measurement, in: Eichhorn, W. (Ed.), Measurement in Economics: Theory and Application of Economics Indices. Springer-Verlag, Heidelberg, pp. 519–532.

Levy, S., Schady, N., 2013. Latin America's social policy challenge: Education, social insurance, redistribution. Journal of Economic Perspectives 27, 193–218.

Llerena Pinto, F.P., Llerena Pinto, M.C., Llerena Pinto, M.A., Perez, G., 2015. Social spending, taxes and income redistribution in Ecuador. CEQ Working Paper 28.

Lopez-Calva, L.F., Lustig, N., Matytsin, M., Popova, D., forthcoming. Who benefits from fiscal redistribution in Russia?, in: Inchauste, G., Lustig, N. (Eds.), The Distributional Impact of Fiscal Policy: Experience from Developing Countries. World Bank, Washington, D.C.

Lustig, N., 2015. The redistributive impact of government spending on education and health: Evidence from 13 developing countries in the Commitment to Equity project, in: Gupta, S., Keen, M., Clements, B., de Mooij, R. (Eds.), Inequality and Fiscal Policy. International Monetary Fund, Washington, D.C.

Makdissi, P., Wodon, Q., 2002. Consumption dominance curves: Testing for the impact of indirect tax reforms on poverty. Economics Letters 75, 227–235.

Martinez-Aguilar, S., Ortiz-Juarez, E., 2015. CEQ Master Workbook for Chile. Mimeo.

Mirrlees, J., Adam, S., Besley, T., Blundell, R., Bond, S., Chote, R., Gammie, M., Johnson, P., Myles, G., Poterba, J., 2011. Tax by Design. Oxford University Press, Oxford.

Mitra, T., Ok, E., 1998. The measurement of income mobility: A partial ordering approach. Economic Theory 12, 77–102.

Nicita, A., 2009. The price effect of tariff liberalization: Measuring the impact on household welfare. Journal of Development Economics 89, 19–27.

Paz Arauco, V., Gray Molina, G., Yáñez Aguilar, E., Jiménez Pozo, W., 2014. Explaining low redistributive impact in Bolivia. Public Finance Review 42, 326–345.

Permanyer, I., 2014. Assessing individuals' deprivation in a multidimensional framework. Journal of Development Economics 109, 1–16.

Plotnick, R., 1982. The concept and measurement of horizontal inequity. Journal of Public Economics 17, 373–391.

Porto, G.G., 2006. Using survey data to assess the distributional effects of trade policy. Journal of International Economics 70, 140–160.

Ravallion, M., 2001. Growth, inequality and poverty: Looking beyond averages. World Development 29, 1803–1815.

Ravallion, M., 2012. Why don't we see poverty convergence? American Economic Review 102, 504–523.

Ravallion, M., 2015. The idea of antipoverty policy, in: Handbook of Income Distribution. North-Holland, Amsterdam. volume 2.

Ravallion, M., Chen, S., 2003. Measuring pro-poor growth. Economics Letters 78, 93–99.

Reynolds, M., Smolensky, E., 1977. Public Expenditures, Taxes and the Distribution of Income: The United States, 1950, 1961, 1970. Academic Press, New York.

Sen, A., 1976. Poverty: An ordinal approach to measurement. Econometrica 44, 219–231.

Sen, A., 1981. Poverty and Famines: An Essay on Entitlement and Deprivation. Oxford University Press, Oxford.

Shimeles, A., Moummi, A., Jouini, N., Lustig, N., forthcoming. Fiscal incidence and poverty reduction: Evidence from Tunisia. CEQ Working Paper 38.

Subramanian, S., 2006. Social groups and economic poverty: A problem in measurement, in: McGillivray, M. (Ed.), Inequality, Poverty, and Wellbeing. Palgrave Macmillan, London.

United Nations, 2015. Addis Ababa Action Agenda of the Third International Conference on Financing for Development. United Nations, New York.

Van Kerm, P., 2009. Income mobility profiles. Economics Letters 102, 93–95.

World Bank, 2013. Financing for Development Post-2015. World Bank, Washington, D.C.

World Bank, 2015. Ethiopia Poverty Assessment 2014. World Bank, Washington, D.C.

Younger, S.D., Khachatryan, A., forthcoming. Fiscal incidence in Armenia, in: Inchauste, G., Lustig, N. (Eds.), The Distributional Impact of Fiscal Policy: Experience from Developing Countries. World Bank, Washington, D.C.

Younger, S.D., Osei-Assibey, E., Oppong, F., 2015. Fiscal incidence in Ghana. CEQ Working Paper 35.

Zheng, B., 1994. Can a poverty index be both relative and absolute? Econometrica 62, 1453–1458.

Zheng, B., 1997. Aggregate poverty measures. Journal of Economic Surveys 11, 123–162.

Appendix 4A

A.1 FI Axioms

Consider pre- and post-fisc incomes y_i^0, $y_i^1 \in \mathbb{R}_+$ for each $i \in S$; denote the vectors of pre- and post-fisc income for these individuals by y^0 and y^1, both ordered by pre-fisc income y_i^0. Now consider income vectors for the same individuals under different pre- and post-fisc scenarios, denoted by x^0 and x^1, both ordered by pre-fisc income x_i^0. The sets of impoverished individuals in scenarios (y^0, y^1) and (x^0, x^1) are denoted $I_y \equiv \{i \in S \mid y_i^1 < y_i^0 \text{ and } y_i^1 < z\}$ and $I_x \equiv \{i \in S \mid x_i^1 < x_i^0 \text{ and } x_i^1 < z\}$. A measure of FI is a function $f : \bigcup_{n=1}^{\infty} \mathbb{R}_+^n \times \bigcup_{n=1}^{\infty} \mathbb{R}_+^n \times \mathbb{R}_+ \to \mathbb{R}$, which takes as arguments the pre- and post-fisc income vectors and the poverty line.

AXIOM 1 (FI Monotonicity). If $y_i^0 = x_i^0$ for all $i \in S$ and there exists $j \in I_y \cup I_x$ such that $y_j^1 > x_j^1$, while $y_k^1 = x_k^1$ for all $k \in I_y \cup I_x \backslash \{j\}$, then $f(y^0, y^1; z) < f(x^0, x^1; z)$.

AXIOM 2 (Focus). If $y_i^0 = x_i^0$ and $y_i^1 = x_i^1$ for all $i \in I_y \cup I_x$, then $f(y^0, y^1; z) = f(x^0, x^1; z)$.

AXIOM 3 (Normalization). $I_y = \varnothing \Rightarrow f(y^0, y^1; z) = 0$.

AXIOM 4 (Continuity). f is jointly continuous in y_i^0, y_i^1, and z.

AXIOM 5 (Permutability), $f(y^0, y^1; z) = f(y_\sigma^0, y_\sigma^1; z)$ for any permutation function $\sigma : S \to S$, where $y_\sigma^0 \equiv (y_{\sigma(1)}^0, \ldots, y_{\sigma|S|}^0)$ and $y_\sigma^1 \equiv (y_{\sigma(1)}^1, \ldots, y_{\sigma(|S|)}^1)$.

AXIOM 6 (Translation Invariance), $f(y^0 + \alpha 1_{|S|}, y^1 + \alpha 1_{|S|}; z + \alpha) = f(y^0, y^1; z)$ for all $\alpha \in \mathbb{R}$, where $1_{|S|}$ denotes a vector of ones with length $|S|$.

AXIOM 7 (Linear Homogeneity), $f(\lambda y^0, \lambda y^1; \lambda_z) = \lambda f(y^0, y^1; z)$ for all $\lambda \in \mathbb{R}_{++}$.

AXIOM 8 (Subgroup Consistency). Partition S into m subsets $S_1, \ldots, S_m$, and denote the vectors of pre- and post-fisc incomes for individuals belonging to subset S_α, $a \in \{1, \ldots, m\}$, by y_σ^0 and y_σ^1 or x_σ^0 and x_σ^1. If $f(y_\sigma^0, y_\sigma^1; z) < f(x_\sigma^0, x_\sigma^1; z)$ for some $a \in \{1, \ldots, m\}$, and $f(y_\sigma^0, y_\sigma^1; z) = f(x_\sigma^0, x_\sigma^1; z)$ for all $b \in \{1, \ldots, m\} \backslash \{a\}$, then $f(y^0, y^1; z) < f(x^0, x^1; z)$.

A.2 FGP Axioms

Let the sets of pre-fisc poor individuals experiencing fiscal gains under two scenarios be denoted $G_y \equiv \{i \in S \mid y_i^0 < y_i^1 \text{ and } y_i^0 < z\}$ and $G_y \equiv \{i \in S \mid x_i^0 < x_i^1 \text{ and } x_i^0 < z\}$. A measure of FGP is a function $g : \bigcup_{n=1}^{\infty} \mathbb{R}_+^n \times \bigcup_{n=1}^{\infty} \mathbb{R}_+^n \times \mathbb{R}_+ \to \mathbb{R}$, which takes as arguments the pre- and post-fisc income vectors and the poverty line.

AXIOM 1′ (FGP Monotonicity). If $y_i^0 = x_i^0$ for all $i \in S$ and there exists $j \in G_y \cup G_x$ such that $y_j^1 > x_j^1$, while $y_k^1 = x_k^1$ for all $k \in G_y \cup G_x \backslash \{j\}$, then $g(y^0, y^1; z) \leq g(x^0, x^1; z)$, with strict inequality if $y_i^1 > z$.

The remaining axioms for FI are desirable for a measure of FGP as well, and carry over directly to FGP after replacing f with g, I_y with G_y, and I_x with G_x.

A.3 Proofs

PROOF OF PROPOSITION 1. We begin with a lemma analogous to one of the propositions in Foster and Shorrocks (1991). To simplify notation, $y_a \equiv (y_a^0, y_a^1)$ for a sub set S_a of a partition of S into m subgroups $a = 1, \ldots, m$; similarly, $x_a \equiv (x_a^0, x_a^1)$. We also define vectors $y_{-a}^t = (y_b^t)_{b \neq a \in \{1, \ldots, m\}}$, $t \in \{0, 1\}$ as the vector of pre- or post-fisc incomes of all $i \notin S_a$ (similarly for x_{-a}^t) and $y_{-a} \equiv (y_{-a}^0, y_{-a}^1)$, $x_{-a} \equiv (x_{-a}^0, x_{-a}^1)$.

LEMMA, $f(y_a, y_{-a}; z) \geq f(x_a, y_{-a}; z)) f(y_a, x_{-a}; z) \geq f(x_a, x_{-a}; z)$.

PROOF. By subgroup consistency, $f(y_a, y_{-a}; z) \geq f(x_a, y_{-a}; z) \Rightarrow f(y_a; z) \geq f(x_a; z)$. (Suppose not. Then $f(y_a; z) < f(x_a; z)$, which by subgroup consistency implies $f(y_a, y_{-a}; z) < f(x_a, y_{-a}; z)$, a contradiction.) $f(y_a; z) \geq f(x_a; z)$ implies either $f(y_a; z) > f(x_a; z)$ or $f(y_a; z) = f(x_a; z)$. In the former case, it immediately follows by subgroup consistency that $f(y_a, x_{-a}; z) \geq f(x_a, x_{-a}; z)$. In the latter case, the implication is shown by contradiction. Suppose that $f(y_a, x_{-a}; z) < f(x_a, x_{-a}; z)$. Then by subgroup consistency we have (since $f(y_a; z) = f(x_a; z)$) $f(y_a, x_{-a}, x_a; z) < f(x_a, y_{-a}, y_a; z)$ which contradicts permutability.

This lemma shows that a subgroup-consistent and permutable measure of FI is separable by group, using a definition of separability analogous to that used for preferences in the utility literature. Because the lemma can be reiterated within any particular subgroup to further separate individuals in that subgroup, we have that each set of individuals is separable (which is analogous to the "each set of sectors is separable" requirement in Gorman (1968, p. 368)). Hence, from Debreu (1960, theorem 3), there exists a continuous FI function determined up to an increasing linear transformation of the form

$$f(y^0, y^1; z) = \alpha + \beta \sum_{i \in S} \phi_i \{y_i^0, y_i^1, z\}).$$

where ϕ_i is a real-valued function for each $i \in S$. The additional requirement for Debreu's (1960) proof that more than two of the $|S|$ elements of S are essential is satisfied as long as $|S| \geq 3$ and f is non-constant on $[0, z]$, which in turn is implied by monotonicity as long as at least one individual is impoverished.[20]

---

[20] The assumptions of at least three individuals in society and at least one impoverished individual are innocuous for any real-world application.

Permutability implies that $\phi_i = \phi_j$ for all $i, j \in S$, so we have $f(y^0, y^1; z) = \alpha + \beta \Sigma \phi\{y_i^0, y_i^1, z\}$). where ϕ is a real-valued function. By the focus and normalization axioms:

$$(4) \qquad \phi(y_i^0, y_i^1, z) = \begin{cases} \tilde{\phi}(y_i^0, y_i^1, z) & \text{if } (y_i^1 < y_i^0 \text{ and } y_i^1 < z) \\ 0 & \text{otherwise.} \end{cases}$$

By the continuity of f, ϕ and $\tilde{\phi}$ must also be continuous. Consider an individual with $y_i^0 > z$ and $y_i^1 = z$. Since y_i^1 is not less than z, i is not impoverished, so by (4), $\phi(y_i^0, y_i^1, z) = 0$. Now consider an alternative situation where $\tilde{y}_i^1 = z - \varepsilon$ for a sufficiently small $\varepsilon > 0$. In this scenario, $\tilde{\phi}$ cannot be a direct function of y_i^0 or ϕ would be discontinuous at z; instead, $\tilde{\phi}$ must be a direct function of just y_i^1 and z so that an infinitesimal decrease in y_i^1 below z results in an infinitesimal increase in ϕ. By a similar argument, for an individual with $y_i^0 > z$, $y_i^1 = y_i^0$, and $\tilde{y}_i^1 = y_i^0 - \varepsilon$, $\tilde{\phi}$ cannot be a direct function of z and instead must directly depend only on y_i^1 and y_i^0 so that an infinitesimal decrease in y_i^1 below $y_i^0 > z$ results in an infinitesimal increase in ϕ.

Given this, we can rewrite $\tilde{\phi}(y_i^0, y_i^1, z) = \tilde{\phi}\min\{y_i^0, z\}, y_i^1)$. Since $\tilde{\phi}$ is only defined for those who are impoverished (i.e., those for whom $\{y_i^0, y_i^1, z\} = y_i^1$), we have

$$(5) \qquad \tilde{\phi}(y_i^0, y_i^1, z) = \tilde{\phi}(\min\{y_i^0, z\}, \min\{y_i^0, y_i^1, z\}).$$
$$(6) \qquad = \tilde{\phi}(\min\{y_i^0, z\} - \min\{y_i^0, y_i^1, z\}, 0)$$
$$(7) \qquad = (\min\{y_i^0, z\} - \min\{y_i^0, y_i^1, z\}\tilde{\phi}(1, 0),$$

where (6) follows from translation invariance and (7) from linear homogeneity. Noting that $\tilde{\phi}(1, 0)$ is a constant (that is positive by monotonicity) and denoting it γ, we have

$$\tilde{\phi}(y_i^0, y_i^1, z) = \begin{cases} (\min\{y_i^0, z\} - \min\{y_i^0, y_i^1, z\})\gamma & \text{if } i \in I_y \\ 0 & \text{otherwise.} \end{cases}$$

For $i \notin I_y$ we can also write $\phi(y_i^0, y_i^1, z) = (\min\{y_i^0, z\} - \min\{y_i^0, y_i^1, z\})\gamma$ since the non-impoverished are either non-poor before taxes and transfers and non-poor after ($\Rightarrow \min\{y_i^0, z\} - \min\{y_i^0, y_i^1, z\} = z$) or poor before taxes and transfers but do not lose income to the fiscal system ($\Rightarrow \min\{y_i^0, z\} - \min\{y_i^0, y_i^1, z\} = y_i^0$). Therefore $f(y^0, y^1; z) = \alpha + \beta\gamma \sum_{i \in S} \min\{y_i^0, z\} - \min\{y_i^0, y_i^1, z\}$). By normalization, $\alpha = 0$, which completes the proof.

PROOF OF PROPOSITION 2. (a) $\Leftrightarrow$ (b) follows immediately from Proposition 1. For (b) $\Leftrightarrow$ (c), we begin by defining Foster and Rothbaum's (2014) second order downward mobility dominance.

DEFINITION, (y^0, y^1) *second order downward mobility dominates* (x^0, x^1) on $[0, z^+]$ if

$$\int_0^z m(y^0, y^1; c)dc < \int_0^z m(x^0, x^1; c)dc \ \forall \ z \in [0, z^+],$$

where $m(y^0, y^1; z) = |S|^{-1} \sum_{i \in S} \mathbb{I}(y_i^1 < z < y_i^0)$ is Foster and Rothbaum's (2014) *downward mobility curve*, measuring the proportion of the population that begins with income above each poverty line and ends with income below the line.

A sufficient condition for (b) $\Leftrightarrow$ (c) is $\int_0^z m(y^0, y^1; z) \propto \int_0^z m(y^0, y^1; c) dc$. For a given poverty line $z = \hat{z}$, partition the set S into four subsets: $S_1 = \{i \in S \mid y_i^1 < y_i^0 < \hat{z}\}$, $S_2 = \{i \in S \mid y_i^1 < \hat{z} < y_i^0\}$, $S_3 = \{i \in S \mid y_i^0 < \hat{z}, y_i^1 > \hat{z}\}$, $S_4 = \{i \in S \mid y_i^0 < \hat{z}, y_i^0 \leq y_i^1\}$. For any subset $S_\alpha \subset S$, denote $f_a(\bullet; z) \equiv \kappa \sum_{i \in S_a} (\min\{y_i^0, z\} - \min\{y_i^0, y_i^1, z\})$ and $m_a(\bullet; z) \equiv |S|^{-1} \sum_{i \in S_a} \mathbb{I}\{y_i^1 < z < y_i^0\}$.

Each $i \in S_1$ experiences downward mobility on the interval $[0, \hat{z}]$ for all $z \in (y_i^0, y_i^1) \Rightarrow$ individual $i \in S_1$ increases $m_1(\bullet; \hat{z})$ by $|S|^{-1}$ for $z \in (y_i^0, y_i^1)$ and by zero for $z \leq y_i^1$ and $z \leq y_i^0 \Rightarrow$ individual $i \in S_1$ increases $\int_0^{\hat{z}} m_1(\bullet; c) dc$ by $|S|^{-1} (y_i^0, y_i^1)$. Summing over all $i \in S_1$, $\int_0^{\hat{z}} m_1(\bullet; c) dc = \sum_{i \in S_1} (y_i^0 - y_i^1)$.

$$y_i^1 < y_i^0 < \hat{z} \; \forall i \in S_1 \Rightarrow f_1(\bullet; \hat{z}) = \kappa \sum_{i \in S_1} (y_i^0 - y_i^1)$$

(8)
$$\Rightarrow f_1(\bullet; \hat{z}) = \kappa |S| \int_0^{\hat{z}} m_1(\bullet; c) dc.$$

Each $i \in S_2$ experiences downward mobility on the interval $[0, \hat{z}]$ for all $z \in (y_i^1, \hat{z}]$, which increases $m_2(\bullet; z)$ by $|S|^{-1}$ for $z \in (y_i^1, \hat{z}]$ and by zero for all other $z \Rightarrow$ individual $i \in S_2$ increases $\int_0^{\hat{z}} m_1(\bullet; c) dc$ by $|S|^{-1} (\hat{z} - y_i^1)$. Summing over all $i \in S_2$, $\int_0^{\hat{z}} m_1(\bullet; c) dc = \sum_{i \in S_2} |S|^{-1} (\hat{z} - y_i^1)$.

$$y_i^1 < \hat{z} < y_i^0 \; \forall i \in S_2 \Rightarrow f_2(\bullet; \hat{z}) = \kappa \sum_{i \in S_2} (\hat{z} - y_i^1)$$

(9)
$$\Rightarrow f_2(\bullet; \hat{z}) = \kappa |S| \int_0^{\hat{z}} m_2(\bullet; c) dc.$$

Each $i \in S_3$ does not experience downward mobility on the interval $[0, \hat{z}]$; summing over all $i \in S_3$ and integrating over our domain, we have $\int_0^{\hat{z}} m_1(\bullet; c) dc = 0$. $y_i^0 \geq \hat{z}$ and $y_i^1 \geq \hat{z} \; \forall i \in S_3 \Rightarrow$

(10)
$$f_3(\bullet; \hat{z}) = \kappa \sum_{i \in S_3} (\hat{z} - \hat{z}) = 0 = \kappa |S| \int_0^{\hat{z}} m_3(\bullet; c) dc.$$

Similarly $\int_0^{\hat{z}} m_4(\bullet; c) dc = 0$ because each $i \in S_4$ does not experience downward mobility on $[0, \hat{z}]$. $y_i^0 < \hat{z}$ and $y_i^0 \leq y_i^1 \; \forall i \in S_4 \Rightarrow$

(11)
$$f_4(\bullet; \hat{z}) = \kappa \sum_{i \in S_4} (y_i^0 - y_i^0) = 0 = \kappa |S| \int_0^{\hat{z}} m_4(\bullet; c) dc.$$

Given the definitions of $f_a(\bullet; z)$ and $m_a(\bullet; z)$ and that $S = S_1 \cup S_2 \cup S_3 \cup S_4$ and $S_1 \cap S_2 \cap S_3 \cap S_4 = \emptyset$, we have $f(y^0, y^1; z) = \sum_{a=1}^4 f_a(\bullet; z)$ and $m(y^0, y^1; z) = \sum_{a=1}^4 m_a(\bullet; z)$. Hence, by (8)–(11), $f(y^0, y^1; \hat{z}) \kappa |S| \int_0^{\hat{z}} m_1(\bullet; c) dc$. This holds for all $\hat{z} \in [0, z^+]$ since the choice of $\hat{z}$ was arbitrary, which completes the proof.

PROOF OF PROPOSITION 3. Analogous to the proof of Proposition 1 for FI.

PROOF OF PROPOSITION 4. Given in text.

Chapter 5

MEASURING THE EFFECTIVENESS OF TAXES AND TRANSFERS IN FIGHTING INEQUALITY AND POVERTY

Ali Enami

Introduction

One of the key questions to be addressed by a *CEQ Assessment* is how effective taxes and government spending in reducing inequality and poverty are. This chapter introduces new Commitment to Equity (CEQ) effectiveness indicators to evaluate the effectiveness of taxes and transfers in reducing inequality and poverty. The main goal of the effectiveness indicators defined here is to provide policymakers with meaningful but easy-to-interpret indexes that measure fiscal interventions' "bang for the buck" in terms of inequality or poverty reduction relative to the amount collected and spent. Special attention has been given to the design of these indicators to fulfill the mathematical requirements of "proper ordering": specifically, the design of the indicators ensures that, keeping the maximum potential of two interventions in reducing inequality (or poverty) constant, an intervention with higher marginal contribution to the reduction of inequality (or poverty) has a higher ranking. By contrast, an intervention with higher potential to reduce inequality (or poverty) but with lower realized effect receives a lower ranking. A brief description of the effectiveness indicators can also be found in chapter 1 by Lustig and Higgins (2022), in this Volume. Also in this Volume, chapter 8 by Higgins and Brest Lopez (2022) describes how these indicators are calculated with the *CEQ Stata Package*. All the effectiveness indicators are calculated by the *CEQ Stata Package* and automatically pasted in section E Output Tables of the *CEQ Master Workbook© (MWB)* (which is in Part IV of this Volume of the Handbook, available online only; CEQ Institute, 2022).

This chapter begins by introducing two general indexes, the Impact and Spending Effectiveness indicators, which are designed to measure the effectiveness of fiscal policies in reducing poverty and inequality. The chapter then reviews the fiscal impoverishment and gains effectiveness indicator (FI/FGP) designed by Enami, Higgins, and Younger (2022) (box 1-3 in this Volume), based on the concepts of fiscal impoverishment (FI) and fiscal gains to the poor (FGP) introduced by Higgins and Lustig (2016). This effectiveness indicator can better capture the poverty-reducing or -increasing effects of fiscal interventions. An application of these indicators for the case of Iran's fiscal system is presented in Enami, Lustig, and Taqdiri (2019) (reproduced in chapter 17 of this Volume).

Before introducing these indicators, the next section will briefly review the concept of marginal contribution (MC), which is central to the construction of the CEQ effectiveness indicators here, as well as the notation used throughout this chapter. Then the shortcomings of the previous CEQ effectiveness indicator are reviewed, and, finally, the new effectiveness indicators are introduced.

1 Notation

This chapter uses T and B to refer to taxes and benefits, where T can refer to any combination of direct and indirect taxes, and B can refer to any combination of direct transfers, indirect subsidies, and in-kind transfers from public spending on health and education. The indicators can also be defined as combinations of taxes and transfers, which is why T *(and/or B)* is used throughout. One can calculate the marginal contribution (MC) of any combination of taxes or benefits as follows:

$$MC_{T(and/or\,B)}^{End\,income} = Index_{End\,income \backslash T(and/or\,B)} - Index_{End\,income}$$

Index refers to any inequality or poverty indexes that may be used to calculate the marginal contribution. For example, this chapter uses the Gini index as a measure of inequality. The subscript of the *Index*, *End income*, refers to the income concept used to calculate the marginal contribution to the index of a tax or benefit. For example, $Gini_{Disposable\,Income}$ refers to the Gini coefficient of Disposable Income, and using $Gini_{Disposable\,Income}$ for $Gini_{End\,Income}$ implies that we are interested in calculating the marginal contribution of a tax or benefit to the Disposable Income Gini. *End income\T (and/or B)* refers to the income concept that is equivalent to *End income* prior to the tax or benefit of interest. For example, *Disposable Income\Direct Taxes* equals Disposable Income plus direct taxes (to find the income concept *prior to* subtracting out direct taxes). Intuitively, $MC_{T(and/or\,B)}^{End\,income}$ is the change in the value of $Index_{End\,income}$ if *T (and/or B)* is removed from the fiscal system or replaced with a tax (or benefit) of the same size that has no effect on inequality (or poverty) when it is added to the fiscal system. It should be noted that *End income* does not have to be one of the CEQ core income concepts. For example, if we wanted to calculate the marginal effect of indirect taxes with respect to Disposable Income, because indirect taxes have not yet been subtracted out of Disposable Income, the end income concept would be *Disposable Income minus Indirect Taxes*. The MC in this case would be calculated as follows:

$$MC_{Indirect\ Taxes}^{Disposable\ Income\ minus\ Indirect\ Taxes} = Index_{Disposable\ Income} - Index_{Disposable\ Income\ minus\ Indirect\ Taxes}$$

On the other hand, if we were calculating the MC of *direct* taxes with respect to Disposable Income, because Disposable Income is already net of direct taxes, the end income would be Disposable Income, whereas the end income without the fiscal intervention would require taking Disposable Income and *adding back in* direct taxes, as follows:

$$MC_{Direct\ Taxes}^{Disposable\ Income} = Index_{Disposable\ Income\ plus\ Direct\ taxes} - Index_{Disposable\ Income}$$

In calculating MC, the important point is that we have two income concepts that are different from each other only because of one component or a bundle of taxes or transfers. In other words, one can use components of a fiscal system separately and also in different combinations (or bundles) to perform a marginal contribution analysis. An example would be to evaluate the inequality-reducing effect of different taxes in a system separately first and then of the whole taxation system together as one entity. Regardless of how a component or bundle is set up, we consider the MC of a fiscal intervention to be the difference between these two income concepts (the *End income* with and without that specific component or bundle) for a particular inequality (or poverty) index.

Although the preceding examples are all related to the Gini index, the concept of MC is applicable to any inequality or poverty index.

2 New CEQ Effectiveness Indicators

Before introducing the new indicators, it is helpful to review why they have replaced the previous CEQ effectiveness indicators. Following this review, the new indicators will be discussed.

2.1 Shortcomings of the 2013 Effectiveness Indicator

The effectiveness indicator introduced in an earlier version of the Handbook (Lustig and Higgins, 2013) was defined as follows:

$$CEQ\ Old\ Effectiveness\ Indicator = \frac{MC_{T(or\ B)}^{End\ income}}{[T(or\ B)]/GDP}$$

This indicator suffers from some shortcomings. The most important one is that it could fail to rank the taxes and transfers properly, or at least it would fail to properly describe how taxes and transfers are performing in comparison to each other. That is because many indicators of inequality and poverty do not have a linear relationship with the size of the taxes and transfers.

An example can help to clarify this point. Assume we are interested in measuring the impact of a tax on reduction in inequality and we allocate that tax in a way that mathematically maximizes the reduction in traditional Gini index. As we increase the size of this tax, despite the fact that we use the most inequality reducing method of allocating the tax, the power of the next dollar to reduce inequality decreases. In other words, doubling the size of a tax does not double its impact on Gini (note that Gini is bounded between zero and one). The point of this example is to show that the "maximum potential" of the next dollar in reducing inequality decreases as the size of a tax (or transfer) increases. Dividing the impact of a tax (i.e., its MC) by the size of that tax implies that the "maximum potential" of that tax is constant. Therefore, everything else being equal, bigger programs would be evaluated as less effective ones.

The second problem with the above-mentioned index relates to the mathematical interpretation of this indicator. The indicator in the equation above states how much the marginal contribution of a tax (or transfer) would change if that tax (or transfer) were scaled up to the size of GDP (note that one can rewrite this indicator to be $\frac{MC_{T(or\ B)}^{End\ income}}{[T(or\ B)]} \times GDP$). Because this is a linear interpolation, the values could easily exceed the reasonable boundaries. For example, values beyond unity (in absolute terms) are meaningless for the power of a tax (transfer) to reduce inequality simply because the change in Gini cannot exceed unity (in absolute terms).

With respect to poverty reduction, the indicator is not problematic in ranking the taxes and transfers individually if a proper indicator (such as poverty gap) is used. However, this indicator is not developed adequately to assess bundles of taxes and transfers. In the case of poverty reduction of a bundle, the two concepts of *fiscal gains to the poor* (FGP) and *fiscal impoverishment* (FI) should be accounted for separately. Note that taxes cannot decrease poverty while transfers cannot increase it.

2.2 Impact and Spending Effectiveness Indicators

The two new CEQ effectiveness indicators are introduced in this section. These indicators have three main properties. First, they rank taxes and transfers properly with regard to how much of their maximum potential in achieving inequality or poverty is in fact achieved. In addition to the proper ranking, the difference between the effectiveness values of two alternative taxes shows how much one is actually performing better than the other one (i.e., the relative difference between various values of these indicators is meaningful). Second, the indicators satisfy the normalization property, meaning that their values equal one when a tax or transfer reaches its maximum effectiveness. Finally, the indicators have an intuitive and independent interpretation. The effectiveness values show not only how well a tax or transfer performs relative to other taxes and transfers, but also how well they do relative to their own maximum potential.

2.2.1 Impact Effectiveness

Impact effectiveness (IE) is defined as the ratio of the observed MC of a tax (transfer) to the optimum MC of that tax (transfer) if it is distributed in a way that maximizes its inequality- or poverty-reducing impact. The following equation shows how this indicator is defined mathematically:

$$Impact\ Effectiveness_{T\,(and/or\,B)}^{End\,income} = \frac{MC_{T\,(and/or\,B)}^{End\,income}}{MC_{T\,(and/or\,B)}^{End\,income^*}},$$

where $MC_{T\,(and/or\,B)}^{End\,income^*}$ is the maximum possible $MC_{T\,(and/or\,B)}^{End\,income}$ if the same amount of T (and/or B) is distributed differently among individuals. For example, for the Gini index we deduct taxes from (add benefits to) the richest (poorest) until her income becomes equal to the second richest (poorest), then deduct taxes from (add benefits to) these two richest (poorest) until their incomes become equal to the third richest (poorest), and we continue this procedure until we end up with the same total value of T (B) that we observe in the actual system.[1] If the indicator of interest is a Gini or S-Gini index, the impact effectiveness indicator is identical to what is proposed by Fellman, Jäntti, and Lambert (1999).[2]

This indicator shows the relative realized power of a tax or transfer in reducing inequality, or of a transfer (or combined tax-transfer system) in reducing poverty. There are two important issues to note. First, the choice of the poverty indicator is crucial. For example, if one chooses to focus on the poverty headcount ratio, then to maximize the IE indicator, the policymakers should focus the financial resources on those who are right below the poverty line and ignore those who are in deep poverty. This is not an optimal policy implication from the social welfare perspective, and we discourage the use of the poverty headcount ratio. Squared poverty gap, on the other hand, encourages targeting the transfer toward the poorest first, and, therefore, it is an indicator that we specially recommend for policymakers to utilize. Second, because taxes can only increase poverty, the poverty-reduction indicator is only defined for benefits and combined tax-transfer systems that have a positive marginal contribution.

An example shows how to interpret this indicator: if the impact effectiveness of a transfer is equal to 0.7, it means the transfer has realized 70 percent of its potential power in reducing inequality. Therefore, the higher the value of this indicator, the more effective a tax (transfer) is in fulfilling its potential to reduce inequality.

One can calculate this indicator for taxes and transfers with both positive and negative MC for inequality. To see why this indicator properly ranks taxes and transfers with a positive MC to inequality or poverty, assume taxes A and B cause the same re-

---

[1] See Fei (1981) for the proof that this method maximizes reduction in Gini.
[2] See Fellman, Jäntti, and Lambert (1999).

duction in inequality but A is larger than B. In this case, B is preferred to A because both taxes do good (by reducing inequality), but A has a higher (unrealized) potential to reduce inequality because it is larger. So when $MC_{T(and/or\,B)}^{End\,income} > 0$, the Impact Effectiveness indicator abides by this ranking because $MC_{T(and/or\,B)}^{End\,income^*}$ is in the denominator and is increasing in the size of T. Now to see why the indicator properly ranks taxes and transfers with a negative MC to inequality (that is, taxes and transfers that cause an *increase* in inequality), assume tax A causes the same increase in inequality as tax B but tax A is larger. This would mean that, while A and B both do harm, tax A at least collects more revenue while doing the same harm.[3] In other words, if tax B were scaled up to collect the same revenue as tax A, its negative effect on inequality would be higher (its MC would be more negative). Thus, tax A is preferred to B, and this is indeed the information given by the Impact Effectiveness indicator because $MC_{T(and/or\,B)}^{End\,income^*}$ is in the denominator and is increasing in the size of T (note that here $MC_{T(and/or\,B)}^{End\,income} < 0$). Note that while the indicator is bounded from above (i.e., one is the maximum possible value for this indicator), it is not bounded from below if MC is negative.

For poverty, one can calculate the impact effectiveness indicator (using the formula above) for benefits or combined tax-benefit systems. For taxes, which can only increase poverty, the denominator will always be zero (so the optimal effect of a tax on poverty is zero). Therefore, the denominator is modified in the following expression to reflect the most harmful way of taxing (taxing the poorest until her income equals zero, then the second poorest until her income equals zero, and so on). We denote this harmful taxation as $MC_{T(or\,B)}^{End\,income^{H}}$ and calculate

$$Poverty\ Impact\ Effectiveness_{T}^{End\,income} = -\frac{MC_{T}^{End\,income}}{MC_{T}^{End\,income^{H}}},$$

where the negative sign is included to ensure that the higher the value of the indicator, the less harmful the tax is relative to its potential to do harm.[4]

2.2.2 Spending Effectiveness

The spending effectiveness (SE) indicator is defined as the ratio of the minimum amount of a tax (transfer) required to be collected (spent) in order to create the observed MC of the tax (transfer), if the tax (transfer) is instead redistributed optimally. The following equation shows how this indicator is calculated:

---

[3] This is not exactly a mathematical property because the MC of taxes A and B is calculated with respect to different reference points, so having different potentials does not necessarily correspond to collecting more revenue.

[4] Note that both numerator and denominator have a negative sign by definition, which will cancel each other, and that therefore, we add a negative sign in front of the ratio to make it a negative value.

$$\textit{Spending Effectiveness}_{T(and/or\,B)}^{End\,income} = \frac{T^*(and/or\,B^*)}{T(and/or\,B)},$$

where T^* ($and/or\ B^*$) is the minimum amount of T (or B) that is needed to create the same $MC_{T(or\,B)}^{End\,income}$ using the same redistribution procedure that was discussed previously to find the maximum MC.

This indicator shows how much less tax (transfer) is required to achieve the same observed outcome (in terms of inequality reduction) if the tax (transfer) is collected (spent) in a way that maximizes the reduction in inequality. For example, a value of 70 percent for spending effectiveness of a transfer means that the same MC could be achieved by spending only 70 percent of the current resources if those resources were spent optimally (if the objective function is to maximize equality).

A higher value of the SE indicator implies that a program is more effective. The following example clarifies this point. Assume two alternative worlds in which we spend $100 in transfers and reduce inequality by 0.1 Gini points. In world A, we can achieve the same level of inequality reduction by spending just $30 but allocating it in the most inequality-reducing way, while in world B we would have to spend $90. In other words, in world A we could achieve just as much inequality reduction by only spending 30 percent as much as we are now; in world B we are already fairly close to the most effective spending. That is because even if we redistribute in the most inequality-reducing way, we would still have to spend 90 percent of what we are currently spending to get the same inequality reduction we observe. Clearly, spending in world B is more effective for inequality reduction.

The spending effectiveness indicator can only be calculated for the taxes and transfers with a positive MC (and as a result, the spending effectiveness of taxes on poverty reduction is undefined). Moreover, and in the context of inequality indices, in order to calculate this indicator for the whole fiscal system (which is a combination of taxes and transfers), one needs to make a normative choice first. There are various inequality-minimizing taxes and transfers that could achieve the same level of reduction in inequality, and a researcher needs to decide between them using a normative criterion. For example, one may choose an optimal fiscal system with the least budget deficit (or surplus), while others may choose an optimal system that keeps the ratio of total taxes to transfers constant (that is, one that scales the current system). For this reason, here we refrain from calculating this indicator for the whole fiscal system.

Spending effectiveness has an important interpretation as a measure of efficiency as well. Because the value of the normative index of interest[5] (for example, the Gini

---

[5] Here we assume that the choice of an index of inequality (e.g., Gini) implies a normative choice in the sense that the society uses this index to evaluate various programs with regard to its social goals. So, for example, the society is indifferent between two alternative taxes as long as they reduce the value of Gini identically. Note that, this is only from the perspective of the social goal stated here, which is reduction in inequality measured by Gini.

index) is kept constant, spending effectiveness shows how the fiscal intervention could have reached the same social goal with less distortion through a smaller size of tax or transfer. Therefore, this indicator not only ranks the effectiveness of different taxes and transfers in reducing inequality and poverty but can also be used to rank alternative taxes and transfers from the view of economic efficiency.

2.3 Fiscal Impoverishment and Gains Effectiveness Indicators

This section reviews the effectiveness indicators introduced by Enami and others.[6] These indicators are specific to the effect of taxes and transfers on fiscal impoverishment (FI) and fiscal gains to the poor (FGP). Axiomatic indicators for FI and FGP are derived by Higgins and Lustig (2016), which is reprinted in chapter 4 in this Volume of the Handbook. Consider a set of policies that may include both benefits and taxes. We measure the effectiveness of these policies at reducing poverty without making many of the poor poorer as

$$Effectiveness_{FI/FGP} = \left[\left(\frac{B}{T+B}\right)\left(\frac{FGP\_MC_{T\,and\,B}^{End\,income}}{B}\right)\right] + \left[\left(\frac{T}{T+B}\right)\left(1 - \frac{FI\_MC_{T\,and\,B}^{End\,income}}{T}\right)\right],$$

where T and B are the size of total taxes and transfers (both positive values), $FGP\_MC_{T\,and\,B}^{End\,income}$ is the marginal contribution of the net system (i.e., T and B) to FGP (always a non-negative value), and $FI\_MC_{T\,and\,B}^{End\,income}$ is the marginal contribution of the net system (i.e., T and B) to FI (always a non-negative value).[7]

Note that T and B are maximum possible reduction or increase in the FGP and FI indicators. In other words, if all taxes are paid by the poor and no benefits reach the poor, $FI\_MC_{T\,and\,B}^{End\,income}$ becomes equal to T. Similarly, if all transfers go to the poor (only up to the point that brings them out of poverty) and the poor pay no taxes, the value of $FGP\_MC_{T\,and\,B}^{End\,income}$ becomes equal to B. As a result, both $\left(\dfrac{FGP\_MC_{T\,and\,B}^{End\,income}}{B}\right)$ and $\left(1 - \dfrac{FI\_MC_{T\,and\,B}^{End\,income}}{T}\right)$ are bounded between zero and 1. Moreover, the higher the value of each of these two components, the more effective the bundle of taxes and transfer is from the poverty reduction perspective. The weights $\left(\text{i.e., } \left(\dfrac{B}{T+B}\right) \text{ and } \left(\dfrac{T}{T+B}\right)\right)$ also add up to one. Therefore, the whole indicator is bounded between zero and one, and the higher the value of the indicator, the more effective the bundle of taxes and transfers

---

[6] See Enami, Higgins, and Younger (2022), box 1-3 in this Volume.

[7] FGP and FI are in Higgins and Lustig (2016), chapter 4 in this Volume. A brief description can be found in chapter 1 of this Volume, and the instructions on how to calculate them with the *CEQ Stata Package* are in chapter 8 of this Volume.

is in reducing poverty. For analyzing bundles that include only taxes, including a single tax, the indicator reduces to

$$Tax\ Effectiveness_{FI} = 1 - \left(\frac{FI\_MC_T^{End\ income}}{T} \right).$$

For policies that include only benefits, it reduces to

$$Transfer\ Effectiveness_{FGP} = \frac{FGP\_MC_B^{End\ income}}{B}.$$

These indicators vary between zero and one and the higher the value of the indicator, the better a tax or transfer is in terms of its effectiveness in reducing poverty. Note that taxes can only hurt and transfers can only help the poor, and even though both of the preceding indicators have positive values, one should not compare the effectiveness of a tax to a transfer in reducing poverty.

3 Conclusion

This chapter introduced two new CEQ effectiveness indicators for evaluating the performance of taxes and transfers in reducing inequality and poverty. The first indicator is the impact effectiveness indicator, which takes the size of a tax or transfer as given and compares the realized reduction in inequality (or poverty) to the maximum possible reduction. The second indicator, spending effectiveness, takes the reduction in inequality (or poverty) as given and compares the actual size of a tax or transfer to the minimum required tax or transfer to create the same reduction in inequality (or poverty). The spending effectiveness index has an interpretation as a measure of efficiency as well because it determines how much unnecessary tax (or transfer) is collected (distributed), which if avoided would have resulted in less distortion. This chapter also reviewed a sub-family of impact effectiveness indicators that is specific to the effectiveness of taxes and transfers in reducing poverty.[8] These indicators are based on the indexes of fiscal impoverishment and fiscal gain to the poor introduced in Higgins and Lustig (2016) (reproduced as chapter 4 in this Volume).

Acknowledgments

I am very grateful to Sean Higgins, Nora Lustig, and Stephen D. Younger for their insightful comments on the previous drafts of this chapter.

---

[8] Enami, Higgins, and Younger (2022), box 1-3 in this Volume.

References

CEQ Institute. 2022. "*CEQ Assessment: CEQ Master Workbook*," available online only in part IV of the *Commitment to Equity Handbook: Estimating the Impact of Fiscal Policy on Inequality and Poverty*, 2nd ed., Vol. 1, edited by Nora Lustig (Brookings Institution Press and CEQ Institute, Tulane University). Free online version available at www.commitmentoequity.org

Enami, Ali, Sean Higgins, and Stephen D. Younger. 2022. "Box 1-3. Fiscal Impoverishment and Gains Effectiveness Indicators," in *Commitment to Equity Handbook: Estimating the Impact of Fiscal Policy on Inequality and Poverty*, Vol. 1, 2nd ed., edited by Nora Lustig (Brookings Institution Press and CEQ Institute, Tulane University). Free online version available at www.commitmentoequity.org.

Enami, Ali, Nora Lustig, and Alireza Taqdiri. 2019. "Fiscal Policy, Inequality, and Poverty in Iran: Assessing the Impact and Effectiveness of Taxes and Transfers." *Middle East Development Journal* 11, no. 1, pp. 49–74.

Fei, John C. H. 1981. "Equity Oriented Fiscal Programs." *Econometrica: Journal of the Econometric Society* 49, no. 4, pp. 869–81.

Fellman, Johan, Markus Jäntti, and Peter J. Lambert. 1999. "Optimal Tax-Transfer Systems and Redistributive Policy." *Scandinavian Journal of Economics* 101, no. 1, pp. 114–26.

Higgins, Sean, and Caterina Brest Lopez. 2022. "Producing Indicators and Results, and Completing Sections D and E of the *CEQ Master Workbook* Using the *CEQ Stata Package*," chap. 8 in *Commitment to Equity Handbook: Estimating the Impact of Fiscal Policy on Inequality and Poverty*, Vol. 1, 2nd ed., edited by Nora Lustig (Brookings Institution Press and CEQ Institute, Tulane University). Free online version available at www.commitmentoequity.org.

Higgins, Sean, and Nora Lustig. 2016. "Can a Poverty-Reducing and Progressive Tax and Transfer System Hurt the Poor?" *Journal of Development Economics* 122, pp. 63–75.

Lustig, Nora, and Sean Higgins. 2013. "Commitment to Equity Assessment (CEQ): Estimating the Incidence of Social Spending, Subsidies and Taxes. Handbook." CEQ Working Paper 1 (New Orleans: Center for Inter-American Policy and Research, Department of Economics, Tulane University, and Inter-American Dialogue).

———. 2022. "The *CEQ Assessment*: Measuring the Impact of Fiscal Policy on Inequality and Poverty," chap. 1 in *Commitment to Equity Handbook. Estimating the Impact of Fiscal Policy on Inequality and Poverty*, Vol. 1, 2nd ed., edited by Nora Lustig (Brookings Institution Press and CEQ Institute, Tulane University). Free online version available at www.commitmentoequity.org.

PART II

Implementation

Chapter 6

ALLOCATING TAXES AND TRANSFERS AND CONSTRUCTING INCOME CONCEPTS

Completing Sections A, B, and C of the *CEQ Master Workbook*©

Ali Enami, Sean Higgins, and Nora Lustig

NOTE TO THE READER: Chapter 6 describes the methods used to allocate taxes and transfers to households and construct each one of the income concepts used to analyze the impact of fiscal policy on inequality and poverty. Since the publication of the first edition in 2018, some of the methodological recommendations have been subject to change and the information included in the CEQ Data Center on Fiscal Redistribution has incorporated them. A key change is that we no longer recommend scaling down spending on education and health as we did in the first edition. Please be sure to use the second edition's chapter in your work.

Introduction

As stated in the introduction, the purpose of Volume 1 of this Handbook is to present a step-by-step guide to applying the incidence analysis used in *Commitment to Equity (CEQ) Assessments*. Developed by the Commitment to Equity Institute at Tulane University, the *CEQ Assessment* is a diagnostic tool that uses fiscal incidence analysis to determine the extent to which fiscal policy reduces inequality and poverty in a particular country. The *CEQ Assessment* is designed to address the following four questions:

1. How much income redistribution and poverty reduction is being accomplished through fiscal policy?[1]
2. How equalizing and pro-poor are specific taxes and government spending?

---

[1] Throughout Volume 1 of this Handbook, "fiscal policy," "fiscal instruments," "taxes and government spending," "revenue collection and government spending," "taxes and transfers," "taxes and benefits," and "net fiscal system" are used interchangeably.

3. How effective are taxes and government spending in reducing inequality and poverty?
4. What is the impact of fiscal reforms that change the size and/or progressivity of a particular tax or benefit?

The introduction orients the reader on how to use this Handbook and specifies the data requirements to implement a study of the kind proposed here. Chapter 1 in this Volume (Lustig and Higgins, 2022) presents a fairly detailed discussion of the theory of fiscal redistribution, describes the method of fiscal incidence and its limitations, and shows how the array of indicators that are produced with the *CEQ Assessment* can be used to answer the questions outlined above.

This chapter describes in detail the methodology to construct the income concepts and, thus, it is one of the key chapters for the reader who wants to implement a fiscal incidence analysis. It is crucial to note that in the second edition of the Handbook we made some important changes to improve the readability of its content. We also made a few methodological changes, and we note below when this happened.

As discussed in chapter 1 in this Volume, the construction of income concepts is the core building block of fiscal incidence analysis. Starting from prefiscal income, the construction of income concepts refers to the method of allocating the burden of taxes and the benefits of government spending to each household. Although this procedure may sound very simple, allocating taxes and transfers to households is among the most—if not the most—challenging tasks of fiscal incidence analysis. Because results can be significantly affected by the allocation methods, it is essential to carefully document all the assumptions made in the allocation process and carry out sensitivity analyses to assess the implications of such assumptions.

The construction of income concepts entails five main steps. The first step is to obtain access to a recent household survey (ideally, an income expenditure survey) for the country of interest.[2] The second step is to obtain budget data from administrative registries (for example, revenues collected by tax category, spending on cash transfers, subsidies, education, health, and housing, and so on) for the same year of the survey. The third step is to select which components of government revenue and spending will be included in the incidence analysis and to obtain detailed information on the qualitative and quantitative characteristics of the selected fiscal interventions. The fourth step is to allocate these fiscal interventions at the household level. By dividing income by the number of household members (or using an equivalence scale), taxes and transfers become allocated at the individual level. Once the allocation process is complete, the fifth step is to construct the income concepts that will be used to assess the impact of fiscal policy on the distribution of income and poverty as well as the contribution of each fiscal intervention to the fiscal policy–induced changes in inequality

---

[2] For details, see the introduction and part IV of Volume 1 (the latter is available only online; CEQ Institute, 2022a).

and poverty. The fifth step may involve the utilization of an input-output matrix (or a Social Accounting Matrix) to incorporate the indirect effects (i.e., through inputs) of indirect taxes and subsidies (described in detail in chapter 7 in this Volume [Jellema and Inchauste, 2022]). Including the indirect effects will affect the amount of taxes and transfers that are allocated to households, and, thus, their postfiscal income.

Once the allocation process is completed, the totals for each fiscal intervention should be compared with administrative totals in sheet B3 of the *CEQ Master Workbook© (MWB)* (available online in part IV of Volume 1 of this Handbook; CEQ Institute, 2022a). Most likely, they will not be equal and this is a common feature in most of these exercises. However, this comparison allows the researcher to decide whether further work is needed in the allocation process. It also informs the users of the study the extent to which the fiscal incidence analysis captures each fiscal intervention. This is obtained by dividing the total obtained from the survey by the administrative total (for example, the total direct taxes obtained from the analysis divided by the total direct taxes in administrative budgetary data or national accounts).

This chapter describes how to construct the income concepts and how to complete sections A, B, and C of the *CEQ MWB)*. Section 1 of this chapter describes the *CEQ MWB*, as well as the data requirements and methodological assumptions that one needs to make in the treatment of the microdata from household surveys, especially; it also explains how to complete sections A and B of the *CEQ MWB*. Section 2 explains the income concepts. Sections 3 and 4 explain how to construct the income concepts, describing the methods used to allocate various fiscal interventions to particular households in microdata from household surveys. In other words, these sections provide information on the process by which taxes, subsidies, and transfers are allocated to each household to assess how incomes—and, thus, inequality and poverty indicators—change with fiscal policy. It also explains how to construct the "income" concepts for surveys that include only consumption. Section 5 explains how to complete section C of the *CEQ MWB* and includes a detailed description of the methodologies used to construct each income concept and a summary of key assumptions made by the team in the process. Part IV, available online only, presents a completed *CEQ MWB* for Mexico and an example of "do files" in Stata for constructing the income concepts with the information from Mexico, which can serve as an example.[3] The data and software requirements and the recommended team composition and timeline are also presented in part IV (CEQ Institute, 2022b and 2022c, respectively).

Before we start, a word on other comparable initiatives. Besides the CEQ Institute at Tulane University, there are other initiatives that monitor the impact of fiscal policy on inequality in a systematic way and for multiple countries using prefisc and postfisc income concepts. EUROMOD at the University of Essex primarily covers the member countries of the European Union and uses microsimulation; its main characteristics are described in appendix B by Daria Popova. Below we highlight some of the main

---

[3] Scott and others (2018).

differences with the methodology followed in *CEQ Assessments*. The Organisation for Economic Cooperation and Development (OECD) also publishes prefiscal and post-fiscal inequality indicators for its member countries and LIS (Cross-National Data Center in Luxembourg) includes prefiscal and postfiscal inequality and poverty indicators among its key figures. One main difference between the CEQ and these three initiatives is the latter include the impact of direct taxes and direct transfers only, while the CEQ indicators also include the impact of indirect taxes and subsidies and transfers in-kind (public education and health). WID.WORLD (the World Inequality Database), based at the Paris School of Economics (with partnering organizations in other places), is focused on generating Distributional National Accounts (DINA) whose main purpose is to add to the income and consumption aggregates their distribution by deciles, both before taxes and transfers and after them. The methodology is described in detail in Alvaredo and others (2016). The main difference between WID/DINA and *CEQ Assessments* is that in the latter, although we rely on administrative data, we do not "force" the scale of the economy (and fiscal interventions) embedded in the household survey to equal the magnitudes found in National Accounts and government budgetary data. We explain the reasons below. Below we also discuss the fact that, in countries where not only the levels but their relative sizes are different in the household survey and administrative registries, this creates a challenge since—essentially—we are implicitly admitting two different economic structures in the same countries.

1 The *CEQ Master Workbook*

The *CEQ MWB*, part IV in Volume 1 (available only online) is a multi-sheet Excel file that houses detailed information on the country's economic, political, and social context, description of microdata, the country's fiscal system and the results of the fiscal incidence analysis used as inputs for policy discussions, academic papers, and policy reports. The *CEQ MWB* consists of six sections: A. "Country Context," B. "Data," C. "Methodology," D. "Summary of Results," E. "Output Tables," and F. "Results by Ethnicity and Race." This chapter focuses on sections A, B, and C. These sections are meant to be filled by the team with information obtained from the household survey, administrative sources, and the methodological assumptions used to estimate the incidence of taxes and public spending. The order of the sections has been chosen having the user of the CEQ exercise in mind. Producers of a *CEQ Assessment* should start with section B, the data and information required to implement an assessment. A *CEQ Assessment* producer can complete section A at the end.

Section A, Country Context, contains information on the macroeconomic, political, and socioeconomic context, as well as the evolution of inequality and poverty over time. It also includes information on whether the country experienced a natural disaster, civil strife, or a financial crisis, and whether there was an election or any other special situation that could have affected fiscal policy in the year of the analysis. Section B, Data, includes a description of the microdata and the fiscal data utilized in the fiscal incidence analysis. For the microdata, section B includes a detailed description of the survey(s) being used to conduct the analysis, such as sample size, coverage, and questionnaire, including, for example, the exact survey questions used to construct each component of the income concepts. In the fiscal data section, the team needs to compile the budget information from administrative registries and summarize the characteristics of the fiscal interventions (such as direct taxes, consumption taxes, excise taxes, cash transfers, subsidies, and in-kind transfers) that will be included in the analysis. Section C, Methodology, presents the methodology followed to construct the income concepts and key assumptions made in the allocation process, and compares survey-based totals with those from administrative registries for validation purposes.

To produce a comprehensive *CEQ Assessment*, one must have access to microdata from a recent household survey, government budget data from fiscal accounts, and a detailed description of the characteristics of fiscal policy instruments that will be included in the analysis. The information on the microdata, budget, and components of the fiscal system are saved in section B of the *CEQ MWB*, in sections B1–B2, B3, and B4–B12, respectively.

We will start with sheets B1 and B2 and subsequently proceed to sheet B3 and then sheets B4–B12.

1.1 The Microdata: Description of the Household Survey and Data Harmonization Assumptions

The available household survey should have, ideally, information on both income and consumption. Since surveys frequently include just one of the two, we will discuss how to adapt the CEQ methodology to cope with this limitation. The characteristics of the household survey used in the analysis should be documented in sheets B1 and B2 of section B of the *CEQ MWB*. Here the researcher will provide details of the household survey such as name, year, sample size, geographic coverage, recall period, and which income, consumption, and fiscal policy variables are included in the survey (sheet B1). To assess cross-country and over time comparability, the researcher should document the specific wording used to retrieve some key variables in the survey questionnaire (Sheet B2). Tables 6G-1 and 6G-2 show the contents of sheets B1 and B2, respectively.

One key goal of the CEQ Institute is to create a Data Center on Fiscal Redistribution to be able to compare the impact of fiscal policy on inequality and poverty across countries and over time. Given this goal, the CEQ methodology considers it very important for the underlying microdata to be as harmonized as possible. In what follows, we discuss a series of definitions (for example, definition of a household, unit of analysis, and so on) and procedures (for example, treatment of missing and zero incomes, top coding, and so on) used by the CEQ for this purpose. We broadly follow the definitions and procedures used by international databases such as LIS, SEDLAC (Socioeconomic Database for Latin America and the Caribbean, Universidad de La Plata and World Bank), and the World Development Indicators (WDI)/Povcal-Net by the World Bank.[4]

1.1.1 Definition of Household

We adopt the definition of a household used by LIS, SEDLAC, and (in most cases) the World Bank's PovcalNet, which excludes external members of the household: boarders, live-in domestic servants, and (if applicable) their families are not considered part of the household, and should not be included in any income calculations. That is, if each observation in the data set is a household (known as wide format), boarders and live-in domestic servants should not be included in the number of members of the household, and their income will not be included in the household aggregate income or consumption.[5] If each observation in your data set is an individual (known as long format), the boarders, live-in domestic servants, and their families should be dropped from the data set.[6] In practice, rather than dropping individuals from the data set, it can be beneficial to create a dummy variable that marks individuals that should be used in calculations, then include an if-condition in the calculations. This allows one to use the "dropped" individuals in other calculations if necessary—for example, to perform a sensitivity analysis of the decision to not include them in the calculations—without having to go back to the original version of the data set before they were dropped. The disadvantage of this approach is that the user has to remember to always include an if-condition for every estimation, restricting the analysis to the "non-dropped" individuals.

When dropping individuals and households (or marking them with a dummy variable equal to 0 to exclude them from all estimations), it is necessary to readjust expansion factors so that the sum of the expansion factors of the non-dropped individuals still sums to the total population in the country, or even better so that the sum of the

---

[4] For a summary of definitions and procedures used by the most renowned international inequality databases, see Ferreira, Lustig, and Teles (2015).

[5] Consider the following example: in an income survey, if the household head earns $100 and then pays the servant $10, the survey data will show us exactly these numbers: $100 and $10. We drop the servant (and his or her income) before making household aggregates because otherwise we would aggregate $100 + 10 = 110, but that would be double counting that $10. In the case of a consumption survey (and ignoring savings), the household (excluding servant) will consume its $100, $10 of which shows up as expenditure on the servant's income. Then the servant also consumes his or her $10 of income. If we aggregate without dropping the servant, we would have $100 + 10 = 110, again double counting the $10 that was "consumed" when the household paid the servant, then consumed again by the servant.

[6] Note that some studies do not drop boarders and domestic servants from the calculations, but instead count them as a *separate household*. The implications of adopting one method rather than the other have yet to be rigorously explored, but "exploratory analysis for some countries suggests that for the most part results are not significantly affected by this decision" (CEDLAS and World Bank 2014, p. 15); a table summarizing this exploratory analysis can be found in appendix 6E.

expansion factors of the non-dropped individuals within each stratum sums to the sum in that stratum prior to dropping individuals. More sophisticated reweighting techniques could also be used.[7]

1.1.2 Unit of Analysis

Unless otherwise specified, all calculations (poverty, inequality, incidence, etc.) will be in terms of individuals rather than households. In other words, the poverty headcount ratio will equal the proportion of individuals below the poverty line, not the proportion of households below the poverty line. If poor households tend to be larger than non-poor households, the former will be higher than the latter. Note that the *CEQ Stata Package* (Higgins, Aranda, and Li, 2022) automatically makes its calculations using the individual as the unit of analysis, and flexibly allows data sets that are at the individual or household level (where the former must include a variable that serves as each individual's household identifier and the latter must include a variable with the number of members in each household).

1.1.3 Missing or Zero Incomes

When a survey respondent reports receiving a certain income source but does not report the value or reports a value of zero as the income from that source, we adopt the convention used by SEDLAC almost in full: missing and zero incomes are regarded as zero, unless the household head's primary income source is missing, in which case the household is excluded from the data.[8] One difference between our treatment and that of SEDLAC is that if the household has zero income after applying the above rules, we include that household in both poverty and inequality measures, whereas SEDLAC includes the household in poverty measures but excludes it from inequality measures. The main argument for excluding them made by SEDLAC is that "some inequality measures collapse when considering zero income."[9] The inequality measure that we focus on, however—the Gini coefficient—has no problem dealing with zero income. (Measures of the Theil, which also appear in the *CEQ MWB*, necessarily exclude households with zero income, but we rarely use these results.) Furthermore, in a fiscal incidence analysis, some households will receive all their income from transfers and thus have zero Market Income but positive Disposable Income. It would be inconsistent to exclude these households from the calculation of Market Income inequality but not that of Disposable Income inequality; on the other hand, excluding those households from *both* measures for consistency would lead us to exclude all households with zero Market Income but positive Disposable Income from our analysis, which is undesirable. Note that when a household is excluded from the data, the expansion factors must be recalculated so that the expanded sample of the nonexcluded households equals the

---

[7] See for example Pacifico (2014); Kolenikov (2014).
[8] CEDLAS and World Bank (2014).
[9] CEDLAS and World Bank (2014, p. 20).

original expanded sample size when they were included (potentially within strata, or using a more sophisticated method, as discussed above).

1.1.4 Top Coding

In some surveys, wage and other income variables are top-coded for very high earners to protect the privacy of respondents. The simplest approach to replace the top-coded value for that variable—which must be done as a precursor to creating any income concepts—is to replace the top-coded values with either the lower bound of the top coding or the maximum non-top-coded value, whichever is available. For example, survey documentation might inform us that every income above $100,000 has been top coded; in this case, we use the lower bound of the top coding which is $100,000 for all the households whose income was subjected to top coding. Alternatively, some surveys (such as the Current Population Survey [CPS] in the United States) do not report what the cut-off for top coding is, but simply inform us that all observations that have a value for that variable of, say, 999999, are top coded. In this case, we find the maximum of the non-top-coded observations (in this example, the observations with a value below 999999 for that variable) and assign it to all of the top-coded variables. For example, suppose the codebook accompanying our household survey data says that 999999 indicates a top-coded value, but does not provide us with information about what income level was used as the cut-off for top coding. We check our data and find that the highest value for the corresponding variable that is below 999999 is $585,400. For all households whose income was subject to top coding, we would assign them with the maximum non-top-coded value, which is $585,400.

If this approach is taken and multiple years or multiple countries are being compared by the same researchers, an adjustment should be made to account for the fact that the top-coding cut-off may be arbitrary and could thus occur at different points of the variable's distribution in the different surveys. Box 6-1 describes how to adjust the top coding in such a way that it becomes comparable across years or countries.

More complex approaches involve imputing values to the top-coded values. (Note that if values are imputed, the methods described in box 6-1 for analyses across multiple years or countries are no longer necessary.) If income and consumption data are both available in the survey, a regression using consumption and other characteristics as explanatory variables can be used to predict the missing income component. Alternatively, the top-coded values could be imputed using assumptions about the distribution of income at the upper end (for example, that it follows a Pareto distribution—see box 6-2). A more complex multiple imputation approach is given in Jenkins and others (2011).

The method chosen in the event of top coding must be made based on the nature of the top coding in the data set and the researchers' preference to employ simpler or more complex solutions. The reasoning behind choosing a particular methodology should always be justified, and ideally, the sensitivity of results to the chosen method should be tested. For a review of methods, see Cowell and Flachaire (2015).

Box 6-1

Top Coding across Multiple Years or Countries

Gary Burtless

To make cross-year or cross-country comparisons comparable, calculate the lowest percentile in the income distribution that the top-code value represents in all of the years or countries being studied. Then, use this top-code percentile to top code each of the years or countries at the same percentile. For example, suppose the top-code value is at the 97th percentile in year or country 1, the 98th percentile in year or country 2, and the 96th percentile in year or country 3. Create a new, uniform top code at the 96th percentile in each of the years or countries. In year or country 1, every respondent with an income value above the 96th percentile is assigned a top code equal to the 96th percentile of the income distribution in year or country 1; and in year or country 2, every respondent with an income value above the 96th percentile is assigned a top code equal to the 96th percentile of the income distribution in year or country 2. The top codes for year or country 3 are left unchanged since that year or country had the lowest percentile at which top coding occurred. This procedure ignores information about incomes between the 96th and 97th percentiles in year or country 1 and between the 96th and 98th percentiles in year or country 2, but the top code procedure makes it feasible to evenhandedly compare income distributions and fiscal incidence across the three years.

1.1.5 Outliers and Extreme Values

In the case of outliers for particular income sources and fiscal interventions, these could reflect real inequality in income from that source, or they could be caused by misreporting or errors in data entry or processing. We recommend that researchers follow standard procedures to carefully examine outliers in their data (a good first pass is to observe extreme values with Nick Cox's user-written Stata command extremes).[10] Then, researchers should apply their discretion to determine whether values could reflect true inequality in income from a particular source, or if they reflect error. If they reflect error, they should be replaced with a zero (not a missing value, which would lead all the income aggregates to be missing as well, essentially equivalent to dropping the household) or imputed using missing data techniques (Cowell and Flachaire, 2015; Little and Rubin, 2014).

In the case of fiscal interventions, determining whether outliers reflect true inequality is often an easier task than for other sources such as labor income, as these

---

[10] Cox (2004).

Box 6-2

Top Incomes and Inequality Measurement

Paolo Verme

The measurement of inequality is susceptible to various statistical problems that relate to the data used for the measurement of inequality such as household income, consumption, or expenditure surveys. It is known that households tend to under-report income (income under-reporting), that some households participating to the survey do not report income at all (item non-response), and that other households do not participate in surveys even when selected in the survey sample (unit non-response). These three phenomena can potentially affect the estimation of inequality seriously, although there is still incomplete evidence on the size of these potential biases. To address the first two issues (income under-reporting and item non-response), scholars have adopted various solutions such as using consumption or expenditure in place of income or imputing income using regression techniques and a set of proxies that are known to predict income well.

The third issue (unit non-response) has only recently been studied in relation to the estimation of inequality. Preliminary findings suggest that this phenomenon can bias the estimation of inequality sharply especially when related to the right-hand side of the distribution, the top incomes. Korinek, Mistiaen, and Ravallion (2006), using U.S. data have, shown how household non-responses can lead to the under-estimation of inequality, while Cowell and Flachaire (2007) have shown how even one observation at the top of the distribution can change the estimation of inequality by several percentage points. These first findings have called for specific solutions to the problem.

Two alternative approaches have been proposed by the authors above to correct for the bias generated by unit non-responses at the top of the distribution. Korinek and others propose a two-stage probabilistic model that, under certain assumptions, provides the true distribution of incomes and allows for the estimation of the correct value of inequality by using a set of weights that correct for unit non-response. Cowell and Flachaire have instead suggested estimating inequality by using a semi-parametric approach whereby inequality is estimated by combining the classic non-parametric measurement for most of the distribution with a parametric measurement applied to top incomes only. In essence, these authors suggest substituting a theoretical distribution for the top incomes—such as the Pareto distribution—which is known to predict top incomes across countries well, and thereby correcting the bias at the top.

A recent paper by Hlasny and Verme (2016) proposed an alternative application of Korinek and others' and Ravallion's models and compared this application with the semi-parametric approach suggested by Cowell and Fla-chaire. They find rather consistent results between the two approaches, although the bias generated by unit non-responses among top incomes is smaller than that found by Korinek and others for the United States. These initial approaches proposed for correcting unit non-response at the top of the distribution are still in an experimental phase and require further tests, but they do provide a first set of tools available to researchers.

fiscal interventions often have rules that determine benefit amounts or tax percentage. Even if these rules are not perfectly applied, they are usually not so broadly misapplied that extreme outliers are possible. When unreasonable outliers are detected, the re-searcher must again use discretion to determine whether these should be replaced by a zero or imputed using missing data techniques, or whether some other approach is appropriate. In the case of Brazil's conditional cash transfer program Bolsa Familia, Higgins and Pereira (2014) found that while the survey asked for benefits received over the past month, most of the outliers had values equal to approximately (and in many cases, exactly) twelve times the monthly benefits that could be received according to program rules. Thus, the authors divided by twelve the benefits received by these outliers—assumed to be mistakenly reported in annual rather than monthly terms.

1.1.6 Under-Reporting and Top Incomes

Household surveys have two serious limitations that bear on the measures of inequality and poverty derived from them, and hence on the results of the fiscal incidence analy-sis: under-reporting of incomes (in particular, income from capital) and under-coverage of the rich. Following what most of the existing international databases do, the CEQ project does not adjust for under-reporting by scaling-up survey totals (for example, wages, disposable income, private consumption, and so on) to totals obtained from ad-ministrative registries.[11] As a result, one ends up with two "economies" for the same country characterized by differences not only in scale (the survey-based usually being considerably smaller in terms of the values of income and consumption than the na-tional accounts totals) but often in structure (for example, the ratio of Disposable to Market Income from the survey may be different from the ratio of Disposable House-hold Income to the closest measure of Market Income from national accounts).[12] The overriding principle followed by the CEQ is that—unless there are good reasons not

---

[11] See Ferreira, Lustig, and Teles (2015, table 2).

[12] When choosing which National Accounts–level income to use a base for comparison with *CEQ Assessment* results (the size of a fiscal instrument with respect to income, for example), the ana-lyst should use National Household Disposable Income. One should not use National Disposable Income from the National Accounts.

to—the information in the surveys is taken as valid and given precedence over the information from administrative registries (see more details on this in section 4.3 on income misreporting and discrepancies between survey and administrative data below). However, whenever the team has sufficient evidence to believe that totals in the survey are less credible than those in administrative registries, the latter should be used and the rationale properly documented in section C of the *CEQ MWB*.

One exception to the above principle might be correcting for the under-reporting and under-coverage of top incomes (or consumption). It is well known that top incomes are not well captured by household surveys. As described in Lustig (2019), the upper-tail issues can be classified into five broad categories.

Sparseness: The chances to capture highly rich individuals are, by definition, low even in stratified samples, so the sampling errors for this group is high.

Unit nonresponse: This involves individuals with a positive ex-ante probability—however small—of being selected into the sample but who do not or would not respond if selected into the sample because of noncontact (e.g., gated communities), refusal, or other reasons.

Item nonresponse: Within the respondent population there may be people who do not provide a response for the income (consumption) variable.

Underreporting: This refers to subjects who are selected and respond to the survey but who report income (consumption) below its actual level.

Top coding (and trimming): This occurs when, for instance, survey administrators top-code reported incomes by design in the data that they make available to researchers (or when questionnaires impose an upper limit to the amount that can be reported).

Upper tail issues can result in serious biases and imprecision of survey-based inequality measures. To avoid these, researchers have developed a series of approaches. These approaches can be distinguished in terms of those that rely on within-survey methods and those that combine survey data with information from external sources such as tax records, National Accounts, rich lists, or other external information. Within each category, the methods can correct by replacing top incomes or increasing their weight (reweighting), or by a combination of replacing and reweighting. In addition, correction methods can be nonparametric and parametric. Lustig (2019) presents a survey of these approaches and a comprehensive list of references that use them. In box 6-2 (and the references therein), Paolo Verme suggests within-survey methods to address unit nonresponse.[13] Led by the eminent late British economist Anthony B. Atkinson, a vast literature has emerged using tax records, combining survey data with tax records, and combining the last two with National Accounts. See, for example, Atkinson

---

[13] See Hlasny (2021a) and Hlasny (2021b).

(2007), Atkinson and Piketty (2010), Atkinson, Piketty, and Saez (2011), Alvaredo and others (2016), Alvaredo and others (2018), and the impressive list of working papers and data housed in the World Inequality Database. Lakner and Milanovic (2016) combine survey and National Account data and a Pareto adjustment to estimate income distribution in 162 countries. An example of applying the replacing method to combined survey and tax data is Jenkins (2017) for the UK. Blanchet, Flores, and Morgan (2018) propose a method that uses both reweighting and replacing on combined survey and tax data. Also see the papers in Cowell, Lustig, and Waldenström (2022). Flachaire, Lustig, and Vigorito (2021) compare how the distribution of income and inequality measures change when replacing, reweighting, and the Blanchet, Flores, and Morgan (2018) combined method are applied.

In the standard fiscal incidence analysis proposed in this Handbook and the results housed in the CEQ Data Center on Fiscal Redistribution, we make no adjustments for upper tail issues. However, we strongly recommend implementing an additional fiscal incidence analysis with incomes at the top corrected for underreporting and under-coverage. Note that results should be presented both ways: correcting and not correcting for under-reporting/under-coverage of top incomes.

1.1.7 Adult Equivalence and Economies of Scale

CEQ generally uses household per capita income or consumption, and thus does not adjust for adult equivalence or economies of scale within households. For each income concept, total household income for the respective concept is divided by the total number of members in the household.[14] The income concept and fiscal intervention variables used with the *CEQ Stata Package* commands should already be expressed in household per capita terms.

The researcher may want to include additional sensitivity analyses to test the sensitivity of the results to different assumptions about economies of scale or adult equivalent units. This is especially important in countries where official estimates of poverty and inequality adjust for economies of scale or adult equivalence units; in that case, the "main results" used for the *CEQ Assessment* may be those that adjust for economies of scale. The sensitivity of incidence results to assumptions about economies of scale—in particular, a comparison of using household per capita income versus the square root scale suggested by Atkinson, Rainwater, and Smeeding (1995)—is discussed in Higgins and others (2015).

For teams who decide to use equivalized income for the CEQ Assessment report, **results using per capita income should be produced as well to facilitate comparisons with other countries.**

---

[14] As explained above, total household income should not include the income of boarders, domestic servants, and their families, and the total number of members in the household should not include them either.

1.1.8 Spatial Price Adjustments

The researchers will have to use their best judgment of whether to adjust for spatial prices based on the spatial price differences in the country and the availability of a spatial price index (SPI) as well as common practice in the country.[15] For teams who decide to use spatially adjusted price indices for the *CEQ Assessment* report, results should be presented both ways: adjusting and not adjusting for spatial price differences.

Spatial price indices are available for many countries, calculated either by the government itself or by an international organization. If an adjustment is made for spatial price differences, a table should be provided showing the value of the SPI in each region. Note that the choice of which region was used to index the SPI may have been arbitrary. Hence, you should re-index your SPI so that 1.0 equals its weighted average. Consider the simple example in table 6-1, where the original SPI was indexed to the country's federal district.

We would re-index the SPI as follows (see table 6-2): first, compute its weighted average as $(0.55 * 1.000 + 0.15 * 0.750 + 0.30 * 0.600) = 0.8425$. Next, divide the original SPI by its weighted average to create a re-indexed SPI.

Finally, all of the income concepts and the variables for each of their components should be adjusted for spatial prices, by dividing the value of those variables by the re-indexed value of the SPI corresponding to a particular household's region. (To see why re-indexing was necessary, note that the above "original SPI" from the above example [tables 6-1 and 6-2] could have instead been arbitrarily indexed to the rural interior, so that it was federal district 1.667; urban interior 1.250; rural interior 1.000. Dividing incomes by the 1.667; 1.250; 1.000 index instead of the 1.000; 0.750; 0.600 index—which tell the exact same story about price differences—would have large implications for poverty. Hence, we re-index for consistency.)

If a reliable SPI is not available, an alternative is to create a SPI using spatial poverty lines, which again might have been calculated by the government or an international organization. Although this solution works well for poverty measures, it is not ideal for inequality measures, since the poverty lines are calculated based on the prices of basic needs, while the prices of other goods may not differ across regions in the same way as basic needs. Nevertheless, it can be better than making no adjustment for the differences in purchasing power experienced by individuals in different regions. Consider the example given in table 6-3.

Treating the regional poverty lines as a (non-indexed) SPI, we calculate the re-indexed SPI the same way (see table 6-4): compute its weighted average as $0.55 * 320 + 0.15 * 250 + 0.30 * 190 = 270.5$, and divide the original SPI (that is, the regional poverty lines) by the weighted average to obtain the re-indexed SPI.

---

[15] Note that CEQ does not do an automatic adjustment of incomes as other datasets do. For instance, SEDLAC adjusts rural incomes downward by 15 percent in all the countries for which indicators are produced.

TABLE 6-1

Example of Re-Indexing: Original Data

Region	Population share (%)	Original SPI
Federal district	55	1.000
Urban interior	15	0.750
Rural interior	30	0.600

TABLE 6-2

Example of Re-Indexing: Calculating the Re-Indexed SPI

Region	Population share (%)	Original SPI	Calculation	Re-indexed
Federal district	55	1.000	1.000/0.8425	1.1869
Urban interior	15	0.750	0.750/0.8425	0.8902
Rural interior	30	0.600	0.600/0.8425	0.7122
Weighted average	. . .	0.8425	. . .	1.0000

. . . = Not applicable

TABLE 6-3

Example of Re-Indexing Using Spatial Poverty Lines: Original Data

Region	Population share (%)	Regional poverty line
Federal district	55	320 local currency per month
Urban interior	15	250 local currency per month
Rural interior	30	190 local currency per month

TABLE 6-4

Example of Re-Indexing Using Spatial Poverty Lines: Calculating the Re-Indexed SPI

Region	Population share (%)	Regional poverty lines	Calculation	Re-indexed
Federal district	55	320	320/270.5	1.1830
Urban interior	15	250	250/270.5	0.9242
Rural interior	30	190	190/270.5	0.7024
Weighted average	. . .	270.5	. . .	1.0000

. . . = Not applicable.

1.1.9 Expressing Values in Annual Terms

Income concept and fiscal intervention variables should be expressed in local currency in annual terms to facilitate the comparison of results from the *CEQ MWB* with results from administrative data. The method to convert local currency into purchasing power parity (PPP) adjusted dollars will be discussed in chapter 8 in this Volume (Higgins and Brest López, 2022).

1.2 Data on Fiscal Systems

To allocate certain taxes and transfers, it is necessary to know the totals that appear in the government budget disaggregated by the categories of interest for the year of the household survey. On sheet B3 of the *CEQ MWB* there is a template for the government budgetary data, which is reproduced here as table 6G-3.

There are four important aspects to note. First, the budgetary data should be for the general government sector following the definition of the International Monetary Fund's *Government Financial Statistics Manual 2014* (GFS). That is, the budgetary data should include revenues from and spending by central, state, provincial, regional, and local governments, as well as social security funds. If for any reason, there is only budgetary information for the central government or central and provincial governments, it should be clearly noted both on sheet B3 and reports. Second, the expenditure categories that are required for the comprehensive fiscal incidence analysis in a *CEQ Assessment* are a combination of what the GFS manual calls "economic" and "functional" categories. For example, while the various categories that comprise social spending on sheet B3 are part of the functional categories,[16] the GFS classifies spending on what in CEQ (and other places) we call "consumption subsidies" under "social benefits" in the economic classification of government expenditures.[17] Third, spending on transfer programs should include administrative costs in the budgetary data but not in the transfers distributed to the population if benefits are simulated. Fourth, for education and health spending, teams should distinguish recurrent from capital expenditures, and present them in separate rows (or columns).

While the categories included in table 6G-3 are quite useful, researchers can of course decide whether they would like to disaggregate categories further (for example, in transfers by type of program; in health, by primary versus hospital care).

As can be observed on sheet B3, the author of a *CEQ Assessment* will need to identify both which components of fiscal policy will be included in the analysis and what proportion of that category is part of the analysis. This will give an idea of how comprehensive the fiscal incidence analysis will be in the country in question. For exam-

---

[16] IMF (2014) table 6.12.

[17] IMF (2014) table 6.1 and p. 1.

ple, for a country that collects most of its revenues, let's say, through corporate taxes, the analysis will capture less of the fiscal system than it will in one in which most of the collection occurs through personal income taxes and/or value-added taxes (VAT).

Sheets B4 through B12 in the *CEQ MWB* provide guidelines to describe the qualitative and quantitative characteristics of the fiscal instruments that will be included in the *CEQ Assessment* (table 6G-4).

Examples of descriptions of fiscal systems can be observed in the country studies included in this Volume's part III, Applications.

2 Income Concepts: Definitions

In the CEQ framework we begin by defining prefiscal income: the income of individuals before taking into account taxes paid and benefits received (henceforth, fiscal policy). Prefiscal income is the income by which individuals are initially ranked to assess the incidence of taxes and transfers across the income distribution. As discussed at length in chapter 1 in this Volume, in the CEQ framework, depending on the assumptions made regarding old-age pensions from a contributory social security system, we define two categories of prefiscal income: Market Income and Market Income plus Pensions. If pensions are treated as deferred income (hereafter, Pensions as Deferred Income, or PDI scenario), the prefiscal income is Market Income plus Pensions; and, if pensions are treated as government transfers (hereafter, Pensions as Government Transfers, or PGT scenario), the prefiscal income is Market Income. Thus, in CEQ there will always be two different prefiscal incomes by which individuals are initially ranked for the same country. And, very importantly, the two are different in terms of which components define them. In fact, Market Income is also different in both scenarios. Figure 6-1 is a stylized representation of the income concepts. It should be noted that regarding the treatment of old-age pensions from the contributory social security system, a third option pursued by some researchers is to treat contributory pensions as a transfer only where the social security system is in deficit. In such cases, the deficit can be allocated as a transfer to individuals in proportion to their pension income, for example.

Note that this figure is different from the first edition of the Handbook (2018). In the first edition of the Handbook, figure 6-1 incorrectly indicated that the two pension scenarios yielded the same concepts of Market Income and Market Income plus Pensions. However, for the PDI scenario the contributions to social insurance old-age pensions need to be subtracted in constructing these two income concepts, and they are not subtracted in PGT. The reasons are explained in chapter 1 of this Volume and below. It should be noted that in the data housed in the CEQ Data Center the income concepts were calculated correctly.

In figure 6-2 we show the eight core income concepts used in the CEQ framework: *Market Income, Market Income plus Pensions, Net Market Income, Gross Income, Taxable*

FIGURE 6-1
Definitions of Income Concepts: A Stylized Presentation

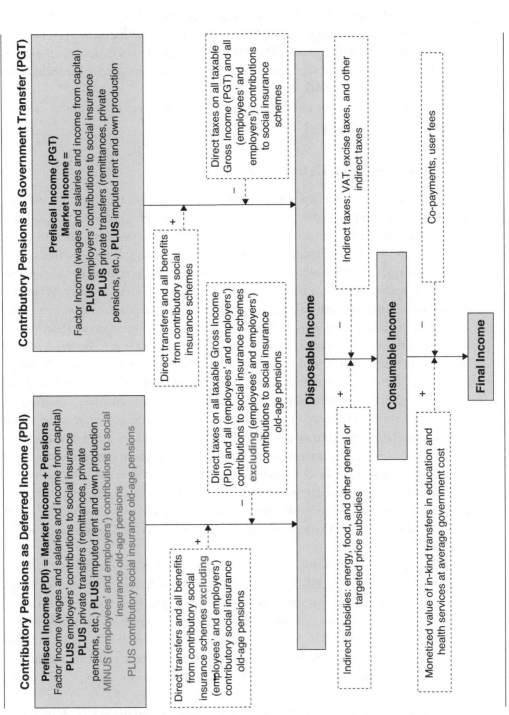

Note that Figure 6-1 here is different from Figure 6-1 in first edition of this Handbook (2018). The changes are discussed in the text throughout.

FIGURE 6-2

Definition of Income Concepts: A Detailed Presentation

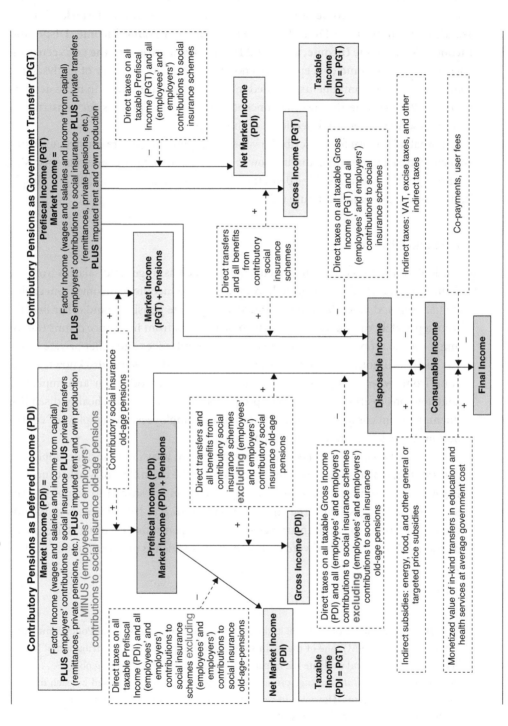

Note that figure 6-2 here is different from figure 6-2 in first edition of this Handbook (2018). The changes are discussed in the text throughout.

Income, Disposable Income, Consumable Income,[18] and *Final Income.* **Note that Market Income, Market Income plus Pensions, Gross Income, and Net Market Income are different under the PDI and the PGT scenarios. Taxable Income, Disposable Income, Consumable Income, and Final Income are identical in the two scenarios.** These eight core income concepts were chosen to allow for a variety of analyses and comparisons.[19] The components included in each concept are shown in more detail in table 6-5. We describe the income concepts here, and the process for constructing them is described in detail in section 2 of this chapter.

In what follows we first describe how these income concepts are constructed using an income-based survey, then discuss how to construct the same income concepts using a consumption-based survey. The definitions are presented in detail in table 6-5. Graphically, they are presented in figure 6-2.

2.1 Market Income

- For PDI: Market Income equals factor income such as wages and salaries from the formal and informal sectors (also known as "earned income"), income from capital (rents, profits, dividends, interest, and so on), private pensions (and other benefits from a privately run benefit system), income received from insurance claims (for example, due to crop failure),[20] private transfers (remittances and other private transfers such as alimony), imputed rent for owner-occupied housing (also known as "income from owner-occupied housing"), the value of own production, and employers' contributions to all social insurance programs (old-age pensions, health, disability, unemployment compensation, and so on) **minus** employees' and employers' contributions to social insurance old-age pensions.

  The last two items may need further explanation. Why do we include employers' contributions to all social insurance programs in the definition of Market Income? Because we assume contributions paid by employers are shifted to workers in the form of lower wages. Thus, the "true" concept of Market Income needs to include the contributions to social insurance (for old-age pensions and other items) made by the employers. In other words, the economic incidence of contributions paid by

---

[18] "Consumable income" is the concept and the name used in Canada's Social Policy Simulation Database Model (SPSD/M), one of the main sources used to produce the distribution of household income accounts and evaluate the impact of changes in tax and spending policies.

[19] The *MWB* and *CEQ Stata Package* produce results with individuals ranked by each of these eight core income concepts. However, in general, the only indicators that are used are those produced by households ranked by prefiscal per capita income.

[20] Note that this concept does not include reimbursements for health expenditures covered by insurance, for example.

TABLE 6-5

Comparison of Income Concepts by Income Source and Fiscal Intervention and by Scenario Pensions as Deferred Income (PDI) and Pensions as Government Transfers (PGT)

Components of Income Concepts	Market income	Market income	Market income plus pensions	Market income plus pensions	Net market income	Net market income	Gross income	Gross income	Disposable income	Consumable income	Final income
	PDI	PGT prefiscal income	PDI prefiscal income	PGT	PDI	PGT	PDI	PGT	PDI = PGT	PDI = PGT	PDI = PGT
Ywk	+	+	+	+	+	+	+	+	+	+	+
Yir	+	+	+	+	+	+	+	+	+	+	+
Ypt	+	+	+	+	+	+	+	+	+	+	+
Ycop	+	+	+	+	+	+	+	+	+	+	+
WSSCp	−		−		−	−	−		−	−	−
ESSCp	+	+	+	+	+	+	+	+	+	+	+
ESSCp	−		−		−	−	−		−	−	−
WSSCo					−	−	−		−	−	−
ESSCo	+	+	+	+	+	+	+	+	+	+	+
ESSCo					−	−	−		−	−	−
Pss	+		+		+		+	+	+	+	+
Oss							+	+	+	+	+
Gd							+	+	+	+	+
Tdpf					−	−			−		
Tdgi										−	−
Ti										−	−
Gs										+	+

(continued)

TABLE 6-5 (continued)

Components of Income Concepts	Market income	Market income	Market income plus pensions	Market income plus pensions	Net market income	Net market income	Gross income	Gross income	Disposable income	Consumable income	Final income
	PDI	PGT prefiscal income	PDI prefiscal income	PGT	PDI	PGT	PDI	PGT	PDI = PGT	PDI = PGT	PDI = PGT
Gk											+
Tuf											−

Notes:

As indicated in the text the fiscal incidence analysis assumes that the burden of contributions from employers is borne by the employees in the form of lower wages.

Recall that "Disposable Income" equals consumption in surveys that only report consumption (or report both but the income variable is less reliable).

The concepts that appear twice are repeated because for some of the income concepts they only need to be added, but in others they should neither be subtracted or added (in essence, they cancel each other out and in the construction of that income concept they are ignored).

Definitions

Income Concepts

Ywk: Factor income (wages and salaries and income from capital) before any contributions by the worker to social security and direct taxes

Yir: Imputed Rents

Ypt: Private Transfers (e.g., remittances)

Ycop: Consumption of Own Production

Pension System

Contributions

WSSCp: Social Security Employee's Contributions for Old-age Pensions

ESSCp: Social Security Employer's Contributions for Old-age Pensions

WSSCo: Social Security Employee's Contributions for Other (e.g., health, unemployment benefits, disability, etc)

ESSCo: Social Security Employer's Contributions for Other (e.g., health, unemployment benefits, disability, etc)

Income

Pss: Benefits from Social Security Old-age Contributory Pensions

Oss: Benefits from Social Security Other (than old-age pensions) Contributory Sytems (e.g., health, unemployment benefits, disability, etc)

Fiscal interventions: spending

Gd: Government Direct Transfers (cash and near cash)

Gs: Indirect Subsidies

Gk: In-kind transfers (e.g., education and health)

Fiscal interventions: revenues

Tdpf: Direct Personal Income Taxes (excluding contributions to social security) on taxable prefiscal incomes

Tdgi: Direct Personal Income Taxes (excluding contributions to social security) on taxable gross incomes

Ti: Indirect Taxes

Tuf: Co-payments and User Fees

employers (also known as "employers' contributions") falls on wage earners.[21] In essence, we are assuming that in the absence of employers' contributions, the market wages would have been higher by the amount of these contributions. It is important to make this adjustment because—under such an assumption—the employers' contributions need to be treated as a tax on gross wages. Note, however, that Market Income is **NOT** the same in the PDI and PGT scenarios. Why do we subtract employees' and employers' contributions to social insurance old-age pensions? Because as mentioned in chapter 1 of this Volume, in the PDI scenario the income from contributory pensions is treated as income coming from savings during working years. Thus, contributions to old-age pensions need to be treated as a form of mandatory savings that are placed "outside" the current household income and that form the funds that later, upon retirement, become income from pensions. Thus, we need to subtract them to avoid double-counting (in an intertemporal context, that is).

- For PGT: Market Income equals the same items listed for PDI up to the "minus", that is, contributions to social insurance old-age pensions are **not** subtracted. There is no double-counting issue here by assumption because contributions to old-age pensions (whether from employer or employee) are considered analogous to any direct tax and income from old-age pensions are considered just like any other government cash transfer. Note that for the PGT scenario, this Market Income is also the **Prefiscal Income** by which households are ranked by (in per capita terms) to carry out the fiscal incidence analysis.

2.2 Market Income plus Pensions

- For PDI: Market Income plus Pensions equals Market Income (as defined for the PDI scenario right above) plus the income from social insurance (public) old-age pensions. Note that for the PDI scenario, this Market Income plus Pensions is also the **Prefiscal Income** by which households are ranked by (in per capita terms) to carry out the fiscal incidence analysis.
- For PGT: Market Income plus Pensions equals Market Income (as defined for the PGT scenario right above) plus the income from social insurance (public) old-age pensions.

2.3 Net Market Income

- For PDI: Net Market Income equals Prefiscal Income (that is, Market Income plus Pensions for PDI described above) minus direct taxes on all taxable Prefiscal Income components (including the income received from contributory social insurance old-age pensions) and contributions to items that differ from old-age social insurance

---

[21] This assumption is commonly made in the literature. See, for example, Hamermesh and Rees (1993), Gruber (1999), Brown, Coronado, and Fullerton (2009).

pensions (e.g., unemployment benefits, disability benefits, health, etc.). Note that direct taxes here do not include direct taxes on government transfers (recall that contributory old-age social insurance pensions are not treated as a government transfer in PDI). The latter is net taxable income, not included in the figure. And, of course, deducted contributions do not include those paid for old-age pensions because these were already subtracted from Market Income. Be careful not to subtract them twice. The usefulness of this income concept is that frequently in income-based surveys Net Market Income as defined here is the reported income and, therefore, the starting point to construct the rest of the income concepts.

- For PGT: Net Market Income equals Prefiscal Income (that is, Market Income for PGT described above) minus direct taxes on all taxable Prefiscal Income components and all contributions to social insurance (old-age pensions and others). Note that, as with Net Market Income for PDI, direct taxes here do not include direct taxes on any government transfers (e.g., old-age pensions, conditional and unconditional cash transfers, social pensions, etc.) even if these items are taxed.

It should be noted that the definition of Net Market Income is somewhat different from the definition in the first edition of this Handbook (2018). In the first edition, there were two inaccuracies. First, the text may have given the wrong impression that Net Market Income was identical for the PDI and PGT scenarios. As shown in table 6-5, the two are not identical. Second, in the first edition it was not clear **which** direct taxes and contributions should be subtracted in both scenarios. This is now clarified in table 6-5.

2.4 Gross Income

- For PDI: Gross Income equals Market Income plus Pensions (as defined for the PDI scenario above) plus direct cash and near-cash (for example, food) transfers and all benefits from contributory social insurance schemes, excluding (employees' and employers') contributory social insurance old-age pensions.
- For PGT: Gros Income equals Market Income (as defined for the PGT scenario above) plus direct cash and near-cash transfers and all benefits from contributory social insurance schemes including contributory social insurance old-age pensions.[22]

2.5 Disposable Income

Disposable Income is the conventional concept of how much "money" households have in their pocket to purchase goods, give away, or save after considering what the state takes away in direct taxes and gives back in direct transfers. Disposable Income is iden-

---

[22] Beneficiary households are assumed to receive the entirety of benefits from these transfers; we ignore spillovers to other households.

tical in the PDI and PGT scenarios, but recall that the preceding income concepts and the direct taxes and direct transfers to be subtracted and added, respectively, are different in each scenario as indicated above and in figure 6-2 and table 6-5. Conventionally, the indicators on poverty and inequality reported by governments and multilateral organizations are calculated using this income concept for income-based surveys. For consumption-based surveys, these indicators are reported with households' expenditures per capita as the welfare indicator. In fact, for a consumption-based survey in our fiscal incidence analysis we assume that the value of consumption (i.e., expenditures) is equivalent to Disposable Income and proceed to construct the other income concepts as if we were using Disposable Income. More details on the specific steps are described later in the chapter.

2.6 Consumable Income[23]

Consumable Income measures how much households can buy of a particular good or service after considering what the state takes away in consumption taxes (for example, value added tax [VAT], excise taxes, and sales taxes) and gives back in consumption subsidies (for example, general or targeted [so-called block tariffs] subsidies on energy consumption). Consumable Income is identical in the PDI and PGT scenarios and it equals Disposable Income minus consumption taxes and plus consumption subsidies. While Consumable Income is not yet a conventional concept, it is widely referred to in the more recent fiscal incidence literature. The indicator used to measure progress in the UN Sustainable Development Goal 10, Target 10.2, also recommends using Consumable Income.[24]

2.7 Final Income

Final Income measures how much households' incomes would need to be adjusted (most frequently, increased) assuming the household had to pay for the free or quasi-free public services in education and health at average government cost net of what the household pays for these services in the form of user fees or co-payments. Final Income is identical in the PDI and PGT scenarios and equals Consumable Income plus government spending on public education and health services minus co-payments and user fees.

An additional income concept that is constructed on its own is **Taxable Income**. *Taxable Income* equals the sum of all the *statutory* taxable income (that is, what the law in a country defines as subject to taxes) from factor income, private transfers,

---

[23] This used to be called "postfiscal income" in the very first online edition of the Handbook (Lustig and Higgins, 2013), which is no longer available to avoid confusion

[24] See SDG indicator metadata for indicator 10.4.2. Consumable Income is mentioned on page 3 of https://unstats.un.org/sdgs/metadata/files/Metadata-10-04-02.pdf.

contributory pensions, and government transfers. By definition, Taxable Income is the same in both scenarios.

In many developing countries, constructing Taxable Income may be quite time consuming, and the values may end up being very similar to Market Income. Teams should exercise judgment about how important it is to calculate Taxable Income depending on the characteristics of the country and the purposes of the *CEQ Assessment*. If the goal is to use the assessment to simulate policy reforms on direct taxes, calculating Taxable Income becomes crucial, for example.

A detailed description of the components included in each CEQ income concept and a comparison with the definitions followed by the most important existing databases on fiscal redistribution is in box 6-3. As can be observed, the CEQ income concepts are similar but not identical to those used by others. In addition, in the online-only part V of this Volume, we present a table "Comparison of Income Concepts in Databases with Indicators of Fiscal Redistribution" (for example, EUROMOD, LIS, the OECD database on income redistribution, and WID.World) so that one is aware of the key differences among them. Appendix 6A presents a description of the income concepts used by the so-called Canberra Group.

3 Constructing Income Concepts: The Art of Allocating Taxes and Transfers

In the process of constructing income concepts, if taxes and transfers are explicitly available in the surveys, one should use this information unless there are reasons to believe that it is not reliable. However, the information on direct and indirect taxes, transfers in cash and in-kind, and subsidies is often not collected in household surveys. To allocate the benefits of transfers and burden of taxation to individuals included in the household surveys, the *CEQ Assessments* make use of administrative data on revenues and government expenditures as well as knowledge about how the tax and transfer programs work and allocates them following methods that are described below. Thus, one of the most important aspects of the CEQ is a detailed description of how each component of income is allocated (for example, directly identified in the survey or simulated) and the methodological assumptions that are made while calculating it. The CEQ relies on local experts as a crucial part of the research team for precisely this reason. In many cases, researchers must exercise judgment based on their knowledge of the country's institutions, spending, and revenue collection, as well as on the availability and quality of the data. *It is of the utmost importance to always describe what method was used for a particular tax or transfer, the reasoning for using this method, and—whenever possible—the sensitivity of the results to using alternative methods.*

We use the following definitions for each allocation method (described in detail in the next section). When taxes and transfers can be obtained directly from the household survey, we call this the *direct identification* method. When this method is not feasible, there are four options: *Inference, Imputation, Simulation,* and *Prediction.*

Box 6-3

Measuring Fiscal Redistribution: Concepts and Definitions in Existing International Databases

Nora Lustig

A number of databases publish indicators of the extent of income redistribution due to taxes and transfers. For example, they publish prefiscal and postfiscal Gini coefficients and other indicators of inequality and poverty. In alphabetical order, the multicountry and multiregional databases most frequently used are the Commitment to Equity (CEQ) Institute's Data Center on Fiscal Redistribution (Tulane University), the Organisation for Economic Cooperation and Development's Income Distribution Database (IDD), the Luxembourg Income Study (LIS) Cross-National Data Center in Luxembourg, and the World Inequality Database (WID.world) (Paris School of Economics). In addition, there are two regional databases: EUROMOD (Institute for Social and Economic Research [ISER], University of Essex), a tax-benefit microsimulation model for the European Union, and the OECD's Eurostat Expert Group on Disparities in a National Accounts Framework (EG DNA).[1]

One feature these databases have in common is that they rely on fiscal incidence analysis, the method used to allocate taxes and public spending to households so that incomes before taxes and transfers can be compared with incomes after them. Standard fiscal incidence analysis just looks at what is paid and what is received without assessing the behavioral responses that taxes and public spending may trigger for individuals or households. This is often referred to as the "accounting approach."

The building block of fiscal incidence analysis is the construction of income concepts. That is, starting from a prefiscal income concept, each new income concept is constructed by subtracting taxes and adding the relevant components of public spending to the previous income concept. While this approach is broadly the same across all five databases mentioned, what differs is the definition of the specific income concepts, the income concepts included in the analysis, and the methods to allocate taxes and public spending. This box focuses on comparing the definition of income concepts—that is, on the types of incomes, taxes, and public spending included in the construction of the prefiscal and postfiscal

---

1. Details on the methodologies applied by each database can be found in the following: CEQ: CEQ Institute, 2022e, chapters 1, 6, and 8; EG DNA: Zwijnenburg, Bournot, and Giovannelli, 2017; EUROMOD: Sutherland and Figari, 2013; IDD: OECD, 2017; LIS: Neugschwender and Espasa-Reig, 2022; WID.World: Alvaredo, Atkinson, Chancel, and others, 2016.

(*continued*)

Box 6-3 (continued)

income concepts. There are important differences, and some can have significant implications for the scale of redistribution observed.

Table B6-3 below compares the definitions of income used by the six databases mentioned above. There are five important differences:

- While all six databases start out with similar definitions of factor income, the additional components included in prefiscal income differs. This is important because the prefiscal income is what each database uses to rank individuals prior to adding transfers and subtracting taxes and will thus affect the ensuing redistribution results (see point on the treatment of pensions below). For example, EUROMOD does not include the value of consumption of own production as part of prefiscal income while the rest of the databases do. EUROMOD, the OECD's IDD, and the LIS do not include the (imputed) value of owner-occupied housing while the other three do. There is also a fundamental difference in the treatment of contributory pensions (see the next paragraph below). Finally, WID.world also includes undistributed profits in its definition of prefiscal income.

- Second, EG DNA, EUROMOD, IDD, and the LIS treat old-age pensions from social security as pure transfers, while WID.world treats them (together with unemployment benefits) as pure deferred income. The CEQ Data Center presents results for both scenarios. This assumption can make a significant difference in countries with a high proportion of retirees whose main or sole income stems from old-age pensions. For example, in the European Union the redistributive effect with contributory pensions as pure transfers is 19.0 Gini points, while it is 7.7 Gini points when old-age pensions are treated as pure deferred income. In the United States the values are 11.2 for pure transfers and 7.2 for pure deferred income.

- Third, EUROMOD, the IDD, and the LIS present information on fiscal redistribution for direct taxes and direct transfers, while CEQ also includes the impact of indirect taxes and subsidies and transfers in kind, and WID.world includes all government revenues and spending. EG DNA does not include indirect taxes and subsidies but does include education, health, and housing.

- Fourth, in the published information on preconstructed variables, the CEQ reports indicators based on income per capita, EG DNA, EUROMOD, IDD, and the LIS report them based on equivalized income, and WID.world reports them based on income per adult.

- Fifth, all but EG DNA and WID.world report incomes as they appear in the microdata, while WID.world adjusts all variables to match administrative totals in tax records and national accounts.

TABLE B6-3

Comparison of Income Concepts across Databases

Income Concepts	CEQ	EG DNA	EUROMOD	IDD (OECD)	LIS	WID.World
	<u>Market income plus pensions</u>	<u>Primary income</u>	<u>Market income</u>	<u>Market income</u>	<u>Market income</u>	<u>Pretax income</u>
	Factor income	Factor income	Factor income	Factor income	Factor income	Factor income
	PLUS Old-age pensions from social security schemes					PLUS Undistributed profits
						PLUS Old-age pensions and unemployment benefits from social security schemes
Prefiscal	PLUS Transfers received from (paid to) nonprofit institutions and other households; payments from employment-related pension schemes; imputed value of owner-occupied housing services; consumption of own production	PLUS Imputed value of owner-occupied housing services; consumption of own production	PLUS Transfers received from (paid to) nonprofit institutions and other households	PLUS Transfers received from (paid to) nonprofit institutions and other households; consumption of own production	PLUS Transfers received from nonprofit institutions and other households; consumption of own production	PLUS Transfers received from nonprofit institutions and other households; payments from employment-related pension schemes; imputed value of owner-occupied housing services; consumption of own production

(continued)

Box 6-3 (continued)

TABLE B6-3 (continued)

Income Concepts	CEQ	EG DNA	EUROMOD	IDD (OECD)	LIS	WID.World
	MINUS Contributions to old-age pensions in social security schemes					MINUS Contributions to old-age pensions and unemployment in social security schemes
	Disposable income	Disposable income	Disposable Income	Disposable income	Disposable income	Post-tax Disposable income
Postfiscal: Disposable	Market income	Primary income	Market income	Market income	Market income	Market income
	PLUS Other cash benefits (excluding old-age pensions) from social security and social assistance benefits	PLUS Old-age pensions and other cash benefits received from social security systems; social assistance benefits; transfers received from (paid to) nonprofit institutions and other households	PLUS Old-age pensions and other cash benefits received from social security systems; social assistance benefits	PLUS Old-age pensions and other cash benefits received from social security systems; social assistance benefits	PLUS Old-age pensions and other cash benefits received from social security systems; social assistance benefits	PLUS Other cash benefits (excluding old-age pensions and unemployment benefits) from public social insurance; social assistance benefits

	MINUS Contributions to other (excluding old-age pensions) social security schemes	MINUS Contributions to old-age pensions, unemployment, and other benefits in social security schemes	MINUS Contributions to old-age pensions, unemployment, and other benefits in social security schemes	MINUS Contributions to old-age pensions, unemployment, and other benefits in social security schemes	MINUS Contributions to old-age pensions, unemployment, and other benefits in social security schemes	MINUS Contributions to other (excluding old-age pensions and unemployment) social security schemes
	MINUS Direct personal income and property taxes	MINUS Direct personal income taxes	MINUS Direct personal income taxes	MINUS Direct personal income taxes	MINUS Direct personal income taxes	MINUS Direct personal income and property taxes
	Consumable income	...	...	...	...	...
Postfiscal: Consumable	Disposable income	Adjusted disposable income	...	...	...	Post-tax national income
	PLUS Indirect consumption subsidies	Disposable income				Post-tax disposable income
	MINUS Indirect consumption taxes (VAT, excise, sales, etc.)					
	Final income					
Postfiscal: including transfers in kind	Consumable income					

(continued)

Box 6-3 (continued)

TABLE B6-3   (continued)

Income Concepts	CEQ	EG DNA	EUROMOD	IDD (OECD)	LIS	WID.World
	PLUS Public spending on education and health	PLUS Public spending on education, health, and housing				PLUS Indirect consumption subsidies MINUS Indirect consumption taxes (VAT, Excise, Sales, etc.); Other taxes. PLUS Public spending on education, health, defense, infrastructure and other public spending

Memo items	CEQ	EG DNA	EUROMOD	IDD (OECD)	LIS	WID.World
Consumption of own production	Included in factor income	Included in factor income	Not included in factor income	Included in factor income	Included in factor income	Included in factor income
Imputed rent	Included in factor income	Included in factor income	Not included in factor income	Not included in factor income	Not included in factor income	Included in factor income
Contributory pensions	Deferred income	Government transfer	Government transfer	Government transfer	Government transfer	Deferred income
Welfare indicator[1]	Income	Income	Income	Income	Income	Income

Memo items	CEQ	EG DNA	EUROMOD	IDD (OECD)	LIS	WID.World
Total values	As implied by microdata	Match National Accounts	As implied by microdata	As implied by microdata	As implied by microdata	Match National Accounts
Unit	Per capita	Equivalized	Equivalized	Equivalized[2]	Equivalized[2]	Per adult[3]

Sources:

CEQ   CEQ Institute, 2022e
EG DNA   Zwijnenburg, Bournot, and Giovannelli, 2017, http://www.oecd.org/officialdocuments/publicdisplaydocumentpdf/?cote=STD/DOC(2016)10&docLanguage=En.
EUROMOD   Sutherland and Figari, 2013, https://www.euromod.ac.uk/publications/euromod-modelling-conventions; https://www.euromod.ac.uk/using-euromod/statistics
LIS   Neugschwender and Espasa-Reig, 2022, https://www.lisdatacenter.org/wps/techwps/12.pdf
IDD   OECD, 2017, http://www.oecd.org/els/soc/IDD-ToR.pdf
WID.World Alvaredo, Atkinson, Chancel, and others, 2016, https://wid.world/document/dinaguidelines-v1/

Notes:

. . . = Not available.

1. CEQ: Commitment to Equity Institute; EG DNA: Expert Group on Distributional National Accounts; LIS: Luxembourg Income Study Database; IDD: Income Distribution Database; WID.World: World inequality Database.

2. When household surveys include only consumption expenditures (no information on income), the Commitment to Equity Institute database assumes that consumption expenditures equal disposable income and constructs the other income concepts as specified above, while the World Inequality Database transforms consumption distributions into income distributions using stylized savings profiles in countries where income data are not available.

2. Equivalized income equals household income divided by the square root of household members (excluding domestic help).

3. An individual is classified as an adult if he or she is older than age 20.

Box 6-3 (continued)

Acknowledgments

This box was constructed with contributions from Carlotta Balestra (Organisation for Economic Co-operation and Development Expert Group on Disparities in a National Accounts Framework), Maynor Cabrera (Commitment to Equity Institute), Lucas Chancel (World Inequality Database, Paris School of Economics), Michael Forster and Maxime Ladaique (Organisation for Economic Co-operation and Development Income Distribution Database), Teresa Munzi (Luxembourg Income Study), Daria Popova (EUROMOD, University of Essex), and Jorrit Zwijnenburg (Organisation for Economic Co-operation and Development Expert Group on Disparities in a National Accounts Framework) for their inputs to the table on the comparison of income concepts. It also appeared in Spotlight 3.3 in United Nations Development Programme (2019).

Note that the word "inference" here is unrelated to the concept of statistical inference. Moreover, the imputation method described below should not be confused with the imputation methods used to treat missing data in statistical analysis. In fact, what we call the "prediction" method belongs to the family of imputation methods used in statistical analysis.

If the primary survey being used for the *CEQ Assessment* does not have the necessary information, the four methods can be used in a different survey and then benefits or taxes can be matched back into the main survey. We refer to this method as *alternate survey*. As a last resort, one can use information from other sources—for example, incidence or concentration shares by quintiles or deciles that have been calculated by other authors. We refer to this approach as *secondary sources*.

We describe the methods in detail below; often, multiple allocation methods are combined for allocating benefits or taxes from a particular fiscal intervention, as evident from the examples included below.

3.1 Methods

3.1.1 Direct Identification

In some surveys, questions specifically ask if households received cash benefits from certain social programs or paid taxes to tax and social security systems, and how much they received or paid. When this is the case, it is easy to identify transfer recipients and taxpayers and to add or remove the value of the transfers and taxes from their income, depending on the definition of income being used.

Many direct transfer programs are directly identified, and direct taxes on labor income are sometimes directly identified as well. For example, in one of our studies for Brazil, the conditional cash transfer program Bolsa Familia, noncontributory pensions, public scholarships, unemployment benefits, and various other direct transfers were directly identified, as were individual income taxes since the survey included a question for each income source not only on the gross amount earned, but also on the amount paid in taxes.[25] Although the majority of surveys do not include direct questions about individual income taxes, various surveys do, including those in Ecuador[26] and Peru.[27]

3.1.2 Inference

In some cases, transfers from social programs are grouped with other income sources (in a category for "other income," for example). In this case, it might be possible to infer which families received a transfer based on whether the value they report in that income category matches a possible value of the transfer in question.

One example of the inference method is the identification of the amount of benefits from noncontributory pensions in Argentina by Lustig and Pessino (2014). Benefits from noncontributory pensions could not be independently identified in the surveys because they were lumped together with contributory pensions. Since benefits from the noncontributory system must be below the minimum pension of the contributory system and cannot exceed a certain amount by law, the amounts of pensions observed for individuals reporting a pension that was either below the minimum in the contributory system or up to the maximum allowed by the law were considered benefits from noncontributory pensions. Another example is milk transfers in Brazil: Higgins and Pereira (2014) used the expenditure module of the survey, which includes a question on the way each consumed good was obtained. For families living in the region of Brazil eligible for this program, the authors assumed that the milk was from the government's milk transfer program if the household reported the milk as having been donated. A creative use of the inference method came from Sri Lanka, where the survey does not include a question as to whether the schools that students attend are public or private, so Arunati-lake, Inchauste, and Lustig (2017) use questions from the consumption module on whether the household paid facility fees to government schools or school fees to private schools to infer whether the household's children attend public or private schools.

3.1.3 Imputation

The imputation method uses information that directly identifies beneficiaries or payers from the survey, such as the respondent reporting attending public school or receiving a direct transfer in a survey that does not ask for the amount received, or purchasing a particular good in a formal market, and some information either from

---

[25] See Higgins and Pereira (2014).

[26] See Llerena and others (2015).

[27] See Jaramillo (2014).

public accounts, such as per capita public expenditure on education by level, or from the program rules, or from consumption tax rates that apply to goods purchased in formal markets. Methods vary depending on the tax or transfer amount to be imputed and are described in detail below. For example, for imputing consumption taxes, one has information on items consumed, and the taxes paid are calculated by applying the effective tax rates (actual collection) to each consumption category. Or, one may have information on children attending public school of a certain level, and the benefit is calculated by imputing a value equal to the per student cost of education spending on that same level. The latter has been applied in all country studies in part III of Volume 1 of this Handbook.

Examples of the imputation method for direct transfers include food aid in Ethiopia;[28] school lunches, uniforms, and textbooks in Ecuador;[29] and school uniforms and textbooks in Sri Lanka.[30] In each of these cases, whether the household receives the benefit is reported in the survey, but not the amount received. Thus, total government spending on the program from national accounts was distributed to those who reported receiving benefits in the survey.

In surveys in which data on personal income taxes are not directly identified but those who work in the formal sector are, we consider this an identification from the survey of who pays the tax, and thus use imputation by combining this information with tax rules to determine the amount paid by those individuals. (If, on the other hand, we do not observe who works in the formal sector, we are not identifying who pays in the survey, and would use the simulation method, described below.)

In many countries, education and health benefits are allocated using imputation. Because surveys include questions about who attends public schools or who uses public health facilities or benefits from public health insurance systems, we use the information from the surveys to determine who benefits, then impute per child, per health visit, or per insured benefits as described in more detail in below.

3.1.4 Simulation

When both the information on beneficiaries (taxpayers) and benefits received (taxes paid) is absent from the survey, one can estimate the latter based on the program (tax) rules. For example, in the case of a conditional cash transfer that uses a proxy means test to identify eligible beneficiaries, one can replicate the proxy means test using survey data, identify eligible families, and simulate the program's impact. However, this method gives an upper bound, as it assumes perfect targeting and no errors of inclusion or exclusion. If possible, it is ideal to incorporate assumptions about program leakages and imperfect take-up, although robustness checks in Argentina (which used imputation and simulation in its main results) and Brazil (which used direct identifi-

---

[28] Hill and others (2017).

[29] Llerena and others (2015).

[30] Arunatilake, Inchauste, and Lustig (2017).

cation in its main results) found similar results when using reported survey transfers and simulating them with perfect targeting and take-up.[31] In lower-income countries, the perfect targeting and take-up assumption would be far less accurate since various programs reach only a small fraction of the eligible; in Uganda, for example, there was a lack of information to simulate imperfect take-up beyond the number of beneficiaries of the program, so Jellema and others (2022) (chapter 19 in Volume 1 of this Handbook) randomly allocated benefits among eligible beneficiaries until the number of *beneficiaries* in the survey matched the number in national accounts. In the case of taxes, estimates usually make assumptions about informality and evasion.[32]

Examples of simulation for direct transfers include targeted transfers in various countries, such as Argentina,[33] Bolivia,[34] and Uganda.[35] For direct taxes, individual income taxes and payroll taxes paid by the employer are often simulated using reported income and the tax code. Most studies also use simulation for indirect taxes and subsidies: even if consumption of particular goods is included in the survey, this does not identify who pays the tax since some may evade it; instead, the details of who pays the tax are simulated (usually by assuming everyone pays the effective tax rates, or making a broad assumption about evasion such as that purchases in informal outlets or rural households do not pay the portion of the tax rate that reflects the good's last stage value added; see, for example, Scott [2014] for Mexico and Jaramillo [2014] for Peru, respectively).

Some studies outside of the CEQ choose to always simulate benefits and taxes rather than using data from surveys, even if the data are there. These are usually referred to as "microsimulation models." There are several different types of microsimulation models, which vary in the types of impact they can be used to assess.[36] Three examples are EUROMOD, LATAX, and SOUTHMOD;[37] EUROMOD is described in appendix 6B[38] and LATAX in appendix 6C.[39] An interesting exercise might be to compare results that come from pure simulation versus those that use information from the survey. The CEQ tool can be used for the purposes of only simulation as well.

----

[31] Rossignolo (2018); Higgins and Pereira (2014).

[32] For more on tax avoidance and evasion in developing countries, see Alm, Bahl, and Murray (1991).

[33] Lustig and Pessino, 2014; Rossignolo (2018).

[34] Paz Arauco and others (2014).

[35] Jellema and others (2018).

[36] For further information on the different types of model that can be developed, and the data requirements for each of these, see O'Donoghue (2014, chapters 1–9).

[37] For SOUTHMOD, see https://www.wider.unu.edu/project/southmod---simulating-tax-and-benefit-policies-development.

[38] Popova (2018).

[39] Abramovsky and Phillips (2018). For LATAX, see also Urzua (2012).

3.1.5 Prediction

Another allocation method is the use of regression to predict benefits, with the most common example being the use of a regression of rental rates on housing characteristics among those who rent their dwellings to predict "imputed rent" for owner-occupied housing. Another example that combines the prediction, imputation, and alternate survey methods (the latter is described below) was implemented by Higgins and others (2015) for education benefits in the United States. Specifically, the main survey (Current Population Survey, CPS) included a question about whether children attended school but not whether they attended public or private school. To predict the probability of attending private school, the authors turned to an alternate survey (American Community Survey; ACS). This survey "includes questions about income, student and household characteristics, and the public vs. private school enrollment. For the subsample that attends primary or secondary school, we use a probit to estimate the probability of choosing public school conditional on covariates common to both surveys. The coefficients from this ACS regression are used to predict the probability of attending public school for each student in CPS who attends primary or secondary school. We then multiply each student's probability of attending public school by the average per pupil spending in the student's state to calculate the expected public spending on education received by that student."[40]

The five methods described above rely on at least some information taken directly from the household survey being used for the analysis. However, in some cases the household survey analyzed lacks the necessary questions to assign benefits or taxes to households. In this case, there are two additional methods.

3.1.6 Alternate Survey

When the survey lacks the necessary questions, such as a question on the use of health services or health services coverage (necessary to impute the value of in-kind health benefits to households), an alternate survey may be used by the researcher to determine the distribution of benefits. In the alternate survey, any of the five methods above could be used to identify beneficiaries and assign benefits. Then, there are various methods to allocate benefits in the main survey. The first is to use matching techniques to match households in the primary and alternate surveys and to assign each household in the main survey the benefit or tax estimated for its matched household in the alternate survey. Another, when the prediction method is used in an alternate survey, is to use only covariates common to both surveys as independent variables in the prediction, then use the coefficients from the alternate survey regression to predict the tax or benefit (or another variable, such as whether a student attended public school) in the main survey. A final method is to estimate the distribution of benefits or taxes by income quantile (for example, percentile) in the alternate survey and assign the average benefit within

---

[40] Higgins and others (2015, p. S30).

each quantile from the alternate survey to individuals in the same quantile in the main survey.

There are various examples of using alternate surveys combined with one of the five methods described above. A combination of an alternate survey with direct identification was used by Indonesia:[41] the 2012 household survey being used for the analysis did not include a question about the main conditional cash transfer, but the 2013 survey did, so the researchers computed the distribution of benefits by region and expenditure decile in the 2013 survey and distributed benefits in the 2012 survey among eligible households within each region-decile pair. A combination of an alternate survey and simulation was used in Bucheli and others (2014), who did not have an expenditure module in their main survey and who thus simulated consumption taxes in an alternate expenditure survey, then allocated taxes into the main survey using the method described later in box 6-5. A combination of an alternate survey and imputation can be used for health benefits when the main survey does not include data on the use of public health facilities, as in Guatemala[42] and South Africa.[43] A combination of an alternate survey, prediction, and imputation was used by Higgins and others (2015) for the United States, as described above.

3.1.7 Secondary Sources

When none of the above methods is possible, secondary sources may be used as a last resort. For example, a secondary source might provide the distribution of benefits (taxes) by quantile. These benefits (taxes) are then imputed to all households in the survey being analyzed; the size of each household's benefits (taxes) depends on the quantile to which the household belongs. This is the approach followed by Goñi, Lopez, and Serven (2011) for most of the fiscal interventions and Scott (2014) for personal income taxes, for instance.

In the next sections, we describe in detail how to construct each income concept used in the *CEQ Assessments*.

3.2 Constructing Market Income and Market Income plus Pensions

In section 2, we described the Market Income and the Market Income plus Pensions concepts for the PDI and PGT scenarios in detail (see also figure 6-2 and table 6-5). When the microdata includes information on incomes, most of the components that are included in these income concepts can be directly extracted from the household survey data. What shall one do if the survey includes only consumption data? If the household survey includes only consumption data, we assume that the latter equals Disposable Income and work backward to construct the "previous" income concepts

---

[41] Jellema, Wai-Poi, and Afkar (2017).

[42] Cabrera, Lustig, and Moran (2015).

[43] Inchauste and others (2017).

(additional methodological details are discussed below). When the analysis relies on income data, we do not include extraordinary income from gifts (outside of remittances), the sale of durables, or any other form of dissaving. As with any other inequality or poverty analysis, the exclusion of these categories introduces a challenge when comparing income-based with consumption-based analyses.

Sometimes, the questions in the survey force the researcher to start at Net Market Income and work backward: for example, if the questions about income are net of taxes, one should construct Net Market Income with data observed in the survey, then "work backward" and simulate the tax code (including contributions to social security) to (after the next step) arrive at Market Income. Since the assumption that has been adopted in the *CEQ Assessments* is that taxes paid by employers are shifted to workers in the form of lower wages, the data on wages recorded in surveys will need to be grossed up. "Grossing up" is the term used to explain how to calculate Market Income of, for example, wage earners given the assumption that the economic incidence of payroll taxes paid by employers (also known as "employers' contributions") also falls on wage earners in the form of lower market wages. In essence, we are assuming that in the absence of employers' contributions, the market wages would have been higher by the amount of these contributions. In the surveys, reported wage income is net of these taxes (compared to the counterfactual in which the tax didn't exist and the employer paid that additional income to the worker). Hence, Market Income must be grossed up by the amount paid in the tax, so that when the tax is subtracted out when moving from Market to Net Market Income, we arrive back at income net of direct taxes.

3.2.1 Grossing Up

Note that these instructions apply regardless of whether income in the survey is reported gross or net of individual income taxes paid by the employee, as grossing up will still need to be done for any employer-paid payroll taxes (since reported wages are always net of taxes paid by the employer), and other taxes that do not constitute a portion of income such as property taxes.[44]

Taking a simple example, suppose employers in the formal sector must pay x percent of the employee's wage as a payroll tax. The amount of the payroll tax is calculated as x percent of the employee's reported wages, and this amount is added to the individual's wage income to arrive at a counterfactual "pre-employer payroll tax wage income." This process is known as "grossing up" because one needs to gross-up "observed" Market Income (recall that the income concept called Market Income is different for the PDI and PGT; see section 2, figure 6-2 and table 6-5 for details). This coun-

---

[44] Payroll taxes and contributions paid by the employer will not appear on the paychecks. Recall, however, that in the CEQ method we assume that the burden of taxes paid by the employer will fall entirely on the employees in the form of lower net wages. In other words, gross wages will equal net wages plus payroll taxes paid by the employee AND the employer.

terfactual pre-employer payroll tax wage income is used in the Market Income aggregate. More concretely, suppose an individual reports wage income from the formal sector of $100 (gross of any taxes or contributions paid by the employee), individual income taxes paid of $10, nonwage sources of Market Income totaling $20, and $0 in pensions. If the employer-paid payroll tax were not considered, we would have Market Income plus pensions = $120, direct taxes = $10, Net Market Income = $110. If we now consider a payroll tax paid by the employer of $8 on the employee's income gross of any taxes paid by the employee (in this case, we have pre-payroll tax counterfactual wage income = $108 and direct taxes = $10 + $8 = $18). This gives Market Income = $128, direct taxes = $18, and as before Net Market Income = $110.

Some surveys include questions on the amounts paid in taxes on extraordinary income such as inheritance. In this case, it is desirable to include that tax in the analysis since the data is available and we might otherwise be missing a highly progressive tax in our analysis. However, since the extraordinary income was not included in income, while the tax is presumably paid out of that extraordinary income rather than the individual's annual income stream, this is another instance in which Market Income must be grossed up: the amount paid in inheritance tax would be added into Market Income (and subtracted back out when moving from Market to Net Market Income).[45] However, following this suggestion implies that the entire inheritance tax was paid out of current income. If it was paid out of savings, then the grossing up of inheritance taxes should not be done. Therefore, if it is not known which portion of the inheritance tax is paid out of current income, for comparison purposes, the researcher should present results without the extraordinary income and taxes as well. The latter would correspond to the scenario in which it is assumed that the entire inheritance tax is paid out of savings.

3.2.2 Negative Farm, Business, and Self-Employed Incomes

In some surveys, farm, business, and self-employment incomes can be reported as negative numbers if the interviewee's business suffered a loss during the reference period. Leaving negative incomes in the data complicates the interpretation of results for many of our measures (for example, imagine trying to draw a Lorenz curve if income for some observations is negative). Hence, we adopt the following convention: the particular variable that has a negative value (for example, farm income) is left as negative, but if total prefiscal ends up being negative once all income components are aggregated at the household level, then that negative prefiscal income is converted to zero. In other words, suppose labor income = $10, farm income = −$12, and other components of Market Income = $0. We would not truncate farm income at $0 (which would give Market Income = 10 + 0 = 10), but rather leave farm income = −$12, and truncate Market Income = 10 − 12 = −2 to 0. The

---

[45] We are grateful to Jorge Martinez-Vazquez for feedback on how to treat taxes on extraordinary income.

researcher should report the proportion of the sample that had negative prefiscal that was then converted to zero.[46]

Having said this, we should add that due to the frequency of economy-wide shocks, natural disasters, and idiosyncratic shocks, negative prefiscal incomes may not be that uncommon, especially in the rural areas in low-income countries (or low-income regions in middle-income countries). In the face of negative prefiscal income, poor households may be forced to sell their meager assets at distressed prices or borrow at very high interest rates. Either one would negatively affect households' long-term welfare. The policy analyst may be interested in determining whether the country's safety net system is able to cushion the poor and near poor from adverse shocks. Thus, it may make sense for teams to first determine the frequency of negative prefiscal income. If the proportion of the population that features negative incomes is, just to state a threshold, above 5 percent, the team may want to run a scenario leaving the negative prefiscal income as such and calculate the poverty indicators and the indicators of fiscal impoverishment (FI) and fiscal gains to the poor (FGP)[47] to assess the extent to which the fiscal system provides an effective cushion against the shocks that leave households with negative Market Income.

3.2.3 Imputed Rent for Owner-Occupied Housing

There are multiple methodologies to impute the value of owner-occupied housing. In some countries, survey questionnaires ask families who own their homes to report the amount they think they would be paying in rent for the same dwelling, or for how much they would rent it out. In the case where there is no such question, or if the researchers feel that survey respondents do not have sufficient information about housing markets to answer this question reasonably accurately, or if they find that the distribution of values in response to this question is suspicious, the regression methodology described below can be used instead.

A standard methodology uses a regression to impute the value of owner-occupied housing. This requires that the survey contains information on how much renters pay per month in rent. For the subset of households that rent, (the log of) their monthly rent is the dependent variable in the regression. Potential independent variables include any characteristics about the dwelling, as well as log income per capita of the household. For instance, after exploring a number of potential independent variables, we end up using the following variables for the case of Brazil: number of bedrooms, number of bathrooms, log household income per capita, rural dummy, state dummies, interaction terms between state dummies and the rural dummy, sets of dummies for whether the dwelling is a house, apartment, or room in a shared building, the material of the walls, type of sewage, presence of piped water, floor material, roofing material, and an

---

[46] We are grateful to David Phillips for confirming that this is the method used by the United Kingdom in its household income statistics.

[47] Higgins and Lustig (2016).

intercept. Alternatively, Paz Arauco and others (2014) perform three separate regressions for houses, apartments, and other housing types, using similar dependent variables. The estimated vector of coefficients for households who are renters of their home is then applied to those variables for owner-occupiers. This generates a predicted rental value for owner-occupiers.

The first method requires a response to a survey question about the value of owner-occupied housing, while the second method requires that families who rent their dwellings report how much they pay in rent. If neither piece of information is available, we resort to the methodology used by SEDLAC for countries in this scenario, which only requires a question as to whether households rent their homes. By this methodology, the incomes of families who own their own homes is increased by x percent; x can be ascertained from national accounts, as it was in the *CEQ Assessment* for Armenia (Younger and Khachatryan, 2017).[48]

3.2.4 Value of Production for Own Consumption

The method used to determine the value of production for own consumption depends on the survey data available. Surveys with consumption data often ask whether that item was produced or purchased. The value of items that were produced by the household, taken from the household's own business inventory, or donated to the household (by someone other than the government) are included in Market Income as production for own consumption. Other surveys simply ask one or more questions about the total value of production for own consumption; in that case this value is added to Market Income. The researcher should perform a sensitivity analysis testing results both including and excluding the value of production for own consumption in the definition of income and make sure that the results including the value of production for own consumption make sense. As an example, including the value of production for own consumption in the case of Bolivia led poverty rates to be lower than in Mexico (a country with a GDP per capita roughly three times higher than Bolivia), which led us to believe that this variable was flawed and should not be used in our income aggregates.

When no variable is available to estimate production for own consumption (which is more common in less rural countries where production for own consumption is less important), it is simply not included in income.

3.3 Constructing Gross Income

Gross income is constructed by adding direct government transfers to the selected pre-fiscal income: Market Income plus Pensions or Market Income.

---

[48] SEDLAC instead sets x to 10 percent for all Latin American countries, which is a value that is "consistent with estimates of implicit rents in the region" (CEDLAS and World Bank, 2014, p. 18).

Direct government transfers include, but are not limited to, conditional cash transfer programs, noncontributory pensions, scholarships, public works programs, and other direct transfers (which may or may not be targeted to the poor). In the case of public works programs (also known as "pay for work" or "welfare to work" programs), we include the full value of wages paid in these programs as direct transfers and do not attempt to subtract the opportunity cost of the individual's time. In the contributory pensions as direct transfers (PGT) scenario, income from contributory pensions is treated as any other government cash transfer. Food transfers, although not cash, are considered a direct transfer because they have a well-defined market value and are close substitutes for cash. Similarly, school uniforms, and other near-cash benefits such as school lunches are treated as direct government transfers. Unemployment benefits and other benefits that might be part of the contributory system but are intended to deal with idiosyncratic shocks are also counted as direct transfers.

3.4 Constructing Taxable Income

We construct a peripheral income concept called Taxable Income, which includes only the portion of gross income that is taxable. This is useful for various reasons. First— although simulations of different taxes will include only the relevant taxable base and not the entire Taxable Income variable—constructing the variable Taxable Income reminds the researcher not to include non-Taxable Income in the simulations of various taxes. Second, analyzing how certain results (such as incidence and concentration) change when the population is ranked by Taxable Income can be interesting. Third, it allows us to easily compare the proportion of gross income that is taxable across countries.

It is worth noting that, although the *CEQ Stata Package* produces all results for Taxable Income since it is one of the CEQ core income concepts, it does not make sense to analyze many of the results for Taxable Income, since Taxable Income in low- and middle-income countries in particular could be zero for a large proportion of the population. For example, the poverty headcount ratio using Taxable Income tends to be extremely high.

3.5 Constructing Net Market Income

One might start with Net Market Income directly because, for example, incomes in the survey are reported net of taxes (including the contributions made by the employee to the social security system). If that is the case, as indicated in section 3.2, Constructing Market Income, work backward to construct Market Income/Market Income plus Pensions. Otherwise, Net Market Income is constructed by subtracting direct taxes and contributions. Direct taxes and contributions are personal income taxes, payroll taxes (paid by both the employer and employee), and property taxes. In the PGT scenario, contributions include contributions to the old-age pension system, while in the PDI scenario these contributions are treated as mandatory saving and subtracted from factor income to generate the prefiscal income that corresponds to this scenario: Market Income plus Pensions. See also section 2 above for additional details.

Corporate taxes and other forms of direct taxes that are not captured by the household survey and cannot be simulated are not included in this analysis.[49] When personal income taxes are not reported in the survey, they should be simulated based on the prevailing tax code and, importantly, tax evasion assumptions. When tax incidence is obtained by the simulation method, the latter should be described in detail, including the evasion assumptions. As a last resort, the incidence of taxes could be obtained from other studies on tax incidence for the same country.

The burden of personal income taxes is assumed to fall entirely on labor in the formal sector, in the form of reduced wages. In other words, if a survey reports gross wages and the amount paid in taxes, the reported amount paid in taxes is subtracted in full from pretax income. If the survey reports net wages and the amount paid in taxes, gross wages are obtained by "working backward" and adding the amount paid in taxes to net wages to obtain gross wages. The burden of payroll taxes is assumed to be borne fully by labor in the formal sector, again recalling that Market Income must be grossed up to create the pre-payroll tax counterfactual.

The burden of property taxes is assumed to fall entirely on the holders of property. If there is a survey question on property taxes paid, we use this information and assume that the tax is borne by those who reported paying it in the survey. (Note that the amount of property taxes paid might be found in the consumption module of surveys that include consumption.) If there is no question on property taxes paid, information on who is a property owner and the value of their property can be used in combination with knowledge of the tax code, again assuming that the tax is borne fully by owners of property. If information about the value of the property is not available, the researcher will have to assess whether there is enough information on property ownership to simulate the tax.

Note that the base income for any tax simulations should always exclude non-Taxable Income, which includes but is not limited to the income we are imputing for owner-occupied housing, production for own consumption, nontaxable fringe benefits, and the value of grossing up for any taxes that the individual did not pay but are assumed to be borne by the individual (for example, payroll taxes paid by employers).

---

[49] For countries that are able to simulate the corporate income tax, the burden of corporate income taxes is assumed to fall entirely on capital income. It is also assumed that all financial assets (not just corporate stock) bear the tax equally. See Piketty and Saez (2007). For a *CEQ Assessment* that included corporate income taxes with alternative assumptions, see Higgins and others (2015) and chapter 5 by Candia and Engel (2022) in Volume 2 of this Handbook.

3.6 Constructing Disposable Income

Disposable Income is the first income concept that is identical for the PDI and PGT scenarios. For details, see section 2 (as well as figure 6-2 and table 6-5).

As we shall see below, when consumption is used instead of income, disposable "income" is set equal to consumption. Then, work backward to construct the "previous" income concepts under each scenario.

3.7 Constructing Consumable Income

From Disposable Income (or consumption if you are using a consumption-based survey), subtract indirect taxes and add indirect subsidies. We provide some detail on estimating and allocating indirect taxes and subsidies below; for more detail, and for a description of estimating the indirect effect of indirect taxes and subsidies, see (chapter 7 in Volume 1 of this Handbook.

3.7.1 Subtract Indirect Taxes

The burden of indirect taxes is assumed to fall entirely on the consumer in the form of higher prices. If you wish to introduce a distinction between the effect of indirect taxes on tradeable and nontradeable goods, follow the methodology discussed in Coady (2006). Indirect taxes should be simulated using consumption—not income—data, which requires that the survey being used contains both income and consumption data or consumption data only (or that an income-only survey is used in conjunction with a consumption survey and a matching or prediction technique to generate consumption totals by category of consumption good for each household in the income-only survey).

Tax rates for the prevailing indirect taxes (such as consumption taxes in the form of a value-added tax) are applied to each household's reported consumption of the corresponding items. Because indirect taxes can apply to both final consumption goods and services and inputs, whenever possible an input-output (IO) table should be used to determine the indirect impact of taxes on inputs on the prices of final consumption goods. For details, see chapter 7 in this Volume. One clarification is in order: although we call them "consumption taxes," strictly speaking we are referring to taxes on current expenditures since we do not include taxes paid on durables purchased before the survey period but partially consumed during the survey period. If an IO table is not available and you are unable to calculate the indirect tax burden including the indirect effects, then just subtract the indirect taxes on final consumption. Note that leaving out the indirect effect of indirect taxes may or may not be of significance, depending on the item. Thus, if the indirect effects are not included, the author should note that the calculated burden may be an underestimation.

Due to tax evasion or informality, which are widespread in developing countries, consumers in rural areas and those who purchase from informal sellers (for example, street vendors, farmers' markets, and so on—when the survey contains a question about place of purchase) might not directly pay indirect taxes. Rajemison, Haggblade, and Younger (2003) show that using statutory rates can overestimate the impact of indirect taxes.[50] Where estimates are available or can be calculated, effective tax rates reflecting the rates paid in reality—rather than the legal rates, which overestimate actual collection of indirect taxes—should be used.

Box 6-4 shows how Aristy-Escuder and others (2022) (chapter 14 in this Volume) included assumptions on the evasion of indirect taxes in their study.

A simpler, but less accurate, option than the one described in box 6-4 is to assume that people who live in rural areas or who purchase from informal sellers do not pay consumption taxes. However, even if they might not directly pay indirect (consumption) taxes, they cannot be assumed to have paid no indirect tax because of the indirect effects of indirect taxes on inputs. Hence, an IO table should be used. For details, see chapter 7 of this Volume, as well as Coady and others (2006) and Coady (2006).[51] Goods that are exempt from consumption taxes should also include the indirect effects of indirect taxes on inputs, again computed using an IO table. Only goods that are taxed at zero-rate can be assumed to involve no indirect taxes since producers are reimbursed for any taxes paid on their inputs.

Once effective rates for different groups of consumption goods have been calculated using an IO table, the next step depends on the type of survey data available—in particular, whether the survey has consumption data only or both consumption and income data. (The latter also includes income-only surveys if they are matched with a consumption survey to generate consumption totals by category for each household, or used in conjunction with a consumption survey to predict consumption of various categories in the income-only survey.) In either case, suppose that consumption goods have been divided into K groups, with tax rates t_k and denote the post-tax (including the cost of taxes) amount spent on consumption of goods in category k by household i as c_k. (We omit the i subscript for simplicity.) Given that we have defined c_k as *post-tax* spending, the amount of spending on category k *net of taxes* is $c_k/(1+t_k)$.

For a survey with consumption data only (or income and consumption data when consumption is being used as the measure of well-being), the total amount spent on indirect taxes is calculated as $\text{IndT} = \sum_{k=1}^{K} t_k c_k/(1+t_k)$, and this amount is subtracted from total consumption when moving from Disposable "Income" (that is, consumption) to Consumable "Income."

For a survey with income and consumption data (or where consumption by category is generated by matching/prediction with an alternate survey), when income is being used as the measure of well-being, subtracting $\sum_{k=1}^{K} t_k c_k/(1+t_k)$ from income

---

[50] See Bachas and others (2020), who show that explicitly including informality makes consumption taxes equalizing.

[51] Sample Stata code for using an IO table is included online in part IV of this Volume (available only online; CEQ Institute, 2022d).

Box 6-4

Inclusion of the Assumptions of Evasion in the Tax on the Transfer of Industrialized Goods and Services (ITBIS) of the Dominican Republic

Jaime Aristy-Escuder, Maynor Cabrera, Blanca Moreno-Dodson, and Miguel E. Sanchez-Martin

E vasion of the ITBIS is a problem to take into account in the Dominican Republic. According to estimates of the General Directorate of Internal Revenue (DGII), for the year 2010, around 29.7 percent of this tax was evaded. Therefore, it is important to incorporate an adjustment for evasion in the estimation of the CEQ.

Following consultations with experts of the DGII, estimates were obtained of the cash payment of taxes for a specific group of products. Nevertheless, the coverage of these estimates was limited. Thus, for the rest of the products, we made assumptions about taxes paid. From this analysis, we identified that for some goods taxes are generally paid in full, while other goods completely evade the taxes, and for other goods, the evasion or payment of taxes depends on the location of the purchase. Therefore, we grouped consumption goods into four categories:

- Highly probable that they will not pay taxes (100 percent evasion in the purchase of these goods);
- Highly probable that they will pay taxes (0 percent evasion in the purchase of these goods);
- Those that have information from the DGII about the proportion of the payment of taxes (we applied the effective rate of the payment of taxes);
- Those for which tax payments are assumed to be conditional on the place of purchase: a different evasion rate was applied to urban and rural consumers.

To realize these adjustments, we used two additional files. The first contains each one of the goods included in the survey and is classified into one of the four previously described categories (code of the product and group of products). The second file defines if the product evades or pays taxes according to the location of the purchase, for those cases where evasion is conditional. With this information we estimated the amount paid in tax (ITBIS) for every good consumed by the households represented in the household income-expenditure survey.

Source: Aristy-Escuder and others (2022) (chapter 14 in this Volume).

when moving from Disposable Income would be problematic for two reasons. First, we would be measuring the incidence of consumption taxes as a percent of income, which could make them appear regressive even if their incidence is progressive when measured as a percent of consumption.[52] Second, some observations in household survey microdata have reported consumption that is much higher than reported income, due either to dissaving or to borrowing. Some of the households with consumption much higher than reported income end up with negative consumable income if we simply subtract $\sum_{k=1}^{K} t_k c_k / (1+t_k)$ from Disposable Income. Thus, for a survey with income and consumption data when income is being used as the measure of well-being, we follow Inter-American Development Bank (2009) and estimate indirect taxes as

$$\text{IndT} = \frac{\sum_{k=1}^{K} t_k \dfrac{c_k}{1+t_k}}{\sum_{k=1}^{K} c_k} \times y^d,$$

where y^d denotes Disposable Income. Note that the first term on the right-hand side of the equation gives the proportion of *post-tax* consumption that is spent on consumption taxes, which is then multiplied by Disposable Income to get an income-based total amount spent on consumption taxes. The denominator of the first term uses total *post-tax* consumption, $\sum_{k=1}^{K} c_k$, as this measure is comparable to Disposable Income (since the Disposable Income spent on consumption must be large enough to also incur consumption taxes on that consumption).

For example, suppose there are two goods: bread and fuel. The effective tax rate (including direct and indirect effects) on bread is 5 percent and on fuel is 10 percent. A household at the lower end of the income distribution has reported Disposable Income of $10, reported consumption of bread as $8, and reported consumption of fuel at $12. Reported consumption exceeds reported income, which often occurs at the lower end of the distribution, perhaps because the household is borrowing or dissaving to meet its consumption needs. Rather than computing indirect taxes as $.05 * 8 + .10 * 12 = \$1.60$, and calculate the rate of paid indirect taxes as $1.60/$10 and hence state that the household pays 16 percent of its income in indirect taxes (which is higher than the effective tax rate for both bread and fuel!), we would calculate the percent of consumption paid in indirect taxes as $(0.05 * 8 + 0.10 * 12)/(8 + 12) = 0.08$ (8 percent) and then multiply this by Disposable Income to arrive at total indirect taxes paid of $0.08 * 10 = \$0.80$. Although this is not the actual amount of indirect taxes paid, it allows us to correctly estimate the progressivity of indirect taxes.

If the difference between consumption and income is due to a measurement error in income or consumption or both variables, then one should consider correcting the error first. For example, in surveys that include both income and consumption, the researcher may choose to use the latter and define it as "disposable income" because he

---

[52] We thank David Phillips for his feedback on this issue.

or she has evidence that consumption is measured more accurately. When this is done, the issue of potentially having negative Consumable Income disappears.

In the absence of consumption data in the main survey, one can resort to an alternate survey and use prediction to generate consumption data. Box 6-5 describes how it was done for the *CEQ Assessment* for Uruguay.

3.7.2 Add Indirect Subsidies

Indirect subsidies can be on final consumption goods and services or on inputs. Consumption subsidies of a fixed percentage can be measured in the same way as consumption taxes described above. Price subsidies on inputs will be passed on to consumers through the cost structure of final consumption goods, both directly and indirectly, which is why we use an IO matrix to measure their impacts on the prices of final goods. Distinctions between tradeables and nontradeables are analogous as well. More details for specific types of subsidies are given below. See chapter 7 of this for a full-fledged discussion on how to incorporate the indirect effects of indirect subsidies.

It is important to note that the definition of subsidy used here is not equivalent, for example, to the definition used by the World Trade Organization.[53] For the purposes of fiscal incidence analysis, a subsidy refers to a benefit that affects the relative price of the subsidized good or service. Although given our assumption of perfectly inelastic demand for goods and services, the effect of a subsidy on a person's income is equivalent to that of a transfer, it is preferable to keep the benefits that operate through the price system separate for two main reasons. First, to facilitate comparability with other indicators of inequality and poverty, which are practically never calculated on an income concept equivalent to our consumable income. Estimates of inequality and poverty are usually done using Disposable Income or private consumption, both of which do not subtract indirect taxes and add indirect subsidies. Second, keeping them separate will facilitate the incorporation of behavioral responses in the future.

Statutory rates can overestimate the impact of indirect subsidies. Where estimates are available or can be calculated, effective subsidy rates reflecting the rates received in reality—rather than the legal rates—should be used.

Fuel subsidies

If the government subsidizes petroleum products, the incidence of these subsidies should be estimated and their value should be added into income when moving from

---

[53] Unlike the Tokyo Round Subsidies Code, the WTO SCM Agreement contains a definition of the term "subsidy." The definition contains three basic elements: (i) a financial contribution (ii) by a government or any public body within the territory of a Member (iii) which confers a benefit. All three of these elements must be satisfied in order for a subsidy to exist. (Source: "Agreement on Subsidies and Countervailing Measures ('SCM Agreement')," https://www.wto.org/english/tratop_e/scm_e/subs_e.htm).

Box 6-5

Example of One Way to Generate Indirect Taxes in the Absence of Consumption Data

Marisa Bucheli

The household survey used for the analysis in Uruguay has data on income only. In order to estimate the indirect taxes paid by each household, we use the National Household Income and Expenditure Survey (Encuesta Nacional de Gastos e Ingresos de los Hogares; EGIH) collected by the National Institute of Statistics (Instituto Nacional de Estadistica; INE) between November 2005 and October 2006. We identify fifty-two consumption baskets using two criteria: each one is composed of goods or services with high substitutability and taxed at the same rate. For each basket we run a multiple regression (52 Tobit models) with household spending on each basket of goods as the dependent variable and a set of independent variables that are available both in EGIH and the household survey, such as the household income, the size of the household, the average years of schooling of the adults of the household, a deprivation index, the total hours worked in the labor market by all the members of the household, the other direct transfers, the participation of age-groups by sex in the household (we consider teenage groups), and a set of regional dummies. The first five variables are introduced as a third-order polynomial to have a more parsimonious functional form. Using the coefficients from these regressions, we predict the consumption basket of households in the household survey using a procedure of matching imputation of missing values embedded in the command *uvis* of Stata. Finally, we then estimate the indirect taxes by applying the scheduled tax rate of each basket and assuming no evasion.

When the survey has income data only and no alternate consumption survey is available, secondary sources may be used. For example, a secondary source might provide the percent of consumption spent on indirect taxes by consumption decile. (Note that for the same reasons discussed above, the secondary source should give the percent of consumption spent on indirect taxes, not the percent of income spent on indirect taxes.) This percent by decile is then applied to the disposable income of each individual in the corresponding consumption decile (not income decile; this may require calculating a new variable that denotes each household's placement in the distribution of consumption) from the CEQ analysis to obtain her spending on indirect taxes. The implicit assumption being made when one uses indirect taxes by consumption decile is that everyone in that consumption decile pays the same proportion of their consumption (equal to the average over the decile) in indirect taxes.

disposable to consumable income. In many cases, the indirect effects of fuel subsidies (through their effect on the prices of goods for which fuel is an input) are larger than the direct effects,[54] so they should be included in the analysis. The method for doing this is described in chapter 7 of this Volume.

Household energy subsidies

In some countries, the government directly subsidizes electricity prices for households who consume low enough amounts of energy, often using an inverted block tariff (IBT) structure. When these subsidies are provided for household energy consumption only, estimating the first-order direct effects is sufficient. Consider the example of Brazil, where the Social Tariff on Electric Energy (TSEE) is an IBT price subsidy on energy. In 2009, eligible households consuming less than 30 kWh per month received a 65 percent discount, households consuming over 30 but less than 100 kWh received a 40 percent discount, and households consuming between 100 kWh and 220 kWh received a 10 percent discount; households consuming more than 220 kWh were charged market price.[55] Note that inverted block tariffs can also require households consuming above a certain amount to pay higher than market price in order to cross-subsidize those who are paying below market price. In this case, the amount each household pays above market price should be calculated using the same method as described below and treated as an indirect tax.

If the survey provides data on the total kilowatt hours consumed by the household, then it is straightforward to classify each household by its consumption level, which determines the proportional subsidy they receive according to the tariff rule. Then, we multiply this proportional subsidy by the amount they spent on electric energy to get the value of the subsidy. If, however, the survey provides data on the total spent on electricity but not the total kilowatt hours consumed, the latter must be calculated. We will illustrate with an example from Brazil.[56] Denote the market price of electricity as $\$p$ per kWh. If households consuming less than 30 kWh per month receive a 65 percent discount as in Brazil, then any household spending less than $(1-0.65)*30p$ a month on electricity would be assumed to have received the 65 percent subsidy. Suppose the household reported spending $c < (1-0.65)*30p$ for the month; the direct effect of the subsidy (the benefit to be allocated to the household) would be calculated as $(0.65/(1-0.65))\,c$. Continuing with the Brazil example, recall that households consuming between 30 and 100 kWh per month receive a 40 percent discount. Thus, any household reporting spending c greater than $(1-0.65)*30p$ per month but less than $(1-.40)*100p$ per month would be assumed to have received the 40 percent subsidy, and the direct

---

[54] Coady and others (2006).

[55] This is a simplification of the actual system for illustrative purposes. See Higgins and Pereira (2014) for more details.

[56] Higgins and Pereira (2014).

effect would be calculated as $(0.40/(1-0.40))$ c.[57] Following this method, the amount of benefits we allocated for household energy subsidies was 77 percent of the amount spent according to national accounts; the discrepancy might be accounted for by leakages—our simulation assumed perfect coverage and no leakages.

Note that a tool for simulating subsidies—which include household energy subsidies with an inverted block tariff structure—is described in Araar and Verme (2012).

Agricultural subsidies

The incidence of benefits of agricultural subsidies will depend on the elasticity of demand for the agricultural products. If demand is perfectly elastic, the benefit will accrue entirely to the producer, in which case benefits would be imputed based on survey questions revealing who produces the subsidized goods. If it is inelastic, it will accrue entirely to the consumer, in which case the benefits can be estimated using an input-output table as they would be for other subsidized goods, using the method described above. The method to impute agricultural subsidies will depend on the nature of these subsidies and the demand for the products whose inputs are subsidized.

Subsidies on agricultural inputs: An exception

When production and consumption decisions are intertwined, as happens with small subsistence farmers in developing countries, subsidies to inputs should be treated as direct transfers rather than a subsidy (even though they are not strictly "cashable"). In essence, we are assuming that the subsidies to agricultural inputs are "inframarginal" (people were going to buy the inputs anyway). Subsidized or free inputs make the net income of farmers/peasants higher than otherwise. This means that the subsidies to inputs need to be added to get the "true" Market Income (which without the "transfer" that comes with these subsidies would have been lower).

Housing subsidy

Impute the in-kind value received by those who live in publicly (fully or partially) subsidized housing. Ideally, the survey will include information on who lives in subsidized housing, and, if it is only partially subsidized, how much they paid in rent. The market value of their subsidized housing can be determined using a regression methodology (similar to the regression methodology described to impute the value of owner-occupied housing under section 3.2.3, Imputed Rent for Owner-Occupied Housing).

---

[57] Note that there are tranches of spending amounts that do not coincide with the IBT schedule: for example, if the household reports spending c such that $(1-0.65) * 30p < c < (1-0.4) * 30p$, their total spending c is not possible given the discontinuous IBT schedule. The value they reported for c could be due to misreporting or, for example, because the survey's reference period does not coincide with the billable month. We have arbitrarily chosen to place individuals in this category with the group who received the 40 percent subsidy; they could also have arbitrarily been placed in the group who received the 65 percent subsidy.

If housing is only partially subsidized, the amount occupants pay in rent should be subtracted from this total. For the observations for which this method results in a negative value, it should be replaced by zero; however, if a negative value results for many observations, this could be an indication that the linear model used to predict housing values is not a good fit and should be revisited.

3.8 Constructing Final Income

3.8.1 Add In-Kind Transfers

Allocating benefits from public spending on government services such as education and health is not straightforward. The options are summarized by Bastagli (2015, p. 12) as follows:

> Studies on the distributive impacts of government services may value these at their production costs, at their opportunity cost in the private sector or at household's willingness to pay. A basic definition utilised for the unit cost of providing a service is as total government spending on a particular service divided by the number of users of that service. An alternative to production costs is to value services by what an individual would have spent if similar services had been bought on the market or on the willingness to pay for them, but the information requirements of these approaches are demanding.

In the current version of the *CEQ Assessment*, the value of in-kind transfers is based on production costs. They are gross benefits. That is, user fees or co-payments are not subtracted, and their incidence is calculated separately by component. They will, of course, be subtracted when constructing Final Income (see figure 6-2 and table 6-5). Note that in the 2018 edition of this Handbook we recommended imputing the net benefits of education and health spending. That is, we recommended subtracting user fees and co-payments. This implied that we were treating in-kind benefits differently from cash benefits. In incidence analysis, one does not deduct taxes paid (when applicable) from cash transfers. The incidence of cash transfers and taxes paid are analyzed separately. We propose the same approach to in-kind transfers. The indicators housed in the CEQ Data Center on Fiscal Redistribution used the gross value, unless otherwise specified.

Details on the imputation method, by category of in-kind transfer, are given below. It is important to note that the concept of Final Income does not include the value of government services that benefit entire communities such as rural roads, water, and sanitation, access to electricity, and other types of infrastructure. While these are clearly very important in terms of enhancing the welfare and productivity of households, it is difficult to impute a monetary value on them. Sergei Soares (2022b) (chapter 4 in

Volume 2 of this Handbook) proposes a method to impute a value to public infra-structure in and illustrates with data from Brazil.

3.8.2 Education

From national accounts, obtain public spending per student by level (pre-school, pri-mary [lower and upper if applicable], secondary [lower and upper if applicable], tertiary [university and technical if applicable]); these totals could be further disaggregated, for example by state if available. The spending amount should include administrative costs and recurring spending. Provide the definition of each level (the corresponding grade levels and age groups). For students who report attending public school, depending on the level they report attending, use the average public spending per student for that level as the valuation of their in-kind benefit from public education, which is added into income when moving from Consumable to Final Income. In addition to having a variable for in-kind education benefits, the researcher should create separate variables for benefits at each level (a variable for preschool education benefits, another for pri-mary education benefits, etc.).

If the main survey being used does not have data on whether school attendance was at public or private institutions, the researcher should search for an alternate sur-vey with data on income and on whether school attendance was public or private. For example, the survey used for our incidence study in the United States[58]—the 2011 Cur-rent Population Survey (CPS)—did not include a question about whether school at-tendance was public or private. We estimated the probability of attending public school for each student attending school in the CPS by using another survey, the 2011 Ameri-can Community Survey (ACS), which contains variables on public and private school enrollment and income. We performed a probit regression on the population of stu-dents attending school, with a dummy variable for attending a public school as the de-pendent variable and per capita income, race, state, age, and highest level of education in the household as independent variables. The coefficients from this regression were then applied to the same variables in the CPS data to estimate the probability of at-tending public school for each student attending school. The average amount of edu-cation spending per pupil by state was then multiplied by the predicted probability of attending public school to get the expected in-kind education transfer for each student attending school; this expected benefit was then scaled down using the method de-scribed above.

Note that in the CPS we do not know which students attended public school, so we are not imputing the full (scaled down) value of per pupil spending to anyone; by multiplying each student's predicted probability of attending public school by per pupil spending, we are assigning each student the expected value of his or her in-kind educa-tion benefit. In checking our method, we verify that the average predicted probability

---

[58] Higgins and others (2015).

from applying the coefficients of the ACS survey to the CPS data is almost identical to the proportion of students attending public school (according to both ACS and administrative data). We also verify that total (scaled down) in-kind education benefits using this method is approximately equal to total (scaled down) education spending in national accounts.

In the 2018 edition of this Handbook, we recommended scaling down education and health spending so that their ratio to Disposable Income from the survey was equal to the ratio of the two variables from National Accounts. The rationale was that if they were not scaled down, the cost of production method would overestimate the redistributive effect of in-kind transfers that households received.[59] While this may be true, there is also an argument in the opposite direction. If in-kind spending is not imputed at actual government cost, the benefit to the household might be underestimated. The researcher may try to estimate the impact on inequality both without and with scaling down to assess the extent to which this assumption affects results. It should be noted that—unless specified otherwise—the results shown in the CEQ Data Center on Fiscal Redistribution do not scale down in-kind transfers.

In previous iterations of CEQ (in particular, in the working papers for Latin American countries published before August 2013 and the special issue of *Public Finance Review*), rather than scaling down in-kind benefits to avoid overestimating their redistributive impact, we scaled up all other income components item by item for calculations of inequality and redistribution (but not poverty).[60] In other words, each component had its own scaling up factor based on total income from that component in the survey compared to total income from that component according to national accounts.

3.8.3 Health

Bastagli (2015) identifies two general approaches to allocate in-kind health benefits to individuals and households: the "actual consumption approach" and the "insurance value approach."[61] The first approach allocates the value of public services to the individuals who are actually using the service. The second approach assigns the same per capita spending to everybody sharing the same characteristic such as age, state, type

---

[59] As the monetary value of the transfers received by households is obtained from the budgetary cost of providing these transfers as reported in national accounts, and while the totals of other taxes and transfers are not "forced" to be equal to the values in national accounts (and tend to be smaller according to the survey), if the in-kind transfers are not scaled down, they will be given a disproportionate effect compared to the other fiscal interventions. Recall, however, that we suggest doing something similar to direct cash transfers; that is, we do not recommend scaling them down.

[60] See Lustig, Pessino, and Scott (2014) and the list of CEQ working papers here: www.commit mentoequity.org.

[61] This section is based largely on O'Donnell and others (2008, chapter 14).

of care, gender, et cetera. One special case of the "insurance value approach" is using eligibility to a specific health system as the shared characteristic (see appendix 6F, section 2.2 "Average Cost and Insurance Value"). The reliance on one approach over the other depends, mainly, on data availability. As Bastagli notes, when identification of beneficiaries is not straightforward, studies "may rely on characteristics of individuals and households rather than actual use of services on the assumption that the probability a person will access these services is the same as that prevailing for others with the same characteristics."[62] Additionally, please note that if the recall period of the actual use of the health service is less than one year on the questionnaire (for example, "How many times in the last three months did you receive service k?"), the "insurance value approach" is more appropriate. Using the "actual consumption approach" in this case will assign zero health benefits to individuals who used the health service during the fiscal year, but not during the recall period.

To impute the value received from public health services, the household survey must have information about the use of health services, and it must distinguish between public care (which is usually services received from the public health system or paid for by public health insurance schemes) and private care. In the absence of information about whether the care received was subsidized by government health spending, a survey question about whether the patient is covered by private insurance can be used as a proxy; patients who received healthcare and report having private health insurance are considered to have received private care, and thus received no in-kind transfer, and patients who report not having private health insurance are considered to have received public care. Ideally, the survey will also contain one or more questions about the type of service received.

If this information is not available in the survey being used, another survey that has information on both income and utilization of public health services—such as a health survey—should be used. In this case, to calculate Final Income one must then treat the results from the alternate survey similarly to a secondary source and impute values by quantiles (for example, ventiles [groups of 5 percent of the population]) back into the original microdata.

In addition to data on the use of public health services and the type of services received, data on total government spending on each of the different types of health services in the household survey is required. Some level of disaggregation by type of service received (at a minimum, distinguishing between in-patient and out-patient care) is required, in order to account for the fact that the value of a medical check-up is different from the value of a hospitalization. This data should also be disaggregated by region or state when possible to account for differences in the quality of health services across regions. Data that is disaggregated as described above is generally not available in the main source of public accounts (for example, from the treasury or ministry of development), but can be obtained instead from national health accounts (for example,

---

[62] Bastagli (2015); Demery (2003); OECD (2015).

from the health ministry). The spending totals should include administrative costs and both recurring and investment spending.

In the event that the care received is partially but not fully subsidized, the amount paid for care by the individual or by private healthcare providers should be subtracted from the total benefit received by that individual. If public healthcare in the country being studied is, in general, not fully subsidized (for example, there is not a universal free healthcare system), but the household survey does not ask how much each individual paid for the service they received or how much was not covered by the public health insurance scheme, each individual's payment can be calculated as the average payment for that service; it is calculated as the total payment from individuals and private health insurers to the state for that service (available in national health accounts) divided by the total number of individuals receiving that service according to the household survey.

The total annualized health benefits received by an individual are thus defined as

$$h_i = \sum_k \alpha_k \left[q_{ki} \left(\frac{S_{kj}}{\sum_{i \in j} \omega_i \alpha_k q_{ki}} \right) \right]$$

where q_{ki} indicates the number of times that individual i received care type k during the recall period, S_{kj} is the total spending (according to national health accounts) on service k in the region j where i resides, $i \in j$ indicates that we are summing over all individuals in region j, ω_i is the expansion factor corresponding to observation i, and α_k is the "annualization factor": for services that have a recall period of one year on the questionnaire (for example, "How many times in the last year did you receive service k?"), $\alpha_k = 1$; for services that have a recall period of four weeks, $\alpha_k = 13$, et cetera.

Note that in the 2018 edition of this Handbook we recommended imputing the net benefits of education and health spending. That is, we subtracted user fees and co-payments in the formula above. This implied that we were treating in-kind benefits differently from cash benefits. In incidence analysis, one does not deduct taxes paid (when applicable) from cash transfers. The incidence of cash transfers and taxes paid are analyzed separately. We propose the same approach to in-kind transfers.

3.8.4 Additional Concerns for In-Kind Transfers

In countries with a contributory public health insurance scheme, we are also interested in knowing the concentration of coverage, so the concentration coefficients and coverage and leakages sheets of the *CEQ MWB* (sheets D8 and D9, respectively) include a row for "contributory public health insurance" in addition to the row for "health spending." The latter is based on use, using the total annualized health benefits, h_i, calculated as explained above. The former is calculated using a variable equal to zero for individuals not covered by the contributory public health insurance schemes and equal to the value of a basic health package for covered individuals.

In the construction of Final Income, the method for education spending consists of imputing a value to the benefit accrued to an individual of going to public school, which is equal to the per beneficiary input costs obtained from administrative data: for example, the average government expenditure per primary school student obtained from administrative data is allocated to the households based on how many children are reported attending public school at the primary level. In the case of health, the approach is analogous: the benefit of receiving healthcare in a public facility is equal to the average cost to the government of delivering healthcare services to the beneficiaries.

The approach to valuing education and healthcare services amounts to asking the following question: How much would the income of a household have to be increased if it had to pay for the free or subsidized public service (or the insurance value in the cases in which this applies to healthcare benefits) at the full cost to the government? The method applied here is equivalent to using a simple binary indicator of whether or not the individual uses the government service.[63] Such an approach ignores the fact that consumers may value services quite differently from what they cost.[64] For the readers who think that attaching a value to education and health services based on government costs is not accurate, Jeremy Barofsky and Stephen Younger (2022) (chapter 1 in Volume 2 of this Handbook) explore alternative options for health (see also appendix 6F in this chapter). For education, see chapter 2 by Sergei Soares (2022c) and chapter 3 by Sergio Urzua (2022), both in Volume 2.

The production costs approach does not take into account variations in need across income groups, does not consider service quality, and may not reflect the actual valuation by beneficiaries.[65] Distributional analysis of in-kind transfers may reveal that poorer households gain larger shares of particular categories of public spending than higher-income households. Since the main beneficiaries of public education services (children) and public healthcare services (elderly) are disproportionately located in the lower half of the income distribution, assessments based on the standard approach of static incidence analysis using per capita income as the underlying welfare measure may show for some countries that in-kind transfers reduce inequality, but ignore the question of demographic and needs variations across socioeconomic groups.

---

[63] This is true only for measures that are independent of monetary units (such as relative inequality measures) and within a level of education. A concentration coefficient for total nontertiary education, for example, where the latter is calculated as the sum of the different spending amounts by level, is not equivalent to the binary indicator method.

[64] By using averages, it also ignores differences across income groups and regions: for example, governments may spend less (or more) per pupil on poorer students. We recommend averaging at as disaggregated of a level as possible (not only by education level but also by state and rural/urban area within states, for example); the level at which it is possible to disaggregate will depend on data from national accounts. Data obtained from the education ministry is likely to be more disaggregated than that obtained from other national accounts.

[65] Atkinson and Bourguignon (1990); OECD (2015); Sahn and Younger (2000).

4 Construction of Income Concepts in Practice: Additional Methodological Challenges

4.1 Using Consumption Instead of Income

In the literature on incidence analysis, both income and consumption have been used as the basic welfare indicator. Typically, the incidence of direct taxes and transfers is calculated using income, while for the incidence of indirect taxes and subsidies, some authors recommend using consumption (for example, Abramovsky, Attanasio, and Phillips, 2012). However, for a comprehensive analysis, one or the other must be chosen as the indicator of well-being.[66] Some thoughts on the choice between income and consumption are given in box 6-6.

Note that in theory, consumption is equal to expenditures on nondurables plus consumption of own production plus the flow value from use of durables owned by the household. In practice, we include imputed rent for owner-occupied housing (explained in greater detail below) but do not calculate the imputed value from use of other durables owned by the household. Although the latter should be included from a theoretical standpoint, doing so requires information about the value and age of assets owned, or at a minimum about assets owned and average prices for these assets. If you have reliable data to estimate the value from use of assets other than housing, you can perform an additional sensitivity analysis including these components in income. If you use consumption, do not include the value of consumer durable purchases (whether in cash or credit) because these are extraordinary expenditures. Similarly, the sale of these items is not included in the income aggregate since it represents extraordinary income.

After equating consumption to Disposable "Income," one must "work backward" to construct Net Market "Income," Gross "Income," Market "Income" plus Pensions, and Market "Income." For example, to obtain Market Income plus Pensions in the PDI scenario (that is, the prefiscal income by which households are ranked), we would start out with Consumption (equals Disposable "Income") and, first, **add** (1) Employee's and Employer's Contributions for Other Contributory Systems, which differs from old-age pensions (unemployment benefits, disability, health, and so on), and (2) Direct Personal Income Taxes (excluding all contributions to social security) on taxable Gross Income.

---

[66] Coudouel, Hentschel, and Wodon (2002) argue that consumption is a better measure for a number of reasons. Although both are underreported (Brewer and O'Dea, 2012), there is substantial evidence that consumption is better measured for the poor (Meyer and Sullivan, 2003). Consumption is smoothed to a greater degree than income (although income is also smoothed, even among the agricultural workers who are often used as an example of people facing volatile incomes; see Murdoch, 1995). A main advantage of income, also noted by Coudouel, Hentschel, and Wodon (2002), is that it can be disaggregated by source, which can be especially appealing for a fiscal incidence analysis.

Box 6-6

On Using Consumption or Income

Gary Burtless

I deally, lifetime consumption (or consumption per year) would be the best measure for an incidence analysis, mainly because it represents our best gauge of long-term well-being. However, this measure is not practical, given the data limitations we face in every country, rich and poor. If we use an annual measure of income or consumption, our choice should be guided by the best (meaning "most accurate available") basic source of data available to us. This will vary by country and probably by income class within a country. The most accurate information is likely to be that which is easiest for household heads to report. In rich countries, a lot of evidence suggests it is easier to report income sources (since most households have few of them) than it is to report consumption (which has many categories and time frames, and consequently is very hard for people to report accurately). In poor countries it is easy to believe that a large proportion of people will find it easier to report consumption than income, since income may fluctuate much more than it does in rich countries and be derived from many sources (including irregular transfers from or to family members outside the household). Of course, in many countries the available distributional information will be constrained by the actual surveys that have been administered. If only consumption surveys are available, that is what the analysis must use; if only income surveys are available, analysts will have to focus on income.

Second, **subtract** (1) Benefits from Other Contributory Systems and (2) Government Direct Transfers (cash and near-cash transfers).

To determine direct taxes paid, information on labor income and property ownership would be necessary. If the survey has consumption data only and does not contain information on labor income, the preferred option is to use an alternate survey that does have data on labor incomes and other characteristics, then map the estimated taxes in the alternate survey back to the primary data set using matching methods.

An alternative, if an alternate survey with reliable labor income data is not available, or if there is no way to reliably match these into the primary data set, is to predict the proportion of Net Market "Income" that comes from wages versus self-employment income. To do this, regress consumption per capita on various household-level variables, including the number of wage earners, average education of wage earners, average age of wage earners, number of self-employed, average education of self-employed, and average age of self-employed. These coefficients can be applied to the corresponding variables in each household to predict the proportion of consumption from wages (this would equal the coefficients for the first three explanatory variables times the values of these variables for the household, divided by their total predicted consumption) and the proportion of consumption from self-employment (this would equal the coefficients for the latter three explanatory variables times the values of these variables for the household). Once the proportion of consumption attributable to wages and self-employment income has been determined, individual income taxes can be estimated to "work backward" to the corresponding prefiscal income, using the rules of the tax rates on wages and self-employment income.

The final option is to use secondary source estimates of direct taxes paid by, for example, consumption decile if they are available and considered reliable.

When only consumption data is available, an alternative to equating consumption to Disposable Income is to attempt to account for savings. Because savings data in developing countries are notoriously bad, we do not attempt to account for savings in the contributory pensions as a deferred income scenario. However, researchers may wish to perform an additional sensitivity analysis in which they do account for savings. If data is available on savings rate by consumption decile (or other population group), one can add the appropriate percentage of imputed savings to households at each consumption decile. Note that when this is done, households' consumption rank should be measured in the same way—to the extent possible—as it was by the secondary source from which the savings rates by decile was obtained. In other words, if the secondary source did not include imputed rent for owner-occupied housing in its consumption variable, researchers should create a new consumption variable to match the secondary source's and determine households' consumption deciles by this new variable, solely for the purpose of allocating indirect taxes (for other calculations, researchers would use the income or consumption variable they had constructed following the instructions in this *CEQ MWB*).

4.2 Underestimation of Beneficiaries

The number of beneficiaries of targeted anti-poverty programs is often underestimated when compared to national accounts. For example, in Brazil, the number of beneficiary households of Bolsa Familia according to the Pesquisa de Orçamentos Familiares is 7.3 million, compared to 12.4 million beneficiary households in 2009 according to the Ministry of Social Development.[67] If the number of beneficiaries according to administrative accounts can be trusted to reflect the true number of beneficiaries (for example, if the government publishes a list of beneficiaries as in Brazil), then the program's coverage and impact will be underestimated by the survey if no correction is made.

Below we recommend a method to adjust for the underestimation of beneficiaries. The choice of whether to use the method will depend on the nature of the program

---

[67] Higgins and Pereira (2014).

and the reliability of national accounts in the country. Ideally, results should be presented both with and without the adjustment as an upper and lower bound on the number of beneficiaries.

To "impute" likely beneficiaries who did not report receiving the benefit, and match the number of beneficiaries in the survey to the number in national accounts, we follow the methodology suggested by Souza, Osorio, and Soares (2011). This method assumes that the beneficiaries who reported receiving the benefit are similar to those who did not report receiving the benefit in terms of the distributions of their incomes and characteristics; if data is available from national accounts or administrative data on the characteristics of all beneficiaries, this assumption can be checked by comparing these characteristics to the ones of the beneficiaries who reported receiving the benefit in the survey. Let the number of recipient households identified using this method be S, and the (larger) number of recipient households in national accounts be N. Finally, let the difference between the number of beneficiaries reported in national accounts and the number reported in the survey be denoted $H \equiv N - S$. The next step is to "identify" the H remaining beneficiary households in the survey. This is done by creating a propensity score for program participation for every household in the survey by running a probit of program participation against household income, possession of various household assets and consumer durables, number of children, race of household head, region or state, rural or urban area, et cetera. Then H households are randomly sampled out of the S beneficiary households, and these H beneficiary households are matched to H nonbeneficiary households with the closest propensity scores. Program benefits are then imputed to the matched households—the amount of benefit imputed is equal to the amount received (reported in the survey) by the household's matched beneficiary household.

Note that for the above method to work, it is necessary that $H < S < N$. It is also necessary that the probit of program participation converges, which means that the method is likely to work for targeted anti-poverty programs such as conditional cash transfers, but unlikely to work for nontargeted programs. In the case of Brazil, the probit converged for the conditional cash transfer program but not the noncontributory pension program, and was thus used for the former anti-poverty program but not the latter.[68] The researcher should also verify that the probit not only converges, but also has sufficiently high predictive power by checking the distribution of the predicted probabilities resulting from the probit.[69]

Sample Stata code to implement this method is included in appendix 6D.

---

[68] See Higgins and Pereira (2014).

[69] A shortcoming of this procedure is that the propensity scores are estimated under the assumption that reported nonparticipants are in fact nonparticipants; however, this is not the case: the entire reason we are undertaking the analysis is that some of the reported nonparticipants must have actually been participants. We are grateful to Gary Burtless for pointing this out.

4.3 Discrepancies between Survey and Administrative Data

Most of the time, totals in surveys for population variables and values of income, consumption, fiscal interventions, and so on will not coincide with totals from administrative accounts. The general principle that we follow is to "believe" in the totals that are in household surveys, unless the teams have a strong reason to think otherwise. First, administrative data on Disposable Income for the household sector may not be available or, if it is, may not be reliable. Second, even if it is, it is not good at telling us what is going on with the incomes of the poor.[70] Suppose the discrepancy comes mostly from surveys failing to capture the richest. We could have everyone in the survey reporting what they actually receive from transfers and accurately reporting their incomes as well, so the absolute amount of transfers matches with the national accounts, but because we are not capturing the rich, total Disposable Income in national accounts is higher than in the survey. If we scale down transfers to make the ratios equal between both sources, we would be falsely deflating the impact of everyone's transfer on their income (both of which they correctly reported). Our recommendation is to look at the absolute amount of the transfer in the survey, not its ratio to Disposable Income; if this is higher than in national accounts, then you have a reason to scale it down so it matches the absolute amount in national accounts (unless you think national accounts have underestimated it for some reason). Also look at the amounts that individual households are reporting from the transfer: Are these amounts accurate given program rules, or are they too high? This is what CEQ authors did in Brazil, and the amounts individual households were reporting was largely accurate according to program rules.

You could make the following counterargument: suppose the household is underreporting income by half and correctly reporting the transfer. Even in this case we think you should not scale down the transfer. Suppose actual Market Income is $1 but the household reports $0.50, and suppose the transfer equals $1 per day, and the poverty line is $1.25. In reality the transfer is pulling it out of poverty, from $1 to $2. If you scale down the transfer, you get income going from $0.50 to $1 as a result of the transfer, whereas if you do not, you would get $0.50 to $1.50 as a result of the transfer. So by scaling down, we do better at estimating the transfer's incidence as a percent of income, but worse at estimating its effect on poverty: we would conclude that transfer did not pull the person out of poverty, but in reality it did! And, conversely, we get the correct result, that the transfer pulled the person out of poverty, when we do not scale it down.

For fiscal interventions in which the totals are NOT in the surveys (for example, VAT, some type of transfers, per capita spending on education and health, and so on), the CEQ methodology recommends scaling down those totals so that ratios between the fiscal intervention of interest and, for example, Disposable Income or private consumption from national accounts equal the ratios for the same variables in the sur-

---

[70] Deaton (2005).

veys. This scaling-down method will yield new totals for the fiscal interventions that need to be analyzed using the imputation method.

For cash transfer programs, the total number of beneficiaries according to the survey is often significantly lower than the total according to national accounts (we are using "national accounts" as a broad term that includes program administrative records, etc.). This occurs even in rich countries.[71] As a result, in a number of CEQ countries, authors have imputed benefits to households that did not report receiving benefits from the program but are similar to households that did receive benefits from the program.[72] The imputation—explained above—uses code adapted from Souza, Osorio, and Soares (2011) included in appendix 6D and causes the number of beneficiary households in the survey to equal the number of beneficiary households from national accounts. This adjustment should be made only if the program administrative accounts are believable (experts agree that they are fairly accurate), as was the case in Brazil.

Regarding the discrepancy in incomes due to underreporting and under-coverage in the upper tail, please see section 1.1.6. above ("Under-Reporting and Top Incomes") and box 6-2.

4.4 Tax Expenditures

Tax expenditures result in people paying less indirect taxes, so they should not be added to income (because that would be double-counting). Nevertheless, if tax expenditures can be estimated reliably, it would be very interesting to analyze their incidence, since tax exemptions are a (sometimes regressive) form of subsidy.

4.5 When the Year of the Survey Does Not Match the Year of Interest of the Analysis

In some countries, household surveys are collected infrequently. When policymakers are interested in a more up-to-date analysis than the year of the available survey, researchers can follow the method proposed in chapter 14 of this Volume for the *CEQ Assessment* for the Dominican Republic. The approach is summarized in box 6-7.

4.6 Infrastructure and Other Public Goods

We do not attempt to impute values for infrastructure and other public goods. Nevertheless, we estimate equity in access to infrastructure (such as electricity, running water, roads). Which components of infrastructure are included here depends on the questions in the survey. To explore alternative approaches, O'Dea and Preston (2012) lay the groundwork for estimating the distributional impact of public goods, but their

---

[71] Meyer and Sullivan (2003).

[72] For example, Higgins and Pereira (2014) for Brazil.

Box 6-7

When the Household Survey Year Is Dated: The CEQ Assessment
for the Dominican Republic

Jaime Aristy-Escuder, Blanca Moreno-Dodson, Miguel E. Sanchez-Martin, and
Maynor Cabrera

Due to a lack of updated household survey data, a set of assumptions was used to estimate the impact of recent policies. The latest household income and expenditure survey, Encuesta Nacional de Ingresos y Gastos de Hogares (ENIGH), was conducted in 2007, and thus the available data do not capture the important policy decisions made between 2007 and 2013. These considerations were incorporated into the CEQ methodology by modifying the major tax rates and bases and by expanding the coverage of direct transfers. The application of the 2013 tax and social program structure to the 2007 survey data enabled a simulation of income and poverty impacts, and 2013 public revenue and spending data were deflated to 2007 prices. Statutory tax rates and income brackets were applied in the estimation of direct tax revenue, similar to other applications of the CEQ methodology (for example, Lustig and others, 2013). Tax evasion assumptions, which were based on discussions with the authorities, were applied only to VAT, not direct or other taxes. This analysis evaluates only the equity effects of the tax system, not its buoyancy or efficiency.

Compared to other country studies using the CEQ methodology, the Dominican Republic is especially challenging because the "departure point," the most recent household income and expenditure survey, dates to 2007. It is necessary to consider that numerous policy decisions were adopted between 2007 and 2013, including the modification of the rates and bases of the main taxes. Furthermore, there has been a notable expansion in the coverage of direct transfers, and the value of certain in-kind transfers, such as education, has been expanded.

In the light of these changes, the methodology applied the tax and public expenditure structures of 2013 to ENIGH 2007. On the tax side, rates and definitions of the 2013 tax base were used. On the expenditure side, the value of the 2013 peso was deflated by the change in the consumer price index (CPI) between 2007 and 2013. In other words, the public revenues and spending vectors of 2013 were used to calculate income poverty—but in 2007 prices. Expenditures were adjusted only for inflation and not by GDP growth. This is because the majority of the recorded public-spending variations were below the growth rate during the period. Overall, the objective was to adapt the CEQ methodology's various definitions of income using the ENIGH 2007 and the public revenue and expenditure structure of 2013, expressed in 2007 prices. We opted for this alternative (instead of inflating to 2013 the variables of the ENIGH 2007) because, besides inflation between 2007 and 2013, relative prices of production factors, structure of employment, and size of households in Dominican Republic could have experienced important changes in income distribution, which we would otherwise not have been able to replicate with available information. The adjustment factor was 42.5 percent inflation between June 2007, the date of the survey, and December 2013.

methods have yet to be implemented empirically as far as we know. See also chapter 4 by Sergei Soares (2022b) in Volume 2 of this Handbook.

4.7 Additional Sensitivity Analyses

We recommend implementing sensitivity analyses and subgroup comparisons to test robustness of results. For example, researchers might test the sensitivity of their results to different assumptions about economies of scale or adult equivalence; to different allocation methods for various tax and transfer programs; to different assumptions about tax avoidance and evasion; to using regression methods versus direct identification for the value of owner-occupied housing; and so on. Subgroup comparisons could compare incidence results by race of the household head, by gender of the household head, by age of the individual (for example, in three groups: below 20, working age 20–65, and retirement age over 65). Other sensitivity analysis will be country-specific (some countries may want to check the implications of adjusting for the underreporting of beneficiaries of a transfer program, using different methods to impute a subsidy, making different assumptions about consumption tax evasion, etc.).

5 Completing Section C of the *CEQ Master Workbook*

The heart of a *CEQ Assessment* is the allocation of taxes and transfers so that one can construct the income concepts for each individual and estimate the impact of fiscal policy on an array of indicators of inequality and poverty both for the system as a whole and by fiscal intervention. Moreover, since one of the key goals of the CEQ Institute was to create a Data Center on Fiscal Redistribution with information that will allow comparisons across countries and over time, painstakingly detailed information on the methods utilized for the allocation process is of the essence. This information should be written up in section C of the *CEQ MWB*. Note that for existing studies, this information is now summarized in the metadata CEQ Metadata Table housed in the CEQ Data Center on Fiscal Redistribution.

Section C of the *CEQ MWB* includes a detailed description of the methodologies used to construct each income concept (sheet C1) and a summary of key assumptions made by the team in the process (sheet C2). In sheet C1 (table 6G-5), Construction of Income Concepts, various income components and fiscal interventions are listed. *CEQ*

Assessment authors should indicate whether these components and fiscal interventions were included in the analysis (column C). In column D, they should indicate which allocation method was used following the taxonomy in section 3.b of this chapter and provide a detailed explanation of the exact process followed. In our experience, authors tend to provide insufficient detail here; the more detail, the better. Columns E through J ask for various statistics about that income component or fiscal intervention, including the total amount received in local currency by all individuals in the survey (using expansion factors, of course) in column E; the share of this as a percent of Disposable Income or private consumption from the survey in column F, where the country authors should specify which of these two was used as the denominator in cell F11 in the online *CEQ MWB* template in part III of this Volume; totals in local currency from administrative accounts in column G; the share of this as a percent of total Disposable Income or private consumption from administrative accounts in column H, where the country authors should specify which of these two was used as the denominator in cell H11; the total population receiving benefits or income from or paying taxes to the particular fiscal intervention or income source based on data from the household survey in column I; the same figure but based on data from administrative accounts in column J; and the total survey's unweighted population receiving benefits or paying taxes in column K.

In sheet C2 in the online *CEQ MWB* in part IV of this Volume (table 6G-6), key assumptions are listed. Specifically, a number of questions are posed in column B of sheet C2 (for example, "Does your survey report income or consumption or both?"), and the answers to these questions should be provided in column C of sheet C2. These answers assist the quality control process by providing the CEQ Institute with information about the survey and assumptions to ensure that the methods employed by the team are the best possible given data constraints and the country-specific context.

Researchers are advised to complete sheets C1 and C2 prior to conducting the analysis (once they have determined the allocation methods and variables from the survey data that will be used for each fiscal intervention and income component) so that these plans can undergo quality control and discussion between the *CEQ Assessment* authors and the CEQ Institute prior to spending the time conducting the analysis.

Acknowledgments

The authors are grateful to Stephen D. Younger for very useful comments on an earlier version of this chapter.

References

Abramovsky, Laura, Orazio Attanasio, Carl Emmerson, and David Phillips. 2011. *The Distributional Impact of Reforms to Direct and Indirect Tax in Mexico. Analytical Report and Results.* Technical Report. External Publications (London: Institute for Fiscal Studies).

Abramovsky, Laura, Orazio Attanasio, and David Phillips. 2012. *The Distributional Impact of Reforms to Direct and Indirect Tax in El Salvador. Analytical Report and Results.* Technical Report. External Publications (London: Institute for Fiscal Studies).

Abramovsky, Laura, and David Phillips. 2015. "LATAX: The Manual" (http://www.ifs.org.uk/uploads/publications/software/LATAX/LATAX%20Manual.pdf).

———. 2022. "Appendix 6C. LATAX: A Multi-Country Flexible Tax Microsimulation Model," in *Commitment to Equity Handbook: Estimating the Impact of Fiscal Policy on Inequality and Poverty*, 2nd. ed., vol. 1, edited by Nora Lustig (Brookings Institution Press and CEQ Institute, Tulane University). Free online version available at www.commitmentoequity.org.

Alm, James, Roy W. Bahl, and Matthew N. Murray. 1991. "Tax Base Erosion in Developing Countries." *Economic Development and Cultural Change* 39, no. 4, pp. 849–72.

Alvaredo, Facundo, Anthony Atkinson, Lucas Chancel, Thomas Piketty, Emmanuel Saez, and Gabriel Zucman. 2016. "Distributional National Accounts (DINA) Guidelines: Concepts and Methods Used in WID.world," WID.World Working Paper 2016/2, June (http://wid.world/document/dinaguidelines-v1/).

Alvaredo, F., L. Chancel, T. Piketty, E. Saez, and G. Zucman. 2018. "Distributional National Accounts in the Context of the WID.World Project," chap. 6 in *For Good Measure: Advancing Research 34 on Well-Being Metrics Beyond GDP*, edited by Martine Durand, Jean-Paul Fitoussi, and Joseph E. Stiglitz, OECD report by the High Level Expert Group on Measuring Economic Performance and Social Progress.

Araar, Abdelkrim, and Paolo Verme. 2012. "Reforming Subsidies: A Toolkit for Policy Simulations." Working Paper 6148 (Washington: World Bank Policy Research).

Aristy-Escuder, Jaime, Maynor Cabrera, Blanca Moreno-Dodson, and Miguel E. Sanchez-Martin. 2022. "The Dominican Republic: Fiscal Policy, Income Redistribution, and Poverty Reduction," chap. 14 in *Commitment to Equity Handbook: Estimating the Impact of Fiscal Policy on Inequality and Poverty*, 2nd ed., Vol. 1, edited by Nora Lustig (Brookings Institution Press and CEQ Institute, Tulane University). Free online version available at www.commitmentoequity.org.

Arunatilake, Nisha, Gabriela Inchauste, and Nora Lustig. 2017. "The Incidence of Taxes and Spending in Sri Lanka," in *The Distributional Impact of Taxes and Transfers: Evidence from Eight Low- and Middle-Income Countries*, edited by Gabriela Inchauste and Nora Lustig (Washington: World Bank).

Atkinson, Anthony B. 2007. "Measuring Top Incomes: Methodological Issues," in *Top Incomes over the Twentieth Century—A Contrast between Continental European and English-Speaking Countries*, edited by A. B. Atkinson, A. B. and T. Piketty (Oxford University Press).

Atkinson, Anthony B., and François Bourguignon. 1990. "Tax-Benefit Models for Developing Countries: Lessons from Developed Countries," in *Tax Policy in Developing Countries*, edited by Javad Khalilzadeh and Anwar Shah (Washington: World Bank).

Atkinson, Anthony B., and Thomas Piketty, eds. 2007. *Top Incomes in the Twentieth Century—A Contrast between Continental European and English-Speaking Countries.* (Oxford University Press).

———. 2010. *Top Incomes. A Global Perspective* (Oxford University Press).

Atkinson, Anthony B., Thomas Piketty, and Emmanuel Saez. 2011. "Top Incomes in the Long Run of History." *Journal of Economic Literature* 49, no. 1, pp. 3–71.

Atkinson, Anthony B., Lee Rainwater, and Timothy M. Smeeding. 1995. "Income Distribution in OECD Countries: Evidence from the Luxembourg Income Study (LIS)." *Social Policy Studies* 18 (Paris: Organization for Economic Cooperation and Development).

Avenir Health. 2014. *Spectrum Manual, Spectrum System of Policy Models: Resource Needs Model* (RNM) (Glastonbury, CT: Avenir Health) (http://avenirhealth.org/Download/Spectrum /Manuals/SpectrumManualE.pdf.)

Bachas, Pierre, Lucie Gadenne, and Anders Jensen. 2020. "Informality, Consumption Taxes and Redistribution." Policy Research Working Paper No. 9267 (World Bank) (https:// openknowledge.worldbank.org/handle/10986/33851 License: CC BY 3.0 IGO).

Bargain, Olivier, Andre Decoster, Mathias Dolls, Dirk Neumann, Andreas Peichl, and Sebastian Siegloch. 2013. "Welfare, Labor Supply and Heterogeneous Preferences: Evidence for Europe and the US." *Social Choice and Welfare* 41, no. 4, pp. 789–817.

Bargain, Olivier, Christina Orsini, and Andreas Peichl. 2014. "Comparing Labour Supply Elasticities in Europe and the US: New Results." *Journal of Human Resources* 49, no. 3, pp. 723–838.

Barofsky, Jeremy, and Stephen Younger. 2022. "Appendix 6F. Comparison of Methods to Value the Distributional Impact of Health Spending," in *Commitment to Equity Handbook: Estimating the Impact of Fiscal Policy on Inequality and Poverty*, 2nd ed., Vol. 1, edited by Nora Lustig (Brookings Institution Press and CEQ Institute, Tulane University). Free online version available at www.commitmentoequity.org.

———. 2022. "The Effect of Government Health Expenditure on Income Distribution: A Comparison of Valuation Methods in Ghana," chap. 1 in *Commitment to Equity Handbook: Estimating the Impact of Fiscal Policy on Inequality and Poverty*, 2nd ed., Vol. 2, edited by Nora Lustig (Brookings Institution Press and CEQ Institute, Tulane University). Free online version available at www.commitmentoequity.org.

Bastagli, Francesca. 2015. "Bringing Taxation into Social Protection Analysis and Planning." Working Paper 421 (London: Overseas Development Institute).

Blanchet, T., I. Flores and M. Morgan. 2018., "The Weight of the Rich: Improving Surveys Using Tax Data," WID.world Working Paper Series No 2018/12, October. To appear in "Finding the Upper Tail," edited by Frank Cowell, Nora Lustig, and Daniel Waldenström, Special issue of the *Journal of Economic Inequality*, forthcoming.

Bourguignon, François, and Amedeo Spadaro. 2006. "Microsimulation as a Tool for Evaluating Redistribution Policies." *Journal of Economic Inequality* 4, no. 1, pp. 77–106.

Brewer, Mike, and Cormac O'Dea. 2012. "Measuring Living Standards with Income and Consumption: Evidence from the UK." Working Paper 12/12 (London: Institute for Fiscal Studies).

Brown, Jeffrey R., Julio Lynn Coronado, and Don Fullerton. 2009. "Is Social Security Part of the Social Safety Net?" NBER Working Paper No. 15070.

Bucheli, Marisa, Nora Lustig, Maximo Rossi, and Florencia Amabile. 2014. "Social Spending, Taxes and Income Redistribution in Uruguay." *Public Finance Review* 42, no. 3, pp. 413–33.

Cabrera, Maynor, Nora Lustig, and Hilcias Moran. 2015. "Fiscal Policy, Inequality and the Ethnic Divide in Guatemala." *World Development* 76 (December), pp. 263–79.

Candia, Bernardo, and Eduardo Engel. 2022. "Taxes, Transfers and Income Distribution in Chiles," in chap. 5 in in The *Commitment to Equity Handbook: Estimating the Impact of Fiscal Policy on Inequality and Poverty*, 2nd ed., Vol. 2, edited by Nora Lustig (Brookings Institution Press and CEQ Institute, Tulane University). Free online version available at www.commitmento equity.org.

CEDLAS (Centro de Estudios Distributivos, Laborales y Sociales at Universidad Nacional de La Plata) and World Bank. 2014. "A Guide to SEDLAC Socio-Economic Database for Latin America and the Caribbean" (http://sedlac.econo.unlp.edu.ar/download.php?file=archivos_upload _items_metodologia/Guide_14_english.pdf).

CEQ Institute. 2022a. "*CEQ Assessment: CEQ Master Workbook*," available online only in part IV of the *Commitment to Equity Handbook: Estimating the Impact of Fiscal Policy on Inequality and Poverty*, 2nd ed., Vol. 1, edited by Nora Lustig (Brookings Institution Press and CEQ Institute, Tulane University). Free online version available at www.commitmento equity.org.

———. 2022b. "Planning for a *CEQ Assessment*: Data and Software Requirements," available online only in part IV of the *Commitment to Equity Handbook: Estimating the Impact of Fiscal Policy on Inequality and Poverty*, 2nd ed., Vol. 1, edited by Nora Lustig (Brookings Institution Press and CEQ Institute, Tulane University). Free online version available at www .commitmentoequity.org.

———. 2022c. "Planning for a *CEQ Assessment*: Recommended Team Composition and Timeline," available online only in part IV of the *Commitment to Equity Handbook: Estimating the Impact of Fiscal Policy on Inequality and Poverty*, 2nd ed., Vol. 1, edited by Nora Lustig (Brookings Institution Press and CEQ Institute, Tulane University). Free online version available at www.commitmentoequity.org.

———. 2022d. "*CEQ Assessment*: Sample Stata Code for Measuring the Indirect Effects of Indirect Taxes and Subsidies," available online only in part IV of the *Commitment to Equity Handbook: Estimating the Impact of Fiscal Policy on Inequality and Poverty*, 2nd ed., Vol. 1, edited by Nora Lustig (Brookings Institution Press and CEQ Institute, Tulane University). Free online version available at www.commitmentoequity.org. Adapted from the International Monetary Fund's (IMF) "Distributional Analysis of Fuel Subsidy Reform (Stata Programs)," available for download from https://www.imf.org/external/np/fad/subsidies/.

———. 2022e. *Commitment to Equity Handbook: Estimating the Impact of Fiscal Policy on Inequality and Poverty*, 2nd ed., vol. 1, edited by Nora Lustig (Brookings Institution Press and CEQ Institute, Tulane University). Free online version available at www.commitmento equity.org.

Coady, David. 2006. "The Distributional Impacts of Indirect Tax and Public Pricing Reforms," in *Analyzing the Distributional Impact of Reforms*, edited by Aline Coudouel and Stefano Paternostro (Washington: World Bank).

Coady, David, Moataz El-Said, Robert Gillingham, Kangni Kpodar, Paulo Medas, and David Newhouse. 2006. "The Magnitude and Distribution of Fuel Subsidies: Evidence from Bolivia, Ghana, Jordan, Mali, and Sri Lanka." Working Paper 06/247 (Washington: International Monetary Fund).

Coudouel, Aline, Jesko Hentschel, and Quentin Wodon. 2002. "Poverty Measurement and Analysis," in *A Sourcebook for Poverty Reduction Strategies. Volume 1: Core Techniques and Cross-Cutting Issues*, edited by Jeni Klugman (Washington: World Bank).

Cowell, Frank A., and Emmanuel Flachaire. 2007. "Income Distribution and Inequality Measurement: The Problem of Extreme Values." *Journal of Econometrics* 141, no. 2, pp. 1044–72.

———. 2015. "Statistical Methods for Distributional Analysis," in *Handbook of Income Distribution*, vol. 2, edited by A. B. Atkinson and F. Bourguignon (North-Holland, Amsterdam: Elsevier).

Cowell, Frank A., Nora Lustig, and Daniel Waldenström. 2022. "Finding the Upper Tail." Special Issue of the *Journal of Economic Inequality* 20, no. 1, March.

Cox, Nick. 2004. "`extremes`: Stata Module to List Extreme Values of a Variable." Boston College Department of Economics, Statistical Software Components S430801.

De Agostini, Paola, Bart Capeau, Andre Decoster, Francesco Figari, Jack Kneeshaw, Chrysa Leventi, Kostas Manios, Alari Paulus, Holly Sutherland, and Toon Vanheukelom. 2017. "EUROMOD Extension to Indirect Taxation: Final Report, EUROMOD Technical Note EMTN 3.0" (Colchester: Institute for Social and Economic Research, University of Essex).

Deaton, Angus. 2005. "Measuring Poverty in a Growing World (or Measuring Growth in a Poor World)." *Review of Economics and Statistics* 87, no. 1, pp. 1–19.

Demery, Lionel. 2003. "Analyzing the Incidence of Public Spending," in *The Impact of Economic Policies on Poverty and Income Distribution*, edited by François Bourguignon and Luis A. Pereira da Silva (World Bank and Oxford University Press).

Ferreira, Francisco H. G., Nora Lustig, and Daniel Teles. 2015. "Appraising Cross-National Income Inequality Databases: An Introduction." *Journal of Economic Inequality* 13, no. 4, pp. 497–526.

Figari, Francesco, and Alari Paulus. 2015. "The Distributional Effects of Taxes and Transfers under Alternative Income Concepts: The Importance of Three 'I's." *Public Finance Review* 43, no. 3, pp. 347–72.

Figari, Francesco, and Holly Sutherland. 2013. "EUROMOD: The European Union Tax-Benefit Microsimulation Model." *International Journal of Microsimulation* 6, no. 1, pp. 4–26.

Finkelstein, Amy, and Robin McKnight. 2008. "What Did Medicare Do? The Initial Impact of Medicare on Mortality and Out of Pocket Medical Spending." *Journal of Public Economics* 92, no. 7, pp. 1644–68.

Flachaire, Emmanuel, Nora Lustig, and Andrea Vigorito. 2021. "Underreporting of Top Incomes and Inequality: An Assessment of Correction Methods Using Linked Survey and Tax Data."

Gertler, Paul, and Jacques van der Gaag. 1990. *The Willingness to Pay for Medical Care: Evidence from Two Developing Countries* (Johns Hopkins University Press).

Goñi, Edwin, J. Humberto Lopez, and Luis Serven. 2011. "Fiscal Redistribution and Income Inequality in Latin America." *World Development* 39, no. 9, pp. 1558–69.

Gruber, Jonathan. 1999. "Social Security and Retirement in Canada," in *Social Security and Retirement Around the World*, edited by Jonathan Gruber and David A. Wise, pp. 73–100. (University of Chicago Press).

Hamermesh, Daniel S., and Albert Rees. 1993. *The Economics of Work and Pay* (New York: Harper Collins College Publishers).

Hammitt, James K., and Lisa A. Robinson. 2011. "The Income Elasticity of the Value per Statistical Life: Transferring Estimates between High and Low Income Populations." *Journal of Benefit-Cost Analysis* 2, no. 1, pp. 1–29.

Hayes, Phillip, and Gerry Redmond. 2014. "Could a Universal Family Payment Improve Gender Equity and Reduce Child Poverty in Australia? A Microsimulation Analysis." Working Paper EM 3/14 (Essex, UK: EUROMOD).

Higgins, Sean. 2022. "Producing Indicators and Results, and Completing Sections D and E of the *CEQ Master Workbook* Using the *CEQ Stata Package*," chap. 8 in *Commitment to Equity Handbook: Estimating the Impact of Fiscal Policy on Inequality and Poverty*, 2nd ed., Vol. 1, edited by Nora Lustig (Brookings Institution Press and CEQ Institute, Tulane University). Free online version available at www.commitmentoequity.org.

Higgins, Sean, Rodrigo Aranda, Caterina Brest Lopez, Ruoxi Li, Beenish Amjad, Patricio Larroulet, Roy McKenzie. 2022. "CEQ Assessment: CEQ Stata Package," in part IV in *Commitment to Equity Handbook: Estimating the Impact of Fiscal Policy on Inequality and Poverty*, 2nd. ed., Vol. 1, edited by Nora Lustig (Brookings Institution Press and CEQ Institute, Tulane University). Available online only at www.ceqinstitute.org.

Higgins, Sean, and Nora Lustig. 2016. "Can a Poverty-Reducing and Progressive Tax and Transfer System Hurt the Poor?" *Journal of Development Economics* 122, pp. 63–75.

Higgins, Sean, Nora Lustig, Whitney Ruble, and Timothy Smeeding. 2015. "Comparing the Incidence of Taxes and Social Spending in Brazil and the United States." *Review of Income and Wealth* 62, no. S1, pp. 22–46.

Higgins, Sean, and Claudiney Pereira. 2014. "The Effects of Brazil's Taxation and Social Spending on the Distribution of Household Income." *Public Finance Review* 42, no. 3, pp. 346–67.

Hill, Ruth, Gabriela Inchauste, Nora Lustig, Eyasu Tsehaye, and Tassew Woldehanna. 2017. "A Fiscal Incidence Analysis for Ethiopia," in *The Distributional Impact of Fiscal Policy: Experience from Developing Countries*, edited by Gabriela Inchauste and Nora Lustig (Washington: World Bank).

Hlasny, Vladimir. 2021a. "Redistributive Effects of Fiscal Policies in Mexico: Corrections for Top Income Measurement Problems." *Latin American Policy* 12, no. 1, pp. 148–80.

———. 2021b. "Parametric Representation of the Top of Income Distributions: Options, Historical Evidence, and Model Selection." *Journal of Economic Surveys* 35, no. 4, pp. 1217–56.

Hlasny, Vladimir, and Paolo Verme. 2016. "Top Incomes and the Measurement of Inequality in Egypt." *The World Bank Economic Review.* lhw031 (https://doi.org/10.1093/wber/lhw031).

Immervoll, Herwig, Henrik J. Kleven, Claus T. Kreiner, and Emmanuel Saez. 2007. "Welfare Reform in European Countries: A Microsimulation Analysis." *Economic Journal* 117, January, pp. 1–44.

Immervoll, Herwig, Horacio Levy, Jose Ricardo Nogueira, Cathal O'Donoghue, and Rozane Bezerra de Siqueira. 2004. "Average and Marginal Effective Tax Rates Facing Workers in the EU. A Micro-Level Analysis of Levels, Distributions and Driving Factors." Working Paper EM6/04 (EUROMOD).

Immervoll, Herwig, and Cathal O'Donoghue. 2002. "Welfare Benefits and Work Incentives: An Analysis of the Distribution of Net Replacement Rates in Europe Using EUROMOD, A Multi-Country Microsimulation Model." Working Paper EM4/01 (EUROMOD).

———. 2009. "Towards a Multi-Purpose Framework for Tax-Benefit Microsimulation: Lessons from EUROMOD." *International Journal of Microsimulation* 2, no. 2, pp. 43–54.

Inchauste, Gabriela, Nora Lustig, Mashekwa Maboshe, Catriona Purfield, Ingrid Woolard, and Precious Zikhali. 2017. "The Distributional Impact of Fiscal Policy in South Africa," in *The Distributional Impact of Fiscal Policy: Experience from Developing Countries*, edited by Gabriela Inchauste and Nora Lustig. (Washington: World Bank).

International Monetary Fund (IMF). 2014. *Government Financial Statistics Manual 2014* (Washington: International Monetary Fund).

Jamison, Dean T., Lawrence H. Summers, George Alleyne, Kenneth J. Arrow, Seth Berkley, Agnes Binagwaho, Flavia Bustreo, and others. 2013. "Global Health 2035: A World Converging within a Generation." *Lancet* 382, no. 9908, pp. 1898–1955.

Jara, H. Xavier, and Alberto Tumino. 2013. "Tax-Benefit Systems, Income Distribution and Work Incentives in the European Union." *International Journal of Microsimulation* 6, no. 1, pp. 27–62.

Jaramillo, Miguel. 2014. "The Incidence of Social Spending and Taxes in Peru." *Public Finance Review* 42, no. 3, pp. 391–412.

Jellema, Jon, Astrid Haas, Nora Lustig, and Sebastian Wolf. 2022. "Uganda: The Impact of Taxes, Transfers, and Subsidies on Inequality and Poverty," chap. 19 in *Commitment to Equity Handbook: Estimating the Impact of Fiscal Policy on Inequality and Poverty*, 2nd ed., Vol. 1, edited by Nora Lustig (Brookings Institution Press and CEQ Institute, Tulane University). Free online version available at www.commitmentoequity.org.

Jellema, Jon, and Gabriela Inchauste. 2022. "Constructing Consumable Income: Including the Direct and Indirect Effects of Indirect Taxes and Subsidies," chap. 7 in *Commitment to Equity Handbook: Estimating the Impact of Fiscal Policy on Inequality and Poverty*, 2nd ed., Vol. 1, edited by Nora Lustig (Brookings Institution Press and CEQ Institute, Tulane University). Free online version available at www.commitmentoequity.org.

Jellema, Jon, Matthew Wai-Poi, and Rythia Afkar. 2017. "The Distributional Impact of Fiscal Policy in Indonesia," in *The Distributional Impact of Fiscal Policy: Experience from Developing Countries*, edited by Gabriela Inchauste and Nora Lustig (Washington: World Bank).

Jenkins, Stephen P. 2017. "Pareto Models, Top Incomes and Recent Trends in UK Income Inequality." *Economica* 84, no. 334, pp. 261–89.

Jenkins, Stephen P., Richard V. Burkhauser, Shuaizhang Feng, and Jeff Larrimore. 2011. "Measuring Inequality Using Censored Data: A Multiple-Imputation Approach to Estimation and Inference." *Journal of the Royal Statistical Society* 174, no. 1, pp. 63–81.

Kolenikov, Stanislav. 2014. "Calibrating Survey Data Using Iterative Proportional Fitting (Raking)." *Stata Journal* 14, no. 1, pp. 22–59.

Korinek, Anton, Johan A. Mistiaen, and Martin Ravallion. 2006. "Survey Nonresponse and the Distribution of Income." *Journal of Economic Inequality* 4 (April), pp. 33–55.

Kremer, Michael, Jessica Leino, Edward Miguel, and Alix Peterson Zwane. 2011. "Spring Cleaning: Rural Water Impacts, Valuation, and Property Rights Institutions." *Quarterly Journal of Economics* 126, no. 1, pp. 145–205.

Lakner, C., and B. Milanovic. 2016. "Global Income Distribution: From the Fall of the Berlin Wall to the Great Recession." *World Bank Economic Review*, 30, no. 2, pp. 203–32 (http://dx.doi.org/10.1093/wber/lhv039).

Li, Ruoxi, and Yang Wang. 2022. "Appendix 6A. Canberra Group: Handbook on Household Income Statistics," in *Commitment to Equity Handbook: Estimating the Impact of Fiscal Policy on Inequality and Poverty*, 2nd ed., Vol. 1, edited by Nora Lustig (Brookings Institution Press and CEQ Institute, Tulane University). Free online version available at www.commitmentoequity.org.

Lietz, Christine, and Daniela Mantovani. 2006. "A Short Introduction to EUROMOD: An Integrated European Tax-Benefit Model." *Research in Labor Economics* 25 (November), pp. 1–26.

Llerena Pinto, Freddy Paul, Maria Christina Llerena Pinto, Roberto Carlos Saa Daza, and Maria Andrea Llerena Pinto. 2015. "Social Spending, Taxes and Income Redistribution in Ecuador." Working Paper 28 (Center for Inter-American Policy and Research, Department of Economics, Tulane University and Inter-American Dialogue).

Little, R. J. A., and D. B. Rubin. 2014. *Statistical Analysis with Missing Data*, 2nd ed., Wiley Series in Probability and Statistics (Hoboken, NJ: John Wiley and Sons, Inc.).

Lustig, Nora. 2019. The "Missing Rich" in Household Surveys: Causes and Correction Approaches CEQ Working Paper 75 (Commitment to Equity (CEQ) Institute, Tulane University).

Lustig, Nora, and Sean Higgins. 2013. "Commitment to Equity (CEQ) Handbook." Working Paper 1 (Commitment to Equity Institute, Tulane University).

———. 2022. "The *CEQ Assessment*: Measuring the Impact of Fiscal Policy on Inequality and Poverty," chap. 1 in *Commitment to Equity Handbook: Estimating the Impact of Fiscal Policy on Inequality and Poverty*, 2nd ed., Vol. 1, edited by Nora Lustig (Brookings Institution Press and CEQ Institute, Tulane University). Free online version available at www.commitmentoequity.org.

Lustig, Nora, and Carola Pessino. 2014. "Social Spending and Income Redistribution in Argentina in the 2000s: The Rising Role of Noncontributory Pensions." *Public Finance Review* 42, no. 3, pp. 304–25.

Lustig, Nora, Carola Pessino, and John Scott. 2014. "The Impact of Taxes and Social Spending on Inequality and Poverty in Argentina, Bolivia, Brazil, Mexico and Peru: An Overview." *Public Finance Review* 42, no. 3, pp. 287–303.

Mani, Anandi, Sendhil Mullainathan, Eldar Shafir, and Jiaying Zhao. 2013. "Poverty Impedes Cognitive Function." *Science* 341, no. 6149, pp. 976–80.

Meyer, Bruce, and James Sullivan. 2003. "Measuring the Well-Being of the Poor Using Income and Consumption." *Journal of Human Resources* 38, Supplement, pp. 1180–220.

Murdoch, Jonathan. 1995. "Income Smoothing and Consumption Smoothing." *Journal of Economic Perspectives* 9, no. 3, pp. 103–44.

Neugschwender, Jörg, and Josep Espasa-Reig. 2022. LIS Technical Working Paper Luxembourg Income Study (LIS). No. 12. Data Access Research Tool (DART) (https://www.lisdatacenter.org/wps/techwps/12.pdf).

O'Dea, Cormac, and Ian Preston. 2012. "The Distributional Impact of Public Spending in the UK." Working Paper 12/06 (London: Institute for Fiscal Studies).

O'Donnell, Owen, Eddy Van Doorslaer, Adam Wagstaff, and Magnus Lindelow. 2008. "Analyzing Health Equity Using Household Survey Data: A Guide to Techniques and their Implementation." WBI Learning Resources Series (Washington: World Bank).

O'Donoghue, Cathal, ed. 2014. *Handbook of Microsimulation* (Bingley: Emerald).

OECD. 2015. *In It Together: Why Less Inequality Benefits All* (Washington: OECD Publishing).

———. 2017. "Terms of Reference: OECD Project on the Distribution of Household Incomes," Income Distribution Database, July (http://oe.cd/idd).

Pacifico, Daniele. 2014. "Sreweight: A Stata Command to Reweight Survey Data to External Totals." *Stata Journal* 14, no. 1, pp. 4–21.

Paz Arauco, Veronica, George Gray Molina, Wilson Jimenez Pozo, and Ernesto Yañez Aguilar. 2014. "Explaining Low Redistributive Impact in Bolivia." *Public Finance Review* 42, no. 3, pp. 326–45.

Piketty, Thomas, and Emmanual Saez. 2007. "How Progressive Is the U.S. Federal Tax System? A Historical and International Perspective." *Journal of Economic Perspectives* 21, no. 1, pp. 3–24.

Popova, Daria. 2013. "Impact Assessment of Alternative Reforms of Child Allowances using RUSMOD—The Static Tax-Benefit Microsimulation Model for Russia." *International Journal of Microsimulation* 6, no. 1, pp. 122–56.

———. 2022. "Appendix 6B. EUROMOD: The Tax-Benefit Microsimulation Model for the European Union," in *Commitment to Equity Handbook: Estimating the Impact of Fiscal Policy on Inequality and Poverty*, 2nd ed., Vol. 1, edited by Nora Lustig (Brookings Institution Press and CEQ Institute, Tulane University). Free online version available at www.commitmentoequity.org.

Rajemison, Harivelo, Steven Haggblade, and Stephen D. Younger. 2003. "Indirect Tax Incidence in Madagascar: Updated Estimates Using the Input-Output Table." Working Paper 147 (Cornell Food and Nutrition Policy Program, Cornell University).

Rossignolo, Dario. 2022. "Argentina: Taxes, Expenditures, Poverty, and Income Distribution," chap. 11 in *Commitment to Equity Handbook: Estimating the Impact of Fiscal Policy on Inequality and Poverty*, 2nd ed., Vol. 1, edited by Nora Lustig (Brookings Institution Press and CEQ Institute, Tulane University). Free online version available at www.commitmentoequity.org.

Sahn, David E., and Stephen D. Younger. 2000. "Expenditure Incidence in Africa: Microeconomic Evidence." *Fiscal Studies* 21, no. 3, pp. 329–47.

Scott, John. 2014. "Redistributive Impact and Efficiency of Mexico's Fiscal System." *Public Finance Review* 42, no. 3, pp. 368–90.

Scott, John, Sandra Martinez-Aguilar, Enrique de la Rosa, and Rodrigo Aranda. 2022. "*CEQ Master Workbook: Mexico (2012)*." Version: February 7, 2018, available online only in part IV of the *Commitment to Equity Handbook: Estimating the Impact of Fiscal Policy on Inequality and Poverty*, 2nd ed., Vol. 1, edited by Nora Lustig (Brookings Institution Press and CEQ Institute, Tulane University). Free online version available at www.commitmentoequity.org.

Soares, Sergei. 2022a. "Appendix 6D. Correcting for Underestimating Number of Beneficiaries," in *Commitment to Equity Handbook: Estimating the Impact of Fiscal Policy on Inequality and Poverty*, 2nd ed., vol. 1, edited by Nora Lustig (Brookings Institution Press and CEQ Institute, Tulane University). Free online version available at www.commitmentoequity.org.

———. 2022b. "The Market Value of Owner-Occupied Housing and Public Infrastructure Services," chap. 4 in *Commitment to Equity Handbook: Estimating the Impact of Fiscal Policy on Inequality and Poverty*, 2nd ed., Vol. 2, edited by Nora Lustig (Brookings Institution Press and CEQ Institute, Tulane University). Free online version available at www.commitmentoequity.org.

———. 2022c. "The Market Value of Public Education: A Comparison of Three Valuation Methods," chap. 2 in *Commitment to Equity Handbook: Estimating the Impact of Fiscal Policy on Inequality and Poverty*, 2nd ed., Vol. 2, edited by Nora Lustig (Brookings Institution Press and CEQ Institute, Tulane University). Free online version available at www.commitmentoequity.org.

Souza, Pedro H. G. F., Rafael G. Osorio, and Sergei Soares. 2011. "Uma metodologia para simular o programa Bolsa Familia." Working Paper (Insituto de Pesquisa Economica Aplicada, Brasilia).

Sutherland, Holly. 2001. "EUROMOD: An Integrated Europan Benefit-Tax Model." Working Paper EM9/01 (EUROMOD).

———. 2014. "Multi-Country Microsimulation," in *Handbook of Microsimulation Modelling*, edited by Cathal O'Donoghue (Bingley: Emerald).

Sutherland, Holly, and Francesco Figari. 2013. "EUROMOD: the European Union Tax-Benefit Microsimulation Model." *International Journal of Microsimulation* 6, no. 1, pp. 4–26.

Sutherland, Holly, Francesco Figari, Orsolya Lelkes, Levy, Horacio, Christine Lietz, Daniela Mantovani, and Alari Paulus. 2008. "Improving the Capacity and Usability of EUROMOD—Final Report." Working Paper EM4/08 (EUROMOD).

United Nations Economic Commission for Europe. 2012. *Canberra Group Handbook on Household Income Statistics. 2011*, 2nd ed. (New York and Geneva: United Nations).

United Nations Development Programme. 2019. *Human Development Report: Beyond Income, Beyond Averages, Beyond Today: Inequalities in Human Development in the 21st Century* (http://hdr.undp.org/sites/default/files/hdr2019.pdf) .

Urzua, Carlos M., ed. 2012. *Fiscal Inclusive Development: Microsimulation Models for Latin America* (Mexico City: Tecnologico de Monterrey).

——. 2022. "Estimating the Value of Education Services," chap. 3 in *Commitment to Equity Handbook: Estimating the Impact of Fiscal Policy on Inequality and Poverty*, 2nd ed., Vol. 2, edited by Nora Lustig (Brookings Institution Press and CEQ Institute, Tulane University). Free online version available at www.commitmentoequity.org.

Viscusi, W. Kip, and Joseph E. Aldy. 2003. "The Value of a Statistical Life: A Critical Review of Market Estimates throughout the World." *Journal of Risk and Uncertainty* 27, no. 1, pp. 5–76.

Wilkinson, Kate. 2009. "Adapting EUROMOD for Use in a Developing Country—The Case of South Africa and SAMOD." Working Paper EM5/09 (EUROMOD).

Younger, Stephen D., and Artsvi Khachatryan. 2017. "Fiscal Incidence in Armenia," in *The Distributional Impact of Taxes and Transfers: Evidence from Eight Low- and Middle-Income Countries*, edited by Gabriela Inchauste and Nora Lustig (Washington: World Bank).

Zarkovic-Rakic, Jelena. 2010. "First Serbian Tax-Benefit Microsimulation Model—SRMOD." *Quarterly Monitor of Economic Trends and Policies in Serbia*, no. 20, January–March.

Zwijnenburg, Jorrit, Sophie Bournot, and Giovannelli Federico. 2017. "OECD Expert Group on Disparities in a National Accounts Framework—Results from the 2015 Exercise." Working Paper No. 76, OECD Statistics Working Paper Series (Paris: Organization for Economic Co-operation and Development), January.

Appendix 6A

Comparing the Definitions of Income Concepts between the United Nations' *Canberra Group Handbook on Household Income Statistics. 2011* and the *CEQ Handbook, Vol. 1*

Ruoxi Li and Yang Wang

The second edition of the *Canberra Group Handbook on Household Income Statistics. 2011* (CGH) establishes a reference for analyzing income distribution statistics across countries.[73] The following review provides a comparison

---

[73] United Nations Economic Commission for Europe (2012). For more information, see http://www.nss.gov.au/nss/home.NSF/pages/NSS%20News%20-%20May%202012%20-%20Canberra%20Group%20Handbook.

of income concepts and methodological assumptions in CGH and Volume 1 of the *CEQ Handbook*.

The most fundamental difference between the two approaches is that CGH does not include consumption taxes and subsidies in the definition of income concepts.

1 Income Definitions, Concepts, and Components

The CGH conceptual definition of total income is "all receipts whether monetary or in kind (goods and services) that are received by the household or by individual members of the household at annual or more frequent intervals, but excludes windfall gains and other such irregular and typically one-time receipts." CGH also excludes receipts that result from a reduction in net worth of a household, with the exception of pension benefits. The *operational* definition of CGH further excludes the value of unpaid domestic services, consumer durables, and social transfers in kind. The practical definition recommended by CGH for international comparison excludes employers' social insurance contribution received and paid, current transfers from nonprofit institutions, and current in-kind transfers from other households compared with the operational definition. The definition of income in CEQ is mostly consistent with the operational definition of CGH but includes in-kind social transfers in the analysis.

The main income concepts established in CGH are total income and disposable income. Adjusted disposable income, primary income, and income from production are also included in the income concept discussion. The four main income concepts constructed in CEQ are Market Income, Disposable Income, Consumable Income, and Final Income.[74] Market Income in CEQ is similar to the operational definition of primary income in CGH except that private transfers (inter-household transfers, for example) are included only in CEQ Market Income. Disposable Income in CEQ in the scenario of contributory pensions as a government transfer is consistent with the operational definition of disposable income in CGH. Final Income in CEQ is similar to adjusted disposable income in CGH, but for a *fundamental difference*: the CEQ definition of Final Income subtracts indirect taxes and adds indirect subsidies.

Both CEQ and the operational definition of CGH income components include paid employment and self-employment income (known as "factor income" in CEQ), property income (known as "income from capital" in CEQ), net (of mortgage payments) value of owner-occupied housing services (known as "imputed rent for owner-occupied housing" in CEQ), and private transfers paid and received. These income components construct Market Income in CEQ (in the scenario of contributory pensions as a government transfer) and form primary income less private transfers paid and received in CGH. The CEQ Market Income in the two scenarios of contributory pensions as deferred income includes contributory pensions and subtracts corresponding contributions. Social assistance and social insurance benefits plus all previous income compo-

---

[74] Lustig and Higgins (2022), chapter 1 in this Volume.

TABLE 6A-1
Comparing Income Components: The Canberra Group and CEQ

Income components	Included in CEQ definition	Included in CGH conceptual definition	Included in CGH operational definition
Employee income	Yes	Yes	Yes
Income from self-employment	Yes	Yes	Yes
Income from financial assets, net of expenses	Yes	Yes	Yes
Royalties	Yes	Yes	Yes
Net value of owner-occupied housing services (imputed rent for owner-occupied housing)	Yes	Yes	Yes
Value of unpaid domestic services	No	Yes	No
Value of services from household consumer durables	No	Yes	No
Social security pensions/schemes	Yes	Yes	Yes
Pensions and other insurance benefits	Yes	Yes	Yes
Social assistance benefits (direct transfers)	Yes	Yes	Yes
Current transfers from nonprofit institutions	Yes	Yes	Yes
Current transfers from other households	Yes	Yes	Yes
Direct taxes, net of refunds	Yes	Yes	Yes
Compulsory fees and fines	Yes	Yes	Yes
Current inter-household transfers paid	Yes	Yes	Yes
Employee's and employers' social insurance contributions	Yes	Yes	Yes
Current transfers to nonprofit institutions	Yes	Yes	Yes
Indirect taxes	Yes	No	No
Indirect subsidies	Yes	No	No
Social transfers in kind (STIK) received	Yes	Yes	No

TABLE 6A-2
Comparing Methodological Assumptions: The Canberra Group and CEQ

Methodological assumptions	CEQ	CGH
	Similar assumptions	
Spatial price differences	Adjustment can be made. Results should be made separately available.	SPI index method is included in discussion.
Treatment of negative income	Adjustment is made.	Included in discussion.
Purchasing power parity	Adjustment is made.	Included in discussion.
Population weighting	Adjustment is made.	Included in discussion.
Construction of indirect taxes through input-output tables	Included in calculation.	Included in discussion.
	Different assumptions	
Public pensions and pension social insurance contributions	Pensions as deferred income scenario: contributory public pensions (or the nonsubsidized component) are treated as part of market income and social insurance contributions are considered not taxes, but lifetime (forced) savings. Pensions as pure government transfer scenario: contributory pensions are treated as government transfers and pension contributions are considered taxes.	Contributory pensions or private funded pensions may represent a form of dissaving.
Employer contributions to social insurance	Employers' contributions are assumed to fall entirely on employees.	In the national accounts, the contributions are treated as part of remuneration.
Equivalence scale	Per capita income in baseline scenario, but some teams use equivalence scales as well.	Several income equivalization methods are included in discussion.
Data source	Surveys as main data sources and administrative accounts as complementary sources when survey data is unreliable.	Administrative income data may be used as an alternative to survey data if suitable data exists.
Missing or zero income	Treats the missing or zero income as zero. Drops the households if the household head's primary	Imputation for missing items is recommended as a common solution.

Methodological assumptions	CEQ	CGH
	income source is missing. House-holds with zero income after applying above procedures are included in both poverty and inequality analyses.	
Dynamic effects	No adjustment is made.	Included in recommendation.
Treatment of imputed rent	Included as part of market income.	Results are suggested to be made separately available.
Measurement of health service transfers in kind	Distribution of aggregate values across individuals according to the health services they indicate as having used in surveys.	Imputation of values based on characteristics of individuals and households rather than the actual use.

	Assumption addressed uniquely by CEQ	
Underestimation of beneficiaries	Adjustment is made.	Not included in discussion.
Discrepancies between survey and administrative data	No adjustment is made.	Not included in discussion.
Grossing up taxes paid by employees	Adjustment is made.	Not included in discussion.
Top coding	Adjustment is made.	Solutions not included in discussion.
Top income under-sampling and under-reporting	No adjustment is made in the main analysis, but methods are discussed so that a sensitivity analysis can be performed.	Not included in discussion.

	Assumption addressed uniquely by CGH	
Relationship matrix	No adjustment is made.	Included in discussion.
PPP choices and comparability across countries and income groups	No adjustment is made.	Included in discussion.
Reference period	No adjustment is made.	Included in discussion.
Adjustment for population weight over extended enumeration period	No adjustment is made.	Included in discussion.

nents, excluding private transfers paid, constitute total income in CGH. Adding private transfers paid, social contributions, direct taxes, and compulsory fees and fines to CGH total income constructs disposable income in CGH. The public transfers are categorized in a much more detailed manner in CEQ because of the different main objectives: while the income components of CGH are categorized to describe the standard of living of households, those of CEQ are constructed to analyze implications of government fiscal policies. Indirect taxes and indirect subsidies are not included in CGH income concepts but are calculated in CEQ. CGH recommends the imputation of social transfers in kind and indirect taxes when analyzing the redistributive effect of government social policies, but indirect taxes as well as indirect subsidies are not included in the income components and concepts.

Table 6A-1 summarizes the differences in income components.

2 Methodology

While CGH is produced for international comparison, it heavily cites examples of developed countries. Meanwhile, CEQ focuses on analyses of low-income and middle-income countries, with very different kinds of data availability and household living conditions.

Table 6A-2 provides a comparison of methodological assumptions applied by CEQ and recommended by CGH.

Appendix 6B

EUROMOD: The Tax-Benefit Microsimulation Model for the European Union

Daria Popova

EUROMOD is a static tax-benefit microsimulation model (MSM) for the European Union, developed and maintained by the Institute for Social and Economic Research at the University of Essex.[75] The construction and development of EUROMOD is documented in a number of publications.[76] The current version of the

---

[75] For more information, see https://www.iser.essex.ac.uk/euromod.

[76] See Figari and Sutherland (2013); Immervoll and O'Donoghue (2009); Lietz and Mantovani (2006); Sutherland (2001); Sutherland and others (2008); Sutherland (2014).

model includes all twenty-eight EU member states. For the majority of countries, it covers policy systems over the period since the mid-2000s to 2017. Both the resulting indicators and the underlying model are openly accessible. Because of its generic structure and flexibility, EUROMOD has been successfully used as a platform on which to build models for non-EU countries, including Australia,[77] Russia,[78] Serbia,[79] South Africa.[80] Models for several other countries[81] in Africa (Ethiopia, Ghana, Mozambique, Tanzania, Zambia) and elsewhere (Ecuador and Vietnam) are being developed.

In general terms, EUROMOD can be used to quantify the consequences, at the micro-level, of changes in tax-benefit policies, given that the characteristics of the underlying population remain constant, and vice versa. By taking full account of interactions among all elements of the tax-benefit system and of the diversity of characteristics in the population, EUROMOD contributes to a better understanding of complex systems, such as contemporary welfare states. Considering several countries over several points in time within the same model framework provides a kind of laboratory for analyzing the effects of similar policy designs in different contexts, and vice versa. In addition, EUROMOD permits analysis at a supranational level (for example for the European Union, the Euro zone, a particular welfare regime, and so on).

In practical terms, EUROMOD represents a software that calculates tax liabilities, benefit entitlements, and disposable income for each micro-unit (individual, family, or household) in a representative sample of the population. Cross-national comparability is provided by using a common, specially developed modeling language, a structured naming convention for variables, and a user interface. When a user runs EUROMOD, the executable reads the policy rules stored in the user interface, applies them to the input micro-data, and produces an individual level output data file containing relevant information from the input data and the tax-benefit simulation, which can be further analyzed using any statistical software. Some preliminary analysis can be performed directly from the user interface (for example summary statistics, marginal tax rates, labor market adjustments, intertemporal policy effects, and so on).

Although EUROMOD aims to simulate as many components of household disposable income as possible, due to data constraints, not all taxes and social benefits are currently simulated. Instruments that are simulated in all countries are cash

---

[77] Hayes and Redmond (2014).

[78] Popova (2013).

[79] Zarkovic-Rakic (2010).

[80] Wilkinson (2009).

[81] See https://www.wider.unu.edu/project/southmod-simulating-tax-and-benefit-policies-development.

transfers, direct taxes, and social insurance contributions. Non-cash transfers are be-yond the scope of the model, although they can be potentially accounted for within the EUROMOD framework.[82] Indirect taxes have been simulated for a selection of countries.[83] The labor market income and other non-simulated income sources (for example, pensions) are taken directly from the micro-data and uprated, if necessary, based on the data about average growth by income source taken from external statistics. The input micro-data for simulations are derived from the EU Survey of Income and Living Conditions (EU-SILC). All simulated and non-simulated variables used in the model and the resulting inequality and poverty measures are validated by using external sources (administrative data, National Accounts, Eurostat, and so on). The model is updated annually in collaboration with national experts from each EU member state.

In the baseline EUROMOD simulations (for example, Macovec and Tammik, 2017) the disposable income is calculated as the sum of original income (gross earnings, private pensions, income from capital, private transfers, in-kind income) and governmental transfers (public pensions, non-means-tested benefits, and means-tested benefits) minus direct taxes (income tax, property taxes) and social insurance contributions (SIC) paid by employees and the self-employed (employers' SIC are simulated but they are not shifted to the employees). It is important to stress, however, that EUROMOD is very flexible and that a user can create a new scenario in which income concepts can be adjusted according to his or her research needs.

Being a static microsimulation model, EUROMOD is intended primarily for the assessment of the first-round effects of changes in taxes and benefits on income distribution. Under certain conditions (namely, if the reform is causing "marginal" changes in the budget constraint faced by agents, and all agents are optimizing under their sole budget constraint), the output of the static model might be a good approximation of a final policy effect.[84] In addition to this, several studies have used EUROMOD as a platform for the analysis of behavioral changes, following the implementation of a policy reform, in particular changes in work incentives and in labor supply.[85]

Table 6B-1 summarizes the main differences in assumptions applied by CEQ and EUROMOD's baseline simulations.

---

[82] Figari and Paulus (2015).

[83] De Agostini and others (2017).

[84] Bourguignon and Spadaro (2006).

[85] See Immervoll and others (2007); Bargain and others (2013); Bargain, Orsini, and Peichl (2014); Immervoll and others (2004); Immervoll and O'Donoghue (2002); Jara and Tumino (2013).

Comparing CEQ and EUROMOD Definitions and Methodological Assumptions

Assumptions	CEQ	EUROMOD's baseline simulations
Public pensions and pension social insurance contributions	Pensions as deferred income scenario: contributory public pensions (or the nonsubsidized component) are treated as part of market income and social insurance contributions are considered not taxes, but lifetime (forced) savings. Pensions as pure government transfer scenario: contributory pensions are treated as government transfers; pension contributions are considered taxes.	All public pensions are treated as government transfers; contributions are treated as a tax and deducted from gross market income.
Employer contributions to social insurance	Employers' contributions are assumed to fall entirely on employees.	Employers' contributions are not shifted to employees and not considered in the analysis, although they are simulated.
Consumption taxes and subsidies	Included and are assumed to be shifted forward to consumers.	Not included in general.
In-kind transfers (education, healthcare)	Included.	Not included in general.
Allocation methods	Direct identification. If information is not directly available in microdata, then other methods such as those described in this chapter.	Simulation. The information is taken directly from the data only if full or at least partial simulation is impossible due to data constraints.
Economic incidence instead of statutory (for example unreported earnings, tax evasion, non-take-up of means-tested benefits)	Included whenever possible.	Included whenever possible, but can be switched off.
Behavioral effects	Not explicitly modeled, but the incidence exercise acknowledges their existence, especially regarding the treatment of pensions: the counterfactual market income in the case of contributory pensions is not zero income for the pensioner, but is the private savings alternative; for consumption taxes, it relies on effective rates and not statutory ones; and, so on.	Not explicitly modeled but are acknowledged. For instance, the model computes MTRs (Marginal Tax Rates).
General equilibrium effects	Not included.	Not included.

(continued)

TABLE 6B-1   (continued)

Assumptions	CEQ	EUROMOD's baseline simulations
Dynamic effects	Not included.	Not included.
How the policy impact is calculated	Mainly average incidence; a few cases with marginal incidence.	Marginal incidence.
Equivalence scale	Per capita income in baseline scenario but some teams use equivalence scales as well.	Equivalized income (the modified OECD equivalence scale).

Appendix 6C

LATAX: A Multi-Country Flexible Tax Microsimulation Model

Laura Abramovsky and David Phillips

LATAX is a multi-country flexible microsimulation model developed by researchers from the Institute for Fiscal Studies (IFS) for the analysis of VAT, excise duties, income tax, and social security contributions, as well as (non-means-tested) price subsidies and (means-tested) cash benefits using a representative cross-section of households from a household survey.[86] It can quantify the revenue and distributional impact of tax reforms under both the assumption that individuals do not change their behavior as a consequence of changes in taxes and the assumption that individuals react to these changes along specific margins. In particular, it has a built-in demand system that can estimate households' consumer spending responses to indirect tax changes; it can also vary the assumptions about the extent to which individuals change their labor supply and the extent to which firms change their final pricing and compensation strategy when taxes change. This allows the sensitivity testing of results to varying behavioral assumptions, helping better inform the policymaking process.

So far, LATAX has been used to assess reforms in Mexico, El Salvador, and Colombia. It is designed to allow researchers with a basic understanding of the statistical software Stata (in which LATAX is written) but limited previous experience of micro-

---

[86] For more information, please see Abramovsky and Phillips (2015).

simulation modeling to adapt it for use in other countries with similar tax and transfer systems. It is designed to be user-friendly, with a separation of the core code, which simulates the tax system, from the main interface module, where the user sets simulation options, file names, directories, and so on, and parameter modules, where the user sets the tax and transfer rates and rules he or she wishes to model. LATAX produces individual and household level data on incomes, expenditures, tax payments and transfer receipts, and summary revenue and distributional tables (such as gains and losses by deciles of the income or expenditure distribution).

LATAX is available for download from the website of the Institute for Fiscal Studies, with an accompanying instruction manual.[87] Please also see the background papers explaining the application of the model to Mexico[88] and El Salvador.[89]

Appendix 6D

Correcting for Underestimating Number of Beneficiaries

The code below to correct for underestimating the number of beneficiaries can also be downloaded from https://github.com/skhiggins/CEQStataPackage /blob/master/handbook_code/correct_underestimate.do.

```
* SAMPLE STATA CODE TO ADJUST FOR UNDERESTIMATION OF
     // BENEFICIARIES
* (Example uses numbers for Bolsa Familia in Brazil)
* Code adapted from code for Souza, Osorio, Soares (2011),
     // provided by Sergei Soares

* preliminaries
scalar S = 7320188 // number of beneficiary households
                   // according to survey
scalar N = 12370915 // number of beneficiary households
                    // according to national accounts
```

---

[87] See Abramovsky and Phillips (2015).

[88] Abramovsky and others (2011).

[89] Abramovsky, Attanasio, and Phillips (2012).

```
scalar H=N-S
scalar prop=H/S // proportion of beneficiaries who reported
                // that needs to be randomly sampled and
                // matched to non-reporters
gen transfer1_h_rep=transfer1_h
    // transfer1_h is a variable with the benefit accruing
    // to the household, and equals that value for all
    // members of the household, not just the member that
    // directly received the benefit

* if dataset is individuals, collapse to households:
tempfile original
save `original', replace
drop if head !=1 // where head==1 denotes household head
    // note other household vars such as dummy for existence
    // of children in household must have already been
    // constructed

* matching
assert !missing(transfer1_h)
generate beneficiary=(transfer1_h>0)
probit beneficiary lny nmemb child age i.race i.state ///
    urban car [pw=s_weight] if incl==1
predict phat if incl==1, p
table beneficiary, c(mean phat p10 phat p25 phat p75 ///
    phat p90 phat)
    // the line above checks distribution of predicted
    // probabilities;
    // the researcher should look at its results
set seed 48490251 // can be any number; set seed so random
                  // sampling of beneficiary HHs doesn't
                  // change upon re-running do file
                  // Randomly sample from beneficiaries the
```

```stata
                        // proportion we need to impute
                        // (then we will match them with most
                        // similar non-beneficiaries)
gen selec=(runiform()<=prop) if beneficiary==1 & phat!=.
tempfile households
save `households', replace
keep if selec==1 | (beneficiary==0 & phat!=.)
        // selec==1 are randomly sampled beneficiaries;
        // (beneficiary==0 & phat!=.) are the "donor pool" of
        // non-beneficiaries from which we will select
        // households to impute benefits to
keep hh_code selec beneficiary phat transfer1_h*
gsort-beneficiary-phat
gen simben=(selec!=.)
gen n=.
count if beneficiary==1
forvalues i=1/`r(N)' { // For each of the randomly selected
                        // beneficiary households
  quietly {
      // Calculate difference between predicted probability
      // of receiving program between each non-beneficiary
      // household and the `i'th beneficiary household
      gen double abs = abs(phat-phat[`i']) if simben==0
      // Then select the closest non-beneficiary household
      // and impute benefits (replace simben = 1)
      summarize abs
      replace simben = 1 if abs==r(min)
      replace n = `i' if abs==r(min)  // n tells you which
                                      // household
                                      // they matched with

      // Then give them the same transfer as the matched
      // household
```

```
        replace transfer1_h=transfer1_h[`i'] if abs==r(min)
        drop abs
  }
}
keep if simben==1 & beneficiary==0 // only keep new imputed
                                   // beneficiaries;
        // we will merge them back in to original data set
rename transfer1_h transfer1_h_imp // to be clear it is the
                                   // imputed value for these
                                   // households
keep hh_code transfer1_h_imp simben
tempfile imputed
save `imputed', replace
        // Now return to original data set to merge in transfer
        // values for "imputed beneficiaries"
use `households',
clear
sort hh_code
merge hh_code using `imputed'
drop _merge
        // Imputation flag:
generate transfer1_is_imputed=(transfer1_h==0 & ///
        simben==1 & beneficiary==0)
        // Replace the transfer value (of 0) with the simulated
        // value for those households:
replace transfer1_h=transfer1_h_imp ///
        if transfer1_is_imputed==1
keep hh_code transfer1_h*
save `households', replace
use `original', clear
drop transfer1_h
merge m:1 hh_code using `households'
drop _merge
```

Appendix 6E

Definition of Household: Sensitivity Tests

Table 6E-1, provided by the Centro de Estudios Distributivos Laborales y Sociales at Universidad Nacional de La Plata (CEDLAS), shows that poverty and inequality results are not very sensitive to the definition of the household (the choice of whether to exclude renters, domestic servants, and their families; to include them as separate households; or to include them as part of the main household).

TABLE 6E-1
Poverty and Inequality with Different Household Definitions

	Households	Observations (individuals)	Members	Average household per capita income	Average household income	Poverty $US2.50 (per day; 2005 PPP)	Poverty $US4.00 (per day; 2005 PPP)	Gini
Argentina 2011								
SEDLAC	34,298	110,785	3.163	2,340.13	7,391.39	4.7	10.8	0.423
Alternative 1	34,298	110,850	3.164	2,337.96	7,400.84	4.7	10.9	0.423
Alternative 2	34,359	110,850	3.158	2,340.21	7,391.13	4.7	10.8	0.422
Brazil 2011								
SEDLAC	117,796	346,021	3.024	824.16	2,487.60	12.6	24.5	0.527
Alternative 1	117,796	346,797	3.031	824.53	2,494.24	12.6	24.4	0.527
Alternative 2	118,453	346,807	3.015	824.56	2,481.36	12.6	24.4	0.527
Mexico 2010								
SEDLAC	27,665	104,493	3.873	2,720.75	10,525.58	12.5	28.0	0.474
Alternative 1	27,665	104,633	3.878	2,717.32	10,525.58	12.5	28.0	0.473
Alternative 2	27,771	104,585	3.862	2,724.90	10,523.00	12.5	28.0	0.474

Source: Centro de Estudios Distributivos Laborales y Sociales at Universidad Nacional de La Plata (2014)

Alternative 1: including domestic servants, their families and renters as household members of the main household.
Alternative 2: domestic servants, their families, or renters as separate households.

Appendix 6F

Comparing Methods to Estimate the Value of Public Health Spending to Its Beneficiaries

Jeremy Barofsky and Stephen D. Younger

This appendix describes four general approaches to valuing the in-kind benefits from public health spending: the average cost approach described in the text of this chapter; willingness-to-pay; health outcomes; and financial risk reduction. Each has advantages and disadvantages, which we highlight. The exercise is complicated by the fact that government health spending is used for a wide variety of health services, including consultations to diagnose medical problems; treatments to address them; information about preventing health problems; medical interventions to prevent health problems; and public health activities like vector control. Moreover, the mere existence of publicly provided health services, funded by general taxation or social insurance contributions, distributes the financial burden of health shocks across the population and so generates insurance value.

In theory, each of the four approaches could treat most or all of these services. In practice, the limitations of the data typically available to an applied researcher mean that each method deals with only some of the services, and it does so with varying degrees of theoretical plausibility and requires more or less sophisticated statistical methods.

1 Average Cost

The average cost approach is by far the most common in benefit incidence analyses and is described in detail in the text of this chapter. We treat the *actual use* and the *insurance value* approach to the average cost method separately.

1.1 Average Cost and Actual Use

The first and most common approach assumes that the value to the recipient of an in-kind health service provided by government is equal to its cost of provision. This variant assigns benefits to actual users of publicly funded health services and nothing to those who do not use them.

The strength of the average cost approach is its ease of implementation. Almost all countries have survey data describing respondents' use of health services, distinguish public from private provision, and have the budgetary information required to calculate spending per patient.

A second strength, in theory, is that this approach can capture the variation in the cost of many different publicly funded health services, thus, for example, assigning large benefits to those having open heart surgery, and small ones to those having a cough diagnosed. In practice, though, most surveys do not ask for much detail on the type of healthcare a respondent received, thereby limiting our ability to get such fine variation. In addition, administrative data often do not include sufficient detail to calculate spending per patient by type of care. In practice, most incidence analyses look only at broad aggregates of services such as inpatient versus outpatient, perhaps broken out by the type of provider.

The main weakness of the average cost approach is that there is no reason to suppose that the value of publicly provided healthcare to its beneficiaries is similar to what government spends to provide it. Revealed preference tells us only that the service is worth more to the recipient than any co-pay or user fee she must make, which might be zero. Governments can spend money inefficiently and corruptly or provide low quality care, thereby increasing the cost of provision to greater than its value to recipients, and beneficiaries will still use the service because they pay less than the full cost. On the other hand, many healthcare services have the unusual characteristic that the marginal benefit of the first unit is high while that of the second is low or zero. A first consultation to diagnose a sinus infection is valuable; a second is worth much less. The same is true for vaccinations, many surgeries, and infectious disease treatments. So the value to the beneficiary of the first and only health service consumed can be greater than its cost, but she will not demand a second unit of the same service. In such instances, the average cost approach will underestimate recipients' benefits.

An extension of this criticism is that the average cost method assumes that all beneficiaries of the same aggregated service value it equally. But clearly one's circumstances matter. Crucially for an incidence analysis, one of those circumstances is income. In addition, the quality of care at different facilities may vary substantially, something the average cost approach ignores.

1.2 Average Cost and Insurance Value

The insurance value method is even easier to implement. It requires information on total health spending from the budget and the total number of eligible citizens in the country. For public health providers, that is usually the entire population. For social insurance systems, it is usually only those who contribute to the system and perhaps their families. In the survey data used for *CEQ Assessments*, we need an indicator of only who is eligible to benefit from that spending, and not even that, if it is the entire population.

In addition to its simplicity, this method has the potential advantage of including all public spending on health, not just that associated with care offered to identifiable beneficiaries, though in practice public goods like vector control, clean water, and sanitation are usually ignored. And implicitly it takes into account variation in need for health services: when the actual use approach increases a beneficiary's Final Income by the value of the healthcare received, it ignores the fact that the health problem necessitating the healthcare may have lowered the beneficiary's welfare, i.e., that she had greater need. The insurance value approach avoids this problem by allocating spending equally across eligible individuals.

Beyond the limitations discussed in the previous section, all of which apply here, an important disadvantage of the insurance value approach is its assumption that all eligible people have equal access to publicly funded healthcare.[90] In many countries, rural populations are both poorer and have a more difficult time accessing health services concentrated in cities. Even if de jure they have an equal right to publicly funded health services, de facto they have less access. In such situations, the insurance value approach will overestimate the equality of healthcare benefits.

2 Willingness to Pay

In economic theory, a monetary measure of the value of a price change to a consumer is the amount of money she would have to give or take to leave her utility equal to its level before the price change. This is the compensating variation (CV), and for a decrease in price, the CV measures how much the user is "willing to pay" for that decrease. If we view publicly funded health services as a price change from their cost of provision to what the user actually pays, then the CV of that price change is an effective measure of its value to users. Compensating variations can be derived from demand functions, so if we can estimate the demand for the healthcare services that government pays for, we can derive a valid monetary value for that service.

This approach has an important advantage over the average cost of provision insofar as it anchors the estimate of the value of care in consumers' preferences and behavior. In addition, because the demand estimates can be conditional on consumers' characteristics, the value we estimate can vary across the population according to those characteristics, including income and need for health services. But as with all the approaches, willingness to pay has limitations.

Conceptually, this approach is applicable only to services that are private goods because we must observe consumer choice to make this estimate. Practically, using survey data to estimate the demand for healthcare services is an order of magnitude more effort than that of the average cost approaches. There certainly are studies that estimate the demand for healthcare services with the single cross-section of data used for a *CEQ Assessment*, but those surveys typically have extra information on the quality of services, usually from a separate survey of healthcare facilities to which the household

---

[90] Indeed, the main concern of many early health incidence studies was to identify lack of access. This is probably why most incidence studies using the average cost approach employ the actual use variation.

survey respondents have access.[91] Because price and quality are correlated, we need good controls for quality to keep it from confounding the estimate of the price's effect on demand. Indeed, a skeptical econometrician could easily cast doubt on whether this approach can successfully estimate ("identify") the demand elasticity. In addition, as in the average cost approach, while it is theoretically possible to estimate willingness to pay for many different publicly funded health services, in practice we are forced to aggregate those services into a few groups, which we assume have the same value. A final criticism of this method is that if there is high income elasticity for healthcare, willingness to pay values health services lower for the poor, who are less able to pay, than the non-poor.

3 Health Outcomes

All of the methods discussed above estimate the value of publicly funded healthcare with information on *spending* by government and/or healthcare consumers, but the real value of publicly funded healthcare services is in the improved health outcomes they produce. Of course, a rational consumer's willingness to pay for healthcare should be closely related to the value of that care's outcomes, but given the limits to consumer sovereignty in healthcare generally, and particularly in low-income settings, many of the rational model's assumptions do not hold. Low-income households experience liquidity constraints that impede decision-making[92] and lack information, or the education to process information, on the returns to healthcare. The limited studies in the developing world that measure willingness to pay find values lower by several orders of magnitude, than estimates in high-income countries.[93] This contradiction between high health burdens (and therefore returns) and low willingness to pay challenges the rational model.

The health outcomes approach begins with an estimate of the effect of healthcare spending on mortality. This estimate must come from a source other than the household survey used for *CEQ Assessments*,[94] typically a medical or epidemiological study whose main purpose is to identify that effect. Since this is a major undertaking, a *CEQ Assessment* must find such estimates in secondary sources. Study results from one nation could be transferred to another, particularly if the two countries share similar socioeconomic, environmental, and disease transmission characteristics. Another option is the Spectrum system of policy models that allows researchers and

---

[91] Gertler and van der Gaag (1990) is the seminal application in developing countries.

[92] Mani and others (2013).

[93] Kremer and others (2011).

[94] Income/expenditure or living standards surveys do not usually ask about mortality, and even when they do, they do not ask about healthcare the deceased may or may not have received.

policymakers to estimate the impact of health interventions on mortality for HIV, malaria, a series of childhood diseases, and cardiovascular conditions.[95]

With these mortality estimates in hand, we then calculate the monetary value of the estimated reduction in mortality using the literature on the *value of a statistical life* (VSL).[96] That literature examines the behavior of people who systematically and voluntarily increase their mortality risk by, say, pursuing an occupation like policing or coal mining, and the additional income they earn for accepting that risk. That additional pay divided by the increased mortality risk gives an estimate of the VSL, which can be understood as the sum of what a cohort would pay for risk reductions that equal one statistical life.

While most survey data used for a *CEQ Assessment* are sufficient to estimate simple wage equations with variables to indicate the premium for risky professions, they do not have sufficient data to estimate the mortality probabilities associated with those professions, so here, too, the health outcomes approach needs secondary sources. The literature estimates that VSL varies substantially with a country's GDP per capita. Hammitt and Robinson (2011) indicate that a reasonable value for a mortality risk reduction of 0.01 percent at age thirty-five is 1.8 percent of annual GDP per capita. This value is then adjusted for remaining life expectancy to give greater values for a child's life saved. VSL has been used to monetize the value of changes in mortality across countries in the developing world.[97]

The most important advantage of the health outcomes approach is the way it deals with health expenditures that have extremely high rates of return in terms of improved health.[98] By estimating an expenditure's benefit rather than the cost to provide it, the health outcomes approach more accurately estimates the impact of health spending and its incidence. This is especially true for spending on public goods, which this method can handle—another advantage.

A disadvantage of this approach is the need for secondary sources to estimate the effect of healthcare services on mortality and the value of a statistical life. If these are not available locally, we may have to import results from other countries with the consequent decrease in credibility.

A second disadvantage of the health outcomes approach is that it may be able to capture the value of only bits and pieces of healthcare spending—those parts for which we can find a secondary source that estimates their impact on mortality. This might be overcome by estimating the effect of all healthcare spending (and similarly, all spending on public goods affecting health) with data that vary over time.[99] Alternatively, for systems like social insurance that do not have universal eligibility, we might esti-

---

[95] Avenir Health (2014).

[96] Viscusi and Aldy (2003).

[97] Jamison and others (2013).

[98] Incidence analyses usually ignore positive (or negative) rates of return to public spending.

[99] For example, many countries have Demographic and Health Surveys spanning three decades.

mate the effect of all social insurance health spending by comparing the mortality out-comes of those in and out of the system at a single point in time. But this approach cannot work for services with universal access. As with the willingness to pay approach, these efforts are an order of magnitude more demanding than the average cost approach.

4 Financial Risk Protection

All public spending on health provides insurance to eligible beneficiaries. This is ob-vious in the case of social insurance schemes, but is equally true of generally provided health services available to all. Both tax everyone and provide benefits to those who draw unfortunate outcomes (fall ill). Since most people are risk averse, this insurance has value to them over and above the cost of providing the health services or the value of their health outcomes. As such, this approach identifies an additional benefit of pub-lic health spending to be added to any of the previous approaches.

To calculate the benefit of financial risk protection, we first estimate what a per-son's risk of spending on healthcare would be in the absence of public provision, and then subtract that spending from her actual income to get a distribution of her net in-come. In countries where only part of the population has access to publicly funded healthcare (as in a social insurance system), we can estimate this difference by com-paring the health spending of those inside and outside the system, usually using the same survey data used for the *CEQ Assessment*. Another option is to examine changes in access to publicly funded health services over time to see how they change the dis-tribution of private health spending.

We then use a stylized risk-averse utility function to evaluate the gain in utility from reduced risk attributable to government health insurance.[100] This is calculated by comparing the distribution of household health spending against the counterfac-tual distribution without coverage. The value of risk reduction is calculated using the change in a household's risk premium with and without coverage. The risk premium represents the quantity of money a risk-averse household would be willing to pay to completely insure against a given set of health shocks. For greater health risks and higher levels of risk aversion, the value of financial risk protection increases.

Because this approach does not need to be traded off against the others, the only consideration in using this method is whether the additional effort required to esti-mate households' counterfactual health spending is worthwhile.

---

[100] Finkelstein and McKnight (2008).

Appendix 6G

The CEQ Master Workbook: Contents

TABLE 6G-1

Sheet B1 of *CEQ Master Workbook*: General Survey Information

	Country:
	Year:
Survey information	
Survey name	
Acronym	
Year	
Link to microdata	
Observations	
Coverage (for example, national or urban only)	
Representative at	
Nonresponse rate	
Data on income and consumption	
Does the survey contain both income and consumption data?	
Consumption or income based analysis?	
Which of the following income components are included in the survey?	
Labor income: wages, salary, self-employment income, commission, tips, vacation pay, overtime bonuses, fringe benefits	
Business income: non-farm and farm income	
Retirement income	
Corporate income: interest, dividends	
Gross property income	

Contributory old-age pensions, survivor's benefits, disability	
Private pensions	
Remittances	
Alimony received	
Child support received	
Other private transfers	
Are both payments in cash and payments in kind accounted for in the survey?	
Are the total amounts of national income coming from each of the above sources available in national accounts or administrative data?	
What is the recall period for consumption?	
Does the survey's consumption data include a question about how each good was obtained, with one of the options being produced for own consumption?	
If not, is there a question about the value of goods produced for own consumption?	
If not, how will auto-consumption be estimated?	
Does the survey include a question for home owners about the estimated rental value of their home such as "If you were renting out this home, how much would you charge?" or "If you were renting this home, how much would you expect to pay?"	
If so, please comment on the reliability of these estimates.	
If not, does the survey ask renters how much they pay in rent per month? If so, what other variables could be used in a regression to predict rental values for owner occupiers?	
Definition of household	
Unit of analysis (individuals/households)	
Treatment of missing or zero Incomes	
Treatment of top coding	

(*continued*)

Treatment of outliers and extreme values	
Do you make corrections for under-reporting/under-sampling for top incomes? Explain.	
Do you adjust for Adult Equivalence or Economies of Scale within households? If your answer is yes, describe the scale that you used.	
Do you use spatial price adjustments? Describe the adjustments that you made.	
Are the income variables expressed in annual terms? Describe the main assumptions that are used to annualize.	
Contributory Pensions	
Contributory pensions programs included:	
Portion of pensions that are subsidized:	
Source of estimations:	
Direct taxes and contributions	
Are wages and salaries reported gross of tax or net of tax?	
Is revenue collection carried out primarily by the federal/central government, or are state/provincial and municipal taxes important in the assessed country as well?	
What direct taxes exist in the assessed country? Potential direct taxes include:	
Individual income taxes paid by employee	
Individual income taxes paid by employer	
Payroll taxes	
Corporate income taxes	
Property taxes	
Others	
Which of the above direct taxes are included in the survey?	

Of those that are not, which can be inferred/imputed/simulated? See the methods described in chapter 6 in Volume 1 of this Handbook. Which method will be used?	
How prevalent is informality and tax evasion in the assessed country? For the direct taxes that are not taken from the survey, what questions in the survey can be used to help identify which workers most likely worked in the informal sector or evaded direct taxes?	
Are total amounts of revenue collected from each of these taxes available in national accounts or administrative data?	
How is taxable income defined?	
Do these totals include revenues at the federal/central government level only, or at the state/provincial and municipal levels as well?	
What public contributions exist in the assessed country? Potential contributions include:	
Contributions to the contributory pension system	
Contributions to the contributory public health insurance system	
Contributions to publicly run unemployment insurance systems, etc.	
Other contributions	
Which of the above contributions are included in the survey?	
If included in the survey, are contributions to the contributory pension system contained in a separate question from the other types of contributions?	
Are social contributions paid by employers included?	
Of those that are not included, which can be inferred/imputed/simulated? See the methods described in chapter 6 in Volume 1 of this Handbook. Which method will be used?	
Are total amounts collected from each of these contributions available in national accounts or administrative data?	
Is alternate assumption used regarding compliance/evasion on social security contributions?	

(continued)

Direct transfers	
Do the following direct transfers exist in the assessed country?	
Non-contributory pension programs	
Conditional cash transfer programs	
Unconditional cash transfer/minimum income programs	
Unemployment benefits	
Cash transfers to farmers	
Publicly funded scholarships	
Other government cash transfers/welfare assistance programs	
Food transfers	
School lunch programs	
Other food/nutrition programs	
Which of the above direct transfers are included in the survey?	
Of those that are not included in the survey, which can be inferred/imputed/simulated? See the methods in Higgins and Lustig (2022). Which method will be used?	
Are total benefits paid by the program (not total spending including administrative costs) available in national accounts or administrative data?	
If not, is total spending (including administrative costs) available in national accounts or administrative data? Are estimates of the size of administrative costs of the program available, either from the government or from secondary sources?	
Are cash transfer programs administered mainly by the federal/central government, or are cash transfers at the state/provincial and municipal levels important as well?	
Are some methods to correct for under-/over-estimation of beneficiaries of direct transfers applied? If yes, explain.	

Indirect subsidies	
Which of the following consumption items are subsidized (for at least a subset of the population) in the assessed country:	
Fuel: gasoline, diesel, natural gas	
Electricity	
Water	
Food	
Communication	
Transportation	
Manufacturing	
Farming inputs	
Interest rates for farmers	
Other agricultural subsidies	
For each of the subsidies in the assessed country, who is eligible to receive the subsidy?	
Is the total spent on each of these subsidies available in national accounts or administrative data?	
Does the survey contain the consumption data necessary to impute recipients of the subsidy and how much they received?	
If fuel subsidies are important, is there an input-output matrix available for the assessed country?	
If utility (water, electricity, communication, transport) subsidies are important, are the tariff structures available?	
If not, is it possible to impute/simulate the benefit in some other way?	

(*continued*)

Indirect taxes	
Is the total amount collected from indirect taxes available in national accounts or administrative data?	
How prevalent is evasion of indirect taxes in the country?	
How does evasion of indirect taxes differ between rural and urban areas?	
Does the survey include consumption data to impute indirect taxes?	
If so, does each item consumed include a question about the place of purchase (for example, supermarket, farmer's market, flea market, etc.)?	
If each item does not include a question about place of purchase, is there a general question about the place where the individual/household normally shops?	
If neither of these is available, how will evasion be incorporated into the analysis?	
If the survey does not include consumption data to impute indirect taxes, is a secondary source available that has estimated the incidence of indirect taxes, for example by Market or Disposable Income decile?	
If a secondary source is used to estimate incidence of indirect taxes, explain which methodology is adopted.	
Does the assessed country have a recent input-output table? Provide year.	
If the answer to the question above was yes, provide source and link if available.	
Are there estimates made for tax expenditures?	
In-kind education	
Does the government provide free public education in the country?	
Are there user fees (direct or indirect in the form of required uniforms and school supplies)?	
Does partially subsidized education exist in the assessed country?	

Does free or partially subsidized pre-school exist in the assessed country?	
Does free or partially subsidized tertiary education exist in the assessed country?	
For those attending school, does the survey include a question specifying what type of school they attend (public, partially subsidized, private)?	
Is the amount of public spending per student available?	
Can this data be disaggregated by education level (pre-school, primary, lower secondary, upper secondary, tertiary)?	
Can this data be disaggregated by sub-national regions for which the survey is representative (for example, spending per student by level in each state, where the survey is representative at the state level)?	

In-kind health

Does the government provide free public health services in the country?	
Are there user fees?	
Who is eligible to receive services?	
What services are covered?	
Do certain facilities offer health services that are partially subsidized by the government?	
Does a public health insurance scheme exist in the country?	
If so, explain how the scheme operates.	
Does the survey include questions about the use of public health services? Specifically:	
What type of service was received?	
What type of facility provided the service (free/fully public, partially subsidized, private)?	
How many visits were made during the recall period?	
Did the patient pay any expenses out of pocket, and if so how much?	

(*continued*)

What is the recall period for the use of health facilities?	
Is the amount of public spending on health services available?	
Can spending on fully public facilities and partially subsidized facilities be distinguished (where applicable)?	
Can spending be disaggregated by type of service received (for example, primary care, in-patient care, and preventative care)?	
Can spending be disaggregated by sub-national regions for which the survey is representative (for example, spending by level in each state, where the survey is representative at the state level)?	
Is the amount of user fees collected from public health facilities available?	
Is there a question on the survey indicating who is covered by the public health insurance scheme?	
If a secondary source is used to estimate incidence of health spending, explain which methodology is adopted.	

Housing subsidies

Does the government subsidize housing?	
Who is eligible to receive government-subsidized housing?	
Is the total spent on each of subsidized housing available in national accounts or administrative data?	
Does the survey include a question on who receives housing subsidies?	
If not, is it possible to impute/simulate the benefit? See the methods described in chapter 6 in Volume 1 of this Handbook.	

Other information

Location (urban/rural)	
Data on race and ethnicity	
Is the year of the survey the same as that of the analysis? If not, please explain the method that is used to overcome this situation.	

Sheet B2 of *CEQ Master Workbook*: Survey Questions and Variable Names

Income	Components	Name of variable in data set	Includes	Survey question	Survey recall period	Notes
Market income	Gross labor income					
	Wages and salary					
	Corporate income					
	Employer contributions to social security					
	Gross property income					
	Private transfers					
	Private pensions					
	Other					
	Remittances					
	Alimony payments					
	Imputed rent from owner-occupied housing					
	Consumption of own production					
	add additional rows as necessary					
Market income + pensions	Old-age contributory pensions					
	Contributions to social security for old-age Pensions					
	Employer contributions to social security for old-age pensions					
	Employee contributions to social security for old-age pensions					
	Self-employed contributions to social security for old-age pensions					
	add additional rows as necessary					

Income	Components	Name of variable in data set	Includes	Survey question	Survey recall period	Notes
Net market income	Direct taxes Income tax Other direct taxes Contributions to social security for health Employer contributions to social security for health Employee contributions to social security for health Self-employed contributions to social security for health Contributions to social security for Other Contributory Programs (such as unemployment insurance) Employer contributions to social security for other contributory programs (such as unemployment insurance) Employee contributions to social security for other contributory programs (such as unemployment insurance) Self-employed contributions to social security for other contributory programs (such as unemployment insurance) *add additional rows as necessary*					

Income	Components	Name of variable in data set	Includes	Survey question	Survey recall period	Notes
Disposable income	Direct cash transfers Non-contributory pensions Conditional cash transfers Scholarships *add additional rows as necessary*					
Consumable income	Indirect subsidies Indirect taxes Sales tax *add additional rows as necessary*					
Final income	In-kind transfers Education Preschool Primary Secondary Other types of education Tertiary Health Primary care Hospitalization School meals and transportation Children's centers Assistance to vulnerable groups Other social services In-kind taxes Co-payments User fees *add additional rows as necessary*					

TABLE 6G-3

Sheet B3 of *CEQ Master Workbook*: General Government Budget and Fiscal Totals Included in Analysis

Year of budget data:	Name of country				
	Currency amounts in administrative accounts (otherwise specified)	Total (% of GDP)	Included in analysis (yes/no)	Total Included in analysis from administrative accounts	Total included in analysis from administrative accounts (% of GDP)
Total Contributions to Social Insurance *of which*					
Total Contributions to social security for old-age pensions *of which*					
Employee					
Employer					
Self-employed					
Total Contributions to social security for health *of which*					
Employee					
Employer					
Self-employed					
Total Contributions to social security for other contributory programs (such as unemployment) *of which*					
Employee					
Employer					
Self-employed					
Indirect taxes *of which*					
VAT					
Sales tax					
Excise taxes					
Customs duties					
Taxes on exports					
Other indirect taxes					
Nontax revenue					
Other taxes					
Grants					

Year of budget data:	Currency amounts in administrative accounts (otherwise specified)	Total (% of GDP)	Included in analysis (yes/no)	Total Included in analysis from administrative accounts	Total included in analysis from administrative accounts (% of GDP)
Name of country					
Total expenditure					
Defense spending					
Social spending					
Social protection					
Social assistance *of which*					
Conditional or unconditional cash transfers					
Noncontributory pensions					
Near cash transfers (food, school uniforms, etc.)					
Other					
social insurance *of which*					
Old-age pensions					
Education *of which*					
Pre-school					
Primary					
Secondary					
Post-secondary non-tertiary					
Tertiary					
Health *of which*					
Contributory					
Noncontributory					
Housing & urban *of which*					
Housing					
Other social spending					

(*continued*)

Year of budget data:	Name of country				
	Currency amounts in administrative accounts (otherwise specified)	Total (% of GDP)	Included in analysis (yes/no)	Total Included in analysis from administrative accounts	Total included in analysis from administrative accounts (% of GDP)
Subsidies *of which*					
Energy *of which*					
Electricity					
Fuel					
Food					
On inputs for agriculture					
Infrastructure *of which*					
Water & sanitation					
Rural roads					
Grants					
Other nonsocial spending					
Fiscal balance and government debt by IMF functional classification					
Primary fiscal balance, including grants					
Primary fiscal balance, excluding grants					
Gross domestic government debt					
Balance of social security administration total and for old-age pensions separately (show deficit with a negative sign)					

TABLE 6G-4

Sheets B4–B12 of *CEQ Master Workbook*: Description of Fiscal System

Sheet name	Contents
B4. Tax system	Describe the tax system in the assessed country and specify which taxes are included in the analysis; for each item, indicate complete reference (including specific page numbers and/or weblink with date of use).
B5. Pension system	Describe the portions of the contributory pensions system that are treated as part of market income in the contributory pensions as deferred income scenario and in the contributory pensions as partial deferred scenario.
B6. Cash transfer programs	Fill in the given table requesting information on program name, type of program, whether the program is taxable, target population, number of beneficiaries (year of survey), year of first implementation, budget (year of survey and local currency per year), targeting mechanism, and estimated impact. For each item, indicate complete reference (including specific page numbers and/or weblink with date of use).
B7. Near cash transfers	Provide a brief description of all near cash transfer programs such as food rations, school uniforms, school feeding programs, and so on. For each item, put complete reference (including specific page numbers and/or weblink with date of use).
B8. Subsidies	Describe the price subsidies in the assessed country and specify which ones are included in the analysis; for each item, indicate complete reference (including specific page numbers and/or weblink with date of use).
B9. Education system	Describe the public education system. For each item, put complete reference (including specific page numbers and/or weblink with date of use).
B10. Health system	Describe the public health system. For each item, put complete reference (including specific page numbers and/or weblink with date of use).
B11. Housing subsidies	Describe other in-kind transfers such as housing, urban infrastructure, etc. For each item, put complete reference (including specific page numbers and/or weblink with date of use). Note that we consider food assistance programs as a direct transfer rather than an in-kind transfer.
B12. Other country-specific additional information	Provide any additional country-specific information that is relevant or that is requested.

	Income concepts and fiscal interventions: definitions, methods, and comparisons with administrative accounts								
	Included (yes/no) [column C in MWB online version]	Description of method [column D in MWB online version]	Totals in local currency from survey [column E in MWB online version]	Share as a % of disposable income or private consumption from survey specify denominator [column F in MWB online version]	Totals in local currency from administrative accounts	Share as a % of disposable income or private consumption from administrative accounts (specify denominator) [column H in MWB online version]	Total population (for example, taxpayers, beneficiaries, enrolled in school) from survey (weighted) [column I in MWB online version]	Total population (for example, taxpayers, beneficiaries, enrolled in school) from administrative accounts [column J in MWB online version]	Total population (e.g., taxpayers, beneficiaries enrolled in school) from survey (unweighted) [column K in MWB online version]
Market income									
Earned and unearned incomes of all possible sources and excluding government transfers									
Gifts, proceeds from sale of durables									
Alimony									
Auto-consumption									
Imputed rent for owner occupied housing									
Other (add more rows if needed)									
Market income plus pensions = market income + pensions – contributions to pensions									
Old-age contributory pensions									

	Income concepts and fiscal interventions: definitions, methods, and comparisons with administrative accounts								
	Included (yes/no) [column C in MWB online version]	Description of method [column D in MWB online version]	Totals in local currency from survey [column E in MWB online version]	Share as a % of disposable income or private consumption from survey specify denominator [column F in MWB online version]	Totals in local currency from administrative accounts [column G in MWB online version]	Share as a % of disposable income or private consumption from administrative accounts (specify denominator) [column H in MWB online version]	Total population (for example, taxpayers, beneficiaries, enrolled in school) from survey (weighted) [column I in MWB online version]	Total population (for example, taxpayers, beneficiaries, enrolled in school) from administrative accounts [column J in MWB online version]	Total population (e.g., taxpayers, beneficiaries, enrolled in school) from survey (unweighted) [column K in MWB online version]
Total Contributions to social security for old-age pensions *of which*									
Employee									
Employer									
Self-employed									

Net market income = market income plus pensions − (direct taxes as well as contributions to social security that are not directed to old-age pensions)

Direct taxes									
Personal income tax									
Corporate income tax									
Payroll tax									
Taxes on property									
Other (add more rows if needed)									
Total Contributions to social security for health *of which*									
Employer contributions to social security for health									

(*continued*)

	Income concepts and fiscal interventions: definitions, methods, and comparisons with administrative accounts									
	Included (yes/no) [column C in MWB online version]	Description of method [column D in MWB online version]	Totals in local currency from survey [column E in MWB online version]	Share as a % of disposable income or private consumption from survey specify denominator [column F in MWB online version]	Totals in local currency from administrative accounts [column G in MWB online version]	Share as a % of disposable income or private consumption from administrative accounts (specify denominator) [column H in MWB online version]	Total population (for example, taxpayers, beneficiaries, enrolled in school) from survey (weighted) [column I in MWB online version]	Total population (for example, taxpayers, beneficiaries, enrolled in school) from administrative accounts [column J in MWB online version]	Total population (e.g., taxpayers, beneficiaries, enrolled in school) from survey (unweighted) [column K in MWB online version]
Employee contributions to social security for health									
Self-employed contributions to social security for health									
Total Contributions to social security for other contributory programs (such as unemployment insurance) *of which*									
Employer contributions to social security for other contributory programs (such as unemployment insurance and others)									

	Income concepts and fiscal interventions: definitions, methods, and comparisons with administrative accounts								
	Included (yes/no) [column C in MWB online version]	Description of method [column D in MWB online version]	Totals in local currency from survey [column E in MWB online version]	Share as a % of disposable income or private consumption from survey specify denominator [column F in MWB online version]	Totals in local currency from administrative accounts [column G in MWB online version]	Share as a % of disposable income or private consumption from administrative accounts (specify denominator) [column H in MWB online version]	Total population (for example, taxpayers, beneficiaries, enrolled in school) from survey (weighted) [column I in MWB online version]	Total population (for example, taxpayers, beneficiaries, enrolled in school) from administrative accounts [column J in MWB online version]	Total population (e.g., taxpayers, beneficiaries, enrolled in school) from survey (unweighted) [column K in MWB online version]
Employee contributions to social security for other contributory programs (such as unemploy-ment insurance and others)									
Self-employed contributions to social security for other contributory programs (such as unemploy-ment insurance and others)									
Gross income = market income plus pensions + direct transfers									
Social protection									
Social assistance									
Conditional and uncondi-tional cash transfers									

(*continued*)

	Income concepts and fiscal interventions: definitions, methods, and comparisons with administrative accounts								
	Included (yes/no) [column C in MWB online version]	Description of method [column D in MWB online version]	Totals in local currency from survey [column E in MWB online version]	Share as a % of disposable income or private consumption from survey specify denominator [column F in MWB online version]	Totals in local currency from administrative accounts [column G in MWB online version]	Share as a % of disposable income or private consumption from administrative accounts (specify denominator) [column H in MWB online version]	Total population (for example, taxpayers, beneficiaries, enrolled in school) from survey (weighted) [column I in MWB online version]	Total population (for example, taxpayers, beneficiaries, enrolled in school) from administrative accounts [column J in MWB online version]	Total population (e.g., taxpayers, beneficiaries, enrolled in school) from survey (unweighted) [column K in MWB online version]
Add one row per program analyzed Noncontributory pensions									
Near cash transfers (food, school uniforms, etc.) Add one row per program analyzed Other (add more rows if needed)									
Taxable income = gross income – nontaxable income									
Add more rows if needed									
Disposable income = net market income + direct government transfers									
Private consumption									
Consumable income = disposable income + indirect subsidies – indirect taxes									

	Income concepts and fiscal interventions: definitions, methods, and comparisons with administrative accounts								
	Included (yes/no) [column C in MWB online version]	Description of method [column D in MWB online version]	Totals in local currency from survey [column E in MWB online version]	Share as a % of disposable income or private consumption from survey specify denominator [column F in MWB online version]	Totals in local currency from administrative accounts [column G in MWB online version]	Share as a % of disposable income or private consumption from administrative accounts (specify denominator) [column H in MWB online version]	Total population (for example, taxpayers, beneficiaries, enrolled in school) from survey (weighted) [column I in MWB online version]	Total population (for example, taxpayers, beneficiaries, enrolled in school) from administrative accounts [column J in MWB online version]	Total population (e.g., taxpayers, beneficiaries, enrolled in school) from survey (unweighted) [column K in MWB online version]
Indirect taxes									
VAT									
Sales tax									
Excise taxes									
Add one row per excise tax analyzed									
Customs duties									
Other (add more rows if needed)									
Indirect subsidies									
Electricity									
Fuel									
Food									
Agricultural inputs									
Other (add more rows if needed)									
Final income = consumable income + government in-kind transfers									
Education									
Preschool									
Primary									

(continued)

	Income concepts and fiscal interventions: definitions, methods, and comparisons with administrative accounts									
	Included (yes/no) [column C in MWB online version]	Description of method [column D in MWB online version]	Totals in local currency from survey [column E in MWB online version]	Share as a % of disposable income or private consumption from survey specify denominator [column F in MWB online version]	Totals in local currency from administrative accounts [column G in MWB online version]	Share as a % of disposable income or private consumption from administrative accounts (specify denominator) [column H in MWB online version]	Total population (for example, taxpayers, beneficiaries, enrolled in school) from survey (weighted) [column I in MWB online version]	Total population (for example, taxpayers, beneficiaries, enrolled in school) from administrative accounts [column J in MWB online version]	Total population (e.g., taxpayers, beneficiaries, enrolled in school) from survey (unweighted) [column K in MWB online version]
Secondary									
Post-secondary									
Non-tertiary									
Tertiary									
School fees									
Education net of fees									
Health									
Contributory									
Noncontributory									
Inpatient									
Outpatient									
Co-payments or fees									
Health net of copay and fees									
Housing									
Total taxes									

	Income concepts and fiscal interventions: definitions, methods, and comparisons with administrative accounts									
	Included (yes/no) [column C in MWB online version]	Description of method [column D in MWB online version]	Totals in local currency from survey [column E in MWB online version]	Share as a % of disposable income or private consumption from survey specify denominator [column F in MWB online version]	Totals in local currency from administrative accounts [column G in MWB online version]	Share as a % of disposable income or private consumption from administrative accounts (specify denominator) [column H in MWB online version]	Total population (for example, taxpayers, beneficiaries, enrolled in school) from survey (weighted) [column I in MWB online version]	Total population (for example, taxpayers, beneficiaries, enrolled in school) from administrative accounts [column J in MWB online version]	Total population (e.g., taxpayers, beneficiaries, enrolled in school) from survey (unweighted) [column K in MWB online version]
Total social spending									
Total subsidies									
Total population									
Side analysis									
Subsidized portion of social security (social security "deficit" as a percent of total social security spending)									
Tax expenditures									

TABLE 6G-6
Sheet C2 of *CEQ Master Workbook*

Key assumptions	
Country name	
Date of MWB on which the following is based	
Name and email of contact person	
Scenario	
General information	
Year of survey	
Name of survey and link if available	
Does the survey report income or consumption or both?	
Does the survey report self-consumption?	
Does the survey report imputed rent for owner-occupied housing?	
Consumption- or income-based analysis?	
Does the income or consumption concept used in incidence analysis include: (1) self-consumption; (2) imputed rent for owner-occupied housing?	
Is the income concept reported in the survey before or after taxes both for wage earners and self-employed? If unspecified, which assumptions were made?	
Which "income concept" is the starting point of the incidence analysis? Note that here authors need to report the income concepts that are lifted directly from the survey as a starting point before adding or subtracting anything.	
Per capita or equivalized consumption/income. If equivalized is used, specify which formula was used.	
Describe any particular assumption in construction of international or national poverty lines used in analysis.	
Government level (see definition of general government on the right-hand side of sheet B5). Ideally, the analysis should include federal, state, and municipal for both revenues and spending.	
List direct taxes included in analysis.	

List contributions to social security included in analysis.	
List cash and near cash (for example, food, school uniforms, etc.) transfers included in Pension as Deferred Income scenario; use actual names of the programs.	
Name of flagship transfer program (if there is one in the country):	
List indirect taxes included in analysis.	
List indirect subsidies included in analysis.	
List levels of schooling included under education transfers and the years that correspond to each (for example, primary 6 years or primary 4 years, etc.).	
List levels of health services included (for example, contributory and noncontributory, primary, etc.).	
List other transfers in kind (housing, etc.) included.	
List any other tax or transfer included in the construction of income concepts not specified above.	
What is defined as a household member (for example, are boarders and domestic servants excluded)?	
Methodological assumptions underlying the incidence of taxes and transfers	
If direct taxes were simulated, which assumptions were made for tax evasion (for example, formal employees, rural vs. urban, etc.)?	
If direct transfers were simulated, which assumptions were made for take-up of program?	
What assumptions were made to take into account the evasion of indirect taxes (for example, by place of purchase, size of locality, rural vs. urban, etc.)?	
What assumptions were made to identify beneficiaries of consumption subsidies?	
Were the indirect effects of indirect taxes included in the incidence analysis? If yes, which method was used? Was an Input and Output Matrix used? If yes, for what year?	
Were the indirect effects of indirect subsidies included? If yes, which method was used? Was an Input and Output Matrix used? If yes, for what year?	

(continued)

List the components that were scaled down (for example, education and health spending).	
List the components (if any) that were scaled up.	
To impute health spending, was the "insurance value" or "usage-based" approach used?	
Do the values of cash and near cash transfers spending used in incidence analysis include administrative costs?	
Does spending on education and health values used in incidence analysis include administrative costs?	
Does spending on education and health values used in incidence analysis include capital expenditures?	
Which definition of coverage was used?	

Add any other assumptions that are relevant for the study below.

Chapter 7

CONSTRUCTING CONSUMABLE INCOME

Including the Direct and Indirect Effects
of Indirect Taxes and Subsidies

Jon Jellema and Gabriela Inchauste

Introduction

How—and from whom—a government collects and replenishes public revenues will make a significant difference to incomes and the consumption patterns among individuals and households. Whether or not a revenue-collection instrument can be targeted also matters a great deal for inequality and impoverishment created by fiscal policy. Indirect taxes on consumption activity—customs duties, value-added taxes, excise taxes, sales taxes—are not usually administered flexibly; that is, all individuals with at least some market-based consumption activity pay indirect taxes.[1] Indirect taxes are popular: the international CEQ database (www.commitmentoequity.org/datacenter) demonstrates that across sixty country-year pairs where GNI per capita measured in purchasing power parity (PPP) terms was less than $PPP 20,000, indirect taxes account for 56 percent of all revenues from taxes. Across fifteen country-year pairs where GNI per capita was less than $PPP 5,000, indirect taxes account for 60 percent of all tax revenues.[2] Accounting for indirect taxes (and subsidies) on consumption activity is critical for fiscal incidence: typical revenue-collection schemes in low- and

---

[1] As long as some part of an individual's consumption attracts at least one of the existing indirect taxes, then the individual will not avoid indirect taxes. An individual (or a household) subsisting exclusively on gifts and inter-household transfers and own-production/own-consumption will consume without directly paying any indirect taxes. See appendix 7A, "Dealing with Taxes on Intermediate Stages of Production and Consumption," for a more detailed discussion of the actors and their activities which may attract taxes.

[2] In eight country-year pairs with GNI per capita greater than $PPP 20,000, indirect taxes account for 44 percent of all tax revenues on average; and in the United States in 2016, where

middle-income countries depend more on indirect taxes, so that the overall magnitude of indirect taxes in the economy will be greater than that of direct taxes, and most households also cannot avoid paying at least some share of the indirect tax burden.

In this chapter, we discuss how to construct Consumable Income,[3] taking into account the direct and *indirect* impacts of indirect taxes and subsidies. If the inputs into production are subject to indirect taxes or subsidies, these may "cascade," or be passed along from producer to producer, until they are borne by consumers in the form of higher or lower prices for consumer goods and services. Higher or lower prices for consumer purchases due to taxes paid or subsidies received (respectively) on producers' inputs are what we call the *indirect* impacts of indirect taxes or subsidies.

Since the previous version of this volume was published, significant methodological advances that build upon the model summarized in this chapter have been made. Specifically, Warwick and others (2022) demonstrate how to extend the basic model to include (a) a differential indirect impacts treatment of imports (in contrast to domestically produced goods); (b) the partitioning of the input-output (IO) matrix to take account of differential tax or subsidy rates or categories on goods within an original product category; and (c) a method for using survey-based information on place of purchase as a proxy for informality to relax the assumption that households across the income distribution spend a similar share of their budgets on goods purchased informally as well as assumptions about which transactions are likely to generate both direct as and indirect tax burdens or subsidy benefits. These extensions are described in brief at the end of section 5 below; the algebra and mechanics of these extensions in our basic model are discussed in the online-only appendix 7B by Maya Goldman. Appendix 7A by James Alm, "Dealing with Taxes on Intermediate Stages of Production and Consumption," provides a more detailed discussion of potential alternatives when estimating the indirect impact of indirect taxes and subsidies.

1 Direct Impacts of Subsidies and Taxes

Taxes and subsidies on goods and services change final retail prices[4] and therefore directly affect household purchasing power and welfare. When consumption expenditure records are available in the household income and expenditure survey, the direct effects of indirect taxes or subsidies can be imputed in a relatively straightforward way. This is typically done by first determining what proportion of total consumption

---

GNI per capita was measured at $PPP 53,442, indirect taxes accounted for 16 percent of all tax revenues.

[3] "Consumable income" is the concept and the name used in Canada's Social Policy Simulation Database Model (SPSD/M), one of the main sources used to produce the distribution of household income accounts and evaluate the impact of changes in tax and spending policies.

[4] See appendix 7A, "Tax Incidence Analysis with Intermediate Goods," for a lengthier discussion of intermediate and final prices (including wages) in the presence of taxes.

expenditure is spent on indirect taxes (or the proportion by which the value of consumption expenditure would increase in the absence of government subsidies), and then creating the Consumable Income concept by subtracting from Disposable Income the loss (gain) in purchasing power or welfare traceable to these taxes (subsidies).

However, a cross-section of consumption expenditure records does not provide evidence of what counterfactual expenditures would be in a world without taxes or subsidies. For example, this year's household budget survey would provide no insight into the distribution of expenditures last year when there was no sales tax on milk. Because a *CEQ Assessment* estimates incomes before ("prefiscal") and after ("postfiscal") the application of fiscal programs, the direct impact of an indirect tax or subsidy instrument is described as the change in income that results from the difference between the pattern of expenditures that would occur in the prefiscal setting, where there are no taxes or subsidies, and the pattern of expenditure that exists in the current, actual postfiscal world reflected in the consumption choices and expenditures recorded in the household survey.

In order to make such an estimate, we therefore need to employ assumptions that help us describe demand or expenditures in a counterfactual no-tax (or no-subsidy) world. Here we discuss two assumptions, inelastic demand and homothetic preferences, that are commonly employed in the welfare analysis of price changes[1] and that allow the CEQ analyst to specify expenditures in a counterfactual, prefiscal world in the absence of a model of consumer demand.[2]

1.1 Inelastic Demand

When demand for any taxed (or subsidized) good or service is inelastic, changes in prices do not lead to changes in quantity demanded. If demand is inelastic, then consumption in the prefiscal counterfactual would be equal to consumption recorded in the current, with-tax regime. If we assume demand is inelastic, we can then calculate the Paasche variation (PV) in the value of the consumption expenditure. The PV measures the value of consumption expenditure at two different points in time—call them "initial" and "final"—using prices from the final period. For our purposes, the PV measures the difference in the value of consumption expenditures in the prefiscal or "no-tax" counterfactual and the value of consumption expenditures in the postfiscal or "with-tax" present reflected in the household survey.

Because we are assuming that demand is inelastic, we are implying that quantities demanded (of the taxed item in question) are constant across the prefiscal counterfactual and the postfiscal present. This simplifying assumption allows us to generate the

---

[1] See Araar and Verme (2016) and their references.

[2] In other words, these assumptions can be used to generate the distribution (among households or individuals) of indirect tax burdens without requiring *more* information than the CEQ analyst already has at hand.

net-of-tax value of consumption expenditure by dividing the current value of consumption expenditure (*CE*) by one plus (minus) the relevant tax (subsidy) rate. That is,

$$(7\text{-}1) \qquad\qquad CE_{t-1} = CE_t/(1+r),$$

where period $t-1$ is the prefiscal period, t is the current period (where with-tax prices are reflected in the household survey), and r is the rate of taxation (expressed as a percent of the net-of-tax price). If we are interested in a subsidy, we can use the same formula as long as we remember that the rate r of taxation on a subsidized good must be negative. Figure 7-1, which is a simple demand schedule with quantity demanded, q (x-axis) at each price, p (y-axis), shows that inelastic demand can be represented by a vertical demand schedule (where the quantity demanded does not change within a certain price range). The Paasche variation can be represented then by the difference (labeled "A" and shaded with hash marks) in the area of two rectangles: $P_t q_t$ and $P_{t-1} q_{t-1}$. Because q_t is equal to q_{t-1} (under the assumption of inelastic demand), the difference between the two rectangles simplifies to

$$(7\text{-}2) \qquad\qquad PV = q_t * P_t/(1+r) * abs(r),$$

which is simply the current, postfiscal value of consumption expenditures valued at prefiscal prices multiplied by the (absolute value) of the rate of taxation (subsidization).

Figure 7-1 also makes clear that the Paasche variation is not a welfare measure: a consumer with inelastic demand is just as well off (in welfare terms) at any price level as long as she is consuming the right quantity. Instead, we can think of the PV as the change in purchasing power experienced when the tax or subsidy is applied. That is, an individual will have to spend more (less) to acquire the same bundle of goods when taxes (subsidies) are imposed. This leaves less (more) room for purchases of other goods, meaning purchasing power declines (increases). It is the decrease (increase) in purchasing power, measured by PV, that is subtracted from (added to) Disposable Income to arrive at Consumable Income.[3] Therefore, when a tax is imposed, we can place a negative sign in front of the first term in equation 7-2 to remind ourselves that an indirect tax *reduces* purchasing power relative to the counterfactual.

1.2 Homothetic Preferences

We can also make headway on the impact of taxes or subsidies in a cross-section of expenditure records if we model consumer demand as described by homothetic pref-

---

[3] The decline (or increase, for a subsidy) in purchasing power can also be expressed as rate$_i$ * (consumption expenditure$_i$/(1 + rate$_i$)), where i indexes the household-consumed good and "rate" refers to an indirect tax or subsidy rate. This formulation makes it easier to understand why we call this a "Paasche welfare variation."

FIGURE 7-1

Paasche Variation in Consumption Expenditure

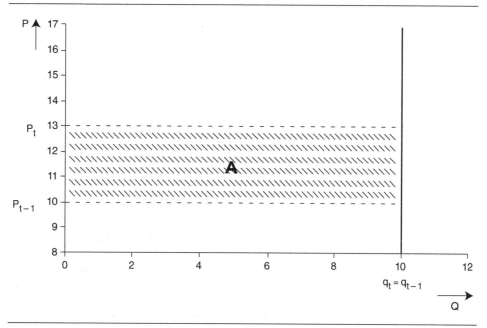

Note: Figure 7-1 is a demand schedule with price on the y-axis and quantity demanded on the x-axis.

erences. When consumers optimize utility (under a budget constraint) described by homothetic preferences, the ratios of goods demanded depend only on their relative prices and not on income or scale.[4] If consumer demand can be described by homothetic preferences,[5] then in the prefiscal counterfactual, quantities demanded are higher (lower) by exactly the amount of the current tax (subsidy): if a good is *currently* taxed at a 20 percent rate, it is assumed that in a no-tax counterfactual, consumption would be 20 percent higher.[6]

Once we have a description of demand in the prefiscal counterfactual, we can proceed as before: compare the consumption expenditure necessary to achieve the optimal bundle of goods in the no-tax (no-subsidy) counterfactual with the consumption expenditure necessary to achieve the optimal bundle in the actual with-tax (with-subsidy) state. Figure 7-2 is a demand schedule under homothetic preferences that shows that the quantity demanded in the prefiscal hypothetical (q_{t-1}) is

---

[4] Varian (1992).

[5] And assuming there are no uncompensated cross-price elasticities.

[6] The expenditure share of the taxed good (evaluated at net-of-tax prices) remains constant in both the no-tax counterfactual and the current, with-tax state. This is a consequence of both homothetic preferences and of treating taxes paid (by individuals or households) as income losses.

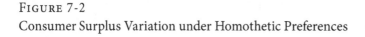

FIGURE 7-2

Consumer Surplus Variation under Homothetic Preferences

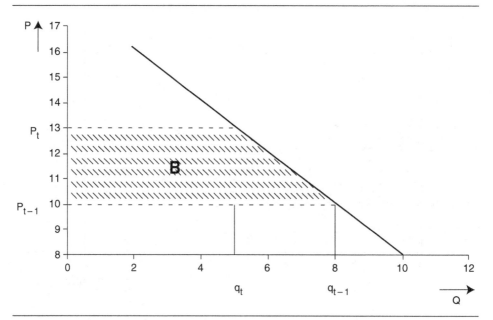

Note: Figure 7-2 is a demand schedule with price on the y-axis and quantity demanded on the x-axis.

greater than the quantity demanded in the postfiscal world by exactly the relative amount by which the price of the good P_t is higher in the postfiscal world.

With demand described by homothetic preferences, the difference in total consumer surplus (CS) can be represented by the area of the polygon $P_t q_t q_{t-1} P_{t-1}$, which is labeled "B" and shaded with hash marks. Figure 7-2 also demonstrates why this is in fact a Consumer Surplus variation (CSV), instead of a variation in purchasing power or a compensating variation, for example: it gives us the amount by which total CS changes when the optimal bundle of goods changes. The area "B" is also described by the following equation:

(7-3) $CS = P_t q_t * r * (1 - 0.5 * r / (1 + r)).$

The *CS* quantity described by equation 7-3 is equivalent to the burden (benefit) created by the indirect tax (subsidy); it is subtracted from Disposable Income to arrive at Consumable Income.

Notice that when we are evaluating the losses (gains) created by the current tax (subsidy) schedules relative to a no-tax (no-subsidy) counterfactual, the Paasche variation (generated by making use of an inelastic demand assumption) will never be greater than the Consumer Surplus variation (generated by making use of a homothetic preferences assumption). The CS variation can only be taken over two optimal demand schedules; optimal demand will be higher (lower) in a no-tax (no-subsidy) state, and the difference between actual recorded demand (which we assume is equal to optimal demand in the current state) and optimal demand in the no-tax or no-subsidy counterfactual must be greater than zero. Araar and Verme (2016) provide both a thorough computational treatment of the size of the differences in these two variations by tax rate and detailed variable-level coding that generates these variations in a cross-section of household-level expenditure.

Notice also that the discussion above has focused on the impacts of taxes or subsidies via a price channel, which means that the CEQ analyst should take care to exclude auto-production and auto-consumption, gifts, in-kind transfers, and other non-market-based acquisition or receipt of goods and services when calculating the impacts of indirect taxes and subsidies. We have presented here two simplifying assumptions—inelastic demand and homothetic preferences—which allow us to calculate incomes in the CEQ prefiscal counterfactual and in the postfiscal environment reflected in the household survey. However, the CEQ analyst may decide that another demand system like Cobb-Douglas demand or the Almost Ideal Demand system better suits a particular country- or household-survey context and may therefore estimate losses (gains) from indirect taxes (subsidies) under the assumptions specified by those alternatives. Araar and Verme provide a computational look at the difference in estimated losses from price changes in different demand systems (including those mentioned above) and note that differences in estimates across demand systems are "minimal as compared to changes in other parameters such as the price change or the budget share."[7]

2 Indirect Impacts of Subsidies and Taxes

The direct impact on purchasing power of sales taxes or subsidies can be traced straightforwardly through consumption expenditure records when simplifying assumptions on consumer demand behavior are allowed. However, these same policies will (more often than not) affect *intermediate* goods and services prices, and therefore producer prices, across the entire economy. If producers pass some of these higher (lower) input prices on to other producers or to final consumers, households will bear more of a total burden (enjoy a larger total benefit) than the direct impact alone would indicate.[8] In fact, a thirty-two country study using micro-datasets to trace the impact of fuel subsidies on household welfare showed that those subsidies produced equal or larger indirect welfare impacts than direct ones.[9] In other words, significant *indirect* effects are the international norm for developing countries.

---

[7] Araar and Verme (2016, p. 6).

[8] See appendix 1, "Dealing with Taxes on Intermediate Stages of Production and Consumption," for a lengthier discussion of intermediate and final prices (including wages) in the presence of taxes.

[9] See Coady, Flamini, and Sears (2015).

CEQ Assessments estimate incomes before and after the application of fiscal policies, including indirect taxes and subsides; when a CEQ analyst can generate the total (direct plus indirect) impact of such policies on purchasing power, she will have a more comprehensive estimate of a fiscal policy's impact on poverty and inequality. When household expenditure levels are recorded with reference to retail prices *including* any subsidies or taxes, which is very common in household surveys, a household's real purchasing power may be overvalued when the price paid includes a portion that finances government consumption (such as with a sales tax) or undervalued when the price paid does not include the amount contributed by the government (such as with a subsidy). Such a misvaluation of purchasing power also occurs when households receive subsidy benefits or bear a sales tax burden indirectly.

3 Theory: The Price-Shifting Model

The following price-shifting model, which describes and quantifies the magnitude of sectoral changes in producer and retail prices resulting from an exogenous shock, provides an estimate of indirect impacts. In section 4, below, we demonstrate how to program such an exogenous shock and solve this model using available statistical software.[10]

The solution to this model can be programmed using information on the current structure of an economy at current levels of production reflected in an input-output (IO) matrix. It makes the following crucial assumption: exogenously generated price changes are either "pushed forward" to output prices or "pushed backward" onto factor payments.[11] Additional assumptions the model exploits are constant returns to scale in production, perfect competition, and reproducible fixed factors of production economy-wide. These assumptions allow the analyst to use the IO matrix, which describes the input shares (of all sectors) in the output of all sectors at a point in time, and given prevailing prices, to generate producer price changes assuming production technologies and production input shares remain *fixed*.

Because the price-shifting model refers to a macroeconomic structure at a point in time and does not specify or generate any behavioral changes (by either households or firms) that result in changes to that macroeconomic structure, it is a static model.

---

[10] The indeterminate "shock" we describe here in the context of a CEQ exercise corresponds to the indirect tax or subsidy in question. For example, "We need to know what the welfare impacts of Country X's electricity subsidy are; let's go about that calculation by using the price-shifting model to determine what would happen if those subsidies were eliminated."

[11] An intermediate solution, where some of the shock to prices is absorbed by output prices and some by factor payments, is possible. However, because (1) *CEQ Assessments* do not attempt to quantify the household welfare impacts from changes in factor prices, and because (2) an input-output matrix does not observe factor payments, such intermediate solutions would manifest themselves here as a less-than-complete shock. See also Araar and Verme (2016, p. 6).

We therefore take results generated as an upper-bound estimate of the impact of any change in government-administered price policy on household welfare. The rest of this section closely follows appendix 3.2 in Coady (2008); additional details can be found there.

Suppose that for any economy at any level of production, there are three types of sectors: cost-push sectors in which higher input prices are pushed fully onto output prices; traded/non-cost-push sectors in which output prices are fixed (possibly because they are determined by world prices) and therefore higher *domestic* input prices are pushed backward onto lower factor prices (or profits); and controlled sectors in which prices are controlled by the government.

For controlled sectors, producer prices are managed (at level $\tilde{p}$) so that retail prices ($\tilde{q}$) and producer prices are equivalent:

$$(7\text{-}4) \qquad\qquad \tilde{q} = \tilde{p},$$

and

$$(7\text{-}5) \qquad\qquad \Delta\tilde{q} = \Delta\tilde{p},$$

where either side of the equation may be specified exogenously (as part of a reform counterfactual, for example).

In the traded sectors (or those that are not cost-push), retail prices are determined by fixed (world) prices (p^w) and taxes (t^*),

$$(7\text{-}6) \qquad\qquad q^* = p^w + t^*,$$

and $q^* = p^* - t^*$ because taxes on domestic production alone must be pushed backwards onto lower producer prices and in turn lower factor payments or profits.[12] Changes in retail prices for traded/non-cost-push sectors are given by

$$(7\text{-}7) \qquad\qquad \Delta q^* = \Delta p^w + \Delta t^*,$$

where both terms on the right-hand side will be specified exogenously.

Finally, in the cost-push sectors, retail and producer prices are related according to

$$(7\text{-}8) \qquad\qquad q^c = p^c + t^c,$$

---

[12] If price shocks are absorbed by factor payments in the traded sectors, there may be an impact on labor incomes and returns to capital in that sector and (potentially all) other sectors. However, this model was not developed to solve for a general equilibrium.

where t^c are sales or excise taxes (which can be negative, for example, for a subsidy). Producer prices are determined by

(7-9) $p^c = p^c(q, w),$

where q are the retail prices for intermediate inputs and w are factor prices. As all cost increases are pushed forward onto retail prices (and factor payments are therefore fixed), then

(7-10) $\Delta q^c = \Delta p^c + \Delta t^c.$

Using equation 7-9 and an input/output (IO) matrix, the change in producer prices is given by

(7-11) $\Delta p^c = \Delta q^c \cdot \alpha \cdot A + \Delta q^* \cdot \beta \cdot A + \Delta \tilde{p} \cdot \gamma \cdot A.$

Here, price changes are $n \times 1$ row vectors (n = the number of sectors in the IO matrix); $\alpha, \beta,$ and γ are $n \times n$ diagonal matrixes representing the proportions of cost-push, traded, and controlled commodities/sectors (respectively) in sectoral outputs; and A is an $n \times n$ technology coefficients matrix.

Further substitution (of equations 7-7 and 7-10 into 7-11) and solving for Δp^c yields

(7-12) $\Delta p^c = \Delta t^c \cdot \alpha \cdot A \cdot K + \Delta p^w \cdot \beta \cdot A \cdot K + \Delta t^* \cdot \beta \cdot A \cdot + K + \Delta \tilde{p} \cdot \gamma \cdot A \cdot K,$

a solution based on exogenously determined changes in taxes on, or prices in, cost-push, traded, and controlled sectors, exogenously determined changes in world prices, and the inverse matrix $K = (I - \alpha \cdot A)^{-1}$, where I is an $n \times n$ identity matrix. The typical element of the inverse matrix K, k_{ij}, captures the combined direct and indirect use of cost-push sector i used to produce one unit of cost-push sector j.

The CEQ analyst is concerned with government policies, so most often $\Delta p^w = 0$. And unless there is good information for any IO sector in particular, or for the entire production economy, the CEQ analyst will most often make the convenient assumption that $\beta = 0$; that is, all sectors are either cost-push or controlled.[13] When those assumptions are made, equation 7-12 becomes

(7-12)' $\Delta p^c = \Delta t^c \cdot \alpha \cdot A \cdot K + \Delta \tilde{p} \cdot (1 - \alpha) \cdot A \cdot K,$

and the change in cost-push retail prices is then given by

(7-13)' $\Delta q^c = \Delta t^c + \Delta t^c \cdot \alpha \cdot A \cdot K + \Delta \tilde{p} \cdot (1 - \alpha) \cdot A \cdot K,$

---

[13] Nonetheless, the software discussed below allow for traded sectors, or sectors where any shock to prices is (implicitly) pushed back onto factor payments instead of forward onto output prices.

which clearly separates the direct effect of the shock (the first term) from the indirect effects arising from changes in producer prices in the cost-push and controlled sectors (the last two terms).

CEQ-generated analytics and results are often disaggregated by specific policy, so the CEQ analyst will most often use the solution in equation 7-12′ for a policy counterfactual that includes *at most* one unique change to price policy. That in turn means running one of the software options described below for the case where, for example, $\Delta t^c \neq 0$ while $\Delta \tilde{p} = 0$ (or vice versa). Theoretically this presents no difficulty because equation 7-12 indicates that changes to producer prices (and therefore to retail prices) are decomposable. Note also that even when $\Delta t^c = 0$, there may still be cost-push price changes arising from a shock to controlled sectors; these price changes arrive exclusively via indirect effects, which will be important to keep in mind for the value-added tax (VAT) discussion below.

This model's solution provides IO-sector by IO-sector changes in producer prices (after a shock). Therefore, the level of detail in the solution corresponds to the level of detail in the IO matrix used. IO matrices do not typically distinguish between, for example, high- and low-quality types of a good, or between informally produced groceries and formally produced groceries. The level of detail in the IO matrix carries over only partially to determination of household-level losses. As we shall see in section 4, calculating the indirect welfare losses (gains) from indirect taxes or subsidies requires knowledge of the amount by which prices are higher or lower in all sectors as a result of the tax (subsidy), as well as of the household budget shares for goods or services from all sectors.

4 Methods for Generating Indirect Effects of Indirect Taxes

In the price-shifting model described in section 3, indirect taxes and indirect subsidies work similarly but with opposite signs: a tax will drive up the final price of a good over its economic cost while a subsidy should drive it down below its economic cost. For example, for any individual good in the price-shifting model, the impact of a 10 percent subsidy will be equal in magnitude (but opposite in sign) to the impact of a 10 percent sales tax.

However, in practice, subsidy impacts on household welfare are often relatively easier to account for. First, it is usually the case that a few easily recognizable and popular *items* (commodities like grains or other dietary staples, fuels, power, and so on) are subsidized; therefore purchases of subsidized goods can often be exclusively and exhaustively identified in the household survey alone and can be exclusively and exhaustively mapped to one aggregated economic sector. In contrast, taxes (VAT, excise, sales, import duties, and so on) typically cover entire *classes* of goods or services while exemptions are specific and narrow. Using the household survey alone, purchases of nonexempt taxed goods may be more difficult to exclusively and exhaustively identify. It may also be more difficult to exclusively map classes of goods to one economic sector. For example, if food is subject to VAT while there is an exemption for "basic commodities," the household survey may not ask households to recall specifically their expenditures on any one of the "basic commodity" items. Moreover, "basic commodities" might map correctly to both the "agriculture products" and "grain mill products" sectors in the IO matrix.[14]

Additionally, economic theory offers few reasons to expect subsidy avoidance; in other words, if the same good is available at both subsidized and nonsubsidized prices, it is reasonable to expect that all household purchases will be made at the subsidized price.[15] In contrast, both in theory and in practice, tax avoidance is to be expected. However, because tax avoidance is "hidden" (except in aggregate) from most of the records that CEQ relies on, it is often difficult for the analyst to acquire enough information to parameterize tax avoidance behavior and the impact of that behavior on household welfare. See section 6, "Taxes versus Subsidies," for additional discussion of these issues and for suggested solutions that can be programmed into the software tools described below. See also appendix 7A for additional discussion of the theoretical impact of tax avoidance on final prices.

4.1 Practical Solutions for Indirect Effects

The CEQ analyst does not need additional software to evaluate the direct effects of indirect taxes; the consumption expenditure records (available in the household survey) together with the formulas for the PV and CSV are enough to generate the item-by-item tax burden within the consumption expenditure survey or within the algorithm that creates CEQ income concepts. For the direct effects of indirect taxes or subsidies, the analyst will likely spend more time poring over the consumption expenditure item list and comparing it with the relevant indirect tax schedules to determine which of the goods or services attract an indirect tax and what the effective rate of taxation[16] and net-of-tax prices (for that item) are likely to be.

The rest of this section instead reviews Stata (a statistical software package) code for calculating indirect effects within the constraints imposed by the price-shifting model and its solution (as described previously), which takes place outside of the household survey. We will discuss general and specific steps the analyst must complete in order to use this code; these steps are as follows:

---

[14] At the end of section 5 and in the online-only, we discuss methods for partitioning the IO matrix of differential tax or subsidy rates on goods within an original IO product category; see also Warwick and others (2022).

[15] Moreover, there is typically only one subsidy per item. While there are several different channels through which subsidies might affect the final retail price (government-managed prices, rebates, input subsidies, and so on), multiple modes of subsidy on the same good are not common. The same good or service may attract more than one tax type, however, each with its own associated tax-avoidance behaviors.

[16] An effective tax rate is calculated as total revenue collection for each tax divided by the tax base. As described in section 6, "Taxes versus Subsidies," in the context of evasion, it is often better to use these rates instead of statutory rates.

1. Prepare the input/output (IO) matrix or Social Accounting Matrix (SAM).
2. Map household consumption expenditures to IO production sectors.
3. Calculate the subsidy (tax) as a percentage of the market or reference price and map the subsidy (tax) schedule to IO sectors.
4. Determine which (if any) IO sectors would continue to have regulated or non-market prices if the price policy under consideration were revised.
5. Read in the IO matrix or the SAM.
6. Enter exogenous price shocks and designate sectors with fixed prices.
7. Solve the model.

We will also provide examples as we go through each of the steps as well as one extended "toy" example at the conclusion of this section.

4.2 Estimating Indirect Impacts with Stata

The International Monetary Fund (IMF) has developed a set of Stata .do files that estimate the direct and indirect effects of indirect taxes (subsidies) using the price-shifting model described above.[17] In order to solve the price-shifting model using the IMF code and to use results to trace the impact of price policy on household welfare, the following steps should be completed.

1. *Prepare the input-output (IO) matrix or Social Accounting Matrix (SAM).*
   Either an IO matrix or a SAM can be used, but the analyst should choose an IO or SAM year closest to the year of the primary household survey.[18] An IO matrix can be created from a SAM or Supply/Use Tables (SUT).[19] Both the OECD and the World Input-Output Database maintain IO databases that are regularly updated.[20]

   IO matrices are usually stated in flows: each row will describe the value of that sector's output by destination (that is, did the sector's output go to other sectors for use as production inputs or to households for consumption?), and each column will contain a complete list of the value of production inputs (from each sector). To calculate the weight of each input in each output, one must calculate the technical coefficients. This is done from the flows in the IO matrix by dividing each cell in

---

[17] The IMF .do files and instructions will be available at www.imf.org/Topics/climate-change/energy-subsidies.

[18] If the IO matrix is relatively old, making use of it would implicitly assume that the structure of the economy has not changed from the time it was assembled.

[19] Appendix 7B, which is only available online, demonstrates methods for creating an IO matrix from either a SAM or Supply/Use Tables (SUT) as well as methods for partitioning the IO matrix of differential tax or subsidy rates on goods within an original IO product category.

[20] The OECD database is available at http://www.oecd.org/trade/input-outputtables.htm, and the World Input-Output Database is available at www.wiod.org.

column j by the row sum (that is, total output) from the final row (where $i = j$). Technical coefficients express the value of inputs (in a sector) as a share of the value of total output from that same sector. The IMF software requires that the analyst create these "technical coefficients" from the IO matrix.

2. *Map household consumption expenditures to IO sectors.*

There will likely be a far more disaggregated category list in the household consumption expenditures questionnaire than in the IO sector list. The analyst will need to use his or her judgment in mapping each household questionnaire item to the relevant IO sector. In cases where an item consumed by the household could plausibly come from more than one sector, it is reasonable to split each household's total consumption of that item among all plausible sectors according to sectoral share in total output (according to the IO table). For example, if expenditures on "grains/cereals/milled wheat/milled rice" from the household survey could plausibly be mapped to either "Agricultural Products" or "Products from Millers" and those two sectors have total output values of 6 million and 4 million (respectively) according to the IO table, the analyst could direct 0.6 of a household's total item expenditures to "Agricultural Products" and the remaining 0.4 of the household's total item expenditures to "Products from Millers."

3. *Calculate the subsidy (tax) as a percentage of the market or reference price and map the subsidy (tax) schedule to IO table (or SAM) sectors.*

The analyst should not expect the tax-schedule-to-IO map to be seamless. The determination of the tax rate to apply may be particularly complicated due to likely evasion or weak enforcement (see section 6, "Taxes versus Subsidies," for a longer discussion of which tax rates to apply). The analyst will need to use his or her judgment for both, although the determination of the correct tax rate to apply should also be discussed among the broader CEQ team.

4. *Determine which (if any) IO sectors would continue to have regulated or nonmarket prices if the price policy under consideration were revised.*

For example, in the case of fuel subsidies, the relevant counterfactual may more likely be one where the government still controls the price of fuel even after eliminating the current subsidy. In such a counterfactual, fuel would be sold at a higher price, but the price at which it was sold would not necessarily be freely determined by market supply and demand.

5. **Read in the IO matrix or the SAM.**

For the IMF software, simply change the following Stata code in order to read the correct "Leontief" or "Technology" coefficients IO matrix into Stata:

```
insheet using iotable.txt
```

6. *Enter exogenous price shocks and designate sectors with fixed prices.*

With the map generated in step 3, enter price change statements (in percent terms) for each sector that describes the counterfactual the analyst wishes to program and solve. For example, "If subsidies were removed, producer prices in this subsidized sector would increase by 20 percent."

In the IMF code, these statements appear as the following steps:

```
** Define price changes
local dpother=0.20; **price change in petrol+diesel
local dpelec='dpother'*(1/3); **assume elec price
increase is 1/3
** of diesel & petrol price increase

** Assign simulated price increases to relevant sectors
matrix dpsim[1,30]= 'dpother'
matrix dpsim[1,36]= 'dpelec'
```

Now use the information from step 4 to designate sectors which would continue to have fixed (or regulated or controlled or administered) prices in the counterfactual. In the IMF code, this happens with the following statement (which occurs just above the previous piece of code):

```
local fixprice "30 36" ; ** these are the sectors whose
prices are fixed
```

All the user needs to do is change the numbers to reflect the IO sectors that will continue to have controlled prices in the counterfactual.

In order to generate the correct *indirect* effects, the price shocks (under the counterfactual) must summarize the change in *producer prices*. For example, there may be different unit subsidy amounts for household and industrial or commercial electricity users when electricity is subsidized. The analyst should use the household subsidy amount for the direct effects of the electricity subsidy and the industrial or commercial subsidy amount for the indirect effects.

7. *Solve the model.*

The user can now run the counterfactual scenario with the IMF code and receive (as Stata output) a list of total price changes (in percent) by IO sector. In order to let the program run, the user has to comment out the rest of the code beginning at section 4:

```
**************************************************************
** 4. Read in the household expenditure data and map
each expenditure
** item to one sector of the IO table. The idea is to
arrive at a new
** mapped dataset having household expenditures by IO
sector.
**************************************************************
```

5 Example Calculations: Steps 1 and 6–7

Suppose the CEQ analyst received the IO matrix (in table 7-1) describing the productive sector in some country-level economy producing food and fuel, in any year.

This IO matrix describes the value of the inputs used in production in all sectors (the columns) and the uses or destinations of all sectoral outputs (the rows) in a double-accounting framework. Step 1 above indicates that we need a technology coefficients matrix, which looks like table 7-2.

The technology coefficients in any sector's column do not sum to 1; we are taking the value of intermediate inputs over the total value of output, but the total value of output also includes payments made to factors (labor, land, capital) in addition to payments made for intermediate inputs.

Suppose the CEQ analyst knows that fuel prices are regulated; in particular, suppose that he finds out that fuel prices are kept 10 percent below the market or reference price through government operations. In other words, the government uses fiscal expenditures to provide fuel at prices that are 10 percent below the price that would occur if the government were not making those expenditures. Suppose also that the government would keep the price of fuels at the reference price even if there were no direct subsidy. The CEQ analyst is interested in the effect of the current subsidy on prices in the food and widget sectors under the cost-push model described above, and so for steps 3, 4, and 6 above, the analyst would enter a 10 percent price change for fuel as well as designate fuel as a "fixed price" sector.

Step 7 asks the analyst to solve the cost-push model of sector prices given the 10 percent shock introduced (representing the no-subsidy counterfactual) in fixed-price fuels. The Stata code discussed above first calculates the matrix $K = (I - \alpha \cdot A)^{-1}$. As stated above (see equations 7-12 and 7-13), the typical element of K captures the combined direct and indirect expenditure on cost-push sector i used to produce one expenditure unit's worth of cost-push sector j and the scalar α demarcates cost-push sectors (sectors 1 [food] and 3 [widgets] in our model) from the controlled sectors (sector 2 [fuel] in our example). For our example, $K =$ (see table 7-3).

We can then create the indirect price changes for each sector (arising as a result of the exogenous shock or shocks) by multiplying the exogenous shock by α post-multiplied by K (following equation 7-13). Because the fuel (sector 2) is controlled, only food (sector 1) and widgets (sector 3) will have indirect price changes. We end up with $\Delta t^c \cdot \alpha \cdot A \cdot K + \Delta \tilde{p} \cdot (1 - \alpha) \cdot A \cdot K =$ (see table 7-4).

In other words, prices would be expected to increase in sector 1 (food) by approximately 1.9 percent and in sector 3 (widgets) by approximately 1.2 percent if the 10 percent fuel subsidy were to be removed. Notice that food's use of fuel (as represented by the technology coefficient in cell [2,1] in the IO matrix) is greater than the widget sector's use of fuel (as represented by the technology coefficient in cell [2,3] in the IO matrix), so it makes sense that the indirect effect is greater for food than for widgets.

TABLE 7-1
Step 1

Sector/commodity	1	2	3	Household consumption
1 = Food	40	5	7	34
2 = Fuel	15	35	7	243
3 = Widgets	2	22	10	120
Output	120	75	80	560

TABLE 7-2
Step 1A

Sector/commodity	1	2	3
1 = Food	0.3333	0.0667	0.0875
2 = Fuel	0.1250	0.4670	0.0875
3 = Widgets	0.0167	0.2930	0.1250

TABLE 7-3
Step 7

	s1	s2	s3
s1	1.5040	0.1444	0.1504
s2	0.0000	1.0000	0.0000
s3	0.0286	0.3380	1.1460

TABLE 7-4
Step 7A

	s1	s2	s3
Indirect price changes	0.0191	0.0000	0.0119

TABLE 7-5
Step 7B

	s1 = food	s2 = fuel	s3 = widgets
Total price changes	0.0191	0.1000	0.0119

We know that fuel was a "fixed price" sector and that the only exogenous shock was in fuel, so we can also list the total (direct plus indirect) price changes for all three sectors. That is, $\Delta t^c + \Delta t^c \bullet \alpha \bullet A \bullet K + \Delta \tilde{p} \bullet (1 - \alpha) \bullet A \bullet =$ (see table 7-5).

This is the vector of sector-by-sector price changes that step 8 (below) calls on. Once the household consumption expenditure survey module is recategorized according to IO sectors (see step 2 above), all consumption expenditure in that IO sector can be revalued according to new prices in that sector by either the "inelastic demand" or "homothetic preferences" scenarios listed above in section 1, on the direct effects of indirect taxes and subsidies.

8. *Apply the sectoral price changes to the microdata.*

   a) Use the map generated in step 2 to determine which consumption items will experience which (IO sector-wide) indirect prices changes.

   b) As for the calculation of the *direct* effects of indirect taxes and subsidies described above, use the formulas for the PV or the CSV to calculate—for each item in a household's consumption basket—the change in purchasing power (or consumer surplus) that the household experiences through purchases of items that have experienced indirect price changes.

Steps 8a and 8b make it clear that a single tax (subsidy) can have both direct and indirect impacts. A fuel subsidy, for example, lowers the price of fuel that a household purchases for vehicles and cooking, but it also lowers the price of agricultural goods and public transport. Under the price-shifting model, households receive the full magnitude of the direct and indirect benefits (burdens) created by a subsidy (tax).

The calculation of indirect effects can also be completed within the IMF code if the user provides (as inputs) the household expenditure records: section 4 through to the end of the program replicates step 8. The code does not estimate PV and CSV in parallel, so we suggest that the CEQ analyst generate the sector-level price changes that would occur if a tax or subsidy were removed using the Stata code and then "import" those price-change vectors into the household consumption expenditure survey to use in calculating the indirect PV and CS magnitudes for the taxes (or subsidies) being analyzed.

Whether the analyst migrates the sectoral price changes "by hand" to the microdata or feeds the microdata into the software to allow the software to complete step 8, she should pause at the completion of step 7 to examine the price changes (listed by sector) for consistency and logic. If, for example, an increase in the price of fuel (due to the removal of a fuel subsidy) has very little impact on the transportation sector, then the analyst should reexamine the price change statements and, if necessary, the IO table to determine the source of the inconsistency.

6 Taxes versus Subsidies

Subsidies—whether they are applied at the point of purchase by the consumer or given to goods and services producers themselves—should lower prices paid. Indirect taxes have the opposite effect. For a good that is subsidized, the retail price is lower than the economic cost while household expenditure on the good (valued at market prices) will reflect only a portion of the economic cost or the price the good would fetch if there were no subsidy. For a good that is taxed, the retail price is higher than the economic cost, and expenditure by a household on that good represents some household consumption and some revenues collected by the government.

However, because businesses and households have reason to avoid taxes and because exemptions or exceptions for subcategories within a taxed class of goods may mean there will be reduced impact on *producer prices*, the CEQ analyst should take care to use empirical facts and judicious discretion in programming and simulating prefiscal counterfactuals for either taxes or subsidies. The CEQ analyst should use all the analytical tools at her disposal to faithfully reflect the *de facto*, rather than the *de jure*, situation. For example, when the statutory VAT rate is 18 percent, but the analyst notes that confirmed revenues from VAT divided by the confirmed sales value of the VAT-able base indicate that the *effective* VAT rate is something less than 18 percent, the analyst should apply the *effective* VAT rate to the household survey. Applying the statutory VAT rate to household purchases would likely overestimate the actual VAT burden on households.

The IMF code accommodates these complications within the price model described above. Take tax avoidance first: when there is no secondary-source data available on tax evasion, the analyst can use effective tax rates calculated from the macro data instead of policy rates. The effective rates implicit in macro data are simply the ratio of (confirmed, verified, or audited) tax revenues divided by the taxable base according to national accounts. Depending on how disaggregated the information used to generate effective rates is, the analyst can then choose to apply one effective rate for all goods or services that attract the tax, or she can differentially apply the various sectoral effective rates, or she can choose to reduce the sectoral policy rates by the same factor by which the global effective rate is lower than the global policy rate. Notice that this approach effectively assumes that all households engage in tax avoidance behavior in the same proportion, when measured as a share of their total consumption, thereby also effectively assuming that the share of goods purchased informally is the same for poorer and richer households.[21]

Whether an indirect tax "cascades" depends on the mechanics of the tax. For instance, an excise tax should compound as prices paid for inputs at any production stage will contain taxes paid during the previous production stage (for cost-push sectors

---

[21] Recent evidence shows that households at the bottom of the consumption distribution typically purchase a larger share of their budgets in informal markets in developing countries, See Bachas and others (2021).

under the assumptions of the price model described above in section 3). In principle, a value-added tax should not compound as producers claim rebates on all VAT paid on inputs. However, exempt items open the door to compounding of VAT, as discussed below. The extent of the compounding may also have to do with the structure of the market for the good or service being taxed; see appendix 7A for a detailed discussion.

The analyst can allow for a compounding tax by *not entering* any fixed price statements; that is, he can let prices in all taxed sectors change by the total (weighted) amount by which all input prices have changed as a result of the initial price shock (for example, the removal of the tax). This will result in the magnitude of the final, total, retail price change in some (possibly all) cost-push sectors being larger than the initial shock.

For a noncompounding tax, the analyst can enter fixed price statements for all sectors in which the counterfactual results in no change to *producer prices*. For example, suppose the counterfactual under consideration is the removal of a VAT system that has no exemptions. Retail prices in the sectors subject to VAT will drop by exactly the VAT rate, but no further: under a VAT system, producers receive rebates on all taxes paid on inputs, so if a VAT is removed, producer prices will not change.

Exemptions within a VAT schedule make it more difficult to put bounds on the minimum and maximum of the actual total change in producer prices. If a VAT schedule designates certain "basic necessity" food items as exempt, for example, then the rebate chain is broken for those items: while consumers will not pay VAT upon purchase, producers of "basic necessity" food items do not receive rebates for any input VAT paid. To the extent that such producers use standard-rated items as inputs, the final price of a "basic necessity" food item will reflect total input costs, which will now include any VAT paid (and not rebated) by the producer on inputs. Therefore, in a VAT system with at least one exempt good, it is no longer true that producer prices will not change if the VAT system is abolished; and as such, indirect effects will need to be calculated.[22]

Another example concerns domestic industrial or commercial users of imported goods, who are often not charged customs duties; in this case producer prices may not change if there is a shock to import duties. Then, as in the case of a VAT system with no exemptions, there will be only direct effects of import duties; there will be no indirect effect that operates through the change in producer prices.

In cases where the indirect tax system in application means that some producer prices would change and some would not in the price-shifting model under the counterfactual, the analyst should break up transmission of higher intermediate prices onto final prices into two steps. As a preliminary, identify the sectors for which *producer prices* will not change *directly*;[23] call the set of those sectors *I* and the set of all remaining

---

[22] For further discussion of the difference between VAT regimes and standard sales or excise taxes (vis-à-vis household welfare impacts), see Newhouse and Coady (2006).

[23] In a VAT system, these are the sectors that are not VAT-exempt (so producers receive a rebate on any VAT paid). In an import duty system, these are the sectors in which producers do not have to pay customs duties.

sectors J. Then (1) enter price shocks (corresponding to the counterfactual) for I only and solve the price model. From the $1 \times (I+J)$ vector of total price changes, select the elements corresponding to J and (2) enter those as (the only) price shocks in a new price model. Once that new price model has been solved, the elements corresponding to I in the $1 \times (I+J)$ vector of total price changes will represent the indirect changes in producer prices that arise when, for example, nonexempt VAT sectors consume some VAT-exempt inputs in the production process. The *indirect* impact on producer prices in I plus the exogenous price shocks in I will be the total change in final prices in the I sectors.

The preceding discussion is meant to sound a gentle alarm: knowing the statutory rate of indirect taxation or the policy subsidy rate is not enough to generate reasonable estimates of the impacts of the indirect tax and subsidy schedule on household purchasing power or welfare. The CEQ analyst will also need to parameterize as completely as possible the *de facto* application of the tax and subsidy schedule, including any weak tax or subsidy administration and tax avoidance as well as how informal purchases from unregistered sellers are to be treated.

7 Relaxing Model Constraints

Relying on IO matrices for empirical solutions to the "cost-push" model of the indirect impacts of indirect taxes and subsidies on producer prices has limitations. The basic model discussed above (a) allows only one tax or subsidy rate per sector whereas in reality goods produced in one aggregated IO sector may attract different rates of taxation; (b) does not distinguish between imported inputs and domestically produced inputs whereas prices of the former should not be directly affected by *domestic* input taxes or subsidies; and (c) does not account for informality or tax evasion on the part of producers and consumers.[24]

There are empirical solutions to the first two limitations. To allow for more than one rate of taxation or subsidization on the multiple goods produced within an IO sector, Warwick and others (2022, p. 7) suggest "partition[ing] the original [IO] product categories into sub-categories subject to different [tax or subsidy] treatments, ensuring that the original input-output accounting identities remain intact." The share of total super-category output (shown in the original IO matrix) accounted for by each subcategory in most cases can be assumed to correspond to the subcategory's share of total expenditure (in the super-category) in the household survey data.[25]

---

[24] Except in an economy-wide aggregate sense, for example when we calculate effective rates of taxation or subsidization.

[25] There are some products—energy products are a good example—for which firms and consumers make use of subcategories in significantly different proportions; in those cases Warwick and others (2022) recommend using estimates of subcategory shares in super-category output from other data.

To account for the *absence* of domestic tax burdens or subsidy benefits on imports (at the point of importation), Warwick and others (2022) suggest partitioning the original IO matrix into imported inputs IO matrix and a domestically produced inputs IO matrix. This and the previous matrix partition steps are described in more detail in the online-only appendix 7B.

With respect to (c), the third limitation: smaller firms that may be officially exempt from remitting taxes on inputs, and informal firms that can successfully evade paying taxes on inputs or remitting taxes on sales, appear (from the point of view of the IO matrix and our cost-push model of producer price formation) to face as large a total burden or total benefit from indirect taxes or subsidies (respectively) as do nonexempt and formal firms. As Warwick and others (2022) point out, however, an empirical solution to this limitation would require a larger information set than is typically available. To wit:

> [I]nput-output tables generally do not contain separate entries for large/tax-compliant and small/tax-evading firms selling the same product. This means if one wanted to utilise [the IO matrix partition] approach, one would need to partition existing product categories into varieties produced by large/tax-compliant and small/tax-evading firms. Both the importance of these two types of firms to overall industry output, and the use of inputs from these two types of firms, is likely to differ by product category (and in the case of input usage, by type of firm. . . .)

Instead, drawing on Bachas, Gadenne, and Jensen (2021), Warwick and others (2022) propose a consumer-side fix to informality in production, based on information on the place of purchase for all transactions as recorded in some household surveys. Household survey information on size and location of firms where producer-consumer transactions are completed are used to classify each transaction as formal or informal, from which one can reduce effective rates of taxation at the level of the household and product. This differentiation allows for more realistic assumptions about the share of goods purchased informally across the distribution. Note that the effective tax rate of an informally purchased item is unlikely to be zero, due to embedded VAT in earlier stages of production. As such, the cost push model described above can be used to estimate the indirect effects of the VAT on goods and services purchased from informal or tax-evading producers.

8 Summary and Conclusion

The impact of indirect taxes (and subsidies) on poverty and inequality can be significant. However, standard poverty headcounts and inequality measures—calculated over a distribution of consumption expenditures—do not typically attempt to apportion the value of household consumption expenditure on goods and services separately from the value of indirect taxes paid while making consumption expenditures.

Accounting for the *direct* impact of indirect taxes (or subsidies) on household welfare and expenditure levels provides an estimate for only one channel by which fiscal policy might affect inequality and poverty. The *indirect* impact of indirect taxes (or subsidies), which is created via the interaction of the production side of the economy with the fiscal system and with consumers, can be larger in magnitude than the direct impact as well as proportionally more important for lower-income consumers.

For example, in a twenty-country study covering Africa, South and Central America, Asia and the Pacific, and the Middle East and Central Asia, the indirect impact of higher fuel prices on welfare accounted for a nearly 60 percent share of the total impact (direct + indirect).[26] On average, the indirect impact was about 1.34 times greater than the direct impact for the poorest population quintile(s). In other words, the burden on the bottom 20 percent of the population created by the removal of fuel subsidies (or the imposition of a fuel tax) in these countries would be on average 134 percent higher if indirect impacts[27] were taken into account than if only direct impacts were taken into account. Including indirect effects, therefore, is likely to have a significant impact on the level of fiscal impoverishment (see Higgins and Lustig [2016], reproduced in chapter 4 in this Volume) generated by fiscal policy.[28]

Low- and middle-income countries raise more in revenue from indirect than from direct taxes (on average), so a fiscal-incidence accounting will be missing an important piece if the burden of indirect taxes is not sensibly estimated. This chapter has provided a practical guide with theoretical underpinnings for calculating the item-by-item and household-by-household burden or benefit of indirect taxes or subsidies. These procedures include steps for calculating both the direct and indirect burdens of indirect taxes so that the CEQ analyst can provide a reasonable description of the prefiscal counterfactual in which taxes or subsidies have been eliminated.

---

[26] See Coady, Flamini, and Sears (2015). Indirect impacts are calculated under the price-shifting model discussed in this chapter and are valued according to the Paasche variation (also discussed in this chapter). The results from two countries, Indonesia and South Africa, in Coady, Flamini, and Sears (2015), are based on *CEQ Assessments* undertaken in collaboration with the World Bank; see Inchauste and Lustig (2017).

[27] Indirect effects created by the price-shifting model and valued by the Paasche welfare variation.

[28] The estimated impact of fiscal policy on inequality is also likely to change if the indirect effects of indirect taxes (or subsidies) are included because the magnitude of the indirect impact (measured as a share of the total impact) on welfare is greater for the poorest than for the richest quintile in all regions included in Coady, Flamini, and Sears (2015).

References

Ahmad, Ehtisham, and Nicholas Stern. 1990. "Tax Reform and Shadow Prices for Pakistan." *Oxford Economic Papers* 42, no. 1, pp. 135–59.

———. 1991. *The Theory and Practice of Tax Reform in Developing Countries* (Cambridge University Press).

Alleyne, Dillon, James Alm, Roy Bahl, and Sally Wallace. 2004. "Tax Burden in Jamaica." Jamaican Tax Reform Project, Working Paper 9 (Atlanta: Andrew Young School of Policy Studies, Georgia State University).

Alm, James, and Sally Wallace. 2007. "Are Jamaica's Direct Taxes on Labor 'Fair'?" *Public Finance Review* 35, no. 1, pp. 83–102.

Araar, Abdelkrim, and Paolo Verme. 2016. "Prices and Welfare." Working Paper 7566 (Washington: World Bank Policy Research).

Bachas, Pierre, Lucie Gadenne, and Anders Jensen. 2021. "Informality, Consumption Taxes and Redistribution." NBER Working Paper No. 27429. https://doi.org/10.3386/w27429.

Ballard, Charles L., Don Fullerton, John B. Shoven, and John Whalley. 1985. *A General Equilibrium Model for Tax Policy Analysis* (University of Chicago Press).

Bird, Richard M., and Barbara Diane Miller. 1989. "The Incidence of Indirect Taxes on Low-Income Households in Jamaica." *Economic Development and Cultural Change* 37, no. 2, pp. 393–409.

Bourguignon, François, and Luiz Pereira da Silva, eds. 2003. *Evaluating the Poverty and Distributional Impact of Economic Policies* (Oxford University Press).

Coady, David. 2008. "The Distributional Impacts of Indirect Tax and Public Pricing Reforms: A Review of Methods and Empirical Evidence," in *Poverty and Social Impact Analysis by the IMF: Review of Methodology and Selected Evidence*, edited by Robert Gillingham (Washington: International Monetary Fund).

Coady, David, Valentina Flamini, and Louis Sears. 2015. "The Unequal Benefits of Fuel Subsidies Revisited: Evidence for Developing Countries," Working Paper 15/250 (Washington: International Monetary Fund).

Fullerton, Don, and Gilbert E. Metcalf. 2002. "Tax Incidence," in *Handbook of Public Economics*, vol. 4, edited by Alan Auerbach and Martin Feldstein (Amsterdam: North Holland).

Fullerton, Don, and Diane Lim Rogers. 1993. *Who Bears the Lifetime Tax Burden?* (Brookings Institution).

Harberger, Arnold C. 1962. "The Incidence of the Corporate Income Tax." *Journal of Political Economy* 70, no. 2, pp. 215–40.

Higgins, Sean, and Nora Lustig. 2016. "Can a Poverty-Reducing and Progressive Tax and Transfer System Hurt the Poor?" *Journal of Development Economics* 122, pp. 63–75.

Inchauste, Gabriela, and Nora Lustig, eds. 2017. *The Distributional Impact of Taxes and Transfers. Evidence from Eight Low- and Middle-Income Countries* (Washington: World Bank).

Kotlikoff, Laurence J., and Lawrence H. Summers. 1987. "Tax Incidence," in *Handbook of Public Economics*, vol. 2, edited by Alan Auerbach and Martin Feldstein (Amsterdam: North Holland).

Leontief, Wassily. 1986. *Input-Output Economics*, 2nd ed. (Oxford University Press).

McLure, Charles E., Jr. 1975. "General Equilibrium Incidence Analysis: The Harberger Model after Ten Years." *Journal of Public Economics* 4, no. 1, pp. 125–61.

Newhouse, David, and David Coady. (2006). "Ghana: Evaluating the Fiscal and Social Costs of Increases in Domestic Fuel Prices," in *Analyzing the Distributional Impacts of Reforms:*

Operational Experience in Implementing Poverty and Social Impact Analysis, edited by A. Coudouel, A. Dani, and S. Paternostro (Washington: World Bank).

Parra, Juan Carlos, and Quentin Wodon. 2011. "SimSIP SAM: A Tool for the Analysis of Input-Output Tables and Social Accounting Matrices" (Washington: World Bank) (http://simsip .org/uploads/SimSIP_SAM.pdf).

Pechman, Joseph. 1985. *Who Paid the Taxes: 1966–1985* (Brookings Institution).

Rajemison, Harivelo, Steven Haggblade, and Stephen D. Younger. 2003. "Indirect Tax Incidence in Madagascar: Updated Estimates Using the Input-Output Table." Cornell University Food and Nutrition Policy Program Working Paper 147.

Rajemison, Harivelo, and Stephen D. Younger. 2000. "Indirect Tax Incidence in Madagascar: Estimations Using the Input-Output Table." Cornell University Food and Nutrition Policy Program Working Paper 106.

Ring, Raymond J., Jr. 1989. "The Proportion of Consumers' and Producers' Goods in the General Sales Tax." *National Tax Journal*, 42, no. 2, pp. 167–79.

———. 1999. "Consumers' and Producers' Shares of the General Sales Tax." *National Tax Journal* 52, no. 1, pp. 79–90.

Sahn, David E., and Stephen D. Younger. 1999. "Fiscal Incidence in Africa: Microeconomic Evidence." Cornell University Working Paper 91.

Varian, Hal. 1992. *Microeconomic Analysis*, 3rd ed. (New York: Norton).

Warwick, Ross, Tom Harris, David Philips, Maya Goldman, Jon Jellema, Gabriela Inchauste, and Karolina Goraus-Tanska. 2022. "The Redistributive Power of Cash Transfers vs VAT Exemptions: A Multi-Country Study." *World Development 151*. https://doi.org/10.1016/j.worlddev .2021.105742.

Wasylenko, Michael. 1987. "Tax Burden in Jamaica before and after Tax Reform." Jamaica Tax Structure Examination Project, Metropolitan Studies Program, Syracuse University, Board of Revenue, Government of Jamaica Staff Paper No. 37.

Appendix 7A

Dealing with Taxes on Intermediate Stages of Production and Consumption

James Alm

All taxes must ultimately be paid by someone, and one of the most basic questions asked by economists is "Who pays the taxes?" Any tax will cause individuals and firms to change their behaviors, and the resulting changes in product and factor prices will affect the incidence, or the distributional effects, of the tax. This appendix discusses the notion of tax incidence, with a focus on a specific and complicating issue in its applied analysis.

Economists have devoted much attention to the question of tax incidence.[29] Much of this work is theoretical. The focus here is on applied, microsimulation work as conducted in other parts of this Volume of the Handbook. Several basic principles of tax incidence emerge from these analyses, which should be kept in mind in the discussion that follows.

A first principle is an obvious but often ignored one: *only individuals can bear the burden of a tax*. Consider, for example, the company income tax. The company is the agent legally responsible for remitting the tax payment to the government, and so bears the "statutory incidence" of the tax. However, the company is merely a legal entity, and it makes little sense to claim that it is the company that bears the "economic incidence" of the tax. Instead, the economic incidence will be borne by one or more of several possible candidates, as produce and factor prices adjust in response to the company tax: the owners of the company, the consumers of the company's product(s), the workers of the company, the individuals who supply other inputs to the company, and even the owners of other companies. To take another example, consider an excise tax on gasoline. The firm that collects the excise tax and remits it to the government will bear the statutory incidence of the tax, but again the economic incidence will depend upon the ways in which product and factor prices adjust to the excise tax. The final burden of the tax will likely be borne by consumers of gasoline via increased gasoline prices or by those who supply inputs to the production of gasoline. And for a final example, consider the employer's share of a payroll tax. The statutory burden of the tax is borne by the legal entity of the firm, but the economic incidence will ultimately be borne by its stockholders via a lower return, by its workers via lower wages, by its input suppliers via lower input prices, or by the consumers of its product via higher product prices. Tax incidence attempts to find ways to assign the burden of a tax to these individuals.

This reasoning suggests that a clear distinction must be made between who is legally responsible for paying a tax and who ultimately bears the true burden of the tax. The process by which the statutory incidence of a tax is moved from those legally responsible to those who bear the economic burden is commonly referred to as "tax shifting." If a tax is shifted to consumers via higher product prices, then the tax is said to be "shifted forward"; if the tax is borne instead by workers or other input suppliers, then the tax is said to be "shifted backward."

A second principle of tax incidence is that *incidence on both the sources of income and the uses of income should be considered*. A tax may affect the prices of the products

---

[29] Much of this work builds on the analysis of Harberger (1962). For comprehensive surveys, see McLure (1975), Kotlikoff and Summers (1987), and Fullerton and Metcalf (2002). For examples of applied work for the United States, see Pechman (1985) and Fullerton and Rogers (1993); for surveys of applied work in developing countries, see Sahn and Younger (1999) and Bourguignon and da Silva (2003), among many others.

that individuals consume (or their "uses" of income). The same tax may also affect factor prices (or the "sources" of income). A full understanding of the incidence of the tax must incorporate both sides. Consider once again the excise tax on gasoline. To the extent that the price of gasoline increases, then individuals who purchase gasoline will pay some of the excise tax. To the extent that individuals who work for the gasoline companies receive lower wages (as, say, the companies reduce their demands for labor), then these individuals will also bear some of the burden of the excise tax. Both the sources and the uses of income must be analyzed in incidence analysis.

A third principle may be less obvious. It is that *incidence depends upon on the nature of the budgetary change; that is, incidence depends upon how the tax revenues are used.* A basic government accounting identity ensures that all government expenditures must be financed from one or more of several sources: tax revenues, borrowing (or the issuance of debt) from the public, or borrowing from the government via money expansion. Any change in tax revenues must be accompanied by a corresponding change in government expenditures, in government debt, in the money supply, or in another tax. The impact of any specific tax change on product and factor prices will clearly depend upon the precise change in these other instruments accompanying the tax change.

The most common assumption here is that another tax (proportional to income) is changed in response to a specific tax change (or "differential tax incidence"), and this is the assumption that is made in the following incidence analysis. Other assumptions are possible.

A fourth principle is that *incidence depends upon market structure.* Tax incidence attempts to trace the impact of a tax on product and factor prices. Clearly, the ways in which prices are determined in these markets will affect the final burden of a tax. An excise tax imposed in a competitive market will have a different impact on prices than the same tax imposed in a market that is a monopoly or an oligopoly. Similarly, a tax imposed in a market in which all demands and supplies come from domestic sources will have a different impact on prices if it is imposed in a market in which international agents participate either on the demand side or on the supply side.

A related subprinciple is that *in a competitive market the incidence of a tax does not depend upon where it is imposed, whether on consumers of the produce or on producers of the product.* The tax simply drives a wedge between the gross-of-tax price paid by consumers and the net-of-tax price received by producers, and the origin of the wedge (for example, from the demand side of the market or from the supply side of the market) is irrelevant.

Finally, and most importantly, when a tax is imposed, individuals will adjust their behavior to reduce their tax liabilities. Those who are better able to adjust their behavior—those who have a larger responsiveness, as measured by the "elasticity"—are better able to shift the tax burden to others and will bear less of the burden of the tax. This leads to a fifth principle: *incidence depends upon elasticities.* For example, if consumers have a low response to gasoline prices, then consumers will bear more of the incidence of an excise tax on gasoline. Similarly, if workers are able to reduce their work effort or to shift their labor to untaxed sectors in response to an individual income tax or a payroll tax, then workers will bear less of the burden of an income or a payroll tax.[30]

How are these basic principles applied in practice? There are various types of incidence analysis. Here, the focus is on microsimulation analyses, as conducted in other parts of the Handbook.

Suppose that we start with pretax/pre-transfer income of unit h, denoted I_h. Define the revenues that tax i collects as T_i and the amount of tax i that is borne by unit h (S_{ih}), so that S_{ih} incorporates the various incidence assumptions that must be made. For example, consider an excise tax on gasoline. If one assumes that an excise tax on gasoline is borne by consumers in proportion to their consumption of gasoline, then S_{ih} will measure the share of total consumption of gasoline for unit h. Similarly, the usual assumption about the incidence of the individual income tax is that it is borne in proportion to income, so that S_{ih} will equal the share of total income for unit h.[31] These S_{ih} terms are sometimes termed "allocators" because they allocate the tax burden of each tax instrument to the relevant units of taxation.

Given this framework, the post-tax/post-transfer income of unit h, or Y_h, is simply

$$(7A\text{-}1) \qquad\qquad Y_h = I_h - \sum_i T_i S_{ih},$$

where the total taxes paid by unit h equal $\sum_i T_i S_{ih}$. From this framework, different measures of taxes can be calculated, in order to characterize "Who pays the taxes?"

This basic framework is a simple one—indeed, a deceptively simple one. For example, application of this framework requires answers to questions about the "unit" of taxation (for example, individual, household, deciles), about the appropriate "income" measure (for example, "comprehensive income," annual versus lifetime income, market versus non-market income, cash versus in-kind income), about the calculation of specific components of income (for example, capital income, rental income, evasion income), about the time frame of analysis (for example, annual versus lifetime), about the specific taxes (and transfers) examined, and about assumptions about the allocators (for example, is there a

---

[30] For example, suppose that an average worker has annual wages of $30,000. If there is an individual income tax of, say, 10 percent and if workers bear the full burden of the tax, then the average worker's net-of-tax wage income falls by $3,000 (= 10 percent × $30,000) to $27,000. However, suppose that the presence of the 10 percent tax causes workers to reduce their supply of labor to the taxed sector, perhaps by working fewer hours in total or by working fewer hours in the taxed sector and more in the untaxed, informal sector. If the average wage rises to, say, $31,000, then labor has been able to shift $1,000 of the $3,000 tax to employers via a higher gross-of-tax wage; employers may in turn shift some of their burden to consumers via higher product prices or to other input suppliers via lower input prices.

[31] Instruments can also include transfers or subsidies, in which case T_i is simply a negative number (for example, the transfer/subsidy increases the post-tax/post-transfer income of unit h).

consensus on incidence?). In most all cases, there are no simple answers, especially for developing countries where data are often limited, even problematic. Even so, answers to these—and many other questions—are discussed at length elsewhere in this Handbook.

Here one specific issue is examined. The basic framework implicitly assumes that each tax T_i is imposed either on *final* consumption of consumers or on *final* income of factor owners; that is, the framework assumes that all taxes are imposed at a final stage of consumption ("uses") or at a final stage of income ("sources"). However, in many cases a tax may be imposed at intermediate stages of consumption or production. This is especially a concern for the analysis of petroleum excise taxes and import duties, even the value-added tax (VAT). For example, import duties (both positive and negative) in developing countries are typically imposed on a wide variety of imported goods, including food, automobiles, petroleum products, beverages, tobacco, clothing, raw materials, and capital goods. As these taxes work their way through the intermediate stages of production, they affect the prices both of the products that are produced (and that become inputs for the succeeding intermediate stages of production) and of the factors that are used to produce these intermediate inputs. Assigning these tax burdens only to final goods and services does not accurately capture the true burden of these taxes. Note that this broad issue is related to the narrower issue that arises in many developing countries: namely, a household is both a consumer of goods and a producer of goods. In this setting, a household may consume some goods in the process of producing other goods, so that taxes at one stage of production or consumption may affect prices of products and factors at other stages of production or consumption.

In one example of this type of "cascading," estimates for the United States indicate that consumers bear on average only about 60 percent of states' general sales taxes, with individual state estimates ranging from 30 to 90 percent (Ring, 1989, 1999), even though it is usually assumed that consumers bear the entire burden of a general sales tax. Put differently, these estimates indicate that businesses pay about 40 percent of general sales tax revenues because many business purchases of (intermediate) goods and services are in fact taxed under the general sales tax, despite the presumed intent of a general sales tax to tax only final goods and services. Estimates for developing countries (Ahmad and Stern, 1990, 1991) show a similar, indeed a more extreme, pattern.

How are these types of taxes incorporated in microsimulation incidence analysis?[32]

---

[32] It should be noted that an alternative to microsimulation analyses is the use of computable general equilibrium (CGE) modeling. Here multiple sectors and so multiple stages of production are introduced, so that the CGE approach is able to examine the incidence of taxes on intermediate inputs on household units. CGE modeling has traditionally been more aggregate in its analysis. For example, the CGE model in Ballard and others (1985) has nineteen production sectors, fifteen consumption goods, and twelve consumer groups. However, more recent models have increased significantly in size, and are able to incorporate multiple production sectors, consumption goods, and consumer groups.

One approach essentially ignores the taxation of intermediate products and attempts to assign the burden of all taxes to final consumers and factor owners. This approach recognizes the bias that is introduced, but believes that the bias is small and is outweighed by the convenience of the approach. For example, Alleyne and others (2004) assume that the incidence of petroleum excise taxes and import duties on petroleum is borne by consumers in proportion to their consumption of cars, even though these taxes are paid in significant amounts by businesses. They also assume that import duties on capital goods are borne by consumers in proportion to their consumption of nonfood items, even though the overlap between capital goods and nonfood items is tenuous. Many other applied incidence studies have often made similarly problematic incidence assumptions.[33]

A second and more recent microsimulation approach attempts to address the taxation of intermediate goods directly, by tracing the impact of taxes on intermediate goods through the various stages of production. This approach leads to more accurate, and more disaggregated, estimates of incidence than most other methods, although at some added cost in complexity and implementation.

This approach proceeds by utilizing input-output tables of a country. As pioneered by Wassily Leontief, an input-output table records the flows of products from each sector considered as a producer to each sector considered as consumers.[34] Application of input-output analysis to tax incidence proceeds by tracking the impact of taxes on intermediate goods through the input-output table to final consumers. For example, some portion of, say, a petroleum excise tax will fall *directly* on households via their consumption of personal transportation and also *indirectly* on households via their consumption of other goods that require transportation as an input. The final incidence of the petroleum excise tax is calculated as the sum of the direct and indirect effects of the tax, so that the incidence calculations will incorporate both the direct price increase in petroleum and the indirect price increases of all other products that use petroleum in production.

To illustrate, suppose that a simple economy consists of n sectors. Suppose that each sector i produces x_i units of a good, and that each sector j requires a_{ij} units of x_i to produce one unit of good x_j. Then the total demand for x_i can be written as:

(7A-2) $$x_i = a_{i1} x_1 + a_{i2} x_2 + a_{i3} x_3 + \cdots + a_{in} x_n + d_i = \sum_j a_{ij} x_j + d_i,$$

where d_i is the final demand for good i. The a_{ij} terms are called "input coefficients." When we consider the entire economy, all n sectors can be represented in matrix form as:

(7A-3) $$x = Ax + d,$$

---

[33] For example, see Wasylenko (1987) and Alm and Wallace (2007), both for the Jamaican tax system.

[34] Leontief's major articles are reprinted in Leontief (1986).

so that

(7A-4) $$x = (I - A)^{-1} d,$$

where x and d are $n \times 1$ vectors, A is an $n \times n$ matrix, I is an $n \times n$ identity matrix, and $(I - A)^{-1}$ denotes the inverse of the $(I - A)$ matrix.

For example, suppose that the economy consists of 3 sectors (x_1, x_2, x_3) with corresponding input coefficients a_{ij} and final demands d_i given by:

$$A = \begin{vmatrix} a_{11} & a_{12} & a_{13} \\ a_{21} & a_{22} & a_{23} \\ a_{31} & a_{32} & a_{33} \end{vmatrix} = \begin{vmatrix} 0.2 & 0.3 & 0.2 \\ 0.4 & 0.1 & 0.2 \\ 0.1 & 0.3 & 0.2 \end{vmatrix}$$

$$d = \begin{vmatrix} 10 \\ 5 \\ 6 \end{vmatrix}.$$

Reading across the rows of the A matrix, we see how the output of each sector is used in the sectors (for example, a_{12} shows that 0.3 units of x_1 are required to produce one unit of x_2). The vector d indicates the final demands for each sector (for example, the final demand for x_3 is six units). Using equation (7A-4) for the solution for x $(= (I - A)^{-1} d)$, the equilibrium in this simple economy requires that

$$x = \begin{vmatrix} 24.84 \\ 20.68 \\ 18.36 \end{vmatrix}.$$

Note that this solution represents a first-order linear approximation. Note also that this framework relies upon a variety of restrictive assumptions, such as constant returns to scale production and fixed and unchanging production requirements.

It is especially the A matrix of input coefficients that is used in the incidence analysis to attribute a tax on intermediate inputs to the final goods.

Applying this approach to tax incidence relies upon a simple price formation equation, which represents a slight variant on the solution for x in equation (7A-4):

(7A-5) $$P_j = \sum_i a_{ij}^d P_i + (1 + \tau_j^d) VA_j + \sum_i (1 + \tau_j^m)(1 + t_i) a_{ij}^m + s_j P_j,$$

where P_j is the price of good j, a_{ij}^d is the input coefficient of *domestic* input i for sector j, a_{ij}^m is the input coefficient of *imported* input i for sector j, τ_j^d is the *domestic* good value-added tax rate for sector j, τ_j^m is the *imported* good value-added tax rate for sector j,

VA_j is value-added in sector j, t_i is the import tariff rate for sector i, and s_j is the excise or other tax rate on sector j. Note that P_j appears on both sides of equation (7A-5), just as x appeared on both sides of equation (7A-4). Accordingly, the equation can be solved for the price P_j that satisfies the various relationships. In particular, the final price of sector j will depend upon the *direct* effects of sector-j specific taxes on sector j (via the value-added tax on good j and the excise/turnover tax on good j) as well as upon the *indirect* effects of all taxes on intermediate goods (via their effects as these taxes work through the complicated input-output relationships). Equation (7A-5) can also be summed across all sectors to derive the solution for all prices in the economy, as functions of direct and indirect effects of all taxes.[35]

The incidence of any particular tax (say, on good i) on the price of good j is then calculated in a straightforward way. The price of good j is calculated with all taxes included, and then the price is calculated when setting tax i equal to zero. The incidence of tax i on good j is simply the difference in prices. The change in P_j can then be used in standard calculations to determine the incidence of the tax at the household level, based on household consumption of the relevant goods, where the incidence now reflects both direct and indirect effects of taxes.

Note that it is straightforward to introduce various constraints reflecting the specific economic environment of the country on the price equation (7A-5). For example, the prices of some goods in a small open economy (such as tradeable goods) are likely to be fixed, determined by international markets and not by domestic markets. In this case, the relevant price is predetermined, and the analysis proceeds by the substitution of the fixed price into the system of equations.

The input-output approach is more cumbersome to apply than the simpler microsimulation approach. In particular, its application requires a detailed input-output table of the relevant economy. The approach also depends upon the validity of the various assumptions underlying the construction of input-output tables, as discussed earlier. Even so, it allows a more accurate assignment of tax liabilities at the household level.

Overall, it should be evident that there are many difficult issues in applied microsimulation incidence studies. As a result, there is no single "best practice" for these studies, and extensive robustness tests are required to test the sensitivity of results to specific assumptions.

---

[35] For detailed applications of this approach, see Bird and Miller (1989), Rajemison and Younger (2000), and Rajemison, Haggblade, and Younger (2003).

Chapter 8

PRODUCING INDICATORS AND RESULTS, AND COMPLETING SECTIONS D AND E OF THE *CEQ MASTER WORKBOOK©* USING THE *CEQ STATA PACKAGE©*

Sean Higgins and Caterina Brest Lopez

Introduction

This chapter describes the indicators and results used in a *CEQ Assessment*, sections D, "Summary of Results," and E, "Output Tables," of the *CEQ Master Workbook©* (MWB) (available online in part IV in Volume 1 of this Handbook; CEQ Institute, 2022), and how the results and indicators can be produced and exported to the *CEQ MWB* using the *CEQ Stata Package* (Higgins, Aranda, Brest Lopez, Li, Amjad, Larroulet, and McKenzie, 2022).

The results in sections D and E of the *CEQ MWB* are designed to answer the following four questions from a *CEQ Assessment*, presented in chapter 1 in Volume 1 of this Handbook (Lustig and Higgins, 2022).

1. How much income redistribution and poverty reduction is accomplished through fiscal policy?[1]
2. How equalizing and pro-poor are specific taxes and government spending?
3. How effective are taxes and government spending in reducing inequality and poverty?
4. What is the impact of fiscal reforms that change the size and/or progressivity of a particular tax or benefit?

---

[1] Throughout this Handbook, "fiscal policy," "fiscal instruments," "taxes and government spending," "revenue collection and government spending," "taxes and transfers," "taxes and benefits," and "net fiscal system" are used interchangeably.

It is important to note that there are two ways that we recommend treating pensions in CEQ (see chapter 1 in Volume 1 of this Handbook). To recapitulate, these are:

1. Contributory pensions as pure deferred income (PDI)
2. Contributory pensions as a pure government transfer (PGT)

Producing results for a *CEQ Assessment* requires completing two sets of section E: one for the scenario in which contributory pensions are considered deferred income (PDI) and one for the scenario in which contributory pensions are considered government transfers (PGT). You need two sets of E sheets because the following income concepts are different for each scenario: Market Income, Market Income plus Pensions, Net Market Income, and Gross Income. Disposable Income, Consumable Income, and Final Income are the same in both. For details, see chapter 6, figure 6-2, and table 6-5 in this Volume (Enami, Higgins, and Lustig, 2022). In the same fashion, two sets of D sheets will be created automatically, one for each scenario. To populate the D section see the general linking Instructions that appear on the sheet called "Linking" in the D section of the *CEQ MWB* and follow the detailed instructions in part IV of this Volume. These instructions are in the same folder where section D is saved in *4. CEQ Master Workbook*. Like everything else, you can download this item from www .ceqinstitute.org and clicking on the Handbook tab.

This chapter is organized as follows. Section 1 presents preliminary definitions. Section 2 describes the structure of sections D and E of the *CEQ MWB* and defines the indicators used in a *CEQ Assessment*. Section 3 describes the suite of user-written Stata commands that make up the *CEQ Stata Package*.

1 Basic Concepts

I begin by overviewing some basic concepts that are necessary to understand the discussions later in this chapter.

1.1 Core Income Concepts

The income concepts presented in figure 6-2 and table 6-5 in chapter 6 in this Volume are the core income concepts and are the primary income concepts used in a *CEQ Assessment*. The income concepts are Market Income, Market Income plus Pensions, Net Market Income, Gross Income, Disposable Income, Taxable Income, Consumable Income,[2] and Final Income. For example, tracing the change in inequality between Market Income and Disposable Income shows how direct taxes and transfers affect in-

---

[2] "Consumable income" is the concept and the name used in Canada's Social Policy Simulation Database Model (SPSD/M), one of the main sources used to produce the distribution of household income accounts and evaluate the impact of changes in tax and spending policies.

equality, while tracing from Market Income to Consumable Income shows how direct and indirect taxes, direct transfers, and indirect subsidies affect inequality.

1.2 Fiscal Interventions

"Fiscal interventions" (also known as "fiscal instruments") refer to any tax, transfer, or subsidy included in a *CEQ Assessment*.

1.3 Income Components

"Income components" refer to elements of income that are not fiscal interventions (they are not collected or provided by the government), such as labor income or production for own consumption.

1.4 Extended Income Concepts

The extended income concepts consist of additional income concepts constructed by adding and subtracting individual fiscal interventions or bundles of fiscal interventions from the core income concepts. For example, one extended income concept would be "Market Income plus Pensions plus conditional cash transfers (CCT)." This extended income concept is useful because, for example, inequality of Market Income plus Pensions can be compared to inequality of this extended income concept to see how CCT affect inequality when we ignore the existence of other direct taxes and transfers. As a second example, another extended income concept would be "Disposable Income minus CCT"; since Disposable Income already includes CCT, Disposable Income *minus* CCT means Disposable Income *prior to* adding in CCT benefits. This extended income concept is useful because, for example, inequality of Disposable Income minus CCT can be compared to inequality of Disposable Income to see how CCT benefits affect inequality when we *do* take into account the existence of other direct taxes and transfers.

1.5 Initial Income

"Initial income" refers to the income concept prior to adding (subtracting) the transfer (tax) we are focusing on. In the first example above, initial income would be "Market Income plus Pensions." In the second, initial income would be "Disposable Income minus CCT."

1.6 End Income

"End income" refers to the post-tax and transfer income concept that we are using in a particular comparison. In the first example above, end income would be "Market

Income plus Pensions plus CCT." In the second, end income would be "Disposable Income."

1.7 Prefiscal Income

"Prefiscal income" refers to income before any taxes and transfers are accounted for. The relevant income concept is generally Market Income or Market Income plus Pensions, depending on the treatment of pensions. In some instances, we also refer to prefiscal income as "original income."

1.8 Postfiscal Income

"Postfiscal income" refers to any income concept after at least some taxes and transfers have been accounted for, such as Disposable Income, Consumable Income, Final Income, or various extended income concepts.

1.9 Marginal Contribution

The "marginal contribution" is defined as the contribution of a particular fiscal intervention to an outcome indicator of interest, such as an inequality or poverty indicator. It is defined explicitly in box 1-2 in chapter 1 in this Volume (Enami, 2022c). Note that if a fiscal intervention's marginal contribution to inequality (poverty) is positive, the intervention is equalizing (poverty-reducing) with respect to whatever end income concept was used, while if it is negative, the intervention is unequalizing (poverty-increasing).

1.10 Progressivity and Pro-Poorness

Since one of the criteria for evaluating the distributive impact of fiscal policy depends on the extent of progressivity of taxes and transfers, this is a good place to review the definitions used in the literature of what constitutes progressive taxes and transfers. To determine if a tax or transfer is progressive, concentration curves, concentration coefficients, and the Kakwani[3] index are commonly used.

Concentration curves are constructed similarly to Lorenz curves but the difference is that the vertical axis measures the proportion of a tax (transfer) paid (received) by each quantile. Therefore, concentration curves (for a transfer targeted to the poor, for example) can be above the diagonal (something that, by definition, could never happen with a Lorenz curve). Concentration coefficients are calculated in the same manner as the Gini but for cases in which the concentration curve is above the diagonal, the difference between the triangle of perfect equality and the area under the

---

[3] Kakwani (1977).

curve is negative, which cannot occur with the Gini for the income distribution by definition. The data used to generate concentration curves and coefficients are derived from incidence analyses. The technical definitions of the Lorenz curve and concentration curve are given in this chapter's sections 2.2.18 Lorenz Curves and 2.2.19 Concentration Curves.

The terms "progressive" and "regressive" are used in two different senses in the literature on taxes and transfers. We borrow Lustig, Pessino, and Scott's (2014) concise summary here:

> The progressivity/regressivity of a transfer can be measured in absolute terms by comparing the amount of transfers across quantiles or it can be defined in relative terms by comparing transfers as a percentage of the (pre-transfer) income of each quantile. In the tax incidence literature, where the fiscal application of the terms *progressive* and *regressive* originated, they are used exclusively in the relative sense. In the benefit (and tax-benefit) incidence literature, it is common practice to use the absolute as well as the relative concepts.[4]

Since the CEQ assesses the progressivity of both taxes and transfers, we have opted for the relative definition. Hence, a transfer is progressive when the proportion received as a percentage of prefiscal income decreases with income. This is consistent with an intuitively appealing principle: in a world with no reranking, a transfer or tax is defined as progressive (regressive) if applying that tax or transfer alone results in a less (more) unequal distribution than that of prefiscal income.

We distinguish between transfers that are progressive in absolute terms and progressive in relative terms. In particular:

1. A tax is everywhere progressive (regressive) if the proportion paid—in relation to prefiscal income—increases (decreases) as income rises.[5] In practice, taxes are not *everywhere* progressive; for example, if one household manages to evade the tax while another household with slightly lower income and another with slightly higher income do not, the definition of being everywhere progressive will be violated. A tax is *globally* progressive (regressive) if its concentration curve lies everywhere below (above) the prefiscal income Lorenz curve. A necessary but not sufficient condition for this is that the concentration coefficient is positive and larger (smaller) than the prefiscal income Gini. This necessary but not sufficient condition is equivalent to saying that the Kakwani index, defined for taxes as the tax concentration coefficient minus the prefiscal income Gini, will be positive (negative) if a tax is globally progressive (regressive).

---

[4] Lustig, Pessino, and Scott (2014, p. 290).

[5] For more on the concept of a tax being everywhere progressive, see Duclos (2008).

Note that the concentration curve of the tax may *cross* the prefiscal income Lorenz curve, in which case it is ambiguous (neither progressive nor regressive). Its concentration coefficient may be either less than or greater than the prefiscal income Gini. Hence, we use concentration curves—and not concentration coefficients or Kakwani indices alone—to determine progressivity.

2. A transfer is everywhere progressive if the proportion received—in relation to prefiscal income—decreases as income rises. There are two types of progressive transfers: absolute and relative. A transfer will be progressive in absolute terms if the per capita amount received decreases as income rises. A transfer will be progressive only in relative terms if the proportion received in relation to prefiscal income decreases as income rises but not so the per capita transfer. Again, transfers in practice are usually not *everywhere progressive* because someone might not receive the transfer, while a slightly poorer and a slightly richer person both do. A transfer is *globally progressive in absolute terms* if its concentration curve lies everywhere above the 45-degree line. A necessary but not sufficient condition for this is that the concentration coefficient is negative, or equivalently that the Kakwani index, defined for transfers as the prefiscal income Gini minus the transfer's concentration coefficient, is positive and higher than the prefiscal income Gini.[6] A transfer is *globally progressive in relative terms* if its concentration curve lies everywhere between the prefiscal income Lorenz curve and the 45-degree line. A necessary but not sufficient condition for this is that the concentration coefficient is positive and lower than the prefiscal income Gini, or equivalently that the Kakwani index is positive if a transfer is progressive in relative terms.

    If the concentration curve of a transfer crosses the 45-degree line (this could be from above or below and any number of times) but still lies everywhere above the prefiscal income Lorenz curve, it is unambiguously progressive, but we cannot say unambiguously whether it is progressive in absolute terms, even if its concentration coefficient is negative.

3. A transfer is everywhere regressive if the proportion received—in relation to initial income—increases as income rises. Again, in practice transfers will not be *everywhere* regressive. A transfer is *globally regressive* if the concentration curve lies everywhere below the prefiscal income Lorenz curve. A necessary but not sufficient condition for this is that the concentration coefficient is positive and greater than the Market Income Gini, or equivalently, that the Kakwani index is negative.

    If the concentration curve of a transfer crosses the prefiscal income Lorenz curve, we cannot unambiguously say that the transfer is progressive or regressive. Its con-

---

[6] The index originally proposed by Kakwani (1977) measures only the progressivity of taxes. It is defined as the tax's concentration coefficient minus the prefiscal income Gini. To adapt to the measurement of transfers, Lambert (1985) suggests that in the case of transfers it should be defined as prefiscal income Gini minus the concentration coefficient (the negative of the definition for taxes) to make the index positive whenever the change is progressive.

centration coefficient may be either less than or greater than the initial income Gini. Hence, we use concentration curves—and not concentration coefficients or Kakwani indices alone—to determine progressivity.

4. A tax or transfer will be neutral (in relative terms) if the distribution of the tax or the transfer coincides with the distribution of prefiscal income. A necessary but not sufficient condition for this is that the concentration coefficient is equal to the prefiscal income Gini. Equivalently, the Kakwani index will equal zero if a tax or transfer is neutral.

The four cases are illustrated in figure 8-1, where we assume that prefiscal income is Market Income.

As shown in Enami, Lustig, and Aranda (2022) (chapter 2 in Volume 1 of this Handbook) and in Enami (2022b) (chapter 3 in Volume 1), however, a progressive tax or transfer is not necessarily equalizing. Furthermore, it is not necessarily poverty-reducing, and Higgins and Lustig (2016) (reproduced in chapter 4 in this Volume), show that even if a tax and transfer system is poverty-reducing *and* progressive, it can still make a substantial portion of the poor poorer, as well as make some non-poor poor.

1.11 Deciles

Each decile represents 10 percent of the population. Individuals are ordered by income from poorest to richest, with the "first decile" referring to the poorest decile, and the "tenth decile" referring to the richest. The *CEQ Stata Package* automatically produces deciles. If you are producing deciles on your own for any additional calculations, note that the division should be done such that the expanded population in each decile, rather than the number of raw observations in each decile, is equal (or approximately equal). The "expanded population" refers to the number of *individuals* (not households) when the appropriate expansion factors are applied to each observation.[7] Individuals in the same household should be kept in the same decile, whereas individuals in different households with the same income may be arbitrarily allocated to different deciles if they are near the cut-off, in order to keep decile sizes approximately equal. This is not possible with Stata's built-in command `xtile`, and is best accomplished with Osorio's (2007) user-written command `quantiles with the keeptog` option.[8] Let the dataset be at the individual level (each observation is an individual rather than household), and let household per capita Market Income be saved as `ym`, the variable containing the identifying code for each household be called `hhcode`, and the variable

---

[7] Expansion factors are a type of sampling weight. Sampling weights re-weight the sample to account for the nonrandom stratified sample design. Expansion factors are sampling weights that are scaled such that they sum to the total population of the country (if the survey is representative at the national level).

[8] To install, type `ssc install quantiles` in Stata's command window.

FIGURE 8-1
Concentration Curves for Progressive and Regressive Transfers and Taxes

Panel A: Transfers

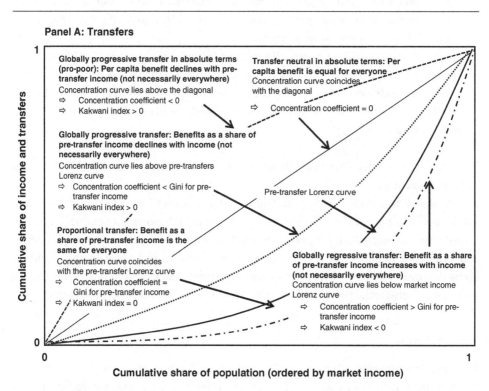

Globally progressive transfer in absolute terms (pro-poor): Per capita benefit declines with pre-transfer income (not necessarily everywhere)
Concentration curve lies above the diagonal
⇨ Concentration coefficient < 0
⇨ Kakwani index > 0

Transfer neutral in absolute terms: Per capita benefit is equal for everyone
Concentration curve coincides with the diagonal
⇨ Concentration coefficient = 0

Globally progressive transfer: Benefits as a share of pre-transfer income declines with income (not necessarily everywhere)
Concentration curve lies above pre-transfers Lorenz curve
⇨ Concentration coefficient < Gini for pre-transfer income
⇨ Kakwani index > 0

Pre-transfer Lorenz curve

Proportional transfer: Benefit as a share of pre-transfer income is the same for everyone
Concentration curve coincides with the pre-transfer Lorenz curve
⇨ Concentration coefficient = Gini for pre-transfer income
⇨ Kakwani index = 0

Globally regressive transfer: Benefit as a share of pre-transfer income increases with income (not necessarily everywhere)
Concentration curve lies below market income Lorenz curve
⇨ Concentration coefficient > Gini for pre-transfer income
⇨ Kakwani index < 0

Cumulative share of income and transfers

Cumulative share of population (ordered by market income)

Panel B: Taxes

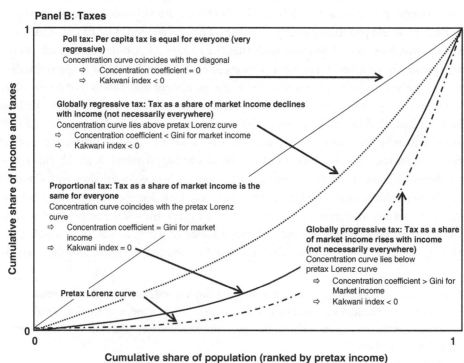

Poll tax: Per capita tax is equal for everyone (very regressive)
Concentration curve coincides with the diagonal
⇨ Concentration coefficient = 0
⇨ Kakwani index < 0

Globally regressive tax: Tax as a share of market income declines with income (not necessarily everywhere)
Concentration curve lies above pretax Lorenz curve
⇨ Concentration coefficient < Gini for market income
⇨ Kakwani index < 0

Proportional tax: Tax as a share of market income is the same for everyone
Concentration curve coincides with the pretax Lorenz curve
⇨ Concentration coefficient = Gini for market income
⇨ Kakwani index = 0

Globally progressive tax: Tax as a share of market income rises with income (not necessarily everywhere)
Concentration curve lies below pretax Lorenz curve
⇨ Concentration coefficient > Gini for Market income
⇨ Kakwani index < 0

Pretax Lorenz curve

Cumulative share of income and taxes

Cumulative share of population (ranked by pretax income)

Source: Enami, Lustig, and Aranda (2022).

containing the expansion factor be called sweight. Then, the following command will create Market Income deciles following the instructions above, and create a new categorical variable called ymdecile containing the decile of each observation (the new variable will be an integer ranging from 1 to 10):

```
quantiles ym [iw=sweight], gen(ymdecile) n(10) keeptog(hhcode)
```

Some output tables are *non-anonymous*; in other words, they follow identified individuals, so that, for example, the first decile always refers to the poorest 10 percent of the population by prefiscal income. Thus, for instance, on the Concentration sheets (e.g., sheets D5, E10) we are looking at the change in incomes caused by various taxes and transfers to the incomes of identified individuals: we want to know by how much the incomes of those who are initially in the poorest 10 percent, etc., changed. On the other hand, other tables are anonymous so we allow reranking between income concepts. For example, on the Lorenz sheets (e.g., sheet E3) we are comparing the Market Incomes of the poorest 10 percent of the population ranked by Market Income to the Disposable Incomes of the poorest 10 percent of the population ranked by Disposable Income, even though these may not be the same individuals.

1.12 Poverty Lines

All poverty lines are absolute and income-[9] or consumption-based. By default, sections D and E use the following poverty lines corresponding to the 2011 International Comparison Program (ICP): the standard international poverty lines of US$1.90 dollars per person per day in purchasing power parity (PPP) adjusted 2011 U.S. dollars (which we call "ultra-poverty"), which is typically used for low-income countries; US$3.20 PPP per person per day ("extreme poverty"), for lower middle-income countries; and US$5.50 PPP per person per day ("moderate poverty"), for upper middle-income countries, such as those in Latin America.[10] These poverty line defaults can be changed using options in the *CEQ Stata Package* commands. For example, if the user is doing a PPP conversion using the 2005 ICP to compare with older fiscal incidence studies and wants to use the World Bank's extreme poverty line of US$1.25 PPP per day in 2005 dollars,[11] she can do this using the options described in sections 3.2.3 and 3.2.5 in this chapter.

---

[9] Strictly speaking, when using Consumable Income, we should adjust the poverty line to take into account the fact that in defining poverty lines the prices that are used implicitly include taxes (subsidies) paid (received). We at CEQ decided to ignore this issue, assuming that the differences it would generate in, for instance, the poverty estimates are small.

[10] See Ferreira and others (2013).

[11] Data based on older fiscal incidence studies housed in the CEQ Data Center on Fiscal Redistribution may have only the poverty measures for poverty lines calculated with PPP 2005.

> **IMPORTANT**
>
> At the time of publication of this Volume, note that the defaults used in the *CEQ Stata Package* use the poverty lines defined in PPP 2011. Since they may be updated in the future to reflect the poverty lines generated with the conversion factors obtained from the 2017 International Comparison Program (or subsequent rounds), periodically update the package and check the help files of the *CEQ Stata Package* to verify the current defaults.[12]

We also include results using national poverty lines, which preferably distinguish between urban and rural areas and possibly by regions, and "other poverty lines," such as those calculated by an international organization for the country. The options for these poverty lines in the *CEQ Stata Package* accept both scalars (if the line is fixed across the country) or variables (for lines that vary, for example, by region or household).

The *CEQ Stata Package* makes PPP conversions automatically, as described in detail in section 3. If the user wishes to manually make PPP conversions for additional calculations, the instructions are as follows.

1.12.1 PPP Conversions Using 2005 ICP

To convert the international poverty lines in PPP adjusted 2005 U.S. dollars per day into poverty lines in local currency per month or year of a specific survey year:

1. Multiply the number that is in 2005 PPP per day by the 2005 PPP conversion rate to convert the international poverty lines into 2005 local currency. The PPP conversion factor should be based on private consumption rather than GDP; this factor can be obtained from the World Development Indicators (WDI) Databank[13] using the series "2005 PPP conversion factor, private consumption (LCU per international dollar)" and selecting the year 2005.
2. Use the country's consumer price index (CPI) to convert the poverty lines in 2005 local currency to survey year local currency. The WDI currently anchors its CPI numbers at the year 2010 (see the series "consumer price index (2010 = 100)"); multiply the poverty line in 2005 local currency by the ratio of the CPI for the survey year divided by the CPI for 2005.
3. If converting the daily poverty lines to monthly currency (for use with monthly income or consumption data), multiply by 365/12. If converting to yearly currency (for use with yearly income or consumption data), multiply by 365.

Please be sure to check the corresponding column for PPP year in the Standard Indicators in www.ceqinstitute.org.

[12] For details on the 2017 program see World Bank (2020).

[13] https://databank.worldbank.org/source/world-development-indicators

In sum, the yearly international poverty line in local currency is equal to the 2005 PPP per day poverty line times the 2005 PPP conversion factor (of 2005 local currency units per 2005 PPP dollar), times the country's CPI of the survey year over the CPI of 2005, times 365 days per year.

For example, in the case of Brazil, the household survey data used for analysis is 2009, its private consumption-based PPP conversion factor for 2005 is 1.571 Brazilian reais (in 2005) = US$1 PPP (in 2005), the CPI for 2009 is 95.203, and the CPI for 2005 (the base year) is 79.560, so the US$4 PPP per day (using the 2005 ICP) international poverty line would be converted into 2009 local currency (reais) per year as follows:

$$\frac{\$4\,PPP}{1\,day} * \frac{1.571\,reais}{\$1\,PPP} * \frac{95.203}{79.560} * \frac{365\,days}{1\,year} = \frac{2745.20\,reais}{1\,year}.$$

Thus, the US$4 PPP per day international poverty line is equivalent to 2,745.20 reais (in 2009) per year.

The *CEQ Stata Package* includes a command to facilitate these conversions: ceqppp, which makes use of the user-written program wbopendata to pull PPP conversion factors and CPI numbers directly from WDI.[14] Thus, both the *CEQ Stata Package* and wbopendata need to be installed; to install them use the following Stata code:

```
update all
ssc install ceq, replace
ssc install wbopendata, replace
```

The advantages of obtaining the necessary statistics for a PPP conversion directly in Stata are efficiency and avoiding rounding error. The syntax of the command is as follows:

```
ceqppp, country(string) baseyear(real) surveyyear(real) locals
```

The command has the following four options:

Option	Description
country(*string*)	Three-letter country code (see help wbopendata)
baseyear(*real*)	Base year for PPP conversion (either 2005 or 2011)
surveyyear(*real*)	Year of household survey
locals	Store these numbers as locals

In Stata, see help ceqppp for more details.

---

[14] Azevedo (2011).

To use ceqppp for the above conversion of the US$4 PPP (using the 2005 ICP) poverty line to local currency for Brazil, the syntax would be:

```
ceqppp, country("bra") baseyear(2005) surveyyear(2009) locals
```

Since the locals command was included, the 2005 local currency to 2005 PPP conversion factor will be saved in the local `ppp`, the CPI for the base year in `cpibase`, and the CPI for the survey year in `cpisurvey`. These can now be used as follows:

```
local z = 4 // PPP poverty line to be converted
local z1CU = `z'*`ppp'*(`cpisurvey'/`cpibase')*365
```

Note that the ceqppp command can also be used to feed the 2005 local currency to the 2005 PPP conversion factor, CPI for the base year, and CPI for the survey year directly into the results-producing commands in the *CEQ Stata Package*, as described in detail in these commands' help files and in section 3.2.3 PPP Conversion Options.

To instead convert numbers from survey-year local currency to 2005 PPP dollars per day (for example, to learn the value of a national poverty line in PPP per day for international comparisons, or to report benefits in PPP dollars per day), follow the reverse sequence. Specifically:

1. If the survey-year local currency numbers are yearly, divide by 365 to obtain local currency per day. If the numbers are monthly, divide by 365/12 to obtain local currency per day.
2. Divide by the ratio of the CPI for the survey year divided by the CPI for 2005, using the series "consumer price index (2010 = 100)" from WDI to convert survey-year local currency per day to 2005 local currency per day.
3. Divide by the consumption-based 2005 PPP conversion factor (using the series "2005 PPP conversion factor, private consumption (LCU per international dollar)" from WDI) to convert 2005 local currency per day to 2005 PPP dollars per day.

1.12.2 PPP Conversions Using 2011 ICP

To convert the international poverty lines in PPP adjusted 2011 U.S. dollars per day into poverty lines in local currency per month or year of a specific survey year:

1. Multiply the number that is in 2011 PPP per day by the 2011 PPP conversion rate to convert the international poverty lines into 2011 local currency. The PPP conversion factor should be based on private consumption rather than GDP; this factor can be obtained from the WDI Databank (http://databank.worldbank.org) using the series "PPP conversion factor, private consumption (LCU per international dollar)" using the year 2011.

2. Use the country's CPI to convert the poverty lines in 2011 local currency to survey year local currency. The WDI now anchors its CPI numbers at the year 2010 (see the series "consumer price index (2010 = 100)"); multiply the poverty line in 2011 local currency by the ratio of the CPI for the survey year divided by the CPI for 2011.

3. If converting to the daily poverty lines to monthly currency (for use with monthly income or consumption data), multiply by 365/12. If converting to yearly currency (for use with yearly income or consumption data), multiply by 365.

In sum, the yearly international poverty line in local currency is equal to the 2011 PPP per day poverty line times the 2011 PPP conversion factor (of 2011 local currency units per 2011 PPP dollar), times the country's CPI of the survey year over the CPI of 2011, times 365 days per year.

For example, in the case of Brazil, the household survey data used for analysis is 2009, its private consumption-based PPP conversion factor for 2011 is 1.6587826 Brazilian reais (in 2011) = US\$1 PPP (in 2011), the CPI for 2009 is 95.203354, and the CPI for 2011 (the base year) is 106.6362, so the US\$1.90 PPP per day (using the 2011 ICP) international poverty line would be converted into 2009 local currency (reais) per year as follows:

$$\frac{\$1.90\,PPP}{1\,day} * \frac{1.6587826\,reais}{\$1\,PPP} * \frac{95.203354}{106.6362} * \frac{365\,days}{1\,year} = \frac{1027.0309\,reais}{1\,year}.$$

Thus, the US\$1.90 PPP per day international poverty line is equivalent to 1027.03 reais (in 2009) per year.

This conversion can also be done efficiently in Stata using the `ceqppp` command by following the example above, replacing <u>b</u>aseyear(2005) with <u>b</u>aseyear(2011) in the `ceqppp` options, and replacing `local z=1.90`.

To instead convert numbers from survey-year local currency to 2011 PPP dollars per day (for example, to learn the value of a national poverty line in PPP per day for international comparisons, or to report benefits in PPP dollars per day), follow the reverse sequence. Specifically:

1. If the survey-year local currency numbers are yearly, divide by 365 to obtain local currency per day. If the numbers are monthly, divide by 365/12 to obtain local currency per day.

2. Divide by the ratio of the CPI for the survey year divided by the CPI for 2011, using the series "consumer price index (2010 = 100)" from WDI to convert survey-year local currency per day to 2011 local currency per day.

3. Divide by the consumption-based PPP conversion factor of 2011 (using the series "PPP conversion factor, private consumption (LCU per international dollar)" from WDI) to convert 2011 local currency per day to 2011 PPP dollars per day.

1.13 Income Groups

We define a set of income groups, beginning (by default, but the cut-offs can be changed using the *CEQ Stata Package* options) with the three poor groups defined above: the ultra-poor (household per capita income less than US$1.90 PPP 2011 per day), the extreme poor (household per capita income greater than or equal to US$1.90 PPP 2011 per day and less than US$3.20 PPP 2011 per day), the moderate poor (household per capita income greater than or equal to US$3.20 PPP 2011 per day but less than US$5.50 PPP 2011 per day). The non-poor income groups are the vulnerable (household per capita income greater than or equal to US$5.50 PPP 2011 per day and less than US$11.50 PPP 2011 per day), the middle class (household per capita income greater than or equal to US$11.50 PPP 2011 per day but less than US$57.60 PPP 2011 per day), and the rich (household per capita income greater than US$57.60 PPP 2011 per day). The naming conventions for these income groups were adopted with middle-income countries, particularly those in Latin America, in mind.

The above income groups were initially generated using the 2005 PPP. The US$1.25 PPP per day line represents approximately the average national poverty line of the bottom fifteen low-income, less-developed countries;[15] thus in the context of middle-income countries we call those living on less than US$1.25 PPP per day the "ultra-poor." The US$2.50 and US$4 PPP per day poverty lines are commonly used as extreme and moderate poverty lines for Latin America and roughly correspond to the median official extreme and moderate poverty lines in those countries.[16] The US$10 PPP per day line is the upper bound of those vulnerable to falling into poverty (and thus the lower bound of the middle class) in three Latin American countries, calculated by Lopez-Calva and Ortiz-Juarez (2014). Ferreira and others (2013) find that an income of around US$10 PPP also represents the income at which individuals in various Latin American countries tend to self-identify as belonging to the middle class and consider this a further justification for using it as the lower bound of the middle class. The US$10 PPP per day line was also used as the lower bound of the middle class in Latin America in Birdsall (2010) and in developing countries in all regions of the world in Kharas (2010). The US$50 PPP per day line is the upper bound of the middle class proposed by Ferreira and others (2013). Since these publications, the World Bank revised the poverty lines using PPP 2011. We kept the analogous thresholds for the ultra-poor, extreme poor, and moderate poverty lines.[17]

At the time of publication of this Volume, note that the defaults in the *CEQ Stata Package* for the income thresholds correspond to the 2011 PPP. However, they can be changed manually if the user wants to use different thresholds (for example, those using

---

[15] Chen and Ravallion (2010).

[16] CEDLAS and World Bank (2012); Ferreira and others (2013).

[17] For the other cutoffs, we simply updated them using the CPI for the United States. The $11.52 was rounded to $11.50.

the 2005 PPP for comparison with older studies or new ones proposed using the PPP conversion factors obtained from the 2017 International Comparison Program). **Note as well that the thresholds may be updated again in the future. Check the help files of the *CEQ Stata Package* to verify the current defaults.**

1.14 Sampling Weights and Stratification

Since most surveys are not simple random samples, calculations must always include sampling weights (specifically, expansion factors). If our expansion factors variable is called `sweight`, we implement this by adding `[pw=sweight]` to our command. Some commands in Stata do not work with `pweights` (sampling weights), so one must instead use `iweights` (importance weights) or `aweights` (analytic weights). For the *CEQ Stata Package* commands, `pweights` should be used. For other commands in the sample Stata code included in this chapter, we always specify which weight is possible with the command being used.

When standard errors are being calculated, the complex stratified sample design must be taken into account. For standard error estimations, using the sampling weights is *not sufficient*. The survey should have, in addition to the commonly used variable for each observation's sampling weight, a variable for the primary sampling unit and the strata (note that in some surveys, particularly those using a two-stage sampling design, the primary sampling unit will be the household). In Stata, the survey sample design variables (sampling weight, strata, and primary sampling unit) can be saved with the dataset using the `svyset` command (followed by the `save` command so that the next time the dataset is opened, Stata will remember the survey sampling design). Once the survey sample design is saved in the dataset, commands that are designed to produce standard errors that account for stratification and clustering can be told to account for them using the `svy:` prefix. In addition, the *CEQ Stata Package* commands and some other user-written commands such as those that are part of the Distributive Analysis Stata Package (DASP)[18] automatically use the information about sampling weights, strata, and primary sampling units. However, for programs not in the *CEQ Stata Package* or DASP, the user should never assume—without consulting the command's help file—that the command automatically incorporates the survey sampling design information.

Let the sampling weight variable in our dataset be saved as `sweight`, the strata be saved as `sstrata`, and the primary sampling unit be saved as `sunit` (in two-stage complex sampling designs, the primary sampling unit is often the household). Then the syntax for saving the sampling information would be:

```
svyset sunit [pw=sweight], strata(sstrata)
```

---

[18] Araar and Duclos (2013).

After saving, closing, and reopening the dataset, one can make sure that the survey sampling design is saved in the dataset by typing `svydes`.

Note that the CEQ Stata commands provide two ways to use the sampling weights and stratification variables: either they can be supplied using `svyset` as described above, or they can be supplied directly to the CEQ Stata commands using the normal weight syntax and the options `psu()` and `strata()` for the primary sampling unit and strata, respectively.

2 The *CEQ Master Workbook* Sections D and E

> **IMPORTANT**
> Always use clean *MWB* sheets with CEQ Stata commands. In other words, do not overwrite an already populated sheet because it will corrupt your output.

This section describes sections D, "Summary of Results," and E, "Output Tables," of the *CEQ Master Workbook* in the part IV (available online) in this Volume of the Handbook (CEQ Institute, 2022).

2.1 Structure

Section E is produced using the *CEQ Stata Package*, a user-written suite of Stata commands. These commands are described in detail in section 3. To automatically transfer the results to Section E of the *CEQ MWB*, Stata 14 or newer is required. Section E contains a wealth of information, which can easily become overwhelming for the user; hence, section D summarizes the main results from section E.

The production of section D is also automated, using Excel formulas to pull the relevant results from section E once the latter is produced using the *CEQ Stata Package*. This linking procedure, written in Visual Basic, is embedded in the section D Excel files and has been tested on both Mac OS and Windows. Instructions for the linking can be found on the CEQ website (www.commitmentoequity.org) and in part IV of the Handbook (available online; CEQ Institute, 2022).[19] Note that it is important to fill in the information for all the listed E sheets. Otherwise, the "macro" for linking the E sheets with the D sheets does not work. If a researcher chooses not to run some of the E sheets, she should still include the E sheets in the *MWB* even if they are left blank.

Tables 8-1 and 8-2 describe the contents of sections D and E of the *CEQ MWB*.

---

[19] It was developed by Maynor Cabrera and Sandra Martinez-Aguilar, with research assistance from Cristina Carrera.

TABLE 8-1
CEQ Master Workbook: Contents of Section D Summary Results

D1. Inequality and poverty; inequality of opportunity; fiscal impoverishment, and fiscal gains to the poor (for core income concepts)

D2. CEQ effectiveness indicators between core income concepts

D3. Vertical inequality and reranking

D4. Incidence and net payers/net beneficiaries by decile and income group, with households ranked by pre-fiscal

D5. Concentration shares and cumulative concentration shares: By decile and income group, with households ranked by pre-fiscal income

D6. Income distribution for core income concepts: By decile and income group

D7. Fiscal profiles for core income concepts (graphs): Net payers and net beneficiaries, fiscal incidence curves, and fiscal mobility curves by decile

D8. Marginal contributions of each fiscal intervention to inequality, and poverty (accordion, for disposable, consumable, and final income)

D9a. Coverage and distribution of benefits and beneficiaries by program ranked by disposable income group (accordion)

D9b. Coverage and distribution of benefits and beneficiaries by program at disposable income (accordion)

D10. Fiscal mobility matrices by income groups

D11. Education enrollment rates ranked by disposable income

D12. Infrastructure access ranked by disposable income

D13. Lorenz curves (graphs)

D14. Concentration curves (graphs)

D15. Cumulative distribution functions of income (graphs)

D16. Comparison over time

D17. Comparison with other studies

2.2 Indicators

Chapter 1 of Volume 1 of this Handbook describes how the indicators fit under each of the four question that a *CEQ Assessment* seeks to answer; the questions are reprinted here for convenience.[20]

1. How much income redistribution and poverty reduction is being accomplished through fiscal policy?
2. How equalizing and pro-poor are specific taxes and government spending?

---

[20] Lustig and Higgins (2022).

TABLE 8-2
CEQ Master Workbook: Contents of Section E Output Tables

E1. Descriptive statistics for core income concepts and fiscal interventions

E2. Population for core income concepts

E2b. Population for extended income concepts (one for each core income concept)

E3. Inequality, poverty and distribution of income for core income concepts

E4. Inequality of opportunity for core income concepts

E5. Fiscal impoverishment for core income concepts

E6. Fiscal gains to the poor between core income concepts

E7. Statistical significance of changes in inequality and poverty between core income concepts

E8. Dominance tests of changes in inequality and poverty between core income concepts

E9. CEQ effectiveness indicators between core income concepts

E10. Incidence and concentration shares for core income concepts with households ranked by each core income concept (one for each core income concept)

E11. Incidence and concentration shares for each fiscal intervention with households ranked by each core income concept (one for each core income concept)

E12. Inequality, poverty, and distribution of income for extended income concepts (one sheet for each core income concept)

E13. Marginal contributions of each fiscal intervention to inequality, vertical equity, reranking and poverty (one for each core income concept)

E14. CEQ effectiveness indicators for each fiscal intervention with respect to each core income concept (one for each core income concept)

E15. Covariance between core income concepts, fiscal interventions and fractional rank (one for each core income concept)

E16. Statistical significance of changes in inequality and poverty for extended income concepts (one for each core income concept)

E17. Dominance tests of changes in inequality and poverty for extended income concepts (one for each core income concept)

E18. Coverage and distribution of benefits and beneficiaries across income groups for each fiscal intervention (one for each core income concept)

E19. Among target population: coverage and distribution of benefits and beneficiaries across income groups for each fiscal intervention (accordion; one for each core income concept)

E20. Educational enrollment by education level and income group (one for each core income concept)

E21. Infrastructure access by income group (one for each core income concept)

E22. Household socio-demographic indicators (one for each core income concept)

E23. Individual socio-demographic indicators (one for each core income concept)

E24. Lorenz and concentration curves for pre and post fisc income concepts (graphs)

E25. Concentration curves of fiscal interventions ranked by each core income concept (graphs)

E26. Cumulative distribution functions of core income concepts (graphs)

E27. Fiscal impoverishment and gains to the poor curves (graphs)

E28. Assumption testing: Test how assumptions used to construct income concepts affect inequality, poverty, distribution

---

3. How effective are taxes and government spending in reducing inequality and poverty?
4. What is the impact of fiscal reforms that change the size and/or progressivity of a particular tax or benefit?

Because the indicators from each category span various sheets of sections D and E of the *CEQ MWB*, and because particular sheets include indicators from various categories, in this section the organization reflects the ordering of sheets in the *CEQ MWB* rather than the categorization based on the four questions above.

The typical indicators of a standard incidence analysis are measures of marginal contributions of fiscal interventions (including both individual interventions and broad aggregates) to inequality and poverty, incidence (the share of taxes paid or transfers received as a proportion of income), concentration coefficients or shares (by decile, income group, quintile, and income bin) of specific or overall taxes and transfers, and measures of progressivity.

One value added by the CEQ framework is the extent of indicators we produce to unpack the redistributive effects seen in the commonly used measures of progressivity, poverty, and inequality; furthermore, these indicators are automatically produced by the *CEQ Stata Package*. The indicators are estimated for each of the CEQ income concepts from Market Income (before any taxes and transfers) to Final Income (after direct and indirect taxes, direct cash and near-cash transfers, indirect subsidies, and benefits from public spending on education and health); in addition, some are computed for extended income concepts, such as the income defined by adding one particular transfer to Market Income. Other indicators are calculated for the fiscal interventions themselves with respect to the distribution of a particular core income concept. Table 8-3 summarizes these indicators.

I now turn to the specific indicators in the results sheets (sections D and E) of the *CEQ MWB*. Expansion factors are omitted from all equations for notational simplicity but are of course included in the estimation of all indicators by the *CEQ Stata Package* as long as the sampling weights are supplied to the command using `svyset` or the standard [pweight = . . .] weights syntax.

2.2.1 Inequality

Sheets D1, D2, E3, E12, and E28 include the following inequality indicators: the Gini, S-Gini, Theil, and 90/10 indices.

Graphically, the Gini is represented by twice the area between the Market Income Lorenz curve and the line of equality. The Market Income Lorenz curve maps the cumulative share of Market Income on the vertical axis against the cumulative share of the population, ordered by Market Income, on the horizontal axis. The Lorenz curve equals $2\int_0^1 (p - L(p))\, dp$, where p is the cumulative proportion of the total population when individuals are ordered in increasing income values using Market Income (graphically, p is also equivalent to the line of perfect equality) and $L(p)$ is the Lorenz curve.

The absolute Gini is equal to the Gini times mean income, $2\mu\int_0^1(p-L(p))dp$, where μ is mean income.

The S-Gini is a single-parameter generalization of the Gini index,[21] which includes an aversion to inequality parameter. It equals

$$1-v(v-1)\int_0^1(1-p)^{v-z}L(p)d(p) \text{ for } 1<v<\infty \text{ and } 0 \text{ for } v=1.$$

When $1<v<2$, the indices place relatively greater weight on individuals ranked at the top of the income distribution. When $v=2$, the index corresponds to the popular Gini coefficient. When v increases toward ∞, more weight is placed on Lorenz ordinates at the lower end of the distribution. In the limit, as $v\to\infty$, all the social weight is focused on the income share of the poorest individual. Geometrically, the difference in the value of S-Gini indices for two income distributions corresponds to the weighted integral of the area between the Lorenz curve and the line of perfect equality, with the weight determined by v.[22]

We include results for various parameters of v: 1, 1.25, 1.5, 2.5, 3, 3.5, 4, 5, 6, 7.5, and 10. These are based on a review of the literature. Using the CPS March Demographic files for 1978, 1988, and 1998, Barrett and Donald (2009) present several members of the S-Gini indices with $v=1.25$, 2, 2.5, 3.5 in order to capture a broad range of normative positions. Based on simulated samples, Demuynck (2012) presents S-Gini indices with $v=1.5$, 2, 5, 7.5 and 10. The parameters employed by Duclos and Araar (2005) for illustration are 1, 2, 3, and 6. The parameters employed in Giorgi, Palmitesta, and Provasi (2006) for illustration are 1.5, 2, 2.5 3, 4, and 5.

The Theil index, also known as the Theil's T index, is a member of the family of generalized entropy inequality measures, with the parameter $\theta=1$. Hence, it is sometimes written as GE(1), and is defined as

$$GE(1)=\frac{1}{n}\sum_{i=1}^{n}\frac{y_i}{\bar{y}}\ln\left(\frac{y_i}{\bar{y}}\right),$$

where y_i is individual i's (household per capita) income, using whichever income concept the Theil is being calculated for, and $\bar{y}$ denotes average income. Note that, because it takes the logarithm of income, the Theil cannot include observations with zero income. This is particularly problematic for fiscal incidence analysis, since some households may have zero Market Income but positive Gross Income (receiving all income from transfers, for example). When this occurs, those with zero Market Income are not included in the Theil for Market Income, but if they have non-zero Gross Income, they are included in the Theil for Gross Income, leading the two to be estimated over different populations. The alternative of not including any households

---

[21] See Donaldson and Weymark (1980, 1983); Kakwani (1980); Yitzhaki (1983).
[22] Barrett and Donald (2009).

TABLE 8-3
Summary of Indicators

Indicator	Core income concepts	Extended income concepts	Fiscal interventions
Descriptive statistics (for example, mean, median, standard deviation, proportion with non-zero values)	X	...	X
Population totals by income decile, group, centile, and bin for various income concepts	X	X	...
Inequality and poverty measures for each income concept	X	...	...
Per capita income, shares, cumulative shares, concentration shares, and fiscal incidence by decile, group, centile, and bin	X	X	X
Inequality of opportunity	X	...	...
Fiscal impoverishment and fiscal gains to the poor[1]	X	...	...
Statistical significance comparing poverty and inequality across income concepts	X	X	...
Effectiveness indicators[2]	X	X	...
Marginal contribution of each fiscal intervention to inequality, poverty, etc.	...	...	X
Dominance tests of income distributions	X	X	...
Coverage of fiscal interventions (e.g., percent of poor receiving a transfer)	...	...	X
Leakage of fiscal interventions (e.g., percent of benefits going to non-poor)	...	...	X
Education enrollment rates by income group	X	...	...
Infrastructure access by income group	X	...	...
Sociodemographic characteristics by income decile, group, centile, and bin	X	...	...
Lorenz curves	X	...	...
Concentration curves	X	...	X
Cumulative distribution functions	X	...	...
Fiscal impoverishment and fiscal gains to the poor curves[3]	X	...	...

1. See Higgins and Lustig (2016).
2. See Enami (2022a) (chapter 5 in Volume 1 of this Handbook).
3. See Higgins and Lustig (2016) (reproduced in chapter 4 in this Volume).
... = Not applicable

with zero Market Income in either inequality estimate is also unsatisfactory. As a result, we estimate but do not focus on the inequality results using the Theil index.

The 90/10 measures how the relatively rich fare compared to the relatively poor. Specifically, after dividing the population into one hundred income percentiles, the 90/10 is calculated as the average income of those in the 90th percentile divided by the average income of those in the 10th percentile.

2.2.2 Inequality of Opportunity

Sheets D1 and E4 measure ex-ante inequality of opportunity based on circumstance sets.[23] First, circumstance sets are identified: for example, one circumstance set could be {female, black, parents were college graduates, urban}: all individuals with those four traits are grouped together in that circumstance set. Circumstances are predetermined factors that are not dependent on an individual's effort, such as race, gender, and parents' education or parents' income. Once each individual's circumstance set has been identified, the mean income of each circumstance set (the mean income of all individuals in that circumstance set) is calculated for each income concept. Contributory pensions as deferred income scenario is used for each income concept. Let s_i^j indicate the mean income for income concept j of everyone in individual i's circumstance set. Each individual is attributed the mean income of his or her circumstance set, and this income distribution is called the "smoothed income distribution." Inequality measured over the smoothed income distribution for each income concept uses the mean log deviation, which gives the measure of inequality of opportunity in levels by income concept. Dividing the resulting measure by the mean log deviation for the original income distribution measures the ratio of inequality due to inequality of opportunity as opposed to inequality of effort. The latter, called "inequality of opportunity" in ratios on Sheet D1 and E4, traces out how each redistributive step affects inequality of opportunity. For example, if the proportion of inequality explained by unequal opportunities decreases from Net Market to Disposable Income but increases from Disposable to Consumable Income, this would indicate that direct transfers have an equalizing impact on ex-ante opportunities, while indirect taxes and subsidies have an unequalizing effect.

The mean log deviation of the smoothed distribution (for income concept j) is calculated as

$$\frac{1}{n} \sum_i \ln\left(\frac{\mu^j}{s_i^j}\right)$$

where μ^j is the mean income of the population for income concept j (either the original or smoothed distribution can be used to calculate μ^j since they have the same mean by definition), and s_i^j is defined above.[1]

---

[23] See Checchi and Peragine (2010); Ferreira and Gignoux (2011).

2.2.3 Poverty

Sheets D1, D2, E3, E12, E13, and E28 include poverty indicators that are members of the FGT class of poverty measures, per Foster, Greer, and Thorbecke (1984). Let households be ranked by y_i, household per capita income for the income variable for which poverty is being measured, from poorest to richest. Let the poverty line being used be denoted z. Then, following Foster, Greer, and Thorbecke (1984), denote $g_i = z - y_i$ the income shortfall of individual i (the increase in income that would be required for individual i to no longer be poor), and let q denote the number of poor individuals and n the total number of individuals. Then the FGT class of poverty measures is a function of the population's ordered income vector $y = (y_1, \ldots, y_n)$ and the poverty line z, and is defined as follows:

$$P_\alpha(y; z) = \frac{1}{n} \sum_{i=1}^{q} \left(\frac{g_i}{z} \right)^\alpha .$$

The headcount index, or the proportion of the population that has income below the poverty line, is equal to the above equation with parameter $\alpha = 0$. The poverty gap, which measures the average shortfall (over the whole population, where non-poor individuals are assigned a shortfall of zero) as a proportion of the poverty line, is equal to the above equation with the parameter $\alpha = 1$. Finally, the squared poverty gap is distribution-sensitive, giving a higher weight to those who are poorer by weighting each individual's shortfall relative to the poverty line by itself (squaring it). It is equal to the above equation with parameter $\alpha = 2$.

2.2.4 Fiscal Impoverishment

Sheets D1 and E5 include measures of fiscal impoverishment (FI) from Higgins and Lustig (2016) while sheet E27 includes FI curves. When using these measures, please cite the Higgins and Lustig (2016) article.

Although Higgins and Lustig (2016) is available open access in the *Journal of Development Economics* and is reprinted as chapter 4 in Volume 1 of this Handbook, we nevertheless include a succinct description of these indicators here.

Let z be the poverty line, y_i^0 be prefiscal income (one of the "before taxes and transfers" income concepts), and y_i^1 be postfiscal income (one of the "after taxes and transfers" income concepts). There is FI if $y_i^1 < y_i^0$ and $y_i^1 < z$ for at least one individual i. In other words, an individual was prefiscal poor and made poorer by the fiscal system, or the individual was prefiscal non-poor and made poor. Let there be n individuals in society, q_0 of whom are prefiscal poor, and q_1 of whom are postfiscal poor. The first measure of fiscal impoverishment in the *CEQ MWB* is the *fiscal impoverishment headcount (out of total population)*, or

$$\frac{1}{n} \sum_{i=1}^{n} 1(y_i^1 < y_i^0) * 1(y_i^1 < z),$$

where $1(\cdot)$ is the indicator function that takes value 1 if its argument is true and 0 otherwise. The second measure, *fiscal impoverishment headcount (out of postfiscal poor)* is defined as

$$\frac{1}{q_1} \sum_{i=1}^{n} 1(y_i^1 < y_i^0) * 1(y_i^1 < z).$$

These measures have undesirable properties, however. First, they violate monotonicity: if a fiscally impoverished individual becomes more fiscally impoverished, the measures do not change. The latter measure also violates *subgroup consistency*: it can increase (show more FI) when an additional transfer is made to a poor person without any additional FI being caused, because—if the additional transfer pulls the poor person out of poverty—this reduces the denominator q_1. In other words, a good transfer that reduces an individual's FI without changing anyone else's FI can *increase* the *fiscal impoverishment headcount (out of postfiscal poor)*.

Higgins and Lustig (2016) thus derive a class of axiomatic measures of FI. The class is given by

$$\kappa \sum_{i=1}^{n} \min(y_i^0, z) - \min(y_i^0, y_i^1, z),$$

where κ is a parameter chosen by the practitioner. Another FI measure included in the *CEQ MWB* is *total fiscal impoverishment* (either in local currency units or PPP dollars), which equals the equation shown right above for $\kappa = 1$. To further illustrate this measure, figure 4-1 in chapter 4 in this Volume (reproduced from Lustig and Higgins, 2016) orders the population by prefiscal incomes on the x-axis, and the y-axis measures income, showing their prefiscal incomes (the increasing curve) and postfiscal incomes (the wavy curve). The dashed horizontal line represents the poverty line. For those who pay more in taxes than they receive in transfers (and hence experience FI if their postfiscal income is below the poverty line), the postfiscal income curve is below the prefiscal income curve. Similarly, for those who receive more in transfers than they pay in taxes, the postfiscal income curve is above the prefiscal income curve. *Total fiscal impoverishment* is given by the sum of the dark-shaded areas in figure 4-1.

Another measure of FI included in the *CEQ MWB* is *fiscal impoverishment per capita*, which equals total fiscal impoverishment divided by the number of individuals in society, or the equation above with $\kappa = \frac{1}{n}$. The final axiomatic measure of FI in the *CEQ MWB* (which meets the axioms from Higgins and Lustig [2016] if we assume z is fixed) is *normalized fiscal impoverishment per capita*, which equals total fiscal impoverishment divided by the number of individuals and normalized by the poverty line (as the poverty gap ratio is), or the equation above with $\kappa = \frac{1}{nz}$.

2.2.5 Fiscal Gains of the Poor

Sheets D1 and E6 also include measures of fiscal gains of the poor (FGP) from Higgins and Lustig (2016), while E27 includes FGP curves. When using these measures, please cite the Higgins and Lustig (2016) article.

There is FGP if $y_i^1 > y_i^0$ and $y_i^0 < z$ for at least one individual i. In other words, an individual was prefiscal poor and gained income from the fiscal system. The measures of FGP in the *CEQ MWB* are analogous to the measures of FI:

The *fiscal gains of the poor headcount (out of total population)* is

$$\frac{1}{n} \sum_{i=1}^{n} 1(y_i^1 > y_i^0) * 1(y_i^0 < z).$$

The *fiscal gains of the poor headcount (out of prefiscal poor)* is

$$\frac{1}{q_0} \sum_{i=1}^{n} 1(y_i^1 > y_i^0) * 1(y_i^0 < z).$$

The axiomatic class of FGP measures is given by

$$\kappa \sum_{i=1}^{n} \min(y_i^1, z) - \min(y_i^0, y_i^1, z),$$

where $\kappa = 1$ gives *total fiscal gains to the poor* (equivalent to the light-shaded area in figure 4-1 in this Volume), $\kappa = \dfrac{1}{n}$ gives *fiscal gains to the poor per capita*, and $\kappa = \dfrac{1}{zn}$ gives *normalized fiscal gains to the poor per capita*.

Higgins and Lustig (2016) also show that the change in a popular poverty measure— the poverty gap ratio—induced by the fiscal system can be decomposed into normalized FGP per capita and normalized FI per capita.

2.2.6 Effectiveness Indicators

Sheets D2, D8, E9, and E14 include effectiveness indicators.

The impact effectiveness indicators measure how much inequality or poverty is reduced by a particular fiscal intervention (or set of fiscal interventions) relative to what could be achieved if the same level of spending on redistribution was "optimal" from an inequality-reduction perspective. The spending effectiveness indicators measure how much was spent or collected to achieve the observed level of inequality or poverty reduction relative to the minimum that could have been spent or collected to achieve the same reduction. These are described and illustrated with an example from Iran in Enami, Lustig, and Taqdiri (2019) (reproduced in chapter 17 in Volume 1 of this Handbook).

In addition, we use a fiscal impoverishment/fiscal gains to the poor effectiveness indicator that assesses the level of FI and FGP caused by the fiscal system or by

FIGURE 8-2
Additional Efficiency Indicators

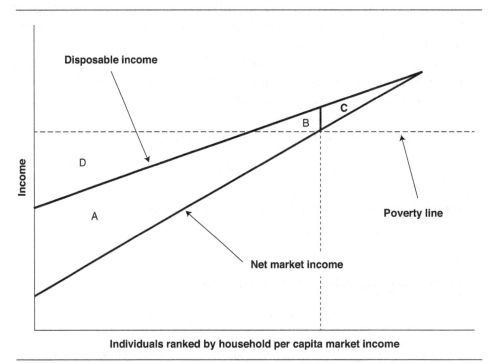

Source: Adapted from Beckerman (1979).

particular fiscal interventions relative to the amount spent and collected. The FI/FGP effectiveness indicator satisfies a number of desirable properties and is summarized in this Volume in box 1-3 of chapter 1, authored by Enami, Higgins, and Younger (2022).

We also estimate additional poverty reduction effectiveness indicators from Beckerman (1979) and Immervoll and others (2009). To define these measures, figure 8-2 shows a stylistic representation of pre- and postfiscal incomes. The diagram is not to scale, nor are the income curves necessarily straight. In the diagram, total direct transfers is A+B+C, direct transfers reaching the Net Market Income poor is A+B, the total Net Market Income poverty gap is A+D, and the total Disposable Income poverty gap is D. Beckerman (1979) then defines:

Vertical expenditure efficiency = (A+B)/(A+B+C);

Spillover index = B/(A+B);

Poverty reduction efficiency = A/(A+B+C).

Immervoll and others (2009) additionally define:

Poverty gap efficiency = A/(A + D).

In more technical notation, we have:

$$Vertical\ Expenditure\ Efficiency = \frac{\sum_{\{i\,|\,y_i^n < z\}}(y_i^d - y_i^n)}{\sum_i(y_i^d - y_i^n)}$$

$$Spillover\ Efficiency = \frac{\sum_{\{i\,|\,y_i^n < z \leq y_i^d\}}(y_i^d - z)}{\sum_{\{i\,|\,y_i^n < z\}}(y_i^d - y_i^n)}$$

$$Poverty\ Reduction\ Efficiency = \frac{\sum_{\{i\,|\,y_i^d < z\}}(y_i^d - y_i^n) + \sum_{\{i\,|\,y_i^n < z \leq y_i^d\}}(z - y_i^n)}{\sum_i(y_i^d - y_i^n)}$$

$$Poverty\ Gap\ Efficiency = \frac{\sum_{\{i\,|\,y_i^d < z\}}(y_i^d - y_i^n) + \sum_{\{i\,|\,y_i^n < z \leq y_i^d\}}(z - y_i^n)}{\sum_{\{i\,|\,y_i^n < z\}}(z - y_i^n)}$$

where y_i^n is individual i's household per capita Net Market Income, y_i^d is individual i's household per capita Disposable Income, and z is the poverty line.[24]

2.2.7 Progressivity Measures

Progressivity measures are included on sheets D3, D8, E10, E11, and E13. A useful summary statistic to measure progressivity is the Kakwani index (however, recall that concentration curves should also be used since the Kakwani index does not tell us when a concentration curve crosses the prefiscal income Lorenz curve or the 45-degree line). For taxes, the Kakwani (1977) index of progressivity can be thought of graphically as twice the area between the initial income Lorenz curve and the tax concentration curve. If the tax concentration curve is above the Lorenz curve, the Kakwani index will be negative, which indicates that taxes are regressive in relative terms. Equivalently, the Kakwani index can be calculated as the tax's concentration coefficient (with the population ranked by initial income) minus the prefiscal income Gini. In other words, $K^{tax} = D_0^{tax} - G_0$, where D_0^{tax} represents the concentration coefficient of a particular tax when the population is ranked by prefiscal income.

To adapt to the measurement of transfers, Lambert (1985) suggests that in the case of transfers, the Kakwani index should be defined as prefiscal income Gini minus the concentration coefficient (the negative of the definition for taxes) to make the index

---

[24] Notice that the Spending Effectiveness Indicator, Fiscal Gains to the Poor Effectiveness Indicator, and Beckerman-Immervoll Poverty Reduction Effectiveness Indicator are equal to each other for all instruments when poverty gap is the index of interest.

positive whenever the change is progressive. Thus, we have $K^{\text{transfer}} = -(D_0^{\text{transfer}} - G_0)$, where D_0^{transfer} represents the concentration coefficient of a particular transfer when the population is ranked by prefiscal income.

Note that, because net taxes (taxes minus transfers) are negative for some individuals and positive for others, the concentration curve for net taxes will not be well behaved.[25] Hence, we calculate Kakwani indices separately for taxes and transfers.

The Reynolds-Smolensky index (1977) is another summary statistic of progressivity, since a globally progressive system will have a positive Reynolds-Smolensky index (although the converse implication is not true). Graphically, the Reynolds-Smolensky of postfiscal income with respect to prefiscal income is twice the area between the prefiscal income Lorenz curve and the concentration curve of postfiscal income with respect to the prefiscal income distribution. Note that the concentration curve of postfiscal income with respect to prefiscal income is not the same as the Lorenz curve for postfiscal income, as the concentration curve does not rerank the population (the population is still ranked by prefiscal income), whereas the Lorenz curve does rerank the population (the population would be ranked by postfiscal income). Equivalently, the Reynolds-Smolensky can be calculated as the prefiscal income Gini minus the concentration coefficient of Consumable Income when the population is ranked by Market Income. In other words, $RS = G_0 - D_0^1$, where D_0^1 represents the concentration coefficient of postfiscal income when the population is ranked by prefiscal income.

2.2.8 Vertical and Horizontal Equity

Sheets D3 and E10 include a decomposition of the change in inequality due to the tax and transfer system into its vertical and horizontal equity components.

A well-recognized form of horizontal inequity is when fiscal interventions arbitrarily alter the relative position of individuals across the distribution: in other words, there is reranking. Reranking occurs if individual A was poorer than individual B before a fiscal intervention, but B is poorer than A after the intervention for no good reason.[26] The definition of horizontal equity postulates that the prefiscal policy income ranking should be preserved.[27] In other words, if individual A was poorer than individual B before fiscal interventions, individual A should continue to be poorer than individual B after the interventions.

From theory, we know that the total redistributive effect (RE) can be decomposed into two elements: the change in vertical inequality (VE) minus reranking (RR).[28] The

---

[25] Lambert (2001).

[26] As an example of a "good reason," an individual could have greater needs due to the health characteristics of the individual, in which case reranking would not be considered a form of horizontal inequity.

[27] See Araar and Duclos (2013).

[28] See Duclos and Araar (2005), Urban (2009).

redistributive effect (RE) is equal to the difference between the Gini coefficient for prefiscal income, G_0, and the Gini coefficient for postfiscal income, G_1, or

$$(8\text{-}1) \qquad\qquad RE = G_0 - G_1.$$

Adding and subtracting D_0^1, the concentration coefficient for incomes after taxes and transfers, equation (8-1) can be decomposed into:

$$(8\text{-}2) \qquad\qquad RE = (G_0 - D_0^1) - (G_1 - D_0^1).$$

Then the redistributive effect can be written as:

$$(8\text{-}3) \qquad\qquad RE = VE - RR,$$

where VE is equal to the difference between the prefiscal Gini coefficient and the concentration coefficient of postfiscal income with respect to prefiscal income; if there is no reranking, $RE = VE$ by definition because the concentration coefficient for postfiscal income with respect to prefiscal income will be identical to the postfiscal Gini coefficient.

RR is equal to the difference between the postfiscal Gini coefficient and the concentration coefficient for postfiscal income with respect to prefiscal income.

The redistributive effect is diminished by reranking, as clearly shown in equation (8-3). The VE measure is the Reynolds-Smolensky progressivity index (RS) and the RR measure is known as the Atkinson-Plotnick index of horizontal inequity.[29]

2.2.9 Incidence and Concentration

Sheets D4, D5, E10, and E11 show the incidence and concentration of fiscal interventions by decile and income group (with income totals also produced by centile and small income bins in section E, which can be used to generate incidence results for these more fine-grained groups as well). Incidence shows the amount each decile or group pays in a particular tax or receives from a particular transfer as a percent of initial income. Concentration shows the percent of a total tax or benefit that is paid or received by each decile or group.

The calculations are non-anonymous, meaning that we do not rerank the population: the totals by decile that we are comparing are always for a particular income concept. On sheets D4 and D5 deciles and income groups are always determined using prefiscal income, which is Market Income plus Pensions for the pensions as deferred income scenario and Market Income for the pensions as government transfers scenario; in section E, there are separate sheets for each core income concept, which show incidence

---

[29] Atkinson (1980); Plotnick (1981).

and concentration shares when deciles and income groups are defined based on that income concept.

2.2.10 Income Distribution

Sheets D6 and E3 provide the income distribution by decile and income group, the income in local currency, and the proportion of income accruing to each decile or group by income concept. The income distribution indicators are anonymous; the deciles are not fixed using prefiscal income. For example, the income distribution for Disposable Income uses deciles and groups defined by Disposable Income.

2.2.11 Fiscal Profiles

Sheet D7 has fiscal profiles, which are graphs that show the difference between each prefiscal decile's postfiscal and prefiscal incomes as a proportion of prefiscal income. When this proportion is positive, members of that decile are net gainers from the fiscal system on average; when it is negative, they are net payers to the fiscal system on average.

2.2.12 Concentration and Kakwani Coefficients

Sheets D8 and E11 provide the concentration coefficients of individual transfer programs with respect to *postfiscal* income, as well as aggregate categories such as total direct transfers and CEQ social spending in incidence analysis. Let p be the cumulative proportion of the total population when individuals are ordered in increasing income values using Market Income, and let $C(p)$ be the concentration curve, the cumulative proportion of total program benefits (of a particular program or aggregate category) received by the poorest p percent of the population. Then, the concentration coefficient of that program or category is defined as $2\int_0^1 (p - C(p))dp$. As discussed above, a program that is progressive in absolute terms will have a concentration curve above the line of perfect equality, and thus the area $2\int_0^1 (p - C(p))dp$ will be negative, implying a negative concentration coefficient. Sheets D3, D8, and E11 also include Kakwani coefficients, defined above in section 2.2.7 on progressivity measures.

2.2.13 Coverage, Errors of Exclusion, Errors of Inclusion, and Errors of Social Programs

Sheets D9a, D9b, E18, and E19 measure the coverage of the poor and those in other income groups by fiscal intervention, errors of exclusion, leakages (errors of inclusion) to the non-poor, and average benefits per capita, per individual in a beneficiary household, and per transfer recipient. The distinction between the latter two depends on how the "average transfer" should be calculated: because the transfer is added to aggregate household income, which is then shared by everyone in the household, an economist would most likely measure the average transfer size among a particular income group as the total benefits received by that group divided by the number of individuals in that group who live in households that received the transfer. On the other hand, when the government reports the average transfer size, it usually reports the total spent on transfers divided by the number of transfer recipients, where a transfer recipient is defined as the individual who physically receives the transfer, not as individuals who live in the same household that receives the transfer.

The following indicators are calculated: the share of benefits going to each income group (which can be used to determine what percent of benefits are leakages to the non-poor), share of individuals in beneficiary households in each income group, percent of individuals in each group who live in beneficiary households (which can be used to determine coverage of the poor), average per capita benefits among beneficiary households by group, average benefits per capita by group, and average benefits per transfer recipient by group. The average benefits are calculated both in local currency and in US$PPP per day.

To link this with the conceptual definitions of coverage, errors of exclusion, and errors of inclusion in chapter 1 of Volume 1 of this Handbook, we follow the same categorization here and elaborate which tables from sheets D9a and D9b have the corresponding results.

To conceptualize the concepts of coverage, leakages, and errors of exclusion, we can think of separating the population into two groups based on poverty status[30] and two groups based on whether they receive benefits. This results in four total groups, which we call group A, B, C, and D and represent with the following 2×2 matrix:

	Receives benefits	Does not receive benefits
Poor	A	B
Non-Poor	C	D

We can then define the indicators of coverage, leakages, and errors of exclusion, where each of these definitions can be measured among *households*, among *direct beneficiaries* (the individuals within the household who directly receive benefits), and among *direct and indirect beneficiaries*, defined as all individuals within a beneficiary household. For example, a household may have five total members and two members who report directly receiving benefits from a particular program. For the household-level calculations, this household counts as one household; for the direct beneficiaries calculation, the household has two direct beneficiaries; and for the individual-level calculation, the household has five individuals who are "direct and indirect beneficiaries."

---

[30] Notice that one can define these concepts separating the population into groups defined by a different criterion, such as income groups (as it is sheets E18 and E19) or eligibility for the program.

The more detailed definitions below include equations using the groups from the above matrix for clarity.

Coverage

Using the groups from the above matrix, coverage $= (A + C)/(A + B + C + D)$.

Of households: defined as the total number of households that receive benefits[31] divided by the total number of households in the country. This can be found in the "Total" column of the "Coverage Rate of Total Households" table in sheet D9a.

Of individuals (direct and indirect beneficiaries): defined as the total number of individuals living in households that receive benefits, divided by the total number of individuals in the country. This can be found in the "Total" column of the "Coverage Rate of Direct and Indirect Individuals" table in sheet D9a.

Of direct beneficiaries: defined as the total number of individuals directly receiving benefits, divided by the total number of individuals in the country. This can be found in the "Total" column of the "Coverage Rate of Direct Beneficiaries" table in sheet D9a.

Of target households: defined as the total number of eligible or "target" households that receive benefits[32] divided by the total number of target households in the country. This can be found in the "Total" column of the "Coverage Rate of Target Direct Individuals" table in sheet D9b.

Of target individuals (direct and indirect beneficiaries): defined as the total number of individuals living in target households that receive benefits, divided by the total number of individuals living in target households in the country. This can be found in the "Total" column of the "Coverage Rate of Target Direct and Indirect Individuals" table in sheet D9a.

Of target direct beneficiaries: defined as the total number of direct target individuals who receive benefits, divided by the total number of direct target individuals in the country. Note that this is defined only for programs that identify eligible *individuals* rather than eligible households. This can be found in the "Total" column of the "Coverage Rate of Target Households" table in sheet D9b.

Coverage of the poor

Using the above matrix, coverage $= A/(A + B)$.

Of households: defined as the total number of poor households that receive benefits divided by the total number of poor households in the country. This can be found

---

[31] For the indicators at the household level, a beneficiary household will be a household that receives a benefit whether one can or cannot identify who within the household is the recipient of the benefit.

[32] Depending on the fiscal intervention, eligibility might be defined at the household level, in which case a target household is a household that meets the criteria, or at the individual level, in which case a target household is defined as a household with at least one target individual.

in the columns corresponding to the poor (in the 2022 version of the *CEQ MWB*, where group cut-offs are based on the 2011 ICP, these columns are "$y < 1.90$," "$y < 3.20$," and "$y < 5.50$") of the "Coverage Rate of Total Households" table in sheet D9a.

Of individuals (direct and indirect beneficiaries): defined as the total number of poor individuals living in households that receive benefits, divided by the total number of poor individuals in the country. This can be found in the columns corresponding to the poor of the "Coverage Rate of Direct and Indirect Individuals" table in sheet D9a.

Of direct beneficiaries: defined as the total number of poor individuals directly receiving benefits, divided by the total number of poor individuals in the country. This can be found in the columns corresponding to the poor of the "Coverage Rate of Direct Beneficiaries" table in sheet D9a.

Of target households: defined as the total number of poor individuals living in eligible or "target" households that receive benefits, divided by the total number of poor individuals living in target households in the country. This can be found in the columns corresponding to the poor of the "Coverage Rate of Target Households" table in sheet D9b.

Of target individuals (direct and indirect beneficiaries): defined as the total number of poor individuals living in target households that receive benefits, divided by the total number of poor individuals living in target households in the country. This can be found in the columns corresponding to the poor of the "Coverage Rate of Target Direct and Indirect Individuals" table in sheet D9a.

Of target direct beneficiaries: defined as the total number of eligible or "target" poor individuals that receive benefits divided by the total number of poor target individuals in the country. Note that this is defined only for programs that identify eligible *individuals* rather than eligible households. This can be found in the columns corresponding to the poor of the "Coverage Rate of Target Direct Individuals" table in sheet D9b.

Errors of exclusion

Using the above matrix, errors of exclusion = $B/(A + B)$.

Of households: defined as the total number of poor households that do *not* receive benefits divided by the total number of poor households in the country. This is not directly reported in the tables, but can be obtained by taking 100 percent minus the coverage of poor households.

Of individuals (direct and indirect beneficiaries): defined as the total number of poor individuals living in households that do *not* receive benefits, divided by the total number of poor individuals in the country. This is not directly reported in the tables, but can be obtained by taking 100 percent minus the coverage of poor individuals.

Of direct beneficiaries: defined as the total number of poor individuals who do *not* directly receive benefits, divided by the total number of poor individuals in the country.

This is not directly reported in the tables, but can be obtained by taking 100 percent minus the coverage of poor individuals.

Of target households: defined as the total number of eligible or "target" poor households that do *not* receive benefits divided by the total number of poor target households in the country. This is not directly reported in the tables, but can be obtained by taking 100 percent minus the coverage of poor target households.

Of target individuals (direct and indirect beneficiaries): defined as the total number of poor individuals living in target households that do *not* receive benefits, divided by the total number of poor individuals living in target households in the country. This is not directly reported in the tables, but can be obtained by taking 100 percent minus the coverage of poor target individuals.

Of target direct beneficiaries: defined as the total number of poor "target" direct beneficiaries who do *not* receive benefits, divided by the total number of target direct beneficiaries in the country. Note that this is defined only for programs that identify eligible *individuals* rather than eligible households. This is not directly reported in the tables, but can be obtained by taking 100 percent minus the coverage of poor target direct beneficiaries.

Errors of inclusion (also known as "leakages")

Using the above matrix, errors of inclusion = $C/(A+C)$.

Of households: defined as the total number of *non*-poor households that receive benefits divided by the total number of households that receive benefits in the country. This can be found in the columns corresponding to the non-poor (in the 2022 version of the *CEQ MWB*, where group cut-offs are based on the 2011 ICP, these columns are "$y > 5.50$," "$y > 11.50$," and "$y > 57.60$") of the "Distribution of Beneficiary Households" table in sheet D9a.

Of individuals (direct and indirect beneficiaries): defined as the total number of *non*-poor individuals living in households that receive benefits, divided by the total number of individuals living in households that receive benefits in the country. This can be found in the columns corresponding to the non-poor columns of the "Distribution of Direct and Indirect Beneficiaries" table in sheet D9a.

Of direct beneficiaries: defined as the total number of *non*-poor individuals directly receiving benefits, divided by the total number of direct beneficiaries in the country. This can be found in the columns corresponding to the non-poor columns of the "Distribution of Direct Beneficiaries" table in sheet D9a.

To non-target households: defined as the total number of *non*-target households that nevertheless receive benefits, divided by the total number of households that receive benefits in the country. This is not directly reported in the tables but can be calculated as 100 percent minus the total coverage of target households.

To non-target individuals (direct and indirect beneficiaries): defined as the total number of individuals living in *non*-target households that nevertheless receive benefits, divided by the total number of individuals that live in households that receive benefits in the country. This is not directly reported in the tables but can be calculated as 100 percent minus the total coverage of target individuals.

To non-target direct beneficiaries: defined as the total number of *non*-target direct beneficiaries who nevertheless receive benefits divided by the total number of direct beneficiaries in the country. Note that this is defined only for programs that identify eligible *individuals* rather than eligible households. This is not directly reported in the tables but can be calculated as 100 percent minus the total coverage of target direct beneficiaries.

Of benefits: defined as the total amount of benefits going to the *non*-poor divided by the total amount of benefits going to all households. This can be found in the non-poor columns of the "Distribution of Benefits" table.

Proportion of beneficiaries that are poor

Using the numbers from the above matrix, proportion of beneficiaries that are poor = $A/(A+C)$.

Of households: defined as the total number of poor households that receive benefits divided by the total number of households that receive benefits in the country. This can be found in the columns corresponding to the poor columns of the "Distribution of Beneficiary Households" table in sheet D9a.

Of individuals (direct and indirect beneficiaries): defined as the total number of poor individuals living in households that receive benefits, divided by the total number of individuals living in households that receive benefits in the country. This can be found in the columns corresponding to the poor columns of the "Distribution of Direct and Indirect Beneficiaries" table in sheet D9a.

Of direct beneficiaries: defined as the total number of poor individuals directly receiving benefits, divided by the total number of direct beneficiaries in the country. This can be found in the columns corresponding to the poor columns of the "Distribution of Direct Beneficiaries" table in sheet D9a.

Of target households: defined as the total number of poor target households that receive benefits divided by the total number of target households that receive benefits in the country. This can be found in the columns corresponding to the poor columns of the "Distribution of Target Beneficiary Households" table in sheet D9b.

Of target individuals (direct and indirect beneficiaries): defined as the total number of poor individuals living in target households that receive benefits, divided by the total number of individuals who live in households that receive benefits in the country. This can be found in the columns corresponding to the poor columns of the "Distribution of Target Direct and Indirect Beneficiaries" table in sheet D9b.

Of target direct beneficiaries: defined as the total number of poor target direct beneficiaries who receive benefits divided by the total number of poor direct beneficiaries in the country. Note that this is defined only for programs that identify eligible *individuals* rather than eligible households. This can be found in the columns corresponding to the poor columns of the "Distribution of Target Direct Beneficiaries" table in sheet D9b.

Of benefits: defined as the total amount of benefits going to the poor divided by the total amount of benefits going to all households. This can be found in the poor columns of the "Distribution of Benefits" table.

Mean benefits
We also calculate mean benefits going to each of the groups identified above.

Target populations
Another measure of interest is the coverage and leakages of these programs among their target population. Sheets D9b and E19 measure coverage among the target population. Table 8-4 defines potential target populations for each type of fiscal intervention; as specified in the table, these definitions may depend on the country context and should depend on the country criteria. For example, for conditional cash transfers among households with children, total pensions (i.e., contributory and noncontributory) in households with a member over age sixty-five, noncontributory pensions in households with a member over age sixty-five and who are not receiving a contributory pension, and education by level in households with children of the corresponding age. For education, the researcher should be sure to specify which ages were used to define the target population for each level of education (e.g., preschool, primary, secondary); see table 8-4 for guidance on age ranges. For tertiary education, the age range used to define target population should be from the theoretical entrance age to the theoretical entrance age plus theoretical duration in years of the first stage of tertiary education according to national criteria; see table 8-4 for more details. For contributory health benefits, the suggested target population is all who are eligible according to national criteria, considering both contributors and dependents. For noncontributory health benefits, the suggested target population is all who are eligible for noncontributory health benefits according to national criteria and not eligible for contributory health benefits; exclude those likely to have private health insurance.

The same measures listed above are calculated, but for the target population only.

2.2.14 Fiscal Mobility Matrices

To see how the income group status of individuals is affected by taxes and transfers, sheet D10 includes fiscal mobility matrices, which are transition matrices that measure the proportion of individuals who move from a before taxes and transfers income group (for example, non-poor) to another income group (for example, poor) after their income is changed by taxes and transfers. A transition matrix was first used to measure transition between income groups before and after taxes and transfers by Atkinson (1980). Note that taxes and transfers can cause individuals to move up or down the income categories. The matrix in percents is row-stochastic, where rows represent prefiscal income groups and columns represent postfiscal income groups. There are multiple matrices for the different possible definitions of postfiscal income: for example, there is a mobility matrix for prefiscal to Disposable Income, as well as a mobility

TABLE 8-4
Fiscal Intervention Target Populations

Fiscal intervention	Target population
Direct taxes	Include those who have taxable income larger than the minimum legal taxable income.
Direct transfers	According to program eligibility rules (if there are defined criteria) or proxies to target the poor. Please explain if the beneficiary is the household or individual.
	If the targeting rules are not defined, do not assume or guess the definition of target population. If you want to know the coverage of poor population, the sheet E18 will answer this question.'
	For example, eligibility criteria could be by: • Age • Attendance to public school • Children in the household • Educational level (of household members or household head) • Ethnic group • Geography • Gender • National socioeconomic groups • Not being part of social security system • Proxy-mean test • Use of public facilities (health or public pharmacies) • Vulnerable population (orphans, widows, etc.)
Pensions	

Old age pensions (contributory and noncontributory)	Population in retirement age (according to national criteria)
	• For example, in some countries, this could be
	  ◦ 65 years for male
	  ◦ 60 years for female

Noncontributory pensions (social or minimum pension)	Population in retirement age (according to national criteria) AND who are not receiving a contributory pension
	• For example, in some countries, this could be
	  ◦ 65 years for male
	  ◦ 60 years for female

Indirect taxes	The concept of a "target population" is not applicable
Indirect subsidies	The concept of a "target population" is not applicable

(*continued*)

TABLE 8-4 (continued)

Fiscal intervention	Target population
Education	
Preschool, primary, secondary	Use age to determine target population:
	• For each educational level, use a definition consistent with the one used to impute the benefits. If it was possible to impute per capita expenditure using International Standard Classification of Education (ISCED), use this classification. Information is available in Unesco Mappings (http://uis.unesco.org/en/isced-mappings).
	• National classification or ISCED theoretical entrance age and theoretical duration in years, according to the definition used for the imputation of the benefits. It is important to use the same levels as in per capita imputations and in coverage indicators.
Tertiary	• Theoretical entrance age + theoretical duration (in years) of first stage of tertiary education according to national criteria.
	• If it *was* possible to impute per capita expenditure using international Standard Classification of Education (ISCED), use this classification instead of national criteria.
Health	
Contributory	All population that is eligible for contributory health system or programs according to national criteria. Consider the contributors and dependents covered by health plan (e.g., wife and children under 5 years).
	If the eligibility criteria for contributory health system is not well specified in the country, do not include target population.
Noncontributory	All population that is eligible for noncontributory health and is not eligible for contributory health system according to national criteria. Exclude those likely to have private and public health insurance.
	If the country does not have specified criteria for targeting, please use all population that is not covered by the public or privatized contributory health system or likely to have private health insurance. If information is available, include programs like vaccinations, prenatal visits, regular checkups for infants, childbirth attention in hospital or specialized health center. To include these programs, you must have information on coverage and per capita expenditure by each type of program.
Housing	According to program eligibility rules, otherwise do not include target population.

matrix for prefiscal to Consumable Income. The mobility matrices have additional rows and columns concatenated to them to show the population shares by income group and the mean Market Income of that income group, for ease of reference.

While the fiscal mobility matrix measures the proportion of the population that loses and gains enough to move to a higher income group, it does not capture the amount lost or gained (except to the extent that the amount lost or gained might be large enough to move more than one income group). Thus, the fiscal mobility matrix is complemented by income loss and income gain matrices, which measure the amount lost by those who lose, and the amount gained by those who gain, respectively. One version of the loss and gain matrices is in average local currency lost or gained, and the other shows the average loss or gain as a proportion of before taxes and transfers income. The matrix also shows the average Market Income of the losers in prefiscal income group i and postfiscal income group j, which serves as a useful reference point.

2.2.15 Education Enrollment Rates

Sheets D11 and E20 show indicators on education enrollment by income group, with sheet D11 defining income groups by Disposable Income and sheet E20 defining income groups by each of the eight core income concepts. Two indicators used to generate other indicators are the target population for each level of education (preschool, primary school, secondary school, and tertiary) and the total population *not* attending school (where the disaggregation by level is determined by the age of the students not attending school).

Other indicators have figures disaggregated not only by education level but also by public or private school (with results for the combination of the two, "public and private school," as well). These indicators include the total population attending school (by education level, regardless of whether the student's age corresponds to that particular education level); the target population—based on age and the corresponding education level—attending school; net enrollment rates, gross enrollment rates, and the share of students belonging to the target population.

Box 8-1 in this Volume (Adam Ratzlaff, 2022) includes a more detailed description of the education enrollment indicators.[33]

2.2.16 Infrastructure Access

Sheets D12 and E21 include statistics on infrastructure access by income group, where income groups are defined either by original (for example, prefiscal) income or by Disposable Income. Although we do not create an income concept with the value of access to infrastructure due to the inherent difficulties of allocating benefits, we use dummy variables on access to examine the distribution of infrastructure access.

The infrastructure items we include are access to running water, electricity, quality walls, floors, and roofs, and access to roads.

---

[33] Ratzlaff (2022).

Box 8-1

Education Enrollment Indicators

Adam Ratzlaff

The provision of public education is an important tool not just in terms of equalizing consumption across income groups, but also toward equalizing the distribution of income in the future and spurring national growth. The two most frequently used measures of educational usage are the net and gross enrollment rates. These indicators should be generated for each individual level of education (primary, secondary, etc.) and for public, private, and total educational enrollment. It is also important to ensure that the target age range for each level of education is well established and does not overlap between educational groups. These indicators may be difficult to produce if data is not available at the individual level or if it is not possible to determine which member of the household is enrolled in a particular level of education. Note that important information on the share of benefits received and the fiscal impact of education spending can be found on other sheets of the *CEQ Master Workbook*.

Educational Enrollment Indicators

Net Enrollment Rate

Numerator: Number of children of school age who are attending school.

Denominator: Total number of children of school age.

Note: It is useful to calculate these figures not only for the population as a whole, but also by gender, race, or ethnicity, by income group, or by other characteristics that may be of interest to your study. Additionally, it is important that the target age range for each level of education is set and identifiable.

Gross Enrollment Rate

Numerator: Total number of individuals who are attending school.

Denominator: Total number of children of school age.

Note: It is useful to calculate these figures not only for the population as a whole, but also by gender, race or ethnicity, income group, or by other characteristics that may be of interest to your study. Additionally, it is important that the target age range for each level of education is set and identifiable. For gross enrollment, it is important to note that it is possible to have rates over 100 percent as there may be a large proportion of students who are not within the target age range.

We measure the number of households with access and the distribution of households with access, as well as the coverage rate (where coverage is defined in 2.2.13) among households. In addition, we measure these indicators at the individual rather than household level in the part marked "weighted households" (where "weighted" here refers to weighting each household by the number of the households; in all calculations sampling weights would of course be used).

2.2.17 Sociodemographic Characteristics

Sheets E22 and E23 include sociodemographic characteristics by decile, income group, centile, and bin, where groups are defined by each core income concept. The columns on this sheet are blank to allow the user to include the variables that are available in the survey being used and relevant in the country for which the *CEQ Assessment* is being conducted. Suggested indicators include assets (including both dummy variables for individual assets and an asset index); geographic variables such as region, urban/ rural, and type of terrain; household expenditures (in various categories); community characteristics such as presence of a school, medical facility, religious institutions, and community activities; household characteristics such as average age of household members, household size, gender of household head, marital status of household head, age of household head, employment status of household head, number of household members of retirement age, number of children in school, education of household head, literacy of household head, race and ethnicity, religion, main language spoken, labor indicators such as hourly salary and sector, access to infrastructure, and number of migrants in household.

2.2.18 Lorenz Curves

To make unambiguous comparisons about whether inequality falls as a result of the fiscal system, sheets D13 and E24 include Lorenz curves; on these sheets, graphs of the Lorenz curves for each core income concept will be included.

The Lorenz curve maps the cumulative share of income (using whichever income concept the curve corresponds to) on the vertical axis against the cumulative share of the population, ordered by income (using whichever income concept the curve corresponds to), on the horizontal axis. Because the horizontal axis is reranked with each income concept, the Lorenz curve is an anonymous measure by definition; its non-anonymous analog would be the concentration curve of each income definition with respect to the prefiscal income rankings. The Lorenz curve is defined as

$$L(p) = \frac{1}{\bar{y}} \int_0^{F^{-1}(p)} y \, dF(y) \quad for \ p \in [0,1],$$

where $\bar{y}$ is mean income, $F(y)$ is the cumulative density function of income, and p is the proportion of the population.

2.2.19 Concentration Curves

Sheets D14 and E25 include graphs of concentration curves (sometimes called "quasi–Lorenz curves"), which map the cumulative share of benefits received or taxes paid from a particular category of transfers or taxes on the vertical axis against the cumulative share of the population, ordered by prefiscal income, on the horizontal axis. The progressivity of a tax or transfer can be determined by comparing its concentration curve to the Market Income Lorenz curve, as shown in figure 8-1 (section 1 of this chapter). Whether a progressive transfer is progressive in absolute terms or in relative terms, can, in turn, be determined by comparing the concentration curve to the 45-degree line. Thus, the concentration curves graph includes the 45-degree line, the prefiscal income Lorenz curve, and concentration curves for the following categories of transfers and taxes: direct taxes, direct transfers, indirect subsidies, indirect taxes, in-kind education, and in-kind health. In the contributory pensions as government transfers scenario, the graph would also include contributory pensions.

For tax or transfer t, the concentration curve with respect to prefiscal income is defined as

$$C(p) = \frac{1}{\bar{t}} \int_0^{F_0^{-1}(p)} t \, dF_0(t) \quad \text{for } p \in [0, 1],$$

where $\bar{t}$ is the mean of the tax or transfer over the population (including those who do not receive the transfer or pay the tax), $F_0(t)$ is the cumulative density function of transfer t with respect to the prefiscal income distribution, and p is the proportion of the population.

2.2.20 Cumulative Distribution Functions of Income

This set of graphs included in sheets D15 and E26 shows the cumulative distribution functions (CDFs) of contributory pensions as deferred income scenario, Net Market, Disposable, and Consumable Income. The CDF of income is then defined as $\int f(y) dy$, where $f(y)$ is the probability density function (PDF) of income. Hence, the CDF is anonymous by definition: the underlying distribution is ranked by whatever income concept is being measured, rather than maintaining the prefiscal income ranking. Following Atkinson (1980) and Foster and Shorrocks (1988), if one income concept first order stochastically dominates another (its CDF lies everywhere below the other's) over a domain of poverty lines, then the headcount index is unambiguously lower for the first income concept over that domain of poverty lines. With respect to other poverty measures beyond the headcount index, if one income concept first order stochastically dominates another over the range of poverty lines from zero to a maximum poverty line, then poverty is unambiguously lower in the first income concept for any poverty measure that is continuous, nondecreasing in income, and additively separable. In the case where first order stochastic dominance is not found (the CDFs of two income concepts cross), poverty can still be unambiguously lower in one of the income concepts if the poverty measure is distribution-sensitive, as with the squared poverty gap. More specifically, if one income concept second order stochastically dominates another (if the integral under its CDF is less than that of the other) from zero to a maximum poverty line, then poverty is unambiguously lower in the first income concept for any poverty measure that is continuous, nondecreasing in income, and (weakly) concave in income (Atkinson, 1980).

2.2.21 Comparison over Time

Although the *CEQ Assessment* is initially completed for a particular year, subsequent analysis can entail completing the analysis for multiple survey years, and there is space for this comparison on sheet D16 of the *CEQ MWB*.[34]

For analyses over time, we propose a simple but new decomposition of the change in the Disposable Income Gini into a change in the pre-intervention (Market Income) Gini and a change in the level of redistribution, as follows:

Let G_0^t and G_1^t be the prefiscal and postfiscal income Gini in year t, respectively; and $G_0^{t'}$ and $G_1^{t'}$ be the prefiscal and postfiscal Gini in year t'. Denoting R^t and $R^{t'}$ the portion of the change from Market Income Gini to Disposable Income Gini for year t and t', we can write:

$$G_1^t = G_0^t - R^t$$

and

$$G_1^{t'} = G_0^{t'} - R^{t'}$$

Subtracting the latter from the former yields:

$$(G_1^{t'} - G_1^t) = (G_0^{t'} - G_0^t) - (R^{t'} - R^t)$$

or

$$(R^{t'} - R^t) = (G_0^{t'} - G_0^t) - (G_1^{t'} - G_1^t).$$

So, $(R^{t'} - R^t)$ is the portion in the change in postfiscal inequality between two points in time, which can be attributed to a change in the redistribution component (in comparison to a change in prefiscal in-equality).

---

[34] Examples of CEQ studies that have completed the analysis for multiple years are Lustig, Pessino, and Scott (2014), and Lopez-Calva and others (forthcoming).

2.2.22 Descriptive Statistics

Sheet E1 includes descriptive statistics about each of the income concepts and fiscal interventions, where the latter are in rows that are originally blank in the *CEQ MWB*, but get filled in automatically by the *CEQ Stata Package* using the labels of the variables included in the command's options, as explained in sections 3.2.1 and 3.2.2. The descriptive statistics include the proportion of the population with non-zero values, as well as the mean, standard deviation, and median of the variable (among those with non-zero values only; in other words, those who have non-zero income or receive benefits from or pay taxes to the corresponding fiscal intervention).

2.2.23 Population

Sheets D6 and E2 include the population by decile, income group, centile, and bin, for each of the core and extended income concepts, for four definitions of population: number of households in sample, number of individuals in sample, number of households in expanded sample, and number of individuals in expanded sample. The first two provide evidence on what occurs in the survey itself before applying sampling weights, and can provide evidence about small cells (for example, some countries may have so few observations with income below US$1.90 per day or above US$57.60 per day that any statistics about these groups are inherently noisy and should not be used). The number of households in the expanded sample shows the total households in the country represented by the sampled households, while the number of individuals in the expanded sample shows the analogue for individuals. Note that deciles and centiles are defined so that the number of individuals in the expanded sample is as equal as possible across groups; as a result, the size of each centile and bin for the other population definitions will *not* be equal.

The population by bin can be useful if an analyst without access to the microdata but with access to *CEQ MWB* wants to use the results produced in a *CEQ MWB* to calculate the poverty headcount ratio for a poverty line not included on sheets D1 and E3. For example, suppose the 2011 ICP was used and the analyst wants to calculate the poverty headcount ratio using the US$3.20 PPP per day poverty line, which is the median of country-specific poverty lines across the world using the 2011 ICP.[35] This could be accomplished by using population results by bin from the "number of individuals in expanded sample" column (for example, column G of the E2 sheets). Specifically, the population in each income bin from the first bin, US$0.00–0.05, to the US$3.15–3.20 bin would be summed, then divided by the total population; the formula to do this would be SUM(G139:G200)/G501.

---

[35] Ferreira and others (2016).

2.2.24 Statistical Significance

Sheet E7 gives point estimates and corresponding p-values for tests of statistical significance between inequality and poverty indices for each possible pair of core income concepts. The point estimates are of the difference between inequality or poverty. Unlike comparing Gini coefficients across countries, comparing across income concepts implies that the incomes being compared come from a bivariate distribution with non-zero covariance (since a household's prefiscal income is highly correlated with its Disposable Income, for example). Thus, the test of statistical significance of the difference in Ginis, G_0 and G_1, relies on

$$Var(G_1 - G_0) = Var(G_1) + Var(G_0) - 2Cov(G_1, G_0),$$

but $2Cov(G_1 - G_0)$ is non-zero and has not been derived in the literature. Thus, statistical significance is determined using a bootstrap procedure (and, as a result, the CEQ Stata commands that produce the statistical significance sheets are slow).

In the matrices of p-values, a p-value of less than 0.05 would mean that the difference between the Ginis of the corresponding income concepts are statistically significantly different than zero, while a p-value above 0.05 would mean that we cannot reject that the difference in Ginis is different than zero (if we have selected a significance level of 5 percent); in other words, a p-value above 0.05 would tell us that the Ginis of the two income concepts are not statistically different from each other.

Sheet E16 gives statistical significance for extended income concepts, defined similarly.

2.2.25 Dominance Tests

Sheets E8 and E17 present results from dominance tests of the CDFs and concentration curves of pairs of income concepts. Using CDFs as an example, if there are no crossings between two CDFs, the reported p-value corresponds to a test with the null hypothesis that the two distributions are the same. If we adopt a significance level of 5 percent, a p-value less than 0.05 would mean that we reject that the two distributions are the same (in other words, we can conclude that one dominates the other); on the other hand, a p-value greater than 0.05 would mean that we fail to reject that the two distributions are the same, and we thus cannot claim that one dominates the other.

2.2.26 Marginal Contributions to Inequality

Sheets D8 and E13 include marginal contributions of each fiscal intervention to poverty and inequality, with respect to each core income concept, progressivity indicators such as the Kakwani index, concentration coefficient, redistributive effect, and vertical equity. Note that the column titles are blank, but are filled in automatically by the *CEQ Stata Package* using the labels of the variables included in the command's options. Marginal contributions are described in chapter 1, box 1-1, in this Volume (Younger, 2022).

2.2.27 Marginal Contributions to Poverty

Marginal contributions to poverty are calculated similarly, but present unique issues. For example, suppose an individual's prefiscal income is US\$10 below the poverty line and the person receives three transfers of US\$6 each. Since marginal contributions are calculated with respect to the end income, the marginal contribution of each program to that individual's poverty status is six, given that the other two programs pushed her out of poverty. This is the issue of path dependence that computations of the Shapley value attempt to circumvent (see appendix 2A).

2.2.28 Marginal Contributions to Vertical Equity and Reranking

The marginal contribution to poverty or inequality is defined based on the fiscal intervention and a particular core income concept; for example, the marginal contribution of Bolsa Familia to inequality, with respect to Disposable Income, is calculated as the Gini of Disposable Income *without (minus) Bolsa Familia* minus the Gini of Disposable Income.[36] For the marginal contribution to vertical equity or reranking, however, both an initial and end income must be defined, so that, for example, the marginal contribution of Bolsa Familia to the vertical equity goes from Market to Disposable Income. Specifically, these more complex marginal contribution indicators are calculated as follows.

Since these can be defined for any initial and end incomes (not necessarily the ones we typically consider prefiscal and postfiscal incomes), we change the notation slightly. Let X denote initial income, Z denote end income, and $Z \backslash T_1$ ($Z \backslash B_1$) be the Z income concept without tax T_1 (without benefit B_1). For example, suppose Z is Final Income, T_1 is personal income taxes, and B_1 is a conditional cash transfer (CCT). Then $Z \backslash T_1$ is constructed by adding personal income taxes to Final Income (by adding them, we get Final Income prior to subtracting out personal income taxes), and $Z \backslash B_1$ is constructed by subtracting CCT benefits from Final Income (by subtracting them, we get Final Income prior to adding in CCT benefits).

The marginal contribution of tax T_1 to vertical equity going from income concept X to income concept Z is calculated as

$$MVE_{T_1} = (G_X - D_Z^X) - (G_X - D_{Z \backslash T_1}^X),$$

where G and D indicate Gini coefficients and concentration coefficients, as before. The marginal contribution of benefit B_1 to vertical equity going from income concept X to income concept Z is calculated as

$$MVE_{B_1} = (G_X - D_Z^X) - (G_X - D_{Z \backslash B_1}^X).$$

---

[36] The indicators in this subsection were derived by Ali Enami.

The analogous marginal contributions to reranking are calculated as

$$MRR_{T_1} = (D_Z^X - G_Z) - (D_{Z\backslash T_1}^X - G_{Z\backslash T_1})$$

and

$$MRR_{B_1} = (D_Z^X - G_Z) - (D_{Z\backslash B_1}^X - G_{Z\backslash B_1}).$$

We can also compute derivatives of these marginal contributions with respect to the size of tax 1 or benefit 1, which can be useful if we want to know if marginally increasing the size of a tax or transfer will increase its marginal contribution. Let the relative size of tax i as a proportion of initial income be g_i and the relative size of transfer j as a proportion of initial income be b_j. The derivative of the marginal contribution of tax T_1 to inequality with respect to its size is

$$\frac{\partial M_{T_1}}{\partial g_1} = \frac{\Pi(X, Z, T_1) + (D_X^Z - G_Z)}{1 - \sum_{i=1}^{n} g_i + \sum_{j=1}^{m} b_j},$$

where $\Pi(X, Z, T_1) = D_{T_1}^Z - D_X^Z$. The derivative of the marginal contribution of benefit B_1 to inequality with respect to its size is

$$\frac{\partial M_{B_1}}{\partial b_1} = \frac{\rho(X, Z, B_1) + (C_X^Z - G_Z)}{1 - \sum_{i=1}^{n} g_i + \sum_{j=1}^{m} b_j},$$

where $\rho(X, Z, B_1) = C_X^Z - C_{B_1}^Z$.

The derivative of the marginal contribution of tax T_1 to vertical equity with respect to its size is

$$\frac{\partial MVE_{T_1}}{\partial g_1} = \frac{\Pi(X, Z, T_1) + (G_X - C_Z^X)}{1 - \sum_{i=1}^{n} g_i + \sum_{j=1}^{m} b_j},$$

and for benefit B_1 it is

$$\frac{\partial MVE_{B_1}}{\partial b_1} = \frac{\rho(X, Z, B_1) - (G_X - C_Z^X)}{1 - \sum_{i=1}^{n} g_i + \sum_{j=1}^{m} b_j}.$$

The derivative of the marginal contribution of tax T_1 to reranking with respect to its size is

$$\frac{\partial MRR_{T_1}}{\partial g_1} = \frac{\partial M_{T_1}}{\partial g_1} - \frac{\partial MVE_{T_1}}{\partial g_1},$$

and for benefit B_1 it is

$$\frac{\partial MRR_{B_1}}{\partial g_1} = \frac{\partial M_{B_1}}{\partial g_1} - \frac{\partial MVE_{B_1}}{\partial g_1}.$$

2.2.29 Covariance

Sheet E15 shows the covariance between each core income concept, as well as each fiscal intervention (whose column titles are currently blank, but are filled in automatically by the *CEQ Stata Package* using the variable labels) with the fractional rank of the same core income concepts, which can be used to manually calculate the Gini coefficient and concentration coefficients. Specifically, Pyatt, Chen, and Fei (1980) and Lerman and Yitzhaki (1984) show that the Gini coefficient can be expressed as $G = (2/\mu)$ $\text{Cov}(y, F(y))$, where $F(y)$ is the fractional income rank in the distribution of income (or, equivalently, the CDF of income) and μ is mean income. Similarly, the concentration coefficient of a tax or transfer t with respect to income concept y can be expressed in terms of the covariance as follows: $C = (2/\mu) \, \text{Cov}(t, F(y))$, where μ is still mean income.

2.2.30 Assumption Testing

Sheet E28 is meant to test various assumptions used to construct the income concepts and quickly compare the implications of these assumptions on a limited number of summary measures (the mean, median, standard deviation, Gini, Theil, 90/10, and poverty using various poverty lines and the headcount, poverty gap, and squared poverty gap, as well as totals by decile and income group). For example, suppose the team is comparing two methods for imputed rent for owner-occupied housing: the first is to use a survey question where respondents report what they think they would rent their house for if it were rented rather than owned, and the second is to use the prediction method, regressing rental rates against housing characteristics among the subset who rent their homes (as described in chapter 3 in Volume 1 of this Handbook]). After creating a prefiscal income variable under each of these two possible methods, these two variables would be used with the `ceqassump` command to quickly compare how the decision of how to allocate imputed rent for owner-occupied housing affects mean income, inequality, and poverty.

3 CEQ Stata Package

Table 8-5 presents the user-written Stata commands that make up the *CEQ Stata Package*, describes the indicators that they compute, the variables for which indicators are estimated, and the sheets of the *CEQ MWB* section E that are automatically populated with results by the *CEQ Stata Package* commands. As described in section 2, section D provides a summary of the results from section E and is populated using the "Fill Results" buttons in the sheets of section D. The *CEQ Stata Package* requires Stata version 14 or newer since it uses the `putexcel` command.

TABLE 8-5
Commands in the *CEQ Stata Package*

Command	Indicators	Variables	Sheet of *CEQ MWB* section E
ceqppp	Preliminary command to obtain numbers needed for PPP conversions	N/A	N/A
ceqdes	Percent with non-zero values for the fiscal intervention or income concept, mean, standard deviation, median, percent of income for the fiscal intervention	Core income concepts and fiscal interventions	E1. Descriptive statistics
ceqpop	Population (number of households, number of individuals, in sample and in expanded sample) by decile, group, centile, and bin (based on core income concepts)	Core income concepts	E2. Population
ceqextpop	Population (number of households, number of individuals, in sample and in expanded sample) by decile, group, centile, and bin (based on extended income concepts)	Extended income concepts	E2b. Ext. population
ceqlorenz	Anonymous summary statistics (mean, median, standard deviation, Gini, S-Gini, Theil, 90/10, poverty headcount index, poverty gap, squared poverty gap), shares, cumulative shares, anonymous incidence by decile, group, centile and bin of core income concepts	Core income concepts	E3. Lorenz
ceqiop	Ex-ante inequality of opportunity using mean log deviation by core income concept	Core income concepts	E4. Inequality of opportunity
ceqfi	Fiscal impoverishment (FI headcount, FI headcount among postfiscal poor, total FI, per capita FI, per capita FI normalized by the poverty line); fiscal gains of the poor (same as above for FGP instead of FI)	Core income concepts (from one income concept to another)	E5. Fisc. impoverishment, E6. Fisc. gains to the poor

(continued)

TABLE 8-5   (continued)

Command	Indicators	Variables	Sheet of *CEQ MWB* section E
ceqstatsig	Statistical significance (p-values) for changes in inequality, poverty, concentration coefficients between core income concepts	Pairs of core income concepts	E7. Statistical significance
ceqdom	Indicators to test dominance for Lorenz curves, concentration curves, etc.; for core income concepts	Core income concepts	E8. Dominance
ceqef	Effectiveness indicators for core income concepts	Core income concepts	E9. Effectiveness
ceqconc	Non-anonymous summary statistics (mean, median, standard deviation, concentration coefficient, redistributive effect, Reynolds-Smolensky index, reranking effect), concentration totals, concentration shares, cumulative shares and non-anonymous incidence by decile, group, centile, bin of each core income concept	Core income concepts; separate sheet for ranking by each core income concept	E10. Concentration (eight sheets E10.m, . . . , E10.f)
ceqfiscal	Summary statistics (mean, median, standard deviation, concentration coefficient, Kakwani index), totals, shares, cumulative shares, non-anonymous incidence for fiscal Interventions by decile, group, centile and bin of each core income concept	Fiscal interventions, separate sheet for ranking by each core income concept	E11. Fiscal interventions (eight sheets E11.m, . . . , E11.f)
ceqextend	Summary statistics (mean, median, standard deviation; inequality, Gini, S-Gini, Theil, 90/10, poverty headcount, poverty gap, squared poverty gap), concentration coefficients, income totals, shares, cumulative shares, anonymous incidence by decile, group, centile and bin of each core income concept	Extended income concepts, separate sheet for extended income concepts with respect to each core income concept	E12. Extended income concepts (eight sheets E12.m, . . . , E12.f)

Command	Indicators	Variables	Sheet of *CEQ MWB* section E
ceqmarg	Marginal contributions to inequality, progressivity, vertical and horizontal equity, poverty	Fiscal interventions, separate sheet for ranking by each core income concept	E13. Marg. contrib. (eight sheets E13.m, . . . , E13.f)
ceqefext	Effectiveness indicators for extended income concepts	Extended income concepts, separate sheet for extended income concepts with respect to each core income concept	E14. Effectiveness (eight sheets E14.m, . . . , E14.f)
ceqcov	Covariance of core income concepts and fiscal interventions	Core income concepts and fiscal interventions	E15. Covariance
ceqextsig	Statistical significance (p-values) for changes in inequality, poverty, concentration coefficients between core and extended income concepts	Core and extended income concepts	E16. Extended income stat. sig. (eight sheets E16.m, . . . , E16.f)
ceqdomext	Indicators to test dominance for Lorenz curves, concentration curves, etc.; for extended income concepts	Extended income concepts	E17. Dominance tests (eight sheets E17.m, . . . , E17.f)
ceqcoverage	Indicators on coverage and leakages for fiscal interventions by income group of each core income concept	Fiscal interventions, separate sheet for ranking by each core income concept	E18. Coverage tables (eight sheets E18.m, . . . , E18.f)
ceqtarget	Indicators on coverage and leakages among target beneficiaries or payers for fiscal interventions by income group of each core income concept	Fiscal interventions, separate sheet for ranking by each core income concept	E19. Coverage (target) (eight sheets E19.m, . . . , E19.f)
ceqeduc	Education enrollment rates by income group	Education enrollment by level; age	E20. Edu. Enrollment rates (eight sheets E20.m, . . . , E20.f)

(*continued*)

TABLE 8-5   (continued)

Command	Indicators	Variables	Sheet of *CEQ MWB* section E
ceqinfra	Coverage and distribution of infrastructure access, for infrastructure access variables (electricity, drinkable water, sanitation, and roads)	Infrastructure access variables	E21. Infrastructure Access
ceqhhchar	Household sociodemographic characteristics (age of the household head, number of rooms, etc.)	Household-level sociodemographic characteristic variables and core income concepts	E22. Group sociodemo. charac. (eight sheets E22.m, . . . , E22.f)
ceqindchar	Individual sociodemographic characteristics (age, years of schooling, etc.)	Individual-level sociodemographic characteristic variables and core income concepts	E23. Indiv. sociodemo. charac. (eight sheets E23.m, . . . , E23.f)
ceqgraph progressivity	Graphs of Lorenz curves	Core income concepts	E24. Lorenz curves
ceqgraph conc	Graphs of concentration curves	Core income concepts	E25. Concentration curves
ceqgraph cdf	Graphs of cumulative distribution functions of each core income concept	Core income concepts	E26. CDF
ceqgraph fi	Graphs of FI and FGP headcounts; FI and FGP per capita; FI and FGP per capita normalized by the poverty line; and total FI and FGP, over different poverty lines	Core income concepts (from one income concept to another)	E27. FIFGP
ceqassump	Tests how assumptions used to construct income concepts affect inequality, poverty, distribution	Any income concept created to test assumptions	E28. Assumptions
ceqrace	Many indicators by race or ethnicity	Core income concepts, extended income concepts, fiscal interventions	Section F see Aranda and Ratzlaff (2022) (chapter 9 in Volume 1 of this Handbook)

CDF = cumulative distribution function; FGP = fiscal gains of the poor; FI = fiscal impoverishment; FIFGP = FI and FGP; *CEQ MWB* = *CEQ Master Workbook*; PPP = purchasing power parity.

3.1 Preliminaries

To install the latest stable release of the *CEQ Stata Package*, include the following Stata code in a .do file or enter it into Stata's command prompt:[37]

```
update all
ssc install ceq, replace
```

Once the package is installed, a short description of each command and links to the help files for each command can be found by typing

```
help ceq
```

Most of the *CEQ Stata Package* commands produce results for specific sheets of section E of the *CEQ MWB*, as shown in table 8-5. These share a common structure, and many share common options, which are described in section 3.2, Structure and Options. There is one preliminary command in the package that is used to extract the numbers necessary to convert local currency units into PPP adjusted dollars, so that income totals can be compared to "international" poverty lines: ceqppp. This command pulls three numbers needed to perform PPP conversions: the consumption-based PPP conversion factor, which converts local currency from the "base year" in which price data was collected by the ICP—usually 2005 or 2011—to dollars for the same year; the country's consumer price index (CPI) for the base year; and the country's CPI for the year of the household survey. The command uses Azevedo's (2011) wbopendata to extract this information from the World Bank's World Development Indicators (WDI).

The syntax of ceqppp is as follows:

```
ceqppp, country(string) baseyear(real) surveyyear(real) [locals]
```

The command's options are described in table 8-6. If locals is specified, the needed numbers are saved in the locals 'ppp', 'cpibase', and 'cpisurvey'.

Consider, for example, the study for Brazil by Higgins and Pereira (2014), which used data from the 2008–09 Family Expenditure Survey (Pesquisa de Orçamentos Familiares). When the survey spans two years, authors must determine whether the data are already deflated to one of the two years; in the case of Brazil, all prices in the

---

[37] In addition to being able to install the *CEQ Stata Package* automatically through Stata, users can access the most recent and previous versions of the commands at https://github .com /skhiggins/CEQStataPackage. The development version of the *CEQ Stata Package* (which sometimes includes updates and bug fixes that have not yet been incorporated into the stable version) can be automatically installed in Stata with net install ceq, from("https://raw .githubusercontent.com/skhiggins/CEQStataPackage/master/")

TABLE 8-6
Options for ceqppp

Option	Description
country(*string*)	Three letter country code (see help wbopendata)
baseyear(*real*)	Base year for PPP conversion (either 2005 or 2011)
surveyyear(*real*)	Year of household survey
locals	Store these numbers as locals

microdata had already been deflated to January 2009 prices by the Brazilian Geographical and Statistical Institute (IBGE), so 2009 was used as the survey year. If the survey spans two years and prices in the microdata are not deflated, the country authors should deflate them to one of the two years before doing PPP conversions. Thus, to convert to 2005 international dollars (using the 2005 ICP):

ceqppp, country("bra") baseyear(2005) surveyyear(2009) locals

The relevant numbers are printed in the Stata results window, and are also saved in the locals `ppp`, `cpibase`, and `cpisurvey`, which can be fed directly into the ppp(), cpibase(), and cpisurvey() options of the relevant *CEQ Stata Package* commands, described below.

Using ceqppp rather than manually obtaining the PPP conversion factor and CPIs from WDI has multiple advantages: it is more efficient, avoids human error, avoids rounding error, and increases the transparency and replicability of one's research. In addition, since the *CEQ Stata Package* commands print these numbers in row 3 of each sheet of section E, ceqppp can be used by those conducting quality control of a *CEQ Assessment* to quickly confirm that the numbers used by a country team for the PPP conversion match those from WDI (and request an explanation from the team if they do not match).

3.2 Structure and Options

The *CEQ Stata Package* commands have a common syntax:

command [*if*] [*in*] [*weight*] [using *filename*], *options*

where command is the name of the command—for example, ceqdes. For most commands, there is no *varlist* specified after the command name because income concept variables, fiscal intervention variables, and other variables are all specified using command options. Exceptions are discussed below in section 3.3 on specific commands.

The optional *if* and *in* arguments allow the user to restrict the analysis to a particular subset of the data. For example, the *if* argument could be used to perform subgroup-specific analyses (e.g., by urban/rural area or region) or to restrict the analysis to "non-dropped" observations if a marker dummy variable is used to mark observations that should be dropped.

For weights, `pweight` is allowed; see `help weight`. Alternatively, weights can be specified using `svyset`.

IMPORTANT

Note that if working with individual-level data, the *CEQ Stata Package* assumes that each member of a household has the same weight.

Results are automatically exported to the *CEQ MWB* if using *filename* is specified, where *filename* is the file of the corresponding sheet of the *CEQ MWB*. (It is a good idea to keep a blank version of each Excel file included in the *CEQ MWB* and create copies for each scenario or sensitivity analysis undertaken as part of the *CEQ Assessment*, adding the three-letter country abbreviation and an abbreviation of the scenario—for example, PDI for pensions as deferred income—as well as the date the analysis was run, to the *CEQ MWB* copies that will be supplied to the command with using *filename*.) There are a number of options that govern this automatic export, which are described in more detail in section 3.2.8, Export Directly to the *CEQ MWB*.

Note that completing the different scenarios for the treatment of pensions[38] requires running the command more than once, with separate *CEQ MWB filenames*, and additional scenarios or sensitivity analyses would require additional runs with other *filenames*. The variables used in the command's options would be different depending on the treatment of pensions, as described in more detail below in 3.2.1, Income Concept Options, and 3.2.2, Fiscal Intervention Options.

3.2.1 Income Concept Options

The first group of options are income concept options, in which the user supplies the variables for each of the core income concepts described in chapter 6 in this Volume. The income concepts should already be adjusted for the number of household members and, if desired, for economies of scale and adult equivalence. In other words, if household per capita income is being used (as is most common in *CEQ Assessments*), these variables should already be in household per capita terms (total household income divided by the number of members of the household). Alternatively, if an equivalence scale is being used, such as the square root scale recommended by Buhmann and others (1988) and used for a *CEQ Assessment* comparing Brazil and the United

---

[38] See chapter 6 in this volume.

TABLE 8-7
Income Concept Options

Option	Description
market(*varname*)	Market Income
mpluspensions(*varname*)	Market Income plus Pensions
netmarket(*varname*)	Net Market Income
gross(*varname*)	Gross Income
taxable(*varname*)	Taxable Income
disposable(*varname*)	Disposable Income
consumable(*varname*)	Consumable Income
final(*varname*)	Final Income

States,[39] these income concepts should already be in equivalized terms, dividing in this case by the square root of the number of household members. They should be in local currency units per year, as the CEQ Stata commands automatically perform PPP conversions to dollars per day for comparison with international poverty lines.[40] When generating the income concept variables during the data preparation stage, these variables should be generated as double-precision variables using generate double, in order to avoid rounding errors (which can be compounded when applying expansion factors and summing across all observations in the sample), and following the Instructions given in part IV of this Volume of the Handbook (CEQ Institute, 2022).

IMPORTANT
Income concepts in local currency should be expressed in annual terms to facilitate the comparison of results from the *CEQ MWB* with results from national accounts.

At least one income concept option must be specified for the command to run. Table 8-7 shows the income concept options, which are used by all commands in the *CEQ Stata Package* (with the exception of the preliminary commands discussed in section 3.1).

---

[39] Higgins and others (2016).

[40] The commands are flexible enough to accommodate local currency per month or day rather than per year, but we highly recommend converting all income concept variables to annual terms so that results can be easily compared to numbers from national accounts.

As described in chapter 6 in this Volume, there are two scenarios for the treatment of pensions. We recapitulate these scenarios, then show how these different scenarios can be subsumed into one set of E sheets using the market(*varname*) and mpluspensions(*varname*) options. Both of these options should be used with the CEQ Stata commands; then the selection of a prefiscal income concept from the results will depend on the scenario:

1. In the *contributory pensions as deferred income* scenario (PDI), the prefiscal income concept used for the analysis should already include contributory pensions; i.e., prefiscal income should be Market Income plus Pensions.
2. Likewise, in the *contributory pensions as a government transfer scenario* (PGT), contributory pensions are excluded from prefiscal income and instead counted as a transfer; i.e., prefiscal income is Market Income.[41]

For details on the prefiscal income in each pensions scenario, please see chapter 6 in this Volume and in particular, figure 6-2 and table 6-5, and the accompanying text.

3.2.2 Fiscal Intervention Options

The second group of options are fiscal intervention options, in which the user supplies each of the variables for particular taxes, transfers, subsidies, and in-kind benefits. These variables should be expressed in the same units as the income concept variables—thus, in local currency per year in household per capita or per adult equivalent terms. Like the income concept variables, these variables should also be created using generate double during the data preparation stage.

The fiscal intervention options are included only in the syntax of commands that provide results by fiscal intervention or extended income concepts: ceqdes, ceqfiscal, and ceqextend. These options are described in table 8-8. All of the fiscal intervention variables fed to these options should be labeled using

label variable *varname* ["*label*"]

since many of the *CEQ Stata Package* commands automatically use these variable labels as the titles of rows or columns of results in the *CEQ MWB*. Examples of these labels are "conditional cash transfers from Bolsa Familia (household per capita)," "noncontributory pensions (household per capita)," and "tobacco excise tax (household per capita)."More detailed variable labeling instructions are provided directly in part IV of Volume 1 of this Handbook (CEQ Institute, 2022).

---

[41] A third potential scenario that could be run would be to treat only the subsidized portion of pensions as a transfer. In this case, a separate set of E sheets would have to be generated, with Prefiscal Income including *only the nonsubsidized portion of contributory pensions.* See chapter 1 in Volume 1 of this Handbook.

TABLE 8-8
Fiscal Intervention Options

Option	Description
pensions(*varlist*)	Contributory pension variable
dtransfers(*varlist*)	Direct transfer variables
dtaxes(*varlist*)	Direct tax variables
contribs(*varlist*)	Contribution variables
subsidies(*varlist*)	Subsidy variables
indtaxes(*varlist*)	Indirect tax variables
health(*varlist*)	Health in-kind transfer variables
userfeeshealth(*varlist*)	Health user fees
education(*varlist*)	Education in-kind transfer variables
userfeeseduc(*varlist*)	Education user fees
otherpublic(*varlist*)	Other public transfers
userfeesother(*varlist*)	Other user fees (corresponding to other public in-kind transfers)

IMPORTANT

Follow the instructions in the document "Constructing the CEQ Harmonized Microdata" in part IV of Volume 1 of this Handbook for a correct functioning of the *CEQ Stata Package*. You should follow these instructions whether or not you plan to produce a harmonized microdata.

Each option accepts a *varlist* so that multiple variables can be included for each program or tax. There might be ten different direct cash transfer programs; each of these would be a variable, and all ten variables would be included with the dtransfers(*varlist*) option.

The pensions(*varlist*) option should include contributory pensions.[42] The contribs(*varlist*) option should include contributions to the contributory pension system.

We now provide some examples of programs included in the fiscal interventions options. dtransfers(*varlist*) commonly includes separate variables for each conditional cash transfer program, unconditional cash transfer program, public scholarship program, noncontributory pension program for the elderly poor, food transfer pro-

---

[42] In the third potential scenario that could be run treating only the subsidized portion of pensions as a transfer, a variable containing only the subsidized portion of pensions would be included in dtransfers(*varlist*).

gram, and other direct transfer programs. dtaxes(*varlist*) commonly includes separate variables for individual income taxes and property taxes. contribs(*varlist*) commonly includes variables for contributions to each contributory program (for example, pensions, unemployment insurance). subsidies(*varlist*) commonly includes variables for each indirect subsidy (for example, the *CEQ Assessment* for Ghana included fertilizer, kerosene, and electricity).[43] indtaxes(*varlist*) commonly includes variables for indirect taxes for various categories. Also, the *CEQ Assessment* for Indonesia included variables for the value-added tax and tobacco excise,[44] while the *CEQ Assessment* for Tanzania included a variable for the value-added tax, a variable for import duties (including their indirect effects), and ten separate variables for excise taxes.[45] health(*varlist*) and userfeeshealth(*varlist*) commonly include variables for different types of care, for example, in-patient, out-patient, and preventative care. education(*varlist*) and userfeeseduc(*varlist*) commonly include variables for different levels of public education spending at the preschool, primary, secondary, and tertiary levels.

In countries with health, education, or other user fees, the transfer benefits supplied to the health(*varlist*), education(*varlist*), and otherpublic(*varlist*) options should be *net* benefits. In other words, in countries where the user fee goes directly to the government and hence the calculated benefits are gross of those user fees, the variables obtained would be those from the imputation method net of user fees; in countries where the user fee goes into the doctor's pocket and thus the imputed benefit based on costs from national accounts does *not* include proceeds from the user fee, this net benefit from national accounts should be used (in other words, the user fee should not be subtracted to obtain the net benefit). Even though the variables supplied to these options should already be net of user fees, we also include userfeeshealth(*varlist*), userfeeseduc(*varlist*), and userfeesother(*varlist*) options so that the user can analyze the concentration of these fees separately, which may be of interest.

Tax, contribution, and user fee variables may be saved as either positive or negative values, as long as one is used consistently for all tax, contribution, and user fee variables.

Figure 8-3 shows how the CEQ income concepts and fiscal interventions map to the CEQ Stata commands.

3.2.3 PPP Conversion Options

Table 8-9 includes the options used to convert from local currency units to PPP-adjusted dollars; the conversion is done automatically by the commands once the PPP conversion factor, CPI for the base year (year of PPP, 2005, 2011, or 2017), and CPI for the survey year are supplied. The PPP conversion options are included only in commands that compare incomes to poverty lines or other income group cut-offs—that is, the commands that have poverty results or results by income group: ceqpop, ceqextpop, ceqlorenz,

---

[43] Younger, Osei-Assibey, and Oppong (2015).

[44] Afkar and others (2017).

[45] Younger, Myamba, and Mdadila (2016).

FIGURE 8-3

Definition of Income Concepts: A Detailed Presentation with Stata Codes

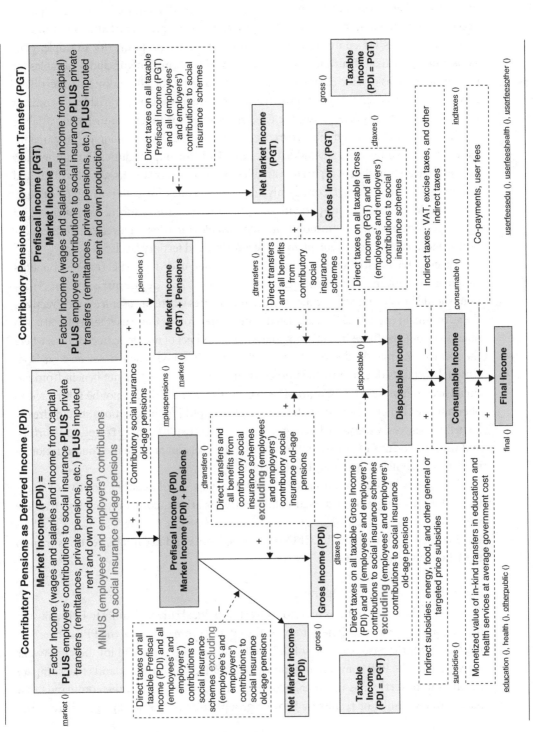

PGT = pensions as government transfer; PDI = pensions as deferred income.

TABLE 8-9
PPP Conversion Options

Option	Description
ppp(*real*)	PPP conversion factor (LCU per PPP-adjusted dollar, consumption-based) from year of PPP (for example, 2005 or 2011) to year of PPP; do not use PPP factor for year of household survey
cpibase(*real*)	CPI of base year (year of PPP, usually 2005 or 2011)
cpisurvey(*real*)	CPI of year of household survey
daily	Indicates that variables are in daily currency
monthly	Indicates that variables are in monthly currency
yearly	Indicates that variables are in yearly currency (the default)

ceqfi, ceqstatsig, ceqef, ceqconc, ceqfiscal, ceqextend, ceqmarg, ceqefext, ceqextsig, ceqcoverage, ceqtarget, ceqinfra, ceqeduc, ceqhhchar, ceqindchar, ceqgraph cdf, ceqgraph fi, and ceqassump.

The *CEQ Stata Package* commands automatically convert local currency variables to PPP dollars, using the PPP conversion factor given by ppp (*real*), the CPI of the year of PPP (2005 or 2011) given by cpibase (*real*), and the CPI of the year of the household survey used in the analysis given by cpisurvey (*real*). The year of PPP, also called "base year," refers to the year of the ICP that is being used, 2005 or 2011. The survey year refers to the year of the household survey used in the analysis. We recommend using ceqppp with the locals option to obtain these figures from WDI, as described in section 3.1; then these can be fed into the *CEQ Stata Package* commands as follows:

command ..., ppp('ppp') cpibase('cpibase') cpisurvey ('cpisurvey')
... *other options*

If obtaining the numbers for the PPP conversion manually from WDI or another source (rather than using the ceqppp command to automatically obtain them from WDI), make sure that the PPP conversion factor is consumption-based: if the year of PPP is 2005, the PPP conversion factor should be the "PPP conversion factor, private consumption (LCU per international dollar)" indicator from the World Bank's WDI for 2005. If the year of PPP is 2011, use the "PPP conversion factor, private consumption (LCU per international dollar)" indicator from WDI for 2011. The PPP conversion factor should convert from year of PPP to year of PPP. In other words, when extracting the PPP conversion factor, it is possible to select any year. **DO NOT select the year of the survey; rather, select the year that the ICP was conducted to compute PPP conversion factors (2005 or 2011 or other).** The base year (year of PPP) CPI, which can also be obtained from WDI, should match the base year chosen for the PPP conversion factor. The survey year CPI should match the year of the household survey.

TABLE 8-10
Survey Information Options

Option	Description
hsize(*varname*)	Number of members in the household (should be used when each observation in the dataset is a household)
hhid(*varname*)	Unique household identifier variable (should be used when each observation in the dataset is an individual)
head(*string*)	Gives the condition identifying the household head (should be used when each observation in the dataset is an individual)
psu(*varname*)	Primary sampling unit; can also be set using svyset
strata(*varlist*)	Strata (used with complex sampling designs); can also be set using svyset

Finally, for the PPP conversion, the user can specify whether the original variables are in local currency units per day (daily), per month (monthly), or per year (yearly, the default assumption). All variables in currency must be in the same units, and we highly recommend using local currency units *per year*, since the figures (total Disposable Income) will then be comparable to analogous figures from national accounts, which are expressed in annual terms.

3.2.4 Survey Information Options

Information about the survey is provided through the survey information options shown in table 8-10.

If the dataset is at the individual level (each observation is an individual), the variable with the identification code of each household (a unique household identifier that takes the same value for all members within a household) should be specified in the hhid(*varname*) option, and the hsize(*varname*) option should not be specified. If the dataset is at the household level (each observation is a household), a variable containing the number of members in each household should be specified in the hsize(*varname*) option, and the hhid(*varname*) option should not be specified. In either case, the *weight* used (or supplied via svyset) should be the household sampling weight and should *not* be multiplied by the number of members in the household, since the program will do this multiplication automatically in the case of household-level data.

There are two options for including information about weights and survey sample design so that the estimates and statistical significance tests are calculated correctly. The sampling weight can be entered in the usual fashion using *weight* or supplied via svyset. Information about complex stratified sample designs can also be entered using svyset since the *CEQ Stata Package* commands automatically use the informa-

TABLE 8-11
Poverty Line Options

Option	Description
pl1(*real*)	Lowest poverty line in PPP dollars per person per day (default is US$1.90)
pl2(*real*)	Second lowest poverty line in PPP dollars per person per day (default is US$3.20)
pl3(*real*)	Third lowest poverty line in PPP dollars per person per day (default is US$5.50)
nationalextremepl(*string*)	National extreme poverty line in same units as income variables (can be a *real* scalar or *varname*)
nationalmoderatepl(*string*)	National moderate poverty line in same units as income variables (can be a *real* scalar or *varname*)
otherextremepl(*string*)	Other extreme poverty line in same units as income variables (can be a *real* scalar or *varname*)
othermoderatepl(*string*)	Other extreme poverty line in same units as income variables (can be a *real* scalar or *varname*)
proportion(*real*)	Proportion of median income used as for the relative poverty line (default is 0.5, or 50 percent of median income)

tion specified using svyset. Alternatively, the primary sampling unit variable can be entered using the psu(*varname*) option, and the strata variable can be entered using the strata(*varlist*) option.

3.2.5 Poverty Line Options

The CEQ Stata commands ceqlorenz, ceqfi, ceqef, ceqextend, ceqmarg, ceqefext, ceqgraph fi, ceqgraph cdf, and ceqassump produce poverty results using three international poverty lines, a national extreme and national moderate poverty line, and—if applicable—an additional extreme and moderate poverty line (for example, poverty lines produced by the regional UN Economic Commission for the country, or the income cut-off used to determine social program eligibility if this differs from the official poverty line). Table 8-11 shows the poverty line options to control what poverty lines are used for these calculations.

The "international" poverty lines in PPP dollars per day can be set using the pl1(*real*), pl2(*real*), and pl3(*real*). As of January 2022, the defaults for these were

US$1.90, US$3.20, and US$5.50 PPP poverty lines.[46] If using 2005 as the base year for PPP conversions (using the 2005 ICP round rather than the 2011 ICP round), the user would likely want to change the lowest poverty line from its default of US$1.90 PPP per day to US$1.25 PPP. Similarly, if using 2005 as the base year for PPP conversions, the user should specify the other two international poverty lines used by the World Bank, $2.50 and $4 per day. To do this, simply use the PPP conversion factor and base year CPI for 2005 and specify options pl1(1.25) pl2(2.50) pl3(4). Notice, however, that as it is explained in the next section, income group cut-off default points are consistent with using the 2011 as base year for PPP conversions. Hence, if the user changes the poverty lines, it is strongly recommended that she changes the income group cut-off points accordingly, following the instructions in the section below. Also, notice that in 2022, the World Bank released new poverty lines based on price data obtained from the 2017 International Comparison Program so the defaults in the *CEQ Stata Package* may have changed. **Since they may be updated in the future to reflect the poverty lines generated with the conversion factors obtained from the 2017 International Comparison Program (or subsequent rounds), periodically update the package and check the help files of the *CEQ Stata Package* to verify the current defaults.**

Poverty lines in local currency can be entered using the national-extremepl(*string*), nationalmoderatepl(*string*), otherextremepl(*string*), and othermoderatepl(*string*) options. Local currency poverty lines can be entered as real numbers (for poverty lines that are fixed for the entire population) or variable names (for poverty lines that vary, for example, across space), and should be in the same units as the income concept variables (preferably local currency units per year).

In addition to the above absolute poverty lines, we also estimate relative poverty using a poverty line equal to x percent of median income (using whichever income concept poverty is being estimated for). By default, the line is set at 50 percent of median income, but this can be changed with the proportion(*real*) option, which takes values between 0 and 1 (and has a default of 0.5).

For the default poverty lines in *the CEQ Stata* Package, the 2011 ICP is used. The $1.90 is the official World Bank extreme poverty line corresponding to the 2011 ICP PPP.[47] Researchers at the World Bank proposed using $3.20 in 2011 PPP for lower-middle income countries and $5.50 in 2011 PPP for upper-middle income countries[48] and a global societal—or weakly relative—poverty line equal to $1 + 0.5$ times the me-

---

[46] For the PPP 2005 poverty lines, see Ravallion, Chen, and Sangraula (2009); Chen and Ravallion (2010). For the PPP 2011 poverty lines, see Ferreira and others (2016). The US$1.90 line is fairly robust to alternate methods of estimating the global poverty line (Lustig and Silber, 2016, table 1), such as taking the median line from a broader set of poor countries (Jolliffe and Prydz, 2016) or a population-weighted average of poverty lines from 101 countries (Kakwani and Son, 2016).

[47] Ferreira and others (2016).

[48] Jolliffe and Prydz (2016).

TABLE 8-12
Income Group Cut-Off Options

Option	Description
cut1(*real*)	Upper bound income for ultra-poor (default is US$1.90 PPP per day)
cut2(*real*)	Upper bound income for extreme poor (default is US$3.20 PPP per day)
cut3(*real*)	Upper bound income for moderate poor (default is US$5.50 PPP per day)
cut4(*real*)	Upper bound income for vulnerable (default is US$11.50 PPP per day)
cut5(*real*)	Upper bound income for middle class (default is US$57.60 PPP per day)

dian consumption (or, in its absence, the median household per capita income) from the country's household survey.[49] All these poverty lines changed in early 2022.

Although the defaults used in the *CEQ Stata Package* are the poverty lines defined in PPP 2011, they may be updated in the future to reflect the new poverty lines. Thus, periodically update the package and check the help files of the *CEQ Stata Package* to verify the current defaults.

For consistency, remember that whenever you change the poverty lines, you should also change the income thresholds cutoffs described in the next section accordingly.

3.2.6 Income Group Cut-Off Options

Some CEQ Stata commands produce results by income bin—for example, total incomes for those with incomes between US$0 and US$1.90 per day, between US$1.90 and US$3.20 per day, etc.; these include ceqpop, ceqextpop, ceqlorenz, ceqconc, ceqfiscal, ceqextend, ceqcoverage, ceqtarget, ceqinfra, ceqeduc, ceqhhchar, ceqindchar, and ceqassump. Like the poverty lines, the income cut-offs can be adjusted, using the income group cut-off options summarized in table 8-12.

These cut-offs are based on 2011 PPP dollars, which are obtained by updating the ones that had been proposed using the 2005 PPP dollars with the US consumer price index. As described in chapter 6 in this Volume, the names were initially based on the context of middle-income countries. For the groups referred to as vulnerable and middle class, the US$10 2005 PPP per day line is the upper bound of those vulnerable to falling into poverty (and thus the lower bound of the middle class) in three Latin American countries, calculated by Lopez-Calva and Ortiz-Juarez (2014). Ferreira and others (2013) find that an income of around US$10 2005 PPP also represents the income at which individuals in various Latin American countries tend to self-identify as belonging to the middle class and consider this further justification for using it as the lower bound of the "middle class." The US$10 2005 PPP per day line was also used as the

---

[49] Jolliffe and Prydz (2017).

lower bound of the middle class in Latin America in Birdsall (2010) and in developing countries in all regions of the world in Kharas (2010). The US$50 2005 PPP per day line is the upper bound of the middle class proposed by Ferreira and others (2013).

Suppose we were converting to 2005 PPP dollars rather than 2011 PPP dollars, and thus wanted to change the cut-off for the lowest income group to US$1.25, one of the World Bank's previous global extreme poverty line, and the cut-off for the second-lowest group and third-lowest groups to $2.50 and $4, which correspond to the national poverty lines typically found in lower- and upper-middle income countries, respectively.[50] We would then specify the options cut1(1.25) cut2(2.50) cut3(4) cut4(10) cut5(50), making the poorest group range from US$0 to US$1.25 PPP per day, the second-poorest group from US$1.25 to US$2.50, and the third-poorest group from US$2.50 to US$4; the vulnerable from US$4 to US$10; the middle class from US$10 to US$50; and, the rich from US$50 and above.[51] If we did not specify every cut-off, that cut-off would remain at its default value; for example, for the cut4 (*real*) option, if we did not write cut4(10), that cut-off would remain at its default value of US$11.50, so the fourth group would then range from US$4 to US$11.50 PPP per day instead of from US$4 to US$10, the correct range.

For consistency, remember that whenever you change the income thresholds cut-offs, you should change the poverty lines accordingly following the instructions presented in the previous section, and viceversa.

3.2.7 Produce a Subset of Results

To increase speed and efficiency for those wishing to produce only a subset of results within a sheet, many commands include options to do so. The commands that produce results by decile, income group, centile, and bin (ceqpop, ceqextpop, ceqlorenz, ceqconc, ceqfiscal, ceqextend, ceqmarg, ceqhhchar, ceqindchar, and ceqassump) have the options nodecile, nogroup, nocentile, and nobin to refrain from producing the corresponding subsets of results summarized in table 8-13.

The ceqfi command also includes the nobin option to not produce results by income bin. Furthermore, to produce results for only some of the fiscal impoverishment (FI) and fiscal gains to the poor (FGP) indicators from Higgins and Lustig (2016), the following options can be specified (where specifying none of the following options is equivalent to specifying all of them, and hence results will be produced for all indicators): headcount to produce results for FI and FGP headcounts, headcountpoor to produce results for FI and FGP headcounts among the poor, total to produce results for total FI and FGP; percapita to produce results for per capita FI and FGP, and normalized to produce results for per capita FI and FGP normalized by the poverty line.

---

[50] Ferreira and others (2016).

[51] Strictly speaking, the upper bound of the cutoffs equal what is shown in the paragraph minus 1 cent of a PPP dollar.

TABLE 8-13
Produce Subset of Results

Option	Description
nodecile	Do not produce results by decile
nogroup	Do not produce results by income group
nocentile	Do not produce results by centile
nobin	Do not produce results by bin

3.2.8 Export Directly to the *CEQ MWB*

As mentioned above, results are automatically exported to the *CEQ MWB* if using *filename* is specified, where *filename* is the file of the corresponding sheet of the *CEQ MWB*. (It is a good idea to keep a blank version of each Excel file included in the *CEQ MWB* and create copies for each scenario or sensitivity analysis undertaken as part of the *CEQ Assessment*, adding the three-letter country abbreviation and an abbreviation of the scenario—e.g., PDI for pensions as deferred income—as well as the date the analysis was run, to the *CEQ MWB* copies that will be supplied to the command with using *filename*.) By default, each command prints to a sheet with a specific name, which is the sheet's default name in the *CEQ MWB*. If you change sheet names, you can inform the *CEQ Stata Package* commands of these changes using the sheet(*string*) option, for commands that print to one sheet; sheetm(*string*), sheetmp(*string*), sheetn(*string*), sheetg(*string*), sheett(*string*), sheetd(*string*), sheetc(*string*), and sheetf(*string*) options for commands that print to eight sheets, one for each core income concept; and the sheetfi(*string*) and sheetfg(*string*) options for the ceqfi command that prints to sheets E5 for fiscal impoverishment and E6 for fiscal gains of the poor.

The options for directly exporting to the *CEQ MWB* are included in table 8-14.

Row 3 of each sheet in section E of the *CEQ MWB* includes information on the country, authors, survey year, the date that the sheet was completed, and—on sheets that require a PPP conversion only—the base year (year of PPP, usually 2005 or 2011), the PPP conversion factor (from base year local currency units to base year PPP dollars), the country's CPI in the base year, its CPI in the survey year, and the resulting PPP conversion factor from survey year local currency units (LCU) to base year PPP.

For the country, survey year, authors, and (if applicable) base year for the PPP conversion to be automatically filled in by the command, the user should include strings with this information in the country(*string*), surveyyear(*string*), authors(*string*), and baseyear(*real*).[52] It Is also strongly recommended that the

---

[52] baseyear(*real*) takes a real number as its argument, whereas surveyyear(*string*) takes a string because the survey year may actually be multiple years. For example, in the case of Brazil we would use the option surveyyear("2008–2009").

TABLE 8-14
Options to Export Directly to the *CEQ MWB*

Option	Description
sheet(*string*)	Name of the sheet (this option can vary as described in text; see help files for each command)
country(*string*)	Country
surveyyear(*string*)	Year of survey
authors(*string*)	Authors of study
baseyear(*real*)	Base year of PPP conversion (for example, 2005 or 2011)
scenario(*string*)	Scenario
group(*string*)	Group
project(*string*)	Project
open	Automatically open *filename* with new results added

user fill the scenario(*string*) option to give information about the treatment of pensions: deferred income (PDI scenario) or government transfer (PGT scenario). These options should be used to provide information for users of the *CEQ MWB*. The ones that should not necessarily be used are group(*string*) to specify the sub-group in analyses done by sub-group; and project(*string*) to give the name of the project, e.g., "CEQ-IDB by Race and Ethnicity."

The date is generated automatically, and the other information about the PPP conversion is generated based on the numbers supplied to the PPP conversion options.

The open option can be used to automatically open *filename* after the results have been exported to the *CEQ MWB*.

3.2.9 Option to Ignore Missing Values

By default, the *CEQ Stata Package* does not allow income concept or fiscal intervention variables to have missing values; if one of these variables has missing values, the commands will produce an error. Other Stata commands (for example, regress) merely exclude observations that have a missing value from the calculations. The *CEQ Stata Package* commands instead produce an error because the missing values are often due to user error: if a household has zero income for an income concept, receives zero from a transfer or a subsidy, or pays zero of a tax, the household should have zero rather than a missing value.[53] For flexibility, however, the *CEQ Stata Package* commands include an ignoremissing option that will drop observations with missing values for any of these variables, thus allowing the command to run even if there are missing values.

---

[53] It is also often the case that household surveys have missing income. As explained in chapter 6 in this Volume, missing and zero incomes are regarded as zero, unless the household head's primary income source is missing, in which case the household is excluded from the data.

3.2.10 Option to Allow Calculations of Indicators with Negative Values

By default, when negative values are included for each core income concept or fiscal intervention, then the concentration coefficient, redistributive effect, Reynolds-Smolensky index and reranking effect are not produced in ceqconc; the concentration coefficient and Kakwani index are not produced in ceqfiscal; Gini coefficient, Theil index, concentration coefficient, poverty gap, and squared poverty gap are not produced in ceqextend. This is because these measures are no longer well behaved when negative values are included. For example, these measures can exceed 1, and other desirable properties of these measures when incomes or fiscal interventions are non-negative no longer hold if negative values are allowed. For flexibility, however, these commands include a negatives option that allows for the calculation of all indicators despite the presence of negative values in core income concepts or fiscal interventions.

3.3 Specific Commands

This section describes the details specific to each command and summarizes the indicators and results that each command produces.

3.3.1 ceqdes

The ceqdes command calculates descriptive statistics for the CEQ core income concepts and fiscal interventions (taxes, transfers, subsidies, and in-kind benefits). It exports these indicators to sheet "E1. Descriptive Statistics" of the *CEQ MWB*.

The descriptive statistics are the percent of individuals in the expanded sample who have positive values for the income concept or non-zero values for the fiscal intervention variables. Among those with positive or non-zero values, the mean, median, and standard deviation of the variable are included. Among all individuals, the total for that variable as a proportion of total income, using each of the core income concepts in the denominator, is included. The results for the core income concepts are included in rows 11 to 18, while the results for fiscal interventions are included in rows 19 in sheet E1 of the *CEQ MWB*. Rows 19 on do not have names of fiscal interventions in column A because these will be filled in automatically using the variable labels of the corresponding variables fed to the fiscal intervention options. Of the categories of options described above, the options for income concepts, fiscal interventions, survey information, exporting, and ignoring missing values are relevant for ceqdes.

3.3.2 ceqpop

The ceqpop command calculates the population by decile, income group, centile, and bin for each of the core income concepts for four definitions of population: number of households in sample, number of individuals in sample, number of households in expanded sample, and number of individuals in expanded sample. It exports them to sheet "E2. Population" of the *CEQ MWB*. The command requires installation of quantiles[54] to assign households to deciles or centiles.

The number of households and individuals in the sample provide evidence on what occurs in the survey itself before applying sampling weights and can provide evidence about small cells (for example, some countries may have so few observations with income below US$1.90 per day or above US$57.60 per day that any statistics about these groups are inherently noisy and should not be used). The number of households in the expanded sample shows the total households in the country represented by the sampled households, while the number of individuals in the expanded sample shows the analogue for individuals. Note that deciles are defined such that the number of individuals in the expanded sample is as equal as possible across groups; as a result, the size of each centile and bin for the other population definitions will *not* be equal. Of the categories of options described above, the options for income concepts, PPP conversions, survey information, income group cut-offs, producing a subset of results, exporting, and ignoring missing values are relevant for ceqpop.

3.3.3 ceqextpop

The ceqextpop command calculates the same definitions of population by decile, income group, centile, and bin as the ceqpop command, except for the extended rather than the core income concepts. It exports results to the "E2b.*y* Ext. Population" sheets where *y* is a letter representing one of the eight core income concepts: m, *m* + *p*, n, g, t, d, c, and f, which respectively denote Market Income, Market Income plus Pensions, Net Market Income, Gross Income, Taxable Income, Consumable Income, and Final Income. The command requires installation of quantiles[55] to assign households to deciles or centiles; to install, ssc install quantiles.

As explained in chapter 6 in this Volume, extended income concepts are constructed by adding or subtracting particular fiscal interventions (or bundles of interventions) from core income concepts. For example, Market Income plus Pensions plus conditional cash transfers is an extended income concept, as is Disposable Income minus conditional cash transfers (Disposable Income prior to adding conditional cash transfers, but with all other direct transfers included). Even though the results produced by ceqextpop are anonymous, and hence do not need a separate sheet for each core income concept ranking, there are eight sheets due to the sheer number of extended income concepts. Continuing the example above, the sheet for Market Income plus Pensions would include these indicators for the Market Income plus Pensions plus conditional cash transfers extended income concept, while the sheet for Disposable Income would include these indicators for the Disposable Income minus conditional cash transfers extended income concept.

---

[54] Osorio (2007). To install, ssc install quantiles.
[55] Osorio (2007).

A description of the definitions of decile, income group, centile, and bin is included under the ceqpop section. Of the categories of options described above, the options for income concepts, PPP conversions, survey information, income group cut-offs, producing a subset of results, exporting, and ignoring missing values are relevant for ceqextpop.

3.3.4 ceqlorenz

The ceqlorenz command calculates anonymous summary statistics and detailed information by income decile, group, centile, and bin for each of the CEQ core income concepts. It exports them to sheet "E3. Lorenz" of the *CEQ MWB*. The command requires installation of quantiles[56] to assign households to deciles or centiles and sgini to calculate S-Gini coefficients.[57]

"Anonymous" means that the ranking is not held fixed: for example, Market Income shares by decile would have deciles defined by Market Income, while Disposable Income shares by decile would have deciles defined by Disposable Income. (An individual in the lowest Market Income decile is not necessarily in the lowest Disposable Income decile if reranking occurs.)

The summary statistics include the mean, median, standard deviation, Gini, absolute Gini, S-Gini with a variety of parameters, Theil, 90/10, and headcount index, poverty gap, and squared poverty gap for a number of poverty lines. The detailed information by income centile and income bin, at a highly disaggregated level (income bins are 5-cent groups, for example, US$0–0.05 dollars per day, US$0.05–0.10 per day, etc.), includes total income in local currency units (per year if the income concept variables supplied to the command are annual). The detailed information by decile and income group (at a more aggregated, but still informative, level), includes these income totals in local currency and the same totals in PPP dollars per day, as well as per capita income in local currency (per year if the income concept variables supplied to the command are annual) and PPP dollars per day, shares of total income, cumulative shares of total income, and fiscal incidence with respect to (income relative to) Market Income, Market Income plus Pensions, Net Market Income, Gross Income, and Disposable Income. Although these latter indicators are not provided at the more disaggregated level by centile and income bin (to make the command faster and the *CEQ MWB* smaller in file size), they can all be generated directly with the total incomes in local currency that *are* produced by centile and bin, in addition to the population information by centile and bin included on sheet E2 and produced by ceqpop.

Of the categories of options described above, the options for income concepts, PPP conversions, survey information, poverty lines, income group cut-offs, producing a subset of results, exporting, and ignoring missing values are relevant for ceqlorenz.

---

[56] Osorio (2007).

[57] Van Kerm (2009). To install, net install sgini, from (http://medim.ceps.lu /stata).

3.3.5 ceqiop

The ceqiop command measures ex-ante inequality of opportunity based on a particular circumstance set specified by users for each of the CEQ core income concepts, following the nonparametric method in Ferreira and Gignoux (2011). Circumstances are predetermined factors that are not dependent on an individual's effort, such as race, gender, parents' education, and parents' income. The command exports results to sheet "E4. Inequality of Opportunity" of the *CEQ MWB*.

The circumstance sets are specified using the groupby(*varlist*) option. For example, one circumstance set could be (female, black, parents were college graduates, urban): all individuals with those four traits are grouped together in one circumstance set. If the dataset is at the individual level (each observation is an individual), the circumstance variables specified in groupby(*varlist*) could be defined at the individual level. In this case, the condition identifying household heads must be specified. For example, if we have a variable called hh_status that takes a value of 1 for the household head, 2 for the spouse, et cetera, we would specify head(hhstatus==1). If a variable name is given rather than a condition, such as head(hhstatus), ceqiop assumes that household heads are individuals for whom that variable is equal to 1. If the dataset is at the household level, the variables given in groupby(*varlist*) should be variables for the household head, for example, a variable for gender would indicate the gender of the household head.

The indicators include levels of inequality of opportunity (mean log deviation of the smoothed distribution as described in 2.2 above), ratios of inequality of opportunity (levels of inequality of opportunity divided by the mean log deviation for the actual income distribution), and Shapley decomposition of contributions of each circumstance. Of the categories of options described above, the options for income concepts, survey information, exporting, and ignoring missing values are relevant for ceqiop.

3.3.6 ceqfi

The ceqfi command calculates the measures of FI and FGP derived in Higgins and Lustig (2016). It exports the FI results to the "E5. Fisc. Impoverishment" sheet and the FGP results to the "E6. Fisc. Gains to the Poor" sheet.

These indicators include the FI and FGP headcounts (where the denominator is the total population); the FI and FGP headcounts among the poor (where the denominator is the total number of postfiscal poor for FI or prefiscal poor for FGP); total FI and FGP (in PPP dollars per day adjusted for PPP); FI and FGP per capita (in PPP dollars per day), where $k = 1/n$ (total FI or FGP is divided by the total population); normalized FI and FGP, where $k = 1/(nz)$ and z is the poverty line (per capita FI or FGP as a proportion of the poverty line). Of the categories of options described above, the options for income concepts, PPP conversions, survey information, poverty lines, producing a subset of results, exporting, and ignoring missing values are relevant for ceqfi. As described above, the options for producing a subset of results in ceqfi are different from those in other commands: the subset options include nobin, headcount, headcountpoor, total, percapita, normalized.

3.3.7 ceqstatsig

The ceqstatsig command tests the statistical significance of the change in inequality or poverty between core income concepts. It exports the p-values of these tests to sheet "E7. Statistical Significance" of the *CEQ MWB*.

The command uses modified versions of the routines from Araar and Duclos's (2013) Distributive Analysis Stata Package to compute p-values for a test of the null hypothesis that the difference between inequality or poverty estimates for two income concepts is zero. Specifically, it uses modified versions of the commands digini, dientropy, dinineq, and difgt; the modified code is included in the *CEQ Stata Package* as ceqdigini, ceqdientropy, ceqdinineq, and ceqdifgt, but these programs run "under the hood" and do not need to be directly used by the researcher.

The included measures are the Gini, absolute Gini, Theil, 90/10, poverty headcount ratio at various poverty lines, poverty gap ratio at various poverty lines, squared poverty gap (also known as "poverty severity") at various poverty lines, and the concentration coefficients of income concepts with respect to each of the eight core income concepts. The ceqstatsig command produces matrices of the difference in point estimates as well as the p-values from the above statistical test. Of the categories of options described above, the options for income concepts, PPP conversions, survey information, poverty lines, exporting, and ignoring missing values are relevant for ceqstatsig.

3.3.8 ceqdom

The ceqdom command calculates the CEQ dominance estimations for the CEQ core income concepts. It exports results to sheet "E8. Dominance Tests" of the *CEQ MWB*.

The command uses a routine from Araar and Duclos's (2013) Distributive Analysis Stata Package, specifically domineq to compute the number of crossings, as well as ksmirnov to test the equality of the two distributions. (However, these two programs run "under the hood" and do not need to be directly used by the researcher.) The command requires installation of glcurve[58] to generate two new variables with the generalized Lorenz ordinates.

Dominance estimations include number of crossings of income CDF curves as well as concentration curves between core income concepts. The estimations also include p-values from bootstrapped Kolmogorov-Smirnov tests between the two distributions if there is no crossing. A set of matrices of estimations is produced for concentration curves ranked by each income concept. Hence, ceqdom produces eight sets of matrices

---

[58] Jenkins and Van Kerm (2004). To install, ssc install glcurve.

for concentration curves and one set of matrices for income CDF curves. Of the categories of options described above, the options for income concepts, survey information, and exporting are relevant for ceqdom.

An option specific to ceqdom is reps(*real*), where users can specify number of iterations for bootstrapped Kolmogorov-Smirnov tests. The default is 10.

3.3.9 ceqef

The ceqef command calculates the CEQ effectiveness indicators (impact and spending effectiveness indicators), Beckerman-Immervoll poverty effectiveness indicators,[59] and the FI/FGP indicators for comparisons of each of the CEQ core income concepts. The command exports results to the sheet "E9. Effectiveness."

Unlike Beckerman-Immervoll and the FI/FGP indicators, CEQ effectiveness indicators are not defined for all combinations of taxes and transfers. While for inequality, the impact effectiveness Indicator is defined for taxes, transfers, and the combined system, for poverty, the indicator is not defined for taxes with a positive marginal contribution, transfers with negative marginal contribution, and the combined system. The Spending Effectiveness Indicator is defined for inequality when taxes or benefits have a positive marginal contribution, and for poverty only for benefits with positive marginal contribution. In no case the Spending Effectiveness indicator can be defined for the combined system (that is, for taxes and transfers combined). For more details see chapter 5 in Volume 1 of this Handbook (Enami, 2022a).

Of the categories of options described above, the options for income concepts, PPP conversions, survey information, poverty lines, income group cut-offs, and exporting are relevant for ceqef.

3.3.10 ceqconc

The ceqconc command calculates non-anonymous summary statistics and detailed information by decile, income group, centile, and income bin for each of the CEQ core income concepts. "Non-anonymous" refers to the fact that deciles, groups, centiles, and bins are defined holding the income concept fixed within each sheet. Hence, ceqconc produces one sheet for each of the CEQ core income concepts; the income concept defining the ranking of each sheet will be referred to as the ranking variable. The command exports results to the "E10.y Concentration," where y is a letter representing one of the eight core income concepts: m, $m+p$, n, g, t, d, c, and f, which respectively denote Market Income, Market Income plus Pensions, Net Market Income, Gross Income, Taxable Income, Consumable Income, and Final Income. The command requires installation of quantiles[60] to assign households to deciles or centiles; to install, ssc install quantiles.

---

[59] Beckerman (1979); Immervoll and others (2009).
[60] Osorio (2007).

Summary statistics include the mean, median, standard deviation, and a number of measures for each core income concept with respect to the ranking variable: its concentration coefficient, redistributive effect, Reynolds-Smolensky index (or vertical equity), and reranking effect. The detailed information by decile, income group, centile, and income bin includes total income in local currency units (preferably per year) and PPP dollars per day, per capita income in local currency (preferably per year) and PPP dollars per day, concentration shares, cumulative concentration shares, and fiscal incidence with respect to the ranking variable.

Of the categories of options described above, the options for income concepts, PPP conversions, survey information, income group cut-offs, producing a subset of results, exporting, ignoring missing values, and allowing negative values for producing indicators are relevant for ceqconc.

3.3.11 ceqfiscal

The ceqfiscal command calculates summary statistics and detailed information by decile, income group, centile, and income bin for fiscal interventions (taxes, transfers, subsidies, and in-kind benefits), where deciles, groups, centiles, and bins are defined holding the income concept fixed within each sheet. Hence, ceqfiscal produces results to eight sheets: one sheet for each of the CEQ core income concepts; the income concept defining the ranking of each sheet will be referred to as the "ranking variable." The command exports results to the "E11.y FiscalInterventions" sheets, where y is a letter representing one of the eight core income concepts: m, $m+p$, n, g, t, d, c, and f, which respectively denote Market Income, Market Income plus Pensions, Net Market Income, Gross Income, Taxable Income, Consumable Income, Consumable Income, and Final Income. The command requires installation of quantiles[61] to assign households to deciles or centiles; to install, ssc install quantiles.

Summary statistics include the mean, median, standard deviation, and measures for each fiscal intervention with respect to the ranking variable: its concentration coefficient and Kakwani coefficient. The detailed information by decile, income group, centile, and income bin includes—for each fiscal intervention—the total received or paid in local currency units (per year if the variables supplied to the command are annual); the detailed information by decile and income group additionally includes totals received or paid in PPP dollars per day, per capita amount received or paid in local currency (per year if the variables supplied to the command are annual) and PPP dollars per day, concentration shares, cumulative concentration shares, and fiscal incidence with respect to the ranking variable.

Of the categories of options described above, the options for income concepts, fiscal interventions, PPP conversions, survey information, income group cut-offs, producing a subset of results, exporting, ignoring missing values, and allowing negative values for producing indicators are relevant for ceqfiscal.

---

[61] Osorio (2007).

3.3.12 ceqextend

The ceqextend command calculates the same anonymous indicators as the ceqlorenz command, except for extended rather than core income concepts. In addition, it calculates concentration coefficients for each extended income concept with respect to the ranking given by each core income concept. It exports results to the "E12.y Extended Income Concepts" sheets, where y is a letter representing one of the eight core income concepts: m, $m+p$, n, g, t, d, c, and f, which respectively denote Market Income, Market Income plus Pensions, Net Market Income, Gross Income, Taxable Income, Consumable Income, Consumable Income, and Final Income. The command requires installation of quantiles[62] to assign households to deciles or centiles and sgini to calculate S-Gini coefficients;[63] to install, ssc install quantiles and net install sgini, from (http://medim.ceps.lu/stata).

As explained above, extended income concepts are constructed by adding or subtracting particular fiscal interventions (or bundles of interventions) to or from core income concepts. For example, Market Income plus Pensions plus conditional cash transfers is an extended income concept, as is Disposable Income minus conditional cash transfers (Disposable Income prior to adding conditional cash transfers, but with all other direct transfers included). Even though the majority of results produced by ceqextend are anonymous, and hence do not need a separate sheet for each core income concept ranking, there are eight sheets due to the sheer number of extended income concepts. Continuing the example above, the sheet for Market Income plus Pensions would include these indicators for the Market Income plus Pensions plus conditional cash transfers extended income concept, while the sheet for Disposable Income would include these indicators for the Disposable Income minus conditional cash transfers extended income concept.

Of the categories of options described above, the options for income concepts, fiscal interventions, PPP conversions, survey information, poverty lines, income group cut-offs, producing a subset of results, exporting, ignoring missing values, and allowing negative values for producing indicators are relevant for ceqextend.

3.3.13 ceqmarg

The ceqmarg command calculates the marginal contributions of fiscal interventions to inequality (redistributive effect), vertical equity, reranking, the derivatives of these marginal contributions with respect to size of the tax or transfer, and marginal contribution to poverty. It exports results to the "E13.y Marg. Contrib." sheets, where y is a letter representing one of the eight core income concepts: m, $m+p$, n, g, t, d, c, and f, which respectively denote Market Income, Market Income plus Pensions, Net Market Income, Gross Income, Taxable Income, Consumable Income, Consumable Income,

---

[62] Osorio (2007).

[63] Van Kerm (2009).

and Final Income. These eight core income concepts identify the income concepts with respect to which the marginal contributions are calculated.

Of the categories of options described above, the options for income concepts, fiscal interventions, PPP conversions, survey information, poverty lines, income group cut-offs, producing a subset of results, exporting, ignoring missing values, and allowing negative values for producing indicators are relevant for ceqmarg.

3.3.14 ceqefext

The ceqefext command calculates the CEQ effectiveness indicators (impact and spending effectiveness indicators), Beckerman-Immerwoll poverty effectiveness indicators,[64] and the FI/FGP indicators for comparisons of each of the extended income concepts. The command exports results to the sheet "E14.*y* Effectiveness" of the *CEQ MWB*, where *y* is a letter representing one of the eight core income concepts: m, *m* + *p*, n, g, t, d, c, and f, which respectively denote Market Income, Market Income plus Pensions, Net Market Income, Gross Income, Taxable Income, Consumable Income, Consumable Income, and Final Income.

Unlike Beckerman-Immervoll and the FI/FGP indicators, CEQ effectiveness indicators are not defined for all combination of taxes and transfers. For a detailed explanation see section 3.3.9 in this chapter. Moreover, this command does not produce indicators for combined systems of taxes and transfers since this information can be found in sheet E9, as explained in section 3.3.9.

Of the categories of options described above, the options for income concepts, fiscal interventions, PPP conversions, survey information, poverty lines, and income group cut-offs are relevant for ceqefext.

3.3.15 ceqcov

The ceqcov command calculates the covariance between core income concepts or fiscal interventions and fractional rank in the distribution of core income concepts. These covariances are useful because they are a building block of the calculation of the Gini coefficient and concentration coefficients. It exports results to the "E15. Covariance" sheet.

Of the categories of options described above, the options for income concepts, fiscal interventions, survey information, exporting, and ignoring missing values are relevant for ceqcov.

3.3.16 ceqextsig

The ceqextsig command tests the statistical significance of the change in the same measures of inequality and poverty as ceqstatsig, except between the extended rather than core income concepts. It exports the p-values of these tests to sheets "E16.y Extended Inc Stat Sig" of the *CEQ MWB*, where *y* is a letter representing one of the

---

[64] Beckerman (1979); Immerwoll and others (2009).

eight core income concepts: m, $m+p$, n, g, t, d, c, and f, which respectively denote Market Income, Market Income plus Pensions, Net Market Income, Gross Income, Taxable Income, Consumable Income, Consumable Income, and Final Income.

The command uses modified versions of the routines from Araar and Duclos's (2013) Distributive Analysis Stata Package to compute p-values for a test of the null hypothesis that the difference between inequality or poverty estimates for extended income concept and core income concept is zero. Specifically, it uses modified versions of the commands `digini`, `dientropy`, `dinineq`, and `difgt`; the modified code is included in the *CEQ Stata Package* as `ceqdigini`, `ceqdientropy`, `ceqdinineq`, and `ceqdifgt`, but these programs run "under the hood" and do not need to be directly used by the researcher.

The construction of extended income concepts is explained under the `ceqextend` section. The command produces matrices of the difference in point estimates as well as the p-values from the above statistical test.

Of the categories of options described above, the options for income concepts, fiscal interventions, PPP conversions, survey information, poverty lines, exporting, and ignoring missing values are relevant for `ceqextsig`.

3.3.17 `ceqdomext`

The `ceqdomext` command calculates the CEQ dominance estimations for the CEQ extended income concepts. It exports results to sheets "E17.y Dominance" of the *CEQ MWB*, where *y* is a letter representing one of the eight core income concepts: m, $m+p$, n, g, t, d, c, and f, which respectively denote Market Income, Market Income plus Pensions, Net Market Income, Gross Income, Taxable Income, Consumable Income, Consumable Income, and Final Income.

The command uses the routines from Araar and Duclos's (2013) Distributive Analysis Stata Package, specifically `domineq` to compute the number of crossings and `ksmirnov` to test the equality of the two distributions. (However, these two programs run "under the hood" and do not need to be directly used by the researcher.) The command requires installation of `glcurve`[65] to generate two new variables with the generalized Lorenz ordinates.

Dominance estimations include number of crossings of income CDFs and concentration curves between each extended income concept and core income concept. The construction of extended income concepts is explained under the `ceqextend` section. The estimations also include p-values from bootstrapped Kolmogorov-Smirnov tests between the two distributions if there is no crossing. A set of matrices of estimations is produced for concentration curves ranked by each income concept. Hence, `ceqdomext` produces one sheet for each of the extended income concepts.

Of the categories of options described above, the options for income concepts, fiscal interventions, survey information, and exporting are relevant for `ceqdomext`. An

---

[65] Jenkins and Van Kerm (2004). To install, `ssc install glcurve`.

option specific to ceqdomext is reps(*real*), where users can specify number of iterations for bootstrapped Kolmogorov-Smirnov tests. The default is 10.

3.3.18 ceqcoverage

The ceqcoverage command calculates coverage and leakage indicators as well as direct beneficiary indicators by income group for fiscal interventions (taxes, transfers, and subsidies), where income groups are defined holding the income concept fixed within each sheet. Hence, ceqcoverage produces one sheet for each of the CEQ core income concepts. The command exports results to sheets "E18.*y* Coverage Tables" of the *CEQ MWB*, where *y* is a letter representing one of the eight core income concepts: m, *m*+*p*, n, g, t, d, c, and f, which respectively denote Market Income, Market Income plus Pensions, Net Market Income, Gross Income, Taxable Income, Consumable Income, Consumable Income, and Final Income.

IMPORTANT

The *CEQ Stata Package* admits up to twelve direct transfers and pensions, twelve direct taxes and contributions, fourteen indirect subsidies, fourteen indirect taxes, and sixteen in-kind transfers. If the user includes more interventions, results will be displayed only for the first twelve, fourteen, or sixteen interventions depending on the case.

The indicators include total benefits[66] by group, the distribution of benefits (what percent of benefits goes to each group), the number of beneficiary households, the number of direct and indirect beneficiaries (members of beneficiary households), the distribution of beneficiary households and direct and indirect beneficiaries (what percent of beneficiaries belongs to each group), coverage within each group (what percent of households or people in that group receive benefits), and mean benefits (per beneficiary household and per beneficiary). The fit between these indicators and conceptual definitions of coverage, errors of exclusion, and errors of inclusion is described in section 2.2.13.

Of the categories of options described above, the options for income concepts, fiscal interventions, PPP conversions, survey information, income group cut-offs, exporting ignoring missing values are relevant for ceqcoverage. In addition, options to directly mark beneficiaries are needed; these are described below.

---

[66] Notice that when calculating, for example, the number of direct beneficiaries of *all* direct transfers, the *CEQ Stata Package* considers the total amount of people who are direct beneficiaries of *at least* one direct transfer. Thus, this number need not coincide with the sum of direct beneficiaries of each individual direct transfer since an individual could receive more than one transfer.

TABLE 8-15

Fiscal Intervention Direct Beneficiary Markers Options

Option	Description
recpensions(*varlist*)	Direct beneficiaries of contributory pension variables
recdtransfers(*varlist*)	Direct beneficiaries of direct transfer variables
paydtaxes(*varlist*)	Direct payers of direct tax variables
paycontribs(*varlist*)	Direct payers of contribution variables
recsubsidies(*varlist*)	Direct beneficiaries of subsidy variables
payindtaxes(*varlist*)	Direct payers of indirect tax variables
rechealth(*varlist*)	Direct beneficiaries of health in-kind transfer variables
payuserfeeshealth(*varlist*)	Direct payers of health user fees
receducation(*varlist*)	Direct beneficiaries of education in-kind transfer variables
payuserfeeseduc(*varlist*)	Direct payers of education user fees
recotherpublic(*varlist*)	Direct beneficiaries of other public in-kind transfers
payuserfeesother(*varlist*)	Direct payers of other user fees (corresponding to other public in-kind transfers)

To estimate the number of direct beneficiaries (the person who directly receives the transfer or directly pays the tax), an additional piece of information is needed: which individuals in the household directly received a particular transfer or directly paid a particular tax. This information cannot be obtained from the fiscal interventions variables described above, since those variables are already at the household per capita level. For example, they would be positive for all direct and indirect beneficiaries (other members of the direct beneficiary's household). Thus, the command ceqcoverage includes the "direct beneficiary marker" options where, for each fiscal intervention variable given in the fiscal intervention options, a variable identifying which individuals are direct beneficiaries (or payers) of that fiscal intervention is given. The options are presented in table 8-15.

For a dataset at the individual level, the variables supplied to the direct beneficiary marker options should be dummy variables that equal 1 if the individual is a direct beneficiary/payer and 0 otherwise.[67] For a dataset at the household level, they should equal the number of household members that are direct beneficiaries/payers. For each category of fiscal intervention, the number of variables supplied to these options must be the same as the number of variables supplied to the corresponding fiscal intervention variables, and they should be supplied in the same order. For example, suppose the dataset is at the individual level, there are two levels of education, primary and sec-

---

[67] For a more detailed description of how to identify beneficiaries, see the "Constructing Harmonized Microdata" document in part IV of this Volume of the Handbook.

ondary, and that household per capita benefits are included in edu_prim_pc and edu_sec_pc, and dummy variables identifying which individuals are the direct beneficiaries are edu_prim_ri and edu_sec_ri. Then the fiscal intervention and direct beneficiary marker options for education would be educ(edu_prim_pc edu_sec_pc) and receduc(are edu_prim_ri edu_sec_ri). For fiscal interventions for which the survey does not specify who is the direct beneficiary (for example, if a question asks only whether anyone in the household receives benefits from a program), mark one member of the household (good practice is to select the household head) as a direct beneficiary.

3.3.19 ceqtarget

The ceqtarget command calculates coverage and leakage indicators among eligible or "target" households and individuals, as well as direct beneficiary indicators by income group for fiscal interventions (taxes, transfers, and subsidies), where income groups are defined holding the income concept fixed within each sheet. Hence, ceqtarget produces one sheet for each of the CEQ core income concepts. The command exports results to sheets "E19.y Coverage (Target)" of the *CEQ MWB*, where y is a letter representing one of the eight core income concepts: m, $m+p$, n, g, t, d, c, and f, which respectively denote Market Income, Market Income plus Pensions, Net Market Income, Gross Income, Taxable Income, Consumable Income, Consumable Income, and Final Income.

IMPORTANT

The *CEQ Stata Package* admits up to twelve direct transfers and pensions, twelve direct taxes and contributions, fourteen indirect subsidies, fourteen indirect taxes, and sixteen in-kind transfers. If the user includes more Interventions, results will be displayed only for the first twelve, fourteen, or sixteen interventions depending on the case.

The syntax is identical to that of ceqcoverage, including the use of the direct beneficiary marker options, with one addition: a set of options to mark the target households or individuals must also be identified. The options are presented in table 8-16.

To identify the target households or individuals, target markers are necessary. For datasets at the individual level and programs that define eligibility at the individual level, these variables should equal 1 for target individuals and 0 otherwise.[68] For datasets at the individual level and programs that define eligibility at the household level, these variables should be equal to 1 for some arbitrary member of the household (good practice is to select the household head) and 0 otherwise. Notice that only *one* member

---

[68] For a more detailed description of how to define the target population, see the "Constructing Harmonized Microdata" document in part IV of this Volume of the Handbook.

TABLE 8-16
Fiscal Intervention Target Household or Individual Markers

Option	Description
trecpensions(*varlist*)	Contributory pension target recipients
trecdtransfers(*varlist*)	Direct transfer target recipients
tpaydtaxes(*varlist*)	Direct tax target payers
tpaycontribs(*varlist*)	Contribution target payers
trecsubsidies(*varlist*)	Subsidy target recipient's subsidy variables
tpayindtaxes(*varlist*)	Indirect tax target payers
trechealth(*varlist*)	Health target recipients
tpayuserfeeshealth(*varlist*)	Health user fees target payers
treceducation(*varlist*)	Education target recipients
tpayuserfeeseduc(*varlist*)	Education user fees target payers
trecotherpublic(*varlist*)	Other public in-kind transfers
tpayuserfeesother(*varlist*)	Other public target fees

of the household should have the target marker equal to 1. *In the case that an arbitrary member of the household is marked as the target beneficiary, the target direct beneficiary results should be ignored; only the target household and target "direct and indirect beneficiary" results should be used.* For datasets at the household level, results for direct beneficiaries of programs that define eligibility at the individual level cannot be produced, but the other indicators can. In this case, these variables should equal 1 for target households (or households with at least one target individual for programs that define eligibility at the individual level) and 0 otherwise.

For programs where the target population is defined at the individual level, the individual targeted should be marked as the target person in the dataset. For programs where the target population is defined at the household level, the head of the targeted household should be marked as the target person in the dataset *and the direct beneficiary results should be ignored*; in other words, for programs defined at the household level, use only the *household beneficiary* and *direct and indirect beneficiary* results.

3.3.20 ceqeduc

The ceqeduc command calculates education enrollment indicators by income group. The dataset for ceqeduc has to be on an individual level. These indicators are calculated at four levels of education: preschool, primary, secondary, and tertiary. The income groups are defined holding the income concept fixed within each sheet. Hence, ceqeduc produces one set of calculations for each of the CEQ core income concepts. The command exports results to the sheet "E20. Edu Enrollment Rates" of the *CEQ MWB*.

TABLE 8-17
Education Enrollment Options

Option	Description
preschool(*varname*)	Dummy variable = 1 if attends preschool
primary(*varname*)	Dummy variable = 1 if attends primary
secondary(*varname*)	Dummy variable = 1 if attends secondary
tertiary(*varname*)	Dummy variable = 1 if attends tertiary
preschoolage(*varname*)	Dummy variable = 1 if preschool age
primaryage(*varname*)	Dummy variable = 1 if primary age
secondaryage(*varname*)	Dummy variable = 1 if secondary age
tertiaryage(*varname*)	Dummy variable = 1 if tertiary age
public(*varname*)	Variable = 0 if attends private; = 1 if attends public; missing if does not attend school

The indicators include target population, total population attending school, target population attending school, target population NOT attending school, net enrollment rates, gross enrollment rates, and share of enrolled students belonging to target population. Of the categories of options described above, the options for income concepts, PPP conversions, survey information, income group cut-offs, exporting, and ignoring missing values options are relevant for ceqeduc. In addition, the user must specify education enrollments using the following options specific to ceqeduc.

The dataset must be at the individual level, and the options should be specified by dummy variables that equal to 1 if the individual attended a particular level of education. In addition, the command includes options that allow for identifying whether the individuals are within the target age cohort for a particular level of school.[69] These options are specified by dummy variables that equal to 1 if the individual's age corresponds to the target age cohort. Finally, there is an option used to indicate whether the individual attends public school (the dummy variable equals to 1), attends private school (equals to 0), or does not attend school (missing value). Table 8-17 provides a list of education enrollment options.

3.3.21 ceqinfra
The ceqinfra command calculates the coverage and distribution of infrastructure access by income group, for infrastructure access variables supplied by users. The income groups are defined holding the income concept fixed within each sheet. Hence, ceqinfra produces one set of calculations for each of the CEQ core income concepts.

---

[69] For a more detailed description of how to define the target population of each educational level, see the "Constructing Harmonized Microdata" document in part IV in Volume 1 of this Handbook.

The command exports results to the sheet "E21. Infrastructure Access" of the *CEQ MWB*.

Infrastructure variables include electricity, drinkable water, sanitation, and roads. These variables should be specified using *varlist* following directly after the command name ceqinfra. Up to eight infrastructure access variables can be used. If the users specify more than eight variables, only the first eight will be taken for calculations.

Indicators include individuals with access to infrastructure, distribution of individuals with access to infrastructure, coverage of direct and indirect recipients of infrastructure, households with access to infrastructure, distribution of households with access to infrastructure, and coverage of infrastructure for households. Of the categories of options described above, the options for income concepts, PPP conversions, survey information, income group cut-offs, exporting, and ignoring missing values are relevant for ceqinfra.

3.3.22 ceqhhchar

The ceqhhchar command calculates mean and median values for household-level sociodemographic characteristic variables supplied by users as well as their standard deviation. In addition, it calculates the mean of these variables by income decile, group, centile, and bin, where these categorization measures are defined holding the income concept fixed within each sheet. Hence, ceqhhchar produces one sheet for each of the CEQ core income concepts. The command exports results to sheets "E22.*y* GroupSociodemoCharac" of the *CEQ MWB*, where *y* is a letter representing one of the eight core income concepts: m, $m+p$, n, g, t, d, c, and f, which respectively denote Market Income, Market Income plus Pensions, Net Market Income, Gross Income, Taxable Income, Consumable Income, Consumable Income, and Final Income.

The household-level sociodemographic characteristic variables are variables defined at household level such as "age of household head," "access to piped water," or "number of rooms." These variables should be specified using *varlist* following directly after the command name ceqhhchar. There is no limit on the number of variables that can be supplied.

Of the categories of options described above, the options for income concepts, PPP conversions, survey information, income group cut-offs, producing a subset of results, exporting, and ignoring missing values are relevant for ceqhhchar.

3.3.23 ceqindchar

The ceqindchar command calculates mean and median values for individual-level sociodemographic characteristic variables supplied by users as well as their standard deviation. In addition, it calculates the mean of these variables by income decile, group, centile, and bin, where these categorization measures are defined holding the income concept fixed within each sheet. Hence, ceqindchar produces one sheet for each of the CEQ core income concepts. The command exports results to sheets "E23.*y* Indiv-SociodemoCharac" of the *CEQ MWB*, where *y* is a letter representing one of the eight core income concepts: m, $m+p$, n, g, t, d, c, and f, which respectively denote Market Income, Market Income plus Pensions, Net Market Income, Gross Income, Taxable Income, Consumable Income, Consumable Income, and Final Income.

The individual-level sociodemographic characteristic variables are defined at an individual level such as "age," "years of schooling," "has a bank account." These variables should be specified using *varlist* following directly after the command name ceqindchar. There is no limit on the number of variables that can be supplied.

Of the categories of options described above, the options for income concepts, PPP conversions, survey information, income group cut-offs, producing a subset of results, exporting, and ignoring missing values are relevant for ceqindchar.

3.3.24 ceqgraph

The ceqgraph command graphs cumulative distribution functions, Lorenz curves, concentration curves, and fiscal impoverishment and gains to the poor. It is used with the sub-commands summarized in table 8-18. The options for the ceqgraph command are summarized in table 8-19.

3.3.25 ceqassump

The ceqassump command calculates the same anonymous indicators as the ceqlorenz command, except for the income concepts constructed by users rather than core income concepts. It is designed to be used to test at a glance how different assumptions used to construct income concepts affect the main inequality, poverty, and distribution indicators used in a *CEQ Assessment*. The command exports results to the "E28. Assumption Testing" sheet. The command requires installation of quantiles[70] to assign households to deciles or centiles and sgini to calculate S-Gini coefficients.[71]

The income concept variables provided by users, which may or may not be CEQ core income concepts, should be specified in *varlist* following directly after the command name ceqassump. For example, suppose the user wants to test the impact of including or excluding own production from the Market Income measure. The user would create two versions of Market Income (at the household per capita or per adult equivalent level) and provide the variables for these two versions of Market Income. Or suppose the user wants to test the impact of tax exemptions. Since income in the survey already includes the benefits of tax exemptions, these cannot be added in the same way as other benefits. Instead, the user could compare "Consumable Income minus tax exemptions" (income that would have existed in the absence of tax exemptions) with Consumable Income to see the marginal contribution of tax exemptions to inequality.

Of the categories of options described above, the options for PPP conversions, survey information, poverty lines, income group cut-offs, producing a subset of results, exporting, and ignoring missing values are relevant for ceqassump.

---

[70] Osorio (2007). To install, ssc install quantiles.

[71] Van Kerm (2009). To install, net install sgini, from(http://medim.ceps.lu/stata).

TABLE 8-18
Sub-Commands of the `ceqgraph` Command

Option	Description
`ceqgraph cdf`	Graphs of cumulative distribution functions
`ceqgraph conc`	Graphs of concentration curves
`ceqgraph fi`	Graphs of fiscal impoverishment and gains to the poor
`ceqgraph progressivity`	Graphs of pre and postfiscal Lorenz and concentration curves to assess progressivity

TABLE 8-19
Graphing Options

Option	Description
`pl1(`*real*`)`	The lowest of three poverty lines to be graphed, expressed in PPP dollars per day (default is $1.90)
`pl2(`*real*`)`	The second of three poverty lines to be graphed, expressed in PPP dollars per day (default is $3.20 PPP per day)
`pl3(`*real*`)`	The highest of three poverty lines to be graphed (and the maximum income included in the graph) expressed in PPP dollars per day (default is $5.50 PPP per day)
`precision(`*real*`)`	Increment for grid-based method to compute FI and FGP (default is $0.01 PPP per day)
`scheme(`*string*`)`	Set the graph scheme (`help scheme`; default is "s1mono")
`path(`*string*`)`	The directory to save the graphs in
`graphname(`*string*`)`	The prefix of the saved graph names (default is "fi")

Acknowledgments

We are grateful to many *CEQ Assessment* authors for testing and pointing out bugs in the user-written commands that make up the *CEQ Stata Package*, particularly Rodrigo Aranda, Maynor Cabrera, Maria Davalos, Luciana De La Flor, Ali Enami, Jon Jellema, Nizar Jouini, Sandra Martinez-Aguilar, Luis Felipe Munguia, Monica Rabayo, Esmeralda Shehaj, Barbara Sparrow, Ernesto Yañez, and Stephen D. Younger. We are also grateful to Rodrigo Aranda, Ali Enami, Nora Lustig, Sandra Martinez-Aguilar, Adam Ratzlaff, and Stephen D. Younger for conversations that helped to shape the structure and features of the commands, to Rodrigo Aranda for writing five of the *CEQ Stata*

Package commands and coauthoring the *CEQ Stata Package*, to Ruoxi Li, Patricio Larroulet, and Roy McKenzie for fixing numerous bugs and making other user-suggested improvements and coauthoring the *CEQ Stata Package*, to Paul Corral Rodas for greatly improving the efficiency of the routine to calculate Gini and concentration coefficients embedded in various commands in the *CEQ Stata Package*, and to Marc Brooks for research assistance. Sections D and E of the *CEQ Master Workbook* were designed together with Nora Lustig, with substantive contributions from Rodrigo Aranda, Maynor Cabrera, Ali Enami, Samantha Greenspun, and Adam Ratzlaff. The linking to automatically export results from Section E to Section D was designed by Maynor Cabrera and Sandra Martinez-Aguilar with research assistance from Cristina Carrera. We are also very grateful to Patricio Larroulet and Federico Sanz for their careful review of this chapter for the second edition of the Handbook.

References

Afkar, Rythia, Jon Jellema, and Matthew Wai-Poi. 2017. "The Distributional Impact of Fiscal Policy in Indonesia," in *The Distributional Impact of Fiscal Policy: Experience from Developing Countries*, edited by Gabriela Inchauste and Nora Lustig (Washington: World Bank).

Araar, Abdelkrim, and Jean-Yves Duclos. 2013. "DASP: Distributive Analysis Stata Package. User Manual, DASP version 2.2" (http://dasp.ecn.ulaval.ca/modules/DASP_V2.2/DASP_MANUAL_V2.2.pdf).

Aranda, Rodrigo, and Ratzlaff Adam. 2022. "Analyzing the Impact of Fiscal Policy on Ethno-Racial Inequality," chap. 9 in *Commitment to Equity Handbook: Estimating the Impact of Fiscal Policy on Inequality and Poverty*, 2nd ed., Vol. 1, edited by Nora Lustig (Brookings Institution Press and CEQ Institute, Tulane University). Free online version available at www.commitmentoequity.org.

Atkinson, Anthony B. 1980. "Horizontal Equity and the Distribution of the Tax Burden," in *The Economics of Taxation* 3, no. 18, edited by H. Aaron and M. Boskin (Brookings Institution Press).

Azevedo, Joao Pedro. 2011. "wbopendata: Stata module to access World Bank databases," Statistical Software Components S457234, Boston College Department of Economics (http://ideas.repec.org/c/boc/bocode/s457234.html).

Barrett, Garry, and Stephen Donald. 2009. "Statistical Inference with Generalized Gini Indices of Inequality, Poverty, and Welfare." *Journal of Business and Economic Statistics* 27, no. 1, pp. 1–17.

Beckerman, Wilfred. 1979. "The Impact of Income Maintenance Payments on Poverty in Britain, 1975." *Economic Journal* 89, no. 354, pp. 261–79.

Birdsall, Nancy. 2010. "The (Indispensable) Middle Class in Developing Countries; or, The Rich and the Rest, Not the Poor and the Rest," in *Equity in a Globalizing World*, edited by Ravi Kanbur and Michael Spence (Washington: World Bank).

Buhmann, Brigitte, Lee Rainwater, Guenther Schmaus, and Timothy M. Smeeding. 1988. "Equivalence Scales, Well-Being, Inequality, and Poverty: Sensitivity Estimates across Ten Countries Using the Luxembourg Income Study (LIS) Database." *Review of Income and Wealth* 34, no. 2, pp. 115–42.

CEDLAS (Centro de Estudios Distributivos, Laborales y Sociales), and World Bank. 2012. "A Guide to the SEDLAC Socio-Economic Database for Latin America and the Caribbean" (http://sedlac.econo.unlp.edu.ar/download.php?file=archivos_upload_items_metodologia/Guide_14_english.pdf).

CEQ Institute. 2022. "*CEQ Assessment: CEQ Master Workbook*," available online only in part IV of the *Commitment to Equity Handbook: Estimating the Impact of Fiscal Policy on Inequality and Poverty*, 2nd ed., Vol. 1, edited by Nora Lustig (Brookings Institution Press and CEQ Institute, Tulane University). Free online version available at www.commitmentoequity.org.

Checchi, Daniele, and Vito Peragine. 2010. "Inequality of opportunity in Italy." *Journal of Economic Inequality* 8, no. 4, pp. 429–50.

Chen, Shaohua, and Martin Ravallion. 2010. "The Developing World Is Poorer Than We Thought, but No Less Successful in the Fight against Poverty." *Quarterly Journal of Economics* 125, no. 4, pp. 1577–625.

Demuynck, Thomas. 2012. "An (Almost) Unbiased Estimator for the S-Gini Index." *Journal of Economic Inequality* 10, no. 1, pp. 109–26.

Donaldson, David, and John Allan Weymark. 1980. "A Single-Parameter Generalization of Gini indices of Inequality." *Journal of Economic Theory* 22, no. 1, pp. 67–86.

———. 1983. "Ethically Flexible Gini Indices for Income Distributions in the Continuum." *Journal of Economic Theory* 29, no. 2, pp. 353–58.

Duclos, Jean-Yves. 2008. "Horizontal and Vertical Equity," in *The New Palgrave Dictionary of Economics*, edited by Steven N. Durlauf and Lawrence E. Blume (London: Palgrave Macmillan).

Duclos, Jean-Yves, and Abdelkrim Araar. 2005. "An Atkinson-Gini Family of Social Evaluation Functions: Theory and Illustration Using Data from the Luxembourg Income Study," LIS Working Paper Series No. 416.

Enami, Ali. 2022a. "Measuring the Effectiveness of Taxes and Transfers in Fighting Inequality and Poverty, chap. 5 in *Commitment to Equity Handbook: Estimating the Impact of Fiscal Policy on Inequality and Poverty*, 2nd ed., Vol. 1, edited by Nora Lustig (Brookings Institution Press and CEQ Institute, Tulane University). Free online version available at www.commitmentoequity.org.

———. 2022b. "Measuring the Redistributive Impact of Taxes and Transfers in the Presence of Reranking," chap. 3 in *Commitment to Equity Handbook: Estimating the Impact of Fiscal Policy on Inequality and Poverty*, 2nd ed., Vol. 1, edited by Nora Lustig (Brookings Institution Press and CEQ Institute, Tulane University). Free online version available at www.commitmentoequity.org.

———. 2022c. "Box 1-2: Marginal Contribution," in *Commitment to Equity Handbook: Estimating the Impact of Fiscal Policy on Inequality and Poverty*, 2nd ed., Vol. 1, edited by Nora Lustig (Brookings Institution Press and CEQ Institute, Tulane University). Free online version available at www.commitmentoequity.org.

Enami, Ali, Sean Higgins, and Nora Lustig. 2022. "Allocating Taxes and Transfers and Constructing Income Concepts: Completing Sections A, B, and C of the *CEQ Master Workbook*," chap. 6 in *Commitment to Equity Handbook: Estimating the Impact of Fiscal Policy on Inequality and Poverty*, 2nd ed, Vol. 1, edited by Nora Lustig (Brookings Institution Press and CEQ Institute, Tulane University). Free online version available at www.commitmentoequity.org.

Enami, Ali, Sean Higgins, and Stephen D. Younger. 2022. "Box 1-3: Fiscal Impoverishment and Gains Effectiveness Indicators," in *Commitment to Equity Handbook: Estimating the Impact of Fiscal Policy on Inequality and Poverty*, 2nd ed., Vol. 1, edited by Nora Lustig (Brookings Institution Press and CEQ Institute, Tulane University). Free online version available at www.commitmentoequity.org.

Enami, Ali, Nora Lustig, and Rodrigo Aranda. 2022. "Analytic Foundations: Measuring the Redistributive Impact of Taxes and Transfers," chap. 2 in *Commitment to Equity Handbook: Estimating the Impact of Fiscal Policy on Inequality and Poverty*, 2nd ed., Vol. 1, edited by Nora Lustig (Brookings Institution Press and CEQ Institute, Tulane University). Free online version available at www.commitmentoequity.org.

Enami, Ali, Nora Lustig, and Alireza Taqdiri. 2019. "Fiscal Policy, Inequality, and Poverty in Iran: Assessing the Impact and Effectiveness of Taxes and Transfers." *Middle East Development Journal* 11, no. 1, pp. 49–74.

Ferreira, Francisco, and Jeremie Gignoux. 2011. "The Measurement of Inequality of Opportunity: Theory and an Application to Latin America." *Review of Income and Wealth* 57, no. 4, pp. 622–57.

Ferreira, Francisco H. G., Shaohua Chen, Andrew Dabalen, Yuri Dikhanov, Nada Hamadeh, Dean Jolliffe, Ambar Narayan, Espen Beer Prydz, Ana Revenga, Prem Sangraula, Umar Serajuddin, and Nobuo Yoshida. 2016. "A Global Count of the Extreme Poor in 2012: Data Issues, Methodology and Initial Results." *Journal of Economic Inequality* 14, no. 2, pp. 141–72.

Ferreira, Francisco, Julian Messina, Jamele Rigolini, Luis Felipe Lopez-Calva, Maria Ana Lugo, and Renos Vakis. 2013. *Economic Mobility and the Rise of the Latin American Middle Class*. Latin America and Caribbean Studies (Washington: World Bank).

Foster, James, Joel Greer, and Erik Thorbecke. 1984. "A Class of Decomposable Poverty Measures." *Econometrica* 52, no. 3, pp. 761–66.

Foster, James, and Anthony F. Shorrocks. 1988. "Poverty Orderings." *Econometrica* 56, no. 1, pp. 173–77.

Giorgi, Giovanni Maria, Paola Palmitesta, and Corrado Provasi. 2006. "Asymptotic and Bootstrap Inference for the Generalized Gini Indices." *International Journal of Statistics* 64, no. 1, pp. 107–24.

Higgins, Sean, Rodrigo Aranda, Caterina Brest Lopez, Ruoxi Li, Beenish Amjad, Patricio Larroulet, and Roy McKenzie. 2022. "CEQ Assessment: CEQ Stata Package," in part IV in *Commitment to Equity Handbook: Estimating the Impact of Fiscal Policy on Inequality and Poverty*, 2nd ed., Vol. 1, edited by Nora Lustig (Brookings Institution Press and CEQ Institute, Tulane University). Available online only at www.ceqinstitute.org.

Higgins, Sean, and Nora Lustig. 2016. "Can a Poverty-Reducing and Progressive Tax and Transfer System Hurt the Poor?" *Journal of Development Economics* 122, pp. 63–75.

Higgins, Sean, Nora Lustig, Whitney Ruble, and Timothy M. Smeeding. 2016. "Comparing the Incidence of Taxes and Social Spending in Brazil and the United States." *Review of Income and Wealth* 62, no. S1, pp. S22–46.

Higgins, Sean, and Claudiney Pereira. 2014. "The Effect of Brazil's Taxation and Social Spending on the Distribution of Household Income." *Public Finance Review* 42, no. 3, pp. 346–67.

Immervoll, Herwig, Horacio Levy, Jose Ricardo Nogueira, Cathal O'Donoghue, Rozane Bezerra de Siqueira. 2009. "The Impact of Brazil's Tax-Benefit System on Inequality and Poverty," in

Poverty, Inequality, and Policy in Latin America, edited by Stephan Klasen and Felicitas Nowak-Lehmann, 271–301 (MIT Press).

Jenkins, Stephen P., and Philippe Van Kerm. 2004. "GLCURVE: Stata Module to Derive Generalized Lorenz Curve Ordinates." Statistical Software Components S366302, Boston College Department of Economics (https://ideas.repec.org/c/boc/bocode/s366302.html).

Jolliffe, Dean, and Espen Beer Prydz. 2016. "Estimating International Poverty Lines from Comparable National Thresholds." *Journal of Economic Inequality* 14, no. 2, pp. 185–98.

———. 2017, May. "Societal Poverty. A Relative and Relevant Measure." Policy Research Working Paper 8073 (World Bank).

Kakwani, Nanak C. 1977. "Measurement of Tax Progressivity: An International Comparison." *Economic Journal* 87, no. 345, pp. 71–80.

———. 1980. "On a Class of Poverty Measures." *Econometrica: Journal of the Econometric Society* 48, no. 2, pp. 437–46.

Kakwani, Nanak C., and Hyun H. Son. 2016. "Global Poverty Estimates based on 2011 Purchasing Power Parity: Where Should the New Poverty Line Be Drawn?" *Journal of Economic Inequality* 14, no. 2, pp. 173–84.

Kharas, Homi. 2010. "The Emerging Middle Class in Developing Countries." OECD Development Centre Working Paper 285 (http://www.oecd.org/dataoecd/12/52/44457738.pdf).

Lambert, Peter. 1985. "On the Redistributive Effect of Taxes and Benefits." *Scottish Journal of Political Economy* 32, no. 1, pp. 39–54.

———. 2001. *The Distribution and Redistribution of Income* (Manchester University Press).

Lerman, Robert I., and Yitzhaki, Shlomo. 1984. "A Note on the Calculation and Interpretation of the Gini Index." *Economics Letters* 15, no. 3, pp. 363–68.

Lopez-Calva, Luis Felipe, and Eduardo Ortiz-Juarez. 2014. "A Vulnerability Approach to the Definition of the Middle Class." *Journal of Economic Inequality* 12, no. 1, pp. 23–47.

Lopez-Calva, Luis Felipe, John Scott, and Andres Castañeda. Forthcoming. "Gasto social, redistribucion del ingreso y reduccion de la pobreza en Mexico: evolucion y comparacion con Argentina, Brasil y Uruguay," in *Politica social y bienestar: Mexico desde el ano 2000*, edited by Rodolfo de la Torre and Eduardo Rodriquez-Oreggia e Isidro Soloaga (Mexico DF: CIDE-FCE).

Lustig, Nora, and Sean Higgins. 2022. "The *CEQ Assessment*: Measuring the Impact of Fiscal Policy on Inequality and Poverty," chap. 1 in *Commitment to Equity Handbook: Estimating the Impact of Fiscal Policy on Inequality and Poverty*, 2nd ed., Vol. 1, edited by Nora Lustig (Brookings Institution Press and CEQ Institute, Tulane University). Free online version available at www.commitmentoequity.org.

Lustig, Nora, Carola Pessino, and John Scott. 2014. "The Impact of Taxes and Social Spending on Inequality and Poverty in Argentina, Bolivia, Brazil, Mexico and Peru: An Overview." *Public Finance Review* 42, no. 3, 287–303.

Lustig, Nora, and Jacques Silber. 2016. "Introduction to the Special Issue on Global Poverty Lines." *Journal of Economic Inequality* 14, no. 2, pp. 129–40.

Osorio, Rafael Guerreiro. 2007. "`quantiles`: Stata Module to Categorize by Quantiles." Boston College Department of Economics Statistical Software Components S456856.

Plotnick, Robert. 1981. "A Measure of Horizontal Inequity." *Review of Economics and Statistics* 63, no. 2, pp. 283–88.

Pyatt, Graham, Chau-Nan Chen, and John Fei. 1980. "The Distribution of Income by Factor Components." *Quarterly Journal of Economics* 95, no. 3, pp. 451–73.

Ratzlaff, Adam. 2022. "Box 8-1: Education Enrollment Indicators," in *Commitment to Equity Handbook: Estimating the Impact of Fiscal Policy on Inequality and Poverty*, 2nd ed., Vol. 1, edited by Nora Lustig (Brookings Institution Press and CEQ Institute, Tulane University). Free online version available at www.commitmentoequity.org.

Ravallion, Martin, Shaohua Chen, and Prem Sangraula. 2009. "Dollar a Day Revisited." *World Bank Economic Review* 23, no. 2, pp. 163–84.

Reynolds, Morgan, and Eugene Smolensky. 1977. "Post-Fiscal Distributions of Income in 1950, 1961, and 1970." *Public Finance Review* 5, no. 4, pp. 419–38.

Scott, John. 2014. "Redistributive Impact and Efficiency of Mexico's Fiscal System." *Public Finance Review* 42, no. 3, pp. 368–90.

Urban, Ivica. 2009. "Indices of Redistributive Effect and Reranking: Reinterpretation." Society for the Study of Economic Inequality Working Paper Series, no. 147.

Van Kerm, Philippe. 2009. "Generalized Gini and Concentration coefficients (with Factor Decomposition) in Stata." MeDIM Project (Advances in the Measurement of Discrimination, Inequality and Mobility), Luxembourg.

World Bank. 2020. *Purchasing Power Parities and the Size of World Economies: Results from the 2017 International Comparison Program.* © World Bank (https://openknowledge.worldbank.org/handle/10986/33623) License: CC BY 3.0 IGO.

Yitzhaki, Shlomo. 1983. "On an Extension of the Gini Inequality Index." *International Economic Review* 64, no. 3, pp. 617–28.

Younger, Stephen D. 2022. "Box 1-1: Ignoring Behavioral Responses to Tax and Expenditure Policies," in *Commitment to Equity Handbook: Estimating the Impact of Fiscal Policy on Inequality and Poverty*, 2nd ed., Vol. 1, edited by Nora Lustig (Brookings Institution Press and CEQ Institute, Tulane University). Free online version available at www.commitmentoequity.org.

Younger, Stephen D., Flora Myamba, and Kenneth Mdadila. 2016. "Fiscal Incidence in Tanzania." CEQ Working Paper No. 36 (Center for Inter-American Policy and Research, Tulane University, Ithaca College, and REPOA).

Younger, Stephen D., Eric Osei-Assibey, and Felix Oppong. 2015. "Fiscal Incidence in Ghana." CEQ Working Paper No. 35 (Center for Inter-American Policy and Research, Tulane University, Ithaca College, University of Ghana, and the World Bank).

Chapter 9

ANALYZING THE IMPACT OF FISCAL POLICY ON ETHNO-RACIAL INEQUALITY

Rodrigo Aranda and Adam Ratzlaff

Introduction

As shown in previous chapters of this Volume, the Commitment to Equity (CEQ) analysis provides researchers with a comprehensive and comparable set of indicators to determine the impacts of fiscal intervention on poverty and inequality.[1] However, inequality may take many different forms and be based on biases that are beyond the control of individuals. Race, gender, location, and parental characteristics can have important implications for the economic and social outcomes of individuals.[2] In Latin America, ethno-racial inequalities are particularly prevalent; indigenous peoples and African descendants are faced with higher rates of poverty, lower average incomes, and lower access to services.[3] In an effort to determine if government fiscal interventions are exacerbating or reducing ethno-racial inequalities in Latin America, the

---

This chapter and the corresponding component of the *CEQ Master Workbook*, section F, "Results by Ethnicity and Race," were prepared as part of the Inter-American Development Bank's technical cooperation "Improving Race and Ethnicity Data Instruments for Policy Analysis and Formulation" (RG-T1906), led by Judith Morrison, Senior Advisor, Gender and Diversity Division (SCL/GDI). Through this technical cooperation, funding was made available for the Inter-American Development Bank–Commitment to Equity Incidence of Taxes and Social Spending by Ethnicity and Race Study for Bolivia, Brazil, Guatemala, and Uruguay.

[1] See especially Lustig and Higgins (2022) (chapter 1 in this Volume of the Handbook); Enami, Higgins, and Lustig (2022) (chapter 6 in this Volume); Jellema and Inchauste (2022) (chapter 7 in this Volume); Higgins and Brest Lopez (2022) (chapter 8 in this Volume).

[2] Molinas Vega and others (2012).

[3] de Ferranti and others (2004); Hall and Patrinos (2006); Ñopo (2012).

Inter-American Development Bank (IDB) has partnered with the CEQ Institute to finance the adoption of the CEQ analysis to explore the impacts of fiscal policies on ethno-racial inequality in the Latin America and Caribbean region (LAC).

A necessary first step in calculating the impact of fiscal policy on reducing ethno-racial inequality is to determine the appropriate indicators for measuring ethno-racial inequalities and what measures should be used to determine the impact of fiscal policy on these indicators. To do this, we will utilize the measures discussed by Lustig.[4] To measure levels of inequality across ethno-racial lines, four different measures will be utilized:

1. *Income gaps*, in terms of the mean incomes or share of income held by different ethno-racial populations, provide for absolute and relative sizes of the ethno-racial inequality at the aggregate level.
2. *Contribution to overall inequality* can be determined using a decomposable measure of inequality such as the Theil coefficient. The benefit to the Theil coefficient is that it can be decomposed to determine the level of national inequality due to inter- and intra-ethno-racial group inequalities. This is particularly important as it provides us with a better understanding of the dynamics not only between ethno-racial groups, but also within these populations. It is important to note here that policies may reduce inequality between groups while exacerbating inequalities within specific populations.
3. *Inequality of opportunity* is a concept popularized by Roemer and further applied in Ferreira and Robalino and Molinas Vega and others to determine the extent to which characteristics or circumstances outside of an individual's control (for example, not due to personal effort or preference) affect his or her economic and social outcomes.[5] These circumstances frequently include characteristics such as gender, location (urban/rural), levels of parental education, and race or ethnicity. In a society that is ethno-racially equal or colorblind, one would expect to see no inequality of opportunity due to ethno-racial differences. Here, inequality of opportunity can be used to assess the extent to which fiscal policy equalizes opportunities and reduces inequality. More details on how this is calculated are provided below.
4. *Poverty* headcounts, gaps, and severity measures can be utilized to provide a better understanding of differences in the well-being of different ethno-racial populations with a particular emphasis on what is happening at the bottom of the income distribution. Having data on the different levels and magnitudes of poverty is particularly important in showing what types of policies are benefiting the most disadvantaged segments of the population.

---

[4] Lustig (2017).

[5] Roemer (1998); Ferreira and Robalino (2010); Molinas Vega and others (2012).

All of the measures indicated above can be calculated using the different income concepts utilized in the CEQ analysis, thereby allowing us to determine the fiscal impact of specific sets of policies on ethno-racial inequality.

In order to determine the effectiveness of programs at reducing ethno-racial inequality, two different measures will be utilized to determine if the impact of specific programs or sets of programs help to reduce ethno-racial inequality:

1. *Progressivity* will be determined by calculating the share of benefits going to different ethno-racial groups relative to their respective shares of the population or their respective share of income. A program is deemed to be relatively progressive if the share of benefits received is greater than the disadvantaged group's share of income (for example, making incomes more equitable) and is considered absolutely progressive if the share of benefits received is greater than their share of the total population.[6]
2. *Pro-disadvantaged group*: While examining progressivity provides a way of measuring if fiscal policy reduces ethno-racial inequality, a targeted poverty reduction policy may appear to be progressive due to the number of individuals of a particular ethno-racial group who are in poverty. Fiscal policy is designated as pro-disadvantaged group if the impact of direct taxes and transfers produces a greater likelihood for members of the disadvantaged group to escape poverty than for advantaged populations.

It is important to note that for a policy to be pro-disadvantaged group, it must violate horizontal equity, or the premise that individuals of equal income should be treated equally. By treating the poor of a particular ethno-racial group differently, a policy violates this criterion.

Section F of the *CEQ Master Workbook© (MWB)* (available online in part IV of this Handbook; CEQ Institute [2022]), "Results by Ethnicity and Race," allows users to produce all of the results necessary to conduct an analysis of the impacts of fiscal policy across ethno-racial lines in one easy-to-use workbook with accompanying Stata ado-file. This workbook presents a compendium of the CEQ main results in a manner that allows for easy interpretation across ethno-racial lines. This chapter describes the different indicators and sheets presented in section F of the *CEQ Master Workbook* (see table 9-1) and details on how to use the ceqrace.ado Stata command to produce these results for each sheet of the workbook.

The ceqrace Stata command is designed to automatically fill in the values for nineteen of the twenty-six Excel sheets listed in table 9-1. The remaining Excel sheets must be filled in manually. The program allows users to estimate the results for each of these sheets separately in Stata and export them to the Excel workbook. It is also

---

[6] The group that has lower per capita incomes is considered the disadvantaged group in this exercise. In all of the four countries analyzed, the disadvantaged group refers to the indigenous or African descendant population.

Table 9-1

Sheets Presented in Section F: Results by Race and Ethnicity

---

1. Background information

F1. Key assumptions*
F2. Ethno-racial definitions*
F3. Ethno-racial populations
F4. Linked information*

---

2. Results

F5. Population composition
F6. Income distribution
F7. Summary poverty rates
F8. Summary poverty gap rates
F9. Summary poverty gap squared rates
F10. Summary inequality indicators
F11. Mean incomes
F12. Incidence by decile
F13. Incidence by income group
F14. Cross-race incidence**
F15. Horizontal equity**
F16. Fiscal profile
F17. Coverage rates (total population)
F18. Coverage rates (target population)
F19. Leakages**
F20. Mobility matrices
F21. Education (totals)
F22. Education (rates)**
F23. Infrastructure access
F24. Theil disaggregation
F25. Inequality of opportunity
F26. Significance

Note: Sheets with an * must be filled in manually. Sheets with an ** are filled in automatically using the results from a different sheet. The remaining sheets can be completed using the ceqrace.ado command in Stata.

designed to be flexible such that it can match the different data and statistical requirements of each country.

In order to utilize the ceqrace, it is necessary to have the basic software requirements of Stata 13.0 (or a more recent version) and Microsoft Excel (.xls or .xlsx format). As for data requirements, the program works on Stata datasets with data at the individual level and includes the main variables used in the CEQ framework such as income concepts, taxes, transfers, as well as sociodemographic characteristics of individuals. While the other sections of the CEQ analysis are designed to utilize either individual or household level data, for the analysis by race and ethnicity only individual-level datasets can be utilized due to the need to identify individuals by race or ethnicity. While some indicators in the analysis are generated at the household level—for example, using the ethno-racial identity of the head of the household for identification purposes—it is preferable to utilize the self-identification method for all individuals in the household.

The main syntax for the command is:

```
ceqrace using filename [weight] [if] [in] [, table(name) options]
```

For each of the different Excel sheets the command asks for the Excel filename, the number of the table, weights, and ethno-racial group identifiers. The race or ethnic group identifiers must be dichotomous variables and should be arranged such that:

- race1: White/non-ethnic population
- race2: Indigenous population
- race3: African descendant population
- race4: Other Races/Ethnicities
- race5: Non-responses

The program requires that at least two different groups have been defined as dichotomous variables. The remaining options for running the analysis are specific to the sheet and will be discussed in detail below. For a summary of variables, their format, and options to be used with this command, see table 9-2.

It is also important to note that this workbook is preset to produce results using the regional income group definitions as well as country-specific poverty results. Where the country-specific poverty lines are used, authors will input the value of the national extreme and moderate poverty lines in their Stata command. The ceqrace command is preset to use the typical poverty lines of US$1.25 purchasing power parity (PPP) per capita per day, US$2.50 PPP per capita per day (extreme poverty), and US$4 PPP per capita per day (moderate poverty), as well as income groupings for the vulnerable (with incomes between US$4 and US$10 PPP per capita per day), for the middle class (with incomes between US$10 and US$50 PPP per capita per day), and for all individuals with per capita per day incomes above US$50 PPP. All of these income groupings utilize the 2005 PPP conversion rate. Although section F of the *CEQ Master Workbook* (available online in part IV of Volume 1; CEQ Institute, 2022) and the ceqrace are preset to utilize these income lines, users may opt to change poverty lines to fit their research needs using the option cut( ).[7] However, it is important to note that this will not change the labels presented in the Excel file. Thus, if users choose to use different

---

[7] As discussed above, the default options are cut1(1.25), cut2(2.50), cut3(4.00), cut4(10.00), and cut5(50.00).

TABLE 9-2
Types of Variables and Options Guide for `ceqrace.ado`

Concept	Option in `ceqrace.ado`	Description

Ethno-racial groups	`race1(varname)`
	`race2(varname)`
	`race3(varname)`
	`race4(varname)`
	`race5(varname)`
		All variables have to be dummies and identify the ethnicity-race of each individual. `race1` is for Indigenous population, `race2` is for White/non-ethnic population, `race3` is for African descendant population, `race4` other races, and `race5` for non-responses.

Income concepts	`original(varname)`
	`market(varname)`
	`mpluspensions(varname)`
	`netmarket(varname)`
	`gross(varname)`
	`taxable(varname)`
	`disposable(varname)`
	`consumable(varname)`
	`final(varname)`
		These variables must have the per capita income concepts in local currency units.

Tax and transfer concepts	`dtax(varname)`
	`contrib(varname)`
	`conypensions(varname)`
	`contpensions(varname)`
	`noncontrib(varname)`
	`flagcct(varname)`
	`otransfers(varname)`
	`isubsidies(varname)`
	`itax(varname)`
	`ikeduc(varname)`
	`ikhealth(varname)`
	`hurban(varname)`
		These variables must have the tax or transfer concepts in per capita local currency units.

PPP conversion options	`ppp(real)`
	`cpibase(real)`
	`cpisurvey(real)`
	`daily`
	`monthly`
	`yearly`
		These options accept only numbers; only one of the daily, monthly, and yearly options can be used.

Poverty lines and income group cut-offs	`nextreme(string)`
	`nmoderate(string)`
	`cut1(real)`
	`cut2(real)`
	`cut3(real)`
		`nextreme( )` and `nmoderate( )` accept numerical values as well as a variable; the values have to be at the same time and currency unit as the income variables.

(continued)

TABLE 9-2 (continued)

Concept	Option in `ceqrace.ado`	Description
	`cut4(real)` `cut5(real)`	The `cut( )` options allow the user to use different thresholds for poverty in daily PPP. If this option is not used, the program automatically uses the income group cut-offs.

Coverage	`cct(varname)`
	`noncontrib(varname)`
	`pensions(varname)`
	`unemploy(varname)`
	`foodtransfers(varname)`
	`otransfers(varname)`
	`health(varname)`
	`pensions(varname)`
	`scholarships(varname)`
		These variables have to be in monetary units at the individual/household level (depending on who receives the benefit) in the same units as income concepts and tax and transfers.

Target population	`tarcct(varname)`
	`tarncp(varname)`
	`tarpen(varname)`
		These variables have to be dummies that identify the target population for each concept.

Education	`age(varname)`
	`edpre(varname)`
	`redpre(varname)`
	`edpri(varname)`
	`redpri(varname)`
	`edsec(varname)`
	`redsec(varname)`
	`edter(varname)`
	`redter(varname)`
	`edpublic(varname)`
	`edprivate(varname)`
	`attend(varname)`
		Age variable has to be the age of the individual. The rest of the variables have to be dummies that identify whether each individual satisfies each condition.

Infrastructure access	`water(varname)`
	`electricity(varname)`
	`walls(varname)`
	`floors(varname)`
	`roof(varname)`
	`sewage(varname)`
	`roads(varname)`
		These variables have to be dummies that identify whether the individual lives in a household with access to each specific concept.

Household	`hhead(varname)` `hhid(varname)`	The dataset to use has to be at the individual level; hhead is the dummy variable that identifies who is the household head for each household, and hhid is the variable that uniquely identifies each household in the data.

Concept	Option in `ceqrace.ado`	Description
Circumstance	`gender(varname)` `urban(varname)` `edpar(varname)`	The gender variable has to take the value of 1 for the gender the user chooses to use. `urban` is a dummy variable that identifies individuals living in an urban context. `edpar` is parents' years of education.
Survey information	`hsize(varname)` `psu(varname)` `strata(varname)`	`hsize` is a variable with the number of members of each household. `psu` and `strata` are variables that identify primary sampling units and strata, respectively.

income groups, they need to manually adjust these labels; not doing so may cause confusion for end users of the workbook.

1 Background Information

The first part of section F of the *CEQ Master Workbook* requires authors to fill in much of the background information necessary to conduct the general CEQ analysis, information on the different ethno-racial populations that are being analyzed, and some of the relevant background information for analyzing the results of the study. Many of these sheets will need to be filled in manually (without the aid of the `ceqrace` command).

1.1 Sheet F1. Key Assumptions

Sheet F1 presents the key assumptions utilized in the CEQ analysis. This sheet is highly important for end users of the data as it is critical to have this information available for interpreting the results of the study. While this sheet will need to be filled in manually by authors, it includes similar information as that presented in the "Key Assumptions" sheet featured in section C, "Methodology of the *CEQ Master Workbook*" (sheet C2). Nonetheless, it is important that authors complete sheet F1 as well, as it allows users to conduct much of the CEQ analysis by race and ethnicity using only the one section of the *CEQ Master Workbook* and ensures that results are interpreted correctly and accurately.

1.2 Sheet F2. Ethno-Racial Definitions

While some countries clearly define ethno-racial categories that should be utilized for the CEQ fiscal incidence analysis, the definitions vary by country and by survey. Most Latin American countries have transitioned to using self-identification as the primary method for determining the ethno-racial categorization of individuals or households, although some countries in the region continue to use maternal language as the determinant of ethno-racial group. Additionally, some populations may have multiple identities depending on the context in which they are being considered. Thus, defining how each study examines ethno-racial populations may be an important factor for providing policy recommendations specific to different segments of society. Further questions on how race and ethnicity should be imputed to individuals who are not asked to self-identify, as well as on how to impute race or ethnicity to the household level, are important and can have profound effects on the results of the analysis. In order to ensure that results are comparable to other studies as well as to verify that the definitions used are understandable to a broader audience, authors should clarify how the different ethno-racial populations are defined for the purpose of their study.

Additionally, this sheet includes information not only on the survey being used, but also on national census results. Differences between the definitions of different ethno-racial categories, the manner in which the question on ethno-racial identity was asked, or how the sample was constructed in the census as compared to the survey being utilized may lead to findings that contradict what would be expected based on census results. Having information on how ethno-racial populations are defined in these two datasets allows users to see if there are differences and if so what these differences may be.

This sheet must be filled in manually by the authors.

1.3 Sheet F3. Ethno-Racial Populations

Sheet F3 expands upon the information presented in the previous sheet by looking at the size of each ethno-racial population and comparing it to census figures. This allows researchers to have a better understanding of the representativeness of the survey being used (when compared to census results) and allows them to express whether they believe that the trends that are seen across ethno-racial lines are truly representative (both in magnitude as well as direction) of national results. Knowing the differences between national surveys and censuses is particularly important given that the sample design in some countries may not take race and ethnicity into account. While most of this sheet is completed using the ceqrace Stata command, data from national censuses must be completed manually by authors.

To fill in this sheet using the ceqrace Stata command, race dummy variables and weights are required. Below is an example of how this can be run:

```
ceqrace [pw=weight] using CEQEthnoRacialMWB.xlsx, race1(indig)
race2(white) race3(afrd) race4(orace) race5(nonrace) table(f3)
```

Where CEQ_Ethno_Racial_MWB.xlsx is the name of the Excel file being used and the race variables are all dichotomous, it is important to note that the table option must include the number of the sheet preceded by an "f" in order to automatically fill in the Excel file.

1.4 Sheet F4. Linked Information

The linked information contained in this sheet provides some additional background information on the different policies that are considered as part of the CEQ analysis. It also allows authors to quickly fill in much of the background information that is necessary to complete tables throughout this workbook. Data that should be filled in by the authors includes information on calculating the conversion rates from local currency units (LCU) to US dollars in 2005 and 2011 purchasing power parity (PPP), information on the national poverty lines used in the country, additional information on the programs that are being analyzed as part of the *CEQ Assessment,* and information on the country's education system. Data for generating the conversion factors between LCU and 2005 or 2011 PPP can be found in the World Bank's World Development Indicators.[8] This information will be used to convert LCU into PPP on several sheets throughout section F of the workbook and to convert national poverty lines in LCU into PPP numbers. Official names of the different programs that are being aggregated or used in this section of the analysis should also be provided so that end users are better able to understand the different elements that are being considered as part of the analysis. For education information, it is important that users input the targeted age ranges for different educational levels as this information has important implications for calculating educational enrollment rates (see sheets F21 and F22).

Authors must complete this sheet manually.

2 Results

Part II of section F of the *CEQ Master Workbook* (available online in part IV of Volume 1; CEQ Institute, 2022) presents the results of the *CEQ Assessment* necessary to conduct the analysis across ethno-racial lines in a user-friendly format. This section includes many of the tables and figures that researchers may want to consider when comparing the impact of fiscal policy across ethno-racial lines.

2.1 Sheet F5. Population Composition

An important element in assessing ethno-racial inequality is understanding how the population is distributed across socioeconomic and ethno-racial lines. This sheet presents the population distribution and magnitude disaggregated by decile and income

---

[8] World Bank (2017).

group across ethno-racial lines for original[9] and Disposable Income concepts. It is important to note that, although national results will be the same, the ethno-racial results by decile will differ from those presented in section D ("Summary of Results") and section E ("Output Tables") of the *CEQ Master Workbook* (available online in part IV of Volume 1; CEQ Institute, 2022) because this worksheet defines deciles nationally and then disaggregates by ethno-racial category rather than presenting the deciles within each ethno-racial group. In other words, the results presented here will express the share of the different population segments in each decile rather than presenting the characteristics of the different ethno-racial groups by decile.

To fill in this sheet using the ceqrace Stata command, it is necessary to have variables generated for original income, Disposable Income, household identifier, consumer price index, purchasing power parity variables, and dummy variables for each ethno-racial category. The syntax should follow:

```
ceqrace [pw=weight] using CEQEthnoRacialMWB.xlsx, race1(indig)
race2(white) race3(afrd) race4(orace) race5(nonrace) table(f5)
o(ym) d(yd) hhid(hhid) ppp(7.65) cpibase(78.661) cpisurvey(105.196)
year
```

Where CEQ_Ethno_Racial_MWB.xlsx is the name of the Excel file being used, the race variables are dichotomous, original(varname) specifies the original income variable in local currency units,[10] disposable(varname) is Disposable Income, hhid(varname) is the variable that uniquely identifies the household, ppp( ) is the purchasing power parity (PPP) conversion factor (local currency units [LCU] per international dollar, consumption-based) from the year of PPP (usually either 2005 or 2011), cpibase( ) is the consumer price index (CPI) of the base year (year of PPP, usually 2005 or 2011), cpisurvey( ) is the CPI for the year of the household survey, and finally, year indicates that income variables are defined in annual terms (although it is preferable to use annualized data, daily and monthly can also be specified if the author chooses).

2.2 Sheet F6. Income Distribution

Sheet F6 builds upon the data in sheet F5 by presenting the distribution of income by ethno-racial group as well as nationally. Results are given using both decile and in-

---

[9] Original income might vary depending on whether one is running an analysis using pensions as deferred income (PDI) or pensions as government transfers (PGT) so Market Income or Market Income plus Pensions variables have to be used for this option depending on the scenario.

[10] Original income might vary depending on whether one is running an analysis using PDI or PGT, so Market Income or Market Income plus Pensions variables have to be used for this option depending on the scenario.

come groups for original and Disposable Income. As with sheet F5, these decile results will differ from the disaggregation presented in sections D and E the *CEQ Master Workbook* (available online in part IV of Volume 1; CEQ Institute, 2022) due to the manner in which deciles are defined in this section of the workbook.[11]

To fill in this sheet using the `ceqrace` Stata command, it is necessary to have variables generated for original income, Disposable Income, household identifier, consumer price index, and purchasing power parity variables, and dummy variables for each ethno-racial category. The syntax should follow:

```
ceqrace [pw=weight] using CEQEthnoRacialMWB.xlsx, race1(indig)
race2(white) race3(afrd) race4(orace) race5(nonrace) table(f6)
o(ym) d(yd) hhid(hhid) ppp(7.65) cpibase(78.661) cpisurvey(105.196)
year
```

Where CEQ_Ethno_Racial_MWB.xlsx is the name of the Excel file being used, the race variables are dichotomous, `original`(*varname*) specifies the original income variable in local currency units,[12] `disposable`(*varname*) is Disposable Income, `hhid( )` is the variable that uniquely identifies the household, `ppp( )` is the purchasing power parity (PPP) conversion factor (LCU per international dollar, consumption-based) from the year of PPP (usually either 2005 or 2011), `cpibase( )` is the consumer price index (CPI) of the base year (year of PPP, usually 2005 or 2011), `cpisurvey( )` is the CPI for the year of the household survey, and finally, `year` indicates that income variables are defined in annual terms (daily and monthly can also be used).

2.3 Sheet F7. Summary Poverty Rates

Poverty headcount rates are key to determining levels of social exclusion and inequality across ethno-racial lines. Sheet F7 presents poverty headcount rates by race and ethnicity as well as nationally for each of the different core income concepts and generates tables that can be used to demonstrate the impacts of fiscal policy on poverty across ethno-racial lines.

To fill in this sheet using the `ceqrace` Stata command, race dummy variables, weights, `market`(*varname*), `mpluspensions`(*varname*), `netmarket`(*varname*), `gross`(*varname*), `taxable`(*varname*), `disposable`(*varname*), `consumable`(*varname*), `nextreme`(*string*), and `nmoderate`(*string*) options are required and the following syntax should be used:

---

[11] For description of why decile results may differ, please refer to the discussion of sheet F5.

[12] Original income might vary depending on whether one is running an analysis using PDI or PGT, so Market Income or Market Income plus Pensions variables have to be used for this option depending on the scenario.

```
ceqrace [pw=weight] using CEQEthnoRacialMWB.xlsx, race1(indig)
race2(white)  race3(afrd)  race4(orace)  race5(nonrace)  table(f7)
m(ym) mplusp(ymp) n(ynm) g(yg) taxab(ytaxab) d(yd) c(yc) ppp(7.65)
cpibase(78.661) cpisurvey(105.196) year next(137) nmod(350)
```

Where CEQ_Ethno_Racial_MWB.xlsx is the name of the Excel file, the race variables are dummies, m(*varname*) specifies the Market Income variable in local currency units, mplusp(*varname*) is Market Income plus Pensions, n(*varname*) is Net Market Income, g(*varname*) is Gross Income, taxab(*varname*) is Taxable Income, d(*varname*) is Disposable Income, and c(*varname*) is Consumable Income. ppp( ) is the PPP conversion factor (LCU per international dollar, consumption-based) from the year of PPP (usually either 2005 or 2011), cpibase( ) is CPI of the base year (year of PPP, usually 2005 or 2011), cpisurvey( ) is the CPI for the year of the household survey, and finally, year indicates that the income variables are annual. next( ) and nmod( ) set the national extreme and moderate poverty lines which should be in LCU and the same periodicity as the income variables.

2.4 Sheet F8. Summary Poverty Gap Rates

This sheet mirrors the results presented on sheet F7, but utilizing poverty gap rates rather than the poverty headcount. In addition to tables and figures presenting the poverty gap results, this sheet also automatically calculates the budget that would be required to completely eliminate poverty assuming that programs were perfectly targeted at each of the core income concepts.

To fill in this sheet using the ceqrace Stata command, race dummy variables, weights, market(*varname*), mpluspensions(*varname*), netmarket(*varname*), gross(*varname*), taxable(*varname*), disposable(*varname*), consumable(*varname*), final(*varname*), poverty line options, nextreme(*string*), and nmoderate(*string*) are required, and the following syntax should be used:

```
ceqrace [pw=weight] using CEQEthnoRacialMWB.xlsx, race1(indig)
race2(white)  race3(afrd)  race4(orace)  race5(nonrace)  table(f8)
m(ym) mplusp(ymp) n(ynm) g(yg) taxab(ytaxab) d(yd) c(yc) f(yf)
ppp(7.65)  cpibase(78.661)  cpisurvey(105.196)  year  next(137)
nmod(350)
```

Where CEQ_Ethno_Racial_MWB.xlsx is the name of the Excel file, the race variables are dummies, m(*varname*) specifies the Market Income variable in local currency units, mplusp(*varname*) is Market Income plus Pensions, n(*varname*) is Net Market Income, g(*varname*) is Gross Income, taxab(*varname*) is Taxable Income, d(*varname*) is Disposable Income, c(*varname*) is Consumable Income, and f(*varname*) is Final Income.

ppp( ) is the PPP conversion factor (LCU per international dollar, consumption-based) from the year of PPP (usually either 2005 or 2011), cpibase( ) is CPI of the base year (year of PPP, usually 2005 or 2011), cpisurvey( ) is the CPI for the year of the household survey, and finally, year indicates that the income variables are annual. next( ) and nmod( ) are the national extreme and moderate poverty lines which should be in LCU and the same periodicity as the income variables.

2.5 Sheet F9. Summary Poverty Gap Squared Rates

Sheet F9 completes the Foster, Greer, and Thorbecke (1984) family of poverty measures by presenting results on poverty severity (poverty gap squared) across ethno-racial lines for each of the core income concepts. Like the previous two sheets, sheet F9 presents the results alongside easy-to-use figures for regional and national extreme and moderate poverty lines.

To fill in this sheet using the ceqrace Stata command, race dummy variables, weights, market(*varname*), mpluspensions(*varname*), netmarket(*varname*), gross(*varname*), taxable(*varname*), disposable(*varname*), consumable(*varname*), final(*varname*), nextreme(*string*), and nmoderate(*string*) are required and the following syntax should be used:

```
ceqrace [pw=weight] using CEQEthnoRacialMWB.xlsx, race1(indig)
race2(white)  race3(afrd)  race4(orace)  race5(nonrace)  table(f9)
m(ym) mplusp(ymp) n(ynm) g(yg) taxab(ytaxab) d(yd) c(yc) f(yf)
ppp(7.65) cpibase(78.661) cpisurvey(105.196) year next(137) nmod(350)
```

Where CEQ_Ethno_Racial_MWB.xlsx is the name of the Excel file, the race variables are dummies, m(*varname*) specifies the Market Income variable in local currency units, mplusp(*varname*) is Market Income plus Pensions, n(*varname*) is Net Market Income, g(*varname*) is Gross Income, taxab(*varname*) is Taxable Income, d(*varname*) is Disposable Income, c(*varname*) is Consumable Income, and f(*varname*) is Final Income. ppp( ) is the PPP conversion factor (LCU per international dollar, consumption-based) from the year of PPP (usually either 2005 or 2011), cpibase( ) is CPI of the base year (year of PPP, usually 2005 or 2011), cpisurvey( ) is the CPI for the year of the household survey, and finally, year indicates that the income variables are annual. next( ) and nmod( ) are the national extreme and moderate poverty lines which should be in LCU and the same periodicity as the income variables.

2.6 Sheet F10. Summary Inequality Indicators

Many different measures are used to calculate income inequality in a given society. This sheet features three of these measures: the Gini coefficient, the Theil coefficient, and the 90/10 index. While the national results presented on this page may be more important than those disaggregated by ethno-racial group since they capture inter- and intra-group inequality rather than just intra-group inequality, it is important to examine these results both at the national level and disaggregated as some policies may decrease inequality nationally while exacerbating inequalities within particular ethno-racial groups. Similarly, programs may increase inequality nationally while decreasing intra-group inequalities. Like sheets F7, F8, and F9, sheet F10 presents results with easy-to-use tables and figures.

To fill in this sheet using the `ceqrace` Stata command, race dummy variables, weights, `market`(*varname*), `mpluspensions`(*varname*), `netmarket`(*varname*), `gross`(*varname*), `taxable`(*varname*), `disposable`(*varname*), `consumable`(*varname*), `final`(*varname*) are required, and the following syntax should be used:

```
ceqrace [pw=weight] using CEQEthnoRacialMWB.xlsx, race1(indig)
race2(white) race3(afrd) race4(orace) race5(nonrace) table(f10)
m(ym) mplusp(ymp) n(ynm) g(yg) taxab(ytaxab) d(yd) c(yc) f(yf)
```

Where CEQ_Ethno_Racial_MWB.xlsx is the name of the Excel file, the race variables are dummies, m(*varname*) specifies the Market Income variable in local currency units, mplusp(*varname*) is Market Income plus Pensions, n(*varname*) is Net Market Income, g(*varname*) is Gross Income, `taxab`(*varname*) is Taxable Income, d(*varname*) is Disposable Income, c(*varname*) is Consumable Income, and f(*varname*) is Final Income.

2.7 Sheet F11. Mean Incomes

In examining inequalities across ethno-racial lines, it is also important to consider gaps in mean incomes held by individuals of different ethno-racial groups. Sheet F11 presents the mean incomes experienced by each ethno-racial population at each of the different income concepts. Results are presented both in 2005 PPP dollars as well as in local currency units. As with the preceding sheets, results are presented as easy-to-use figures and tables.

To fill in this sheet using the `ceqrace` Stata command, race dummy variables, weights, `market`(*varname*), `mpluspensions`(*varname*), `netmarket`(*varname*), `gross`(*varname*), `taxable`(*varname*), `disposable`(*varname*), `consumable`(*varname*), `final`(*varname*) are required, and the following syntax should be used:

```
ceqrace [pw=weight] using CEQEthnoRacialMWB.xlsx, race1(indig)
race2(white) race3(afrd) table(f11)m(ym) mplusp(ymp) n(ynm) g(yg)
taxab(ytaxab) d(yd) c(yc) f(yf)
```

2.8 Sheet F12. Incidence by Decile

When conducting the CEQ fiscal incidence analysis, one of the most important elements is determining the incidence of different fiscal interventions on household income. When analyzing the effects of fiscal policy across ethno-racial lines the same holds true. Sheet F12 presents the magnitude of interventions in each decile, disaggregated by ethno-racial group as well as nationally, measured in local currency units. Results are also presented as a share of original income for each population. While the results shown on this sheet should be the same as those on sheet D4 of the *CEQ Master Workbook* and in section E for the national level, when disaggregated by ethno-racial group, results will be different from those shown for particular groups' respective sections D and E of the *CEQ Master Workbook* as deciles are defined differently.

To fill in this sheet using the ceqrace Stata command, race dummy variables, weights, hhid(*varname*), original(*varname*), market(*varname*), mpluspensions(*varname*), netmarket(*varname*), gross(*varname*), taxable(*varname*), disposable(*varname*), consumable(*varname*), final(*varname*), dtax(*varname*), contributions(*varname*), contpensions (*varname*), contypensions(*varname*), noncontributory(*varname*), flagcct(*varname*), otransfers(*varname*), isubsidies(*varname*), itax(*varname*), ikeducation(*varname*), ikhealth(*varname*), and hurban(*varname*) are required, and the following syntax should be used:

```
ceqrace [pw=weight] using CEQEthnoRacialMWB.xlsx,race1(indig)
race2(white) race3(afrd) race4(orace) race5(nonrace) table(f12)
hhid(hhid) o(ym) m(ym) contp(contp) conyp(conyp) mplusp(ymp)
dtax(dtax) n(ynm) nonc(nonc) flagcct(fcct) otran(otran) g(yg)
taxab(ytaxab) d(yd) isub(isub) itax(itax) c(yc) ike(ike)
ikh(ikh) hu(hu) f(yf)
```

Where CEQ_Ethno_Racial_MWB.xlsx is the name of the Excel file, the race variables are dummies, hhid( ) is the variable that uniquely identifies the household, o(*varname*) specifies the original income variable in local currency units, m(*varname*) is Market Income, contp(*varname*) are contributions to pensions, conyp(*varname*) are contributory pensions, mplusp(*varname*) is Market Income plus Pensions, dtax(*varname*) are direct taxes, n(*varname*) is Net Market Income, nonc(*varname*) are noncontributory pensions, flagcct(*varname*) is the Flagship Conditional Cash Transfer Program (CCT), otran(*varname*) are other direct transfers, g(*varname*) is Gross Income, taxab(*varname*) is Taxable Income, d(*varname*) is Disposable Income, isub(*varname*) and itax(*varname*) are indirect subsidies and taxes, respectively, c(*varname*) is Consumable Income, ike(*varname*), ikh(*varname*), and hu(*varname*) are in-kind education, in-kind health, and in-kind housing and urban benefits respectively, and f(*varname*) is Final Income.

2.9 Sheet F13. Incidence by Income Group

While Sheet F12 presents the incidence results of the analysis by decile, sheet F13 complements this by conducting the same analysis by income group. This allows researchers to utilize populations that have the same income or to examine the impact of policies on particular income groups within the different ethno-racial groups. These results will be the same as those presented on sheet D4 of the *CEQ Master Workbook* (available online in part IV of Volume 1; CEQ Institute, 2022) for each respective ethno-racial group.

To fill in this sheet using the ceqrace Stata command, race dummy variables, weights, original(*varname*), market(*varname*), mpluspensions(*varname*), netmarket(*varname*), gross(*varname*), taxable(*varname*), disposable(*varname*), consumable(*varname*), final(*varname*), dtax(*varname*), contributions(*varname*), contpensions(*varname*), contypensions (*varname*), noncontributory(*varname*), flagcct(*varname*), otransfers (*varname*), isubsidies(*varname*), itax(*varname*), ikeducation(*varname*), ikhealth(*varname*), hurban(*varname*), and poverty line options are required, and the following syntax should be used:

```
ceqrace [pw=weight] using CEQEthnoRacialMWB.xlsx, race1(indig)
race2(white) race3(afrd) race4(orace) race5(nonrace) table(f13)
o(ym) m(ym) contp(contp) contyp(contyp) mplusp(ymp) dtax(dtax)
n(ynm) nonc(nonc) flagcct(fcct) otran(otran) g(yg) taxab(ytaxab)
d(yd) isub(isub) itax(itax) c(yc) ike(ike) ikh(ikh) hu(hu) f(yf)
ppp(7.65) cpibase(78.661) cpisurvey(105.196) year
```

Where CEQ_Ethno_Racial_MWB.xlsx is the name of the Excel file, the race variables are dummies, o(*varname*) specifies the original income variable in local currency units, m(*varname*) is Market Income, contp(*varname*) are contributions to pensions, conyp(*varname*) are contributory pensions, mplusp(*varname*) is Market Income plus Pensions, dtax(*varname*) are direct taxes, n(*varname*) is Net Market Income, nonc(*varname*) are noncontributory pensions, flagcct(*varname*) is the CCT, otran(*varname*) are other direct transfers, g(*varname*) is Gross Income, taxab(*varname*) is Taxable Income, d(*varname*) is Disposable Income, isub(*varname*) and itax(*varname*) are indirect subsidies and taxes respectively, c(*varname*) is Consumable Income, ike(*varname*), ikh(*varname*), and hu(*varname*) are in-kind education, in-kind health, and housing and urban benefits, respectively, and f(*varname*) is Final Income.

2.10 Sheet F14. Cross-Race Incidence

While sheets F12 and F13 present the results of the fiscal incidence analysis across ethno-racial lines, these results may be difficult to read. Sheet F14 utilizes the analysis presented on Sheet F12 to show the findings of the incidence analysis by ethno-racial group in an easy-to-read table. The results reveal the share of benefits (or payments) received (paid out) by each ethno-racial group as a share of total benefits (or payments). When this is compared to the population (row 8) or income (rows 9, 15, and 18 for Market, Disposable, and Consumable, respectively) shares, the progressivity of different policy interventions can be examined. As discussed above, policies are considered to be regressive when the share of benefits (taxes) being received (paid) by the disadvantaged population is less (more) than its share of national income, relatively progressive when the share of benefits (taxes) being received (paid) by the disadvantaged population is more (less) than its share of national income, and absolutely progressive when the share of benefits being received by the disadvantaged population is more than its share of the population.

This sheet is filled in automatically using the results calculated from sheet F12.

2.11 Sheet F15. Horizontal Equity

The impact of the fiscal policies targeted to the poor may appear to be ethno-racially progressive due to greater poverty rates among the disadvantaged population(s). This can lead to questions about whether the program benefits the poor of a particular group more or less than other segments of the population. Sheet F15 examines the incidence of different policy interventions among the poor of each ethno-racial group relative to its population and income shares. This allows us to examine whether policies are disproportionately benefiting the poor of a particular ethno-racial group or whether certain polices appear to be ethno-racially progressive or regressive due to differences in the socioeconomic status of the different populations. If the share of benefits going to a particular population is equal to its share of the poor, policies are considered to be colorblind; that is, they do not violate horizontal equity by benefiting the poor of particular populations more than others.

This sheet is filled in automatically using the results calculated on sheet F13.

2.12 Sheet F16. Fiscal Profile

In addition to looking at the share of benefits going to each ethno-racial population, it is important to see the impact on incomes within each of these populations. Looking at the fiscal profile sheet allows us to see these changes in mean income, in terms of local currency units and as a share of the different income concepts. In addition to looking at the impacts on mean income among individuals of each race or ethnicity, this sheet looks at the differences that occur in households headed by members of different races or ethnicities. This allows us to see if there are differences between inter-racial households and single-race households.

To fill in this sheet using the `ceqrace` Stata command, race dummy variables, weights, `original(varname)`, `disposable(varname)`, `consumable(varname)`, `final(varname)`, `age(varname)`, `pensions(varname)`, `hhe(varname)`, `hhid(varname)`, and poverty line options are required, and the following syntax should be used:

```
ceqrace [pw=weight] using CEQEthnoRacialMWB.xlsx, race1(indig)
race2(white) race3(afrd) race4(orace) race5(nonrace) table(f16)
o(ym)  d(yd)  c(yc)f(yf)  pens(pensions)  hhe(hheid)  hhid(hhid)
ppp(7.65) cpibase(78.661) cpisurvey(105.196) year
```

Where CEQ_Ethno_Racial_MWB.xlsx is the name of the Excel file, the race variables are dummies, and o(*varname*) specifies the original income variable in local currency units. Original income is used in order to assert whether the analysis that is being run uses pensions as deferred income (PDI) or pensions as government transfers (PGT). d(*varname*) is Disposable Income, c(*varname*) is Consumable Income, f(*varname*) is Final Income, pens(*varname*) are pensions, hhe(*varname*) is a dummy variable that identifies the household head, hhid(*varname*) is the household identifier, ppp( ) is the PPP conversion factor (LCU per international dollar, consumption-based) from the year of PPP (usually either 2005 or 2011), cpibase( ) is CPI of the base year (year of PPP, usually 2005 or 2011), cpisurvey( ) is the CPI for the year of the household survey, and finally, year indicates that the income variables are annual.

2.13 Sheet F17. Coverage Rates (Total Population)

In addition to looking at the impacts of fiscal policy between ethno-racial groups on the aggregate, it is important to look at what share of each ethno-racial population is receiving benefits from the different fiscal interventions. The coverage rates of the different populations allow researchers to have a better understanding of the targeting of programs, in addition to seeing their impact on incomes and poverty. Sheet F17 looks at the coverage rates of the total population, regardless of whether all individuals making up the population are the desired targets of particular fiscal interventions. These results are disaggregated by ethno-racial group as well as by income group.

There are multiple ways that one can calculate coverage rates. For the purpose of the CEQ analysis, coverage rates of direct beneficiaries, indirect beneficiaries, and households may all be interesting and can be calculated for each of these distinct populations. In order to understand the differences between the different coverage rates, it is necessary to understand what populations are being considered as part of each group.

1. *Direct beneficiaries* are those who report being recipients of a particular intervention. In cases where benefits are directed at the household, direct beneficiaries will be imputed to the head of the household or to all members of the household de-

pending on the targeting method being utilized. In some cases, households may have more than one direct beneficiary.

2. *Beneficiary households* are households in which at least one direct beneficiary resides.

3. *Direct and indirect beneficiaries* are all individuals who reside within a beneficiary household.

To calculate the coverage rates using these different methods requires dividing the number of beneficiaries by the total population in the case of direct and indirect beneficiaries and by the total number of households in the case of beneficiary households. For additional information on how to calculate each of the different coverage rates, please refer to chapter 8 in Volume 1 of this Handbook (Higgins and Brest Lopez, 2022).

To fill in this sheet using the `ceqrace` Stata command, race dummy variables, weights, `original`(*varname*), `cct`(*varname*), `noncontrib`(*varname*), `unemploy`(*varname*), `foodtransf`(*varname*), `otransfers`(*varname*), `health`(*varname*), `pensions`(*varname*), `hhe`(*varname*), `hhid`(*varname*), and poverty lines are required, and the following syntax should be used:

```
ceqrace [pw=weight] using CEQEthnoRacialMWB.xlsx, race1(indig)
race2(white) race3(afrd) race4(orace) race5(nonrace) table(f17)
o(ym)   cct(cct)   nonc(nonc)   unem(unemployment)   foodt(ftran)
otran(otran)  hea(health)  pen(pensions)  hhe(hheid)  hhid(hhid)
ppp(7.65) cpibase(78.661) cpisurvey(105.196) year
```

Where CEQ_Ethno_Racial_MWB.xlsx is the name of the Excel file, the race variables are dummies, o(*varname*) specifies the original income variable in local currency units, cct(*varname*) are conditional cash transfers, nonc(*varname*) are noncontributory pensions, unem(*varname*) are unemployment benefits, foodt(*varname*) are food transfers, otran(*varname*) are other direct transfers, hea(*varname*) are health transfers, pen(*varname*) are pensions, hhe(*varname*) is a dummy variable that identifies the household head, hhid(*varname*) is the household identifier, ppp( ) is the PPP conversion factor (LCU per international dollar, consumption-based) from the year of PPP (usually either 2005 or 2011), cpibase( ) is the CPI of the base year (year of PPP, usually 2005 or 2011), cpisurvey( ) is the CPI for the year of the household survey, and finally, year indicates that the income variables are annual.

2.14 Sheet F18. Coverage Rates (Target Population)

Building upon the results of sheet F17, this sheet examines the coverage rates among the population that is the desired target of specific interventions. The target population is likely to differ by intervention. For example, pensions may be targeted to individuals over a particular age, while some social cash transfers may be targeted to heads of households with children within a particular age range. These targeted coverage rates are calculated using the same three population definitions given above. However, the coverage rates presented on this sheet do not include recipients who are not part of the desired population. In the case of households, the denominator includes all households where at least one individual with the desired characteristics resides, while for direct and indirect beneficiaries, the denominator includes all individuals who reside in a household where at least one individual with the desired characteristics resides.

To fill in this sheet using the ceqrace Stata command, race dummy variables, weights, original(*varname*), cct(*varname*), noncontrib(*varname*), pensions(*varname*), hhe(*varname*), hhid(*varname*), tarcct(*varname*), tarncp(*varname*), tarpen(*varname*), and poverty line options are required and the following syntax should be used:

```
ceqrace [pw=weight] using CEQEthnoRacialMWB.xlsx, race1(indig)
race2(white) race3(afrd) race4(orace) race5(nonrace) table(f18)
o(ym) cct(cct) nonc(nonc) pen(pensions) hhe(hheid) hhid(hhid)
tarncp(tncp) tarcct(tcct) tarpen(tpen) ppp(7.65) cpibase(78.661)
cpisurvey(105.196) year
```

Where CEQ_Ethno_Racial_MWB.xlsx is the name of the Excel file, the race variables are dummies, o(*varname*) specifies the original income variable in local currency units, cct(*varname*) are conditional cash transfers, nonc(*varname*) are noncontributory pensions, pen(*varname*) are pensions, hhe(*varname*) is a dummy variable that identifies the household head, hhid(*varname*) is the household identifier, tarncp(*varname*) is a dummy variable that identifies noncontributory pensions target population, tarcct(*varname*) is a dummy variable that identifies CCT's target population, tarpen(*varname*) is a dummy variable that identifies pensions target population, ppp( ) is the PPP conversion factor (LCU per international dollar, consumption-based) from the year of PPP (usually either 2005 or 2011), cpibase( ) is the CPI of the base year (year of PPP, usually 2005 or 2011), cpisurvey( ) is the CPI for the year of the household survey, and finally, year indicates that the income variables are annual.

2.15 Sheet F19. Leakages

Programs are often likely to direct some benefits to a segment of the population that does not meet the desired targeting characteristics. Using the results of the two different coverage sheets (F17 and F18), this sheet seeks to explain if the leakages from these programs benefit a particular ethno-racial group more than another. These are calculated by taking the total size of benefits and subtracting the amount of benefits that are received by the target population. Results are calculated in both 2005 PPP values and local currency, as well as in terms of a percentage of total spending on a particular intervention.

This sheet is filled in automatically using the results presented on sheets F17 and F18.

2.16 Sheet F20. Mobility Matrices

In order to determine if a program is "pro-disadvantaged group," it is necessary to determine if the impact of fiscal policies leads to a higher probability of escaping poverty for the disadvantaged population than for the advantaged population. To calculate this, this workbook utilizes the mobility matrices discussed in Lustig and Higgins (2013). These matrices look at the population that is in or out of poverty at two different income concepts. This sheet presents these mobility matrices for each of the different ethno-racial populations and calculates the probability of an individual living in poverty at Market Income escaping poverty through fiscal interventions. Probabilities of escaping poverty are calculated from Consumable, Disposable, and Final Income, all with respect to Market Income for each of the different ethno-racial populations using the regional poverty lines of $2.50 PPP per capita per day and $4 PPP per capita per day. The results represented in the mobility matrices on this sheet should match those found on sheet D10 for each of the ethno-racial groups.

To fill in this sheet using the ceqrace Stata command, race dummy variables, weights, original(*varname*), disposable(*varname*), consumable(*varname*), final(*varname*), and poverty lines are required, and the following syntax should be used:

```
ceqrace [pw=weight] using CEQEthnoRacialMWB.xlsx, race1(indig)
race2(white) race3(afrd) race4(orace) race5(nonrace) table(f20)
o(ym) d(yd) c(yc) f(yf) ppp(7.65) cpibase(78.661) cpisurvey(105.196)
year
```

Where CEQ_Ethno_Racial_MWB.xlsx is the name of the Excel file, the race variables are dummies, o(*varname*) specifies the original income variable in local currency units, mplusp(*varname*) is Market Income plus Pensions, n(*varname*) is Net Market Income, g(*varname*) is Gross Income, taxab(*varname*) is Taxable Income, d(*varname*) is Disposable Income, c(*varname*) is Consumable Income, and f(*varname*) is Final Income, ppp( ) is the PPP conversion factor (LCU per international dollar, consumption-based) from the year of PPP (usually either 2005 or 2011), cpibase( ) is the CPI of the base year (year of PPP, usually 2005 or 2011), cpisurvey( ) is the CPI for the year of the household survey, and finally, year indicates that the income variables are annual.

2.17 Sheet F21. Education (Totals)

One area that is commonly cited as a source of ethno-racial inequality is educational outcomes. This is also where government provision of services is an important tool in closing ethno-racial inequalities. Thus, looking at the differences in educational attainment and enrollment can be crucial to explaining ethno-racial inequalities. This sheet looks at the size of different ethno-racial populations that are attending public and private educational institutions in order to see the impacts of government services at closing inequalities in access to education.

To fill in this sheet using the ceqrace Stata command, race dummy variables, weights, original(*varname*), edpre(*varname*), edpri(*varname*), edsec(*varname*), edter(*varname*), redpre(*varname*), redpri(*varname*), redsec(*varname*), redter(*varname*), edpublic(*varname*), edprivate(*varname*), and attend(*varname*) are required, and the following syntax should be used:

```
ceqrace [pw=weight] using CEQEthnoRacialMWB.xlsx, race1(indig)
race2(white) race3(afrd) race4(orace) race5(nonrace) table(f21)
o(ym)   edpre(edpre)   edpri(edpri)   edsec(edsec)   edter(edter)
attend(attendschool)      redpre(redpre)      redpri(redpri)
redsec(redsec)    redter(redter)    hhe(idhhead)    hhid(idhh)
edpriv(private) edpub(public)
```

Where CEQ_Ethno_Racial_MWB.xlsx is the name of the Excel file, the race variables are dummies, o(*varname*) specifies the original income variable in local currency units; edpre(*varname*), edpri(*varname*), edsec(*varname*), edter(*varname*) are preschool, primary, secondary, and tertiary level of education dummies respectively; redpre(*varname*), redpri(*varname*), redsec(*varname*), redter(*varname*) are preschool, primary, secondary, and tertiary age ranges dummies, respectively;[13] attend(*varname*) is a dummy that defines whether the individual attends school; hhe(*varname*) is a dummy variable that identifies the household head, hhid(*varname*) is the household identifier; edpriv(*varname*) and edpub(*varname*) are dummies that identify whether the individual attends a private or public school; ppp( ) is the PPP conversion factor (LCU per international dollar, consumption-based) from the year of PPP (usually either 2005 or 2011); cpibase( ) is the CPI of the base year (year of PPP, usually 2005 or 2011); cpisurvey( ) is the CPI for the year of the household survey; and finally, year indicates that the income variables are annual.

2.18 Sheet F22. Education (Rates)

Utilizing the population numbers presented on sheet F21, this sheet calculates different education rates and presents them in easy-to-use tables. Both gross and net enrollment rates are calculated for each ethno-racial population at each level of education that is available for analysis, ranging from preschool through tertiary

---

[13] If an individual is between the age range of each education level, then the variable takes the value of one.

education. These rates are further disaggregated by income group at Disposable Income.

This sheet is filled in automatically using the results presented on sheet F21.

2.19 Sheet F23. Infrastructure Access

Another element of ethno-racial inequality comes from the nonmonetary deprivations that may be experienced by different populations. These may include access to key services that are often considered to be connected to economic performance, such as access to potable water or electricity. This sheet presents the different coverage rates experienced by individuals of different ethno-racial populations for access to running water, electricity, sewage, and roads as well as to well-constructed walls, floors, and roofs. These results are calculated using two different methods, one that examines the coverage rate of the population (weighted households) and one that looks at the coverage rate of households. In addition to showing the coverage rates, this sheet presents the distribution of beneficiaries, both by household and population.

To fill in this sheet using the ceqrace Stata command, race dummy variables, weights, original(*varname*), hhid(*varname*), hhead(*varname*), water(*varname*), electricity(*varname*), walls(*varname*), floors(*varname*), roof(*varname*), sewage(*varname*), roads(*varname*), and poverty lines are required. If one of the infrastructure variables is not included in the dataset, the ado-file will leave those observations blank.

Example:

```
ceqrace [pw=weight] using CEQEthnoRacialMWB.xlsx, race1(indig)
race2(white) race3(afrd) race4(orace) race5(nonrace) table(f23)
o(ym) hhid(idhh) hhe(idhhead) water(water) electricity(elect)
walls(walls) floors(floors) roof(roof) sewage(sewage) roads(roads)
ppp(7.65) cpibase(78.661) cpisurvey(105.196) year
```

Where CEQ_Ethno_Racial_MWB.xlsx is the name of the Excel file, the race variables are dummies, o(*varname*) specifies the original income variable in local currency units, hhe(*varname*) is a dummy variable that identifies the household head, hhid(*varname*) is the household identifier, water(*varname*), electricity(*varname*), walls(*varname*), floors(*varname*), roof(*varname*), sewage(*varname*), and roads(*varname*) are all dummies for having running water, electricity, walls, floors, roof, sewage, and roads, respectively. ppp( ) is the PPP conversion factor (LCU per international dollar, consumption-based) from the year of PPP (usually either 2005 or 2011), cpibase( ) is the CPI of the base year (year of PPP, usually 2005 or 2011), cpisurvey( )is the CPI for the year of the household survey, and finally, year indicates that the income variables are annual.

2.20 Sheet F24. Theil Decomposition

As discussed above, one of the ways that one can determine the effect of fiscal policy and the magnitude of ethno-racial inequality is to use a decomposable inequality indicator to determine what share of inequality is due to differences in income between income groups. This sheet does just that and uses the decomposable Thiel coefficient to determine what share of inequality is due to differences in incomes between groups and what share of inequality is due to intra-group inequalities. These results are calculated for each of the eight core income concepts. These can be compared to see if the share of inequality due to ethno-racial differences declines as a result of fiscal interventions.

To fill in this sheet using the ceqrace Stata command, race dummy variables, weights, market(*varname*), mpluspensions(*varname*), netmarket(*varname*), gross(*varname*), taxable(*varname*), disposable(*varname*), consumable(*varname*), final(*varname*), gender(*varname*), urban(*varname*), and edpar(*varname*) are required.

Example:

```
ceqrace [pw=weight] using CEQEthnoRacialMWB.xlsx, race1(indig)
race2(white) race3(afrd) race4(orace) race5(nonrace) table(f24)
m(ym) mplusp(ymp) n(ynm) g(yg) taxab(ytaxab) d(yd) c(yc) f(yf)
gender(sex) urban(rururb) edpar (parentsed)
```

Where CEQ_Ethno_Racial_MWB.xlsx is the name of the Excel file, the race variables are dummies, m(*varname*) specifies the Market Income variable in local currency units, mplusp(*varname*) is Market Income plus Pensions, n(*varname*) is Net Market Income, g(*varname*) is Gross Income, taxab(*varname*) is Taxable Income, d(*varname*) is Disposable Income, c(*varname*) is Consumable Income, and f(*varname*) is Final Income; gender(*varname*) is a dummy variable specifying the gender of the individual (1 for women and 0 otherwise), urban(*varname*) is also a dummy specifying whether the individual lives in an urban or a rural area, and edpar(*varname*) specifies the years of education of the head of the household.

2.21 Sheet F25. Inequality of Opportunity

As discussed above, one of the ways in which one can measure ethno-racial inequality is through inequality of opportunity. This measure seeks to explain if differences in outcomes are due to characteristics or circumstances outside of an individual's control rather than being due to personal preferences or effort. In this case, the characteristics that are considered part of the analysis are the individuals' gender, location (urban/rural), and race or ethnicity. The CEQ race and ethnicity analysis looks specifically at how these characteristics affect inequality of income at each of the different income concepts. By considering the mean incomes of the different combinations of individuals with these characteristics, one can calculate to what extent each of the different characteristics describes the differences in mean incomes. By considering the change in the share of inequality of opportunity explained by race and ethnicity, one can determine if fiscal policy reduces the share of inequality of opportunity explained by race and ethnicity.

To fill in this sheet using the `ceqrace` Stata command, race dummy variables, weights, `market`(*varname*), `mpluspensions`(*varname*), `netmarket`(*varname*), `gross`(*varname*), `taxable`(*varname*), `disposable`(*varname*), `consumable`(*varname*), `final`(*varname*), `gender`(*varname*), `urban`(*varname*) are required.

Example:

```
ceqrace [pw=weight] using CEQEthnoRacialMWB.xlsx, race1(indig)
race2(white) race3(afrd) race4(orace) race5(nonrace) table(f25)
m(ym) mplusp(ymp) n(ynm) g(yg) taxab(ytaxab) d(yd) c(yc) f(yf)
gender(sex) urban(rururb)
```

Where CEQ_Ethno_Racial_MWB.xlsx is the name of the Excel file, the race variables are dummies, m(*varname*) specifies the Market Income variable in local currency units, mplusp(*varname*) is Market Income plus Pensions, n(*varname*) is Net Market Income, g(*varname*) is Gross Income, taxab(*varname*) is Taxable Income, d(*varname*) is Disposable Income, c(*varname*) is Consumable Income, and f(*varname*) is Final Income, gender(*varname*) is a dummy variable specifying the gender of the individual (1 for women and 0 otherwise), and urban(*varname*) is a dummy specifying if the individual lives in an urban or a rural area.

2.22 Sheet F26. Significance

In order to determine whether there are in fact differences in the incomes of different ethno-racial populations, it is necessary to verify that these values are statistically significant. To do this, one can calculate p-values comparing the different indicators across ethno-racial lines. This sheet looks at the p-values for the poverty headcounts (US$2.50 and US$4 PPP/day), Gini coefficient, and Theil coefficient between each pairwise set of ethno-racial groups to determine if the differences between each ethno-racial group are statistically significant for each indicator. These are calculated for each of the eight core income concepts.

To fill in this sheet using the `ceqrace` Stata command, race dummy variables, weights, `market`(*varname*), `mpluspensions`(*varname*), `netmarket`(*varname*), `gross`(*varname*), `taxable`(*varname*), `disposable`(*varname*), `consumable`(*varname*), `final`(*varname*), `psu`(*varname*), `strata`(*varname*), and poverty line options are required.

Example:

```
ceqrace [pw=weight] using CEQEthnoRacialMWB.xlsx, race1(indig)
race2(white) race3(afrd) race4(orace) race5(nonrace) table(f26)
m(ym) mplusp(ymp) n(ynm) g(yg) taxab(ytaxab) d(yd) c(yc) f(yf) psu
(upm) strata(strata) ppp(7.65) cpibase(78.661) cpisurvey(105.196)
year
```

Where CEQ_Ethno_Racial_MWB.xlsx is the name of the Excel file, the race variables are dummies, m(*varname*) specifies the Market Income variable in local currency units, mplusp(*varname*) is Market Income plus Pensions, n(*varname*) is Net Market Income, g(*varname*) is Gross Income, taxab(*varname*) is Taxable Income, d(*varname*) is Disposable Income, c(*varname*) is Consumable Income, and f(*varname*) is Final Income; gender(*varname*) is a dummy variable specifying the gender of the individual (1 for women and 0 otherwise), urban(*varname*) is also a dummy specifying if the individual lives in an urban or a rural area, psu(*varname*) is the primary sampling unit, strata(*varname*)is the strata variable, ppp( ) is the PPP conversion factor (LCU per international dollar, consumption-based) from the year of PPP (usually either 2005 or 2011), cpibase( ) is the CPI of the base year (year of PPP, usually 2005 or 2011), cpisurvey( )is the CPI for the year of the household survey, and finally, year indicates that the income variables are annual.

References

CEQ Institute. 202022. "*CEQ Assessment: CEQ Master Workbook*," available online only in part IV of the *Commitment to Equity Handbook: Estimating the Impact of Fiscal Policy on Inequality and Poverty*, 2nd ed., vol. 1, edited by Nora Lustig (Brookings Institution Press and CEQ Institute, Tulane University). Free online version available at www.commitmentoequity.org.

de Ferranti, David, Guillermo E. Perry, Francisco Ferreira, and Michael Walton. 2004. *Inequality in Latin America: Breaking with History?* (Washington: World Bank).

Enami, Ali, Sean Higgins, and Nora Lustig. 2022. "Allocating Taxes and Transfers and Constructing Income Concepts: Completing Sections A, B, and C of the *CEQ Master Workbook*," chap. 6 in *Commitment to Equity Handbook: Estimating the Impact of Fiscal Policy on Inequality and Poverty*, 2nd ed., Vol. 1, edited by Nora Lustig (Brookings Institution Press and CEQ Institute, Tulane University). Free online version available at www.commitmentoequity.org.

Ferreira, Francisco H. G., and David Robalino. 2010. "Social Protection in Latin America: Achievements and Limitations." Policy Research Working Paper 5305 (Washington: World Bank, Latin America and Caribbean Region Office of the Chief Economist, and Human Development Network Social Protection and Labor Unit).

Foster, J., J. Greer, and E. Thorbecke, 1984. "A Class of Decomposable Poverty Measures." *Econometrica: Journal of the Econometric Society* 52, no. 3, 761–66.

Hall, Gillette, and Harry Patrinos. 2006. *Indigenous Peoples, Poverty and Human Development in Latin America, 1994–2004* (London: Palgrave Macmillan).

Higgins, Sean, and Caterina Brest Lopez. 2022. "Producing Indicators and Results, and Completing Sections D and E of the *CEQ Master Workbook* Using the *CEQ Stata Package*," chap. 8 in *Commitment to Equity Handbook: Estimating the Impact of Fiscal Policy on Inequality and Poverty*, 2nd ed., Vol. 1, edited by Nora Lustig (Brookings Institution Press and CEQ Institute, Tulane University). Free online version available at www.commitmentoequity.org.

Jellema, Jon, and Gabriela Inchauste. 2022. "Constructing Consumable Income: Including the Direct and Indirect Effects of Indirect Taxes and Subsidies," chap. 7 in *Commitment to Equity Handbook: Estimating the Impact of Fiscal Policy on Inequality and Poverty*, 2nd ed., Vol. 1, edited by Nora Lustig (Brookings Institution Press and CEQ Institute, Tulane University). Free online version available at www.commitmentoequity.org.

Lustig, Nora. 2017. "Fiscal Redistribution and Ethnoracial Inequality in Bolivia, Brazil and Guatemala," *Latin American Research Review. Special Issue: Enduring and/or New Forms of Inequality in a Globalizing World* 52, no. 2, pp. 208–20 (doi:http://doi.org/10.25222/larr.90).

Lustig, Nora, and Sean Higgins. 2013. "Measuring Impoverishment: An Overlooked Dimension of Fiscal Incidence." Department of Economics Working Paper 1315 (Tulane University).

———. 2022. "The *CEQ Assessment*: Measuring the Impact of Fiscal Policy on Inequality and Poverty," chap. 1 in *Commitment to Equity Handbook: Estimating the Impact of Fiscal Policy on Inequality and Poverty*, 2nd ed., Vol. 1, edited by Nora Lustig (Brookings Institution Press and CEQ Institute, Tulane University). Free online version available at www.commitmentoequity.org.

Molinas Vega, Jose R., Ricardo Paes de Barros, Jaime Saavedra Chanduvi, Marcelo Giugale, Louise J. Cord, Carola Pessino, and Amer Hasan. 2012. *Do Our Children Have a Chance? A Human Opportunity Report for Latin America and the Caribbean* (Washington: World Bank).

Ñopo, Hugo. 2012. *New Century, Old Disparities: Gender and Ethnic Earnings Gaps in Latin America and the Caribbean* (Washington: World Bank and the Inter-American Development Bank).

Roemer, John E. 1998. *Equality of Opportunity* (Harvard University Press).

World Bank. 2017. *World Development Indicators* (Washington: World Bank).

PART III

Applications

Chapter 10

FISCAL POLICY, INCOME REDISTRIBUTION, AND POVERTY REDUCTION IN LOW- AND MIDDLE-INCOME COUNTRIES

Nora Lustig

Introduction

Two key indicators of a government's (or society's) commitment to equalizing opportunities and reducing poverty and social exclusion are the share of total income devoted to social spending and how equalizing and pro-poor this spending is.[1] Typically, redistributive social spending includes cash benefits[2] and benefits in-kind such as spending on education and health.[3] As shown in chapter 2 by Enami, Lustig, and

---

[1] Because national and international agencies often update their data series, the information included here may be subject to change. For updates, the reader is referred to the CEQ Standard Indicators, available online in the CEQ Institute's website, http://www.commitmentoequity.org/datacenter. Lindert (2004) and Barr (2012).

[2] "Cash" benefits typically include cash transfers and near-cash transfers such as school feeding programs and free uniforms and textbooks. Depending on the analysis, cash benefits also include consumption subsidies (for example, on food) and energy consumption and housing subsidies. The studies included here include cash and near-cash transfers as well as (in most cases) consumption subsidies.

[3] Social spending as a category frequently includes spending on pensions funded by contributions. Following Lindert (1994), the sum total of social spending does not include pensions. Strictly speaking, one should include the subsidized portion of these pensions as part of redistributive social spending (for example, the portion of contributory pensions that is paid out of general revenues and not from contributions). However, estimates of these subsidies are hard to produce. As an alternative, the analysis here is presented for the two extreme scenarios: pensions as pure deferred income (also called replacement income) and pensions as pure government transfer. Noncontributory pensions (also known as social or minimum pensions) are treated as any other cash transfer.

Aranda (2022) and chapter 3 by Enami (2022) in Volume 1 of this Handbook, the redistributive potential of a country does indeed depend on the size and composition of government spending and how it is financed, as well as the progressivity of all the taxes and government spending combined.

Analogously, the impact of fiscal policy on poverty will depend on the size and incidence of government spending and revenues. Recall that, in theory, a fiscal system can be inequality-reducing but poverty-increasing. How so? If every individual in the system pays more in taxes than he or she receives in transfers but the proportion of net tax payments (as a share of prefiscal or Market Income) is higher for the rich than for the poor, the system would be inequality-reducing but poverty-increasing. As we shall see, this result is not uncommon in actual fiscal systems, especially when we focus on the cash portion of the fiscal systems (the analysis that does not include the impact of the monetized value of government services). Given the importance of the size and composition of government revenues and spending, we start by showing the patterns observed in the twenty-nine countries analyzed here.

The main objective here is to analyze the impact of fiscal policy on inequality and poverty in twenty-nine low- and middle-income countries from around 2010.[4] The studies apply the same fiscal incidence methodology described in detail in chapter 1 (Lustig and Higgins, 2022), chapter 6 (Enami, Higgins, and Lustig, 2022), chapter 7 (Jellema and Inchauste, 2022), and chapter 8 (Higgins and Brest Lopez, 2022) in Volume 1 of this Handbook.[5] With a long tradition in applied public finance, fiscal incidence analysis is designed to respond to the question of who benefits from government transfers and who ultimately bears the burden of taxes in the economy.[6] The fiscal policy instruments included here are personal income and payroll taxes, direct transfers, consumption taxes, consumptions subsidies, and transfers in-kind in the form of education and healthcare free or subsidized services.

The data utilized here is based on the *CEQ Assessments* available in the Commitment to Equity Institute's[7] database on fiscal redistribution for twenty-nine low- and

---

[4] At the time this chapter was written, the World Bank classified countries as follows. Low-income: US$1,025 or less; lower middle-income: US$1,026–4,035; upper-middle-income: US$4,036–12,475; and, high-income: US$12,476 or more. The classification uses Gross National Income per capita calculated with the World Bank Atlas Method, June 2017 (see http://data.worldbank.org/about /country-and-lending-groups). Using the World Bank classification, the group includes three *low-income* countries: Ethiopia, Tanzania, and Uganda; ten *lower-middle-income* countries: Armenia, Bolivia, El Salvador, Ghana, Guatemala, Honduras, Indonesia, Nicaragua, Sri Lanka, and Tunisia; fourteen *upper-middle-income* countries: Argentina, Brazil, Colombia, Costa Rica, Dominican Republic, Ecuador, Georgia, Iran, Jordan, Mexico, Peru, Russia, South Africa, and Venezuela; and two *high-income* countries: Chile and Uruguay.

[5] Strictly speaking, the studies reviewed here were produced using Lustig and Higgins (2013), an earlier version of this Handbook, which is available upon request.

[6] Musgrave (1959); Pechman (1985); Martinez-Vazquez (2008).

[7] Launched first as a project in 2008, the Commitment to Equity Institute (CEQ) at Tulane University was created in 2015 with the generous support of the Bill and Melinda Gates Foundation.

middle-income countries and the United States: Argentina, Armenia, Bolivia, Brazil, Chile, Colombia, Costa Rica, Dominican Republic, Ecuador, El Salvador, Ethiopia, Georgia, Ghana, Guatemala, Honduras, Indonesia, Iran, Jordan, Mexico, Nicaragua, Peru, Russia, South Africa, Sri Lanka, Tanzania, Tunisia, Uganda, United States, Uruguay, and Venezuela. The *CEQ Assessments* for Bolivia, Brazil, Mexico, Peru, and Uruguay are published in a *Public Finance Review* special issue by Lustig, Pessino, and Scott.[8] The results for Ghana and Tanzania, as well as the United States, are published in other peer-reviewed journals.[9] The *CEQ Assessments* for Armenia, Ethiopia, Georgia, Indonesia, Jordan, Russia, South Africa, and Sri Lanka appear in the World Bank volume edited by Inchauste and Lustig.[10] The *CEQ Assessments* for Argentina, Chile, Dominican Republic, El Salvador, Tunisia, and Uganda are chapters in this Volume of the Handbook.[11] The studies for Costa Rica, Ecuador, Guatemala, Honduras, Iran, and Nicaragua are available in the CEQ Working Paper series at www .commitmenttoequity.org.[12] The results for Colombia and Venezuela are in the CEQ Data Center on Fiscal Redistribution (same website).[13] The household surveys used in the country studies include either income or consumption as the welfare indicator.[14]

---

[8] Lustig, Pessino, and Scott (2014). Bolivia: Paz Arauco and others (2014a); Brazil: Higgins and Pereira (2014); Mexico: Scott (2014); Peru: Jaramillo (2014); and Uruguay: Bucheli and others (2014a).

[9] Ghana: Younger, Osei-Assibey, and Oppong (2017); Tanzania: Younger, Myamba, and Mdadila (2016a); and United States: Higgins and others (2016).

[10] Inchauste and Lustig (2017). Armenia: Younger and Khachatryan (2017); Ethiopia: Hill and others (2017); Georgia: Cancho and Bondarenko (2017); Indonesia: Jellema, Wai-Poi, and Afkar (2017); Jordan: Alam, Inchauste, and Serajuddin (2017); Russia: Lopez-Calva and others (2017); South Africa: Inchauste and others (2017); and Sri Lanka: Arunatilake, Inchauste, and Lustig (2017).

[11] Argentina: Rossignolo (2022); Chile: Martinez-Aguilar and others (2022); Dominican Republic: Aristy-Escuder and others (2022); El Salvador: Beneke de Sanfeliu, Lustig, and Oliva Cepeda (2022); Tunisia: Jouini and others (2022); and, Uganda: Jellema and others (2022).

[12] Costa Rica: Sauma and Trejos (2014a); Ecuador: Llerena and others (2015); Guatemala: ICEFI (2017a); Honduras: ICEFI (2017b); Iran: Enami, Lustig, and Taqdiri (2017a); and, Nicaragua: ICEFI (2017c).

[13] Colombia: Melendez and Martinez (2015); and, Venezuela: Molina (2016).

[14] The household surveys are (the letters "I" and "C" refer to income and consumption-based data, respectively): Argentina (I): Encuesta Nacional de Gasto de los Hogares, 2012–13; Armenia (I): Integrated Living Conditions Survey, 2011; Bolivia (I): Encuesta de Hogares, 2009; Brazil (I): Pesquisa de Orçamentos Familiares, 2008–09; Chile (I): Encuesta de Caracterizacion Social, 2013; Colombia (I): Encuesta Nacional de Calidad de Vida, 2010; Costa Rica (I): Encuesta Nacional de Hogares, 2010; Dominican Republic (I): Encuesta Nacional de Ingresos y Gastos de los Hogares, 2006–07; Ecuador (I): Encuesta Nacional de Ingresos y Gastos de los Hogares Urbano y Rural, 2011–12; El Salvador (I): Encuesta de Hogares de Propositos Multiples, 2011; Ethiopia (C): Household Consumption Expenditure Survey, 2010–11 and Welfare Monitoring Survey, 2011; Georgia (I): Integrated Household Survey, 2013; Ghana (C): Living Standards Survey, 2012–13; Guatemala (I): Encuesta Nacional de Ingresos y Gastos Familiares, 2009–10 and Encuesta Nacional de Condiciones de Vida, 2011; Honduras (I): Encuesta Permanente de Hogares de Propositos Multiples, 2011; Indonesia (C): Survei Sosial-Ekonomi Nasional, 2012; Iran (I): Iranian Urban and Rural Household Income and Expenditure Survey, 2011–12; Jordan (C): Household Expenditure and Income Survey, 2010–11; Mexico (I):

As explained in chapter 1 in this Volume of the Handbook, given that contributory pensions are part deferred income and part government transfer, results were calculated under both scenarios (that is, as pure deferred income and pure government transfers).

While fiscal policy unambiguously reduces income inequality, this is not always true for poverty. In Ethiopia, Tanzania, Ghana, Nicaragua, Uganda, and Guatemala the extreme poverty headcount ratio is higher after taxes and transfers than before.[15] In addition, to varying degrees, in all countries a portion of the poor are net payers into the fiscal system and are thus impoverished by the fiscal system.[16] While all taxes can be poverty-increasing as long as the poor and near poor have to pay taxes, consumption taxes are the main culprits of fiscally induced impoverishment. As for the impact of specific instruments on inequality, net direct taxes and spending on education and health are always equalizing, and net indirect taxes are equalizing in nineteen countries of the twenty-nine. An examination of the relationship between prefiscal inequality and social spending (as a share of GDP) and fiscal redistribution suggests that there is no evidence of a "Robin Hood paradox"; the more unequal countries tend to spend more on redistribution and show a higher redistributive effect, but the coefficient for the latter is not always significant. (Preliminary results of regression-based analysis indicate that the positive association between initial inequality and the size of the redistributive effect is not robust across the board. When one controls for income per capita and leaves out the "outliers" or measures redistribution in percent change instead of Gini points, the coefficient is often not statistically significant).

Several caveats are in order. The fiscal incidence analysis used here is point-in-time and does not incorporate behavioral or general equilibrium effects. That is, no claim is made that the prefiscal equals the true counterfactual income in the absence of taxes and transfers. The analysis is a first-order approximation that measures the average incidence of fiscal interventions. However, the analysis is not a mechanically applied accounting exercise. The incidence of taxes is the economic rather than the statutory incidence. It is assumed that individual income taxes and contributions by both employees and employers, for instance, are borne by labor in the formal sector. Individuals who are not contributing to social security are assumed to pay neither direct taxes

---

Encuesta Nacional de Ingresos y Gastos de los Hogares, 2010; Nicaragua (I): Encuesta Nacional de Medicion de Nivel de Vida, 2009; Peru (I): Encuesta Nacional de Hogares, 2009; Russia (I): Russian Longitudinal Monitoring Survey of Higher School of Economics, 2010; South Africa (I): Income and Expenditure Survey, 2010–11; Sri Lanka (C): Household Income and Expenditure Survey, 2009–10; Tanzania (C): Household Budget Survey, 2011–12; Tunisia (C): National Survey of Consumption and Household Living Standards, 2010; Uganda (C): Uganda National Household Survey, 2012–13; United States (I): Current Population Survey, 2011; Uruguay (I): Encuesta Continua de Hogares, 2009; Venezuela (I) Encuesta Nacional de Hogares por Muestreo (ENHM), third quarter 2012.

[15] Because most of the studies were completed before the latest revision of the World Bank's global poverty line, the line used here is the *old* poverty line of US$1.25 per day in purchasing power parity of 2005. Estimates with the new poverty line of US$1.90 in purchasing power parity of 2011 will be available in due course at CEQ Data Center.

[16] Higgins and Lustig (2016) (reproduced as chapter 4 of this Volume of the Handbook).

FIGURE 10-1

Size and Composition of Government Revenues (as a % of GDP; circa 2010)

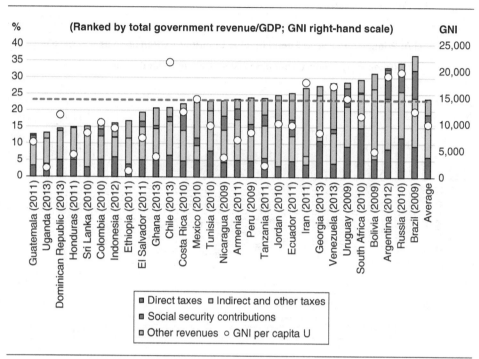

Source: CEQ Data Center on Fiscal Redistribution. Based on the following *Master Workbooks of Results:* Argentina (Rossignolo, 2017); Armenia (Younger and Khachatryan, 2014); Bolivia (Paz Arauco and others, 2014b); Brazil (Higgins and Pereira, 2017); Chile (Martinez-Aguilar and Ortiz-Juarez, 2016); Colombia (Melendez and Martinez, 2015); Costa Rica (Sauma and Trejos, 2014b); Dominican Republic (Aristy-Escuder and others, 2016); Ecuador (Llerena and others, 2017); El Salvador (Beneke de Sanfeliu, Lustig, and Oliva Cepeda, 2014); Ethiopia (Hill, Tsehaye, and Woldehanna, 2014); Georgia (Cancho and Bondarenko, 2015); Ghana (Younger, Osei-Assibey, and Oppong, 2016); Guatemala (Cabrera and Moran, 2015a); Honduras (Castaneda and Espino, 2015); Indonesia (Afkar, Jellema, and Wai-Poi, 2015); Iran (Enami, Lustig, and Taqdiri, 2017b); Jordan (Abdel-Halim and others, 2016); Mexico (Scott, 2013); Nicaragua (Cabrera and Moran, 2015b); Peru (Jaramillo, 2015); Russia (Malytsin and Popova, 2016); South Africa (Inchauste and others, 2016); Sri Lanka (Arunatilake and others, 2016); Tanzania (Younger, Myamba, and Mdadila, 2016b); Tunisia (Jouini and others, 2015); Uganda (Jellema and others, 2016); Uruguay (Bucheli and others, 2014b); and Venezuela (Molina, 2016).

Notes: The year for which the analysis was conducted is in parenthesis. Data shown here is administrative data as reported by the studies cited; the numbers do not necessarily coincide with those found in databases from multilateral organizations (e.g., World Bank's WDI). Bolivia does not have personal income taxes. For Tanzania, fiscal year runs from July 2011 to June 2012. Gross National Income per capita on right axis is in 2011 PPP from World Development Indicators, August 29, 2016, http://data.worldbank.org/indicator/NY.GNP.PCAP.PP.CD. The dotted line in red is the average for the 29 countries.

nor contributions. Consumption taxes are fully shifted forward to consumers. In the case of consumption taxes, the analyses take into account the lower incidence associated with own-consumption, rural markets, and informality.

1 Taxes and Public Spending: Levels and Composition

Figure 10-1 shows government revenues as a share of GDP for around 2010. The revenue collection patterns are heterogeneous. In general, indirect taxes are the largest

FIGURE 10-2

Size and Composition of Primary and Social Spending plus Contributory Pensions (as a % of GDP; circa 2010)

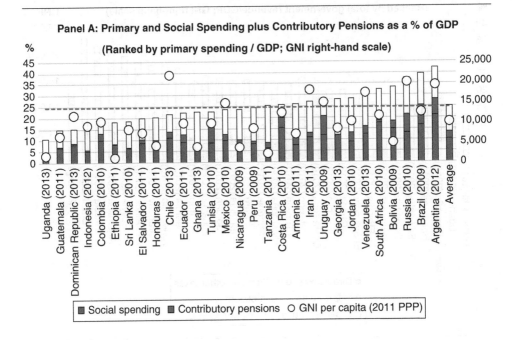

Panel A: Primary and Social Spending plus Contributory Pensions as a % of GDP

(Ranked by primary spending / GDP; GNI right-hand scale)

■ Social spending   ■ Contributory pensions   ○ GNI per capita (2011 PPP)

component of government revenues (as a share of GDP), except for Iran, Mexico, and Venezuela, where nontax revenues from oil-producing companies are the largest, and South Africa, where the share of direct taxes is the largest. Iran, Venezuela, and Mexico rely very heavily on oil-related nontax revenues; these revenues represent around 50 percent or more of total revenues.

Figure 10-2 shows the level and composition of primary and social spending plus contributory pensions (panel A), and the composition of social spending for the following categories: direct transfers, education, health, other social spending, and contributory pensions around 2010 (panel B). On average, and excluding contributory pensions, the twenty-nine low-income and middle-income countries analyzed here allocate 10.3 percent of GDP to social spending, while the advanced countries in the OECD group allocate 18.8 percent of GDP—that is, almost twice as much. The twenty-nine countries on average spend 1.8 percent of GDP on direct transfers, 4.4 percent on education, and 3.1 percent on health. In comparison, the OECD countries spend on average 4.4 percent of GDP on direct transfers, 5.3 percent on education, and 6.2 percent on health.[17] The largest difference between the OECD group and our sample occurs in

---

[17] The difference between the sum of these three items and the total in previous sentence is "Other social spending."

FIGURE 10-2 (continued)

Panel B: Composition of Social Spending plus Contributory Pensions as a % of GDP

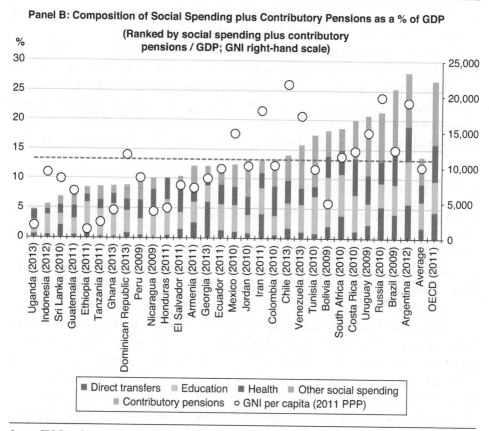

(Ranked by social spending plus contributory pensions / GDP; GNI right-hand scale)

■ Direct transfers ■ Education ■ Health ■ Other social spending
■ Contributory pensions o GNI per capita (2011 PPP)

Source: CEQ Data Center on Fiscal Redistribution. Based on the following *Master Workbooks of Results.* Argentina (Rossignolo, 2017); Armenia (Younger and Khachatryan, 2014); Bolivia (Paz Arauco and others, 2014b); Brazil (Higgins and Pereira, 2017); Chile (Martinez-Aguilar and Ortiz-Juarez, 2016); Colombia (Melendez and Martinez, 2015); Costa Rica (Sauma and Trejos, 2014b); Dominican Republic (Aristy-Escuder and others, 2016); Ecuador (Llerena and others, 2017); El Salvador (Beneke de Sanfeliu, Lustig, and Oliva Cepeda, 2014); Ethiopia (Hill, Tsehaye, and Woldehanna, 2014); Georgia (Cancho and Bondarenko, 2015); Ghana (Younger, Osei-Assibey, and Oppong, 2016); Guatemala (Cabrera and Moran, 2015a); Honduras (Castaneda and Espino, 2015); Indonesia (Afkar, Jellema, and Wai-Poi, 2015); Iran (Enami, Lustig, and Taqdiri, 2017b); Jordan (Abdel-Halim and others, 2016); Mexico (Scott, 2013); Nicaragua (Cabrera and Moran, 2015b); Peru (Jaramillo, 2015); Russia (Malytsin and Popova, 2016); South Africa (Inchauste and others, 2016); Sri Lanka (Arunatilake and others, 2016); Tanzania (Younger, Myamba, and Mdadila, 2016b); Tunisia (Jouini and others, 2015); Uganda (Jellema and others, 2016); Uruguay (Bucheli and others, 2014b); and Venezuela (Molina, 2016).

Notes: The year for which the analysis was conducted is in parenthesis. Data shown here is administrative data as reported by the studies cited; the numbers do not necessarily coincide with those found in databases from multilateral organizations (e.g., World Bank's World Development Indicators [WDI]). The scenario for South Africa assumed free basic services are direct transfers. For Tanzania, fiscal year runs from July 2011 to June 2012. Figure for OECD average (includes only advanced countries) was directly provided by the statistical office of the organization. Other social spending includes expenditures on housing and community amenities; environmental protection; and recreation, culture, and religion. The only contributory pensions in South Africa are for public servants who must belong to the Government Employee Pension Fund (GEPF). The government made no transfers to the GEPF in 2010/11. The only contributory pensions in Sri Lanka are for public servants, and income from pensions has been considered as part of the public employees' labor contract, rather than a transfer in spite of the fact that the funding comes from general revenues. Gross National Income per capita on right axis is in 2011 PPP from World Development Indicators, August 29, 2016, http://data.worldbank.org/indicator/NY.GNP.PCAP.PP.CD.

direct transfers. Regarding spending on contributory pensions (which includes contributory pensions only and not social or noncontributory pensions, which are part of direct transfers), the twenty-nine low-income and middle-income countries spend 3.2 percent of their GDP, while OECD countries, spend 7.9 percent.

Given the size of social spending (excluding contributory pensions), Argentina, South Africa, and Brazil (from highest to lowest) show the largest amount of resources at their disposal to engage in fiscal redistribution. At the other end of the spectrum are Uganda, Indonesia, Sri Lanka, and Guatemala (from lowest to highest). Whether the first group achieves its higher redistributive potential, however, depends on how the burden of taxation and the benefits of social spending are distributed. This shall be discussed below.

2 Fiscal Policy and Inequality

Recall that in order to measure the redistributive effect, each *CEQ Assessment* constructs four income concepts: Market Income or Market Income plus Pensions (depending on the treatment of contributory pensions), Disposable Income, Consumable Income, and Final Income. To refresh the reader's memory, we replicate the figure presented in chapter 1 in Volume 1 of this Handbook as 10-3.

A typical indicator of the redistributive effect of fiscal policy is the difference between the Market Income Gini and the Gini for income after taxes and transfers, where "after" can refer to just direct taxes and transfers as in Disposable Income, to the latter plus the effect of net indirect taxes as in Consumable Income, and to the latter plus the effect of education and health spending as in Final Income.[18] If the redistributive effect is positive (negative), fiscal policy is equalizing (unequalizing). Figure 10-4 presents the Gini coefficient for Market Income and the other three income concepts shown in figure 10-3: Disposable, Consumable and Final Income.[19] In broad terms, Disposable Income measures how much income individuals may spend on goods and services (and save, including mandatory savings such as contributions to a public pensions system that is actuarially fair). Consumable Income measures how much individuals are able to actually consume. For example, a given level of Disposable Income—even if consumed in full—could mean different levels of actual consumption depending on the size of indirect taxes and subsidies. Final Income includes the value of public services in education and health if individuals would have had to pay for those services at the average cost to the government. Based on the fact that contributory pensions can be treated as de-

---

[18] All the theoretical derivations that link changes in inequality to the progressivity of fiscal interventions have been derived based on the so-called family of S-Gini indicators, of which the Gini coefficient is one case. See, for example, Duclos and Araar (2006). While one can calculate the impact of fiscal policy on inequality using other indicators (and one should), it will not be possible to link them to the progressivity of the interventions.

[19] Other measures of inequality such as the Theil index or the 90/10 ratio are available in the individual studies. Requests should be addressed directly to the authors.

FIGURE 10-3
Basic Income Concepts

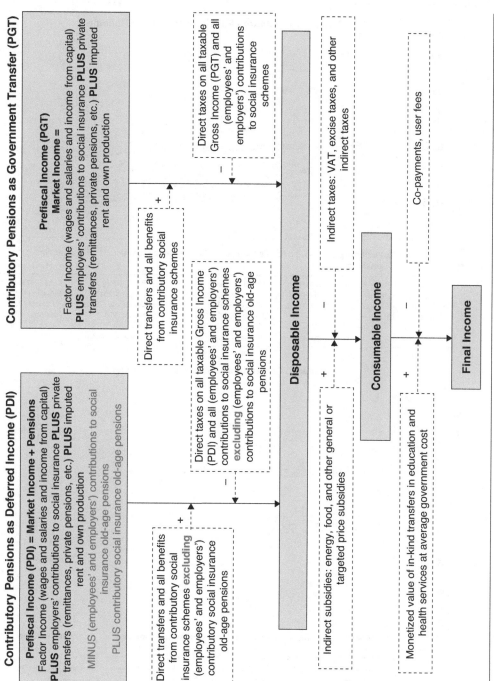

FIGURE 10-4

Fiscal Policy and Inequality (circa 2010): Gini Coefficient for Market, Disposable, Consumable, and Final Income

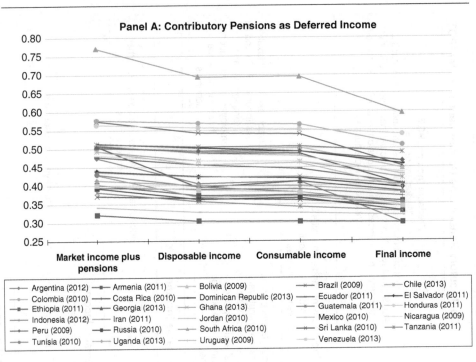

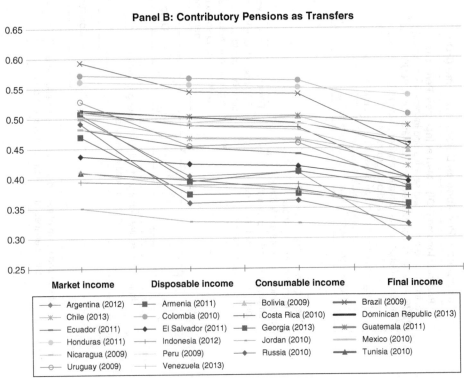

ferred income or as a direct transfer, here all the calculations are presented for two scenarios: one with contributory pensions included in Market Income and another with them as government transfers. For consistency, remember that in the first scenario contributions to the system are treated as mandatory savings and in the second as a tax.

If figure 10-4 proves difficult to read, actual numbers can be downloaded from the CEQ Data Center. As can be observed, in Ethiopia, Jordan, Guatemala, and Indonesia, fiscal income redistribution is quite limited, while in Argentina, Georgia, South Africa, and Brazil, it is of a relevant magnitude. One can observe that Argentina and South Africa are the countries that redistribute the most; South Africa, however, remains the most unequal even after redistribution. It is interesting to note that although Brazil and Colombia start out with similar Market Income inequality, Brazil reduces inequality considerably, while Colombia does not. Similarly, Mexico, Costa Rica, and Guatemala start out with similar levels of Market Income inequality, but Mexico and

Source: CEQ Data Center on Fiscal Redistribution. Based on the following *Master Workbooks of Results.* Argentina (Rossignolo, 2017); Armenia (Younger and Khachatryan, 2014); Bolivia (Paz Arauco and others, 2014b); Brazil (Higgins and Pereira, 2017); Chile (Martinez-Aguilar and Ortiz-Juarez, 2016); Colombia (Melendez and Martinez, 2015); Costa Rica (Sauma and Trejos, 2014b); Dominican Republic (Aristy-Escuder and others, 2016); Ecuador (Llerena and others, 2017); El Salvador (Beneke de Sanfeliu, Lustig, and Oliva Cepeda, 2014); Ethiopia (Hill, Tsehaye, and Woldehanna, 2014); Georgia (Cancho and Bondarenko, 2015); Ghana (Younger, Osei-Assibey, and Oppong, 2016); Guatemala (Cabrera and Moran, 2015a); Honduras (Castaneda and Espino, 2015); Indonesia (Afkar, Jellema, and Wai-Poi, 2015); Iran (Enami, Lustig, and Taqdiri, 2017b); Jordan (Abdel-Halim and others, 2016); Mexico (Scott, 2013); Nicaragua (Cabrera and Moran, 2015b); Peru (Jaramillo, 2015); Russia (Malytsin and Popova, 2016); South Africa (Inchauste and others, 2016); Sri Lanka (Arunatilake and others, 2016); Tanzania (Younger, Myamba, and Mdadila, 2016b); Tunisia (Jouini and others, 2015); Uganda (Jellema and others, 2016); Uruguay (Bucheli and others, 2014b); and Venezuela (Molina, 2016).

Notes: In Ethiopia, Ghana, Indonesia, Jordan, Sri Lanka, Tanzania, Tunisia, and Uganda, consumption expenditure is the primary income measure, and all other income concepts including Market Income are derived assuming that consumption expenditure is equal to Disposable Income. For Argentina, Ethiopia, Ghana, Indonesia, Jordan, Russia, South Africa and Tanzania, the study includes indirect effects of indirect taxes and subsidies. Bolivia does not have personal income taxes. In Bolivia, Costa Rica, Ecuador, Honduras, South Africa, and Sri Lanka, Market Income does not include consumption of own production because the data was either not available or not reliable. For Brazil, the results for the analysis presented here differ from the results published in Higgins and Pereira (2014) because the latter include taxes on services (ISS), on goods and services to finance pensions (CONFINS), and to finance social workers (PIS), while the results presented here do not include them. Post-publishing the mentioned paper, the authors concluded that the source for these taxes was not reliable. Gini coefficients for Chile are estimated here using total income and thus differ from official figures of inequality, which are estimated using monetary income (i.e., official figures exclude owner's occupied imputed rent). In South Africa, the results presented here assume that free basic services are a direct transfer. In Armenia, Costa Rica, Iran, Peru, South Africa, Uruguay, and Venezuela, there are no indirect subsidies. Poverty headcount ratios and inequality rates for Uganda were estimated using adult equivalent income. For the rest of the countries, the indicators were estimated using per capita income. For the Dominican Republic, the study analyzes the effects of fiscal policy in 2013, but the household income and expenditure survey dates back to 2006–07. For Indonesia, the fiscal incidence analysis was carried out adjusting for spatial price differences. Personal income taxes are assumed to be zero because the vast majority of households have implied Market Incomes below the tax threshold. The only contributory pensions in South Africa are for public servants who must belong to the Government Employees Pension Fund (GEPF). Since the government made no transfers to the GEPF in 2010/11, there is no scenario with contributory pensions as transfer. The only contributory pensions in Sri Lanka are for public servants, and income from pensions has been considered as part of the public employees' labor contract, rather than a transfer in spite of the fact that the funding comes from general revenues. For Ethiopia, Ghana, Iran, South Africa, Sri Lanka, Tanzania, and Uganda, there is no scenario in which contributory pensions are considered as a transfer. Georgia has a noncontributory public pension scheme only, and therefore they are treated only as a transfer. In all these cases, the scenario is the same in both panels. The scenario for pensions as deferred income for Iran defines Market Income as proposed in Volume 1 of this Handbook while all the other studies define Market Income as proposed in the *CEQ Handbook* (2013). The results for Iran's pensions as deferred income scenario used the new definition of prefiscal income: factor income plus old-age contributory pensions MINUS contributions to old-age pensions. In the rest of the countries, the latter had not been subtracted. For Ethiopia, while the distributional results presented here incorporate the indirect effects of indirect taxes and subsidies, the results in the World Bank Poverty Assessment and chapter by Hill and others. (2017) include the direct effects only. For South Africa, the Gini coefficient for Final Income differs from the chapter by Inchauste and others (2017).

Costa Rica reduce inequality by more. Ethiopia is the less unequal of all twenty-nine countries, and fiscal redistribution is also the smallest in order of magnitude. In almost all cases, the largest change in inequality occurs between Consumable and Final Income. This is not surprising given the fact that governments spend more on education and health than on direct transfers and pensions. However, one should not make sweeping conclusions from this result because—as explained in chapter 1 and chapter 6 in this Volume of the Handbook—in-kind transfers are valued at average government cost, which is not really a measure of the "true" value of these services to the individuals who use them.

As indicated in chapter 1 in this Volume, contributory pensions are in many cases a combination of deferred income and government transfer. Given that at present the CEQ methodology does not include a way to estimate which portion of a contributory pension is deferred income and which is a government transfer (or a tax, if the individual receives less than what he or she should have received given his or her contributions), the *CEQ Assessments* produce results for both "extreme" assumptions: contributory pensions as pure deferred income (in which contributions are a form of mandatory savings) and as pure government transfer (in which contributions are treated as any other direct tax). Panels A and B in figure 10-4 show that the patterns of inequality decline are similar whether one looks at the scenario in which contributory pensions are considered deferred income (and, thus, part of Market Income) or with pensions as transfers. In Argentina, Armenia, Brazil, Russia, and Uruguay, the redistributive effect is considerably larger when contributory pensions are treated as a transfer. These are countries with higher coverage and an older population. In Chile, Costa Rica, Ecuador, Jordan, and Venezuela, the effect is larger, but only very slightly. Interestingly, in Bolivia, Colombia, El Salvador, Honduras, Mexico, Nicaragua, and Tunisia, the redistributive effect is smaller when contributory pensions are considered a government transfer versus deferred income.

3   Measuring the Marginal Contribution of Taxes and Transfers

As discussed in chapter 1 in this Volume, the CEQ methodology measures the impact of a tax or a transfer by relying on the marginal contribution, which, as formally discussed in chapter 2 in this Volume. is equal to the difference between the Gini (or other inequality measures) for a postfiscal income concept *without* the fiscal intervention of interest (for example, a particular tax) and the postfiscal income which includes it. Figure 10-5 shows the marginal contribution on net direct taxes (direct taxes net of direct transfers), net indirect taxes (indirect taxes net of subsidies), and spending on education and health. (Existing fiscal redistribution studies frequently stop at direct taxes and direct transfers.[20]) Note that an equalizing (unequalizing) effect is presented

---

[20] For example, the data published by the EUROMOD project at the University of Essex presents results up to disposable income for the European Union (https://www.euromod.ac.uk/).

FIGURE 10-5
Marginal Contribution of Taxes and Transfers (circa 2010)

Panel A: Marginal Contributions of Net Direct Taxes
(contributory pensions as deferred income)

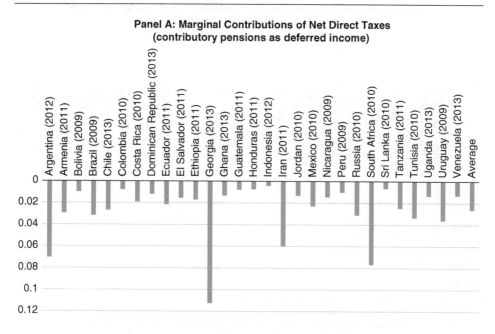

Panel B: Marginal Contributions of Net Indirect Taxes
(contributory pensions as deferred income)

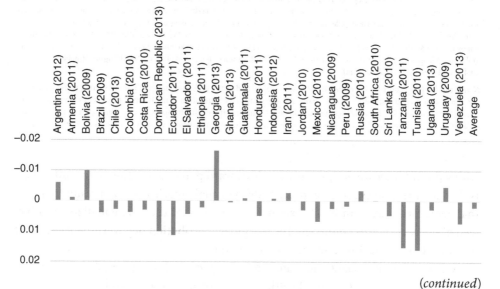

(continued)

FIGURE 10-5   (continued)

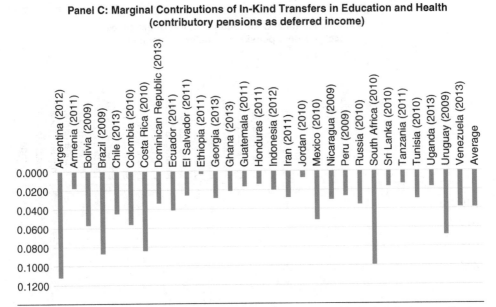

Panel C: Marginal Contributions of In-Kind Transfers in Education and Health (contributory pensions as deferred income)

Source: CEQ Data Center on Fiscal Redistribution. Based on the following *Master Workbooks of Results*. Argentina (Rossignolo, 2017); Armenia (Younger and Khachatryan, 2014); Bolivia (Paz Arauco and others, 2014b); Brazil (Higgins and Pereira, 2017); Chile (Martinez-Aguilar and Ortiz-Juarez, 2016); Colombia (Melendez and Martinez, 2015); Costa Rica (Sauma and Trejos, 2014b); Dominican Republic (Aristy-Escuder and others, 2016); Ecuador (Llerena and others, 2017); El Salvador (Beneke de Sanfeliu, Lustig, and Oliva Cepeda, 2014); Ethiopia (Hill, Tsehaye, and Woldehanna, 2014); Georgia (Cancho and Bondarenko, 2015); Ghana (Younger, Osei-Assibey, and Oppong, 2016); Guatemala (Cabrera and Moran, 2015a); Honduras (Castaneda and Espino, 2015); Indonesia (Afkar, Jellema, and Wai-Poi, 2015); Iran (Enami, Lustig, and Taqdiri, 2017b); Jordan (Abdel-Halim and others, 2016); Mexico (Scott, 2013); Nicaragua (Cabrera and Moran, 2015b); Peru (Jaramillo, 2015); Russia (Malytsin and Popova, 2016); South Africa (Inchauste and others, 2016); Sri Lanka (Arunatilake and others, 2016); Tanzania (Younger, Myamba, and Mdadila, 2016b); Tunisia (Jouini and others, 2015); Uganda (Jellema and others, 2016); Uruguay (Bucheli and others, 2014b); and Venezuela (Molina, 2016).

Notes: The marginal contribution of net direct taxes is calculated as the difference between Gini of market income plus contributory pensions and disposable income (panel A). The marginal contribution of net indirect taxes is calculated as the difference between Gini of disposable income and consumable income (panel B). The marginal contribution of in-kind transfers is calculated as the difference between Gini of consumable income and final income (panel C). Also, see notes to figure 10-4.

with a positive (negative) sign but with downward point bars.[21] The first result to note is that net direct taxes are, as expected, always equalizing. The second result to note is that net indirect taxes (indirect taxes net of indirect subsidies) are equalizing in nineteen of the twenty-nine countries. The marginal contribution of government spending on education and health combined is always equalizing.

Country specific results indicate that, as expected, direct taxes, direct transfers, and spending on education and health are equalizing. However, contrary to expecta-

---

[21] Note that for the reasons mentioned in chapter 2 in this Volume, one cannot strictly compare the orders of magnitude between marginal contributions calculated based on the redistributive effect for different categories of income.

tions, indirect taxes, indirect subsidies, and spending on tertiary education are more frequently equalizing than unequalizing. Results also show the presence of Lambert's conundrum (see chapter 1 and chapter 2 in this Volume) in the case of Chile, where the VAT is regressive—the Kakwani coefficients is negative—and yet its marginal contribution is equalizing.[22]

4 Is There Evidence of a Robin Hood Paradox?

One of the most important findings in Lindert's[23] pathbreaking work is that both across countries and over time, resources devoted to the poor are lower in the nations in which poverty and inequality are greater.[24] According to Lindert,

> History reveals a "Robin Hood paradox," in which redistribution from rich to poor is least present when and where it seems most needed. Poverty policy within any one polity or jurisdiction is supposed to aid the poor more, . . . the greater the income inequality. Yet over time and space, the pattern is usually the opposite. While there are exceptions to this general tendency, the underlying tendency itself is unmistakable, both across the globe and across the past three centuries.[25]

An examination of the relationship between prefiscal inequality and social spending suggests that there is no evidence of a "Robin Hood paradox": as it is shown in figure 10-6, the more unequal countries devote more resources to tax-based redistribution measured by the size of social spending as a share of GDP (even if we leave out "outliers," this result holds).

Second, as shown in figure 10-7, redistribution from rich to poor is greater in countries where Market Income inequality is higher—a result that seems consistent with the prediction of the Meltzer and Richard median-voter hypothesis.[26]

Could the above results be driven because more unequal countries tend to be richer and therefore have higher capacity to raise revenues and afford higher levels of spending? Preliminary results from regressing the redistributive effect (measured as change in the Gini coefficient from Market to Final Income in Gini points) on GNI per capita and the Market Income Gini show that the coefficient for the latter is positive: that is, the more unequal, the more redistribution. The coefficient for GNI per capita is

---

[22] These results are available upon request. For a description of Lambert's conundrum, see chapter 1 in this Volume.

[23] Lindert (2004).

[24] Lindert (2004).

[25] Lindert (2004, p. 15).

[26] Meltzer and Richards (1981). An OECD (2011) study illustrates that more Market Income inequality tends to be associated with higher redistribution, for a subset of OECD countries, both within countries (over time) and across countries.

FIGURE 10-6

Initial Inequality and Social Spending, circa 2010 (social spending/GDP and Market Income plus Pensions inequality [contributory pensions as deferred income])

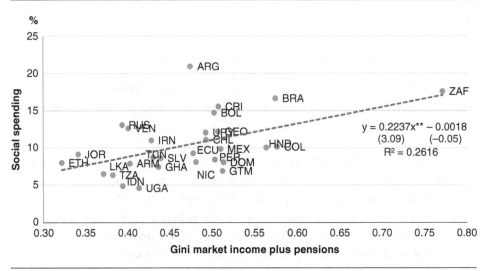

$y = 0.2237x** - 0.0018$
(3.09)   (-0.05)
$R^2 = 0.2616$

Source: Author's estimates. CEQ Data Center on Fiscal Redistribution. Based on the following *Master Workbooks of Results*: Argentina (Rossignolo, 2017); Armenia (Younger and Khachatryan, 2014); Bolivia (Paz Arauco and others, 2014b); Brazil (Higgins and Pereira, 2017); Chile (Martinez-Aguilar and Ortiz-Juarez, 2016); Colombia (Melendez and Martinez, 2015); Costa Rica (Sauma and Trejos, 2014b); Dominican Republic (Aristy-Escuder and others, 2016); Ecuador (Llerena and others, 2017); El Salvador (Beneke de Sanfeliu, Lustig, and Oliva Cepeda, 2014); Ethiopia (Hill, Tsehaye, and Woldehanna, 2014); Georgia (Cancho and Bondarenko, 2015); Ghana (Younger, Osei-Assibey, and Oppong, 2016); Guatemala (Cabrera and Moran, 2015a); Honduras (Castaneda and Espino, 2015); Indonesia (Afkar, Jellema, and Wai-Poi, 2015); Iran (Enami, Lustig, and Taqdiri, 2017b); Jordan (Abdel-Halim and others, 2016); Mexico (Scott, 2013); Nicaragua (Cabrera and Moran, 2015b); Peru (Jaramillo, 2015); Russia (Malytsin and Popova, 2016); South Africa (Inchauste and others, 2016); Sri Lanka (Arunatilake and others, 2016); Tanzania (Younger, Myamba, and Mdadila, 2016b); Tunisia (Jouini and others, 2015); Uganda (Jellema and others, 2016); Uruguay (Bucheli and others, 2014b); and Venezuela (Molina, 2016).

Notes: The dotted line in red is the slope obtained from a simple regression with social spending/GDP as a dependent variable. Social spending includes direct transfers, spending on education and health, and other social spending. In parentheses are t statistics. * p < 0.1, ** p < 0.05, ***p < 0.01. Also, see notes to figure 10-4.

significant, but small. The coefficient for Market Income inequality, however, is not statistically significant when the redistributive effect is measured from Market to Disposable Income only, or when the redistributive effect is measured in percent (instead of Gini points). In a few cases, the coefficient for the Market Income Gini is even negative but not significant.[27]

Differences in redistribution change the ranking of countries by inequality level. Panel A of figure 10-8 displays the levels of income inequality before (horizontal axis) and after (vertical axis) accounting for fiscal policies. Since all data points fall below the diagonal, fiscal policies reduce inequality in all countries. South Africa continues to be the most unequal country and Ethiopia the least unequal country based on income (for

---

[27] Results are available upon request.

FIGURE 10-7

Initial Inequality and Fiscal Redistribution, circa 2010 (redistributive effect and Market Income plus Pensions inequality [contributory pensions as deferred income])

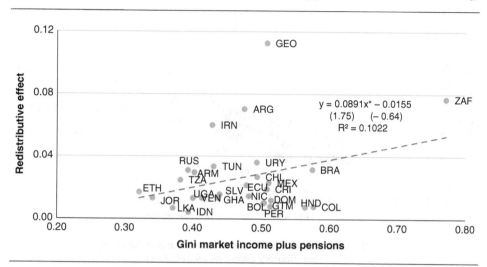

Source: Author's estimates. CEQ Data Center on Fiscal Redistribution. Based on the following *Master Workbooks of Results*: Argentina (Rossignolo, 2017); Armenia (Younger and Khachatryan, 2014); Bolivia (Paz Arauco and others, 2014b); Brazil (Higgins and Pereira, 2017); Chile (Martinez-Aguilar and Ortiz-Juarez, 2016); Colombia (Melendez and Martinez, 2015); Costa Rica (Sauma and Trejos, 2014b); Dominican Republic (Aristy-Escuder and others, 2016); Ecuador (Llerena and others, 2017); El Salvador (Beneke de Sanfeliu, Lustig, and Oliva Cepeda, 2014); Ethiopia (Hill, Tsehaye, and Woldehanna, 2014); Georgia (Cancho and Bondarenko, 2015); Ghana (Younger, Osei-Assibey, and Oppong, 2016); Guatemala (Cabrera and Moran, 2015a); Honduras (Castaneda and Espino, 2015); Indonesia (Afkar, Jellema, and Wai-Poi, 2015); Iran (Enami, Lustig, and Taqdiri, 2017b); Jordan (Abdel-Halim and others, 2016); Mexico (Scott, 2013); Nicaragua (Cabrera and Moran, 2015b); Peru (Jaramillo, 2015); Russia (Malytsin and Popova, 2016); South Africa (Inchauste and others, 2016); Sri Lanka (Arunatilake and others, 2016); Tanzania (Younger, Myamba, and Mdadila, 2016b); Tunisia (Jouini and others, 2015); Uganda (Jellema and others, 2016); Uruguay (Bucheli and others, 2014b); and Venezuela (Molina, 2016).

Notes: The dotted line in red is the slope obtained from a simple regression with the redistributive effect as a dependent variable. Redistributive effect is defined as the difference between Gini of Market Income plus Pensions and Disposable Income. In parentheses are t statistics. * $p < 0.1$, ** $p < 0.05$, ***$p < 0.01$. Also, see notes to figure 10-4.

Ethiopia, consumption) before or after fiscal policy. However, due to lower redistribution, Peru ends up being more unequal than Brazil once fiscal policies are considered while the opposite is true when inequality is measured with Market Income.

5 Redistributive Effect: A Comparison with Advanced Countries

How do these twenty-nine countries compare with the fiscal redistribution that occurs in advanced countries? Although the methodology is somewhat different, one obvious comparator is the analysis produced by EUROMOD for the twenty-eight countries in the European Union.[28] Given that EUROMOD covers only direct taxes, contributions to social security, and direct transfers, the comparison can be done for the

---

[28] The data for the EU-28 is from EUROMOD (2017).

FIGURE 10-8
Market Income plus Contributory Pensions Gini versus Final Income Gini, circa 2010

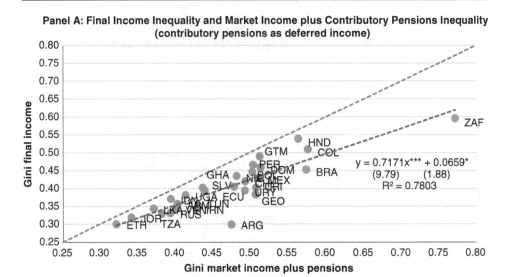

Panel A: Final Income Inequality and Market Income plus Contributory Pensions Inequality (contributory pensions as deferred income)

$y = 0.7171x^{***} + 0.0659^*$
(9.79)   (1.88)
$R^2 = 0.7803$

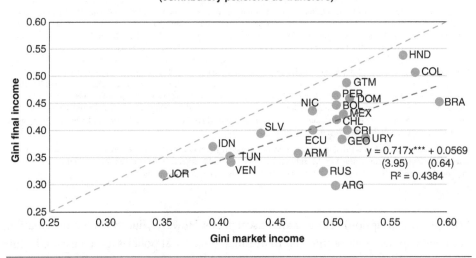

B: Final Income Inequality and Market Income Inequality (contributory pensions as transfers)

$y = 0.717x^{***} + 0.0569$
(3.95)   (0.64)
$R^2 = 0.4384$

Source: Author's estimates. CEQ Data Center on Fiscal Redistribution. Based on the following *Master Workbooks of Results*: Argentina (Rossignolo, 2017); Armenia (Younger and Khachatryan, 2014); Bolivia (Paz Arauco and others, 2014b); Brazil (Higgins and Pereira, 2017); Chile (Martinez-Aguilar and Ortiz-Juarez, 2016); Colombia (Melendez and Martinez, 2015); Costa Rica (Sauma and Trejos, 2014b); Dominican Republic (Aristy-Escuder and others, 2016); Ecuador (Llerena and others, 2017); El Salvador (Beneke de Sanfeliu, Lustig, and Oliva Cepeda, 2014); Ethiopia (Hill, Tsehaye, and Woldehanna, 2014); Georgia (Cancho and Bondarenko, 2015); Ghana (Younger, Osei-Assibey, and Oppong, 2016); Guatemala (Cabrera and Moran, 2015a); Honduras (Castaneda and Espino, 2015); Indonesia (Afkar, Jellema, and Wai-Poi, 2015); Iran (Enami, Lustig, and Taqdiri, 2017b); Jordan (Abdel-Halim and others, 2016); Mexico (Scott, 2013); Nicaragua (Cabrera and Moran, 2015b); Peru (Jaramillo, 2015); Russia (Malytsin and Popova, 2016); South Africa (Inchauste and others, 2016); Sri Lanka (Arunatilake and others, 2016); Tanzania (Younger, Myamba, and Mdadila, 2016b); Tunisia (Jouini and others, 2015); Uganda (Jellema and others, 2016); Uruguay (Bucheli and others, 2014b); and Venezuela (Molina, 2016).

Notes: The dotted line in red is the slope obtained from a simple regression with the final income Gini as a dependent variable. The dotted line in blue is a 45-degree line. In parentheses are t statistics. * $p < 0.1$, ** $p < 0.05$, *** $p < 0.01$. The number of countries in panel B is smaller because it does not include the countries for which—for different reasons—there is no additional scenario in which contributory pensions were considered a transfer: namely, Ethiopia, Ghana, Iran, South Africa, Sri Lanka, Tanzania, and Uganda. Also, see notes to figure 10-4.

redistributive effect from Market (and Market Income plus Pensions) to Disposable Income. A comparison is also made with the United States.[29]

There are three important differences between the advanced countries and the twenty-nine analyzed here. First, Market Income inequality tends to be somewhat higher for the twenty-nine countries.[30] However, the difference is most striking when pensions are treated as transfers. The average prefiscal Gini coefficient for the twenty-nine countries for the scenario in which pensions are treated as deferred income and the scenario in which they are considered transfers is 47.0 and 48.8 percent, respectively. In contrast, in the European Union, the corresponding figures are 35.6 and 46.3 percent, respectively; and in the United States, they are 44.8 and 48.4, respectively. One important aspect to note, however, is that in the European Union, pensions include both contributory and noncontributory social pensions while in the twenty-nine countries and the United States, the category of pensions includes only contributory pensions. Thus, the prefiscal income in the European Union when pensions are treated as deferred income is likely to be more equally distributed (than in the United States, for example) because the prefiscal income includes social pensions as well as contributory ones.

Second, as expected and shown in figure 10-9, the redistributive effect is larger in the E.U. countries and, to a lesser extent, in the United States if pensions are considered a government transfer. Except for Argentina, Armenia, Brazil, Russia, and Uruguay—countries with large contributory pension systems—in the rest of the low- and middle-income countries, whether pensions are treated as deferred income or a transfer makes a relatively small difference. This is not the case in the E.U. countries where the difference is huge. In the European Union, the redistributive effect with contributory pensions as deferred income and contributory pensions as a transfer is 7.7 and 19.0 Gini points, respectively. In the United States, the numbers are less dramatically different: 7.2 and 11.2, respectively. In the twenty-nine countries, the numbers are 2.6 and 3.7 Gini points, respectively. Clearly, the assumption made about how to treat incomes from pensions, again, can make a big difference. The results for the scenario with pensions as transfers for the European Union and the United States are influenced by what in chapter 1 in this Volume we called the presence of "false poor": that is, many households composed of retirees appear, by definition, with zero or near zero Market Income. However, as discussed in chapter 1 in this Volume, strictly speaking the counterfactual income should not be zero but what these households would have been able to spend during retirement based on the history of their contributions and market returns.

While in low- and middle-income countries pensions can be equalizing at some times and unequalizing at other times, in no European country nor in the United States are contributory pensions unequalizing. On the contrary, vis-à-vis *Market Income without pensions*, they exert a large equalizing force in the European Union and

---

[29] Higgins and others (2016).

[30] South Africa pulls the average up, but Indonesia pulls it down.

FIGURE 10-9
Redistributive Effect: Comparing Developing and Advanced Countries (change in Gini points; circa 2010)

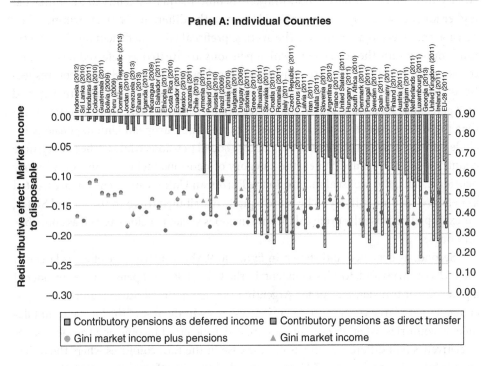

Panel A: Individual Countries

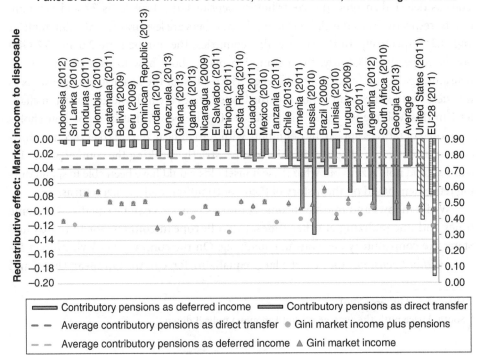

Panel B: Low- and Middle-Income Countries, the United States, and Average for EU-28

Source: CEQ Data Center on Fiscal Redistribution. Based on the following *Master Workbooks of Results*: Argentina (Rossignolo, 2017); Armenia (Younger and Khachatryan, 2014); Bolivia (Paz Arauco and others, 2014b); Brazil (Higgins and Pereira, 2017); Chile (Martinez-Aguilar and Ortiz-Juarez, 2016); Colombia (Melendez and Martinez, 2015); Costa Rica (Sauma and Trejos, 2014b); Dominican Republic (Aristy-Escuder and others, 2016); Ecuador (Llerena and others, 2017); El Salvador (Beneke de Sanfeliu, Lustig, and Oliva Cepeda, 2014); Ethiopia (Hill, Tsehaye, and Woldehanna, 2014); European Union (EUROMOD version no. G3.0); Georgia (Cancho and Bondarenko, 2015); Ghana (Younger, Osei-Assibey, and Oppong, 2016); Guatemala (Cabrera and Moran, 2015a); Honduras (Castaneda and Espino, 2015); Indonesia (Afkar, Jellema, and Wai-Poi, 2015); Iran (Enami, Lustig, and Taqdiri, 2017b); Jordan (Abdel-Halim and others, 2016); Mexico (Scott, 2013); Nicaragua (Cabrera and Moran, 2015b); Peru (Jaramillo, 2015); Russia (Malytsin and Popova, 2016); South Africa (Inchauste and others, 2016); Sri Lanka (Arunatilake and others, 2016); Tanzania (Younger, Myamba, and Mdadila, 2016b); Tunisia (Jouini and others, 2015); Uganda (Jellema and others, 2016); United States (Higgins and others, 2016); Uruguay (Bucheli and others, 2014b); and Venezuela (Molina, 2016).

Notes: The year for which the analysis was conducted is in parenthesis. For definition of income concepts see chapter 1 and chapter 6 in this Volume of the Handbook. Redistributive effect is defined as the difference between Gini of Market Income plus Pensions and Disposable Income with contributory pensions treated as deferred income and the difference between Gini of market income and disposable income with contributory pensions treated as transfers. The graph is ranked from the smallest to the largest by redistributive effect with contributory pensions treated as deferred income. The number of countries in the scenario in which contributory pensions are treated as a transfer is smaller because it does not include the countries for which—for different reasons—there is no additional scenario in which contributory pensions were considered a transfer: namely, Ethiopia, Ghana, Iran, South Africa, Sri Lanka, Tanzania, and Uganda. Also, see notes to figure 10-4.

less so in the United States. Using data for 2011, for example, the difference between the Market Income Gini and the Market Income Gini plus contributory pensions is 10.7 percentage points in the European Union and 3.6 in the United States.

How does social spending in today's developing countries compare with that of today's advanced countries but when their income per capita was similar to that of the former (that is, when today's rich countries were as poor as today's developing countries)? Around 2010, El Salvador was among the countries that spent the least on education: 2.9 percent of GDP. According to Angus Maddison's estimates, in 1990 international dollars, El Salvador's GDP per capita in 2008 was similar to that of the United States in 1880, and Guatemala's and Peru's were similar to the United States' around 1900. The United States, a pioneer in public education, devoted only 0.74 percent of GDP in 1880 and 1.24 percent in 1900, according to Lindert.[31] That is, the lowest spenders on public education of the twenty-nine countries in this chapter spent more than twice the amount spent by the United States when it was approximately equally poor. Sweden was as rich as today's El Salvador around 1910, at which time Sweden spent 1.26 percent of GDP on public education, or about half as much as El Salvador in 2010. Around 2010, Indonesia showed among the lowest spending on health: 0.9 percent of GDP; the figure for Ethiopia was 1.25 percent and for Brazil above 5 percent. When the United States (around 1900) was as rich as Indonesia in the early twenty-first century (2008), it spent about 0.17 percent of GDP in government subsidies for healthcare.[32] When the United States was as rich as Brazil was in 2008, it spent only 0.4 percent of GDP in health subsidies.[33]

---

[31] Appendix C in Lindert (2004).

[32] Table 1D in Lindert (1994).

[33] The United States in about 1925 was as rich as Brazil in 2008. The health spending figure corresponds to 1920 (Lindert, 1994).

6 Fiscal Policy and the Poor

The above discussion has concentrated on the impact of fiscal policy on inequality. As important is the impact of fiscal policy on poverty, particularly because the results do not necessarily go in the same direction: in other words, an inequality-reducing fiscal system could be poverty-increasing. The effect of fiscal policy on poverty can be measured using the typical indicators such as the headcount ratio for Market Income and income after taxes and transfers. Another measure that one can use to assess the impact of fiscal policy on the poor is the extent to which Market Income poor end up being net payers to the fiscal system in cash terms (leaving out in-kind services). A third measure is that of fiscal impoverishment,[34] or the extent to which fiscal policy makes the poor (non-poor) poorer (poor).

When analyzing the impact of fiscal interventions on poverty, it is useful to distinguish between the net benefits in cash from the benefits received in the form of free government services in education and health. The cash component of fiscal policy impact is measured by comparing the indicators for Consumable Income with the same indicators using Market Income. The level of Consumable Income will tell whether the government has enabled an individual to be able to purchase private goods and services above his or her original Market Income. As shown in figure 10-10 (panel A), using the $1.25 (PPP 2005 per day) poverty line,[35] fiscal policy reduces the headcount ratio for Consumable Income in most countries. However, there is a startling result. In the scenario in which pensions are considered deferred income, the Consumable Income headcount ratio for Ethiopia, Ghana, Guatemala, Nicaragua, Uganda, and Tanzania is *higher* than the headcount ratio for Market Income. This is a worrisome result. Poverty should not be higher as a result of fiscal policy. Note that this result occurs despite the fact that the net fiscal system (even without including in-kind transfers) reduces inequality. This emphasizes the fact that the impact of fiscal interventions on inequality and poverty should be studied separately, as indicated in chapter 1 in this Volume. Of course, at the higher $2.50 a day poverty line, the number of countries in which the headcount for Consumable Income is higher than that for Market Income rises.[36]

In principle, it would be desirable for the poor—especially the extreme poor—to be net receivers of fiscal resources in cash so that poor individuals can buy/consume the minimum amounts of food and other essential goods embedded in the selected poverty line. Figure 10-11 shows at which Market Income category, individuals—on average—

---

[34] Higgins and Lustig (2016) (reproduced in chapter 4 of this Volume).

[35] The $1.25 is the World Bank global extreme poverty line until 2015, when it was updated with the 2011 PPP to $1.90 per day. The $2.50 a day poverty line is considered to be a reasonable international extreme poverty line for middle-income countries: for example, in the case of Latin America, this poverty line is close to the average of the local extreme poverty lines.

[36] Results for the scenario in which contributory pensions are treated as a pure government transfer are available upon request.

FIGURE 10-10

Fiscal Policy and Poverty Reduction (circa 2010): Change in Headcount Ratio from Market to Disposable and Consumable Income (in %)

Panel A: Contributory Pensions as Deferred Income
(ranked by poverty reduction in %; poverty line $1.25 2005 PPP/day)

	Disposable	Consumable
Average	−29.1	−35.0
Uruguay (2009)	−82.6	−97.0
Iran (2011)	−90.5	92.5
Argentina (2012)	−65.4	−78.7
Georgia (2013)	−54.2	−70.7
Chile (2013)	−66.2	−69.8
Jordan (2010)	−76.4	−69.6
South Africa (2010)	−42.7	−56.4
Brazil (2009)	−36.2	−50.6
Ecuador (2011)	−54.1	−46.0
Costa Rica (2010)	−22.7	−45.5
Russia (2010)	−37.8	−44.9
Tunisia (2010)	−53.8	−34.6
Mexico (2010)	−35.0	−33.9
El Salvador (2011)	−15.7	−31.8
Venezuela (2013)	−36.0	−29.0
Armenia (2011)	−7.5	−24.9
Colombia (2010)	−24.6	−18.5
Dominican Republic (2013)	−14.1	−18.0
Sri Lanka (2010)	−14.1	−16.5
Bolivia (2009)	−2.3	−16.1
Honduras (2011)	−8.8	−11.5
Indonesia (2012)	−12.7	−10.3
Guatemala (2011)	2.4	−8.3
Ethiopia (2011)	1.7	−3.3
Ghana (2013)	12.0	−1.8
Uganda (2013)	0.7	−1.3
Tanzania (2011)	17.8	−0.2
Nicaragua (2009)	2.6	1.7

■ Market income plus pensions to disposable income   ■ Market income plus pensions to consumable income

(continued)

FIGURE 10-10 (continued)

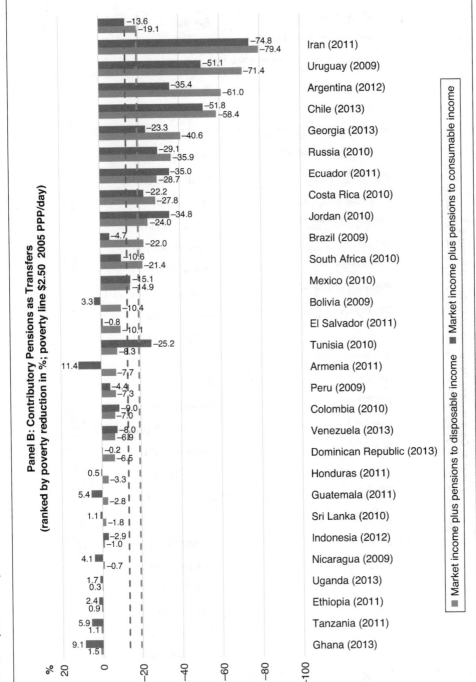

Panel B: Contributory Pensions as Transfers
(ranked by poverty reduction in %; poverty line $2.50 2005 PPP/day)

■ Market income plus pensions to disposable income
■ Market income plus pensions to consumable income

Source: CEQ Data Center on Fiscal Redistribution. Based on the following Master Workbooks of Results: Argentina (Rossignolo, 2017); Armenia (Younger and Khachatryan, 2014); Bolivia (Paz Arauco and others, 2014b); Brazil (Higgins and Pereira, 2017); Chile (Martinez-Aguilar and Ortiz-Juarez, 2016); Colombia (Melendez and Martinez, 2015); Costa Rica (Sauma and Trejos, 2014b); Dominican Republic (Aristy-Escuder and others, 2016); Ecuador (Llerena and others, 2017); El Salvador (Beneke de Sanfeliu, Lustig, and Oliva Cepeda, 2014); Ethiopia (Hill, Tsehaye, and Woldehanna, 2014); Georgia (Cancho and Bondarenko, 2015); Ghana (Younger, Osei-Assibey, and Oppong, 2016); Guatemala (Cabrera and Moran, 2015a); Honduras (Castaneda and Espino, 2015); Indonesia (Afkar, Jellema, and Wai-Poi, 2015); Iran (Enami, Lustig, and Taqdiri, 2017b); Jordan (Abdel-Halim and others, 2016); Mexico (Scott, 2013); Nicaragua (Cabrera and Moran, 2015b); Peru (Jaramillo, 2015); Russia (Malytsin and Popova, 2016); South Africa (Inchauste and others, 2016); Sri Lanka (Arunatilake and others, 2016); Tanzania (Younger, Myamba, and Mdadila, 2016); Tunisia (Jouini and others, 2015); Uganda (Jellema and others, 2016); Uruguay (Bucheli and others, 2014b); and Venezuela (Molina, 2016).

Notes: Percentage of poverty reduction is defined as percentage change in headcount ratio from Market Income (or Market Income plus Contributory Pensions) to Consumable Income. For South Africa, the poverty reduction is defined as percentage change in headcount ratio from Market Income plus Contributory Pensions) to Consumable Income. For South Africa, the poverty reduction is defined as percentage change in headcount ratio from Market Income plus Contributory Pensions) to Consumable Income. For South Africa, the poverty reduction is defined as percentage change in headcount ratio from Market Income plus Contributory Pensions) to Consumable Income. For South Africa, the poverty reduction is defined as percentage change in headcount ratio from Market Income plus Contributory Pensions) to Consumable Income. For South Africa, the poverty reduction is defined as percentage change in headcount ratio from Market Income plus Contributory Pensions) to Consumable Income. For South Africa, the poverty reduction is defined as percentage change in headcount ratio from Market Income plus Contributory Pensions) to Consumable Income. For South Africa, the poverty reduction is defined as percentage change in headcount ratio from Market Income plus Contributory Pensions) to Consumable Income.

FIGURE 10-11

Net Payers to the Fiscal System by Income Groups (contributory pensions as deferred income)

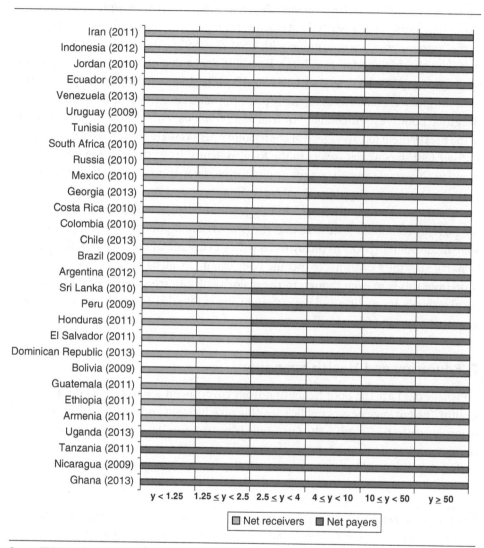

Source: CEQ Data Center on Fiscal Redistribution. Based on the following *Master Workbooks of Results:* Argentina (Rossignolo, 2017); Armenia (Younger and Khachatryan, 2014); Bolivia (Paz Arauco and others, 2014b); Brazil (Higgins and Pereira, 2017); Chile (Martinez-Aguilar and Ortiz-Juarez, 2016); Colombia (Melendez and Martinez, 2015); Costa Rica (Sauma and Trejos, 2014b); Dominican Republic (Aristy-Escuder and others, 2016); Ecuador (Llerena and others, 2017); El Salvador (Beneke de Sanfeliu, Lustig, and Oliva Cepeda, 2014); Ethiopia (Hill, Tsehaye, and Woldehanna, 2014); Georgia (Cancho and Bondarenko, 2015); Ghana (Younger, Osei-Assibey, and Oppong, 2016); Guatemala (Cabrera and Moran, 2015a); Honduras (Castaneda and Espino, 2015); Indonesia (Afkar, Jellema, and Wai-Poi, 2015); Iran (Enami, Lustig, and Taqdiri, 2017b); Jordan (Abdel-Halim and others, 2016); Mexico (Scott, 2013); Nicaragua (Cabrera and Moran, 2015b); Peru (Jaramillo, 2015); Russia (Malytsin and Popova, 2016); South Africa (Inchauste and others, 2016); Sri Lanka (Arunatilake and others, 2016); Tanzania (Younger, Myamba, and Mdadila, 2016b); Tunisia (Jouini and others, 2015); Uganda (Jellema and others, 2016); Uruguay (Bucheli and others, 2014b); and Venezuela (Molina, 2016).

Note: See notes to figure 10-4.

become net payers to the fiscal system (again, this calculation takes into account only the cash portion of the fiscal system and excludes in-kind transfers such as access to free public education and healthcare).[37] In Ghana, Nicaragua, Tanzania, and Uganda, net payers to the fiscal system begin in the "ultra-poor" income category with US$0–US$1.25/day in purchasing power parity. In Armenia, Ethiopia, and Guatemala, net payers begin in the "extreme poor" income group with US$1.25–US$2.50/day. In Bolivia, the Dominican Republic, El Salvador, Honduras, Peru, and Sri Lanka, net payers to the fiscal system begin in the income category US$2.50–US$4/day in purchasing power parity—that is, in the group classified as moderately poor. In twelve countries, the net payers start in the group known as "vulnerable." In Iran and Indonesia, only the "rich" are net payers to the fiscal system (on average).[38] If contributory pensions are considered a government transfer (not shown), net payers to the fiscal system start in the extreme poor income group in Guatemala and Nicaragua and in the moderately poor group in Armenia, Bolivia, the Dominican Republic, El Salvador, Honduras, and Peru.

Using the measures discussed in Higgins and Lustig (2016) (reproduced in chapter 4 of this Handbook), we find that the proportion of poor (non-poor) people who were made poorer (poor) of the by fiscal policy as a share of the total population and, in particular, the Consumable Income poor is not trivial, as table 10-1 demonstrates. Moreover, this is so even though in the majority of countries shown on the table, the fiscal system is inequality- and poverty-reducing as revealed by the change in the headcount ratio and the Gini coefficient.

7 Education and Health Spending[39]

To what extent are the poor benefiting from government spending on education and health? The pro-poorness of public spending on education and health here is measured using concentration coefficients (also called "quasi-Ginis").[40] In keeping with conventions, spending is defined as regressive whenever the concentration coefficient is higher than the Gini for Market Income. When this occurs, it means that the benefits

---

[37] Note that this graph presents a non-anonymous result: it looks at the extent to which the Market Income poor become net payers to the fiscal system on average. This information cannot be extrapolated from the typical poverty measures where winners and losers are not tracked.

[38] These income categories are based on Lopez-Calva and Ortiz-Juarez (2014) and Ferreira and others (2012).

[39] Section based on Lustig (2015).

[40] A concentration coefficient is calculated in a way analogous to the Gini coefficient. Let p be the cumulative proportion of the total population when individuals are ordered in increasing income values using Market Income, and let $C(p)$ be the concentration curve; the cumulative proportion of total program benefits (of a particular program or aggregate category) received by the poorest p percent of the population. Then, the concentration coefficient of that program or category is defined as $2\int_0^1 (p - C(p))dp$.

TABLE 10-1

Fiscal Impoverishment (circa 2010): Contributory Pensions as Deferred Income (in %)

Country (survey year)	Market Income plus Pensions poverty headcount (%)	Change in poverty headcount (p.p.)	Market Income plus Pensions inequality (Gini)	Reynolds-Smolensky	Change in inequality (◇Gini)	Fiscally impoverished as % of population	Fiscally impoverished as % of consumable income poor
Panel A: Upper-middle-income countries, using a poverty line of $2.50 2005 PPP per day							
Brazil (2009)	16.8	-0.8	57.5	4.6	-3.5	5.6	34.9
Chile (2013)	2.8	-1.4	49.4	3.2	-3.0	0.3	19.2
Ecuador (2011)	10.8	-3.8	47.8	3.5	-3.3	0.2	3.2
Mexico (2012)	13.3	-1.2	54.4	3.8	-2.5	4.0	32.7
Peru (2011)	13.8	-0.2	45.9	0.9	-0.8	3.2	23.8
Russia (2010)	4.3	-1.3	39.7	3.9	-2.6	1.1	34.4
South Africa (2010)	49.3	-5.2	77.1	8.3	-7.7	5.9	13.3
Tunisia (2010)	7.8	-0.1	44.7	8.0	-6.9	3.0	38.5
Panel B: Lower-middle-income countries, using a poverty line of $1.25 2005 PPP per day							
Armenia (2011)	21.4	-9.6	47.4	12.9	-9.3	6.2	52.3
Bolivia (2009)	10.9	-0.5	50.3	0.6	-0.3	6.6	63.2
Dominican Republic (2013)	6.8	-0.9	50.2	2.2	-2.2	1.0	16.3
El Salvador (2011)	4.3	-0.7	44.0	2.2	-2.1	1.0	27.0
Ethiopia (2011)	31.9	2.3	32.2	2.3	-2.0	28.5	83.2
Ghana (2013)	6.0	0.7	43.7	1.6	-1.4	5.1	76.6
Guatemala (2010)	12.0	-0.8	49.0	1.4	-1.2	7.0	62.2
Indonesia (2012)	12.0	-1.5	39.8	1.1	-0.8	4.1	39.2
Sri Lanka (2010)	5.0	-0.7	37.1	1.3	-1.1	1.6	36.4
Tanzania (2011)	43.7	7.9	38.2	4.1	-3.8	50.9	98.6

Source: Higgins and Lustig (2016) (reproduced in chapter 4 of this Volume).

from that spending as a share of Market Income *tend* to rise with Market Income.[41] Spending is progressive whenever the concentration coefficient is lower than the Gini for Market Income. This means that the benefits from that spending as a share of Market Income tend to fall with Market Income. Within progressive spending, spending is neutral in absolute terms—spending per capita is the same across the income distribution—whenever the concentration coefficient is equal to zero. Spending is defined as *pro-poor* whenever the concentration coefficient not only is lower than the Gini but also its value is negative. Pro-poor spending implies that the *per capita* government spending on the transfer *tends* to fall with Market Income.[42] Any time spending is pro-poor or neutral in absolute terms, it is by definition progressive. The converse, of course, is not true.[43] The taxonomy of transfers is synthesized in figure 1-3 in chapter 1 of this Volume.

A clarification is in order. In the analysis presented here, households are ranked by per capita Market Income, and no adjustments are made to their size because of differences in the composition by age and gender. In some analyses, the pro-poorness of education spending, for example, is determined using children—not all members of the household—as the unit of analysis. Because poorer families have, on average, a larger number of children, the observation that concentration curves are pro-poor is a reflection of this fact. It does not mean that poorer families receive more resources per child.

Table 10-2 summarizes the results regarding the pro-poorness of government spending on education (total and by level) and health. Total spending on education is pro-poor (that is, per capita spending declines with income) in upper-middle-income and high-income countries except for South Africa and Iran, where it is (approximately) neutral in absolute terms. Total per capita spending on education tends to be the same (neutral in absolute terms) across different income groups in low-income and lower-middle-income countries, except for Armenia and El Salvador, where it is pro-poor, and Ethiopia, Ghana, Tanzania, and Uganda, where it is progressive only in relative terms. Preschool tends to be pro-poor in all countries for which there is data except for Georgia. Primary school is pro-poor in all countries other than Ethiopia. For secondary school, spending is pro-poor in all upper-middle-income countries for which there is data. In Mexico, lower secondary is pro-poor and upper secondary is progressive only in relative term. Secondary-school spending is neutral in most low-income and lower-middle-income countries other than Bolivia (pro-poor), as well as Ethiopia, Ghana, and Uganda (progressive only in relative term). Government spending on ter-

---

[41] I say "tend" because for global regressivity/progressivity to occur, it is not a necessary condition for the share of the benefit to rise/fall at each and every income level. When the latter occurs, the benefit is regressive/progressive *everywhere*. Whenever a benefit is *everywhere* regressive/progressive, it will be *globally* regressive/progressive, but the converse is not true.

[42] This case is also sometimes called "progressive in absolute terms."

[43] As mentioned above, care must be taken not to infer that any spending that is progressive (regressive) will automatically be equalizing (unequalizing).

TABLE 10-2
Progressivity and Pro-Poorness of Education and Health Spending, Summary of Results

	Education total			Preschool			Primary			Secondary			Tertiary				Health		
	A	B	C	A	B	C	A	B	C	A	B	C	A	B	C	D	A	B	C
Argentina (2012)	+	+		+			−			−		+			+		+		
Armenia (2011)	+			+			+			−					+			+	
Bolivia (2009)		+		+			+			+					+			+	
Brazil (2009)	+			+			+			+					+		+		
Chile (2013)	+			+			+			+					+		+		
Colombia (2010)	−			+			+			+					+		−		
Costa Rica (2010)	−			+			+			+					+		−		
Dominican Republic (2013)	+			+			+			−					+		+		
Ecuador (2011)	+			−			+			+			−				+		
El Salvador (2011)	+			+			+				+				+				+
Ethiopia (2011)			+	−				+		−		+				+			+
Georgia (2013)			+	+	+		+					+			+		+		
Ghana (2013)		+		+			+				+	+			+	+		+	
Guatemala (2011)		+		+			+				+				+	+			+
Honduras (2011)		+		+			+				+				+			+	
Indonesia (2012)		+		−			+				+				+	+			+
Iran (2011)		+		−			+			+					+			+	
Jordan (2010)	+			+			+			+					+				+
Mexico (2010)	+			+			+					+			+			+	
Nicaragua (2009)		+		+			+				+				+			+	

(continued)

TABLE 10-2 (continued)

	Education total			Preschool			Primary			Secondary			Tertiary				Health		
	A	B	C	A	B	C	A	B	C	A	B	C	A	B	C	D	A	B	C
Peru (2009)	+			+			+			+					+				+
Russia (2010)	+			−			−			−			−					+	
South Africa (2010)		+		+			+			+					+		+		
Sri Lanka (2010)		+		+			−				−				+			+	
Tanzania (2011)			+	+			+					+				+		+	
Tunisia (2010)		+		−			−					+			+			+	
Uganda (2013)	+		+	−			+			+					+		+		
Uruguay (2009)	+			+												+	+		
Venezuela (2013)	+			+			+			+				+					

Source: CEQ Data Center on Fiscal Redistribution. Based on the following *Master Workbooks of Results:* Argentina (Rossignolo, 2017); Armenia (Younger and Khachatryan, 2014); Bolivia (Paz Arauco and others, 2014b); Brazil (Higgins and Pereira, 2017); Chile (Martinez-Aguilar and Ortiz-Juarez, 2016); Colombia (Melendez and Martinez, 2015); Costa Rica (Sauma and Trejos, 2014b); Dominican Republic (Aristy-Escuder and others, 2016); Ecuador (Llerena and others, 2015); El Salvador (Beneke de Sanfeliu, Lustig, and Oliva Cepeda, 2014); Ethiopia (Hill, Tsehaye, and Woldehanna, 2014); Georgia (Cancho and Bondarenko, 2015); Ghana (Younger, Osei-Assibey, and Oppong, 2016); Guatemala (Cabrera and Moran, 2015a); Honduras (Castaneda and Espino, 2015); Indonesia (Afkar, Jellema, and Wai-Poi, 2015); Iran (Enami, Lustig, and Taqdiri, 2017b); Jordan (Abdel-Halim and others, 2016); Mexico (Scott, 2013); Nicaragua (Cabrera and Moran, 2015b); Peru (Jaramillo, 2015); Russia (Malytsin and Popova, 2016); South Africa (Inchauste and others, 2016); Sri Lanka (Arunatilake and others, 2016); Tanzania (Younger, Myamba, and Mdadila, 2016b); Tunisia (Jouini and others, 2015); Uganda (Jellema and others, 2016); Uruguay (Bucheli and others, 2014b); and Venezuela (Molina, 2016).

Notes: A = Pro-poor, concentration coefficient is negative. B = Same per capita for all, concentration coefficient equals zero. C = Progressive, concentration coefficient positive but lower than market income plus contributory pensions Gini. D = Regressive, concentration coefficient positive and higher than market income plus contributory pensions Gini. If the concentration coefficient is higher or equal to −0.5 but not higher than 0.5, it was considered equal to 0. Also, see notes to figure 10-4.

— = Not available

tiary education is regressive in Ethiopia, Ghana, Guatemala, Indonesia, Uganda, and Tanzania, and progressive only in relative terms in various degrees in the rest.

Health spending is pro-poor (that is, per capita spending declines with income) in Argentina, Brazil, Chile, the Dominican Republic, Ecuador, Georgia, South Africa, Uruguay, and Venezuela. In Armenia, Bolivia, Ghana, Honduras, Iran, Mexico, Nicaragua, Russia, Sri Lanka, Tunisia, and Uganda, the per capita benefit is roughly the same across the income scale. In El Salvador, Ethiopia, Guatemala, Indonesia, Jordan, Peru, and Tanzania, health spending per person is progressive only in relative terms.

While the results regarding the pro-poorness of spending on education and health are quite encouraging, a caveat is in order. Guaranteeing access to and facilitating usage of public education and health services for the poor is not enough. As long as the quality of schooling and healthcare provided by the government is low, distortive patterns such as those observed in Brazil and South Africa (for example, mostly the middle classes and the rich benefiting from free tertiary education[44]) will be a major obstacle to the equalization of opportunities. However, with the existing information, one cannot disentangle to what extent the progressivity or pro-poorness of education and health spending is a result of differences in family composition (the poor have more children and, therefore, poor households receive higher benefits in the form of basic education transfers) or frequency of illness (the poor have worse health than the non-poor) versus the "opting-out" of the middle classes and the rich.

8 Conclusions

In order to analyze the impact of fiscal policy on income inequality, it is useful to separate the "cash portion" of the system. The cash portion includes direct taxes, direct transfers, indirect taxes, and indirect subsidies. The noncash, or "in-kind," portion includes the monetized value of the use of government education and health services. The results show that the reduction in inequality induced by the cash portion of the fiscal system in the twenty-nine countries analyzed here is quite heterogeneous. Redistributive success is broadly determined primarily by the amount of resources and their combined progressivity. Net direct taxes are always equalizing. The effect of net indirect taxes is equalizing in nineteen of the twenty-nine countries.

While the cash portion of the net fiscal system is always equalizing, the same cannot be said for poverty. In Ethiopia, Ghana, Guatemala, Nicaragua, Uganda, and Tanzania, for instance, the headcount ratio measured with the international extreme poverty line of US$1.25 (PPP 2005 per day) is higher for Consumable Income than for Market Income. In these countries, fiscal policy *increases* poverty, meaning that a larger number of the Market Income poor (non-poor) are made poorer (poor) by taxes and

---

[44] Among the reasons for this outcome is the fact that children of poor households tend to drop out of high school more, and the rich children who receive enough quality (often private) education are better equipped to pass the entrance examination.

transfers than the number of people who escape poverty.[45] This startling result is primarily the consequence of high consumption taxes on basic goods.

Turning now to the in-kind portion of the fiscal system, spending on education and health is equalizing, and its contribution to the reduction in inequality is rather large. This result is not surprising given that the use of government services is monetized at a value equal to average government cost. While the results concerning the distribution of the benefits of in-kind services in education and health are encouraging from the equity point of view, it is important to note that they may be due to factors one would prefer to avoid. The more intensive use of services in education and health on the part of the poorer portions of the population, for example, may be caused by the fact that in their quest for quality, the middle classes (and, of course, the rich) chose to use private providers. This situation leaves the poor with access to second-rate services. In addition, if the middle classes opt out of public services, they may be much more reluctant to pay the taxes needed to improve both the coverage and the quality of services than they would be if services were used universally.

An important result to note is that there is no evidence of a "Robin Hood paradox:" the more unequal countries tend to spend more on redistribution and show a higher redistributive effect. However, regression-based analysis indicates that this last result is not robust across the board when one controls for income per capita, leaves out the "outliers," or measures redistribution in percent change instead of Gini points. While the sign of the slope shows that the more unequal a country is before taxes and transfers, the more redistribution occurs, the coefficient is often not statistically significant.

There are a few lessons that emerge from the analysis. Let's start with those pertaining to the diagnostic of fiscal redistribution. First, the fact that specific fiscal interventions can have countervailing effects underscores the importance of taking a coordinated view of both taxation and spending rather than pursuing a piecemeal analysis. Efficient regressive taxes (such as the value-added tax) when combined with generous well-targeted transfers can result in a net fiscal system that is equalizing. Even more, because a net fiscal system with a regressive tax could be more equalizing than without it (Lambert's conundrum), policy recommendations—such as eliminating the regressive tax—based on a piecemeal analysis could be flatly wrong. Second, to assess the impact of the fiscal system on people's standard of living, it is crucial to measure the effect of taxation and spending not only on inequality but also on poverty: the net fiscal system can be equalizing but poverty-increasing.

Regarding policy prescriptions, one fundamental lesson emerges: governments should design their tax and transfers system so that the after taxes and transfers incomes (or consumption) of the poor are not lower than their incomes (or consumption) before fiscal interventions. Leaving out in-kind transfers, the so-called cash portion of the fiscal system should not impoverish the poor (or make the non-poor poor). The results indicate that, on average, the ultra-poor in Ghana, Nicaragua, Tanzania, and Uganda, the ex-

---

[45] Higgins and Lustig (2016) (reproduced in chapter 4 of this Volume of the Handbook).

treme poor in Armenia, Ethiopia, and Guatemala, and the moderate poor in Bolivia, the Dominican Republic, El Salvador, Honduras, Peru, and Sri Lanka are net payers into the fiscal system. In the case of Brazil, the cause is the high consumption taxes paid on staple goods. In the case of Peru, cash transfers are too small to compensate for what the poor pay in taxes. Furthermore, as shown in Higgins and Lustig (2016) (reproduced as chapter 4 in this Volume of the Handbook), fiscal impoverishment can be quite pervasive and, in low-income countries, larger in magnitude than fiscal gains to the poor.

The current policy discussion (and the literature) focuses primarily on the power of fiscal policy to reduce inequality and much less (and often not at all) on the impact of fiscal policy on the standard of living of the poor. If the policy community is seriously committed to eradicating income poverty, governments will need to explore ways to redesign taxation and transfers so that the poor do not end up as net payers. This could become an overriding principle in the design of fiscal systems that could be explicitly added to the frameworks proposed by Atkinson (2015) and Stiglitz (2012) to build more equitable societies.

Acknowledgments

I am very grateful to Israel Martinez and Cristina Carrera for their valuable research assistance. All errors and omissions remain my sole responsibility.

References

Abdel-Halim, Morad, Shamma A. Alam, Yusuf Mansur, Umar Serajuddin, and Paolo Verme. 2016. "*CEQ Master Workbook*: Jordan. Version: March 8, 2016," CEQ Data Center on Fiscal Redistribution (CEQ Institute, Tulane University, and the World Bank).

Afkar, Rythia, Jon Jellema, and Matthew Wai-Poi. 2015. "*CEQ Master Workbook*: Indonesia. Version: February 26, 2015," CEQ Data Center on Fiscal Redistribution (CEQ Institute, Tulane University, and the World Bank).

Alam, Shamma A., Gabriela Inchauste, and Umar Serajuddin. 2017. "The Distributional Impact of Fiscal Policy in Jordan," in *The Distributional Impact of Taxes and Transfers: Evidence from Eight Low- and Middle-Income Countries*, edited by Gabriela Inchauste and Nora Lustig (Washington: World Bank).

Aristy-Escuder, Jaime, Maynor Cabrera, Blanca Moreno-Dodson, and Miguel Sanchez-Martin. 2016. "*CEQ Master Workbook*: Dominican Republic. Version: August 4, 2016," CEQ Data Center on Fiscal Redistribution (CEQ Institute, Tulane University, and the World Bank).

———. 2022. "The Dominican Republic: Fiscal Policy, Income Redistribution, and Poverty Reduction," chap. 14 in *Commitment to Equity Handbook: Estimating the Impact of Fiscal Policy on Inequality and Poverty*, 2nd ed., Vol. 1, edited by Nora Lustig (Brookings Institution Press and CEQ Institute, Tulane University). Free online version available at www.commitmentoequity.org.

Arunatilake, Nisha, Camilo Gomez, Nipuni Perera, and Kaushalya Attygalle. 2016. "*CEQ Master Workbook*: Sri Lanka. Version: March 10, 2016," CEQ Data Center on Fiscal Redistribution (CEQ Institute, Tulane University, and the World Bank).

Arunatilake, Nisha, Gabriela Inchauste, and Nora Lustig. 2017. "The Incidence of Taxes and Spending in Sri Lanka," in *The Distributional Impact of Taxes and Transfers: Evidence from Eight Low- and Middle-Income Countries*, edited by Gabriela Inchauste and Nora Lustig (Washington: World Bank).

Atkinson, Anthony B. 2015. *Inequality: What Can Be Done?* (Harvard University Press).

Barr, Nicholas. 2012. *Economics of the Welfare State* (Oxford University Press).

Beneke de Sanfeliu, Margarita, Nora Lustig, and Jose Andres Oliva Cepeda. 2014. "*CEQ Master Workbook*: El Salvador. Version: June 26, 2014," CEQ Data Center on Fiscal Redistribution (CEQ Institute, Tulane University, and Inter-American Development Bank).

———. 2022. "El Salvador: The Impact of Taxes and Social Spending on Inequality and Poverty," chap. 15 in *Commitment to Equity Handbook: Estimating the Impact of Fiscal Policy on Inequality and Poverty*, 2nd ed., Vol. 1, edited by Nora Lustig (Brookings Institution Press and CEQ Institute, Tulane University). Free online version available at www.commitmentoequity.org.

Bucheli, Marisa, Nora Lustig, Maximo Rossi, and Florencia Amabile. 2014a. "Social Spending, Taxes and Income Redistribution in Uruguay," in *The Redistributive Impact of Taxes and Social Spending in Latin America*, edited by Nora Lustig, Carola Pessino, and John Scott, special issue, *Public Finance Review* 42, no. 3, pp. 413–33 (doi:10.1177/1091142113493493).

———. 2014b. "*CEQ Master Workbook*: Uruguay. Version: August 18, 2014," CEQ Data Center on Fiscal Redistribution (CEQ Institute, Tulane University).

Cabrera, Maynor, and Hilcias E. Moran. 2015a. "*CEQ Master Workbook*: Guatemala. Version: May 6, 2015," CEQ Data Center on Fiscal Redistribution (CEQ Institute, Tulane University, Instituto Centroamericano de Estudios Fiscales [ICEFI], and International Fund for Agricultural Development [IFAD]).

———. 2015b. "*CEQ Master Workbook*: Nicaragua. Version: October 14, 2015," CEQ Data Center on Fiscal Redistribution (CEQ Institute, Tulane University, Instituto Centroamericano de Estudios Fiscales [ICEFI], and International Fund for Agricultural Development [IFAD]).

Cancho, Cesar, and Elena Bondarenko. 2015. "*CEQ Master Workbook*: Georgia. Version: December 31, 2015," CEQ Data Center on Fiscal Redistribution (CEQ Institute, Tulane University, and the World Bank).

———. 2017. "The Distributional Impact of Fiscal Policy in Georgia," in *The Distributional Impact of Taxes and Transfers: Evidence from Eight Low- and Middle-Income Countries*, edited by Gabriela Inchauste and Nora Lustig (Washington: World Bank).

Castaneda, Ricardo, and Ilya Espino. 2015. "*CEQ Master Workbook*: Honduras. Version: August 18, 2015," CEQ Data Center on Fiscal Redistribution (CEQ Institute, Tulane University, Instituto Centroamericano de Estudios Fiscales [ICEFI], and International Fund for Agricultural Development [IFAD]).

Duclos, Jean-Yves, and Abdelkrim Araar. 2006. *Poverty and Equity: Measurement, Policy and Estimation with DAD*. Economic Studies in Inequality, Social Exclusion and Well-Being 2 (New York: Springer, IDRC).

Enami, Ali. 2022. "Measuring the Redistributive Impact of Taxes and Transfers in the Presence of Reranking," chap. 3 in *Commitment to Equity Handbook: Estimating the Impact of Fiscal Policy on Inequality and Poverty*, 2nd ed., Vol. 1, edited by Nora Lustig (Brookings Institution Press and CEQ Institute, Tulane University). Free online version available at www .commitmentoequity.org.

Enami, Ali, Nora Lustig, and Rodrigo Aranda. 2022. "Analytical Foundations: Measuring the Redistributive Impact of Taxes and Transfers," chap. 2 in *Commitment to Equity Handbook: Estimating the Impact of Fiscal Policy on Inequality and Poverty,* 2nd ed., Vol. 1, edited by Nora Lustig (Brookings Institution Press and CEQ Institute, Tulane University). Free online version available at www.commitmentoequity.org.

Enami, Ali, Nora Lustig, and Alireza Taqdiri. 2017a. "Fiscal Policy, Inequality and Poverty in Iran: Assessing the Impact and Effectiveness of Taxes and Transfers," CEQ Working Paper 48 (CEQ Institute, Tulane University and the Economic Research Forum), September.

———. 2017b. "*CEQ Master Workbook*: Iran. Version: May 5, 2017," CEQ Data Center on Fiscal Redistribution (CEQ Institute, Tulane University, and Economic Research Forum).

EUROMOD. 2017. "Statistics on Distribution and Decomposition of Disposable Income," using EUROMOD version no. G3.0+ (http://euromod.ac.uk/using-euromod/statistics).

Ferreira, Francisco H. G., Julian Messina, Jamele Rigolini, Luis Felipe Lopez-Calva, Maria Ana Lugo, and Renos Vakis. 2012. *Economic Mobility and the Rise of the Latin American Middle Class* (Washington: World Bank).

Higgins, Sean, and Caterina Brest Lopez. 2022. "Producing Indicators and Results, and Completing Sections D and E of the *CEQ Master Workbook* Using the *CEQ Stata Package*," 2nd ed., Vol. 1, chap. 8 in *Commitment to Equity Handbook: Estimating the Impact of Fiscal Policy on Inequality and Poverty*, edited by Nora Lustig (Brookings Institution Press and CEQ Institute, Tulane University). Free online version available at www.commitmentoequity.org.

Higgins, Sean, and Nora Lustig. 2016. "Can a Poverty-Reducing and Progressive Tax and Transfer System Hurt the Poor?" *Journal of Development Economics* 122, pp. 63–75.

———. 2022. "Allocating Taxes and Transfers and Constructing Income Concepts: Completing Sections A, B, and C of the *CEQ Master Workbook*," chap. 6 in *Commitment to Equity Handbook: Estimating the Impact of Fiscal Policy on Inequality and Poverty*, 2nd ed., Vol. 1, edited by Nora Lustig (Brookings Institution Press and CEQ Institute, Tulane University). Free online version available at www.commitmentoequity.org.

Higgins, Sean, Nora Lustig, Whitney Ruble, and Timothy M. Smeeding. 2016. "Comparing the Incidence of Taxes and Social Spending in Brazil and the United States." *Review of Income and Wealth* 62, pp. S22–46.

Higgins, Sean, and Claudiney Pereira. 2014. "The Effects of Brazil's Taxation and Social Spending on the Distribution of Household Income," in *The Redistributive Impact of Taxes and Social Spending in Latin America,* edited by Nora Lustig, Carola Pessino, and John Scott, special issue, *Public Finance Review* 42, no. 3, pp. 346–67 (doi:10.1177/1091142113501714).

———. 2017. "*CEQ Master Workbook*: Brazil. Version: April 19, 2017," CEQ Data Center on Fiscal Redistribution (CEQ Institute, Tulane University).

Hill, Ruth, Gabriela Inchauste, Nora Lustig, Eyasu Tsehaye, and Tassew Woldehanna. 2017. "Fiscal Incidence Analysis for Ethiopia," in *The Distributional Impact of Taxes and Transfers. Evidence from Eight Low- and Middle-Income Countries*, edited by Gabriela Inchauste and Nora Lustig (Washington: World Bank).

Hill, Ruth, Eyasu Tsehaye, and Tassew Woldehanna. 2014. "*CEQ Master Workbook*: Ethiopia. Version: September 28, 2014," CEQ Data Center on Fiscal Redistribution (CEQ Institute, Tulane University, and the World Bank).

Inchauste, Gabriela, and Nora Lustig, eds. 2017. *The Distributional Impact of Taxes and Transfers: Evidence from Eight Low- and Middle-Income Countries*, edited by Gabriela Inchauste and Nora Lustig (Washington: World Bank).

Inchauste, Gabriela, Nora Lustig, Mashekwa Maboshe, Catriona Purfield, and Ingrid Woolard. 2017. "The Distributional Impact of Fiscal Policy in South Africa," in *The Distributional Impact of Taxes and Transfers: Evidence from Eight Low- and Middle-Income Countries*, edited by Gabriela Inchauste and Nora Lustig (Washington: World Bank).

Inchauste, Gabriela, Nora Lustig, Mashekwa Maboshe, Catriona Purfield, Ingrid Woolard, and Precious Zikhali. 2016. "*CEQ Master Workbook*: South Africa. Version: March 6, 2016," CEQ Data Center on Fiscal Redistribution (CEQ Institute, Tulane University, and the World Bank).

Instituto Centroamericano de Estudios Fiscales (ICEFI). 2017a. "Incidencia de la politica fiscal en la desigualdad y la pobreza en Guatemala," CEQ Working Paper 50 (CEQ Institute, Tulane University, International Fund for Agricultural Development [IFAD], and Instituto Centroamericano de Estudios Fiscales), May.

———. 2017b. "Incidencia de la politica fiscal en la desigualdad y la pobreza en Honduras," CEQ Working Paper 51 (CEQ Institute, Tulane University, International Fund for Agricultural Development [IFAD], and Instituto Centroamericano de Estudios Fiscales), April.

———. 2017c. "Incidencia de la politica fiscal en la desigualdad y la pobreza en Nicaragua," CEQ Working Paper 52 (CEQ Institute, Tulane University, International Fund for Agricultural Development [IFAD], and Instituto Centroamericano de Estudios Fiscales), May.

Jaramillo, Miguel. 2014. "The Incidence of Social Spending and Taxes in Peru," in *The Redistributive Impact of Taxes and Social Spending in Latin America*, edited by Nora Lustig, Carola Pessino, and John Scott, special issue, *Public Finance Review* 42, no. 3, pp. 391–412 (doi:10.1177/1091142113496134).

———. 2015. "*CEQ Master Workbook*: Peru. Version: August 7, 2015," CEQ Data Center on Fiscal Redistribution (CEQ Institute, Tulane University).

Jellema, Jon, Astrid Haas, Nora Lustig, and Sebastian Wolf. 2016. "*CEQ Master Workbook*: Uganda. Version: July 28, 2016," CEQ Data Center on Fiscal Redistribution (CEQ Institute, Tulane University, and International Growth Center).

———. 2022. "Uganda: The Impact of Taxes, Transfers, and Subsidies on Inequality and Poverty," chap. 19 in *Commitment to Equity Handbook: Estimating the Impact of Fiscal Policy on Inequality and Poverty*, 2nd ed., vol. 1, edited by Nora Lustig (Brookings Institution Press and CEQ Institute, Tulane University). Free online version available at www.commitmentoequity.org.

Jellema, Jon, and Gabriela Inchauste. 2022. "Constructing Consumable Income: Including the Direct and Indirect Effects of Indirect Taxes and Subsidies," chap. 7 in *Commitment to Equity Handbook: Estimating the Impact of Fiscal Policy on Inequality and Poverty*, 2nd ed., vol. 1, edited by Nora Lustig (Brookings Institution Press and CEQ Institute, Tulane University). Free online version available at www.commitmentoequity.org.

Jellema, Jon, Matthew Wai-Poi, and Afkar, Rythia. 2017. "The Distributional Impact of Fiscal Policy in Indonesia," in *The Distributional Impact of Taxes and Transfers: Evidence from Eight Low- and Middle-Income Countries*, edited by Gabriela Inchauste and Nora Lustig (Washington: World Bank).

Jouini, Nizar, Nora Lustig, Ahmed Moummi, and Abebe Shimeles. 2015. "*CEQ Master Workbook*: Tunisia. Version: October 1, 2015," CEQ Data Center on Fiscal Redistribution (CEQ Institute, Tulane University, and African Development Bank).

———. 2022. "Tunisia: Fiscal Policy, Income Redistribution, and Poverty Reduction," chap. 18 in *Commitment to Equity Handbook: Estimating the Impact of Fiscal Policy on Inequality and Poverty*, 2nd ed., vol. 1, edited by Nora Lustig (Brookings Institution Press and CEQ Institute, Tulane University). Free online version available at www.commitmentoequity.org.

Lindert, Peter H. 1994. "The Rise of Social Spending, 1880–1930." *Explorations in Economic History* 31, no. 1, pp. 1–37.

———. 2004. *Growing Public. Social Spending and Economic Growth since the Eighteenth Century*, vols. 1–2 (Cambridge University Press).

Llerena Pinto, Freddy Paul, Maria Cristhina Llerena Pinto, Roberto Carlos Saa Daza, and Maria Andrea Llerena Pinto. 2015. "Social Spending, Taxes and Income Redistribution in Ecuador," CEQ Working Paper 28 (Center for Inter-American Policy and Research and Department of Economics, Tulane University, and Inter-American Dialogue), February.

———. 2017. "*CEQ Master Workbook*: Ecuador. Version: January 5, 2017," CEQ Data Center on Fiscal Redistribution (CEQ Institute, Tulane University).

Lopez-Calva, Luis Felipe, Nora Lustig, Mikhail Matytsin, and Daria Popova. 2017. "Who Benefits from Fiscal Redistribution in the Russian Federation?," in *The Distributional Impact of Taxes and Transfers: Evidence from Eight Low- and Middle-Income Countries*, edited by Gabriela Inchauste and Nora Lustig (Washington: World Bank).

Lopez-Calva, Luis Felipe, and Eduardo Ortiz-Juarez. 2014. "A Vulnerability Approach to the Definition of the Middle Class." *Journal of Economic Inequality* 12, 1, pp. 23–47.

Lustig, Nora. 2015. "The Redistributive Impact of Government Spending on Education and Health: Evidence from 13 Developing Countries in the Commitment to Equity Project," in *Inequality and Fiscal Policy*, edited by Sanjeev Gupta, Michael Keen, Benedict J. Clements, and Ruud A. de Mooij (Washington: International Monetary Fund).

———, ed. 2022. *Commitment to Equity Handbook: Estimating the Impact of Fiscal Policy on Inequality and Poverty*, 2nd ed., vol. 1, (Brookings Institution Press and CEQ Institute, Tulane University). Free online version available at www.commitmentoequity.org.

Lustig, Nora, and Sean Higgins. 2013. "Commitment to Equity Assessment (CEQ): Estimating the Incidence of Social Spending, Subsidies and Taxes. Handbook," CEQ Working Paper 1 (Center for Inter-American Policy and Research, Department of Economics, Tulane University, and Inter-American Dialogue), September.

———. 2022. "The *CEQ Assessment*: Measuring the Impact of Fiscal Policy on Inequality and Poverty," chap. 1 in *Commitment to Equity Handbook: Estimating the Impact of Fiscal Policy on Inequality and Poverty*, 2nd ed., Vol. 1, edited by Nora Lustig (Brookings Institution Press and CEQ Institute, Tulane University). Free online version available at www.commitmentoequity.org.

Lustig, Nora, Carola Pessino, and John Scott, eds. 2014. *The Redistributive Impact of Taxes and Social Spending in Latin America*, special issue, *Public Finance Review* 42, no 3.

Malytsin, Mikhail, and Daria Popova. 2016. "*CEQ Master Workbook*: Russia. Version: March 17, 2016," CEQ Data Center on Fiscal Redistribution (CEQ Institute, Tulane University, and the World Bank).

Martinez-Aguilar, Sandra, Alan Fuchs, Eduardo Ortiz-Juarez, and Giselle Del Carmen. 2022. "Chile: The Impact of Fiscal Policy on Inequality and Poverty," chap. 13 in *Commitment to Equity Handbook: Estimating the Impact of Fiscal Policy on Inequality and Poverty*, 2nd ed., Vol. 1, edited by Nora Lustig (Brookings Institution Press and CEQ Institute, Tulane University). Free online version available at www.commitmentoequity.org.

Martinez-Aguilar, Sandra, and Eduardo Ortiz-Juarez. 2016. "*CEQ Master Workbook*: Chile. Version: October 7, 2016," CEQ Data Center on Fiscal Redistribution (CEQ Institute, Tulane University, and the World Bank).

Martinez-Vazquez, Jorge. 2008. "The Impact of Budgets on the Poor: Tax and Expenditure Benefit Incidence Analysis," in *Public Finance for Poverty Reduction: Concepts and Case Studies from Africa and Latin America*, edited by Blanca Moreno-Dodson and Quentin Wodon (Washington: World Bank).

Melendez, Marcela, and Valentina Martinez. 2015. "*CEQ Master Workbook*: Colombia. Version: December 17, 2015," CEQ Data Center on Fiscal Redistribution (CEQ Institute, Tulane University, and Inter-American Development Bank).

Meltzer, Allan H., and Scott F. Richards. 1981. "A Rational Theory of the Size of Government." *Journal of Political Economy* 89, no. 5, pp. 914–27.

Molina, Emiro. 2016. "*CEQ Master Workbook*: Venezuela. Version: November 15, 2016," CEQ Data Center on Fiscal Redistribution (CEQ Institute, Tulane University).

Musgrave, Richard A. 1959. *The Theory of Public Finance* (New York: McGraw-Hill).

OECD. 2011. "Changes in Redistribution in OECD Countries over Two Decades," in *Divided We Stand: Why Inequality Keeps Rising* (Paris: OECD Publishing) (http://dx.doi.org/10.1787/9789264119536-en).

Paz Arauco, Veronica, George Gray-Molina, Wilson Jimenez, and Ernesto Yañez. 2014a. "Explaining Low Redistributive Impact in Bolivia," in *The Redistributive Impact of Taxes and Social Spending in Latin America*, edited by Nora Lustig, Carola Pessino, and John Scott, special issue, *Public Finance Review* 42, no. 3, pp. 326–45 (doi:10.1177/1091142113496133).

———. 2014b. "*CEQ Master Workbook*: Bolivia. Version: September 22, 2014," CEQ Data Center on Fiscal Redistribution (CEQ Institute, Tulane University).

Pechman, Joseph A. 1985. *Who Paid the Taxes, 1966–1985* (Washington: Brookings Institution).

Rossignolo, Dario. 2017. "*CEQ Master Workbook*: Argentina. Version: May 19, 2017," CEQ Data Center on Fiscal Redistribution (CEQ Institute, Tulane University).

———. 2022. "Argentina: Taxes, Expenditures, Poverty, and Income Distribution," chap. 11 in *Commitment to Equity Handbook: Estimating the Impact of Fiscal Policy on Inequality and Poverty*, 2nd ed., Vol. 1, edited by Nora Lustig (Brookings Institution Press and CEQ Institute, Tulane University). Free online version available at www.commitmentoequity.org.

Sauma, Pablo, and Juan D. Trejos. 2014a. "Social Public Spending, Taxes, Redistribution of Income, and Poverty in Costa Rica," CEQ Working Paper 18 (Center for Inter-American Policy and Research and Department of Economics, Tulane University, and Inter-American Dialogue), March.

———. 2014b. "*CEQ Master Workbook*: Costa Rica. Version: February 14, 2014," CEQ Data Center on Fiscal Redistribution (CEQ Institute, Tulane University).

Scott, John. 2013. "*CEQ Master Workbook*: Mexico. Version: September 2, 2013," CEQ Data Center on Fiscal Redistribution (CEQ Institute, Tulane University).

———. 2014. "Redistributive Impact and Efficiency of Mexico's Fiscal System," in *The Redistributive Impact of Taxes and Social Spending in Latin America*, edited by Nora Lustig, Carola Pessino, John Scott, special issue, *Public Finance Review* 42, no. 3, pp. 368–90 (doi:10.1177/1091142113497394).

Stiglitz, Joseph E. 2012. *The Price of Inequality* (New York: W. W. Norton).

Younger, Stephen D., and Artsvi Khachatryan. 2014. "*CEQ Master Workbook*: Armenia. Version: May 31, 2014," CEQ Data Center on Fiscal Redistribution (CEQ Institute, Tulane University, and the World Bank).

———. 2017. "Fiscal Incidence in Armenia," in *The Distributional Impact of Taxes and Transfers: Evidence from Eight Low- and Middle-Income Countries*, edited by Gabriela Inchauste and Nora Lustig (Washington: World Bank).

Younger, Stephen D., Flora Myamba, and Kenneth Mdadila. 2016a. "*CEQ Master Workbook*: Tanzania. Version: June 1, 2016," CEQ Data Center on Fiscal Redistribution (CEQ Institute, Tulane University).

———. 2016b. "Fiscal Incidence in Tanzania." *African Development Review* 28, no. 3, pp. 264–76 (doi:10.1111/1467-8268.12204).

Younger, Stephen D., Eric Osei-Assibey, and Felix Oppong. 2016. "*CEQ Master Workbook*: Ghana, February 10, 2016," CEQ Data Center on Fiscal Redistribution (CEQ Institute, Tulane University).

———. 2017. "Fiscal Incidence in Ghana." *Review of Development Economics*, January 11 (doi:10.1111/rode.12299).

Chapter 11

ARGENTINA

Taxes, Expenditures, Poverty, and Income Distribution

Dario Rossignolo

Introduction

Starting in 2003, tax collection and public expenditures experienced exceptional growth in Argentina. In 2014, the tax burden reached 32.5 percent of GDP. This increase was due to several factors. Taxes that were sporadically levied in previous periods such as export duties and taxes on financial transactions were significantly expanded. The economic recovery, as expected, resulted in a boon to tax collection. In addition, no adjustments for inflation to financial reporting and thresholds impacted the burden of corporate income tax (CIT) and personal income tax (PIT).[1] Additional revenues were obtained through the (re)nationalization of the pension system.

On the expenditures side, public spending at the federal, provincial, and municipal levels increased from 26 percent of GDP in 2004 to around 45 percent in 2013. The most important changes in social spending were the expansion of the so-called Pension Moratorium, which is a sort of early retirement program with a moratorium for those who did not complete the thirty-year contributions requirement, the Educational Financing Law, which required education spending to increase to 6 percent of GDP, and the expansion of the Universal Allowance per Child, which extended the benefits to include not only formal sector workers but also workers in the informal sector

---

[1] Fiscal drag, or "bracket creeping," furthermore, contributed to the increase in tax revenues from PIT. This fiscal drag is illustrated by the fact that in 1997, roughly 12.5 percent of taxable income was concentrated in the highest tax bracket, subject to the highest marginal tax rate, which in 2011 was 58 percent. Gomez Sabaini and Rossignolo (2014).

and the unemployed.[2] Aside from the increase in social spending, expenditures on subsidies—in particular, electricity, gas, and transportation subsidies—increased greatly and reached around 6 percent of GDP in 2013.

With this extraordinary expansion during the last decade, the size of the state in Argentina reached a level similar to that in many advanced countries. To what extent did the government use this additional fiscal space to reduce inequality and poverty through taxes and transfers? This chapter applies the CEQ methodology described in previous chapters in this Volume of the Handbook to estimate the impact of taxes and public expenditures on income distribution and poverty. It uses data from the National Household Survey on Expenditures (Encuesta Nacional de Gastos de los Hogares; ENGHo), which was conducted by the National Bureau of Statistics in Argentina (INDEC) from March 2012 to February 2013.[3]

While several studies have jointly or separately analyzed the impact of taxes and expenditures on income distribution, very few have analyzed their impact on poverty. Gasparini (1998), for example, analyzed the distributional impact of the tax system for 1996, taking per capita income and per capita consumption expenditures as welfare indicators. In the former case, the author found that taxes were highly regressive, whereas in the latter, the incidence was moderately progressive. Gomez Sabaini, Santiere, and Rossignolo (2002) analyzed the impact of taxes on income distribution for 1997, considering per capita income adjusted for underreporting as a welfare measure. The incidence was regressive in this case, chiefly because of the value added tax (VAT) and other indirect taxes. Gomez Sabaini and Rossignolo (2009) analyzed the incidence of taxes for 2006, again considering per capita income adjusted for under-reporting. When measured with the Gini coefficient, the redistributive impact of taxes was moderately progressive, mainly as the result of export taxes and the increasing importance of income tax and payroll taxes. However, when inequality was measured with the ratio of average incomes of the richest to poorest deciles, it increased. On the spending side, the Secretary of Economic Policy ([SPE] 2002) and the Secretary of Economic and Regional Programming ([SPER] 1999) estimated the incidence of public expenditures, with results that show an unequivocal reduction in inequality. Similarly, Gasparini (1999) concluded that benefits of public expenditures were received more strongly by lower income brackets.[4] The net effect of taxes (both direct and indirect) and public expenditures (cash transfers and spending on education and health) on income distribution has been calculated in Gasparini (1999), SPE (2002), and Gomez Sabaini, Harriague, and Rossignolo (2013).[5]

---

[2] In Spanish, these programs are called Moratoria Previsional, Ley de Financiamiento Educativo, and Asignacion Universal por Hijo, respectively.

[3] No official statement has been made about the reliability of this survey.

[4] Several studies have analyzed the impact of specific programs on poverty reduction. For example, Maurizio (2009) explored the impact of different cash transfers on poverty, while Marchionni and others (2008) examined the impact of simulated subsidy schemes.

[5] See Gasparini (1999), SPE (2002), and Gomez Sabaini and others (2013).

Although the methodologies differ to a certain extent, all the studies find that the two highest income quintiles transfer resources to the lowest ones. All of the studies also note a significant equalizing effect, though the magnitude of the redistributive impact varies. The only study that has looked at the effect of social spending on both income distribution and poverty is by Lustig and Pessino (2014). Following CEQ methodology, the authors find that the inequality- and poverty-reducing impact of social spending in Argentina was quite high due to a large extent to the growing importance of noncontributory pensions in the last decade and to a lesser extent to the expansion of other cash transfers such as the Universal Allowance per Child.

The analysis presented here differs from the above studies in that it measures the impact of taxes and spending combined not only on inequality but also on poverty. In addition, except in one case, the existing studies rely on information by decile rather than the entire distribution, and, except in one case, they do not include the analysis of price subsidies. Another important difference is that existing studies that look at both taxes and expenditures assume a balanced budget and scale up the totals by decile to equal totals for the same items from budgetary data. In contrast, following CEQ, in this study I neither scale up totals nor assume a balanced budget.

As recommended by the CEQ methodology, I produced two scenarios of the fiscal incidence analysis: one in which contributory pensions are treated as pure government transfers (and contributions as a form of direct taxation) and another in which contributory pensions are treated as deferred income (and contributions as mandatory saving). The results show that the impact of direct taxes net of direct transfers on inequality is quite significant. In the scenario in which pensions are considered a transfer, the Gini coefficient for Disposable Income is 19.5 percent lower than the Market Income Gini. The impact of consumption taxes net of subsidies is equalizing. When the monetized value of education and health spending is included, the Gini coefficient for Final Income is 40.7 percent lower than the Market Income Gini coefficient. While the numbers are smaller, the redistributive effect in the scenario in which pensions are deferred income are also quite significant. However, in terms of poverty reduction, the results are less auspicious. While the headcount ratio for Disposable Income is 78 percent lower than the Market Income headcount ratio, with the moderate poverty line, the headcount ratio for Consumable Income is *higher* than the Market Income headcount ratio. This result indicates that a relatively large number of poor individuals are net payers to the fiscal system. This happens because consumption taxes weigh heavily on many of the poor.

1 The Fiscal System in Argentina: Taxes and Expenditures

Table 11-1 shows taxes and public expenditures by category as a share of GDP. The direct taxes analyzed are personal income tax (PIT), payroll taxes, and other taxes on income. The indirect taxes considered are the value added tax (VAT), excise taxes, fuel

TABLE 11-1

Government Spending and Revenue Structure in Percentage of GDP for Argentina 2012

Government spending and revenue	Percentage of GDP
Total government spending	44.1
Social spending (excludes contributory pensions)	20.9
Direct transfers (total cash & near-cash transfers)	5.8
Flagship cash or near-cash transfer program	0.5
Noncontributory pensions	2.9
Other cash & near-cash transfers	2.4
Total in-kind transfers	13.1
Education	7.4
Basic (primary and secondary)	7.5
Tertiary and university	4.6
Science, culture, and education not distinguished	1.5
Health	5.6
Contributory	3.2
Noncontributory	2.5
Housing and urban	0.6
Other social spending	1.3
Contributory pensions	7.1
Nonsocial spending	14.1
Indirect subsidies	5.9
Agriculture	0.3
Energy, fuel, and mining	2.6
Industry	0.1
Transportation	2.4
Communication	0.2
Other indirect subsidies	0.3
Other nonsocial spending	8.2
Debt servicing	
Interest payments	2.1
Total tax revenue	32.7
Direct taxes	2.2
Personal income tax	2.1
Simplified tax regime (Monotributo)	0.1
VAT and other indirect taxes	12.3
Other taxes	18.1
of which social security contributions with pensions	8.8

Source: Author's calculations based on data from the Argentine Ministerio de Hacienda (2017).

taxes, and the provincial turnover tax. Together, these taxes represent about 71 percent of total national and provincial tax revenues for 2012; of that 71 percent, 80 percent were simulated with the methods described in sections 1.1 and 1.2.[6] On the expenditure side, direct transfers include the flagship cash transfer program, Universal Allowance per Child; the two noncontributory pensions under the so-called Pension Fund Inclusion Plan (in Spanish, Plan de Inclusion Previsional) the Pension Moratorium (Moratoria Previsional); the Early Retirement Program (Jubilacion Anticipada); and other cash and near-cash transfers, which are described in sections 1.3, 1.4, and 1.5. Subsidies include subsidies to electricity, domestic gas, and transportation. Transfers in-kind include spending on public education and health. In total, these spending categories represent 65 percent of total national and provincial public spending for 2012, from which around 74 percent were imputed and simulated.[7]

1.1 Direct Taxes

PIT is a global-type tax, structured with progressive rates. Its taxable base has been expanded by several pieces of legislation. The Income Tax Act identifies four categories of income based on their source: land rent, capital gains, corporate income, and personal income. A single taxpayer may receive income from one or more income categories at the same time. The calculation of taxable income is based on the income and expenses corresponding to the four categories and a few other items on income derived from businesses and other activities. Several income categories are also exempt.[8]

In the analyzed period, PIT is determined by taxable net income bracket, based on a sliding scale consisting of a fixed amount plus a rate increasing from 9 to 35 percent on the excess of each income bracket bottom level. Individuals paying income tax are classified as either self-employed taxpayers or salaried workers. Self-employed taxpayers (that is, independent workers registered as income taxpayers) must pay income tax each fiscal year in five bimonthly advance payments.

---

[6] Export duties have been excluded from this analysis. Gomez Sabaini and Rossignolo (2009) and Gomez Sabaini and others (2013), following a different methodology than the one used here, conclude that these taxes are progressive following the standard Gini and concentration coefficients.

[7] Several expenditure items such as housing, urban services, water and sanitation programs, science and culture, discretionary pensions, and other nonsocial items could not be allocated because of lack of adequate information in the household survey.

[8] There are numerous exemptions. The most important are those on interest accrued on saving accounts deposits, special saving accounts, and term deposits; income derived from securities, shares, bonds, bills of exchange, notes, and other securities issued or to be issued in the future by a governmental authority; and the rental value of the residence when occupied by its owners. The following items are not exempt: pensions, retirement payments, other compensations, and salaries received during medical leave.

One group of taxpayers, consisting primarily of the self-employed and small businesses, is subject to a simplified tax regime called "single tax" (Monotributo). This regime replaces the PIT and VAT with a monthly fixed tax plus social security and health insurance contributions. The tax levied is a fixed amount established according to specific categories mapped onto income brackets in which the taxpayer falls. These categories are determined based on invoicing, the surface area of the facilities, or the amount of electricity consumed during production. No deductions for dependents or any other special deductions apply.

Taxes on wages are analyzed as part of the tax system, including contributions made by both the employee and the employer. In both cases, the amount collected is deposited into the Federal Tax Administration and that revenue is distributed according to the corresponding legal provisions.

For formal sector employees, we consider contributions to the social security system (11 percent), health insurance (3 percent), and the national pension fund (3 percent, up to a ceiling of Arg$21,248 monthly, the maximum taxable base), for a total rate of 17 percent.

For employers, we consider contributions to the social security system (12.71 percent), health insurance (6 percent), the national pension fund (1.62 percent), the fund for family allowances (5.56 percent), and the national employment fund (1.11 percent), which amounts to 27 percent of earnings in the formal sector. This rate pertains to employers whose activity is concentrated in the services sector; for other employers, the rate is 23 percent.

For the self-employed workers, we consider their contributions to the social security system (27 percent) and the national pension fund (5 percent). These rates are applied to a scaled tax base that is progressive and differs between professionals and traders. These workers have been identified in the household survey by years of education.

1.2 Indirect Taxes

VAT is a consumption tax on all stages of the production and distribution of goods and services. It is not cumulative and uses the "tax against tax" system, where the balance between tax credits (charged to sales) and tax debits (charged to purchases) is paid to the seller every month. This procedure is equivalent to applying the tax on the value added at every elaboration stage. It is levied on imports in a similar way to domestic production, but exports are zero rated.

The general VAT rate is 21 percent. There are few exemptions because most have been eliminated in successive reforms.[9] There are also differential rates: the highest is

[9] Among exemptions with considerable tax collection importance in 2012 were books, brochures, and similar printed material; noncarbonated water; and milk without additives, when the purchasers are end users or tax exempt; medicines, at the resale stage and for which the tax has been paid at the import or manufacturer's stage; medical services rendered through health insurance

27 percent on the invoices of public services provided to companies that are liable for the tax; the lowest is 10.5 percent on new home sales and a very limited list of goods and services.[10]

Excise taxes apply to the domestic sale and import of specific kinds of goods and transactions: alcoholic beverages (20 percent), beer (8 percent), soft drinks and other nonalcoholic beverages (4 to 8 percent), automobiles and diesel engines (10 percent), and insurance (2.5 percent).

For all taxes on goods, the taxable basis includes the tax itself. The taxable basis is the net price billed by the responsible party, defined as the remainder after discounts and bonuses, financing interest, and the VAT generated by the operation are deducted. In the case of cigarettes, the taxable basis is the sale price to the end user, excluding the VAT. In the case of insurance, the taxable basis does not include the tax itself, which is the only case in domestic taxes where the legal or nominal rate is applied to the taxable basis.

In 2012, liquid fuel and natural compressed gas were taxed (at 62 to 70 percent). The fuel tax is applied to all forms of gasoline: solvent, turpentine, gas oil, diesel oil, and kerosene. The tax also falls on compressed natural gas for motor vehicles, which is distributed through pipelines. The tax must be applied in a single circulation stage for the sale of national or imported products. Importers of liquid fuel and companies that refine or market it are subject to the fuel tax, as are distributors of gas before it enters the pipeline. Fuel tax is therefore calculated by applying the rate to the net sales price listed on the invoice for resellers at the dispatching plant.[11]

The so-called provincial tax on Gross Incomes is an important source of revenue for the subnational governments and is applied by all provinces. It is a cascading tax because it falls on all stages of production and distribution of goods and services. It taxes Gross Income without deducting the tax already paid and accumulated through previous purchases in the production process. Because it forces vertical integration of firms and discriminates in favor of imports that do not contain taxes paid on every production stage, the provincial turnover tax alters neutrality.

---

services by trade unions; theater performances; international passenger and cargo transportation; and life insurance.

[10] The lowest tax rate includes some basic foods (meat, fruit, vegetables, bread); newspapers, magazines and periodicals; goods at the selling stage to the general public; and domestic transportation services for passengers by land, water, or air, except for taxis and rental car services on routes less than 100 km. In the case of exempt goods, the 1997 input-output table was used, with data from 1993. The taxable input proportion was estimated for each exempt good: the incidence of taxable inputs was estimated for the sales amount of exempt goods, and the same structure was applied to the total of VAT purchases deriving from the consumption of exempt goods.

[11] Alternatively, although there is no reliable study at present in Argentina determining the percentage of fuel cost that is part of the transportation cost transferred to the consumer, and because transportation and fuel subsidies distort relative values, we assumed that 30 percent of the tax is transferred.

Although tax rates follow similar patterns across the country, rates vary considerably due to differences in economic activities and corresponding jurisdictions. In general, the highest rates appear in commerce and services, intermediate rates are applied to industrial activities, and the lowest rates occur in the primary sector.

In order to calculate tax incidence, we applied the tax rates described in this section to the data on consumption reported in the household survey. According to several authors, effective tax rates are about twice as high as rates on final consumption.[12] Consequently, rates on retail consumption have increased 150 percent in every province in order to account for the taxes included at every production stage. The methodology applied is the same as that for VAT and excise taxes. Because the tax base excludes VAT, excises, and fuel tax, the provincial turnover tax is the closest to input costs and should be included in the tax base of the previously mentioned taxes.

1.3 Flagship Cash Transfer Program: The Universal Allowance per Child

The target population for the Universal Allowance per Child is parents who have dependent children under the age of eighteen and are either informal workers with an income lower than the minimum salary of the formal sector, unemployed people without unemployment benefits, or domestic service workers.

The targeting mechanism consists of a monthly transfer of Arg$270 per child in 2012, raised to Arg$340 in September 2012. Parents receive benefits for each of up to five children. The first 80 percent of the benefit is received by direct deposit; the remaining 20 percent is transferred with proof that the children are attending school and have received the mandatory vaccines. This benefit includes a means testing mechanism in the sense that beneficiaries cannot receive other social benefits while receiving the Universal Allowance per Child.

1.4 Noncontributory Pensions

In 2005, the government instituted a retirement program through a moratorium for those who had not completed thirty years of service known as the Pension Moratorium (Moratoria Previsional). In 2007, the government added a program that allowed workers who had completed the required thirty years of service but who were at least five years younger than the official retirement age (sixty-five for men, sixty for women) to receive an Early Retirement pension (Jubilacion Anticipada). In the case of the Pension Moratorium, beneficiaries receive their transfer net of a reduction that corresponds to the number of years the person has not contributed to the system. For the Early Retirement pension, the transfer is 50 percent of the benefit that the person would receive at full retirement age, although the amount cannot be lower than the minimum pension.

---

[12] See, for instance, Rossignolo (2015).

1.5 Other Cash and Near-Cash Transfers

This category includes the following programs: Family Allowances (Asignaciones Familiares), Employment and Training Insurance (Seguro de Capacitacion y Empleo), Families for Social Inclusion Program (Programa Familias por la Inclusion Social), University Scholarships (Becas Universitarias), Youth with More and Better Jobs (Programa Jovenes con Mas y Mejor Trabajo), Unemployment Insurance (Seguro de Desempleo), and School Feeding Programs and Community Kitchens (Comedores Escolares y Comunitarios).

Family Allowances provides benefits to households based on the number of dependents (spouses, children, adopted children, and disabled children) and in support of school attendance for children living in the household. Eligible beneficiaries include wage earners in the formal sector who have children up to eighteen years of age and wages below a maximum threshold, as well as pensioners and unemployment compensation beneficiaries with children under eighteen. Benefits are determined based on income and the reported number of eligible beneficiaries. For instance, the fixed amount for every child in June 2012 was Arg$270 if the worker's wage was between Arg$100 and Arg$2,800; the amount decreased to Arg$204 for a wage between Arg$2,800 and Arg$4,000, and to Arg$136 for a wage between Arg$4,000 and Arg$5,200. These amounts were higher in the southern region of the country. A household might be excluded from this benefit in there are no children, or if the head of household is not working in the formal sector, is retired, is unemployed and receiving unemployment benefits, or is earning an income higher than the maximum allowed for the benefit (Arg$5,200 per month in 2012).

The beneficiaries of the Heads of Household Program, a safety net program launched in 2002 to help households cope with the surge in unemployment resulting from the financial crisis, were divided in two groups according to their employability potential. Those considered more "employable" were incorporated in the Training and Employment Insurance program, a twenty-four-month transfer of Arg$225 for the first eighteen months and Arg$200 for the remaining six months. The beneficiaries must attend training courses to increase their skills. Workers whose employability potential was considered low, received benefits from the Families for Social Inclusion Program. Benefits are based on the number of dependent children under age eighteen, from two to six children. The benefit starts at Arg$155 per child and increases to Arg$380 for six children or more for families below the poverty line.

The National Program of University Scholarships is for college-level students attending an officially recognized program of any national university. Beginning in 2009, students receive AR$3000 in ten installments throughout the year.[13] The target popu-

---

[13] There are other two additional scholarship programs: Bicentennial Scholarships (Programa de Becas Bicentenario), for students preparing for scientific careers, and National Program of Scholarships (Programa Nacional de Becas de Grado), for students of information technology. The

lation of the Youth with More and Better Jobs Program is people between eighteen and twenty-four years of age who neither work nor study. The beneficiaries must be unemployed, with incomplete primary or secondary education. The amount of the transfer is Arg$150 a month for two to eighteen months; in addition, transfers are made against the presentation of a small entrepreneur project for which the beneficiary receives Arg$4,000 per project (in 2012).

Workers who have lost their jobs through no fault of their own and have been unemployed for at least thirty-six months are entitled to receive unemployment insurance, which consists of a transfer of between Arg$250 and Arg$400, calculated as a percentage of the highest previous salary. Maximum coverage lasts one year.

Schools, clubs, and other organizations that serve meals to children or the unemployed receive a transfer under the School Feeding Program and Community Kitchen, which consists of a cash transfer related to the cost of milk or a basic food basket provided to feed children or adults below the poverty line.

1.6 Subsidies

Subsidies are directed to transportation, communications, energy and fuel, industry and agriculture, and other sectors. The most important subsidies are those for transportation and for energy and fuel; transportation subsidies are mainly oriented to supply, whereas energy and fuel are oriented to both supply and demand. Subsidies to energy include fuel, gas, and electricity; subsidies to transportation comprise tariffs for trains, subways, airplanes, and buses.

Argentina has become a net importer of fuel after being a net exporter of fuel in the 1990s and at the beginning of the 2000s. The price of the imported gas oil is subsidized through a fiduciary fund, and the consumer receives the difference between the price of fuel within the internal market and the same product at international prices. For gas, there are two kinds of subsidy: for those who receive gas through a pipeline, the subsidy is included in the reduced cost of imported gas, which is included in the tariff; those who buy bottled gas pay a subsidized price in which the government gives the producers the difference between the market price and the subsidized price. The total amount paid varies depending on the volume of the previous year's gas consumption. For electricity, the government created a fiduciary fund to subsidize tariffs for households. The subsidy depends on the volume of the previous year's electricity consumption.

1.7 Education and Health

In 2006, the National Education Law was passed following the Education Financing Law, which extended compulsory education to the end of secondary school. Data show

---

study presented here might overestimate the amount received by students somewhat because it cannot establish in which program the beneficiaries are studying.

that when compulsory education is extended, attendance increases but that students also continue to drop out at the same ages as before the law was passed.[14]

There are two educational systems at every level in Argentina: a free, public education system and a subsidized, private system. Primary education is managed by the municipalities, secondary education is the responsibility of the provinces, and university is administered at a national level (with several exceptions at all levels). The public education system served 73 percent of total students in 2012, of which 28.2 percent were enrolled in primary public schools. Public universities enrolled 79 percent of university students. Because there is no reliable information on public spending by level, the results for the distributional impact of education expenditures will be classified in aggregated terms in basic education, including initial, primary and secondary school, and tertiary and university education.[15]

The Argentine health system is split into several parts because different population groups access different providers. One component of health insurance covers the population dependent on formal wage earners or retired pensioners. Populations that are not covered have access to the public health system. The high-income population has access to the private system.

For formal workers in both the private and public sectors as well at national and provincial levels, health benefits are delivered mainly through the health insurance systems of trade unions. These workers comprise the greatest share of beneficiaries. Pensioners are covered by the health insurance system known as the INSSJyP (Instituto Nacional de Servicios Sociales para Jubilados y Pensionados, or, National Institute for Social Services for Retirees and Pensioners, also known as PAMI), a subsystem that finances private health service providers. The public health system (hospitals) covers those who are not covered by a health insurance system.

It is worth noting that the population covered by the private system can also receive public system benefits. Public expenditures for health have risen to 5.4 percent of GDP, 2.4 percent of which belongs to health insurance systems. Low-complexity hospitals were decentralized to the provinces and municipalities in the 1990s, while the high-complexity ones still remain under federal administration.

2 Data Sources and Methodological Assumptions

The main source of information for this report was the National Household Expenditure Survey (ENGHo), which collects information on households' incomes and expenditures and was conducted by the Federal Statistics and Census Institute (INDEC; Instituto Nacional de Estadistica y Censos) between March 2012 and February 2013.

---

[14] See Gomez Sabaini and others (2013).

[15] For each educational level, the results for public and private subsidized education can be shown and are available from the author upon request.

The ENGHo is a large-scale survey that obtains detailed answers from approximately 20,960 households across the country.

For the purposes of the survey, households are units made up of any person or group of people, related or unrelated, living in the same home under a family system and consuming food paid for by the same budget.

The ENGHo is a representative sample of 86.8 percent of the population, mainly urban. Rural towns with fewer than five thousand inhabitants were excluded.

Regarding macroeconomics aggregates, as of the completion of this study, Argentina did not have a consolidated GDP series. The official information consists of two series with different base years, 1993 and 2004. The series with base year 1993 was used for the first three quarters and the 2004 series was substituted in the fourth quarter of 2013. The 2004 series shows higher nominal GDP values than the 1993 series, around 22 percent for the same period, which is a reflection of the previous government's effort to avoid measuring inflation rates accurately.[16]

The 2012–2013 survey used for this study was published before the base year was changed, so the nominal values are from base year 1993. The amounts of public spending and taxes used here, in contrast, correspond to base year 2004. So, if we had maintained the nominal values for incomes and expenditures as they appear in the survey, the redistributive impact would have been overestimated. In order to avoid such a distortion, the nominal values for taxes and transfers were adjusted downward on the order of 22 percent (the ratio of GDP with 1993 as the base year and GDP with 2004 as the base year).

There was also no national accounts information on Disposable Income, which, according to the CEQ methodology, should be used to generate the coefficient to scale down public spending in education and health to the level of Disposable Income found in the survey. Thus, a new macroeconomic available income calculation was made (ad hoc) to use for scaling down the budget values on education, health, and economic benefits expenditure. These available income values were calculated according to the methodology of previous work on replacing official data.[17] With these calculations, available income represents only 67 percent of 2012 official GDP rather than the official 97 percent.

With regard to consolidated public spending, after 2009 there is no information covering the three jurisdictional levels: national, provincial, and municipal. To estimate this amount, we projected the components of aggregate spending by objective and function, based on the evolution of some partial components of expenditure included in the budgets of jurisdictions and different agencies such as the National Administration of Social Security and the Ministry of Education, among others. Because information is

---

[16] For reference, the annual inflation officially recognized by INDEC was around 9.5 percent on average for the 2007–2014 period, whereas unofficial estimates (from an average of seven to nine provinces from Centro de Estudios para el Desarrollo Argentino, Fundacion de Investigaciones Economicas Latinoamericanas) showed annual averages of 23 percent.

[17] See Gomez Sabaini and others (2002) and Gasparini (1998).

not available on each of the existing programs for every jurisdiction, the most representative programs were identified and were then used to calculate the impact of public spending on social inequality and poverty.

The calculation of the effect on equity of the following direct transfer programs—Universal Allowance per Child, Family Allowances, Employment and Training Insurance, Families for Social Inclusion Program, Youth with More and Better Jobs, Unemployment Insurance, School Feeding Programs and Community Kitchens, and college scholarships—was carried out through using one of the methods described in chapter 6 in this Volume of the Handbook by Enami, Higgins, and Lustig (2022). Because the household survey reported only the value of total cash transfers, including both private and government transfers, the incidence of the Universal Allowance per Child and Unemployment Insurance had to be imputed. This was done by imputing the amounts that would have corresponded to households that included members who reported receiving benefits from one or both of these programs. The imputed amounts were subtracted from the total reported cash transfers; the remaining ones were assumed to be private transfers and thus were included as part of Market Income. It should be noted that, since the self-employed were not included as beneficiaries in the Universal Allowance per Child program in 2012–13, I made sure that the self-employed did not appear as beneficiaries of these cash transfers. In order to assess how sensitive the results are to these specific assumptions, I estimated the incidence of cash transfers assuming that the entire amount reported as transfers came from government transfers to obtain an "upper bound." The redistributive and poverty effects are not so different from the ones reported here, which can be taken as evidence that results are quite robust to alternative assumptions. For the rest of the transfers, the benefits were simulated based on the statutory rules.

The incidence of the noncontributory pension programs known as the Pension Moratorium and Early Retirement was inferred.[18] The household survey reports "pensions" as a total without specifying whether they are pensions from the contributory system, these two noncontributory pension programs, or private pensions.[19] The survey does indicate whether a household member received a pension, although it does

---

[18] It should be noted that the term "noncontributory" pensions in Argentina refers to other forms of noncontributory pensions. Here, I always refer to the two programs mentioned in this paragraph.

[19] In particular, the household survey reports incomes by source, as follows: wages and salaries, self-employed income, employer's income, rents, retirement pensions, and cash transfers. The survey does not distinguish whether pensions or transfers are public or private. The survey does, however, ask whether the household received benefits from the Universal Allowance per Child and the Unemployment Insurance, private transfers, and pensions from the national or provincial systems. These responses to these questions are "yes" or "no." Thus, strictly speaking, one cannot determine whether the reported amounts (in total or in part) for transfers and pensions should be classified as government transfers. Hence, the various assumptions that were made to obtain an estimate of their incidence.

not state whether that income corresponds to one of the two noncontributory pensions or to a contributory pension. Here, I assumed that noncontributory pensions were included in the reported amount. In order to determine the amount corresponding to contributory pensions, I subtracted from the pensions reported by households the pensions whose amount was below the minimum in the contributory system (for the Pension Moratorium) and the pensions received by beneficiaries whose age was at least five years earlier than the legal retirement age (for the Early Retirement program).

Since Argentina did not have reliable estimates of the Consumer Price Index, in order to convert the values of income thresholds expressed in 2005 and 2011 purchasing power parity into 2012 prices, I used the implicit GDP deflator.

Also, since the government did not report consolidated expenditures on subsidies for transport services, gas, and electricity, to generate these totals I used data reported by the Argentine Public Spending Association on the amounts that were transferred from the public sector to private companies to keep prices unchanged.

For the inclusion of taxes paid on inputs, we partially adapted the information aggregated from the input-output matrix of 1997, which is particularly relevant for the case of VAT exemptions or the fuel tax.

Information on direct taxes is rarely collected directly by surveys; instead, surveys report earnings, and the incidence of taxes needs to be simulated. Wage earners in the formal sector report income after taxes. For wage earners in the informal sector, the self-employed, capital income earners, and people receiving pensions and transfers, the assumption is that reported income reflects earnings before taxes. In this study, as in the majority of studies based on a partial equilibrium framework, I assume that the burden generated by taxes/subsidies on goods and services is fully shifted to consumers via a higher/lower price and that the burden of PIT and other income taxes falls on the person required to pay them (the income earner). Tax evasion here is taken into account in two ways: for purchases made in informal markets, I assume that no consumption taxes have been paid; regarding wage earners in the informal sector (for example, those who do not contribute to the social security system), I assume that they do not pay PIT.

3 Main Results

This section presents several results of the CEQ analysis of the impact of taxes and public spending on poverty and inequality in Argentina. The main results focus on the benchmark case, in which pensions are a part of Market Income. Results from the sensitivity analysis, where pensions are treated as a government transfer, are presented as well.

3.1 Impact on Inequality and Poverty

The evolution of the Gini coefficient and headcount ratio (using the international poverty lines of US$2.50 purchasing power parity [PPP] and US$4.00 PPP per day—extreme

TABLE 11-2

Gini and Headcount Index by Income Concept for Argentina 2012

	Market income	Net market income	Disposable income	Consumable income	Final income
Benchmark case: Pensions are part of market income					
Gini	0.475	0.436	0.405	0.411	0.299
Headcount index					
US$2.50 PPP (%)	4.7%	5.1%	1.8%	3.0%	
US$4.00 PPP (%)	12.3%	13.9%	7.3%	12.5%	
National moderate poverty line	10.3%	12.0%	5.6%	9.7%	
Other moderate poverty line	28.8%	33.1%	28.4%	37.8%	
Sensitivity analysis: Pensions are a government transfer					
Gini	0.502	0.459	0.404	0.410	0.298
Headcount index					
US$2.50 PPP (%)	8.5%	9.0%	1.8%	3.1%	
US$4.00 PPP (%)	17.3%	19.0%	7.3%	12.5%	
National moderate poverty line	14.7%	16.8%	5.6%	9.8%	
Other moderate poverty line	33.8%	39.3%	28.5%	37.9%	

Source: Author's calculations based on ENGHo (2012–2013).

PL = Poverty line.
National moderate PL. *Source:* INDEC (2017).
Other moderate PL. *Source:* FIEL (2017).

and moderate, respectively—and the national moderate poverty lines)[20] for the scenario with contributory pensions as deferred income (also called "benchmark" scenario) and with pensions as a government transfer (also called "sensitivity analysis") are presented in table 11-2 and figures 11-1 and 11-2.

As shown, the impact of direct taxes and direct transfers combined is equalizing and poverty-reducing. In the scenario with contributory pensions as deferred income, the Disposable Income Gini declines by around 14.8 percent and extreme poverty falls by 61 percent (figures 11-1 and 11-2, respectively). Because contributory pensions are progressive, the declines are considerably higher in the scenario in which contributory pensions are treated as a transfer (remember that the noncontributory Pension Moratorium and Early Retirement are always treated as government transfers).

---

[20] The national extreme poverty line is calculated by INDEC and refers to the minimum consumption basket necessary to meet adult daily food needs; the moderate poverty line adds to the former other minimum daily expenditures.

FIGURE 11-1

Evolution of Inequality through Different Income Concepts

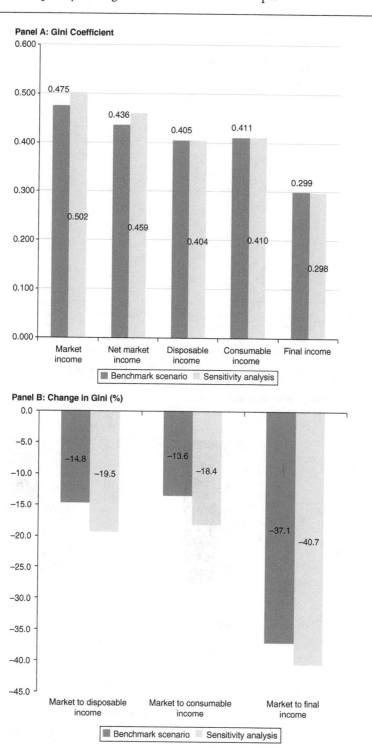

Source: Author's calculations based on ENGHo (2012–2013).

FIGURE 11-2
Evolution of Poverty through Different Income Concepts

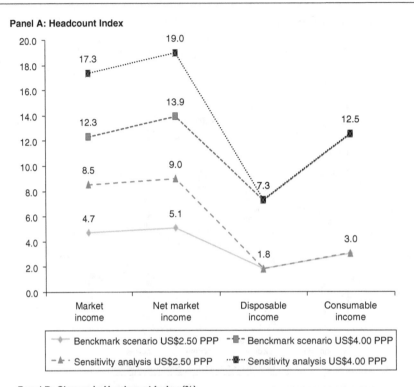

Panel A: Headcount Index

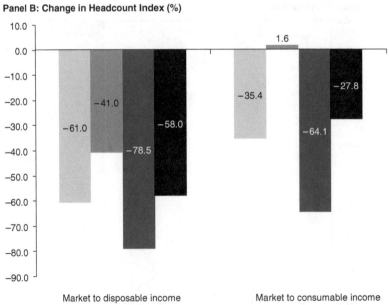

Panel B: Change in Headcount Index (%)

Source: Author's calculations based on ENGHo (2012–2013).

Consumable Income adds the net effect of indirect taxes and economic subsidies to Disposable Income. The high impact of subsidies more than compensates for the unequalizing effect of taxes (see 11.1 and 11.2). With the international poverty line of $2.50, the Consumable Income headcount ratio is lower than Market Income poverty (though higher than Disposable Income poverty). However, with the $4.00 line, the Consumable Income headcount ratio is above Market Income poverty. Except for the very poor, low-income consumers pay more in indirect taxes than what they receive in subsidies.

In-kind transfers in education and health are quite equalizing, as shown when calculating the Gini index with Final Income. The Final Income Gini (compared to the Market Income Gini) declines by 37 percent when pensions are considered deferred income. When pensions are considered a government transfer, the impact is—as expected—considerably higher.

3.2 Coverage and Effectiveness of Direct Transfers

Table 11-3 presents indicators that measure the extent to which direct transfers are effective and efficient in reducing poverty (using both international and national poverty lines) for the scenarios with contributory pensions as deferred income and as transfers.

The vertical expenditure efficiency (VEE) indicator measures the amount of direct transfers that go to the poor. This indicator shows that 11 percent of direct transfers reach the extreme poor, while 31 percent of direct transfers reach the total poor population (using international poverty lines). (The results were 43 percent and 50 percent in the sensitivity analysis.) The spillover index (S) indicates how much of the spending that reached the poor was in excess of the strictly necessary amount required for the beneficiaries to reach the poverty line. As shown, the spillovers are high. The poverty reduction efficiency (PRE) indicator is the product of VEE × S. Finally, the poverty gap efficiency (PGE) measures the transfers' effectiveness in reducing the poverty gap. PGE estimates indicate that direct transfers are more efficient in reducing extreme poverty gaps than in reducing total poverty gaps.

Table 11-4 shows coverage levels and the distribution of benefits for every disaggregated area of public spending. The table shows that Universal Allowance per Child, Families for Social Inclusion Program, and the Pension Moratorium (and hospitals, among in-kind transfers) are the programs most targeted to the extreme poor. Meanwhile, tertiary education and indirect subsidies concentrate their benefits more heavily on the non-poor (that is, those who exceed the US$4.00 PPP per day line).

3.3 Incidence Analysis

The incidence analysis has been calculated through the ratio of benefits to Market Income by Market Income deciles (see tables 11-5 and 11-6). The effect of direct taxes and

TABLE 11-3

Poverty Reduction Efficiency and Effectiveness Indicators of Direct Transfers
for Argentina 2012 in Percentages

	Benchmark case (national accounts)	Sensitivity analysis (national accounts)
Inequality		
Change in Gini (direct transfers)	0.58	1.11
Poverty		
Change in headcount index (US$2.50 PPP per day)	0.58	0.58
Change in headcount index (US$4.00 PPP per day)	1.20	0.95
Effectiveness indicators		
US$2.50 PPP per day		
Vertical expenditure efficiency	0.11	0.43
Poverty reduction efficiency	0.04	0.07
Spillover index	0.62	0.85
Poverty gap efficiency	0.71	0.94
US$4.00 PPP per day		
Vertical expenditure efficiency	0.31	0.50
Poverty reduction efficiency	0.14	0.13
Spillover index	0.55	0.74
Poverty gap efficiency	0.62	0.85
National extreme poverty line		
Vertical expenditure efficiency	0.05	0.40
Poverty reduction efficiency	0.02	0.04
Spillover index	0.67	0.90
Poverty gap efficiency	0.78	0.97
National moderate poverty line		
Vertical expenditure efficiency	0.28	0.49
Poverty reduction efficiency	0.11	0.11
Spillover index	0.60	0.77
Poverty gap efficiency	0.64	0.88

Source: Author's calculations based on ENGHo (2012–2013).

direct transfers leads to a reduction in inequality: the highest decile by Market Income ranking is the one that bears the highest proportion of direct taxes. Meanwhile, in the case of direct transfers, the effect is the inverse, because the lowest Market Income deciles receive the highest proportion of transfers.

The analysis of indirect taxes shows that the lowest Market Income deciles pay a higher proportion of their Market Income in taxes than other deciles, although this effect is partially mitigated by the indirect subsidies. In-kind transfers (health and education) benefit heavily on the lowest Market Income deciles.

As expected, when pensions are considered a government transfer, the impact is outstanding for the lowest deciles of income distribution (table 11-6). However, such

TABLE 11-4

Coverage and Distribution of Benefits and Beneficiaries by Program in Argentina 2012

	Benchmark scenario groups			Sensitivity analysis groups		
	y < 2.5 (%)	2.5 < y < 4 (%)	y > 4 (%)	y < 2.5 (%)	2.5 < y < 4 (%)	y > 4 (%)
Health: hospitals	14.7	15.5	69.8	39.9	15.2	44.9
Health: contributory	1.0	3.8	95.2	2.3	4.7	93.0
Health: contributory elderly (INSSJyP)	2.3	4.8	93.0	5.8	5.5	88.7
Education: basic	5.6	8.6	85.8	7.7	9.5	82.8
Education: tertiary and university	0.4	1.3	98.2	2.3	1.9	95.9
Transportation	1.1	2.6	96.2	5.0	2.9	92.1
Subsidies on bus tariffs	1.5	3.0	95.5	5.9	3.7	90.4
Subsidies on train tariffs	1.0	2.8	96.2	4.6	2.7	92.8
Subsidies on subway tariffs	0.0	1.8	98.2	7.1	1.8	91.0
Subsidies on airplane tariffs	0.0	0.0	100.0	3.2	0.0	96.8
Electricity	2.3	3.2	94.5	14.0	3.0	83.0
Gas provision by pipeline	0.8	1.1	98.1	7.7	1.0	91.3
Bottled gas	3.5	8.1	88.4	13.3	9.0	77.7
Total gas provision	1.1	1.9	97.0	8.3	1.8	89.9
Direct fuel subsidies	0.1	0.2	99.7	1.0	0.2	98.8
Indirect fuel subsidies	2.0	3.0	95.0	8.2	3.6	88.2
Family Allowances	2.9	6.6	90.5	13.7	9.4	76.9
Universal Allowance per Child	16.2	21.7	62.1	20.4	23.0	56.6
Pension Fund Moratorium and Early Retirement Program	12.2	22.5	65.2	48.3	3.6	48.1

(continued)

TABLE 11-4   (continued)

	Benchmark scenario groups			Sensitivity analysis groups		
	y < 2.5 (%)	2.5 < y < 4 (%)	y > 4 (%)	y < 2.5 (%)	2.5 < y < 4 (%)	y > 4 (%)
Employment and Training Insurance	4.1	2.8	93.1	17.5	5.6	76.9
Family Social Inclusion Program	20.1	36.7	43.1	24.4	39.1	36.4
University grants	0.0	0.0	100.0	0.0	0.0	100.0
Youth Program for More and Better Work	3.3	4.0	92.7	3.4	4.0	92.6
Unemployment Insurance	7.4	15.6	77.1	9.0	15.8	75.2
School and Community Kitchens	7.2	14.6	78.2	12.2	14.5	73.3
Direct cash transfers	10.6	18.4	71.0	41.7	6.4	51.9
Total non-contributory pensions	12.2	22.5	65.2	48.3	3.6	48.1
Total contributory pensions	0.5	1.2	98.3	45.8	4.7	49.4
Total education spending	4.3	6.9	88.8	6.4	7.7	86.0
Total health spending	6.8	8.7	84.5	18.2	9.1	72.6
Total CEQ social spending	6.4	9.6	84.0	25.3	7.5	67.2
Income shares	0.3	0.9	98.8	0.4	1.2	98.4
Population shares	4.1	6.0	89.9	10.7	6.5	82.7

Source: Author's calculations based on ENGHo (2012–2013).

y < 2.5. Income below US$2.50 PPP.

2.5 < y < 4. Income between US$2.50 PPP and US$4.00 PPP.

y > 4. Income higher than US$4.00 PPP.

INSSJyP. Instituto Nacional de Servicios Sociales para Jubilados y Pensionados (National Institute for Social Services for Retirees and Pensioners).

an impact is not a measure of the pensions' targeting, because by definition retirees will have zero or near zero Market Income.

3.4 Progressivity

Figure 11-3 presents social spending by program, total social spending, and indirect expenditures, sorted by their degree of progressivity. The concentration coefficient for social spending shows progressivity in absolute terms (a pro-poor characteristic).

Most direct cash transfers, education expenditures, and health benefits are progressive in absolute terms. Spending in tertiary and university education, however, is "pro-rich," because it benefits wealthier households more than poorer ones (in absolute terms). This result coincides with those of other studies.[21] By contrast, expenditures that are regressive in absolute terms (pro-rich) are dominated by indirect subsidies (public transfers designed to keep tariffs low). Transportation, electricity, and gas are among these expenditures, because richer households receive a higher benefit in absolute terms than low-income individuals do.

Income distribution by decile for the benchmark case and the sensitivity analysis is presented in table 11-7. For instance, the first decile concentrates 1.2 percent of Market Income for the benchmark case and 0.3 percent of Market Income when pensions are considered a government transfer. After government intervention, the first decile concentrates 3.9 percent of Final Income.

The richest decile concentrates 35.7 percent of Market Income in the benchmark case and 38.5 percent in the sensitivity analysis, although taxes and public expenditures reduce its share to 27.3 percent of Final Income.

Figure 11-4 presents Lorenz and concentration curves for aggregate public expenditures and Market Income. Social expenditures, direct transfers, and noncontributory expenditures are progressive in absolute (pro-poor) and relative terms, whereas indirect subsidies benefit the rich in absolute terms.

Figure 11-5 shows these curves for every income concept and expresses the redistribution through taxes and public expenditures. The Lorenz curve corresponding to Final Income lies above that of Market Income, showing that public intervention improves income distribution.

3.5 Poverty

Tables 11-8 and 11-9 show the results for poverty. The picture is roughly similar to that of inequality in that most poor households benefit strongly from direct and in-kind transfers (health and education) and the richest receive a greatly reduced proportion of these benefits. The impact on the lowest deciles is much higher when

---

[21] See, for example, Gomez Sabaini and others (2013).

TABLE 11-5

Incidence of Taxes and Transfers on Income Distribution in Percentages
for Argentina 2012 (benchmark case)

Deciles	Direct taxes (%)	Contributions excluding contributions to pensions (%)	Non-contributory pensions (%)	Flagship conditional cash transfers (%)	Other direct transfers (targeted or not) (%)
1	−0.4	−3.1	40.1	18.6	20.4
2	−0.3	−5.5	5.4	6.8	9.1
3	−0.3	−9.0	3.4	2.7	4.4
4	−0.2	−11.8	2.9	1.0	2.9
5	−0.3	−12.3	1.8	0.7	2.3
6	−0.2	−13.6	2.0	0.1	1.8
7	−0.2	−15.2	0.9	0.1	1.0
8	−0.4	−15.9	0.6	0.0	0.7
9	−1.9	−17.0	0.3	0.0	0.3
10	−10.9	−19.6	0.2	0.0	0.2
Total population	−4.4	−16.1	1.4	0.6	1.3

Source: Author's calculations based on ENGHo (2012–2013).

TABLE 11-6

Incidence of Taxes and Transfers on Income Distribution in Percentages
for Argentina 2012 (sensitivity analysis)

Deciles	Direct taxes (%)	Contributions to social security (%)	Contributory pensions (%)	Non-contributory pensions (%)	Flagship conditional cash transfers (%)
1	−0.8	−2.3	1501.4	226.0	36.3
2	−0.4	−4.4	42.8	6.2	11.8
3	−0.3	−6.5	19.6	4.0	5.0
4	−0.3	−10.8	16.0	2.3	1.9
5	−0.3	−13.2	12.5	2.0	0.8
6	−0.3	−15.2	6.7	1.7	0.5
7	−0.2	−17.7	6.3	1.0	0.1
8	−0.6	−18.3	6.9	0.5	0.0
9	−1.7	−19.2	4.0	0.3	0.0
10	−11.5	−21.2	1.5	0.1	0.0
Total population	−4.9	−18.0	11.0	1.6	0.7

Source: Author's calculations based on ENGHo (2012–2013).

All direct transfers (%)	Indirect subsidies (%)	Indirect taxes (%)	Net indirect taxes (%)	In-kind education (%)	In-kind health (%)	In-kind transfers (%)
79.1	15.1	−41.1	−26.0	76.9	94.2	171.1
21.3	9.3	−28.4	−19.2	40.2	46.6	86.7
10.5	7.5	−24.1	16.5	25.4	25.0	50.4
6.8	7.8	−23.0	−15.3	18.3	16.7	35.0
4.8	6.5	−22.1	−15.7	14.4	13.0	27.4
3.9	6.5	−21.8	−15.3	11.0	9.8	20.8
2.0	5.3	−21.0	−15.7	8.5	6.7	15.2
1.3	7.2	−19.9	−12.6	6.5	4.4	11.0
0.7	4.5	−18.9	−14.4	4.1	2.7	6.8
0.3	3.0	−15.0	−12.0	2.2	0.9	3.2
3.4	5.2	−19.1	−14.0	8.5	7.5	16.0

Other direct transfers (targeted or not) (%)	All direct transfers (%)	Indirect subsidies (%)	Indirect taxes (%)	Net indirect taxes (%)	In-kind education (%)	In-kind health (%)	In-kind transfers (%)
57.9	1821.6	142.1	−432.3	−290.2	161.5	435.7	597.2
15.9	76.7	13.1	−14.2	−28.2	57.7	62.4	120.1
6.4	35.0	11.0	−30.9	−20.0	33.9	43.0	76.9
4.0	24.2	7.9	−27.1	−19.2	23.8	19.6	43.5
3.0	18.3	8.2	−24.8	−16.6	16.9	14.4	31.3
2.0	10.8	5.9	−22.9	−17.0	14.5	11.8	26.3
1.3	8.7	5.6	−22.0	−16.4	11.2	7.0	18.2
0.8	8.2	8.1	−21.3	−13.2	7.8	4.3	12.1
0.3	4.8	4.4	−19.6	−15.2	5.3	2.5	7.8
0.2	1.8	3.2	−14.9	−11.7	2.4	0.9	3.3
1.5	14.8	5.8	−21.2	−15.4	9.5	8.4	17.9

FIGURE 11-3

Concentration Coefficient by Spending Category with Respect to Market Income, Argentina 2012

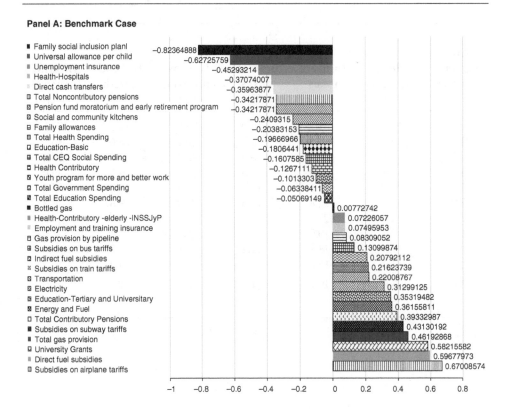

Panel A: Benchmark Case

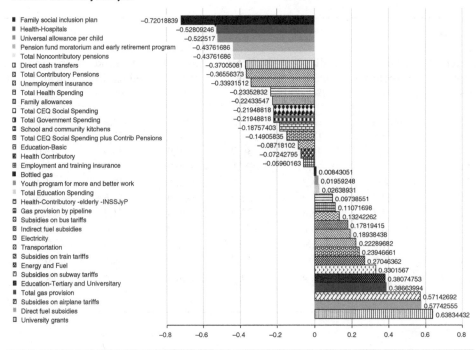

Panel B: Sensitivity Analysis

Source: Author's calculations based on ENGHo (2012–2013).

Note: The phrase "health contributory elderly" refers to the health coverage received by elderly people through INSSJyP. Instituto Nacional de Servicios Sociales para Jubilados y Pensionados (National Institute for Social Services for Retirees and Pensioners).

TABLE 11-7

Income Distribution by Decile for Argentina 2012

Decile	Benchmark case					Sensitivity analysis				
	Market income (%)	Net market income (%)	Disposable income (%)	Consumable income (%)	Final income (%)	Market income (%)	Net market income (%)	Disposable income (%)	Consumable income (%)	Final income (%)
1	1.23	1.46	2.08	2.06	3.85	0.33	0.41	2.10	2.08	3.88
2	2.43	2.84	3.39	3.34	4.97	1.88	2.28	3.41	3.36	5.00
3	3.62	4.04	4.41	4.35	5.76	3.03	3.59	4.44	4.38	5.79
4	4.84	5.28	5.55	5.50	6.53	4.33	4.90	5.58	5.52	6.56
5	6.18	6.68	6.85	6.68	7.40	5.68	6.29	6.86	6.69	7.40
6	7.57	8.15	8.19	8.04	8.40	7.33	7.94	8.18	8.05	8.40
7	9.36	9.95	9.85	9.70	9.60	9.23	9.85	9.81	9.66	9.57
8	12.15	12.64	12.36	12.22	11.51	12.18	12.72	12.34	12.17	11.46
9	16.97	17.02	16.52	16.25	14.70	17.51	17.61	16.47	16.20	14.68
10	35.65	31.92	30.80	31.86	27.28	38.50	34.39	30.83	31.90	27.27
Total	100.00	100.00	100.00	100.00	100.00	100.00	100.00	100.00	100.00	100.00

Source: Author's calculations based on ENGHo (2012–2013).

FIGURE 11-4
Lorenz and Concentration Curves for Aggregate Public Expenditures, Argentina 2012

Panel A: Benchmark Case

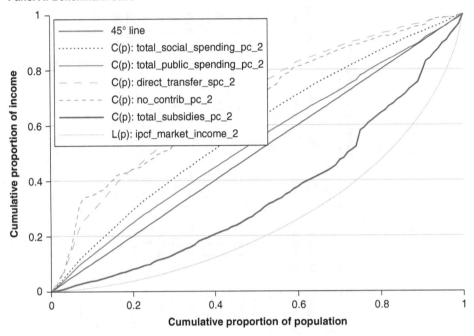

Panel B: Sensitivity Analysis

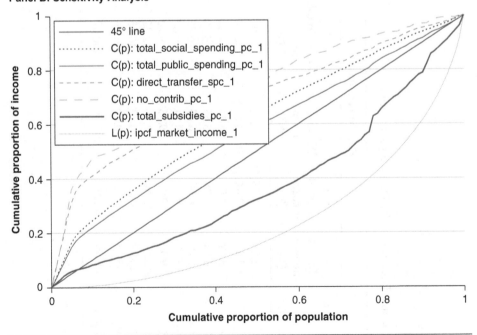

Source: Author's calculations based on ENGHo (2012–2013).

FIGURE 11-5
Redistributional Effect of Taxes and Public Expenditures, Argentina 2012

Panel A: Benchmark Case

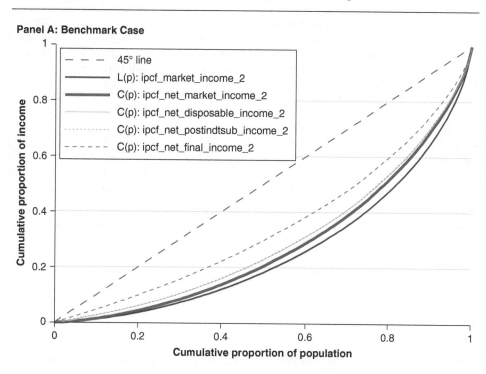

Panel B: Sensitivity Analysis

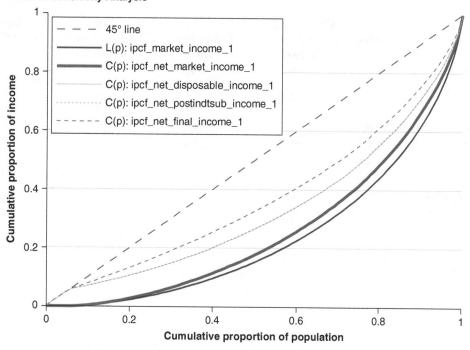

Source: Author's calculations based on ENGHo (2012–2013).

TABLE 11-8
Incidence of Taxes and Transfers on Poverty in Percentages in Argentina 2012 (benchmark case)

Group	Direct taxes (%)	Contributions excluding contributions to pensions (%)	Non-contributory pensions (%)	Flagship conditional cash transfers (%)	Other direct transfers (targeted or not) (%)
y < 1.25	−0.9	−1.1	60.8	98.9	86.5
1.25 ⇐ y < 2.50	−0.4	−1.6	57.4	24.4	20.8
2.50 ⇐ y < 4.00	−0.3	−3.5	33.7	13.9	17.9
4.00 ⇐ y < 10.00	−0.3	−8.3	4.1	3.5	5.6
10.00 ⇐ y < 50.00	−1.2	−15.5	0.9	0.2	1.0
50.00 ⇐ y	−11.7	−19.8	0.1	0.0	0.2
Total population	−4.4	−16.1	1.4	0.6	1.3

Source: Author's calculations based on ENGHo (2012–2013).

y < 2.5. Income below US$2.50 PPP.
2.5 < y < 4. Income between US$2.50 PPP and US$4.00 PPP.
y > 4. Income higher than US$4.00 PPP.

TABLE 11-9
Incidence of Taxes and Transfers on Poverty in Percentages in Argentina 2012 (sensitivity analysis)

Group	Direct taxes (%)	Contributions to social security (%)	Contributory pensions (%)	Non-contributory pensions (%)	Flagship conditional cash transfers (%)
y < 1.25	−1.5	−2.4	6779.0	949.7	77.3
1.25 ⇐ y < 2.50	−0.5	−2.4	89.8	29.1	23.7
2.50 ⇐ y < 4.00	−0.4	−4.4	44.8	4.9	13.5
4.00 ⇐ y < 10.00	−0.3	−9.0	18.5	3.0	3.2
10.00 ⇐ y < 50.00	−1.6	−18.1	5.7	0.8	0.2
50.00 ⇐ y	−12.5	−21.2	1.4	0.1	0.0
Total population	−4.9	−18.0	11.0	1.6	0.7

Source: Author's calculations based on ENGHo (2012–2013).

y < 2.5. Income below US$2.50 PPP.
2.5 < y < 4. Income between US$2.50 PPP and US$4.00 PPP.
y > 4. Income higher than US$4.00 PPP.

All direct transfers (%)	Indirect subsidies (%)	Indirect taxes (%)	Net indirect taxes (%)	In-kind education (%)	In-kind health (%)	In-kind transfers (%)
246.2	36.6	−81.3	−44.7	321.3	437.1	758.3
102.6	18.5	−47.3	−28.8	98.3	136.5	234.8
65.5	13.3	−37.7	−24.4	61.9	69.1	131.0
13.2	8.1	−25.3	−17.2	28.3	29.6	57.9
2.1	5.9	−20.2	−14.3	7.8	6.2	13.9
0.3	2.6	−14.6	−12.0	2.1	0.8	2.9
3.4	5.2	−19.1	−14.0	8.5	7.5	16.0

Other direct transfers (targeted or not) (%)	All direct transfers (%)	Indirect subsidies (%)	Indirect taxes (%)	Net indirect taxes (%)	In-kind education (%)	In-kind health (%)	In-kind transfers (%)
171.5	7977.4	569.3	−1809.7	−1240.5	371.4	1498.1	1869.6
24.7	167.4	25.0	−62.8	−37.8	98.2	137.2	235.4
18.1	81.3	13.4	−41.2	−27.8	62.8	65.9	128.7
5.2	30.0	9.4	−29.0	−19.6	27.6	28.7	56.2
0.9	7.5	6.1	−20.8	−14.8	8.6	5.5	14.1
0.2	1.6	2.4	−14.4	−11.9	2.2	0.8	2.9
1.5	14.8	5.8	−21.2	−15.4	9.5	8.4	17.9

pensions are considered a public transfer, because under this scenario, retirees who by definition have zero or near zero Market Income in the household survey are classified as poor.

Like the income distribution analysis by decile, table 11-10 presents the distribution by socioeconomic group based on poverty analysis and shows that the greatest proportion of the population lies in the fifth bracket (US$10.00 to US$50.00 PPP). The fiscal system reduces the percentage of the population below the poverty lines, even in the highest bracket. For the benchmark case, 30.9 percent of the population was below US$50.00 PPP when considering Market Income in the benchmark case, whereas when considering Consumable Income, that percentage dropped to 13 percent. In the sensitivity analysis, 7.1 percent of the population was below US$50.00 PPP considering Market Income, but when considering Consumable Income, that proportion decreased to 2.4 percent.

3.6 Fiscal Mobility

Table 11-11 and table 11-12 display the fiscal mobility matrixes for the benchmark case and the sensitivity analysis, respectively. For the benchmark case, around 27 percent of the population under extreme poverty in the Market Income group remains in that condition in the Disposable Income classification, which means that around 73 percent of that population can rise out of that condition into a group with between US$1.25 and US$10.00 PPP when considering Disposable Income.

Analyzing Consumable Income, we see that 38.1 percent of the population is in the group below US$1.25 PPP. This is an increase from the percentage in the Disposable Income analysis and indicates the effect of indirect taxes and transfers.

When comparing Market Income and Final Income groups, about 80 percent of the population that was below the extreme poverty threshold considering Market Income move into groups between US$4.00 to US$10.00 PPP when considering Final Income due to the effect of in-kind taxes and transfers.

In the sensitivity analysis, around 4 percent of the population under extreme poverty in the Market Income group remains in that condition in the Disposable Income classification. Around 63 percent can move out of that condition and into the group with between US$10.00 and US$50.00 PPP when considering Disposable Income.

When analyzing Consumable Income, we find that 6 percent of the population is below US$1.25 PPP; the effect of indirect taxes and transfers increases this proportion compared to Disposable Income.

In comparing Market Income and Final Income groups, we see that about 24 percent of the population that was below the extreme poverty threshold considering Market Income rise to between US$4.00 to US$10.00 PPP when considering Final Income due to the effect of in-kind taxes and transfers.

TABLE 11-10

Income Distribution by Socioeconomic Group in Argentina 2012

Group	Benchmark case				Sensitivity analysis			
	Market income	Net market income	Disposable income	Consumable income	Market income	Net market income	Disposable income	Consumable income
$y < 1.25$	0.03	0.05	0.02	0.03	7.24	7.38	0.32	0.51
$1.25 \Leftarrow y < 2.50$	0.27	0.36	0.13	0.27	3.50	3.72	1.21	2.01
$2.50 \Leftarrow y < 4.00$	0.95	1.36	0.80	1.61	6.54	7.45	4.13	6.96
$4.00 \Leftarrow y < 10.00$	8.12	12.22	12.46	17.91	25.50	30.89	31.33	38.10
$10.00 \Leftarrow y < 50.00$	59.77	69.24	70.11	67.15	50.09	47.41	59.24	50.01
$50.00 \Leftarrow y$	30.87	16.77	16.47	13.03	7.13	3.16	3.77	2.41
Total	100.00	100.00	100.00	100.00	100.00	100.00	100.00	100.00

Source: Author's calculations based on ENGHo (2012–2013).

$y < 2.5$. Income below US$2.50 PPP.

$2.5 < y < 4$. Income between US$2.50 PPP and US$4.00 PPP.

$y > 4$. Income higher than US$4.00 PPP.

TABLE 11-11

Fiscal Mobility Matrices (benchmark case): Market to Disposable, Consumable, and Final Income

Disposable income groups

Market income groups	y<1.25	1.25⇐y<2.50	2.50⇐y<4.00	4.00⇐y<10.00	10.00⇐y<50.00	50.00⇐y	Percent of population
y<1.25	27.39	41.66	17.08	13.88	0.00	0.00	1.16
1.25⇐y<2.50	0.07	24.43	48.36	25.10	2.04	0.00	2.89
2.50⇐y<4.00	0.00	0.26	37.53	51.24	10.97	0.00	6.05
4.00⇐y<10.00	0.00	0.00	1.04	91.10	7.86	0.00	24.54
10.00⇐y<50.00	0.00	0.00	0.00	8.07	91.80	0.13	57.50
50.00⇐y	0.00	0.00	0.00	0.00	51.23	48.77	7.86

Consumable income groups

Market income groups	y<1.25	1.25⇐y<2.50	2.50⇐y<4.00	4.00⇐y<10.00	10.00⇐y<50.00	50.00⇐y	Percent of population
y<1.25	38.15	38.10	19.56	4.19	0.00	0.00	1.16
1.25⇐y<2.50	2.41	40.40	32.86	23.50	0.83	0.00	2.89
2.50⇐y<4.00	0.00	6.11	53.60	34.91	5.38	0.00	6.05
4.00⇐y<10.00	0.00	0.03	10.38	86.02	3.56	0.00	24.54
10.00⇐y<50.00	0.00	0.00	0.00	23.68	76.08	0.23	57.50
50.00⇐y	0.00	0.00	0.00	0.00	70.52	29.48	7.86

Final income groups

Market income groups	y < 1.25	1.25 ⇐ y < 2.50	2.50 ⇐ y < 4.00	4.00 ⇐ y < 10.00	10.00 ⇐ y < 50.00	50.00 ⇐ y	Percent of population
y < 1.25	0.00	0.00	13.11	80.49	6.41	0.00	1.16
1.25 ⇐ y < 2.50	0.00	0.00	1.85	84.17	13.99	0.00	2.89
2.50 ⇐ y < 4.00	0.00	0.00	0.61	72.43	26.96	0.00	6.05
4.00 ⇐ y < 10.00	0.00	0.00	0.00	53.42	46.58	0.00	24.54
10.00 ⇐ y < 50.00	0.00	0.00	0.00	3.48	96.24	0.28	57.50
50.00 ⇐ y	0.00	0.00	0.00	0.00	66.09	33.91	7.86

Source: Author's calculations based on ENGHo (2012–2013).

y < 2.5. Income below US$2.50 PPP.

2.5 < y < 4. Income between US$2.50 PPP and US$4.00 PPP.

y > 4. Income higher than US$4.00 PPP.

TABLE 11-12
Fiscal Mobility Matrices (sensitivity analysis): Market to Disposable, Consumable, and Final Income

Disposable income groups

Market income groups	y < 1.25	1.25 ⇐ y < 2.50	2.50 ⇐ y < 4.00	4.00 ⇐ y < 10.00	10.00 ⇐ y < 50.00	50.00 ⇐ y	Percent of population
y < 1.25	4.40	6.85	4.08	19.78	63.37	1.52	7.24
1.25 ⇐ y < 2.50	0.06	19.86	42.02	25.25	12.81	0.00	3.50
2.50 ⇐ y < 4.00	0.00	0.24	32.53	58.37	8.52	0.34	6.54
4.00 ⇐ y < 10.00	0.00	0.00	0.92	81.13	17.86	0.09	25.50
10.00 ⇐ y < 50.00	0.00	0.00	0.00	9.00	90.44	0.57	50.09
50.00 ⇐ y	0.00	0.00	0.00	0.00	53.22	46.78	7.13

Consumable income groups

Market income groups	y < 1.25	1.25 ⇐ y < 2.50	2.50 ⇐ y < 4.00	4.00 ⇐ y < 10.00	10.00 ⇐ y < 50.00	50.00 ⇐ y	Percent of population
y < 1.25	6.13	7.15	4.93	28.64	51.91	1.24	7.24
1.25 ⇐ y < 2.50	1.99	33.15	28.71	26.79	9.36	0.00	3.50
2.50 ⇐ y < 4.00	0.00	4.96	50.22	39.17	5.47	0.17	6.54
4.00 ⇐ y < 10.00	0.00	0.03	9.07	79.42	11.43	0.05	25.50
10.00 ⇐ y < 50.00	0.00	0.00	0.00	24.50	75.01	0.49	50.09
50.00 ⇐ y	0.00	0.00	0.00	0.00	71.21	28.79	7.13

Final income groups

Market income groups	y<1.25	1.25⇐y<2.50	2.50⇐y<4.00	4.00⇐y<10.00	10.00⇐y<50.00	50.00⇐y	Percent of population
y<1.25	0.00	0.00	2.11	24.27	72.29	1.34	7.24
1.25⇐y<2.50	0.00	0.00	1.52	73.23	25.24	0.00	3.50
2.50⇐y<4.00	0.00	0.00	0.56	71.92	27.17	0.34	6.54
4.00⇐y<10.00	0.00	0.00	0.00	47.55	52.40	0.05	25.50
10.00⇐y<50.00	0.00	0.00	0.00	3.83	95.61	0.57	50.09
50.00⇐y	0.00	0.00	0.00	0.00	66.85	33.15	7.13

Source: Author's calculations based on ENGHo (2012–2013).

y<2.5. Income below US$2.50 PPP.

2.5<y<4. Income between US$2.50 PPP and US$4.00 PPP.

y>4. Income higher than US$4.00 PPP.

4 Conclusions

This chapter has introduced the CEQ methodology to analyze the impact of public expenditures and taxes on income distribution and poverty in Argentina using ENGHo survey data from 2012–2013. The results show that fiscal policy had a very high impact on inequality. However, while fiscal policy reduces extreme poverty, moderate poverty increases mainly as a result of the impact of indirect taxes. Indirect subsidies and programs like Family Allowances in the formal sector transfer a significant portion of fiscal resources to the non-poor. That is, there is room for reallocating resources from the higher income deciles to the poor. In addition, given the fact that tax collection reached its peak, it is unlikely that this magnitude of redistribution could be sustained and simultaneously keep macroeconomic balance and incentives to invest in place.

Acknowledgments

This chapter was possible thanks to the generous support of the Center for Inter-American Policy and Research at Tulane University.

References

Enami, Ali, Sean Higgins, and Nora Lustig. 2022. "Allocating Taxes and Transfers and Constructing Income Concepts: Completing Sections A, B, and C of the *CEQ Master Workbook*," chap. 6 in *Commitment to Equity Handbook: Estimating the Impact of Fiscal Policy on Inequality and Poverty*, 2nd ed., Vol. 1, edited by Nora Lustig (Brookings Institution Press and CEQ Institute, Tulane University). Free online version available at www.commitmentoequity.org.

Fundacion de Investigaciones Economicas Latinoamericanas (FIEL). 2017. "Informes sobre canasta basica alimentaria y canasta basica total" (http://www.fiel.org/canasta).

Gasparini, Leonardo. 1998. "Incidencia distributiva del sistema impositivo argentino," in *La reforma tributaria en la Argentina,* edited by Fundacion de Investigaciones Economicas Latinoamericanas (Buenos Aires: Fundacion de Investigaciones Economicas Latinoamericanas).

———. 1999. "Incidencia distributiva del gastopublico social y de la politica tributaria argentina," in *La distribucion del ingreso en la Argentina,* edited by Fundacion de Investigaciones Economicas Latinoamericanas (Buenos Aires: Fundacion de Investigaciones Economicas Latinoamericanas).

Gomez Sabaini, Juan Carlos, Marcela Harriague, and Dario Rossignolo. 2013. "Argentina. La situacion fiscal y los efectos en la distribucion del ingreso." *DesarrolloEconomico* 52, pp. 207–08.

Gomez Sabaini, Juan Carlos, and Dario Rossignolo. 2001. "Analisis de la incidencia de los impuestos y de la politica fiscal sobre la distribucion del ingreso en Argentina," in *Noveno Congreso Tributario del Consejo Profesional de Ciencias Economicas de la Ciudad Autonoma de Buenos Aires* (Buenos Aires: Consejo Profesional de Ciencias Economicas de la Ciudad Autónoma de Buenos Aires).

———. 2009. "Argentina. Analisis de la situacion tributaria y propuestas de reformas impositivas destinadas a mejorar la distribucion del ingreso," in *Reflexiones y propuestas para mejorar la distribucion del ingreso en Argentina*, edited by Saul Keifman (Buenos Aires: Oficina de la Organizacion Internacional del Trabajo).

———. 2014. "La tributacion sobre las altas rentas en America Latina." Serie Estudios y Perspectivas No. 13 (Economic Commission for Latin America and the Caribbean Montevideo Office).

Gomez Sabaini, Juan Carlos, Juan Santiere, and Dario Rossignolo. 2002. "La equidad distributiva y el sistema tributario: Un análisis para el caso argentino." Serie Gestion Publica No. 20 (Instituto Latinoamericano de Planificacion Economica y Social—Comision Economica para America Latina y el Caribe [ILPES-CEPAL]).

INDEC (Instituto Nacional de Estadistica y Censos). 2012. "Muestra Maestra Urbana de Viviendas de la Republica Argentina. 2011, Documento Metodologico." *I Reunion del Grupo de Trabajo Sobre Encuestas a Hogares de la Conferencia Estadistica de las Americas*, Buenos Aires (https://www.cepal.org/deype/noticias/noticias/6/48356/2012-10_GTEH-AR-Muestra-maestra-urbana2011.pdf).

———. 2013. Encuesta Nacional de Gastos de los Hogares 2012–2013 (ENGHo) (http://www.indec.gob.ar/bases-de-datos.asp).

———. 2017. Canasta basica alimentaria y total (https://www.indec.gob.ar/nivel4_default.asp).

Lustig, Nora, and Carola Pessino. 2014. "Social Spending and Income Redistribution in Argentina in the 2000s: The Rising Role of Noncontributory Pensions." *Public Finance Review* 42, no. 3, pp. 304–25.

Marchionni, Mariana, Walter Sosa Escudero, and Javier Alejo. 2008. "La incidencia distributiva del acceso, gasto y consumo en los servicios publicos." Documento de Trabajo Centro de Estudios Distributivos, Laborales y Sociales, Universidad Nacional de La Plata, Argentina No. 67.

Maurizio, Roxana. 2009. "Politicas de transferencias monetarias en Argentina: Evaluacion de su impacto sobre la pobreza y la desigualdad, y evaluacion de sus costos," in *Reflexiones y propuestas para mejorar la distribucion del ingreso en Argentina*, edited by Saul Keifman (Buenos Aires, Argentina: Oficina de la Organización Internacional del Trabajo).

Ministerio de Hacienda. 2017. Gasto Publico Consolidado (https://www.minhacienda.gob.ar/secretarias/politica-economica/programacion-macroeconomica/gasto-publico-consolidado/).

———. 2017. Recaudacion Tributaria Anual (https://www.economia.gob.ar/sip/basehome/rectrib.htm).

Rossignolo, Dario. 2015. "Competencia tributaria vertical: Una estimación empirica en impuestos sobre los consumos en Argentina." *Urban Public Economic Review* 21, no. 1, pp. 84–135.

SPE (Secretaria de Politica Economica), Direccion Nacional de Programacion del Gasto Social. 2002. "El impacto redistributivo de la Politica Social en Argentina." Serie: Gasto Publico, Documento de trabajo: No. GP/ 12.SPE (Secretaria de Politica Economica).

SPER (Secretaria de Programacion Economica y Regional), Direccion Nacional de Programacion del Gasto Social. 1999. "El impacto redistributivo del gasto publico en los Sectores Sociales. Resultados provisorios." Serie: Gasto Publico, Documento de trabajo: No. GP/ 08.SPER (Secretaria de Programacion Economica y Regional).

Chapter 12

BRAZIL

Fiscal Policy and Ethno-Racial Poverty and Inequality

Claudiney Pereira

Introduction

Historically, Brazil has had one of the highest levels of inequality in the world; in 1989, for example, Brazil had a Gini coefficient of 0.63, making it the second most unequal country in the world, narrowly behind Sierra Leone.[1] However, inequality has fallen in Brazil every year since 2001. The recent decline is due largely to increased public cash transfers[2] and a more equitable distribution of educational attainment resulting from expanded access to education in the 1990s.[3] Social spending has become both larger and more progressive.[4] Poverty decreased every year since 2003, whether measured by the headcount index, poverty gap index, or squared poverty gap index. Brazil's conditional cash transfer program, Bolsa Familia, is very effective at reducing poverty,[5] especially in rural areas.[6] There is also evidence that the racial divide has declined; as shown by Soares (2008) and Blackman and others (2014), the income ratio between whites and non-whites (blacks and pardos) decreased between 1987 and 2012, albeit slowly.

Despite its relative success in reducing overall income inequality and poverty, Brazil's ethno-racial divide is still substantial. Afro-Brazilians lag behind in almost every

[1] Ferreira, Leite, and Litchfield (2008).

[2] Barros and others (2010).

[3] Gasparini and Lustig (2011).

[4] Silveira and others (2011).

[5] Soares (2012).

[6] Higgins (2012).

social indicator.[7] Afro-Brazilian poverty rates are twice those of white Brazilians.[8] Afro-Brazilian unemployment rates are typically 35 percent higher than those of whites, income per capita is about 50 percent less than that received by whites, and according to Blackman and others (2014), it would take forty-one years to equalize following the same trend as 2001–12.[9] Lower Afro-Brazilian educational attainment is one explanation for the income divide. In 2012, less than 13 percent of the Afro-Brazilian population over sixteen had tertiary education compared to almost 28 percent of whites. However, even if we consider the same level of education, Afro-Brazilians with tertiary education earned only 70 percent (men) and 41 percent (women) compared to whites. According to Campante, Crespo, and Leite (2004), discrimination may explain up to 25 percent of the wage gap between whites and Afro-Brazilians.

Given these facts, the extent to which governments use fiscal policy to reduce inequality and poverty differentials between Afro-Brazilians and other ethno-racial groups is of great relevance. Most Brazilian fiscal incidence studies do not disaggregate the results by such socially relevant groups.[10] This chapter summarizes the results of applying a standard benefit-tax incidence analysis to estimate the effect of taxes and social spending on inequality and poverty among ethnic groups using the Brazilian Consumer Expenditure Survey (POF in Portuguese, 2009). In particular, I use the methodology described in chapter 1 (Lustig and Higgins, 2022), chapter 6 (Enami, Higgins, and Lustig, 2022), chapter 8 (Higgins and Brest Lopez, 2022), and chapter 9 (Aranda and Ratzlaff, 2022) in this Volume of the Handbook to estimate the effects of taxation (direct and indirect) as well as cash transfers, indirect subsidies, and in-kind benefits on income distribution and poverty among ethnic groups in Brazil. The rich detail of our dataset allows us to single out the effects of each direct tax and transfer without needing to simulate most taxes or benefits.

The chapter is organized as follows. The next section describes the social spending and taxation systems in Brazil in addition to describing the data and methodology used. Section 2 summarizes the main results of our incidence analysis. Conclusions are presented in section 3.

1 Methodology

In addition to describing the social spending and taxation systems in Brazil, this section focuses on the aspects of methodology that are unique to the country.

---

[7] Blackman and others (2014).

[8] Paixão and others (2010).

[9] Blackman and others (2014).

[10] Recent incidence analyses for Brazil include Immervoll and others (2009); Nogueira, Siqueira, and Souza (2012); Silveira and others (2011); Higgins and Pereira (2014). However, as far as we know, there is no fiscal incidence analysis accounting for the ethno-racial divide.

1.1 Definitions and Measurements

The fiscal incidence analysis is based on the CEQ methodology as described in chapters 1, 6, 8, and 9 in this Volume of the Handbook.[11] As described in chapter 1 of this volume, we use four income concepts in our incidence analyses: Market, Disposable, Consumable, and Final Income.[12] Market Income is total current income before direct taxes. It is equal to the sum of gross (pretax) wages and salaries in the formal and informal sectors (also known as "earned income"), income from capital (dividends, interest, profits, rents, etc.) in the formal and informal sectors (excludes capital gains and gifts), auto-consumption, imputed rent for owner-occupied housing, private transfers (remittances and other private transfers such as alimony), and old-age and other pensions from the contributory social security system. Disposable Income equals Market Income minus direct personal income taxes on all income sources (included in Market Income) that are subject to taxation and all contributions to social security except for the portion going toward pensions,[13] plus direct government transfers (mainly cash transfers, but can include food transfers). Consumable Income is defined as Disposable Income plus indirect subsidies minus indirect taxes (for example, value added tax, sales tax, etc.). Final Income is defined as Consumable Income plus government in-kind transfers in the form of free or subsidized services in education, health, and housing, minus co-payments or user fees.[14]

In the fiscal incidence literature, pensions from contributory systems are sometimes treated as part of deferred income or at other times as government transfers.[15] Since this is an unresolved issue, we estimate both scenarios in our study. In the deferred income scenario, contributory pensions are part of Market Income. In the government transfer scenario, contributory pensions are treated as any other government transfer. The results presented here are for the scenario in which pensions are deferred income.[16]

---

[11] Although this chapter was based on an earlier version of the *CEQ Handbook* (Lustig and Higgins, 2013), the relevant reading is chapters 1, 6, 8, and 9 in this Volume of the Handbook.

[12] For more details on concepts and definitions, see Lustig and Higgins (2013).

[13] Since here we are treating contributory pensions as part of Market Income, the portion of the contributions to social security going toward pensions is treated as "savings."

[14] One may also include participation costs such as transportation costs or foregone incomes because of use of time in obtaining benefits. In our study, they were not included.

[15] See Lustig and Higgins (2013) for more details.

[16] For an explanation of why it might be more appealing to choose this scenario, see chapter 1 in this Volume of the Handbook.

1.2 Social Spending and Taxation in Brazil

Social spending used in our analysis accounts for about 15 percent of GDP in Brazil in 2009.[17] This figure includes social assistance (direct transfers and other social assistance), health spending, and education spending at the federal, state, and municipal levels. Direct transfers include conditional cash transfer programs, noncontributory pensions, food transfers, unemployment benefits, special circumstances pensions, and others. In-kind transfers are benefits received from universal free public education and health systems.[18]

There are more than eighty-five taxes in Brazil.[19] Total tax revenues at the federal, state, and municipal levels were about 35 percent of GDP in 2009. Direct taxes represent 45 percent of the taxes levied by the government and indirect taxes 55 percent. The Brazilian tax system is exceedingly complex, and the "cascading effect" is one of its major distortions[20] as taxes (federal, state, and municipal) become compounded and are applied to the final sales price of the good, not the pretax sales price. The cascading effect was estimated to be 18 percent of the tax collected in 2003,[21] and the overall cost of the distortions created by it was about 2 percent of GDP.[22]

The distortions generated by the Brazilian tax system are even more important in our study due to the effects of indirect taxes on the purchasing power of poorer families. The cascading effect and lack of exemptions, even for a basic basket of goods and services, can have detrimental effects on those who spend a larger proportion of their income on food.

1.3 Data

Ethno-racial groups[23] in Brazil considered in our study are whites, pardos, blacks, and indigenous peoples. The self-reported information is collected by the Brazilian national statistical office (IBGE). In the 2010 census, the proportions of whites, pardos, blacks, and indigenous peoples were 48.8, 43.1, 7.7, and 0.4 percent, respectively. In some studies such as Soares (2008)[24] and Paixão and others (2010), pardos and blacks are aggregated as blacks, but they are kept separated here.

---

[17] Social spending including contributory pensions is about 26 percent of GDP. The complete table with all different groups of social spending and their share of GDP is available on Higgins and Pereira (2014, p. 349).

[18] A complete description of the transfer and tax systems is given on Higgins and Pereira (2014).

[19] Portal Tributario (2012).

[20] Amaral, Olineike, and Amaral Viggiano (2007).

[21] Nogueira, Siqueira, and Souza (2012).

[22] Amaral, Olenike, and Amaral Viggiano (2007).

[23] Asian descendants accounted for about 1 percent and undeclared individuals 0.003 percent. Both groups were counted as whites.

[24] Soares (2008).

The data on household incomes, taxes, and transfers come from the most recent Pesquisa de Orçamento Familiares (POF, Family Expenditure Survey) from 2008–09.[25] This survey has national coverage, sampling 56,091 households using a two-stage stratified sample design, and is conducted approximately once every five years. It contains detailed information about many labor and nonlabor income sources, direct taxes paid, transfers received, use of public education, and consumption. Data on the use of public health services come from the Pesquisa Nacional por Amostra de Domicilios (PNAD, National Household Sample Survey, 2008), which contains income data and a detailed supplemental health survey containing the necessary information regarding the use of public health services. Both POF and PNAD are representative at the state level.[26] In-kind education benefits are equal to the average spending per student by level (early childhood development, preschool, primary, lower secondary, upper secondary, and tertiary), which is obtained from national accounts and imputed to students who attend public school.

Data on government revenues and spending, which are used to scale up household survey data for the inequality (but not poverty) calculations, come from Brazil's national accounts. In general, the amounts received from direct transfers are directly identified from the survey. On the tax side, individual income taxes (e.g., household income taxes, or IRPF, and the portion of municipal service taxes, or ISS paid by workers) and property taxes (e.g., urban property tax, or IPTU, and rural property tax, or ITR)[27] are directly identified in the survey. By using the values reported in the survey, we are implicitly assuming that the incidence of individual income tax is borne entirely by labor (specifically, those workers who report paying the taxes in the household survey) and that property taxes are borne entirely by the owners of property (specifically, those who report them in the survey). Consumption taxes are imputed by applying effective tax rates to the very detailed consumption data available from the survey. We assume that the incidence of consumption taxes falls fully on consumers.

To impute indirect subsidies, we use the total spent on electricity, in combination with income, to determine who was eligible for the electricity subsidy. We assume that all eligible households received the subsidy.

2 Results

Figure 12-1 shows the distribution of ethnic groups according to their income (Market, Disposable, and Consumable).[28] Their income ranges from less US$1.25 to greater

---

[25] A new issue of the POF has been delayed due to budget problems and is expected to be released in 2019.

[26] See IBGE (2008, 2012) for more information on PNAD and POF, respectively.

[27] IRPF is "imposto de renda da pessoa física" (household's income tax), ISS is "imposto sobre serviços" (municipal service tax), IPTU is "imposto predial e territorial urbano" (urban property tax), and ITR is "imposto territorial rural" (rural property tax).

[28] Tables and graphs are based on Higgins and Pereira (2013).

FIGURE 12-1
Brazil's Great Divide: Distribution of the Population by Ethnic Groups, Market
Income (___), Disposable Income (_ _ _), and Consumable Income (. . . . .)

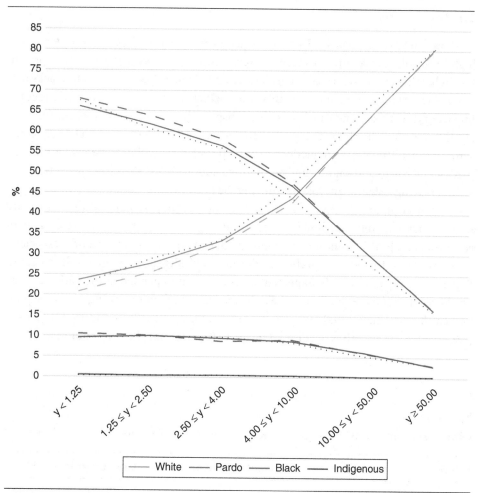

y. Income in US$ (PPP).

than US$50. There is clearly a great divide between whites and non-whites. The vast
majority of those living with less than US$4.00 are pardos and blacks. On other end,
whites are the overwhelming majority of those living with more than US$4.00 daily,
with an increasing representation as income rises. In addition, Brazil's great divide per-
sists after accounting for taxes and transfers (Consumable Income).

Fiscal policy played an important role in reducing poverty and inequality in
Brazil,[29] but how much redistribution and poverty reduction is being accomplished

---

[29] Higgins and Pereira (2014).

across ethnic groups? How was the ethno-racial divide affected by fiscal policy? The results are shown in sections 2.1 and 2.2.

2.1 Inequality

As shown in table 12-1, Market Income inequality at the national level is considered very high in Brazil, with a Gini coefficient of 0.579. Indigenous peoples and whites present the highest inequality with a Gini coefficient of 0.588 and 0.558, respectively. Blacks present the lowest level of inequality with a Gini coefficient of 0.525. When we consider the impact of direct taxes and direct transfers (Disposable Income vs. Market Income), inequality falls for all ethnic groups, but the effects of fiscal policy are relatively equal across groups. The average reduction in the Gini coefficient is about 3 percent for whites, pardos, and blacks and slightly higher for indigenous peoples. Therefore, direct transfers are not playing a significant role in reducing the great divide.

When compared with Disposable Income inequality, net indirect taxes are slightly unequalizing. As shown in table 12-1, when adding the monetized value of education and health spending, the Gini coefficient falls more significantly, especially for non-whites. Income inequality for pardos and indigenous peoples falls by about 17 percent compared to only 10 percent for whites and 13 percent at the national level. The lower effect on inequality may be only a reflection of whites opting out of the public health and educational systems. In fact, according to the Educational Census (IBGE, 2005), non-whites accounted for just 30 percent of those attending a private school.

TABLE 12-1
Gini Coefficient and Its Change with Respect to Market Income by Ethnic Groups

Ethnicity	Gini/Change	Market	Disposable	Consumable	Final
White	Gini	0.558	0.527	0.528	0.45
	Change	...	−0.031	−0.029	−0.107
Pardo	Gini	0.552	0.512	0.515	0.376
	Change	...	−0.039	−0.037	−0.175
Black	Gini	0.525	0.486	0.488	0.36
	Change	...	−0.038	−0.036	−0.165
Indigenous	Gini	0.588	0.536	0.541	0.408
	Change	...	−0.051	−0.046	−0.179
National	Gini	0.579	0.544	0.546	0.439
	Change	...	−0.035	0.033	−0.139

... = Not applicable.

FIGURE 12-2
Distribution of Income between Whites and Non-Whites

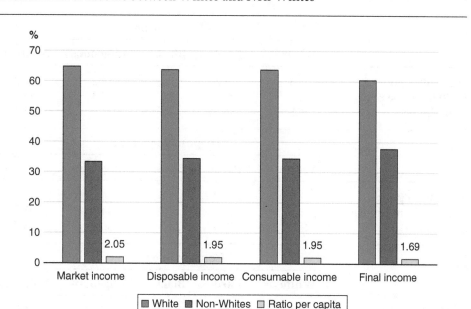

In spite of the apparent improvement, the per capita income of non-whites is still about 50 percent of whites (figure 12-2). The fiscal system is reducing the gap, but only moderately and only after monetized values for public health and education are added.

2.2 Poverty

To measure the impact of fiscal policy on poverty, we use three poverty lines: US$1.25 PPP per day (ultra-poverty), US$2.50 PPP per day (extreme poverty), and US$4.00 PPP per day (moderate poverty).[30] Results are showed in table 12-2.

Market Income poverty shows a wide difference between whites and non-whites. For any poverty line, prevalence of poverty among pardos, blacks, and indigenous peoples is at least twice as high as that of whites, with the largest difference occurring among the ultra-poor.

At the national level, ultra-poverty is reduced by 54 percent by direct transfers (net of any direct taxes paid), extreme poverty by 26 percent, and moderate poverty by 11 percent. Nonetheless, when indirect taxes are considered, the reduction in ultra-poverty is weakened, and extreme and moderate poverty actually increase when one compares Market

---

[30] The poverty lines are in 2005 purchasing power parity.

TABLE 12-2
Headcount, Poverty Lines (in US$)

	Market income				
	White	**Pardo**	**Black**	**Indigenous**	**National**
$1.25 (ultra poor)	2.8	8.8	7.1	8.2	5.8
$2.50 (extreme poor)	8.2	22.1	19.2	18.3	15.1
$4.00 (poor)	15.8	36.6	32.8	32.6	26.2

	Disposable income				
	White	**Pardo**	**Black**	**Indigenous**	**National**
$1.25 (ultra poor)	1.2	5.2	3.6	4	2.7
$2.50 (extreme poor)	5.6	16.7	14.7	14.1	11.2
$4.00 (poor)	13.7	32.9	28.3	30	23.2

	Consumable income				
	White	**Pardo**	**Black**	**Indigenous**	**National**
$1.25 (ultra poor)	2.1	7	5.4	5	4.5
$2.50 (extreme poor)	9.2	23.6	20.6	20.4	16.3
$4.00 (poor)	19.3	42.5	39	42.7	31

Income with Consumable Income. In other words, the number of near-poor who are pushed into moderate poverty by paying more in taxes than they receive in benefits (direct transfers and indirect subsidies) is higher than the number of poor who escape poverty by receiving more in transfers and subsidies than they pay in taxes.

Ultra-poverty is reduced for all four ethnic groups, anywhere from 40 to 57 percent. However, whites had a considerably higher reduction at 57 percent compared to pardos and blacks with a 40 percent and 49 percent reduction, respectively. A similar result is also found on extreme poverty (US$2.50) and poverty (US$4.00), with whites having a significantly higher reduction than other ethnic groups. In all poverty lines, whites had a higher poverty reduction than the national average. Considering net indirect taxes, Consumable Income (compared to Market Income) poverty reduction is tempered for the ultra-poor and increased for the other two poverty lines across all groups. After accounting for all taxes and transfers, the prevalence of poverty between non-whites and whites stayed practically unchanged; however, the headcount ratio between pardos and whites increased from 3.1 to 3.3 for those living under US$1.25.

At the national level, the moderate success of direct transfers at reducing poverty can be attributed to high coverage of the poor: 85 percent of the poor live in households receiving at least one direct transfer. This figure is even higher among the extreme poor (93 percent) and ultra-poor (98 percent). Table 12-3 shows the percent of individuals living in beneficiary households across different ethnic groups. The ultra-poor (white, pardo, and black) have similar coverage, which is also comparable to the national average. The overall coverage for the extreme poor and poor is higher for pardos and blacks than whites.

While non-whites have higher overall coverage, table 12-3 on the next page shows that the per capita transfer for whites is higher for all income groups. The table also shows difference being higher on the two extremes (below $1.25 and above $50). The average benefit for pardos living under $1.25 is just 60 percent of the amount received by whites. For those living above $50, whites are receiving more than twice the amount per capita received by pardos.

This unwelcome result occurs because coverage for two particularly generous programs is considerably higher for the white population than for the non-white. Coverage for Special Circumstances Pensions and Scholarships programs is higher for whites than pardos and blacks at any poverty line (U$1.25, US$2.50, and US$4.00). The coverage for the Scholarships program is twice as high for whites living on less than US$1.25. Special Circumstances Pensions have a significantly higher coverage for whites at any poverty line.

The reasons why whites have better coverage than non-whites on those programs are still not completely understood. The Special Circumstance Pensions program benefits those living in urban areas and working in the formal sector more than their counterparts in rural areas and the informal sector because individuals must be enrolled in the social security system to be eligible. If pardos and blacks comprise a majority of the informal sector and/or rural areas, then they will be underrepresented. The data available corroborates such a possibility. According to Araujo and Lombardi (2013), who use 2009 data, about 56 percent of all pardos and blacks were working in the informal sector versus 44 percent of all whites.

The fact that poverty is not reduced further despite Brazil's high spending on direct transfers is also due to high leakages to the non-poor (in addition to the deleterious effect of indirect taxes): 73 percent of total direct transfer benefits go to the population that is above the US$4.00 poverty line.[31]

3 Conclusions

This chapter summarizes the results of applying a standard benefit-tax incidence analysis to estimate the effect of taxes and social spending on inequality and poverty among ethnic groups in Brazil.

Direct transfers through fiscal intervention had similar effects on inequality across ethnic groups. The average reduction of the Gini coefficient is 3 percent for whites, pardos, and blacks and slightly higher for indigenous peoples. Adding monetized in-kind benefits, health, and education, the reduction in inequality for pardos is significantly higher than for whites (17 percent vs. 10 percent). However, the income ratio between whites and non-whites is virtually unchanged from Market Income to Final Income.

---

[31] Higgins and Pereira (2014).

TABLE 12-3

Percent of Individuals Living in Beneficiary Households

White groups	Percent of individuals living in beneficiary HH						
	y < 1.25	1.25 < y < 2.5	2.5 < y < 4	4 < y < 10	10 < y < 50	y > 50	Total
Bolsa Familia (CCT)	84.40	70.90	53.40	18.50	2.40	0.20	16.90
Scholarships	1.50	2.50	1.20	0.90	1.20	2.00	1.30
BPC (non-contributory pensions)	7.00	4.20	3.30	2.40	0.40	0.20	1.60
Unemployment	2.40	3.30	3.20	5.70	4.70	0.90	4.50
Special circumstances pensions	18.10	16.40	12.40	12.50	10.50	5.70	11.40
Other transfers	1.30	2.50	2.30	2.40	2.80	2.20	2.50
All above	98.40	84.50	67.20	37.70	20.70	10.70	34.20
Pardo groups	**y < 1.25**	**1.25 < y < 2.5**	**2.5 < y < 4**	**4 < y < 10**	**10 < y < 50**	**y > 50**	**Total**
Bolsa Familia	93.20	87.30	69.00	30.90	5.10	1.00	42.20
Scholarships	0.80	2.10	1.80	1.30	1.00	1.00	1.30
BPC	7.30	4.50	3.70	2.30	0.60	0.40	2.80
Unemployment	2.60	3.40	3.40	5.60	5.10	2.70	4.50
Special circumstances pensions	12.00	9.30	9.40	9.80	9.20	5.00	9.60
Other transfers	1.30	2.60	2.40	3.30	3.00	0.90	2.80
All above	98.30	93.10	77.50	22.20	46.20	10.50	54.70

y < 1.25. Income below US$1.25 PPP.
1.25 < y < 2.5. Income between US$1.25 PPP and $2.5 PPP.
y < 2.5. Income below US$2.50 PPP.
2.5 < y < 4. Income between US$2.50 PPP and US$4.00 PPP.
4 < y > 410. Income between US$4.00 PPP and US$10 PPP.
10 < y < 50. Income between US$10 PPP and US$50 PPP.
y > 50. Income above US$50 PPP.
BPC = Benefício de Prestação Continuada; CCT = Conditional Cash Transfer

Non-whites' incomes are still about half of that of whites. The fiscal system reduces the divide, but only very slightly. The higher effect in the Gini coefficient for pardos may be only a reflection of whites opting out of the public health and educational systems. According to the Educational Census, about 70 percent of those attending private schools were whites.[32] In addition, the proportion of pardos and blacks with private health insurance is less than 18 percent, compared to over 32 percent for whites.[33]

---

[32] IBGE (2005).
[33] IBGE (2009).

Benefits per capita in daily US$ PPP dollars (PPP 2005)						
y<1.25	1.25<y<2.5	2.5<y<4	4<y<10	10<y<50	y>50	Total
0.31	0.26	0.18	0.06	0.01	0.00	0.06
0.19	0.02	0.01	0.02	0.03	0.10	0.03
0.17	0.09	0.08	0.05	0.01	0.00	0.04
0.01	0.02	0.02	0.04	0.05	0.01	0.04
0.62	0.62	0.49	0.56	0.68	1.82	0.71
0.00	0.01	0.01	0.01	0.01	0.02	0.01
1.30	1.02	0.77	0.73	0.79	1.96	0.89
y<1.25	1.25<y<2.5	2.5<y<4	4<y<10	10<y<50	y>50	Total
0.36	0.32	0.24	0.10	0.02	0.01	0.15
0.00	0.01	0.01	0.01	0.02	0.01	0.15
0.16	0.08	0.08	0.05	0.01	0.00	0.06
0.01	0.01	0.02	0.03	0.05	0.06	0.03
0.26	0.23	0.21	0.33	0.54	0.71	0.36
0.00	0.01	0.01	0.01	0.01	0.01	0.01
0.80	0.66	0.57	0.54	0.65	0.84	0.62

Poverty rates are at least twice as high for non-whites for any poverty line (US$1.25, $2.50, and $4.00). The fiscal system reduces poverty across all ethnic groups and poverty lines after accounting for direct transfers. However, consistent with Higgins and Pereira (2014), such positive effects are offset by a deleterious effect from indirect taxes, which reverses the benefits accrued by all ethnic groups. In fact, the results for ultra-poverty are weakened, and those for extreme and moderate poverty actually increased.

In addition, we found another unwelcomed result. While direct transfers have a high coverage of the poor especially for pardos and blacks, per capita transfers are on average higher for whites, and benefits can be twice as large as those for non-whites.

Brazil has experienced a significant decrease in income inequality and poverty over the last fifteen years. Fiscal policy played an important role, especially in reducing inequality at the national level.[34] However, our study shows that fiscal interventions did not have a significant impact in reducing the divide between whites and non-whites.

---

[34] Higgins and Pereira (2014).

References

Amaral, Gilberto Luiz, João Eloi Olenike, and Leticia Mary Fernandes do Amaral Viggiano. 2007. "Estudo sobre o verdadeiro custo da tributação brasileira." Working paper (Instituto Brasileiro de Planejamento Tributario Working Paper, São Paulo, Brazil).

Aranda, Rodrigo, and Adam Ratzlaff. 2022. "Analyzing the Impact of Fiscal Policy on Ethno-Racial Inequality," chap. 9 in *Commitment to Equity Handbook: Estimating the Impact of Fiscal Policy on Inequality and Poverty*, 2nd ed., Vol. 1, edited by Nora Lustig (Brookings Institution Press and CEQ Institute, Tulane University). Free online version available at www.commitmento equity.org.

Araujo, Angela Maria Carneiro, and Maria Rosa Lombardi. 2013. "Trabalho Informal, Genero e Raça no Brasil do Inicio do Seculo XXI." *Cadernos de Pesquisa* 43, no. 149, pp. 452–77.

Barros, Ricardo, Mirela de Carvalho, Samuel Franco, and Rosane Mendonça. 2010. "Markets, the State, and the Dynamics of Inequality in Brazil," in *Declining Inequality in Latin America: A Decade of Progress?*, ed. Luis Felipe Lopez-Calva and Nora Lustig (Brookings Institution Press).

Blackman, Ana Elisa De Carli, Fernanda Lira Goes, Milko Matijascic, and Tatiana Dias Silva. 2014. "Igualdade Racial," chap. 8 in *Politicas Sociais: Acompanhamento e Analise number v. 22*. (Brasilia: IPEA).

Campante, Felipe R., Anna R. V. Crespo, and Phillippe G. P. G. Leite. 2004. "Desigualdade salarial entre raças no mercado de trabalho urbano brasileiro: aspectos regionais." *Revista Brasileira de Economia* 58, no. 2, pp. 185–210.

Enami, Ali, Sean Higgins, and Nora Lustig. 2022. "Allocating Taxes and Transfers and Constructing Income Concepts: Completing Sections A, B, and C of the *CEQ Master Workbook*," chap. 6 in *Commitment to Equity Handbook: Estimating the Impact of Fiscal Policy on Inequality and Poverty*, 2nd ed., Vol. 1, edited by Nora Lustig (Brookings Institution Press and CEQ Institute, Tulane University). Free online version available at www.commitmentoequity.org.

Ferreira, Francisco H. G., Phillippe G. Leite, and Julie A. Litchfield. 2008. "The Rise and Fall of Brazilian Inequality: 1981–2004." *Macroeconomic Dynamics* 12, no. 2, pp. 199–230.

Gaspirini, Leonardo, and Nora Lustig. 2011. "The Rise and Fall of Income Inequality in Latin America," in *The Oxford Handbook of Latin American Economics*, edited by Jose Antonio Ocampo and Jaime Ros (Oxford University Press).

Higgins, Sean. 2012. "The Impact of Bolsa Familia on Poverty: Does Brazil's Conditional Cash Transfer Program Have a Rural Bias?" *Journal of Politics and Society* 23, no. 1, pp. 88–125.

Higgins, Sean, and Caterina Brest Lopez. 2022. "Producing Indicators and Results, and Completing Sections D and E of the *CEQ Master Workbook* Using the *CEQ Stata Package*," chap. 8 in *Commitment to Equity Handbook: Estimating the Impact of Fiscal Policy on Inequality and Poverty*, 2nd ed., Vol. 1, edited by Nora Lustig (Brookings Institution Press and CEQ Institute, Tulane University). Free online version available at www.commitmentoequity.org.

Higgins, Sean, and Claudiney Pereira. 2013. "Fiscal Incidence by Race and Ethnicity: Master Workbook for Brazil," prepared by the Commitment to Equity Project for the Inter-American Development Bank, Programa para Mejorar Las estadisticas de Raza y Etnicidad para el analisis y formulacion de Politicas, New Orleans, La.

———. 2014. "The Effects of Brazil's Taxation and Social Spending on the Distribution of Household Income," in "The Redistributive Impact of Taxes and Social Spending in Latin America," edited by Nora Lustig, Carola Pessino, and John Scott, special issue, *Public Finance Review* 42, no. 3, pp. 346–67.

IBGE (Instituto Brasileiro de Geografia e Estatistica). 2005. "Censo Escolar." Rio de Janeiro.

———. 2008. "Pesquisa Nacional por Amostra de Domicilios 2008, Notas Metodologicas." Rio de Janeiro.

———. 2009. "Pesquisa Nacional por Amostra de Domicilios, Sintese de Indicadores 2008." Rio de Janeiro.

———. 2012. "Pesquisa de Orçamentos Familiaries 2008–2009: Perfil das Despesas no Brasil, Indicadores Selecionados." Rio de Janeiro.

Immervoll, Herwig, Horacio Levy, Jose Ricardo Nogueira, Cathal O'Donoghue, and Rozane Bezerra de Siqueira. 2009. "The Impact of Brazil's Tax-Benefit System on Inequality and Poverty," in *Poverty, Inequality, and Policy in Latin America*, edited by Stephan Klasen and Felicitas Nowak-Lehmann (MIT Press).

Lustig, Nora, and Sean Higgins. 2013. "Commitment to Equity Assessment (CEQ): Estimating the Incidence of Social Spending, Subsidies and Taxes." Handbook, CEQ Working Paper No. 1, July 2011; revised January 2013 (CEQ Institute, Tulane University).

———. 2022. "The *CEQ Assessment*: Measuring the Impact of Fiscal Policy on Inequality and Poverty," chap. 1 in *Commitment to Equity Handbook: Estimating the Impact of Fiscal Policy on Inequality and Poverty*, 2nd ed., vol. 1, edited by Nora Lustig (Brookings Institution Press and CEQ Institute, Tulane University). Free online version available at www.commitmentoequity .org.

Nogueira, Jose Ricardo Bezerra, Rozane Bezerra de Siqueira, and Evaldo Santana de Souza. 2012. "A Brazilian Tax-Benefit Microsimulation Model," in *Microsimulation Models for Latin America*, edited by Carlos M. Urzua (Mexico, D.F.: ITESM).

Paixão, Marcelo, Irene Rossetto, Fabiana Montovanele, and Luiz M. Carvano. 2010. *Relatorio anual das desigualdades raciais no Brasil, 2009–2010* (Rio de Janeiro: Editora Garamond).

Portal Tributario. 2012. Os tributos no Brasil (http://www.portaltributario.com.br/tributos.htm).

Silveira, Fernando Gaiger, Johnatan Ferreira, Joana Mostafa, and Jose A. Carlos Ribeiro. 2011. "Qual o impacto da tributação e dos gastos publicos sociais na distribuição de renda no Brasil?," in *Progressividade da Tributação e Desoneração da Folha de Pagamentos*, edited by Jose A. Carlos Ribeiro, Alvaro Luchiezi Jr., and Sergio E. Arbulu Mendonça (Brasilia: IPEA).

Soares, Sergei. 2008. "A demografia da cor: a composicao da populacao brasileira de 1890 a 2007," in *As Politicas Publicas e a desigualdade racial no Brasil: 120 anos apos a abolicao*, edited by M. Theodoro (Brasilia: IPEA).

———. 2012. "Bolsa Familia: Its Design, Its Impacts and Possibilities for the Future," Working paper (International Policy Centre for Inclusive Growth Working Paper, Brasilia).

Chapter 13

CHILE

The Impact of Fiscal Policy on Inequality and Poverty

Sandra Martinez-Aguilar, Alan Fuchs, Eduardo Ortiz-Juarez,
and Giselle Del Carmen

Introduction

Since the early 2000s, Chile has adopted an integral approach to social policy, gradually incorporating a set of multi-sectorial programs and interventions to serve as a buffer against negative shocks. The introduction in 2002 of Chile Solidario as a strategy to overcome extreme poverty, the health reform of 2004 that created the Plan for Universal Access to Explicit Health Guarantees (Plan Acceso Universal a Garantias Explicitas), also known as General Regime of Explicit Health Guarantees (Regimen General de Garantias Explicitas en Salud), to reduce horizontal inequalities in access to health care,[1] the social security reform of 2008 that introduced a noncontributory component of the pension system (Pensiones Solidarias), the creation of a subsystem for comprehensive early childhood protection (Chile Crece Contigo), and the launch of a subsystem of social protection and opportunities (Ingreso Etico Familiar)[2]—all have contributed to a social protection system with a life-cycle perspective, combining universal and targeted coverage for specific groups with certain degrees of vulnerability. Through 295 social programs, 130 actions related to scholarships, pensions, and subsidies, and a budget of around 10 percent of the GDP as of the end of 2015, Chile's social policy delivers direct and in-kind transfers, family allowances, noncontributory

---

[1] The Plan AUGE (Universal Access to Explicit Guarantees), now called GES (Explicit Guarantees in Health), guarantees the coverage of 80 diseases by the public National Health Fund (FONASA) and the private health system (ISAPRE).

[2] This program was introduced to replace and extend the benefits of Chile Solidario.

pensions, and other types of social spending, including psychosocial support, technical advice, training, and credit and funding for productive projects.

The significance given to social policy is evidenced by the increase of per capita public social expenditure during the last decade, which occurred at an annual rate of 6.8 percent in real terms.[3] During this period, the incidence of income-based poverty in Chile has significantly declined.[4] The headcount for extreme poverty reduced from 12.6 percent in 2006 to 3.5 percent in 2015, equivalent to an average decline of 1 percentage point yearly, whereas the incidence of moderate poverty changed from 29.1 to 11.7 percent for an annual average decline of 1.9 percentage points. In the case of income inequality, changes in the Gini coefficient show a declining trend, although they were not statistically significant between 2006 (0.499) and 2013 (0.491), and it was not until 2015 that inequality registered a significant reduction (0.482).[5]

In order to estimate the effects that public social spending, along with the tax system, exert on poverty and inequality indicators in Chile, this chapter engages in a comprehensive tax-benefit incidence analysis using household-level data and administrative records for 2013. Specifically, the analysis presented in the next sections evaluates the concentration and incidence of several fiscal instruments in Chile—including direct and indirect taxes, contributory and noncontributory pensions, direct transfers, indirect subsidies, and in-kind government transfers in the form of health and education—to address five questions. First, who bears the tax burden and who receives the benefits from social spending? Second, are fiscal interventions in Chile equalizing? Third, are they poverty-reducing? Fourth, does Chile's fiscal system either hurt or benefit the poor, and in what magnitude? And finally, how do Chile's redistributive effects compare to those of Bolivia, Brazil, Colombia, Costa Rica, Dominican Republic, Guatemala, Mexico, Peru, and Uruguay?

The contribution of this chapter to the empirical fiscal incidence literature and public debate in Chile is threefold. First, it focuses on the redistributive effects of fiscal policy using a standardized approach that allows the results to be compared across countries using the same methodology. For that purpose, the effects are computed not only at the national level and among the poor according to national official standards, but also across predefined income groups by international standards—namely poor,

---

[3] This rate of change was calculated using the OECD social expenditure database (OECD, 2016a).

[4] In 2015, a multidimensional poverty measure was officially introduced to assess nonmonetary deprivations of households. This measure considers four equally weighted dimensions, each measured through three indicators: education (school attendance, years of schooling, and underachievement), health (child malnutrition, access to the health system, and medical care), labor and social security (access to social security, employment status, and retirement), and housing (overcrowding, dwelling conditions, and access to basic services).

[5] Official figures on poverty incidence and income inequality are taken from Ministerio de Desarrollo Social (2016).

vulnerable, middle-class, and wealthy individuals.[6] Second, this chapter presents results for innovative measures related to income-based poverty and inequality—namely "fiscal impoverishment" and "fiscal gains to the poor," per Higgins and Lustig (2016) (reproduced in chapter 4 of this Volume of the Handbook), and "marginal contributions" to poverty and inequality, per Enami, Lustig, and Aranda (2022) (chapter 2 in this Volume). Finally, the chapter offers evidence of a counterintuitive but possible (and frequently overlooked) result: Chile's fiscal system features regressive, yet equalizing indirect taxes. This conundrum involving the redistributive effects of indirect taxes in Chile shows that sound and robust fiscal incidence analyses should assess the redistributive impacts of fiscal interventions as part of a whole system, and not as isolated tools, which in turn could lead to misleading policy conclusions.

The chapter is structured as follows. Section 1 provides a brief description of Chile's social spending and tax systems and the main interventions included in the incidence analysis. Section 2 describes the methodology, the data sources exploited, and the assumptions made in estimating the benefits received and the taxes paid by individuals. Section 3 presents the main results, and finally, the concluding remarks are presented in section 4.

1 Social Spending and Taxes in Chile

In 2013, the year for which the incidence analysis is carried out, public social spending defined as the sum of social protection, education, health, and housing accounted for 10.7 percent of the country's GDP, and for 13.7 percent if contributory pensions are included in the definition, as is often done (table 13-1). Education, health, and social assistance are the three core concepts of social spending analyzed in this and twenty-nine other assessments applying the same fiscal incidence methodology. The three concepts account, respectively, for 4.3, 3.8, and 1.6 percent of Chile's GDP, which are around the average levels of the other 29 countries shown by Lustig (2022a) in chapter 10 in this Volume, but well below the comparable averages for the Organization for Cooperation and Development (OECD), countries which are 5.3, 6.2, and 4.4 percent, respectively. Regarding contributory pensions, there is no agreement in the fiscal incidence literature: these pensions can be treated either as a government transfer or as deferred income—for example, as part of the Market Income. This chapter takes a neutral stance on the issue given that the fiscal incidence analysis was carried out for both scenarios. The results using either option, however, do not affect the conclusions derived because of the small size of the pay-as-you-go system. This chapter thus presents the analysis considering contributory pensions as deferred income.

There are several categories of social spending. The first includes all public expenditure on all levels of education, including government spending on both public and private educational institutions. Expenditure on health considers all public spending

---

[6] For a definition of these income groups, see the end of section 2 of this chapter.

TABLE 13-1
Structure of Chile's Government Spending, 2013

Government spending	% of total expenditure	% of GDP	Included in analysis
Total expenditure	**100.00**	**21.65**	
Social spending	**63.14**	**13.67**	
Social protection	21.10	4.57	
Social assistance	7.59	1.64	
Conditional/unconditional cash transfers	1.96	0.42	Yes
Noncontributory pensions	4.05	0.88	Yes
Near-cash transfers	1.47	0.32	Yes
Other	0.11	0.02	No
Social security	13.51	2.93	
Old-age pensions	10.15	2.20	Yes
Bonos de reconocimiento	3.36	0.73	No
Education	19.80	4.29	
Preschool	2.38	0.51	Yes
Primary	7.05	1.53	Yes
Secondary	4.03	0.87	Yes
Adults	0.31	0.07	Yes
Diferencial	1.23	0.27	Yes
Tertiary	4.11	0.89	Yes
Non-separable by level	0.69	0.15	Yes
Health	17.59	3.81	
Primary FONASA	3.36	0.73	Yes
Secondary/tertiary FONASA, MLE, FF.AA.	10.32	2.23	Yes
Sectoral investment	0.81	0.18	Yes
Supply of the national health system	0.04	0.01	Yes
Other	3.06	0.66	No
Housing and urban services	4.65	1.01	No
Subsidies	**2.26**	**0.49**	
Energy	-	-	No
Water	0.20	0.04	Yes
Gas in the Magallanes region	0.09	0.02	Yes
Public transportation	1.96	0.42	Yes
Infrastructure	**1.46**	**0.32**	
Water and sanitation	0.55	0.12	No
Rural roads	0.92	0.20	No
Defense spending	**4.72**	**1.02**	**No**
Other spending	**(7,058.59)**	**6.15**	**No**

Source: Authors' elaboration based on the 2013 executed budget published by Chile's Budget Office (Direccion de Presupuestos, DIPRES).

Notes: Other spending includes, for instance, legislative spending, or expenditures on culture and sports.
MLE = Modalidad Libre Eleccion (free-choice modality); FF.AA. = Armed forces.
The figures shown do not necessarily coincide with those published by multilateral organizations due to differences in concepts and definitions.

on primary, secondary, and tertiary healthcare of the three systems in place in Chile: the National Health Fund (FONASA)[7] and those for the armed forces (CAPREDENA) and the police (DIPRECA).

The third category, social assistance, is composed of unconditional and conditional cash transfers, noncontributory pensions, and near-cash transfers. Cash transfers include the cash benefits from Chile's conditional cash flagship program (Chile Solidario/ Ingreso Etico Familiar), the family allowances scheme of the subsystem for comprehensive early childhood protection (Chile Crece Contigo), noncontributory pensions (Pensiones Solidarias), and other allowances and special scholarships.[8] Near-cash transfers include complementary support for food, school texts, clothes, and school supplies.[9] An additional aspect of public spending that is taken into account, but not as part of social spending, is that of subsidies, particularly for water, public transportation, and gas in the Magallanes region, which account for 0.49 percent of the GDP. The water subsidy is targeted to low-income families who face difficulties paying for running water services; that for public transportation is a generalized subsidy, benefiting all the user population; and that for gas is applied to all families living in the aforementioned region of the country.

Regarding Chile's income structure, in 2013 total government revenues represented 21 percent of the GDP, of which tax revenues accounted for about 80 percent (or 16.7 percent of the country's GDP) with a relatively higher dependence on indirect taxes on sales of goods and services (9.8 percent) than on direct taxes on income (6.6 percent)[10] (table 13-2). For direct taxes, the incidence analysis considers only those on personal

---

[7] This considers the two modalities of FONASA: institutional and free-choice.

[8] The following allowances of the flagship cash transfers program—related to social protection, child health, school attendance, school achievement, and female work—are considered in the analysis: Bono de proteccion social y egreso, Bono base familiar, Bono por control del niño sano, Bono por asistencia escolar, Bono por logro escolar, and Bono al trabajo de la mujer. In the case of Chile Crece Contigo, the following child, maternity, disability, and mental disability allowances are included: Subsidio familiar al menor o recien nacido, Subsidio de asistencia maternal, Subsidio familiar a la madre, Subsidio familiar por invalidez, and Subsidio discapacidad mental. Cash transfers for old-age and disabled population (Pensiones Solidarias) include Pension Basica Solidaria de Vejez e Invalidez, Aporte Previsional Solidario de Vejez e Invalidez, and Pensiones de Leyes Especiales de Reparacion. Other benefits in cash include: Bono bodas de oro, Bono de invierno, Bono marzo, Asignacion Familiar, Subsidio empleo joven, Aporte estatal Fondo de Censatia Solidario, Descuento Cotizaciones de Salud, Beca Indigena, Beca Retencion Escolar, and Beca Presidente de la Republica.

[9] The near-cash transfers included in the analysis are Progama Nacional de Alimentacion Complementaria, Progama Nacional de Alimentacion Complementaria para el Adulto Mayor, Programa de Alimentacion Escolar, Yo elijo mi PC, and Utiles Escolares.

[10] Chile's tax burden of 16.7 percent of GDP, as reported by administrative data, does not necessarily coincide with the figures published by multilateral organizations due to differences in concepts and definitions. Using revenue statistics of the OECD (2016b), we find that the tax burden

TABLE 13-2

Structure of Chile's Government Revenues, 2013

Government revenues, contributions to social security and grants	% of total	% of GDP	Included in analysis
Total	**100.00**	**21.01**	
Revenues	**92.92**	**19.53**	
Tax revenues	79.60	16.73	
Direct taxes:	31.51	6.62	
Personal income tax	6.28	1.32	Yes
Corporate income tax	17.57	3.69	No
Adicional	5.44	1.14	No
Others	2.22	0.47	No
Indirect taxes:	46.69	9.81	
VAT	37.81	7.95	Yes
Sales tax (alcoholic/nonalcoholic beverages)	0.89	0.19	Yes
Sales tax (luxury goods, cars and others)	0.05	0.01	No
Excise taxes	6.89	1.45	Yes
Foreign trade taxes	1.05	0.22	No
Others	1.49	0.31	No
Nontax accounts	−0.10	−0.02	No
Nontax revenues	13.32	2.80	No
Contributions to social security	**6.83**	**1.43**	
From employees	6.62	1.39	Yes
From employees	0.21	0.04	No
Grants	**0.25**	**0.05**	**No**

Source: Authors' elaboration based on Direccion de Presupuestos (2014) and the 2009–15 data on annual tax revenue published by Chile's Servicio de Impuestos Internos, SII (2015).

income: (1) the Second Category Tax (SCT), which is a monthly tax levied on income derived from labor income such as salaries, contributory pensions, and other remuneration; and (2) the Complementary Global Tax (CGT), which is levied on annual total income obtained by an individual, with any SCT paid or First Category Tax (FCT)[11] related to dividends received being creditable against it. The rates for both SCT and CGT range from 0 to 40 percent.

---

in Chile in 2013 is close to the Latin American average, but well below (by about 12 percentage points) the tax burden of Argentina, Brazil, and the OECD average.

[11] The FCT is levied on income from capital and from enterprises that undertake commercial, industrial, and other activities. The FCT paid by an enterprise can be used as a credit against the CGT to which its owners, shareholders, partners, or managers are liable when they receive dividends.

For indirect taxes, the analysis includes: (1) the value-added tax (VAT), which is levied at a rate of 19 percent on sales of goods and services; (2) special taxes on nonalcoholic and alcoholic beverages, which are charged in addition to the VAT and on the same tax base as that for VAT with varying rates depending on the alcohol content; (3) excise taxes levied on tobacco, which are charged on the value of the sale to the final consumer with varying rates depending on the product (for example, cigars, processed tobacco, and cigarettes); and (4) excise taxes on fuels, with a base determined by the amount of fuel expressed in cubic meters. Finally, social contributions from employees to healthcare, unemployment insurance, and contributory pensions are also included in the analysis. Contributions to health include FONASA, and the health systems of the armed forces (CAPREDENA) and police (DIPRECA).

2 Methodology, Data, and Assumptions

The analysis follows the CEQ methodology described in Lustig and Higgins (2013) to assess the distributional impact of taxes, transfers, and subsidies across income groups in Chile in 2013 based on household-level data and administrative records on taxes and social spending. Basically, the methodology consists of defining income concepts first, and then allocating taxes, social contributions, subsidies, and public social spending to individuals included in the household survey in a consistent and methodologically sound way, so that it is possible to compare incomes and income-based measures of well-being before and after taxes and public transfers.

The methodology has two standard scenarios depending on how contributory pensions are treated: as deferred income or as government transfers. In the analysis for Chile, both scenarios can be constructed by using two definitions of income that are employed in the estimation of official figures of income inequality and income-based poverty. The measurement of inequality in Chile uses a *monetary income* definition, which is composed of wages and salaries (monetary and in-kind), earnings from self-employment, self-provision of goods produced by the household, rents, interest, dividends, retirements, pensions, private transfers, and public monetary transfers. In the case of poverty, the measurement is based on a *total income* definition, which is equivalent to monetary income plus imputed rent. It is important to highlight that the methodology for measuring income changed in 2013 and that the new approach is the one employed in this chapter. Specifically, household income is no longer adjusted to national accounts, and the new estimation of the imputed rent considers not only owner-occupied dwellings, but also dwellings that were donated or given as work benefit, or dwellings in usufruct.[12]

---

[12] The official methodology for the measurement of poverty also changed. The new method incorporated new poverty lines based on updated values of both basic food and basic nonfood baskets, equated the value of the poverty lines between urban and rural areas, and adjusted the poverty lines based on equivalence scales.

This chapter uses the 2013 National Socioeconomic Characterization Survey (CASEN) carried out by the Ministry of Social Development, which is a nationally representative sample collecting detailed information on household incomes, as well as on individual and dwelling characteristics. This survey is employed as the primary source of data in the incidence analysis as it is the official data set to measure the levels of poverty and income inequality in Chile. Since the CASEN does not collect information on household spending, the Family Budget Survey (EPF) for 2011–12 is employed as a secondary source to estimate indirect taxes on household consumption. This survey was carried out by the National Institute of Statistics and is aimed at identifying the structure and characteristics of final consumption of urban households in the regional capitals of the country. In addition, the analysis considers official data on government revenues and expenditures from the 2013 executed budgets reports published by the Ministry of Finance's Budget Office, the Ministry of Social Development, the National Institute of Statistics, and the National Audit Office.

In order to assess the distributional effects of fiscal interventions, the core building block of the fiscal incidence analysis is the definition and construction of the income concepts using the previous data sources (figure 13-1). The allocation of fiscal interventions to individuals in the CASEN, depending on the income concept, is based on the following methods: *direct identification*, when the survey contains information on who receives (pays) benefits (taxes), as well as the amount received (paid); *imputation*, when the survey informs who receives (pays) benefits (taxes), but the amount received (paid) is retrieved from administrative records or program (tax) rules; *simulation*, when neither direct identification nor imputation can be used, so that the beneficiaries (taxpayers) and the amount received (paid) is simulated based on the program (tax) rules; and imputation based on *secondary sources*.[13]

The income reported in the CASEN is the income after direct taxes and social contributions, which is equivalent to the Net Market Income concept—composed of wages and salaries from the formal and informal sectors, income from capital, private transfers such as remittances and alimonies, pensions, and imputed rent—and is therefore the baseline for constructing the other income concepts. In order to construct Market Income, a "reverse engineering" process from Net Market Income is implemented by simulating and adding direct taxes and social contributions based on fiscal rules.

For direct taxes paid by each individual, taxes on salaries and remunerations (Second Category Tax, SCT) and taxes on other personal income (Complementary Global Tax, CGT) are allocated using simulation. This method applies the statutory rate and discount of each Taxable Income bracket defined by the Internal Revenue Service (IRS) to the Taxable Income reported by each individual in the CASEN. The Taxable Income for salaried workers is Gross Income minus bonuses for Christmas and national festivities and social security contributions, while for independent workers who report

---

[13] For a detailed description of these and other allocation methods, see Higgins and Lustig (2018).

FIGURE 13-1
Definition of Income Concepts in Chile's Incidence Analysis

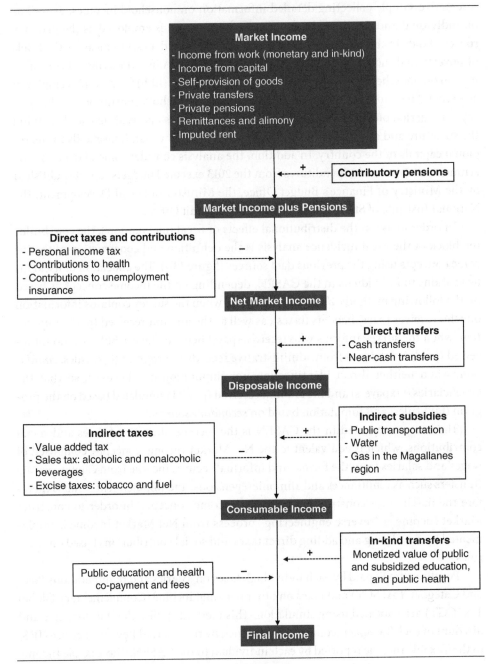

Source: Authors' elaboration based on Lustig and Higgins (2013).

issuing invoices or receipts, the Taxable Income is 70 percent of total annual Gross Income. For all the individuals, all rents before taxes are added up to calculate the CGT. Finally, given that the CASEN contains information on who receives income from profits withdrawal as well as the amount received, the tax paid on business income (First Category Tax, FCT) is calculated and used as a tax credit to the CGT. It is important to highlight that the following concepts are not included in the Taxable Income: tips, per diems, in-kind income, and auto-consumption. In addition, it is assumed that incomes from rental of nonagricultural properties,[14] vacation rentals, and self-employment in the informal sector do not pay income taxes. In the case of social contributions, the CASEN identifies who contributes to health care and to what system, and the amount of the contribution is allocated using simulation based on the level of income before taxes, the stipulated rates of each system, and the maximum and minimum taxable limits.

The construction of the Market Income plus Pensions concept requires adding contributory pensions to Market Income. In Chile different contributory pension systems coexist: an individual capitalization system and two pay-as-you-go schemes—namely, the police and armed forces system and the old pension system of the former Cajas de Prevision Social. The individual capitalization is a system with compulsory, forced savings, and it is part of the Market Income concept—since the pension is the product of the individual's savings—while the two pay-as-you-go systems can be treated either as deferred income or as government transfer—since the share contributed by both the individual and the government is unknown. For the Market Income plus Pensions concept, contributory pensions from the two pay-as-you-go schemes are treated as deferred income, and the allocation method is direct identification.

The Disposable Income concept is constructed by adding direct cash and near-cash transfers to Net Market Income. For all cash transfers the allocation method is direct identification, while for all near-cash transfers the allocation method is imputation since although the CASEN identifies who receives the benefit, the amount is taken from administrative accounts.[15] The addition of subsidies to and the discount of indirect taxes from Disposable Income yields the Consumable Income concept. In the first case, the analysis considers subsidies to water consumption, public transportation, and gas for the Magallanes Region. The allocation method for water subsidies is direct identification, whereas public transportation and gas subsidies are allocated using simulation. For each of the two latter subsidies, the total executed expenditure is divided by the total targeted population, and the result is then scaled down to prevent overestimation bias.[16] Regarding indirect taxes, it is assumed that they are paid entirely by

---

[14] Either properties under the Decree-Law No. 2, or for the use of the owner and her or his family, or whose rents are less than 11 percent of the property valuation.

[15] In the case of the scholarships Beca Indigena, Beca Retencion Escolar, and Beca Presidente de la Republica, although they are considered as cash transfers, the allocation method is imputation.

[16] For a detailed description of the scaling down procedure, see Enami, Higgins, and Lustig (2022) (chapter 6 in this Volume).

the consumers, and their estimation is based on the EPF, which is used to calculate, by consumption decile, the shares of consumption spent on indirect taxes. Since these shares must be imputed to each individual's Disposable Income in the corresponding consumption decile, it is necessary to rank individuals in the CASEN by consumption decile, which requires both the CASEN and EPF surveys to interlock.

The estimation of indirect taxes in the EPF and the survey-to-survey imputation follows the hot-deck procedure used by Larrañaga and others (2012) in their tax-benefit microsimulation model for Chile. In order to avoid a potential overestimation of the actual VAT rate paid and to be consistent with the CEQ methodology, a distinct feature in the treatment of the VAT between that microsimulation model and the incidence analysis presented in this chapter is that the latter does not use the statutory rate (19 percent); instead, it uses the effective rate (14.3 percent), which is based on the estimate of evasion (24.5 percent) in 2013.[17] For the estimation of the VAT, the analysis considers fiscal exemptions, the most important being those on health, education, insurance and financial operations, gambling, and cultural services. It also considers special sale taxes such as those on alcoholic and nonalcoholic beverages and excise taxes such as those on tobacco and fuel.

The last income concept, Final Income, is constructed by adding the monetized value of in-kind transfers on education and health to Consumable Income and by subtracting the corresponding copayments and fees for the use of such services from Consumable Income. For both education and health, the allocation method is imputation. In the first case, the CASEN allows us to identify who attends an educational institution, the educational level attended, and the financing scheme of the institution—public, subsidized, or private—so that it is possible to impute the average cost of education disaggregated by level of education, by financing scheme, and, in the case of tertiary education, by whether the benefit is received by the institution or by the student. If the student is the recipient, the imputation is disaggregated by benefit, scholarship, or credit, with the latter considering only the fee paid for the credits bought by the government under the *Credito con Garantia Estatal* scheme (credit guaranteed scheme). In the case of health, the CASEN identifies who is affiliated with FONASA, DIPRECA, or CAPREDENA systems, respectively, so that the analysis imputes the average cost based on the use of health services.

The assessment presented in this chapter offers the most comprehensive tax-benefit incidence analysis available for Chile to date and allows for the results to be comparable with other developing countries by applying the same methodology. Yet, since the results presented are point-in-time and do not account for behavioral, general equilibrium, or lifecycle effects, they do not take into account the long-term effects of fiscal policy on well-being indicators. In addition, we acknowledge the potential presence of

---

[17] The magnitude of VAT evasion was estimated by Chile's internal revenue service (Servicio de Impuestos Internos, 2015).

measurement errors due to under-reporting of certain income categories and under-sampling of the top incomes in the household surveys.

The evidence presented in the next section, as mentioned before, corresponds to the scenario that considers contributory pensions as deferred income instead of as government transfer, and for comparability purposes with other countries the analysis uses the total income definition, instead of the monetary income definition, to account for the imputed rent. In pursuance of a better understanding of the incidence of fiscal policy in Chile, the following income groups are used: *poor*, defined as those individuals with per capita income below the US$4 a day poverty line and including within this group the "ultra-poor" (living with less than US$1.25/day), the "extreme poor" (living on US$1.25–US$2.50/day), and the "moderate poor" (living on US$2.50–US$4/day); *vulnerable*, defined as those with per capita income between US$4 and US$10 a day; *middle class*, defined as those living on US$10–US$50/day; and *wealthy*, defined as those with per capita income above US$50/day.[18] The analysis also considers the incidence on the extreme and moderate poor as defined using the official poverty lines in Chile, as well as on income deciles.

3 Main Results

3.1 Redistributive Effects of Chile's Fiscal System

Are fiscal interventions in Chile equalizing? Figure 13-2 shows that income inequality in Chile, as measured by the Gini coefficient, declines from 0.494 to 0.467 when moving from Market Income plus Pensions to Disposable Income[19]—that is, after the intervention of direct taxes, social contributions to health and unemployment insurance, and direct transfers.

When analyzed independently, social contributions to health and unemployment insurance are found to be regressive with respect to Market Income plus Pensions, with a Kakwani progressivity index of −0.17, whereas both direct taxes and direct transfers

---

[18] The poverty line of $1.25/day is the standard used by the World Bank to measure the incidence of poverty globally; its value corresponds to the average of the poverty lines of some of the poorest countries in the world. The $2.50/day and $4.00/day poverty lines are equivalent to the conditional mean of the national extreme and moderate poverty lines, respectively, across Latin American countries (conditional on GDP per capita). The thresholds to define the vulnerable, middle-class, and upper-class groups are those proposed by Lopez-Calva and Ortiz-Juarez (2014). All these figures are expressed in 2005 PPP prices.

[19] The Gini coefficients shown in figure 13-2 are different from the official estimates because the latter uses the monetary income definition, which excludes the imputed rent, whereas this chapter uses the total income definition in order to include it and thereby allow for cross-country comparisons. If the imputed rent is excluded from the analysis, for instance, the Gini coefficient for Disposable Income would be 0.490 instead of 0.467, which is virtually the same value as that reported by the Ministerio de Desarrollo Social (2016): 0.491.

FIGURE 13-2

Effects of Fiscal Interventions on Income Inequality (Gini coefficients)

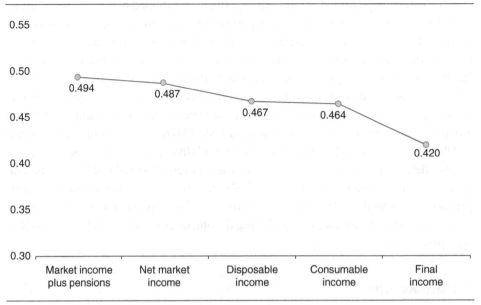

Source: Authors' elaboration based on Martinez-Aguilar and Ortiz-Juarez (2016).

are progressive with a Kakwani index of 0.45 and 0.82, respectively.[20] This is not a surprising result given the design of the two latter interventions. As figure 13-3 shows, the lion's share of total direct taxes (89 percent) is paid by the wealthy (who comprise 6.7 percent of Chile's population), and the remaining 11 percent is paid almost entirely by the middle-class group that accounts for more than half of the country's population. The share of direct taxes paid is negligible (0.02 percent) for the third of the population identified as vulnerable, whereas the 7.5 percent of the poor population likely do not pay these kinds of taxes.[21] Regarding the concentration of direct transfers— that is, who receives the benefits—figure 13-3 shows that almost two-thirds of the total amount is received by the poor (18.4 percent) and the vulnerable (44.6 percent), whereas the middle-class accounts for most of the remaining share (35.3 percent).

The Kakwani index, however, cannot tell if these and other fiscal interventions make the whole fiscal system more (un)equal,[22] because the effect of a tax or transfer

---

[20] The Kakawani index for all fiscal interventions analyzed is shown in table 13A-1 in the appendix.

[21] If the concentration of direct taxes is analyzed by income deciles instead of income groups, the results are strongly consistent with findings by Engel, Galetovic, and Raddatz (1999) and by Castelletti (2013).

[22] When taxes or transfers are seen as single, independent interventions, the Kakwani index is sufficient to unambiguously establish that a progressive (regressive) tax or transfer is equalizing (unequalizing). In a multitax/multitransfer setting, however, this direct relationship does not neces-

FIGURE 13-3

Concentration of Total Direct Taxes Paid on Personal Income and Total Direct Transfers Received, by Income Group

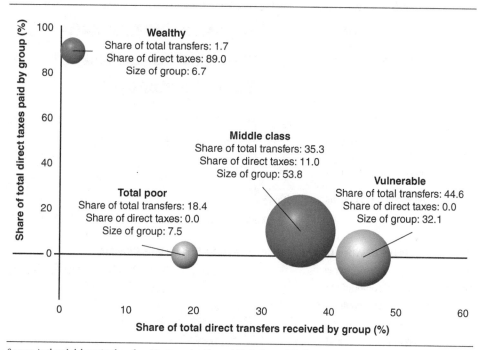

Source: Authors' elaboration based on Martinez-Aguilar and Ortiz-Juarez (2016).

Notes: The "Total poor" group includes the share of the population living in ultra (0.8 percent), extreme (2 percent), and moderate (4.7 percent) poverty, based on the total Market Income plus Pensions concept. The income thresholds to define the groups are the following: less than US$1.25/day for the ultra-poor, US$1.25–US$2.50/day for the extreme poor, US$2.50–US$4.00/day for the moderate poor, US$4–US$10/day for the vulnerable, US$10–US$50/day for the middle class, and above $50/day for the wealthy. The size of the bubbles is relative to the size of each group as measured with total Market Income plus Pensions.

is not independent from the effect of other interventions. Therefore, in order to answer the initial question, marginal contributions are used, which are equivalent to the difference in inequality with and without a specific tax or transfer.[23] Taking Disposable Income as the relevant end income concept, the marginal contributions of most of the

---

sarily hold (Lambert 2001). The Kakwani (1977) index for taxes is defined as the difference between the concentration coefficient of a tax and the Gini coefficient of pretax income. The index for transfers is defined as the difference between the Gini coefficient of pre-transfer income and the concentration coefficient of a transfer.

[23] As shown in chapter 2 in this Volume, the marginal contribution of a tax (transfer) to inequality is calculated by taking the difference between the Gini coefficient of the relevant end income concept without the tax (transfer) and the Gini coefficient of the relevant end income concept with the tax (transfer). Because of path dependency, the sum of the marginal contributions of each fiscal intervention will not be equal to the total change in inequality.

FIGURE 13-4

Marginal Contributions of Fiscal Interventions to Income Inequality (Gini points)

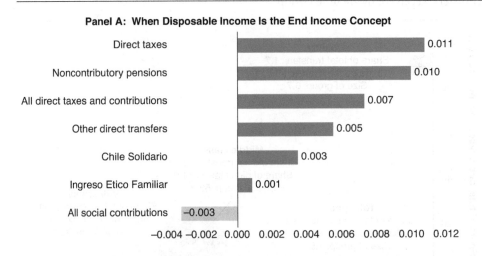

Panel A: When Disposable Income Is the End Income Concept

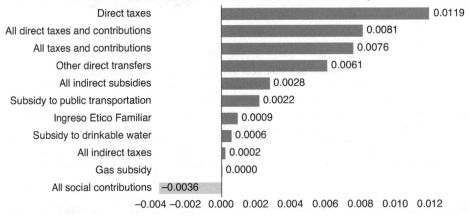

Panel B: When Consumable Income Is the End Income Concept

Source: Authors' elaboration based on Martinez-Aguilar and Ortiz-Juarez (2016).

fiscal interventions are equalizing; the only exception is social contributions to health and unemployment insurance, which show an unequalizing effect. Specifically, direct taxes and noncontributory pensions have the largest impact on the decline in inequality, with a marginal contribution of about 0.01 Gini points (figure 13-4, panel A).

Moving from Disposable Income to Consumable Income further reduces the Gini coefficient to 0.464 (figure 13-2, which is indicative of a remarkable finding: the net effect of adding indirect subsidies to and subtracting indirect taxes from Disposable Income is equalizing. As panel B of figure 13-4 shows, this is due not only to the positive marginal contribution of indirect subsidies to inequality reduction, but also to the fact that indirect taxes have a slightly positive effect despite their regressivity, as indicated by a Kakwani index of −0.03. The latter result is referred to in the literature as the "Lambert's conundrum" (Lambert, 2001), which states that "if taxes are regressive in relation to the original income, but progressive with respect to the less unequally distributed post-transfers (and subsidies) income, regressive taxes exert an equalizing effect over and above the effect of progressive transfers."[24]

As noted, indirect taxes in Chile are regressive with respect to Market Income plus Pensions (the original income), but they are progressive with respect to Disposable Income (the less unequally distributed post-transfers income), as indicated by a Kakwani index of 0.09. Indirect taxes, therefore, exert an equalizing effect over and above the effect of progressive direct taxes and direct transfers. This finding indicates that the redistributive impact of fiscal interventions must be assessed by considering the whole system and not as isolated tools, which in turn could lead to misleading policy conclusions.[25] Overall, when taking Consumable Income as the end concept, only social contributions and the subsidy to gas exhibit, respectively, a negative and neutral effect on inequality, whereas both direct taxes and transfers account for the largest positive marginal contributions (figure 13-4, panel B). The overall equalizing effect of taxes and direct transfers is unambiguous as the Lorenz curve for Consumable Income lies completely above the Lorenz curve for Market Income plus Pensions (figure 13-5).

Finally, in-kind transfers in the form of education and health services have an even larger positive effect on inequality when moving from Consumable Income to Final Income: the Gini coefficient reduces to 0.420, equivalent to a 15 percent decline relative to Market Income plus Pensions (figure 13-2). The marginal contributions to inequality reach 0.032 Gini points for education and 0.014 Gini points for health, and the equalizing effect holds for all levels of education, as indicated by their positive marginal contribution to inequality (figure 13-6).[26] The large effect of in-kind transfers on inequality is not surprising given that Chile spends significantly more on education and healthcare (roughly 8.1 percent of the GDP) than on direct transfers and pensions (1.6 percent of the GDP). Yet, such a result must be interpreted with caution because in-kind transfers are monetized at average government cost, which does not necessarily reflect the actual value of the education and health services provided, and there are no adjustments for differences in quality across the distribution. The method assumes that a poor person living in a rural area receives the same benefit as an urban middle-class person, for instance.

While most fiscal interventions in Chile are found to be equalizing, a second fundamental question then emerges: Are fiscal interventions also poverty-reducing? While

---

[24] See chapter 2 in this Volume). The authors Enami, Lustig, and Aranda offer a detailed theoretical explanation for this counterintuitive result.

[25] Recently, Eduardo Engel, using the same data exploited in Engel, Galetovic, and Raddatz (1999), found the same Lambert's conundrum in the Chilean system.

[26] A summary of the marginal contributions for all fiscal interventions analyzed is shown in table 13A-1 in the appendix.

FIGURE 13-5
Concentration and Lorenz Curves

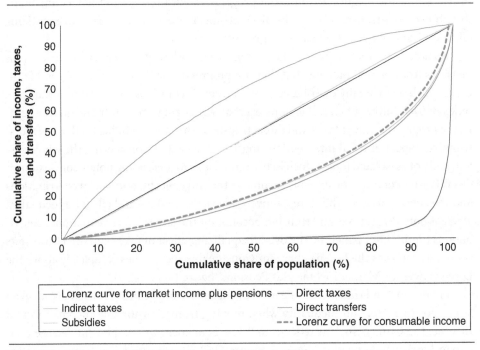

Source: Authors' elaboration based on Martinez-Aguilar and Ortiz-Juarez (2016).

FIGURE 13-6
Marginal Contributions of In-Kind Transfers to Income Inequality (Gini points)

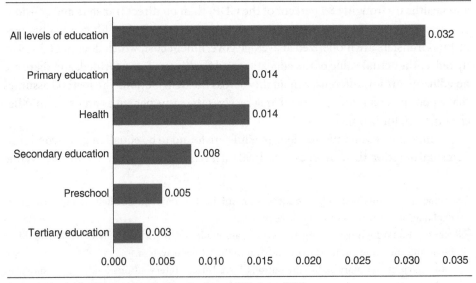

Source: Authors' elaboration based on Martinez-Aguilar and Ortiz-Juarez (2016)

the combined effect of direct taxes and social contributions does increase the incidence of poverty (figure 13-7, panel A)—an effect that is driven mostly by social contributions given that the population in poverty likely does not pay direct taxes—direct transfers more than compensate this effect. Specifically, poverty headcounts decline by nearly 3 percentage points (or around 40 percent) with respect to Market Income plus Pensions for both the official extreme and $4/day poverty lines, and by 4 percentage points (or 24 percent) for the official moderate poverty line.

While indirect taxes, as expected, increase the incidence of poverty when moving from Disposable Income to Consumable Income, the effect is not large enough to nullify the gains from direct transfers—and also from subsidies, which exhibit a positive marginal contribution to poverty (figure 13-8); therefore Consumable Income–based poverty still remains below the incidence measured with Market Income plus Pensions: 1.8 percentage points (or 24 percent) below using the $4/day poverty line, 1.9 points (or 27 percent) below using the official extreme line, and half a point (or 3 percent) below using the official moderate line.[27] Moreover, after the intervention of taxes, subsidies, and direct transfers, not only does the incidence of poverty decline, but also the depth of poverty (intensity) and the magnitude of inequality among the poor (severity) fall remarkably (figure 13-7, panel B).

A breakdown of the fiscal system after the intervention of taxes, subsidies, and direct transfers reveals that the latter have the largest positive marginal contributions to the reduction of the incidence of poverty: between 3.9 and 5.3 percentage points, depending on the poverty line used. In particular, noncontributory pensions account for between 1.7 and 2.5 percentage points of the poverty decline, whereas Chile Solidario and Ingreso Etico Familiar are responsible for 0.9 and 0.2 percentage points, respectively (figure 13-8). The contribution of indirect subsidies to the poverty decline is positive overall, yet modest for public transport and water subsidies, and virtually neutral for gas subsidies in the Magallanes region. Finally, and not surprisingly, indirect taxes exert an important adverse effect on the incidence of poverty, although in a magnitude that it is significantly lower than that of the positive contributions exerted by direct transfers.

The underlying significance of the previous results is that the net effect of fiscal interventions favors upward economic mobility, especially among the poorest. Of the total ultra-poor, 39 percent move to extreme poverty, 16 percent to moderate poverty, and 14 percent to vulnerability. Among those initially identified as extreme poor, 45 percent experience upward mobility to moderate poverty and 24 percent to vulnerability, whereas

---

[27] The official extreme and moderate poverty rates in 2013 are, respectively, 4.5 and 14.4 percent, and these figures are conceptually comparable with the poverty rates resulting from the Disposable Income concept in this chapter: 3.9 and 12.5 percent, respectively. The differences occur because the methodology implemented here includes near-cash transfers as part of direct transfers, whereas near-cash transfers are not considered in the income used by the Ministry of Social Development in the estimation of national poverty rates.

Figure 13-7
Effects of Fiscal Interventions on Poverty

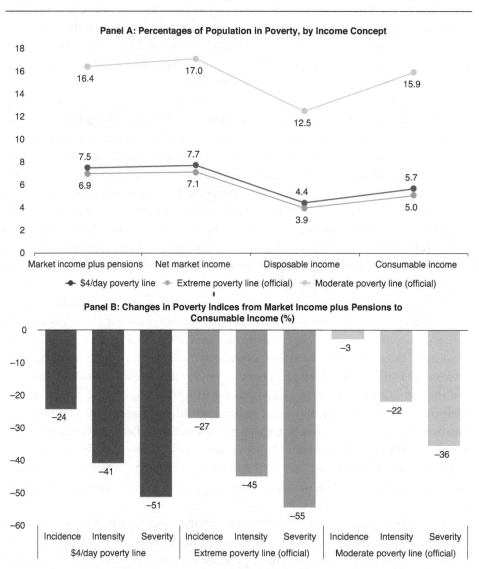

Source: Authors' elaboration based on Martinez-Aguilar and Ortiz-Juarez (2016).

Notes: The indices measuring the incidence, intensity, and severity of poverty correspond to the FGT family of poverty indices (Foster, Greer, and Thorbecke, 1984). The incidence represents the percentage of population under the poverty line; the intensity index, also known as the poverty gap, measures the shortfall from the poverty line as a share of the same poverty line; and the severity index measures the magnitude of inequality among the poor.

FIGURE 13-8

Marginal Contributions of Fiscal Interventions to Poverty (percentage points)

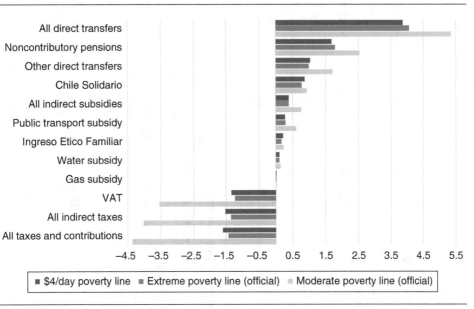

Source: Authors' elaboration based on Martinez-Aguilar and Ortiz-Juarez (2016).

53 percent of the moderate poor exit poverty. Conversely, 2 and 6 percent of those initially identified as middle class and wealthy, respectively, experience downward mobility (table 13-3, panel A). A different way to appreciate the overall effect of fiscal policy is that if the country's population is reduced to 100 individuals, then the number of people living with less than $4/day declines from 8 to 4; that of vulnerable increases from 32 to 34; that of middle class also increases, from 54 to 55; and that of the wealthy reduces from 7 to 6 individuals (table 13-3, panel B).

Overall, the net effect of fiscal interventions in Chile is both equalizing and poverty-reducing, yet the extent to which such interventions make the prefiscal poor either poorer or better off is unknown. In order to explore the extent to which a fiscal system like Chile's hurts and benefits the poor, Higgins and Lustig (2016) (reproduced in chapter 4 of this Volume) developed a set of innovative measures to capture the magnitude of fiscal impoverishment (FI) and fiscal gains to the poor (FGP). The authors define an individual as fiscally impoverished if she is poor according to her postfiscal income (that is, after taxes and transfers) and such income is lower than her prefiscal income (that is, the amount paid in taxes is higher than the amount received in transfers). On the other hand, an individual experiences fiscal gains when he is poor according to his prefiscal income (that is, before taxes and transfers) and such income is lower than his postfiscal income (that is, the amount received in transfers is higher than the amount paid in taxes). In addition to the headcounts, the monetary amounts of FI and FGP

TABLE 13-3

Fiscal Mobility Matrices from Market Income plus Pensions to Consumable Income

A. Row percentage distribution of population

Initial/ending income concept and income groups	Consumable income						
	Ultra-poor	Extreme poor	Moderate poor	Vulnerable	Middle class	Wealthy	Total
Market income plus pensions Ultra-poor	30	39	16	14	0	—	100
Extreme poor	—	31	45	24	0	—	100
Moderate poor	—	0	47	53	0	—	100
Vulnerable	—	—	0	93	7	—	100
Middle class	—	—	—	2	98	0	100
Wealthy	—	—	—	—	6	94	100

B. Total percentage distribution of population

Initial/ending income concept and income groups	Consumable income						
	Ultra-poor	Extreme poor	Moderate poor	Vulnerable	Middle class	Wealthy	Total
Market income plus pensions Ultra-poor	0.2	0.3	0.1	0.1	0.0	—	0.8
Extreme poor	—	0.6	0.9	0.5	0.0	—	2.0
Moderate poor	—	0.0	2.2	2.5	0.0	—	4.7
Vulnerable	—	—	0.0	29.8	2.4	—	32.2
Middle class	—	—	—	0.9	52.7	0.0	53.6
Wealthy	—	—	—	—	0.4	6.3	6.6
Total	0.2	0.9	3.3	33.8	55.5	6.3	100.0

Source: Authors' elaboration based on Martinez-Aguilar and Ortiz-Juarez (2016).

Figure 13-9

Headcounts and Amounts of Fiscal Impoverishment and Fiscal Gains to the Poor
(percentages of population and US$ millions adjusted by PPP)

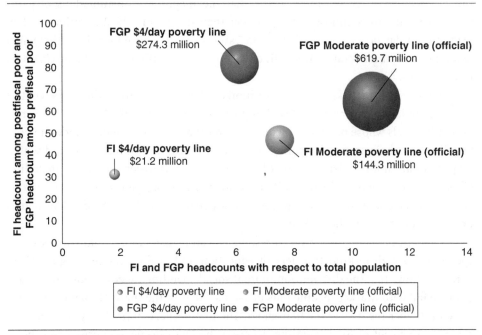

Source: Authors' elaboration based on Martinez-Aguilar and Ortiz-Juarez (2016).

Notes: The size of the bubbles is relative to the total monetary amounts of FI and FGP. The amounts are annual and expressed in millions of dollars adjusted by PPP at 2005 prices. The headcounts and amounts of FI and FGP for the official extreme poverty line are close to those for the $4/day poverty line and are therefore excluded from the graph in order to avoid an overlapping of the bubbles.

can be computed. The first amount equals the sum of the fall in income for the prefiscal poor, plus the difference between the poverty line and the income (also known as the poverty gap) for those prefiscal non-poor but postfiscal poor. The second amount is calculated as the sum of the increase in income for the prefiscal poor who remain poor after taxes and transfers, plus the prefiscal poverty gap for the prefiscal poor who escaped poverty after taxes and transfers.

Using both the $4/day and official moderate poverty lines, figure 13-9 draws both the FI and FGP headcounts with respect to the country's population over the x-axis, whereas the y-axis reflects the FI headcount among the postfiscal (Consumable Income) poor and the FGP headcount among the prefiscal (Market Income plus Pensions) poor; the size of the bubbles is relative to the total monetary amounts of both FI and FGP. One finding is that fewer individuals are impoverished in comparison to the number of fiscal gainers after the intervention of taxes, subsidies, and direct transfers. Using the $4/day poverty line, 1.8 percent of Chile's population (or 31.6 percent of the postfiscal poor) are impoverished, whereas 6.1 percent of the total population (or 82 percent of the prefiscal poor) are fiscal gainers. If the official moderate poverty line is employed instead, the proportion of impoverished (7.5 percent of the total, or 47.1 percent of the postfiscal poor) is lower than that of the fiscal gainers (10.6 percent of the total, or 65.1 percent of the prefiscal poor). A second result is that the magnitude of annual fiscal gains (US$274.3 million) is almost 13 times larger than that of FI (US$21.2 million) when using the $4/day poverty line, whereas the ratio is slightly above four times that when using the official moderate poverty line (with US$619.7 million of FGP and US$144.3 million of FI).[28]

The previous analysis yields an additional interesting finding. The 7.5 percent of Chile's population experiencing fiscal impoverishment—equivalent to nearly 1.3 million individuals whose postfiscal income is lower than both the official moderate poverty line and their prefiscal income—lives in 0.37 million households out of which 69 percent are not recipients of any of the main direct transfers analyzed, including Chile Solidario, Ingreso Etico Familiar, or noncontributory pensions. This is significant as 84 percent of the fiscal impoverished are members of households identified as poor according to the official definition.

A last, fundamental question to resolve is who benefits more from Chile's social spending through in-kind transfers of education and health services? Figure 13-10, panel A, shows that the distribution of total social spending on education and health tends to fall with Market Income plus Pensions—that is, the share of total benefits received is higher the poorer the household. The first decile, comprised by the poor, receives 13.6 percent of total spending, whereas the tenth decile, comprised mostly by wealthy individuals, receives just above 5 percent. Moreover, half of total spending is distributed among the bottom 40 percent of Chile's population, which is composed entirely by poor and vulnerable individuals.[29] That pattern holds when total spending is disaggregated by component, with the only exception being social spending on tertiary education, which seems disproportionally distributed among the upper deciles.

---

[28] When using the $4/day poverty line, these annual amounts are equivalent in Chilean pesos to roughly 137,700 million for fiscal gains and around 10,660 million for FI. For the official moderate poverty line the amounts are nearly 311,300 and 72,470 million of Chilean pesos, respectively. The headcounts and amounts of FI and FGP for the official extreme poverty line are relatively similar to those for the $4/day poverty line. The proportion of impoverished reaches 1.6 percent of the total population (or 31.2 percent of the postfiscal poor), whereas that of fiscal gainers reaches 5.7 percent of the total population (or 82.9 percent of the prefiscal poor). Regarding the amounts, annual fiscal gains are US$296.7 million (or roughly 149,000 million Chilean pesos) and annual FI is US$19.2 million (or nearly 9,600 million Chilean pesos).

[29] The values of the ultra-poor ($1.25/day), extreme ($2.5/day), and moderate ($4/day) poverty lines lie, respectively, at the first, third, and eighth percentiles of the income distribution. The value of the $10/day threshold dividing the vulnerable and the middle class lies at the fortieth percentile, whereas the $50/day line dividing the middle-class and the wealthy lies at the ninety-fourth percentile.

FIGURE 13-10

Distribution of Total Social Spending on Education and Health and Concentration and Incidence of Social Spending on Tertiary Education (percentages by deciles of market income plus pensions)

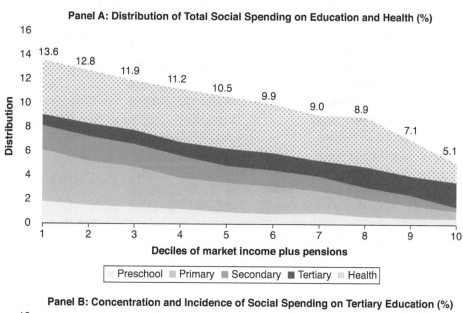

Panel A: Distribution of Total Social Spending on Education and Health (%)

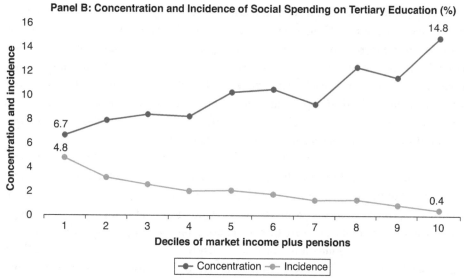

Panel B: Concentration and Incidence of Social Spending on Tertiary Education (%)

Source: Authors' elaboration based on Martinez-Aguilar and Ortiz-Juarez (2016).

Note: The sum of the areas measured in panel A equals 100 percent.

FIGURE 13-11

Concentration Coefficients of Social Spending and Public Spending on Subsidies

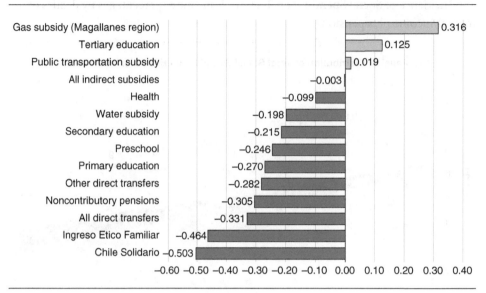

Source: Authors' elaboration based on Martinez-Aguilar and Ortiz-Juarez (2016).

In fact, when looking at its concentration, almost 15 percent of the total spending on tertiary education in Chile goes to the tenth decile, which is more than twice the share (6.7 percent) received by the bottom 10 percent of the population (figure 13-10, panel B). In terms of its incidence, when social spending on tertiary education is analyzed as share of income in each decile, this share is higher for the first decile (4.8 percent) than for the tenth decile (0.4 percent); the result, which is consistent with the positive marginal contribution to inequality (0.003) found previously, indicates that this component of social spending exerts a slightly equalizing effect.

While social spending on tertiary education is slightly equalizing, this intervention is not pro-poor as indicated by its positive concentration coefficient (figure 13-11). In fact, most of the interventions through public spending analyzed in this chapter are equalizing (positive marginal contributions). Among them, the most pro-poor (negative concentration coefficients) are direct transfers followed by primary education, preschool, and secondary education. The water subsidy and social spending on health are also somewhat pro-poor. In the case of the subsidy to public transportation, it is slightly equalizing but not pro-poor, whereas the subsidy to gas exerts a neutral effect on inequality (zero marginal contribution) and is also not pro-poor.[30] (The latter is not sur-

---

[30] The concentration coefficients for all fiscal interventions analyzed are shown in table 13A-1 in the appendix.

FIGURE 13-12

Redistributive Effects and Social Spending on Direct Transfers in Select Latin American Countries

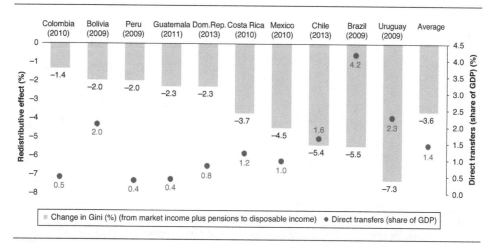

Source: Authors' elaboration based on the following works: Bolivia (Paz Arauco and others, 2014); Brazil (Higgins and Pereira, 2014); Chile (Martinez-Aguilar and Ortiz-Juarez, 2016); Colombia (Melendez and Martinez, 2015); Costa Rica (Sauma and Trejos, 2014); Dominican Republic (Aristy-Escuder and others, 2022) (chapter 14 in this Volume of the Handbook); Guatemala (Cabrera and Moran, 2016); Mexico (Scott, 2014); Peru (Jaramillo, 2014); and Uruguay (Bucheli and others, 2014).

Notes: The year for which the country analysis was conducted is shown in parentheses in each bar of the graph. The average is the simple mean of the percent changes by country. The figures shown in the graph may differ slightly from those originally published in the works cited due to recent updates of the CEQ methodology.

prising given that the gas subsidy uses geographical targeting and does not consider the poverty status of the population.)

3.2 Fiscal Redistribution in Chile: A Comparative Perspective

The redistributive effect of direct transfers, measured as the percent change in the Gini coefficient from Market Income plus Pensions to Disposable Income, is considerably larger in Chile (5.4 percent) than in other Latin American countries with a comparable fiscal incidence analysis: it is well above the average, and between 2.3 and 4 times larger than the effect found in the Dominican Republic, Guatemala, and the Andean countries. A salient result is that although spending on direct transfers as a share of GDP is lower in Chile (1.6 percent) than in Bolivia (2 percent), the redistributive gains are as much as 2.7 times larger in the former. Moreover, Chile achieves the same redistributive gains as Brazil (5.5 percent) with a significantly lower volume of direct transfers relative to GDP (figure 13-12). At the same time, however, Chile's redistributive effect of direct transfers is well below the effect observed in Uruguay (7.3 percent), and in all the Eastern European countries shown in figure 13-13 for which the comparison is possible.

For instance, in Georgia, a country with a similar Gini coefficient for Market Income plus Pensions (0.483) as Chile's (0.494), the redistributive effect reaches 18.4 percent

FIGURE 13-13

Inequality Dynamics in Chile and Select Countries in Eastern Europe

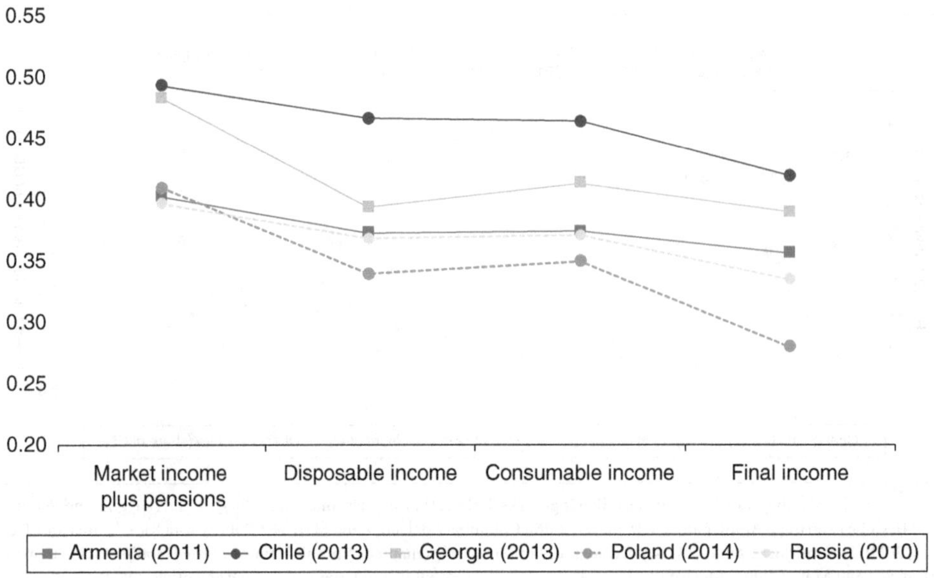

Source: Authors' elaboration based on the following works: Armenia (Younger and Khachatryan, 2017); Chile (Martinez-Aguilar and Ortiz-Juarez, 2016); Georgia (Cancho and Bondarenko, 2017); Poland (Goraus and Inchauste, 2016); and Russia (Lopez-Calva and others, 2017).

Note: The year for which the country analysis was conducted is shown in parentheses in each country label of the graph.

after deducting (adding) direct taxes (transfers) from/to Disposable Income, placing the Gini coefficient at 0.349. The magnitude of the redistributive effect is also similar in Poland (17.1 percent), although this country exhibits a Gini coefficient for Market Income plus Pensions that is significantly lower (0.410). When social spending on education and health is considered, the inequality-reducing effect in Chile (15 percent)—relative to Market Income plus Pensions—surpasses that of Armenia (11.4 percent), is on par with that of the Russian Federation (15.6 percent), and remains well below the effect found in Georgia (19.3 percent) and Poland (31.7 percent). (It is worth noting that when moving from disposable to Consumable Income—for example, when considering indirect taxes and subsidies—only Chile exhibits a decline in the Gini coefficient, which is the result of the aforementioned Lambert's conundrum.)

Regarding the influence of direct transfers on poverty, figure 13-14 shows that they can reduce the incidence of poverty in Chile by 41.2 percent with respect to the Market Income plus Pensions concept, a change that is similar to that observed in Uruguay (42 percent) and threefold the average of the selected Latin American countries (12.6 percent). The intervention of indirect taxes and subsidies in Chile halves the magnitude of such reduction (24.2 percent), although it remains large enough to position

FIGURE 13-14

Poverty-Reducing Effects in Select Latin American Countries

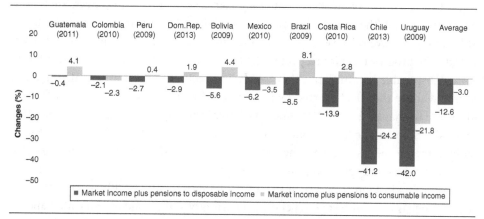

Source: Authors' elaboration based on the following works: Bolivia (Paz Arauco and others, 2014); Brazil (Higgins and Pereira, 2014); Chile (Martinez-Aguilar and Ortiz-Juarez, 2016); Colombia (Melendez and Martinez, 2015); Costa Rica (Sauma and Trejos, 2014); Dominican Republic (Aristy-Escuder and others, 2022) (chapter 14 in this Volume); Guatemala (Cabrera and Moran, 2016); Mexico (Scott, 2014); Peru (Jaramillo, 2014); and Uruguay (Bucheli and others, 2014).

Notes: The incidence of poverty is measured according to the $4/day poverty line. The year for which the country analysis was conducted is shown in parentheses in each bar of the graph. The average is the simple mean of the percent changes by country. The figures shown in the graph may differ slightly from those originally published in the works cited due to recent updates of the CEQ methodology.

Chile as the best performer among the Latin American countries with a comparable assessment. In startling contrast, in countries like Bolivia, Brazil, Costa Rica, the Dominican Republic, and Guatemala, the effect of indirect taxes and subsidies on poverty more than compensates for the gains from direct transfers.

4 Conclusions

The results from the fiscal incidence analysis presented here indicate, in general, that fiscal interventions in Chile exert a positive net effect in reducing poverty and inequality and favor upward economic mobility, especially among the poorest. In particular, subsidies for public transportation and water exert a positive, yet modest effect on poverty and inequality, whereas the effects of gas subsidy are mostly neutral. Direct transfers are progressive (that is, the benefits as share of prefiscal income decline with income), as well as equalizing and poverty-decreasing (that is, direct transfers show positive marginal contributions to both inequality and poverty). In terms of their effect on poverty, for instance, direct transfers reduce the incidence by 4–5 percentage points, depending on the poverty line used, with noncontributory pensions and the flagship cash transfer scheme (Chile Solidario, Ingreso Etico Familiar) accounting for the lion's share of such reduction. Direct transfers are also pro-poor, as indicated by their negative concentration coefficient (for example, per capita benefits from direct transfers decline with income).

On the other hand, direct taxes on personal income are found to be equalizing and poverty-neutral; social contributions are unequalizing and poverty increasing; and indirect taxes are poverty increasing, but they exert a slight equalizing effect. This counterintuitive result (the so-called Lambert's conundrum) occurs because indirect taxes, although regressive relative to prefiscal income (Market Income plus Pensions), are found to be progressive with respect to the less unequally distributed post-transfer income (Disposable Income). In other words, indirect taxes exert an equalizing effect over and above the effect exerted by progressive direct taxes and direct transfers. As discussed in chapter 2 of this Volume), the latter is not equivalent to ascertaining that regressive taxes can be fine as long as the net effect of the whole fiscal system is equalizing; rather, it means that such net effect with a regressive tax, relative to pre-fiscal income, can be more equalizing than without the tax.

Regarding in-kind transfers in the form of education and health, all the interventions are equalizing, with social spending on primary and secondary education and on health having the largest effect on inequality. The latter is not surprising given that Chile spends more on education and health (8.1 percent of the country's GDP) than in direct transfers (1.6 percent). Yet, this result must be interpreted with caution because in-kind transfers are monetized at average government cost, which does not necessarily reflect the actual value of the education and health services provided, and there are no adjustments for differences in quality across the distribution. It is important to emphasize that although social spending on tertiary education is slightly equalizing, this intervention is not pro-poor as indicated by its positive concentration coefficient. Conversely, social spending on basic (preschool and primary) and secondary education and health is not only equalizing but also pro-poor (negative concentration coefficients).

Four additional results are worth noting. First, after the intervention of taxes, subsidies, and direct transfers, not only is the incidence of poverty reduced, but also the depth of poverty and the magnitude of inequality among the poor decrease remarkably. Second, when using the official moderate poverty line, the net effect of the whole fiscal system leaves fewer individuals impoverished (7.5 percent of Chile's population, or 47.1 percent of the postfiscal poor) in comparison to the number of fiscal gainers (10.6 percent of the total, or 65.1 percent of the prefiscal poor), and the magnitude of monetary fiscal gains is as much as four times larger than that of fiscal impoverishment. Third, the 7.5 percent of Chile's population that experiences fiscal impoverishment lives in 0.37 million households out of which the 69 percent are not recipients of any of the main direct transfers analyzed. This is significant as 84 percent of the fiscally impoverished are members of households identified as poor according to the official definition; it also indicates that additional efforts are required to improve the targeting and expand the coverage of direct transfers among the poor population, in particular because direct transfers have a considerable effect on reducing inequality and poverty.

Finally, when put into a regional perspective, the redistributive effect of direct transfers (that is, the decline in inequality from prefiscal income to post-transfers income) is particularly greater in Chile than in other Latin American countries with a comparable fiscal incidence analysis. A remarkable result is that with 1.6 percent of the GDP being spent on direct transfers, the redistributive gains in Chile are as much as 2.7 times larger than in Bolivia, where direct transfers account for 2 percent of the GDP, and virtually the same as in Brazil, where they account for 5.5 percent of the GDP. In terms of the effect on poverty, as measured by the $4/day poverty line, direct transfers in Chile reduce the incidence by 41.2 percent with respect to prefiscal income, placing the country as a top performer in the region.

As part of its efforts to address persistently high levels of income inequality, the government of Chile enacted a comprehensive tax reform in 2014 aimed at generating additional tax revenues (amounting to around 3 percent of the GDP) to finance social spending, especially on education; improving neutrality and equity of the tax system; improving the efficiency of tax incentives on savings and investment; and reducing tax evasion and avoidance.[31] Even though the effect of such reform is not quantified in this chapter, further spending on education could potentially contribute to income inequality decline in the medium and long term. Moreover, an ex ante evaluation of the reform using the 2013 fiscal records suggested that the tax reform would likely increase the effective tax burden for the top 1 percent of the income distribution by 6 percentage points (equivalent to an increase from 2.4 to 3.5 percent of the GDP, with 80 percent of the latter figure being paid by the top 0.1 percent), while for most of the population the tax burden is expected to remain roughly constant, thereby eventually making the tax system more progressive.[32]

Acknowledgments

We are very grateful to Nora Lustig, consultant to the *CEQ Assessment* for Chile, for her valuable advice and insights from the very beginning and throughout the project, for solving many methodological issues, and for her helpful comments to an earlier draft of this paper. We are also grateful to Alberto Arenas de Mesa, former Minister of Finance of Chile, for providing detailed comments on the results shown in this chapter; Gustavo Cabezas, economist at the United Nations Development Programme Chile, for his valuable help in estimating the indirect taxes; and Maynor Cabrera, Technical Coordinator at the CEQ Institute, for his quality oversight of the results presented. We would also like to thank Oscar Calvo-Gonzalez, Lidia Ceriani, Gabriela Inchauste, and Alberto Rodriguez from the World Bank, who provided comments that greatly benefited this chapter. The findings, interpretations, and conclusions, as well as any errors or omissions, are entirely the authors' responsibility and may not represent those of the institutions with which they are associated.

---

[31] Arenas de Mesa (2016).
[32] World Bank (2016).

References

Arenas de Mesa, Alberto. 2016. *Sostenibilidad fiscal y reformas tributarias en America Latina* (Santiago: Comision Economica para America Latina y el Caribe [CEPAL]).

Aristy-Escuder, Jaime, Maynor Cabrera, Blanca Moreno-Dodson, and Miguel E. Sanchez-Martin. 2022. "The Dominican Republic: Fiscal Policy, Income Redistribution, and Poverty Reduction in the Dominican Republic," chap. 14 in *Commitment to Equity Handbook: Estimating the Impact of Fiscal Policy on Inequality and Poverty*, 2nd ed., Vol. 1, edited by Nora Lustig (Brookings Institution Press and CEQ Institute, Tulane University). Free online version available at www.commitmentoequity.org.

Bucheli, Marisa, Nora Lustig, Maximo Rossi, and Florencia Amabile. 2014. "Social Spending, Taxes and Income Redistribution in Uruguay," in "The Redistributive Impact of Taxes and Social Spending in Latin America," edited by Nora Lustig, Carola Pessino, and John Scott, special issue, *Public Finance Review* 42, no. 3, pp. 413–33.

Cabrera, Maynor, and Hilcias E. Moran. 2016. *"CEQ Master Workbook*. Guatemala" (CEQ Institute, Instituto Centroamericano de Estudios Fiscales, and International Fund for Agricultural Development).

Cancho, Cesar, and Elena Bondarenko. 2017. "The Distributional Impact of Fiscal Policy in Georgia," in *The Distributional Impact of Taxes and Transfers: Evidence from Eight Low- and Middle-Income Countries*, edited by Gabriela Inchauste and Nora Lustig (Washington: World Bank).

Castelletti, Barbara. 2013. "How Redistributive Is Fiscal Policy in Latin America? The Case of Chile and Mexico." OECD Development Centre Working Papers, No. 318 (OECD).

Direccion de Presupuestos. 2014. *Estadisticas de las Finanzas Publicas 2004–2013* (Santiago: Ministerio de Hacienda).

Enami, Ali, Sean Higgins, and Nora Lustig. 2022. "Allocating Taxes and Transfers and Constructing Income Concepts: Completing Sections A, B, and C of the *CEQ Master Workbook*," chap. 6 in *Commitment to Equity Handbook: Estimating the Impact of Fiscal Policy on Inequality and Poverty*, 2nd ed., Vol. 1, edited by Nora Lustig (Brookings Institution Press and CEQ Institute, Tulane University). Free online version available at www.commitmentoequity.org.

Enami, Ali, Nora Lustig, and Rodrigo Aranda. 2022. "Analytic Foundations: Measuring the Redistributive Impact of Taxes and Transfers," chap. 2 in *Commitment to Equity Handbook: Estimating the Impact of Fiscal Policy on Inequality and Poverty*, 2nd ed., Vol. 1, edited by Nora Lustig (Brookings Institution Press and CEQ Institute, Tulane University). Free online version available at www.commitmentoequity.org.

Engel, Eduardo M. R. A., Alexander Galetovic, and Claudio E. Raddatz. 1999. "Taxes and Income Distribution in Chile: Some Unpleasant Redistributive Arithmetic." *Journal of Development Economics* 59, no. 1, pp. 155–92.

Foster, James, Joel Greer, and Erik Thorbecke. 1984. "A Class of Decomposable Poverty Measures." *Econometrica* 3, no. 52, pp. 761–66.

Goraus, Karolina, and Gabriela Inchauste. 2016. "The Distributional Impact of Taxes and Transfers in Poland," Policy Research Working Paper 7787 (Washington: World Bank).

Higgins, Sean, and Nora Lustig. 2016. "Can a Poverty-Reducing and Progressive Tax and Transfer System Hurt the Poor?" *Journal of Development Economics* 122, pp. 63–75.

Higgins, Sean, and Claudiney Pereira. 2014. "The Effects of Brazil's Taxation and Social Spending on the Distribution of Household Income," in "The Redistributive Impact of Taxes and Social Spending in Latin America," edited by Nora Lustig, Carola Pessino, and John Scott, special issue, *Public Finance Review* 42, no. 3, pp. 346–67 (doi:10.1177/1091142113501714).

Jaramillo, Miguel. 2014. "The Incidence of Social Spending and Taxes in Peru," in "The Redistributive Impact of Taxes and Social Spending in Latin America," edited by Nora Lustig, Carola Pessino, and John Scott, special issue, *Public Finance Review* 42, no. 3, pp. 391–412 (doi:10.1177/1091142113496134).

Kakwani, Nanak C. 1977. "Measurement of Tax Progressivity: An International Comparison." *Economic Journal* 87, no. 345, pp. 71–80.

Lambert, Peter. 2001. *The Distribution and Redistribution of Income*, 3rd ed. (Manchester University Press).

Larrañaga, Osvaldo, Jenny Encina, and Gustavo Cabezas. 2012. "A Microsimulation Model of Distribution for Chile," in *Fiscal Inclusive Development: Microsimulation Models for Latin America*, edited by Carlos M. Urzua (Mexico City: IDRC-UNDP-ITESM).

Lopez-Calva, Luis Felipe, Nora Lustig, Mikhail Matytsin, and Daria Popova. 2017. "Who Benefits from Fiscal Redistribution in Russia?," in *The Distributional Impact of Taxes and Transfers: Evidence from Eight Low- and Middle-Income Countries*, edited by Gabriela Inchauste and Nora Lustig (Washington: World Bank).

Lopez-Calva, Luis Felipe, and Eduardo Ortiz-Juarez. 2014. "A Vulnerability Approach to the Definition of the Middle Class." *Journal of Economic Inequality* 12, no. 1, pp. 23–47.

Lustig, Nora. 2022a. "Fiscal Policy, Income Redistribution, and Poverty Reduction in Low- and Middle-Income Countries," chap. 10 in *Commitment to Equity Handbook: Estimating the Impact of Fiscal Policy on Inequality and Poverty*, 2nd ed., Vol. 1, edited by Nora Lustig (Brookings Institution Press and CEQ Institute, Tulane University). Free online version available at www.commitmentoequity.org.

———, ed. 2022b. *Commitment to Equity Handbook: Estimating the Impact of Fiscal Policy on Inequality and Poverty*, 2nd ed., Vol. 1 (Brookings Institution Press and CEQ Institute, Tulane University). Free online version available at www.commitmentoequity.org.

Lustig, Nora, and Sean Higgins. 2013. "Estimating the Incidence of Social Spending, Subsidies and Taxes. Handbook." CEQ Working Paper No. 1 (CEQ Institute, Tulane University).

Martinez-Aguilar, Sandra, and Eduardo Ortiz-Juarez. 2016. "*CEQ Master Workbook*. Chile" (CEQ Institute, Tulane University, and World Bank).

Melendez, Marcela, and Valentina Martinez. 2015. "*CEQ Master Workbook*. Colombia" (CEQ Institute, Tulane University, and Inter-American Development Bank).

Ministerio de Desarrollo Social. 2016. *Informe de Desarrollo Social 2016* (Santiago: Gobierno de Chile).

OECD. 2016a. "Social Expenditure: Aggregated Data." OECD Social Expenditure Statistics (https://stats.oecd.org/Index.aspx?DataSetCode=SOCX_AGG).

———. 2016b. "Revenue Statistics: Comparative Tables." OECD Tax Statistics (https://stats.oecd.org/Index.aspx?DataSetCode=REV).

Paz Arauco, Veronica, George Gray Molina, Wilson Jimenez Pozo, and Ernesto Yañez Aguilar. 2014. "Explaining Low Redistributive Impact in Bolivia," in "The Redistributive Impact of Taxes and Social Spending in Latin America," edited by Nora Lustig, Carola Pessino, and

John Scott, special issue, *Public Finance Review* 42, no. 3, pp. 326–45 (doi:10.1177/109114
2113496133).

Sauma, Pablo, and Juan Diego Trejos. 2014. "Social Public Spending, Taxes, Redistribution of In-
come, and Poverty in Costa Rica." CEQ Working Paper No. 18 (Center for Inter-American
Policy and Research and Department of Economics, Tulane University and Inter-American
Dialogue).

Scott, John. 2014. "Redistributive Impact and Efficiency of Mexico's Fiscal System," in "The Redistributive Impact of Taxes and Social Spending in Latin America," edited by Nora Lustig,
Carola Pessino, and John Scott, special issue, *Public Finance Review* 42, no. 3, pp. 368–90
(doi:10.1177/1091142113497394).

Servicio de Impuestos Internos. 2015. "Serie de evasion de IVA 2003–2015. Base MIP 2008." Sub-
direccion de Gestion Estrategica y Estudios Tributarios (Santiago: Servicio de Impuestos
Internos).

World Bank. 2016. "Chile. Distributional Effects for the 2014 Tax Reform." Working Paper 104099
(Washington).

Younger, Stephen D., and Artsvi Khachatryan. 2017 "Fiscal Incidence in Armenia," in *The Distributional Impact of Taxes and Transfers. Evidence from Eight Low- and Middle-Income Countries*, edited by Gabriela Inchauste and Nora Lustig (Washington: World Bank).

Appendix 13A

Marginal Contributions to Inequality by End Income Concept, Concentration Coefficients, and Kakwani Indexes for All Fiscal Interventions

TABLE 13-A1

Marginal Contributions to Inequality by End Income Concept, Concentration Coefficients, and Kakwani Indexes for All Fiscal Interventions

	Marginal contributions to inequality	Concentration coefficients	Kakwani index
When disposable income is the end income concept			
Direct taxes	0.011	0.946	0.452
Noncontributory pensions	0.010	−0.305	0.799
All direct taxes and contributions	0.007	0.637	0.143
Other direct transfers	0.005	−0.282	0.775
Chile Solidario	0.003	−0.503	0.997
Ingreso Etico Familiar	0.001	−0.464	0.958
All social contributions	−0.003	0.327	−0.166
When consumable income is the end income concept			
Direct taxes	0.012	0.946	0.452
All direct taxes and contributions	0.008	0.637	0.143
All taxes and contributions	0.008	0.518	0.025
Other direct transfers	0.006	−0.282	0.775
All indirect subsidies	0.003	−0.003	0.497
Subsidy to public transportation	0.002	0.019	0.475
Ingreso Etico Familiar	0.001	−0.464	0.958
Subsidy to drinkable water	0.001	−0.198	0.692
All indirect taxes	0.000	0.466	−0.027
Gas subsidy	0.000	0.316	0.177
All social contributions	−0.004	0.327	−0.166
Chile Solidario	n.a.	−0.503	0.997
Noncontributory pensions	n.a.	−0.305	0.799

(continued)

TABLE 13-A1 (continued)

	Marginal contributions to inequality	Concentration coefficients	Kakwani index
When final income is the end income concept			
All education	0.032	−0.171	0.664
Primary education	0.014	−0.270	0.763
Health	0.014	−0.099	0.593
All direct taxes	0.012	0.946	0.452
All direct taxes and social contributions	0.009	0.637	0.143
Secondary education	0.008	−0.215	0.708
Preschool	0.005	−0.246	0.739
All indirect taxes	0.004	0.466	−0.027
Tertiary education	0.003	0.125	0.369
All indirect subsidies	0.002	−0.003	0.497
All direct transfers	n.a.	−0.331	0.824

Source: Authors' elaboration based on Martinez-Aguilar and Ortiz-Juarez (2016).

Notes: The values of the concentration coefficient and Kakwani index for each fiscal intervention are the same regardless of the end income concept because such coefficients and indexes are calculated with respect to the Market Income plus Pensions concept. The "n.a." label represents the cases where the Gini coefficient is not calculated without the corresponding fiscal intervention because without it the income of some households becomes negative.

Chapter 14

THE DOMINICAN REPUBLIC
Fiscal Policy, Income Redistribution, and Poverty Reduction

Jaime Aristy-Escuder, Maynor Cabrera,
Blanca Moreno-Dodson, and Miguel E. Sanchez-Martin

Introduction

In spite of sustained economic growth over the past two decades, the population in the Dominican Republic did not achieve significant welfare improvements until recently. Economic growth averaged 5.7 percent a year in 1991–2013 and was among the highest rates in the region. This performance enabled the country's GNI per capita (US$5,520 in 2012) to rise from 52 percent to 78 percent of the Latin America and the Caribbean (LAC) region's average. From 2000 to 2013, a slight improvement in income inequality occurred, with the Gini index falling from 0.549 to 0.514. Disaggregation by area suggests that most of the inequality reduction took place in the rural parts of the country; inequality in urban areas did not decline significantly.[1]

After a sharp rise in the early 2000s, poverty rates have been falling in recent years, and one possible explanation is that fiscal policy may not be redistributive enough. According to the official poverty measurement methodology for the Dominican Republic,[2] moderate poverty incidence soared from 32 percent in 2000 to almost 50 percent in 2004, a period that included a severe banking crisis. It then declined gradually to around 41 percent in 2013 and about 35 percent by October 2014. Rapid poverty reduction in 2014,[3] a year of 7.3 percent economic growth, has been attributed to rising wages, increased employment in school construction, public support to agriculture,

---

[1] World Bank (2014a).

[2] See ONE and MEPyD (2012).

[3] According to ONE and MEPyD, poverty headcount index fell from 41.2 percent in 2013 to 35.8 percent in 2014.

credit to small and medium enterprises, and allocating more public investment to disadvantaged areas.

At least until recently, the pace of poverty reduction has been slower in the Dominican Republic than in other countries with similar growth rates. Several studies have tried to explain the pre-2014 puzzle of slow poverty reduction at a time of rapid growth. Aristy-Escuder (2017) analyzes whether the typical consumption basket for the poor differs significantly from that used to calculate the general consumer price index and the GDP deflator, but does not find statistical distortions in the measure of poverty headcount. Other hypotheses include: (1) stagnant real wages (real earnings per hour of both self-employed and private-sector wage workers were about 27 percent lower in 2011 than in 2000) despite rising labor productivity (around 30 percent increase between 2000 and 2010[4]); (2) the enclave nature of the economy, with activity in special economic zones and tourist poles relatively isolated from the rest of the country; and (3) the lack of redistributive capacity of the public sector.[5] To explore the latter hypothesis, this chapter uses the Commitment to Equity (CEQ) methodology[6] to perform a fiscal incidence analysis on the poverty and equity implications of the Dominican Republic's fiscal system, including current taxes, subsidies, and overall public spending.

The Dominican Republic's tax policy has become more reliant on indirect taxes. Public revenues averaged 14.3 percent of GDP in 2004–14, with tax collections at 13.4 percent of GDP, which is below the LAC average.[7] It is worth noting that the government responded to a fall in fiscal revenues (partly related to declining trade taxes in the context of the implementation of the Dominican Republic-Central America Free Trade Agreement [DR-CAFTA] with the United States) by adopting a total of six tax reforms between 2004 and 2012. A country heavily dependent on indirect taxation, the Dominican Republic repeatedly increased value-added tax (VAT) rates—from 12 percent to 16 percent and then to 18 percent.[8] This, together with the introduction of selective taxes on telecommunication services, has been the most far-reaching re-

---

[4] See Abdullaev and Estevao (2013).

[5] Carneiro and others (2015).

[6] Lustig and Higgins (2013). Led by Nora Lustig since 2008, the Commitment to Equity (CEQ) project is an initiative of the Center for Inter-American Policy and Research (CIPR) and the Department of Economics, both at Tulane University, along with the Center for Global Development and the Inter-American Dialogue. The CEQ project is housed in the Commitment to Equity Institute at Tulane. For more detail visit www.commitmentoequity.org.

[7] When both tax and nontax revenue are considered, the Dominican Republic trails only Guatemala for the lowest revenue level in Latin America, according to ECLAC Statistics. When social security contributions are excluded, Dominican Republic tax revenue is similar to the regional average.

[8] Laws 288-04 and 253-12.

form. However, the tax bases have remained narrow, and persistent extensive tax exemptions have eroded the effective revenue base, since a large portion of the population (including both individuals and special economic zones) have so far opposed an integral fiscal reform.[9] Despite recent improvement, at 15.1 percent of GDP in 2014, fiscal revenues remain below their level in 2007 (16.6 percent). Revenue collection capacity is partly hampered by high levels of informality and existing tax exemptions, with tax expenditure amounting to an estimated 6.6 percent of GDP in 2014, including 3.2 percent of GDP in VAT exemptions.[10]

The Dominican Republic has made notable efforts to increase social spending. As mandated by law and demanded by the citizenry, public outlays for education doubled in recent years—from around 2.2 percent of GDP in 2011 to close to 4 percent in 2013. In a social security reform, some health services were privatized, and lower income households began to receive insurance under a subsidized scheme. However, a large part of the population remains uninsured. In addition, indirect subsidies on electricity (and technical and commercial losses) take a big toll on the public budget, equaling about 2 percent of GDP. Finally, a relatively large number of targeted social assistance programs represent around 0.5 percent of GDP. The structure of revenue and expenditure in the Dominican Republic is presented in more detail in the appendix to this chapter.

A few existing fiscal incidence studies are relevant to the Dominican Republic: Santana and Rathe (1993),[11] Lindert, Skoufias, and Shapiro (2006), and Barreix, Bes, and Roca (2009). Lindert, Skoufias, and Shapiro (2006) find low levels of social spending in the Dominican Republic. They measure the extent to which social assistance and social security spending, consumption subsidies, and education and health spending favor the poor in eight Latin American countries (LAC). For the Dominican Republic, they use the National Survey on Living Conditions (ENCOVI) for 2004. At that time, the country had the lowest levels of social spending in the sample, and social insurance had negligible poverty impacts. The results reflect a combination of factors: (1) some programs had relatively low (net) unit subsidies and weak targeting and coverage of the poor and vulnerable, and (2) social assistance programs like the school-based attendance transfer and school feeding ranked fairly high in terms of social welfare impact per dollar spent, but were quite small in terms of budget and subsidy per person.

Barreix, Bes, and Roca (2009) examine the impact of fiscal policy (social spending and taxation) on inequality and find Dominican fiscal policy to have been progressive in 2004. Their work is based on a collection of studies for Central America and the

---

[9] World Bank (2014b).

[10] DGII (2014).

[11] This study used 1989 household income data and found "a degree of progressivity" in direct and indirect taxation (Chu, Davoodi, and Gupta, 2000, p. 38).

Dominican Republic written by various authors who followed a common methodology.[12] The analysis uses ENCOVI 2004 and covers direct and indirect taxes, spending on education, health, and social assistance programs, and subsidies on electricity and gas. They find that fiscal policy in 2004 was progressive, and inequality was overall reduced thanks to a progressive social spending and despite a regressive tax system at that time. In addition, health and education spending was pro-poor, meaning it was progressive in absolute terms.[13] Some social assistance programs, like the general subsidies on electricity (Programa de Reduccion de Apagones) and liquified petroleum gas (LPG), which were in place prior to the shift to targeted subsidies in 2008, were progressive.[14]

In January 2013, a series of microsimulation exercises looked at the impact of selected fiscal policy tools on poverty and inequality; the results were mixed. The analysis found that: (1) the tax reform of November 2012[15] had a neutral impact on poverty and inequality; (2) the freezing of the lower exemption threshold on individual income taxes had a positive impact in terms of redistribution; and (3) the VAT rate increases were regressive.[16] A parallel microsimulation exercise showed that an RD$125 increase in the amount allocated to beneficiaries under the Comer es Primero conditional cash transfer (CCT) program would result in a 0.22 percent reduction in moderate poverty and a 0.0013 reduction in inequality (Gini index). Similarly, the expansion in the number of beneficiaries of the subsidized health regime would contribute to better equity outcomes.

This chapter goes beyond previous exercises. Using the CEQ methodology, it analyzes the impact of fiscal policy in 2013, including several fiscal instruments and social programs targeting the poor (direct and indirect taxes, transfers, CCTs, public services in education and health). Some taxes (like the corporate income tax [CIT]) and public spending categories (like some infrastructure and rural development items) are not included due to the difficulty of assessing their effects on the Disposable Income of citizens, specially the poor.

The chapter's main contributions are that, first, it provides insight into how selected taxes and transfers programs affect income distribution in the Dominican Republic by introducing an innovative approach to address the time gap between the current fiscal structure (2013) and the year of the latest household survey (2007). Second, it compares the Dominican Republic's results with a number of countries in which the CEQ methodology has been applied,[17] including some with similar incomes per capita, such

---

[12] For the Dominican Republic analysis, the background study was prepared by Diaz (2008).

[13] A transfer will be progressive in absolute terms if the per capita amount received decreases as income rises (Lustig and Higgins, 2013).

[14] Gallina and others (2015). Progressive in relative terms: subsidy increases as a percentage of income but per capita subsidy declines as income rises.

[15] Law 253-12.

[16] MEPyD (2013).

[17] The common methodology is described in Lustig and Higgins (2013).

as Costa Rica[18] and Peru.[19] Third, it considers a series of alternative scenarios that would help enhance the redistributive capacity of the state.

1 Methodology and Sources of Information

1.1 CEQ Methodology

The goal of the analysis is to estimate the impact of taxes and transfers on income inequality and poverty in the Dominican Republic. We use the CEQ methodology, applying the fiscal incidence analysis described in Lustig and Higgins (2013). This starts with the individual's Market Income and adds transfers and subtracts taxes at different stages (figure 14-1).

Market Income is a measure of pretax income that does not include the effects of government policies. It consists of pretax wages, salaries, self-employed income, income from capital (dividends, interest, and rent), and pensions.[20]

We estimate three scenarios, concerning how to take into consideration contributory pensions in income definition (i.e., benchmark vs. sensitivity analysis 1) and which is the impact of the increase in public education expenditure (i.e., sensitivity analysis 1 and sensitivity analysis 2). The difference between the benchmark and sensitivity analysis 2 scenarios is that, in order to estimate the impact of the significant increase in public education expenditures in 2013, an alternative sensitivity analysis 2 featuring the lower expenditure level of 2011 is built. Since there is no theoretical consensus on whether contributory pensions are part of Market Income or a government transfer, the scenario sensitivity analysis 1 does not include public pensions in Market Income and instead makes them a transfer contained in Disposable Income, in contrast with benchmark and sensitivity analysis 2, in which contributory pensions are considered to be part of Market Income.

Net Market Income subtracts direct taxes. Personal income taxes on wages, dividends, and interest are included in the analysis. Because the Dominican Republic's old public pension system was privatized, social security contributions are not included as direct taxes. Disposable Income adds direct cash and food transfers to Net Market Income. As explained in the previous section, we include CCTs for nutrition and education; nonconditional cash transfers; goods transfers like food, shoes, uniforms, and backpacks; and the alphabetization program for adults implemented by the government (Quisqueya Aprende Contigo).

---

[18] Sauma and Trejos (2014).

[19] Jaramillo (2014).

[20] It is worth mentioning that the question asked in the National Survey of Household Income and Expenditure ENIGH 2007 (Encuesta Nacional de Ingresos y Gastos de Hogares) is about labor income gross of taxes.

FIGURE 14-1

Income Concepts Used in Fiscal Incidence Analysis

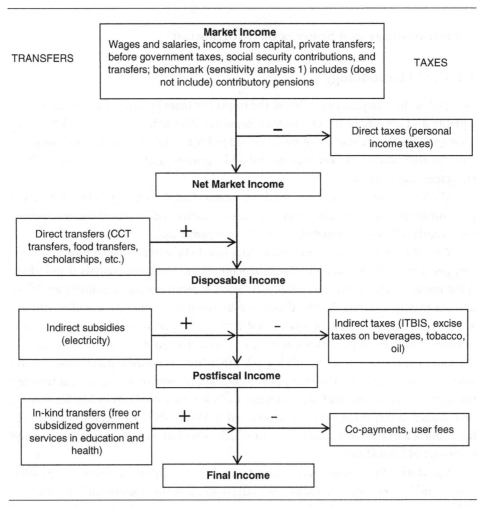

Source: Lustig and Higgins (2013).

Postfiscal income adds implicit subsidies on electricity and subtracts indirect taxes. These levies include the tax on the transfer of industrialized goods and services (ITBIS), a value-added tax (VAT) applied to domestic and imported goods and services, and excises on alcoholic beverages, beer, tobacco, and oil derivatives.

Final Income includes in-kind transfers. These are measured by the monetized value of public expenditures in health (Ministry of Health, social security, and others) and education (preschool, primary, lower-secondary, upper-secondary, and tertiary). It is important to take into consideration that contributive health insurance is not included in the analysis, since it works de facto as a private insurance.

1.2 Data Sources

This fiscal incidence analysis uses several sources of information. The main one is the National Survey of Household Income and Expenditure 2006–07 (ENIGH), which was collected by the National Office of Statistics (ONE) between January 2007 and January 2008 for 22,000 households and 80,131 individuals. It is representative at the national level and for four main domains: Metropolitan (or Ozama), North (or Cibao), South, and East. ENIGH contains data on income, expenditures, auto-consumption, remittances, and use of educational services. To account for changes in health coverage, we complement ENIGH with the Demographic and Health Survey (ENDESA 2013). This survey has a nationally representative sample of 11,464 households, 9,372 women ages fifteen to forty-one, and 10,306 men ages fifteen to fifty-nine.

Additionally, data on government revenues were obtained from the General Directorate for Internal Taxation and the Ministry of Finance. Data on direct transfers come from Administradora de Subsidios Sociales (ADESS), the Ministry of Finance, and the Ministry of Education. Information on electricity subsidies was facilitated by the Ministry of Finance. Finally, data on public health expenditures were obtained from the Ministry of Finance, the Ministry of Health, and Seguro Nacional de Salud (SENASA).

1.3 Main Assumptions

Compared to other countries' studies using the CEQ methodology, the Dominican Republic is especially challenging because the "departure point," the most recent household income and expenditure survey, dates back to 2007. It is necessary to take into account the fact that numerous policy decisions were adopted between 2007 and 2013, including the modification of the rates and bases of the main taxes (for example, ITBIS, ISR, ISC).[21] Furthermore, there has been a notable expansion in the coverage of direct transfers (for example, Comer es Primero, Bonogas Hogar, and Bonogas Chofer),[22] and the value of certain in-kind transfers, such as education, has been expanded.

In light of these changes, the methodology applied the tax and public expenditure structures of 2013 to ENIGH 2007. On the tax side, rates and definitions of the 2013 tax base were used. On the expenditure side, the value of the 2013 peso was deflated by the change in the consumer price index (CPI) between 2007 and 2013. In other words, the public revenues and spending vectors of 2013 were used to calculate income poverty—but

---

[21] ITBIS stands for Impuesto sobre Transferencias de Bienes Industrializados y Servicios: ISR, Impuesto sobre la renta; and ISC, Impuesto Selectivo al Consumo.

[22] Comer es Primero (Eating Is First) grants a monthly financial aid to each beneficiary family to purchase food according to a determined basic basket. Bonogas Hogar grants a monthly payment to each beneficiary family to purchase Liquefied Petroleum Gas (LPG). Bonogas Chofer grants a monthly payment to public car drivers to purchase LPG.

in 2007 prices. Expenditures were adjusted only for inflation and not by GDP growth. This is because the majority of the recorded public-spending variations were below the growth rate during the period. Overall, the objective was to adapt the CEQ methodology's various definitions of income using the ENIGH 2007 and the public revenue and expenditure structure of 2013, expressed in 2007 prices. We opted for this alternative (instead of inflating to 2013 the variables of the ENIGH 2007) because, besides inflation between 2007 and 2013, relative prices of production factors, structure of employment, and size of households in the Dominican Republic could have affected important changes in income distribution, which we would otherwise not have been able to replicate with available information. The adjustment factor was 42.5 percent, which is inflation between the June 2007 date of the survey and December 2013.

The following analysis evaluates the tax system along only one dimension—its impact on equity. It does not assess other important features of a tax system, such as its efficiency (which measures the amount collected given the rate), buoyancy (that is, the response of tax collections to economic growth), simplicity, and ease of administration.

An estimation of direct taxes was made by applying statutory rates and income brackets from 2012 (in 2007 prices) to the salaries and wages declared in ENIGH 2007. Individuals have to pay direct taxes out of Market Income. Because income tax payments in 2013 were made taking into consideration income from 2012, we deflate from 2012 to 2007 prices. Due to the fact that income brackets were adjusted by inflation from 2008 to 2012, mismatch between effective income brackets is expected to be minimal. As pointed out by Dominican authorities, tax evasion among the self-employed is considered significant. However, we were unable to gain access to profiles of payments of independent businesses or official estimations of evasion, so we do not calculate personal income taxes for those groups. In addition, we do not use assumptions regarding informality of wage earners or other assumptions regarding tax evasion on personal income tax. In order to ensure that the incidence analysis is not detached from reality due to our assumptions, we contrasted simulated collections applying statutory tax rates and actual collections and discussed results with the tax authority in the Dominican Republic to ensure consistency.

The personal income tax is levied on individuals with income above the exemption threshold. The system uses three rates that rise with tax brackets: 15 percent, 20 percent, and 25 percent. Dividends and interest income are taxed at 10 percent. It is assumed that informal self-employed workers do not pay income taxes. The corporate income tax is also not included in the analysis. Two caveats apply: (1) using statutory rates does not measure taxes actually paid, and (2) even if the survey's simulated total income tax payment is similar to actual collection, the incidence by quintile could be over or under the estimated values. We assume the household survey includes labor income gross of taxes because the ENIGH 2007 survey asks for gross salary without deductions.

Indirect taxes were estimated using the simulation method. We include ITBIS, excises, a tax on telecommunications, and the insurance tax. ENIGH 2007 has a detailed list of household purchases of goods and services, categorized according to the Classification of Individual Consumption According to Purpose (COICOP).[23] We separate each good or service into one of three groups: (1) those exempt in 2007 and 2013, (2) those exempt in 2007 but not in 2013, and (3) those taxable by both ITBIS and excises.

Within ITBIS, it was necessary to distinguish between goods that were and were not exempt. To avoid overestimating the taxes paid by low-income earners, we decided, after discussion with authorities, to include tax evasion in all scenarios. We incorporated the assumption of tax evasion by creating four groups of goods and services: (1) high propensity for evasion; (2) high propensity to pay ITBIS; (3) products with estimated compliance rates, according to the General Directorate for Internal Taxation;[24] and (4) products on which the VAT was paid as a condition of purchase.[25] Indirect taxes were down-scaled to prevent overestimation, using the method in Lustig and Higgins (2013). For example, we adjust VAT payments to equalize the ratio of total VAT to Disposable Income in the survey to the ratio of VAT collection to private consumption in the national accounts in 2013. Also, we take into account exemptions and reduced rates on each kind of good and service according to statutory rates.

Direct transfers received were assigned if the household fell into a Sistema Unico de Beneficiarios (SIUBEN) category that indicates eligibility for each program—for example, categories "poor 1" and "poor 2" in the case of Comer es Primero. Ultimately, beneficiaries were randomly selected as a subgroup of the household, based on coverage statistics. A series of steps were taken: (1) we adjusted the population of ADESS beneficiaries in 2013, taking into consideration the variation in the population between 2007 and 2013; (2) we calculated transfers at 2007 prices; and (3) we adjusted the coverage in terms of SIUBEN categories to reproduce the number of beneficiaries and coverage as a percent of the population. When the household survey and the national accounts differed on the ratio of direct transfers to national income, we down-scaled the value of the transfer to make the ratios comparable. Other transfers, like those on shoes, uniforms, and backpacks, plus the alphabetization program, were imputed using average costs estimated by the Ministry of Education and UNICEF—once again, with 2013 values adjusted to 2007 prices.

Implicit electricity transfers were calculated by applying existing tariffs. Using 2007 prices, we estimated the implicit kwh consumed by each household and applied the subsidy to users consuming less than 700 kwh a month. For those in the ENIGH survey who consume electricity but do not pay the bill, an implicitly standard subsidy is calculated.

Education benefits depend on the number of students and the average cost of education. The survey identifies individuals who attend school, their levels of education,

---

[23] See the explanatory notes of the Classification of Individual Consumption According to Purpose as presented at the United Nations Statistics Division, http://unstats.un.org/unsd/cr/registry/regcst.asp?Cl=5.

[24] DGII provided a list with estimated compliance rates for VAT payments.

[25] We estimated a detailed list of goods and services according to these assumptions.

and whether the schools are private or public. The education benefit is based on the cost per student by level, estimated by UNESCO and the Dominican Republic Ministry of Education. We adjust these figures to 2007 prices. Following Lustig and Higgins (2013), we prevent overestimation by adjusting the ratio of education expenditures to Disposable Income, making it equal the ratio calculated using national accounts.

An alternative analysis examines the impact of a larger budget for public education. To account for the significant increase in public education expenditures in 2013, from 1.9 percent of GDP in 2011 to 3.8 of GDP in 2013, we estimated the alternative sensitivity analysis 2, featuring the lower expenditure level of 2011. Because gross coverage rates did not significantly change in primary schools and changed little in elementary and secondary schools between 2007 and 2013, the different scenarios assume coverage did not change.[26]

Finally, we account for in-kind health transfers by estimating the impact of the subsidized social security regime only, which is free for the poor and vulnerable, and not the contributory regime, which works as a private insurance.[27] We use the Demographics and Health Survey (ENDESA 2013) to determine whether individuals with health insurance belong in social security's subsidized regime. For the uninsured, we identify only those who use the services of public hospitals or ambulatory centers. It is also possible to identify those who are insured by the Dominican Institute of Social Security (IDSS). Finally, public spending under the Essential Medicines Program (PROMESE) is also computed; this includes spending to purchase medicines and medical supplies for public health institutions as well as the distribution of subsidized medicines to the population. Drawing from information in the ENDESA 2013 survey, we use matching-score analysis to identify beneficiaries in the ENIGH 2007 survey.

For beneficiaries of the subsidized regime, we impute an insurance value based on the average transfer by insured (per capita) from the government to SENASA. For IDSS affiliates, we estimated an average insurance value by dividing the government transfer by the total number of insured. For the uninsured who report using public facilities, we impute an average cost per user at hospital and ambulatory centers. This figure is estimated by dividing total expenditure on each level of health services from National Health Accounts[28] by users of health public services in the survey, identified using matching-score analysis from ENDESA 2013. For PROMESE, once we selected the beneficiaries of this program, we estimated an average benefit by dividing the program's expenditures in 2013 by the number of users reported in ENDESA 2013. As with educa-

---

[26] The rise in spending went mostly for construction and repair of classrooms, extension of school hours from five to eight, higher salaries for teachers, and hiring new teachers.

[27] The contributive system is actuarially fair. In the case of the subsidized regime, workers do not make contributions. This regime, financed by the Dominican state, covers the self-employed, disabled, and the extreme poor (as defined by the national poverty line).

[28] Ministry of Health (2014).

tion, the ratio of health expenditure to Disposable Income under the survey is adjusted to match the ratio calculated using national accounts.

In sum, using data from a dated household survey in the Dominican Republic required making a number of additional assumptions for the purposes of applying the CEQ methodology. Overall, the validity of results depends on the fact that changes in income distribution between 2007 and 2013 have been observed, but are not dramatic (for example, a decline in Gini from 0.487 to 0.471, according to World Development Indicators); this is the most relevant caveat in our analysis. In the case of education, since no significant change in enrollment is observed between 2007 and 2013 (except for pre-primary education), and given that the team accessed official data detailing the cost of delivery of education services, we are confident that incidence analysis for this sector is relatively precise. In the case of health services, using ENDESA 2013—a specialized survey collected during the year of analysis, which details information on the insurance beneficiaries and effective use of health services by income level—helps ensure the robustness of results. In addition, a matching-scores technique has been applied, and results should be thus as robust as those in other CEQ exercises using a specialized health survey. With respect to CCTs, a careful revision of the indicators was performed to ensure consistency with actual population coverage, transfers per capita, and budget for the different programs in 2013. In the case of indirect electricity subsidies, results should be interpreted with caution, since administrative registries do not adequately identify beneficiaries, and the analysis was performed on the basis of a profile of beneficiaries described by authorities of the sector.

Some mitigation measures in potentially problematic areas were taken and include the use of sources of information in addition to the household survey, discussions with authorities, and revision of results by the developers of the CEQ methodology. Discussions with authorities helped ensure results are consistent with existing evidence and knowledge. This includes discussions with the General Directorate for Internal Taxation, the Ministry of Finance, and the Electricity Distribution Holding Corporation (CDEEE), the Social Cabinet and the ADESS, the Ministry of Education, the Ministry of Health, and SENASA. Finally, estimations have gone through two thorough review rounds by Tulane University, to verify results, correct for mistakes, and ensure both consistency with CEQ methodology and comparability to similar analyses.

2 Main Results

As a departure point for the fiscal incidence analysis, population and income shares in total Market Income by socioeconomic group are presented. As illustrated in table 14-1, 5.7 percent of the total population lives below US$1.25 PPP a day and has a share of only 0.5 percent of total Market Income. Around 19.5 percent of the population in 2013 lived below US$ 2.50 PPP at 2005 prices. The poor represent about 37 percent of the population, whereas 40 percent of the population remains vulnerable according to Ferreira et al. (2013).

TABLE 14-1
Benchmark Scenario: Population and Income Shares of Market Income

Group	% Population	% Income
Ultra-poor (y < 1.25)	5.7	0.5
Extreme poor (1.25 ⇐ y < 2.50)	13.8	3.1
Moderate poor (2.50 ⇐ y < 4.00)	17.4	6.6
Vulnerable poor (4.00 ⇐ y < 10.00)	40.0	29.6
Middle class (10.00 ⇐ y < 50.00)	21.6	46.6
Upper class (50.00 ⇐ y)	1.4	13.6
Total population	100.0	100.0

Source: Authors' estimates based on ONE (2007).

Note: Income definition is US$ PPP at 2005 prices.

2.1 The Redistributional Impact of Taxes

The Dominican Republic imposes a variety of taxes that affect Final Income under the CEQ analysis. As previously mentioned, the country depended on indirect taxes for 63 percent of total tax revenues (8.8 percent of GDP) in 2013.[29] The most important sources were the ITBIS (4.4 percent of GDP), a VAT on the transfer of industrialized goods and services, and the excise tax on oil derivatives (1.7 percent of GDP). Excise taxes on alcoholic beverages, beer, and tobacco added up to 0.9 percent of GDP. Direct taxes amounted to only 5.2 percent of GDP. Corporate income taxes (2.4 percent of GDP) were the principal direct tax. Taxes on wages and personal income represented 1.3 percent of GDP, and other direct taxes, including property taxes and lottery taxes, accounted for 1.5 percent of GDP.

According to the results of the CEQ analysis, and using the Lorenz curves estimates, both direct and indirect taxes appear to be progressive.[30] As shown in figure 14-2, the concentration curves for direct and indirect taxes lie below the Lorenz curve for Market Income. As expected, direct taxes are much more progressive than indirect taxes.

Direct taxes have a significant average incidence on the Market Income of individuals in only the middle and upper classes, although it is perhaps smaller than what might be expected (2.1.1).[31] Direct taxes reduce the Market Income of the upper class (per capita income above US$50 PPP a day) by 4.1 percent.

---

[29] This figure includes taxes on imported goods, which are not included in the incidence analysis on poverty and income distribution.

[30] A tax is everywhere progressive (regressive) if its concentration curve lies everywhere below (above) the Market Income Lorenz curve.

[31] For benchmark and sensitivity analysis 2, the results are the same and for sensitivity analysis 1 are very similar. For this reason, we include only the benchmark results.

FIGURE 14-2

Progressivity of Direct and Indirect Taxes: Concentration and Lorenz Curves for Market Income

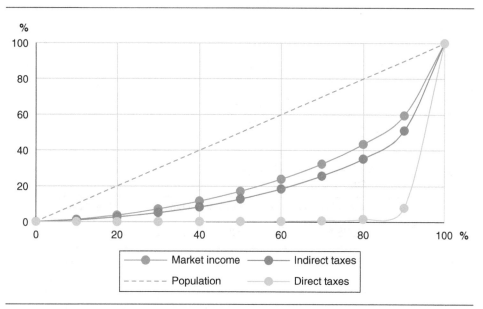

Source: Authors' estimates based on ENIGH (2007).

TABLE 14-2

Benchmark Scenario: Incidence of Direct and Indirect Taxes by Socioeconomic Group (% of market income)

Group	Direct taxes	Indirect taxes
Ultra-poor (y < 1.25)	0.0	4.7
Extreme poor (1.25 ⇐ y < 2.50)	0.0	5.4
Moderate poor (2.50 ⇐ y < 4.00)	0.0	5.4
Vulnerable poor (4.00 ⇐ y < 10.00)	0.0	6.3
Middle class (10.00 ⇐ y < 50.00)	1.6	7.8
Upper class (50.00 ⇐ y)	4.1	10.4
Total population	1.3	7.5

Source: Authors' estimates based on ENIGH (2007).

Note: Income definition is US$ PPP at 2005 prices.

Indirect taxes reduce the Market Income of the total population, but the incidence is progressive in absolute terms. The Market Income of the ultra-poor is reduced 4.7 percent, while the upper classes' income is reduced by 10.4 percent. This is explained by the higher levels of consumption by the upper class, especially on goods that are outside the basic consumption basket (currently exempt) (table 14-2).

FIGURE 14-3

Progressivity of Direct Taxes: Concentration and Lorenz Curves for Market Income

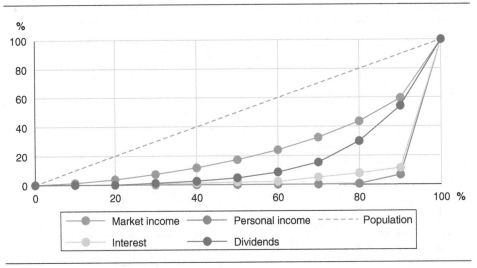

Source: Authors' estimates based on ENIGH (2007).

2.1.1 Direct Taxes

Direct taxes (that is, taxes on wages and personal income, interest income, and dividends) are found to be progressive (figure 14-3). They represent 1.3 percent of total Market Income. Concentration shares show that the top decile of the population pays 92 percent of direct taxes, while it receives 40.5 percent of total Market Income. Direct taxes decrease Market Income 3 percent for the top decile; they decrease the Market Income of the seventh decile by only 0.1 percent. In terms of socioeconomic groups, middle-class households (per capita income between US$10 and US$50 a day) pay 56.3 percent of direct taxes, and the richest (above US$50 a day per capita income) pay 42.5 percent. It is important to take into account the fact that the middle class accounts for 21.6 percent of total population and 46.6 percent of Market Income. Meanwhile, the richest group represents 1.4 percent of population and 13.6 percent of Market Income. This means that the relative tax burden is much higher for the rich.

Personal income taxes—which account for 90.6 percent of the direct taxes in the analysis—are highly progressive in the Dominican Republic. These taxes reduce the Market Income of the top decile by 2.75 percent and the ninth decile by 0.46 percent. In terms of socioeconomic groups, personal income taxes reduce the average Market Income of the middle class by 1.5 percent and the richest segment of the population by 3.6 percent. The middle class represent 58.3 percent of total personal income tax payments, and the highest income group represents 41.6 percent (figure 14-4). It is worth noting that the mean dividend tax in the upper class is higher than that on the middle class, but since the latter group has more individuals, the share of tax paid by the middle

FIGURE 14-4
Direct Taxes, Concentration Shares per Socioeconomic Group

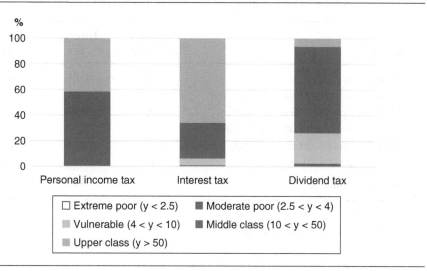

Source: Authors' estimates based on ENIGH (2007).

y = Income, in US$ PPP at 2005 prices.

class over total collections is larger. In addition, there could be some under-reporting of income dividends in the household survey by high-income individuals.

The tax on interest income affects the middle and upper socioeconomic groups. Established by the November 2012 tax reform, this tax represents 7.8 percent of total direct tax revenues. It reduces the Market Income of the population by 0.09 percent. The top decile's income is reduced by 0.2 percent due to the 10 percent tax on interest earnings. The middle class pays 27.6 percent of the total interest tax and the upper class 65.9 percent. In terms of socioeconomic groups, the data show that some people within the vulnerable population are paying tax on interest, resulting in a 0.02 percent reduction of their Market Income.

Dividend-tax payments reduce the average Dominican's Market Income by 0.03 percent. The top three deciles account for 84.8 percent of total dividend tax payments. In terms of socioeconomic groups, the middle class pays 67.3 percent of dividend taxes, a much higher proportion than the rich pay (6.3 percent). Those taxes reduce the Market Income of the middle class by 0.04 percent, while the toll on the rich was only 0.01 percent (table 14-3).

Figure 14-5 suggests that direct taxes could be more progressive in the Dominican Republic than in other countries. Of the selected cases, Jordan and Peru have similar or higher progressivity. Low-income households in other countries, such as Armenia, Brazil, and Uruguay, pay much higher percentages of their Market Income as direct taxes. At the same time, the Dominican Republic's high exemption threshold results in the lowest share of direct taxes to GDP among surveyed countries. A decrease in

TABLE 14-3

Benchmark Scenario: Incidence of Personal Income, Interest, and Dividend Taxes by Socioeconomic Group (% of market income)

Group	Personal income tax	Interest tax	Dividend tax
Ultra-poor (y < 1.25)	0.00	0.00	0.00
Extreme poor (1.25 ⇐ y < 2.50)	0.00	0.01	0.00
Moderate poor (2.50 ⇐ y < 4.00)	0.00	0.01	0.01
Vulnerable poor (4.00 ⇐ y < 10.00)	0.01	0.02	0.02
Middle class (10.00 ⇐ y < 50.00)	1.49	0.06	0.04
Upper class (50.00 ⇐ y)	3.65	0.45	0.01
Total population	1.19	0.09	0.03

Source: Authors' estimates based on ENIGH (2007).

Note: Income definition is US$ PPP at 2005 prices.

FIGURE 14-5

Direct Taxes, Concentration Shares per Decile: Country Comparison

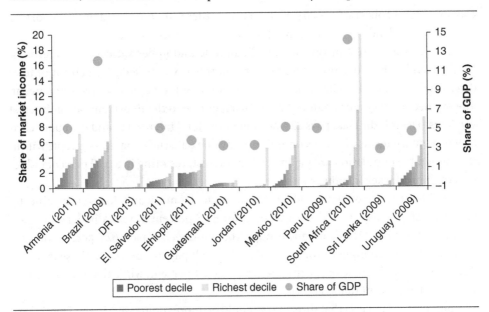

Source: Authors' estimates for the Dominican Republic, and based on CEQ Standard Indicators (www.commitmentoequity .org): Armenia (Younger and Khachatryan, 2017); Brazil (Higgins and Pereira, 2014); Ethiopia (Hill and others, 2017); Guatemala (Cabrera, Lustig, and Moran, 2015); Jordan (Alam, Inchauste, and Serajuddin, 2017); Mexico (Scott, 2014), Peru (Jaramillo, 2014); South Africa (Inchauste and others, 2017); Sri Lanka (Arunatilake, Inchauste, and Lustig, 2017); Uruguay (Bucheli and others, 2014).

informality, which currently accounts for 56 percent of labor activity, could also have a positive effect on personal income tax revenues. Nonetheless, the high amounts of foregone revenue can probably be explained by evasion among the richest. All these cross-country comparisons are based on the same estimation methodology;[32] nonetheless, since the taxes, rates, and exemptions may differ across countries, results should be interpreted with caution.

2.1.2 Indirect Taxes

The analysis includes the ITBIS and several excise taxes paid by Dominican Republic residents. The indirect taxes are subtracted from Disposable Income (that is, Net Market Income plus direct government transfers) to calculate postfiscal incomes (once indirect subsidies are also added). The indirect taxes considered in the analysis are the ITBIS; excise taxes on alcoholic beverages, beer, and cigarettes; excise taxes on oil products, telecommunications, and insurance services; and excise taxes on several imported goods.

Rates vary on the Dominican Republic's indirect taxes. The ITBIS is a VAT, which had two tax rates in 2013. The general tax rate was 18 percent and the reduced tax rate, levied on a group of primary goods, was 8 percent.[33] The excise taxes on consumption are a single-stage sales tax. The excise taxes on alcoholic beverages, beer, and cigarettes include specific taxes and ad valorem taxes.[34] Telecommunications services are taxed at 10 percent, and insurance services at 16 percent.

In terms of concentration, the share of indirect tax payments of the first eight deciles (35.3 percent) is below their share of Market Income (43.5 percent). By socioeconomic groups, the concentration share of those living on less than US$4 a day is lower for indirect taxes (7.3 percent) than for Market Income (10.2 percent). The middle class (per capita income between US$10 and US$50 a day)[35] has a higher share in indirect taxes (48.9 percent) than Market Income (46.6 percent).

Indirect taxes have reduced the Market Income across all deciles; at the same time, their incidence is higher on the richer deciles, which makes these taxes progressive. Indirect taxes reduce the Market Income of the poorest decile by 5.1 percent, compared to 9.0 percent in the top decile. In terms of the socioeconomic groups, indirect taxes reduce middle-class Market Income (per capita income between US$10 and US$50 a day) by 7.8 percent.

---

[32] Lustig (2013).

[33] Law No. 253-12 of November 2012 states that the reduced tax rates would be increasing annually until 16 percent in 2016. It was also stated that the general tax rates would be reduced to 16 percent if the tax income achieves 16 percent of GDP in 2015.

[34] See Title IV of the Law No. 11-92 Tax Code of the Dominican Republic. Ad valorem taxes are 10 percent on alcoholic beverages and beer and 20 percent on cigarettes. In this analysis, only ad valorem excise taxes are included because there is not enough information to map fixed excise taxes onto consumption of alcoholic beverages and cigarettes.

[35] For a definition of middle class specific to the Dominican Republic, see Guzman (2011).

FIGURE 14-6

Progressivity of Indirect Taxes: Concentration and Lorenz Curves for Market Income

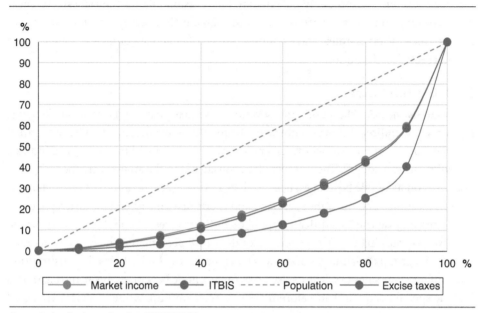

Source: Authors' estimates based on ENIGH (2007).

In terms of tax revenue, the ITBIS is the most important indirect tax, representing 58.6 percent of total indirect taxes included in this study. ITBIS is just slightly progressive, as depicted in figure 14-6, where the concentration curves and Lorenz curve for Market Income are almost on top of each other. The top decile income population accounts for 41.2 percent of total ITBIS paid, just above its share of Market Income (40.5 percent). Average Market Income is reduced 4.4 percent by ITBIS incidence (table 14-4). Among population segments, the ultra-poor suffer a 3.5 percent reduction of Market Income and the extreme poor a 4.0 percent reduction. The tax reduces Market Incomes by 4.5 percent for both the middle and upper classes.

Excise taxes account for 41.4 percent of the indirect taxes included in this chapter. These taxes are more progressive than ITBIS. Almost 60 percent of excise taxes are paid by the top decile of the population. In terms of socioeconomic groups, the middle class receives 46.6 percent of total Market Income and pays 51.1 percent of excise taxes (figure 14-7). The 1.4 percent richest population (per capita income above US$50 PPP a day) accounts for 14.6 percent of total Market Income and pays 26 percent of excise taxes. Excise taxes reduce the Market Income received by the upper class by 5.9 percent, which is significantly higher than the reduction for the ultra-poor (1.2 percent).

As a percentage of GDP, indirect taxes provide the Dominican Republic with a relatively high level of revenue. Such indirect-tax revenues are higher in the Dominican

TABLE 14-4

Benchmark Scenario: Incidence of ITBIS and Excises Taxes by Socioeconomic Group (% of market income)

Group	ITBIS	Excises
Ultra-poor (< 1.25 PPP)	3.50	1.19
Extreme poor (1.25–2.5 PPP)	3.95	1.48
Moderate poor (2.5–4 PPP)	4.06	1.36
Vulnerable (4–10 PPP)	4.38	1.92
Middle class (10–50 PPP)	4.45	3.39
Upper class (> 50 PPP)	4.47	5.91
Total population	4.38	3.09

Source: Authors' estimates based on ENIGH (2007).

Note: Income definition is US$ PPP at 2005 prices.

FIGURE 14-7

Indirect Taxes, Concentration Shares per Socioeconomic Group

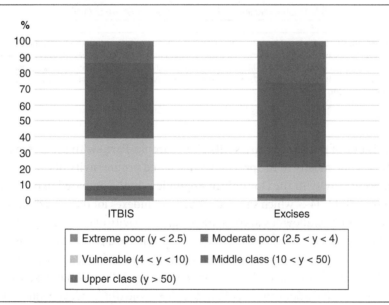

Source: Authors' estimates based on ENIGH (2007).

Note: Socioeconomic income groups are defined in US$ PPP at 2005 prices.

Republic than in select countries that include Mexico, Indonesia, Guatemala, Sri Lanka, Peru, and Ethiopia (figure 14-8). At the same time, the Dominican Republic's VAT tax rate is also high (18 percent) by international standards.[36] In addition, the Dominican

---

[36] The average nominal VAT rate in Latin America is around 15.6 percent.

FIGURE 14-8

Indirect Taxes, Concentration Shares per Decile

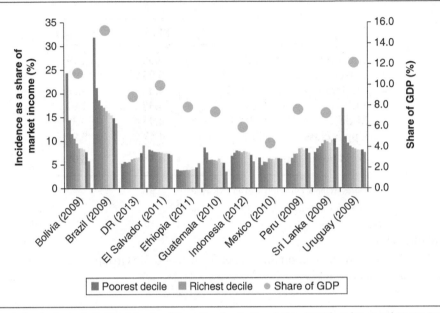

Source: Authors' estimates for the Dominican Republic; and based on Lustig and others (2013) for Bolivia, Brazil, Mexico, Peru, and Uruguay; and CEQ Standard Indicators (www.commitmentoequity.org): El Salvador (Beneke de Sanfeliu, Lustig, and Oliva Cepeda, 2022) (chapter 15 in this Volume); Ethiopia (Hill and others, 2017); Guatemala (Cabrera, Lustig, and Moran, 2015); Indonesia (Jellema, Wai-Poi, and Afkar, 2017); Mexico (Scott, 2014); Peru (Jaramillo, 2014); and Sri Lanka (Arunatilake, Inchauste, and Lustig, 2017).

Republic is one of the few countries (like, for example, Peru) with progressive indirect taxes. This is due mostly to the previously discussed progressivity of excise taxes.

Tax progressivity in the Dominican Republic is high compared to other developing countries. Table 14-5, which shows the Kakwani indexes for direct and indirect taxes in selected countries, allows us to compare the progressivity of taxes. This index is equal to the difference between the concentration coefficients of a particular tax and the Gini coefficient of the reference income. When the Kakwani index is above zero, the tax is progressive. If it is below zero, the tax is regressive. And if it is equal to zero, the tax is neutral. The Reynolds-Smolensky (RS) index shows the difference in value of Gini coefficient after direct or indirect Taxes. Among the selected countries, the Dominican Republic has one of most progressive direct taxes, with a Kakwani index of 0.42. Only Jordan, Sri Lanka, and Peru have more progressive direct-tax systems. In the Dominican Republic, indirect taxes are slightly progressive, with a Kakwani index of 0.05. International practice dictates that a Kakwani index between −0.1 and 0.1 could be considered neutral; however, looking at this group of countries, we conclude that the Dominican Republic has the second most progressive indirect tax system, just behind Ethiopia.

TABLE 14-5

Progressivity Indices for Direct and Indirect Taxes: Country Comparisons

	Kakwani index for direct taxes	Direct taxes as share of GDP	RS index	Kakwani index for indirect taxes	Indirect taxes as share of GDP	RS index
	(1)	(2)	(3) = (1) * (2) * 100	(1)	(2)	(3) = (1) * (2) * 100
Armenia (2011)	0.23	5.2%	1.19	−0.04	12%	−0.48
Bolivia (2009)	n.c.	n.c.	n.c.	−0.13	11%	−1.46
Brazil (2009)	0.27	4.2%	1.13	−0.03	14%	−0.46
Costa Rica (2010)	n.a.	n.a.	0.00	n.a.	n.a.	0.00
Dominican Republic (2013)	0.42	1.3%	0.54	0.05	7%	0.37
El Salvador (2011)	n.a.	n.a.	0.00	n.a.	n.a.	0.00
Ethiopia (2011)	0.28	3.9%	1.11	0.06	8%	0.50
Indonesia (2012)	. . .	. . .	. . .	−0.05	4%	−0.22
Jordan (2010)	0.63	3.3%	2.09	−0.06	11%	−0.60
Mexico (2010)	0.30	3.9%	1.14	0.01	4%	0.05
Peru (2009)	0.43	1.5%	0.65	0.02	7%	0.14
South Africa (2010)	0.13	14.3%	1.79	−0.08	10%	−0.86
Sri Lanka (2009)	0.53	2.9%	1.52	0.00	7%	0.02
Uruguay (2009)	0.25	4.7%	1.18	−0.05	7%	−0.37

Sources: Authors' estimates for the Dominican Republic and based on: for Armenia (Younger and Khachatryan, 2017); Bolivia (Paz Arauco and others, 2014); Brazil (Higgins and Pereira, 2014); Costa Rica (Sauma and Trejos, 2014); El Salvador (Beneke de Sanfeliu, Lustig, and Oliva Cepeda, 2022) (chapter 15 in this Volume); Ethiopia (Hill and others, 2017); Indonesia (Jellema, Wai-Poi, and Afkar, 2017); Jordan (Alam, Inchauste, and Serajuddin, 2017); Mexico (Scott, 2014); Peru (Jaramillo, 2014); South Africa (Inchauste and others, 2017); Sri Lanka (Arunatilake, Inchauste, and Lustig, 2017); Uruguay (Bucheli and others, 2014).

. . . = Not applicable; n.a. = Not available.
0. Value is zero.
n.c. Value was not calculated.

2.2 Social Spending in the Dominican Republic

This section assesses the incidence of direct transfers. These include the conditional cash transfer (CCT) food program Comer es Primero, CCT programs related to education, targeted transfers for LPG and electricity consumption, transfers to policemen and marines, indirect subsidies (mainly on electricity), and health and education services. The aim is to gain a better understanding of the extent to which Dominican social spending is progressive, using other countries as a benchmark for comparison.

2.2.1 Direct Transfers

Total concentration shares from the fiscal incidence analysis show that some of the Dominican Republic's direct transfers do better than others in reaching the poor. Around

FIGURE 14-9

Distribution of Direct Transfer Spending by Level: Concentration Curves (left) and Distribution by Socioeconomic Group (right)

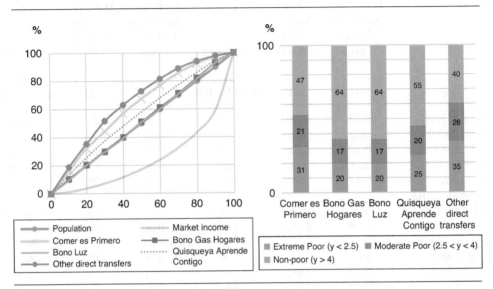

Source: Authors' elaboration using the CEQ methodology.

Note: Socioeconomic income groups are defined in US$ PPP at 2005 prices.

52 percent of the public expenditures under Comer es Primero reaches poor households (per capita income below US$4 a day), 38 percent goes to the vulnerable (between US$4 and US$10 a day), and less than 10 percent benefits middle-class households (above US$10 a day per capita). For Bonogas Hogar and Bono Luz,[37] more than 60 percent of total spending goes to the non-poor (earning more than US$4 a day); as previously explained, this relates to the fact that, unlike the case with CCTs, a group of the non-poor according to the SIUBEN life-quality index can be beneficiaries of these programs. This makes Bonogas Hogar and Bono Luz the only programs progressive in relative terms (figure 14-9, left panel). In contrast, Comer es Primero and the aggregate of other direct transfers are progressive in both relative and absolute terms, since, apart from representing a larger share of Market Income for poor households than for non-poor households, total transferred amounts in aggregate terms are also larger for the former group. The CCT incentivizing school attendance, Incentivo a la Asistencia Escolar (ILAE), is the most progressive direct transfer program in the Dominican Republic.

In terms of incidence, Comer es Primero is the program with the largest impact. These direct transfers represent 5.5 percent of Market Income among the ultra-poor (less than US$1.25 a day) and 2.1 percent for the extremely poor (below US$2.50 a day) (table 14-6). This has to do with the amount of the transfer, which is significantly larger

---

[37] Bono Luz is a grant to help poor families pay their electricity bill.

TABLE 14-6

Incidence of Direct Transfer Programs on Socioeconomic Class Income (percentages)

Group	Comer es Primero	Bono Luz	Quisqueya Aprende Contigo	Bono Gas Hogares	Other direct transfers
Ultra-poor (<1.25 PPP)	5.55	1.14	1.15	1.18	5.92
Extreme poor (1.25–2.5 PPP)	2.15	0.51	0.57	0.52	2.29
Moderate poor (2.5–4 PPP)	1.00	0.28	0.31	0.27	1.15
Vulnerable (4–10 PPP)	0.39	0.16	0.17	0.11	0.32
Middle class (10–50 PPP)	0.06	0.05	0.05	0.03	0.04
Upper class (>50 PPP)	0.00	0.00	0.01	0.00	0.00
Total population	0.31	0.11	0.12	0.09	0.29

Source: Authors' estimates based on ENIGH (2007).

Note: Income definition is US$ PPP at 2005 prices.

for Comer es Primero than for ILAE; the latter is included in the "other direct transfers" category. The incidence of Bonogas Hogar, Bono Luz, and Quisqueya Aprende Contigo[38] is more limited due to the relatively modest amount transferred and the fact that some of the funds go to the non-poor population.

Although the Dominican Republic's direct transfers are progressive, international comparisons suggest more could be done to help the poor. The Dominican Republic exhibits declining concentration shares for direct transfers by deciles, indicating that public spending in this category was progressive in relative terms in 2013 (unlike in Bolivia or Brazil in 2009). Nonetheless, as shown in figure 14-10, the decline in shares from the poorest to the richest decile is less steep than in the rest of the countries.[39] This suggests that there would be room for a more pronounced income redistribution strategy using direct transfers.

The Dominican Republic is less able to reduce inequality through direct transfer programs than most of these other countries (figure 14-10). The incidence of direct transfers as a share of Market Income for individuals in the first decile (11 percent) is similar in the Dominican Republic and Peru, although the Andean country invests only a third of the Dominican Republic's budget. Incidence is much smaller in the Dominican Republic than in Argentina (247 percent), Brazil (107.3 percent), Uruguay (61.9 percent), Bolivia (33.2 percent), and Mexico (31.4 percent). The main explanation is that half of the Dominican Republic's spending on direct transfers benefits the non-poor.

---

[38] Quisqueya Aprende Contigo is a national literacy plan assumed by the Dominican government since 2012.

[39] These cross-country comparisons are based on the same estimation methodology (Lustig, 2013); nonetheless, results need to be interpreted with caution because taxes, rates, and exemptions may differ across countries.

FIGURE 14-10

Concentration Shares of Direct Transfers, by Deciles: Country Comparison

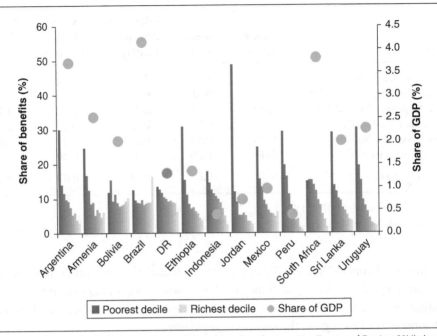

Source: Authors' estimates for the Dominican Republic and based on: for Argentina (Lustig and Pessino, 2014); Armenia (Younger and Khachatryan, 2017); Bolivia (Paz Arauco and others, 2014); Brazil (Higgins and Pereira, 2014); Ethiopia (Hill and others, 2017); Indonesia (Jellema, Wai-Poi, and Afkar, 2017); Jordan (Alam, Inchauste, and Serajuddin, 2017); Mexico (Scott, 2014); Peru (Jaramillo, 2014); Sri Lanka (Arunatilake, Inchauste, and Lustig, 2017); Uruguay (Bucheli and others, 2014).

Overall, the amounts granted under CCTs and other targeted and untargeted programs in the Dominican Republic are relatively modest. On one hand, a small grant may prevent the search for work from being discouraged. On the other hand, small CCT amounts may be insufficient to mitigate a sharp economic shock. In a microsimulation exercise, Valderrama et al. (2013) assessed ex ante the planned increase in monthly Solidaridad CCT grants from RD$700 to RD$830 (around US$3 more). According to the results, this would have resulted in a decrease of 0.22 percent in moderate poverty and 0.65 percent in extreme poverty.

In sum, cash transfers in the Dominican Republic are generally well targeted and benefit the poor and vulnerable more than proportionately. Most direct transfer programs are built on three transparent mechanisms or institutions: the debit card, the SIUBEN census of beneficiaries, and ADESS as independent administrator for transferring funds. Comer es Primero and Incentivo a la Asistencia Escolar[40] are highly pro-

---

[40] Incentivo a la Asistencia Escolar (ILAE) grants a monthly financial aid during the period of classes to each beneficiary family for each child up to a maximum of four, between the ages of six and sixteen, enrolled at a public school.

gressive programs. On the other hand, 60 percent of public spending on Bono Luz and Bonogas Hogar goes to the non-poor (vulnerable and middle class), making them barely progressive. Compared to other countries, the impact of direct transfers on poverty and equity is modest due to the fact that, while coverage has noticeably expanded over the past eight years, the amount of individual transfers is relatively small, and part of public spending is directed to the non-poor.

2.2.2 Indirect Subsidies

In addition to targeted direct transfer mechanisms, generalized subsidies remain in place—for electricity. As previously mentioned, both subsidies have in common a structure of explicit (tariffs below costs) and implicit (irregular connections, fraud, nonpayment) components. Given this partly informal nature, few studies have analyzed the distributional impact of utility subsidies in the Dominican Republic. In what is probably the most comprehensive of them, Actis (2012) estimated that 83 percent of electricity subsidies were directed to non-poor households. Following a similar approach, we have prepared an analysis consistent with the CEQ methodology (see box 14-1).

Results confirm that around 81 percent of total spending on electricity in 2013 benefited non-poor individuals. As in many countries, indirect subsidies were progressive only in relative terms (improving the distribution relative to Market Income) and were regressive in absolute terms (remaining below the 45 degree line in figure 14-11, left

FIGURE 14-11

Distribution of Indirect Subsidies Spending: Concentration Curves (left) and Incidence on Market Income by Level (right)

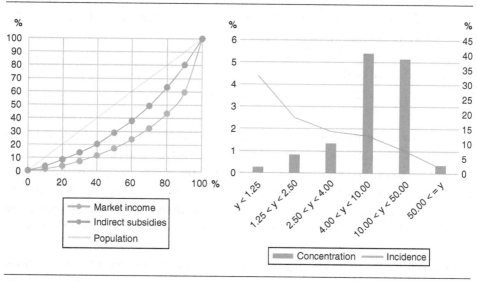

Source: Authors' estimates based on ENIGH (2007).

Note: Socioeconomic income groups are defined in US$ PPP at 2005 prices.

Box 14-1

Electricity Subsidy Estimation

The Dominican Republic has a fixed electricity fee for households that have not been yet provided with a meter and an electricity tariff for metered households. The official reference table of the Dominican Superintendence for Electricity established different tariffs by energy consumption intervals, and it is used to determine consumption.

The ENIGH 2007 survey distinguishes between these two groups of households. However, it does not provide information on the consumption of those declaring they are subject to the variable tariff. For this analysis, the following method was developed to estimate energy consumption: (1) depart from the official reference table of the Dominican Superintendence for Electricity containing consumption intervals and tariffs to be applied; (2) take the value of the electricity invoice of the household (data in ENIGH 2007); (3) apply a multi-tier algorithm that divides the value of the invoice paid by the household by the tariff in each of the different consumption intervals (the tariff varies as kwh consumption increases); (4) make calculations for both the fixed and variable tariffs set by the Superintendence for Electricity.

Given that not all households report paying for electricity, energy consumption was applied to households that have not paid for service. The average consumption of households paying for electricity was applied to these individuals, depending on their SIUBEN life conditions category.

Once consumption estimates were computed for all households, the electricity subsidy was estimated as the energy cost per kwh minus the average tariff according to the consumption interval. The assigned energy cost was RD$8.75 per kwh in 2013, or RD$6.16 per kwh in 2007 prices.

Finally, to monetize the subsidy at the household level, the subsidy per kwh was multiplied by the energy consumption of the household.

---

panel). Most spending on indirect subsidies is concentrated on the vulnerable and middle class. Nonetheless, indirect subsidies represent 4.4 percent of the Market Income of the ultra-poor and around 2.5 percent of the Market Income of the extreme poor (figure 14-11, right panel). So if these subsidies were eliminated, compensatory mechanisms to shield the poor from a deterioration in their purchasing power would be required. This could be done through well-targeted and formally established mechanisms, such as Bono Luz.

Indirect subsidies are also regressive in absolute terms in these other countries—except for Brazil, where concentration shares decline toward the richer deciles (figure 14-12, left panel). In Jordan, Mexico, and Sri Lanka, these subsidies help by

FIGURE 14-12

Concentration Shares (left) and Incidence of Indirect Subsidies (right)
in Comparable Countries

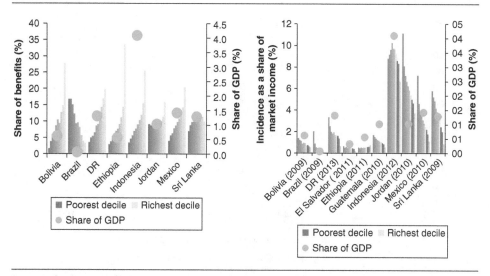

Source: Authors' estimates for the Dominican Republic and based on: for Bolivia (Paz Arauco and others, 2014); Brazil (Higgins and Pereira, 2014); El Salvador (Beneke de Sanfeliu, Lustig, and Oliva Cepeda, 2022) (chapter 15 in this Volume); Ethiopia (Hill and others, 2017); Guatemala (Cabrera, Moran, and Lustig, 2015); Indonesia (Jellema, Wai-Poi, and Afkar, 2017); Jordan (Alam, Inchauste, and Serajuddin, 2017); Mexico (Scott, 2014); and Sri Lanka (Arunatilake, Inchauste, and Lustig, 2017).

improving the income of the bottom deciles significantly more than the rest of the distribution (figure 14-12, right panel). In the Dominican Republic, with a similar level of spending to GDP, the incidence on the bottom deciles is more modest.[41]

2.2.3 In-Kind Transfers: Education and Health

While the effects of inequality of taxes, direct transfers, and subsidies have been small in the Dominican Republic, public expenditures on education and health seem to have greater contributions in terms of inequality reduction. This is because both categories of social spending are progressive in absolute terms—i.e., the per capita amount received declines as income increases. As a result, the accumulated shares of public expenditure in health and education are higher than their accumulated percentage of the total population (figure 14-13). In fact, the bottom 40 percent of the population receives around 52 percent of spending for education and 58 percent for health.

We estimate the incidence of education spending on inequality at its 2013 level and simulate an alternative scenario to try to assess a counterfactual with spending levels remaining at 2011 levels. By contrasting the impact of these two different levels of

---

[41] These cross-country comparisons are also based on the same estimation methodology (Lustig and Higgins, 2013); nonetheless, results need to be interpreted with caution because taxes, rates, and exemptions differ across countries.

FIGURE 14-13
Progressivity of Health and Education Spending: Concentration and Lorenz Curves
for Market Income

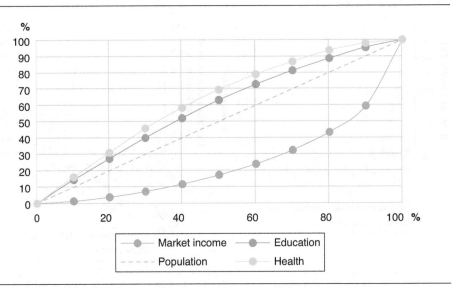

Source: Authors' estimates based on ENIGH (2007).

spending on poverty and inequality, we conclude that the size of social spending
matters. In the benchmark scenario, which includes the increased education expenditures (to 3.8 percent of GDP), Gini-coefficient inequality was reduced by 5.6 points.
This reduction compares favorably with a scenario in which public education expenditures stay at the 2011 level of 1.9 percent of GDP, reducing the Gini by only 4.5 points.
Using the same logic, the impact of health spending in reducing inequality is lower
because health spending levels are half those for education, even if health spending
is more progressive.

The monetized value of in-kind transfers is more significant for the lower income
strata. Education spending increases overall Market Income by 3.3 percent; however,
the effect of education is equivalent to more than 10 percent of income for the extremely
and moderately poor. In sensitivity analysis 2, the scenario of lower spending of education, it is important to note that benefits increased by a greater proportion for poor
households (table 14-7). The impact on Market Income is lower for health spending than
for education. Moreover, these expenditures do not significantly affect the middle class
and upper classes.

Progressivity benefits the poorest segments of population, but it could be an indicator of other social trends in education and health care. Those with higher incomes
might be opting for private education and participating in contributive health insurance schemes. For example, more than 90 percent of ultra-poor or extreme-poor

TABLE 14-7

Distribution of Health and Education Spending by Socioeconomic Group
(% of market income)

Group	Education 2011*	Education 2013	Health
Ultra-poor (<1.25 PPP)	25.2	50.9	28.4
Extreme poor (1.25–2.5 PPP)	9.9	19.9	12.0
Moderate poor (2.5–4 PPP)	5.5	11.1	6.4
Vulnerable (4–10 PPP)	2.1	4.2	2.2
Middle class (10–50 PPP)	0.5	0.9	0.3
Upper class (>50 PPP)	0.0	0.1	0.0
Total population	1.7	3.3	1.7

Source: Authors' estimates based on ENIGH (2007).

Note: Income definition is US$ PPP at 2005 prices.
* Sensitivity analysis 2

children in primary school (ages seven to twelve years) went to public schools. In contrast, around 33 percent of middle-class children went to public schools.[42]

Education

Total public education expenditures are progressive in absolute terms, according the CEQ analysis, but only preschool, primary, and lower-secondary levels achieve this standard of progressivity. For these levels, the bottom 40 percent of the population receives close to two-thirds of spending (figure 14-14, left panel). Upper secondary expenditure is progressive in relative terms and almost proportional to population, which means that the proportion received in relation to Market Income decreases with income. As in other countries, tertiary education is the least progressive, with more that 20 percent of public spending going to non-poor students.

Educational failure and opting-out reduce participation of the poor in higher levels of education. In lower levels such as preschool and primary almost 60 percent of total expenditures go to poor households. The share shrinks to 40 percent for secondary levels and less than 20 percent for tertiary levels (figure 14-14, right panel). This may be caused by quality concerns about public education, which leads those who can afford to opt out from the public system to instead choose private schools. As Sanchez-Martin and Senderowitsch (2012) explain, "The education sector in the DR presents faulty public service delivery, which originates a private offer that is more of a reactive upshot to deficiencies in state education than a high quality alternative (at least not in every case)."[43]

---

[42] See Sanchez-Martin and Senderowitsch (2012, pp. 10–20).

[43] Sanchez-Martin and Senderowitsch (2012, p. 13).

FIGURE 14-14

Distribution of Education Spending by Level: Concentration Curves (left) and
Distribution by Socioeconomic Group (right)

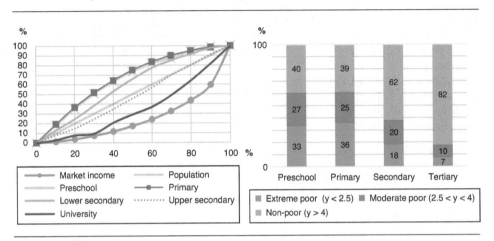

Source: Authors' estimates based on ENIGH (2007).

Note: Socioeconomic income groups are defined in US$ PPP at 2005 prices.

For the poor, the benefits of education are high for primary schooling but not at
other levels. Figure 14-15 shows that almost all children from extremely poor households
are enrolled in primary education. This declines to two-thirds in secondary education,
less than a quarter in preschool, and only 6 percent in university.[44] Second, public
primary-school enrollment declines as income increases, while it increases for secondary school and university. For the lower levels, this decline could be the result of opting-
out of public schools for quality concerns. Finally, preschool enrollment is low in public
schools. Around three-quarters of students go to public schools;[45] however, close to
90 percent of students in the first quintile go to public schools, compared to 34 percent
and 42 percent of fifth-quintile students in Basico and Medio, respectively.

At more than 30 percent, the monetized value of primary education is large compared to Market Income for the ultra-poor (figure 14-16, left panel). It is smaller for the
extreme poor and moderate poor but still important. However, it is almost negligible for
the vulnerable non-poor, middle, and upper classes for two reasons: they attend less
primary and lower-secondary public education, and the impact of public spending per
capita is low relative to their income level. Tertiary education has only a small impact on
income, and it is almost proportional or neutral in relation to income. Because pre-

---

[44] According to the Ministry of Education, which used a different classification, net enrollment
rates in 2012–13 were 44.0 percent for Inicial, 92.6 percent for Basico, and 54.1 percent for Medio.
[45] According to administrative records, this figure is 75 percent of Basica students and 77 percent
of Medio students in 2012–13. In our analysis, 74 percent of students of Basica and 70 percent of
Medio go to public schools.

Figure 14-15
Enrollment in Public Education by Level for School-Age Children

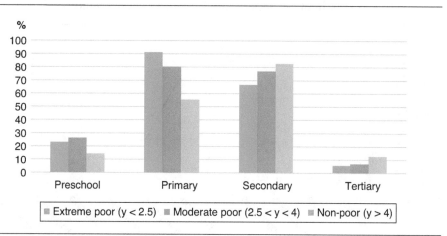

Source: Authors' estimates based on ENIGH (2007).

Note: Socioeconomic income groups are defined in US$ PPP at 2005 prices.

school has low coverage, it has a lower impact than secondary education, even though both are progressive (figure 14-16, right panel). In particular, upper-secondary incidence is significant for the vulnerable non-poor population, even more important than lower-secondary and pre-school.

The middle and upper classes make up around 23 percent of the population, and they hardly use the public education services, with the exception of higher and upper-secondary education. However, education reform has been implemented and not only increases school hours but also provides breakfast, lunch, and snacks. It also includes improvements in education infrastructure, postgraduate programs for teachers, innovative teaching practices, and curricular offerings in foreign languages and technology.[46] As a result, public education use probably will increase in non-poor households, especially among the vulnerable and middle class in the near future.

The Dominican Republic compares favorably with other countries in education spending's incidence on the income of the poorest deciles. For example, countries with similar levels of education spending, like Indonesia and Armenia, have smaller income impacts on the poorest decile (figure 14-17). In contrast, education expenditures have a higher incidence on the poorest deciles in Uruguay than in the Dominican Republic. Peru spends less on education, but it has almost the same spending incidence as the Dominican Republic.[47]

---

[46] OECD (2015).

[47] These cross-country comparisons are based on the same estimation methodology (Lustig and Higgins, 2013); nonetheless, the results need to be interpreted with caution because taxes, rates, and exemptions may differ across countries.

FIGURE 14-16

Incidence of Education Expenditures by Level for School-Age Children: Primary Level (left) and Preschool, Secondary, and University Levels (right)

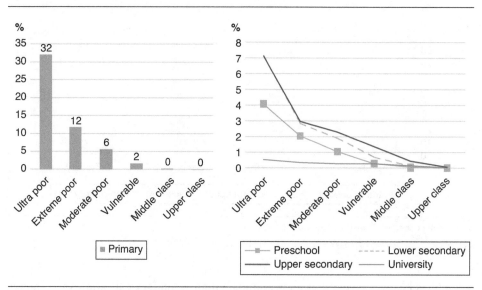

Source: Authors' estimates based on ENIGH (2007).

Note: Socioeconomic income groups are defined in US$ PPP at 2005 prices.

FIGURE 14-17

Incidence of Education Expenditure per Decile, Country Comparison

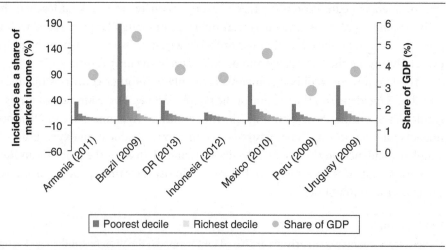

Source: Authors' estimates for the Dominican Republic and based on: for Armenia (Younger and Khachatryan, 2017); Brazil (Higgins and Pereira, 2014); Indonesia (Jellema, Wai-Poi, and Afkar, 2017); Mexico (Scott, 2014); Peru (Jaramillo, 2014); and Uruguay (Bucheli and others, 2014).

FIGURE 14-18

Distribution of Health Spending by Level: Concentration Curves (left) and
Distribution by Socioeconomic Group (right)

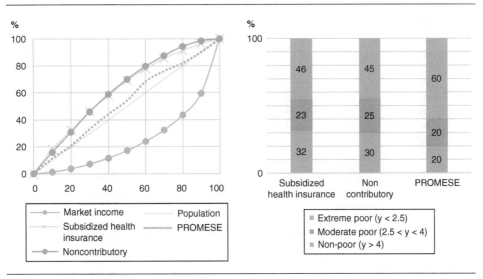

Source: Authors' estimates based on ENIGH (2007).

Note: Socioeconomic income groups are defined in US$ PPP at 2005 prices.

Health

Health expenditures are even more progressive than education, according to the
CEQ results. Due to the limited resources devoted to health, however, the redistributive effect is lower. All components of public health in the analysis are progressive in
absolute terms. Subsidized health insurance covers a large portion of the extreme poor,
and noncontributory programs (hospital and outpatient care) reach a big portion of
the moderate poor. In contrast, the Essential Medicines Program (PROMESE), which
includes spending to purchase medicines and medical supplies for public health institutions as well as the distribution of subsidized medicines, is just barely progressive
(figure 14-18, left panel).

Many people in the low-income strata are still not covered by subsidized or noncontributory health insurance, despite their progressivity. Figure 14-19 shows coverage is low in poor households. The finding is consistent with information from ENDESA
2013,[48] wherein the poorest two quintiles had coverage of less than 25 percent in the
subsidized regime and less than 21 percent in the noncontributory regime. In the lowest quintile, two-thirds of the population does not report having health insurance.
Hence, substantial challenges remain in terms of increasing health insurance coverage. Despite the progress already made, further increases could benefit poor households.

---

[48] CESDEM/ICF (2014).

FIGURE 14-19

Individuals Who Live in Beneficiary Households by Health Program and Socioeconomic Ranking

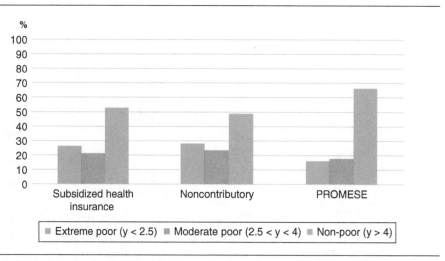

Source: Authors' estimates based on ENIGH (2007).

Note: Socioeconomic income groups are defined in US$ PPP at 2005 prices.

Valderrama and others (2013) analyze the impact of the projected increase in SENASA coverage to 4 million in 2016. Using the Encuesta Nacional de Fuerza de Trabajo (ENFT) household survey to simulate the impact on income, they conclude that this policy could reduce extreme poverty by 0.78–1.18 percent.

The incidence of noncontributory health is the most important because the amount of health insurance granted under the noncontributory health regime is six times larger than under the subsidized scheme. As designed, the subsidized regime benefits only the extreme poor and ultra-poor, not the non-poor and moderate poor (figure 14-20). Finally, PROMESE expenditures—related to cheaper medicines that can be acquired by poor and non-poor at the so-called Boticas Populares[49]—is small compared to Market Income. However, pharmaceutical products are very important, accounting for 2.6 percent of household budget (CPI basket).

In the Dominican Republic, spending policies vary greatly in their impact on the poor. To better understand the effects of the different lines of social spending on equity, figure 14-21 adds to the previously presented concentration curves by presenting concentration coefficients for each fiscal instrument.[50] Most social programs are progressive in absolute terms, with a coefficient below −0.1. This includes most components of

---

[49] The Essential Medicines Program (PROMESE) has a network of pharmacies (Boticas Populares) in which it sells drugs at subsidized prices.

[50] Concentration coefficients are calculated in the same manner as the Gini; when the concentration coefficient is above the diagonal, the difference between the triangle of perfect equality and

FIGURE 14-20
Incidence of Health Expenditures by Coverage Regime

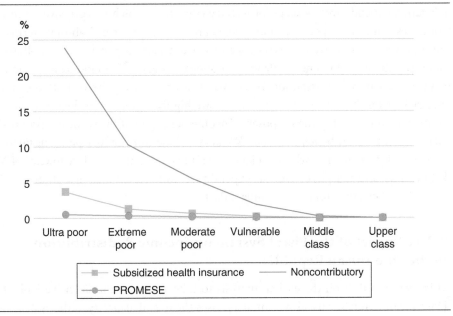

Source: Authors' estimates based on ENIGH (2007).

Note: Socioeconomic income groups are defined in US$ PPP at 2005 prices.

FIGURE 14-21
Concentration Coefficients with Respect to Market Income, by Fiscal Instrument

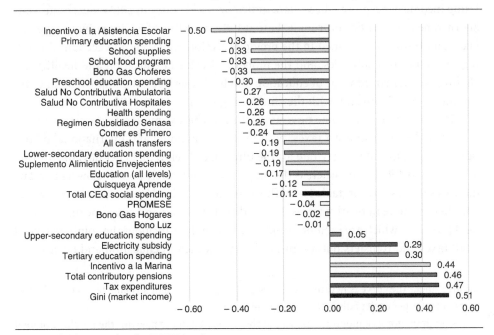

Source: Authors' estimates based in ENIGH (2007).

education expenditures—except for tertiary education, which is regressive, as in most countries. All health-spending components are also progressive in absolute terms. The most progressive cash transfer is the Incentivo a la Asistencia Escolar (−0.5), followed by Bonogas Chofer and Comer es Primero. Bonogas Hogar and Bono Luz are practically neutral in terms of redistribution; Incentivo a la Marina[51] is regressive. Both the indirect electricity subsidy and the tax expenditure are highly regressive in the sense that they contribute to increasing the Disposable Income per capita of the wealthier proportionately more than they benefit the poor. We also include contributory pensions (analyzed in Sensitivity Analysis 2), whose incidence is almost neutral (very close to Gini of Market Income), and analysis of VAT tax expenditure, which is detailed in section 4.1, Alternative VAT Scenarios for a Fiscal Impact Pact.

3 Net Impact of the Fiscal System on Income Redistribution in the Dominican Republic

This section builds on the earlier analysis to take a more comprehensive look at the Dominican Republic's fiscal system. It assesses the overall capacity of the system to redistribute income, as well as such related aspects as vertical and horizontal equity, efficiency, and coverage of public spending.

3.1 Fiscal Policy Instruments, Poverty, and Inequality

Dominican Republic fiscal policy contributes to reducing Market Income inequality. Using income per capita as the welfare indicator, fiscal policy in 2013 reduced the Market Income Gini coefficient from 0.514 to 0.458—a decline of 5 Gini points—when all taxes and transfers examined in the previous section are taken into account (including CCTs, indirect subsidies, and the monetized value of education and health). Excluding the monetized value of education and health services, the improvement in inequality is still significant, with the Gini falling from 0.514 to 0.492.

The incidence of extreme poverty declines, whereas moderate poverty remains slightly higher after indirect taxes, both under the national and international definitions. The headcount poverty rate for the ultra-poor (below $1.25 per day) drops from 5.7 percent to 4.9 percent, whereas the rate for the moderately poor (below $4 per day) increases to 37.6 percent (table 14-8). This is partly explained by the fact that the ultra-poor benefit more in relative terms from indirect subsidies and consume mainly basic food products, which are exempt from VAT. The analysis includes the combined effect of all taxes and transfers but not in-kind services such as education and health. It is

---

the area under the curve is negative, and spending is progressive in absolute terms (i.e., the size of the transfer per capita falls with per capita income).

[51] This program grants a monthly payment to those enlisted in the navy for the purchase of food in the establishments affiliated with the Social Supply Network (Red de Abastecimiento Social).

TABLE 14-8
Dominican Republic: Poverty and Inequality Indicators at Each Income Concept

	Market income (1)	Net market income (2)	Disposable income (3)	Postfiscal income (4)	Final income (5)
		(2) = (1) − Direct taxes	(3) = (2) + Cash transfers	(4) = (3) − Indirect taxes	5 = 4 + In-kind transfers
Inequality indicators					
Gini coefficient	0.514	0.509	0.502	0.492	0.458
Theil index	0.521	0.506	0.495	0.468	0.413
90/10	10.41	10.34	9.69	9.28	7.13
Headcount poverty indicators					
National extreme poverty line*	13.8%	13.8%	12.5%	13.1%	...
National moderate poverty line*	41.2%	41.2%	40.1%	42.3%	...
US$1.25 PPP per day	5.7%	5.7%	4.7%	4.9%	...
US$2.50 PPP per day	19.5%	19.5%	18.2%	19.5%	...
US$4.0 PPP per day	37.0%	37.0%	35.9%	37.6%	...

Source: Authors' estimates based in ENIGH (2007).

* Official poverty estimates based on ONE and MEPyD (2012). The lower bound poverty line was set at RD$1,397 per month in 2005–06 using March 2006 prices for rural areas and RD$1,458 for urban areas. The upper bound poverty line was set at RD$2,883 per month in 2005–06 using March 2006 prices for rural areas and RD$3,238 for urban areas.

. . . = Not applicable.

n.a. Data is not available.

0. Value is zero.

n.c. = Not calculated.

TABLE 14-9
Average per Capita Income in Each Market Income Decile, in Dominican Pesos per Year

Decile	Market income (1)	Net market income (2)	Disposable income (3)	Postfiscal income (4)
Poorest	9,456	9,456	10,454	10,251
2	17,977	17,972	18,924	18,361
3	25,507	25,503	26,339	25,429
4	32,515	32,512	33,282	32,066
5	40,341	40,334	41,033	39,387
6	49,635	49,628	50,251	47,934
7	62,468	62,447	63,047	60,021
8	80,991	80,941	81,466	77,422
9	117,220	116,510	116,953	109,930
Richest	296,428	287,676	287,939	263,070

Source: Authors' estimates based in ENIGH (2007).

also more common to see the incidence of poverty calculated with Disposable Income (before ITBIS); in this case, direct taxes and transfers reduce moderate poverty incidence by about 1 percentage point.

The analysis allows us to measure the impact of fiscal policy on postfiscal income. In monetary terms, people in the first decile see their per capita incomes increase from RD\$9,456 to RD\$10,251 a year (an 8.4 percent increase), still far from the average Market Income per capita of the second decile. Netting out the impact of indirect taxes would take postfiscal income to RD\$10,454 (table 14-9). Fiscal policy reduces incomes for 8 deciles because the burden of progressive direct and indirect taxes rises with income, and direct transfers are concentrated in lower deciles. It modestly raises incomes for only two deciles because of the limited amounts granted under direct transfers.

3.2 Is Fiscal Policy More or Less Redistributive and Pro-Poor than in Other Countries?

Compared to other countries, the Dominican Republic achieves a modest poverty reduction, although it performs better once education and healthcare are included. One of the advantages of applying the CEQ methodology is that it allows for international comparison (Lustig and Higgins, 2013). This helps us to understand how the Dominican Republic compares to other middle-income countries in terms of fiscal redistribution. Direct taxes, cash transfers, indirect taxes, and health and education spending all contribute to inequality reduction, a desirable result. Relative to its peers, fiscal policy in the Dominican Republic, when looking at Disposable Income, attains a modest reduction

FIGURE 14-22

Change in Inequality: Disposable and Final Income versus Market Income (in Gini points)

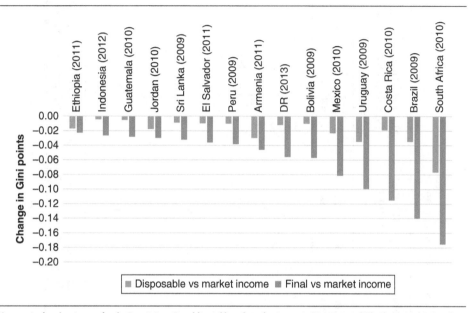

Source: Authors' estimates for the Dominican Republic and based on: for Armenia (Younger and Khachatryan, 2017); Bolivia (Paz Arauco and others, 2014); Brazil (Higgins and Pereira, 2014); Costa Rica (Sauma and Trejos, 2014); El Salvador (Beneke de Sanfeliu, Lustig, and Oliva Cepeda, 2022) (chapter 15 in this Volume); Ethiopia (Hill and others, 2017); Guatemala (Cabrera, Lustig, and Moran, 2015); Indonesia (Jellema, Wai-Poi, and Afkar, 2017); Jordan (Alam, Inchauste, and Serajuddin, 2017); Mexico (Scott, 2014); Peru (Jaramillo, 2014); South Africa (Inchauste and others, 2017); Sri Lanka (Arunatilake, Inchauste, and Lustig, 2017); Uruguay (Bucheli and others, 2014).

in inequality—a drop of 0.012 in the Gini. The results are similar to those in Bolivia, Peru, and Sri Lanka and only higher than Guatemala and Indonesia (figure 14-22). Once in-kind education and health spending are monetized, the Dominican Republic compares much more favorably in terms of inequality reduction (0.056) because public spending is much larger than the budgeted-for direct transfers, and the poor are more likely to use these public services. Brazil, Costa Rica, and South Africa, the countries with the most redistributive fiscal policies, achieve their inequality reductions through significantly higher levels of social spending than the Dominican Republic. In addition, South Africa has the most equitable fiscal policy in the sample.[52]

Poverty incidence, using the standard of $2.50 per day, does not significantly change when considering postfiscal income in the Dominican Republic (table 14-10). In other countries, even those where the incidence of direct taxes and cash transfers on poverty

---

[52] These cross-country comparisons are based on the same estimation methodology (Lustig, 2013); nonetheless, results need to be interpreted with caution because taxes, rates, and exemptions may differ across countries.

TABLE 14-10
Poverty Headcount Rate for the US$2.50 PPP a Day for Each Income Concept (in percentages)

	Market income (1)	Net market income (2) 2 = 1 − Direct taxes	Disposable income (3) 3 = 2 + Cash transfers	Postfiscal income (4) 4 = 3 − Indirect taxes	Net variation (postfiscal to market) = 4 − 1	Net variation (disposable to market) = 3 − 1
Armenia (2011)	31.3	32.0	28.9	34.9	3.6	−2.4
Bolivia (2009)	19.6	19.6	17.6	20.2	0.6	−2.0
Brazil (2009)	15.1	15.7	11.2	16.3	1.2	−3.9
Costa Rica (2010)	5.4	5.7	3.9	4.2	−1.2	−1.5
Dominican Republic (2013)	**19.5**	**19.5**	**18.2**	**19.5**	**0.0**	**−1.3**
El Salvador (2011)	14.7	15.1	12.9	14.4	−0.2	−1.8
Ethiopia (2011)	81.7	82.7	82.4	84.2	2.6	0.7
Guatemala (2010)	35.9	36.2	34.6	36.5	0.6	−1.3
Indonesia (2012)	56.4	56.4	55.9	54.8	−1.6	−0.5
Jordan (2010)	4.2	4.2	2.4	1.8	−2.4	−1.8
Mexico (2010)	12.6	12.6	10.7	10.7	−1.9	−1.9
Peru (2009)	15.2	15.2	14.0	14.5	−0.7	−1.1
South Africa (2010)	46.2	46.4	33.4	39.0	−7.2	−12.8

Source: Authors' estimates for the Dominican Republic and, based on CEQ Standard Indicators (www.commitmentoequity.org): for Armenia (Younger and Khachatryan, 2017); Bolivia (Paz Arauco and others, 2014); Brazil (Higgins and Pereira, 2014); Costa Rica (Sauma and Trejos, 2014); El Salvador (Beneke de Sanfeliu, Lustig, and Oliva Cepeda, 2022) (chapter 15 in this Volume); Ethiopia (Hill and others, 2017); Guatemala (Cabrera, Lustig, and Moran, 2015); Indonesia (Jellema, Wai-Poi, and Afkar, 2017); Jordan (Alam, Inchauste, and Serajuddin, 2017); Mexico (Scott, 2014); Peru (Jaramillo, 2014); and South Africa (Inchauste and others, 2017).

Notes: Year of the survey in parenthesis. Bolivia and Indonesia include indirect taxes only.

reduction is slightly below average, indirect taxes have a lower incidence on the income of the poor. For example, Brazil and Bolivia significantly reduce poverty incidence through cash transfers; however, when looking at postfiscal income (after indirect taxes), extreme poverty incidence has increased in those countries.

Fiscal policy reduces poverty in the Dominican Republic. Overall, when looking at postfiscal income in the Dominican Republic, we observe a decline in the share of population living on less than US$1.25 a day, while the percentages of extremely poor, moderately poor, and vulnerable increase. At the same time, we see a reduction in the size of the middle and upper classes (figure 14-23). Nonetheless, it is worth noting that poverty incidence figures do not give a sense of the total impact on the poor. When using the non-anonymous measure of fiscal impoverishment, 27 percent of the postfiscal poor were impoverished using the US$1.25 line (poor made poorer and non-poor made poor). However, these results do not consider the effects that the monetized value of in-kind education and health services have on household income (Final Income).

It is also important to consider the extent to which fiscal policy boosts the income of the poor. In the Dominican Republic, households in the poorest decile receive transfers and indirect subsidies that are worth 9.2 percent of their Market Income, which is relatively low compared to most countries (figure 14-24, left panel). This may be due to two causes: the lowest decile in terms of Market Income per capita is not as poor in the Dominican Republic as in other countries; and the amounts granted under CCT programs are probably smaller than in Brazil, South Africa, or Uruguay. Including monetized value of public spending in health and education, households in the poorest decile see an increase of 68 percent relative to Market Income, about half the average for the selected group of countries, excluding South Africa (figure 14-24, right panel).

Households' net cash position after taxes and transfers is positive for the bottom 30 percent of the population, which is similar to other middle-income countries. The fact that the line is flatter for the Dominican Republic than for similar countries reflects an overall lower income per capita redistribution across deciles. Once the monetized value of in-kind spending on education and health are included, only the top 30 percent are net contributors in fiscal terms in the Dominican Republic.

3.3 Income Redistribution: Vertical and Horizontal Equity and Effectiveness Indicators

A fiscal system can generate horizontal inequity by generating different impacts on the Disposable Income of similar households.[53] For example, imagine two poor individuals, A and B, who have similar consumption patterns. The Market Income is just 100 Dominican pesos higher for B than for A. Both households should be entitled to conditional cash transfers, but B does not receive these benefits due to limitations in coverage of the social programs. As a result, Disposable Income after intervention will be

---

[53] Duclos and Araar (2006).

FIGURE 14-23

Percentage of Population by Socioeconomic Class in the Dominican Republic

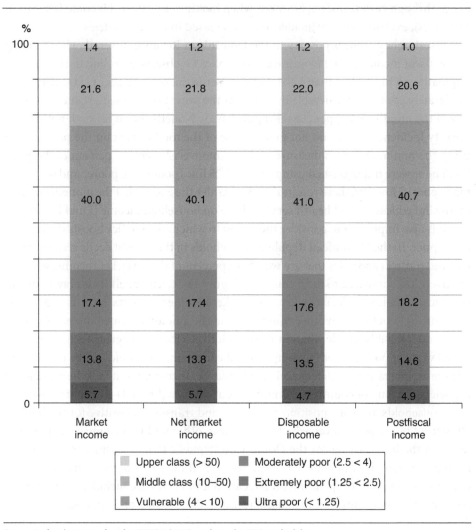

Source: Authors' estimates based in ENIGH (2007), applying the CEQ methodology.

Note: Socioeconomic income groups are defined in US$ PPP at 2005 prices.

lower for B than for A. In this hypothetical case, the fiscal system would be generating horizontal inequality.

Fiscal policy's overall redistributive effect is defined as the change in inequality associated with direct and indirect taxes as well as direct transfers and subsidies. This effect can be decomposed into vertical equity and reranking effects. The latter postulates that the prefiscal policy income ranking of individuals should be preserved. If not, there is a loss of horizontal equity. Results for five middle-income countries are presented in table 14-11. An extreme case of horizontal inequity induced by fiscal policy is

FIGURE 14-24

Postfiscal (left) and Final Income (right) as a Share of Market Income

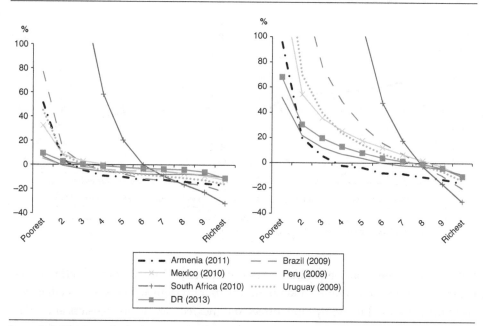

Source: Authors' estimates for the Dominican Republic and based on for Armenia (Younger and Khachatryan, 2017); Brazil (Higgins and Pereira, 2014); Mexico (Scott, 2014); Peru (Jaramillo, 2014); South Africa (Inchauste and others, 2017); and Uruguay (Bucheli and others, 2014).

TABLE 14-11

Taxes, Transfers, and Subsidies: Overall Redistributive Effect (decline in Gini points; shown as positive)

	South Africa (2010)	Bolivia (2009)	Brazil (2009)	DR (2013)	Indonesia (2012)
Gini (market income)	0.771	0.503	0.579	0.514	0.418
Gini (postfiscal income)	0.695	0.503	0.546	0.492	0.416
Redistributive effect[1]	0.077	0.000	0.033	0.023	0.002
Vertical equity (VE)[2]	0.083	0.003	0.048	0.025	0.007
Reranking effect (RR)[3]	0.006	0.003	0.014	0.001	0.005
RR/VE	0.075	1.000	0.300	0.026	0.706

Source: Authors' estimates for the Dominican Republic and based on: for Bolivia (Paz Arauco and others, 2014); Brazil (Higgins and Pereira, 2014); Indonesia (Jellema, Wai-Poi, and Afkar, 2017); and South Africa (Inchauste and others, 2017).

Notes: 1. Redistributive effect calculated as the difference between Market Income and postfiscal income Gini.
2. Reynolds-Smolensky index.
3. Atkinson-Plotnick index.

FIGURE 14-25

Fiscal Incidence Curves (left) and Fiscal Mobility Profiles (right), by Deciles

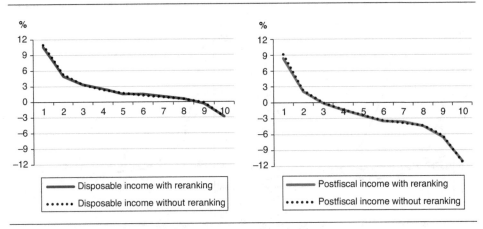

Source: Authors' estimates based in ENIGH (2007), applying the CEQ methodology.

Bolivia, where the reranking of individuals completely wipes out the reduction in vertical inequity. In the Dominican Republic, the fiscal system achieves intermediate levels of inequality reduction through direct and indirect taxes and transfers and subsidies, and it generates very little horizontal inequality. The country's reranking as a proportion of vertical inequality is by far the lowest among the five countries. As figure 14-25 shows, disposable and postfiscal income incidence curves in the Dominican Republic hardly vary when the reranking effect is considered. It is worth noting that geographical disparities in income distribution in the Dominican Republic are observed, although they remain beyond the scope of this analysis.

Effectiveness indicators[54] suggest the Dominican Republic has space to improve the effectiveness of direct transfers by focusing them on the extreme poor. According to table 14-12, the share of direct transfers that contribute to eliminating extreme poverty is low—8 percent for US$1.25 PPP, 29 percent for US$2.50 PPP, and 20.7 percent for extreme national poverty.[55] The effectiveness for moderate poverty is better because vertical efficiency and poverty-reduction efficiency increase with the level of the poverty line. Although direct transfers are not very good at reducing extreme poverty, the spillover index shows that there are few impacts on the non-poor. In moderate poverty, only 2 percent of direct transfers received by the poor raise their incomes above the poverty-line threshold. In contrast, direct transfers reduce a bigger share of the poverty gap in extreme poverty (19.2 percent for US$1.25 PPP, 10.9 percent for US$2.50 PPP, and 13.5 percent for extreme national poverty) than in moderate poverty (less than 6 percent).

---

[54] Beckerman (1979); Immervol and others (2009).

[55] The extreme poverty line under the official poverty measurement methodology (ONE and MEPyD, 2012) is US$2.07 PPP a day for urban households and US$2.00 PPP a day for rural ones.

TABLE 14-12
Beckerman and Immervoll Effectiveness Indicators

	$1.25 PPP per day	$2.50 PPP per day	$4.00 PPP per day	National extreme poverty level	National moderate poverty level
Vertical expenditure efficiency	0.088	0.289	0.503	0.207	0.549
Poverty reduction efficiency	0.059	0.243	0.469	0.162	0.515
Spillover index	0.128	0.049	0.026	0.063	0.020
Poverty gap efficiency	0.192	0.109	0.062	0.135	0.056

Source: Authors' estimates based in ENIGH (2007), applying the CEQ methodology.

Note: Socioeconomic income groups are defined in US$ PPP at 2005 prices.

3.4 Resource Needs to Fill In Coverage Gaps

The relatively high efficiency of Dominican public education and health expenditures in reducing inequality has to do with their high levels of progressiveness in terms of coverage. The Dominican Republic has a subsidized health regime targeted to the poor; it is estimated that 90 percent of the extreme poor and 83 percent of the moderately poor benefit from public health services. Compared with other countries, the Dominican middle and upper classes participate less in subsidized healthcare because they usually benefit from the contributory health regime or private health insurance. As a result, the percentage of beneficiaries declines markedly by socioeconomic strata as daily Market Income increases (figure 14-26, left panel). This is a distinguishing feature of the Dominican Republic when compared with the other surveyed countries.

Turning to education expenditures, markedly declining percentages of beneficiaries by socioeconomic strata are more common as daily Market Income increases (figure 14-26, right panel). Yet, only about 65 percent of the extreme poor in the Dominican Republic benefit from public education spending—a low figure compared to other middle-income countries for which results are available. This may be due to the perceived low quality of public education, which compels household heads (even in poor families) to send their children to private schools.[56] However, this opting-out behavior may have declined with the significant increases of education expenditures after 2012, which would, of course, not be reflected in the ENIGH 2007 survey used in this analysis.

Using calculations drawn from the CEQ methodology, it is possible to quantify the resources that would be needed to lift all Dominicans out of poverty and cover

---

[56] Sanchez-Martin and Senderowitsch (2012).

FIGURE 14-26

Percentage of Individuals Benefiting from Health (left) and Public Education (right)
Services, by Daily Income

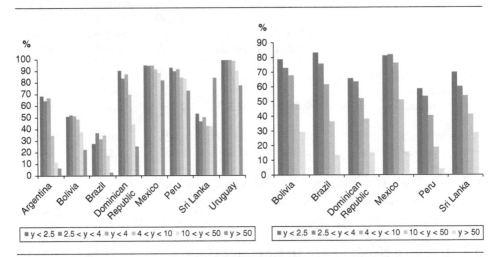

Source: Authors' estimates for the Dominican Republic and based on: for Argentina (Lustig and Pessino, 2014); Bolivia (Paz Arauco and others, 2014); Brazil (Higgins and Pereira, 2014); Mexico (Scott, 2014); Peru (Jaramillo, 2014); Sri Lanka (Arunatilake, Inchauste, and Lustig, 2017); and Uruguay (Bucheli and others, 2014).

education and health coverage gaps. Closing the extreme poverty gap (below US$2.50 PPP per capita a day) would require from an additional RD$18.3 billion in cash transfers, the equivalent to 4.9 percent of government revenue and 0.7 percent of GDP in 2013 (table 14-13). This would mean doubling the current level of spending on direct transfers. Closing the human-capital gap, defined by public education and health coverage needs for the moderately poor (US$4 PPP a day), would require RD$28.4 billion, or 1.1 percent of 2013 GDP. To fill in the overall poverty gap (US$4 PPP a day), additional resources equivalent to a quarter of total government revenue would be needed, other policies (e.g., taxation) being equal. These results are in Dominican pesos of 2013 and take into account population growth since 2007. One caveat: this exercise assumes that the government has the capacity to manage and efficiently allocate the higher funding, which may not be always the case because of administrative bottlenecks encountered when scaling up public spending.

4 Options for Enhancing the Equity Outcomes of Fiscal Policy in the Dominican Republic

4.1 Alternative VAT Scenarios for a Fiscal Impact Pact

Dependence on indirect taxes remains a challenge for the Dominican Republic. As previously mentioned, tax expenditures derived from ITBIS exemptions amount to around

TABLE 14-13
Estimated Resource Needs to Close Existing Social Gaps in the Dominican Republic

	Gap in millions of RD$ 2013	Total spending	Required increase to close gap		
			Primary spending	Gov. revenue	2013 GDP
Spending or revenues in millions of LCU	—	515,562	391,884	370,573	2,558,585
Income poverty gap					
$2.50 PPP per day	18,325	3.6%	4.7%	4.9%	0.7%
$4 PPP per day	65,941	12.8%	16.8%	17.8%	2.6%
Education coverage gap	7,757	1.5%	2.0%	2.1%	0.3%
$2.50 PPP per day					
$4 PPP per day	14,608	2.8%	3.7%	3.9%	0.6%
Health coverage gap	6,864	1.3%	1.8%	1.9%	0.3%
$2.50 PPP per day					
$4 PPP per day	13,778	2.7%	3.5%	3.7%	0.5%
Human capital gap	14,621	2.8%	3.7%	3.9%	0.6%
$2.50 PPP per day					
$4 PPP per day	28,386	5.5%	7.2%	7.7%	1.1%
Overall poverty gap	32,946	6.4%	8.4%	8.9%	1.3%
$2.50 PPP per day					
$4 PPP per day	94,327	18.3%	24.1%	25.5%	3.7%

Source: Authors' estimates based in ENIGH (2007), applying the CEQ methodology.

Note: Income definition is US$ PPP at 2005 prices

FIGURE 14-27

Beneficiaries of VAT Tax Expenditure for Different Product Categories

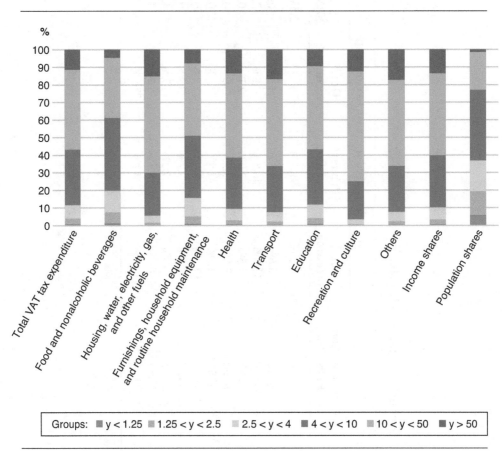

Source: Authors' estimates based in ENIGH (2007) and DGII (2014).

Note: Socioeconomic income groups are defined in US$ PPP at 2005 prices.

3 percent of GDP.[57] The estimations in figure 14-27 suggest that the bulk of total tax expenditures (88 percent) benefits non-poor households. The share of tax expenditures held by the poor (US$4 PPP a day definition) would be largest in the case of exemptions relating to food (around 20 percent) and household furnishings (16 percent).

Taking as a starting point the analysis of the World Bank (2006), we estimate alternative ITBIS reform scenarios, with the purpose of exploring the likely effects on revenue collection, poverty, and inequality that would follow total or partial elimination of ITBIS exemptions. As a caveat, it is important to note that this estimate is based on a static incidence analysis, and simulations do not consider potential changes in the behavior of taxpayers due to the changes in ITBIS. The four scenarios simulated are:

---

[57] DGII (2015).

(1) total elimination of ITBIS exemptions; (2) elimination of all exemptions except for health, education, and electricity; (3) partial elimination of exemptions, preserving those in the basket of basic goods and services; and (4) partial elimination of exemptions except for electricity, health, education, and basic goods—a combination of (2) and (3).

In the first scenario, we simulate the elimination of all exemptions (i.e., all exempted goods and those with reduced rate would pay a rate of 18 percent). This exercise also takes into account ITBIS tax evasion, drawing from information by the General Directorate of Internal Taxation for 2010 by different product lines (see box 14-2). So we assume that tax payments on ITBIS goods that had been exempted will have an average evasion rate about 29.7 percent in 2010, equal to what was estimated by DGII (2015).

The second scenario retains exemptions for some products. The World Bank (2006) warns that some goods and services are hard to tax for political and efficiency reasons, like educational, health, and electricity supply services. The second simulation is also ambitious in broadening the tax base by eliminating all exemptions except for those relating to these sectors.

In the third scenario, only exemptions on the basic basket products will remain. In cooperation with public-sector institutions and international agencies, ONE (2012) drafted a report identifying the basket of basic goods, and we use it to select the goods that remain exempt goods in this scenario.[58] The final scenario for dealing with ITBIS combines the previous two and is more conservative in that it maintains exemptions on politically sensible goods and the basket of basic consumption.[59]

The simulations show that ITBIS changes would not have a significant impact on the Gini coefficient. Elimination of all exemptions slightly increases inequality. However, the second scenario has the greatest inequality increases because of the elimination of exemptions in some basic goods and services (including food products). The third and fourth scenarios preserve basic food exemptions, and inequality remains unchanged.

Eliminating all exemptions would increase poverty. In the first scenario, moderate poverty incidence would increase by 1.3 percentage points and extreme poverty incidence by 0.7 percentage points. If only politically sensitive goods were exempt, moderate poverty increase would be lower but still significant. By contrast, extreme poverty incidence would not increase if ITBIS exemptions on the basket of basic goods are kept in place (figure 14-28), which seems to indicate that the poor purchase products in this basket almost exclusively. This is not surprising, since the national poverty definitions are according to country specific patterns of consumption and caloric requirements.[60]

In the first scenario, with all exemptions removed, revenue collection would increase the most—around 2.2 percent of Disposable Income, assuming other things

---

[58] See annex 5 in ONE (2012).

[59] The World Bank (2006) considered a fourth scenario with reduced rates for basic food. However, we do not consider this scenario because the Dominican Republic has been phasing out reduced rates.

[60] ONE and MEPyD (2012).

Box 14-2

Including VAT Evasion Assumptions in the Dominican Republic

Value-added tax (VAT) evasion is a problem in the Dominican Republic. According to General Directorate of Internal Taxation (DGII) estimates for 2010, about 29.7 percent of this tax was evaded.

Therefore, it was important to include an adjustment for evasion in the CEQ analysis.

In consultation with DGII experts, we obtained estimates of actual tax payments for a limited group of products. It was necessary to make assumptions of tax evasion for the products not covered by DGII data. The evidence suggests that taxes on some goods are either regularly evaded or paid in full, while evasion or payment depends on place of purchase for another group of goods. With this in mind, goods were clustered in the following four groups:

1. Highly probable that no tax is paid (100 percent evasion on the purchases of these goods).

2. Highly probable that taxes are paid (0 percent evasion on the purchases of these goods).

3. For those on which the DGII has information on the proportion of tax paid, the effective tax rate was applied.

4. For those on which tax payments are conditional on place of purchase, a different evasion rate was applied to urban and rural consumers.

To make these adjustments, we created two auxiliary files. The first includes each of the goods contained in the ENIGH 2007 and classified in one of the four categories described above (product code and product group). The second defines whether the tax on the product is evaded or paid according to the place of purchase for those cases where evasion is conditional.

With the information on tax evasion, and taking into account the nominal tax rate for 2007 (16 percent), we calculated the VAT tax base for each household, given the level of consumption for each good in 2007. Then we applied the nominal tax rates for 2013 (18 percent and a reduced rate of 8 percent for some goods) for each type of good, adjusted by evasion levels. This allowed us to estimate the VAT payment for each good consumed by households in the survey.

being equal (and no change in the behavioral response of economic agents). In the second scenario, with all exemptions but those on education, health, and electricity removed, revenue collection would increase by 1.7 percent of Disposable Income. Finally, if basic food were also exempt, tax revenue would increase by only about 0.3 percent of Disposable Income (figure 14-29). Note that the incidence analysis simulated using the

FIGURE 14-28

Effects on Inequality (left) and Poverty (right) of Alternative ITBIS Exemption
Scenarios

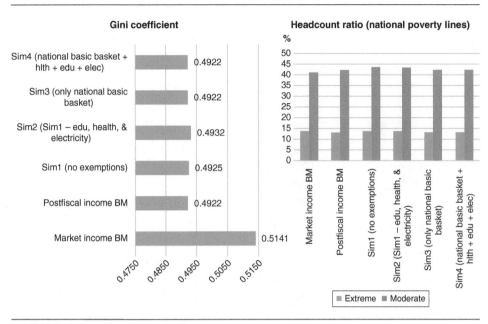

Source: Authors' estimations based on ENIGH (2007).

ENIGH 2007 has been adjusted to reflect the amount of tax expenditure estimated by
official sources in 2013.

According to our analysis, eliminating exemptions would result in improved tax
collection. In all scenarios, inequality would not increase significantly, but income poverty would be sensitive to changes in ITBIS exemptions under simulation scenarios 1
and 2. There seems to be an important trade-off in terms of revenue collection (most
improved under first and second scenarios) and poverty incidence (less affected under
the third and fourth scenarios).

4.2 Policy Options and Conclusion

Fiscal incidence analysis applying the CEQ methodology shows that, as of 2013, the Dominican Republic's fiscal policy was progressive overall. Compared to other countries
subject to the same methodology, the Dominican fiscal system achieves intermediate
levels of inequality reduction through direct and indirect taxes as well as transfers and
subsidies, and it generates very little horizontal inequality. Reranking of households as a
proportion of vertical inequality is by far the lowest among similar countries. When
income per capita is used as the welfare indicator, fiscal policy in 2013 reduced the Market Income Gini coefficient from 0.514 to 0.458—a decline of 5 Gini points—when all

FIGURE 14-29

Effects on Revenue Increase in Scenarios of ITBIS (as percentage of total disposable income)

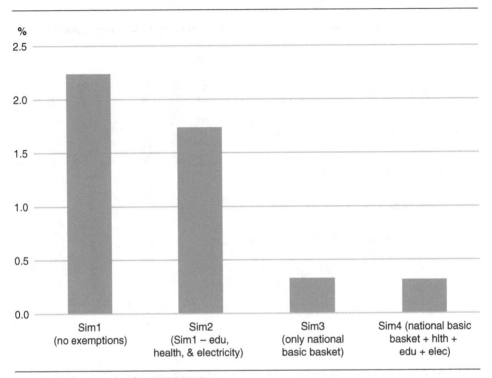

Source: Authors' estimates based on ENIGH (2007).

taxes and transfers (including the monetized value of education and health) are taken into account. Excluding the monetized value of education and health services, the improvement in inequality is more modest, with the Gini falling to 0.492. The incidence of extreme poverty also declines when comparing Market Income and postfiscal income (excluding education and health), whereas moderate poverty would remain slightly higher after indirect taxes, both under the national and international definitions.

In terms of poverty reduction, the incidence of direct transfers is modest. This is due to the fact that households in the poorest decile receive transfers and indirect subsidies worth 10 percent of their Market Income, which is relatively low compared to most countries (see figure 14-24, left panel). This likely relates to the amounts granted under CCT programs being smaller than in Brazil, South Africa, or Uruguay.

For the Dominican Republic, resources amounting to 1.3 percent of GDP would be needed to lift the extreme poor who are under the international poverty line of

US$2.50 PPP a day. Ending extreme poverty and ensuring the poor have access to public education and health would require an increase in public resources to social services equivalent to 1.3 percent of GDP, other things remaining equal. This section presents a series of policy options that could help in further improving equity outcomes using fiscal policy.

On the education front, the challenge will be increasing the quality of education through measures included in the Education Pact.[61] The Dominican Republic has already significantly boosted public spending, from 2.2 percent of GDP in 2011 to around 4 percent of GDP in 2013 and beyond. This has had a significant effect in terms of inequality reduction, given that education spending is highly progressive. In the analysis, we are monetizing the value of public spending in education to estimate changes in inequality. However, if the quality of the service provided is not good, the de facto welfare improvement would be smaller. Enrollment in primary school is higher among the poor than among the non-poor; this is probably because the latter have the resources to opt out and choose private education because of the perception that the quality of public education remains mediocre. Thus, the priority in the sector at the moment should be increasing the quality of education through implementation of the measures included in the Education Pact. In addition, authorities could try to improve access and coverage among the poor, especially in pre-primary and secondary education, where enrollment remains low among the extreme poor (23 percent in pre-primary and 67 percent in secondary). Finally, introducing a series of grants to support top performers among the poor could help mitigate school dropout and improve access to and equity in tertiary education.

Unlike education, health will require significant increases in expenditures in the Dominican Republic. The country's public health resources remain low by international standards at around 1.7 percent of GDP, half the amount spent by South Africa and Brazil and a third of Costa Rica's outlays. The Dominican Republic has had noticeable improvements in terms of coverage, with the percentage of the population with health insurance increasing from 27 percent in 2007 to 55 percent in 2013, according to the ENDESA of 2013.[62] However, the bottom 40 percent of the population has coverage of less than 25 percent in the subsidized regime and less than 21 percent in the noncontributory regime. In the first quintile, two-thirds of the population does not report having health insurance. In fact, a number of people who do not have insurance are using the Ministry of Health's hospitals and clinics in emergency situations. A strategy to increase the subsidized regime's coverage while improving the quality of services would likely result in substantial equity gains and may also require upgrading in public facilities in order to attract non-poor individuals into the contributory regime as well.

---

[61] The Pact for Education (Pacto por la Educacion) was signed in 2014 by representatives of the civil society and the government to improve the quality of and access to public education.
[62] CESDEM/ICF (2014).

As discussed in section 3.4, health spending would need to be increased by around 0.3 percent of GDP to extend coverage to the population living under US$2.50 PPP a day per capita. All the analyzed components and programs of health spending are highly progressive except for PROMESE, which is barely progressive and could be revised to focus resources and medicines on the poor and vulnerable. The non-poor could pay for these health services.

A revision of tax policies could be considered to finance the 1.3 percent of GDP in additional resources needed to fill the above-mentioned gaps. Personal income taxes make up the lion's share of direct tax collections; yet, according to our simulations, effective rates of 3.5 percent among upper-class earners (more than US$40 a day PPP) are far from the 15 percent called for in the tax schedule. A positive impact on personal income tax revenue would come from tax administration measures to reduce evasion by the upper class and measures to decrease informality among independent workers, who currently account for 56 percent of the active workforce.

In the Dominican Republic, the challenge will be raising added revenue while maintaining the tax system's progressivity. The country's tax progressivity seems high compared to other countries. Of the selected countries, only Jordan, Sri Lanka, and Peru have more progressive direct tax systems. On income taxes, it bears repeating that we have applied statutory rates, and preliminary evidence would need to be contrasted with actual data on collections by income level.

The Dominican Republic could raise additional revenue by reforming its system of indirect taxes, focusing on the ITBIS exemptions. The indirect taxes are slightly progressive, mostly due to the progressivity of excise taxes; ITBIS is almost neutral. The ITBIS exemptions represent close to 3 percent of GDP,[63] and the majority of tax expenditures from these exemptions are related to the consumption of middle- and upper-class households. At the same time, phasing out certain exemptions would have negative impacts on poverty and inequality. With that in mind, a possible option could be for goods in the basic consumption basket (based on the national poverty measurement methodology) to remain taxed at a zero rate, along with health and education services. Other exemptions, especially those that are regressive, could be removed, potentially granting up to 0.5 percent of GDP in additional revenue collection. The impact of the removal of ITBIS exemptions on electricity for the poor could be mitigated through the Bono Luz program.

Electricity subsidies could be withdrawn from the non-poor, while taking care of the poor through Bono Luz. Explicit electricity subsidies (tariffs below costs) and implicit ones (irregular connections, fraud, nonpayment) are equalizing in absolute terms but not in relative terms. Simulations applying the CEQ methodology confirm evidence presented by Actis (2012), who estimated that 83 percent of electricity subsidies benefited non-poor households. Fostering a culture of payment by improving service quality and reducing blackouts and adjusting tariffs to market rates are among the mea-

---

[63] Ministerio de Hacienda (2012).

sures that could help reduce the deficit in the electricity sector (more than 1.5 percent of GDP in 2013). At the same time, the poor and vulnerable could be shielded from decreases in purchasing power through Bono Luz.

Bono Luz and Bonogas Hogar are among the programs that could be slightly reshaped since at the moment they are just barely progressive in relative terms. One way would be to phase out the eligibility of beneficiaries in the SIUBEN quality-of-living index category 3 (non-poor). The savings, totaling around 0.1 percent of GDP, could be used to expand both programs' coverage among the poor. Since these programs are functioning pretty much as universal transfers, another policy alternative would be maintaining non-poor as beneficiaries but focusing future coverage expansions on the poor. According to ADESS, 843,000 would be beneficiaries of Bonogas Hogar in 2013 and 533,000 for Bono Luz, compared to a universe of up to 2.4 million potential beneficiaries.

Finally, conditional cash transfers have been effective in reaching the poor and could be further strengthened. These programs, such as Comer es Primero and Incentivo a la Asistencia Escolar, are highly progressive, with less than 10 percent of public expenditures seeming to go to the middle class. Comer es Primero is fruitful in terms of reducing poverty and inequality, representing 5.5 percent of Market Income for the ultra-poor (living on less than US$1.25 a day) and 2.1 percent for the extremely poor (below US$2.50 a day). Even so, authorities could consider increasing the individual cash amounts transferred through these well-targeted instruments, or at least make sure they are indexed to prevent an erosion of purchasing power. The past decade's success in putting both conditional and nonconditional cash transfers under the SIUBEN single-targeting mechanism and ADESS administration should be continued. At the same time, the more recent proliferation of small incentive programs may need to be limited to attain more powerful outcomes. Some promising steps are being taken by establishing support schemes and facilitating labor-market integration to those households that have reached non-poor status and will graduate from Progresando con Solidaridad, thus enabling other poor households to become beneficiaries of the CCT in a context of still limited coverage and resources.

All in all, overall fiscal policy in the Dominican Republic is already progressive. Going forward, the challenge is raising revenue collection without affecting the poor and vulnerable, at the same time that public service delivery is improved. Compared to other countries, the fiscal system achieves intermediate levels of inequality reduction (5 Gini points) through direct and indirect taxes, transfers, and subsidies, and it generates very little horizontal inequality. Some European states are able to reduce the Gini by more than 15 percentage points, but by reinvesting large revenue collection in social programs and public services. In this sense, enhancing the quality of public services would be a priority in the Dominican Republic, as it would not only help achieve social outcomes but also improve citizen trust in institutions, which could ultimately lead toward formalization of economic activity and improved revenue collection.

Acknowledgments

The authors are obliged to the following World Bank colleagues for their substantive contributions: Javier Eduardo Baez, Alan Fuchs, Juan Baron, Omar Arias, Luis Felipe Lopez-Calva, Francisco Galrao Carneiro, Gabriela Inchauste, and McDonald Benjamin. Special thanks to Nora Lustig and Samantha Greenspun (Tulane University) for the exceptional help in validating the accuracy of results when applying the Commitment to Equity methodology.

The authors are also grateful to the following government and donor counterparts in the Dominican Republic for their collaboration: Magdalena Lizardo, Antonio Morillo, Alexis Cruz, and Martin Francos (Ministry of Economy, Planning and Development); Luis Madera, Augusto de los Santos, and Mabely Diaz (National Office for Statistics); Jose Luis Actis (Ministry of Finance); Guarocuya Felix, Marvin Cardoza, and Hamlet Gutierrez (General Directorate for Internal Taxation, Ministry of Finance); Matilde Chavez (Social Cabinet); Tirsis Quezada and Rafael Montero (Ministry of Public Health); Chanel Rosa (SENASA); Pedro Castellanos and Ayacx Mercedes (DIGEPEP, Presidency); Rafael Perez (National Council for the Social Security); Ramon Gonzalez Hernandez (Central Bank of the Dominican Republic); Rita Mena (UNDP); and Javier Casasnovas (European Union).

References

Abdullaev, Umidjon, and Marcello Estevao. 2013. "Growth and Employment in the Dominican Republic: Options for a Job-Rich Growth," IMF Working Papers 13/40 (International Monetary Fund).

Actis, Jose Luis. 2012. "Una evaluacion de la eficacia de los subsidios al consumo residencial de energia electrica en la Republica Dominicana." Mimeo. Dominican Republic.

ADESS (Administradora de Subsidios Sociales). 2017. "Reportes y Graficos Estadisticos: Subsidios otorgados por año y mes" (http://adess.gov.do/v2/Reportes/ReportView2.aspx).

Alam, Shamma A., Gabriela Inchauste, and Umar Serajuddin. 2017. "The Distributional Impact of Fiscal Policy in Jordan," in *The Distributional Impact of Taxes and Transfers: Evidence from Eight Low- and Middle-Income Countries*, edited by Gabriela Inchauste and Nora Lustig (Washington: World Bank).

Aristy-Escuder, Jaime. 2017. "Income Definition, Price Indexes, and the Poverty Headcount in the Dominican Republic," in *When Growth Is Not Enough*, ed. Francisco Galrao Carneiro and Sophie Sirtaine (Washington: World Bank Group).

Arunatilake, Nisha, Gabriela Inchauste, and Nora Lustig. 2017. "The Incidence of Taxes and Spending in Sri Lanka," in *The Distributional Impact of Taxes and Transfers: Evidence from Eight Low- and Middle-Income Countries*, edited by Gabriela Inchauste and Nora Lustig (Washington: World Bank).

Barreix, Alberto, Martin Bes, and Jeronimo Roca. 2009. *Equidad fiscal en Centroamerica, Panama y Republica Domicana* (Washington: Interamerican Development Bank/Eurosocial).

Beckerman, Wilfred. 1979. "The Impact of Income Maintenance Payments on Poverty in Britain, 1975." *Economic Journal* 89, pp. 261–79.

Beneke de Sanfeliu, Margarita, Nora Lustig, and Jose Andres Oliva Cepeda. 2022. "El Salvador: the Impact of Taxes and Social Spending on Inequality and Poverty," chap. 15 in *Commitment to Equity Handbook: Estimating the Impact of Fiscal Policy on Inequality and Poverty*, 2nd ed., Vol. 1, edited by Nora Lustig (Brookings Institution Press and CEQ Institute, Tulane University). Free online version available at www.commitmentoequity.org.

Bucheli, Marisa, Nora Lustig, Maximo Rossi, and Florencia Amabile. 2014. "Social Spending, Taxes, and Income Redistribution in Uruguay." *Public Finance Review* 42, no. 3, pp. 413–33.

Cabrera, Maynor, Nora Lustig, and Hilcias Moran. 2015. "Fiscal Policy, Inequality and the Ethnic Divide in Guatemala." *World Development*, 76 (C), pp. 263–79.

Carneiro, Francisco Galrão, Aleksandra Iwulska, Jose-Daniel Reyes, and Miguel Eduardo Sanchez-Martin. 2015. "Resilient Growth, Persisting Inequality: Identifying Potential Factors Limiting Shared Prosperity in the Dominican Republic." World Bank Other Operational Studies 21499 (World Bank).

CESDEM/ICF. 2014. "Encuesta demografica y de Salud Republica Dominicana 2013" (ENDESA) (http://countryoffice.unfpa.org/dominicanrepublic/drive/DRDHS2013-Final02-10-2013 .pdf).

Chu, Ke Young, Hamid Davoodi, and Sanjeev Gupta. 2000. "Income Distribution and Tax and Government Social Spending Policies in Developing Countries," Working Paper No. 00/62 (International Monetary Fund).

CNSS (Consejo Nacional de la Seguridad Social). 2013. "Informe Mensual del Sistema Dominicano De Seguridad Social (SDSS)" (Consejo Nacional de Seguridad Social), December.

DGII. 2014. "Gastos Tributarios en Republica Dominicana. Estimacion para el Presupuesto General del Estado del año 2015" (Direccion General de Impuestos Internos, Ministerio de Hacienda), September.

———. 2015. "Sistema tributario en Republica Dominicana" (Direccion General de Impuestos Internos, Ministerio de Hacienda), April.

Diaz, Magin. 2008. "Equidad Fiscal en la República Dominicana: Análisis de la Incidencia Distributiva de la Política Fiscal." Mimeo. Interamerican Development Bank.

Duclos, Jean-Yves, and Abdelkrim Araar. 2006. *Poverty and Equity: Measurement, Policy, and Estimation with DAD* (New York: Springer and International Development Research Centre).

Ferreira, Francisco H. G, Julian Messina, Jamele Rigolini, Luis Felipe Lopez-Calva, Maria Ana Lugo, and Renos Vakis. 2013. "Economic Mobility and the Rise of the Latin American Middle Class" (Washington: World Bank).

Gallina, Andrea, Gabriela Inchauste, Pavel Isa, Catherine Lee, and Migeul Sanchez-Martin. 2015. "Political Economy of Subsidy Reform Case Study for the Dominican Republic." Mimeo.

Guzman, Rolando. 2011. "Composicion economica Dominicana. El Estrato de Ingresos Medios en el Umbral del Siglo XXI." Document prepared for the Ministry of Economy, Planning, and Development of the Dominican Republic.

Higgins, Sean, and Claudiney Pereira. 2014. "The Effects of Brazil's Taxation and Social Spending on the Distribution of Household Income." *Public Finance Review* 42, no. 3, pp. 346–67.

Hill, Ruth, Gabriela Inchauste, Nora Lustig, Eyasu Tsehaye, and Tassew Woldehanna. 2017. "Fiscal Incidence Analysis for Ethiopia," in *The Distributional Impact of Taxes and Transfers:*

Evidence from Eight Low- and Middle-Income Countries, edited by Gabriela Inchauste and Nora Lustig (Washington: World Bank).

Immervoll, Herwig, Horacio Levy, Jose Ricardo Nogueira, Cathal O'Donoghue, and Rozane Bezerra de Siqueira. 2009. "The Impact of Brazil's Tax-Benefit System on Inequality and Poverty," in *Poverty, Inequality, and Policy in Latin America*, edited by Stephan Klasen and Felicitas Nowak-Lehmann (MIT Press).

Inchauste, Gabriela, Nora Lustig, Mashekwa Maboshe, Catriona Purfield, and Ingrid Woolard. 2017. "The Distributional Impact of Fiscal Policy in South Africa," in *The Distributional Impact of Taxes and Transfer: Evidence from Eight Low- and Middle-Income Countries*, edited by Gabriela Inchauste and Nora Lustig (Washington: World Bank).

Jaramillo, Miguel. 2014. "The Incidence of Social Spending and Taxes in Peru," *Public Finance Review* 42, no. 3, pp. 391–412.

Jellema, Jon, Matthew Wai-Poi, and Rythia Afkar. 2017. "The Distributional Impact of Fiscal Policy in Indonesia," in *The Distributional Impact of Taxes and Transfers: Evidence from Eight Low- and Middle-Income Countries*, edited by Gabriela Inchauste and Nora Lustig (Washington: World Bank).

Law 288-04. On Tax Reform. National Congress of the Dominican Republic. September 28, 2004.

Law 253-12. On Strengthening the State's Collecting Capacity for Fiscal Sustainability and Sustainable Development. National Congress of the Dominican Republic. November 13, 2012.

Lindert, Kathy, Emmanuel Skoufias, and Joseph Shapiro. 2006. "Redistributing Income to the Poor and the Rich: Public Transfers in Latin America and the Caribbean," Social Protection Discussion Paper 0605 (Washington: World Bank).

Lustig, Nora, Florencia Amabile, Marisa Bucheli, George Gray Molina, Sean Higgins, Miguel Jaramillo, Wilson Jimenez Pozo, Veronica Paz Arauco, Claudiney Pereira, Carola Pessino, Maximo Rossi, John Scott, and Ernesto Yañez Aguilar. 2013. "The Impact of Taxes and Social Spending on Inequality and Poverty in Argentina, Bolivia, Brazil, Mexico, Peru, and Uruguay: An Overview," CEQ Working Paper No. 13 (Tulane University), August.

Lustig, Nora, and Sean Higgins. 2013. "*Commitment to Equity Assessment* (CEQ): Estimating the Incidence of Social Spending, Subsidies and Taxes. Handbook," CEQ Working Paper No. 1, July 2011; revised September 2013.

Lustig, Nora, and Carola Pessino. 2014. "Social Spending and Income Redistribution in Argentina in the 2000s: The Rising Role of Noncontributory Pensions." *Public Finance Review* 42, no. 3, pp. 304–25.

MEPyD. 2013. "El efecto de la Ley de fortalecimiento de la capacidad recaudadora del Estado (Ley 253-12) sobre la pobreza y desigualdad." Ministerio de Economia Planificacion y Desarrollo y Oficina Nacional de Estadistica. Documento de Trabajo. Enero de 2013.

Ministerio de Hacienda. 2012. "Gastos Tributarios en Republica Dominicana, Estimacion para el Presupuesto General del Estado del año 2013." Informe de la Comision Interinstitucional Coordinada por la Direccion General de Politica y Legislacion Tributaria.

———. 2017. "Ejecucion presupuestaria del Gobierno Central. Clasificacion Funcional" (http://www.digepres.gob.do/wp-content/uploads/2017/02/Funcional-Anual-1990-2016-VF.xlsx).

Ministry of Education. 2014. "Gastos en Establecimientos Publicos periodo 2013 (En millones de RD$) Formulario de UNESCO" (http://www.ministeriodeeducacion.gob.do/transparencia/file/descarga?fileNombre=Datos+Formulario+UNESCO+2013&fileExt=pdf&fileName=datos

-formulario-unesco-2013.pdf&category=presupuesto&subcategory=resultados-de-la-inversion-por-estudiante).

Ministry of Health. 2014. "Gasto Nacional en Salud," Powerpoint presentation, unpublished.

OECD (Organisation for Economic Co-operation and Development). 2015. *Latin American Economic Outlook 2015: Education, skills and innovation for development* (Paris: OECD).

ONE. 2007. National Survey of Household Income and Expenditure 2006–07 (ENIGH). Dominican Republic.

———. 2012. *Estimacion de la Canasta Basica y las Lineas de Pobreza* (Dominican Republic Poverty Committee, July) (www.one.gob.do/Multimedia/Download?ObjId=1935).

ONE and MEPyD. 2012. *Metodologia para el calculo de la medicion oficial de la pobreza monetaria en la Republica Dominicana* (Dominican Republic Poverty Committee, July) (http://www.one.gob.do/Multimedia/Download?ObjId=1936).

Paz Arauco, Veronica, George Gray Molina, Wilson Jimenez Pozo, and Ernesto Yañez Aguilar. 2014. "Explaining Low Redistributive Impact in Bolivia." *Public Finance Review* 42, no. 3, pp. 326–45.

Sanchez-Martin, Miguel Eduardo, and Roby Senderowitsch. 2012. "The Political Economy of the Middle Class in the Dominican Republic: Individualization of Public Goods, Lack of Institutional Trust and Weak Collective Action." Policy Research Working Paper Series 6049 (World Bank).

Santana, Isidoro, and Magdalena Rathe. 1993. "The Distributive Impact of Fiscal Policy in the Dominican Republic," in *Government Spending and Income Distribution in Latin America*, edited by Ricardo Hausmann and Roberto Rigobon (Washington: Inter-American Development Bank).

Sauma, Pablo, and Juan Diego Trejos. 2014. "Social Public Spending, Taxes, Redistribution of Income, and Poverty in Costa Rica." CEQ Working Paper No. 18 (Economics Department and Center for Inter-American Policy and Research, Tulane University).

Scott, John. 2014. "Redistributive Impact and Efficiency of Mexico's Fiscal System." *Public Finance Review* 42, no. 3, 368–90.

SENASA. (2014). "Reconversion del IDSS y Red Publica unica." Mimeo.

Valderrama, Daniel, Martin Francos, Mariano Jimenez, Magdalena Lizardo, and Antonio Morillo. 2013. "El efecto de un programa de transferencias condicionadas sobre la pobreza y desigualdad en el corto plazo: El caso de Progresando con Solidaridad en Republica Dominicana." MEPyD and ONE. Mimeo.

Valderrama, Daniel, Martin Francos, Magdalena Lizardo, and Antonio Morillo. 2013. "Seguro Familiar de Salud en el Regimen Subsidiado: Sus efectos de corto plazo sobre la pobreza y desigualdad" (Santo Domingo, Dominican Republic: ONE and MEPyD).

World Bank. 2006. "Achieving More Pro-Poor Growth," Poverty Assessment Report No. 32422-DO (World Bank, October 30).

———. 2014a. "When Prosperity Is Not Shared: The Puzzle of the Weak Links between Growth and Equity in Dominican Republic," Equity Assessment Report No. 85760 (World Bank).

———. 2014b. "Patronage or Reform? The Political Economy of Reform in the Dominican Republic," Institutional and Governance Review Report No. 91312 (Washington: World Bank).

Younger, Stephen D., and Artsvi Khachatryan. 2017. "Fiscal Incidence in Armenia," in *The Distributional Impact of Taxes and Transfers: Evidence from Eight Low- and Middle-Income Countries*, edited by Gabriela Inchauste and Nora Lustig (Washington: World Bank).

Appendix 14A

Structure of Revenue and Expenditure

TABLE 14A-1
Composition of Taxes in the Dominican Republic (2013)

Revenue	Included in analysis	Estimation method	% of total taxes	% of GDP
Total Revenue				14.5
Total Taxes			100.0	13.8
Direct taxes			37.0	5.1
Direct taxes on individuals			9.4	1.3
On wages & income on personal income	Yes	Simulation	5.7	0.8
On dividends	Yes	Simulation	1.7	0.2
On interest	Yes	Simulation	0.6	0.1
Other personal income tax	No		1.3	0.2
Corporate income tax	No		16.5	2.3
Other direct taxes	No		11.1	1.5
VAT and other indirect taxes			63.0	8.7
ITBIS (VAT)	Yes	Simulation with assumptions of tax evasion and tax expenditures	32.0	4.4
Excises on alcoholic beverages	Yes	Simulation	2.4	0.3
Excises on beer	Yes	Simulation	2.7	0.4
Excises on tobacco	Yes	Simulation	1.2	0.2
Excises on oil derivatives	Yes	Simulation	12.2	1.7
Other indirect taxes	No		12.4	1.7
Other taxes	No		0.0	0.0

Contributions	Included in analysis		% of total taxes	% of GDP
Contributions to social security	No		0.4	0.1
Total Taxes and Contributions			100.0	13.9

Source: Authors' calculations based on Ministry of Finance data.

TABLE 14A-2
Composition of Expenditures in the Dominican Republic (2011 and 2013)

	Included in analysis	Estimation method	2011 (SA2)		2013 (benchmark & SA1)	
			% of total gov. spending	% of GDP	% of total gov. spending	% of GDP
			100.0	18.0	100.0	20.2
Total Government Spending (A + B)						
A. Primary government spending (a+b+c)			74.2	13.3	76.0	15.3
a. Social spending (excludes contrib. pensions) (1+2+3+4)			32.7	5.9	39.9	8.0
1. Total cash transfers			2.3	0.4	4.0	0.8
Cash transfers (excluding all pensions)	Yes	Imputation	2.3	0.4	4.0	0.8
Noncontributory pensions	n.a.	n.a.	0.0	0.0	0.0	0.0
2. Total in-kind transfers			20.9	3.7	27.8	5.6
Education	Yes	Imputation	10.5	1.9	18.7	3.8
Tertiary	Yes	Imputation	1.2	0.2	1.3	0.3
Health			10.4	1.9	9.1	1.8
Social security	Partially (only subsidized)	Imputation using alternate survey Demographic Health Survey Endesa 2013 (CESDEM/ICF, 2014)	1.7	0.3	1.5	0.3
Ministry of Health	Yes	Imputation using alternate survey Demographic Health Survey Endesa 2013 (CESDEM/ICF, 2014)	7.2	1.3	6.2	1.3
Other (including PROMESE)	Partial	Imputation using alternate survey Demographic Health Survey Endesa 2013 (CESDEM/ICF, 2014)	1.5	0.3	1.4	0.3

(continued)

TABLE 14A-2   (continued)

	Included in analysis	Estimation method	2011 (SA2)		2013 (benchmark & SA1)	
			% of total gov. spending	% of GDP	% of total gov. spending	% of GDP
Total Government Spending (A + B)			100.0	18.0	100.0	20.2
3. Housing and urban 1/	No		4.3	0.8	3.4	0.7
4. Other social spending	No		5.3	1.0	4.7	1.0
b. Contributory pensions	Yes	Direct identification	4.9	0.9	4.2	0.8
c. Nonsocial spending (1 + 2)			36.6	6.6	31.9	6.4
1. Indirect subsidies			7.0	1.3	6.7	1.3
on final goods	Yes	Simulation	7.0	1.3	6.7	1.3
on inputs	No		0.0	0.0	0.0	0.0
2. Other nonsocial spending	No		29.6	5.3	25.2	5.1
Memo			0.0	0.0	0.0	0.0
Social spending plus contributory pensions			38.2	6.8	44.1	8.9
Debt Servicings	No		25.8	4.6	24.0	4.8
Interest payments	No		11.2	2.0	11.5	2.3
Amortization payments	No		14.5	2.6	12.5	2.5

Source: Authors' calculations based on Ministry of Finance data.

Table 14A-3

Composition of Public Education Expenditure in the Dominican Republic (2013)

Spending component	% of GDP	% GDP in analysis
Total	**3.8**	**3.5**
Preschool (3 to 5 years)	0.2	0.2
Primary (from 6 to 11 years, 1st to 6th *Basico*)	1.8	1.8
Lower econdary (12 to 13 years, 7th and 8th *Basico*)	0.5	0.5
Upper Secondary (14 to 17 years, 1st to 4th *Medio*)	0.8	0.8
Tertiary	0.3	0.3
Other expenses in education	0.2	0.0

Sources: Ministry of Education (2014) and Ministerio de Hacienda (2017).

Note: Levels of education in this table are equivalent to International Standard Classification of Education categories.

Table 14A-4

Composition of Public Health Expenditure in the Dominican Republic (2013)

Spending component	% of GDP	% GDP in analysis
Total	**1.8**	**1.6**
Ministry of Public Health	**1.3**	**1.3**
Outpatient services[a]	0.3	0.3
Hospitals[a]	0.9	0.9
Social Security System	**0.3**	**0.3**
Subsidized Regime Social Security[b]	0.2	0.2
Dominican Institute for Social Security (IDSS)[c]	0.1	0.1
Retired (SENASA)[b]	0.0	0.0
Others	**0.2**	**0.1**
PROMESE 2012[ad]	0.1	0.1
Others: Military and Police Hospital, National VIH Commission (CONAVIHSIDA), Health reform commission (CERS)[ad]	0.2	0.0

Sources: a. Authors' calculations based on Ministry of Health (2014); b. CNSS (2013); c. SENASA (2014) d. Ministerio de Hacienda (2017).

TABLE 14A-5
Direct Transfers Programs in the Dominican Republic (2013)

Categories of direct transfers	Programs	# of Beneficiaries	% of 2013 GDP
CCT food program	Comer es Primero (CEP)	698,196	0.24%
Education CCT programs	Incentivo a la Asistencia Escolar (ILAE)	299,111	0.03%
	Bono Estudiando Progreso (BEEP)	45,982	0.01%
	Incentivo a la Educacion Superior (IES)	25,795	0.01%
Targeted non-CCT transfers on utilities and commodities	Gas bonus to households: Bono Gas Hogar (BGH)	843,439	0.08%
	Electricity: *Bonus Bono Luz* (BL)	533,766	0.09%
	Gasoline bonus to public transport drivers: Bono Gas Choferes (BGC)	15,726	0.03%
Other transfers	Programa de Incentivo a la Policia Preventiva (PIPP)	22,493	0.01%
	Programa de Incentivo a la Marina de Guerra (PIAMG)	-	0.00%
	Contributive pensions from old regime	99,802	0.01%

Source: ADESS (2017) and authors' calculations.

Chapter 15

EL SALVADOR

The Impact of Taxes and Social
Spending on Inequality and Poverty

Margarita Beneke de Sanfeliu, Nora Lustig,
and Jose Andres Oliva Cepeda

Introduction

El Salvador is a middle-income country with a population of 6.2 million and an average per capita income of US$7,441.70 in purchasing power parity (PPP) in 2012.[1] In that year, the Gini coefficient was 0.425 and the poverty rate, measured using the international poverty line of US$2.50 a day PPP 2005, was 14.7 percent. With growing debt and a persistent fiscal deficit, El Salvador faces major fiscal policy challenges. In this context, it is essential to know the impact of fiscal policy on inequality and poverty in order to have a basis for evaluating alternative courses of action to achieve fiscal stability.

To this end, we present here a fiscal impact study to estimate the effect of taxes, social spending, and subsidies on inequality and poverty. To determine the distribution of the fiscal burden and the benefits of social spending, we developed concepts of income before and after fiscal interventions, by category and as a whole based on data from the 2011 Multi-Purpose Household Survey (Encuesta de Hogares y Propositos Multiples [EHPM]),[2] and administrative data from various sources. The study uses the methodology proposed by the Commitment to Equity (CEQ) Institute,[3] so that the results for El

This paper is based on the *CEQ Assessment* for El Salvador prepared by the authors and the CEQ Institute for the Inter-American Development Bank.

[1] Equivalent to US$3,819 in current dollars.

[2] Ministry of Economy (Ministerio de Economia [MINEC]), 2011.

[3] See, especially, chapter 1 (Lustig and Higgins, 2022), chapter 2 (Enami, Lustig, and Aranda, 2022), chapter 6 (Enami, Higgins, and Lustig, 2022), and chapter 8 (Higgins and Brest Lopez,

Salvador can be compared with countries that have similar income levels in Latin America and outside the region, where the same methodology has been applied.

Some fiscal incidence studies available for El Salvador analyze only a subset of fiscal policy components; for example, Acevedo and Gonzalez Orellana (2003) analyzed the impact of taxes on inequality, but did not consider public spending. The Central American Institute for Fiscal Studies (ICEFI, 2009)[4] analyzed the impact of taxes and public spending on inequality in the social area, but did not include the effect of subsidies. Barreix, Martin, and Roca (2009) and Cubero and Hollar (2010) dealt with progressivity and regressivity of taxes and spending for education and health for the Central American countries, including El Salvador, but neither considered the effects on poverty.

In contrast to existing literature, this study analyzes the incidence of the various components of fiscal policy not only on inequality, but also on poverty. Social spending includes direct cash transfers, such as the Rural Solidarity Communities (RSC) or the Temporary Income Support Program (PATI), as well as transfers in kind. These include school lunches and farm and school packages, subsidies for gas, water, electricity, and public transportation, education services (preschool, primary, secondary, and tertiary), and health services provided by the state. With respect to taxes paid by individuals, we considered direct and indirect taxes as well as contributions to health systems. We also analyzed contributory pensions.

The analysis shows that the direct transfer programs (sometimes also called "social programs") are generally aimed at lower-income households, but since the budget dedicated to them is small, their impact on inequality and poverty is limited. The analysis also shows that a large part of the resources used to subsidize liquid petroleum gas (LPG), electricity, water, and public transportation reaches households in the upper deciles of income distribution, so although their budget is larger, their impact on poverty is small. These taxes are progressive as a whole, but their impact on equality is also limited. The analysis also shows that the component with the greatest effect on inequality is (the monetized value of) social spending for education and health services provided by the government.

Direct transfers reduce the incidence of poverty, measured at both national and international poverty lines. However, this effect is almost completely offset when we take into account indirect taxes net of subsidies. The state's net fiscal action—in terms of purchasing power—results in a higher percentage of individuals living under said poverty lines. In fact, starting with the second poorest decile, the population is a net payer; it pays more in direct and indirect taxes than it receives in direct transfers and subsidies.

In summary, El Salvador's fiscal policy, has little, no, or even a negative effect on poverty reduction, depending on the line used. Using the international poverty line of US\$2.50 (PPP), El Salvador fares relatively well in comparison with other countries with

---

2022) in this Volume. The methodology used here is based on an earlier version of the *CEQ Handbook* (Lustig and Higgins, 2013).

[4] ICEFI (2009).

similar per capita income, such as Armenia and Guatemala. El Salvador, however, redistributes relatively less in comparison to the general trend in countries both inside and outside of the region with similar per capita income.

The analysis makes it possible to identify areas in which fiscal policy could be changed to obtain better results. For example, since electricity subsidies to households that use more than 99 kilowatt hours (kWh) represent a low percentage of the income that they receive, this resource could be redirected to strengthen coverage in preschool or middle school.

1 Taxes and Public Spending

The following is a detailed description of the taxes and fiscal spending used in this research. The government's total revenue was 18.2 percent of Gross Domestic Product (GDP); net fiscal revenue was 13.8 percent of GDP, and gross was 15.1 percent. Direct taxes were 5.2 percent of GDP, of which 1.97 percent was individual income tax. Indirect taxes accounted for 10 percent, with 7.8 percent coming from the value added tax (VAT). Non-taxed income totaled 3.5 percent, and external grants equaled 1 percent of GDP. In 2011, public expenditures[5] in El Salvador represented 22.3 percent of GDP; primary spending was 19.9 percent, and social spending 8.6 percent of GDP, respectively (table 15-1).

It is important to clarify that the CEQ concepts and definitions standardize social spending and do not correspond exactly with the classification used in El Salvador's national budget. CEQ social spending is defined as the sum of direct transfers from the state to the population, plus the monetary value of education, health, and other services provided directly to the population (for example, Women's City [Ciudad Mujer]). Direct transfers include both those made in cash and those made in-kind (for example, food, uniforms, etc.) if they have a defined market value and are near substitutes for cash. Indirect subsidies to public services are not considered direct transfers, because they do not contribute to available household income.

1.1 Fiscal Revenue: Taxes and Contribution Fees

The two main taxes in El Salvador are the income tax and the VAT. Specific taxes apply to select articles, such as automobiles (tax on the first registration), liquor and beer, cigarettes, firearms, and ammunition. In addition, there are special fees for special

---

[5] Includes spending by the nonfinancial public sector (NFPS)—for example, the central government, city governments, and nonfinancial decentralized and autonomous institutions. It does not include the public financial sector Central Reserve Bank (Banco Central de Reserva [BCR]), Mortgage Bank (Banco Hipotecario [BH]), the Development Bank of El Salvador (Banco de Desarrollo de El Salvador [BANDESAL]), the National Fund for Popular Housing (Fondo Nacional de Vivienda Popular [FONAVIPO]), the Social Fund for Housing (Fondo Social para la Vivienda [FSV]), and the Agricultural Development Bank (Banco de Fomento Agropecuario[BFA]).

TABLE 15-1
El Salvador: Composition of Spending and Fiscal Revenue (2011)

Item	Amount (millions of US$)	% of GDP Total	% of GDP In analysis*
TOTAL REVENUE	**4,220.20**	**18.24**	**11.6**
A. Net tax collection (A.1–A.2)	**3,206.52**	**13.86**	**9.40**
A.1 Tax collection (gross)	3,499.92	15.13	9.40
A.1.1 Direct taxes (income tax)	1,192.81	5.15	1.11
A.1.1.1 Income tax—individuals	455.58	1.97	1.11
A.1.1.1.1 Salaried workers	256.12	1.11	1.11
A.1.1.1.2. Nonsalaried individuals	199.46	0.86	...
A.1.1.2 Income tax—corporations	630.5	2.72	...
A.1.1.3 Tax withholding (corporations and individuals)	106.7	0.46	...
A.1.2 Indirect taxes	2,307.12	9.97	8.30
A.1.2.1 Value-added tax	1,801.32	7.78	7.80
A.1.2.2 Duties	167.31	0.72	...
A.1.2.3 Specific taxes on products	140.39	0.61	0.50
A.1.2.4 FEFE, FOVIAL, and public transportation (gasoline)	116.40	0.50	0.50
A.1.2.5 Other indirect taxes and contributions	81.70	0.35	...
A.2. Refunds	293.40	1.27	...
B. Nontax revenue	799.78	3.46	1.66
B.1. Contributions to social security (health)	385.20	1.66	1.66
B.2. Public corporations	169.00	0.73	...
B.3. Others (includes capital income, excludes FEFE)	245.58	1.06	...
C. Donations	**213.90**	**0.92**	**0.00**
TOTAL SPENDING OF THE NONFINANCIAL PUBLIC SECTOR	**5,126.80**	**22.16**	**13.88**
Interest on the debt	517.90	2.24	...
Primary spending (A + B + C + D)	**4,608.90**	**19.92**	**11.15**
A. Social spending (A.1 + A.2)	**1,989.06**	**8.60**	**8.43**
A.1. Direct transfers (in cash or goods)	317.16	1.37	1.36
A.1.1. Cash transfers	195.27	0.84	0.84
A.1.1.1 Rural Solidarity Partnership Communities	17.12	0.07	0.07
A.1.1.2 Temporary Income Support Program (PATI)	14.65	0.06	0.06
A.1.1.3 Direct subsidy to gas (in cash)	163.50	0.71	0.71
A.1.2. Non-contributory pensions (Universal Basic Pension)	7.10	0.03	0.03

TABLE 15-1   (continued)

Item	Amount (millions of US$)	% of GDP	
		Total	In analysis*
A.1.3. Other direct transfers (in goods)	114.79	0.50	0.49
A.1.3.1 School package	71.05	0.31	0.31
A.1.3.2 School lunch	15.30	0.07	0.07
A.1.3.3 Glass of milk	1.90	0.01	...
A.1.3.4 Agricultural package	26.54	0.11	0.11
A.2. Social services	1,671.90	7.23	7.08
A.2.1. Education	677.60	2.93	2.93
A.2.2. Health	991.70	4.29	4.15
A.2.2.1 Health—noncontributory (MINSAL)	532.70	2.30	2.30
A.2.2.2 Health—contributory (ISSS)	358.10	1.55	1.55
A.2.2.3 Health—contributory (Teachers' Well-being)	50.10	0.22	0.22
A.2.2.4 Health—contributory (Military Health Command, COSAM)	19.20	0.08	0.08
A.2.2.5 Health - others	31.60	0.14	...
A.2.3. Women's City	2.6	0.01	...
B. Indirect subsidies	**224.30**	**0.97**	**0.97**
B.1. Electricity	115.20	0.50	0.50
B.2 Water	56.50	0.24	0.24
B.3. Public transportation	52.60	0.23	0.23
C. Other spending	**1,989.94**	**8.60**	...
C.1. Administrative direction	460.40	1.99	...
C.2 Administration of justice and citizen security	625.60	2.70	...
C.3. Others	903.94	3.91	...
D. Contributory pensions	**405.60**	**1.75**	**1.75**
Deficit	−906.60	−3.92	...

Source: Prepared by the authors with information from the Ministry of the Treasury (Ministerio de Hacienda [MH]), Central Reserve Bank (Banco Central de Reserva [BCR]), and administrative data from the respective institutions.

* This column lists the categories that are included in the impact analysis.

... = Not applicable

purposes, of which the most important are those applied to fuel. Here is a description of the taxes and contributions considered in this analysis.

1.1.1 Income Tax

El Salvador has a progressive tax on personal income. Corporations are subject to a 25 percent tax rate on declared earnings up to US$150,000. Above that amount the rate is 30 percent.

In 2011, there were four levels for the personal income tax: exemption for income below US$2,514.30 and three levels with progressive rates of 10, 20, and 30 percent, respectively. Taxable income excluded alimony payments, compensation for death or disability, payments received for services abroad, rental income from the house of residence, and interest on investment funds abroad. Individuals with an annual income of less than US$5,714.29 could take a standard deduction of US$1,371.43. Those with high incomes could take this deduction only with evidence of expenditures for health or education.

As of 2012, with the tax reform that took effect that year, the annual income exemption was increased to US$4,064.00. Also, if an individual's income did not exceed US$9,100 for the year, they could take a standard deduction of US$1,600.00.

1.1.2 Value-Added Tax

VAT is collected for each transaction at the various stages of production for a taxed good or service, generating a tax credit to the next stage, so that finally the end user pays the tax. The VAT rate is 13 percent. Exported goods are not exempt from the law, but they have a 0 percent rate. Taxes paid for the production of export goods are reimbursed, with a few exceptions.

Corporations or individual vendors whose sales are less than US$5,714.29 per year, or US$476.19 per month, and have assets less than US$2,285.71 are not obliged to charge VAT to their clients. However, they are subject to the tax for the purchase of inputs. In other words, they are exempt from the VAT generated at the last link of the chain.

1.1.3 Special Fees: Fuel

Three different fees are applied to fuel consumption. In total, US$0.46 is collected for each gallon of gasoline, and US$0.30 for each gallon of diesel.

1. In 1981, the Economic Development and Stabilization Fund (Fondo de Estabilizacion y Fomento Economico [FEFE]) was established. Currently, the earnings are used to pay part of the subsidy for LPG. This fund's budget comes from a fee of US$0.16 collected for each gallon of gasoline purchased; diesel purchases are excluded. From July to December 2011, this fee was temporarily suspended to compensate for the high cost of gasoline. In 2011, the FEFE collected US$13.6 million.
2. In 2001, a compulsory contribution was established to generate funds for highway maintenance and repairs through the Highway Conservation Fund (Fondo de Conservacion Vial [FOVIAL]). The fee is US$0.20 per gallon of gasoline or diesel. In 2011, the amount collected was US$68.9 million.
3. In 2007, another fee was added to generate funds to pay the public transportation subsidy, the Special Contribution to Stabilize Public Transportation Fares (Contribucion Especial para la Estabilizacion de las Tarifas del Servicio de Transporte Colectivo de Pasajeros [COTRANS]). The fee is US$0.10 per gallon of gasoline or diesel. In 2011, the amount collected was US$33.9 million.

1.1.4 Contributions to Social Security (Health)

Contributions to the Salvadoran Social Security Institute (Instituto Salvadoreño del Seguro Social [ISSS]) cover the general health system and professional risks inherent in the specific work. Workers contribute 3 percent of their wages, while the employer contributes 7.5 percent. For both, the maximum taxable salary is US$685.70 per month. Contributions are deducted directly from the employee's pay.

1.2 Social Spending

In El Salvador, social spending falls into two main categories: (1) *direct transfers* to households, in cash or in-kind, either through *social programs* for specific population groups, which are currently part of the Universal Social Protection System, or through cash transfers, such as the subsidy for cooking gas; and (2) *social services* provided by the state, principally education and health services. In 2011, direct transfers represented 1.4 percent of GDP, and social services 7.2 percent of GDP. In that year, social spending was 8.6 percent of GDP.

Other public resources spent on household benefits include *indirect subsidies* and *pensions*, which represented 0.97 percent and 1.75 percent of GDP, respectively.

1.2.1 Social Programs

Social programs in El Salvador include direct cash transfers and transfers of goods. Some programs provide different services within the same infrastructure to facilitate access. Table 15-2 lists these programs, the number of beneficiaries, and the corresponding expenditure.

1.2.2 Cash Transfers

Rural Solidarity Communities (RSC)

This program was created in 2005 as the Solidarity Network that includes cash transfers based on public education and health services usage in households in the poorest hundred municipalities of the country, according to the Social Investment Fund for Local Development (Fondo de Inversion Social para el Desarrollo Local [FISDL], 2004). These municipalities account for about 12 percent of total of households nationwide.[6] Households are eligible if they meet the following criteria when the program starts in their community: for the education transfer, they were eligible if they had children between the ages of six and eighteen who had not completed primary school; for the health transfer, they were eligible if the household included a pregnant woman or any child aged zero to five. The education transfer is contingent upon enrollment

---

[6] According to the Census of Population and Housing (Censo de Poblacion y Vivienda, 2007), prepared by the Ministry of Economy (Ministerio de Economia [MINEC]) 2008.

TABLE 15-2
Social Programs

Program	Responsable institution	Year implemented	Beneficiaries			
			2008	2009	2010	2011
Cash transfers			**83,654**	**112,311**	**110,030**	**120,822**
Rural Solidarity partnership communities	FISDL	2005	83,654	105,824	98,378	90,997
Universal Basic Pension	FISDL	2009	0	6,487	8,019	15,300
PATI	FISDL	2010	0	0	3,633	14,525
Urban bonus	FISDL	2012	0	0	0	0
Veterans' pensions	FISDL	2012	0	0	0	0
Transfers of goods			**1,314,039**	**1,860,289**	**3,231,903**	**3,386,480**
School package	MINED	2010	0	0	1,377,113	1,386,767
School lunch programs	MINED	1992	877,041	1,310,286	1,316,779	1,334,044
Glass of milk	MINED/MAG	2011	0	0	0	246,072
Agricultural package	MAG	1997	436,998	550,003	538,011	419,597
Integrated services			**0**	**0**	**0**	**35,614**
Women's City	Secretaríat for Inclusion	2011	0	0	0	35,614

Source: Technical Secretariat of the Office of the President (2013, table 3, pp. 86–87) and (2014).

and school attendance to complete primary school. The health transfer is contingent upon monitoring the children's development, their timely vaccination, and prenatal care for pregnant women. The amount of the transfer is US$15 per month if the household is only eligible for either the education or health transfer and US$20 per month if it is eligible for both. The payments do not vary depending on the number of eligible children in the household and the amount has not changed since 2005.

In rural areas, all households in a municipality that met the eligibility requirements when the census was conducted by the implementing agency (FISDL) were registered in the program. In urban areas, all eligible households entered the program in municipalities with "severe" extreme poverty. However, in urban municipalities with "high" extreme poverty, a means test with proxy variables was applied to selected beneficiaries. It is important to note that the only way a household could get into the RSC program was to meet the requirements at the time the FISDL census was conducted in a given municipality. This means that if a household met the eligibility criteria *after* the program started in a community (for example, due to the birth of their first baby), that household was not eligible. For that reason, new families have not been incorporated,

	Beneficiaries		Expenditure, % PIB					
Program	2012	2013	2008	2009	2010	2011	2012	2013
Cash transfers	**141,370**	**133,998**	**0.05**	**0.09**	**0.11**	**0.17**	**0.17**	**0.19**
Rural Solidarity partnership communities	83,128	75,385	0.05	0.09	0.09	0.07	0.06	0.06
Universal Basic Pension	25,477	28,200	0.0	0.00	0.02	0.03	0.04	0.08
PATI	27,992	23,456	0.0	0.00	0.00	0.06	0.06	0.04
Urban bonus	2,691	4,837	0.0	0.00	0.00	0.00	0.003	0.01
Veterans' pensions	2,082	2,120	0.0	0.00	0.00	0.00	0.003	0.01
Transfers of goods	**3,701,173**	**4,109,649**	**0.19**	**0.21**	**0.58**	**0.50**	**0.49**	**0.51**
School package	1,386,767	1,299,358	0.0	0.00	0.36	0.31	0.30	0.30
School lunch programs	1,339,726	1,453,118	0.08	0.06	0.10	0.07	0.06	0.08
Glass of milk	499,819	821,036	0.0	0.00	0.00	0.01	0.01	0.02
Agricultural package	474,861	536,137	0.11	0.15	0.12	0.11	0.11	0.10
Integrated services	**82,874**	**315,000**	**0.0**	**0.00**	**0.00**	**0.01**	**0.09**	**0.05**
Women's City	82,874	315,000	0.0	0.00	0.00	0.01	0.09	0.05

and as a result, the number of beneficiaries has decreased as households leave the program (when the children complete primary school or reach the age of eighteen) or when they no longer meet the criteria.

In total there were 75,385 households benefiting from the program in 2013 (equal to about 5 percent of total households and about 14 percent of the poor households). These beneficiaries received approximately US$14.6 million that year. In 2011, the year analyzed for this study, there were 90,997 total household beneficiaries, and the average transfer per household was US$15.65 per month.

Universal Basic Pension

This noncontributory pension was established in 2009 for older adults in municipalities with "severe" and "high" extreme poverty. This is an unconditional transfer of US$50 per month given to anyone over the age of seventy who does not receive any other pension. There can be more than one beneficiary per household.

In 2013 there were 28,200 beneficiaries in the program (accounting for about 7 percent of all the senior adults in the country and 20 percent of those living in poverty). That year they received about US$18.8 million. In 2011, the year analyzed in this study, the total number of beneficiaries was 15,300.

FMLN Veterans' Pension

This is a program of noncontributory pensions that began in 2012 for ex-combatants consisting of a monthly pension of US$50 paid to about 2,000 veterans.[7]

Temporary Income Support Program (PATI)

PATI was designed to protect the income of vulnerable households that face adverse situations of various kinds by means of a monetary transfer of US$100 per month for six months in exchange for their participation in community projects and their attendance at eighty hours of training (sixty-four hours of technical training and sixteen hours on job hunting and skills to start a business). The amount of the transfer is less than half the minimum urban wage, so it is not a disincentive for beneficiaries to participate in the labor market. Beneficiaries can participate in it only once and for a maximum of six months. There is no limit on the number of beneficiaries in the same household.

PATI is implemented in informal urban settlements (Asentamientos Urbanos Precarios [AUP])[8] classified with levels of extreme or high poverty in the Urban Poverty Map (Mapa de Pobreza Urbana).[9] It has been implemented in thirty-seven municipalities: eleven that were ravaged by tropical storm Ida and twenty-six that have the highest number of persons living in AUP. The program is designed for youth ages sixteen to twenty-four, as well as female heads of household. However, since it is a program of self-selection, any person at least sixteen years old who lacks a formal job and is not studying during the day is eligible and can participate. In 2011, there were 14,525 participants.[10]

Urban Bonus

This program, which is designed to increase the demand for secondary education, was implemented in 2012. It consists of a cash transfer that covers part of school transportation costs and is contingent upon the individual's continued class attendance. The program seeks to include vulnerable groups. Therefore, the amount of the transfer is higher for women, adolescent mothers, and disabled students. In addition, it provides an incentive to attend technical schools. To encourage students to complete secondary education, the amount of the transfer increases as they progress; when students graduate, they get an additional bonus. In 2012 there were 2,691 beneficiaries.

---

[7] Technical Secretary of the Presidency (Secretaria Tecnica de la Presidencia [STP]), 2013.

[8] In English, Precarious Urban Settlements.

[9] Facultad Latinoamericana de Ciencias Sociales (FLACSO), Ministry of Economy (Ministerio de Economia [MINEC]), United Nations Development Program (UNDP) (2010).

[10] Secretaria Tecnica de la Presidencia (2014).

Liquid Petroleum Gas Subsidy

Liquid petroleum gas (LPG) Liquid Petrolum Gas, or cooking gas, has been subsidized for many years. Previously, to compensate for the difference between the market price and the fixed price, the government would transfer this difference in cost to distributors. All consumers, regardless of their income, could buy gas at the regulated price.

This system changed in 2011, when the subsidy began to be paid directly to the households. At that time, the price of a twenty-five-pound canister, which was US$5.10, increased to a market price calculated at US$14.70, and households began to receive a cash transfer of US$9.10, provided that they used less than 199 kWh of electricity per month. The transfer was given when the consumers paid their electric bill. Households without electric service had to register to receive a "subsidy card" that permitted them to receive the monthly cash transfer in offices located throughout the country. In December 2011 there were 1.2 million beneficiaries, or 80 percent of the total households in the country.

A different mechanism was implemented in the middle of 2013. Households had to register as beneficiaries using the head of household's sole identity document (Documento Unico de Identidad [DUI]). When consumers bought gas, they had to show their DUI and the vendor would then key in that information on a mobile device connected to the beneficiary system, resulting in a payment of US$9.10 toward the bill. The beneficiary had to pay only the difference. However, the number of beneficiaries remained at 1.2 million.[11]

Starting in January 2014, registered consumers received a subsidy card called the "Solidarity Card" (Tarjeta de Solidaridad), which they had to present when making a purchase, instead of their DUI. In March 2014, the amount of the subsidy varied with the real cost of the gas, so that the amount paid by the consumer would remain constant. The total amount that a household received in 2014 could be less than in previous years, because the subsidy is no longer a fixed amount of cash per month, but is applied at the time of purchase, which might not be made every month.

Part of the money used to fund this subsidy comes from the gasoline tax, though the amount collected is insufficient. For example, in 2011 the government transferred US$163.0 million to consumers, while the gasoline tax only collected US$18.6 million.

1.2.3 Direct Transfers In-Kind

School package

Since 2010 all students from preschool to ninth grade in the public schools receive two complete uniforms, a pair of shoes, and school supplies. The cost of the uniforms is about 60 percent of the total cost of the package. In 2011 there were 1,386,767 beneficiaries.

---

[11] Information from the Ministry of Economy (Ministerio de Economia [MINEC]).

School lunch program

This program, dating back more than twenty years, provides a meal to all students from preschool to sixth grade in rural public schools. The program was expanded to the ninth grade in 2008. Urban public schools have been included since the beginning of 2010.

"Glass of Milk" program

The Ministry of Agriculture and Livestock (Ministerio de Agricultura y Ganaderia [MAG]) buys milk from local producers, and the Ministry of Education (Ministerio de Educacion [MINED]) distributes a glass of milk twice a week to students from preschool to ninth grade in public schools in sixty-three municipalities in four departments: Ahuachapan, Santa Ana, Sonsonate, and La Libertad. In 2011, an estimated 250,000 students benefited. The program was expanded to other municipalities to benefit about 500,000 students in 2012 and more than 800,000 in 2013.

Agricultural packages

This subsidy includes the distribution, without cost, of seeds and fertilizer to producers of corn and beans who have less than 2.25 hectares of land. Each package includes twenty-five pounds of corn seed and one hundred pounds of fertilizer, enough to cultivate 0.7 hectares. In addition, some farmers receive twenty-five pounds of beans for seed, enough to cultivate 0.2 hectares. Those who receive beans generally also receive packages of corn. The content of the individual packages has been the same for the past five years.

Theoretically, all corn producers who cultivate small parcels are eligible to receive packages for this crop. For beans, the packages are given to the small producers in geographical areas selected as being best suited for bean production. It is estimated that all producers of corn or beans received packages in 2011. The lists of eligible beneficiaries have historically been compiled by extension agents, producers' organizations, and municipal authorities, although the farmers can also sign up directly. The number of recipients varies; in the case of corn, the number of beneficiaries doubled between 2007 and 2013, but prior to 2008, the number of bean producers who received the subsidy was insignificant.

1.3 Subsidies

In El Salvador, subsidies take the form of government assistance with consumer goods widely used by the population. The main goods include electricity, liquid petroleum gas, public transportation, and water service when it is provided by the public water supply agency (the National Administration of Aqueducts and Sewerage, Administracion Nacional de Acueductos y Alcantarillados [ANDA]). In total, these subsidies represent 1.7 percent of GDP and account for 19.5 percent of social spending.

1.3.1 Electricity

The state regulates the price of electricity to the consumer, and electric companies receive transfers from the state to cover any difference. The subsidy has two levels: one for households with monthly consumption of up to 99 kWh and the other for consumption between 99 and 200 kWh, funds for which come from earnings generated by the public electric company (Comision Ejecutiva del Rio Lempa, Lempa River Executive Hydroelectric Commission [CEL]). Between April and October 2011, up to 300 kWh were subsidized. During 2011, 80 percent of households received the subsidy: 60 percent at the level of lower consumption, which in total represented US$88.1 million, and 20 percent at the higher consumption level, which was US$27.1 million.

1.3.2 Water

Residential water service has an indirect and implicit subsidy through regulation of the price when the service is provided by the public entity ANDA. The rates per cubic meter increase as more water is consumed. However, in general, the amount collected from the official tariffs does not cover the cost of operation and maintenance, so there is an implicit subsidy for the consumer. ANDA serves only about half of the population. In 2011 the subsidy was US$56.2 million.

In rural areas and small urban zones, water service and sanitation are provided by local providers who receive a discount on their electric bill from the state electric company to subsidize the pumping and repumping of water. This way, their consumers also receive a subsidy, indirectly. In 2011 this subsidy was US$6.9 million.

1.3.3 Public Transportation

Public transportation is provided by private operators who receive permits from the Vice Ministry of Transportation (Viceministerio de Transporte [VMT]) for each of the established routes. The price of transportation is regulated. To compensate the operators, the government pays a fixed monthly amount for each vehicle that they operate regardless of the number of passengers served. This system was established in 2007 to compensate operators for the high prices of gasoline so they could continue to charge users the regulated fares. In 2007 the transfers were $400 per bus and $200 per minibus. In 2009, the amounts increased to $500 and $250, respectively. The amount was increased again in 2011, to $750 and $375, respectively. Finally, in 2013, the amounts reverted to the original $400 and $200.

1.4 Social Services: In-Kind Transfers

Transfers in-kind considered are related to the services provided by the state in two particular areas: education and health.

1.4.1 Education

El Salvador has the following educational levels: initial education (zero–three years); preschool (four–six years); basic education (seven–fifteen years) divided into primary (grades one to six, seven–twelve years) and third cycle (lower secondary, grades seven to nine, thirteen–fifteen years); middle education (sixteen–eighteen years) divided into general (grades ten and eleven) or technical-vocational (grades ten to twelve); and higher education, which includes university and nonuniversity. Basic education is compulsory; basic and middle education are free in public schools.

In 2011 there were 1.7 million students enrolled, excluding higher education. Of these, 87 percent were in the public sector. In basic education, nearly 90 percent of the students were in public schools. In preschool that percentage was about 84 percent, and in middle education it was 75 percent.

According to statistics from MINED (2011), the primary education net enrollment rate is higher than 92 percent. The other levels have greater problems with access. Net enrollment rates are 0.6 percent in initial education, 54 percent in preschool, 62 percent in lower secondary (third cycle), and 35.4 percent in upper secondary (middle education).

1.4.2 Health

El Salvador's public health system has a noncontributory component, with services provided by the Ministry of Health and Social Protection (Ministerio de Salud y Proteccion Social [MINSAL]), and a contributory component with services provided by three institutions: ISSS, which provides services to workers in the formal sector and employers; the Salvadoran Institute for Teachers' Well-Being (Instituto Salvadoreño de Bienestar Magisterial [ISBM]), which provides services to teachers in the public sector; and the Military Health Command (Comando de Sanidad Militar [COSAM]), which provides services to military personnel.

MINSAL covers all those not affiliated with public contributory programs or covered by private insurance, which is estimated to be 4.5 million persons, or 73 percent of the population. ISSS, ISBM, and COSAM cover 23 percent, 1.6 percent, and 1.2 percent, respectively, and includes affiliated workers, spouses, and children to a certain age.

The distribution of the budget among the public health institutions is not equal. In 2011, according to the National Health Accounts, the per capita budget available for the MINSAL[12] was US$118; for ISSS, US$242; for ISBM, US$484; and for COSAM, US$251.

1.4.3 Women's City

Women's City (Ciudad Mujer) is a program that provides women with health services, services related to domestic violence, legal services, labor training, and more, all within

---

[12] According to Ministry of Health and Social Protection (Ministerio de Salud y Proteccion Social [MINSAL]), 2013.

the same facility. This program began in 2011 with a facility in the municipality of Colon. During that first year it provided assistance to 35,614 women, with services valuing a total of US$2.6 million. In 2012 another facility was opened in Usulutan, and in 2013 three more were opened in San Miguel, Santa Ana, and San Martin, respectively. In 2013, the program benefited 82,874 women, with services valuing US$22 million. This program does not include any type of transfer in cash or goods.

1.4.4 Contributory Pensions

Before 1998, a joint contributory pension system with withholding, called the Public Pension System (Sistema Publico de Pensiones [SPP]), covered disability and old-age pensions. Starting in June of that year, a reform established a system of individual capitalization called the Pension Savings System (Sistema de Ahorro para Pensiones [SAP]) managed by private Pension Fund Administrator (Administradora de Fondos de Pensiones [AFP]). At that time, all men between the ages of thirty-six and fifty-five and all women between thirty-six and fifty could opt to remain in the old system or change to the new one. These workers were given a guarantee that their pensions would be similar to those that they could have obtained in the public sector. All workers under age thirty-six were transferred to the SAP, while workers above the given age bracket had to remain in the SPP. With SAP, all contributions go directly to the individual's account.

Currently, pensions are for workers who remained in the SPP or opted for SAP. Public system pensions are fully funded by the government. Other workers' pensions come in part from their contributions to SAP and in part from government funds. Upon retirement, the government transfers a matching amount to an individual's AFP. In both systems, the pensions cannot be less than US$207.60. The government may transfer an additional amount to the AFP to guarantee the minimum pension (known as a "complementary transfer certificate [Certificado de Traspaso Complementario, or CTC])"

During 2011, about 101,000 people received pensions from SPP and 42,000 from SAP. That year the government issued bonds equivalent to US$405.6 million[13] to pay benefits; this included pensions paid directly to beneficiaries of SPP and the Transfer Certificate (Certificado de Traspaso [CT]) and CTC transferred to SAP. Public spending for pensions was 1.75 percent of GDP.

2 Data

The analysis in this study uses the results of the 2011 Multi-Purpose Household Survey (EHPM), carried out by the Ministry of the Economy (Ministerio de Economia [MINEC]). The EHPM was conducted from January to December, with a sample of

---

[13] Information from the Development Bank of El Salvador (Banco de Desarrollo de El Salvador [BANDESAL]), 2012.

21,413 households. These households were representative at various levels: country-wide, urban, rural, within the metropolitan area of San Salvador (Area Metropolitana de San Salvador [AMSS]), the departmental level, as well as within the fifty largest municipalities. The survey compiled information on each member of the household, altogether 85,291 individuals. For the 77,929 individuals five years of age or older, detailed information was collected on their workforce participation, consumption, and pensions. Additionally, data was collected regarding usage of education and health services, as was information from each household on income from a variety of sources, such as remittances. In addition, the survey included a detailed module on household consumption. Before 2011, the survey did not take into direct account the value of cash transfers from the government such as the LPG subsidy, the payments of RSCs, and noncontributory pensions. Additional information comes from official budget reports of various agencies.

3 Methodology

The impact analysis is based on CEQ methodology presented in the previous chapters in this Volume of the handbook. This method basically consists of generating concepts of income that include taxes and transfers to create a menu of indicators that measure the progressivity of the system of taxes and transfers and its impact on inequality and poverty in a quantifiable manner (without considering changes in the behavior of the stakeholders or the effects of general balance). Next we present an explanation of how each component was constructed for El Salvador.

3.1 Market Income

All necessary components to estimate Market Income can be calculated using *direct identification methods* with information included in the EHPM. The survey has sufficient detail to permit estimation of the individual components of income: pretax gross labor income (formal or informal), self-consumption, capital income, and imputed rent for owner-occupied housing. Private transfers (including remittances and others), gifts, and contributory pensions can be identified directly; the survey reports the dollar amount for each individual. In the sensitivity analysis, pensions from the contributory system are excluded from Market Income and are treated as government transfers.

3.2 Disposable Income

Disposable income is equal to Market Income less direct taxes on personal income from all taxable sources (including Market Income) and all contributions to social security, except for the portion earmarked for old-age pensions. Using information included in the EHPM, taxes and direct contributions can be estimated using imputation methods.

Direct taxes paid are not reported directly to the EHPM. Given that income tax is paid mainly by formal workers,[14] the amount of the tax was estimated taking into account the gross monthly salary reported by formal workers as a baseline and then applying the rules and rates determined by the income tax law. However, income taxes paid by nonsalaried workers could not be identified using the EHPM, so they are not included in the analysis.

Contributions to health systems are also not reported directly in the EHPM. However, the survey does include information on the health system to which the worker belongs. Contributions were thus estimated by taking the gross monthly salary reported and applying the official rates.

Currently, since most contributions to pension funds in El Salvador go to individual workers' accounts[15] they are considered savings, and therefore are not deducted in the sensitivity analysis.

Plus all direct government transfers in cash or in-kind. In the sensitivity analysis, contributory pensions are included. The EHPM has questions on the types of benefits received from social programs, so it is possible to estimate direct transfers using imputation methods.

Direct cash transfers depend on:

- If the household reported receiving conditioned payments (RSCs), US$15 or US$20 per month was assigned to the household based on the rules of the program.
- If the household reported receiving noncontributory pensions, US$50 per month was assigned to eligible adults.
- If the household reported receiving PATI benefits, US$100 per month was assigned for a period of six months.
- If the household reported receiving LPG subsidy, US$9.10 per month was assigned to the household.

Direct transfers of goods are considered as follows:

- The EHPM reports whether each individual attends school, his or her level of education, and the type of institution attended (public or private). Each public school student from preschool to ninth grade receives a school package and a meal. The annual cost per capita of both programs for each student was assigned to the household: for uniforms and supplies, the figure was US$50.77 for preschool and US$53.26 for the rest, and for the lunches US$11.40 was assigned for all.

---

[14] The survey has a question that makes it possible to determine whether employees are formal or informal.

[15] In 2011, the SAP covered 602,382 persons, while the SPP had only 14,788. Information gathered in the EHPM does not identify to which of the two systems the worker belongs.

- The EHPM asks questions about agricultural activities. If a household meets the eligibility requirements, the average cost of the corresponding package is added: US\$64.50 for corn and US\$48.50 for beans.[16] The EHPM does not have enough information to determine whether the students in the household benefit from the "Glass of Milk" program, so this was not included in the analysis; its budget is very small.

3.3 Consumable Income

Consumable income is Disposable Income plus the indirect subsidies received, less indirect taxes and contributions paid.

Regarding indirect subsidies, the EHPM contains questions on the amount spent for each of the subsidized services, so indirect subsidies can be estimated using imputation methods.

- The electricity subsidy was imputed estimating the kWh used based on the expenditure reported, using the rates current at the time of the survey. The subsidy received is estimated as the difference between the real amount paid and the total of the nonsubsidized amount.[17]
- The water subsidy was imputed using the household expenditure reported by households that receive service from ANDA, the public provider. Cubic meters used were estimated based on reported spending using the rate schedule, and then the real cost per cubic meter was applied to estimate the nonsubsidized cost. The estimated subsidy received is the difference between the actual amount paid and the nonsubsidized amount.[18]
- The public transportation subsidy was imputed using the reported household spending for public transportation; the number of trips was estimated based on the ex-

---

[16] Information from the Ministry of Agriculture and Livestock (MAG).

[17] The rules for the subsidy for 2011 were as follows: each quarter a rate sheet was established and remained in force for three months. Households that used less than 99 kWh paid fixed tariffs for electricity, and the subsidy they received was the difference between the rate sheet in force (full rate) and the fixed rate. Households that used more than 99 kWh paid the full rate during the first quarter of the year, so they did not receive a subsidy. In the second and third quarters, households that used between 99 kWh and 300 kWh paid the rate in effect during the first quarter, receiving a subsidy for the difference between the full rate and the rate that they had during the previous quarter; in the fourth quarter, the maximum amount subsidized was reduced to 200 kWh. All these aspects were taken into account for the imputation, using the amount of the bill paid and the date when the household survey was conducted.

[18] Similarly, the amount reported as paid in the survey was used to estimate the quantity of cubic meters consumed, based on the rate sheet in effect at the time of the survey. The subsidy was the difference between the amount paid and the cost per cubic meter of water reported by ANDA.

penditure reported. The subsidy was calculated by multiplying the estimated number of trips by US$0.09 outside the AMSS and by US$0.092 inside it.[19]

Greater detail about these subsidies can be found in the appendix.

Indirect taxes and contributions are also estimated using imputation methods:

- VAT: The EHPM has detailed information on consumption, including place of purchase. Using this, total consumption subject to VAT was estimated (omitting exempt articles and food purchases in informal establishments[20]). Then the amount of VAT was imputed multiplying the "effective rate" by Disposable Income, according to the CEQ manual.[21]
  - Special contribution fees, fuel: Fees applied to fuel consumption were imputed estimating the number of gallons consumed based on the reported spending, using the average fuel price in the month of the survey. To calculate the taxes and contributions, the number of gallons was multiplied by US$0.46.[22]

3.4 Final Income

Final income is Consumable Income plus the monetary value of social services provided by the state. With information included in the EHPM, these in-kind transfers can be estimated using imputation methods.

For education, the EHPM reports whether an individual attends school, the level of education, and the type of institution (public or private). The amount of the benefit is estimated as an average annual cost per student if he or she attends public school: US$314.50 at the preschool level, US$416.70 during basic education (first to ninth grade), US$567.70 in middle education, and US$788.60 in tertiary education.

---

[19] In 2011, the public transportation subsidy was US$750 for each bus and US$375 for each minibus. On average, each bus has sixty seats and each minibus has twenty-five. On average, a seat on a bus has a daily subsidy of US$0.5, and a seat on a minibus has a daily subsidy of US$0.41. A study done by the Vice Ministry of Transportation (Viceministerio de Transporte [VMT], 2010) found that on average each bus makes 4.6 trips per day and each minibus 5.4 trips. As a result, the subsidy per bus seat is estimated at US$0.0905 per trip, and the subsidy per minibus seat is US$0.0925 per trip. The same study found that in the metropolitan area 60 percent of the public transportation units are minibuses. By contrast, outside the metropolitan area 80 percent are buses. Based on the foregoing, the weighted amount of the subsidy in the metropolitan area was estimated at US$0.09178, and in other areas it was US$0.0909.

[20] Informal establishments include dining hall, chalet, itinerant cart, and informal store.

[21] Lustig and Higgins (2013).

[22] Including the following contributions: FOVIAL (US$0.20), FEFE (US$0.16), COTRANS (US$0.10). The FEFE does not apply to diesel consumption, but the EHPM does not specify the type of fuel used. In practice, most vehicles for domestic use are gasoline-powered.

For public health, the EHPM has information on the type of contributory health system to which the household has access (ISSS, ISBM, or COSAM). It is assumed that everybody without access to contributory health systems or private health insurance uses public health services. For each individual in the household, the average cost per patient per type of provider is imputed[23]: US$117 for public health, US$242 for ISSS, US$484 for Teachers' Well-Being, and US$251 for COSAM.[24]

For Women's City, the EHPM does not have sufficient information to determine if a woman in the household is a beneficiary in this program, so it is not included in the analysis. In 2011, this program's budget was very small.

4 Impact of Fiscal Policy on Inequality and Poverty

As shown in table 15-3, direct taxes and transfers have an equalizing effect of 0.0156 Gini points. The combined effect of indirect taxes net of indirect subsidies is equalizing. Adding the impact of transfers in kind (public spending on education and health), the Gini coefficient is reduced by 0.0455 points. With respect to poverty reduction, fiscal policy has achieved very little, in both rural and urban areas. Table 15-3 shows that direct transfers reduce the incidence of poverty measured with Disposable Income (and compared with the incidence measured with Market Income plus Pensions) using any of the national and international poverty lines. However, this effect is almost null when considering indirect taxes net of subsidies.[25] In other words, the incidence of poverty with Consumable Income is practically equal to the one that prevails with Market Income, at both national and international extreme poverty lines. In the case of moderate poverty, measured with either the international or national poverty lines, the incidence of poverty for Consumable Income is higher than for Market Income. In other words, fiscal policy results in a greater proportion of individuals being below the moderate poverty lines.[26] The poverty gap remains almost unchanged. However, the squared poverty gap declines, so at least the poorest individuals are less poor even after the effect of net indirect taxes. It should be noted, though, that this last indicator can

---

[23] According to National Health Accounts registered in Ministry of Health and Social Protection (Ministerio de Salud y Proteccion Social [MINSAL]), 2013.

[24] The imputation of average costs does not include in the analysis the differences in access to health services that may apply to individuals with different income levels, owing to factors such as the institutional organization or personal decision. That analysis was not possible because the information reported by the survey was insufficient.

[25] All differences with respect to incidence measured with Market Income are statistically significant.

[26] With the poverty gap or the poverty gap squared index this does not occur: both indicators decrease slightly. This means that although fiscal policy can increase the proportion of poor when taking into account the effect of net indirect taxes, at least the poorest in these groups experience some improvement (something already registered with the incidence measured with the extreme poverty lines).

TABLE 15-3

Impact of Fiscal Policy on Inequality and Poverty (contributory pensions as deferred income)

	Level	Market plus pensions	Disposable	Consumable	Final	Change (from market to disposable)	Change (from market to consumable)	Change (from market to final)
Gini	National	0.4396	0.424	0.4197	0.3941	−0.0156	−0.0199	−0.0455
	Rural	0.3991	0.382	0.3786	0.3453	−0.0171	−0.0205	−0.0538
	Urban	0.4171	0.4042	0.3984	0.3773	−0.0129	−0.0187	−0.0398
Poverty headcount ratio			**In percent**				**Changes in percent**	
Poverty US$2.5 PPP	National	19.2	17.3	19.1	...	−10.1	−0.8	...
	Rural	34.8	32.0	34.9	...	−8.2	0.3	...
	Urban	9.8	8.4	9.5	...	−14.3	−3.0	...
Poverty US$4 PPP	National	39.3	38.3	40.8	...	−2.7	3.8	...
	Rural	60.1	58.7	62.0	...	−2.2	3.2	...
	Urban	8.5	7.1	7.8	...	−16	−7.9	...
Extreme poverty National line*	National	11.6	9.6	10.8	...	−17.4	−7.0	...
	Rural	16.9	13.7	15.8	...	−18.7	−6.3	...
	Urban	8.5	7.1	7.8	...	−16	−7.9	...
Moderate poverty National line*	National	40.5	39.3	42.6	...	−2.9	5.2	...
	Rural	49.0	46.6	50.9	...	−4.9	3.9	...
	Urban	35.3	34.9	37.5	...	−1.2	6.3	...
Poverty gap								
Poverty US$2.5 PPP	National	6.2	5.0	5.7	...	−18.5	−7.3	...
	Rural	12.3	10.1	11.6	...	−17.9	−6.1	...
	Urban	2.4	1.9	2.2	...	−20.5	−11.1	...

(continued)

TABLE 15-3 (continued)

	Level	Market plus pensions	Disposable	Consumable	Final	Change (from market to disposable)	Change (from market to consumable)	Change (from market to final)
Poverty US$4 PPP	National	14.9	13.7	15.0	...	−8.5	0.2	...
	Rural	25.8	23.6	25.8	...	−8.5	0.2	...
	Urban	8.4	7.6	8.4	...	−8.7	0.1	...
Extreme poverty National line*	National	3.2	2.3	2.7	...	−28.7	−16.2	...
	Rural	5.1	3.4	4.2	...	−32.8	−18.2	...
	Urban	2.1	1.6	1.8	...	−22.0	−12.7	...
Moderate poverty National line*	National	14.6	13.3	14.7	...	−8.9	0.3	...
	Rural	19.3	17.0	19.0	...	−11.8	−1.6	...
	Urban	11.8	11.1	12.1	...	−6	2.1	...
Poverty gap squared								
Poverty US$2.5 PPP	National	2.9	2.1	2.5	...	−26.3	−13.7	...
	Rural	6.0	4.5	5.3	...	−26	−12.6	...
	Urban	0.9	0.7	0.8	...	−26.9	−17.2	...
Poverty US$4 PPP	National	7.9	6.6	7.4	...	−15.8	−6	...
	Rural	14.3	12.3	13.8	...	−13.8	−3.4	...
	Urban	3.7	3.2	3.5	...	−13.6	−4.4	...
Extreme poverty National line*	National	1.3	0.8	1.0	...	−38.2	−25.2	...
	Rural	2.2	1.3	1.6	...	−43.2	−28.2	...
	Urban	0.8	0.5	0.6	...	−29.9	−19.5	...
Moderate poverty National line*	National	7.2	6.2	6.9	...	−14.5	−4.1	...
	Rural	10.1	8.3	9.5	...	−18.3	−6.7	...
	Urban	5.5	4.9	5.4	...	−10.4	−1.6	...

Source: CEQ Master Workbook for El Salvador, July 10, 2015, based on data from the Multi-Purpose Household Survey (2011)

Note: All changes with respect to market income are statistically significant. For inequality, changes are in Gini points, while for poverty they are changes in percent.

*The moderate poverty line is twice the amount of the extreme poverty line; the latter is equivalent to the market value of the basic food basket. In local currency, the extreme poverty line is equal to $49 and $33.90 per month for urban and rural areas, respectively, and the moderate poverty line is equal to $98.20 and $67.90 for urban and rural areas, respectively. The local currency value of the PPP lines is $51.10 per month for US$2.50 a day and $83.10 per month for the US$4 a day.

lead to unwarranted complacency because starting with the second poorest decile, the population is a net payer, meaning it pays more in direct and indirect taxes than it receives in direct transfers. Furthermore, using the fiscal impoverishment indicators developed by Higgins and Lustig (2016) (reproduced in chapter 4 of this Volume), even with the ultra-poverty line of US$1.25/day in 2005 PPP, close to 30 percent of the poor population was made poorer by taxes net of cash transfers and subsidies. Table 15-4 shows the same indicators but for the scenario in which contributory pensions are treated as pure government transfers; in table 15-3, pensions are treated as pure deferred income.

4.1 Coverage and Leakages

Why does fiscal policy have practically no effect on the incidence of poverty? To answer this question, it is important to analyze the targeting effectiveness of direct transfers. Table 15-5 presents several relevant indicators.[27] The vertical efficiency indicator measures the percentage of spending on direct transfers that goes to the poor population for different poverty lines. As seen in table 15-5, the percentage channeled toward the population in extreme poverty under international and national lines is between 25 and 16 percent, respectively. For the total poor population (extreme and moderate), the resources allocated are between 47 percent and 49 percent, respectively.

The spillover amount measures the percentage destined for the poor population in excess of what would be needed to bring it to the income of the corresponding poverty line. This number is quite small, which means that the average size of the benefits received is not excessive.

The efficiency indicator for the poverty gap shows the percentage of the total gap that is covered with direct transfers. As can be seen, the extreme poverty gap is closed by only roughly 20 percent. In part this is because resources are not concentrated on the poorest, as noted in the indicator on vertical efficiency. However, as table 15-6 shows, this is not because money is being spent on the middle or upper class. An important share of benefits from direct transfers goes to households with income of between US$4 and US$10 PPP, or what has come to be known as the "vulnerable groups."[28] This is important because it means that improving the targeting of cash transfers to the poor could be at the expense of increasing the vulnerability of groups that are only slightly above the poverty line.

In addition, as can be seen in table 15-6, of the total number of people receiving direct transfers, only 26.6 percent are individuals with income below the extreme poverty line of US$2.50 PPP. For example, of the beneficiaries of RSCs and PATI, 50.9 percent have income below the international extreme poverty line of US$2.50. The same holds true with beneficiaries of the rest of the programs, which cover 29.4 percent. Only 12.5 percent of the beneficiaries of indirect subsidies are among the extreme poor.

---

[27] Beckerman (1979).

[28] Lopez-Calva and Ortiz-Juarez (2011); Ferreira and others (2012).

TABLE 15-4
Impact of Fiscal Policy on Inequality and Poverty (contributory pensions as government transfers)

	Level	Market	Disposable	Consumable	Final	Change (from market to disposable)	Change (from market to consumable)	Change (from market to final)
Gini	National	0.4369	0.424	0.4197	0.3941	-0.0129	-0.0172	-0.0428
	Rural	0.3992	0.382	0.3786	0.3453	-0.0172	-0.0206	-0.0539
	Urban	0.416	0.4042	0.3984	0.3773	-0.0118	-0.0176	-0.0387
Poverty headcount ratio			In percent				Changes in percent	
Poverty US$2.5 PPP	National	20.2	17.3	19.1	...	-14.3	-5.4	...
	Rural	35.3	32.0	34.9	...	-9.4	-1.0	...
	Urban	11.0	8.4	9.5	...	-23.9	-14.0	...
Poverty US$4 PPP	National	40.4	38.3	40.8	...	-5.2	1.1	...
	Rural	60.5	58.7	62.0	...	-2.9	2.5	...
	Urban	28.2	25.9	28.0	...	-8.1	-0.6	...
Extreme poverty National line	National	12.5	9.6	10.8	...	-23.2	-13.6	...
	Rural	17.4	13.7	15.8	...	-20.9	-8.9	...
	Urban	9.6	7.1	7.8	...	-26.0	-18.9	...
Relative poverty National line*	National	41.6	39.3	42.6	...	-5.5	2.4	...
	Rural	49.4	46.6	50.9	...	-5.6	3.1	...
	Urban	36.8	34.9	37.5	...	-5.3	1.8	...

Source: CEQ Master Workbook for El Salvador, July 10, 2015, based on data from the Multi-Purpose Household Survey (2011)

Note: All changes with respect to market income are statistically significant. For inequality, changes are in Gini points while for poverty they are changes in percent.

*The moderate poverty line is twice the amount of the extreme poverty line; the latter is equivalent to the market value of the basic food basket. In local currency, the extreme poverty line is equal to $49 and $33.90 per month for urban and rural areas, respectively, and the moderate poverty line is equal to $98.20 and $67.90 for urban and rural areas, respectively. The local currency value of the PPP lines is $51.10 per month for the US$2.50 a day and $83.10 per month for the US$4 a day.

. . . = Not applicable

TABLE 15-5

Direct Transfers, Efficiency, and Efficacy in Poverty Reduction, El Salvador 2011

	Headcount poverty effictiveness indicators	Vertical Expenditure Efficiency (VEE)	Spillover (s)	Poverty Reduction Efficiency (PRE)	Poverty Gap Efficiency (PGE)
Benchmark: Contributory pensions as part of market income					
US$ 2.5 PP	1.784	0.252	0.084	0.231	0.204
US$ 4 PP	1.248	0.473	0.030	0.459	0.105
Extreme National Poverty Line	1.733	0.165	0.146	0.141	0.303
Moderate national Poverty line	1.577	0.491	0.038	0.018	0.004
Sensitivity analysis: Pensions are treated as government transfer					
US$ 2.5 PP	1.082	0.218	0.423	0.126	0.256
US$ 4 PP	0.877	0.361	0.277	0.261	0.141
Extreme National Poverty Line	1.063	0.175	0.510	0.086	0.374
Moderate national Poverty line	1.051	0.399	0.257	0.058	0.030

Source: CEQ Master Workbook for El Salvador, May 12, 2015, prepared by the authors based on data from the Multi-Purpose Household Survey (2011)

Although the subsidies partially offset the effect of indirect taxes, their impact is limited for reducing consumable poverty (table 15-6).

As shown in table 15-7, coverage for some of the programs is also rather low among the extreme and moderate poor.

5 Conclusions

Fiscal policy affects inequality and poverty, but its impact is limited. When compared with other countries inside and outside the region, El Salvador has a medium- to small-size government. However, in comparing the results with those of economies with a similar level of per capita income in purchasing power, the reduction in poverty and inequality is relatively small. There is room for greater influence and to increase the incidence with current resources. In this regard, the results on poverty and inequality could be made stronger by reorienting funds from other public spending items or from transfers and subsidies that go to higher income households and channeling them toward social spending. At the same time, the effectiveness and efficiency of the programs and direct transfers should be increased to ensure better focus.

TABLE 15-6

Distribution of Benefits and Beneficiaries by Income Group

El Salvador (2011)	Share of benefits by income group (%)						
	y < 2.5	2.5 < y < 4	y < 4	4 < y < 10	10 < y < 50	y > 50	Total
Direct transfers	**24.7**	22.0	**46.7**	40.0	13.2	0.1	100.0
Rural Solidarity Partnership Communities and PATI	**48.3**	23.2	**71.5**	25.2	3.3	0.0	100.0
Non-contributory pensions (older adults)	**42.4**	19.6	**62.0**	20.9	17.1	0.0	100.0
Gas subsidy (cash)	**12.1**	17.5	**29.5**	47.4	22.8	0.2	100.0
Remaining direct transfers*	**30.3**	25.7	**56.1**	37.3	6.7	0.0	100.0
Indirect subsidies (transportation, electricity, and water)	**8.2**	13.4	**21.7**	44.4	32.6	1.3	100.0
Transportation	**4.4**	10.1	**14.5**	46.4	37.8	1.3	100.0
Electricity	**13.7**	18.7	**32.5**	45.6	21.6	0.4	100.0
Water	**4.4**	10.1	**14.5**	46.4	37.8	1.3	100.0
In-kind transfers	**19.2**	20.4	**39.6**	42.7	17.4	0.2	100.0
Education (total)	**23.9**	23.7	**47.6**	41.8	10.5	0.0	100.0
Preschool Education	**26.7**	25.0	**51.8**	40.3	8.0	0.0	100.0
Basic Education	**28.1**	26.1	**54.2**	38.8	7.0	0.0	100.0
Middle Education	**14.5**	20.7	**35.2**	50.9	13.9	0.0	100.0
Tertiary Education	**1.5**	6.1	**7.7**	53.6	38.7	0.1	100.0
Health (total)	**15.8**	18.0	**33.8**	43.4	22.4	0.4	100.0
Contributory pensions	**1.0**	4.1	**5.1**	25.2	62.1	7.7	100.0
Income	**4.7**	9.4	**14.1**	38.8	43.5	3.6	100.0
Population	**19.2**	20.1	**39.3**	42.5	17.8	0.3	100.0

Source: CEQ Master Workbook for El Salvador May, 12, 2015 based on data from the Multi-Purpose Household Survey (2011).

* Includes the Agricultural Package, School Package, and School Lunch Program.

El Salvador redistributes slightly less than the general trend in countries with the same purchasing power of per capita income. Together transfers and direct taxes reduce inequality by 1 percentage point. When the effect of indirect subsidies and taxes on consumption is added, the result is slightly more equalizing. Finally, factoring in the impact of public spending on education and health, the Gini coefficient is reduced by 3.6 percent. This means the country redistributes slightly less than the trend line predicts for a country with similar gross per capita income, measured in PPP.

	Share of beneficiaries by income group (%)					
y<2.5	2.5<y<4	y<4	4<y<10	10<y<50	y>50	Total
26.6	24.0	50.6	40.0	9.4	0.0	100.0
50.9	23.2	74.1	23.2	2.7	0.0	100.0
44.0	21.2	65.2	19.6	15.2	0.0	100.0
15.7	20.6	36.3	46.8	16.8	0.1	100.0
29.4	25.4	54.8	38.3	6.8	0.0	100.0
12.5	18.3	30.8	47.5	21.4	0.3	100.0
9.2	17.9	27.0	50.2	22.4	0.4	100.0
17.8	20.9	38.8	44.8	16.3	0.1	100.0
6.6	13.3	19.9	49.0	30.5	0.6	100.0
19.1	21.0	40.1	43.8	16.0	0.2	100.0
24.4	24.3	48.7	42.2	9.0	0.0	100.0
30.4	25.3	55.6	37.9	6.5	0.0	100.0
26.6	25.8	52.4	40.4	7.2	0.0	100.0
16.4	22.3	38.8	49.6	11.6	0.0	100.0
2.1	7.7	9.8	57.1	33.1	0.0	100.0
15.7	18.9	34.6	44.7	20.3	0.3	100.0
4.7	11.0	15.7	42.1	41.0	1.2	100.0
4.7	9.4	14.1	38.8	43.5	3.6	100.0
19.2	20.1	39.3	42.5	17.8	0.3	100.0

In general, on the income side, direct taxes on individuals and contributions to social security for health are progressive. Indirect taxes as a whole are neutral from the distributive perspective. On the spending side, direct transfers—taking into consideration the social programs evaluated, such as RSCs, Universal Basic Pension, PATI, the School Package, the School Lunch Program, and the Agricultural Packet—are progressive in absolute terms. This means the amount per individual decreases with income. However, spending on these programs is small, amounting to 1.3 percent of primary spending and 0.3 percent of GDP.

TABLE 15-7
Percent of Beneficiaries in Each Income Group

El Salvador (2011)	Percent of beneficiaries in each income group (%)					
	y < 2.5	2.5 < y < 4	y < 4	4 < y < 10	10 < y < 50	y > 50
Rural Solidarity Partnership Communities and PATI	18.2	7.9	12.9	3.7	1.0	0.0
Non-contributory pensions (older adults)	1.0	0.5	0.7	0.2	0.4	0.0
Gas subsidy (cash)	42.3	53.1	47.9	57.0	48.7	14.2
Remaining direct transfers*	85.2	76.8	80.9	57.9	25.8	2.8
Transportation	27.7	51.6	39.9	68.5	72.9	64.7
Electricity	73.7	82.6	78.2	83.6	72.7	32.7
Water	13.1	25.3	19.4	44.1	65.3	70.6
Preschool Education	74.2	79.2	76.4	72.2	52.5	0.0
Basic Education	95.6	93.7	94.6	85.6	54.4	44.6
Middle Education	27.6	40.9	34.0	46.7	38.1	0.0
Tertiary Education	1.3	4.2	2.8	14.4	26.0	2.7
Contributory pensions	1.4	3.1	2.2	5.5	12.8	20.2
Population	19.2	20.1	39.3	42.5	17.8	0.3

Source: CEQ Master Workbook for El Salvador May, 12, 2015, based on data from the Multi-Purpose Household Survey (2011).

Note: Except for education, coverage for each income group here is defined as the total number of individuals from that group who live in households where there is at least one beneficiary divided by the total population in that same group. In case of education, for each income group and school level, coverage refers to the total number of individuals living in households where at least one child is enrolled in that school level regardless of her age, divided by the population living in households for that income group where at least one child has the corresponding school age for that particular school level.

* Includes the Agricultural Package, School Package, and School Lunch Program.

Subsidies are progressive in relative terms, due in mainly to the electricity and gas subsidies. However, the water subsidy, up to the fifth decile, or for the half of the population that has lower income, is regressive, as is the public transportation subsidy. However, the latter finding must be taken with caution due to the concentration of beneficiaries in urban areas where the cost of living is higher.

With respect to health, the amount assigned is progressive only in relative terms. Noncontributory public health spending is progressive in absolute terms. With regard to education, basic and preschool education are progressive in absolute terms, while middle education is neutral in absolute terms. In other words, all receive about the same amount per pupil. Tertiary education is neutral in relative terms, and its percentage of incidence is low.

Fiscal policy has little impact on poverty reduction. Although the direct transfers are properly focused, their coverage among the poorest is low, and they represent only a small percentage of primary spending. In this regard, including the effect of indirect taxes net of subsidies, extreme poverty is practically equal while total poverty is increasing, when compared with what is obtained from Market Income using both international and national poverty lines.

Despite the limited effect observed in the reduction of extreme poverty measured with after-tax income, the country comes out fairly well when comparing the results of other economies in the region that used the same methodology. For example, poverty increased in other countries, including one country with considerably more income per capita, Brazil, while remaining practically the same in El Salvador.

A significant part of the benefits of direct transfers reaches households with income between US$4 and US$10 per day in PPP, the so-called vulnerable groups. However, the main cause of the low impact of direct transfers on poverty reduction is the relatively low coverage. This is due to the limited percentage of beneficiaries with income below the international poverty line of US$2.5 per day in PPP; only 26.6 percent receive some direct transfer.

6 Recommendations

Expand the beneficiaries and coverage of targeted social programs that have proved effective. As has been noted, the weak impact on poverty reduction is due to the nature of direct transfers which, although concentrated, do not have wide coverage among the poorest.

Improve subsidy targeting to reorient resources to the poorest. Although subsidies are progressive in relative terms, they have limited impact on the reduction of poverty and inequality owing to the fact that a major portion of the subsidies goes to people who are not poor. Therefore, it is possible to improve the outcome by reorienting resources to programs that reach lower-income households. For example, since the electricity subsidies for households using more than 99 kWh represent a low percentage of the income they receive, meaning their relative incidence is low, a consideration could be eliminating this subsidy to those consumers with high incomes and diverting it to social spending, such as expanding education coverage.

Improve the coverage and quality of health services provided by the Ministry of Health, as well as education coverage for preschool and middle education levels, especially for the poorest. Due to the large public social spending budget for health and education services, these services have a strong effect on reducing inequality. Therefore, improving their coverage and quality, especially amongst the poorest, would improve the impact of fiscal policy on this population. For example, increasing the supply of preschool and middle education, which are the levels with the lowest net enrollment rates, and increasing resources for noncontributory health services, would have a greater impact on the reduction of inequality.

Acknowledgments

The authors are grateful for the research assistance received from Sean Higgins, Nicole Florack, and Yang Wang.

References

Acevedo, Carlos, and Mauricio Gonzalez Orellana. 2003. "El Salvador: Diagnostico del sistema tributario y recomendaciones de politica para incrementar la recaudacion." Serie de Estudios Economicos y Sectoriales. Region II (Washington: Inter-American Development Bank).

Barreix Alberto, Bes Martin, and Jeronimo Roca. 2009. "Equidad fiscal en Centroamerica, Panama y Republica Dominicana" (Washington: Inter-American Development Bank).

Beckerman, Wilfred. 1979. "The Impact of Income Maintenance Payments on Poverty in Britain, 1975." *Economic Journal* 89, no. 354, pp. 261–79.

Central American Institute of Fiscal Studies (Instituto Centroamericano de Estudios Fiscales [ICEFI]). 2009. "Analisis de incidencia fiscal de la politica fiscal en 2006" (Guatemala).

Cubero, Rodrigo, and Ivanna Vladkova Hollar. 2010. "Equity and Fiscal Policy: The Income Distribution Effects of Taxation and Social Spending in Central America." IMF Working Paper (Washington: International Monetary Fund).

Development Bank of El Salvador (Banco de Desarrollo de El Salvador [BANDESAL]). 2012. "Informe Operativo Anual Fideicomiso de Obligaciones Previsionales" (San Salvador).

Duclos, Jean-Yves, and Adbelfrim Araar. 2006. *Poverty and Equity: Measurement, Policy, and Estimation with DAD* (New York: Springer and International Development Research Centre).

Enami, Ali, Sean Higgins, and Nora Lustig. 2022. "Allocating Taxes and Transfers and Constructing Income Concepts: Completing Sections A, B, and C of the *CEQ Master Workbook*," chap. 6 in *Commitment to Equity Handbook: Estimating the Impact of Fiscal Policy on Inequality and Poverty*, 2nd ed., Vol. 1, edited by Nora Lustig (Brookings Institution Press and CEQ Institute, Tulane University). Free online version available at www.commitmentoequity.org.

Enami, Ali, Nora Lustig, and Rodrigo Aranda. 2022. "Analytic Foundations: Measuring the Redistributive Impact of Taxes and Transfers," chap. 2 in *Commitment to Equity Handbook: Estimating the Impact of Fiscal Policy on Inequality and Poverty*, 2nd ed., Vol. 1, edited by Nora Lustig (Brookings Institution Press and CEQ Institute, Tulane University). Free online version available at www.commitmentoequity.org.

Facultad Latinoamericana de Ciencias Sociales (FLACSO), Ministerio de Economia (MINEC), and Programa de las Naciones Unidas para el Desarrollo (PNUD). 2010. "Mapa de pobreza urbana y exclusion social." Volume 2. Atlas. Localizacion de asentamientos urbanos precarios (San Salvador).

Ferreira, Francisco, Julian Messina, Jamele Rigolini, and Renos Vakis. 2012. *Socio-Economic Mobility and the Rise of the Middle Class in Latin America and the Caribbean*. Regional Flagship Report for Latin America and the Caribbean (Washington: World Bank).

Higgins, Sean, and Caterina Brest Lopez. 2022. "Producing Indicators and Results, and Completing Sections D and E of the *CEQ Master Workbook* Using the *CEQ Stata Package*," chap. 8 in *Commitment to Equity Handbook: Estimating the Impact of Fiscal Policy on Inequality and Poverty*, 2nd ed., Vol. 1, edited by Nora Lustig (Brookings Institution Press and CEQ Institute, Tulane University). Free online version available at www.commitmentoequity.org.

Higgins, Sean, and Nora Lustig. 2016. "Can a Poverty-Reducing and Progressive Tax and Transfer System Hurt the Poor?" *Journal of Development Economics* 122, pp. 63–75.

Lambert, Peter. 1985. "On the Redistributive Effect of Taxes and Benefits." *Scottish Journal of Political Economy* 32, no. 1, pp. 39–54.

Lopez-Calva, Luis Felipe, and Ortiz-Juarez, Eduardo. 2011. "A Vulnerability Approach to the Definition of the Middle Class." Policy Research Working Paper 5902 (Washington: World Bank).

Lustig, Nora, and Sean Higgins. 2013. *"Commitment to Equity Assessment* (CEQ): Estimating the Incidence of Social Spending, Subsidies and Taxes," CEQ Working Paper 1 (Center for Inter-American Policy and Research and Department of Economics, Tulane University, and Inter-American Dialogue).

———. 2022. "The *CEQ Assessment*: Measuring the Impact of Fiscal Policy on Inequality and Poverty," chap. 1 in *Commitment to Equity Handbook: Estimating the Impact of Fiscal Policy on Inequality and Poverty*, 2nd ed., Vol. 1, edited by Nora Lustig (Brookings Institution Press and CEQ Institute, Tulane University). Free online version available at www.commitment oequity.org.

Ministry of Economy (Ministerio de Economia [MINEC]). 2008. "Censo de Poblacion y Vivienda. 2007" (San Salvador).

———. 2011. "Encuesta de Hogares de Propositos Multiples [EHPM]" (San Salvador).

Ministry of Education (Ministerio de Educacion [MINED]). 2011. "Cifras actualizadas de la educacion de El Salvador. Direccion de Planificacion, Gerencia de Monitoreo, Evaluacion y Estadistica" (San Salvador).

Ministry of Health and Social Protection (Ministerio de Salud y Proteccion Social [MINSAL]). 2013. "Informe de Labores 2012–2013" (San Salvador).

Ministry of Treasury (Ministerio de Hacienda [MH]). 2011. "Informe de la gestion financiera del Estado. Ejercicio Financiero Fiscal" (San Salvador).

Social Investment Fund for Local Development (Fondo de Inversion Social para el Desarrollo Local [FISDL]). 2004. "Mapa de pobreza" (San Salvador).

Technical Secretary of the Presidency (Secretaria Tecnica de la Presidencia [STP]). 2012. "El camino del cambio en El Salvador, creando las bases de una sociedad democratica, incluyente y equitativa" (San Salvador).

———. 2013. "El camino del cambio en El Salvador, Legados de cuatro years de gestion" (San Salvador).

———. 2014. "Balance Social 2009–2013" (San Salvador).

Vice Ministry of Transportation (Viceministerio de Transporte [VMT]). 2010. "Estrategia para la Planificacion del Nuevo Sistema de Transporte Publico," Informe 1, Diagnostico de consultoria individual internacional No. CO 022/2010 (San Salvador).

Appendix 15A

Estimating the Incidence of Consumption Subsidies

1 Electricity Subsidy

The subsidy for electricity consumption in El Salvador is indirect. A significant portion of households pays less than market value for electricity, so this subsidy was incorporated in this exercise to calculate consumable income.

To estimate the value of the electricity subsidy for households, the database of the Household Multi-Purpose Survey (EHPM) was used. The EHPM reports monthly electricity expenditure in US dollars, including any discount for the subsidy in eligible households plus the value-added tax (VAT). The monthly expenditure was adjusted using institutional rules for the subsidy, as given by the laws and regulations applied to the sector.

The elements that affect the amount of the subsidy are electricity consumption of households, expressed in kilowatt hours (kWh), the level of rates in force as established in the tariff schedule dictated by the General Superintendency of Electricity and Telecommunications (Super intendencia General de Electricidad y Telecomunicaciones [SIGET]), and the kWh threshold set by policy to qualify for the subsidy.

Because the survey does not contain the amount of kWh consumed, and this is an important parameter, the first step was to estimate the kWh consumed from the bill paid with subsidy and VAT. The tariff schedule corresponded to the month in which the household was surveyed. In the exercise conducted for 2011, the tariff schedule changed every quarter, or four times during the year, and corresponded to the month in which the survey was taken.

The electricity tariff schedule was divided into four ranges: from 0 to 50 kWh, from 51 to 99 kWh, from 100 up to 200 kWh, and over 200 kWh. With the data from the tariff schedule, sixteen regressions (four calendar quarters multiplied by four tariff ranges) were performed, using as an explanatory variable the amount payable including subsidy and VAT, and as an outcome variable the number of kWh consumed, and the slope or subsidized price per kWh was calculated. The regressions based on the tariff schedule are accurate ($R^2 = 99$, or with a total sum of squared errors of zero). The amount of kWh charged was obtained by substituting these equations into the monthly cost of electricity reported by the household survey.

The second step was to calculate the subsidy. In El Salvador the subsidy is granted in two tranches. The first, between 0 and 99 kWh, is where households pay a fixed price stipulated by regulations in the Law of the National Investment Fund in Electricity and Telephony (Fondo de Inversion Nacional en Electricidad y Telefonia [FINET]), adopted in May 1999, particularly Article 16, which determines a rate of US$0.067/kWh. In these cases, the subsidy is 89.5 percent, the difference between the price of US$0.067 and the average market price or rate schedule set out in the corresponding month excluding VAT. The state delivered the subsidy via a transfer directly to the electric distribution company, and it was reflected in consumers' electricity bills. For the second tranche, above 99 kWh, the maximum threshold for subsidy is set by policy. For 2011, during the first quarter, consumers above 99 kWh paid the rate of January 2011. However, in April 2011, the rate was scheduled to increase an average of 16.4 percent, so the maximum threshold to receive the subsidy was increased to 300 kWh. With the price change in April, a legislative decree was approved to keep prices at their January 2011 level for part of the household's consumption. For the last quarter of 2011, the threshold was decreased to 200 kWh.

If the household was surveyed between April and July 2011, its consumption between 99 and 300 kWh received the subsidy (paying at the January 2011 price), while consumption over 300 kWh paid 100 percent of the new, higher rate. If the household was surveyed after October 2011, the consumption between 99 and 200 kWh reflected the subsidized rate, while excess was calculated as paying the higher, nonsubsidized rate. Finally, the amount required to cover the subsidy is transferred by government to the electricity distribution companies.

In general, when analyzing the amount of kWh, we observed that if a household paid US$10 in the month for electricity, it was located below the 99 kWh threshold and was paying the fixed price from May 1999. After April 2011, if the household paid between US$10 and US$46, it consumed less than 200 kWh, and the price paid per kWh was that of January 2011. The subsidies covered 91 percent of residential users, of which 69.7 percent were up to 99 kWh consumption, 21.3 percent between 99 and 200 kWh, and 4.9 percent between 200 and 300 kWh.

2 Public Transportation Subsidy

The subsidy operates as an indirect transfer, since the users of public transport pay a fixed price. The service is subject to state regulation, which establishes the rates to be charged by companies that offer the service and are licensed for specific bus routes.

The government has subsidized the system of public transportation since 1974. Due to the increase in oil prices in 2007, the Transitional Law for the Stabilization of Tariffs for Public Transportation (Ley transitoria para la estabilizacion de tarifas) was passed and has been extended to present day. The subsidy is granted to the supply side and operates by delivering a fixed amount of money per unit of transport.

According to the parameters of the law, the state transferred the following to entrepreneurs: US$375 per month per full-sized bus and US$750 per month for each smaller bus during 2011. In addition, according to a study by the Israeli Institute for Transport Planning and Research in 2000, full-size buses cover an average of 4.6 trips on their routes per day, while smaller buses cover 5.4 trips a day. Taking the daily average amount of monthly allowance commensurate with the amount of travel, each full-size bus receives US$5.43 and each smaller bus US$2.31 per trip. Then, according to the number of seats of each unit (sixty in full-size buses and twenty-five in smaller buses), each seat allowance amounts to US$0.0905 in full-size buses and $0.0925 in smaller buses.

The same study found that in the metropolitan area of San Salvador (Area Matropolitana de San Salvador [AMSS]), 40 percent of public transportation units were full-size buses and 40 percent were smaller buses. Conversely, outside the AMSS, 80 percent were full-size and 20 percent were smaller. Taking this into account, and the per seat amounts on both size buses, the weighted average subsidy per seat on every trip was US$0.09178 in AMSS and US$0.0909 outside AMSS.

On the demand side, the price paid by the population is fixed. According to Agreement No. 292 from the Transportation Ministry, tariffs of service for passengers in public transportation are US$0.25 for full-size buses and US$0.28 for smaller buses. The EHPM collected the monthly amount allocated to public transport. This expenditure was divided by the weighted average rate of US$0.261 to calculate the number of trips made in each household. To impute the subsidy, the number of trips was multiplied by the parameters indicated above, US$0.09178 in AMSS and US$0.0909 outside the AMSS.

3 Water Subsidy

The public sector is the principal potable water supplier, through the autonomous National Administration of Aqueducts and Sewers (Administracion Nacional de Acueductos y Alcantarrillados [ANDA]). The law gives ANDA the authority to propose tariffs to the executive, which will be approved by the Ministry of the Economy. The current tariff schedule was approved by the Ministry of the Economy in June 2011. These rates are exempt from VAT.

Like the electricity subsidy, the tariff schedule throughout the year 2011 was approved on February 24, 2010, and was separated into thirteen levels. Consistent with this rate schedule, thirteen regressions were performed, where the explanatory variable was the amount to pay including the subsidy and the result variable was the volume consumed in cubic meters, while the slope or price per cubic meter with subsidy was calculated. Similarly, regressions based on the tariff schedule are accurate ($R^2 = 99$, or with a total sum of squared errors of zero). Using these equations for the monthly spending per household on potable water reported in the survey, the number of cubic meters consumed was calculated.

The estimated volume consumed was calculated for each household based on the reported expense using information from households that received service directly from ANDA, according to the EHPM survey. Also, according to ANDA records, the cost of providing 1 cubic meter of potable water was US$0.85, which was used to calculate the nonsubsidized water bill by multiplying by the volume of water consumed by each household. Finally, the subsidy was the difference between the water cost without subsidy and the bill actually paid.

4 LP Gas Subsidy

Before 2011, the gas subsidy was transferred directly to the supply side, to companies that imported liquefied petroleum gas (LPG) into the country. Previously, the domestic price was fixed.

The price of a twenty-five-pound tank, which is widely used for cooking, stood at US$5.10. This was the lowest price in Central America, and all El Salvadorians paid the same price. On the other hand, the US$0.16 per gallon tax on gasoline consumed was used to finance the LPG subsidy.

However, increases in the price of petroleum products pushed the difference between the market price and that facing consumers, which, in turn, increased the amount that the government had to subsidize.

During 2011, several changes were made in how the gas subsidy was delivered. The government began a program known as the Plan for Comprehensive Management and Market Transparency for LPG, with which changes in the regulation of gas prices were made. First, it allowed the price of tanks to rise to their market value, reaching US$14.60 for twenty-five pounds, and went on to deliver the subsidy directly to households, with a fixed monthly amount of US$9.10 if the household consumed less than 99 kWh of electricity per month. Also, the Ministry of the Economy engaged in efforts to reduce exclusion errors by granting the subsidy to other households in poverty without an electrical connection, to subsistence businesses, and to nongovernmental charities. To impute the subsidy, the EHPM identified whether a household was a subsidy recipient through a direct question. If awarded, the subsidy of US$9.10 was linked to the household.

Chapter 16

GHANA AND TANZANIA

The Impact of Reforming Energy Subsidies, Cash Transfers, and Taxes on Inequality and Poverty

Stephen D. Younger

Introduction

A Commitment to Equity (CEQ) analysis aims to give as comprehensive a description as possible of the distributional consequences of government's fiscal policy, focusing on the status quo. This chapter shows how one can use methods similar to the CEQ's to analyze the distributional consequences of prospective policy changes. Those changes may be driven by a desire to increase redistribution, but it is more common for policymakers to make changes to close budget deficits while trying to minimize the poverty impact. In both situations, simulations of policy changes provide useful information.

Particularly for poorer countries, it is common for a *CEQ Assessment* to find that redistribution is minimal, often much less than policymakers expect. This is certainly true in Ghana and Tanzania, where the taxation and expenditure measured in this study reduce the Gini coefficient by 0.035 and 0.037, respectively. Results for poverty reduction are even less encouraging. Were it not for the in-kind benefits from health and education spending, the taxation and social expenditure would actually increase poverty in Ghana and Tanzania by 0.022 and 0.025, respectively, for the headcount index at the national poverty lines. This effect is almost entirely because poor people pay indirect taxes, as in every other country. Assuming that the governments of Ghana and Tanzania would like their taxation and social expenditure policies to be more re-

This study is based on Younger, Osei-Assibey, and Oppong (2015) and Younger, Myamba, and Mdadila (2016). The Commitment to Equity Institute collaborated with the University of Ghana and the World Bank in Ghana and REPOA in Tanzania. These studies were possible thanks to the generous support of the Bill & Melinda Gates Foundation.

distributive than is currently the case, what can they do? This chapter simulates several policy changes and analyzes their impact on inequality and poverty.

Both Ghana and Tanzania also face chronic budget deficits, which limit their ability to reduce poverty by simply increasing social expenditures. Faced with such strictures, both governments would like to find ways to reduce expenditures and increase taxes in ways that are the least hurtful to the poor. The chapter also simulates policy changes directed at budgetary savings to assess their distributional consequences.

The methods used here are descriptive, like the methods in a standard CEQ analysis. But because the simulated policies are hypothetical, we cannot simply describe those policies' beneficiaries as observed in the data but must rather make some assumptions about who would benefit from each of the proposed policies. Some changes mainly affect existing payers of a tax or beneficiaries of an expenditure. In other words, these changes refer to what is known as a policy's intensive margin, as opposed to the extensive margin, which would involve increasing the number of taxpayers or beneficiaries. Modeling these changes is straightforward because survey data indicate who the existing taxpayers and expenditure beneficiaries are. For example, because the consumers of items subject to VAT are already known, if the value-added tax (VAT) rate were increased, their tax burden would simply be increased by the amount of the proposed change. This approach is applicable to any policy reform that changes the rate on an existing direct or indirect tax or an indirect subsidy. In the examples that follow, we consider changes to indirect subsidies to electricity and petroleum products and changes to direct and indirect tax rates.

On the other hand, some policy proposals change an extensive margin: they expand taxes or benefits to people who are not currently affected. For these changes, stronger assumptions must be made about who the new taxpayers or beneficiaries would be, and those people must be identified in some way in the survey data. Take, for instance, expanding the VAT to informal enterprises that currently evade it. It might be possible to identify in the survey the households with informal enterprises, but it is difficult to know which of these households is likely to be captured by the reform efforts and which will continue to evade them. Still, for some extensive margins, it is possible to model the households affected by the change. For example, governments sometimes fund campaigns to ensure that vaccination rates are 100 percent. Surveys often record data on childhood vaccinations, allowing us to identify the unvaccinated as the likely beneficiaries of such a campaign. In the examples that follow, we focus on expansion of conditional cash transfer (CCT) programs to previously unaffected households. In most cases, the targeting mechanism for these programs is well defined, usually including a proxy means test (PMT). The kinds of data that such a test uses are usually available in household surveys, allowing us to calculate a proxy means score for the survey households and thus identify the likely beneficiaries of a program expansion on the extensive margin.

As with the main CEQ analysis, the results of these simulations provide a first-order approximation of the actual distributional consequences of the policy changes, ignoring behavioral and general equilibrium effects.

1 Examples

The following section estimates the effects of four possible policy changes that involve eliminating energy subsidies and, in some cases, expanding conditional cash transfers.

1.1 Eliminating Energy Subsidies

Governments looking for ways to trim expenditures face a difficult task. Large parts of the budget go to items that are difficult or impossible to cut, such as health and education spending, debt service, and public employees' compensation. One line item that stands out for both its size and economic inefficiency is the subsidy for electricity and petroleum products.[1] This is the case in both Ghana and Tanzania. In Ghana in 2013, the year of this study, the government spent 1.1 billion cedis (1.2 percent of GDP) on electricity subsidies and indirectly subsidized fuel imports by offering the bulk oil companies an artificially low exchange rate, saving them about 600 million cedis that year. In Tanzania in 2011–12, the government spent 0.5 percent of GDP on electricity subsidies and 0.4 percent on fuel subsidies. In both countries, then, removing these subsidies would offer significant savings. Nevertheless, subsidy removal is unpopular, often bringing protesters to the streets. The strongest complaint against subsidy removal is that it hurts the poor. A distributional analysis allows us to assess the validity of that complaint.

Table 16-1 shows the results of four separate simulations of the elimination of electricity subsidies in Ghana and Tanzania. These subsidies existed at the time that we performed the original CEQ analyses, so we had already calculated the benefits to each household. These four simulations remove those benefits in different ways. The original studies first calculated the rate that each household paid for electricity based on its reported total consumption. The subsidy benefit is the difference between that rate and one that was estimated to be sufficient to cover all generation and distribution costs.

The first simulation removes this subsidy completely, requiring every household to pay a new, higher rate sufficient to cover all electricity costs. This measure saves the government a considerable amount of money: 1.4 percent of GDP in Ghana and 0.4 percent in Tanzania.[2] Eliminating the subsidy also reduces inequality in both countries, but only by a very small amount. Poverty increases, however, especially in Ghana, as critics of these removal policies have claimed.

Both Ghana and Tanzania have lifeline tariffs for electricity, which are low rates for the first 50 kilowatt hours (kWh) of consumption and are meant to concentrate electricity subsidies among those who consume low amounts of electricity and who might be presumed to be poorer than people who consume more. The second simulation

---

[1] Coady and others (2015).

[2] The effect on the budget comes from the fact that central government must make transfers to the electricity providers to cover the losses they incur by charging rates below full cost recovery.

TABLE 16-1

Simulated Effects of Eliminating Electricity Subsidies in Ghana and Tanzania

Change	Simulation			
	(1)	(2)	(3)	(4)
Ghana				
Extreme poverty	0.0044	0.0036	−0.0108	−0.0032
Poverty	0.0088	0.0053	−0.0128	0.0001
Inequality	−0.0011	0.0004	−0.0101	−0.0051
Budgetary savings (percent GDP)	1.36	0.71	0.00	0.82
Tanzania				
Extreme poverty	0.0007	0.0005	−0.0185	−0.0053
Poverty	0.0029	0.0024	−0.0148	−0.0004
Inequality	−0.0036	−0.0020	−0.0108	−0.0055
Budgetary savings (percent GDP)	0.43	0.27	0.00	0.34

Sources: Younger, Osei-Assibey, and Oppong (2015); Younger, Myamba, and Mdadila (2016). Simulations are based on data from annual household surveys in GSS (Ghana Statistical Service) (2014) and National Bureau of Statistics (2014).

Note: Results are for Consumable Income (see chapter 1 [Lustig and Higgins, 2022] and chapter 6 [Enami, Higgins, and Lustig, 2022] in this Volume of the Handbook). Changes in poverty are measured as the difference between the headcount ratio obtained under the corresponding policy simulation and the headcount ratio before any policy simulation. Analogously, changes in inequality are measured as the difference between the Gini coefficient obtained under the corresponding policy simulation and the Gini coefficient before any policy simulation. Poverty lines are nationally determined.

Simulation descriptions:
(1) Eliminates the electricity subsidy with no compensation.
(2) Eliminates subsidy except for lifeline tariff for the first 50kWh, which is held constant.
(3) Eliminates electricity subsidy and uses all the funds to expand CCT coverage by raising PMT threshold.
(4) Eliminates electricity subsidy and uses enough funds to expand CCT to leave poverty roughly unchanged.

maintains the lifeline tariff in each country but increases other rates to full cost recovery, thus removing the subsidy on marginal (but not infra-marginal) consumption for heavier users. This measure reduces the fiscal savings by about half in Ghana and less in Tanzania, but it also reduces the (negative) poverty impact in Ghana by almost half, though by much less in Tanzania. In Tanzania and to a lesser extent in Ghana, the lifeline tariff seems not to benefit the poor very much, most likely because the poor do not have access to the electricity mains.

One possible response to the small but negative impact on poverty is to make an offsetting increase in another poverty-reducing expenditure: the conditional cash transfer. In both Ghana and Tanzania, this transfer is one of the most progressive government expenditures and should therefore be more efficient in reducing poverty than expenditure on electricity subsidies. The third simulation completely eliminates electricity subsidies and uses all of the funds saved to expand each country's CCT program. These amounts are huge increases to the CCT budgets of both countries, so it is not reasonable to allocate them only to existing beneficiaries. Instead, we expand the pool of recipients in each country, or in other words, we increase the extensive margin of the CCTs. In Ghana, we did this by calculating the proxy means formula for each household and using its benefit cutoff plus the other criteria for CCT benefits applicable in 2013 to identify all eligible households in the country. Even with this expanded pool, we could not exhaust the savings from the elimination of the electricity subsidy, so we also increased each recipient's benefit by 89 percent. In Tanzania, we expanded the pool of recipients by starting with the lowest proxy means scores and working our way up until all the electricity savings were exhausted. By design, these simulations have zero net benefit for the budget, but they do show large reductions in poverty, especially in Tanzania, despite the elimination of the electricity subsidies.

The fourth simulation takes a slightly different tack. Here, we eliminate the subsidy entirely but increase the CCT just enough to keep poverty from increasing, providing smaller poverty and inequality reductions than in the third simulation but generating substantial fiscal savings: 0.8 percent of GDP in Ghana and 0.3 percent in Tanzania.[3] Ultimately, then, both Ghana and Tanzania would do better to remove the electricity subsidies, which are poorly targeted, and offset the poverty consequences with an increase in a well-targeted expenditure like CCTs if poverty is the main objection to electricity subsidy removal.

1.2 Expanding Conditional Cash Transfers

Both Ghana and Tanzania had nascent CCT programs at the time our survey data were collected. In Ghana the program operated only in some districts selected for relatively high poverty rates, whereas in Tanzania, a pilot program was operational in three districts only. Because these programs have among the lowest concentration coefficients of any government expenditure (−0.29 in Ghana and −0.50 in Tanzania), they are prime candidates for increased expenditures meant to reduce poverty and inequality.

Both countries use a PMT along with additional criteria to target households. In Ghana, the CCT targets households in eligible districts headed by a child, an elderly person, or a disabled person and those that include an elderly person or a vulnerable child (including children who have lost one or both parents or who are disabled). Within this household category, funds available to the district are allocated to the households with the lowest proxy means score. After the survey date, Ghana updated its PMT

---

[3] Because the poverty increase is different for each income concept and poverty line, we would need to run a slightly different simulation for each one if we want to have poverty stay constant. Instead, we targeted the income and poverty line that showed the worst poverty increase in the first simulation and held it to zero, which implies small poverty reductions for the other income/ poverty line combinations.

because there was some concern that the previous test was not targeting poor households effectively. In Tanzania, the pilot CCT targets the vulnerable elderly (those who have no caregivers, are in poor health, or are very poor) and vulnerable children (those who have lost one or more parents, whose parents are chronically ill, or who are chronically ill themselves). The program relies on local communities to identify households that include such vulnerable people, applies a PMT to the identified households, and makes the CCT payment to all households that fall below the cutoff level for the PMT.

Although we took slightly different approaches in the two countries, in general, we simulated several options for expanding each country's CCT to a budget of 0.5 percent of GDP, an amount that is fairly typical for countries with new CCTs. Unlike in many similar simulations, we pay for these additional transfers by increasing the VAT, which offsets the poverty reduction impact somewhat. Table 16-2 shows the results for Ghana, and table 16-3 shows those for Tanzania.

For Ghana, we ran five simulations. The first expands the CCT to all eligible persons in the entire country using the old PMT and represents a complete expansion of the existing program. To keep the total cost to 0.5 percent of GDP, this expansion requires scaling down the benefit to each recipient by 30 percent.

The second simulation changes the targeting to the new PMTs, allocating transfers to all people found to be extremely poor by that test's criteria. This change greatly improves the targeting from a concentration coefficient of −0.29 to −0.65, which is better than most middle-income countries.[4] In this simulation, everyone who is extremely poor receives a transfer, not just the elderly, handicapped, and vulnerable children currently targeted. Keeping the total cost to 0.5 percent of GDP requires scaling down the benefit to each recipient by 49 percent in this simulation.

The third simulation targets transfers to the poorest people as judged by the new PMT at current benefit rates (no scaling down), until total payments are 0.5 percent of GDP. This method is in one sense perfect targeting: the money goes to the poorest people in the sample as identified by the PMT (though not, perhaps, the absolutely poorest people because the PMT is not a perfect predictor).

The fourth simulation increases benefits to current beneficiaries only until total transfer payments reach 0.5 percent of GDP—that is, it uses only the current targeting. Because current (2013) beneficiaries are so few, this increase produces a huge and unrealistic payment to them, one that is sixteen times larger than the current 24 cedis per person per month.

The fifth simulation keeps the program size constant at the 2013 level of 0.02 percent of GDP, much smaller than the other simulations, and changes the targeting to the new PMT.

---

[4] In practice, the new PMT will not work this well. Because it is estimated using the same Ghana Living Standards Survey 6 (GLSS-6) data that we use here, it is particularly well suited to identifying the poor in this sample, but because of sampling error, it will do less well in the general population.

TABLE 16-2
Simulated Effects of Expanding Conditional Cash Transfers in Ghana

Change		Simulation				
		(1)	(2)	(3)	(4)	(5)
Extreme poverty	Disposable income	−0.0065	−0.0173	−0.0188	−0.0066	−0.0015
	Consumable income	−0.0032	−0.0157	−0.0175	−0.0044	−0.0006
Poverty	Disposable income	−0.0085	−0.0159	−0.0124	−0.0077	−0.0004
	Consumable income	−0.0044	−0.0112	−0.0081	−0.0042	−0.0002
Inequality	Disposable income	−0.0035	−0.0082	−0.0081	−0.0040	−0.0002
	Consumable income	−0.0039	−0.0088	−0.0087	−0.0043	−0.0002
Scaling factor		0.70	0.70	0.51	1.00	16.29

Source: Younger, Osei-Assibey, and Oppong (2015). Simulations are based on data from the 2013 household survey in GSS (Ghana Statistical Service) (2014).

Note: Results are for Disposable and Consumable Income (see chapter 1 [Lustig and Higgins, 2022] and chapter 6 [Enami, Higgins, and Lustig, 2022] in this Volume of the Handbook). Changes in poverty are measured as the difference between the headcount ratio obtained under the corresponding policy simulation and the headcount ratio before any policy simulation. Analogously, changes in inequality are measured as the difference between the Gini coefficient obtained under the corresponding policy simulation and the Gini coefficient before any policy simulation. Poverty lines are nationally determined. In all simulations except (5), VAT is increased to pay for the increased program size.

Simulation descriptions:
(1) Expands program to all eligible persons in the entire country using the old PMT, then scales benefits down so the total expenditure is 0.5 percent of GDP.
(2) Expands program to all people judged to be extremely poor using the new PMT, then scales benefits down so the total expenditure is 0.5 percent of GDP.
(3) Expands program to the poorest people as judged by the new PMT at current benefit rates until total payments are 0.5 percent of GDP.
(4) Increases benefits to current beneficiaries only until total payments are 0.5 percent of GDP.
(5) Keeps program payments constant, but converts to the new PMT.

Note that all of these simulations except the fourth require us to identify an extensive margin—that is, new beneficiaries who are not receiving benefits at the time of the survey. In the case of cash transfers in these two countries, identifying new beneficiaries is relatively easy because the eligibility criteria are clear and rely on information collected in the survey—age, disability, and orphan status—and a proxy means test that also uses variables readily available in the survey.[5] Accordingly, we can identify the extensive margin in the survey without recourse to any behavioral analysis.

_____

[5] In fact, the proxy means test is usually estimated on a survey very similar to the ones we use.

TABLE 16-3

Simulated Effects of Expanding Conditional Cash Transfers in Tanzania

Change		Simulation		
		(1)	(2)	(3)
Extreme poverty	Disposable Income	−0.0113	−0.0172	−0.0212
	Consumable Income	−0.0110	−0.0183	−0.0229
Poverty	Disposable Income	−0.0148	−0.0163	−0.0236
	Consumable Income	−0.0104	−0.0138	−0.0146
Inequality	Disposable Income	−0.0045	−0.0073	−0.0087
	Consumable Income	−0.0063	−0.0094	−0.0108
Scaling factor		0.55	1.00	1.00

Source: Younger, Myamba, and Mdadila (2016). Simulations are based on data from the 2011 household survey in National Bureau of Statistics (2014).

Note: Changes in poverty are measured as the difference between the headcount ratio obtained under the corresponding policy simulation and the headcount ratio before any policy simulation. Analogously, changes in inequality are measured as the difference between the Gini coefficient obtained under the corresponding policy simulation and the Gini coefficient before any policy simulation. Poverty lines are nationally determined.
In all simulations VAT is increased to pay for the increased program size.

Simulation descriptions:
(1) Expands CCT to all eligible persons, then scales benefits down so the total CCT expenditure is 0.5 percent of GDP.
(2) Expands CCT at current benefit rates to the poorest eligible people according to the proxy means test until total CCT payments are 0.5 percent of GDP.
(3) Expands CCT at current benefit rates to the poorest people regardless of vulnerable children or elderly according to the proxy means test until total CCT payments are 0.5 percent of GDP.

That said, our simulations may be overly optimistic if in practice the selection process fails to choose according to the eligibility criteria.

In interpreting the results, recall that Disposable Income is measured prior to incorporating the effect of VAT, so the impact shown for Disposable Income reflects the impact of the CCT increase only, whereas impacts for Consumable Income account for both the additional transfer and its assumed financing via additional VAT.[6]

The first simulation shows that increasing the transfer to nationwide coverage using existing targeting criteria while holding the overall budget to 0.5 percent of GDP would reduce Disposable Income poverty by 0.85 percentage points and extreme poverty by 0.65 percentage points. Including the effect of the VAT increase (the Consumable Income row) reduces the gains to 0.32 and 0.44 percentage points. Reductions in the Gini are small: 0.39 percentage points.

The second simulation does much better, demonstrating the advantages of better targeting. Here, Disposable Income poverty declines by 1.59 percentage points and

---

[6] See chapter 1 in this Volume by Lustig and Higgins (2022) and especially chapter 6 in this Volume by Enami, Higgins, and Lustig (2022) for a description of income concepts.

extreme poverty by 1.73 percentage points. Including the losses from imposing additional VAT, the gains are still much larger: 1.12 and 1.57 percentage points, respectively.

The third simulation reflects "perfect targeting," but it does only about as well as the second. In fact, it does a little worse on some of the measures. How can this be? Here, transfers are perfectly targeted to the PMT value, not the actual incomes used to calculate the poverty rates, and the rank correlation of the PMT and incomes is therefore not perfect. The fact that the third simulation does not do much better than the second indicates that the PMT does not predict household consumption per adult equivalent perfectly and also that there is not that much difference between the poorest of the extremely poor and the rest of the extremely poor when we use actual household expenditures per adult equivalent to measure well-being.

Results for the fourth simulation are very similar to the first because both use the old PMT. It is interesting to note, though, that the poverty and inequality effects are broadly similar for an expansion of the transfer's extensive margin (adding new beneficiaries as in the first simulation) and intensive margin (increasing benefits to existing beneficiaries as in the fourth simulation).

Finally, the fifth simulation shows almost no change in poverty or inequality measures, despite the switch to the better targeting of the new PMT, because the program size does not change here. Thus even greatly improved targeting of a small program cannot have much impact on poverty and inequality. Larger program size is essential.

Table 16-3 simulates three possible ways of scaling up Tanzania's CCT so that its total expenditures would be 0.5 percent of GDP. The first simulation expands the CCT to all vulnerable children and elderly people, regardless of their score on the PMT. This expansion would require almost 1 percent of GDP in additional expenditures, so to keep the budget to 0.5 percent of GDP, we scale down the benefits for each recipient. The second simulation expands the program to eligible participants by raising the PMT threshold until the additional expenditures total 0.5 percent of GDP. The third simulation opens the CCT to all people, not just vulnerable children and the elderly, and raises the PMT threshold until the additional expenditures total 0.5 percent of GDP.

The first simulation would seem to be the least effective approach to an expansion, both because some of the vulnerable children and the elderly are not poor to begin with and because the additional VAT and reduced benefits levels used to finance the program expansion would impoverish some people. Nevertheless, this simulation does reduce extreme poverty by about one percentage point, and poverty by a little more.

The second simulation has a larger effect on both poverty and inequality, which is to be expected because it limits benefits to those with the lowest PMT scores. The third simulation does even better, suggesting that the government could improve the CCT's targeting by eliminating the restriction of benefits to vulnerable children and the elderly and focusing instead only on those with low PMT scores. But regardless of the approach, a fairly limited expansion of the CCT to 0.5 percent of GDP would have significant effects on poverty and inequality in Tanzania, given this program's excellent targeting.

2 Making Taxation More Progressive

In Ghana and Tanzania, as in most countries, direct taxation is more progressive than indirect (with the exception of some excise taxes). This is especially true in countries with large informal sectors because direct taxes fall only on formal sector employees who tend to be much wealthier than the rest of the population. Thus, the government might consider shifting from the use of indirect to direct taxation. To explore this possibility, we simulated two very extreme tax policy changes in Ghana and Tanzania. In Ghana, we eliminate both VAT and import duties, replacing the revenue with higher taxes on earned income in the formal sector (pay as you earn [PAYE]) and presumptive taxes on small businesses. In Tanzania, we removed import duties and offset the revenue loss with increased taxes on formal sector earnings (also PAYE) and presumptive taxation.[7] Clearly, neither of these simulations is practical or even possible. Formal sector employees are already heavily taxed, especially in Tanzania, so considerable tax increases would induce a large shift to informality. We pursue these policy changes to show that even shifting very large amounts of revenue, 5.9 percent of GDP in Ghana and 1.2 percent in Tanzania, from indirect to direct taxes has a relatively modest overall effect on poverty and inequality. Table 16-4 gives the results.

Why are the effects so small? Even though direct taxes are more progressive than indirect, concentration coefficients for indirect and direct taxes are not so different. In Ghana, they are 0.42 for import duties, 0.44 for VAT, and 0.73 for PAYE, which is by far the largest source of direct taxation in this study. The difference between these is about 0.3, whereas the difference between the concentration coefficients for electricity

TABLE 16-4

Simulated Effects of Replacing Indirect with Direct Taxation in Ghana and Tanzania

Change	Extreme poverty headcount	Poverty headcount	Gini coefficient
Ghana	−0.0031	−0.0056	−0.0034
Tanzania	−0.0049	−0.0071	−0.0037

Sources: Younger, Osei-Assibey, and Oppong (2015); Younger, Myamba, and Mdadila (2016). Simulations are based on data from annual household surveys in GSS (Ghana Statistical Service) (2014) and National Bureau of Statistics (2014).

Note: Results are for Consumable Income (see chapter 1 [Lustig and Higgins, 2022] and chapter 6 [Enami, Higgins, and Lustig, 2022] in this Volume of the Handbook). Changes in poverty are measured as the difference between the headcount ratio obtained under the corresponding policy simulation and the headcount ratio before any policy simulation. Analogously, changes in inequality are measured as the difference between the Gini coefficient obtained under the corresponding policy simulation and the Gini coefficient before any policy simulation. Poverty lines are nationally determined.

---

[7] In Tanzania, the VAT is actually quite progressive, so the difference between VAT and direct taxes is not as dramatic as the difference between import duties and direct taxes.

subsidies and Ghana's CCT studied in the previous section is 0.76. In Tanzania, the concentration coefficients are 0.38 for import duties and 0.91 for PAYE, the latter being the highest concentration coefficient for a tax we have ever observed. Still, that difference of about 0.5 is less than the difference of 1.2 between electricity subsidies and the CCT.

This result is important for policymakers in two ways. First, broad-based indirect taxes like the VAT are generally considered to be more efficient than direct taxes, whereas direct taxes are more equitable. Thus, there is a trade-off between equity and efficiency when choosing tax instruments. But the results here suggest that the trade-off is not too severe. The governments of Ghana and Tanzania can continue to rely on broad-based indirect taxes, knowing that their use of direct taxation instead has only a minor effect on poverty and inequality. Second, the result suggests that to have a large redistributional impact, governments need to consider combinations of taxes with large positive concentration coefficients and expenditures with large negative concentration coefficients, which are usually those like CCTs that explicitly target the poor.

References

Coady, David, Ian Parry, Louis Sears, and Baoping Shang. 2015. "How Large Are Global Energy Subsidies?" IMF Working Paper WP/15/105 (Washington: International Monetary Fund).

Enami, Ali, Higgins, Sean, and Nora Lustig. 2022. "Allocating Taxes and Transfers and Constructing Income Concepts: Completing Sections A, B, and C of the *CEQ Master Workbook*," chap. 6 in *Commitment to Equity Handbook: Estimating the Impact of Fiscal Policy on Inequality and Poverty*, 2nd ed., Vol. 1, edited by Nora Lustig (Brookings Institution Press and CEQ Institute, Tulane University). Free online version available at www.commitmentoequity.org.

GSS (Ghana Statistical Service). 2014. *Ghana Living Standards Survey 6 (GLSS 6): Main Report*. Accra.

Lustig, Nora, and Sean Higgins. 2022. "The *CEQ Assessment*: Measuring the Impact of Fiscal Policy on Inequality and Poverty," chap. 1 in *Commitment to Equity Handbook: Estimating the Impact of Fiscal Policy on Inequality and Poverty*, 2nd ed., Vol. 1, edited by Nora Lustig (Brookings Institution Press and CEQ Institute, Tulane University). Free online version available at www.commitmentoequity.org.

National Bureau of Statistics. 2014. *Household Budget Survey: Main Report, 2011/12*. Dar es Salaam.

Younger, Stephen D., Flora Myamba, and Kenneth Mdadila. 2016. "Fiscal Incidence in Tanzania," CEQ Working Paper 36 (New Orleans: CEQ Institute, Tulane University, Ithaca College, and REPOA).

Younger, Stephen D., Eric Osei-Assibey, and Felix Oppong. 2015. "Fiscal Incidence in Ghana," CEQ Working Paper 35 (New Orleans: CEQ Institute, Tulane University, Ithaca College, University of Ghana, and World Bank).

Chapter 17

FISCAL POLICY, INEQUALITY, AND POVERTY IN IRAN

Assessing the Impact and Effectiveness of Taxes and Transfers

Ali Enami, Nora Lustig, and Alireza Taqdiri

This chapter is a reprint of an article published in the *Middle East Development Journal*, which can be accessed in its published form at https://doi.org/10.1080/17938120.2019.1583510. The article is published Open Access funded by the Economic Research Forum (Egypt) and the Bill & Melinda Gates Foundation, under Creative Commons license CC BY 4.0. If you use material from this chapter, please cite the following article: Enami, Ali, Nora Lustig, and Alireza Taqdiri. 2019. "Fiscal policy, inequality, and poverty in Iran: assessing the impact and effectiveness of taxes and transfers." *Middle East Development Journal* 11, no. 1. pp. 49.

Abstract

Using the Iranian Household Expenditure and Income Survey for 2011/12, we estimate the impact and effectiveness of various components of Iran's fiscal system on reducing inequality and poverty. We utilize the marginal contribution analysis to determine the impact of each component, and we introduce newly developed indicators of effectiveness to calculate how well various taxes and transfers are operating to reduce inequality and poverty. We find that the fiscal system reduces the poverty-head-count-ratio by 10.5 percentage points and inequality by 0.0854 Gini points. Transfers are generally more effective in reducing inequality than taxes while taxes are especially effective in raising revenue without causing poverty to rise. Although transfers are not targeted toward the poor, they reduce poverty significantly. The main driver is the Targeted Subsidy Program (TSP), and we show through simulations that the poverty reducing impact of TSP could be enhanced if resources were more targeted to the bottom deciles.

Note: Appendices A, B, and C mentioned in this chapter are available online: https://www.tandfon line.com/doi/suppl/10.1080/17938120.2019.1583510?scroll=top

1 Introduction

In December 2010, Iran's government replaced its energy and bread subsidies with a lump-sum cash transfer known as the Targeted Subsidy Program (TSP) (Guillaume, Farzin, & Zytek, 2011).[1] The removal of (mainly, energy) subsidies resulted in an increase of about 21% in prices. Had the reforms stopped there, the poor would have been hurt. At the same time, to garner political support for the reform, the nonpoor had to be awarded a certain degree of protection from the rise in prices of previously subsidized goods. Hence the rationale for a universal cash transfer rather than a targeted one (Guillaume et al., 2011; Mostafavi-Dehzooei & Salehi-Isfahani, 2017; Salehi-Isfahani, Stucki, & Deutschmann, 2015).[2]

This paper analyzes to what extent the TSP reduces poverty under the new scenario of higher prices. By using information from a household survey collected several months after the reform, one can assume that the ensuing increase in prices due to this reform is already embedded in the survey. Likewise, one can assume that the survey has captured the adjustment in consumption patterns that the reform might have induced. To answer this question, we measure the impact of TSP on inequality and poverty by comparing it to a counter factual world in which the reform did not include the cash transfer component.[3] Although Salehi-Isfahani et al. (2015) find that TSP reduced inequality and poverty when compared to the hypothetical case of households receiving neither TSP nor a consumption subsidy, they only looked at the impact of this reform three months into its implementation.[4] Moreover, they relied on

---

[1] Energy here refers to subsidies on electricity, water, natural gas, and oil-based fuels.

[2] The government justified this reform on two main grounds: the high fiscal burden of the energy subsidies, which amounted to 20% of GDP in 2010 (or $70 billion US dollars), and the fact that fiscal resources disproportionately were benefitting the non-poor given that the latter consume much more of the subsidized goods (Guillaume et al., 2011; Salehi-Isfahani et al., 2015; Mostafavi-Dehzooei & Salehi-Isfahani, 2017). In addition to the fiscal burden and the failure of the energy subsidies to target the poor, other justifications also have been used to gain public support for this reform: the excessive amount of energy consumption per GDP as compared to Iran's neighbors and other developing countries, the excessive waste in the use of subsidized goods, the environmentally negative side effects of cheap fossil fuels, the problem of smuggling subsidized fuel out of the country, and the fear of a potential international embargo on importing gasoline (a main fuel for cars) precipitating a need to reduce consumption of this product (Guillaume et al., 2011; Salehi-Isfahani et al., 2015).

[3] For a more general equilibrium analysis of the effect of removing subsidies see Gahvari and Taheripour (2011).

[4] Atamanov, Mostafavi, Salehi Isfahani, and Vishwanath (2016) and Salehi-Isfahani (2017) also find a decrease in inequality and poverty in the first couple of years following the reform. However, their analysis describes general trends of these indicators and not exclusively the role of the subsidy reform.

indirect methods to determine who received TSP because the survey they used did not include an explicit question about this program. After their paper was published, Iran released the Household Expenditure and Income Survey (HEIS) for 2011/12 (1390 by the Iranian calendar) which did include specific questions on how much the household received in TSP transfers and how many people in the household received them. Therefore, we can estimate the impact of TSP transfers with actual data on benefits, rather than relying on the indirect method. This is the first contribution of this paper.

As Salehi-Isfahani et al. (2015) indicate, the reform did increase the fiscally-induced reduction in inequality and poverty from the start, but it did not reduce the government's fiscal burden. Spending on TSP exceeded the additional revenue generated from the increase in the prices of previously subsidized energy goods in large part because energy consumption was lower without the subsidies, but also because of the reduction in international oil prices (Salehi-Isfahani et al., 2015). In the first eighteen months of this reform, spending on TSP was almost twice the amount of the increase in government revenue that resulted from eliminating the energy subsidies (Iranian Labour News Agency, 2013).[5] To address this problem, the Iranian government decided in 2014 to switch from a universal cash transfer to one that prevented the top 20% of the population from receiving TSP. The government called this change the 'Second Phase' of the subsidy reform, but it was not able to properly implement it to this day due to the pressure from the public. The government has only been able to remove the cash transfer from a very small percentage of the rich population. Here, we analyze what would have been the impact on inequality and poverty, and the fiscal resources saved, if the design of the transfer had excluded the top 20% from the start. In a way, one can consider the extra budgetary outlays as an estimate of the fiscal cost associated with making the reform politically palatable to the population as a whole. This is the second contribution of this paper.

While eliminating the cash transfer from the rich households can reduce the financial burden of the program without hurting the poor, its effectiveness in reducing poverty can increase if it is distributed in a more targeted way. Therefore, a third contribution of this paper is an assessment of the extent to which making the TSP more targeted would be more effective in protecting the poor and would reduce fiscal outlays. Specifically, we analyze how much the contribution of this program to reducing inequality and poverty, and TSP's overall effectiveness, would change if in addition to the elimination of the cash transfer from the top two decile, deciles VII and VIII were also no longer eligible and the resulting savings from the latter two deciles

---

[5] The estimated total cash transfer for this period (December 2010–June 2012) is about 62,000 billion Rials (about $5.4 billion) and the government revenue from the increase in prices is about 30,000 billion Rials (about $2.7 Billion). The dollar values in parentheses are based on the average exchange rate for this period from the Central Bank of Iran (CBI, 2014).

were transferred to the remaining income deciles (policy simulation 1) or to the bottom 30% (policy simulation 2).[6]

To estimate the impact of both the universal and 'Second Phase' of TSP, as well as policy simulations 1 and 2, we rely on standard fiscal incidence analysis as described in Lustig (2018). Fiscal incidence analysis is used to assess the distributional impacts of a country's taxes and transfers.[7] Essentially, it consists of allocating taxes (particularly the personal income tax and consumption taxes) and public spending (particularly social spending) to households or individuals in order to compare incomes before taxes and transfers to incomes after taxes and transfers. Transfers include: direct cash transfers; in-kind benefits, such as free government education and health care services, and consumption subsidies, including food, electricity, and fuel subsidies. Our analysis includes: personal income taxes and contributions to health insurance and social security, Social Assistance, TSP and other direct transfers, sales taxes, and in-kind transfers in education and health (net of user fees). Because standard fiscal incidence analysis, such as the one applied here, ignores behavioral responses and general equilibrium effects, our exercise estimates the direct effects of subsidies (and their removal) only. Thus, it is a useful first-order approximation of the effects of this fiscal policy. Furthermore, this analysis is one of the very few available for Iran, especially since its sweeping energy subsidy reform.

To measure the contribution of taxes and transfers to fiscally-induced changes in inequality and poverty, we use the marginal contribution approach (Enami, Lustig, & Aranda, 2018; Lambert, 2001). By this method, the contribution of a tax or a transfer to a change in inequality is measured by comparing the existing fiscal system to a counter-factual that excludes the tax (or transfer) of interest.[8] This approach is supe-

---

[6] Note that in both policy simulations, the cash transfer of the top two deciles is completely removed from the fiscal system and not redistributed to the other deciles.

[7] The tax incidence literature includes a long list of studies with empirical estimates going back more than half a century (Musgrave, 1959; Musgrave, Carroll, Cook, & Frane, 1951; Musgrave, Case, & Leonard, 1974; Pechman & Okner, 1974). Similarly, on the expenditure side, there are decades of work using the traditional approach (Meerman, 1979; Selowsky, 1979) and a behavioral approach (Gertler & Glewwe, 1990; Gertler & van der Gaag, 1990; Younger, Sahn, Haggblade, & Dorosh, 1999). For more recent work see, for example: Alm and Wallace (2007), Martinez-Vazquez (2008), Förster and Whiteford (2009), Immervoll and Richardson (2011), Bucheli, Lustig, Rossi, and Amábile (2014), Higgins and Pereira (2014), Jaramillo (2014), Lustig and Pessino (2014), Arauco, Molina, Pozo, and Aguilar (2014), Scott (2014), Cabrera, Lustig, and Morán (2015), Higgins and Lustig (2016), Higgins, Lustig, Ruble, and Smeeding (2016), Lustig (2015, 2016a, 2016b), Younger, Myamba, and Mdadila (2016), and Younger, Osei-Assibey, and Oppong (2017).

[8] For example, the marginal contribution of direct taxes to reducing inequality is measured by comparing the Gini of the system with direct taxes to the Gini of the same system without direct taxes. One also can think of this counter factual as having the tax or transfer replaced with an alternative tax or transfer of the same size but with no effect on inequality or poverty.

rior to using progressivity indicators (such as the Kakwani index) for determining whether a tax (or transfer) is inequality-increasing (or decreasing). This is because standard progressivity indicators can yield the wrong prediction, in terms of the impact of a particular intervention, when the number of fiscal instruments is greater than one. When a fiscal system is composed of multiple taxes and transfers, a progressive tax (or transfer) can actually increase inequality and a regressive tax (transfer) can reduce inequality.[9]

While a specific tax (transfer) can have a large effect on reducing inequality (or poverty), one key concern for economists and policymakers is to determine whether that tax (transfer) is effective. In this paper, we follow Fellman, Jäntti, and Lambert (1999) and Enami (2018b), and define effectiveness by comparing how close the actual marginal contribution of a tax (transfer) comes to achieving its maximum potential. We show, for example, that despite its relatively large effect on poverty and inequality, TSP is relatively less effective compared to some other components of the fiscal system in Iran. This finding highlights the importance of better targeting of cash subsidies, and motivates our policy simulations.

Our results show that the fiscal system in Iran (including direct and indirect taxes, direct transfers, and in-kind transfers for education and health) reduces the Gini coefficient by 0.0854 points, or 20%, compared to the Market Income Gini. Excluding the in-kind transfers for education and health, the reduction equals 0.0574 Gini points, or 13% of the Market Income Gini. Moreover, Iran's fiscal system is quite powerful in reducing poverty. The headcount ratio falls from about 21% to 11%.[10,11]

We also find that taxes are very effective in raising revenue without increasing poverty, and are moderately effective in reducing inequality. In contrast, because transfers are universal and not targeted to poor households, they realize only about 16% of their potential to reduce poverty. In terms of inequality, transfers are more similar to taxes: they moderately realize their potential. The 'Social Assistance' program leads other interventions, with a realized power of about 40% to 42%. Among taxes, only the Income Tax displays an effectiveness of this magnitude (about 34% to 36%).

Based on the size of its marginal contribution, TSP has the greatest impact in reducing inequality and poverty. TSP actually reduced inequality by about 0.0552 Gini points. Without TSP, the poverty headcount ratio would have been about 22% rather

---

[9] Lambert (2001) and Enami et al. (2018) show this mathematically. Also, Enami (2018a) shows what happens when taxes and transfers end up reranking individuals.

[10] Unless otherwise specified, throughout this paper we use $4 per day in 2005 purchasing power parity (PPP) as the poverty line.

[11] We calculate the poverty indices using the international poverty lines defined without accounting for the 'consumption' of education and health. To be consistent with the definition of these poverty lines, we do not include the in-kind transfers for education and health as part of the fiscal system when evaluating its effect on poverty.

than 12%. This reduction in poverty comes mainly from the large effect of this program in rural areas. Without it, the headcount ratio in rural areas would have been about 44%, not the observed 23% (while the headcount ratio in urban areas would have been 13%, not the observed 6%).[12] However, TSP's 'success' is mainly due to its size. Because it is basically universal, it is not effective in the sense that much more could be achieved in terms of reducing inequality and poverty if the resources were better targeted to the poor.

Given the importance of the TSP, we also evaluate two alternative scenarios of allocating its resources. We show that removing the subsidy from deciles VII and VIII, and allocating the additional savings to the bottom 60% (policy simulation 1), or just to the bottom 30% (policy simulation 2), would significantly reduce inequality and poverty. This is mainly because the program is already very successful in reaching the low-income groups, especially in rural areas.

The rest of this paper is organized as follows: section 2 briefly reviews Iran's fiscal system and lists the programs that are included in the analysis. It also explains the method and assumptions used to construct items not directly observed in the household survey. Section 3 discusses the data and methodology used in this paper, specifically the marginal contribution approach to calculating the effect of different taxes and transfers on reducing (increasing) inequality and poverty. We also describe the effectiveness indicators used in our analysis. Section 4 presents the results of our inequality and poverty analysis. We pay special attention to the Target Subsidy Program because of its significant role in reducing inequality and poverty. Finally, Section 5 concludes and presents policy recommendations for moving forward in managing the TSP in Iran.

2 Overview of Iran's Fiscal System and the Taxes and Transfers Included in This Analysis

Iran's fiscal system is composed of taxes, transfers, subsidies, and pensions which are briefly described in appendix A. In this appendix, we indicate which components are included in the analysis and what assumptions are used to construct their values if they are not directly observed in the household survey. Note that the information in this appendix closely relates to figure 17-1 and section 3 on methodology.

To provide some context here, table 17-1 presents a summary of the revenue sources and expenditure areas of Iran's budget (2011/12). Total revenues and spending are roughly the same: about 164 billion dollars, which is about 27% of GDP. The main source of revenue is natural resources (mainly oil), followed by capital and financial assets (55.23% of budget), and finally by tax revenues (24.0% of budget). Government expen-

---

[12] Note that these estimates rely on the concept of Consumable Income which is described later in section 3.

FIGURE 17-1

A Framework to Define Income Concepts and Combine Fiscal Interventions

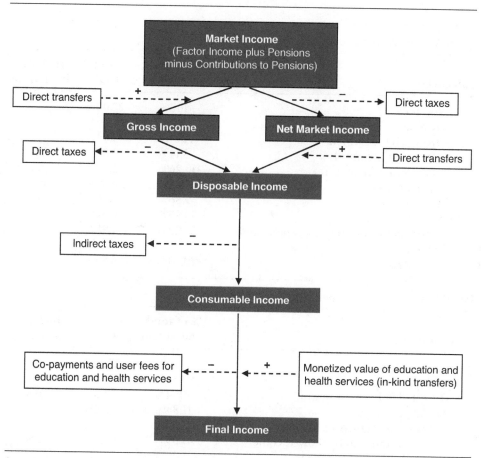

Source: Lustig (2018) with some adaptation.

Note: Core Income Concepts in dark blue background, Fiscal Interventions in white background.

ditures are divided equally into social expenditures and all other types of expenditures (e.g. defense). Education, social protection, TSP, and health expenditures are the main categories of social expenditures with 16.58%, 11.84%, 10.91%, and 9.24% of the budget allocated to them respectively. Table 17-1 also shows the categories that were included in the analysis.

3 Methodology and Data

Fiscal incidence analysis begins with constructing basic income concepts. Figure 17-1 presents the generally defined income concepts. In the Methodological Appendix

TABLE 17-1

Iranian Government Revenues and Expenditures (1390 Iranian calendar, equivalent to 2011–12)

Panel A. Government revenues

Categories	% of total revenue	% of GDP	Included in analysis
Total Revenues	100%	**27.00%**	
Tax revenues	24.07%	6.50%	
Direct taxes, of which:	14.21%	3.84%	
Personal Income Tax	3.14%	0.85%	Yes
Corporate Income Tax	10.26%	2.77%	No
Wealth Tax	0.81%	0.22%	No
Indirect Taxes	9.86%	2.66%	Yes
Non-tax revenues	75.93%	20.50%	
Sales of natural resources, capital, and financial assets	55.23%	14.91%	No
Other Revenues	20.70%	5.59%	No

Panel B. Government expenditures

Categories	% of total expenditure	% of GDP	Included in analysis
Total expenditure	100%	27.00%	
Social spending	50.68%	13.69%	
Targeted Subsidy Program	10.91%	2.95%	Yes
Social protection	11.84%	3.20%	
Social assistance, of which:	3.85%	1.04%	
Assistance to the Low-Income Families and Orphans	1.59%	0.43%	Yes
Assistance to the Families of Martyrs and wounded soldiers	2.23%	0.60%	Yes
Other	0.03%	0.01%	Yes
Social security, of which:	7.99%	2.16%	
Retirement Pensions: Civilians	4.49%	1.21%	Yes
Retirement Pensions: Armed Forces	3.50%	0.95%	Yes
Education, of which:	16.58%	4.48%	
12-K (Primary and Secondary)	7.79%	2.10%	Yes
Adult Literacy	0.14%	0.04%	No
Tertiary	7.89%	2.13%	Yes
Other	0.76%	0.20%	No
Health	9.24%	2.50%	Yes
Housing (urban and rural)	2.12%	0.57%	No
Other expenditures	49.32%	13.32%	No

Source: Own calculations using Adlband (2011) and SCI (2015).

Note: The total revenues and expenditures are equal to each other and equal to 1,697,255 billion Rials (about 163.76 billion dollars). The raw data is from Iran's budget in which total revenues and expenditures are equal, but that is due to the elements such as borrowing from the public and banks as well as the sales of public firms which close the deficit gap. The GDP of Iran for this period is 6,285,255 billion Rials (about 606.45 billion dollars).

(appendix B), we describe in greater detail how these income concepts are constructed for Iran. In broad terms, we begin with Market Income,[13] then subtract direct taxes and add cash transfers to obtain Disposable Income. Next, we subtract indirect taxes to generate Consumable Income. Because TSP replaced consumption subsidies, there are no consumption subsidies in our model. Finally, we add the monetized value (at average government cost) of In-kind transfers (i.e. health and education), net of user fees, to obtain Final Income.

This study relies on the concept of marginal contribution to estimate the contribution of taxes and transfers to reducing inequality and poverty. Theoretically, marginal contribution analysis asks what the distribution of income would have been in the absence of a tax[14] (or transfer), defining the difference between this counter factual and the actual distribution of income as the marginal contribution of that tax (or transfer). This is shown in the equation below:

$$MC_{T(or\ B)}^{End\ income} = Index_{End\ income \backslash T(or\ B)} - Index_{End\ income},$$

where $MC_{T(or\ B)}^{End\ income}$ is the marginal contribution of tax or transfer to the inequality or poverty index of an 'end income' concept (such as the disposable income). $Index_{End\ income \backslash T(or\ B)}$ is the value of that index for the same end income concept but when T (or B) is excluded. Similarly, $Index_{End\ income}$ is the value of that index when T (or B) is included. For example, the marginal contribution of direct taxes to the redistributive effect from market income to disposable income equals the difference between the Gini of disposable income including the direct taxes and the Gini coefficient of disposable income alone. In this paper, we focus on the first order effects of removing a tax or transfer and therefore ignore the behavioral responses. As is clear from the equation above, the order in which other fiscal interventions are added has no effect on the value of the $Index_{End\ income \backslash T(or\ B)}$.

One important feature of the marginal contribution approach is that it does not rely on the order in which other taxes and transfers (besides the tax or transfer of interest) are incorporated into the calculation. However, there is no guarantee that the sum of the marginal contributions of all components of a fiscal system is equal to the overall redistributive effect. This mathematical constraint has no implication for policy makers. Policy questions are all about changing the characteristics of a particular tax or transfer, adding a tax or transfer, or eliminating a tax or transfer, and how such changes potentially would affect the redistributive and poverty indicators. Only the marginal contribution approach provides the correct answer to these questions by comparing the fiscal system before and after a tax, transfer, or particular reform.

---

[13] The survey actually includes pre-tax income for employees. For the self-employed, market income is generated by subtracting Business Costs from Sales since both items are in the survey.

[14] Or replacing that tax (or transfer) with another tax (or transfer) that is neutral in reducing inequality (or poverty).

We use 'Impact and Spending Effectiveness Indicators' to evaluate how well taxes and transfers reduce inequality. In order to assess the effectiveness of taxes, transfers, or changes in them, we rely on the notion of 'optimal tax (transfer)' (Fellman et al., 1999),[15] using the indicators proposed in Enami (2018b) which are described below.

Mathematically, a given amount of taxes (or transfers) can be collected (allocated) in such a way to maximize the impact on inequality (or poverty) reduction. For example, in the case of the Gini coefficient, the maximum effect is obtained by collecting taxes from the richest individual until his/her income becomes equal to the second richest, then taxing both of them until their income becomes equal to the third richest person, and to continue this process until all of the tax has been collected. This procedure maximizes the reduction in Gini while keeping the size of taxes constant. An 'optimal' transfer would follow a similar procedure, but start with the poorest individual and move him/her up in the income distribution. This indicator is defined as follows:

$$Inequality\ Impact\ Effectiveness_{T(or\ B)}^{End\ income} = \frac{MC_{T(or\ B)}^{End\ income}}{MC_{T(or\ B)}^{End\ income^*}},$$

where $MC_{T(or\ B)}^{End\ income^*}$ is the maximum possible $MC_{T(or\ B)}^{End\ income}$ if the same amount of Tax (or Benefit) is levied on (distributed among) individuals optimally. The 'end income' in our analysis can refer to one of three income concepts: Disposable Income, Consumable Income, and Final Income (defined in figure 17-1). The value of this Inequality Impact Effectiveness indicator lies between -1 and $+1$ (the higher the indicator, the more effective).

Alternatively, one can keep the change in inequality constant and estimate the minimum size of a tax or a transfer that would be required to achieve the same marginal contribution. This reduction in the size of a tax or transfer is obtained through the same optimal redistribution process described above. This indicator is defined as follows:

$$Inequality\ Spending\ Effectiveness_{T(or\ B)}^{End\ income} = \frac{T^*(or\ B^*)}{T(or\ B)};$$

where $T^*(or\ B^*)$ is the minimum amount of T (or B) that is needed to create the same $MC_{T(or\ B)}^{End\ income}$ if the tax or transfer were optimally redistributed. Note that the Spending Effectiveness Indicator is only calculated for taxes and transfers with a positive $MC_{T(or\ B)}^{End\ income}$ because it is meaningless to calculate the optimum size of a tax or transfer that increases inequality. As a result, the value of this indicator lies between 0 and 1 (the higher the indicator, the more effective).

---

[15] Fellman et al. (1999) call a tax (transfer) optimal when it optimizes the social welfare index of interest (e.g. Gini index or poverty head count ratio) comparing to the class of all taxes (transfers) that raise (distribute) an identical amount of funds.

We use Impact and Spending Effectiveness Indicators to evaluate the performance of taxes and transfers in reducing inequality. Although we have shown results using the Gini coefficient, the indicators can be calculated with any other inequality measure.

To evaluate how taxes and transfers reduce poverty, we need a different index. Higgins and Lustig (2016) show that fiscal policies usually create both fiscal gain to the poor (FGP) and fiscal impoverishment (FI). Thus, one should differentiate between the two effects. Therefore, we use FI-FGP effectiveness indicators to account for these two effects. Although FI-FGP indicators are conceptually similar to our Impact Effectiveness indicators, one should not compare the FI-FGP effectiveness of taxes to transfers. Taxes can only hurt the poor (i.e. by increasing FI), while transfers can only benefit the poor (i.e. by increasing FGP). The FI-FGP indicators are defined so that the higher their value, the better a tax or transfer is. But the interpretations are different: the higher the value of the FI-FGP indicator for a tax, the more successful that tax is in raising revenue without increasing poverty; the higher the value of this indicator is for a transfer, the more successful it is in reducing poverty.

The FI-FGP indicators are calculated as follows:

$$FI\_FGP_T = \frac{T - FI\_MC_T^{End\,income}}{T},$$

$$FI\_FGP_B = \frac{FGP\_MC_B^{End\,income}}{B},$$

$$FI\_FGP_{Total\,system} = \left[\left(\frac{B}{T+B}\right)\left(\frac{FGP\_MC_B^{End\,income}}{B}\right)\right] + \left[\left(\frac{T}{T+B}\right)\left(\frac{T - FI\_MC_T^{End\,income}}{T}\right)\right],$$

where $FI\_MC_T^{End\,income}$ is the marginal contribution of tax T to the Fiscal Impoverishment (FI) index of the end income of interest and $FI\_MC_B^{End\,income}$ is the marginal contribution of transfer B to the Fiscal Gain to Poor (FGP) index of the end income of interest. The FI indicator measures how much poor individuals become worse off and non-poor become poor as a result of a tax. The FGP indicator measures how much poor individuals are made better off as a result of a transfer. Following Higgins and Lustig (2016), the change in the poverty gap is the index used to calculate the FI-FGP indicators.

All FI_FGT indicators vary between zero and one (the higher the indicator, the better). However, one cannot compare the effectiveness of taxes to transfers because taxes can only increase poverty. So, their effectiveness is calculated with respect to how much they do not increase poverty while raising revenue. On the other hand, transfers can only reduce poverty, so their effectiveness is calculated with respect to their performance in reducing poverty. The total fiscal system, which is the combination of all taxes and transfers, can increase or decrease poverty. Therefore, it should be only compared to alternative fiscal systems that have both taxes and transfers.

TABLE 17-2

Distribution of Individuals and Households According to Socio-Economic Group

In Daily US 2005 PPP	Socio-Economic Group	Number of individuals (% share)	Number of households (% share)	Average size of household
0–1.25	Ultra Poor	2,875,462 (3.62%)	729,004 (3.45%)	3.9
1.25–2.5	Extreme Poor	5,284,959 (6.65%)	1,305,675 (6.17%)	4.0
2.5–4	Moderate Poor	8,586,729 (10.80%)	1,930,893 (9.13%)	4.4
4–10	Vulnerable	32,281,101 (40.60%)	7,810,339 (36.91%)	4.1
10–50	Middle Class	29,755,312 (37.42%)	9,026,572 (42.66%)	3.3
50 or more	High Income Class	728,130 (0.92%)	356,549 (1.69%)	2.0
Total		79,511,694	21,159,033	3.8

Source: Own calculations using the Iranian household survey (1390 Iranian calendar, equivalent to 2011–12).

Note: The total population slightly exceeds the actual population for this year due to the application of survey weights. Socio-Economic group is determined according to the 'Market Income'. PPP stands for Purchasing Power Parity. In calculating PPP values, we use the 2005 round of ICP (International Comparison Program) as reported in the World Development Indicators (WDI) published by the World Bank. To change monetary values from the year of survey to 2005, we use the CPI index from the WDI.

The main data base for this study is the Iranian Household Expenditure and Income Survey (HEIS) for the calendar year 1390 (2011–12).[16] The Statistical Center of Iran conducts this survey every year, and its sample represents all rural and urban areas of Iran. In the survey year that we use, there are 18,727 urban and 19,786 rural households in the sample. These households represent about 56.4 million urban and 23.1 million rural individuals. For each of the households in the sample, we follow figure 17-1 and construct the core income concepts as well as income components (i.e. taxes and transfers) as described in table 17B-1 in the Methodological Appendix. As mentioned earlier, the marginal contribution technique used in this paper is not sensitive to the order of adding taxes and transfers.

Table 17-2 shows the distribution of individuals and households based on their income group and the average household size in each income group. About 21% of the population live in poverty and 41% are economically vulnerable. Together, about 62% of Iranians are considered low-income. The middle class is also large and includes about 37% of the population. The remaining 1% belong to the high-income group.

---

[16] Most of the survey data is available at goo.gl/MnYB23. Please note that the online database does not include the survey weight variables. These variables are, however, available for researchers who visit the Statistical Center of Iran in person.

4 Results

In this section, we first analyze each component of the fiscal system and evaluate its marginal contribution to reducing inequality and poverty, as well as its effectiveness in doing so. then, we focus on the 'Targeted Subsidy Program,' and evaluate how much it would contribute to the change in poverty and inequality (in terms of marginal contribution) and its effectiveness in different policy scenarios. It is important to note that throughout our analysis, all income values are in per capita terms and poverty lines are appropriately adjusted to reflect the per capita nature of the data.

4-1 Contribution of Fiscal Interventions to Changes in Inequality and Poverty

Table 17-3 shows the progressivity of each income component of the fiscal system, as well as its marginal contribution to reducing (or increasing) inequality for three of the main income concepts (i.e. Disposable, Consumable, and Final Incomes). The interpretation of marginal contributions is as follows: how much the Gini of an income concept would have been higher (or lower) if a specific income component (i.e. a tax or transfer) were removed from the fiscal system. Positive values mean that the Gini would have been higher; therefore, removing that component increases inequality. Put differently, positive values for the marginal contribution mean that an income component has a positive effect in increasing equality (or reducing inequality). Among all the income components, Semi-cash Transfers (Food), indirect taxes (i.e. Sales Taxes), and Health User-fees have a negative effect on equality. As expected, direct transfers make the highest marginal contribution to reducing inequality in all three income concepts. However, the main contribution comes from the Targeted Subsidy Program with a marginal contribution of about 0.05 Gini points. This is in line with findings of Cockburn, Robichaud, and Tiberti (2018), that utilize ex-ante simulations of energy subsidy reform proposals in Egypt and Jordan (two countries that are also in the Middle East region) to show that using cash transfers to reallocate part of the freed-up resources would have a significant effect on reducing poverty in these two countries.

Table 17-3 also reveals two examples of a phenomenon known as the Lambert Conundrum (Enami et al., 2018). The commonly used rule of thumb regarding the effect of a tax or transfer on reducing inequality states that a progressive tax or transfer (as measured by the Kakwani index) reduces inequality and a regressive tax or transfer increases it. However, this rule is not always correct, because adding a regressive tax (or transfer) can result in higher equality, or adding a progressive tax (or transfer) can increase inequality. In Iran's case, the Semi-Cash Transfer (Food) and Health User-fees are progressive (have a positive Kakwani index) but their marginal contributions to the inequality of Final Income (and other Income concepts for the Semi-Cash Transfer) are negative. In other words, removing these progressive

TABLE 17-3
Marginal Contribution of Taxes and Transfers to Inequality

Fiscal Intervention		Marginal contribution to the Gini index of			
		Progressivity (Kakwani Index)	Disposable Income (0.3686)	Consumable Income (0.3712)	Final Income (0.3432)
Direct Taxes and Contributions	Income Tax	0.2274	0.0018	0.0018	0.0019
	Employee contributions to the health insurance	0.0002	0.0003	0.0002	0.0004
	Employer contributions to the health insurance	0.0455	0.0008	0.0007	0.0009
	Total Direct Taxes and Contributions	0.0855	0.0029	0.0028	0.0032
Direct Transfers	Targeted Subsidy Program	0.4164	0.0527	0.0552	0.0465
	Social Assistance	0.8205	0.0043	0.0045	0.0040
	Semi-cash Transfers (Food)	0.3018	<0.0000	<0.0000	<0.0000
	Total Direct Transfers	0.4384	0.0583	0.0611	0.0516
Indirect Taxes (Sales Taxes)		−0.1363	–	−0.0026	−0.0025
In-kind Transfers	Education Transfers	0.3485	–	–	0.0226
	Education User-fees	0.0682	–	–	0.0018
	Health Transfers	0.4171	–	–	0.0177
	Health User-fees	0.1611	–	–	−0.0075
	Total In-kind Transfers	0.5886	–	–	0.0290

Source: Own calculations using the Iranian household survey (1390 Iranian calendar, equivalent to 2011–12).

Note: The Kakwani index is calculated with respect to the "Market Income."

interventions would result in lower (instead of higher) inequality over the whole income distribution.[17]

Table 17-4 does the same marginal contribution analysis for the poverty headcount ratio. In this table, positive values have a positive connotation, similar to that of the previous table. In other words, a transfer with a positive marginal contribution would reduce poverty; if it is removed from the fiscal system, the result would be an increase

---

[17] Results related to education and health in-kind transfers should be interpreted with caution as the quality of service that a household receives is not incorporated in imputation of these two transfers (please see appendix A for more detail). However, this has no impact on the fact that given the current values used in this analysis, we observe a Lambert Conundrum in our database.

TABLE 17-4

Marginal Contribution of Taxes and Transfers to Poverty

Fiscal Intervention		Marginal contribution to the $4 PPP poverty headcount index of		Marginal contribution to the Urban-Rural Poverty headcount index of	
		Disposable Income (0.0939)	Consumable Income (0.1057)	Disposable Income (0.2581)	Consumable Income (0.2805)
Direct Taxes and Contributions	Income Tax	−0.0004	−0.0005	−0.0031	−0.0029
	Employee contributions to the health insurance	−0.0013	−0.0014	−0.0044	−0.0059
	Employer contributions to the health insurance	−0.0008	−0.0005	−0.0045	−0.0053
	Total Direct Taxes and Contributions	−0.0024	−0.0021	−0.0119	−0.0138
Direct Transfers	Targeted Subsidy Program	0.1131	0.1190	0.1473	0.1513
	Social Assistance	0.0104	0.0111	0.0099	0.102
	Semi-cash Transfers (Food)	0.0001	0.0002	0.0002	0.0004
	Total Direct Transfers	0.1217	0.1277	0.1554	0.1591
Indirect Taxes (Sales Taxes)		–	−0.0118	–	−0.0224

Source: Own calculations using the Iranian household survey (1390 Iranian calendar, equivalent to 2011–12).

Note: PPP stands for Purchasing Power Parity. In calculating PPP values, we use the 2005 round of ICP (International Comparison Program) as reported in the World Development Indicators (WDI) published by the World Bank. To change monetary values from the year of survey to 2005, we use the CPI index from the WDI. Urban-Rural poverty lines are based on Negahdari et al. (2014, 2015) which differentiate between households based on their size and whether they are located in an Urban/Rural area.

in the poverty headcount ratio equal to the size of the marginal contribution. As expected, taxes always can do harm, i.e. increase poverty, but they are not a concern in the case of Iran except for the Sales Taxes. With respect to Consumable Income and $4PPP poverty line, Direct Taxes increase the poverty headcount ratio by about 0.2 percentage points and Sales Taxes increase it by about 1.2 percentage points. On the other hand, direct transfers reduce this poverty index by about 12.8 percentage points. Most of this effect is due to the Targeted Subsidy Program, which reduces poverty by about 11.9 percentage points. To put this value in context, note that the poverty headcount ratio of Consumable Income is about 10.6%, so without the Targeted Subsidy Program, the value of this indicator would have been about 22.5%. The general results remain unchanged when the Urban-Rural poverty lines are used instead of the $4PPP. The former poverty lines are based on Negahdari, Piraee, Keshavarz Haddad, and Haghighat (2014, 2015) which differentiate between households based on their size and whether they are located in an Urban/Rural area.[18]

Now we turn to measuring the effectiveness of taxes and transfers in reducing inequality and poverty. The previous analysis focused on the observed outcome of these fiscal interventions, but what follows provides a context for evaluating the observed marginal contributions. As was mentioned before, these indicators show how effective taxes and transfers are in reducing poverty and inequality when compared to their full potential. Tables 17-5 and 17-6 present the results for Impact Effectiveness and Spending Effectiveness, and FI-FGP Effectiveness indices, respectively.

Focusing on table 17-5, and with respect to Consumable Income, the Income Tax has the highest Impact Effectiveness of the direct taxes, fulfilling about 34% of its potential in reducing inequality. However, the highest effectiveness belongs to Social Assistance (a direct transfer), which fulfills about 42% of its potential. Among interventions with a positive marginal contribution the lowest Impact Effectiveness belongs to Employee Contributions to the Health Insurance, about 4% of its potential. Health User-fees are the worst: they have an increasing effect on inequality, but compared to Semi-Cash Transfers (Food) and Sales Taxes, which also increase inequality, they have relatively more potential to reduce it.

With regard to Spending Effectiveness, and focusing on the Consumable Income column, Social Assistance (with about 41%) and Income Tax (with about 34%) are the two most effective interventions. Employee Contributions to the Health Insurance are worst, with almost zero effectiveness. That means that with a very small fraction of Employee Contributions to the Health Insurance, one can achieve the same level of reduction in inequality as is currently produced by these contributions. This outcome is expected given the small size of the Marginal Contribution of this intervention (see table 17-3).

Table 17-6 presents FI-FGP effectiveness indicators. As was mentioned earlier, we should not compare Taxes and Transfers because taxes can only increase poverty while transfers can only reduce it. All taxes are highly efficient in raising revenue without significantly increasing poverty, while direct transfers are not very efficient in reducing poverty. Focusing on $4PPP poverty line and among transfers, Social Assistance has the highest effectiveness (about 21% with respect to Consumable Income) and Semi-Cash Transfers have the lowest (about 4% with respect to Consumable Income). The Targeted Subsidy Program's poverty reduction effectiveness is about 15%. One may question these results for TSP given the high marginal contribution of this program

---

[18] We use the equivalent US 2005 $PPP of poverty lines in Negahdari et al. (2014, 2015) in our analysis. Depending on the size of a household, the poverty line for an urban household ranges from $7.14 PPP to $8.93 PPP. For the rural households, the range of values is from $3.19 PPP to $3.51 PPP. The exact poverty line used for each size of household in urban and rural areas is available upon request.

TABLE 17-5
Impact and Spending Effectiveness Indicators for Taxes and Transfers in Iran

Fiscal Intervention		Impact Effectiveness with respect to			Spending Effectiveness with respect to		
		Disposable Income	Consumable Income	Final Income	Disposable Income	Consumable Income	Final Income
Direct Taxes and Contributions	Income Tax	0.3445	0.3384	0.3611	0.3461	0.3399	0.3625
	Employee contributions to the health insurance	0.0476	0.0357	0.0765	0.0479	0.0359	0.0770
	Employer contributions to the health insurance	0.1243	0.1152	0.1388	0.1252	0.1161	0.1397
	Total Direct Taxes and Contributions	0.1701	0.1613	0.1901	0.1725	0.1636	0.1925
Direct Transfers	Targeted Subsidy Program	0.3603	0.3648	0.3353	0.2848	0.2872	0.2623
	Social Assistance	0.4122	0.4172	0.4061	0.4022	0.4069	0.3969
	Semi-cash Transfers (Food)	−0.0377	−0.0381	−0.0543	N/A	N/A	N/A
	Total Direct Transfers	0.3747	0.3795	0.3498	0.2943	0.2969	0.2721
Indirect Taxes (Sales Taxes)		—	−0.1284	−0.1250	—	N/A	N/A
In-kind Transfers	Education Transfers	—	—	0.2163	—	—	0.1713
	Education User-fees	—	—	0.1514	—	—	0.1530
	Health Transfers	—	—	0.3002	—	—	0.2660
	Health User-fees	—	—	−0.2361	—	—	N/A

Source: Own calculations using the Iranian household survey (1390 Iranian calendar, equivalent to 2011–12).

Note: Fiscal interventions with an N/A are the ones with a negative marginal contribution, so it is mathematically impossible to calculate the spending effectiveness for them.

TABLE 17-6

FI-FGP Effectiveness Indicators for Taxes and Transfers in Iran

Fiscal Intervention		FI-FGP Effectiveness with respect to ($4PPP)		FI-FGP Effectiveness with respect to (Urban-Rural poverty lines)	
		Disposable Income	Consumable Income	Disposable Income	Consumable Income
Direct Taxes and Contributions	Income Tax	0.9984	0.9964	0.9349	0.9245
	Employee contributions to the health insurance	0.9879	0.9837	0.8719	0.8550
	Employer contributions to the health insurance	0.9964	0.9955	0.9226	0.9075
	Total Direct Taxes and Contributions	0.9945	0.9923	0.9144	0.9009
Direct Transfers	Targeted Subsidy Program	0.1340	0.1492	0.3099	0.3343
	Social Assistance	0.1827	0.2069	0.3589	0.3840
	Semi-cash Transfers (Food)	0.0344	0.0387	0.1293	0.1383
	Total Direct Transfers	0.1464	0.1619	0.3213	0.3456
Indirect Taxes (Sales Taxes)		–	0.9567	–	0.8387
Total System		0.2838	0.4018	0.4174	0.5015

Source: Own calculations using the Iranian household survey (1390 Iranian calendar, equivalent to 2011–12).

Note: PPP stands for Purchasing Power Parity. In calculating PPP values, we use the 2005 round of ICP (International Comparison Program) as reported in the World Development Indicators (WDI) published by the World Bank. To change monetary values from the year of survey to 2005, we use the CPI index from the WDI. The FI-FGT effectiveness indicators are bounded between zero and one and the higher the value of an indicator, the better the tax is in not increasing poverty and a transfer is in reducing poverty. Urban-Rural poverty lines are based on Negahdari et al. (2014, 2015) which differentiate between households based on their size and whether they are located in an Urban/Rural area.

to reducing poverty, as established in the previous sections. But the explanation is in the properties of TSP. The TSP's cash transfers are made to all Iranians (i.e. poor and non-poor equally), so the total cash transfer is very large, but not specifically targeted toward the poor. As a result, its poverty effectiveness diminishes substantially. Poverty would be reduced significantly if the Targeted Subsidy Program were allocated more toward low-income households. We explore this idea further in the next subsection. Finally, it is worth noting that the fiscal system as a whole is not very effective in reducing poverty. With respect to Disposable Income and Consumable Income, the fiscal system only realizes about 28% and 39% of its potential, respectively.

The results are generally robust when Urban-Rural poverty lines are used. One should note that these poverty lines are higher than the $4PPP in the urban areas and as a result the effectiveness of the direct transfers, for example, would be automatically higher. However, even with this higher poverty line, direct transfers do not achieve anything more than 35% of their potential to reduce poverty.

4-2 Alternative Scenarios for Implementation of the "Targeted Subsidy Program"

Since the TSP makes the largest marginal contribution to the reduction of inequality and poverty, it is important to analyze it further. This cash transfer program (in the survey year used in this paper) offers an identical amount to every Iranian regardless of income (Baseline scenario). In order to be sure our results are not driven by how the income concepts are set up in the Baseline scenario (which uses the income portion of the survey), we reconstruct the same income concepts using the expenditure (of nondurable goods and imputed rent) portion of the survey. We call this Alternative Baseline scenario.

As was mentioned before, the Iranian government has proposed a plan known as the 'Second Phase' of the energy subsidies reform (but not yet successfully implemented it) to eliminate eligibility for receiving cash transfer from the top two deciles. What if this new policy had been in place from the beginning? We consider that (i.e. the 'Second Phase' policy) as well as two alternative policy scenarios with fiscally neutral effects as compared to the Second Phase policy, asking how much larger the marginal contribution of TSP would be in reducing inequality and poverty.[19] In the first scenario, we remove the subsidy for the top 40%, but increase transfers to the bottom 60% by about 30% ('Policy Simulation 1'). In the second scenario, we again eliminate transfers for the top 40%, but increase the cash transfer to those at the bottom 30% by about 60% ('Policy Simulation 2'). It is important to note that for the two alternative policy simulations, we do not redistribute the cash transfer of the top two deciles so that these two scenarios are fiscally similar to the 'Second Phase' scenario.

Panel A in Table 17-7 shows how the Targeted Subsidy Program's marginal contribution to reducing inequality changes in different scenarios. The results of the 'Baseline' and 'Alternative Baseline' cases are very similar indicating that using income or expenditure portions of the household survey to set up the income concepts produces very similar results. As expected as the transfer to the top income groups are removed and the transfer to the low-income group is increased, inequality decreases significantly. Focusing only on Consumable Income, the marginal contribution of TSP to reducing inequality is about 0.0655, 0.0868, and 0.0953 Gini points in the Second Phase and the two alternative scenarios, respectively. To put this in context, note that in the Baseline case the marginal contribution of TSP to the Gini of Consumable Income is about

---

[19] These microsimulations follow the 'arithmetical approach' that ignores the behavioral responses. For more information about this type of simulation see Bourguignon and Spadaro (2006).

0.0552. Therefore, from the inequality perspective, there is not a big difference between the Baseline scenario and the Second Phase, but the two alternative scenarios produce significantly more reduction in inequality.

Panel B in Table 17-7 performs a similar analysis under each scenario using the poverty headcount ratio for the change in poverty. The Baseline and the Second Phase are not different, given that the top 20% would not become poor if they lose this cash transfer. The Baseline and Alternative Baseline scenarios have very similar values, especially when the Urban-Rural poverty lines are used. For simulated scenarios and with respect to Consumable Income and $4PPP poverty line, Policy Simulation 1 and 2 improve the marginal contribution of this cash transfer from 11.90 percentage points in the Baseline to 14.69 percentage points and 16.79 percentage points respectively. The poverty headcount ratio decreases from about 11% in the Second Phase case to about 6% in Policy Simulation 2; that is a significant reduction in poverty for a fiscally neutral policy alternative. The change in poverty line from $4PPP to the Urban-Rural poverty lines do not change our conclusions and the results are very similar as is clear in Panel B of Table 17-7.

The poverty-reducing effect of an additional cash transfer to low income deciles is significant. To get at that effect, we analyze how different policy scenarios change the poverty headcount index of urban versus rural areas. These results are presented in appendix C. Overall, TSP substantially benefits the rural areas.

Table 17-8 presents the effectiveness of TSP under different scenarios, taking the values reported for the Baseline scenario from the previous tables for comparison purposes. The Baseline and Alternative Baseline produce a very similar set of results. With regard to all measures of effectiveness, eliminating the cash transfer from the top deciles and allocating it to the low-income groups improves the performance of the TSP significantly. In fact, Policy Simulation 2, which has the most focused approach to allocating the cash transfer to low-income households, almost doubles the effectiveness of the Baseline scenario in reducing inequality. Still, the FI-FGP effectiveness indicator reveals that even this scenario has significant room for improvement, because it only reaches about 22% of its potential when the $4PPP poverty line is used. Changing the poverty line to the Urban-Rural poverty lines increases the effectiveness of TSP in all scenarios but this is a byproduct of the fact that the Urban-Rural poverty lines are higher than the $4PPP line in the urban areas.

5 Conclusion

This paper analyzes the effect of different components of the fiscal system in Iran on reducing inequality and poverty. Using the marginal contribution approach, we show that direct transfers in general, and the (cash component of the) Targeted Subsidy Program in particular, play the most significant role in creating a more equal distribution of income and reducing poverty in Iran. The system as a whole reduces the inequality of income distribution by about 20% (comparing Market Income to Final Income) and the poverty head count ratio by about 50% (comparing Market Income to Consum-

TABLE 17-7

Alternative Policies for How to Manage Targeted Subsidy Program and Their Effect on Inequality and Poverty

Panel A. Inequality

Policy	Marginal contribution to the Gini index of		
	Disposable Income (DI)	Consumable Income (CI)	Final Income (FI)
Baseline (All income deciles receive the subsidy)	0.0527 (Gini of DI: 0.3686)	0.0552 (Gini of CI: 0.3712)	0.0465 (Gini of FI: 0.3432)
Alternative Baseline: (Baseline with income concepts calculated using reported household expenditure)	0.0647 (Gini of DI: 0.3570)	0.0680 (Gini of CI: 0.3570)	0.0532 (Gini of FI: 0.3140)
Second Phase: No subsidy for top 20%	0.0628 (Gini of DI: 0.3586)	0.0655 (Gini of CI: 0.3609)	0.0559 (Gini of FI: 0.3336)
Policy Simulation 1: No subsidy for top 40% and an extra 30% for bottom 60%	0.0834 (Gini of DI: 0.3379)	0.0868 (Gini of CI: 0.3397)	0.0742 (Gini of FI: 0.3153)
Policy Simulation 2: No subsidy for top 40% and an extra 60% for bottom 30%	0.0916 (Gini of DI: 0.3297)	0.0953 (Gini of CI: 0.3312)	0.0816 (Gini of FI: 0.3080)

Panel B. Poverty

Policy	Marginal contribution to the $4 PPP poverty headcount index (PHI) of		Marginal contribution to the Urban-Rural poverty headcount index (PHI) of	
	DI	CI	DI	CI
Baseline (All income deciles receive the subsidy)	0.1131 (PHI of DI: 0.0939)	0.1190 (PHI of CI: 0.1057)	0.1473 (PHI of DI: 0.2581)	0.1513 (PHI of CI: 0.2805)
Alternative Baseline (Baseline with income concepts calculated using reported household expenditure)	0.1501 (PHI of DI: 0.1211)	0.1602 (PHI of CI: 0.1348)	0.1578 (PHI of DI: 0.3662)	0.1586 (PHI of CI: 0.3923)

(continued)

TABLE 17-7   (continued)

Policy	Marginal contribution to the $4 PPP poverty headcount index (PHI) of		Marginal contribution to the Urban-Rural poverty headcount index (PHI) of	
	DI	CI	DI	CI
Second Phase: No subsidy for top 20%	0.1131 (PHI of DI: 0.0939)	0.1190 (PHI of CI: 0.1057)	0.1473 (PHI of DI: 0.2581)	0.1512 (PHI of CI: 0.2806)
Policy Simulation 1: No subsidy for top 40% and an extra 30% for bottom 60%	0.1387 (PHI of DI: 0.0682)	0.1469 (PHI of CI: 0.0778)	0.1832 (PHI of DI: 0.2222)	0.1908 (PHI of CI: 0.2410)
Policy Simulation 2: No subsidy for top 40% and an extra 60% for bottom 30%	0.1578 (PHI of DI: 0.0492)	0.1679 (PHI of CI: 0.0568)	0.1819 (PHI of DI: 0.2236)	0.1837 (PHI of CI: 0.2481)

Source: Own calculations using the Iranian household survey (1390 Iranian calendar, equivalent to 2011–12).

Note: PPP stands for Purchasing Power Parity. In calculating PPP values, we use the 2005 round of ICP (International Comparison Program) as reported in the World Development Indicators (WDI) published by the World Bank. To change monetary values from the year of survey to 2005, we use the CPI index from the WDI. Urban-Rural poverty lines are based on Negahdari et al. (2014, 2015) which differentiate between households based on their size and whether they are located in an Urban/Rural area.

able Income). The Targeted Subsidy Program alone reduces the inequality and poverty of Consumable Income by about 0.0552 Gini points and 12 percentage points respectively (using $4PPP as the poverty line). The main reduction in poverty comes from the rural areas: this program reduces the poverty headcount ratio from about 44% to 23%. The urban areas only experience a moderate 8 percentage point reduction in poverty (i.e. from 13% to 5%) due to this program.

We find mixed results for how effective taxes and transfers are in reducing inequality and poverty compared to their potential. Taxes are very effective in raising revenue without increasing poverty and are moderately effective in reducing inequality. On the other hand, transfers exhibit a similar, moderate effectiveness in reducing inequality to that of taxes, but they are not focused on poor households, and realize less than 17% of their potential power to reduce poverty.

We evaluate different policy scenarios about how to proceed with the current Targeted Subsidy Program in Iran. We find that if the Iranian government's current plan to eliminate the cash transfer of top deciles were extended from the top 20% to the top 40%, and were combined with a moderate increase in the cash transfer to the bottom deciles, the additional reduction in poverty and inequality would be considerable. If the cash transfer of the top 40% is eliminated and the cash transfer to the bottom 60% is increased by only 30%, inequality and poverty would be reduced by an additional

TABLE 17-8

Effectiveness of Targeted Subsidy Program in Alternative Policy Scenarios

Panel A. Impact Effectiveness

Policy	Impact Effectiveness with respect to		
	Disposable Income	Consumable Income	Final Income
Baseline	0.3603	0.3648	0.3353
Alternative Baseline	0.3804	0.3852	0.3468
Second Phase	0.4850	0.4891	0.4586
Policy Simulation 1	0.6447	0.6479	0.6103
Policy Simulation 2	0.7077	0.7108	0.6709

Panel B. Spending Effectiveness

Policy	Spending Effectiveness with respect to		
	Disposable Income	Consumable Income	Final Income
Baseline	0.2848	0.2872	0.2623
Alternative Baseline	0.2874	0.2890	0.2572
Second Phase	0.4111	0.4133	0.3852
Policy Simulation 1	0.5747	0.5764	0.5377
Policy Simulation 2	0.6435	0.6452	0.6025

Panel C. FI-FGP Effectiveness

Policy	FI-FGP Effectiveness with respect to ($4PPP)		FI-FGP Effectiveness with respect to (Urban-Rural poverty lines)	
	Disposable Income	Consumable Income	Disposable Income	Consumable Income
Baseline	0.1340	0.1492	0.3099	0.3343
Alternative Baseline	0.2050	0.1138	0.4574	0.3444
Second Phase	0.1586	0.1766	0.3669	0.3957
Policy Simulation 1	0.1798	0.2012	0.4393	0.4747
Policy Simulation 2	0.1921	0.2160	0.4769	0.5103

Source: Own calculations using the Iranian household survey (1390 Iranian calendar, equivalent to 2011–12).

Note: The description of policy scenarios are as follows. Baseline: all income deciles receive the subsidy; Alternative Baseline: The same as Baseline with income concepts calculated using reported household expenditures; Second Phase: No subsidy for top 20%; Policy Simulation 1: No subsidy for top 40% and an extra 30% for bottom 60%; Policy Simulation 2: No subsidy for top 40% and an extra 60% for bottom 30%. PPP stands for Purchasing Power Parity. In calculating PPP values, we use the 2005 round of ICP (International Comparison Program) as reported in the World Development Indicators (WDI) published by the World Bank. To change monetary values from the year of survey to 2005, we use the CPI index from the WDI. Urban-Rural poverty lines are based on Negahdari et al. (2014, 2015) which differentiate between households based on their size and whether they are located in an Urban/Rural area.

8.5% and 26.4%, respectively (compared to the current Gini and poverty headcount ratio of Consumable Income). This poverty reduction effect would not be the same for rural versus urban areas. An extra 30% going to the bottom 60% of the income distribution would reduce the poverty headcount ratio of Consumable Income to 16.7% (from 22.8%) in rural areas. In urban areas, the reduction in the poverty head count ratio would be only 1.4 percentage points (i.e. 4.2% from 5.6% now). The power of the Targeted Subsidy Program in reducing inequality and poverty stems from the ability of the program to reach the bottom deciles of the income distribution in rural areas of Iran. Therefore, the main policy recommendation of this paper is to not just remove the cash transfers from the top 20% (as it was implemented recently in Iran), but extend it to the top 40% and to allocate part of the resulting extra funds to the bottom deciles, especially in the rural areas.

Acknowledgements

This paper was produced under the research program on fiscal incidence in low and middle income countries of the Commitment to Equity Institute at Tulane University (www.commitmentoequity.org) and the Economics Research Forum (ERF grant number 2015–006). An earlier version of this work was published as ERF Working Paper Number 1020. The authors are very grateful to ERF for its financial and intellectual support. The contents and recommendations are of the authors' (and not their affiliations) and do not necessarily reflect ERF's views. Any remaining errors are the sole responsibility of the authors. The authors are thankful of the Statistical Center of Iran for providing additional documents and data beyond what is available online and to the editor and two anonymous referees for their insightful comments on the previous version of this paper.

Disclosure statement

No potential conflict of interest was reported by the authors.

Funding

This work was supported by Bill and Melinda Gates Foundation [grant number OPP1135502]; Economic Research Forum (Egypt) [grant number 2015–006].

References

Adlband, T. (2011). 1390 Budget Bill from the Education Perspective (tentative translation from Farsi title: Layehe-ye Boodje-ye Saal-e 1390-e Kol-e KeshvarazNegah-e Amoozeshva-Parvaresh). Barname weekly, Year 9, Number 405, 1–9.

Alm, J., & Wallace, S. (2007). Which elasticity? Estimating the responsiveness of taxpayer reporting decisions. *International Advances in Economic Research, 13*(3), 255–267.

Arauco, V. P., Molina, G. G., Pozo, W. J., & Aguilar, E. Y. (2014). Explaining low redistributive impact in Bolivia. *Public Finance Review, 42*(3), 326–345.

Atamanov, A., Mostafavi, M.-H., Salehi Isfahani, D., & Vishwanath, T. (2016). *Constructing robust poverty trends in the Islamic Republic of Iran: 2008–14* (Policy Research working paper; no. WPS 7836). Washington, DC: World Bank Group.

Bourguignon, F., & Spadaro, A. (2006). Microsimulation as a tool for evaluating redistribution policies. *The Journal of Economic Inequality, 4*(1), 77–106.

Bucheli, M., Lustig, N., Rossi, M., & Amábile, F. (2014). Social spending, taxes and income redistribution in Uruguay. *Public Finance Review, 42*(3), 413–433.

Cabrera, M., Lustig, N., & Morán, H. E. (2015). Fiscal policy, inequality, and the ethnic divide in Guatemala. *World Development, 76*, 263–279.

Central Bank of Iran (CBI), Reference Exchange Rates. (2014, November 23). Retrieved from http://www.cbi.ir/exrates/rates_en.aspx

Cockburn, J., Robichaud, V., & Tiberti, L. (2018). Energy subsidy reform and poverty in Arab countries: A comparative CGE-microsimulation analysis of Egypt and Jordan. *Review of Income and Wealth, 64*, S249–S273.

Enami, A. (2018a). Measuring the redistributive impact of taxes and transfers in the presence of reranking. In N. Lustig (Ed.), *Commitment to equity handbook: Estimating the impact of fiscal policy on inequality and poverty* (pp. 116–174). Washington, DC: Brookings Institution Press and CEQ Institute, Tulane University.

Enami, A. (2018b). Measuring the effectiveness of taxes and transfers in fighting inequality and poverty. In N. Lustig (Ed.), *Commitment to equity handbook: Estimating the impact of fiscal policy on inequality and poverty* (pp. 207–216). Washington, DC: Brookings Institution Press and CEQ Institute, Tulane University.

Enami, A., Lustig, N., & Aranda, R. (2018). Analytic foundations: Measuring the redistributive impact of taxes and transfers. In N. Lustig (Ed.), *Commitment to equity handbook: Estimating the impact of fiscal policy on inequality and poverty* (pp. 56–115). Washington, DC: Brookings Institution Press and CEQ Institute, Tulane University.

Fellman, J., Jäntti, M., & Lambert, P. J. (1999). Optimal tax-transfer systems and redistributive policy. *Scandinavian Journal of Economics, 101*(1), 115–126.

Förster, M., & Whiteford, P. (2009). How much redistribution do welfare states achieve? The role of cash transfers and household taxes. *CESifo DICE Report, 7*(3), 34–41.

Gahvari, F., &Taheripour, F. (2011). Fiscal reforms in general equilibrium: Theory and an application to the subsidy debate in Iran. *The B.E. Journal of Economic Analysis & Policy, 11*(1), 1–54.

Gertler, P., & Glewwe, P. (1990). The willingness to pay for education in developing countries: Evidence from Rural Peru. *Journal of Public Economics, 42*(3), 251–275.

Gertler, P., & van der Gaag, J. (1990). *The willingness to pay for medical care: Evidence from two developing countries*. Baltimore: Johns Hopkins University Press for the World Bank.

Guillaume, D. M., Farzin, M. R., & Zytek, R. (2011). *Iran: The chronicles of the subsidy reform* (Working paper no. 11-167). Washington, DC: International Monetary Fund.

Higgins, S., & Lustig, N. (2016). Can a poverty-reducing and progressive tax and transfer system hurt the poor? *Journal of Development Economics, 122*, 63–75.

Higgins, S., Lustig, N., Ruble, W., & Smeeding, T. (2016). Comparing the incidence of taxes and social spending in Brazil and the United States. *Review of Income and Wealth, 62*(S1), S22–S46. doi:10.1111/roiw.12201

Higgins, S., & Pereira, C. (2014). The effects of Brazil's taxation and social spending on the distribution of household income. *Public Finance Review, 42*(3), 346–367.

Immervoll, H., & Richardson, L. (2011). *Redistribution policy and inequality reduction in OECD countries: What has changed in two decades?* (Discussion Paper No. 6030). Bonn: Institute for the Study of Labor (IZA).

Iranian Labour News Agency. (2013). *Pumping strong liquidity into the economy/ the second phase of [targeted subsidy reform] should be operationalized when there is economic stability (tentative translation from Farsi).* Retrieved from http://goo.gl/rz3a6V

Jaramillo, M. (2014). The incidence of social spending and taxes in Peru. *Public Finance Review, 42*(3), 391–412.

Lambert, P. (2001). *The distribution and redistribution of income.* Manchester: Manchester University Press.

Lustig, N. (2015). The redistributive impact of government spending on education and health: Evidence from thirteen developing countries in the commitment to equity project. In *Inequality and the role of fiscal policy: Trends and policy options,* edited by Benedict Clements, Ruud de Mooij, Sanjeev Gupta, and Michael Keen. Washington, DC: International Monetary Fund.

Lustig, N. (2016a). *Fiscal policy, inequality and the poor in the developing world* (Commitment to Equity (CEQ) Working Paper No. 23, CEQ Institute). New Orleans: Tulane University.

Lustig, N. (2016b). Inequality and fiscal redistribution in middle income countries: Brazil, Chile, Colombia, Indonesia, Mexico, Peru and South Africa. *Journal of Globalization and Development, 7*(1), 17–60. doi:10.1515/jgd-2016-0015

Lustig, N. (Ed.). (2018). *Commitment to equity handbook: Estimating the impact of fiscal policy on inequality and poverty.* Washington, DC: Brookings Institution Press and CEQ Institute, Tulane University.

Lustig, N., & Pessino, C. (2014). Social spending and income redistribution in Argentina during the 2000s: The increasing role of noncontributory pensions. *Public Finance Review, 42*(3), 304–325.

Martinez-Vazquez, J. (2008). The impact of budgets on the poor: Tax and expenditure benefit incidence analysis. In B. Moreno-Dodson & W. Quentin (Eds.), *Public finance for poverty reduction: Concepts and case studies from Africa and Latin America* (pp. 113–162). Washington, DC: World Bank.

Meerman, J. (1979). *Public expenditure in Malaysia: Who benefits and why.* New York: Oxford University Press for the World Bank.

Mostafavi-Dehzooei, M. H., & Salehi-Isfahani, D. (2017). Consumer subsidies in the Islamic Republic of Iran: Simulations of further reforms. In *The quest for subsidy reforms in the Middle East and North Africa region* (pp. 259–289). Cham: Springer.

Musgrave, R. (1959). *The theory of public finance.* New York: McGraw-Hill.

Musgrave, R. A., Carroll, J. J., Cook, L. D., & Frane, L. (1951). Distribution of tax payments by income groups: A case study for 1948. *National Tax Journal, 4,* 1–53.

Musgrave, R., Case, K., & Leonard, H. (1974). The distribution of fiscal burdens and benefits. *Public Finance Quarterly, 2*(3), 259–311.

Negahdari, E., Piraee, K., Keshavarz Haddad, G., & Haghighat, A. (2014). Economy of scale and poverty line: A case study of Iranian urban households (2006–2011). *The Journal of Planning and Budgeting, 19*(1), 3–30. Retrieved from http://jpbud.ir/article-1-1134-fa.html

Negahdari, E., Piraee, K., Keshavarz Haddad, G, & Haghighat, A. (2015). Estimating poverty line of Iranian rural households with respect to household size, 2006–2011. *Quarterly Journal of Roosta Va Towse'e. 3, 17*(4), 155–172. Retrieved from http://rvt.agri-peri.ir:8080/browse.php ?a_id=642&sid=1&slc_lang=en

Pechman, J. A., & Okner, B. A. (1974). *Who bears the tax burden?* Washington, DC: Brookings Institution.

Salehi-Isfahani, D. (2017). Poverty and income inequality in the Islamic Republic of Iran. *Revue Internationale des Etudes du Développement, 229*(1), 113–136.

Salehi-Isfahani, D., Stucki, B. W., & Deutschmann, J. (2015). The reform of energy subsidies in Iran: The role of cash transfers. *Emerging Markets Finance and Trade, 51*(6), 1144–1162.

Scott, J. (2014). Redistributive impact and efficiency of Mexico's fiscal system. *Public Finance Review, 42*(3), 368–390.

Selowsky, M. (1979). *Who benefits from government expenditures? A case study of Colombia.* New York: Oxford University Press.

Statistical Center of Iran (SCI). *National accounts: National health accounts of 1390.* Information extracted on August 5, 2015. Retrieved from http://www.amar.org.ir/Default.aspx?tabid=104

World Development Indicator (WDI). The World Bank. Data extracted on August 5, 2015. Retrieved from http://data.worldbank.org/data-catalog/world-development-indicators

Younger, S. D., Myamba, F., & Mdadila, K. (2016). Fiscal incidence in Tanzania. *African Development Review, 28*(3), 264–276.

Younger, S., Osei-Assibey, E., and Oppong, F. (2017). Fiscal incidence in Ghana. *Review of Development Economics.* Published electronically January 11, 2017. doi:10.1111/rode.12299

Younger, S., Sahn, D., Haggblade, S., & Dorosh, P. (1999). Tax incidence in Madagascar: An analysis using household data. *The World Bank Economic Review, 13*(2), 303–331.

Chapter 18

TUNISIA

Fiscal Policy, Income Redistribution, and Poverty Reduction

Nizar Jouini, Nora Lustig, Ahmed Moummi, and Abebe Shimeles

Introduction

In 2011 Tunisia went through a profound political transformation involving the democratization of its institutions. This political reform coincided with the period of the global Great Recession and its aftershocks. Coping with this adverse external environment while simultaneously responding to heightened social demands generated fiscal imbalances: the fiscal deficit rose from 1 percent of GDP in 2010 to 6.8 percent in 2013. Due to the combination of this reduced fiscal space and political demands for a more equitable society, fiscal policy is at the heart of the reform agenda. In this context, it is essential to know who benefits from transfers and subsidies and who bears the burden of taxation. This chapter estimates the impact of Tunisia's tax and transfers system on inequality and poverty reduction and assesses who benefits from public spending on education and health. Using the National Survey of Consumption and Household Living Standards for 2010, the most recent survey data available, we apply standard fiscal incidence analysis as described in Lustig and Higgins (2013) and in this Volume of the Handbook in chapter 1 by Lustig and Higgins (2022), chapter 6 by Enami, Higgins, and Lustig (2022), and chapter 8 by Higgins and Brest Lopez (2022).[1] Because this methodological framework has been applied to other middle-income countries under the

---

This chapter is part of a collaborative effort between the African Development Bank and the Commitment to Equity (CEQ) Institute. The study was carried out under the guidance of CEQ advisor Jean-Yves Duclos.
[1] It should be noted that this chapter uses primarily Lustig and Higgins (2013).

Commitment to Equity (CEQ) project, we will be able to compare the results for Tunisia with those of other countries.[2]

Existing studies have looked at the equity implications of specific fiscal interventions in Tunisia. One study that examined cash transfers and subsidies, for example, found that they reduced poverty from 16.5 percent to 15.5 percent when poverty was measured with the national poverty line and that 48.8 percent of the poor were not covered.[3] The same study also found that subsidies were not well targeted: the poor received only 9.2 percent of total subsidies and 12 percent of food subsidies in particular. A World Bank study on energy subsidies found that 13 percent were allocated to the poorest quintile while the richest quintile received 29 percent of these subsidies.[4] Currently, however, no studies have analyzed the incidence of fiscal policy from both the spending and revenue sides. The purpose of our chapter is to fill this gap.

Our results show that when taxes and transfers (including the monetized value of education and health services) are taken together, Tunisia's fiscal policy reduces the Gini coefficient from 0.44 to 0.35. Thus, fiscal policy is quite redistributive in Tunisia.[5] The impact of fiscal policy on rates of poverty depends on the poverty line. For the lower poverty lines of US$1.25 and US$2.50 per day in 2005 purchasing power parity (PPP), the combined effect of taxes, transfers, and subsidies reduces poverty. However, this is not true when one uses Tunisia's national poverty line (Tunisian Dinar 5.02 per day, equivalent to US$3.40 in 2005 PPP) or the middle-income international poverty line of US$4.00 per day (in 2005 PPP). After taking into account all taxes, direct cash transfers, and indirect subsidies and using Tunisia's national poverty line, the rate of poverty increases from 15.2 percent to 17.86 percent. This increase is due particularly to the high burden of direct taxes and social contributions on those at relatively low income levels.

Spending on primary and secondary education is progressive in absolute terms ("pro-poor"): the concentration coefficient is negative. Spending on tertiary education, however, is progressive in relative terms only and not pro-poor, but because its concentration coefficient is much lower than Market Income Gini, it is equalizing. Health spending is progressive in absolute terms, except for hospitalization.

We think that our results remain relevant even during the post-revolutionary period because the structure of social programs remains the same. Some of these programs have benefited from additional resources, including subsidies, which increased by almost 300 percent between 2010 and 2013 (energy subsidies in particular experienced a fivefold increase), and cash transfers, which increased by 50 percent during the same period.

---

[2] The results are based on the Commitment to Equity Assessment Master Workbook from September 9, 2015, which is available upon request.

[3] INS, CRES, AfDB (2013).

[4] World Bank (2013).

[5] For comparisons with other countries, see the redistributive effects in the CEQ Data Center, http://www.commitmentoequity.org/datacenter.

1 Taxation and Social Spending in Tunisia

With a Gini coefficient of 0.39, Tunisia is one of the most equal countries in the Middle East and North Africa region. Many consider Tunisia a success story, given its sustained rate of growth between 4 and 5 percent since 1990. In 2010, the year of the survey used in this study, the population was estimated at about 10.5 million and gross national income (GNI) per capita in current dollars was US$4,160 (9,700 in 2011 PPP international dollars). The World Bank classifies Tunisia in the upper-middle income group. With primary spending at around 29.1 percent of its GDP in 2010, Tunisia's government spending is above the average of other developing countries.[6] Poverty measured with the official poverty line of US$4.30 per day in 2011 PPP decreased from 32.4 percent in 2000 to 15.5 percent in 2010. Within the country, disparities exist regionally and by population density: rural poverty is almost twice as high as urban poverty, and the poorest regions are the West Central and the North West followed by the southern sub-regions, compared to the wealthier littoral and the north.[7] Although the decline in poverty has been driven by economic growth, it is also due to increased government transfers and subsidies. Tunisia created an array of programs following the structural adjustment program (SAP) led by the International Monetary Fund (IMF) in 1986. The current Tunisian safety net system includes programs that have been in place since then.

1.1 Taxation

The Tunisian tax system is composed of two main categories: direct taxes and indirect taxes. Direct taxes include the personal income tax (PIT) and corporate tax, whereas indirect taxes include value-added tax (VAT) and consumption duties. As reported in table 18-1, the ratio of total tax revenue to GDP was about 20 percent in 2010, which is comparable to other middle-income countries. Indirect taxes are the main source of tax revenue (almost two-thirds of total tax revenue), and the share of other consumption taxes to GDP is the same as VAT. Even so, direct taxes represent a high burden on labor in particular if we add social contribution to PIT. Despite this high burden, the amount of tax collected remains below the standards of developed and emerging countries.

1.1.1 Personal Income Tax

PIT is levied on different sources of income such as labor, pensions, interest, and dividends. The tax rates imposed start at 15 percent and rise to 35 percent as indicated in table 18-2. PIT is paid primarily via a source withholding tax on wages on amounts greater than TD1,000 (US$696) paid by the state and public authorities or greater

---

[6] Lustig (2015).

[7] INS-AfDB-WB (2012).

Table 18-1

Tunisian General Government Revenue Collection, 2010

	National accounts 2010 (% of GDP)	Incidence analysis (% of GDP)
Total general government revenue	24.3	10.29
Tax revenue	*20.9*	*10.29*
Direct taxes	*8.3*	*4.29*
Personal income tax	4.29	4.29
Corporate income tax	4.01	. . .
Indirect taxes	*12.6*	*6.1*
VAT	6.1	6.1
Customs taxes	1.0	. . .
Consumption duties	2.6	. . .
Others indirect taxes	2.9	. . .
*Non-tax revenue**	*3.1*	. . .

Source: Calculation based on data from the Tunisian Ministry of Finance (2011), accessible at http://www .finances.gov.tn/index.php?option=com_content&view=article&id=121&Itemid=302&lang=fr.

Notes: "Nontax revenue" includes oil and gas revenue and revenue from privatization of public enterprises and participation in private companies.

. . . = Not applicable.

Table 18-2

Taxable Income Brackets in Tunisia, 2010

Taxable income brackets (TD, annual)	US$	Rate (%)
0–1,500	0–1,044	0
1,500–5,000	1,044–3,480	15
5,000–10,000	3,480–6,960	20
10,000–20,000	6,960–13,920	25
20,000–50,000	13,920–34,800	30
More than 50,000	More than 34,800	35

Source: Tunisian Ministry of Finance (2011), accessible at http://www.finances.gov.tn /index.php?option=com_content&view=article&id=75&Itemid=258&lang=fr.

TD = Tunisian dinar.

than TD5,000 (US$3,480) paid by corporations and individuals. Several deductions are permitted, including for employees earning the minimum wage, salaries of foreign consuls, interest from deposits in foreign currency, interest on housing savings or special savings accounts, premiums on life insurance, and for marital status and dependents.

1.1.2 Social Security Contributions

The Tunisian social security system is a contributory system administrated completely by the government. Compulsory social security covers pensions and family benefits, as well as illness, accidents at work, and occupational diseases. All benefits were provided either by the National Social Security Fund (Caisse Nationale de Securite Sociale [CNSS]) or the National Pension and Social Security Fund (Caisse Nationale de Retraite et de Prevoyance Sociale [CNRPS]); CNSS covers workers from the private sector whereas the CNRPS covers all employees of the state and local public authorities and public institutions. Since 2007, the National Health Insurance Fund (Caisse Nationale d'Assurance Maladie, CNAM) has administered the health insurance component. Social security contributions vary depending on whether the worker belongs to an agricultural or a nonagricultural sector. Self-employed workers are required to join the National Social Security Fund (CNSS). They may voluntarily insure against work accidents and illnesses. The contribution rates and social protections vary across regimes: for example, nonagricultural employees do not receive family allowances. Agricultural workers, independent operators, and self-employed workers in agriculture benefit from different rates.

Under CNSS and CNRPS, the main benefit for contributors is a retirement pension. The pension is based on wages, subject to contributions that the insured has made during the ten years prior to reaching retirement age. For 120 months of contributions, the pension rate is 40 percent of salary; beyond this level, the pension is increased by 0.5 percent for every three months of additional contribution and may not exceed 80 percent of salary after thirty years of work. The types of social security contributions are summarized in table 18-3.

1.1.3 Indirect Taxes

Indirect taxes are collected mainly through VAT, which represents almost 50 percent of total indirect tax revenues. Other taxes include customs taxes (7.3 percent) and consumption taxes, including excise taxes (20.3 percent). VAT is collected using the credit invoice method, and the rate varies from 6 percent for fertilizer, handicrafts, medical activities, canned food, and compound feed for cattle, to 12 percent for computers, computer services, hospitality, food, equipment not produced locally, and four-horsepower cars, to an 18 percent general rate for products and services not subject to another rate. Exports are zero rated. There are a number of exempt goods, the most important ones being primary foods, nurseries, schooling (primary, secondary, tertiary, vocational), equipment for the agriculture sector, air transport, and interest from banks. Consumption taxes are also applied to alcoholic beverages, wine, tobacco, personal vehicles, and fuels. Rates are applied as ad valorem rates or as specific taxes, in particular for alcoholic beverages and tobacco.

Other indirect taxes include customs taxes and registration fees, which are applied to the sale of property (rates range from 2 to 5 percent of the value), professional train-

TABLE 18-3

Social Security Contributions by Regime in Tunisia, 2010

	Employer contribution (%)	Employee contribution (%)	Total (%)
Nonagricultural regime			
Pension	7.76	4.73	12.50
Sickness, maternity	4.61	2.90	7.60
Family allowances	2.21	0.88	3.10
Accidents, occupational diseases	0.40–4.00	. . .	0.40–4.00
Welfare workers: special state fund	1.51	0.38	1.90
Total	16.97–20.57	9.18	26.15–29.75
Agricultural regime			
Pension	3.50	1.75	5.25
Sickness, maternity	4.18	2.80	6.98
Accidents, occupational diseases	0.04	0.01	0.05
Total	7.72	4.56	12.28
Independent regime			
Pension	. . .	7.00	7.00
Sickness, maternity	. . .	7.26	7.26
Accidents, occupational diseases	. . .	0.45	0.45
Total	. . .	14.71	14.71

Source: Statistics department, Centre des Recherches et des Etudes Sociales.

. . . = Not applicable.

ing tax (1 percent of gross payroll for manufacturing industries), and tax on insurance contracts (5 percent for contracts in maritime and air transport and 10 percent for others).

In our incidence analysis, we include VAT, excise taxes on alcohol, cigarettes, coffee, tea, Coke, gas oil, jewelry, and some transport services, and import duties on dried fruits, bananas, air conditioning, and perfume.

1.1.4 Corporate Taxes

Corporate income tax is imposed on companies established in Tunisia. The tax rate amounts to 30 percent of profits, except for small businesses and agriculture (10 percent) and firms dealing with the financial, telecommunications, insurance, oil production, refining, transportation, and distribution sectors (35 percent). It is worth noting that 97 percent of companies are microenterprises with between zero and five employees.

Most of these enterprises do not pay taxes and are part of the informal sector, which highlights the problem of tax evasion.

1.2 Social Spending

Social spending excluding contributory pensions (our benchmark scenario in the fiscal incidence analysis is presented in table 18-4) accounts for 10 percent of GDP. This amount includes direct cash transfers and in-kind spending on education and health. Direct transfers include the cash transfer program PNAFN (Programme National des Familles Necessiteuses [National Needy Families Assistance Program]) and scholarship assistance given to students. These two programs amounted to 0.3 percent of GDP in 2010. Other cash transfers represent a combined 0.5 percent of GDP and include grants distributed to local communities, youth activities, nongovernmental organizations (NGOs), and special treasury funds.

In-kind transfers are benefits received from the universal free public education and health systems. The main programs are described below, and their budget sizes are given in table 18-4. Contributory pensions amount to 8.7 percent of GDP; thus, if contributory pensions are included, total social spending equals 18.7 percent of GDP.

TABLE 18-4

General Government Expenditure for Tunisia, 2010

	2010 (% of GDP)	Incidence analysis (% of GDP)
Total General Government Expenditure	29	
Primary government spending	23	
Social spending	18.7	17.7
Total Cash Transfers	1.30	0.30
PNAFN	0.15	0.15
Scholarships	0.15	0.15
Other cash transfers	0.5	—
Subsidies	2.4	2.4
In-kind Transfers	6.2	6.2
Education	4.6	4.6
Health	1.6	1.6
Housing and Urban	0.03	0.03
Contributory Pensions	8.7	8.7

Source: Tunisia, Ministry of Finance (2011) public finance report.

PNAFN = Programme National des Familles Necessiteuses (National Needy Families Assistance Program); ... = Not applicable.

1.2.1 Direct Transfers

Created in 1986, the PNAFN is the main cash transfer program for monthly cash assistance to low-income households. This national program was designed to mitigate the adverse effects of the IMF-led structural adjustment program, particularly in areas with high numbers of poor families. In 2010, this program covered 520,337 beneficiaries (135,000 households) for a total of about TD100 million, compared to 1986, when it covered 250,000 beneficiaries (74,000 households). The monthly amount paid per beneficiary was around TD70 (US$48.80) per household in 2010. Household eligibility for the PNAFN is based on social surveys conducted by the Ministry of Social Affairs[8]; criteria include income below the poverty threshold, inability to work, absence of head of household, lack of family support, or the presence of disabled or chronically ill family members. Although no evaluation of the program was conducted before the revolution, it has now been recognized as suffering from both poor identification of families in need and subjective criteria.

Direct social assistance also includes a scholarship program for students in tertiary education. The number of beneficiaries was 98,533 in 2010 (according to a 2010 report from the Ministry of Higher Education)[9] and the total amount of grants is equivalent to TD56 million (US$38.9 million) per year. The head of household's total income cannot exceed the official minimum wage for a student to be eligible to receive the scholarship.

Other cash transfers account for 0.5 percent of GDP and include grants distributed to local communities, NGOs, nurseries, and cultural activities in the local areas.[10]

1.2.2 Indirect Subsidies

The subsidy system in Tunisia has long been directed at basic consumption products, energy, and transportation. These subsidies were equal to 2.4 percent of the GDP in 2010, which was lower than in 1988, when subsidies equaled 8.5 percent of GDP.[11] Since the Tunisian revolution, subsidies have risen again to reach 6.9 percent of GDP in 2013. In 2010, the composition of subsidies was 1.2 percent for food, 1 percent for energy consumption, and 0.3 percent for transportation.[12] Existing studies point to the need for reform of the subsidy system because subsidies are relatively regressive.[13] However, these subsidies play a key role in maintaining purchasing power for vulnerable groups who spend almost all their revenue on food consumption.

---

[8] Tunisia, Ministry of Social Affairs (2011).

[9] Tunisia, Ministry of Education (2010).

[10] Other programs such as the national fund for employment (Fond National de l'Emploi [FNE]), microcredits of Banque Tunisienne de Solidarite (BTS) to reduce unemployment, and a public agency to improve housing for vulnerable families in urban settings are not considered social spending, and their incidence was not analyzed here.

[11] At that time, almost half of the subsidy costs were related to hard and soft wheat.

[12] World Bank (2013).

[13] AfDB, CRES (2013); World Bank (2013).

The composition and the weight of each product or group of products in the subsidized basket witnessed many changes between the 1990s and 2010. Although subsidies on primary products and transport were established in the 1990s, the energy subsidy was introduced for the first time in 2003, following increases in energy prices in the international market, in order to promote the competitiveness of the private sector and support the purchasing power of the middle class.

1.2.3 In-Kind Transfers

The next section describes the education and health systems in Tunisia as part of the in-kind transfers analyzed in this chapter.

Education

At all levels of education, there are two systems: public and private. Tunisia's public education system includes mandatory basic, secondary, and tertiary education. Mandatory basic education consists of two cycles: six years of primary school and three years of lower secondary school, or a preparatory cycle. Upper secondary school is four years. Public primary and secondary education is almost free (beneficiaries pay only US$3 per year). Tertiary education is also considered free as students pay about US$25 per year for undergraduate education and US$50 for graduate education. Primary and secondary education spending amounted to 5 percent of GDP in 2010, and tertiary education accounted for 1.7 percent.

Since 2002, primary school gross enrollment has been almost universal, averaging 100 percent for both sexes. The net enrollment rate for individuals ages six to sixteen years has increased by 3.3 percent, reaching 93.4 percent. Access to basic and secondary education has mainly benefited girls, who have made up the majority of enrollment since 2005. In terms of net enrollment of youth between twelve and eighteen years, girls represented 84.5 percent compared to 75.8 percent for boys. Greater enrollment, however, has not been accompanied by improvements in the quality of education. Scores from the Program for International Student Assessment (PISA) in 2007 and 2011 show almost no change in rankings, with fewer Tunisian students passing the low international baseline for fourth and eighth grade in mathematics and science than the international average.[14]

The enrollment rate in tertiary education for individuals between twenty and twenty-four years rose from 25 percent to 37 percent between 2000 and 2010, an increase of about 139,876 students. The number of students in 2010 reached 346,876 as the result of a state effort to increase the number of enrolled students through a budget share expansion from 3.7 percent of GDP to 6.1 percent. Of these students, girls were the majority (61 percent). Despite this quantitative surge in the number of students,

---

[14] The number of students enrolled in primary and lower secondary school has been declining since 2002, from 1.8 million students in 2002 to 1.4 million students in 2012. Secondary education enrollment increased until 2005, but has been falling since, from 508,790 students in 2005 to 453,090 students in 2012.

the quality did not improve at the same rate, which is reflected in international rankings (for example, not a single Tunisian university was included in the Shanghai ranking of the 500 best universities in the world[15]). Tunisian students also had limited prospects for finding employment after graduation.

Health

Healthcare in Tunisia is provided through two systems: a contributory national health insurance program for the non-poor and a free or subsidized system for low-income individuals and households. The first of the two low-income programs, the Free Health Care (Aide Medicale Gratuite, AMG1) program, targets poor families and provides a five-year assistance program. Decree number 98-1812 establishes the conditions for allocating the "free healthcare card" to complying beneficiaries for a period of five years. The second program is the Subsidized Health Care (AMG2) program, which grants "healthcare discount cards" to families based on income and family size. For two-member households, annual family income cannot exceed an amount equal to the guaranteed minimum wage (Salaire Minimum Interprofessionnel Garanti, SMIG). Annual income cannot exceed 1.5 times the minimum wage for families with three to five members or twice the minimum wage for families with more than five members. Beneficiaries receive a lump-sum payment based on the costs of the service. The healthcare discount card is also issued for a period of five years and needs to be validated every year at a cost of TD10 (US$7).

In 2010, the contributory system had 2,202,447 affiliates, and the free and subsidized systems had 197,411 and 448,810, respectively. Public expenditure on healthcare was equivalent to 1.66 percent of GDP in 2010.

2 Methodology and Data

This study uses the CEQ methodology as presented in Lustig and Higgins (2013) and in this Volume of the Handbook in chapters 1, 6, and 8. Essentially, the method consists of allocating taxes and transfers to derive five income concepts, including Market Income, Net Market Income, Disposable Income, Consumable Income, and Final Income, and then assessing the effectiveness of inequality and poverty reduction.

This study is data intensive and requires many categories of macro- and microdata. We focused on using as much official data as possible to minimize judgment and ad-hoc estimation. In the case of Tunisia, surveys on income are not available, and the only existing module on income data is not related to the consumption survey (that is, surveyed households are not the same). For this reason, we use the consumption survey to estimate the income concepts in the incidence analysis. As recommended in chapter 6 in this Volume, we assume that consumption is equivalent to Disposable Income and work backward to construct Market Income. The consumption variable includes expenditures on nondurable goods, consumption of own production, and imputed rent for

---

[15] See Academic Ranking of World Universities, www.shanghairanking.com.

owner-occupied housing. We used the National Survey of Consumption and Household Living Standards of 2010 from the National Institute of Statistics (Institut National de Statistiques). It includes three components: expenditures, living standards, and food. In our analysis, we included only individuals who simultaneously appear in all three components. The final sample is national in scope and is statistically representative for large cities, medium-sized cities, and small towns and rural areas. This sample has 23,764 individuals and 5,456 households, which represents about half of the households in the full expenditure component.

To estimate the incidence of taxes and transfers, we used macroeconomic data from the Ministry of Finance. Data on indirect taxes and subsidies for primary products and energy was taken from the statistics department of the DGELF (La Direction Generale des Etudes et de la Legislation Fiscale [General Directorate of Tax Studies and Legislation]) of the Ministry of Finance. Data on direct taxes includes only income tax and was imputed according to the tax rate of each income level. Here we assume that formal workers are defined as those who contribute to social security and do not evade taxes. Information on which individuals contribute to the social security system is reported in the survey, and contributions were imputed according to whether the household head is salaried or nonsalaried and works in the agricultural or nonagricultural sector. The number of beneficiaries of the PNAFN program (for poor families) and of the scholarship program for students was obtained from the surveys. The amount transferred to each individual or household was imputed. For the PNAFN, the total benefits came from CRES (Centre de Recherches et des Etudes Sociales), and for scholarships, the total benefits came from the Ministry of Higher Education.

In-kind transfers were calculated from data included in the budget of the Ministry of Higher Education for tertiary education, the Ministry of Education[16] for primary and secondary education, and the Ministry of Health[17] for health expenditures. Imputed spending amounts include current and capital expenditures for 2010.

3 Main Assumptions

Because the survey used in the incidence analysis reported expenditures but not income, we followed the recommendation in Lustig and Higgins (2013) to obtain the different revenue concepts. Following their recommendation, we started by assuming that consumption equals Disposable Income and worked backward to obtain Net Market Income and Market Income. Because our consumption survey did not include the imputed rent for owner-occupied housing, we used an estimation from the National Institute of Statistics.[18] We estimated the imputed rent through a log linear regression model, including variables controlling for the characteristics of the housing and geo-

---

[16] Tunisia, Ministry of Education (2010).
[17] Tunisia, Ministry of Health (2010).
[18] See INS-AfDB-WB (2012).

graphic locations. According to these estimations, the housing rent is valued at TD211 (US$147) per month per household in cities, TD129 (US$90) in small- and medium-sized towns, and TD119 (US$83) in noncommunal cities.

Regarding taxation, because the consumption survey in Tunisia does not include information on personal income tax, the tax burden had to be simulated. We adopted two different tax rates following Tunisian tax law: a regular regime for salaried workers and a flat regime for independent workers. Under both regimes, we assumed that taxpayers include only those individuals who reported affiliation with the social security system. In order to have similar proportions, we adjusted the level of direct taxes downward to match their ratio to private consumption in administrative accounts and the household survey. The rate of tax evasion, calculated from the survey as the percentage of workers who do not pay income tax, was found to be 40 percent, and the percentage of tax revenue paid by salaried workers reached 73 percent. These ratios are comparable to the data reported in national accounts for salaried workers (75 percent of total PIT) and for the informal sector (40 percent according to some studies). The simulation of VAT is more straightforward and uses detailed consumption data on consumption products, energy products, transportation, and health. The VAT rates vary between 6, 12, and 18 percent, plus special rates on imported products.

The survey directly reports the number of workers who contribute to each social security regime. The imputed contributions to social security are simulated as a percentage of Market Income and include pension contributions, health contributions, and death benefits. The contributions include both employee and employer contributions, and the rate depends on three factors: whether the worker is in the public sector (Caisse Nationale de Retraite et de Prevoyance Sociale [CNRPS]) or the private sector (Caisse Nationale de Securite Sociale [CNSS]), under the salaried regime or nonsalaried regime, and in the agricultural or nonagricultural sector.

Regarding spending, the third part of the survey, called "Quality of Life," reports information on cash transfer recipients by inquiring whether the individual received free healthcare and therefore benefited automatically from the PNAFN monthly allocation for poor families. The survey also reports information on recipients of the scholarship program for students from low-income families. The amount of cash transfer for each beneficiary equals the mean of the total annual amount paid divided by the number of beneficiaries in the survey (the number of beneficiaries in the survey is almost equal to the number reported by the ministry).

Direct transfers in this study do not take into account all programs executed by the government because information related to these programs is missing in the survey. The programs that were included in the survey are the PNAFN and scholarships allocated to students. The survey, however, reports only the number of recipients and not the amount of the transfers. The total number of beneficiaries in the surveys for the analyzed programs is very similar to that in the administrative data. The amount of the benefits was imputed by taking the values from the administrative accounts for each of the programs. In order to keep the transfers in line with the income reported in the surveys, they were scaled down so that the ratio of transfers to Disposable Income in the survey matched that of the national accounts.

To estimate the in-kind benefits derived from government spending on education and health, the average cost of the service was imputed from the budget of each ministry. This cost includes administrative and capital expenditures divided by the number of beneficiaries. For education, we separated the cost of primary and secondary education from the average cost of tertiary education, because those services are administered by two different ministries with independent budgets. In the second stage, we scaled down spending for the different levels of education so that the ratio of total spending by level divided by Disposable Income in the survey was the same as administrative accounts. The survey reports whether individuals attend school (and if so, whether public or private school) and their level of education. The number of beneficiaries was aggregated from the household survey. The annual cost per capita is the ratio between the annual budget and the number of beneficiaries.

The health benefit is equal to Ministry of Health budget data on capital and current expenditures incurred in public hospitals and health centers. By dividing the total budget by the number of beneficiaries from the survey, we determined the average spending per individual. Following survey categorizations, we split health expenditures into normal care spending, expenditures related to maternity care, and hospital spending. Hospital spending represents five times the average cost of normal care or maternity care, which is taken here as a metric unit. Each category of spending is a multiplier of the unit average cost of normal care. The total multiplier coefficient for each individual is a function of the type of care the patient received and the number of times the individual received services. The average cost unit was calculated by dividing the Ministry of Health's budget by the total multiplier coefficient of all patients reported in the survey.

Subsidies in this study were calculated based on information reported on food and nonfood consumption. They include subsidies on primary consumption products, energy subsidies, and transport subsidies. The amount of subsidies was adjusted downward to match their ratio to Disposable Income in administrative accounts and the household survey.

4 The Impact of Fiscal Policy on Inequality and Poverty

Under the benchmark scenario in which contributory pensions are treated as deferred income, fiscal policy in Tunisia reduces Market Income inequality quite significantly: the Gini coefficient for Market Income per capita declines from 0.44 to a Final Income Gini of 0.35, a decline of 0.09 Gini points (see table 18-5). When in-kind transfers to public education and health are excluded, the Gini declines by 0.05 points, which means that two-thirds of inequality reduction is accounted for by taxes, cash transfers, and subsidies. Compared to other middle-income countries, the total redistributive effect of taxes, cash transfers, subsidies, and in-kind transfers (from Market to Final Income) is somewhat lower than in Argentina, Brazil, Costa Rica, Georgia, Iran, Mexico, South Africa, and Uruguay, but it is higher than in other middle-income countries such as

TABLE 18-5

Inequality and Poverty Indicators for Each Income Concept, Tunisia 2010

	Market income	Disposable income	Consumable income	Final income
Inequality indicators				
Gini coefficient	0.44	0.39	0.38	0.35
Theil index	0.35	0.27	0.26	0.22
90/10	7.91	5.98	5.67	4.65
Headcount poverty indicators (%)				
National poverty line	15.20	15.61	17.86	. . .
US$1.25 per day at 2005 PPP	0.65	0.41	0.38	. . .
US$2.50 per day at 2005 PPP	6.18	5.58	5.65	. . .
US$4.00 per day at 2005 PPP	17.01	18.90	19.23	. . .

Source: Data from National Institute of Statistics (2010), Tunisian National Survey of Consumption and Household Living Standards; calculations from CEQ Tunisia Master Workbook (2015).

Notes: TD5.026 per day is equivalent to US$3.40 in 2005 PPP.

. . . = Not applicable.

Chile, Colombia, Russia, and Venezuela, and much higher than in Indonesia, Jordan, and Peru. The combined redistributive effect of direct taxes and direct cash transfers only is higher in Tunisia than in twenty-four of the remaining twenty-nine countries included in the CEQ Data Center (http://www.commitmentoequity.org/datacenter). The redistributive effect of in-kind transfers is higher in fifteen of the remaining twenty-nine countries included in the CEQ Data Center, so Tunisia does not stand out one way or the other. Where Tunisia really differs from the rest is in the combined effect of consumption taxes and subsidies. The decline in inequality induced by the latter is not only higher in Tunisia than in every other country included in the Data Center but for as many as one-third of the thirty countries, consumption taxes and subsidies increase inequality (when compared with disposable income inequality) while in Tunisia consumption taxes and subsidies are quite equalizing.

The redistributive effect generates a low rate of horizontal inequality in the sense of reranking. For example, considering the redistributive effect of Market Income to Consumable Income, the extent of horizontal inequity is evaluated at 0.0069, which represents 12 percent of the vertical equity (see table 18-6).

Table 18-5 shows that the impact of fiscal policy on poverty rates depends on the poverty line. For the lower poverty lines of US$1.25 and US$2.50 per day (in 2005 PPP), the combined effect of taxes, transfers, and subsidies reduces poverty. However, this is not true using Tunisia's national poverty line (TD5.02 per day, equivalent to US$3.40 in 2005 PPP) or the middle-income international poverty line of US$4.00 per day (in 2005 PPP). In relation to the national poverty line, the rate of poverty increases from 15.20 percent to 17.86 percent after taking into account all taxes, direct cash transfers, and

TABLE 18-6
Overall Redistributive Effect of Taxes, Transfers, and Subsidies in Bolivia, Brazil, Indonesia, South Africa, and Tunisia*

	Tunisia (2010)	South Africa (2010)	Bolivia (2009)	Brazil (2009)	Indonesia (2012)
Gini (market income)	0.44	0.771	0.503	0.579	0.394
Gini (postfiscal income)	0.38	0.695	0.503	0.546	0.391
Redistributive effect	n.a.	0.077	0.000	0.033	0.003
Vertical equity (VE)	0.05	0.083	0.003	0.048	0.006
Reranking effect (RR)	0.006	0.006	0.003	0.014	0.003
RR/VE	0.12	0.075	1.000	0.300	0.451

Sources: Tunisian figures are based on data from the 2010 National Survey of Consumption and Household Living Standards; calculations from CEQ Tunisia Master Workbook (2015). Other figures: Bolivia, Paz Arauco and others (2014); Brazil, Higgins and Pereira (2014); Indonesia, Jellema, Wai-Poi, and Afkar (2017); South Africa, Inchauste and others (2017).

Notes: *Decline shown as positive.

n.a. = Data not available.

indirect subsidies. This increase is due particularly to the high burden of direct taxes and social contributions on relatively low income levels, as shown in table 18-7. For people in the bottom 40 percent, direct taxes and social contributions amount to roughly 4 percent of Market Income, which cannot be compensated by direct transfers, except for those in the poorest decile. In fact, an unusual result for the case of Tunisia is that individuals become net payers to the fiscal system after direct taxes and transfers from the *second* decile onward. After considering the impact of indirect taxes net of indirect subsidies (on which Tunisia relies heavily as a redistributive instrument), net payers in cash terms start at higher income levels: the third decile. Nevertheless, in spite of the large amount of subsidies, the headcount ratio based on Consumable Income is still a bit higher than the one for Market Income with the national poverty line due to indirect taxes.

In sum, the poorest decile is the only decile that does relatively well. The poorest decile receives transfers equivalent to its Market Income (90 percent), including in-kind transfers, mainly imputed to education (50.3 percent) and indirect subsidies (12.3 percent), and to a lesser extent, health (20 percent) and cash transfers (6.2 percent). Moreover, this category is supported by a low burden of direct taxes, which stands at 0.6 percent of its Market Income, although indirect taxes amount to 13 percent of Market Income. Overall, the poorest decile's Market Income is increased by 74.7 percent.

4.1 Who Benefits from Direct Transfers and Subsidies and Who Bears the Burden of Taxes?

In table 18-8, we show the concentration shares of each component of fiscal policy analyzed here. Several results stand out. The share of benefits of the PNAFN and "other

TABLE 18-7

Fiscal Incidence by Decile in Tunisia, 2010

Decile	Direct taxes	Contributions	Direct taxes and contributions to SS	Net market income	Flagship CCT	Other direct transfers (targeted or not)	All direct transfers	Disposable income	Indirect subsidies	Indirect taxes	Net indirect taxes	Consumable income	In-kind education	In-kind health	Housing and urban	Final income
1	-0.6%	-1.1%	-1.7%	-1.8%	3.3%	2.9%	6.2%	4.5%	12.3%	-13.1%	-0.8%	3.7%	50.3%	20.0%	0.4%	74.7%
2	-1.2%	-2.5%	-3.7%	-4.5%	1.4%	1.6%	3.0%	-1.5%	9.3%	-12.4%	-3.1%	-4.7%	35.7%	8.6%	0.2%	40.6%
3	-1.3%	-3.2%	-4.6%	-4.7%	0.8%	1.1%	1.9%	-2.7%	8.1%	-13.1%	-5.0%	-7.8%	22.4%	7.8%	0.0%	22.7%
4	-2.1%	-4.9%	-6.9%	-9.3%	0.6%	1.0%	1.6%	-7.7%	7.3%	-12.8%	-5.6%	-13.3%	17.6%	4.7%	0.1%	11.4%
5	-3.1%	-7.3%	-10.3%	-11.0%	0.5%	0.7%	1.2%	-9.8%	6.1%	-13.0%	-6.9%	-16.8%	14.3%	3.4%	0.0%	1.7%
6	-3.9%	-9.3%	-13.2%	-14.1%	0.4%	0.6%	0.9%	-13.2%	5.4%	-12.4%	-7.0%	-20.2%	13.5%	2.6%	0.0%	-3.1%
7	-5.0%	-11.5%	-16.5%	-16.8%	0.2%	0.5%	0.8%	-16.0%	5.0%	-11.1%	-6.1%	-22.2%	12.9%	3.1%	0.0%	-5.8%
8	-6.1%	-13.5%	-19.7%	-20.3%	0.2%	0.2%	0.4%	-19.9%	4.2%	-11.2%	-7.0%	-26.9%	8.6%	2.0%	0.0%	-15.5%
9	-7.3%	-15.2%	-22.5%	-23.4%	0.1%	0.1%	0.2%	-23.1%	3.4%	-10.3%	-6.9%	-30.0%	5.7%	1.3%	0.0%	-22.2%
10	-11.4%	-20.2%	-31.6%	-30.2%	0.1%	0.1%	0.2%	-30.0%	2.3%	-8.6%	-6.2%	-36.2%	3.2%	1.2%	0.0%	-33.3%
Total Population	-7.0%	-13.8%	-20.8%	-20.8%	0.3%	0.4%	0.7%	-20.0%	4.3%	-10.6%	-6.3%	-26.3%	10.0%	2.8%	0.0%	-13.5%

Source: Data from the 2010 National Survey of Consumption and Household Living Standards. Calculations from CEQ Tunisia Master Workbook (2015).

SS = Social security.

TABLE 18-8
Concentration Shares of Taxes and Transfers by Decile in Tunisia, 2010

Decile	Direct taxes (%)	Contributions (%)	Flagship CCT (%)	Other direct transfers (%)	Indirect subsidies (%)	Indirect taxes (%)	In-kind education (%)	In-kind health (%)	Housing and urban spending (%)
1	0.20	0.10	19.20	13.20	5.20	2.30	9.20	13.30	28.20
2	0.50	0.60	13.30	12.20	6.50	3.60	10.90	9.60	19.80
3	0.80	0.90	10.60	11.10	7.60	5.00	9.30	11.50	6.60
4	1.50	1.80	9.70	12.30	8.30	6.20	9.00	8.80	11.30
5	2.70	3.30	9.50	10.80	8.70	7.70	9.00	7.70	6.30
6	4.20	5.20	8.60	10.40	9.30	8.90	10.30	7.10	13.10
7	6.60	7.80	7.10	11.90	10.70	9.80	12.00	10.40	13.00
8	10.50	11.90	6.60	7.20	11.80	12.80	10.40	8.90	0.00
9	17.60	18.60	7.20	4.40	13.70	16.40	9.50	8.00	0.60
10	55.40	49.80	8.20	6.60	18.30	27.50	10.90	14.60	1.10
Total population	100.00	100.00	100.00	100.00	100.00	100.00	100.00	100.00	100.00

Source: Data from the 2010 National Survey of Consumption and Household Living Standards. Calculations from CEQ Tunisia Master Workbook (2015).

Note: "Other direct transfers" includes targeted and nontargeted transfers.

TABLE 18-9
Concentration Coefficients by Specific Category for Tunisia, 2010

Program	Concentration coefficient with respect to benchmark case market income
Conditional cash transfer	−0.17
Primary & secondary education spending	−0.08
Subsidy	0.21
Other scholarships	−0.18
Tertiary education spending	0.21
Health spending	0.04
Hospitalization	0.07
Contributory pensions	0.56
Direct cash transfers	−0.17
Total contributory pensions	0.56
Total education spending	−0.01
Total health spending	0.04
Total CEQ social spending	0.00
Total CEQ social spending plus contributory pensions	0.20

Source: Data from the 2010 National Survey of Consumption and Household Living Standards. Calculations from CEQ Tunisia Master Workbook (2015).

direct transfers" received by the poorest 20 percent is 32.5 percent and 25 percent, respectively. In other words, spending on these direct transfers appears to be pro-poor. However, the richest 10 percent also benefit from these transfers: they receive 8.2 percent and 6.6 percent, respectively. Most importantly, indirect subsidies, which account for 2.3 percent of government spending as shown above, are not pro-poor at all. The bottom 20 percent of the population receives 11.7 percent of indirect subsidies, whereas the richest 10 percent receives 18.3 percent.

Spending on education is fairly even across deciles. Our results show that spending on primary and secondary education is progressive in absolute terms: the concentration coefficient is negative (see table 18-9). This result is expected because enrollment rates are becoming almost universal in Tunisia, including among people in vulnerable categories.[19] Spending on tertiary education is progressive in relative terms only, however, but because its concentration coefficient is much lower than the Market Income Gini, it is equalizing, if not pro-poor. The number of students in tertiary education from the poorest decile was low, roughly 0.1 percent of the total, compared to 0.8 percent for primary and secondary school.[20]

---

[19] The net enrollment rate for individuals aged 6 to 16 years has reached 92.6 percent.

[20] The figure 0.1 percent represents the proportion of pupils from the first decile as a percentage of the total number of pupils in primary and secondary; 0.8 percent represents the number of students from the first decile as a percentage of the total number of students in the survey.

Health spending is progressive in absolute terms, except for hospitalization. The monetized value of health spending is distributed fairly equally across all deciles, increasing Market Income for the poorest decile by 20 percent compared to 1 percent for the richest decile (see table 18-7).

The observed distribution of benefits from direct transfers and subsidies indicates that there is room for improving the situation of the poorest and most vulnerable groups (those with incomes from US$4.00 to US$10.00 in 2005 PPP per day) through better targeting. Furthermore, once taxation is taken into account, the combination of direct and indirect taxes puts a significant burden on the vulnerable, who represent 37 percent of the population and are net payers into the fiscal system. On average, this income group pays 8 percent of their Market Income when only the cash components of fiscal policy are taken into account (that is, without considering the imputed value of in-kind transfers in education and health). This group receives 34.6 percent of total subsidies and 46.7 percent of total direct transfers, however. Adding the in-kind benefits, they are net gainers: Final Income is on average 17.3 percent higher than Market Income for the vulnerable.

5 Conclusions

This chapter estimates the incidence of the government's taxation and spending in Tunisia. Fiscal analysis has been applied to three subcomponents of the 2010 consumption survey: spending, food, and quality of life. On the tax side, the analysis includes direct tax (only for personal income) and indirect tax (VAT on consumption goods and services). On the expenditure side, we have analyzed the incidence of 43 percent of general government expenditures, including direct cash transfers (PNAFN and scholarships), contributory pensions, subsidies, and health and education spending.

Taking into account net cash transfers, only the bottom two deciles receive more in transfers than they pay in direct and indirect taxes. When basic services are included, this proportion increases in the bottom seven deciles while the three richest top deciles bear the brunt of redistribution of income. In fact, this redistribution goes from the richest to the poorest, with 43 percent of the top two deciles moving into a lower income class and 40 percent of the three bottom deciles rising to a higher income class. Ninety-five percent of the vulnerable, with an income ranging between US$4.00 and US$10.00 a day, remain in the same class. When all transfers and taxes are taken into account, the distance between the average per capita income between the top decile and the poorest decile decreases from 18 to 6 times.

The Gini coefficient falls from 0.44 (before taxes and transfers) to 0.35 (after taxes and transfers), due mainly to taxes (30 percent of the decrease) and in-kind services (30 percent of the decrease). Most of the equalization is produced by personal income taxes and contributions to social security. Direct taxes are progressive, and the VAT is regressive. Cash transfers contribute little to redistribution. Although direct transfers are strongly progressive and equalizing, their share in the budget remains very limited (only 0.2 percent). Subsidies are equalizing, though much less so than cash transfers because benefits to the non-poor are higher than their population share (that is, subsidies are progressive but only in relative terms). Primary and secondary education are strongly redistributive and equalizing, whereas tertiary education is progressive only in relative terms because the poor still have limited access. Health spending is progressive and equalizing for primary healthcare, whereas hospitalization services are progressive in relative terms.

In light of the areas of Tunisian fiscal policy in need of improvement, we make the following policy recommendations:

1. Reinforce direct transfer programs to target the segments of the population that do not benefit from the basic services of education and health, especially programs related to tertiary education (scholarship programs for the poor) and hospitalization.
2. Strengthen and improve the existing PNAFN cash transfer program through revision of the allocation criteria.
3. Reduce energy subsidies and replace them with more targeted programs for the poor. The less vulnerable groups could receive a decrease in tax burden against the removal of the subsidy.

Acknowledgments

The authors are very grateful to Mustapha Nabli for his invaluable comments and insights, and Yassine Jmal from the National Institute of Statistics, Nidhal Bechikh from Centre de Recherches et des Etudes Sociales, and Imed Zair from Direction Generale des Etudes et de la Legislation Fiscales for their outstanding help with statistical information. The authors also wish to thank Ali Enami and Sean Higgins for their valuable help in the preparation of the *CEQ Assessment* for Tunisia.

References

Academic Ranking of World Universities (www.shanghairanking.com).

Enami, Ali, Sean Higgins, and Nora Lustig. 2022. "Allocating Taxes and Transfers and Constructing Income Concepts: Completing Sections A, B, and C of the *CEQ Master Workbook*," chap. 6 in *Commitment to Equity Handbook: Estimating the Impact of Fiscal Policy on Inequality and Poverty*, 2nd ed., Vol. 1, edited by Nora Lustig (Brookings Institution Press and CEQ Institute, Tulane University). Free online version available at www.commitmentoequity.org.

Higgins, Sean, and Caterina Brest Lopez. 2022. "Producing Indicators and Results, and Completing Sections D and E of the *CEQ Master Workbook* Using the *CEQ Stata Package*," chap. 8 in *Commitment to Equity Handbook: Estimating the Impact of Fiscal Policy on Inequality and Poverty*, 2nd ed., Vol. 1, edited by Nora Lustig (Brookings Institution Press and CEQ Institute, Tulane University). Free online version available at www.commitmentoequity.org.

Higgins, Sean, and Claudiney Pereira. 2014. "The Effects of Brazil's Taxation and Social Spending on the Distribution of Household Income," in "The Redistributive Impact of Taxes and Social Spending in Latin America," edited by Nora Lustig, Carola Pessino, and John Scott, special issue, *Public Finance Review* 42, no. 3, pp. 346–67 (doi:10.1177/1091142113501714).

Inchauste, Gabriela, Nora Lustig, Mashekwa Maboshe, Catriona Purfield, and Ingrid Woolard. 2017. "The Distributional Impact of Fiscal Policy in South Africa," in *The Distributional Impact of Taxes and Transfers: Evidence from Eight Low- and Middle-Income Countries*, edited by Gabriela Inchauste and Nora Lustig (Washington: World Bank).

INS (National Institute of Statistics), CRES (Centre de recherche et d'etudes sociales), AfDB (African Development Bank), and World Bank. 2013. *Analyse de l'impact des subventions alimentaires et des programmes d'assistance sociale sur la population pauvre et vulnerable* (Tunis, Tunisia: INS, CRES, AfDB, and World Bank).

INS-AfDB-WB (National Institute of Statistics, African Development Bank, and World Bank). 2012. *Measuring Poverty, Inequality and Polarization in Tunisia* (Tunis: National Institute of Statistics).

Jellema, Jon, Matthew Wai-Poi, and Rythia Afkar. 2017. "The Distributional Impact of Fiscal Policy in Indonesia," in *The Distributional Impact of Taxes and Transfers: Evidence from Eight Low- and Middle-Income Countries*, edited by Gabriela Inchauste and Nora Lustig (Washington: World Bank).

Lustig, Nora. 2015. "The Redistributive Impact of Government Spending on Education and Health: Evidence from 13 Developing Countries in the Commitment to Equity Project," in *Inequality and Fiscal Policy*, edited by Sanjeev Gupta, Michael Keen, Benedict Clements, and Ruud de Mooij (elibrary, International Monetary Fund).

Lustig, Nora, and Sean Higgins. 2013. "*Commitment to Equity Assessment* (CEQ): Estimating the Incidence of Social Spending, Subsidies and Taxes. Handbook," CEQ Working Paper 1 (Center for Inter-American Policy and Research, Department of Economics, Tulane University, and Inter-American Dialogue). This version was replaced by Lustig, 2017 (2018).

———. 2022. "The *CEQ Assessment*: Measuring the Impact of Fiscal Policy on Inequality and Poverty," chap. 1 in *Commitment to Equity Handbook: Estimating the Impact of Fiscal Policy on Inequality and Poverty*, 2nd ed., Vol. 1, edited by Nora Lustig (Brookings Institution Press and CEQ Institute, Tulane University). Free online version available at www.commitmentoequity.org.

National Institute of Statistics (Institut National de Statistiques). 2010. National Survey of Consumption and Household Living Standards for 2010 (Enquete Nationale sur le Budget, la Consommation et le Niveau de Vie 2010).

Nizar, Jouini. September 2015. "Tunisia Master Workbook," unpublished Excel files. Available from authors by request.

Paz Arauco, Veronica, George Gray Molina, Ernesto Yañez Aguilar, and Wilson Jimenez Pozo. 2014. "Explaining Low Redistributive Impact in Bolivia." *Public Finance Review* 42, no. 3, pp. 287–303 (doi:10.1177/1091142113506931).

Statistics department, Centre des Recherches et des Etudes Sociales (http://www.cres.tn/index.php?id=3).

Tunisia, Ministry of Education. 2010. *Annual Report* (Tunis).

Tunisia, Ministry of Finance. 2011. *Annual Report of Public Finance* (Tunis).

Tunisia, Ministry of Health. 2010. *Annual Report* (Tunis).

Tunisia, Ministry of High Education and Scientific Research. 2010. *Annual Report* (Tunis).

Tunisia, Ministry of Social Affairs. 2011. "Les programmes sociaux de lutte contre la pauvrete et d'amelioration des conditions de vie." *Annual Report* (Tunis).

World Bank. 2013. *Towards Greater Equity: Energy Subsidies, Targeting and Social Protection in Tunisia*, World Bank Report (Washington: World Bank).

Chapter 19

UGANDA

The Impact of Taxes, Transfers, and Subsidies on Inequality and Poverty

Jon Jellema, Nora Lustig, Astrid Haas, and Sebastian Wolf

Introduction

Over the last twenty-five years Uganda has made great strides in reducing poverty. It is one of the few Sub-Saharan African countries that achieved the Millennium Development Goal of halving the proportion of people living in poverty between 1990 and 2015, and it reached this goal five years ahead of time.[1] Even so, figure 19-1 indicates that high income inequality remains: as measured by the Gini coefficient—where a coefficient of 0 represents perfect equality and a coefficient of 1 perfect *in*equality— inequality has fluctuated around 0.4 since the beginning of this millennium.[2] A growing body of international evidence suggests that high income inequality may slow growth[3] and can also have negative effects on socioeconomic stability.[4] In recognition of the negative effects of income inequality, the Ugandan government has repeatedly declared the reduction of income inequality a priority policy goal.[5]

However, the overall impact of fiscal policy on inequality in income, consumption, savings, and other outcomes is often poorly understood. This study provides policy makers with an assessment of the redistributive impact of Ugandan fiscal policy— both its individual elements as well as the composite whole—using an internationally

The *CEQ Assessment* in Uganda was generously supported by the International Growth Center.

[1] Duponchel, McKay, and Ssewanyana (2015).

[2] MoFPED (2014b).

[3] Berg and Ostry (2011); Ostry, Berg, and Tsangarides (2014).

[4] Bardhan (2005).

[5] See the Uganda National Development Plans I and II (Republic of Uganda, 2010; Republic of Uganda, 2015), for example.

FIGURE 19-1
Gini Index of Inequality in Uganda, 1992–2013

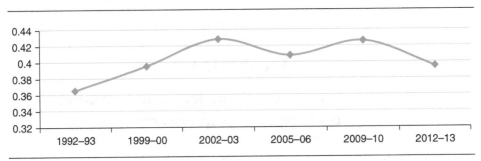

Source: MoFPED (2014b).

recognized methodology developed by the CEQ Institute.[6] This study estimates the impact of fiscal revenue collections (taxes) and fiscal expenditures—direct cash and near-cash transfers, in-kind benefits, subsidies—on household-level income inequality and poverty. By using an internationally consistent methodology, the results from the Uganda *CEQ Assessment* can be compared with results from other CEQ countries.

To our knowledge, fiscal incidence has so far not been studied systematically in Uganda. The assessment summarized in this report comes at a crucial time for Ugandan fiscal policy. On the revenue side, the government wants to raise the tax-to-GDP ratio from 13.9 percent in 2014–15 to 16.3 percent in 2020–21.[7] This implies new directions in tax policy and tax collection, which may have negative impacts on poor and non-poor households alike, depending on which tax instrument the government intends to use to generate the bulk of the revenue increase. On the expenditure side, the government has committed to large infrastructure projects that will leave little fiscal space for other social spending, for targeted spending on social protection, or for introducing new initiatives to reduce income inequality. Gaining a clear understanding of the impact of the current fiscal system will be crucial in the design of a pro-poor fiscal system for the years to come.

The Ugandan government's strategy to tackle poverty and income inequality over the last twenty-five years can be broken down in two periods. The first period was characterized by an expansion of the provision of in-kind education, healthcare, water, and sanitation benefits. After a period of civil war and chaos, the new National Resistance Movement government's extensive liberalization agenda, combined with disciplined monetary and fiscal policy reforms, triggered a period of sustained economic growth and trade in the early 1990s. Alongside gains from increased economic activity,

---

[6] For details on the methodology, please see the Introduction to Volume 1 in this Handbook and chapter 1 by Lustig and Higgins (2022), chapter 6 by Enami, Higgins, and Lustig (2022), chapter 7 by Jellema and Inchauste (2022), and chapter 8 by Higgins and Brest Lopez (2022), all in Volume 1.
[7] MoFPED (2016).

the establishment of the semiautonomous Uganda Revenue Authority led to large improvements in domestic revenue collections. The tax-to-GDP ratio rose from 6 to 13 percent in between 1990 and 2000. In 2007, with additional resources at hand, the government formulated a comprehensive Poverty Reduction Plan that would increase service delivery drastically. The centerpiece of the plan was the introduction of universal primary education. Delivery of many of these services was to be managed in a decentralized fashion, funded by transfers from central government. Donors aided these efforts with budget support.[8]

When the growth of taxes relative to GDP began to level off in the early 2000s, the government refocused. Infrastructure and investments in productive sectors were prioritized over further expenditure increases on service delivery transfers, arguably shifting fiscal policy away from the pro-poor, redistributive agenda that had been taken on in the 1990s to focus more directly on economic growth. This policy shift meant that in real terms, service delivery transfers largely peaked around 2003, with later adjustments mainly covering increases in the wage bill.[9]

The second period was characterized by the introduction of targeted cash and in-kind benefits. Responding to chronic inequality among regions caused by political instability and conflict, the government shifted to smaller programs specifically targeted to reduce regional imbalances in the early 2000s. The first Northern Uganda Social Action fund was introduced in 2003 and was followed by the introduction of the Social Assistance Grants for Empowerment programs in 2009 and the second Northern Uganda Social Action fund in 2010. These regionally focused programs are still ongoing, but given the large infrastructure investments the government is undertaking, it is unclear whether there will be sufficient fiscal space to expand them from their current rather small size. Furthermore, first evaluations have raised concerns about these projects' effectiveness.[10]

The government foresees large infrastructure investments going forward. These commitments leave little space to expand targeted poverty-reduction or income-equality programs and require intensified tax and other revenue collection efforts. In this context, the government is embarking on a reform to improve the efficiency of the service delivery transfer systems already in place. As part of these reforms, the government is reformulating transfer amounts and spending regulations to achieve a more equitable transfer distribution among districts and a more efficient delivery of in-kind education, healthcare, water, and sanitation benefits. The introduction of performance conditionality and transparency initiatives will, it is hoped, increase the accountability of decentralized government units.

Income inequality has a complex set of drivers, including educational opportunities, access to healthcare, water, and sanitation, availability of infrastructure, financial

---

[8] Kuteesa and others (2009).

[9] Aziz and others (2016).

[10] Ssewanyana and Kasirye (2015).

inclusion, and gender inequality. Not all of these are influenced by fiscal policy, but the progressivity of taxes and government expenditures is undisputedly significant. It is important to note that the assessment summarized in this report aims to uncover only the extent of redistribution achieved by the fiscal system and remains silent on fiscal policy's dynamic and long-term effects on income inequality. These issues are beyond the scope of the study, and the interested reader is referred to the 2015 issue of the International Monetary Fund's *Regional Economic Outlook for Sub-Saharan Africa* (IMF, 2015) for an overview. Furthermore, this study focuses solely on the fiscal year 2012–13, because this is the latest year in which the Uganda National Household Survey was carried out (UBOS, 2014). Additional assessments of earlier or later periods are required to uncover trends, so further research is called for.

The Ugandan *CEQ Assessment* demonstrates that fiscal policy in Uganda is equalizing and does not increase poverty. However, the redistributive impact is quite small, especially when compared with similar low-income countries such as Ethiopia and Tanzania and with the trend observed for twenty-nine low- and middle-income countries (including Uganda).[11] The small effect is driven primarily by low social spending (as a share of GDP), which in turn may be driven by low revenues from domestic collections and low revenues overall. Tax revenues in the year 2012–13 were just under 12 percent of GDP (provisional figures), lower than in Ethiopia and Tanzania, for example. At just over 12 percent, fiscal expenditures were also small (as a proportion of GDP), and the social expenditures that were executed at least partly to redistribute income accounted for approximately one-third of the total.

Within the social expenditures, education and health had the largest effect in reducing national income inequality, achieving a reduction of 1.6 Gini points (education and health make up a reduction of about 1.0 and 0.6 Gini points each). These in-kind transfers also constituted the largest proportion of social expenditure (at 2.4 and 1.6 percent of GDP, respectively). Direct transfers have provided meaningful income to the poor, but geographical coverage of these transfers is very limited, and thus they have led to only a modest reduction in income inequality of 0.1 Gini points. Indirect

---

[11] Argentina (Rossignolo, 2022) (chapter 11 in this Volume); Armenia (Younger and Khachatryan, 2017); Bolivia (Paz Arauco and others, 2014); Brazil (Higgins and Pereira, 2014); Chile (Martinez-Aguilar and others, 2022) (chapter 13 in this Volume); Colombia (Melendez and Martinez, 2015); Costa Rica (Sauma and Trejos, 2014); Dominican Republic (Aristy-Escuder and others, 2022); (chapter 14 in this Volume) Ecuador (Llerena and others, 2015); El Salvador (Beneke de Sanfeliu, Lustig, and Oliva Cepeda, 2022) (chapter 15 in this Volume); Ethiopia (Hill and others, 2017); Georgia (Cancho and Bondarenko, 2017); Ghana (Younger, Osei-Assibey, and Oppong, 2017); Guatemala (Icefi, 2017a); Honduras (Icefi, 2017b); Indonesia (Jellema, Wai-Poi, and Afkar, 2017); Iran (Enami, Lustig, and Taqdiri, 2017); Jordan (Alam, Inchauste, and Serajuddin, 2017); Mexico (Scott, 2014); Nicaragua (Icefi, 2017c); Peru (Jaramillo, 2014); Russia (Lopez-Calva and others, 2017), South Africa (Inchauste and others, 2017); Sri Lanka (Arunatilake, Inchauste, and Lustig, 2017); Tanzania (Younger, Myamba, and Mdadila, 2016); Tunisia (Jouini and others, 2022) (chapter 18 in this Volume); Uruguay (Bucheli and others, 2014); and Venezuela (Molina, 2016).

subsidies of water, electricity, and agricultural inputs had a negligible equalizing re-distributive impact in the period studied, reducing inequality by only 0.05 Gini points. On the tax side, VAT and excise taxes are neutral to slightly equalizing in distributive terms, in part due to their exemption schedule. Income taxes, which do not affect the poorest 50 percent of the population, help reduce inequality in Disposable Income by 1.2 Gini points.

Uganda's fiscal system leaves the incidence of poverty virtually unchanged: when the impact of indirect taxes and indirect subsidies is taken into account, Uganda's "no change" is the third-best result in a seven-country comparator group (Bolivia, Ethiopia, Ghana, Honduras, Nicaragua, Tanzania, and Uganda). Furthermore, Uganda is the only low-income country in Africa in which the poverty headcount *after* taking into account the effect of indirect taxes and subsidies does not rise above the Market Income (or "prefiscal") poverty headcount. This remarkable outcome has as much to do with the value of nonmarket consumption (auto-production, auto-consumption) in rural areas where the majority of the poor are located as with the set of indirect tax exemptions and indirect subsidies on the provision of water, electricity, and agricultural inputs. *These results are relevant when considering options to increase domestic resource mobilization in Uganda. Whatever path is chosen, it is important to assess the impact of reforms on the tax and subsidy system on the poor.*

The rest of this chapter is organized in the following manner: section 1 will provide an overview of the main transfers and taxes in Uganda; section 2 will explain the methodology behind the assessment and a description of the data sources; section 3 will provide an overview of the main findings from the Uganda assessment together with international benchmark comparisons; and section 4 will conclude and spell out the implications the results have for policy in Uganda.

1 Social Spending and Taxation in Uganda

The following sections examine the level and composition of public social expenditures and revenue collection.

1.1 Social Spending and Subsidies

Social spending in Uganda can be divided in three categories: in-kind transfers, direct transfers, and indirect subsidies. As outlined above, in-kind transfers were the government's main instrument to address income inequality until around 2003, and they remain today the largest transfer item (in terms of expenditure magnitudes) in the government's portfolio of expenditures. Beginning in the early 2000s, however, the government shifted focus to concentrate on more targeted direct transfers aimed at reducing regional inequalities as their main inequality reduction tool. Targeted, direct transfers may see their share of public expenditures decrease as the government has declared that, going forward, it intends to focus on reducing poverty and inequality

TABLE 19-1
Uganda Government Expenditures, 2012–2013

	UGX (billions)	% of GDP	Included?
Total expenditure	7,454	12.1	. . .
Defense spending	749	1.2	No
Social spending	2,817	4.6	Yes
Social protection	344	0.6	. . .
Social assistance	84	0.14	Yes
Cash transfers	84	0.14	Yes
Non-contributory pensions	. . .	. . .	. . .
Near-cash transfers	. . .	. . .	. . .
Other	. . .	. . .	. . .
Social insurance	260	0.4	Yes
Education	1,504	2.4	. . .
Preschool	n.c.	n.c.	. . .
Primary	750	1.2	Yes
Secondary	528	0.9	Yes
Post-secondary non-tertiary	n.c.	n.c.	. . .
Tertiary	202	0.3	Yes
Health	969	1.6	Yes
Contributory	n.c.	n.c.	. . .
Non-contributory	n.c.	n.c.	. . .
Housing & Urban	24	0.04	No
Subsidies	129	0.21	. . .
Energy	. . .	. . .	. . .
Inputs for agriculture	18	n.c.	Yes
Water	91	n.c.	Yes
Rural electrification	9	n.c.	Yes
Infrastructure	2,595	4.21	No

Source: Republic of Uganda (2014).

Note: Expenditures (and revenues) included in Uganda's CEQ Assessment may not be fully allocated within the Uganda National Household Survey (UNHS) for various reasons; see section 2 for more detail on the allocative methods and assumptions.

. . . = Not applicable; n.c. = Not calculated; UGX = Uganda shilling.

by boosting agricultural productivity and by increasing investment in other productive sectors.[12]

Table 19-1 provides a snapshot of expenditures in the fiscal year 2012–13. Social expenditures—social protection, education, health, and housing and urban spending—account for nearly two-fifths of total expenditures; infrastructure approximately one-third; defense spending one-tenth; and other sectors (for example, energy and mineral

---

[12] MoFPED (2016).

development, information and communications technology, tourism, trade, and industry; these are not shown in table 19-1), the remaining 17 percent.

Table 19-1 also provides a snapshot of the fiscal expenditures covered by Uganda's *CEQ Assessment*. Defense spending ("security" in Uganda budget-report terminology) and infrastructure are not covered, while most of the social protection portfolio is incorporated. The only "in-kind" social spending that is not covered by this *CEQ Assessment* is "housing/urban" spending, of which there is very little in Uganda as a whole and virtually none undertaken outside of the capital, Kampala.

1.1.1 In-Kind Transfers

Education

The main education expenditure is for capitation grants for primary and secondary school students, which are allocated to schools based on their current enrollment figures. At a primary level, schools receive a grant of about 7,000 Ugandan shillings (UGX) in 2012–13 (currently about US$2.11) per student per year. For secondary school the amount was about 41,000 UGX (currently about US$12.35) for government schools and 47,000 UGX for public-private partnership schools (currently about US$14.16) per student per year enrolled in one of the identified schools under Uganda's Universal Secondary Education Program.[13] At a tertiary level, the government allocates scholarships for study at public institutions.

Health

Uganda abolished user fees in public health facilities in 2001 in support of the government's overall aim of attaining universal healthcare coverage. Health transfers are made through grants to a district government level. These transfers include payments of wages for health workers at all district health facilities, funding for service delivery operations by the health departments, as well as a development grant for constructing and rehabilitating health facilities.[14]

1.1.2 Direct Transfers

Social Assistance Grants Transfer for Empowerment (SAGE)

This program, which began as a pilot in 2011 and is targeted at the poorest and most vulnerable members of society with an aim of providing them a minimum level of income security, is currently being delivered in fourteen districts in Northern Uganda. As part of the SAGE program, regular cash transfers are made to individuals or households under two separate schemes. The first is the Senior Citizen Grant (SCG) targeting individuals who are above sixty-five years of age (or in the case of the Karamoja region, above sixty years). The second is the Vulnerable Family Support Grant

---

[13] Uganda Ministry of Education and Sports (2013).
[14] MoFPED (2016).

(VFSG) which targets households with low labor capacity as a result of age or physical disability and high dependency ratios, with district specific thresholds. The exact eligibility is determined through a targeting exercise that takes place every two to three years. Under both schemes, each individual or family receives about 25,000 UGX (approximately US$7.50) per month. This figure is revised on an annual basis to ensure it is in line with inflation.

Northern Uganda Social Action Fund (NUSAF)

The second round of this program (NUSAF II) began in 2009 under the auspices of the Office of the Prime Minister. It was established to support communities in previously war-torn Northern Uganda, which remains one of the poorest regions of the country. Two programs under NUSAF are focused on transferring cash and assets to vulnerable individuals: the Household Income Support Programme (HISP) and the Public Works Programme (PWP). The HISP finances income-generating activities and supports livelihood and skills-development initiatives that create further opportunities for self-employment. Under this program, transfers of livestock or other productive assets are made to groups of up to fifteen individuals. To be eligible, groups have to include the most vulnerable members of society, determined by a community participatory wealth-ranking exercise, and they have to be comprised of at least 50 percent women. The overall value of the transfer can be up to US$5,000 per group. The government aims to target 8,000 groups with these transfers.

The PWP targets beneficiaries geographically based on a set of predetermined poverty and socioeconomic indicators. This program supports labor-intensive interventions to provide poor households with additional income support that can help them weather the impact of rising food prices. On average, each project employs up to 250 people for the period of one month. The maximum funding is US$20,000 per district and US$10,000 per project. The target under NUSAF II is to fund 1,000 such projects, generating about 5.5 million employment days, over a period of five years.

1.1.3 Indirect Subsidies

Water and Electricity

In urban areas, heavy direct subsidies of water and electricity consumption had been phased out by the time of the Uganda National Household Survey (UNHS) 2012–13 (our primary source for microdata; see below), but both utility sectors still receive indirect subsidies in the form of infrastructure investment contributions. In the case of water, tariffs in urban areas are set to cover operating and maintenance costs, so consumption of water in urban areas is subsidized only indirectly by lowering the investment cost component that would otherwise have to be recovered through higher tariffs. In rural areas, water supply is directly subsidized from the national budget, which funds part of the operating costs of water delivery.

The situation is slightly different in the case of electricity, where some cross-subsidization occurs; while serving rural customers is more expensive than serving urban customers, both pay the same tariff, and no direct government subsidies of operating costs are in place, not even in rural areas. This cross-subsidization (enforced by government contracting, but not funded from government revenues directly) is not included in the Uganda *CEQ Assessment*. As with the water sector, the government also provides indirect subsidies of infrastructure to expand rural electrification. These expenditures are counted as indirect subsidies and are included in the Uganda *CEQ Assessment*.

National Agricultural Advisory Services (NAADS)

NAADS, a semiautonomous public agency under the Ministry of Agriculture, Animal Industries, and Fisheries, is responsible for the provision of extension services to farmers across the country. NAADS organizes the distribution of a range of agricultural inputs to support interventions along the value chain—for example seeds, seedlings, and farming equipment such as hoes. The government is currently planning an expansion of NAADS, so it is likely that the importance of indirect subsidies of agricultural inputs will increase in the years to come.

1.2 Revenues

Table 19-2 provides a snapshot of public revenue sources in the fiscal year 2012–13. Uganda's revenues come largely from indirect taxes like VAT, excise taxes (including on petroleum products), and trade taxes. Direct taxes—the pay as you earn (PAYE) personal income tax and various corporate income taxes (including on capital gains and a withholding tax)—make a contribution to public revenues that is approximately half as large as the contribution from indirect taxes.

The Uganda *CEQ Assessment* covers the majority of indirect taxes and the personal income tax (including the PAYE component, which is essentially personal income tax withholding). We do not have enough information to allocate corporate income tax burdens to UNHS households; nor do we have enough administrative information to allocate social insurance contributions. The paragraphs below provide further detail on the taxes included in Uganda's *CEQ Assessment*.

1.2.1 Taxes

Uganda's tax-to-GDP ratio, provisionally at 11.6 percent of GDP[15] in the 2012–13 fiscal year, is one of the lowest in Sub-Saharan Africa. The tax compliance gap in Uganda is large, and collections rest on a very small base. In light of this, the government has

---

[15] Official government reports, such as the "Annual Economic Performance Report 2012–13," (MoFPED, 2014a) indicate total domestic revenues from taxes at 12.9 percent of GDP while giving the same Ugandan shilling figure as we report here for total revenues from taxes. Our measure of GDP comes from the World Bank's database (http://data.worldbank.org/); we are unable to locate the GDP denominator used in these other reports. The GDP figure may have been rebased and/or revised after the publication of the 2012–13 noted above.

TABLE 19-2
Uganda Government Revenues, 2012–2013

	UGX (billions)	% of GDP	Included?
Total revenue and grants revenue	9,213	14.9	...
	8,277	13.4	...
Tax revenue	7,150	11.6	...
Direct taxes	2,407	3.9	...
Personal income tax	1,197	1.9	Yes
Corporate income tax	598	1.0	No
Corporate withholding tax	389	0.06	No
Taxes on property	n.c.	n.c.	...
Contributions to social insurance	n.c.	n.c.	...
Indirect taxes	4,712	7.6	...
VAT	2,353	3.8	Yes
Sales tax	...	...	...
Excise taxes	1,466	2.4	Yes
Customs Duties	753	1.2	...
Taxes on exports	0	0.0	No
Nontax revenue	191	0.3	No
Grants	936	1.5	Yes

Source: Republic of Uganda (2014).

Note: Revenue collections (and expenditures) included in Uganda's CEQ Assessment may not be fully allocated within the Uganda National Household Survey (UNHS) for various reasons; see section 2 for more detail on the allocative methods and assumptions.

... = Not applicable; n.c. = Not calculated; UGX = Uganda shilling.

declared increasing its domestic revenue base as a policy priority. Under the National Budget Framework, the government declared the goal to raise the tax-to-GDP ratio at a rate of 0.5 percent per annum with the aim of achieving a ratio of 16.3 percent by the 2020–21 fiscal year. To achieve this goal, reforms targeted at improving efficiency (rather than increasing rates) are planned: increasing investment in revenue collection, saving on costs and modernizing systems, and integrating tax systems operating at different levels of government (inter alia).

The main domestic taxes in Uganda are the following:

Income taxes:
- The personal income tax (including PAYE withholding): marginal rates range from 0 to 40 percent;[16]

---

[16] Technically, the PAYE rate converges to 40 percent with income; the 40 percent marginal rate is applied only to income over 120 million UGX.

- Corporate tax: the standard rate is 30 percent;
- Withholding tax on corporate income: 6 percent;
- Presumptive income tax: 1.5 percent of gross turnover or a flat fee depending on the bracket.

Consumption taxes:
- VAT: 18 percent;
- Excise duties (including on fuels);
- Customs duties.

Although the VAT has a uniform rate, there are various exemptions and zero-rated products. These are targeted at goods that have been identified as consumed by the poor and represent an attempt to make the consumption tax less regressive. Examples of exempt goods are unprocessed foodstuffs and agricultural products (except for wheat grain) and supply of various agricultural inputs. Customs duties are applied at common external tariff (CET) rates specified in the East African Community (EAC) framework; the EAC-CET specifies 0 percent rates for raw materials, capital goods, agricultural inputs, and medicines and medical equipment and lower rates (than the CET rate) for intermediate goods and other essential industrial inputs and for finished goods.

1.3 International Perspective on Fiscal Magnitudes and Composition

Figures 19-2 and 19-3 show that Uganda's domestic revenue collection efforts are below similar low-income countries such as Ethiopia and Tanzania (figure 19-2) and the broader trend for twenty-nine low- and middle-income countries (figure 19-3). In fact, Uganda raises revenues below the trend on every revenue source except personal income and payroll taxes (as shown in figure 19-4).

Given comparatively low revenue collections, it is not surprising that figures 19-5 and 19-6 demonstrate that Uganda's total spending and redistributive spending (spending on direct transfers, education, health, other social spending, and indirect subsidies) is lower than that of Ethiopia and Tanzania, and significantly below the trend of the twenty-nine low- and middle-income countries. Ethiopia, though poorer, dedicates more fiscal resources to redistributive spending than Uganda. In terms of the composition of social spending (direct transfers, education, health, and other social spending), Uganda allocates a share of GDP to direct transfers that is similar to that allocated in Ghana, Nicaragua, and Tanzania, but much less than allocated in Ethiopia (figure 19-7). The same is true for education spending. For health, however, Uganda spends a share similar to Ghana's and Tanzania's, and a slightly higher share than Ethiopia's.

FIGURE 19-2
Composition of Total Government Revenues (as % of GDP): Bolivia, Ethiopia, Ghana, Honduras, Nicaragua, Tanzania, and Uganda (circa 2010)

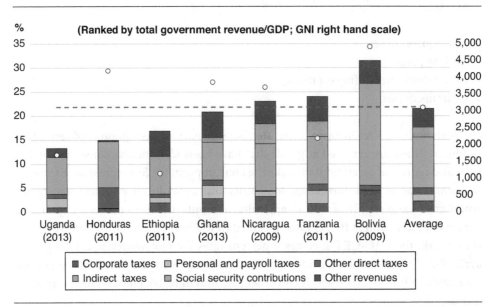

Source: CEQ Data Center on Fiscal Redistribution. Based on Bolivia (Paz Arauco and others, 2014); Ethiopia (Hill and others, 2017); Ghana (Younger, Osei-Assibey, and Oppong, 2017); Honduras (Icefi, 2017b); Nicaragua (Icefi, 2017c); and Tanzania (Younger, Myamba, and Mdadila, 2016).

Notes: The year for which the analysis was conducted is in parenthesis. Data shown here is administrative data as reported by the studies cited; the numbers do not necessarily coincide with those found in databases from multilateral organizations (e.g., World Bank's WDI). Gross National Income per capita on right axis is in 2011 PPP from World Development Indicators, August 29, 2016, http://data.worldbank.org/indicator/NY.GNP.PCAP.PP.CD.

2 Methods and Data

The following sections describe the CEQ fiscal incidence assessment methodology in general as well as the specific methodological choices made for the Uganda *CEQ Assessment*.

2.1 Methodological Summary

The *CEQ Assessment* takes specific fiscal policy elements, programs, expenditures, or revenue collections—such as those described above—and allocates them to individuals and households appearing in a micro-level socioeconomic survey. Once the allocations are made, the CEQ analytical program consists of calculating different measures of poverty and impoverishment, inequality and progressiveness, and the amount of redistribution accomplished (inter alia) on the measures of income—or "income concepts"—that exclude ("prefiscal") and include ("postfiscal") these fiscal policy elements. Figure 19-8 summarizes the construction of these income concepts.

FIGURE 19-3

Total Revenue (as % of GDP) versus Gross National Income per Capita (circa 2010)

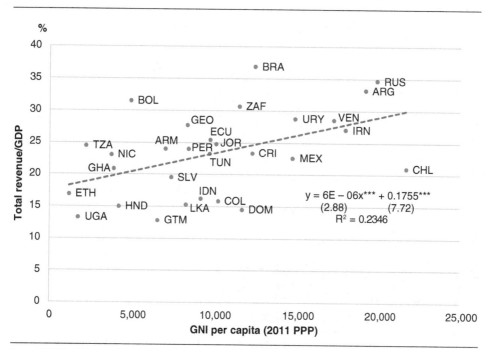

Source: CEQ Data Center on Fiscal Redistribution. Based on Argentina (Rossignolo, 2022) (chapter 11 in this Volume); Armenia (Younger and Khachatryan, 2017); Bolivia (Paz Arauco and others, 2014); Brazil (Higgins and Pereira, 2014); Chile (Martinez-Aguilar and others, 2022) (chapter 13 in this Volume); Colombia (Melendez and Martinez, 2015); Costa Rica (Sauma and Trejos, 2014); Dominican Republic (Aristy-Escuder and others, 2022) (chapter 14 in this Volume); Ecuador (Llerena and others, 2015); El Salvador (Beneke de Sanfeliu, Lustig, and Oliva Cepeda, 2022) (chapter 15 in this Volume); Ethiopia (Hill and others, 2017); Georgia (Cancho and Bondarenko, 2017); Ghana (Younger, Osei-Assibey, and Oppong, 2017); Guatemala (Icefi, 2017a); Honduras (Icefi, 2017b); Indonesia (Jellema, Wai-Poi, and Afkar, 2017); Iran (Enami, Lustig, and Taqdiri, 2017); Jordan (Alam, Inchauste, and Serajuddin, 2017); Mexico (Scott, 2014); Nicaragua (Icefi, 2017c); Peru (Jaramillo, 2014); Russia (Lopez-Calva and others, 2017), South Africa (Inchauste and others, 2017); Sri Lanka (Arunatilake, Inchauste, and Lustig, 2017); Tanzania (Younger, Myamba, and Mdadila, 2016); Tunisia (Jouini and others, 2022) (chapter 18 in this Volume); Uruguay (Bucheli and others, 2014); and Venezuela (Molina, 2016).

Notes: The dotted line is the slope obtained from a simple regression with total revenue/GDP as the dependent variable, t statistics in parentheses *p < 0.1, **p < 0.05, ***p < 0.01. Gross National Income per capita is in 2011 PPP from World Development Indicators, August 29, 2016, http://data.worldbank.org/indicator/NY.GNP.PCAP.PP.CD.

The Uganda *CEQ Assessment* incorporates every type of fiscal policy element listed in figure 19-8. However, as the income module in the UNHS was judged to be unreliable and would likely lead to under-reporting of income for those with little-to-no income from the sources listed in the UNHS as well as for those with very high incomes (from any source), we chose to use consumption expenditure as our measure of primary income.[17] We assumed total consumption expenditures—including the value of imputed rent for those living in owner-occupied housing as well as the implied value

---

[17] See Bollinger and Hirsch (2013) and Bollinger and Hirsch (2007). These examples include thorough treatments of the difficulties created by recall error and item nonresponse in socioeconomic survey income modules.

FIGURE 19-4

Personal and Payroll Taxes (as % of GDP) versus Gross National Income per Capita (circa 2010)

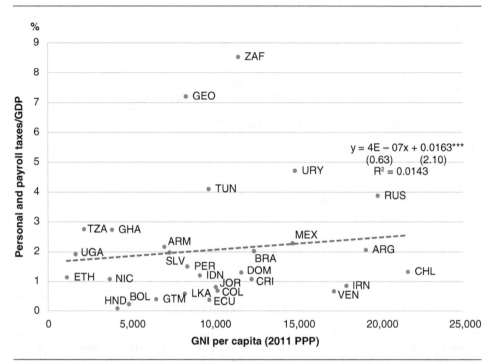

Source: CEQ Data Center on Fiscal Redistribution. Based on Argentina (Rossignolo, 2022) (chapter 11 in this Volume); Armenia (Younger and Khachatryan, 2017); Bolivia (Paz Arauco and others, 2014); Brazil (Higgins and Pereira, 2014); Chile (Martinez-Aguilar and others, 22022) (chapter 13 in this Volume); Colombia (Melendez and Martinez, 2015); Costa Rica (Sauma and Trejos, 2014); Dominican Republic (Aristy-Escuder and others, 2022) (chapter 14 in this Volume); Ecuador (Llerena and others, 2015); El Salvador (Beneke de Sanfeliu, Lustig, and Oliva Cepeda, 2022) (chapter 15 in this Volume); Ethiopia (Hill and others, 2017); Georgia (Cancho and Bondarenko, 2017); Ghana (Younger, Osei-Assibey, and Oppong, 2017); Guatemala (Icefi, 2017a); Honduras (Icefi, 2017b); Indonesia (Jellema, Wai-Poi, and Afkar, 2017); Iran (Enami, Lustig, and Taqdiri, 2017); Jordan (Alam, Inchauste, and Serajuddin, 2017); Mexico (Scott, 2014); Nicaragua (Icefi, 2017c); Peru (Jaramillo, 2014); Russia (Lopez-Calva and others, 2017), South Africa (Inchauste and others, 2017); Sri Lanka (Arunatilake, Inchauste, and Lustig, 2017); Tanzania (Younger, Myamba, and Mdadila, 2016); Tunisia (Jouini and others, 2022) (chapter 18 in this Volume); Uruguay (Bucheli and others, 2014); and Venezuela (Molina, 2016).

Notes: The dotted line is the slope obtained from a simple regression with personal and payroll taxes/GDP as the dependent variable, t statistics in parentheses $^*p < 0.1$, $^{**}p < 0.05$, $^{***}p < 0.01$. The year for which the analysis was conducted is in parenthesis. Data shown here is administrative data as reported by the studies cited; the numbers do not necessarily coincide with those found in data bases from multilateral organizations (e.g., World Bank's WDI). Gross National Income per capita is in 2011 PPP from World Development Indicators, August 29, 2016, http://data.worldbank.org/indicator/NY.GNP.PCAP.PP.CD.

of any auto-production/auto-consumption—were equal to the CEQ Disposable Income concept (approximately in the middle of the flowchart in figure 19-8) and work "backward" and "forward" from Disposable Income to other CEQ income concepts.[18]

---

[18] As consumption expenditure is our primary income measure, and as all other income concepts including Market Income are derived from consumption expenditure, we do not create a taxable income concept; other *CEQ Assessments* do produce this income concept when relevant. Creating a

FIGURE 19-5

Total Primary and Redistributive Spending plus Contributory Pensions (as % of GDP): Bolivia, Ethiopia, Ghana, Honduras, Nicaragua, Tanzania, and Uganda (circa 2010)

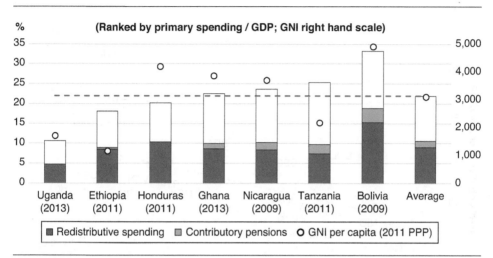

Source: CEQ Data Center on Fiscal Redistribution. Based on Bolivia (Paz Arauco and others, 2014); Ethiopia (Hill and others, 2017); Ghana (Younger, Osei-Assibey, and Oppong, 2017); Honduras (Icefi, 2017b); Nicaragua (Icefi, 2017c); and Tanzania (Younger, Myamba, and Mdadila, 2016).

Notes: The year for which the analysis was conducted is in parenthesis. Redistributive spending includes: direct transfers, spending on education and health, other social spending and indirect subsidies. Data shown here is administrative data as reported by the studies cited; the numbers do not necessarily coincide with those found in data bases from multilateral organizations (e.g., World Bank's WDI). Gross National Income per capita on right axis is in 2011 PPP from World Development Indicators, August 29, 2016, http://data.worldbank.org/indicator/NY.GNP.PCAP.PP.CD.

2.2 Data Sources

The primary micro-level dataset providing the individual- and household-level information necessary to allocate fiscal policy elements is the UNHS 2012–13.[19] The Uganda Bureau of Statistics carries out two nationally representative surveys that cover consumption and income behavior on a regular basis, the Uganda National Panel Survey (UNPS) and the UNHS. The UNHS has twice the sample size of the UNPS (6,887 households surveyed in the UNHS vs. 3,188 households in the UNPS) and provides better statistical power at sub-national levels, which is especially important for allocating

taxable income concept requires knowledge of the composition of Market Income, but a Ugandan household's expenditure profile (in the UNHS) cannot provide any information in the composition of income. Likewise, we are unable to say anything about the savings or current asset profile of UNHS households for the same reason: a current consumption expenditure profile does not provide any information on investment spending nor on the returns accruing to any household's assets.

[19] The allocations—including the assumptions and choices implicit in them—are described in section 2.3.

FIGURE 19-6

Redistributive Spending (as % of GDP) versus Gross National Income per Capita (circa 2010)

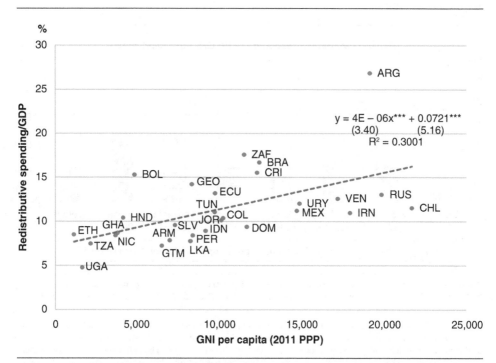

Source: CEQ Data Center on Fiscal Redistribution. Based on Argentina (Rossignolo, 2022) (chapter 11 in this Volume); Armenia (Younger and Khachatryan, 2017); Bolivia (Paz Arauco and others, 2014); Brazil (Higgins and Pereira, 2014); Chile (Martinez-Aguilar and others, 2022) (chapter 13 in this Volume); Colombia (Melendez and Martinez, 2015); Costa Rica (Sauma and Trejos, 2014); Dominican Republic (Aristy-Escuder and others, 2022) (chapter 14 in this Volume); Ecuador (Llerena and others, 2015); El Salvador (Beneke de Sanfeliu, Lustig, and Oliva Cepeda, 2022) (chapter 15 in this Volume); Ethiopia (Hill and others, 2017); Georgia (Cancho and Bondarenko, 2017); Ghana (Younger, Osei-Assibey, and Oppong, 2017); Guatemala (Icefi, 2017a); Honduras (Icefi, 2017b); Indonesia (Jellema, Wai-Poi, and Afkar, 2017); Iran (Enami, Lustig, and Taqdiri, 2017); Jordan (Alam, Inchauste, and Serajuddin, 2017); Mexico (Scott, 2014); Nicaragua (Icefi, 2017c); Peru (Jaramillo, 2014); Russia (Lopez-Calva and others, 2017); South Africa (Inchauste and others, 2017); Sri Lanka (Arunatilake, Inchauste, and Lustig, 2017); Tanzania (Younger, Myamba, and Mdadila, 2016); Tunisia (Jouini and others, 2022) (chapter 18 in this Volume); Uruguay (Bucheli and others, 2014); and Venezuela (Molina, 2016).

Notes: The dotted line is the slope obtained from a simple regression with Redistributive spending/GDP as the dependent variable, t statistics in parentheses *p < 0.1, **p < 0.05, ** p < 0.01. Redistributive spending includes: direct transfers, spending on education and health and indirect subsidies. The year for which the analysis was conducted is in parenthesis. Data shown here is administrative data as reported by the studies cited; the numbers do not necessarily coincide with those found in data bases from multilateral organizations (e.g., World Bank's WDI). Gross National Income per capita is in 2011 PPP from World Development Indicators, August 29, 2016, http://data.worldbank.org/indicator/NY.GNP.PCAP.PP.CD.

direct transfers in Uganda (see below). The UNHS is conducted approximately every three years using a two-stage stratified sample design that allows for reliable estimations of key indicators at the national, rural-urban, regional, and sub-regional levels. Apart from coverage of in-kind transfers received, the survey contains detailed information about income sources and consumption levels, which enable imputations of effective taxation, as well as the imputation of effective indirect transfers and subsidies.

FIGURE 19-7

Composition of Social Spending (as % of GDP): Bolivia, Ethiopia, Ghana, Honduras, Nicaragua, Tanzania, and Uganda (circa 2010)

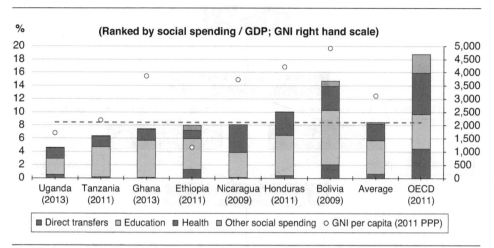

Source: CEQ Data Center on Fiscal Redistribution. Based on Bolivia (Paz Arauco and others, 2014); Ethiopia (Hill and others, 2017); Ghana, (Younger, Osei-Assibey, and Oppong, 2017); Honduras, (Icefi, 2017b); Nicaragua (Icefi, 2017c); and Tanzania, (Younger, Myamba, and Mdadila, 2016).

Notes: The year for which the analysis was conducted is in parenthesis. Data shown here is administrative data as reported by the studies cited; the numbers do not necessarily coincide with those found in data bases from multilateral organizations (e.g., World Bank's WDI). Figure for OECD average (includes only advanced countries) was directly provided by the statistical office of the organization. Other social spending includes expenditures in housing and community amenities; environmental protection; and recreation, culture and religion. Gross National Income per capita on right axis is in 2011 PPP from World Development Indicators, August 29, 2016, http://data.worldbank.org/indicator/NY.GNP.PCAP.PP.CD.

The source for total revenues collected by the government from households—via the PAYE, VAT, and excise taxes—is the Annual Budget Performance Report (ABPR) 2012–13 published by the Ministry of Finance, Planning and Economic Development (MoFPED). To impute "effective" or actually prevailing rates (which may differ from statutory rates), we first scale down the expected tax take from UNHS households so that the ratio of VAT (for example) revenues in the ABPR to Private Final Household Consumption Expenditure in Uganda National Accounts data is equivalent to the ratio of VAT collections from UNHS households to the value of cumulative UNHS household consumption expenditure. For the VAT and excise taxes, the total revenue figure from the ABPR we use includes revenues via the application of those taxes (when applicable) to domestically produced goods and services.[20]

Government expenditure on indirect subsidies for water and electricity and in-kind transfers of healthcare and education services are also taken from the ABPR 2012–13.

---

[20] While imported goods also attract VAT and excise (potentially), we are unable to determine which UNHS household expenditures are for imported goods and which for domestic goods.

FIGURE 19-8
CEQ Income Concepts and Fiscal Policy Elements

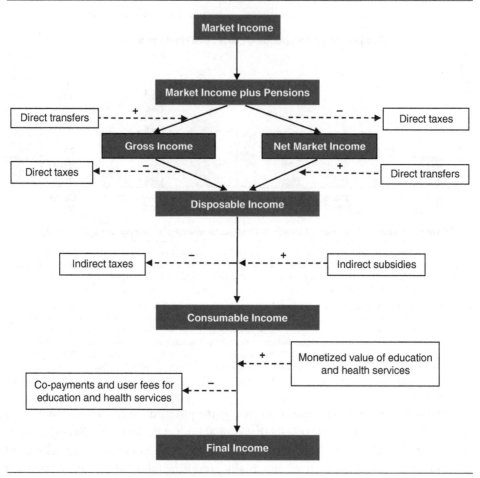

Source: Enami, Higgins, Lustig (2022) (chapter 6 in this Volume).

Expenditures on agricultural input subsidies (delivered by the NAADS agency—see above in section 1.1.3) were provided by the MoFPED. These subsidies and in-kind transfers are scaled in a manner equivalent to the scaling of taxes. The ABPR also provides aggregate expenditure information for the government agency responsible for the two programs that feature direct transfers, NUSAF and SAGE (as explained in section 1.1.2). We use operational reports, program characteristics, and rules to allocate uniform transfer magnitudes to all households that are imputed to be eligible (or to households deemed to host at least one eligible individual) for these programs. The total amount of direct transfer expenditure allocated, then, is not scaled in the way that the other fiscal policy elements described above are.

2.3 Allocation Assumptions

When and where possible, *CEQ Assessments* allocate fiscal policy elements to individuals or households based on direct observation. For example, when an individual queried in a socioeconomic survey is asked to recall how much she has paid in VAT on all her purchases in the last seven days or is asked to provide receipts detailing VAT payments, then we directly "observe" the total VAT collection from that individual. These VAT payments recorded by individuals are then assumed to be the same VAT revenues listed in the executive, administrative, and other budget reporting for the same year. In Uganda, however, very few fiscal policy elements could be allocated via direct observation; the subsections below provide a summary of allocation assumptions and decisions for various fiscal policy elements.

2.3.1 Personal Income Taxes

PAYE income tax collections allocated in the UNHS were scaled such that the ratio of total PAYE revenues in administrative records to National Accounts Household Final Consumption Expenditure was equivalent to the ratio of PAYE collected from UNHS households to total UNHS Consumption Expenditures. The PAYE rate schedule was adjusted so that the marginal change in PAYE rates between PAYE brackets remained intact while total PAYE collections remained equal to the amount described above. Taxpayer status was imputed based on a combination of (1) having recorded taxable income above the PAYE policy threshold; (2) the respondent indicating positively that he or she had made either PAYE payments or social security payments (or had them made on his or her behalf); and (3) the respondent having a score of 2 or greater on a "formality of employment" scale if and when there were no definitive answers to the questions listed in (2). The "formality of employment" score was generated within the household survey and is additive across seven characteristics including the receipt of paid sick leave and vacation, the duration of the contract, and other benefits.

2.3.2 Simulated Direct Transfers

Both of the umbrella programs under which Uganda's direct transfers are executed—the Social Assistance Grants for Empowerment and the Northern Uganda Social Action Fund—operate in limited areas. Since there is no question in the UNHS that records receipts of any direct transfers, we use program reports (from the Ugandan executing agency as well as multilateral development agencies) to understand eligibility, (annual) coverage, and (annual) benefit levels. We then parameterize eligibility and generate transfer-eligible populations within the household survey and randomly allocate program-specific benefits to program-specific eligible household pools until we reach (approximately) the average number of beneficiaries and benefits delivered yearly according to program reporting.

2.3.3 VAT, Excise, and Fuel Excise: Based on Expenditure Records

We cannot directly identify VAT or excise tax amounts paid, so instead we back out, for each purchased item, the share of the item's value that is a VAT or excise charge. In order to determine this share, these taxes are scaled in two ways. The first scale factor involves selecting the proportion of the total tax collection we expect to be generated by household expenditure. For VAT, nonfuel excise, and fuel excise, these first scale factors are 0.5, 1.0, and 0.1, respectively.[21] When this first scale factor is less than 1, it indicates our assumption that the tax in question is not collected exclusively from households. For example, the 0.1 factor on the fuel excise indicates we assume that 90 percent of the fuel excise collection total (listed in table 19-1) is coming from the commercial/industrial/enterprise and government/NGO sectors. We do not assume the fuel excise collected from the nonhousehold sectors does not create a burden for households (through higher prices of other goods and services consumed); however, in this report we allocate only the direct burden of indirect taxes like VAT and the excise tax.[22]

The second scale factor is generated in the following way: we calculate the ratio of revenues collected (per indirect tax) in the ABPR to Household Final Consumption Expenditure in the National Accounts and set it equal to the ratio of revenues collected from UNHS households (per tax) to cumulative UNHS consumption expenditure. We then create categories of goods in the UNHS consumption module, which, according to tax statutes, attract the tax in question. For example, in the UNHS consumption module the only good that attracts the fuel excise tax is fuel itself; only UNHS households that record non-0 expenditure on fuel are allocated a fuel excise tax.[23] For

---

[21] These first factors are not chosen arbitrarily. For VAT we had a preview of estimates (generated by the Uganda Revenue Authority) of sector-level VAT collections: over 80 percent of VAT collections (in the 2012–13 fiscal year) were generated from just two sectors: manufacturing and electricity/gas/steam and air-conditioning supply. As final consumers in these sectors need not be exclusively households or private citizens, we guessed that less than 100 percent of VAT collections were coming from direct purchases by households. We then chose a proportion of VAT to allocate to households based on the effective rate that it implied (14.6 percent) compared with the statutory rate (18 percent). For the fuel excise, we knew that only 6 percent of UNHS households recorded positive fuel purchases. As for VAT, we chose the first fuel excise factor, 0.1, based on the effective rate of taxation (on fuel) that it implied (217 percent) compared to the statutory rate (217 percent). The nonfuel excise is collected primarily from alcoholic beverages, tobacco, chewing gum, sweets, chocolate, and other comestibles, as well as from furniture, cosmetics and perfumes, banking fees and money transfers, and cement. All of these items (save for cement) are plausibly purchased by households.

[22] See Jellema and Inchauste (2022) (chapter 7 in this Volume of the Handbook), for a theoretical model and estimation tools and procedures for estimating the *indirect effects* of indirect taxes within the *CEQ Assessment* framework.

[23] We do not have access to the sales value of the VAT-able base by sector or good/service category, so we instead assume that VAT was collected at the same rate (proportional to net-of-VAT

the VAT, we create within the UNHS consumption expenditure records a measure of "VAT-able" consumption expenditure, and apply our imputed effective VAT rate to those expenditures only. We decided which items are "VAT-able" according to policy and statutes.

We then determine the share of the tax in the total expenditure value of the taxed good (or good category). From this share we determine what "effective" rate of taxation would, when applied to the value of the good, net of the indirect tax paid, give us back the actual sales value of the good as recorded by households in the UNHS.

The "effective" rate, or the on-average actual rate, so calculated allows us to take care not to allocate indirect taxes to purchases of goods or services that are exempt from the tax. We also implicitly exclude any informal purchases that are not included in the sales over which an indirect tax is collected. However, because we do not directly observe informal purchases, the reduction in taxes collected (and therefore the reduction in taxes allocated to UNHS households) due to informal purchases or weak tax administration is allocated to all households purchasing the good (or category of goods) that is taxed.

2.3.4 Electricity and Water Subsidies

As the previous section indicates, water and electricity tariffs are not directly subsidized, but the Rural and Urban Water Supply programs and the Rural Electrification program provide (to the utility operators) a fixed, on-budget sum annually, which is meant to cover network maintenance, investment, and upgrading costs. In other words, without this budget support, utility operators would raise prices so that total revenues collected privately covered these costs as well. For these programs, we divide the total (scaled) expenditure on these programs by the total number of eligible users in the UNHS to get a per-user subsidy. We are allocating to eligible households an amount that would cover, for example, a fixed "connection charge"; this in turn means more intensive utility users receive the same total subsidy as less intensive users.

2.3.5 Agricultural Input Subsidy

The NAADS Agricultural Input Subsidy provides beneficiaries with (some) free agricultural inputs. The UNHS does not record the source of the purchase for those individuals who purchase agricultural inputs. We turn to Uganda's National Service Delivery Survey (NSDS) to generate a propensity score (at the household level) for acquiring NAADS-subsidized inputs (conditional on having purchased any agricultural inputs).

---

price) over all goods that attract the VAT. Uganda's excise tax applies to sugar, alcoholic beverages, tobacco, cell phone minutes, cement, cosmetics, and the statutory excise rates occupy a range, but because excise collections are not available by sector, the total excise collection from UNHS households is accomplished in a manner similar to that for VAT; that is, we assume that excise is collected at the same rate (proportional to net-of-excise price) over all goods attracting the excise.

We then generate that propensity score (again at the household level) for UNHS households and select households with the highest propensity scores until the number of NAADS-subsidy beneficiaries in the UNHS (as a percent of the agricultural-input-purchasing pool of households in the UNHS) matches the number of NAADS-subsidy beneficiaries in the NSDS (as a percent of agricultural-input-purchasing pool of households in the NSDS). Given the technique we use to allocate NAADS expenditures, this allocation can be described as the expected allocation of expected benefits available under the NAADS program.

2.3.6 In-Kind Transfers

Uganda's expenditures on education and health are allocated to those UNHS households where at least one member utilizes either the public education or the public healthcare service system. As for the water and electricity subsidies, scaled in-kind spending is divided by the total number of UNHS users in order to get a "per-student" or "per-patient" subsidy; this uniform subsidy amount is then allocated to all directly identified users. So a single household with an enrolled primary school student, an enrolled secondary school student, one visit to a (public) hospital, and two visits to the (public) outpatient clinic would receive five different in-kind subsidies for the five service types utilized.

3   Results

The following sections summarize the impact of Ugandan fiscal policy on contemporaneous poverty and inequality.

3.1   Does Fiscal Policy Have an Impact on Inequality and Poverty?

Overall, inequality would be higher in Uganda if the fiscal policy elements covered here (see tables 19-1 and 19-2) were eliminated; in other words, *Uganda fiscal policy does reduce inequality.* For example, table 19-3 demonstrates that the Gini coefficient estimated over incomes that do not include direct taxes, pension benefits and contributions, and other direct transfers (Market Income in CEQ nomenclature) is 0.413, or 1.3 Gini points higher than the Gini coefficient of 0.400 estimated over incomes that include those elements (Disposable Income). The Gini coefficient measured at Final Income—which includes indirect taxes, subsidies, and in-kind benefits in addition to the fiscal policy elements included in Disposable Income—is 0.381; therefore the *total impact of fiscal policy on inequality is a reduction of approximately 3 Gini points,* from 0.413 to 0.381.

Fiscal policy does not increase poverty rates significantly (nor does the poverty gap or the squared poverty gap change). For example, the poverty headcount rate at the national poverty line stays at approximately 20 percent when moving from Market

TABLE 19-3

Inequality and Poverty before and after Fiscal Policy

Income concept	Gini coefficient	Poverty headcount (%)
Market income	0.413	19.9
Market income + pensions	0.414	19.8
Net market income	0.401	19.8
Disposable income	0.400	19.7
Consumable income	0.398	19.9
Final income	0.381	. . .

. . . = Not applicable

Income to Consumable Income (which includes pensions, all taxes, direct transfers, and subsidies[24]). Likewise, at the US$1.25 PPP (2005) international poverty line, the poverty headcount hovers right at 18 percent in between Market Income and Consumable Income.

Fiscal policy is therefore modestly inequality-reducing, while there is essentially no change in poverty (due to fiscal policy). Among the set of countries with low fiscal expenditures, the estimated impact of Ugandan fiscal policy on inequality is approximately average. As seen in figure 19-9, the redistributive effect (measured as the absolute difference between the Gini for Market Income and the Gini for Final Income) is larger in Uganda than in Ethiopia and Honduras, but noticeably smaller than in Bolivia, Nicaragua, and Tanzania. In figure 19-10, one can observe that, although starting from a higher Market Income (prefiscal) inequality level, Uganda's redistributive effect is below the trend. In contrast, while Ethiopia and Tanzania start from a lower Market Income inequality, their corresponding redistributive effect is practically on trend. Figure 19-11 demonstrates that Uganda's redistributive effect is slightly above trend, given the share of social spending to GDP; therefore, the modest redistributive effect is associated with low overall tax collections and social spending, rather than ineffective social spending. Among the same set of countries, Uganda generates only modest poverty reduction to Disposable Income but at the same time generates only a small increase in the poverty headcount to Consumable Income (figure 19-12). In other words, relatively low expenditures combined with relatively low revenue collection means poor and vulnerable households are neither much helped nor harmed (on net) from fiscal policy.

---

[24] Consumable income does not include in-kind transfers; in-kind transfers are difficult to value appropriately in terms of household purchasing power.

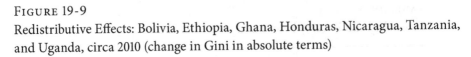

FIGURE 19-9

Redistributive Effects: Bolivia, Ethiopia, Ghana, Honduras, Nicaragua, Tanzania, and Uganda, circa 2010 (change in Gini in absolute terms)

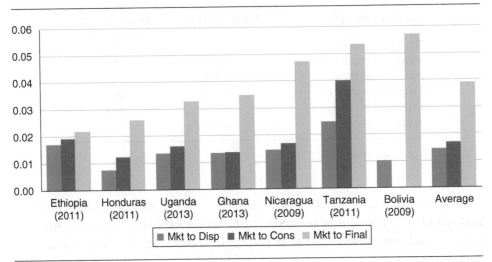

Source: CEQ Data Center on Fiscal Redistribution. Based on Bolivia (Paz Arauco and others, 2014); Ethiopia (Hill and others, 2017); Ghana (Younger, Osei-Assibey, and Oppong, 2017); Honduras (Icefi, 2017b); Nicaragua (Icefi, 2017c); and Tanzania (Younger, Myamba, and Mdadila, 2016).

Notes: The year for which the analysis was conducted is in parentheses. The graph is ranked from the smallest to the largest by redistributive effect (from Market Income plus Pensions to Final Income). In Ethiopia, Ghana, and Uganda, consumption expenditure is the primary income measure, and as all other income concepts including Market Income are derived assuming that consumption expenditure is equal to Disposable Income. For Ethiopia and Ghana, the study includes indirect effects of indirect taxes and subsidies. Poverty headcount ratios and inequality rates for Uganda were estimated using adult equivalent income. For the rest of the countries, the indicators were estimated using per capita income. Bolivia does not have personal income taxes. In Bolivia, Market Income does not include consumption of own production because the data was either not available or not reliable.

3.2 How Many Ugandans Are Impoverished by Taxes, Transfers, and Subsidies?

Calculating the poverty headcount before and after fiscal policy elements are applied gives us a broad indication of the advantage or disadvantage created by that policy: if the poverty headcount is higher after the policy is allocated, then the policy has disadvantaged some individuals. However, anyone receiving (as benefits) a fiscal expenditure sees his or her income increase; and anyone paying a tax (or other revenue collection) sees his or her income decrease. We can summarize those individual losses and gains through the fiscal impoverishment (FI) and fiscal gains to the poor (FGP) indices, first proposed by Higgins and Lustig (2016) (reproduced in chapter 4 in this Volume of the Handbook).

The FI index "tracks" each individual who becomes poor upon the execution of a fiscal policy (or a collection of fiscal policies) to determine how much his income decreased and therefore by how much he was impoverished. Table 19-4 shows that in

FIGURE 19-10

Initial Inequality and Redistributive Effect (circa 2010)

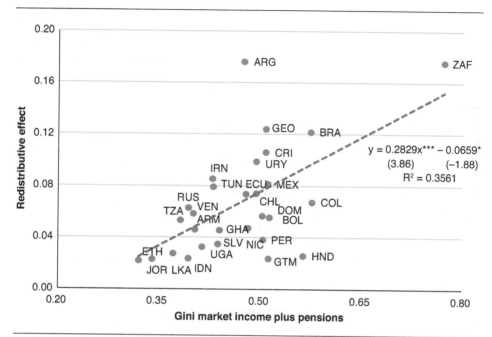

Source: CEQ Data Center on Fiscal Redistribution. Based on Argentina (Rossignolo, 2022) (chapter 11 in this Volume); Armenia (Younger and Khachatryan, 2017); Bolivia (Paz Arauco and others, 2014); Brazil (Higgins and Pereira, 2014); Chile (Martinez-Aguilar and others, 2022) (chapter 13 in this Volume); Colombia (Melendez and Martinez, 2015); Costa Rica (Sauma and Trejos, 2014); Dominican Republic (Aristy-Escuder and others, 2022) (chapter 14 in this Volume); Ecuador (Llerena and others, 2015); El Salvador (Beneke de Sanfeliu, Lustig, and Oliva Cepeda, 2022) (chapter 15 in this Volume); Ethiopia (Hill and others, 2017); Georgia (Cancho and Bondarenko, 2017); Ghana (Younger, Osei-Assibey, and Oppong, 2017); Guatemala (Icefi, 2017a); Honduras (Icefi, 2017b); Indonesia (Jellema, Wai-Poi, and Afkar, 2017); Iran (Enami, Lustig, and Taqdiri, 2017); Jordan (Alam, Inchauste, and Serajuddin, 2017); Mexico (Scott, 2014); Nicaragua (Icefi, 2017c); Peru (Jaramillo, 2014); Russia (Lopez-Calva and others, 2017); South Africa (Inchauste and others, 2017); Sri Lanka (Arunatilake, Inchauste, and Lustig, 2017); Tanzania (Younger, Myamba, and Mdadila, 2016); Tunisia (Jouini and others, 2022) (chapter 18 in this Volume); Uruguay (Bucheli and others, 2014); and Venezuela (Molina, 2016).

Notes: The year for which the analysis was conducted is in parentheses. The dotted line is the slope obtained from a simple regression with redistributive effect as the dependent variable. Redistributive effect is defined as the difference between Gini of Market Income plus contributory pensions and Final Income. In parentheses are t statistics. *p < 0.1, *p < 0.05, ***p < 0.01. Also, see notes to figure 19-9.

Uganda, the net position of all households after the addition of the PAYE income tax, direct transfers, the indirect VAT, excise, and fuel excise taxes, and the water, electricity, and agricultural input subsidies to Market Income is such that 12 percent of the population is impoverished (column 4) if poverty is measured using the US$1.25 PPP (2005) line. In other words, 12 percent of the population would not have become impoverished (on net) had there been no net fiscal policy adjustment to their Market Incomes.[25]

---

[25] That additional 12 percent of the Ugandan population represents approximately 68 percent of the Consumable-Income poor.

FIGURE 19-11
Social Spending (as % of GDP) versus Redistributive Effect (circa 2010)

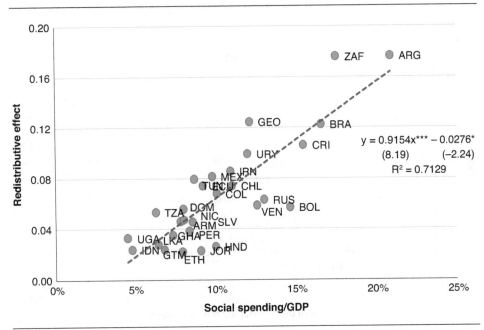

Source: CEQ Data Center on Fiscal Redistribution. Based on Argentina (Rossignolo, 2022) (chapter 11 in this Volume); Armenia (Younger and Khachatryan, 2017); Bolivia (Paz Arauco and others, 2014); Brazil (Higgins and Pereira, 2014); Chile (Martinez-Aguilar and others, 2022) (chapter 13 in this Volume); Colombia (Melendez and Martinez, 2015); Costa Rica (Sauma and Trejos, 2014); Dominican Republic (Aristy-Escuder and others, 2022) (chapter 14 in this Volume); Ecuador (Llerena and others, 2015); El Salvador (Beneke de Sanfeliu, Lustig, and Oliva Cepeda, 2022) (chapter 15 in this Volume); Ethiopia (Hill and others, 2017); Georgia (Cancho and Bondarenko, 2017); Ghana (Younger, Osei-Assibey, and Oppong, 2017); Guatemala (Icefi, 2017a); Honduras (Icefi, 2017b); Indonesia (Jellema, Wai-Poi, and Afkar, 2017); Iran (Enami, Lustig, and Taqdiri, 2017); Jordan (Alam, Inchauste, and Serajuddin, 2017); Mexico (Scott, 2014); Nicaragua (Icefi, 2017c); Peru (Jaramillo, 2014); Russia (Lopez-Calva and others, 2017), South Africa (Inchauste and others, 2017); Sri Lanka (Arunatilake, Inchauste, and Lustig, 2017); Tanzania (Younger, Myamba, and Mdadila, 2016); Tunisia (Jouini and others, 2022) (chapter 18 in this Volume); Uruguay (Bucheli and others, 2014); and Venezuela (Molina, 2016).

Notes: The year for which the analysis was conducted is in parentheses. The dotted line is the slope obtained from a simple regression with redistributive effect as the dependent variable. Redistributive effect is defined as the difference between Gini of Market Income plus contributory pensions and Final Income. In parentheses are t statistics. *$p < 0.1$, **$p < 0.05$, ***$p < 0.01$. Also, see notes to figure 19-9.

Table 19-4 indicates that Uganda's FI index (for poverty measured at the US$1.25 PPP [2005] line) puts it in the middle of the distribution of FI performance in lower middle-income countries. Sri Lanka and the Dominican Republic generate significantly less FI through their fiscal systems, while Ghana and Ethiopia generate significantly more; Armenia, Bolivia, and Guatemala all have somewhat lower levels of FI through their fiscal systems. Column 5, which presents FI among the individuals who are poor (rather than in the population at large), shows that even in Sri Lanka, where FI is negligible when measured as a percent of the total population, about one-third of the Consumable-Income poor have been impoverished by the (net) fiscal system.

FIGURE 19-12

Percent Change, Poverty Headcount: Bolivia, Ethiopia, Ghana, Honduras, Nicaragua, Tanzania, and Uganda (circa 2010)

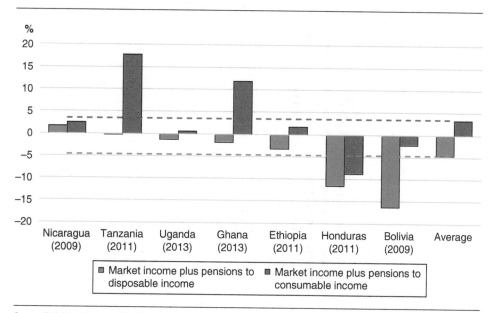

Source: CEQ Data Center on Fiscal Redistribution. Based on Bolivia (Paz Arauco and others, 2014); Ethiopia (Hill and others, 2017); Ghana (Younger, Osei-Assibey, and Oppong, 2017); Honduras (Icefi, 2017b); Nicaragua (Icefi, 2017c); and Tanzania (Younger, Myamba, and Mdadila, 2016).

Notes: Percentage of poverty reduction is defined as percentage change in headcount ratio from Market Income plus contributory pensions to Consumable Income. The graph is ranked from the smallest to the largest by poverty reduction in % (from Market Income plus Pensions to Disposable Income). Also, see notes to figure 19-9.

3.3 How Many Poor Ugandans Experience Income Gains via Fiscal Expenditures?

The FGP index is the mirror of FI: it tracks prefisc poor households receiving (net) benefits to determine by how much their incomes are increased from this receipt. At Consumable Income, and using the same US$1.25 PPP (2005) poverty line as in table 19-4, 28.4 percent of the prefisc poor—those whose Market Income (including pensions) is below the poverty line—receive (net) benefits from the Ugandan fiscal policy. *The fiscal system adds about 8 percent (on average) to the prefisc-income of the poor individuals who receive net transfers.*

Overall, then, the fiscal system adds more income to fewer of the prefisc poor and takes away less income from more of the postfisc poor. The result is by now familiar: on net, the poverty headcount is basically unchanged in between Market Income plus Pensions and Consumable Income.

TABLE 19-4
Fiscal Impoverishment (circa 2010)

Country (survey year)	(1) Market income plus contributory pensions poverty headcount (%)	(2) Change in poverty headcount (percentage points)	(3) Market income plus contributory pensions inequality (Gini)	(4) Fiscally impoverished as % of population	(5) Fiscally impoverished as % of consumable income poor
Armenia (2011)	21.4	−9.6	47.4	6.2	52.3
Bolivia (2009)	10.9	−0.5	50.3	6.6	63.2
Dominican Republic (2013)	6.8	−0.9	50.2	1.0	16.3
Uganda (2012/13)	7.1	0.1	41.3	12.2	67.7
Ethiopia (2011)	31.9	2.3	32.2	28.5	83.2
Ghana (2013)	6.0	0.7	43.7	5.1	76.6
Guatemala (2010)	12.0	−0.8	49.0	7.0	62.2
Indonesia (2012)	12.0	−1.5	39.8	4.1	39.2
Sri Lanka (2010)	5.0	−0.7	37.1	1.6	36.4
Tanzania (2011)	43.7	7.9	38.2	50.9	98.6

Source: Higgins and Lustig (2016) (reproduced in chapter 4 in this Volume). Uganda data from authors' own calculations.

3.4 Market to Disposable Income: Pensions, Personal Income Taxes, and Direct Transfers

The addition of pensions, personal income taxes, and direct transfers to Market Income creates Disposable Income (see figure 19-1).[26] Table 19-5, which presents the marginal impact of fiscal policy elements on inequality and poverty, demonstrates that *pensions reduce inequality and poverty slightly*, thereby indicating that some pension benefits are received by poorer households.[27]

Uganda's *PAYE personal income tax also reduces inequality slightly while leaving the poverty headcount unchanged*. As any tax collection from an individual necessarily reduces that individual's purchasing power over all other goods and services, then a tax (whether direct or indirect) considered individually will always *at best* leave the poverty headcount unchanged (relative to the pretax poverty headcount), so the Ugandan PAYE result could not be any better. The lack of an impact on poverty is likely a result of the decision to impute taxpayer status by developing a "formality" scale for contracted labor and allocating simulated tax amounts only to those who claim to have paid PAYE (or to have had it deducted) or who score high on the formality scale and have reported taxable income above the tax threshold. There are very few poor or near-poor households that either are formally employed or claim to have paid PAYE with taxable income greater than the tax threshold.[28]

Direct transfers in Uganda are minimal and thinly spread. The direct transfers covered here—the HISP and the PWP, both delivered under the NUSAF, and the SCG and the VFSG under the SAGE—cover few individuals or households. The cumulative value of these transfers is approximately 0.1 percent of cumulative Market Income. NUSAF is, as its name implies, targeted to a specific region while the SAGE program was still a pilot in 2012. As a result, there is no significant impact of any one of these programs on either poverty or inequality (table 19-5); their joint impact is to reduce both poverty and inequality but by very small amounts.

The bottom two deciles are estimated to receive over 50 percent of the transfers available; transfers received represent about 7 percent of the prefisc income of transfer beneficiaries or 9.5 percent of the prefisc income of poor beneficiaries. In other words, *direct transfers in Uganda are well-targeted and make a significant difference to those*

---

[26] Pension contributions are not allocated in this Uganda *CEQ Assessment* because of a lack of data on both the household side and the budget and administrative side.

[27] In the UNHS, we find one poor household that records receipt of pension income.

[28] Our imputation gave us only two observations where a household was poor and paid PAYE; they were both rural households, and they were imputed to be in the lowest tax bracket, where the effective marginal rate was determined to be about 8.5 percent. Both these households are also estimated to be poor households at Market Income and Market Income plus Pensions concepts, meaning they would have been poor whether or not there was a PAYE system and whether or not they *actually* contributed to PAYE revenues.

TABLE 19-5
Marginal Impacts on Inequality and Poverty (at final income): Direct Taxes and Direct Transfers

	Inequality	Poverty
Market income		
Contributions to pensions	. . .	. . .
Contributory pensions	−0.0001	−0.001
PAYE personal income taxes (imputed)	−0.013	0.000
Net market income		
All direct transfers (excl. contrib. pensions)	−0.001	0.001
PWP	0.000	0.000
HISP	0.000	0.000
SCG	0.000	0.000
VFSG	0.000	0.000
Disposable income		

. . . = Not applicable.

who receive them, but overall less than 3 percent of Ugandan households receive these transfers (in a given year). The nationwide distribution of income is largely unchanged even after these programs are executed, meaning that though they do reduce poverty and inequality, their impact on nationwide indicators is minimal.

3.5 Disposable to Final Income: Indirect Taxes and Subsidies, In-Kind Health, and Education Expenditures

Inequality decreases slightly from Disposable to Consumable Income, meaning that once we add income received as indirect subsidies and subtract income that represents indirect taxes paid, the resulting distribution is more equal.[29] The indirect taxes included here are the VAT and the excise tax (including the fuel excise); the revenue collections allocated under these taxes are equivalent to approximately 2 percent of cumulative

---

[29] The Disposable Income concept, based on consumption expenditures valued at prevailing prices, does not explicitly contain the expenditure done by the government on behalf of the consumer (in the form of a subsidy) nor does it explicitly ignore expenditure done by the consumer on behalf of the government (in the form of indirect taxes paid).

TABLE 19-6

Marginal Impacts on Inequality and Poverty (at final
income): Indirect Taxes, Subsidies, and Spending on
Education and Health

	Inequality	Poverty
Disposable income		
Indirect subsidies	−0.0005	−0.002
Water	−0.0003	−0.001
Electricity	0.0000	0.000
NAADS—ag. inputs	−0.0002	0.000
Indirect taxes	−0.002	0.005
VAT	−0.0013	0.0032
Excise	−0.0007	0.0025
Fuel excise	−0.0003	0.0000
Consumable income		
In-kind spending	−0.017	n.c.
Education	−0.010	n.c.
Primary	−0.010	n.c.
Secondary	−0.002	n.c.
Tertiary	0.002	n.c.
Health	−0.006	n.c.
Clinic-based care	−0.005	n.c.
Hospital-based care	−0.001	n.c.
Final income		

n.c. = Not calculated.

Market Income plus Pensions. VAT, the nonfuel excise, and the fuel excise account for approximately 52, 45, and 3 percent, respectively, of the total indirect taxes allocated.[30] The indirect subsidies included here are the Rural Electrification Program, the Water Supply Program, and the Agricultural Input Subsidy Program; these three subsidies together provide benefits equal to approximately 0.2 percent of cumulative Market Income. The Water Supply Program is the largest indirect subsidy (in terms of expenditure), while the Rural Electrification Program and the Agricultural Input Subsidy Program transfer approximately the same benefit totals. Table 19-6 provides the marginal impacts of these fiscal policy instruments on inequality and poverty (at Final Income).

[30] We generate "effective" rates of taxation within the UNHS of 14.6, 20.2, and 245 percent for the VAT, nonfuel excise, and fuel excise taxes. The statutory VAT rate is 18 percent, the statutory nonfuel excise rate varies, and the statutory fuel excise is a fixed nominal amount per liter.

Most households pay more in indirect taxes than they receive in indirect subsidies, but enough poor households receive enough subsidies such that the poverty rate actually stays constant when indirect taxes and subsidies are allocated. Rural households, primarily, may be lifted out of poverty when the government spends to deliver goods and services (water, electricity, and agricultural inputs) at below market prices (table 19-6). Among poor households only, total subsidies received represent about 0.8 percent of their (cumulative) Disposable Income, but the share of total subsidies received rises with income. Subsidies can have a poverty-reduction impact, but relative to direct transfers they are an inefficient way to assist poor and vulnerable households as subsidies are targeted toward higher-volume users by design.

In the CEQ framework, only those who utilize the public service provision system can benefit from publicly financed outputs in health and education. Even so, in Uganda, *these "in-kind" services make the largest impact on inequality*: the Gini index of inequality drops by 1.7 points in between Consumable and Final Income, and the marginal contribution of in-kind spending is approximately double that of the fiscal policy element with the next largest marginal contribution (personal income taxes). *Education makes a larger marginal contribution to inequality reduction*—see the international comparisons in table 19-7—but there are higher total expenditures in the public education system.

The impact of public education expenditures depends on rates of enrollment: Is enrollment higher in poorer or in richer households, and does the difference vary across schooling levels? The impact of public education expenditure also depends on the generosity of the benefits provided—typically, the education benefit level rises with the level of schooling, such that public university enrollees will receive an in-kind transfer with a larger monetary value than will primary school enrollees. In Uganda, education benefits do rise with education levels: the capitation grant (alone) is five to six times as large for secondary school students as for primary school students, for example (see section 1 above).[31] However, poorer household enrollment is weighted heavily toward primary school, so poorer households have a larger share of the available primary school benefits but smaller shares of the available secondary and tertiary school benefits. Overall, the public education benefit share of the poorest decile (ranked by Market Income) is roughly 7.5 percent, while the same share for the middle and richest deciles are 9.5 and 15.5 percent, respectively. Compare this to health benefits, where the poorest decile has a 10.5 percent share of the total public

---

[31] It is encouraging that we find that total education expenditures per pupil—including capital spending and other supplies, administrative costs, teacher salaries, and others—are approximately five times as large for a secondary school student as for a primary school student, and approximately three times as large for a tertiary school student as for a secondary school student. In the Uganda *CEQ Assessment*, we allocate to each household with one or more students enrolled in public school a uniform benefit equal to total education expenditure (by schooling level) per enrolled student (at that level).

TABLE 19-7
Inequality-Reduction Profile of In-Kind Spending, by Country (circa 2010)

	Education (total)	Preschool	Primary	Secondary	Tertiary	Health
Argentina (2012)	A	A	n.a.	n.a.	C	A
Armenia (2011)	A	A	A	n.a.	C	B
Bolivia (2009)	B	A	A	A	C	B
Brazil (2009)	A	A	A	A	C	A
Chile (2013)	A	A	A	A	C	A
Colombia (2010)	n.a.	A	A	A	C	n.a.
Costa Rica (2010)	n.a.	A	A	A	C	n.a.
Dominican Republic (2013)	A	A	A	n.a.	C	A
Ecuador (2011)	A	...	A	A	n.a.	A
El Salvador (2011)	A	A	A	B	C	C
Ethiopia (2011)	C	...	B	C	D	C
Georgia (2013)	B	B	A	n.a.	C	A
Ghana (2013)	C	A	A	C	D	B
Guatemala (2011)	B	A	A	B	D	C
Honduras (2011)	B	A	A	B	C	B
Indonesia (2012)	B	n.a.	A	B	D	C
Iran (2011)	B	n.a.	A	A	C	B
Jordan (2010)	A	A	A	A	C	C
Mexico (2010)	A	A	A	C	C	B
Nicaragua (2009)	B	A	A	B	C	B
Peru (2009)	A	A	A	A	C	C
Russia (2010)	A	n.a.	n.a.	n.a.	n.a.	B
South Africa (2010)	B	A	A	A	C	A
Sri Lanka (2010)	B	A	n.a.	n.a.	C	B
Tanzania (2011)	C	A	A	C	D	C
Tunisia (2010)	B	n.a.	n.a.	n.a.	C	B
Uganda (2012/13)	C	n.a.	A	C	D	B
Uruguay (2009)	A	A	A	A	C	A
Venezuela (2013)	A	A	A	A	B	A

Legend

A   Pro-poor and equalizing, per capita spending declines with income
B   Neutral in absolute terms and equalizing, same per capita spending for all
C   Equalizing, not pro-poor, per capita spending as a share of market income declines with income
D   Unequalizing, per capita spending as a share of Market Income increases with income

Source: CEQ Data Center on Fiscal Redistribution. Based on Argentina (Rossignolo, 2022) (chapter 11 in this Volume); Armenia (Younger and Khachatryan, 2017); Bolivia (Paz Arauco and others, 2014); Brazil (Higgins and Pereira, 2014); Chile (Martinez-Aguilar and others, 2022) (chapter 13 in this Volume); Colombia (Melendez and Martinez, 2015); Costa Rica (Sauma and Trejos, 2014); Dominican Republic (Aristy-Escuder and others, 2022); (chapter 14 in this Volume) Ecuador (Llerena and others, 2015); El Salvador (Beneke de Sanfeliu, Lustig, and Oliva Cepeda, 2022) (chapter 15 in this Volume); Ethiopia (Hill and others, 2017); Georgia (Cancho and Bondarenko, 2017); Ghana (Younger, Osei-Assibey, and Oppong, 2017); Guatemala (Icefi, 2017a); Honduras (Icefi, 2017b); Indonesia (Jellema, Wai-Poi, and Afkar, 2017); Iran (Enami, Lustig, and Taqdiri, 2017); Jordan (Alam, Inchauste, and Serajuddin, 2017); Mexico (Scott, 2014); Nicaragua (Icefi, 2017c); Peru (Jaramillo, 2014); Russia (Lopez-Calva and others, 2017), South Africa (Inchauste and others, 2017); Sri Lanka (Arunatilake, Inchauste, and Lustig, 2017); Tanzania (Younger, Myamba, and Mdadila, 2016); Tunisia (Jouini and others, 2022); (chapter 18 in this Volume) Uruguay (Bucheli and others, 2014); and Venezuela (Molina, 2016).

Notes: If the concentration coefficient was higher or equal to per −0.5 but not higher than 0.5, it was considered equal to 0. Also, see notes to figure 19-9.

... = Not applicable; n.a. = Not available.

health benefits available, the middle decile a 9.7 percent share, and the top decile a 10.3 percent share.

However, the education benefits received by the poorest decile represent 6.7 percent of Market Income in that group, while the education benefits received by the richest decile represent 1.1 percent of Market Income in that group. For health benefits the analogous numbers are 6.5 percent (for the poorest decile) and 0.5 percent (for the richest decile). Even though shares of total public health spending are more equitably distributed (than education benefits), nonetheless public health benefits are of smaller magnitude (than education benefits), and the total impact on inequality from public health is less than that from public education spending.

As can be seen from table 19-7, the profile of impacts from in-kind spending in Uganda is slightly better than average: primary education is pro-poor in that per capita amounts spent fall as income rises, secondary education is progressive only in relative terms, and health is (approximately) neutral in absolute terms. In Uganda, only tertiary education is unequalizing (benefits as a share of Market Income rise as income rises), but that is true in Ethiopia, Ghana, and Tanzania as well.

3.6 Redistribution, Reranking, and the Total Impact on Inequality

Not all redistribution is created equal. Imagine two different fiscal scenarios in a two-person economy with one poor individual having $48 and one rich individual having $52 in income (so that total income in this economy is $100). In the first scenario, fiscal policy taxes all income from non-poor individuals at 3.85 percent and then executes an omnibus transfer to poor households such that the rich individual has a Final Income of $50.01 and the poor individual a Final Income of $49.99 (and the government funds its operations with external aid). In this scenario, redistribution is limited, but the impact on inequality is large. In the second scenario, fiscal policy (overall) taxes all income from any individual at 100 percent and then executes transfers such that the (formerly) rich individual ends up with $48 and the (formerly) poor individual ends up with $52 (and again the government receives external aid to fund its operations). In this scenario, redistribution is extensive but there is essentially zero impact on inequality.

The reranking (RR) index summarizes—for any pre- and postfiscal distribution of income—the impact that any redistributive program has on "horizontal" equity due to reranking (as described intuitively above). Horizontal equity here captures the degree to which households who are "near" each other (in terms of their ranking in the income distribution) are treated equally. In the first scenario above, horizontal equity was complete, in that the first- and second-ranked individuals remained the first- and second-ranked individuals after the government had completed its fiscal policy. In the second scenario, horizontal equity was incomplete as the top-ranked individual fell to the bottom rank in the postfiscal income distribution. In lay terms, the RR index summarizes how much "place-swapping" there is for any amount of redistribution of income.

Uganda's RR index is quite small absolutely as well as when measured relative to the total amount of redistribution accomplished by fiscal policy. For example, total redistribution (or the vertical equity component) from Market Income to Final Income is 3.2 Gini points, while 0.3 points of that redistribution contributed to place-swapping. In other words, approximately 8 percent of the total redistribution that occurred (and is attributable to fiscal policy) had no impact on inequality. From Market Income to Disposable Income, approximately 7 percent of the total redistribution that occurred and is attributable to the execution of fiscal policy had no impact on inequality.

4 Conclusions and Policy Implications

Fiscal policy—including many of its constituent elements—is inequality-reducing in Uganda. For example, inequality including personal income tax is lower than inequality would be if there were no personal income tax. Likewise, inequality is reduced when the SAGE and NUSAF direct transfers are received, and inequality is reduced after public healthcare services are accessed. The only fiscal policy element in Uganda (among those included in Uganda's *CEQ Assessment*) that increases inequality is tertiary education spending, but this result, too, would be overturned if there were a greater number of students from poor households in upper education levels.

However, the impact of fiscal policy on current-year inequality is modest: fiscal policy achieves a reduction of approximately 3 Gini points in Uganda. The impact magnitude is tied to low levels of spending in Uganda generally. For example, Ethiopia,[32] a country with a similar per capita income level, spends approximately twice as much as Uganda does overall, twice as much on redistributive spending (so that Ethiopia's redistributive spending as a share of total spending is approximately equal to Uganda's), and approximately twice as much on direct transfers as well as education (relative to GDP). The impact of fiscal policy in Ethiopia (relative to prefisc inequality levels) is approximately average, while in Uganda the impact of fiscal policy (relative to prefisc inequality levels) is below average. In other words, the redistributive spending that Uganda executes, and the targeting of both social expenditures as well as the revenue collections that support them, help reduce inequality. The small impact is due to low revenue collection and spending overall.

The impact of fiscal policy on poverty is negligible. While an insignificant number of poor or near-poor households are burdened by the personal income tax, it is also true that very few households receive any of the direct transfers available under the SAGE or NUSAF programs. The net income position of most households after indirect taxes are paid and indirect subsidies are received is slightly lower than before those fiscal policy elements are allocated. However, the poor households that do receive net additions to their incomes receive more (as a percent of their prefiscal income) than the poor households that become net payers into the fiscal system.

---

[32] 2011 Ethiopia (Uganda) GNI per capita (2011 PPP factor): $1,160 ($1,620).

Poverty-neutral fiscal policy looks very good relative to African countries with similar income levels. The execution of fiscal policy in Ethiopia, Ghana, and Tanzania (for example) leaves the postfiscal poverty rate higher than the prefiscal poverty rate.

Recent directions in fiscal policy have focused on increasing revenues without concurrent social spending increases. For example, the tax-to-GDP ratio has risen since the 2012–13 fiscal year, but total direct and indirect benefit expenditure has increased at a slower rate during the same period. Since 2012–13-era personal income tax thresholds were high enough to protect poor households, if the increased revenues have come primarily from more efficient personal income tax collection, then it is likely that poor households are no worse off in 2015–16 than in 2012–13.

On the other hand, in 2012–13, Uganda's tax collections came primarily from VAT, excise, and customs duties. If the increase in revenues (from taxes) since 2012–13 has proceeded proportionally to 2012–13 tax instrument shares—if, in other words, most of the increase to 2015–16 is coming from the indirect tax instruments mentioned above—then it is likely the case that poor and near-poor households face greater disadvantage today. The VAT and excise taxes were widespread—over 95 percent of households paid at least one of the indirect taxes—and the burden they create is approximately neutral with respect to consumption expenditure. So if the increase in revenues has been achieved by closing exemptions for particular goods—unprocessed agricultural goods, for example, or health and education services—then poor households will face a proportionally greater burden in 2015–16 than in 2012–13.

If in the future indirect taxes on "luxury goods"—or a set of products and services consumed primarily by non-poor households—can contribute the bulk of marginal revenues from indirect taxes, then poor households may remain (marginally) unaffected by the drive to increase revenues. For example, the fuel excise does not create a direct burden for poor or near-poor households, and therefore does not contribute to an increase in the poverty headcount, because lower-income households in Uganda purchase no fuel directly. Targeting marginal revenue increases from indirect taxes to "luxury" good purchases would similarly protect poor households and, unlike fuel, would not create an indirect burden for households as long as the luxury goods targeted were not themselves important inputs for the production of other goods and services.

Recent budgets have allocated more resources toward investment in the productive sectors and infrastructure. If this focus on infrastructure were broadened to include human-capital-enhancing infrastructure like schools, health facilities, and low-cost, high-quality housing, the impact on inequality of fiscal policy would likely be enhanced. As the Uganda *CEQ Assessment* has demonstrated, the equalization of access to public education and healthcare services provides over half of the reduction in inequality from fiscal policy overall.

However, public services alone cannot create a more equal future for Ugandans; despite relatively high enrollment numbers, Uganda's results in standardized assessments of education performance are below average. In addition, tertiary education appears to be out of reach for most low- and middle-income households in Uganda.

Likewise, current investments in electricity should continue increasing the rate of access among poor and disadvantaged households, but the impact of this access on inequality will depend on the (regulated) tariff-setting procedures that the government decides on. Increasing public service provision reduces inequality in the short term, but longer-term impacts will depend also on how the public service delivery and public capital investment are managed.

Capital spending (or other infrastructure investment) may also have a salutary effect on poverty and inequality in the short term when it is channeled through a broad-coverage PWP like the Productive Safety Net Program in Ethiopia, the Vision 2020 Program in Rwanda, or the Program Nasional Pemberdayaan Masyarakat (PNPM, or the National Program for Community Empowerment) community-driven development program in Indonesia. These programs allocate public expenditures for infrastructure investment at least partially to poor or vulnerable households through the payment of wages for labor contributions on the infrastructure projects themselves. While in the longer term the areas receiving infrastructure and other physical capital may benefit more generally, in the short term poor and vulnerable individuals benefit directly from paid employment for labor contributed. Uganda already has experience with such a program—the community-based PWP in NUSAF II—and could adapt operational lessons learned to a national, broad-coverage PWP program.

These recent fiscal policy developments—increased revenue collections and an emphasis on infrastructure spending—are general in that they affect nearly all Ugandans. Specifically disadvantaged populations (the elderly poor; the jobless or underemployed poor) may require specifically targeted programs, and Uganda already has a few such instruments in place. The planned increases in the SAGE program—for example—will likely further reduce inequality as well as the poverty headcount. However, as SAGE was previously donor-financed, any increase in SAGE expenditures will require a concurrent increase in revenue collections (at least in present-value terms), and the source of these additional revenues will determine whether on net the fiscal system is poverty- and inequality-reducing.

Acknowledgments

The *CEQ Assessment* in Uganda was generously supported by the International Growth Center. The authors are grateful to Richard Newfarmer for comments on an earlier draft.

References

Alam, Shamma A., Gabriela Inchauste, and Umar Serajuddin. 2017. "The Distributional Impact of Fiscal Policy in Jordan," in *The Distributional Impact of Taxes and Transfers: Evidence from Eight Low- and Middle-Income Countries*, edited by Gabriela Inchauste and Nora Lustig (Washington: World Bank).

Aristy-Escuder, Jaime, Maynor Cabrera, Blanca Moreno-Dodson, and Miguel Sanchez-Martin. 2022. "The Dominican Republic: Fiscal Policy, Income Redistribution, and Poverty Reduction," chap. 14 in *Commitment to Equity Handbook: Estimating the Impact of Fiscal Policy on Inequality and Poverty*, 2nd ed., vol. 1, edited by Nora Lustig (Brookings Institution Press and CEQ Institute, Tulane University). Free online version available at www.commitmento equity.org.

Arunatilake, Nisha, Gabriela Inchauste, and Nora Lustig. 2017. "The Incidence of Taxes and Spending in Sri Lanka," in *The Distributional Impact of Taxes and Transfers: Evidence from Eight Low- and Middle-Income Countries*, edited by Gabriela Inchauste and Nora Lustig (Washington: World Bank).

Aziz, Imran, Edward Hedger, Fiona Davies, and Tim Williamson. 2016. *Budget Support to Uganda 1998–2012: A Review*. Overseas Development Institute Draft Research Report (London), March.

Bardhan, Pranab K. 2005. *Scarcity, Conflicts, and Cooperation: Essays in the Political and Institutional Economics of Development* (MIT Press).

Beneke de Sanfeliu, Margarita, Nora Lustig, and Jose Andres Oliva Cepeda. 2022. "El Salvador: The Impact of Taxes and Social Spending on Inequality and Poverty," chap. 15 in *Commitment to Equity Handbook: Estimating the Impact of Fiscal Policy on Inequality and Poverty*, 2nd ed., Vol. 1, edited by Nora Lustig (Brookings Institution Press and CEQ Institute, Tulane University). Free online version available at www.commitmentoequity.org.

Berg, Andrew G., and Jonathan D. Ostry. 2011. "Inequality and Unsustainable Growth: Two Sides of the Same Coin?," Staff Discussion Note SDN/11/09 (Washington: International Monetary Fund).

Bollinger, Christopher, and Barry Hirsch. 2007. "How Well Are Earnings Measured in the Current Population Survey? Bias from Nonresponse and Proxy Respondents," Working Paper (University of Kentucky and Trinity University).

———. 2013. "Is Earnings Nonresponse Ignorable?" *Journal of Labor Economics* 24, no. 3 (doi:10.2139/ssrn.1717151).

Bucheli, Marisa, Nora Lustig, Maximo Rossi, and Florencia Amabile. 2014. "Social Spending, Taxes and Income Redistribution in Uruguay," in *The Redistributive Impact of Taxes and Social Spending in Latin America*, edited by Nora Lustig, Carola Pessino, and John Scott, special issue, *Public Finance Review* 42, no. 3, pp. 413–33 (doi:10.1177/1091142113493493).

Cancho, Cesar, and Elena Bondarenko. 2017. "The Distributional Impact of Fiscal Policy in Georgia," in *The Distributional Impact of Taxes and Transfers. Evidence from Eight Low- and Middle-Income Countries*, edited by Gabriela Inchauste and Nora Lustig (Washington: World Bank).

Duponchel, Marguerite, Andy McKay, and Sarah Ssewanyana. 2015. "Poverty Dynamics in Uganda (2005/6 to 2011/12)," IGC presentation to Ministry of Finance (Kampala), February.

Enami, Ali, Sean Higgins, and Nora Lustig. 2022. "Allocating Taxes and Transfers and Constructing Income Concepts: Completing Sections A, B, and C of the *CEQ Master Workbook*," chap. 6 in *Commitment to Equity Handbook: Estimating the Impact of Fiscal Policy on Inequality and Poverty*, 2nd ed., Vol. 1, edited by Nora Lustig (Brookings Institution Press and CEQ Institute, Tulane University). Free online version available at www.commitmentoequity.org.

Enami, Ali, Nora Lustig, and Alireza Taqdiri. 2017. "Fiscal Policy, Inequality and Poverty in Iran: Assessing the Impact and Effectiveness of Taxes and Transfers," CEQ Working Paper 48 (CEQ Institute, Tulane University and the Economic Research Forum), September.

Higgins, Sean, and Caterina Brest Lopez. 2022. "Producing Indicators and Results, and Completing Sections D and E of the *CEQ Master Workbook* Using the *CEQ Stata Package*," chap. 8 in *Commitment to Equity Handbook: Estimating the Impact of Fiscal Policy on Inequality and Poverty*, 2nd ed., Vol. 1, edited by Nora Lustig (Brookings Institution Press and CEQ Institute, Tulane University). Free online version available at www.commitmento equity.org.

Higgins, Sean, and Nora Lustig. 2016. "Can a Poverty-Reducing and Progressive Tax and Transfer System Hurt the Poor?" *Journal of Development Economics* 122, pp. 63–75.

Higgins, Sean, and Claudiney Pereira. 2014. "The Effects of Brazil's Taxation and Social Spending on the Distribution of Household Income," in *The Redistributive Impact of Taxes and Social Spending in Latin America*, edited by Nora Lustig, Carola Pessino, and John Scott, special issue, *Public Finance Review* 42, no. 3, pp. 346–67 (doi:10.1177/1091142113501714).

Hill, Ruth, Gabriela Inchauste, Nora Lustig, Eyasu Tsehaye, and Tassew Woldehanna. 2017. "Fiscal Incidence Analysis for Ethiopia," in *The Distributional Impact of Taxes and Transfers: Evidence from Eight Low- and Middle-Income Countries*, edited by Gabriela Inchauste and Nora Lustig (Washington: World Bank).

Inchauste, Gabriela, Nora Lustig, Mashekwa Maboshe, Catriona Purfield, and Ingrid Woolard. 2017. "The Distributional Impact of Fiscal Policy in South Africa," in *The Distributional Impact of Taxes and Transfers: Evidence from Eight Low- and Middle-Income Countries*, edited by Gabriela Inchauste and Nora Lustig (Washington: World Bank).

Instituto Centroamericano de Estudios Fiscales (Icefi). 2017a. "Incidencia de la politica fiscal en la desigualdad y la pobreza en Guatemala," CEQ Working Paper 50 (CEQ Institute, Tulane University, International Fund for Agricultural Development [IFAD], and Instituto Centroamericano de Estudios Fiscales), May.

———. 2017b. "Incidencia de la politica fiscal en la desigualdad y la pobreza en Honduras," CEQ Working Paper 51 (CEQ Institute, Tulane University, International Fund for Agricultural Development, and Instituto Centroamericano de Estudios Fiscales), April.

———. 2017c. "Incidencia de la politica fiscal en la desigualdad y la pobreza en Nicaragua," CEQ Working Paper 52 (CEQ Institute, Tulane University, International Fund for Agricultural Development, and Instituto Centroamericano de Estudios Fiscales), May.

International Monetary Fund (IMF). 2015. *Regional Economic Outlook: Sub-Saharan Africa*. (Washington: International Monetary Fund).

Jaramillo, Miguel. 2014. "The Incidence of Social Spending and Taxes in Peru," in *The Redistributive Impact of Taxes and Social Spending in Latin America*, edited by Nora Lustig, Carola Pessino, and John Scott, special issue, *Public Finance Review* 42, no.3, pp. 391–412 (doi:10.1177/1091142113496134).

Jellema, Jon, and Gabriela Inchauste. 2022. "Constructing Consumable Income: Including the Direct and Indirect Effects of Indirect Taxes and Subsidies," chap. 7 in *Commitment to Equity Handbook: Estimating the Impact of Fiscal Policy on Inequality and Poverty*, 2nd ed., Vol. 1, edited by Nora Lustig (Brookings Institution Press and CEQ Institute, Tulane University). Free online version available at www.commitmentoequity.org.

Jellema, Jon, Matthew Wai-Poi, and Rythia Afkar. 2017. "The Distributional Impact of Fiscal Policy in Indonesia," in *The Distributional Impact of Taxes and Transfers. Evidence from Eight Low- and Middle-Income Countries*, edited by Gabriela Inchauste and Nora Lustig (Washington: World Bank).

Jouini, Nizar, Nora Lustig, Ahmed Moummi, and Abebe Shimeles. 2022. "Tunisia: Fiscal Policy, Income Redistribution, and Poverty Reduction," chap. 18 in *Commitment to Equity Handbook: Estimating the Impact of Fiscal Policy on Inequality and Poverty*, 2nd ed., Vol. 1, edited by Nora Lustig (Brookings Institution Press and CEQ Institute, Tulane University). Free online version available at www.commitmentoequity.org.

Kuteesa, Florence, Emmanuel Tumusiime-Mutebile, Alan Whitworth, and Tim Williamson. 2009. *Uganda's Economic Reforms: Insider Accounts* (Oxford University Press).

Llerena Pinto, Freddy P., Maria C. Llerena Pinto, Roberto C. Saa Daza, and Maria Andrea Llerena Pinto. 2015. "Social Spending, Taxes and Income Redistribution in Ecuador," CEQ Working Paper 28 (Center for Inter-American Policy and Research and Department of Economics, Tulane University, and Inter-American Dialogue), February.

Lopez-Calva, Luis Felipe, Nora Lustig, Mikhail Matytsin, and Daria Popova. 2017. "Who Benefits from Fiscal Redistribution in the Russian Federation?," in *The Distributional Impact of Taxes and Transfers: Evidence from Eight Low- and Middle-Income Countries*, edited by Gabriela Inchauste and Nora Lustig (Washington: World Bank).

Lustig, Nora, and Sean Higgins. 2022. "The CEQ Assessment: Measuring the Impact of Fiscal Policy on Inequality and Poverty," chap. 1 in *Commitment to Equity Handbook: Estimating the Impact of Fiscal Policy on Inequality and Poverty*, 2nd ed., Vol. 1, edited by Nora Lustig (Brookings Institution Press and CEQ Institute, Tulane University). Free online version available at www.commitmentoequity.org.

Martinez-Aguilar, Sandra, Alan Fuchs, Eduardo Ortiz-Juarez, and Giselle Del Carmen. 2022. "Chile: The Impact of Fiscal Policy on Inequality and Poverty," chap. 13 in *Commitment to Equity Handbook: Estimating the Impact of Fiscal Policy on Inequality and Poverty*, 2nd ed., Vol. 1, edited by Nora Lustig (Brookings Institution Press and CEQ Institute, Tulane University). Free online version available at www.commitmentoequity.org.

Melendez, Marcela, and Valentina Martinez. 2015. "CEQ Master Workbook: Colombia. Version: December 17, 2015," CEQ Data Center on Fiscal Redistribution (CEQ Institute, Tulane University, and Inter-American Development Bank).

Ministry of Finance, Planning, and Economic Development (MoFPED). 2014a. "Annual Economic Performance Report 2012–13" (Uganda), December.

———. 2014b. "Poverty Status Report 2014—Structural Change and Poverty Reduction in Uganda" (Uganda), November.

———. 2016. "National Budget Framework Paper FY 2016/17" (Uganda), December.

Molina, Emiro. 2016. "CEQ Master Workbook: Venezuela. Version: November 15, 2016," CEQ Data Center on Fiscal Redistribution (CEQ Institute, Tulane University).

Ostry, Jonathan D., Andrew Berg, and Charalambos G. Tsangarides. 2014. "Redistribution, Inequality, and Growth," IMF Staff Discussion Note SDN/14/02 (Washington: International Monetary Fund).

Paz Arauco, Veronica, George Gray-Molina, Wilson Jimenez, and Ernesto Yañez. 2014. "Explaining Low Redistributive Impact in Bolivia," in *The Redistributive Impact of Taxes and Social Spending in Latin America*, edited by Nora Lustig, Carola Pessino, and John Scott, special issue, *Public Finance Review* 42, no 3, pp. 326–45 (doi:10.1177/1091142113496133).

Republic of Uganda. 2010. "National Development Plan (2010/11-2014/15)" (Uganda), December.

———. 2014. "Annual Budget Performance Report FY 2012/13" (Uganda), December.

———. 2015. "Second National Development Plan 2015/16-2019/20" (Uganda), December.

Rossignolo, Dario. 2022. "Argentina: Taxes, Expenditures, Poverty, and Income Distribution," chap. 11 in *Commitment to Equity Handbook: Estimating the Impact of Fiscal Policy on Inequality and Poverty*, 2nd ed., Vol. 1, edited by Nora Lustig (Brookings Institution Press and CEQ Institute, Tulane University). Free online version available at www.commitmentoequity .org.

Sauma, Pablo and Juan D. Trejos. 2014. "Social Public Spending, Taxes, Redistribution of Income, and Poverty in Costa Rica," CEQ Working Paper 18 (Center for Inter-American Policy and Research and Department of Economics, Tulane University, and Inter-American Dialogue), January.

Scott, John. 2014. "Redistributive Impact and Efficiency of Mexico's Fiscal System," in *The Redistributive Impact of Taxes and Social Spending in Latin America*, edited by Nora Lustig, Carola Pessino, John Scott, special issue, *Public Finance Review* 42, no. 3, pp. 368–90 (doi:10.1177/1091142113497394).

Ssewanyana, Sarah, and Ibrahim Kasirye. 2015. "Progressivity or Regressivity in Uganda's tax system: Implications for the Fy2014/15 Tax Proposals," Economic Policy Research Centre Research Series no. 123 (Kampala, Uganda), June.

Uganda Bureau of Statistics (UBOS). 2014. "Uganda National Household Survey 2012/2013" (Kampala, Uganda: UBOS).

Uganda Ministry of Education and Sports. 2013. "2012 Education Statistical Abstract" (Kampala, Uganda).

Younger, Stephen D., and Artsvi Khachatryan. 2017. "Fiscal Incidence in Armenia," in *The Distributional Impact of Taxes and Transfers: Evidence from Eight Low- and Middle-Income Countries*, edited by Gabriela Inchauste and Nora Lustig (Washington: World Bank).

Younger, Stephen D., Flora Myamba, and Kenneth Mdadila. 2016. "Fiscal Incidence in Tanzania." *African Development Review* 28, no. 3, pp. 264–76 (doi:10.1111/1467-8268.12204).

Younger, Stephen D., Eric Osei-Assibey, and Felix Oppong. 2017. "Fiscal Incidence in Ghana." *Review of Development Economics* 21, no. 4, pp. e47–e66 (doi:10.1111/rode.12299).

Chapter 20

CHINA

The Impact of Taxes and Transfers on Income Inequality, Poverty, and the Urban-Rural and Regional Income Gaps in China

Nora Lustig and Yang Wang

Introduction

After far-reaching economic reforms were introduced in 1978, China has experienced fast economic growth and social development.[1] The rapid growth significantly improved the overall well-being of the Chinese population and lifted an enormous number of people out of poverty. Using the international poverty line of $1.9 PPP (purchasing power parity) a day, we find that the headcount ratio declined from 88.3 percent in 1978 to 0.73 percent in 2015 (PovcalNet, World Bank). At the same time, income inequality increased dramatically over the past three decades. The Gini coefficient rose from 0.33 in 1988 (Ravallion and Chen, 2007) to a range between 0.52 and 0.63 in 2010–12 (Xie and Zhou, 2014). In addition to high overall inequality, there is a significant divide between urban and rural areas, as well as between regions.[2] As shown in figure 20-1, the absolute difference between urban and rural per capita Disposable Income has grown between 1978 and 2018. In addition to the rural-urban gap, there has been a significant and persistent disparity between the Eastern, Central, and

---

[1] The average annual GDP growth between 1978 and 2018 rate has been estimated at 9.6 percent.

[2] Rural and urban residents are kept separated by the household registration system (Hukou; see Song [2014] for more details regarding the Hukou system in China), and the main economic activities of rural and urban households are different: most urban residents participate in the production and service industries as employees, while most rural households rely on agricultural production. Due to migration, the proportion of rural residents has declined from 89.4 percent in 1949 to 41.5 percent in 2017 (authors' own calculation using information from the *2018 China Statistical Yearbook* [National Bureau of Statistics of China, 2018]).

FIGURE 20-1

Urban/Rural per Capita Disposable Income (Unit: Yuan), 1978–2018

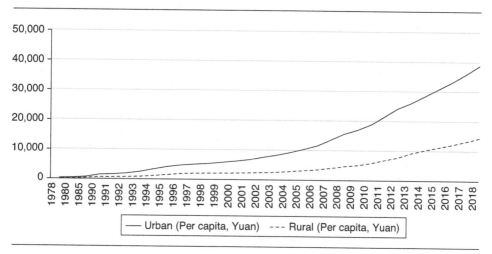

Western regions.[3] Figure 20-2 shows average per capita Disposable Income by region between 2013 and 2017.

In this chapter, we analyze the extent to which the fiscal system reduces inequality and poverty overall at the country-wide level. We also assess how much the fiscal system closes the income gap between rural and urban areas and between regions, and how much it reduces inequality and poverty within geographic locations. We do this by applying standard fiscal incidence analysis to the China Family Panel Studies 2014 survey data. On the tax system, our analysis includes personal income tax, contributions to social security, value-added tax (VAT), and consumption tax. On the spending side, our analysis covers social security benefits, the urban and rural Minimum Living Standard Scheme (MLSS), the rural Five Guarantees System, the agricultural subsidy, as well as the health and education systems.

The fiscal incidence method we apply here is described in detail in Lustig (2022a) (chapter 1 in Volume 1 of the Handbook) and Enami, Higgins, and Lustig (2022) (chapter 6 in Volume 1). Known in the literature as the "accounting approach" because it ignores behavioral responses and general equilibrium effects, fiscal incidence analysis is designed to respond to the question of who benefits from government spending

---

[3] Provinces are classified into three regions based on level of development and geographical location. The Eastern region is the most well developed, followed by the Central and the Western. The Eastern region includes Beijing, Tianjin, Hebei, Liaoning, Shanghai, Jiangsu, Zhejiang, Fujian, Shandong, Guangdong, Guangxi, and Hainan; the Central region includes Shanxi, Inner Mongolia, Heilongjiang, Jilin, Anhui, Jiangxi, Henan, Hubei, and Hunan; the Western region includes Chongqing, Sichuan, Guizhou, Yunnan, Tibet, Shaanxi, Gansu, Qinghai, Ningxia, and Xinjiang.

FIGURE 20-2

Average per Capita Disposable Income by Region (Unit: Yuan), 2013–2017

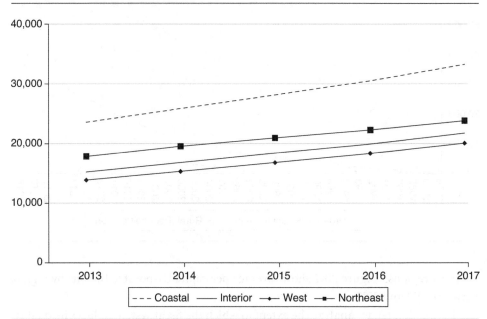

Source: Generated by authors based on data collected from National Bureau of Statistics of China (2019).

(social spending, in particular) and who bears the burden of taxes. With a long tradition in applied public finance, fiscal incidence analysis is considered an adequate instrument to evaluate the first-round impact of fiscal policy on inequality and poverty (Martinez-Vazquez, 2008).

In addition to measuring the impact of taxes and social spending on overall inequality and poverty, we also quantify the effect of fiscal policy on the urban-rural gap and regional inequality. In order to do this, we decompose the Theil index into the contributions of "within group" inequality and "between group" inequality with the formula originally proposed by Shorrocks (1984). This decomposition allows us to measure the contribution of "between-group" component to overall inequality. By comparing the "between-group" contribution to prefiscal Theil and postfiscal Theil, we can see if the fiscal system has contributed to lower the rural-urban gap and regional disparity. Although we use the Theil index for the decomposition instead of the Gini coefficient because the latter is not perfectly decomposable, for the rest of the analysis, we use Gini coefficients. We do this mainly to be able to compare the results for China with those for other countries.[4]

---

[4] The results using the Theil index are qualitatively the same as those obtained with the Gini coefficient.

Regarding inequality, the results show that the fiscal system has been effective in reducing prefiscal inequality in China, in both the rural and urban areas, as well as in each economic region. This reduction was driven mainly by direct taxes (including personal income tax and contributions to social security), direct transfers (including direct cash transfers and contributory pensions), and in-kind health and education transfers. For the marginal contribution of each fiscal intervention, on the tax side, personal income tax, contributions to social security and VAT are equalizing for all groups, while the consumption tax is quite unequalizing for all groups. On the spending side, direct cash transfers, contributory pensions, indirect subsidies, and in-kind transfers are always equalizing for all groups. In addition, the fiscal system reduced inequality between regions primarily because the Eastern region—the richest—paid a higher proportion of taxes (25.8 percent of Market Income) and received the least benefits (15.7 percent), while the poorest Western region paid the smallest proportion of taxes (20.9 percent) and received the largest share of prefiscal income in transfers (direct and in-kind) and subsidies (20.2 percent).

In contrast to our findings concerning the reduction of fiscal inequality, our results show that the fiscal system widened the urban-rural income gap. This undesirable outcome is driven mainly by the fact that urban residents receive significantly more income from contributory pensions than rural residents. On average, urban residents receive 11.4 percent of Market Income in pensions, while rural residents receive only 3.1 percent. This indicates that although the "basic pension insurance for rural residents" has been in place since 2009, pensions received by rural residents are still significantly lower than those received by urban residents in 2013.[5] Regarding poverty and using the headcount ratio as the indicator, we find that the fiscal system reduced poverty in urban areas. However, for one of the poverty lines, the fiscal system increased poverty in the poorer rural areas and in all three regions, which means that the fiscal system has driven some people who were not poor into poverty in larger numbers than it has helped the poor escape their condition (and become non-poor). When we use the squared poverty gap index, however, the fiscal system is poverty-reducing throughout. This is reassuring in the sense that it is telling us that the fiscal system reduces poverty for the poorest of the poor (even though it makes some of the non-poor poor).

This chapter makes three main contributions. First, while there are studies that evaluate the distributional impact of a specific fiscal instrument or part of the fiscal system, our analysis is more comprehensive. In particular, our study includes the impact of the "monetized" benefits of transfers in kind such as public spending on education and health. Second, this is the first study that assesses to what extent the tax

---

[5] According to the 2013 Statistical Bulletin of Development of Human Resources and Social Security (Ministry of Human Resources and Social Security, 2014), coverage and total expenditure of "pension insurance for urban and rural residents" are 497.5 million and CN¥134.8 billion, respectively, while coverage and total expenditure of "pension insurance for employees" are 322.2 million and CN¥1,847 billion.

and social spending systems reduce the urban-rural and regional gaps. Third, by applying a standard methodological framework developed by the Commitment to Equity (CEQ) Institute,[6] our results can be compared with those of other countries with similar levels of income per capita as China.

With regard to the first contribution, most of the literature on this topic (both in English and in Chinese) has focused on analyzing the impact of either one specific policy or part of the system.[7] Two papers have produced a relatively comprehensive assessment of the Chinese fiscal system on income distribution. One, by Li, Zhu, and Zhan (2017), carried out a standard fiscal incidence analysis to assess the redistributive effect of the personal income tax, the social security system, direct transfer and subsidy using the 2013 China Household Income Project Survey (CHIPS). They found that these fiscal interventions reduced poverty and inequality, with the impact being more pronounced in urban areas. The other, by Xie (2018), implemented a fiscal incidence analysis of the personal income tax, contributions to social security, and government transfers to assess their impact on the distribution of income using the 2013 China Health and Retirement Longitudinal Study (CHARLS). The author found that the combination of these fiscal instruments was equalizing, with government transfers contributing more than 90 percent of the redistributive effect while personal income taxes and contributions to social security contributed less than 10 percent.

However, neither Li, Zhu, and Zhan (2017) nor Xie (2018) includes the impact of spending on education and health. Furthermore, both focus on the distribution of in-

---

[6] Founded in 2015 at Tulane University, the Commitment to Equity Institute (CEQI) works to reduce inequality and poverty through comprehensive and rigorous tax and benefit incidence analysis, and active engagement with the policy community. For more information, please visit http://commitmentoequity.org/. See also Lustig (2022b).

[7] Among those writing in English, Wagstaff and others (2009) and Lei and Lin (2009) studied the impact of the New Cooperative Medical Scheme on rural residents' health service utilization and out-of-pocket payments. Alm and Liu (2013, 2014) analyzed the impact of rural Tax-for-Fee reform on rural residents' net income/welfare and village inequality. Gao, Garfinkel, and Zhai (2009) analyzed the effectiveness of the urban Minimum Living Standard Scheme on reducing urban poverty rate. Golan, Sicular, and Umapathi (2017) studied the effectiveness of the rural Minimum Living Standard Scheme in alleviating poverty and simulated how alternative program designs can improve the poverty reduction outcome. Among those writing in Chinese, Yue and others (2012) and Xu, Ma, and Li (2013) found that the personal income tax has been progressive, but its overall redistributive impact was small due to low tax rates; Mi, Liu, and Liu (2012) and Yue, Zhang, and Xu (2014) found that the tax system has been regressive; Wang and Kang (2009) found an equalizing effect of contributory pensions; Wang and others (2016) found the social security system had an equalizing impact, while Cai and Yue (2017) found an unequalizing impact of the social security benefits; Tan and Zhong (2010) found the New Rural Cooperative Medical Scheme had reduced inequality; Li and Yang (2009) found the Minimum Living Standard Scheme had reduced poverty incidence of the urban areas, and Chen, Ma, and Qin (2010) found the Minimum Living Standard Scheme had reduced inequality of urban areas as well as inequality of rural areas.

come at the country-wide level. Given the large income gaps between rural and urban areas and between the richer and poorer regions, the question of how much these gaps are narrowed through fiscal redistribution is also of great importance. Although China's urban-rural gap and regional disparity have been studied, the current literature focuses predominantly on documenting levels and trends of these gaps and identifying the key reasons behind them during different time periods. To the best of our knowledge, the impact of taxes and government spending on the urban-rural gap or regional disparity has not been analyzed before.

The rest of this chapter is organized as follows. Section 1 presents the methodology. The data and assumptions for allocating taxes and social spending are described in section 3. Section 4 discusses the main findings. Section 5 concludes. A detailed description of the fiscal system is in appendix A. Appendix B shows the consumption tax rates by item.

1 Methodology

1.1 Fiscal Incidence Analysis: Construction of Income Concepts

In order to estimate the distributional impact of the fiscal system in China, we apply a standard fiscal incidence analysis to the China Family Panel Studies 2014 survey data using the framework developed by the Commitment to Equity Institute (CEQ) (Lustig, 2022b). The fiscal incidence analysis starts from a prefiscal income and constructs postfiscal income concepts by allocating the taxes and transfers under analysis to each individual. Once the prefiscal and postfiscal incomes are constructed, various indicators can be generated to evaluate the distributive impact, progressivity, and effectiveness of the fiscal intervention.[8] We can also observe how taxes and benefits impact different geographic groups, such as urban and rural areas, as well as different regions. For the latter, we chose three main economic regions that are widely employed in China to analyze patterns of development. These are (from richest to poorest) the Eastern, the Central and the Western regions.[9]

Construction of the income concepts is the fundamental building block in any incidence analysis. In this study, we define four income concepts: Market Income, Disposable Income, Consumable Income, and Final Income (see figure 20-3). Market Income includes wages and salaries, income from business operation, property income, private transfers, auto-consumption and imputed rent of owner-occupied housing.[10] We obtain Disposable Income by subtracting direct taxes (mainly personal

---

[8] See Higgins and Brest Lopez (2022) (chapter 8 in Volume 1 of the Handbook).

[9] For details, see note 3 above.

[10] Our analysis presents results for the scenario in which contributory pensions are treated as government transfers and contributions to social security are treated as a direct tax. For details explaining the difference between this scenario and the scenario in which pensions are treated as deferred income, please see chapter 1 in this Volume of the Handbook.

FIGURE 20-3
Construction of Income Concepts

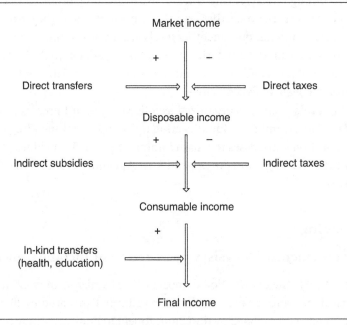

Source: Based on Lustig (2022a) (chapter 1 in Volume 1 of the Handbook).

income tax and contributions to social security) and adding direct transfers (mainly cash transfers and contributory pensions). Consumable Income equals Disposable Income plus indirect subsidies and minus indirect taxes. Finally, adding the monetized value (at average cost to government) of in-kind transfers (mainly, education and health) to Consumable Income yields Final Income.

As in any standard fiscal incidence analysis, behavioral responses and general equilibrium effects are not considered. Although these are clear limitations of any fiscal incidence analysis, if the primary interest is to assess progressivity of the overall tax and social spending system or to compare the progressivity of each specific tax and social spending program, existing research indicates that not much value can be added by going beyond an accounting approach.[11]

1.2 Decomposition of Theil Index

In order to quantify the contribution of taxes and transfers to inequality between urban and rural areas and between regions, we rely on the decomposition of the Theil index using prefiscal and postfiscal income concepts. The Theil index can be decomposed into

---

[11] See references in chapter 1 in this Volume.

the contribution of "within group" inequality and "between group" inequality based on the formula originally proposed by Shorrocks (1984). This decomposition allows us to measure the contribution of the "between-group" component to overall inequality. By comparing the "between-group" contribution to prefiscal Theil and postfiscal Theil, we can see if the fiscal system has contributed to lower the rural-urban gap and regional disparity. In our analysis, the groups are rural/urban and three regions. Thus the formula can be written as

$$T = [v_U \lambda_U T^U + v_R \lambda_R T^R]_{WITHIN} + [v_U \lambda_U \ln(\lambda_U) + v_R \lambda_R \ln(\lambda_R)]_{BETWEEN},$$

where U denotes urban and R denotes rural,

$$T = [v_E \lambda_E T^E + v_C \lambda_C T^C + v_W \lambda_W T^W]_{WITHIN} + [v_E \lambda_E \ln(\lambda_E) + v_C \lambda_C \ln(\lambda_C) \\ + v_W \lambda_W \ln(\lambda_W)]_{BETWEEN},$$

where E denotes Eastern, C denotes Central and W denotes Western, in which $v_U = n_U/n$ is the population share of the urban group, $\lambda_U = \mu_U/\mu$ is the average income of the urban group over the average income of the overall group, and (v_R, λ_R), (v_E, λ_E), (v_C, λ_C), and (v_W, λ_W), are similarly defined for the rural areas, the Eastern region, the Central region, and the Western region.

2 Data and Assumptions

2.1 Data

The primary source employed for the incidence analysis is the China Family Panel Studies (CFPS) 2014 survey data. The CFPS is an annual nationally representative longitudinal survey of Chinese communities, families, and individuals launched in 2010 by the Institute of Social Science Survey (ISSS) of Peking University. The CFPS 2014 dataset contains 37,147 adults and 8,616 children from 13,946 households in 29 provinces,[12] in which 25,530 individuals reported living in urban areas. The survey collects necessary and important information relevant to incidence analysis, including household income, expenditures, received government transfers, and use of education and health services.

According to the survey's metadata documents, wages/salaries and business operation income reported in the survey is the after-tax measure. Thus personal income tax and contributions to social security should be added when constructing the prefiscal Market Income.

---

[12] Hong Kong, Macao, Qinghai, Taiwan, and Tibet are not covered.

The unit of analysis here is the individual, and the welfare concept is household income per capita.[13] The classification of individuals by urban-rural and by region is based on the reported place of residence by individuals (as opposed to by households).[14] Out of the 45,276 individuals in the sample, there were 3,599 for whom the place of urban-rural residency as an individual was different than the households'. However, our results are not sensitive if we switch the place of residency for this group of individuals to that of the households they belong to. Similarly, there are 146 individuals whose reported province of residency is different from the households' province of residency. Our results are not sensitive if we change the province to that ascribed to the household.

In addition, when an important fiscal component is not directly identifiable in the survey, it can be simulated or imputed based on known policy rules, together with other available information in the survey and administrative data (Enami, Higgins, and Lustig, 2022).

2.2 Allocation of Taxes and Social Spending: Assumptions

2.2.1 Taxes

On the tax side, our analysis includes personal income tax, contributions to social security, VAT, and consumption tax.[15] When analyzing the incidence of taxes, we consider economic incidence rather than statutory incidence. Following the conventional practice of the accounting approach of fiscal incidence analysis, we assume the personal income tax to be borne entirely by income earners in the formal sector. The VAT and consumption tax are assumed to be fully borne by consumers.

Imputation of personal income tax

The CFPS survey reports annual post-tax wages and salaries. To impute corresponding tax, annual wages/salaries are divided by twelve to get the average monthly wages/salaries. The Chinese State Taxation Administration provides the rates that apply to brackets for both gross and net (of taxes) incomes. With the latter, we can calculate the estimated tax paid by each individual and aggregate to the household level to obtain the per capita tax payments. We assume that there is no tax evasion. In this sense, the burden of taxes is based on *de jure* rules, and it may be an upper bound. For tax of business operation income, the tax code can be applied directly to household annual business operation income (which is also a post-tax measure) to obtain the tax payment. The imputed household annual payment to personal income tax is the sum of the two.

---

[13] Following convention, missing and zero incomes are included in the analysis as zero, except for households with a primary income reported as zero, which are excluded from the analysis.

[14] The Hukou classification does not necessarily coincide with reported place of residence.

[15] Only part of the consumption tax that is related to consumption of tobacco, alcoholic beverage, and cosmetic products is included in this analysis due to data limitations.

Imputation of employers' contributions to social security

The CFPS survey reports the contributions of employees to social security (including the "contributions to the five insurances" and the "contributions to the housing fund").

The contributions to social security from employers need to be imputed. The compulsory contribution rates by employee and employer to each social security program varies across cities. In order to calculate employers' contribution, we collected the contribution schemes of the capital city of each province in 2013. For simplicity we assume employees and employers of each province pay according to the scheme of the capital city. The corresponding employer's payment to social security can be calculated by multiplying the reported employee's payment to the ratio of employer's total contribution rate over employee's total contribution rate.

Imputation of VAT and simulation of consumption tax

Household annual expenditures are reported by thirty-one categories. For each category, a VAT rate is assigned according to the VAT code, and then the household yearly payment on VAT is imputed.

For consumption taxes, given that expenditures are not sufficiently detailed, we need to rely on a combination of methods. Consumption tax on cosmetic products can be imputed using the tax rate that applies and the total annual expenditure on cosmetic products reported in the survey.

For consumption of tobacco and alcohol, we use an alternative survey (China Family Panel Studies 2012) to estimate two types of regressions. In one, the dependent variables are whether the individual is a smoker and whether he or she drinks alcoholic beverages, and the independent variables are the individual's characteristics such as education level, gender, marital status, rural-urban residency, province of residency, age, number of children, health status, and income. In the second set of regressions, the dependent variables are the amount smoked, the price of the cigarette chosen, and the amount of alcohol drunk. With the estimates, we predict spending on alcoholic beverages and tobacco products using the information from our main survey (CFPS 2014). We then proceed to apply the rates to estimate the consumption taxes paid on those products.

2.2.2 Social Spending

Social security benefits, minimum living standard schemes, rural Five Guarantees System, and agricultural subsidy

Social security benefits, the urban and rural minimum living standard scheme, the rural Five Guarantees System, and the agricultural subsidy are reported in the survey, and no adjustments are made.

Imputation of in-kind education transfer

In the survey, available information includes "whether currently attending school," "current education level," and "whether attending a public or private school." For all students attending public schools, we assume the amount of in-kind education transfer they received equals the provincial level per student education spending by education level. The latter is obtained from the Announcement of 2013 Education Expenditure Statistics (Ministry of Education, National Bureau of Statistics, and Ministry of Finance, 2014) issued by the Ministry of Education, the National Bureau of Statistics, and the Ministry of Public Finance.[16] Thus, the in-kind education transfer varies across provinces and education level.

Imputation of in-kind health transfer

Since the 2014 yearbook, total government health expenditures by province have been collected and the provincial-level per capital government health expenditure has been calculated. In the survey, each sample has a province ID, and the corresponding provincial-level health in-kind transfer is assumed for everyone who reported usage of health services. Thus, the in-kind health transfer varies across provinces

3   Main Findings

In this section we show the impact of fiscal policy on inequality and poverty overall, for urban and rural areas and for the three economic regions. Since the impact of fiscal policy on inequality and poverty depends on the size of fiscal interventions and their progressivity, we first present a snapshot of taxes and government spending in tables 20-1 and 20-2. A detailed description of each item can be found in the appendix 20A. In the last column of tables 20-1 and 20-2, we indicate the taxes and spending items that were included in our fiscal incidence analysis.

3.1   Size of Taxes and Government Spending

According to data from the *2014 Statistical Yearbook of China* (National Bureau of Statistics of China, 2014), total government tax revenues of 2013 (not including contributions to social security) amounted to 11,053 billion yuan RMB (CN¥),[17] equal to 19.4 percent of China's 2013 GDP. Of the total tax revenue, 51.2 percent was reserved by the central government with the rest going to local governments. According to the *2013 Statistical Bulletin of Development of Human Resources and Social Security* (Ministry of Human Resources and Social Security, 2014), total revenue from social security programs was CN¥3,525.2 billion in 2013.

As shown in table 20-2, in 2013 total social spending equaled 7.3 percent of GDP, in which social security outlays were 4.9 percent of GDP, in-kind education and health

---

[16] In addition, there is question in the survey that asks "Among the total education expenditure during last 12 months, how much was paid by the government, the school or any other organization?" This is also added into the in-kind education transfer.

[17] Equal to US$1,785.6 billion at the 2013 average exchange rate of CN¥6.19 per US dollar.

TABLE 20-1

Chinese Government Revenues, 2013 (Billion CN¥ [Billion US$])

Categories	Currency amount	% of total gov. revenue	% of GDP	In analysis
Total government revenue	**¥12,921 (US$2,087.4)**	**100.0**	**22.7**	
Total tax revenue	*¥11,053.1 (US$1,785.6)*	*85.5*	*19.4*	
Direct taxes	¥4,106.9 (US$663.5)	31.8	7.2	
Personal income tax	¥653.2 (US$105.5)	5.1	1.1	Yes
Corporate income tax	¥2,242.7 (US$362.3)	17.4	3.9	No
Other direct taxes	¥1,211 (US$195.6)	9.4	2.1	No
Indirect taxes	¥6,946.2 (US$1,122.2)	53.8	12.2	
VAT	¥2,881 (US$465.4)	22.3	5.1	Yes
Consumption tax	¥823.1 (US$133)	6.4	1.4	Yes
Business tax	¥1,723.3 (US$278.4)	13.3	3.0	No
Other indirect taxes	¥1,518.7 (US$245.4)	11.8	2.7	No
Total non-tax revenue	*¥1,867.9 (US$301.8)*	*14.5*	*3.3*	

Source: National Bureau of Statistics of China (2014).

Note: Other direct taxes include house property tax, tax on vehicles and boat operation, tax on ship tonnage, vehicle purchase tax, deed tax, tobacco leaf tax, city maintenance and construction tax. Other indirect taxes include VAT and consumption tax on imports, VAT and consumption tax rebate on exports, resource tax, tariffs, land appreciation tax, urban land use tax, farm land occupation tax, and stamp tax.

Currency amount in 2013 US$ is converted based on 2013 average exchange rate of CN¥6.19 per US dollar. Total revenue from social security programs in 2013 was CN¥3525.2 billion according to the Ministry of Human Resources and Social Security of the People's Republic of China (2014).

TABLE 20-2

Chinese Government Spending, 2013 (Billion CN¥ [Billion US$])

Categories	Currency amount	% of total gov. spending	% of GDP	In analysis
Total government spending	**¥1,4021.2 (US$2,265.1)**	**100.0**	**24.6**	
Primary government spending	*¥13,715.6 (US$2,215.8)*	*97.8*	*24.1*	
Social spending	¥4,170.5 (US$673.8)	29.7	7.3	
Social assistance, *of which*	¥427.7 (US$69.1)	3.1	0.8	
Urban MLSS	¥75.7 (US$12.2)	0.5	0.1	Yes
Rural MLSS	¥86.7 (US$14)	0.6	0.2	Yes
Rural Five Guarantees	¥17.2 (US$2.8)	0.1	0.03	Yes
Other social assistance	¥248.1 (US$40.1)	1.8	0.4	No
Social security	¥2791.6 (US$451)	19.9	4.9	Yes
In-kind education transfers	¥2,448.8 (US$395.6)	17.5	4.3	Yes
In-kind health transfers	¥843.2 (US$136.2)	6.0	1.5	Yes
Housing	¥448.1 (US$72.4)	3.2	0.8	No
Non–social spending	¥9545.1 (US$1,542.0)	68.1	16.8	No
Debt Servicing	*¥305.6 (US$49.4)*	*2.2*	*0.5*	

Source: National Bureau of Statistics of China (2014); Ministry of Civil Affairs of the People's Republic of China (2014);Ministry of Education of the People's Republic of China (2015); National Health Commission of the People's Republic of China (2014); Ministry of Human Resources and Social Security of the People's Republic of China (2014).

Note: Currency amount in 2013 US$ is converted based on 2013 average exchange rate of CN¥6.19 per US dollar.

transfers were 4.3 percent and 1.5 percent of GDP, respectively, and the social assistance programs (including the rural and urban Minimum Living Standard Scheme [MLSS]) accounted for 0.8 percent of GDP.

3.2 Results

Table 20-3 presents summary statistics of household per capita income and expenditure for the overall, urban, rural, and regional (Eastern, Central, and Western) samples. As expected, average per capita Market Income was higher in urban than rural areas and in the Eastern region compared with the other two. Table 20-3 also reveals that the combination of direct and indirect taxes and direct and in-kind transfers slightly increased the urban-rural income gap, an outcome that goes in the opposite direction of the desired one if the goal is to reduce urban-rural inequality. The main factor behind this result is that urban areas receive much more income (in absolute term and in proportion to Market Income) from contributory pensions; we shall return to this below. In contrast, the regional income gap between the richer Eastern region and the other two was narrowed primarily as a result of the fact that the former paid much more in direct taxes.

3.2.1 Impact on Inequality

Country-wide and within rural, urban, and regions

Table 20-4 shows a set of inequality indicators for Market Income, Disposable Income, Consumable Income, and Final Income for each sample group. For Market Income (prefiscal income), the urban areas exhibit higher inequality compared to the rural areas, and the inequality level is the highest in the Central region, followed by the Eastern and the Western regions. The inequality indicators of Disposable Income for each sample group decreased compared to the corresponding indicators of Market Income: the urban Gini declined by 0.052 Gini points and the rural Gini declined by 0.025 Gini points; the Gini coefficients for the Eastern, Central and Western regions declined by 0.047, 0.031 and 0.025 Gini points, respectively. This means that the combined effect of direct taxes and direct transfers was equalizing overall and within each geographical category. In contrast, the combined effect of indirect taxes and subsidies was unequalizing as the inequality measures using Consumable Income are higher—albeit slightly—than those using Disposable Income. In-kind transfers (education and health spending) were equalizing for all geographic categories. In comparing the inequality indicators for Final Income with those of Market Income, we can observe that the fiscal system decreased inequality in urban areas by 0.081 Gini points, in rural areas by 0.073 Gini points, and in the Eastern, Central and Western regions by 0.076, 0.069, and 0.081 Gini points, respectively.

What do these orders of magnitude mean? If we compare the change in the Gini coefficient for the whole country with that found in other countries with similar Mar-

TABLE 20-3
Household per Capita Income by Concept (averages and as % of Market Income) (RMB)

	All	Urban	Rural	Eastern	Central	Western
Market Income (pre-fiscal income) of which:	20,677	24,772	16,396	24,228	20,281	15,133
1. Wages/salaries after tax	10,201 (49.3%)	12,456 (50.3%)	7,539 (46.0%)	12,542 (51.8%)	9,488 (46.8%)	7,179 (47.4%)
2. Business income after tax	2,252 (10.9%)	2,182 (8.8%)	2,425 (14.8%)	2,510 (10.4%)	2,211 (10.9%)	1,871 (12.4%)
3. Personal inc. tax + contrib. to soc. Security	2,118 (10.2%)	3,214 (13.0%)	960 (5.9%)	3,030 (12.5%)	1,768 (8.7%)	1,012 (6.7%)
4. Property income	291 (1.4%)	495 (2.0%)	94 (0.6%)	334 (1.4%)	280 (1.4%)	232 (1.5%)
5. Private transfers	2,478 (12.0%)	2,457 (9.9%)	2,462 (15.0%)	2,831 (11.7%)	2,402 (11.8%)	1,976 (13.1%)
6. Imputed rent for owner-occupied housing	2,807 (13.6%)	3,670 (14.8%)	2,132 (13.0%)	2,557 (10.6%)	3,659 (18.0%)	2,076 (13.7%)
7. Auto consumption	530 (2.6%)	298 (1.2%)	784 (4.8%)	424 (1.8%)	473 (2.3%)	787 (5.2%)
Disposable Income, starting from Market Income:	20,314 (98.2%)	24,520 (99.0%)	16,090 (98.1%)	23,311 (96.2%)	20,159 (99.4%)	15,417 (101.9%)
1. Direct cash transfers (added)	140 (0.7%)	145 (0.6%)	141 (0.9%)	109 (0.4%)	126 (0.6%)	212 (1.4%)
2. Contributory pensions (added)	1,613 (7.8%)	2,817 (11.4%)	511 (3.1%)	2,005 (8.3%)	1,519 (7.5%)	1,080 (7.1%)
3. Personal inc. tax + contrib. to soc. security (subtracted)	2,118 (10.2%)	3,214 (13.0%)	960 (5.9%)	3,030 (12.5%)	1,768 (8.7%)	1,012 (6.7%)
Consumable Income, starting from Disposable Income:	17,616 (85.2%)	21,210 (85.6%)	13,992 (85.3%)	20,204 (83.4%)	17,493 (86.3%)	13,371 (88.4%)
1. Indirect subsidies (added)	133 (0.6%)	75 (0.3%)	181 (1.1%)	125 (0.5%)	163 (0.8%)	104 (0.7%)
2. Indirect taxes (VAT, consumption tax) (subtracted)	2,831 (13.7%)	3,385 (13.7%)	2,279 (13.9%)	3,232 (13.3%)	2,829 (13.9%)	2,149 (14.2%)
Final Income, starting from Consumable Income:	19,150 (92.6%)	22,828 (92.2%)	15,451 (94.2%)	21,778 (89.9%)	18,891 (93.1%)	15,025 (99.3%)
1. In-kind education transfer (added)	1,143 (5.5%)	1,222 (4.9%)	1,068 (6.5%)	1,182 (4.9%)	1,049 (5.2%)	1,206 (8.0%)
2. In-kind health transfer (added)	391 (1.9%)	396 (1.6%)	391 (2.4%)	392 (1.6%)	348 (1.7%)	449 (3.0%)
Number of observations	**45,276**	**19,534**	**22,638**	**19,057**	**13,726**	**12,478**

Source: Author's calculation using China Family Panel Studies 2014 survey data.

Note: For each sample group, percentage of each income category with respect to market income is shown in parenthesis.

TABLE 20-4
Inequality Indicators for China, 2013

Indicator	Market Income	Disposable Income	Consumable Income	Final Income
Overall				
Gini coefficient	0.545	0.509	0.509	0.470
Theil index	0.684	0.595	0.596	0.514
90/10	17.934	12.755	12.899	8.731
Urban				
Gini coefficient	0.547	0.495	0.497	0.466
Theil index	0.672	0.548	0.552	0.488
90/10	16.783	11.485	11.356	8.340
Rural				
Gini coefficient	0.529	0.504	0.505	0.456
Theil index	0.675	0.626	0.625	0.522
90/10	17.214	13.043	13.273	8.000
Eastern				
Gini coefficient	0.536	0.489	0.491	0.460
Theil index	0.601	0.484	0.487	0.429
90/10	17.104	12.245	12.182	9.104
Central				
Gini coefficient	0.537	0.506	0.506	0.468
Theil index	0.757	0.700	0.695	0.607
90/10	16.568	11.191	11.276	7.874
Western				
Gini coefficient	0.527	0.502	0.503	0.446
Theil index	0.684	0.631	0.634	0.514
90/10	16.157	12.459	12.533	7.290

Source: Authors' calculation using China Family Panel Studies 2014 survey data.

ket Income inequality (all in Latin America), we find that the redistributive effect is larger than in Honduras but somewhat smaller than in Panama and considerably smaller than in Brazil and Uruguay.[18]

---

[18] The results for these other countries can be found at http://commitmentoequity.org/datacenter. See the analysis for Brazil by Higgins and Pereira (2014), for Honduras by Instituto Centroameri-

Marginal contribution of specific fiscal interventions

The marginal contribution of a specific fiscal intervention measures how much it contributes to the fiscally induced changes in inequality. The marginal contribution of a certain fiscal intervention in redistributing income equals the Gini coefficient of the income measure with the intervention, minus the Gini coefficient of the income measure without the intervention.[19] A positive marginal contribution indicates an equalizing impact, while a negative marginal contribution means the fiscal intervention is unequalizing.

Table 20-5 shows the marginal contributions of fiscal interventions in reducing inequality for the entire country as well as for each geographical category. Excluding the non-cash portion (i.e., in-kind transfers in education and health) of the fiscal system, the marginal contribution measures the impact of each fiscal intervention on the observed change from the Market Income Gini to the Consumable Income Gini. The results on the tax side are as follows. Personal income tax and contributions to social security are always equalizing. The VAT is unequalizing for the country as a whole, the urban areas, and the Eastern region but is equalizing for the rest of the categories. The consumption tax is quite unequalizing for all categories. On the spending side, direct transfers and indirect subsidies are always equalizing. In order to consider both the cash and non-cash portions together, we use the marginal contribution to measure the impact of each fiscal intervention on the observed change from the Market Income Gini to the Final Income Gini. In this case, personal income tax and contributions to social security are still always equalizing and now so is the VAT. The consumption tax, however, is still always unequalizing. Direct cash transfers, contributory pensions, indirect subsidies, and in-kind transfers are always equalizing.

The above results are similar to what one tends to find in other countries. Usually, the only unequalizing component are indirect taxes (and also subsidies), while the rest of the fiscal interventions are always equalizing.

Impact on the urban-rural gap and inequality between regions

The decomposition results are shown in table 20-6. As we can see, "within-urban and rural" inequality contributes about 95.5 percent–96 percent (for different income measures) to overall inequality, and the "between urban and rural" component contributes 4.0 percent–4.3 percent for different income measures. Similarly, inequality within regions contributes about 96.6 percent–96.8 percent to the overall Theil index, and between-region inequality accounts for 3.2 percent–3.4 percent of overall inequality. From the decomposition results, we see that although the fiscal system decreased total inequality, within-urban inequality, and within-rural inequality, it resulted in an *increase* in the urban-rural gap. As we can see, the "between urban and rural" component

cano de Estudios Fiscales (2017), for Panama by Martinez-Aguilar (2018), and for Uruguay by Bucheli and others (2014).

[19] See chapter 1 in this Volume and Enami, Lustig, and Aranda (2022) (chapter 2 in this Volume).

TABLE 20-5

Marginal Contribution of Fiscal Interventions in Reducing Inequality in China, 2013

Fiscal intervention	Overall	Urban	Rural	Eastern	Central	Western
Total from Market Income to Consumable Income						
All taxes and contributions to social security	0.0198	0.0182	0.0112	0.0273	0.0076	0.0096
All taxes (direct & indirect)	0.0014	0.0023	−0.0003	0.0023	0.0000	−0.0002
Personal income tax	0.0036	0.0053	0.0012	0.0059	0.0013	0.0013
VAT	−0.0001	−0.0008	0.00001	−0.0011	0.0006	0.00001
Consumption tax	−0.0019	−0.0017	−0.0017	−0.0020	−0.0021	−0.0016
All contributions to social security	0.0134	0.0108	0.0056	0.0181	0.0041	0.0060
All direct transfers incl. contributory pensions	0.0306	0.0548	0.0203	0.0362	0.0362	0.0247
All contributory pensions	0.0244	0.0491	0.0131	0.0318	0.0306	0.0148
All direct transfers excl. contributory pensions	0.0054	0.0046	0.0068	0.0034	0.0050	0.0093
All indirect subsidies	0.0017	0.0008	0.0010	0.0016	0.0014	0.0007
Total from Market Income to Final Income						
All taxes and contributions to social security	0.0224	0.0215	0.0128	0.0299	0.0101	0.0117
All taxes (direct & indirect)	0.0058	0.0059	0.0049	0.006	0.0044	0.0059
Personal income tax	0.0036	0.0053	0.0013	0.0058	0.0013	0.0014
VAT	0.0040	0.0025	0.0048	0.0021	0.0046	0.0056
Consumption tax	−0.0015	−0.0014	−0.0012	−0.0017	−0.0016	−0.001
All contributions to social security	0.0155	0.0138	0.0065	0.0204	0.0061	0.0075
All direct transfers incl. contributory pensions	0.0256	0.0485	0.0169	0.0316	0.0316	0.0191
All contributory pensions	0.0204	0.0437	0.0109	0.0278	0.0269	0.0111
All direct transfers excl. contributory pensions	0.0046	0.0039	0.0057	0.0030	0.0043	0.0075
All indirect subsidies	0.0013	0.0007	0.0004	0.0014	0.0011	0.0000
In-kind transfers	0.0391	0.0312	0.0486	0.0306	0.0384	0.0571
Health	0.0279	0.0229	0.0341	0.0224	0.0276	0.0399
Education	0.0099	0.0074	0.0125	0.0072	0.0097	0.0144

Source: Author's calculation based on China Family Panel Studies 2014 survey data.

Note: The unit of numbers reported in the table is Gini points. The marginal contribution = Gini of Consumable Income/Final Income without the specific fiscal intervention—Gini of Consumable Income/Final Income with the specific fiscal intervention.

TABLE 20-6
Decomposition of Theil Index for China, 2013

	Overall Theil	Within urban-rural component	Between urban-rural component
Market Income	0.685	0.658 (96.0%)	0.027 (4.0%)
Disposable Income	0.608	0.581 (95.5%)	0.027 (4.5%)
Consumable Income	0.609	0.583 (95.7%)	0.026 (4.3%)
Final Income	0.526	0.503 (95.7%)	0.023 (4.3%)

	Overall Theil	Within region component	Between region component
Market Income	0.672	0.649 (96.6%)	0.023 (3.4%)
Disposable Income	0.595	0.575 (96.6%)	0.020 (3.4%)
Consumable Income	0.596	0.576 (96.8%)	0.019 (3.2%)
Final Income	0.514	0.497 (96.8%)	0.016 (3.2%)

Source: Author's calculation based on China Family Panel Studies 2014 survey data, following method for decomposing Theil index proposed by Shorrocks (1984).

Note: When decomposing between urban and rural, only samples with non-missing indicator of urban/rural residency are kept, and when decomposing between regions, only samples with non-missing indicator of province of residency are kept. Thus there are minor differences of overall Gini of each income concept.

accounts for 4.0 percent of overall Market Income Theil, while it contributes 4.5 percent to the Disposable Income Theil and 4.3 percent to Consumable Income and Final Income Theil. This somewhat surprising result stems from the fact mentioned above—namely, that combination of direct taxes and direct transfers exacerbate rather than diminish the income gaps between rural and urban areas. The main driver of this undesirable outcome is the income from contributory pensions, which is much higher in urban than rural areas (see table 20-3).[20]

For regional inequality, the decomposition results show that the fiscal system has been effective in reducing regional inequality. As we can see, the "between-region" component accounts for 3.4 percent of overall Market Income Theil, while it contributes 3.2 percent to the Final Income Theil. This would still be the case if we considered just the cash component of the fiscal system. Again, if we look at table 20-3, we can notice that the richest Eastern region pays the highest proportion of taxes (25.8 percent of Market Income) and receives the least benefits (15.7 percent), while the poorest Western region pays the smallest tax (20.9 percent) and gets the largest benefits (20.2 percent);

[20] As shown in table 20-3, urban residents pay 13 percent of Market Income as direct taxes, and the total direct transfers they received is equal to 12 percent of Market Income, while rural residents pay 6 percent of Market Income as direct taxes and their direct transfers are equal to 4 percent of Market Income.

these figures suggest the possibility that the fiscal system has an effective role in reducing regional inequality.

3.2.2 Impact on Poverty

As shown in table 20-7, based on a US$1.9 PPP/day poverty line (in 2011 PPP dollars), the headcount ratio of Market Income poverty in China in 2013 was 12.3 percent, 9.6 percent in the urban areas, and 15.7 percent in the rural areas. The poverty rate was the highest in the Western region (16.3 percent) relative to the Central (12.9 percent) and the Eastern (9.4 percent) regions. In comparing poverty indicators measured based on Market Income and those based on Disposable Income, we find that direct transfers net of personal income tax and contributions to social security are poverty reducing: the headcount ratios of all groups decreased (see table 20-7). When we add the impact of indirect taxes net of indirect subsidies, the headcount ratio for Consumable Income is *still lower* than the headcount ratio of Market Income in many cases and for many of the poverty lines used here, but not for all. In urban areas, the headcount ratio of Consumable Income is always lower than the headcount ratio of Market Income.[21] However, we noticed an undesirable result: the fiscal system increased vulnerable poverty in the poorer rural areas and also in the three regions, which means that the fiscal system has driven some people who were not vulnerable poor into vulnerable poverty in larger numbers than helping the vulnerable poor escape their condition (and become non-poor).

What drives this undesirable result? By looking at table 20-3, one can observe that the main difference between the urban and rural areas is the (relative) amount of contributory pensions received by their respective residents. In urban areas, it is much higher (as a proportion of Market Income, 11.4 percent versus 3.1 percent in rural areas). However, it is important to note that if one uses the squared poverty gap instead of the headcount ratio, poverty measured with Consumable Income is always lower than prefiscal (Market Income) poverty. In other words, the poorest of the poor do not appear to be harmed by the net fiscal system.

4 Conclusion

This chapter provides a comprehensive assessment of how fiscal policy affected overall income inequality and poverty in China, as well as inequality and poverty within rural and urban areas and within each economic region. In addition, it analyzes whether the fiscal system has contributed to lowering the urban-rural income gap and regional inequality.

Our results show that the fiscal system has been inequality-reducing at the country level, as well as in rural and urban areas and in each economic region. On the tax

---

[21] We observe the same pattern if we use the poverty gap ratio or squared poverty gap ratio (results available upon request).

TABLE 20-7

Headcount Ratios for China, 2013

Headcount ratios	Market Income %	Disposable Income %	Consumable Income %
Overall			
1.9 $PPP/Day	12.28	9.25	10.90
3.2 $PPP/Day	19.87	16.70	19.48
5.5 $PPP/Day	32.21	29.30	33.80
National poverty line	11.11	8.15	9.73
Urban			
1.9 $PPP/Day	9.55	6.05	7.44
3.2 $PPP/Day	16.43	12.12	14.39
5.5 $PPP/Day	26.40	21.70	25.68
National poverty line	8.64	5.21	6.52
Rural			
1.9 $PPP/Day	15.71	13.04	15.09
3.2 $PPP/Day	24.31	22.09	25.42
5.5 $PPP/Day	39.02	37.69	42.69
National poverty line	14.24	11.64	13.56
Eastern			
1.9 $PPP/Day	9.43	6.87	8.21
3.2 $PPP/Day	16.23	13.55	16.16
5.5 $PPP/Day	26.82	24.36	28.31
National poverty line	8.57	5.99	7.22
Central			
1.9 $PPP/Day	12.93	8.84	10.23
3.2 $PPP/Day	19.82	15.59	18.62
5.5 $PPP/Day	32.53	28.96	33.40
National poverty line	11.70	7.82	9.31
Western			
1.9 $PPP/Day	16.25	13.86	16.40
3.2 $PPP/Day	26.14	23.59	26.29
5.5 $PPP/Day	40.94	38.16	43.69
National poverty line	14.66	12.27	14.56

Source: Authors' calculation using China Family Panel Studies 2014 survey data.

Note: The National Poverty Line is CN¥2,300/Year in 2011 CN¥.

side, personal income tax, contributions to social security, and VAT are equalizing for all groups, while consumption tax is quite unequalizing for all groups. On the spending side, direct transfers, indirect subsidies, and in-kind transfers are always equalizing for all groups. In addition, the fiscal system reduced inequality between regions primarily because the Eastern region—the richest—paid a higher proportion of taxes and received the least benefits, while the poorest Western region paid the smallest proportion of taxes and received the largest share of prefiscal income in transfers (direct and in-kind) and subsidies. However, our results also show that the fiscal system widened the urban-rural income gap. This undesirable outcome is driven mainly by the fact that the urban residents receive significantly more income from contributory pensions than rural residents.

We find that the fiscal system is poverty-reducing in the urban areas. However, for the international poverty line applicable to middle-income countries, the fiscal system increases poverty in the poorer rural areas and also in the three regions, which means that the fiscal system has driven some people who were not poor with prefiscal income into poverty in larger numbers than helping the poor escape their condition (and become non-poor). When we use the squared poverty gap index, the fiscal system is poverty-reducing throughout. This is reassuring in the sense that it is telling us that the fiscal system reduces poverty for the poorest of the poor (even though it makes some of the non-poor poor).

Our analysis seems to support the Chinese government's diagnosis of the limitations that prevailed in the fiscal system and its efforts to address entrenched income inequality across geographic locations. In fact, as a response to rising overall and urban-rural inequality and the persistence of poverty pockets, in 2013 the government committed itself to reducing them through taxation, the social security system and cash transfers (State Council, 2013).[22] In 2014, the government launched the Targeted Poverty Alleviation program, which aims to lift all rural poor and impoverished counties out of extreme poverty by 2020. The Targeted Poverty Alleviation program seeks to precisely identify households in poverty and to customize support according to local and household conditions to effectively help them. In 2019, the government also initiated the personal income tax reform and VAT reform to reduce the tax burden and improve income redistribution through the fiscal system. For the personal income tax reform, higher personal deductions, adjusted tax brackets, and more deductible items were introduced, and for the VAT reform, lower tax rates were introduced. To assess how much these reforms ultimately accomplish in terms of inequality and poverty reduction goals through the fiscal system, it is important to have a benchmark to which these reforms can be compared. Thus, the main contribution of this chapter is both to estimate how much redistribution was being accomplished through

---

[22] In particular, the government stated that it would "accelerate the improvement of the redistribution adjustment mechanism with taxation, social security, and transfer payments as the main means" (translation by authors).

the pre-reform fiscal system and for this exercise to serve as a benchmark against which one can compare fiscal redistribution in the future using information from new household surveys.

References

Alm, J., and Y. Liu. 2013. "Did China's Tax-for-Fee Reform Improve Farmers' Welfare in Rural Areas?" *Journal of Development Studies* 49, no. 4, pp. 516–32.

———.2014. "China Tax-for-Fee Reform and Village Inequality." *Oxford Development Studies* 42, no. 1, pp. 38–64.

Bucheli, M., N. Lustig, M. Rossi, and F. Amabile. 2014. "Social Spending, Taxes, and Income Redistribution in Uruguay," in "Analyzing the Redistributive Impact of Taxes and Transfers in Latin America," edited by Nora Lustig, Carola Pessino, and John Scott, Special Issue, *Public Finance Review* 42, no. 3, pp. 413–33.

Cai, M., and X. Yue. 2017. "The Redistributive Role of Government Social Security Transfers on Inequality in China." Centre for Human Capital and Productivity Working Papers, 2017-21 (London, ON: Department of Economics, University of Western Ontario).

Chen, J., X. Ma, and Q. Qin. 2010. "The Impact of Minimum Living Standard Scheme on Income Distribution," vol. 4, pp. 62–65. (In Chinese)

Chen, S., M. Ravallion, and Y. Wang. 2006. "Di Bao: A Guaranteed Minimum Income in China's Cities?" World Bank Policy Research Working Paper No. 3805.

Enami, Ali, Sean Higgins, and Nora Lustig. 2022. "Allocating Taxes and Transfers, Constructing Income Concepts, and Completing Sections A, B, and C of CEQ Master Workbook," chap. 6 in *Commitment to Equity Handbook: Estimating the Impact of Fiscal Policy on Inequality and Poverty*, 2nd ed., Vol. 1, edited by Nora Lustig (Brookings Institution Press and CEQ Institute, Tulane University). Free online version available at www.commitmento equity.org.

Enami, Ali, Nora Lustig, and Rodrigo Aranda. 2022. "Analytic Foundations: Measuring the Redistributive Impact of Taxes and Transfers," chap. 2 in *Commitment to Equity Handbook: Estimating the Impact of Fiscal Policy on Inequality and Poverty*, 2nd ed., Vol. 1, edited by Nora Lustig (Brookings Institution Press and CEQ Institute, Tulane University). Free online version available at www.commitmentoequity.org.

Golan, J., T. Sicular, and N. Umapathi. 2017. "Unconditional Cash Transfers in China: Who Benefits from the Rural Minimum Living Standard Guarantee (Dibao) Program?" *World Development* 93, pp. 316–36.

Gao, Q., I. Garfinkel, and F. Zhai. 2009. "Anti-Poverty Effectiveness of the Minimum Living Standard Assistance Policy in Urban China." *Review of Income and Wealth*, Series 55, Special Issue 1, pp. 630–55.

Higgins, Sean, and Caterina Brest López. 2022. "Producing Indicators and Results, and Completing Sections D and E of *CEQ Master Workbook* using the *CEQ Stata Package*," chap. 8 in *Commitment to Equity Handbook: Estimating the Impact of Fiscal Policy on Inequality and Poverty*, 2nd ed., Vol. 1, edited by Nora Lustig (Brookings Institution Press and CEQ Institute, Tulane University). Free online version available at www.commitmento equity.org.

Higgins, S., and C. Pereira. 2014. "The Effects of Brazil's Taxation and Social Spending on the Distribution of Household Income," in "Analyzing the Redistributive Impact of Taxes and Transfers in Latin America," edited by Nora Lustig, Carola Pessino, and John Scott, Special Issue, *Public Finance Review* 42, no. 3, pp. 346–67.

Instituto Centroamericano de Estudios Fiscales. 2017. "Incidencia de la politica fiscal en la desigualdad y la pobreza en Honduras." CEQ Working Paper 51 (CEQ Institute, Tulane University, IFAD and Instituto Centroamericano de Estudios Fiscales), April.

Lei, X., and W. Lin. 2009. "The New Cooperative Medical Scheme in Rural China: Does More Coverage Mean More Service and Better Health?" Working Paper, Peking University.

Li, S., C. Luo, and T. Sicular. 2013. "Overview: Income Inequality and Poverty in China, 2002–2007," in *Rising Inequality in China: Challenge to a Harmonious Society*, edited by Li Shi, Hiroshi Sato, and Terry Sicular (Cambridge University Press).

Li, S., and S. Yang. 2009. "Impact of the Minimum Living Standard Guarantee on Income Distribution and Poverty Reduction in Urban China." *Chinese Journal of Population Science*, no. 5, pp. 19–27. (In Chinese)

Li, S., M. Zhu, and P. Zhan. 2017. "Redistributive Effects of the Social Security System in China." *Chinese Social Security Review* 1, no. 4, pp. 3–20. (In Chinese)

Lustig, N. 2022a. "The *CEQ Assessment*: Measuring the Impact of Fiscal Policy on Inequality and Poverty," chap. 1 in *Commitment to Equity Handbook: Estimating the Impact of Fiscal Policy on Inequality and Poverty*, 2nd ed., Vol. 1, edited by Nora Lustig (Brookings Institution Press and CEQ Institute, Tulane University). Free online version available at www.commitmentoequity.org.

———, ed. 2022b. *Commitment to Equity Handbook: Estimating the Impact of Fiscal Policy on Inequality and Poverty*, 2nd ed., Vol. 1 (Brookings Institution Press and CEQ Institute, Tulane University). Free online version available at www.commitmentoequity.org.

Martinez-Aguilar, S. 2018. "CEQ Master Workbook: Panama (2016)." CEQ Data Center on Fiscal Redistribution (CEQ Institute, Tulane University and the Economic Co-operation and Development), November 2.

Martinez-Vazquez, J. 2008. "The Impact of Budgets on the Poor: Tax and Expenditure Benefit Incidence Analysis," in *Public Finance for Poverty Reduction: Concepts and Case Studies from Africa and Latin America*, edited by Blanca Moreno-Dodson and Wodon Quentin (Washington World Bank).

Mi, Z., X. Liu, and Q. Liu. 2012. "Economic Growth and Income Inequality: Study of the Fiscal Policies of Balanced Incentive." *Economic Research Journal* 47, no. 12, pp. 43–54. (In Chinese)

Ministry of Civil Affairs of the People's Republic of China. 2014. "2013 Statistical Communique of Social Service Development"., Beijing.

Ministry of Education, National Bureau of Statistics, and Ministry of Finance, 2014. "Statistical Announcement on the Implementation of National Education Funding in 2013," Beijing (http://www.moe.gov.cn/srcsite/A05/s3040/201410/t20141031_178035.html).

Ministry of Education of the People's Republic of China. 2015. *2014 Educational Statistical Yearbook of China* (Beijing: People's Education Press).

Ministry of Human Resources and Social Security of the People's Republic of China. 2014. "2013 Statistical Bulletin of Development of Human Resources and Social Security."

National Bureau of Statistics of China. 2000. *China Statistical Yearbook 2000* (Beijing: China Statistics Press).

———. 2014. *China Statistical Yearbook 2014* (Beijing: China Statistics Press).

———. 2018. *China Statistical Yearbook 2018* (Beijing: China Statistics Press).

———.2019. *China Statistical Yearbook 2019* (Beijing: China Statistics Press).

National Health Commission of the People's Republic of China. 2015. *2015 Health Statistical Yearbook of China* (Beijing: Peking Union Medical College Press).

The National People's Congress. 2011. "Individual Income Tax Law of the People's Republic of China" (amended version), Beijing.

Ravallion, M., and S. Chen. 2007. "China's (Uneven) Progress against Poverty." *Journal of Development Economics* 82, no. 1, pp. 1–42.

Shorrocks, A. F. 1984. "Inequality Decomposition by Population Subgroups." *Econometrica* 52, no. 6, pp. 1369–85.

Song, Y. 2014. "What Should Economists Know about the Current Chinese Hukou System?" *China Economic Review* 29, pp. 200–12.

State Council. 2008. "State Council Order No. 538," Beijing.

———. 2013. "Notice of the State Council on the Approval of the Development and Reform Commission and Other Departments on Deepening the Reform of the Income Distribution System," Beijing (http://www.gov.cn/zwgk/2013-02/05/content_2327531.htm).

State Taxation Administration. 2011. "State Taxation Administration Announcement No. 46 of 2011," Beijing.

Wagstaff, A., M. Lindelow, J. Gao, L. Xu, and J. Qian. 2009. "Extending Health Insurance to the Rural Population: An Impact Evaluation of China's New Cooperative Medical Scheme." *Journal of Health Economics* 28, no. 1, pp. 1–19.

Wang, X., and B. Kang. 2009. "Redistribution in the Current Social Pension System in China." *Statistical Research* 26, no. 11, pp. 75–81. (In Chinese)

Wang, Y., Y. Long, C. Jiang, and Q. Xu. 2016. "Research on Social Security Income Redistribution Effect in China." *Economic Research Journal* 51, no. 2, pp. 4–15. (In Chinese).

World Bank. Povcal.Net (portal; no specific date).

Xie, E. 2018. "Effects of Taxes and Public Transfers on Income Redistribution." *Economics Research Journal* 53, no. 8, pp. 116–31. (In Chinese)

Xie, Y., and X. Zhou. 2014. "Income Inequality in Today's China." *PNAS* 111, no. 19, pp. 6928–33.

Xu, J., G. Ma, and S. Li. 2013. "Has the Personal Income Tax Improved China's Income Distribution? A Dynamic Assessment of the 1997–2011 Micro Data." *Social Science in China* 6, pp. 53–71. (In Chinese)

Yue, X., J. Xu, Q. Liu, S. Ding, and L. Dong. 2012. "Evaluation of Redistributive Effects of the Personal Income Tax Reform in 2011." *Economic Research Journal* 2, no. 3, pp. 113–24. (In Chinese)

Yue, X., B. Zhang, and J. Xu. 2014. "Measuring the Effect of the Chinese Tax System on Income Distribution." *Social Science in China* 6, pp. 96–117. (In Chinese)

Appendix 20A

The Fiscal System in China

The main types of taxes commonly used around the world are also used in China. In particular, direct taxes equaled 37.2 percent of total tax revenue in 2013, of which personal income tax was 5.9 percent of total tax revenue. About 62.8 percent of the total tax revenue in 2013 was from indirect taxes, of which the VAT was 26.1 percent, the consumption tax was 7.4 percent, and the business tax was 15.6 percent. The taxes included in the incidence analysis below are personal income tax, VAT, and consumption tax.

A1 Direct Taxes

A1.1 Personal Income Tax

China's personal income tax system sees different types of income subject to various gradual tax rates. Wages and salaries income are taxed monthly. Contributions to social security programs and the housing fund are deducted from earnings to obtain taxable income subject to personal income tax as are the first CN¥3,500 of net monthly wages/salaries income, such that total taxable wages/salaries equal "wages/salaries minus payment to the five social security programs and the housing fund, then minus 3,500" (State Taxation Administration, 2011). Table 20A-1 shows the seven-level progressive tax rate on wages/salaries income.

Individual business income (production and operation income) is taxed on an annual basis. The taxable income is gross income deducting costs, expenses, losses, and other taxes (State Taxation Administration, 2011). The five-level tax rate is shown in table 20A-2.

Individual services and capital income are also subject to tax (The National People's Congress, 2011). For capital gains from the transfer of property (e.g., financial securities, real estate, equipment, land use rights), original property value and reasonable fees can be deducted, and then 20 percent of the net gain is taxed. Capital gains from the stock market and interest on bank deposit and government bonds are taxed at 20 percent. With regard to income from remunerations for services, from authorships and royalties, and from leasing property, if a single payment is no more than CN¥4,000, CN¥800 can be deducted; if a single payment is above CN¥4,000, 20 percent of the payment can be deducted. Then, 20 percent of the taxable amount should be paid. When the taxable remuneration income is higher than CN¥20,000, the excess amount is taxed based on the gradual tax rates shown in table 20A-3. The full amount of occasional income is subject to a tax rate of 20 percent.

Table 20A-1

Tax Rates on Wages/Salaries Income

Grade	Monthly taxable income, CN¥ (2013 US$)	% Tax rate
1	CN¥0–1,500 (US$0–242)	3
2	CN¥1,500–4,500 (US$242–727)	10
3	CN¥4,500–9,000 (US$727–1,454)	20
4	CN¥9,000–35,000 (US$1,454–5,654)	25
5	CN¥35,000–55,000 (US$5,654–8,885)	30
6	CN¥55,000–80,000 (US$8,885–12,924)	35
7	> CN¥80,000 (>12,924)	45

Source: State Taxation Administration (2011).

Note: equivalence in 2013 US$ is converted based on 2013 average exchange rate of 6.19 Yuan per US dollar.

Table 20A-2

Tax Rates on Individual Business Income

Grade	Annual taxable income, CN¥ (2013 US$)	% Tax rate
1	CN¥0–15,000 (US$0–2,423)	5
2	CN¥15,000–30,000 (US$2,423–4,847)	10
3	CN¥30,000–60,000 (US$4,847–9,693)	20
4	CN¥60,000–100,000 (US$9,693–16,155)	30
5	> CN¥100,000 (>US$16,155)	35

Source: State Taxation Administration (2011).

Note: Equivalence in 2013 US$ is converted based on 2013 average exchange rate of CN¥6.19 per US dollar.

A2 Indirect Taxes

The two main types of indirect taxes in China are the VAT and consumption tax. The VAT applies to all sale and importation of goods and services in China. According to the Provisional Regulations on Value Added Tax of the People's Republic of China (amended version since 2008),[23] the standard VAT rate was 17 percent and applied to the sale and importation of most goods, the provision of processing, repair, or replacement services, and the leasing of movable and tangible assets. A reduced rate of 13 percent applied to certain types of goods, including (1) grain, vegetable oil; (2) tap water, heating, air conditioning, hot water, gas, liquefied petroleum gas, natural gas, biogas, coal products for residential use; (3) books, newspapers, magazines; (4) feed, fertilizer, pesticides,

---

[23] It was further amended in 2016.

TABLE 20A-3

Tax Rates on Remuneration Income

Grade	Taxable income, CN¥ (2013)	% Tax rate
1	CN¥0–20,000 (US$0–3,231)	20
2	CN¥20,000–50,000 (US$3,231–8,078)	25
3	> CN¥50,000 (>US$8,078)	35

Source: National People's Congress. 2011.

Note: Equivalence in 2013 US$ is converted based on 2013 average exchange rate of CN¥6.19 per US dollar.

agricultural machinery, agricultural film; (5) other goods prescribed by the State Council (State Council, 2008). In 2012, the government initiated the reform of replacing the business tax with a VAT: an 11 percent VAT rate was applied to transportation services, postal services, basic telecommunication services, construction services, and the leasing and sale of real estate/land use right, while a 6 percent VAT rate applied to value-added telecommunications services, financial services, lifestyle and other modern services, and sale of intangible assets (except land use rights).

According to the Provisional Regulations on Consumption Tax (2008 revision), the consumption tax targets mainly fifteen types of luxury goods, including tobacco, alcohol, cosmetics, jewelry, fireworks, gasoline, diesel oil, tires, motorcycles, automobiles, golf equipment, yachts, luxury watches, disposable chopsticks, and wooden floorboards. The tax is computed based on sale price and/or sale volume.[24]

A3 The Social Protection System: Social Security and Social Assistance

A3.1 Social Security

China's social security system consists of five social security programs (including basic contributory pensions, health insurance, unemployment insurance, on-the-job injury insurance, and maternity insurance) and a housing fund. Enrollment in the "5 insurances & 1 fund" is legally required for all formal employment. Basically, urban employees, who comprise the majority of the urban residents, and those of the rural residents who have a formal job, are covered by the social security system. Both employer and employee insurance premiums are tax-deductible under corporate income tax and personal income tax law. All income received by the beneficiaries of these mandatory social security programs is also tax-exempt. The contributions paid by employers and employees for each social security program varies across provinces as well as has changed with time.

---

[24] See appendix 20B for detailed consumption tax rates.

Table 20A-4

Social Security Contributions as Percentage of Monthly Wages/Salaries, Beijing/Shanghai

Social security type	% Employee's contribution	% Employer's contribution
Pension insurance for employees	8/8	20/21
Health insurance for employees	2/2	10/11
Unemployment insurance	0.2/0.5	1/1.5
On-job injury insurance	0/0	0.5, 1 or 2/0.5
Maternal insurance	0/0	0.8/1
Housing fund	12/7	12/7

Source: Beijing/Shanghai Municipal Human Resources and Social Security Bureau, Beijing/Shanghai Housing Fund Management Center.

Table 20A-4 summarizes the contribution rates paid by employers and employees in Beijing and Shanghai for 2013.[25]

Many efforts have been made to extend the social security system in order to benefit the urban unemployed and rural residents, including the initiation of new rural cooperative medical insurance in 2003,[26] medical insurance for urban residents in 2007, basic pension insurance for rural residents in 2009, and basic pension insurance for urban unemployed residents in 2011.

Further expansion of social security coverage remains to be achieved in China. In 2013, total social security revenue was CN¥3,525 billion (equal to US$569 billion), while total social security expenditure was CN¥2,792 billion (equal to US$451 billion). Table 20A-5 documents the coverage, revenue, and expenditure of each of the five social security programs.[27]

A3.2 Social Assistance: The Minimum Living Standard Scheme (Dibao Program)

Launched in 1993, the Minimum Living Standard Scheme (MLSS) is a direct transfer program that aims to improve the economic well-being of the new urban poor. Urban residents whose household per capita income is lower than the threshold of the local minimum living standard are eligible for basic assistance from the local government. There are two main groups of beneficiaries. One comprises those without an income source, working capability, or legal guardian, who previously were recipients of social

---

[25] There are minor variations of the contribution rates across provinces. The rates of Beijing and Shanghai are reported here as representative cases.

[26] See section 1.3.4 for details.

[27] See also Ministry of Human Resources and Social Security of the People's Republic of China (2014).

TABLE 20A-5

Coverage, Revenue and Expenditure of Social Security Programs (2013)

Social Security Program	Coverage (million CN¥)	Revenue (billion CN¥)	Expenditure (billion CN¥)
Pension insurance for employees	322.2	2,268	1,847
Health insurance for employees & urban residents	570.7	824.8	680.1
Unemployment insurance	164.2	128.9	53.2
On-job injury insurance	199.2	61.5	48.2
Maternal insurance	163.9	36.8	28.3
Pension Insurance for urban & rural residents	497.5	205.2	134.8

assistance. This group can receive the full amount of benefits equal to the local assistance line. The other is made up of the new urban poor whose household per capita income is lower than the local assistance line, including families with temporary financial difficulties due to unemployment and families with limited income. The benefit amount for this group is the gap between the local assistance line and their overall household income. There were 2.7 million beneficiaries in 1999 (National Bureau of Statistics, 2000); the number rose to 20.6 million (in 11 million households) in 2013 (Ministry of Civil Affairs, 2014). The average transfer amount per urban beneficiary in 2013 was CN¥264/month (Ministry of Civil Affairs, 2014).

Since 2003, the MLSS, which was originally aimed at the urban poor, has been extended to rural areas. According to the Ministry of Civil Affairs, the system covers 29.3 million rural households, or a total of 53.9 million rural residents. It operates similarly to that described above for urban areas. Local governments are responsible for the operation and financing of the system, with subsidies from the central government. The average transfer amount per rural beneficiary in 2013 was CN¥116/month (Ministry of Civil Affairs, 2014).

The MLSS thresholds for assistance are set by local governments, according to the local minimum standard of living, local average per capita income, and local cost of basic consumption needs. These thresholds are also often set in consideration of local governments' financing capacities. As a result, the thresholds in many less developed cities are lower than actual basic needs. Gao, Garfinkel, and Zhai (2009) find that 2.3 percent of all urban residents are eligible for MLSS, but only slightly less than half of them are actual beneficiaries. Although the poverty rate decreased among the participants, due to limited coverage, poverty is still an issue among eligible households.

A3.3 Social Assistance: The Rural Five Guarantees System

In rural China, the Five Guarantees System aims to provide the most vulnerable rural residents (i.e., the elderly, disabled, children under sixteen who are not dependents, those unable to work) with basic means of support, including food, clothing, housing, education (only for children), medical care, and proper burial. Since its initiation in 1956, the system has undergone several reforms, which were made necessary in part by the fact that it was financed by local villages, whose funds were reduced by agricultural tax reform. Thus, in 2006, the central government issued the "New Guidelines on Rural Five Guarantees System," which explicitly states that the living standards of the beneficiaries of the Five Guarantees should be higher than average local villagers, that local governments should include Five Guarantees expenditure in their fiscal budgets, and that the central government should subsidize local governments with financial shortages. According to the Ministry of Civil Affairs, at the end of 2013 a total of 5.4 million rural citizens were covered by the Five Guarantees System, and total spending in 2013 equaled CN¥17.2 billion. Annual expenditure per beneficiary was CN¥4,685 for those staying in the support centers and CN¥3,499 for those living at home (Ministry of Civil Affairs, 2014).

A4 The Health System

Total government health expenditure in China during the year 2013 was CN¥828 billion (National Bureau of Statistics, 2014), which amounted to 1.5 percent of the total GDP. An aging population has seen a rapid increase in demand for care and has required the expansion and development of the health care system. This has been especially challenging in rural areas and has revealed sharp urban-rural disparities in health insurance coverage and related healthcare services and costs. Through decades of efforts, the Chinese government has developed three health insurance systems, which provide coverage for more than 90 percent of the population: Basic Medical Insurance for Urban Employees was launched in 1998, Basic Medical Insurance for Rural Residents in 2003, and Basic Medical Insurance for Urban Residents in 2007.

A4.1 Basic Medical Insurance for Urban Employees

This insurance is compulsory based on employment and forms part of the social security system described above. It provides basic medical coverage for urban employees in both the public and private sectors. Local governments, mainly at the municipal level, set the levels for deductibles, co-payments, and reimbursement caps according to local economic levels. The system is financed by premiums from both employers and employees.

A4.2 Basic Medical Insurance for Urban Residents

This insurance provides medical coverage for primary and secondary school students, young children, and other unemployed urban residents on a voluntary basis. The primary purpose is to provide coverage for urban residents without formal employment and to eliminate impoverishment resulting from catastrophic expenditures. This insurance system was expanded nationwide, until it gradually extended to all unemployed urban residents by 2010. It is financed mostly by participant premiums, although the government also provides some subsidies. The premium of the policy is determined by local governments according to local economic and medical care expense levels.

A4.3 New Rural Cooperative Medical Insurance

In 2003, the New Cooperative Medical Scheme (NCMS) was launched in rural China following a period of time (since 1985) when the majority of rural residents were not covered by any kind of health insurance. The NCMS is completely voluntary, administrated by county (which has resulted in diversified programs in terms of premiums, coverage, co-payments and deductibles), and funded by both individual contributions and government subsidies. The primary goal of the NCMS is to protect rural households from becoming impoverished due to catastrophic health expenditures. Inpatient services have been covered since its inception. More recently, general outpatient services as well as large outpatient expenses due to certain chronic diseases have started to be reimbursed from the pooling revenue. The NCMS was initially implemented in several pilot counties. By 2013, 802 million rural people were enrolled in the NCMS, accounting for about 98.7 percent of the total rural population. In addition, average per capita funding reached CN¥370.6 per year, the reimbursement rate of inpatient expenses rose to more than 75 percent, and the rate of outpatient expenditure to more than 50 percent. The total number of beneficiaries was 1.9 billion people (National Bureau of Statistics, 2014).

A5 The Education System

The school system of China includes preschool, primary school, junior middle school, senior middle school, college, and graduate school. The majority of schools at and above the primary school level are public schools.

Children normally enroll in primary school at age six or seven following some preschool. Primary school normally lasts five to six years, junior middle school is normally three to four years, senior middle school is three years, college is normally four years (medical school is normally five years), and it takes two to three years to get a master's degree and three additional years to get a doctoral degree. In parallel with senior middle schools, there are secondary professional schools: vocational schools usually provide three or four years of schooling, and technical schools provide three years of schooling. Primary and junior middle schools are free and obligatory in China and

TABLE 20A-6

Government Expenditure on Education in China, 2013

Level of Education	Total enrollment	Total expenditure (unit: CN¥ million)	Expenditure per student (unit: CN¥)
Preschool	40,507,145	86,237.2	2,129
Primary school	95,674,926	764,219.9	7,988
Junior middle school	43,846,297	488,232.3	11,135
Senior middle school	24,004,723	249,962.3	10,413
Tertiary	33,855,900	493,339.1	14,572

Source: Ministry of Education of the People's Republic of China (2014).

are known as "free nine-year compulsory education." There is, however, considerable discrepancy between urban and rural areas in terms of educational attainment. While illiteracy has been virtually eliminated in urban areas since the adoption of "free nine-year compulsory education" and the strict prohibition of child labor, a lack of satisfactory financial support and consequent insufficient educational resources has meant that illiteracy in rural China remains high. Table 20A-6 documents the total enrollment and total expenditure by education level for the year of 2013.

Another reason for relatively poor scholastic attainment in rural China is that although nine-year compulsory education is basically free for all children, textbooks and miscellaneous fees associated with schooling remained unaffordable for many rural parents with multiple children. In response, the Ministry of Finance and the Ministry of Education began jointly to provide free textbooks for children from poor families. In 2001, the government started subsidizing the compulsory education of students from rural poor households with a yearly per capita income lower than CN¥882 yuan. Fees for textbooks and supplies, as well as other miscellaneous fees (e.g., CN¥70 per student per semester for primary school and CN¥90 per student per semester for junior middle school) were exempted. In addition, boarders began to receive subsidies for their living expenditures, initially CN¥750 per student per year and then adjusted to CN¥1,000 per year for primary school students and CN¥1,250 per year for junior middle school students. In 2005, central and local governments together spent more than CN¥7 billion on funding 34 million students from poor rural families (Ministry of Education of the People's Republic of China). Up until 2007, all poor rural households were covered by this program.

A6 Agricultural Subsidy

So as to increase farmers' income levels, beyond the abolition of agricultural tax, the central government provides subsidies to farmers, mainly in the form of grain and agricultural input subventions. In 2002, grain subsidy policies were implemented in several major grain-producing areas, including the provinces of Jilin, Anhui, Henan, and Hubei. The grain subsidy is either fixed, based on historical grain plantings, or tied to current market prices or yearly production. In most areas, the fixed subsidy is adopted. There is also an agricultural input subvention that subsidizes high-quality seeds and agricultural machines. The input subsidy is paid to companies selling agricultural inputs, through which the subsidies are supposed to be passed on to farmers.

Appendix 20B

Consumption Tax Rate

TABLE 20B-1
Consumption Tax Rates (2013)

Taxable items	Tax rates
Tobacco	
Grade A cigarettes	56% + CN¥0.003/item
Grade B cigarettes	36% + CN¥0.003/item
Cigars	36%
Cut tobacco	30%
Wholesale process of cigarettes	5%
Alcoholic drinks and alcohol	
White spirit	20% + CN¥0.5/500ml
Yellow wine	CN¥240/ton
Type A beer	CN¥250/ton
Type B beer	CN¥220/ton
Other alcoholic drinks	10%
Alcohol	5%
Cosmetics	30%
Fine jewelry and precious gems	
Gold, silver and platinum jewelry; diamond and diamond jewelry	5%
Other fine jewelry and precious stones	10%
Firecrackers and fireworks	15%
Refined oil	
Leaded gasoline	CN¥0.28/liter
Unleaded gasoline	CN¥0.20/liter
Diesel, aviation kerosene, fuel oil	CN¥0.10/liter
Naphtha, solvent oil, lubricating oil	CN¥0.20/liter
Auto tires	3%

Taxable items	Tax rates
Motorcycle	
Cylinder capacity <= 250ml	3%
Cylinder capacity > 250ml	10%
Automobile	
Cylinder capacity <= 1 liter	1%
1 < cylinder capacity <= 1.5 liter	3%
1.5 < cylinder capacity <= 2 liter	5%
2 < cylinder capacity <= 2.5 liter	9%
2.5 < cylinder capacity <= 3 liter	12%
3 < cylinder capacity <= 4 liter	25%
cylinder capacity > 4 liter	40%
Light/medium bus	5%
Golf and golf club	10%
High-end watch	20%
Yacht	10%
Disposable wood chopstick	5%
Hardwood floor	5%

Source: State Council Order No.539 (Regulations on Consumption Tax, revised version since November 2008); Notice on Adjusting the Consumption Tax Policy of Tobacco Products, 2009, State Taxation Administration.

Note: The table reports effective consumption tax rates for 2013. Grade A cigarettes are those with a transfer price above CN¥70/carton. Grade B cigarette are those with a transfer price below CN¥70/carton. Type A Beer are those with an ex works price above CN¥3,000/ton. Type B Beer are those with an ex works price below CN¥3,000/ton. High-end watch is one that is priced above CN¥10,000 (excluding VAT).

Chapter 21

ARGENTINA

Fiscal Policy, Income Redistribution, and Poverty Reduction in Argentina

Juan Cruz Lopez Del Valle, Caterina Brest Lopez,
Joaquin Campabadal, Julieta Ladronis, Nora Lustig,
Valentina Martinez Pabon, and Mariano Tommasi

Introduction

Argentina is an upper-middle-income country with relatively low levels of inequality and poverty by Latin American standards. In 2017 the Gini coefficient was 0.418 and the poverty rate 6 percent. The averages for Latin America were 0.486 and 23.7 percent, respectively.[1] Applying the methodology described in Volume 1 of this Handbook (Lustig, 2022b), we carry out a fiscal incidence analysis to assess the extent to which the fiscal system reduces inequality and poverty in Argentina. We present indicators of the effects of fiscal policy on inequality and poverty at the aggregate level and for specific taxes and transfers, including in-kind transfers.

Our analysis addresses the impact of taxes and government transfers on inequality and poverty. It tries to identify who wins and who loses and which taxes and spending categories are more or less equalizing. We explore how progressive government spending on cash transfers, education, and health services is and consider the leakages to the non-poor of the different spending programs.

The Argentine fiscal system reduces the Gini coefficient from 0.477 to 0.308 (a 16.9 Gini points reduction) and the incidence of poverty from 12.4 to 6 percent (a reduction of 6.4 percentage points).[2] To put these results in perspective, we compare with other countries with similar levels of development: Brazil, Chile, Mexico, Poland, Rus-

---

[1] CEQ data and the US$5.5 per day (2011 PPP) poverty line are used to calculate these indexes.

[2] The results reported here correspond to the case in which we treat Pensions as Deferred Income (PDI). We also carry the analysis treating Pensions as Government Transfers (PGT), which can be

sia, and Uruguay.[3] The average decline in inequality and poverty for the Latin American countries is 12 Gini and −0.6 percentage points; for the other comparator countries, 10.1 and 1.1.[4]

Thus, Argentina is an outlier in how much inequality and poverty are reduced through fiscal redistribution. However, one's enthusiasm is curbed as soon as one compares the amount of government spending it takes to achieve it. In 2017, public spending was 42.9 percent of GDP, while the average for the comparator Latin American and other upper-middle-income countries was 20.7 percent and 37.5 percent. The Argentine state is the largest in Latin America and similar to that observed in advanced countries with large welfare states. In fact, the large redistributive impact in Argentina is the result mainly of its size and not of its overall progressivity. While there are spending items that are quite progressive and even pro-poor, taxes are unequalizing, and a number of subsidies benefit mainly the rich.

Even though purely macroeconomic implications are not the focus of this study, in order to put redistributive policies in adequate perspective, we must recognize that such high levels of spending have had large macroeconomic costs and that such poor macroeconomic performance has had a heavy toll in terms of poverty. Revenues have not kept up with spending, and, thus, fiscal deficit and indebtedness are high. Between 2007 and 2017, the fiscal deficit went up 7 GDP points (from −1 percent to almost 6 percent), the external debt grew 45 percent, and GDP per capita grew only 5 percent! The large fiscal deficit has caused recurrent crises and high inflation rates (the annual inflation rate was never lower than 10 percent, reaching tops of over 48 percent). High inflation is a tax whose incidence is known to be unequalizing given that the affluent have better ways to cope and avoid such a tax (Ahumada and others, 1993; Canavese and others, 1999). High tax burdens have caused distortions and inefficiencies, while large government transfers have created disincentives to work. All these factors have hampered growth. Gasparini, Cicowiez, and Sosa Escudero (2012) and Gasparini, Tornarolli, and Gluzmann (2019) convincingly show that economic growth is strongly correlated with poverty reduction, suggesting that economic growth is the main driver of changes in poverty in the long term. A counterfactual exercise suggests that, had Argentina grown the last several decades like the average country in Latin America, poverty (by the national poverty line), would have been 14 percent instead of 35 percent. Had it grown like the fastest growing country in the region, Chile, it would have been only 5 percent.

---

found in the online appendix. For the PGT scenario, the inequality reduction is of 21.1 Gini points from 0.519 to 0.308, and poverty reduction of 11.8 percentage points from 17.9 to 6.1 percent.

[3] The information for the rest of the countries is available in the CEQ Data Center on Fiscal Redistribution that has results for over fifty countries applying the *same* methodology worldwide.

[4] For the PGT scenario, the decline for Latin American countries' Gini and poverty rate is 13.7 and 3.4 percentage points. For the other comparator countries, the analogous numbers are 21.9 and 15.9.

Given the inefficiencies and unsustainable nature associated with the Argentine fiscal system, a logical follow-up question is, what needs to change? In particular, how should taxes, transfers, and subsidies be reformed to reduce their costs, while at the same time protecting the poor and keeping the system as equalizing as possible? This crucial question is beyond the scope of this chapter. Nevertheless, on first approximation, it would seem that price subsidies that benefit the rich are promising candidates for reform.

There have been a few other fiscal incidence studies for Argentina—for example, Gasparini (1998, 1999), SPE (2002), SPER (1999), Gomez Sabaini and Rossignolo (2009), Gomez Sabaini and others (2013), Lustig and Pessino (2014), Rossignolo (2022) (chapter 11 in Volume 1 of this Handbook), and Cruces and others (2018)—on which the present work is based. Given the significant differences in dates, scope, methodologies, and indicators, a review of results from previous studies would not be a useful exercise: we would unable to assess whether the system became more or less redistributive over time or to identify the methodological assumptions that most affect results since so many of them change in tandem. Thus, no attempt is made to compare our findings with those of previous studies.

1 Fiscal Incidence Analysis: Methodological Highlights

This chapter uses incidence analysis, a description of who benefits from government spending and who is burdened by taxation, following the methods developed by the Commitment to Equity (CEQ) Institute and detailed in Volume 1 of the *Commitment to Equity Handbook* (Lustig, 2022b). Although it is possible to use incidence analysis to examine one particular expenditure or tax, the thrust of the CEQ analysis is to get a comprehensive picture of the redistributive effect of as many tax and expenditure items as possible. Since this analysis has been performed in many countries, it enables cross-country comparisons.

In order to do that, it is necessary to construct income concepts that incorporate the effect of fiscal interventions. Figure 21-1 shows the four core income concepts used: prefiscal income, Disposable Income, Consumable Income, and Final Income.

The analysis is carried out for two concepts of prefiscal income depending on the treatment of contributory pensions. If pensions are treated as a pure *government transfer* (PGT), the prefiscal income is Market Income. If pensions are treated as *deferred income* (PDI), the prefiscal income is Market Income + Pensions. These two scenarios are shown on the right- and left-hand sides of figure 21-1. Choosing which scenario best suits the reality of a country requires analyzing the deficit of the pension system. Systems with large deficits tend to think of pensions as government transfers. In the PDI scenario pensions are thought of as forced savings made by individuals during their working years. Individuals in this setting "defer" a part of their current income to the moment they enter retirement. For this to be true, pensions received by individuals must be financed mostly by past contributions. When a pension system's deficit be-

FIGURE 21-1
CEQ Income Concepts

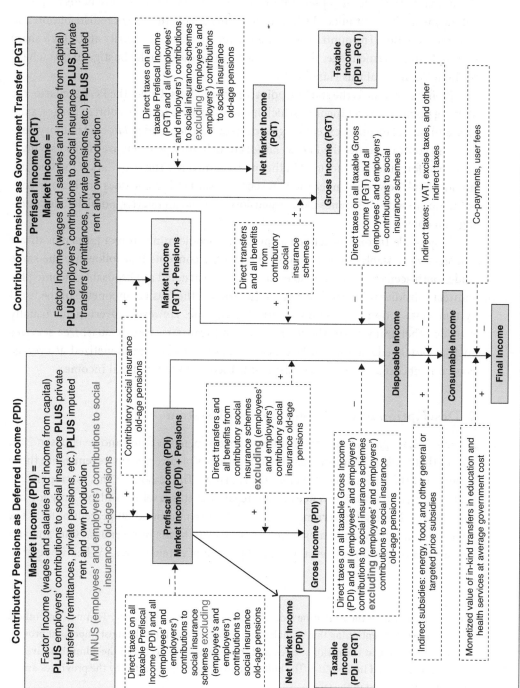

Source: Adapted from Lustig and Higgins (2022) (chapter 1 in this Volume).

come large, this mechanism ceases to hold. The importance of which scenario is used lies in that both the level of prefiscal income and the ranking of households by prefiscal income is different under PGT and PDI. This affects the size of redistribution and poverty reduction. In countries with high coverage of social security and a high share of people in retirement age, this difference can be quite high (Lustig, 2022a) (chapter 10 in Volume 1 of this Handbook).

Prefiscal income is the starting point for the analysis. Under the PGT scenario, the starting point is Market Income, which includes income from all sources (wages, salaries, and capital income), except for government transfers and *public* contributory pensions. In contrast, under the PDI scenario, contributory pensions are "forced savings" and, therefore, they *are* included in the prefiscal income. The two Market Incomes are not identical, however. Under the PDI scheme, Market Income does not include contributions to social insurance old-age pensions to avoid an intertemporal double counting of income.

Disposable Income is defined as prefiscal income minus direct taxes plus direct transfers. Disposable Income and all the income concepts that follow are the same under both scenarios. Consumable Income is constructed as Disposable Income plus indirect subsidies minus indirect taxes. In terms of the "cash component" of the fiscal system, state action ends with Consumable Income. However, governments usually provide other transfers in the form of in-kind transfers: free or quasi-free services such as public education and healthcare. These transfers are monetized at average government cost and added to Consumable Income to obtain Final Income.

2 Description of the Argentine Fiscal System

In table 21-1, we present the composition of government spending and revenues in 2017. Notice that while expenditure data include all levels of government, revenues are those collected at the national level (before tax sharing). The reason for this discrepancy is that information on tax revenues disaggregated at this level is available only for national taxes. National government revenues represent around 80 percent of total tax collection and include the most important taxes in terms of revenues.[5] Our analysis captures 53 percent of tax revenue and 70 percent of expenditures.[6] When we refer to

---

[5] For the intricacies of the Argentine federal fiscal system see, for instance, Tommasi and others (2001). It is worth mentioning that a small share of Ingresos Brutos, the most important provincial tax, is collected at the national level, and this is what is reflected in the administrative accounts' data reported in table 21-1. The bulk of its revenues are collected by the provinces and is therefore not included in the table.

[6] These figures are somewhat lower than the, on average, 84 percent and 81 percent captured by the analyses carried in the comparator countries. This difference may be due to the greater level of precision of our allocation methodology.

TABLE 21-1
Revenues and Expenditure (% of GDP)

	% Administrative	% Analysis	Methodology
Tax Revenues			
Direct taxes	14.4	8.2	. . .
Social security contributions	6.8	5.6	S
Corporate income tax	3.2	n.c.	n.c.
Personal income tax	1.6	0.9	S
Health contributions	1.3	1.2	S
Payroll taxes	0.8	0.5	S
Other income taxes	0.5	n.c.	n.c.
Other direct taxes	0.2	n.c.	n.c.
Indirect taxes	10.3	5.9	. . .
VAT	7.2	3.9	AS and I
Customs duties	1.3	n.c.	n.c
Fuel tax	1.0	0.3	AS and I
Excise taxes	0.7	0.5	AS and I
Ingresos Brutos	0.2	1.1	AS and I
Other indirect taxes	0.0	n.c.	n.c.
Other tax revenues	1.9	n.c.	n.c.
Expenditures			
Pensions	7.9	5.2	. . .
Contributory pensions	7.9	5.2	AS and I
Direct transfers	7.3	4.9	. . .
Moratoria	2.9	2.4	AS and I
Other direct transfers	1.8	n.c.	. . .
PNC	1.0	1.1	AS and I
AAFF	0.8	0.7	S and I
AUH	0.6	0.5	S and I
Progresar	0.1	0.1	S and I
Community kitchens	0.1	0.1	AS and I
Unemployment insurance	0.0	0.0	S and I
Educational scholarships	0.0	0.0	DI and I
JMyMT	0.0	0.0	S and I
Capacitacion y Empleo	0.0	0.0	S and I
Subsidies	4.9	2.1	. . .
Electricity	n.a.	1.1	DI, AS and I
Gas	n.a.	0.4	DI, AS and I
Bus	n.a.	0.4	DI, AS and I
Bottled gas	n.a.	0.1	DI, AS and I
Train	n.a.	0.1	DI, AS and I
Education	5.2	4.8	. . .
Initial			
Primary	3.9	3.9	DI and I
Secondary			
Tertiary	1.3	0.9	DI and I

(*continued*)

TABLE 21-1   (continued)

	% Administrative	% Analysis	Methodology
Health	6.7	6.9	. . .
PAMI	3.0	3.1	AS and I
Social security health insurance	2.7	2.8	AS and I
Public health care	0.9	0.9	AS and I
Other expenditures	2.2	n.c.	. . .

Source: Administrative: Ministry of Economy, AFIP, and National Social Security Administration (ANSES). Analysis: Authors' own calculations.

Notes: n.a. = not available; . . . = not applicable; n.c. = not calculated. PNC = Pensiones No Contributivas. AAFF = Asignaciones Familiares. AUH = Asignacion Universal por Hijo. JMyMT = Jovenes con Mas y Mejor Trabajo. PAMI = Programa de Atencion Medica Integral. S = Simulation. AS = Alternate Survey. DI = Direct Identification. I = Imputation. Methodology follows taxonomy described in Enami, Higgins, and Lustig (2022) (chapter 6 in Volume 1 of this Handbook). Expenditure data includes all central, state, provincial, regional, and local government units, among others, while tax revenues are those collected at the national level before fiscal co-participation.

"size" below, we mean revenue and taxes as they come from administritative accounts, with some exceptions.

2.1 Tax Revenues

Revenues from **direct taxes** (14.4 percent of GDP) seem high compared to similar countries.[7] However, when we exclude social security and health contributions, they are not particularly high (6.3 percent) compared to those of similar countries (4.9 percent) or to the overall size of the Argentinean government. The most important components of tax revenues are social security contributions (6.8 percent), corporate income tax (3.2 percent), and personal income tax (1.6 percent).

The personal income tax is a global tax with progressive rates, based on a scale of a fixed amount plus a rate that increases up to 35 percent. Two categories of individuals pay income tax: salaried workers and the self-employed. Self-employed taxpayers can be classified as *monotributistas* or *autónomos*. *Monotributistas* are subject to a simplified tax regime. They pay a unique monthly contribution that includes contributions to social security and health. Federal Administration of Public Revenues (Administración Federal de Ingresos Públicos, AFIP) classifies part of the revenues from the *monotributo* as "social security revenues" and the rest as "tax revenues." For our analysis, *autónomos* are sole owners or partners of companies, with several categories depending on type of activity and annual gross income.

---

[7] The data is supplied by the Federal Administration of Public Revenues (Administración Federal de Ingresos Públicos, AFIP). Based on information availability, some taxes (such as corporate) were not included in our analysis.

Payroll taxes (0.8 percent of GDP) are taxes levied on salaries. Given the size of social security, contributions to the system (8.1 percent) are a particularly important source of revenue.

There are several types of **indirect taxes**, levied on the purchases of goods and services. The value-added tax (VAT) is the most significant (7.2 percent of GDP). There is an almost universal 21 percent rate applied to most goods. Lower rates, from 0 percent to 10.5 percent, are applied to certain foods and electronics, while a higher rate of 27 percent is applied to telecommunications and electricity. There are some exempt items such as books and newspapers.

Another important group of indirect taxes are fuel taxes (1 percent of GDP). There are three main fuel taxes: one on diesel oil at 22 percent, one on gasoline at 4 percent, and, most important, one on fuel transfer and import. The rate for the latter—from 17.1 percent to 63 percent—depends on the type of fuel. Excise taxes (0.7 percent of GDP) are levied on goods such as tobacco-related products, alcoholic beverages, and vehicles.

Ingresos Brutos (0.2 percent of GDP) is a percentage of firm/personal invoicing, independently of profit collected by provinces. Rates vary from 1.5 percent to 5 percent, with 3.5 percent average. Even though it is an important source of provincial income, it has a cascading effect and double counting problems, which make it a very inefficient tax.

2.2 Expenditures

As can be seen in figure 21-2, Argentina ranks first in social spending among the comparator sample of upper-middle-income countries. The social security system consists of contributory pensions, non-contributory pensions, and other direct transfers.

2.2.1 Pensions

The Argentine **contributory pensions** system is one of the oldest in the region, and it has suffered a series of fundamental changes, including privatization in 1994 and renationalization in 2008. It consists of an Integrated Retirement and Pension System (Sistema Integrado Previsional Argentino, SIPA) administered by the National Social Security Administration (Administración Nacional de la Seguridad Social, ANSES), as well as a number of pensions regimes not included in SIPA, such as pensions for several armed and security forces, and some remaining provincial workers' pension regimes. Contributory pensions amounted to 7.9 percent of GDP in 2017 (figure 21-3).

In 2005, the government relaxed the conditions to get a pension through a number of laws collectively known as the Moratoria. These laws allowed people of retirement age who had not contributed to social security for the required thirty years of

FIGURE 21-2

Social Spending and Taxes (% of GDP) by Country and Year

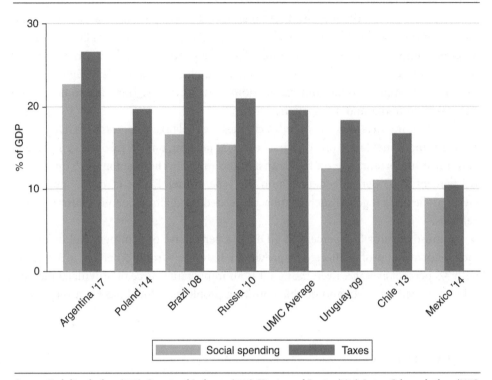

Sources: Bucheli and others (2013); Goraus and Inchauste (2016); Higgins and Pereira (2014); Lopez-Calva and others (2017); Martinez-Aguilar (2019); and Scott and others (2017).

Notes: Social spending includes expenditure on direct transfers, education, and health, as well as other social spending. It does not include contributory pensions or indirect subsidies. UMIC = upper middle income countries.

formal employment—even those who had never contributed—to receive a pension. The beneficiaries of these programs usually receive a transfer equivalent to the minimum pension of the contributory system minus a deduction based on the period of unpaid contributions.[8] Additionally, since Law 27,260 (Reparación Histórica) was passed in 2016, a benefit is offered to anyone over sixty-five who does not meet the requirements for a contributory pension. These programs amounted to 2.9 percent of GDP in 2017 (figure 21-3).

---

[8] In appendix 21A we show that the Moratoria was behind a number of cases of households with zero income. This is due not only to the fact that the beneficiaries of Moratoria were pensioners at the time but also to the fact that they were mainly woman who had informal jobs or were housewives.

FIGURE 21-3

Old-Age Pensions (% of GDP) by Country and Year

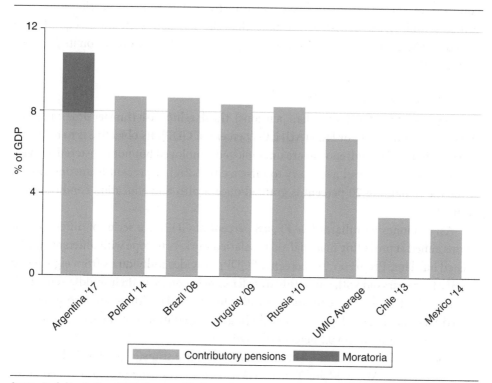

Sources: Bucheli and others (2013); Goraus and Inchauste (2016); Higgins and Pereira (2014); Lopez-Calva and others (2017); Martinez-Aguilar (2019); and Scott and others (2017).

Note: UMIC = upper middle income countries.

There are also social assistance programs, which in Argentina are called Pensiones No Contributivas (PNCs). The bulk of these PNCs are disability pensions and pensions for mothers of seven children or more, but there are also special laws for former soldiers and political prisoners, and *ex-gratia* pensions granted by Congress. The size of these programs, which are administered in a more discretionary manner, has been increasing since 2004, and in 2017 there were almost 1.5 million beneficiaries, amounting to 1.0 percent of GDP.

As we will explain in the next section on methodology, in the incidence analysis we treat the contributory pensions as deferred income and the Moratoria pensions as direct transfers. In spite of that, from a macroeconomic perspective and from the point of view of intergenerational dynamics, they have similar effects. Considering both types of old-age pensions jointly, we find that the total amount spent climbs up to 10.8 percent, making Argentina the country that spends the most in pensions among comparator countries (figure 21-3).[9] Considering Argentina's pension system as a whole, we find that the size of expenditures exceeds not only those of similar countries but also the system's revenues (mostly social security contributions). Cetrangolo and Grushka (2020) estimate that the pension system's disequilibrium would still be of around 3 percent of GDP by 2050, which casts doubts on its financial sustainability.

2.2.2 Other Direct Transfers

Among direct transfers (other than pensions), the flagship cash transfer program is the Asignacion Universal por Hijo (AUH; 0.6 percent of GDP). Its objective is to help parents of school-age children who are unemployed, employed but not registered, or have earnings below the level necessary to raise a child. Eighty percent is unconditional, while the remaining 20 percent is granted once health and education conditions are verified.

Asignaciones Familiares (AAFF; 0.8 percent of GDP) is a series of different programs aimed at providing financial aid to salaried workers to cope with different family-related burdens. Progresar (0.1 percent of GDP) provides individuals from eighteen to twenty-four years old with a monthly transfer to help complete their middle-school education. The transfer has conditions similar to the AUH's. There are also programs aimed at combating food insecurity, including aiding community kitchens, and related programs that amount to 0.1 percent of GDP.

There exists a fixed-sum unemployment insurance transfer (with very low coverage). Jovenes con Mas y Mejor Trabajo (JMyMT) is a training program aimed at including young adults in the labor market. Capacitacion y Empleo is another fixed-sum transfer for unemployed individuals, compatible with programs like the AUH but not with the unemployment insurance.

2.2.3 Indirect Subsidies

Indirect subsidies (4.9 percent of GDP) are benefits in the form of reduced prices for specific goods and services, mainly electricity, gas, and transportation. While many of them are across-the-board price subsidies, Tarifa Social provides additional targeted financial help, conditional on some eligibility requirements.

There are several consumption-price subsidies for electricity and gas. One is a fund financed through charge on the consumer price of gas. These funds are distributed unevenly across regions, with some subsidized, and others taxed. There are also direct subsidies to gas companies to cover the cost of price controls. Bottled gas consumption

---

[9] To the best of our knowledge, none of the comparator countries has any program with characteristics similar to the Moratoria. In Argentina 3.2 out of 6.3 million pension benefits correspond to the Moratoria.

is subsidized for families who do not have access to the gas network, depending on income and other vulnerability conditions.[10]

Transportation by train and bus is subsidized. In the case of train, as the state owns the company, it charges artificially low prices. In 2017, the state subsidized 50 pesos for each train ticket.

2.2.4 In-Kind Transfers

Education

Public schools and universities are financed entirely by the government, and the service is free to students. Private schools also receive a subsidy from the state, intended to cover professors' salaries, which are the main cost of the whole system. Primary and secondary education are in the hands of the provinces, but some financing, such as said subsidies to private schools, comes from national funds. Seventy percent of primary schools across the country receive some kind of state subsidy, and these institutions account for 93 percent of primary students. Seventy-seven percent of high schools, accounting for 95 percent of high school students, received aid. State financing of education is vast. At 5.2 percent, Argentina ranks second in expenditure in education as a percentage of GDP in the sample of upper-middle-income countries, as shown in figure 21-4.

Health

In-kind public transfers in health belong to two broad categories: the coverage of the formal protection system and the public healthcare subsystem.[11]

The social insurance subsystem includes the National Institute of Social Services for Retirees and Pensioners (Instituto Nacional de Servicios Sociales para Jubilados y Pensionados, INSSJyPJ). This institute offers a Comprehensive Medical Assistance Program (Programa de Atencion Medica Integral, PAMI) to the elderly.

The second component is the coverage of the formal social protection system—that is, the coverage for formal workers—through the social security health insurance system (Obras Sociales), including both provincial and national plans. Workers (and their employers) also finance this system through their contributions. As a result, formal workers are entitled to receive a health insurance plan.

The public healthcare subsystem consists of subsidized medical attention services provided by government entities. This is accomplished in two ways: (1) by a supply subsidy structure, which includes hospitals and primary care clinics throughout the

---

[10] There are also supply-side subsidies to gas, which we are not able to calculate due to the obsolescence of accessible data, in particular the fact that the most recent input matrix available is from more than a decade ago.

[11] For a more detailed description see Gragnolati and others (2015).

FIGURE 21-4

Education Expenditure (% of GDP) by Country and Year

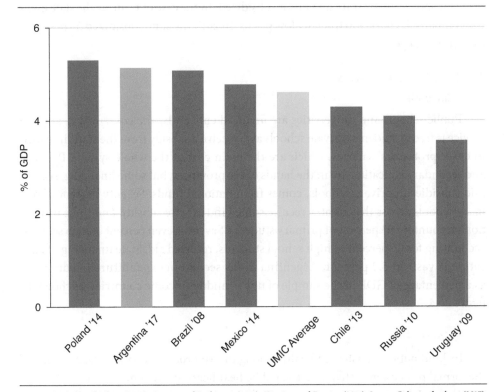

Sources: Bucheli and others (2013); Goraus and Inchauste (2016); Higgins and Pereira (2014); Lopez-Calva and others (2017); Martinez-Aguilar (2019); and Scott and others (2017).

Note: UMIC = upper middle income countries.

country, and (2) by a program called Include Health, former Federal Health Care Program (PROFE), which provides coverage to beneficiaries of non-contributory pensions.

This complex system amounts to nearly 7 percent of GDP. As we can see in figure 21-5, Argentina ranks first in the size of health spending among comparable countries.

3 Data and Methodology

3.1 Data

The main source of information of the analysis is the household survey Encuesta Permanente de Hogares (EPH). The EPH is an urban survey that covers 63 percent of the population and includes information on household and individual income, cash transfers, and personal characteristics including education and employment status. It does not include information on consumption. Since our exercise needs to cover the entire

FIGURE 21-5
Health Expenditure (% of GDP) by Country and Year

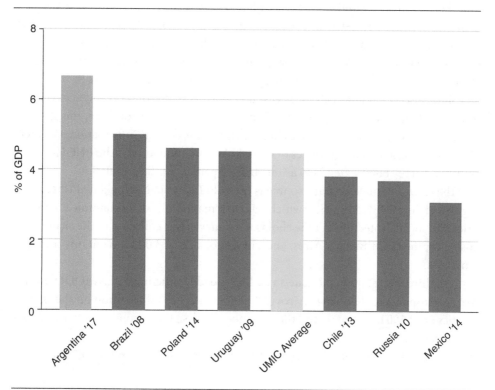

Sources: Bucheli and others (2013); Goraus and Inchauste (2016); Higgins and Pereira (2014); Lopez-Calva and others (2017); Martinez-Aguilar (2019); and Scott and others (2017).

Note: UMIC = upper middle income countries.

population, we assume that the remaining 37 percent of the population is similar to those individuals in the survey. We adjust the sampling weights to make the total population in the survey equal the total population in the country.[12]

Since Argentina has a medium-high inflation regime, purchasing power can change significantly throughout the time the data is being surveyed. To adjust for inflation, we convert all prices to December 2017 values.

There is significant item nonresponse for incomes in the EPH.[13] To deal with item nonresponse, we imputed the missing data applying hot-deck methodology. This

---

[12] This strong assumption is the same approach followed by previous similar efforts (Cruces and others, 2018; Rossignolo, 2022). We leave for future research to explore alternative ways of obtaining information from the population that is not covered by the EPH.

[13] For instance, depending on individual characteristics, the proportion of individuals who did not respond to the question on main source of income ranges from 12.5 percent (for salaried workers) to as much as 30.9 percent (for employers).

method consists of imputing a missing value from a randomly selected record of individuals with similar characteristics.[14]

There are also a number of cases of households with zero income. We analyzed their characteristics to determine whether the income reported is plausible or if it is an error. Most of these households are inactive individuals, students, under-age, and pensioners who receive the Moratoria or a non-contributory pension (see appendix 21A). Hence, we conclude that these reported zero prefiscal incomes are correct.

Since we cannot obtain all the necessary information for the core income concepts from the EPH, we resort to three complementary surveys. One of them, the 2017–018 Encuesta Nacional de Gastos de los Hogares (ENGHo), collects information on expenditure, income, and characteristics of households and individuals. The ENGHo is also an urban survey but it extends to as much as 92 percent of the population.

The second complementary source is the 2015 Encuesta Nacional de Proteccion y Seguridad Social (ENAPROSS), which has information on socioeconomic characteristics and social protection of households. This survey was collected in the city of Buenos Aires, the Great Buenos Aires, and villages of at least 5,000 inhabitants from five provinces.

The third is the 2009–10 Encuesta de Movilidad Domiciliaria (ENMODO) for the Área Metropolitana de Buenos Aires (AMBA), which has information on the characteristics of 22,500 households and their members and on their mobility and use of public transportation.

Finally, we use national administrative and fiscal information for 2017.

3.2 Methodology

For some taxes and transfers, the information for how much a household pays or receives is reported in the EPH. However, direct identification is not always available, so we resort to other allocation methods as suggested in Enami, Lustig, and Higgins (2022) (chapter 6 in Volume 1 of the Handbook). The methods used for each category are summarized in table 21-1 and explained below. In all cases, taxes and transfers were aggregated at the household level to obtain per capita amounts. For more details, see appendix 21B.

3.2.1 Tax Allocation

It is assumed that salaried workers and pensioners report their income net of both pension and non-pension social insurance contributions and personal income tax. For independent workers, it is assumed that they report income net of only non-pension

---

[14] This was the method used by the Instituto Nacional de Estadísticas y Censos (INDEC)—the Argentine statistical institute—prior to 2016. Since missing values are imputed, there is no need to reweight the observations, so we use the uncorrected base weights (called PONDERA). See also Tornarolli (2018).

social insurance contributions. Therefore, it is not possible to directly identify the burden of direct taxes in the EPH, and we simulate them based on the contribution and tax rules.

Since the EPH does not have consumption data, direct identification for indirect taxes is not possible. We use the ENGHo to estimate the burden of the different indirect taxes. Consumption taxes are assumed to be shifted forward to consumers. Evasion is implicitly taken into account by using effective rates rather than statutory rates.

3.2.2 Pensions as Deferred Income or Government Transfer (PDI or PGT)

Deciding which way pensions should be treated in Argentina's case is not straightforward. The system's disequilibrium (expenditure minus revenues as a share of revenues) is around 40 percent (Cetrangolo and Grushka, 2020). However, 57 percent of this disequilibrium is explained solely by Moratoria, while the remaining 43 percent is due to contributory pensions and special regimes. In fact, if we only consider contributory pensions, the disequilibrium is around 7 percent.

For practical purposes, in this analysis we take the PDI scenario as closer to Argentina's situation in 2017—provided we treat the Moratoria as non-contributory and hence as a transfer—but we believe the reality lies somewhere in between the two extreme scenarios. For this reason, we run both scenarios (PGT results can be found in the online appendix) and leave the development of a tool that allows for an incidence analysis in a more realistic hybrid scenario for future research.

3.2.3 Public Spending Allocation

In the EPH, one can identify if an individual is receiving a pension, but since contributory and non-contributory pensions are lumped together, it is not possible to independently distinguish one from the other.[15] Thus, we resort to the ENAPROSS to identify the beneficiaries of each type of pension and then match the pension markers back to the main survey. The amount received is then imputed according to the law's rules.

It is not possible to directly identify the beneficiaries of cash transfers in the EPH, and the availability of information necessary to simulate the impact of each program varies. One question on the amount received from social programs lumps all of them together. Hence, we take different approaches and assumptions for each program. Below, we summarize the two most important direct transfers; for the rest of the programs see appendix 21B.

For the AUH we make use of the program's rules to identify recipients in EPH and simulate the impact of the program.[16] Once they are identified, we use information on the statutory amount of the program given to beneficiaries to impute the corresponding value. We impute only the 80 percent unconditional part.

---

[15] Fewer than 1 percent received both pensions, so we assume that individuals have only one.

[16] This has the problem of assuming perfect targeting and no errors of inclusion or exclusion.

For the Moratoria we resort to the ENAPROSS to identify the eligible individuals by decile of the household per capita income and calculate the ratio of beneficiaries to total amount of pensioners per decile. Then, for pensioners in each decile in the EPH, we draw a number from a Bernoulli distribution with probability of success equal to the ratio estimated in the ENAPROSS. The 1s are considered the beneficiaries of the Moratoria. We also identify as beneficiaries those who declare that they receive a pension if the amount reported is significantly lower than the minimum pension (using 4,000 pesos as the cut-off). We take the reported amount as valid.

It is possible to directly identify students from different levels of education in the EPH. Expenditure per student is imputed using administrative data on expenditure and on the number of students. Expenditure per student varies depending on the type of institution (private or public), province, and education level, and it is calculated for each combination of these dimensions.

Since it is not possible to directly identify the type of health insurance in the EPH, we use the ENGHo, where one can determine whether an individual has any form of insurance. We consider all the individuals reporting having no form of insurance as going to public hospitals. Then, we estimate the proportion of individuals who have access to each type of health insurance per quintile of per capita household income. With these proportions, we estimate in the EPH the (rounded) number of people who have each kind of insurance per quintile of the income per capita distribution.

In the EPH, we assign a random number from a uniform distribution over (0, 1) by which we order the individuals in each quintile; we then sequentially assign a form insurance until we cover the estimated proportion of each type. Expenditure per capita is imputed using administrative data on expenditure, and, since there are no official numbers regarding health insurance beneficiaries, we use the total beneficiaries estimated in the ENGHo (with weights corrected to represent the total population).

In order to simulate the amount of subsidy (both general and the Tarifa Social) received in each service, we use the ENGHo in conjunction with the EPH. We first simulate in the EPH potential beneficiaries of these subsidies by ventile of income per capita and classify them according to whether or not they are eligible for the Tarifa Social. If they are eligible, we classify them further by the eligibility condition they meet, the number of eligibility conditions they meet, and the region in which they reside. Then we estimate the quantity of gas and electricity that households consume in the ENGHo. Since there was considerable noise in the reported quantities consumed, we estimated the mean quantities consumed by income ventile and region. The size of the subsidies was estimated as the product of the quantity and imputed subsidy for both the general and the Tarifa Social component.

4 Results

In this section, we quantify the extent to which the fiscal system impacts overall inequality and poverty and identify which components drive the results. To give perspec-

TABLE 21-2

Inequality and Poverty by Income Concept

Measure	Market Income + Pensions	Disposable Income	Consumable Income	Final Income
Gini coefficient	0.477	0.418	0.408	0.308
Theil index	0.371	0.308	0.293	0.173
90/10	12.80	7.643	7.204	3.735
US$5.5 per day (2011 PPP) poverty line				
Headcount index	12.4%	6.0%	6.1%	. . .
Poverty gap	7.2%	2.2%	2.1%	. . .
Sq. poverty gap	5.7%	1.2%	1.1%	. . .
National poverty line				
Headcount index	29.5%	22.2%	24.1%	. . .
Poverty gap	14.3%	8.1%	8.6%	. . .
Sq. poverty gap	9.7%	4.3%	4.4%	. . .

Source: Authors' own calculations.

Note: . . . = not applicable. These measures are calculated for the PDI scenario. Poverty calculations for Final Income are not calculated since they would require a significantly different poverty line. See Lustig and Higgins (2022) (chapter 1 in this Volume).

tive, we compare Argentina with other upper-middle-income countries from the CEQ Data Center of similar income per capita: Brazil, Chile, Mexico, Poland, Russia, and Uruguay.[17]

4.1 The Impact of Fiscal Policy on Inequality and Poverty

To show the impact of taxes and transfers on inequality and poverty, table 21-2 shows inequality measures (Gini coefficient, Theil index, and the 90/10 ratio) and poverty indicators (headcount ratio, poverty gap index, and squared poverty gap index) with standard international poverty lines and the national poverty line.

Argentina's fiscal system features two characteristics that are desirable for equity in the income dimension in the short-run. It is overall progressive (reduces inequality), and it lowers poverty.

The redistributive effect of direct and indirect taxes, direct transfers, and subsidies combined is positive and relatively large, compared with that of other countries. When pensions are treated as deferred income, the Gini coefficient declines by 6.9 Gini

---

[17] Unless otherwise noted, we present results for the scenario of pensions as deferred income. The results for pensions as transfers is available in the online appendix.

points.[18] Most of the decline occurs through the effect of direct transfers net of direct taxes. While the combined effect of indirect taxes and subsidies is still equalizing (which does not happen in many countries), the size of the impact is small in comparison. If one also contemplates the impact of transfers in-kind, the fiscal system is even more equalizing. Compared to the Gini coefficient for Consumable Income, the Gini coefficient for Final Income is 10 points lower. The combined effect of all taxes and all transfers (including in-kind transfers) leads to a reduction of 16.9 Gini points.

The headcount ratio falls significantly for all poverty lines considered. Generous cash transfers are the main driver of this result. Even net of direct taxes, the headcount ratio with the US$5.5 per day (2011 power purchasing parity, PPP) poverty line falls by half of its prefiscal level when pensions are treated as deferred income, and to one third of its prefiscal level when pensions are treated as transfers. The marginal effect of indirect taxes and subsidies on poverty (the difference between Disposable and Consumable Income headcount) is nil when using the international poverty lines. When poverty is measured with the national poverty line, the effect is that poverty increases.

Net payers to the fiscal system are those who live in households that receive less in transfers and subsidies than they pay in taxes—i.e., those whose Consumable Income is lower than their prefiscal income. Net payers in Argentina start at the 6th decile and the more-than US$10 per day (2011 PPP) income category, which means that the extreme poor, moderate poor, and vulnerable to poverty groups are net receivers.[19] Argentina stands out by this high number of net receivers compared with Brazil 2009 (3rd decile), Mexico 2014 (4th decile), and Uruguay 2009 (3rd decile). In Chile and Russia, net payers also start at the middle class.

The estimated reduction in inequality and poverty is quite large, especially compared with the other upper-middle-income countries, as table 21-3 shows. While these results put Argentina seemingly in a bright spot, we will see that the main factor behind these results is the amount of public spending and not its overall progressivity. Tax revenues are quite high, and yet not enough to keep up with problematic spending levels. Even though they are not the direct focus of our analysis, we cannot finish a section on the impact of fiscal policy on poverty without taking these effects into consideration.

Fiscal imbalances have been a key cause in subsequent recessions in recent Argentine macroeconomic history.[20] In the two-year period 2018–19, GDP per person fell by 3 percent. The incidence of poverty rose 8.2 percentage points from 27.3 to 35.5 percent between the first semester of 2018 and the second semester of 2019 (Instituto Nacional de Estadísticas y Censos, 2020). Using the same metric of the national poverty line and Disposable Income, the headcount ratio fell by 6.4 percentage points

---

[18] If pensions are considered a government transfer, the redistributive effect rises to 11.1 Gini points.

[19] Income categories income are standard definitions based on dollars per day (2011 PPP).

[20] See, for instance, Gerchunoff and Llach (2018), Mussa (2002), and Sturzenegger (2019).

TABLE 21-3

Inequality and Poverty by Country and Year

Country	Market Income + Pensions	Disposable Income	Consumable Income	Final Income
Gini coefficient				
Argentina '17	0.477	0.418	0.408	0.308
Brazil '08	0.573	0.545	0.542	0.430
Chile '13	0.494	0.467	0.464	0.419
Mexico '14	0.528	0.494	0.492	0.393
Poland '14	0.412	0.345	0.355	0.291
Russia '10	0.379	0.348	0.351	0.299
Uruguay '08	0.505	0.467	0.468	0.377
US$5.5 per day (2011 PPP) poverty line				
Argentina '17	12.4%	6.0%	6.1%	. . .
Brazil '08	32.0%	30.3%	35.7%	. . .
Chile '13	8.3%	5.3%	6.7%	. . .
Mexico '14	36.3%	36.1%	37.4%	. . .
Russia '10	6.9%	4.9%	5.9%	. . .
Uruguay '08	15.9%	11.5%	15.0%	. . .

Sources: Bucheli and others (2013); Goraus & Inchauste (2016); Higgins & Pereira (2014); Lopez-Calva and others (2017); Martinez-Aguilar (2019); and Scott and others (2017).

Note: . . . = not applicable. Data for Poland not available.

as a result of direct transfers (net of taxes). That is, the recession caused poverty to rise in two years by more than the fiscal system reduced it in 2017. This suggests that redistributive policies can be self-defeating if not anchored in a fiscally prudent framework.

4.2 Determinants: Size, Progressivity, and Reranking

The extent of fiscal redistribution and poverty reduction depends on the size and progressivity of the fiscal system. To see which factor is more important in the Argentine case, we use Lambert's (2001) equation for the overall progressivity of the fiscal system, which equals a weighted sum of the progressivity of taxes and transfers:

$$\Pi_N^{RS} = \frac{(g\,\Pi_T^K + b\,\rho_B^K)}{(1 - g + b)},$$

where Π_N^{RS} is the Reynolds-Smolensky (RS) index of progressivity of the fiscal system ("vertical equity"). In the absence of reranking, RS is identical to the difference

FIGURE 21-6

Social Spending and Subsidies (% of GDP) by Country and Year

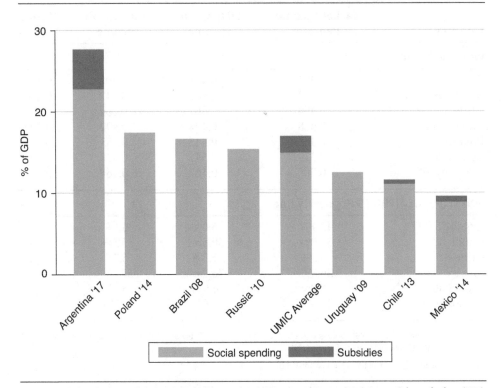

Sources:. Bucheli and others (2013); Goraus and Inchauste (2016); Higgins and Pereira (2014); Lopez-Calva and others (2017); Martinez-Aguilar (2019); and Scott and others (2017).

Notes: Social spending includes expenditure on direct transfers, education, and health, as well as other social spending. It does not include contributory pensions. Subsidies are not available for Poland, Brazil, Russia, and Uruguay. UMIC = upper middle income countries.

between the postfiscal and prefiscal Gini coefficients; g and b are the ratio of taxes and transfers to prefiscal income; and Π_T^K and ρ_B^K are the Kakwani indexes for total taxes and total transfers.[21] This equation can be used to compare the relative importance of size versus progressivity (in the absence of reranking, which we shall assume away for now in analyzing the drivers of fiscal redistribution).

Measured by the ratio of social spending to GDP (even leaving out contributory pensions), Argentina's fiscal system is the largest among similar countries (figure 21-6).

Regarding progressivity as measured by the Kakwani index, table 21-4 shows that direct taxes in Argentina are the least progressive except for those in Russia. Indirect

---

[21] The Kakwani index for tax (transfer) is defined as the (negative of the) difference between the concentration coefficient for the tax (transfer) in question and the Gini coefficient. A positive (negative) Kakwani index means that the tax or transfer is progressive (regressive).

TABLE 21-4
Kakwani Index by Country and Year

Country	Gini coefficient	Direct taxes	Direct transfers	Indirect taxes	Subsidies	All taxes	Education	Health	SS + subsidies
						Kawkani Index			
Argentina '17	0.477	0.132	0.738	-0.088	0.352	-0.021	0.633	0.489	0.578
Brazil '08	0.573	0.169	0.464	-0.025	0.712	0.046	0.711	0.690	0.647
Chile '13	0.494	0.143	0.824	-0.027	0.497	0.025	0.664	0.592	0.674
Mexico '14	0.528	0.167	0.852	-0.005	0.060	0.104	0.608	0.466	0.539
Russia '10	0.379	0.116	0.594	-0.066	0.173	0.020	0.510	0.371	0.472
Uruguay '09	0.505	0.151	0.979	-0.050	n.a.	0.042	0.668	0.608	0.684
Average	**0.493**	**0.146**	**0.742**	**-0.043**	**0.359**	**0.036**	**0.633**	**0.536**	**0.599**

Sources: Bucheli and others (2013); Goraus & Inchauste (2016); Higgins & Pereira (2014); Lopez-Calva and others (2017); Martínez-Aguilar (2019); and Scott and others (2017).

Notes: n.a. = Not available. Gini coefficient is calculated for Market Income + Pensions. Data for Poland not available.

taxes are the most regressive in Argentina. All taxes combined are regressive only for Argentina.[22] Direct transfers are relatively progressive but less so than in Uruguay, Mexico, and Chile, while subsidies are the least progressive. In the case of education spending, Argentina is among the most progressive. For health, the country is among the less progressive group.

Thus, the large impact on inequality and poverty observed in Argentina is driven primarily by the large amount of resources devoted to social spending and subsidies. The poor performance in terms of progressivity on some of the spending components must mean that a nontrivial portion of resources is spent on the non-poor. As we shall see, this is particularly true for subsidies.

Beyond low progressivity, another factor that can weaken the redistributive power of taxes and transfers is the presence of reranking. Reranking, the swapping of individuals in the distribution, is considered a measure of horizontal inequity and of "waste" in the redistributive machinery. The reranking effect for all taxes and transfers equals 0.022. To put this in perspective, we take the ratio of this effect to the redistributive and the vertical equity effects. These ratios equal 13 percent and 12 percent. Comparing these with other countries in table 21-5, we observe that the extent of reranking is much lower than Russia's, much higher than Uruguay's, and similar to Brazil's, Chile's, and Mexico's. Argentina's fiscal system does not seem to feature more reranking than comparable countries.[23]

4.3 Components of the Fiscal System: Marginal Contributions, Pro-Poorness, and Leakages to the Non-Poor

The previous section analyzed the determinants of the broad redistributive effect of the Argentine fiscal system. In this section, using marginal contributions,[24] we focus on identifying which specific taxes, transfers, and subsidies contribute the most to the reduction in inequality and poverty and which ones are most unequalizing. We also assess which specific transfers are more targeted to the poor and which ones allocate an inordinate amount of resources to the non-poor. For this purpose, we look at the concentration coefficients and concentration shares by income category.

Table 21-6 shows that the spending interventions that contribute more to reducing inequality are the Moratoria, the PNC, and the AUH. These are also the programs

---

[22] We carried out a sensitivity analysis to uncover the reasons behind this seemingly odd feature and found that a main driver of this result is the existence of a special program: the Moratoria. For more details, see appendix 21A.

[23] There are countries in which the reranking effect is so large that it takes away the entire redistributive effect. In the CEQ Data Center sample, this occurs in Bolivia and Indonesia.

[24] The marginal contribution of a tax (transfer) is calculated by taking the difference between inequality (or poverty) indicator *without* the tax (transfer) and *with* it.

TABLE 21-5

Redistributive, Vertical Equity, and Reranking Effects by Country and Year

Country	Redistributive Effect (RE)	Vertical Equity Effect (VE)	Reranking Effect	% Reranking over RE	% Reranking over VE
Argentina '17	0.169	0.192	0.022	13	12
Brazil '08	0.143	0.158	0.015	10	9
Chile '13	0.075	0.084	0.009	12	10
Mexico '14	0.135	0.151	0.016	12	11
Russia '10	0.080	0.105	0.025	32	24
Uruguay '09	0.128	0.135	0.007	5	5
Average	**0.122**	**0.137**	**0.010**	**14**	**12**

Sources: Bucheli and others (2013); Goraus & Inchauste (2016); Higgins & Pereira (2014); Lopez-Calva and others (2017); Martinez-Aguilar (2019); and Scott and others (2017).

Note: Data for Poland not available.

that contribute the most to reduce poverty. These results are not surprising because the first two programs are non-contributory pensions whose beneficiaries are likely to have zero or very low prefiscal incomes.[25]

Subsidies are equalizing but to a much lower extent. They are also poverty reducing. One aspect to note is that the marginal contribution of subsidies to poverty reduction increases as we measure it with higher poverty lines. This is telling us that subsidies benefit the moderate poor relatively more than the extreme poor. Regarding in-kind transfers, the most equalizing is public health care and primary and secondary education, in that order. The least equalizing is spending on tertiary education.[26]

On the tax side, excise taxes, fuel taxes, and VAT are outright unequalizing. The most equalizing tax is personal income tax. All taxes by definition are poverty increasing, but the VAT has the highest marginal contribution and by a nontrivial difference from the next in line. The VAT is significantly poverty- increasing for poverty measured by low or higher poverty lines, as shown in the table 21-6.

Regarding payroll taxes, there are concerns about its progressivity. Despite being less so than personal income tax, they are progressive and equalizing, unlike indirect taxes. Figure 21C-10 in the appendix 21C shows that the higher deciles are the ones who pay most of these taxes.

---

[25] Incidence of these programs is broken down by deciles in figures 21C-1 through 21C-3 in appendix 21C. Although incidence as a percentage of prefiscal income declines with income for all three programs, incidence in dollars per capita falls only monotonically with income for the AUH and remains constant after the first decile for the PNC and the Moratoria.

[26] See figures 21C-4 through 21C-9 in appendix 21C.

TABLE 21-6
Marginal Contributions by Program

Budget item	Size (% of Market Income + Pensions)	Concentration coefficient	Kakwani index	Redistribution	Poverty reduction		
				Marginal Contribution (MC)	MC US$3.2	MC US$5.5	MC national
Disposable Income	105.2						
Direct transfers	11.0	−0.261	0.738	0.051	0.056	0.065	0.082
Moratoria	5.4	−0.338	0.815	0.021	0.023	0.026	0.035
PNC	2.5	−0.222	0.699	0.013	0.017	0.019	0.021
AAFF	1.5	0.076	0.401	0.005	0.000	0.001	0.010
AUH	1.1	−0.533	1.010	0.011	0.019	0.021	0.012
Progresar	0.2	0.053	0.424	0.001	0.001	0.001	0.001
Community kitchens	0.2	−0.002	0.479	0.001	0.001	0.000	0.002
Unemployment insurance	0.1	−0.046	0.523	0.000	0.001	0.001	0.001
Scholarships	0.0	−0.221	0.698	0.000	0.000	0.001	0.001
JMyMT	0.0	−0.248	0.725	0.000	0.000	0.000	0.000
Capacitacion y Empleo	0.0	−0.287	0.764	0.000	0.000	0.000	0.000
Direct taxes	5.8	0.609	0.132	0.008	−0.000	−0.002	−0.010
Personal income tax	2.1	0.762	0.285	0.006	0.000	0.000	−0.001
Health contributions	2.6	0.524	0.047	0.001	−0.000	−0.001	−0.007
Payroll taxes	1.1	0.524	0.047	0.000	−0.000	−0.000	−0.003
Consumable Income	96.7						
Subsidies	4.6	0.125	0.352	0.015	0.023	0.018	0.027
Electricity	2.5	0.177	0.300	0.007	0.007	0.007	0.015
Gas	0.9	0.214	0.263	0.002	0.002	0.002	0.005
Bus	0.8	−0.016	0.493	0.004	0.004	0.005	0.007

Bottled gas	0.2	−0.317	0.794	0.002	0.003	0.003	0.004
Train	0.2	0.139	0.338	0.007	0.001	0.000	0.001
Indirect taxes	13.1	0.389	−0.088	−0.014	−0.015	−0.032	−0.063
VAT	8.7	0.382	−0.095	−0.009	−0.008	−0.0194	−0.041
Fuel taxes	0.7	0.279	−0.198	−0.001	−0.001	−0.002	−0.004
Excise taxes	1.1	0.307	−0.170	−0.002	−0.001	−0.002	−0.007
Ingresos Brutos	2.5	0.477	−0.000	−0.000	−0.001	−0.0023	−0.009
Final Income	122.4						
In-kind transfers	25.3	−0.072	0.549	0.106	…	…	…
Initial education	1.0	−0.230	0.708	0.007	…	…	…
Primary education	3.5	−0.264	0.741	0.023	…	…	…
Secondary education	4.1	−0.195	0.672	0.024	…	…	…
Tertiary education	1.9	0.160	0.317	0.005	…	…	…
PAMI	2.0	0.033	0.444	0.008	…	…	…
Social security health insurance	6.7	0.106	0.372	0.023	…	…	…
Public health care	6.0	−0.155	0.632	0.035	…	…	…

Source: Authors' own calculations.

Notes: . . . = not applicable. PNC = Pensiones No Contributivas. AAFF = Asignaciones Familiares. AUH = Asignacion Universal por Hijo. JMyMT = Jovenes con Mas y Mejor Trabajo. PAMI = Programa de Atencion Médica Integral. These measures are calculated for the PDI scenario. Poverty calculations for final income are not calculated since they would require a significantly different poverty line. See Lustig and Higgins (2022).

We consider pro-poor those spending categories that have negative concentration coefficients—per person spending declining with income. The more a program is targeted to the poor, the more negative the concentration coefficient will be. In table 21-6 we see that the pro-poor spending categories are (in decreasing order) the AUH, Moratoria, bottled gas subsidy, Capacitacion y Empleo, JMyMT (youth program), scholarships, PNC, unemployment insurance, community kitchens, and bus subsidies.

While the concentration coefficient gives us a summary measure of pro-poorness, it does not allow us to see the extent to which resources are allocated to the non-poor. In table 21-7 we show the concentration shares by income category—the ultra, extreme, and moderate poor, those vulnerable to poverty, the middle class, and the rich. While the ultra-poor receive a large portion of direct transfers, especially when compared to their population share, the middle class and the rich receive almost 54 percent of what is spent on direct transfers. Thus, there is a considerable amount of "leakage" to the non-poor. Subsidies stand out with their pro-rich spending patterns.[27] The poor and the vulnerable comprise 30 percent of the population and receive only 23.7 percent of subsidies. The middle class is 61 percent of the population and receives 60 percent of subsidies. The rich are 10 percent of the population but receive 16.4 percent of subsidies!

From a public policy point of view, one may wonder how effectively government resources are spent. Figure 21-7 highlights some features that may help answer the question. The circles indicate the size and progressivity for each spending item. The horizontal axis shows the amount of spending as a share of GDP. The vertical axis shows the Kakwani index of progressivity. The size of the circles reflects the magnitude of the marginal contribution: larger marginal contributions are represented by larger circles.[28]

Figure 21-7 raises some important questions regarding the allocation of government resources. Larger programs tend to be more equalizing (larger circles), even if the programs (such as social security health insurance or PAMI) are less progressive. On the other end, there are a number of relatively small (labor and education) programs that are not particularly equalizing—despite being quite progressive—because of their small size. Various utility subsidies (gas, electricity) and tertiary education stand out as the least progressive in spite of being slightly equalizing. AUH, while relatively small, is an outlier in terms of progressivity and manages to be among the most equalizing programs.

5 Conclusions

Argentina is an outlier in how much inequality and poverty are reduced through fiscal redistribution. The fiscal system overall reduces the Gini coefficient by 16.9 points

---

[27] See, for instance, electricity subsidies in figure 21C-11.

[28] Recall that a positive marginal contribution means that the item is equalizing. In this case, all items that are progressive according to the Kakwani index are also equalizing. As discussed in Lustig and Higgins (2022) (chapter 1 in this Volume), this is not necessarily always the case.

TABLE 21-7

Concentration Shares of Taxes and Transfers by Market Income + Pensions Group

Market Income + Pensions group	% Market Income + Pensions	% Direct transfers	% Direct taxes	% Disposable Income	% Indirect taxes	% Subsidies	% Consumable Income	% Health	% Education	% Final Income	% Population by group
Income < $1.9	0.1	21.8	0.0	2.3	2.5	7.6	2.6	5.5	4.7	3.1	5
US$1.9 ≤ Income < US$3.2	0.2	2.4	0.0	0.5	0.5	1.5	0.5	2.5	3.8	1.0	2
US$3.2 ≤ Income < US$5.5	0.7	4.3	0.1	1.1	1.1	2.7	1.2	4.7	7.0	2.1	5
US$5.5 ≤ Income < US$10	5.3	18.1	2.0	6.8	6.8	11.9	7.1	17.2	22.7	9.7	17
US$10 ≤ Income < US$50	59.9	48.7	53.5	59.0	59.1	60.0	59.1	60.4	57.3	59.1	61
US$50 ≤ Income	33.8	4.8	44.3	30.2	30.0	16.4	29.6	9.7	4.5	24.9	10
Total population	**100**	**100**	**100**	**100**	**100**	**100**	**100**	**100**	**100**	**100**	**100**

Source: Authors' own calculations.

FIGURE 21-7
Size, Progressivity, and Marginal Contribution

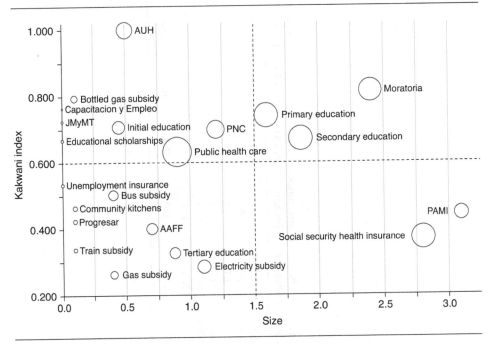

Source: Authors' own calculations.

Note: Circle sizes correspond to marginal contribution.

and poverty by 5 or 6 percentage points, depending on the line used. Direct cash transfers are the main driver of this result.

The large redistributive impact in Argentina is the result mainly of its size and not its overall progressivity. The state in Argentina is the largest in Latin America and similar to that observed in some advanced countries with large welfare states. However, some of the spending components exhibit a poor performance in terms of progressivity and spend nontrivial resources on the non-poor: the middle class and the rich receive almost 54 percent of what is spent on direct transfers and as much as 76.4 percent of subsidies. Furthermore, such high levels of spending have large costs in terms of macroeconomic stability, efficiency, and growth, which in turn feed back into higher poverty and thereby make some of this distributive effort self-defeating.

The spending programs with the highest contributions to reducing inequality and poverty are the Moratoria, PNC, and AUH. There is an interesting contrast between the AUH and PNC. Both reduce inequality by 1 Gini point. However, while the AUH represents 0.5 percent of GDP, spending on the PNC is more than twice as much (1.1 percent of GDP). Their impact on inequality is similar because the AUH compensates its lower spending with a higher progressivity.

Regarding in-kind transfers, the most equalizing are public health care and primary and secondary education, in that order. The least equalizing is spending on tertiary education.

Subsidies go disproportionally to the rich. Despite being (marginally) equalizing and progressive, they are concentrated in the higher deciles of the income distribution. This pattern stems from mainly electricity subsidies, which represent over half of the spending on subsidies. An exception is the bottled gas subsidy, which is the third most progressive spending item.

Some small programs as scholarships and youth and training programs are well targeted and hence progressive, but given their trivial size, they are barely equalizing.

Unlike in the comparator countries, taxes are regressive overall, due to indirect taxes. Excise taxes, fuel taxes, and VATs are outright unequalizing. Personal income taxes, on the contrary, are progressive. Payroll taxes, usually identified as a burden on the lower deciles, are actually progressive and equalizing, since they are paid by formal workers who are not typically in the low end of the income distribution. For the same reason, spending programs associated with formal employment as health care programs have low progressivity and take up lots of resources.

In conclusion, Argentina has a large redistributive state with many leakages and inefficiencies that pose a threat to macroeconomic stability, growth, and the very sustainability of the redistributive effort. Thus, it is of upmost importance to think how taxes, transfers, and subsidies should be reformed to reduce those costs, while at the same time protecting the poor and keeping the system as equalizing as possible. Addressing this issue is beyond the scope of this chapter. Nevertheless, on first approximation, it would seem that promising candidates for reform are the subsidies that disproportionately benefit the rich, as well as large programs that are not effectively redistributive.

Acknowledgments

This paper was prepared as part of the Commitment to Equity Institute's country-cases research program and benefited from the generous support of the Bill & Melinda Gates Foundation (www.ceqinstitute.org). We would like to thank the Center for Inter-American Policy and Research and the United Nations Development Programme for their support. Our thanks to Juan Pablo Romero for his outstanding research assistance and to José Luis Machinea, Jorge Paz, Maynor Cabrera, Stephen Younger, and Jon Jellema as well as participants in seminars and presentations for their valuable comments. We especially acknowledge the insightful work of Guillermo Cruces, Federico Sanz, Maria Josefina Baez, Pascuel Plotkin, María Pia Brugiafredo, and Leopoldo Tornarolli on which this analysis has built. Last but not least we want to thank the peer-reviewers, Jim Alm and Luis Beccaria, for their valuable comments on an earlier draft.

References

Ahumada, H., A. Canavese, P. Sanguinetti, and W. Sosa Escudero. 1993. "Efectos distributivos del impuesto inflacionario: Una estimacion del caso argentino." *Economia Mexicana 2*, no. 2, pp. 329–83.

Bucheli, M., N. Lustig, M. Rossi, and F. Amabile. 2013. *Social Spending, Taxes and Income Redistribution in Uruguay* (Washington: World Bank).

Canavese, A., W. Sosa Escudero, and F. G. Alvaredo. 1999. "El impacto de la inflacion sobre la distribucion del ingreso: El impuesto inflacionario en la Argentina en la decada del ochenta," in *La Distribucion Del Ingreso En La Argentina,* edited by Fundacion de Investigaciones Economicas Latinoamericanas (Buenos Aires: Fundacion de Investigaciones Economicas Latinoamericanas).

Cetrangolo, O., and C. Grushka. 2020. "El sistema de pensiones en la Argentina: Institucionalidad, gasto publico y sostenibilidad financiera" (Santiago, Chile: Comision Economica Para America Latina y el Caribe).

Cruces, G., V. Anauati, D, Cerisoli, J. Baez, E. Battistotti, P. Brugiafreddo, P. Plotkin, J. Puig, and F. Sanz, F. 2018. "Incidencia del sistema fiscal argentino en 2016" (Buenos Aires: Secretaria de Politica Economica, Ministerio de Hacienda de Argentina).

Enami, A., N. Lustig , and S. Higgins. 2022. "Allocating Taxes and Transfers and Constructing Income Concepts: Completing Sections A, B, and C of the *CEQ Master Workbook,*" chap. 6 in *Commitment to Equity Handbook: Estimating the Impact of Fiscal Policy on Inequality and Poverty,* 2nd ed., Vol. 1, edited by Nora Lustig (New Orleans: Brookings Institution Press and CEQ Institute). Free online version available at www.commitmentoequity.org.

Gasparini, L. 1998. "Incidencia distributiva del sistema impositivo argentine," in *La reforma tributaria en la Argentina. Tomo II* (Buenos Aires: Fundacion de Investigaciones Economicas Latinoamericanas).

———. 1999. "Incidencia distributiva del gasto publico social y de la politica tributaria en la Argentinam" in *La distribucion del ingreso en la Argentina* (Buenos Aires: Fundacion de Investigaciones Economicas Latinoamericanas).

Gasparini, L., M. Cicowiez, and W. Sosa Escudero. 2012. *Pobreza y desigualdad en America Latina* (Buenos Aires: Temas Grupo Editorial).

Gasparini, L., L. Tornarolli, and P. Gluzmann. 2019. "El desafio de la pobreza en Argentina" (Buenos Aires: Centro de Implementacion de Politicas Publicas para la Equidad y el Crecimiento).

Gomez Sabaini, J., M. Harriague, and D. Rossignolo. 2013. "Argentina. La situacion fiscal y los efectos en la distribucion del ingreso." *Desarrollo Economico, 52*, nos. 207–8), pp. 341–82.

Gomez Sabaini, J., and D. Rossignolo. 2009. "Argentina. Analisis de la situacion tributaria y propuestas de reformas impositivas destinadas a mejorar la distribucion del ingreso," in *Reflexiones y propuestas para mejorar la distribucion del ingreso en Argentina* (Buenos Aires: Oficina Internacional del Trabajo).

Goraus, K., and G. Inchauste. 2016. *The Distributional Impact of Taxes and Transfers in Poland* (Washington: World Bank).

Gragnolati, M., R. Rofman, I. Apella, and S. Troiano. 2015. *As Time Goes by in Argentina: Economic Opportunities and Challenges of the Demographic Transition* (Washington: World Bank Publications).

Higgins, S., and C. Pereira. 2014. "The Effects of Brazil's Taxation and Social Spending on the Distribution of Household Income." *Public Finance Review 42*, no. 3, pp. 346–67.

Instituto Nacional de Estadisticas y Censos. 2020. "Incidencia de la pobreza y la indigencia en 31 aglomerados urbanos. Primer semestre de 2020." *Informes Tecnicos 4*, no. 13.

Lambert, P. 2001. *The Distribution and Redistribution of Income* (Manchester: Manchester University Press).

Gerchunoff, P., and L. Llach, 2018. *El ciclo de la ilusion y el desencanto: Politicas economicas argentinas de 1880 a nuestros dias* (Buenos Aires: Critica).

Goraus-Tanska, K., and G. Inchauste. 2016. "The Distributional Impact of Taxes and Transfers in Poland." *World Bank Policy Research Working Paper No. 7787.*

Lopez-Calva, L. F., N. Lustig, M. Matytsin, and D. Popova. 2017. "Who Benefits from Fiscal Redistribution in the Russian Federation?" in *The Distributional Impact of Taxes and Transfers: Evidence From Eight Developing Countries*, edited by G. Inchauste and N. Lustig (Washington: World Bank).

Lustig, N. 2022a. "Fiscal Policy, Income Redistribution, and Poverty Reduction in Low- and Middle-Income Countries," chap. 10 in *Commitment to Equity Handbook: Estimating the Impact of Fiscal Policy on Inequality and Poverty*, 2nd ed., Vol. 1, edited by Nora Lustig (New Orleans: Brookings Institution Press and CEQ Institute). Free online version available at http://www.commitmentoequity.org.

———, ed. 2022b. *Commitment to Equity Handbook: Estimating the Impact of Fiscal Policy on Inequality and Poverty*, 2nd ed., Vol. 1, edited by Nora Lustig (New Orleans: Brookings Institution Press and CEQ Institute). Free online version available at www.commitmentoequity.org.

Lustig, N., and S. Higgins. 2022. "The CEQ Assessment: Measuring the Impact of Fiscal Policy on Inequality and Poverty," chap. 1 in *Commitment to Equity Handbook: Estimating the Impact of Fiscal Policy on Inequality and Poverty*, 2nd ed., Vol. 1, edited by Nora Lustig (New Orleans: Brookings Institution Press and CEQ Institute). Free online version available at www .commitmentoequity.org.

Lustig, N., and C. Pessino. 2014. "Social Spending and Income Redistribution in Argentina during the 2000s: The Increasing role of Noncontributory Pensions." *Public Finance Review 42*, no. 3, pp. 304–25.

Martinez-Aguilar, S. 2019. "CEQ Master Workbook: Panama (2016)" *CEQ Data Center on Fiscal Redistribution.*

Mussa, M. 2002. *Argentina and the Fund: From Triumph to Tragedy* (Washington: Peterson Institute).

Rossignolo, D. 2018. "Taxes, Expenditures, Poverty and Income Distribution in Argentina," chap. 11 in *Commitment to Equity Handbook: Estimating the Impact of Fiscal Policy on Inequality and Poverty*, 2nd ed., Vol. 1, edited by Nora Lustig (New Orleans: Brookings Institution Press and CEQ Institute). Free online version available at www.commitmentoequity.org.

Scott, J., S. Martinez-Aguilar, E. De la Rosa, E., and R. Aranda. 2017. "CEQ Master Workbook: Mexico (2014)." *CEQ Data Center on Fiscal Redistribution.*

Secretaria de Política Economica. 2002. "El impacto redistributivo de la Politica Social en Argentina" (Buenos Aires: Secretaria de Politica Economica, Ministerio de Hacienda de Argentina).

Secretaria de Programacion Economica y Regional. 1999. "El impacto redistributivo del gasto publico en los Sectores Sociales. Resultados provisorios" (Buenos Aires: Secretaria de Programacion Economica, Ministerio de Hacienda de Argentina).

Sturzenegger, F. (2019). "Macri's Macro: The Meandering Road to Stability and Growth." *Brookings Papers on Economic Activity*, Fall (https://www.brookings.edu/wp-content/uploads/2020/10/Sturzenegger-final-draft.pdf).

Tommasi, M., S. Saiegh, P. Sanguinetti, E. Stein, and M. Cárdenas. 2001. "Fiscal Federalism in Argentina: Policies, Politics, and Institutional Reform." *Economia* 1, no. 2, pp. 157–211.

Tornarolli, L. 2018. "Series Comparables de Indigencia y Pobreza: Una Propuesta Metodologica" (La Plata, Argentina: Centro de Estudios Distributivos, Laborales y Sociales).

Appendix 21A

Zero Income

Over the whole sample, 3.5 percent of the prefiscal incomes are zero. To understand this peculiar feature of Argentina's microdata, we consider employment status in figure 21A-1. It seems that these zero incomes in the first four centiles come from inactive individuals. The share of inactives in the first four centiles is 78.7 percent, whereas the share for the other 96 centiles is 39.4 percent. Zooming into the first ten centiles and turning to inactivity status in figure 21A-2, one can see that the lion's share of inactive individuals comes from the Moratoria and non-contributory pension receivers, who represent 60.3 percent of the first four centiles and 10.3 percent of the other 96 centiles.

Given its characteristics, we treat the Moratoria as a direct transfer. Nevertheless, it is an important part of the pensions system and therefore represents the main source of income for a big part of the population. That is why there is a large share of the first decile with zero prefiscal income, making incidence of taxes and expenditures huge. This drives some our results.

Take the regressivity of Argentina's taxes as an example. As explained above, zero incomes make incidence's denominator quite low. Furthermore, people spend and therefore pay indirect taxes once they have received direct transfers (particularly, the Moratoria), that is, with their Disposable Income, which is what makes the numerator quite high. Hence, indirect taxes' first decile incidence explodes, leading to the large regressivity of indirect taxes, which, combined with direct taxes' low progressivity, makes all taxes regressive.

We conducted two sensitivity analyses on our results: one in which we considered the Moratoria as part of the prefiscal income and one in which we excluded the households with individuals that both receive the Moratoria and have zero income. In both cases, the regressivity of taxes, for instance—which was a seemingly odd feature—faded out (0.010 and 0.001 Kakwani indexes, respectively). Nonetheless, Argentina keeps having the most regressive taxes, and the main results as Argentina's large inequality reduction hold (14.3 and 15.4 Gini points, respectively).

FIGURE 21A-1

Distribution of Employment Status (%) by Centile of Prefiscal Income

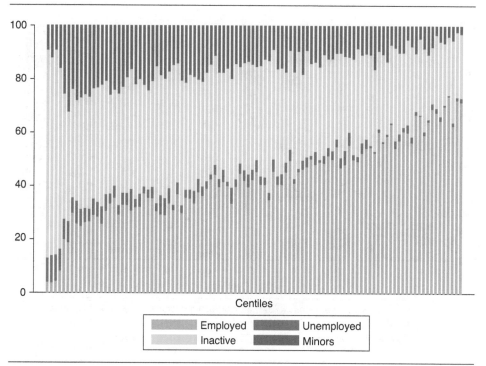

Source: Authors' own calculations.

Appendix 21B

Methodology

1 Direct Taxes

In Argentina, there are two broad categories of independent workers. The first is *mono-tributistas*, who pay a unique monthly contribution that includes social insurance contributions. For them, we take the reported income in the EPH and simulate the gross income by means of the contribution and tax rules. The other type of independent workers are *autónomos*. They are typically owners or partners of companies. These workers also pay a fixed monthly amount that includes social insurance contributions. For *autónomos*, as well as for salaried workers and pensioners, we created a synthetic database for each combination of number of children (0–9) and marital status {1,0}. We created twenty synthetic databases per working condition (salaried workers, *autónomos*, and pensioners), each of which has a simulated gross and net monthly income and a corresponding burden of contributions and personal income tax. We simulate

FIGURE 21A-2
Distribution of Inactives (%) by Centile of Prefiscal Income

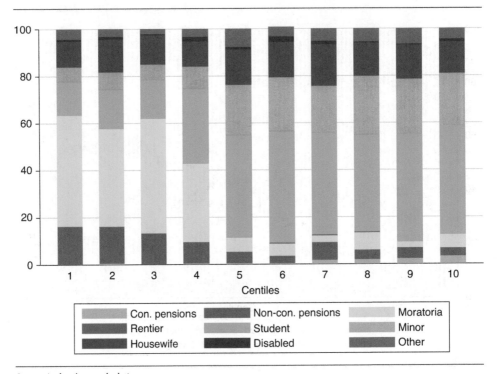

Source: Authors' own calculations.

these burdens using the rules for each contribution and tax. Then, for each working condition and the corresponding number of children and marital status, we (near) merge the synthetic datasets back to the EPH using net income as a merging variable, since it is assumed that reported income is equal to labor income net of contributions and personal income tax.

Tax avoidance and informal employment are pervasive in Argentina. Therefore, we estimated effective rate per percentile of the income distribution from administrative data. These effective rates are different depending on whether the contribution corresponds to the employee or to the employer. Moreover, for the first eight deciles, we apply the average of the percentiles per decile. For the ninth and tenth deciles, since there is a higher dispersion of income, we keep the effective rates at the percentile level. Hence, we have twenty-eight estimated effective rates.[29]

---

[29] Unfortunately, it is not possible to estimate the effective rates for pension and nonpension social insurance contributions separately from administrative data.

2 Pensions

The first step for calculating pensions is to identify those who receive any kind of pension in the EPH. Second, we use the ENAPROSS's questions to identify those who receive each type of pension and calculate the ratio of non-contributory pension beneficiaries to contributory pension beneficiaries per decile of per capita household income. Finally, to match this ratio back to the main survey, for pensioners in each decile in the EPH, we draw a number from a Bernoulli distribution with probability of success equal to the ratio estimated in the ENAPROSS. The 1s are considered the beneficiaries of the Moratoria. Non-contributory pensions can be received under five regimes: mother of seven children or more, old-age, disability, special laws, and *ex-gratia* granted by Congress. Each regime receives a different amount of pension. Hence, we need to distinguish which kind of non-contributory pension each pensioner receives. To do so, we estimate the distribution of pensioners among the five categories by randomly assigning, per decile, individuals to each category.

For those at least seventy years old who are identified as receiving a non-contributory pension, we consider the regime to be the old-age pension. In the remaining cases, for each decile of the per capita household income in the EPH and for each pensioner not previously identified with some category, we draw a number from a Bernoulli distribution with probability of success equal to the previously estimated percentage of individuals who receive that type of pension in that decile.

Once all non-contributory pensions are classified, we impute the amounts according to the law.

3 Direct Transfers

Although it is possible to directly identify who receives he unemployment insurance, the total amount of individuals captured by the EPH is almost half of what the administrative data indicate. Therefore, we simulate the unemployment program using the program's rules. We identify the potential beneficiaries of the unemployment insurance and then impute the value according to the relevant rules.

Regarding Asignaciones Familiares, we simulate the program's impact by using its rules to identify eligible individuals in the survey. To correct for errors of inclusion or exclusion, we calculate the ratio of the number of the AAFF beneficiaries reported in the administrative data and the number estimated in the survey. For each eligible individual of each program, we draw a number from a Bernoulli distribution with probability of success equal to that ratio. The 1s are considered beneficiaries. We impute the amount received by beneficiaries using the program's rules. An analogous procedure is used to simulate the impact of the Progresar, Capacitacion y Empleo, and JMyMT.

As for educational scholarships, it is possible to directly identify the beneficiaries in the EPH, but given substantial differences in administrative data, we decided to impute the amount received using administrative data.

Finally, regarding economic aid by community kitchens, we resort to the ENAPROSS to directly identify the proportion of beneficiaries per decile. Then, for each individual in each decile of the EPH, we draw a number from a Bernoulli with probability of success equal to the proportion estimated in ENAPROSS. The 1s are identified as beneficiaries. We assume that only individuals from the first three deciles attend community kitchens. Hence, we re-scale the number of beneficiaries per decile and make it consistent with administrative data. Once the corrected distribution of beneficiaries per decile is estimated, we calculate the proportion of beneficiaries per decile. For everyone in each decile, we repeat the Bernoulli procedure. The amount received is estimated based on administrative expenditure data for feeding programs and the expenditure of the provinces toward the Plan Nacional de Seguridad Alimentaria.

4 Indirect Subsidies

The bottled gas subsidy is targeted to families who do not have access to the gas network. In the EPH, it is possible to identify if a household has access to the gas network and if it buys bottled gas, but not the amount bought. Hence, we simulate potential beneficiaries of the program following the program's rules and assume each household receives the maximum amount of bottled gas, as determined by law, according to region and number of children. The subsidy is calculated as the product of this quantity and the amount subsidized per bottle of gas according to the law.

Direct identification of train subsidies is not possible since transportation data are not available in the EPH or the ENGHo. Hence, we resort to the 2010 Home Mobility Survey (ENMODO) for the Metropolitan Area of Buenos Aires. There we calculate the proportion of people who travel by train in each quintile of income per capita. This proportion is matched back to the EPH by quintile. The amount of the subsidy is calculated using administrative data on the total expenditure on the transportation subsidy and the number of train passengers.

There is one general bus subsidy that applies only to beneficiaries of the Tarifa Social. Expenditure data on bus transportation at the household level are available in the ENGHo. We use the ENGHo to identify the expenditure on bus transportation and the number of household members who travel by bus to estimate per capita spending per household. We also estimate the average per capita expenditure per region and income decile. Then, we estimate the proportion of households with more than one member and the proportion of households that use the bus, per region and decile. To match this proportion back to the EPH, we use the Bernoulli procedure for household heads and for households with at least two people who travel by bus, by region and income decile. For those now identified in the EPH as traveling by bus, we impute their average expenditure on bus transportation calculated according to their region and decile. Then, we calculate the ventiles of the per capita expenditure on bus transportation and the average expenditure by region. Using SUBE—the public transport card—data, we estimate the number of bus trips made on average by individuals in each region. We combine this with the ENGHo data to calculate the average number of trips by individual per region and ventile rescaling to match SUBE data. Similarly, this dataset allows us to identify the proportion of individuals who travel by bus and are beneficiaries of the Tarifa Social by region. We use this proportion to estimate the corresponding amount of people in the EPH, differentiating the Metropolitan Area of Buenos Aires from the rest of country. The subsidy is imputed using the legal rules.

Appendix 21C

Incidence

FIGURE 21C-1
Moratoria

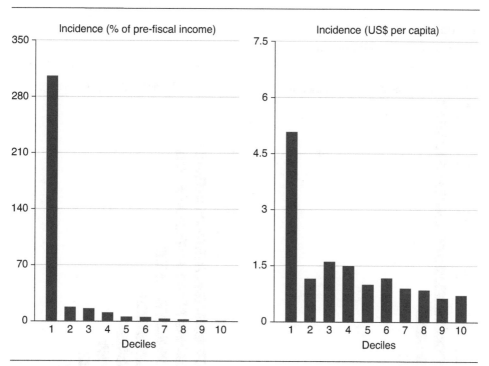

Source: Authors' own calculations.

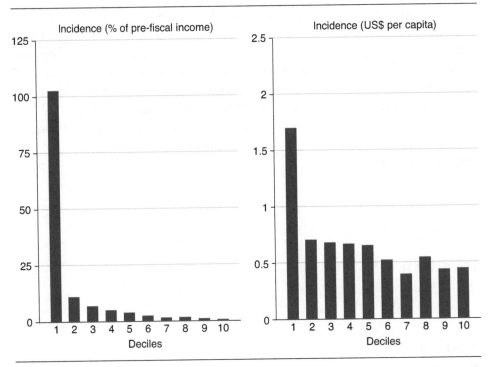

Source: Authors' own calculations.

FIGURE 21C-3
Asignacion Universal por Hijo

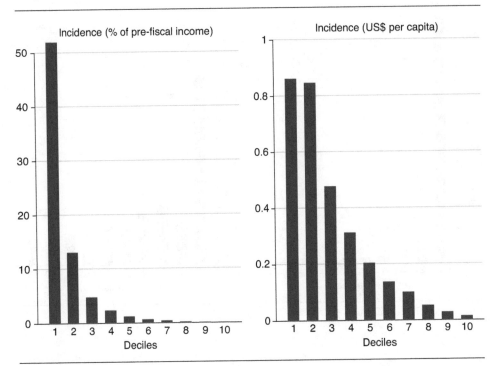

Source: Authors' own calculations.

FIGURE 21C-4

Social Security Health Insurance

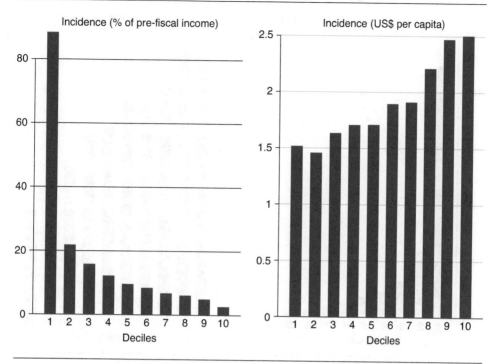

Source: Authors' own calculations.

FIGURE 21C-5

Programa de Atencion Medica Integral

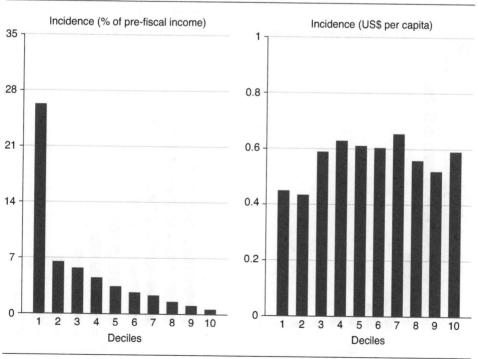

Source: Authors' own calculations.

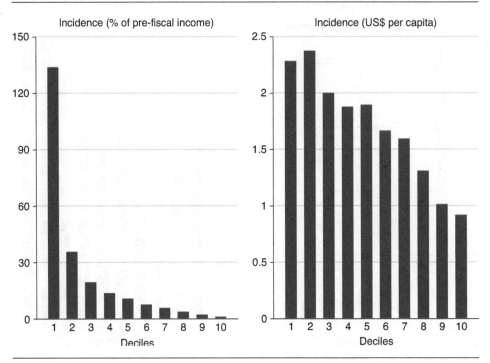

Source: Authors' own calculations.

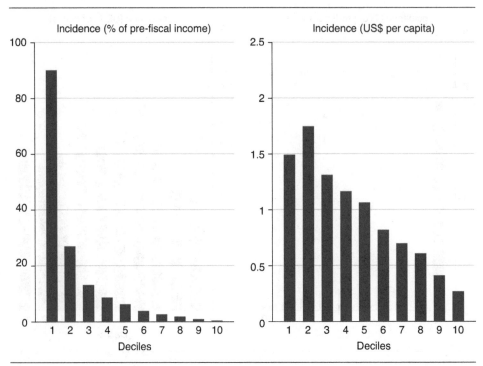

Source: Authors' own calculations.

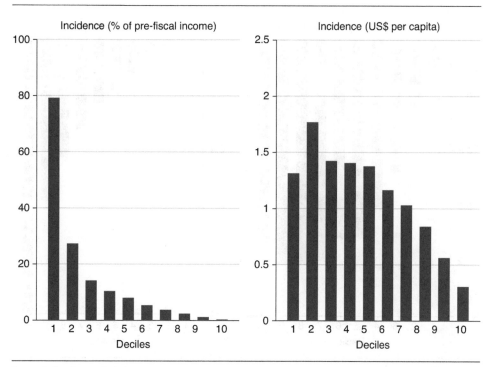

Source: Authors' own calculations.

FIGURE 21C-9
Tertiary Education

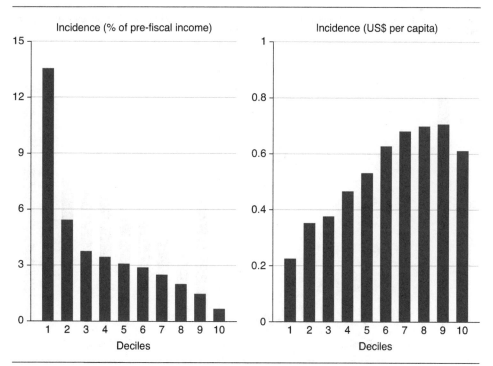

Source: Authors' own calculations.

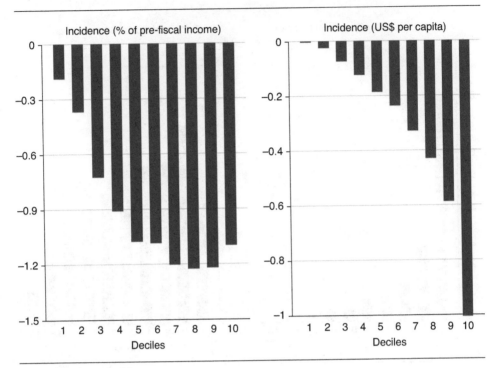

FIGURE 21C-11
Electricity Subsidies

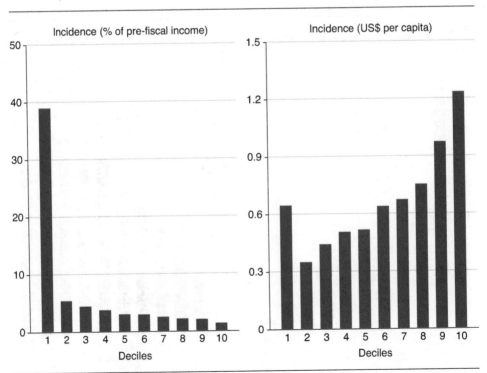

The *CEQ (Commitment to Equity) Assessment* Tools

Available only online at
www.ceqinstitute.org, under "Handbook."

CEQ Data Center on Fiscal Redistribution

Available only online at
www.ceqinstitute.org, under "Handbook."

PART VI

CEQ Microsimulation Tools

Available only online at
www.ceqinstitute.org, under "Handbook."

PART VI

CCQ Microsimulation Tools

Available only online at

www.cqpress.org, under "Handbook."

ABOUT THE AUTHORS

LAURA ABRAMOVSKY is an independent economic consultant and researcher, and a research associate at the Institute for Fiscal Studies (IFS) in the United Kingdom. She has more than fifteen years of experience in microeconomic research and public policy evaluation. Her current work focuses on tax and social protection policy and program and impact evaluation in developing countries. She is one of the founders of the IFS's UK Department for International Development–funded Centre for Tax Analysis in Developing Countries (TAXDEV). This program aims at generating new research, analysis, and in-country analytical capacity in the area of tax and benefit policy and administration in a range of developing countries. She obtained her Ph.D. in economics from University College London.

JAMES ALM is Professor Emeritus of Economics at Tulane University, after recently stepping down as chair of the department. Previously, he was Regents Professor in the Department of Economics at the Andrew Young School of Policy Studies at Georgia State University, where he served as chair of the department and dean of the school. He has also taught at Syracuse University and the University of Colorado-Boulder. He earned his master's degree in economics at the University of Chicago and his doctorate at the University of Wisconsin-Madison. Much of his research has focused on the effects of taxes, in such areas as tax compliance, the marriage tax, opportunity zones, tax reform, and tax incidence. He has also worked on fiscal and decentralization reforms domestically and internationally. He has been editor of *Public Finance Review*, and he has served as President of the Southern Economic Association and of the National Tax Association.

RODRIGO ARANDA is a Postdoctoral Research Scholar at the Center for Economic and Social Research (CESR) in University of Southern California and University of Wisconsin - Milwaukee. He became a Research Associate of the CEQ Institute in 2017. He is an applied microeconomist with interest in health economics, crime economics, and development economics. He holds a Ph.D. from the Economics Department at Tulane University.

JAIME ARISTY-ESCUDER is an economist and mathematician in the Dominican Republic. He is a professor of mathematical economics at Instituto Tecnologico de Santo Domingo (INTEC) and has been a consultant for numerous international organizations. He is the author of conference papers that have been presented at the Massachusetts Institute of Technology, Harvard, and the University of London. In 2011, he received the INTEC Outstanding Alumni Award. He is a member of the American Economic Association and the Econometric Society. He became a nonresident Research Associate of the CEQ Institute in 2017. He holds a master of science in financial mathematics from the University of Chicago.

JEREMY BAROFSKY is the Vice President of Applied Research and Evaluation at ideas42 and a Nonresident Fellow in Governance Studies at the Brookings Institution. Barofsky is interested in the intersection between poverty and health and also studies how behavioral models of decision-making can increase well-being and human capital. His work has been published in the *Journal of Health Economics*, the *Lancet*, and *Health Affairs*. He became a nonresident Research Associate of the CEQ Institute in 2017. He received his doctorate in global health and population (economics) from Harvard University's T. H. Chan School of Public Health and holds a master of arts in economics from Boston University.

MARGARITA BENEKE DE SANFELIU is the director of the Center for Research and Statistics at Fundacion Salvadoreña para el Desarrollo Economico y Social (FUSADES). With more than twenty-five years of experience coordinating interdisciplinary research teams and designing, implementing, and analyzing social and economic research, she has directed and conducted empirical quantitative and mixed methods research, including surveys (household, individuals, enterprises, and so on). Recent research and publications have focused on women's economic empowerment; labor market; youth, poverty, and vulnerability; household income dynamics; migration and remittances; crime prevention; fiscal incidence of social programs; and impact evaluation of social programs. She became a nonresident Research Associate of the CEQ Institute in 2017. Beneke de Sanfeliu holds a master of science in industrial engineering from the University of Oklahoma, with a concentration on math modeling.

CATERINA BREST LOPEZ is a Ph.D. candidate in Economics at Universidad de San Andrés in Argentina. She is Coordinator of the Fiscal Equity Lab Argentina of the Center of Studies for Human Development (CEDH, for its Spanish acronym). Her research interests include macroeconometrics, public finance focused on inequality and poverty, and applied microeconomics focused on labor and gender inequality.

MARISA BUCHELI is a professor in the Department of Economics of the Faculty of Social Sciences at Universidad de la Republica in Uruguay. Her research focuses on income inequality, poverty, discrimination, and the role of private transfers and social policies. She is also interested in several areas of population studies. Her work has been published in *Economics and Philosophy*, the *Journal of Pension Economics and Finance*, the *Journal of Interpersonal Violence*, and *Latin American Politics and Society*, among others. She became a nonresident Research Associate of the CEQ Institute in 2017. She received her doctorate in economics from the University of Granada.

GARY BURTLESS is a Senior Fellow (Emeritus) in Economic Studies at the Brookings Institution in Washington, DC. His research focuses on issues connected with aging, income distribution, labor markets, social insurance and pension policy, and the behavioral effects of government policy. Burtless has coauthored six books and edited or coedited five additional volumes. He served five years as coeditor of the *Brookings-Wharton Papers on Urban Affairs* and earlier served as associate editor of the *Journal of Human Resources*. Burtless graduated from Yale College in 1972 and received a Ph.D. in economics from the Massachusetts Institute of Technology in 1977.

MAYNOR CABRERA is an economist with expertise in fiscal policy, human development, and macroeconomics, he was Secretary of the Commission of the Fiscal Pact of Guatemala and has worked as an adviser to government agencies and as a consultant to international organizations. He is the author of articles published in leading development journals and international organizations. He holds a master's degree in applied economics from the Catholic University of Chile and studied tax policy at the Harvard Kennedy School of Government. He is a Research Associate of the CEQ Institute.

JOAQUIN CAMPABADAL is a research assistant at the CEQ Institute since February 2020 where he has contributed to both the 2017 and 2020 versions of the Argentina's CEQ Assessment. He holds a MSc and a BSc. in economics from Universidad de San Andrés. His interests focus on macroeconomics, international economics and political economy.

CRISTINA CARRERA worked as a research assistant at the CEQ Institute where, among other functions, she built expertise on data automation tools for the systematization and quality assurance of results from the *CEQ Assessments*. She has served as a survey coder at the Mexican Institute of Statistics and Geography (INEGI). She holds a Masters from the University of Sussex.

ENRIQUE DE LA ROSA is a Ph.D. student in Development Studies at King's College London. His research focuses on living standards, inequality, and economic development in Mexico. He has also held several positions in Mexican public administration including Advisor to the President of Mexico and Economic Deputy Director at the Federal Telecommunications Commission. He is a Research Associate of the CEQ Institute.

GISELLE DEL CARMEN is a consultant in the Poverty and Equity Global Practice at the World Bank, where she focuses on Latin America and the Caribbean. She has been working on poverty, inequality, and labor market analysis. Before joining the World Bank, she worked at the Ministry of Finance of Honduras. She holds a master's degree in public administration from the London School of Economics and Political Science.

ALI ENAMI is an Assistant Professor of Economics at The University of Akron. His research focuses on the socioeconomic effects of fiscal policies on poverty, inequality, migration, educational achievement, and business activities. His work has been published in *Economics of Education Review, Atlantic Journal of Economics, Middle East Development Journal, Applied Economics Quarterly, Regional Science and Urban Economics, Party Politics,* and *Journal of Policy Modeling.* He is a Research Associate of the CEQ Institute.

ALAN FUCHS is a senior economist in the Poverty and Equity Global Practice of the World Bank. He has led operations and analytical work on social inclusion, risk management, and fiscal incidence in Chile, Colombia, the Dominican Republic, and Uruguay. His research focuses on development economics, applied microeconomics, insurance, and energy and has peer-reviewed publications in the *American Economic Review,* the *American Economic Journal: Economic Policy,* and the *American Journal of Agricultural Economics.* Prior to joining the World Bank, he worked for the United Nations Development Program (UNDP) and the Mexican Government. Fuchs holds a Ph.D. from the University of California, Berkeley.

MAYA GOLDMAN is a non-resident associate at the CEQ and a senior research economist at the Southern African Labour and Development Research Unit. As a CEQ consultant, she led the second CEQ assessment of South Africa and Uzbekistan; has contributed to CEQs on numerous countries, including Uganda, and Tajikistan; and has been involved in work on the indirect effects of VAT since 2017. Prior to the CEQ, she worked as an ODI Fellow in the Ministry of Finance in East-Timor, and the Central Bank of Burundi. She has a Masters in Economics from Toulouse School of Economics. She is a Research Associate of the CEQ Institute.

ASTRID HAAS is an urban economist currently working as a long-term consultant with the African Development Bank where she is supporting cities strengthen their financial systems and unleash new opportunities for subnational financing. Her previous roles include Policy Director and Head of the Cities that Work initiative at the International Growth Centre. Astrid has worked extensively with city governments across Africa and Asia. In 2016, she was nominated by the University of Cape Town as one of Africa's Young Leaders and in 2020 she received Johns Hopkins University's Outstanding Recent Graduate Award, for her work on urbanisation. For more information: www.astridrnhaas.com

SEAN HIGGINS is an Assistant Professor of Finance at the Kellogg School of Management at Northwestern University. His research studies how technology reduces barriers to financial inclusion, and the effect of reducing these barriers on households and small businesses. He received a BS and PhD in Economics from Tulane University. Prior to joining Kellogg, he was a Post-Doctoral Fellow at the Haas School of Business at the University of California, Berkeley. He is a Research Associate of the CEQ Institute.

GABRIELA INCHAUSTE is a lead economist in the Poverty and Equity Global Practice at the World Bank, where she focuses on Eastern Europe and Central Asia. In addition, she is the Global Lead on Fiscal and Social Policies for Poverty Reduction and Shared Prosperity, and in this role she has been working on the distributional impact of fiscal policy and on ex ante analysis of the distributional impacts of policy reforms. Before joining the World Bank, she worked at the Inter-American Development Bank and the International Monetary Fund. She holds a doctorate in economics from the University of Texas at Austin.

JON JELLEMA is the CEQ Institute's Director of Projects, Advisory Services, and Training. He is leading the CEQ Assessments in the Comoros, Indonesia, Namibia, Uganda, and Vietnam, and has participated in the CEQ effort in Ethiopia, Jordan, and South Africa. He previously worked as a poverty economist and social development specialist in the World Bank's Jakarta, Indonesia, office. He received his doctorate in economics from the University of California, Berkeley. He is a Research Associate of the CEQ Institute.

NIZAR JOUINI is an Assistant Professor and program head of the Public Policy program at the Doha Institute for high graduates. He served as a full-time economic consultant at the African Development Bank between 2007 and 2015. His current research focuses on fiscal issues, trade policy, education inequality, and more. He became a nonresident Research Associate of the CEQ Institute in 2017. He received his Ph.D. in economics from the François Rabelais University in Tours, France.

JULIETA LADRONIS is a research analyst at the Fiscal Affairs Department of the International Monetary Fund (IMF). She previously worked at the Poverty and Equity Global Practice at the World Bank. Her research interests focus on tax policy, especially regarding how it affects people's choices and wellbeing. She holds a Bachelor's Degree in Economics from Universidad de Buenos Aires (Magna cum laude) and a Master's Degree in Economics from Universidad de San Andres, Argentina.

PATRICIO LARROULET has been a Research Assistant at the CEQ Institute since 2019. He has been in charge of curating the CEQ Data Center on Fiscal Redistribution and has collaborated in several projects, including estimating the impact of COVID-19 on poverty and inequality in Guatemala, Honduras and El Salvador using microsimulation methods. He is completing his Master's degree in Economics at the Universidad de San Andres, Argentina

RUOXI LI was a Research Assistant of the CEQ Institute. She is a PhD student in economics at Yale University.

JUAN CRUZ LOPEZ DEL VALLE is a research associate at Centro de Estudios para el Desarrollo Humano (CEDH). His research interests span political economy, macroeconomics and behavioral economics. He holds a BSc in economics from Universidad Nacional de Rosario and a MSc in economics from Universidad de San Andrés, Argentina.

NORA LUSTIG is Samuel Z. Stone Professor of Latin American Economics and founding director of the CEQ Institute at Tulane University. She is also a nonresident fellow at the Brookings Institution, the Center for Global Development and the Inter-American Dialogue. Her research on economic development, inequality and social policies has been published in more than 70 articles, close to 90 chapters, and 25 books and edited volumes. She is president-elect of the Society for the Study of Economic Inequality (ECINEQ), a founding member and president emeritus of the Latin American and Caribbean Economic Association (LACEA) and was a codirector of the *World Bank's World Development Report 2000/2001: Attacking Poverty*. She is the editor of the *Journal of Economic Inequality Forum*, and she is a member of the Inter-American Dialogue, and the Society for the Study of Economic Inequality (ECINEQ)'s Executive Council. Professor Lustig earned her Ph.D. in Economics from the University of California, Berkeley.

SANDRA MARTINEZ-AGUILAR has worked as consultant on poverty and inequality analysis for international organizations such as the World Bank and UNDP, and has been the lead author of CEQ Assessments for Latin-American and African countries. She served as the CEQ Institute's Data Center Director and as an analyst at the Ministry of Finance of Chile. She holds a master's degree in Public Policy from Columbia University and BSc in Economics from the Universidad de Chile. Currently, she is a doctoral student at the Social Research Institute at UCL. She is a Research Associate of the CEQ Institute.

VALENTINA MARTINEZ PABON is a Ph.D. candidate in Economics at Tulane University. Her research is in applied microeconomics, focusing on development economics, economics of education, inequality, and poverty. She has worked as a consultant of the

Inter-American Development Bank and has participated in the CEQ Assessments of Argentina and Colombia. Her research has been published in Economia and Estudios Economicos.

BLANCA MORENO-DODSON is an experienced development macroeconomist with twenty-five years of World Bank service. She has published three books: *Reducing Poverty on a Global Scale* (2005), Public *Finance for Poverty Reduction* (2007), and *Is Fiscal Policy the Answer? A Developing Country Perspective* (2012), as well as numerous articles on macroeconomics, public expenditures, tax policy and growth, and other development issues. She obtained her Ph.D. in international economics and finance from the Aix-Marseille University II, France.

AHMED MOUMMI joined the United Nations Economics and Social Commission for Western Asia (UN-ESCWA) in 2017 as First Economic Affairs Officer in the Modeling and Forecasting Section, Economic Development and Globalization Division. Prior to this appointment, he built up over twenty-four years of experience as a head of research, senior economist, and associate professor in economics. He was also senior research economist at the Development Research Department of the African Development Bank and Task Manager of several projects and flagship studies on fiscal policy, inclusive growth, employment, and the impact of economic policies. He holds a Ph.D. in economics from the University of Tlemcen, Algeria, and CERDI (Centre d'Etudes et de Recherches sur le Developpement International), Clermont-Ferrand, France.

JOSE ANDRES OLIVA CEPEDA is an economist at the Foundation for Economic and Social Development in El Salvador (FUSADES). His main research is in public finance and labor economics. He has elaborated analyses and studies related to fiscal policy, poverty, and inclusive growth in El Salvador. Since 2012, he has conducted research and implemented CEQ methodologies in El Salvador. He became a nonresident Research Associate of the CEQ Institute in 2017. He holds a master's degree in finance (2007) from the Central American University, Jose Simeon Cañas, in El Salvador.

FELIX OPPONG works in the Independent Evaluation Group of the World Bank. Before joining the Bank in 2010, he worked as a Senior Economist in the Ministry of Finance and Economic Planning of Ghana for nearly 10 years. He holds a PhD in Tax Policy from University of Pretoria, South Africa.

ERIC OSEI-ASSIBEY is an Associate Professor and Dean of International Programmes Office in the Department of Economics at the University of Ghana. His research interests include Development and Small Business Financing, Monetary Economics, Sustainable Development, Poverty Reduction and Progress towards the MDGs. He holds a Ph.D. in International Development from Nagoya University, Japan.

Eduardo Ortiz-Juarez is a Lecturer (Assistant Professor) in Development Economics at the Department of International Development, King's College London; Economist at the Strategic Policy Unit, UNDP; and Research Associate at the Commitment to Equity Institute (CEQ). He is interested in the study of poverty, inequalities, and social policy. He has worked as Economist and Senior Economist at the UNDP Latin America, as Deputy Director of Economic and Social Analysis at the Mexican Ministry of Social Development, and as consultant for international organisations and governments, including the World Bank, IDB, UNU-WIDER, and SEGIB.

Claudiney Pereira is a clinical associate professor in the Department of Economics at Arizona State University. He has served as a faculty member of Tulane University and Catholic University of Brasilia and senior economic researcher and adviser at the National Confederation of the Industry in Brazil. His research focuses on monetary policy and the role of the financial sector in Brazil, as well as fiscal policy effects on poverty and income distribution there. He became a nonresident Research Associate of the CEQ Institute in 2017. He received his doctorate in economics from North Carolina State University.

David Phillips is an associate director at the Institute for Fiscal Studies (IFS) in London. He leads the UKAID-funded Centre for Tax Analysis in Developing Countries' (TAXDEV) work in Ethiopia and Ghana, where the IFS is helping the governments undertake and improve tax policy analysis, and carries out further work on tax policy issues in developing countries. Other research interests include sub-national public finance, labor supply, and consumer demand responses to taxation, as well as UK income and poverty statistics. He has produced both academic publications and policy reports and has been a member of various government and parliamentary advisory groups for public finance issues in recent years. He has a master's degree in economics from University College London (UCL).

Daria Popova is a research fellow at the Institute for Social and Economic Research at the University of Essex (United Kingdom) and a developer for EUROMOD, the tax-benefit microsimulation model for the European Union. Her research areas include the comparative analysis of welfare states, distributional issues, and family dynamics. She is also a research associate at the Higher School of Economics (Moscow) and has previously worked as a lecturer at the University of Michigan, Ann Arbor. She became a nonresident Research Associate of the CEQ Institute in 2017. She received her doctorate in political science from the European University Institute.

Adam Ratzlaff is a Ph.D. candidate in International Relations at Florida International University. He has conducted political and economic analysis for several groups, including the World Bank and the Inter-American Development Bank. He holds a master of arts in international studies from the Josef Korbel School of International Studies (University of Denver) as well as a bachelor of arts from Tulane University, where he triple-majored in international relations, economics, and Latin American studies.

HALEY RENDA has been engaged with the CEQ Institute since mid-2018, first as a research assistant and then as a long-term consultant. She has worked in collaboration with other CEQI members, partners in the World Bank and IMF, and independently in conducting CEQ Assessments of the impact of fiscal policy in Uganda, Namibia, eSwatini, Tajikistan, Uzbekistan, and the USA, among others. Haley received her Master of Science in Applied Econometrics from Eastern Michigan University in 2020.

DARIO ROSSIGNOLO is a Professor of Macroeconomics, Public Finance, and Political Economy at the University of Buenos Aires. He is a professor at the Master of Public Economics at the National University of Cordoba and at the Master of Generation and Analysis of Statistical Information at the National University of Tres de Febrero. He has been a consultant for international organizations and has specialized in the evaluation of the economic effects of public policies and taxation in Latin America. He is a Research Associate of the CEQ Institute. Professor Rossignolo holds a PhD. in Economics from University of La Plata in Argentina.

MIGUEL E. SANCHEZ-MARTIN is the World Bank senior country economist for Ethiopia, where he leads the economic reform dialogue. Since joining the World Bank in 2010, he has worked in Latin America, South-East Asia, and Africa on issues including growth and diversification, foreign direct investment attraction, fiscal policy and redistribution, and tax expenditure. He has published peer reviewed articles on these topics and is a reviewer of academic journals. Miguel holds a MsC in Political Economy of Development by the University of London, SOAS, and a PhD in Economics by Universidad Autónoma de Madrid.

JOHN SCOTT is professor-researcher in the Economics Department at the Centro de Investigacion y Docencia Economicas (CIDE) in Mexico City and Academic Researcher of the Consejo Nacional de Evaluacion de la Politica de Desarrollo Social (CONEVAL), a public institution responsible for poverty measurement and the evaluation of social programs in Mexico. His principal research areas include the distributive incidence of social spending, poverty and inequality analysis, and evaluation of social policy, rural development policies, agricultural and energy subsidies, and health and social security. He holds a master of philosophy in economics from Oxford University.

ABEBE SHIMELES is the Director of Research in the African Economic Research Consortium (AERC). Previously he worked for the African Development Bank, the

United Nations Economic Commission for Africa, the World Bank, ActionAid, and Addis Ababa University in different capacities. His recent research interests include labor market integration, migration issues in Africa, and impact evaluation of policy interventions. He became a nonresident Research Associate of the CEQ Institute in 2017. He holds a Ph.D. in economics from the University of Goteborg, Sweden.

MARIANO TOMMASI is Professor of Economics at Universidad de San Andrés and Director of the Center of Studies for Human Development. He is a Fellow of the Econometric Society. He specializes in Political Economy, Institutions, Poverty, and Social Policies. He was President of the Latin American and Caribbean Economic Association. He has published more than 50 articles in some of the top academic journals such as the *American Economic Review, American Journal of Political Science, American Political Science Review, Journal of Development Economics, Journal of Law, Economics and Organization*, and *Journal of Economic Inequality*. From 2015 to 2017 he worked as an advisor to the Chief of Staff Office, Presidency of Argentina, in the coordination of social policies. Professor Tommasi holds a Ph.D. in Economics from the University of Chicago.

PAOLO VERME is a lead economist and manager of the Research Program on Forced Displacement at the World Bank. He was a visiting professor at Bocconi University and the University of Torino between 2003 and 2010. For a period of two decades prior to joining the World Bank, he served as senior adviser and project manager for the European Union, the United Nations, private consulting groups, and governments specializing in the design, implementation, and evaluation of welfare and labor reforms. His research covers labor markets, poverty, and income distribution. He holds a Ph.D. from the London School of Economics.

YANG WANG is an assistant professor in economics at Tianjin University of Finance and Economics. Her research focuses on earning inequality and human capital, as well as the impacts of economic conditions and fiscal policies on poverty and income distribution. She has worked as a consultant for the Inter-American Development Bank and the World Bank. Her research has been published in the *Journal of Economic Inequality*, among others. She became a nonresident Research Associate of the CEQ Institute in 2017. She received her Ph.D. in economics from Tulane University.

SEBASTIAN WOLF is an economist and public financial management specialist. He has worked as an adviser with the Overseas Development Institute in the Ministries of Finance in Uganda and South Sudan and as Country Economist for Uganda for the London School of Economics and the University of Oxford's International Growth Centre. He holds a master of philosophy degree in economics from the University of Cambridge.

STEPHEN D. YOUNGER is a consultant to the CEQ Institute and worked previously at Williams College, Cornell University, the Vrije Universiteit Amsterdam, the Facultad Latinoamericana de Ciencias Sociales (Quito, Ecuador), and Ithaca College. His research focuses on the distributional consequences of public policy in developing countries, especially the nonincome dimensions of well- being, as well as multidimensional poverty and inequality. He earned his doctorate in economics from Stanford University.

INDEX